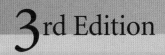

3rd Edition

TEXTBOOK OF
Gastrointestinal Radiology

Richard M. Gore, MD
Professor of Radiology
Northwestern University Feinberg School of Medicine
Chief, Gastrointestinal Radiology Section
Evanston Northwestern Healthcare
Evanston, Illinois

Marc S. Levine, MD
Professor of Radiology
Advisory Dean
University of Pennsylvania School of Medicine
Chief, Gastrointestinal Radiology Section
University of Pennsylvania Medical Center
Philadelphia, Pennsylvania

VOLUME **2**

SAUNDERS

ELSEVIER

SAUNDERS
ELSEVIER

1600 John F. Kennedy Blvd.
Ste. 1800
Philadelphia, PA 19103-2899

TEXTBOOK OF GASTROINTESTINAL RADIOLOGY

Copyright © 2008, 2000, 1994 by Saunders, an imprint of Elsevier Inc.

Set ISBN: 978-1-4160-2332-6
Volume 1 Part No. 9996008037
Volume 2 Part No. 9996007553

Notice

Knowledge and best practice in this field are constantly changing. As new research and experience broaden our knowledge, changes in practice, treatment, and drug therapy may become necessary or appropriate. Readers are advised to check the most current information provided (i) on procedures featured or (ii) by the manufacturer of each product to be administered, to verify the recommended dose or formula, the method and duration of administration, and contraindications. It is the responsibility of the practitioner, relying on his or her experience and knowledge of the patient, to make diagnoses, to determine dosages and the best treatment for each individual patient, and to take all appropriate safety precautions. To the fullest extent of the law, neither the Publisher nor the Editors assume any liability for any injury and/or damage to persons or property arising out of or related to any use of the material contained in this book.

The Publisher

Library of Congress Cataloging-in-Publication Data

Textbook of gastrointestinal radiology/[edited by] Richard M. Gore,
    Marc S. Levine.—3rd ed.
        p. ; cm.
    Includes bibliographical references and index.
    ISBN 1-4160-2332-1
    1. Gastrointestinal system—Radiography. I. Gore, Richard M.
II. Levine, Marc S.
    [DNLM: 1. Gastrointestinal Diseases—diagnosis. 2. Diagnostic
Imaging—methods. 3. Digestive System—pathology. WI 141 T355 2008]
    RC804. R6T46—2007   616.3'307572—dc22   2006030686

Acquisitions Editor: Rebecca Schmidt Gaertner
Developmental Editor: Jean Nevius
Publishing Services Manager: Linda Van Pelt
Project Managers: Joan Nikelsky, Melanie Johnstone
Design Direction: Ellen Zanolle

Printed in China

Last digit is the print number: 9 8 7 6 5 4 3 2 1

To Margaret and our children,
Diana, Elizabeth, and George

RICHARD M. GORE

To my parents, Wilfred and Helen Levine,
and to Deborah and our children,
Daniel, Amy, Kevin, and Laura

MARC S. LEVINE

Contributors

SECTION EDITOR

STEPHEN E. RUBESIN, MD
Professor of Radiology, University of Pennsylvania School of
Medicine; Radiologist, Hospital of the University of
Pennsylvania, Philadelphia, Pennsylvania

SAMUEL NATHAN ADLER, MD
Chief, Department of Gastroenterology, Bikur Holim
Hospital, Jerusalem, Israel

STEPHEN R. BAKER, MD, MPHIL
Professor and Chairman, Department of Radiology, UMDJ
New Jersey Medical School; Chief, Department of Radiology,
The University Hospital, Newark, New Jersey

APARNA BALACHANDRAN, MD
Assistant Professor, Department of Radiology, Division of
Diagnostic Imaging, University of Texas MD Anderson
Cancer Center, Houston, Texas

DENNIS M. BALFE, MD
Professor of Radiology, Department of Diagnostic Radiology,
Washington University in St. Louis School of Medicine;
Radiologist, Department of Diagnostic Radiology, Barnes-
Jewish Hospital, St. Louis, Missouri

EMIL J. BALTHAZAR, MD
Professor Emeritus, Department of Radiology, New York
University School of Medicine; Attending Consultant,
Department of Radiology, Bellevue Hospital, New York,
New York

STUART A. BARNARD, MB, BS, MA, MRCS, FRCR
Radiologist, Department of Radiology, Middlemore Hospital,
Auckland, New Zealand

CLIVE BARTRAM, MD, FRCS, FRCP, FRCR
Honorary Professor of Gastrointestinal Radiology, School of
Medicine, Imperial College Faculty of Medicine, London;
Emeritus Consultant, Department of Radiology, St. Mark's
Hospital, Harrow, United Kingdom

GENEVIEVE L. BENNETT, MD
Assistant Professor of Radiology, Department of Radiology,
Abdominal Imaging Division, New York University School
of Medicine, Bellevue Hospital Medical Center, New York,
New York

JONATHAN W. BERLIN, MD, MBA
Associate Professor of Radiology, Northwestern University
Feinberg School of Medicine, Evanston; Radiologist, Body
Imaging Section, Evanston Northwestern Healthcare,
Evanston; Lecturer, Department of Radiology, Rosalind
Franklin University of Medicine and Science, North Chicago,
Illinois

GEORGE S. BISSETT III, MD
Professor of Radiology and Pediatrics, Vice Chairman,
Department of Radiology, Duke University School of
Medicine, Durham, North Carolina

PEYMAN BORGHEI, MD
Visiting Research Scholar, Department of Diagnostic
Radiology, University of California Irvine Medical Center,
Orange, California

JAMES L. BUCK, MD
Professor, Department of Diagnostic Radiology, University of
Kentucky College of Medicine, Lexington, Kentucky

CARINA L. BUTLER, MD
Assistant Professor, Department of Diagnostic Radiology,
University of Kentucky College of Medicine, University
of Kentucky Chandler Medical Center, Lexington, Kentucky

MARC A. CAMACHO, MD, MS
Chief, Emergency Radiology, Department of Radiology, Beth
Israel Deaconess Medical Center, Boston, Massachusetts.
Formerly: Assistant Professor, Department of Radiology,
Virginia Commonwealth University College of Medicine;
Chief, Emergency Radiology, Department of Radiology,
Virginia Commonwealth University Health System, Medical
College of Virginia Hospital, Richmond, Virginia

DINA F. CAROLINE, MD, PHD
Professor, Department of Radiology, Temple University
School of Medicine, Temple University Hospital,
Philadelphia, Pennsylvania

CAROLINE W. T. CARRICO, MD
Assistant Clinical Professor, Departments of Radiology and
Pediatrics, Duke University School of Medicine, Durham,
North Carolina

RICHARD I. CHEN, MD
Assistant Professor, Department of Interventional Radiology, Northwestern University Feinberg School of Medicine; Medical Director, Department of Interventional Radiology, Northwestern Memorial Hospital, Chicago, Illinois

BYUNG IHN CHOI, MD
Professor of Radiology, Department of Radiology, Seoul National University College of Medicine, Seoul National University Hospital, Seoul, Republic of Korea

HOWARD B. CHRISMAN, MD
Associate Professor, Department of Radiology, Northwestern University Feinberg School of Medicine, Northwestern Memorial Hospital, Chicago, Illinois

PETER L. COOPERBERG, MDCM, FRCPC, FACR
Professor and Vice Chairman, Department of Radiology, University of British Columbia Faculty of Medicine, St. Paul's Hospital, Vancouver, British Columbia, Canada

ABRAHAM H. DACHMAN, MD
Professor, Director of Fellowship Programs, Department of Radiology, University of Chicago Pritzker School of Medicine, Chicago, Illinois

SUSAN DELANEY, MD, FRCPC
Lecturer, Department of Radiology, Dalhousie University Faculty of Medicine, Halifax; Staff Radiologist, Department of Radiology, Dartmouth General Hospital, Dartmouth, Nova Scotia, Canada

GERALD D. DODD III, MD
Professor and Chairman, Department of Radiology, University of Texas School of Medicine at San Antonio, University Hospital System, San Antonio, Texas

RONALD L. EISENBERG, MD
Department of Radiology, Beth Israel Deaconess, Harvard Medical School, Boston, Massachusetts. *Formerly*: Clinical Professor of Radiology, University of California, San Francisco, School of Medicine, San Francisco; University of California, Davis, School of Medicine, Davis, California

SUKRU MEHMET ERTURK, MD, PHD
Lecturer in Radiology, Harvard Medical School; Research Fellow, Department of Radiology, Brigham and Women's Hospital, Boston, Massachusetts; Radiologist, Department of Radiology, Sisli Etfal Training and Research Hospital, Istanbul, Turkey

SANDRA K. FERNBACH, MD
Professor of Radiology, Northwestern University Feinberg School of Medicine, Chicago; Pediatric Radiologist, Department of Radiology, Evanston Northwestern Healthcare, Evanston, Illinois

JULIA R. FIELDING, MD
Associate Professor, Director of Abdominal Imaging, Department of Radiology, University of North Carolina Medical Center, Chapel Hill, North Carolina

ELLIOT K. FISHMAN, MD
Professor of Radiology and Oncology, Johns Hopkins University School of Medicine; Attending Radiologist, Department of Radiology, Johns Hopkins Hospital, Baltimore, Maryland

FRANS-THOMAS FORK, MD, PHD
Associate Professor of Radiology, Department of Clinical Sciences/Medical Radiology, Lund University Faculty of Medicine; Consultant Radiologist, Department of Radiology, Malmo University Hospital, Malmo, Sweden

MARTIN C. FREUND, MD
Associate Professor, Department of Radiology, Medical University Innsbruck, Innsbruck, Austria

ANN S. FULCHER, MD
Professor and Chairman, Department of Radiology, Virginia Commonwealth University School of Medicine, Medical College of Virginia Hospitals and Physicians, Richmond, Virginia

EMMA E. FURTH, MD
Professor of Pathology and Laboratory Medicine, Department of Pathology, University of Pennsylvania School of Medicine, Hospital of the University of Pennsylvania, Philadelphia, Pennsylvania

HELENA GABRIEL, MD
Associate Professor, Department of Radiology, Northwestern University Feinberg School of Medicine; Director, Division of Ultrasound, Department of Radiology, Northwestern Memorial Hospital, Chicago, Illinois

ANA MARIA GACA, MD
Clinical Associate, Department of Radiology, Duke University Medical Center, Durham, North Carolina

GABRIELA GAYER, MD
Senior Lecturer, Department of Radiology, Sackler Faculty of Medicine, Tel Aviv University, Tel Aviv; Chief, CT Division, Department of Diagnostic Imaging, Assaf Harofeh Medical Center, Ramat-Gan, Israel

GARY G. GHAHREMANI, MD, FACR
Clinical Professor of Radiology, Department of Radiology, University of California, San Diego, School of Medicine, La Jolla, California; Emeritus Professor of Radiology, Northwestern University Feinberg School of Medicine, Chicago, Illinois

SETH N. GLICK, MD
Clinical Professor of Radiology, Department of Radiology, University of Pennsylvania School of Medicine, Philadelphia, Pennsylvania

MARGARET D. GORE, MD
Assistant Professor, Department of Radiology, Northwestern University Feinberg School of Medicine, Senior Attending Radiologist, Department of Radiology, Evanston Northwestern Healthcare, Evanston, Illinois

RICHARD M. GORE, MD
Professor of Radiology, Northwestern University Feinberg School of Medicine; Chief, Gastrointestinal Radiology Section, Evanston Northwestern Healthcare, Evanston, Illinois

NICHOLAS C. GOURTSOYIANNIS, MD
Professor, Department of Radiology, University of Crete Medical School; Chairman, Department of Radiology, University Hospital of Heraklion, Heraklion, Crete, Greece

DAVID HAHN, MD
Assistant Professor, Department of Radiology, Northwestern University Feinberg School of Medicine, Chicago; Section Chief, Department of Interventional Radiology; Director, ENH Endovascular Lab, Evanston Northwestern Healthcare, Evanston, Illinois

ROBERT A. HALVORSEN, MD, FACR
Professor, Department of Radiology, Division of Abdominal Imaging, Virginia Commonwealth University School of Medicine; Staff Radiologist, Medical College of Virginia Hospitals, Richmond, Virginia

NANCY A. HAMMOND, MD
Assistant Professor, Department of Radiology, Northwestern University Feinberg School of Medicine, Northwestern Memorial Hospital, Chicago, Illinois

MARJORIE HERTZ, MD
Professor Emeritus, Department of Radiology, Sackler Faculty of Medicine, Tel Aviv University, Tel Aviv; Attending Staff Radiologist, Department of Diagnostic Imaging, Sheba Medical Center, Maccabim, Israel

FREDERICK L. HOFF, MD
Associate Professor, Department of Radiology, Northwestern University Feinberg School of Medicine; Staff Radiologist, Department of Diagnostic Radiology, Northwestern Memorial Hospital, Chicago, Illinois

CAROLINE L. HOLLINGSWORTH, MD, MPH
Assistant Professor, Department of Radiology, Division of Pediatric Radiology, Duke University School of Medicine, Durham, North Carolina

KAREN M. HORTON, MD
Associate Professor, The Russell H. Morgan Department of Radiology and Radiological Sciences, Johns Hopkins University School of Medicine, Baltimore, Maryland

JILL E. JACOBS, MD
Associate Professor of Radiology, New York University School of Medicine; Chief of Cardiac Imaging, Department of Radiology, New York University Medical Center, New York, New York

WERNER R. JASCHKE, MD, PHD
Professor and Chairman, Department of Radiology, Medical University Innsbruck, Innsbruck, Austria

BRUCE R. JAVORS, MD
Professor of Clinical Radiology, Department of Radiology, New York Medical College, Valhalla; Chairman, Department of Radiology, St. Vincent's Hospital–Manhattan, New York, New York

BRONWYN JONES, MD, FRACP, FRCR
Professor of Radiology, The Russell H. Morgan Department of Radiology and Radiological Sciences, Johns Hopkins University School of Medicine; Radiologist, Department of Radiology; Director, Johns Hopkins Swallowing Center, Johns Hopkins Hospital, Baltimore, Maryland; Editor-in-Chief, *Dysphagia*, Springer Publishers, New York, New York

MANNUDEEP K. KALRA, MD
Clinical Fellow, Department of Radiology, Harvard Medical School/Massachusetts General Hospital, Boston, Massachusetts

ANA L. KEPPKE, MD
Radiology Resident, Department of Radiology, Advocate Illinois Masonic Medical Center, Chicago, Illinois

STANLEY TAESON KIM, MD
Instructor, Department of Radiology, Northwestern University Feinberg School of Medicine; Interventional Radiologist, Department of Radiology, Northwestern Memorial Hospital; Interventional Radiologist, Department of Medical Imaging, Children's Memorial Hospital, Chicago, Illinois

MICHAEL L. KOCHMAN, MD, FACP
Professor of Medicine, Department of Medicine, Gastroenterology Division, University of Pennsylvania School of Medicine, Hospital of the University of Pennsylvania, Philadelphia, Pennsylvania

JOHN C. LAPPAS, MD
Professor, Department of Radiology, Indiana University School of Medicine; Chief of Abdominal Imaging, Indiana University Medical Center/Clarian Health, Wishard Memorial Hospital, Indianapolis, Indiana

THOMAS C. LAUENSTEIN, MD
Assistant Professor, Department of Radiology, Emory University School of Medicine, Emory University Hospital, Atlanta, Georgia

IGOR LAUFER, MD
Professor of Radiology, Department of Radiology, University of Pennsylvania School of Medicine; Staff, Gastrointestinal Radiology Section, Hospital of the University of Pennsylvania, Philadelphia, Pennsylvania

JEONG MIN LEE, MD
Associate Professor, Department of Radiology, Seoul National University College of Medicine, Seoul National University Hospital, Seoul, South Korea

KANG HOON LEE, MD
Staff Radiologist, Body Imaging Section, Department of
Radiology, University of North Carolina Medical Center,
Chapel Hill, North Carolina

MARC S. LEVINE, MD
Professor of Radiology, Advisory Dean, University of
Pennsylvania School of Medicine; Chief, Gastrointestinal
Radiology Section, University of Pennsylvania Medical
Center, Philadelphia, Pennsylvania

RUSSELL N. LOW, MD
Medical Director, Sharp and Children's MRI Center,
Department of Radiology, Sharp Memorial Hospital, San
Diego, California

MICHAEL MACARI, MD
Associate Professor, Section Chief, Department of Radiology,
New York University School of Medicine; Tish Hospital,
New York, New York

ROBERT L. MACCARTY, MD, FACR
Professor, Department of Radiology, Mayo Clinic College of
Medicine; Consultant, Mayo Clinic, Mayo Foundation,
Rochester, Minnesota

DEAN D. T. MAGLINTE, MD, FACR
Professor, Department of Radiology, Indiana University
School of Medicine; Attending Radiologist, Indiana
University Medical Center, Indianapolis, Indiana

CHARLES S. MARN, MD
Associate Professor of Radiology and Gastroenterology,
Medical College of Wisconsin; Chief, Gastrointestinal
Radiology, Department of Radiology, Froedtert Memorial
Lutheran Hospital, Milwaukee, Wisconsin

GABRIELE MASSELLI, MD
Staff Radiologist, Consultant, Abdominal and Pelvic MRI,
Radiology Department, Umberto I Hospital, La Sapienza
University, Rome, Italy

ALAN H. MAURER, MD
Professor of Radiology and Internal Medicine, Department
of Radiology, Temple University School of Medicine; Director
of Nuclear Medicine, Department of Radiology, Temple
University Hospital, Philadelphia, Pennsylvania

JOSEPH PATRICK MAZZIE, DO
Chief Resident, Department of Radiology, St. Vincent's
Hospital and Medical Center, New York, New York

ALEC J. MEGIBOW, MD, MPH, FACR
Professor, Department of Radiology, New York University
School of Medicine, New York, New York

UDAY K. MEHTA, MD
Assistant Professor of Radiology, Department of Radiology,
Northwestern University Feinberg School of Medicine;
Diagnostic Radiologist, Evanston Hospital, Evanston, Illinois

JAMES M. MESSMER, MD, MED
Professor, Senior Associate Dean for Medical Education,
Department of Radiology, Virginia Commonwealth
University School of Medicine, Richmond, Virginia

MORTON A. MEYERS, MD, FACR, FACG
Distinguished Professor, Departments of Radiology and
Internal Medicine, Stony Brook School of Medicine, Stony
Brook, New York

FRANK H. MILLER, MD
Professor, Department of Radiology, Northwestern University
Feinberg School of Medicine; Director, Body Imaging Section
and Fellowship, Chief, Gastrointestinal Radiology,
Northwestern Memorial Hospital, Chicago, Illinois

KOENRAAD J. MORTELE, MD
Associate Professor, Department of Radiology, Harvard
Medical School; Associate Director, Division of Abdominal
Imaging and Intervention; Director, Abdominal and Pelvic
MRI, CME, Department of Radiology, Brigham and Women's
Hospital, Boston, Massachusetts

KAREN A. MOURTZIKOS, MD
Assistant Professor, Department of Radiology, Division of
Nuclear Medicine, New York University School of Medicine,
New York, New York

SARAVANAN NAMASIVAYAM, MD, DNB, DHA*
Research Fellow, Department of Radiology, Division of
Abdominal Imaging and Intervention, Harvard University/
Massachusetts General Hospital, Boston, Massachusetts
*Deceased

VAMSI R. NARRA, MD, FRCR
Associate Professor of Radiology, Co-Chief, Body MRI, Co-
Director, Body MRI Fellowship, Mallinckrodt Institute of
Radiology, Washington University in St. Louis School of
Medicine; Chief, Clinical Operations, Barnes-Jewish West
County Hospital, St. Louis, Missouri

RENDON C. NELSON, MD
Professor and Vice-Chair, Department of Radiology, Duke
University School of Medicine, Durham, North Carolina

ALBERT A. NEMCEK, JR., MD
Professor, Department of Radiology, Northwestern University
Feinberg School of Medicine; Attending Staff, Department of
Radiology, Northwestern Memorial Hospital, Chicago, Illinois

GERALDINE MOGAVERO NEWMARK, MD
Assistant Professor, Department of Radiology, Northwestern
University Feinberg School of Medicine; Chief, Section of
Body Imaging, Department of Radiology, Evanston
Northwestern Healthcare, Evanston, Illinois

PAUL NIKOLAIDIS, MD
Associate Professor of Radiology, Department of Radiology,
Northwestern University Feinberg School of Medicine;
Chicago, Illinois

DAVID J. OTT, MD
Professor of Radiology, Department of Radiologic Sciences, Wake Forest University School of Medicine; Staff Radiologist, Section of Abdominal Imaging, Wake Forest University Baptist Medical Center, Winston-Salem, North Carolina

NICKOLAS PAPANIKOLAOU, PHD
Biomedical Engineer, Research Associate, Department of Radiology, University of Crete Medical School, Heraklion, Crete, Greece

ERIK K. PAULSON, MD
Professor, Department of Radiology, Duke University School of Medicine; Chief, Abdominal Imaging Division, Department of Radiology, Duke University Medical Center, Durham, North Carolina

F. SCOTT PERELES, MD
Salinas Valley Radiologists, Director, Magnetic Resonance Imaging, Coastal Valley Imaging, Salinas, California

CHRISTINE M. PETERSON, MD
Clinical Instructor, Mallinckrodt Institute of Radiology, Washington University in St. Louis School of Medicine, St. Louis, Missouri

VIKRAM A. RAO, MD
Instructor of Radiology, Department of Radiology, Northwestern University Feinberg School of Medicine, Chicago; Staff Radiologist, Evanston Northwestern Healthcare, Evanston, Illinois

RICHARD D. REDVANLY, MD
Radiologist, MR Body Imaging Section, Charlotte Radiology, Charlotte, North Carolina

PABLO R. ROS, MD, MPH
Professor of Radiology, Department of Radiology, Harvard Medical School; Executive Vice Chair, Department of Radiology, Brigham and Women's Hospital; Chief, Department of Radiology, Dana Farber Cancer Institute, Boston, Massachusetts

SANJAY SAINI, MD
Professor of Radiology, Harvard Medical School; Vice Chairman, Department of Radiology, Massachusetts General Hospital, Boston, Massachusetts

RIAD SALEM, MD, MBA
Associate Professor, Department of Radiology, Northwestern University Feinberg School of Medicine; Director of Interventional Oncology, Department of Radiology, Northwestern Memorial Hospital, Chicago, Illinois

KUMARESAN SANDRASEGARAN, MD
Assistant Professor, Department of Radiology, Indiana University School of Medicine, Indianapolis, Indiana

KENT T. SATO, MD
Assistant Professor, Department of Interventional Radiology, Northwestern University Feinberg School of Medicine, Chicago, Illinois

CHRISTOPHER D. SCHEIREY, MD
Clinical Instructor, Department of Diagnostic Radiology, Tufts University School of Medicine, Boston; Staff Radiologist, Department of Diagnostic Radiology, Lahey Clinic Medical Center, Burlington, Massachusetts

FRANCIS J. SCHOLZ, MD
Clinical Professor, Department of Radiology, Tufts University School of Medicine, Boston; Radiologist, Department of Diagnostic Radiology, Lahey Clinic Medical Center, Burlington, Massachusetts

ALI SHIRKHODA, MD
Clinical Professor of Radiology, Department of Radiology, University of California, Irvine, Irvine, California; Clinical Professor of Radiology, Department of Radiology, Wayne State University School of Medicine, Detroit; Director, Division of Diagnostic Imaging, William Beaumont Hospital, Royal Oak, Michigan

PAUL M. SILVERMAN, MD
Department of Radiology, Division of Diagnostic Imaging, MD Anderson Medical Center, Houston, Texas

STUART G. SILVERMAN, MD
Professor, Department of Radiology, Harvard Medical School; Director, Abdominal Imaging and Intervention, Director, CT scan, Director, Cross-sectional Imaging Service, Department of Radiology, Brigham and Women's Hospital, Boston, Massachusetts

JOVITAS SKUCAS, MD
Professor Emeritus, Department of Imaging Science, University of Rochester School of Medicine and Dentistry; Attending Radiologist, Department of Imaging Science, Strong Memorial Hospital, Rochester, New York

WILLIAM C. SMALL, MD, PHD
Associate Professor, Director of Abdominal Imaging, Department of Radiology, Emory University School of Medicine, Atlanta, Georgia

CLAIRE H. SMITH, MD, FACR
Professor, Rush Medical College; Senior Attending Radiologist, Section Director, Gastrointestinal Radiology, Department of Diagnostic Radiology and Nuclear Medicine, Rush University Medical Center, Chicago, Illinois

ROBERT H. SMITH, MD
Director, Department of Vascular and Interventional Radiology, Roper St. Francis Healthcare, Charleston, South Carolina

SAT SOMERS, MBCHB, FRCPC, FFRRCSI
Professor, Department of Radiology, Michael G. DeGroote School of Medicine, McMaster University Faculty of Health Sciences, Hamilton, Ontario, Canada

ALLISON L. SUMMERS, MD
Instructor in Radiology, Department of Radiology, Northwestern University Feinberg School of Medicine, Northwestern Memorial Hospital, Chicago, Illinois

RAJEEV SURI, MD
Assistant Professor, Department of Radiology, University of Texas School of Medicine at San Antonio; Associate Director, Radiology Residency Program, University of Texas Health Sciences Center at San Antonio; Interim Section Chief, Department of Interventional Radiology, University Hospital System; Director, Department of Interventional Radiology, Audie L. Murphy Veterans Affairs Medical Center, San Antonio, Texas

RICHARD A. SZUCS, MD
Clinical Assistant Professor of Radiology, Virginia Commonwealth University School of Medicine; Chairman, Department of Radiology, Bon Secours St. Mary's Hospital, Richmond, Virginia

MARK TALAMONTI, MD
Associate Professor, Chairman, Department of Surgery, Northwestern University Feinberg School of Medicine, Evanston Northwestern Healthcare, Chicago, Illinois

ANDREW J. TAYLOR, MD
Professor of Radiology, Department of Radiology, University of Wisconsin School of Medicine and Public Health, Chief of Gastrointestinal Radiology, University of Wisconsin Hospital and Clinics, Madison, Wisconsin

RUEDI F. THOENI, MD
Professor, Department of Radiology, University of California, San Francisco, School of Medicine; Chief, Department of Abdominal Imaging, San Francisco General Hospital; Staff Radiologist, Moffitt-Long Hospital, San Francisco, California

WILLIAM MOREAU THOMPSON, MD
Professor, Department of Radiology, Duke University School of Medicine, Durham, North Carolina

RANISTA TONGDEE, MD
Clinical Fellow, Department of Body MR Imaging, Mallinckrodt Institute of Radiology, St. Louis, Missouri; Instructor in Radiology, Department of Diagnostic Radiology, Abdominal Section, Siriraj Hospital, Bangkok, Thailand

MITCHELL E. TUBLIN, MD
Associate Professor, Department of Radiology, University of Pittsburgh School of Medicine; Chief, Ultrasound Section, Department of Radiology Abdominal Imaging, University of Pittsburgh Medical Center, University of Pittsburgh Hospital, Pittsburgh, Pennsylvania

MARY ANN TURNER, MD
Professor, Department of Radiology, Virginia Commonwealth University School of Medicine; Director, Gastrointestinal Radiology, Virginia Commonwealth University Medical Center, Richmond, Virginia

SEAN M. TUTTON, MD, FSIR
Associate Professor, Department of Radiology, Medical College of Wisconsin, Milwaukee, Wisconsin

ROBERT L. VOGELZANG, MD
Professor, Department of Radiology, Northwestern University Feinberg School of Medicine; Chief of Interventional Radiology, Department of Radiology, Northwestern Memorial Hospital, Chicago, Illinois

PATRICK M. VOS, MD
Clinical Instructor, Department of Radiology, University of British Columbia Faculty of Medicine; Hospital Staff, Department of Radiology, St. Paul's Hospital, Vancouver, British Columbia, Canada

DAPHNA WEINSTEIN, MD
Surgeon, Surgery B, Assaf-Harofeh Medical Center, Zrifin, Ramat-Hasharon, Israel

NOEL N. WILLIAMS, MD
Director, Bariatric Surgery Program, Department of Gastrointestinal Surgery, Hospital of the University of Pennsylvania, Philadelphia, Pennsylvania

STEPHANIE R. WILSON, MD
Department of Diagnostic Imaging, Foothills Medical Center; Professor of Radiology, University of Calgary, Calgary, Alberta, Canada. *Formerly*: Professor of Diagnostic Imaging, University of Toronto; Head, Section of Ultrasound, Department of Medical Imaging, Toronto General Hospital, Toronto, Ontario, Canada

ELLEN L. WOLF, MD
Professor of Clinical Radiology, Albert Einstein College of Medicine; Chief of Gastrointestinal Radiology, Department of Radiology, Montefiore Medical Center, Bronx, New York

VAHID YAGHMAI, MD, MS
Associate Professor, Department of Radiology, Northwestern University Feinberg School of Medicine; Medical Director of CT, Department of Radiology, Northwestern Memorial Hospital, Chicago, Illinois

SILAJA YITTA, MD
Resident, Department of Radiology, New York University Medical Center, New York, New York

RIVKA ZISSIN, MD
Senior Lecturer, Department of Radiology, Sackler Faculty of Medicine, Tel Aviv University, Tel Aviv; Head, CT Unit, Department of Diagnostic Imaging, Meir Medical Center, Kochav Yair, Israel

Preface

Since the publication in 1994 of the first edition of *Textbook of Gastrointestinal Radiology,* much has changed in our discipline. Technological advances have dramatically improved the capabilities of computed tomography (CT), magnetic resonance imaging (MRI), ultrasonography, fluoroscopy, and positron emission tomography (PET) for abdominal and pelvic imaging. CT has evolved from a single-detector row to multidetector rows that permit isotropic volumetric imaging, greatly expanding the clinical utility of this imaging technique. Multidetector CT has become the gold standard for evaluating the acute abdomen, as well as most abdominal and pelvic infectious, inflammatory, neoplastic, ischemic, vascular, and hemorrhagic disorders. CT colonography, CT enterography, and CT enteroclysis are now well-established methods for evaluating the colon and small bowel. CT angiography and venography are currently the preferred means for noninvasively evaluating the splanchnic circulation.

Innovations in software and hardware technology, such as faster pulse sequences, the development of parallel imaging, and improved coil design, have encouraged the growth of MRI. Magnetic resonance cholangiopancreatography (MRCP) has largely replaced diagnostic endoscopic retrograde cholangiopancreatography (ERCP), and at many institutions, MRI also has been increasingly performed as the primary staging examination for hepatic and pancreatic malignancies. MR angiography and venography also are widely used to assess the patency of abdominal and pelvic blood vessels, as well as for tumor invasion of these vessels.

The usefulness of abdominal ultrasound examination has been enhanced by the increasing application of color and power Doppler techniques and harmonic imaging, improvements in high-resolution transducers with greater fields of view, and identification of wider indications for the use of ultrasound contrast agents.

Digital radiography and digital fluoroscopy have dramatically altered the practice of gastrointestinal fluoroscopic procedures and barium studies, and the dissemination of picture archiving and communication systems (PACS) in most radiologic departments has transformed the abdominal radiologist's workday.

PET/CT has emerged as one of the most exciting applications of new technology in gastrointestinal radiology. Both functional and anatomic data can now be provided in a single image. This technique has gained wide acceptance for the initial staging and follow-up evaluation of primary colorectal and esophageal neoplasms and for the detection of lymph node and hepatic malignancies from other primary tumors.

To keep pace with these technological and scientific advances, every chapter of the third edition has been updated and revised. In addition, several chapters have been added (and a few were deleted), and nearly one third of the chapters have new authors to provide their topics with fresh insight and perspective.

Throughout this new edition, we have taken great care to maintain the fundamental goals of the first two editions for providing complete and up-to-date coverage of the state of the art in gastrointestinal radiology in a practical and usable form. As in the first two editions, our basic organizing principle is the integration of rapidly changing information, common sense, and good judgment in an orderly and useful approach for radiologic diagnosis and treatment. To this end, the text contains sections on general radiologic principles for evaluating the hollow viscera and solid organs and for performing and applying specific imaging and therapeutic techniques. Other sections present the clinical, radiologic, and pathologic aspects of disease in the various gastrointestinal organs. The chapters in these sections are designed to illustrate and integrate the spectrum of abnormalities seen with all diagnostic modalities available to the radiologist, including conventional radiography, barium studies, cholangiography, multidetector CT, ultrasonography, MRI, PET, PET/CT, and angiography. To make the book even more user friendly, the contributing authors have worked diligently—as have we—to eliminate redundancies and produce a shorter, more compact text. With the addition of color graphics and images, the book's format has been redesigned to facilitate reading and review.

Once again, we have been able to assemble an outstanding group of internationally recognized and renowned authors for the third edition. Their time, effort, cooperation, and expertise are greatly appreciated. As editors, we have tried to strike a balance between uniformity of style and individuality of author contributions, so that each contributor is able to speak in his or her own unique voice.

We hope that the collective efforts of the authors of the 130 chapters, as well as our own, have accomplished our goal of providing students and practitioners of gastrointestinal radiology with a valuable educational resource that is clear, interesting, and enjoyable to read.

Richard M. Gore, MD
Marc S. Levine, MD

Contents

VOLUME 1

Pharynx   STEPHEN E. RUBESIN, SECTION EDITOR

Esophagus

Stomach and Duodenum

Small Bowel   STEPHEN E. RUBESIN, SECTION EDITOR

Colon

VOLUME 2

General Radiologic Principles for Imaging and Intervention of the Solid Viscera

Gallbladder and Biliary Tract

Liver

Pancreas

Spleen

XIII Peritoneal Cavity

XIV Pediatric Disease

Common Clinical Problems

DVD Contents

VIII

General Radiologic Principles for Imaging and Intervention of the Solid Viscera

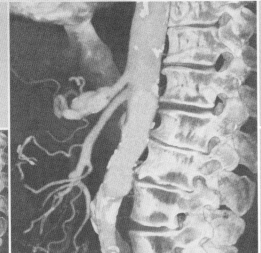
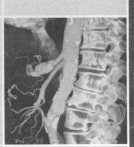

Computed Tomography of the Solid Abdominal Organs

Frederick L. Hoff, MD

HISTORICAL PERSPECTIVE

The practice of medicine was transformed by CT. Recognizing the importance of this technique, Cormack and Hounsfield were awarded The Nobel Prize in 1979 for their role in its development.[1] The first clinical CT unit was placed at Atkinson Morley's Hospital in England on October 1, 1971.[1] Each image took 4 minutes to acquire, and 2 days were needed to reconstruct the series. The clinical importance of CT was immediately appreciated; by 1976, 22 companies were manufacturing CT scanners, and in 1979, more than 1000 scanners were in use throughout the world. Since then, there has been continuous and dramatic improvement in both spatial and temporal resolution as a result of advances in both hardware and software design, particularly the development of helical and multidetector helical CT.

CREATING THE COMPUTED TOMOGRAPHY IMAGE

The fundamental concept of CT is to use multiple projections of an object to reconstruct the internal structure of that object.[2,3] The creation of a CT image can be divided into three steps. *Data acquisition* involves the actual exposure to radiation (scanning of the patient) with the creation of raw data; *image reconstruction* involves processing the raw data into a numerical matrix revealing the internal structure; and *image display* involves converting the numerical data matrix to a gray-scale image. Each of these will be discussed using conventional CT, and then the changes created by the advent of helical and multidetector helical CT will be described.

Data Acquisition

A radiographic tube and an array of detectors, as well as the associated electronics, are mounted on a track or frame called a *gantry*. The x-ray tube produces a fan-shaped beam of x-rays that interact with the patient via absorption or scattering; some of the x-rays pass through the patient to interact with the detector array. During data acquisition, the tube and detectors rotate around the patient, and the detectors repeatedly measure the number of x-rays transmitted through the patient. The amount of radiation transmitted to each detector and the gantry angle at the time of the measurement are recorded (Fig. 69-1). Typically, the detector array contains

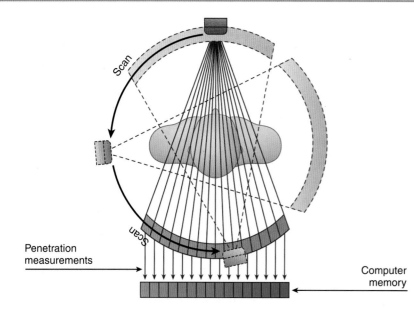

Figure 69-1. Three sample positions of data measurement in obtaining a single image. Data are collected from approximately 1000 positions during each revolution. At each position, measurements are obtained from each detector in the array; although the example shows 16 detectors, in actuality, 500 to 1000 are used. The entire group of measurements forms the raw data used to reconstruct the internal structure of the scanned object. (Modified from Sprawls P: Physical Principles of Medical Imaging. Gaithersburg, MD: Aspen, 1987.)

500 to 1000 detectors, each of which is sampled approximately 1000 times per revolution.[3] Each line of this information reflects the summation of the attenuation coefficients of all structures in that x-ray path. The entire data set forms the "raw data" from which an image is reconstructed. Conventional or incremental scanning is obtained by performing a series of individual scans during suspended respiration. After each scan, the patient breathes; the patient table is advanced; and in most machines, the tube and detector apparatus rewinds to begin another scan.[4]

Image Reconstruction

From the raw data, a digital image is created. A variety of techniques can be used to accomplish this; these rely on the principles of back projection, iterative formulas, or analytic formulas, either with or without Fourier transformation.[5] The result is a matrix of numbers; generally, a 512 × 512 matrix is used in abdominopelvic CT. Each number in this matrix is called a *pixel,* or picture element. Each pixel corresponds to a volume of tissue or voxel within the patient; the average density of the tissue within the voxel is represented by the pixel value. The difference in attenuation of the contents of a voxel relative to water is defined as the CT attenuation number and expressed in Hounsfield units (HU).[6]

Image Display

This digital image or number matrix is converted to a visual format for interpretation. A gray scale is used with the densest materials, such as bone (highest HU), being assigned lighter shades, whereas the least dense, such as air (most negative HU), are assigned darker shades. A problem arises in that display devices are limited to demonstrating approximately 60 shades of gray, and the human eye may distinguish as few as 30 shades; the 4096 CT numbers cannot be simply mapped without conversion. The wide range of numbers is converted for display by window width and level controls. The window level specifies the centering of the gray scale, and the choice of width specifies the numbers over which the gray scale is

to extend. For example, if the window level is set to 0 and the width is set to 500, every pixel number below −250 will be black and every pixel greater than 250 will be white; if there are 50 shades of gray, each would be assigned a range of 10 numbers with the middle gray used for the numbers adjacent to 0.

HELICAL COMPUTED TOMOGRAPHY

Helical or spiral CT involves a continuous rotation of the gantry as the patient is advanced at a steady rate thorough it, dispensing with the discrete steps of data acquisition in conventional CT.[4,7] This continuous rotation creates a volume set of raw data, which must then be segmented to create planar images. Introduced in 1989, the technology was rapidly accepted and distributed. The major advantages of helical scanning include rapid acquisition, unlimited ability to obtain overlapping images without increased radiation exposure, high-quality multiplanar reconstruction, and absence of respiratory misregistration.[8]

Helical CT introduced several unique new concepts that the physician must understand. The first reflects the relationship between the speed of the table and the speed of the gantry. This is described as the *pitch* and is defined as the table feed per 360-degree tube revolution divided by the width of the collimated beam (Fig. 69-2). When the patient movement is equal to the beam collimation, the pitch is 1. Increasing the pitch allows increased coverage in the z direction but with some increase in image noise. Use of pitches greater than 1 also decreases the radiation dose to the patient.[7]

A second important new concept introduced by helical CT is that of reconstruction increment and overlapping reconstructions. As with conventional CT, once the scan has been obtained, the image thickness cannot be changed. However, because the data acquisition is continuous, the location of the image center along the z-axis may be altered. This has two practical applications: it allows overlapping reconstructions for use in postprocessing without any increase in radiation dose to the patients, and it reduces volume averaging effect, which may lead to improved detection of small lesions[9] (Fig. 69-3).

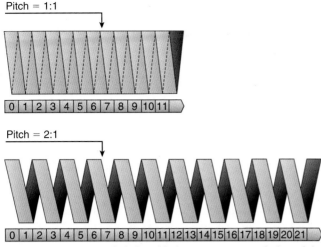

Figure 69-2. **Concept of pitch (table increment per revolution of the gantry over collimation).** Pitch of 1:1. The table increment is a constant 1 cm/s with a collimation of 1 cm (*top*). Pitch of 2:1 (*bottom*). The table increment is 2 cm/s with the 1-cm collimation. Advantages of pitches greater than 1 include increased coverage (20 cm versus 10 cm in this example with a 10-second acquisition) and decreased radiation exposure. However, there is increased noise and slice profile broadening with increased pitches. In clinical scanning of the abdomen, pitches of 1.3 to 2.0 are frequently used with single detector helical CT. (Modified from Zeman RK, Fox SH, Silverman PM, et al: Helical [spiral] CT of the abdomen. AJR 160:719-725, 1993.)

The demand to scan faster continued despite the dramatic improvement resulting from helical CT. This demand was met by increasing the rotational speed of the gantry and increasing the number of slices obtained with each revolution.[10] Rotation speed has been reduced to a fraction of a second with most high-end scanners having speeds of less than 0.5 sec/rotation. Increasing the number of slices obtained per revolution was the next evolution of CT technology: multidetector helical CT (MDCT), also called multidetector-row CT and multislice CT (MSCT).[11]

MULTIDETECTOR COMPUTED TOMOGRAPHY

MDCT machines segment the detector array along the *z*-axis of the patient, allowing multiple rows of data in this plane to be obtained simultaneously. Elscint (Haifa, Israel) introduced the first MDCT, a dual-slice unit, in 1992. However, it was not until several manufacturers introduced four-channel machines in 1998 that the technology exploded. The technology behind MDCT is fascinating but largely beyond the scope of this chapter. Several reviews and books have been published to which the interested reader is referred.[12-15] As with other improvements in CT technology, the major advantage of multiple detector rows is an increase in performance that can be used to shorten scan duration, increase scan range, and improve resolution. In imaging, the solid abdominal organs radiologists have exploited both the improved resolution and speed afforded by this new technology.[16] A significant portion of the performance gain has been used to obtain images of the organs multiple times during a single bolus of contrast material.[17]

When discussing MDCT, it is important to distinguish between the number of channels and the number of detector rows. Manufacturers and radiologist often refer to, for example, "four-row" or "16-row" MDCT; however, this is a misnomer, and referring to "four-channel" or "16-channel" MDCT is more accurate. The number of data *channels* determines the number of data streams that can be acquired simultaneously from the detector. The number of detector rows is the number of segmented detectors in the z-axis; this number is often greater than the number of channels[18] (Fig. 69-4). However, as the number of channels increases, this discrepancy decreases.

Another important new concept must be considered with MDCT: acquisition thickness versus image thickness. Prior to MDCT, image thickness was an acquisition parameter. Once this was chosen and the patient was scanned, it could not be altered. However, with multidetector machines, image

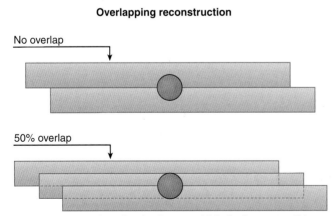

Figure 69-3. **Use of overlapping images with helical CT.** A small lesion may be difficult to visualize because of volume averaging effects if it is centered between two adjacent images as demonstrated on the *upper example* where the "nodule" is centered between the top and bottom images. With the use of a 50% overlap, the nodule would be well visualized on the middle of the three images (*lower example*). There is no additional scanning time or radiation exposure to the patient.

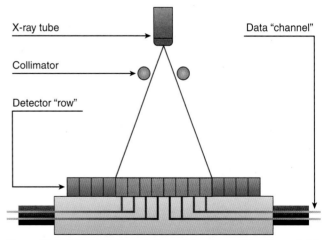

Figure 69-4. **Differentiation of channel from row: Four-channel, 16-row MDCT.** In this example the gray boxes represent the 16 detector rows. The x-ray beam is collimated to expose the central eight rows. The radiation information obtained from each pair of central detector rows is combined electronically behind the detector to create four data streams, one for each of the four channels. The bold yellow lines demonstrate the channels. Common usage is to refer to this as a "four-row" MDCT, meaning "four-channel" MDCT.

thickness is a reconstruction parameter; that is, one can change the image thickness after the patient has been scanned. Various reconstructed section widths are available; the number of choices varies by the manufacturer. It is important to remember that an image cannot be created with an image width thinner than the acquisition collimation. As long as the raw data are available, additional images can be created at a different thickness.

Multidetector row CT has been used in imaging of the solid abdominal organs in several ways. There has been a reduction in slice width and scan acquisition time for routine abdomen and pelvis imaging. Scanning of a single organ, such as the liver or the pancreas, at multiple times during the rapid administration of intravenous contrast (*multiphase studies*) is much easier to accomplish than on single-detector helical CT and has become part of the routine armamentarium of the radiologist. Finally, the use of very thin images during the arterial phase of injection has become helpful in CT angiography, often combined with routine images of the organ of interest.

DOSIMETRY AND DOSE REDUCTION

There has been a significant increase in both the public and professional awareness of radiation dose in medical imaging.[19] As CT is a relatively high-dose procedure and is used for a widening array of applications, it has received a large share of the attention.[20] CT scanning is now the highest single contributor to manmade radiation exposure to the population, second only to background radiation.[20] The National Radiological Protection Board in Great Britain estimated that in 1999 while only 4% of diagnostic procedures were CTs, they contributed to 40% of overall medical radiation exposure.[21] Unfortunately, calculating the radiation dose in CT is complex, leading to difficulty is providing simple answers to questions of dose.[22] Important principles include the following: the dose is administered only to a certain volume of the body, not to the entire patient; the dose can vary considerably from scanner to scanner and from image to image depending on the

technical parameters set; and the percentage of the dose delivered centrally compared with the skin dose is much greater with CT than with conventional radiography.[2,3]

Absorbed dose is the energy absorbed per unit mass; it is measured in Gray (Gy) and its subunit milliGray (mGy). Fundamental CT absorbed dose descriptors include *volume CT dose index (mGy)* ($CTDI_{vol}$), which reflects the average radiation dose within a scan volume, and the *dose-length product (mGy cm)* (DLP), which reflects the radiation dose over the entire scan length. One or both of these values is displayed on the operator console of newer CT machines. The other descriptor of importance is the *effective dose (mSv)*, which estimates biological risk. This is almost always the number a clinician or patient wants to know when they ask, "What is the radiation dose?" of a CT examination. Determining the effective dose quickly is difficult, as it requires consideration of the body part scanned as well as the size of the patient, in addition to the absorbed dose. Typical effective dose values for abdominopelvic CT scans range from 8 to 16 mSv.[20,23] It is often helpful to remember that the range of background radiation in the United States is from 1 to 10 mSv with an average of about 3.6 mSv. Several excellent reviews are available for those interested in further information.[24-26]

The underlying geometry and physics of MDCT impart a larger radiation dose than single-slice helical or conventional CT.[27] This is due in part to the radiation penumbra. In MDCT, the penumbra contributes to radiation dose but not the image and therefore is considered "wasted" radiation exposure. On a positive note, the relative contribution of the penumbra to dose decreases as the number of simultaneously obtained slices increases; thus, a 16-channel machine is more efficient than a four-channel if other factors are held constant (Fig. 69-5).

The recent interest by the public as well as regulatory agencies has prompted development of several innovative technical advances that decrease radiation exposure.[24] However, the most important potential way to decrease dose is appropriate adaptation of the technique to patient size.[28] This is particularly important when scanning pediatric

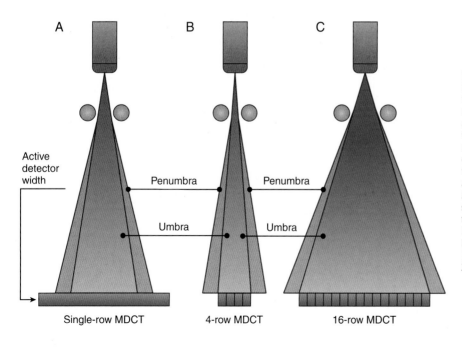

Figure 69-5. Dose efficiency related to penumbra. A. Single row helical CT. All of the radiation falls on active detector (blue in all examples) for maximum efficiency using both the beam umbra and penumbra. **B.** With MDCT as demonstrated for a four-channel scanner, the penumbra does not fall on the active detectors, leading to decreased efficiency. The increase in dose ranges from 10% to 100% depending on the scanner and the slice width chosen. **C.** For 16-channel MDCT, the penalty is decreased as the penumbra stays constant but the portion of the beam used to create the images is greater. (Modified from Nagal HD: Radiation dose issues with MSCT. In Reiser MF, Takahashi M, Modic M, Becker CR [eds]: Multislice CT, 2nd ed. Berlin, Springer, 2004, pp 17-26.)

patients.[29,30] Manufacturers have taken this basic concept and extrapolated it to within the individual patient. CT scanners are now able to modulate tube current continuously during the examination. This modulation occurs in both the x and y planes and throughout the scan length (z-axis). In the xy plane, many portions of the human body are elliptical. Therefore, lower doses may be used when the x-ray transverses the body in the thinner anteroposterior plane as opposed to the larger laterorostral plane without significant increase in the resultant image noise. Likewise, in the z-axis the body varies in volume and density. Less radiation will produce good images through the chest, which is mostly air compared with the abdomen. Different manufacturers have approached the problem in slightly different ways and the operator choices regarding milliampere settings are now significantly different from scanner to scanner.[31]

The tendency to use MDCT to scan greater distances or scan the same area multiple times is an additional and important source of increased radiation dose in MDCT.[25] It is important that the radiologist consider the scan dose when creating and assigning protocols. Except when high quality thin (less than 2 mm) images are required, the newest MDCT units generally require less dose than conventional CT or a dose similar to helical single-channel CT obtained with a pitch of 2.[15]

INTRAVENOUS CONTRAST PRINCIPLES

Iodine-based intravenous contrast material should be routinely used in CT of the solid abdominal organs. When properly used, such contrast material improves lesion detection and characterization. However, when used improperly, contrast can actually decrease lesion detection.[32] In the early days of conventional CT, abdominal enhancement was described as consisting of three phases: bolus, nonequilibrium, and equilibrium.[33,34] While these phases are no longer as critical in protocol planning as they were with conventional CT, it is important to remember that scanning of the liver should be completed before the equilibrium phase, which generally begins about 90 to 120 seconds after injection.[35] This could be relevant when either patient or technical problems cause an unplanned increase in the scan delay.

With helical and MDCT, enhancement characteristics of abdominal structures have been more completely studied[36] (Fig. 69-6). The *early arterial phase* is a common name given to the period when a significant amount of contrast is in the arterial system but little to no contrast is in the venous system or organs. In the abdomen, this generally occurs 15 to 25 seconds after the initiation of injection in most patients. The *late arterial phase* describes the time when contrast is entering hypervascular tumors and vascular organs in significant amounts; this is generally from 30 to 45 seconds after the beginning of the injection. Some have termed this the *portal inflow phase*, as contrast is generally seen in the portal vein also, but not the hepatic veins; however, the enhancement of the liver parenchyma in this phase is primarily due to hepatic arterial flow. Finally, the period from 50 to 80 seconds after the injection is referred to as the *portal venous phase* and is the time during which the liver is maximally enhanced; this delay reflects the predominate portal venous supply of the liver. Contrast reaches the liver via the portal vein only after it transverses the mesentery and bowel. This phase has

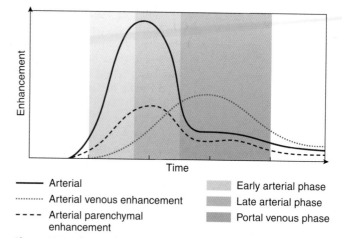

Figure 69-6. Phases of enhancement. The curves display the density of arteries, arterial parenchymal enhancement (such as seen in hypervascular tumors or the pancreas) and portal venous enhancement of the liver. The boxes demonstrate the timing of acquisition of each phase for a hypothetical scanner. Each of the three phases is acquired while contrast enhancement difference is greatest between the desired structure and other structures.

also been called the *hepatic parenchymal phase* and the *hepatic venous phase*.[36]

Iodinated contrast is available in varying concentrations. Sixty percent iodine concentrations (300 mg/mL) are most commonly used for abdominal applications. However, varying concentrations have been studied with a recent trend in using higher concentrations.[37] One rationale for use of higher concentrations (350 to 370 mg/mL available in the United States; 400 mg/mL elsewhere) is the ability to get a greater number of iodine atoms into the organ of interest with the same injection rate.[38] Lower injections rates may be safer and easier to use.[39] Use of higher concentrations has been shown to improve detection of hypervascular hepatocellular carcinoma compared with 300 mg/mL preparations.[40]

Injection of contrast material should always be performed with a power injector. This ensures that the desired injection rates and timing are achieved. Both the rate at which the contrast material should be administered and the length of the scan delay (time from initiation of contrast injection to time of initiation of scanning) have been studied extensively.[41] As the rapidity of acquisition increased with helical and MDCT, a complete reevaluation of contrast administration strategies has been required.[35] Prior to helical CT, the greatest concern was administering the contrast so to maximize the time to equilibrium phase in order to allow scan completion before equilibrium began. This is now easily accomplished, and the focus has been on determining the strategies to maximize visualization of various normal and pathologic structures at certain points of enhancement.

There are two additional questions to be answered with regard to intravenous contrast administration: the amount and method of administration. All currently used iodine-based contrast agents distribute rapidly into the extracellular space. Thus, the enhancement of vessels and organs depends not only on the dose but also on the rate of injection and the length of time from the beginning of the injection to imaging (scan delay) (Fig. 69-7).

The dose of contrast administered depends on scanner type and the specific organ of interest. Because of the various concentrations available, dose is best considered in grams of iodine. The increased speed of helical CT and MDCT has allowed dose reductions when the primary purpose of contrast is vascular opacification. However, adequate opacification of the hepatic parenchyma to optimize detection of focal lesions probably is not as dependent on speed; it has been recommended that a minimum dose of 38 g (125 mL of a 300 mg/mL formulation) should be used with helical scanning.[42] For general parenchymal organ imaging, a dose of 120 to 150 mL of 300 mg/mL to 370 mg/ml contrast is generally used.[43] The volume of contrast administered to adults undergoing CT has routinely been held constant regardless of the patient size. By adjusting the dose according to patient weight, a lower overall amount of contrast material may be used creating a cost savings while maintaining image quality. A weight-based dose of 1.5 mL/kg was found acceptable in most patients for routine survey examinations.[44]

In general, contrast material is injected at relatively high rates to obtain rapid opacification of vessels and organs and avoid imaging during the equilibrium phase. The degree of enhancement as well as the time of maximum enhancement are both directly related to the injection rate.[45] Rates for routine abdominal studies generally are from 2 to 3 mL/s; this is adequate to image the abdomen during the portal venous phase of enhancement. With multiphasic imaging a more rapid bolus helps to separate the different phases; for example, with a higher rate a greater volume of contrast is administered to obtain a high degree of hepatic arterial enhancement in the liver before portal venous contamination begins.[46] Rates for hepatic examinations generally range from 3 to 6 mL/s.

The scan delay is defined as the time between the initiation of injection and the initiation of image acquisition. The delay chosen depends primarily on the phase of enhancement one wishes to image. Routine abdominal studies are ideally performed during the portal venous phase; CT angiographic images are obtained during the early arterial phase and hepatic parenchymal arterial studies during the late arterial phase. The scan delay also depends on how fast the scanner is—one must consider the contrast enhancement at the end of the scan as well as at the beginning. Ideally the scan is centered at the peak of the desired phase. Thus, with the slowest scanners one might have to begin before the ideal opacification is reached to insure that at the end of the scan the enhancement phase is still appropriate; conversely, with the fastest scanners, the delay is greater to center the acquisition at the desired enhancement peak (Fig. 69-7). The optimal scan delay depends on the injection rate and volume administered; when the rate is changed, the delay may require adjustment as well.[47-50]

The terminology used to describe the contrast administration in CT varies in the literature, by local custom and with the organ of interest. Multiphase studies are usually referred to by the number of series obtained after the injection of contrast; for example a "biphasic" CT of the liver would usually include two contrast-enhanced scans; it may or may not include a precontrast scan. If a precontrast scan were included, some would term this a triphasic examination while others would not.

As the science of contrast administration has progressed, patient-dependent factors have become more obvious. Most institutions use nearly the same technique for most adult patients. However, differences in cardiac output, weight, time

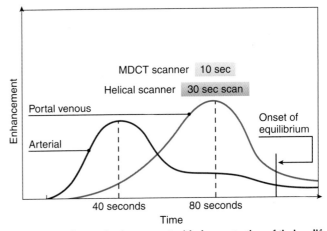

Figure 69-7. Phases of enhancement with demonstration of timing differences based on machine type. If a series of images through the liver is desired at peak parenchymal enhancement, the scan delay will vary with the length of time the scanner takes to image the entire organ. Shown are two examples: a four-channel MDCT that requires 10 seconds to scan the liver and a single-channel helical scanner that requires 30 seconds to complete the images.

from last meal, and fluid status affect the actual enhancement obtained on the images.[51,52] In an effort to tailor the examination to the specific patient, automated systems are available that initiate scanning when the optimal enhancement has been reached.[53,54] In general, these systems use a series of low-dose scans obtained at a single location within the abdomen. A region of interest cursor is placed on the aorta or liver, and a threshold density level is set. After the beginning of the contrast administration, scans are obtained every second or so until the density measured within the region of interest reaches a threshold value. At that time, the diagnostic scan is begun.

Another technique becoming more popular, particularly with the use of 64-channel CT machines and in CT angiography, is the use of a "saline chaser." This was originally described with a technique of placing both the contrast and saline in one injector chamber, but now dual bore (one piston for the contrast and one for the saline) injectors are available as well.[55] The saline serves two functions: it increases the efficiency of the contrast used as no contrast will remain in the tubing or in the peripheral circulation of the arm at the end of the injection, and it maintains high concentrations of contrast in the circulation longer by preserving the bolus shape. This in turn has been used to decrease the total dose of contrast administered.[56]

Other intravenous contrast agents are being explored, primarily to image the liver with the goal of improving lesion detection and characterization. These contrast agents target either the reticuloendothelial system (Kupffer cells) or hepatocytes. However, iodine is the only intravenous agent currently used routinely in abdominopelvic CT.

INTERPRETATION PRINCIPLES

The conventional approach to CT interpretation is based on "hard-copy" film. A number of forces have changed interpretation from a film-based environment to "soft-copy" or monitor-based environment. The number of images obtained in abdominal studies is climbing as multidetector techniques allow the creation of more (usually thinner) images. Multiple phase acquisitions and use of multiplanar reformatations leads to the creation of even more images. Filming this number of images is not practical. Picture archiving and communications system (PACS) methods have helped manage these images as well as allowed enterprise wide simultaneous visualization of images with central secure data storage. Interpretation from a monitor in a cine-based format leads to an increased rate of pulmonary nodule detection as well as improved visualization of the pancreas.[57,58] CT interpretation is moving from image analysis to volumetric analysis; this has been defined as the treatment of data not as a stack of images but as a volume of voxels.[59]

Certain principles are the same with both film and monitor interpretation. Images should be displayed with window width and level settings appropriate for differentiation of solid-containing, fluid-containing, and air-containing structures ("body window," level = 40-70, width = 380-550). Many radiologists find narrower width ("liver window," level = 60-80, width = 125-150) images of the upper abdomen helpful, and viewing of these windows is suggested to aid in identification of lesions with minimal density difference from normal liver.[60,61] Varieties of measurements are made to clarify findings and include objective data in the radiology report. Regions of interest are created to obtain the average density of the contents inscribed to help lesion characterization. Size measurements on conventional CT images should be performed in only the scanned plane (generally axial), but measurements from helical data sets are also accurate in the longitudinal or z-axis.[62] Bidimensional measurements are made by determining the longest single diameter, then the longest dimension that is perpendicular to the first.[63]

POSTPROCESSING

One of the important advantages of helical acquisition is that a true volume data set is obtained. Planar reformations in sagittal, coronal, or oblique planes are the simplest of the postprocessing techniques and with the newest machines can be obtained automatically. These can be helpful in localizing masses or disease to a specific space or organ. For example, the origin of a mass located between the liver, adrenal, and right kidney may be more convincingly demonstrated on a longitudinal reformation. Clinicians particularly appreciate coronal images, which they can quickly assimilate as it more closely replicates the anatomy seen on physical exam and at surgery. Curved planar reformations may be helpful in placing the entire extent of a single object with a tortuous or curving course on a single image. This technique is commonly used to display the pancreatic duct or a vessel on a single image and is particularly helpful in communicating with referring physicians.[64] The term three-dimensional is used to describe such techniques such as maximum-intensity projection (MIP) and volume rendering (VR). MIP techniques are simple and particularly suited for angiographic simulation procedures.[65] VR adds a variety of effects, such as semitransparent views, improved surface definition, which enables simultaneous visualization of the vessels and parenchyma.[66] Minimum-intensity projections (MinIP) techniques are also available and helpful in imaging the biliary system. Applications of these postprocessing techniques in CT of the solid abdomen organs includes presurgical planning and staging of tumors in the biliary tree, liver, and pancreas.[67,68] Preoperative evaluation of patients undergoing hepatic transplantation with CT angiography is as accurate as conventional angiography.[69] Preoperative evaluation in pancreatic cancer can provide both staging and preoperative planning information.[70]

SCANNING PROTOCOLS

Exact scanning protocols depend on many variables including purpose of imaging, patient related factors such as weight and venous access as well as scanner type and manufacturer. Scanning protocols should be tailored for the specific clinical indication.[71] Some basic principles are provided below from which exact protocols may be derived.

Abdominopelvic Survey

Survey examinations of the abdomen are often obtained for conditions such as abdominal pain, possible abscess, and possible mass. If available, helical scanning should be used for all abdominopelvic applications. For a general survey examination, the study is best performed with both oral and intravenous contrast material unless contraindicated. Unenhanced, precontrast images are required only in specific situations and are not routinely used in survey studies of the abdomen. Sample Abdominopelvic survey protocols can be found in Table 69-1.

If only conventional equipment is available, dynamic scanning should be used to attempt to image the entire liver before the onset of equilibrium phase. The use of 10-mm-thick images obtained every 10 mm through the abdomen is standard. A biphasic injection of 150 mL of 60% contrast material is used. The first 50 mL is injected at a rate of 1.5 to 2.0 mL/s, with the remainder injected at 0.5 to 1.0 mL/s. A scan delay of 30 to 40 seconds is used for most patients.

Table 69-1
Abdominal CT Survey Protocols

	Conventional	Single Slice	4-Slice	16-Slice	64-Slice
Intravenous contrast (300 mg/mL)*	150 mL	125-150 mL	125 mL	125 mL	125 or 100 mL + 50 mL saline chaser
Injection rate	50 mL at 1.5-2 mL/s; 100 mL at 0.5-1.0 mL/s	2 mL/s	2-3 mL/s	2-3 mL/s	2-4 mL/s
Scan delay	30 s	50-60 s	60-70 s	60-70 s	60-70 s
Detector collimation	10 mm²	7 mm†	2.5-5 mm	1-1.5 mm	0.5-0.625 mm
Image thickness	10 mm²	7 mm†	5 mm	5 mm	5 mm

Oral and intravenous contrast should be used unless contraindicated.
*Other contrast concentrations may be used; the volume can be adjusted to keep grams of iodine constant.
†Detector collimation and image thickness are the same by definition in conventional and single-channel helical CT.

Using a single detector helical machine, the scan should be obtained in the portal venous phase using a 50- to 60-second scan delay after the injection of 125 mL of 60% iodinated contrast material at a rate of 2 to 3 mL/s. If possible, a slice thickness should be chosen such that the abdomen and pelvis can each be scanned in one or two breath holds; this is generally 5 to 7 mm. Many centers perform delayed images through the kidneys to identify small renal masses that may be missed during earlier phases; however, this may not be cost-effective and exposes the patient to additional radiation.[71]

With MDCT, acquisition section thickness may range from 2.5 mm on a four-slice unit to 0.5 mm on a 64-slice machine. Usually the images created for interpretation are thicker, from 3 to 5 mm.[17] As long as the raw data are still in the scanner memory, additional thinner images can be created later if needed. Contrast material injection is similar to that used for single detector helical units usually with a delay of 60 to 70 seconds. One should be cognizant of the length of time of the injection versus scanning speed. This is usually only an issue in patients with poor intravenous access requiring lower injection rates. For example, if the injection rate is reduced to 1.5 mL/s, the injection will last about 90 seconds. Depending on the acquisition collimation and gantry rotation speed, a scan initiated at 70 seconds could easily be complete before all the contrast has entered the abdominal circulation. To avoid this one may increase the delay, slow the scanner, and/or reduce the volume of contrast.

Hepatic Protocols

Specific CT techniques to better evaluate the liver have become routine with helical and especially MDCT (Table 69-2). Conentional CT cannot be used for specific hepatic imaging protocols. While certain principles of hepatic CT imaging exist, the specific techniques used will vary slightly by the exact indication. Specific protocols may focus on lesion characterization, screening for hepatocellular carcinoma in high-risk

individuals, evaluation of cholangiocarcinoma or preoperative staging and planning. In addition, there are also special techniques involving catheter angiography with CT.

The general principle from which most specific protocols are derived is based on the dual blood supply of the liver.[72] The normal liver receives approximately 25% of its blood supply from the hepatic artery and 75% from the portal vein. The hepatic arteries will receive contrast after a peripheral venous injection first, generally beginning at 15 to 25 seconds, depending on contrast injection rate and the patient's circulation time.[73] Contrast reaches the portal venous system later as it must first transverse the mesenteric vessels and bowel capillaries. The portal vein begins to enhance about 35 to 40 seconds after the contrast injection begins. Finally, at about 60 to 70 seconds, contrast is identified in the hepatic veins. In distinction from the hepatic parenchyma, most hepatic tumors are supplied by the hepatic artery exclusively. The appearance of a focal hepatic mass depends upon its vascularity and the delay after contrast administration.[74] Hepatic tumors that are hypervascular are generally best seen on late arterial phase images which are obtained near the end of the phase of exclusive enhancement of the liver by the hepatic arteries, that is to say when the contrast just reaches the portal vein, at about 35 to 40 seconds (Fig. 69-8). Images obtained at this time have been referred to in the literature as "arterial," "late arterial," or "portal venous inflow" images.[74] Hepatic tumors that are hypovascular are generally best seen when there is good opacification of the liver by both the hepatic artery and portal vein, but before the onset of equilibrium. This is at 60 to 70 seconds and is identified by contrast in the hepatic veins. Images obtained at this time may be varyingly referred to as "portal venous," "parenchymal," or 'hepatic venous" phase images. However, these tumors may not be visualized during earlier phases (Fig. 69-9). This is because the hypovascular tumor receiving a large amount of contrast may become isodense to the hypervascular liver which is only receiving contrast from a portion of its blood supply.

Table 69-2
Hepatic CT Protocols

		Single Slice	4-Slice	16-Slice	64-Slice
Precontrast images	Detector collimation	7-10 mm†	5 mm	1.5 mm	0.5-0.625 mm
	Image thickness	7-10 mm†	5 mm	5 mm	5 mm
Injection	Contrast volume (300 mg/mL)	150 mL	125 mL	125 mL	125 mL
	Injection rate	3-4 mL/s	3-4 mL/s	3-4 mL/s	3-4 mL/s
	Scan delay	20 s	15 s	15 s	15 s
Early arterial phase* (CTA)	Detector collimation	3 mm	1-1.25 mm	0.75 mm	0.5-0.625 mm
	Image thickness	3 mm	2 mm	1 mm	1 mm
Late arterial phase (arterial, portal venous inflow)	Scan delay	25 s	30 s	35 s	35 s
	Detector collimation	7 mm†	1-2.5 mm	0.75 mm	0.5-0.625 mm
	Image thickness	7 mm†	2-4 mm§	2 mm§	2 mm§
Portal venous phase (hepatic venous, parenchymal)	Scan delay	60 s	60-70 s	70 s	70 s
	Detector collimation	7-10 mm†	5 mm	1.5 mm	0.5-0.625 mm
	Image thickness	7-10 mm†	5-7 mm	2-5 mm	2-5 mm
Delayed phase‡	Scan delay	10-20 min	10-20 min	10-20 min	10-20 min
	Detector collimation	7-10 mm†	5 mm	0.75 mm	0.5-0.625 mm
	Image thickness	7-10 mm†	5-7 mm	2-5 mm	2-5 mm

For most indications three phases are chosen, generally precontrast, late arterial and portal venous phases. Early arterial images may be performed if desired for surgical planning and delayed phase images are generally added in evaluation of cholangiocarcinoma.
*With single channel cannot be combined with arterial phase. Positive enteric contrast material should not be used; neutral or negative enteric contrast may be administered. A 50% image overlap should be used (reconstruction interval equal to one half image thickness).
†Image thickness is a scan parameter determined by the detector collimation.
‡For use in identification or evaluation of cholangiocarcinoma.
§Thinner slice images with a softer kernel are created for use in MIP and VR angiographic images.

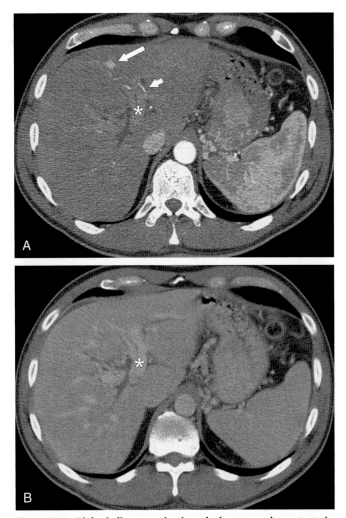

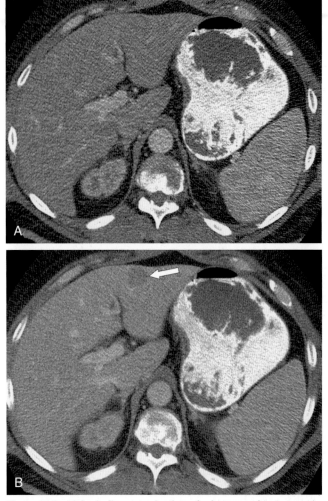

Figure 69-8. Biphasic liver examination of a hypervascular metastasis. **A.** On this late arterial phase image a 1 cm hypervascular metastasis is identified in the medial segment of the left lobe (*long arrow*). Note that portions of the hepatic artery (*short arrow*) are well seen and contrast is just entering the portal vein (*asterisk*). **B.** On this portal venous phase image obtained at the same location as the image in **A**, the lesion cannot be easily identified (*asterisk*).

Figure 69-9. Biphasic liver examination of a hypovascular metastasis. **A.** On this late arterial phase image in a patient with metastatic colon cancer, no hepatic lesion can be identified. **B.** On the portal venous phase image obtained at the same location, the hypovascular metastasis on the lateral segment of the left lobe is easily seen (*arrow*).

The exact timing of each phase in a particular patient may be determined by a test bolus technique.[72]

The specific acquisition collimation, pitch, gantry rotation and table speed will vary by scanner type and manufacturer. In general, these parameters are adjusted such that each phase can be accomplished within a 10- to 15-second breath hold. Increasing pitch decreases the radiation dose but increases image noise; in general pitch should vary from 0.75 to 1.5 for most protocol phases. The reconstruction interval is generally equal to the image thickness resulting in contiguous images, with the exception of early arterial images to be used for CT angiographic reconstruction in which the reconstruction interval is generally 50% of the image thickness.

The usefulness of precontrast images has been the subject of some debate. Proponents note the increased sensitivity for certain malignant lesions.[75] They can also be helpful in the identification of focal calcifications. Detractors focus on the relatively small incremental advantages compared to the additional cost and radiation exposure.[76] On single-channel machines, the slice thickness should be 5 to 7 mm; the param-

eters and pitch are often chosen to reduce radiation dose and prevent excessive heating of the tube. With MDCT, acquisition collimation is also generally kept relatively large and image thickness is usually kept at 3 to 5 mm (see Table 69-2) provides more specifics.

Early arterial phase images can be separately obtained for 3D reconstructions of the upper abdominal and hepatic arterial trees for use in surgical planning. When these are desired, a high rate of injection (4 to 6 mL/s) is important. As thin an acquisition collimation and as rapid a gantry speed as possible are used. If 3D reconstructions are anticipated, positive oral contrast material should not be given as it interferes with reconstructions.

Late arterial phase images are used for identification of hypervascular lesions as well as lesion characterization.[36] This requires high injection rates of 4 to 6 mL/s to get adequate amounts of iodine into the liver before portal venous contamination. It is important to remember that with higher concentrations of contrast slightly slower injection rates introduce the same amount of iodine per unit time. The limiting factors for single-channel CT machines are coverage and anode overheating. Image thickness on single-channel helical machines is generally kept at 5 to 7 mm; a pitch greater than 1.5 can allow improved coverage with an acceptable increase in noise. MDCT acquisition thickness ranges from 2.5 mm on four-channel units to 0.5 mm on 64-channel units. The general principle used is to obtain as thin of a collimation as possible that will allow completion of the scan before a large amount of contrast has entered the liver via the portal vein. This allows excellent spatial resolution that can be exploited to evaluate the arterial tree during this phase, negating the need for early arterial images. Image thickness of 2.5 to 5 mm may be used. Thinner images may help with small vessel identification; however, one study demonstrated no improvement in the detection of hypervascular hepatocellular carcinoma with images thinner than 5 mm.[77]

Portal venous phase images are obtained with parameters similar to those used for routine survey examination of the abdomen. Single-channel helical scanning is begun at 50 to 60 seconds after contrast initiation with a collimation of 7 mm and MDCT is begun at 60 to 70 seconds with an acquisition collimation of 0.5 to 5 mm, depending on the number of channels. With MDCT, the image thickness is generally larger than the collimator thickness, usually 3 to 5 mm. Results from several studies comparing different image thickness have had varying results. A study of small lesions (defined as ≤10 mm) found that 2.5-mm image thickness was more sensitive than 5-, 7.5-, or 10-mm images.[78] However, a later study comparing images of 5-, 3.75-, and 2.5-mm thickness showed no improvement is detection of small metastasis with the thinner image thickness, possibly due to increased noise on the thinner images.[79] Finally, one must consider that 80% of small (10 mm) liver lesions in patients with known malignancy are benign and differentiating small benign from small malignant lesions can be difficult or impossible.[80] It is possible that when evaluating for small and very small metastases, an approach different from the routine anatomic one, such as perfusion imaging, will be required.[81]

Delayed scanning at 10 to 20 minutes after the injection of scanning can be performed, particularly for the detection or evaluation of cholangiocarcinoma.[82,83] At this time contrast persists in fibrous, dense structures but is decreasing in concentration in most tissues due to renal excretion. Such a delayed acquisition generally would have the same parameters as the portal venous phase sequence.

Additional specialized hepatic CT imaging techniques exist but are not routinely used at most institutions. Delayed images at 6 hours following injection demonstrate focal lesions as slightly hypodense as the liver is slightly increased in density due to active excretion of the contrast material by the hepatocytes into the bile.[84] CT angiography and CT portography employ the use of an arterial catheter placed in the hepatic, splenic or superior mesenteric artery. Images are obtained either during the direct arterial opacification of the liver (CT hepatic angiography, CTHA) or during the first pass of contrast through the portal venous system of the liver (CT arterial portography, CTAP).[85,86] These techniques have been shown to be most sensitive for focal lesion detection; however, most comparisons predate MDCT.[87]

Pancreatic Protocols

Helical and MDCT protocols may be tailored to evaluate the pancreas (Table 69-3). Conventional CT does not have the capability to perform specialized pancreatic imaging. Protocols used vary by the exact indication and images can be obtained before or at various times following the administration of intravenous contrast. Precontrast images can be helpful in identifying pancreatic calcifications and calcified common bile duct stones. CT angiography as part of the protocol can be useful to the surgeon for surgical planning.[88] Images obtained at maximum pancreatic enhancement can be particularly helpful in identifying both hypervascular and hypovascular pancreatic lesions or vascular involvement by tumor or inflammation[89] (Fig. 69-10).

Table 69-3
Pancreatic CT Protocols

		Single Slice	4-Slice	16-Slice	64-Slice
Precontrast*§	Detector collimation	7-10 mm†	5 mm	1.5 mm	0.5-0.625 mm
	Image thickness	7-10 mm†	5 mm	5 mm	5 mm
Injection	Contrast volume (300 mg/mL)	150 mL	125 mL	125 mL	125 mL
	Injection rate	3-4 mL/s	4-6 mL/s	4-6 mL/s	4-6 mL/s
Arterial phase (CTA)	Scan delay	20 s	15 s	15 s	15 s
	Detector collimation	2-3 mm†	1-1.25 mm	0.75 mm	0.5-0.625 mm
	Image thickness	2-3 mm†	1.25 mm	1 mm	1 mm
Parenchymal phase‡‖	Scan delay	30 s	35-45 s	35-45 s	35-45 s
	Detector collimation	3-7 mm†	2.5 mm	0.75 mm	0.5-0.625 mm
	Image thickness	3-7 mm†	2-3 mm	2 mm	2 mm
Portal venous phase¶	Scan delay	60 s	60-70 s	70 s	70 s
	Detector collimation	7-10 mm†	5 mm	0.75 mm	0.5-0.625 mm
	Image thickness	7-10 mm†	5-7 mm	2-3 mm	2-3 mm

Up to four phases may be obtained through the pancreas; however, most institutions will perform only three (choosing either the arterial phase or parenchymal phase) to limit radiation dose. Enteric contrast should be neutral or negative.
*Most useful in evaluating patients with chronic pancreatitis or biliary obstruction, not generally used for routine mass evaluation.
†Image thickness is a scan parameter determined by the detector collimation.
‡In many circumstances can also be used for vascular assessment and reconstructions (CTA) with minimal venous contamination. The raw data can be reconstructed into an additional data set with image thickness equal to detector collimation and with 50% overlap.
§This may be restricted in the z-axis to only cover the pancreas.
‖In cases of known or suspected hypervascular pancreatic tumor (i.e., neuroendocrine) this phase can be expanded to include the liver for assessment for metastasis.
¶Generally includes the entire abdomen.

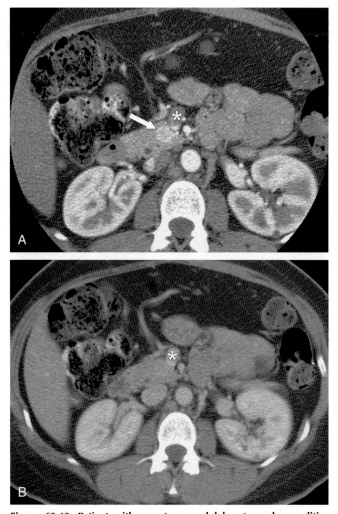

Figure 69-10. Patient with symptoms and laboratory abnormalities consistent with an insulinoma. A. Image obtained during the pancreatic phase clearly demonstrates the hypervascular tumor (*arrow*) in the pancreatic head adjacent to the superior mesenteric vein (*asterisk*). **B.** The tumor is almost impossible to identify on the portal venous phase image obtained at the same level.

Water or low-density commercial oral contrast material is generally given prior to the procedure. If water is used, approximately 1000 to 1500 cc is given 30 minutes prior to scanning.[90] Negative contrast material, as opposed to positive contrast material, will not obscure common bile duct stones and helps in assessing bowel wall involvement as well as identifying gastric varices.

Precontrast images are of value in identifying pancreatic calcifications in chronic pancreatitis and occasionally in identifying calcified common bile duct stones. These are therefore often included in pancreatic studies for suspected or known acute and chronic pancreatitis; they are less commonly used in pancreatic mass evaluation. If performed, the slice thickness varies from 5 to 7 mm on single channel machines; the parameters and pitch are often chosen to reduce radiation dose and prevent excessive tube heating. With MDCT, acquisition collimation is generally kept relatively large, from 2.5 to 5 mm. Image thickness is usually kept at 5 mm.

True *arterial phase* images are used primarily when CT angiography is desired, primarily for surgical planning. The technique is identical to that used in hepatic CT angiography

described previously. Some authors recommend true arterial phase images for identification of hypervascular tumors.[91] However, others have found that during the early arterial phase there is not enough contrast present within the pancreas for identification of hypervascular or hypovascular lesions.[88,92]

Images obtained during the maximal enhancement of the pancreas are useful for identifying both hypervascular neuroendocrine tumors and hypovascular adenocarcinomas.[88,93] This *parenchymal phase* is achieved by using a scan delay of approximately 30 to 40 seconds after the initiation of contrast at a rate of 4 to 6 mL/s.[94] With single detector helical CT this is generally performed with 2- to 5-mm collimation and a pitch of 1.5. With MDCT acquisition collimation is generally kept at or near the limits of the machine, from 0.5 to 1.25 mm while the image thickness may be slightly greater, from 2 to 4 mm to decrease noise.

Portal venous phase images are also useful for the identification of focal lesions as well as assessment of the portal venous structures (involvement by tumor; patency) and liver for metastatic disease. Single-channel helical scanning is begun at 50 to 60 seconds after contrast initiation with a collimation of 5 to 7 mm and MDCT is begun at 60 to 70 seconds with an acquisition collimation of 0.5 to 5 mm, depending on the machine capabilities.

Due to the complex regional anatomic relationships, imaging of the pancreas may be helped by various reconstructions.[95] Using MDCT and curved planar reformation, one group demonstrated an accuracy of 99% (109 of 110 vessels) and a negative predictive value of 100% (108 of 108 vessels) in predicting vascular invasion of tumor in 25 patients.[89] Others have questioned the usefulness of the reformations.[98] MinIP images can be helpful in visualization of the pancreatic duct.

FUTURE DIRECTIONS

The history of CT has been one of continuous improvement, usually measured in resolution and speed. Several significant leaps forward have occurred, most notably the introduction of helical and multidetector technologies. While one major goal, the isotropic voxel, has been achieved with 64-channel machines, the demand for continued improvement persists. The number of channels available on a MDCT has been the most recent measure of the progress of CT: from 2 to 4 to 8 to 16 to 32 and, at the time of this writing, 64. How much longer will competing manufacturers continue to develop machines with greater numbers of channels? Probably as likely as a 128- or 256-channel machine is another major generational change in CT technology, perhaps to a machine with a digital acquisition device such as an area detector or a unit using dual radiation sources. Obviously, either development would require yet another reevaluation of scanning protocols.

Another area of active interest is the development of perfusion CT in the abdomen and pelvis, particularly of the liver.[97,98] Following the pathway of many CT innovations, this technique is becoming increasingly important in neuroradiology and applications in the body (where cardiac and respiratory motion as well as greater z-coverage present additional challenges) may not be far behind. Perfusion is an area of great research interest that may have practical clinical benefits as well. Comparison with MR perfusion techniques will have to be made, particularly in light of the potentially high radiation dose of perfusion CT. Another tool that may improve image quality is respiratory gating.

There are many practical questions that still have not been answered: Does a low-dose noncontrast abdominopelvic CT become the KUB (kidney, ureter, bladder radiograph) of the 21st century? How can new larger data sets in abdominal examinations be interpreted efficiently? How is the data to be stored: as raw data that can be reconstructed in multiple ways in the future or as end product digital images, as in the past? It is clear that as the acquisition capabilities improve, data display techniques will be driven toward change as well.[99] Approaching 35 years of age, CT technology continues to evolve and continues to change the way medicine is practiced.

References

1. Friedland GW, Thurber BD: The birth of CT. AJR 167:1365-1370, 1996.
2. Miraldi F: Imaging principles in computed tomography. In Haaga JR, Lanzieri CF (eds): CT and MR Imaging of the Whole Body, 4th ed. Philadelphia, Lippincott, 2002, pp 3-36.
3. Bae KT, Whiting BR: Basic principles of computed tomography physics and technical considerations. In Lee JKT, Sagel SS, Stanley RJ, et al (eds): Computed Tomography with MRI Correlation. Philadelphia, Lippincott Williams & Wilkins, 2006, pp 1-29.
4. Heiken JP, Brink JA, Vannier MW: Spiral (helical) CT. Radiology 189: 647-656, 1993.
5. Seeram E: Computed Tomography: Physical Principles, Clinical Applications and Quality Control. Philadelphia, WB Saunders, 1994, pp 125-138.
6. Barnes JE: Characteristics and control of contrast in CT. RadioGraphics 12:825-837, 1992.
7. Kalender WA, Seissler W, Klotz E, Vock P: Spiral volumetric CT with single-breath-hold technique, continuous transport, and continuous scanner rotation. Radiology 176:181-183, 1990.
8. Herts BR, Einstein DM, Paushter DM: Spiral CT of the abdomen: Artifacts and potential pitfalls. AJR 161:1185-1190, 1993.
9. Urban BA, Fishman EK, Kuhlman JE, et al: Detection of focal hepatic lesions with spiral CT: Comparison of 4- and 8-mm interscan spacing. AJR 160:783-785, 1993.
10. Foley WD: Technology/contrast: Current state of the art. In Fishman EK, Federle MP (eds): Body CT Categorical Course Syllabus. Reston, VA, American Roentgen Ray Society, 1994, pp 1-4.
11. Silverman PM, Kalender WA, Hazle JD: Common terminology for single and multislice helical CT. AJR 176:1135-1136, 2001.
12. Flohr TG, Schaller S, Stierstorfer K, et al: Multi-detector row CT systems and image-reconstruction techniques. Radiology 235:756-773, 2005.
13. Prokop M: Principles of CT, spiral CT and multislice CT. In Prokop M, Galanski M (eds): Spiral and Multislice Computed Tomography of the Body. Stuttgart, Thieme, 2003, pp 1-43.
14. Fishman EK, Jeffrey RB (eds): Multidetector CT: Principles, Techniques, and Clinical Applications. Philadelphia, Lippincott Williams & Wilkins, 2004.
15. Prokop M: General principles of MDCT. Eur J Radiol 45:S4-S10, 2003.
16. Ros PR, Hoon J: Multisection (multidetector) CT: Applications in the abdomen. RadioGraphics 22:697-700, 2002.
17. Saini S: Multi-detector row CT: Principles and practice for abdominal applications. Radiology 233:323-327, 2004.
18. Napel S: Basic principles of MDCT. In Fishman EK, Jeffrey RB (eds): Multidetector CT: Principles, Techniques, and Clinical Applications. Philadelphia, Lippincott Williams & Wilkins, 2004, pp 3-13.
19. Kalra MK, Maher MM, Toth TL, et al: Strategies for CT radiation dose optimization. Radiology 230:619-628, 2004.
20. Kalra MK, Maher MM, Rizzo S, Saina S: Radiation exposure and projected risks with multidetector-row computed tomographic scanning. J Comput Assist Tomogr 28:S46-S49, 2004.
21. Crawley MT, Booth A, Wainwright A: A practical approach to the first iteration in the optimization of radiation dose and image quality in CT: Estimates of the collective dose savings achieved. Br J Radiol 74:607-614, 2001.
22. Rothenberg LN, Pentlow KS: AAPM tutorial: radiation dose in CT. RadioGraphics 12:1225-1243, 1992.
23. Huda W: Radiation dosimetry in diagnostic radiology. AJR 169:1487-1488, 1997.
24. Kalra MK, Maher MM, Toth TL, et al: Techniques and applications of automatic tube current modulation for CT. Radiology 233:649-657, 2004.
25. Nagel HD (ed): Radiation Exposure in Computed Tomography: Fundamentals, Influencing Parameters, Dose Assessment, Optimization, Scanner Data, Terminology, 2nd ed. Frankfurt, COCIR, 2000.
26. McNitt-Gray MF: Radiation dose in CT. RadioGraphics 22:1541-1553, 2002.
27. Flohr T, Ohnesorge B, Schaller S: Design, technique, and future perspective of multislice CT scanners. In Reiser MF, Takahashi M, Modic M, Becker CR (eds): Multislice CT, 2nd ed. Berlin, Springer, 2004, pp 3-16.
28. Kalra MK, Prasad S, Saini S, et al: Clinical comparison between standard dose and 50% reduced dose abdominal CT: Effect on image quality. AJR 179:1101-1106, 2002.
29. Donelly LF, Emery KH, Brody AS, et al: Minimizing radiation dose for pediatric body applications of single-detector helical CT: Strategies at a large children's hospital. AJR 176:303-306, 2001.
30. Frush T, Soden B, Frush KS, et al: Improved pediatric multidetector body CT using a size based color-coded format. AJR 178:721-726, 2002.
31. Kulama E: Scanning protocols for multislice CT scanners. Br J Radiol 77:S2-S9, 2004.
32. Burgener FA, Hamlin DJ: Contrast enhancement in abdominal CT: Bolus versus infusion. AJR 137:351-358, 1981.
33. Foley WD, Berland LL, Lawson TL, et al: Contrast enhancement technique for dynamic hepatic computed tomographic scanning. Radiology 147:797-803, 1983.
34. Foley WD: Dynamic hepatic CT. Radiology 170:617-622, 1989.
35. Silverman PM: Pharmacokinetics of contrast enhancement in body CT: Implications for spiral (helical) scanning. In Fishman EK, Jeffrey RB (eds): Spiral CT: Principles, Techniques and Clinical Applications. New York, Raven, 1995, pp 11-23.
36. Foley WD, Mallisee TA, Hohenwalter MD: Multiphase hepatic CT with a multirow detector CT scanner. AJR 175:679-685, 2000.
37. Hanninen EL, Vogl TF, Felfe R: Detection of focal liver lesions at biphasic spiral CT: Randomized double-blind study of the effect of iodine concentration in contrast material. Radiology 216:403-409, 2000.
38. Fleischman D: Use of high concentration contrast media: Principles and rationale. Eur J Radiol 45:S88-S93, 2003.
39. Harris JP, Nelson RC: Abdominal imaging with multidetector computed tomography. J Comput Assist Tomogr 28:S1-S19, 2004.
40. Yagyu Y, Awai K, Inoue M, et al: MDCT of hypervascular hepatocellular carcinomas: A prospective study using contrast materials with different iodine concentrations. AJR 184:1535-1540, 2005.
41. Laghi A: Multidetector CT (64 slices) of the liver: Examination techniques. Eur Radiol 17:675-683, 2007.
42. Small WC, Nelson RC, Bernardino ME: Contrast-enhanced spiral CT of the liver: Effect of different amounts and injection rates of contrast material on early contrast enhancement. AJR 163:87-92, 1994.
43. Jeffrey RB: Multidetector CT of hepatic tumors. In Fishman EK, Jeffrey RB (eds): Multidetector CT: Principles, Techniques, and Clinical Applications. Philadelphia, Lippincott Williams & Wilkins, 2004, pp 185-198.
44. Megibow AJ, Jacob G, Heiken JP, et al: Quantitative and qualitative evaluation of volume of low osmolality contrast medium needed for routine helical abdominal CT. AJR 176:583-589, 2001.
45. Tublin ME, Tessler FN, Cheng SL, et al: Effect of injection rate of contrast medium on pancreatic and hepatic helical CT. Radiology 210:97-101, 1999.
46. Kim T, Murakami T, Takahashi S, et al: Effects of injection rates of contrast material on arterial phase hepatic CT. AJR 171:429-432, 1998.
47. Oliver JH, Baron RL: Helical biphasic contrast-enhanced CT of the liver: Technique, indications, and pitfalls. Radiology 201:1-14, 1996.
48. Garcia PA, Bonaldi VM, Bret PM, et al: Effect of rate of contrast medium injection on hepatic enhancement at CT. Radiology 199:185-189, 1996.
49. Chambers TP, Baron RL, Lush RM. Hepatic CT enhancement: Part I. Alterations in the volume of contrast material within the same patients. Radiology 193:513-517, 1994.
50. Chambers TP, Baron RL, Lush RM. Hepatic CT enhancement: Part II. Alterations in the contrast material volume and rate of injection within the same patients. Radiology 193:518-522, 1994.
51. Sheafor DH, Keogan MT, DeLong DM, et al: Dynamic helical CT of the abdomen: Prospective comparison of pre- and post-prandial contrast enhancement. Radiology 206:359-363, 1998.

52. Bae KT, Heiken JP, Brink JA: Aortic and hepatic contrast medium enhancement at CT: Part II. Effect of a reduced cardiac output in a porcine model. Radiology 207:657-662, 1998.

53. Silverman PM, Roberts SC, Ducic I, et al: Assessment of a technology that permits individualized scan delays on helical hepatic CT: A technique to improve efficiency of contrast material. AJR 167:79-84, 1996.

54. Silverman PM, Brown B, Wray H, et al: Optimal contrast enhancement of the liver using helical (spiral) CT of the liver: Value of SmartPrep. AJR 164:1169-1171, 1995.

55. Dorio PJ, Lee FT, Henseler KP, et al: Using a saline chaser to decrease contrast media in abdominal CT. AJR 180:929-934, 2003.

56. Haage P, Schmitz-Rode T, Hubner D, et al: Reduction of contrast material dose and artifacts by a saline flush using a double power injector in helical CT of the thorax. AJR 174:1049-1053, 2000.

57. Tillich M, Kammerhuber F, Reittner P: Detection of pulmonary nodules with helical CT: Comparison of cine and film-based viewing. AJR 169:1611-1614, 1997.

58. Bonaldi VM, Bret PM, Atri M, et al: Helical CT of the pancreas: A comparison of cine display and film-based viewing. AJR 170:373-376, 1998.

59. Rubin GD, Napel S, Leung AN: Volumetric analysis of volumetric data: Achieving a paradigm shift. Radiology 200:312-317, 1996.

60. Federle MP: Liver windows in body CT. AJR 163:1525, 1994.

61. White T: A plea for narrow windows. AJR 165:1307-1308, 1995.

62. Van Hoe L, Van Cutsem E, Vergote I, et al: Size quantification of liver metastasis in patients undergoing cancer treatment: Reproducibility of one-, two- and three-dimensional measurements determined with spiral CT. Radiology 202:671-675, 1997.

63. Fornage BD: Measuring masses on cross-sectional images [letter]. Radiology 189:289, 1993.

64. Desser TS, Sommer FG, Jeffrey RB: Value of curved planar reformations in MDCT of abdominal pathology. AJR 182:1477-1484, 2004.

65. Prokop M, Shin HO, Schanz A, et al: Use of maximum intensity projections in CT angiography: A basic review. RadioGraphics 17:433-451, 1997.

66. Fishman EK, Magid D, Ney DR, et al: Three-dimensional imaging. Radiology 181:321-337, 1991.

67. Van Beers BE, Lacrosse M, Trigaux JP, et al: Noninvasive imaging of the biliary tree before or after laparoscopic cholecystectomy: Use of three-dimensional spiral CT cholangiography. AJR 162:1331-1335, 1994.

68. Cheng YF, Lee TY, Chen CL, et al: Three-dimensional helical computed tomographic cholangiography: Application to living related hepatic transplantation. Clin Transplant 11:209-213, 1997.

69. Winter TC, Freeny PC, Nghiem HV: Hepatic arterial anatomy in transplantation candidates: Evaluation with three-dimensional CT angiography. Radiology 195:363-370, 1995.

70. Zeman RK, Davros WJ, Berman P, et al: Three-dimensional models of the abdominal vasculature based on helical CT: Usefulness in patients with pancreatic neoplasms. AJR 162:1425-1429, 1994.

71. Zeman RK, Baron RL, Jeffrey RB, et al: Helical body CT: Evolution of scanning protocols. AJR 170:1427-1437, 1998.

72. Foley WD: Multidetector CT: Abdominal visceral imaging. RadioGraphics 22:701-709, 2002.

73. Bader TR, Prokesch RW, Grabenwoger F: Timing of the hepatic arterial phase during contrast enhanced computed tomography of the liver: Assessment of normal values in 25 volunteers. Invest Radiol 35:486-492, 2000.

74. Kopp AF, Heuschmid M, Claussen CD: Multidetector helical CT of the liver for tumor detection and characterization. Eur Radiol 12:745-752, 2002.

75. Kanematsu M, Kondo H, Goshima S, et al: Imaging liver metastases: Review and update. Eur J Radiol 58:217-228, 2006.

76. Miller FH, Butler RS, Hoff FL, et al: Using triphasic helical CT to detect focal hepatic lesions in patients with neoplasms. AJR 171:643-649, 1998.

77. Kawata S, Murakami T, Kim T, et al: Multidetector CT: Diagnostic impact of slice thickness on detection of hypervascular hepatocellular carcinoma. AJR 179:61-66, 2002.

78. Weg N, Scheer MR, Gabor MP: Liver lesions: Improved detection with dual-detector-array CT and routine 2.5-mm thin collimation. Radiology 209:417-426, 1998.

79. Haider MA, Amitai MM, Rappaport DC, et al: Multi-detector row helical CT in preoperative assessment of small (≤1.5 cm) liver metastasis: Is thinner collimation better? Radiology 225:137-142, 2002.

80. Schwartz LH, Gandras EJ, Colangelo SM, et al: Prevalence and importance of small hepatic lesions found at CT in patients with cancer. Radiology 210:71-74, 1999.

81. Robinson PJA: Imaging liver metastasis: Current limitations and future prospects. Br J Radiol 73:234-241, 2000.

82. Keogan MT, Seabourn JT, Paulson EK, et al: Contrast-enhanced CT of intrahepatic and hilar cholangiocarcinoma: Delay time for optimal imaging. AJR 169:1493-1499, 1997.

83. Lacomis JM, Baron RL, Oliver JH, et al: Cholangiocarcinoma: Delayed CT contrast enhancement patterns. Radiology 203:98-104, 1997.

84. Miller DL, Simmons JT, Chang R, et al: Hepatic metastasis detection: Comparison of three CT contrast enhancement methods. Radiology 165:785-790, 1987.

85. Bluemke DA, Soyer PA, Chan BW, et al: Spiral CT during arterial portography: Techniques and applications. RadioGraphics 15:623-637, 1995.

86. Lupetin AR, Cammisa BA, Beckman I, et al: Spiral CT during arterial portography. RadioGraphics 16:723-724, 1996.

87. Hori M, Murakami T, Oi H, et al: Sensitivity in detection of hypervascular hepatocellular carcinoma by helical CT with intra-arterial injection of contrast medium, and by helical CT and MR imaging with intravenous injection of contrast medium. Acta Radiol 39:144-151, 1998.

88. Schima W, Ba-Ssalamah A, Kolblinger C, et al: Pancreatic adenocarcinoma. Eur Radiol 17:638-649, 2007.

89. Vargas R, Nino-Murcia M, Trueblood W, et al: MDCT in pancreatic adenocarcinoma: Prediction of vascular invasion and resectability using a multiphasic technique with curved planar reformations. AJR 182:419-425, 2004.

90. Tunaci M: Multidetector row CT of the pancreas. Eur J Radiol 52:18-30, 2004.

91. Sheth S, Hruban R, Fishman EK: Helical CT of islet cell tumors of the pancreas: Typical and atypical manifestations. AJR 179:725-730, 2002.

92. Satoi S, Yamamoto H, Takai S, et al: Clinical impact of multidetector row computed tomography on patients with pancreatic cancer. Pancreas 34:175-179, 2007.

93. Fidler JL, Fletcher JG, Reading CC, et al: Preoperative detection of pancreatic insulinomas on multiphasic helical CT. AJR 181:775-780, 2003.

94. Schima W, Ba-Ssalamah A, Plank C, et al: Pancreas. Part II: Tumors. Radiology 46:421-437, 2006.

95. Nino-Murcia M, Tamm EP, Charnsangavej C, et al: Multidetector-row helical CT and advanced postprocessing techniques for the evaluation of pancreatic neoplasms. Abdom Imaging 28:366-377, 2003.

96. Kondo H, Kanematsu M, Goshima S, et al: MDCT of the pancreas: Optimizing scanning delay with a bolus-tracking technique for pancreatic, peripancreatic vascular, and hepatic contrast enhancement. AJR 188:751-756, 2007.

97. Pollard RE, Broumas AR, Wisner ER, et al: Quantitative contrast enhanced ultrasound and CT assessment of tumor response of antiangiogenic therapy in rats. Ultrasound Med Biol 33:235-245, 2007.

98. Pandharipande PV, Krinsky GA, Rusinek H, et al: Perfusion imaging of the liver: Current challenges and future goals. Radiology 234:661-673, 2005.

99. Hashimoto K, Murakami T, Dono K, et al: Quantitative tissue blood flow measurement of the liver parenchyma: Comparison between xenon CT and perfusion CT. Dig Dis Sci 52:943-949, 2007.

Ultrasound Examination of the Solid Abdominal Organs

Stuart A. Barnard, MB, BS • Patrick M. Vos, MD • Peter L. Cooperberg, MDCM

The use of diagnostic medical ultrasound (US) has expanded rapidly over the past four decades. This expansion has paralleled the improvements in US technology, which have enabled detailed, rapid, and reproducible examinations to be performed in a number of areas including the abdomen. CT and MRI of the solid abdominal viscera have also been developed over the past three decades, and the cross-sectional imaging modalities are often complementary. US has several advantages over CT and MRI, including cost (and hence ease of access), real-time imaging, portability, lack of ionizing radiation, and absence of contraindications. Further advances in US technology will ensure that it retains a central role in abdominal imaging for the foreseeable future.

Medical US was developed in the 1950s, building on innovations in the fields of sonar, radar, and ultrasonic flaw detection in metals. Several technological innovations were necessary to drive forward US as the commonplace medical imaging technique we know today. Early scans used the "A mode" technique, where the amplitude of returning echoes along a single line was displayed on an oscilloscope screen. Later, "B mode" compound scan images were composed of only black and white. Gray-scale imaging improved interpretation and is now the standard for abdominal imaging. The first static arm commercial medical scanners were marketed in the 1960s, but the technique was slow and the machines were cumbersome. Real-time scanners soon replaced static arm scanners. The development of the transistor and later the integrated circuit improved signal generation and amplifica-

tion. All modern machines now use digital signal processing techniques, and improvements in the design and manufacture of probes have allowed the development of compact, robust, and versatile probes for a variety of applications.

The real-time nature of imaging with US lends itself particularly well to problem solving. Movement with respiration can be examined, tubular structures can be followed, and structures can be examined in different planes. US is an ideal method of guiding intervention such as fine needle aspiration, core biopsy, and drain placement.[1]

The real-time nature of US requires competence on the part of the ultrasonographer performing the examination. Although the examination is performed in real-time with up to 30 frames per second, only a fraction of these are saved as representative images for future review. Thus, the experience of the operator is important, as he or she will decide on the images to store. Picture archiving and storage (PACS) systems have enabled more still images to be stored without incurring the cost of printing film and may also allow the storage of cine loops to show dynamic processes.

US enables blood flow to be easily demonstrated without the need for nephrotoxic contrast agents, and neither the patient nor the operator is exposed to ionizing radiation. The ability of US to differentiate between solid and cystic structures is a particular strength. In the near future, it may be possible to examine the behavior of fluid within cystic structures in response to energy from the US beam and to characterize the cyst contents based on this behavior.[2]

BASIC PHYSICS

Medical US uses short pulses of sound waves that are transmitted and received by the transducer (Fig. 70-1). A coupling gel is used to facilitate the transmission of sound waves to and from the probe. This matches the acoustic impedance of the probe to that of tissue and eliminates air gaps between the probe and the skin. The basic element of most current transducers is a piezoelectric crystal that emits a sound wave when a voltage is applied to it (transmission) and generates a voltage when the reflected sound wave returns to the crystal (reception). Future transducer designs may use alternative methods of transducer construction,[3] but the principles of sound wave generation and reception will remain the same. The probe contains multiple crystals arranged in a strip or a grid. There are typically 128 individual crystals within a transducer array, and they can be independently activated; this allows the US beam to be electronically steered and focused. Earlier designs used mechanical devices to steer and focus the beam, but these have been superseded by electronic controls. The best resolution of an image is within the focal zone and focusing allows the focal zone to be varied according to the area of interest being examined. The beams of array transducers can be focused on both transmit and receive. Some transducers allow multiple focal zones to be selected in order to increase the effective focal zone, but this will reduce the frame rate or temporal resolution of the scan. The voltages produced by each crystal when receiving reflected sound waves are converted into digital signals by an analogue to digital signal converter and processed by the US machine to form the image.

Several factors have to be taken into account when choosing a transducer for a given application. Modern transducers suitable for abdominal imaging include linear arrays, curved linear arrays, and sector scanners. Linear arrays (typically

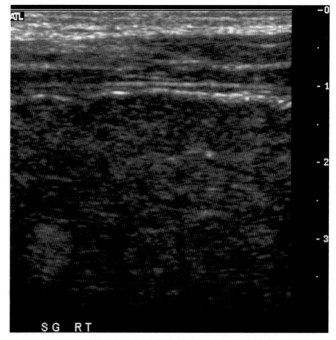

Figure 70-2. Hepatic cirrhosis. Superficial aspect of the liver scanned with a 7-MHz linear transducer showing nodular surface due to cirrhosis.

7-12 MHz) provide excellent resolution at the expense of penetration and field of view. They are ideal for superficial lesions or for examining the surface of abdominal viscera such as the liver (Fig. 70-2). The field of view can be extended by the use of trapezoidal imaging (Fig. 70-3) or compound (or extended field of view) imaging, where the probe is moved across a structure and the US machine "stitches together" the images to produce a panoramic image. This is useful for large superficial lesions such as soft tissue tumors (Fig. 70-4). Curved linear (or curvilinear) arrays are less effective for the examination of superficial structures but provide better penetration (due to their lower frequencies) and a wider field of view. Sector scanners have a limited role in routine abdominal

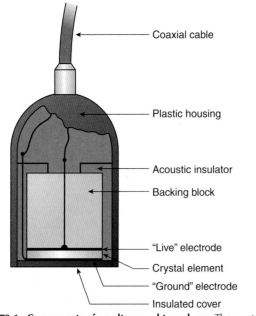

Figure 70-1. Components of an ultrasound transducer. The crystal element has piezoelectric properties. (From Curry TS. Dowdey JE, Murry RC: Christensen's Physics of Diagnostic Radiology, 2nd ed. Philadelphia, Lea & Febiger, 1990, p 328.)

- Coaxial cable
- Plastic housing
- Acoustic insulator
- Backing block
- "Live" electrode
- Crystal element
- "Ground" electrode
- Insulated cover

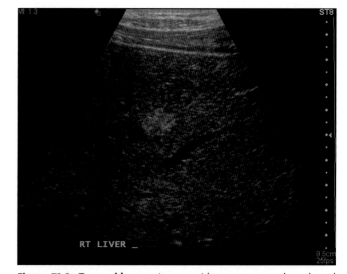

Figure 70-3. Trapezoid scan. A trapezoid scan area can be selected using some linear transducers to extend the field of view but maintain the resolution of a high-frequency linear transducer.

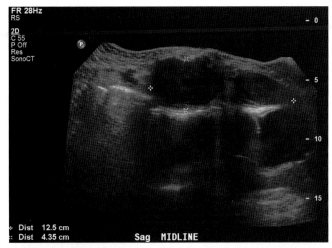

FR 28Hz
RS

2D
C 55
P Off
Res
SonoCT

P

× ×

− 0

− 5

− 10

− 15

✛ Dist   12.5 cm
: Dist   4.35 cm   **Sag   MIDLINE**

Figure 70-4. Extended field of view demonstration of abdominal wall desmoid tumor.

US but do provide a wide field of view with a small footprint, which can be useful when access is limited. A compromise must be reached between penetration and resolution, which are inversely proportional. Raising the frequency of the transmitted US pulse will improve resolution due to shortening of the wavelength, but it will also decrease the penetration as high frequencies are attenuated more than are low frequencies. The attenuation of a sound wave is proportional to its frequency. Many modern transducers allow the operator to vary the transmitted frequency within a certain range (2-5 MHz) without having to change probes. Most modern US machines will select the transmitted frequency based on the user's selection of presets, optimizing the image for detail or resolution (high frequency) or penetration (low frequency).

Sound waves interact with the tissues of the body in three main ways: reflection, absorption, and scatter. The terminology used to describe US findings is a description of the brightness of the structure; the more sound energy reflected back to the transducer, the brighter is the object. Objects are described as hypoechoic (darker), isoechoic (the same brightness), or hyperechoic (brighter) than adjacent structures. Anechoic structures appear black and indicate fluid. Internal echoes may be due to debris, septations, or artifacts. Often the liver is chosen as a reference in the abdomen, but care must be taken to ensure that the reference organ is of normal reflectivity and not abnormal due to fatty infiltration, cirrhosis, or hepatitis. The amount of energy reflected back to the transducer depends on several factors. The simplest form of reflection occurs when sound waves encounter a flat interface perpendicular to the beam with a large disparity in the velocity of sound be-

tween the adjacent tissues; this is termed a specular reflector and will appear as a well-defined bright line (Fig. 70-5). Smaller interfaces (0.1-1 mm in diameter) may cause scattering in all directions. Only a small fraction of the transmitted energy is returned to the probe, but when multiple such structures are present, the interference pattern between echoes produces a visible texture. This process is responsible for the US appearance of liver, spleen, and kidney parenchyma.

Sound waves propagate through tissues at different velocities, and when there is an interface between different tissues, the sound may be reflected or refracted (just as light may be reflected or refracted by a glass prism). The greater the difference in velocity between the adjacent tissues, the greater proportion is reflected (if the incident angle of the beam is large) or the more the beam is refracted (if the incident angle of the beam is smaller) (Fig. 70-6).

RECENT DEVELOPMENTS

US machines continue to rapidly evolve with the introduction of new technology. Although the principles of physics remain the same, manufacturers have developed new methods of probe construction, US generation, and postprocessing algorithms. Often these are assigned brand-specific trademarked titles that may be rather opaque to the user.

Many US machines now allow the user to select a real-time compound imaging mode, whereby the area to be examined is insonated from several different directions by electronic beam steering for transmission and reception. This facility is now available on linear and curvilinear probes. The multiple images are combined to form a single image, which is displayed on the monitor. This has been shown to improve overall image quality, increase lesion conspicuity, and reduce artifacts.[4]

A recent development that is now standard on most machines is tissue harmonic imaging (THI). "Conventional" imaging without harmonics is known as fundamental imaging because only the fundamental transmitted frequency is used for transmission and reception. THI was originally proposed for use with US contrast agents, but it has been shown to improve visualization of abdominal structures without the use of contrast agents.[5,6] The shape of the transmitted waveform changes as a sound wave is propagated through tissue, particularly in the focal zone where the intensity is high. Tissues resist compression more than expansion. This is termed "nonlinear" behavior. The waveform of the reflected pulse is altered and contains higher frequencies than the transmitted pulse. The higher frequencies are multiples of the transmitted fundamental frequency, called harmonic frequencies. At present, it is usually the second harmonic (twice the fundamental frequency) that is used for imaging, but higher

Figure 70-5. Specular versus non-specular echoes. Specular reflectors are large interfaces that must be close to the perpendicular of the beam path for the reflected wave in many directions. Some of the wave returns to the transducer. (From Sarti DA: Diagnostic Ultrasound: Text and Cases, 2nd ed. Chicago, Year Book Medical, 1987, p 10.)

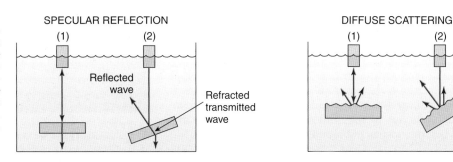

SPECULAR REFLECTION

(1)   (2)

Reflected
wave

Refracted
transmitted
wave

DIFFUSE SCATTERING

(1)   (2)

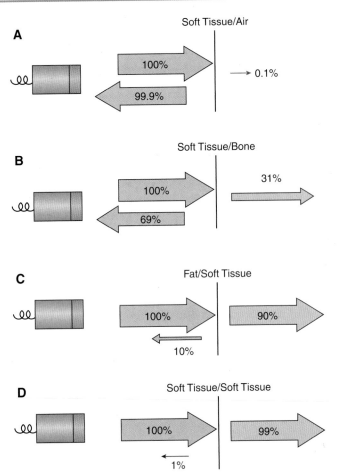

Figure 70-6. Sound wave transmission and reflection. The percentages of sound transmission and reflection at different interfaces (**A–D**) are illustrated. This is for the amplitude of a wave. (From Sarti DA: Diagnostic Ultrasound: Text and Cases, 2nd ed. Chicago, Year Book Medical, 1987, p 8.)

multiples may also be used. The fundamental frequencies are electronically filtered out after reception leaving only the harmonic frequencies. The harmonic frequencies only travel through the tissues once on the return to the probe and therefore are attenuated half as much as an identical frequency transmitted and received by the probe. There is less scatter, particularly in obese patients, where subcutaneous fat and superficial muscle layers cause scatter and attenuation of the fundamental frequencies, which may cause a haze of echoes degrading the image on fundamental imaging. Artifacts such as side and grating lobe artifacts that degrade fundamental images are also reduced because the weak side and grating lobes are not powerful enough to produce harmonic frequencies. The images are clearer and THI may improve diagnostic ability in challenging patients.[7]

Phase inversion imaging also exploits the nonlinear behavior of tissues but uses a different technique from frequency-based THI.[8,9] Two pulses are sent with 180-degree phase difference. If the pulse is reflected in a linear fashion, the reflected waves will cancel each other out. If the waves are reflected in a nonlinear fashion, the waves will not cancel out and are used to form the image. Phase inversion harmonic imaging reduces the frame rate due to the need to transmit twice as many pulses, but the spatial resolution is better than frequency-based THI.

The use of three-dimensional (3D) and 4D US is established in obstetric US,[10] but their value has yet to be proved in abdominal imaging.[11] Improvements in processing and probe technology have made real-time 3D volume-rendered and multiplanar reconstruction (MPR) imaging possible. Conventional 2D US does have an advantage over other cross-sectional imaging techniques by virtue of its ability to image in the axial and sagittal planes, with an infinite number of oblique planes in between. It is not possible to image abdominal structures in the coronal plane sonographically unless MPR techniques are used. An acquisition of a volume of data in a fashion akin to helical CT allows retrospective reconstruction of MPR views and surface-rendered images.

DOPPLER ULTRASOUND

The examination of blood flow with Doppler techniques is a valuable addition to real-time gray-scale abdominal US. The wavelengths of a transmitted sound pulse and the received pulse differ when sound waves are reflected from a moving surface. The wavelength shortens when the reflector is moving toward the transducer and lengthens when it is moving away. The change in wavelength is accompanied by a change in frequency and phase. The Doppler frequency (or phase) shift is measured, and the velocity and direction of blood flow can be calculated. One method of displaying the information is as color flow, where a color map of flow is superimposed upon a gray-scale real-time image. Convention dictates that blood flow toward the transducer is red and that away from the transducer is blue, although the operator may invert this. Color flow Doppler is used in the abdomen to examine the arterial tree, the portal venous system, and the systemic veins (Fig. 70-7). It may also be used to examine vascularity within the solid organs, for example, within or surrounding a mass lesion. The box displaying the color information can be resized and moved to include different parts of the image. A compromise between the color box size and the refresh rate of the image must be reached as an increased color box size will slow down the refresh rate of the image and create a "jumpy" appearance.

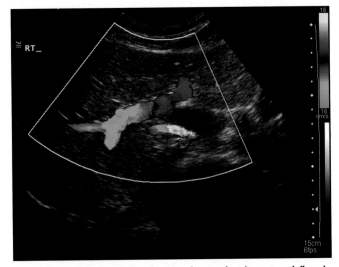

Figure 70-7. Color Doppler ultrasound scan showing normal flow in the left and right branches of the portal vein. Red represents flow toward the transducer, and blue, flow away from the transducer.

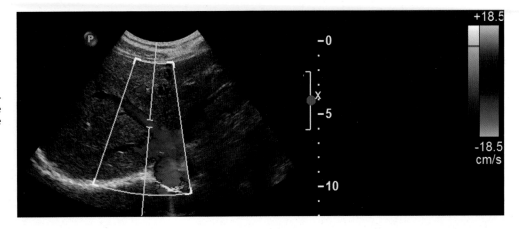

Figure 70-8. Color and pulsed-wave Doppler examination of the liver illustrating normal flow in the middle hepatic vein.

Power Doppler is a similar technique, but the total power of the reflected Doppler signal is displayed. There are no velocity data and therefore no indication of the direction of flow, but there are some advantages of power Doppler over color-flow Doppler in certain situations.[12] Power Doppler is more sensitive to slow flow and, unlike color Doppler, can display flow that is almost perpendicular to the beam. Background noise appears as brightly colored speckles in color Doppler that can be distracting, whereas in power Doppler, the background noise is dark, allowing higher gains to be used. It is thus a useful technique when the demonstration of low flow is needed but the direction of flow is not important.

The waveform and the direction of flow in vessels may change in disease states such as portal hypertension. Pulsed-wave Doppler displays the flow velocity as a waveform, and this is often combined with gray-scale imaging as duplex imaging (Fig. 70-8). The flow is measured in a small sample volume that can be placed on the region of interest. The operator can adjust the position and the size of the sample volume. If quantitative measurement of flow is required, a correction has to be made as the Doppler beam is at an angle to the blood flow. The angle between the blood flow and the interrogating Doppler beam should be kept as small as possible; it is not possible to obtain a reliable Doppler velocity measurement if this angle exceeds 60 degrees.[13] This quantitative data can be used to assess vascular resistance, for example, within a transplanted liver.

ULTRASOUND CONTRAST MEDIA

Conventional US does have limitations in the detection and characterization of liver lesions, and CT and MRI have often been used to complement US and overcome these limitations. US contrast agents have been developed to increase the sensitivity of US to small liver lesions and to improve the characterization when lesions are detected, based on their perfusion properties. The first-generation US contrast agents were based on air-filled bubbles and required high acoustic pressures (high mechanical index) in order to break the bubbles. Contrast enhancement was short lived. Second-generation contrast agents are now available. These form small bubbles filled with gases other than air such as sulfur hexafluoride[14] and allow real-time scanning at a low mechanical index, depicting the different phases of blood flow, which is particularly useful in the liver. The appearances of a lesion in

arterial, portal venous and sinusoidal phases (15-35, 35-90, and 90-240 seconds, respectively) can be observed.[15]

Most modern US machines include technology that will allow imaging with contrast agents, but an estimated 60% of US machines in use worldwide do not have the capability.[11] The contrast is administered via an intravenous cannula as a rapid bolus followed by a saline flush. The area is then scanned continuously to depict the different vascular phases, and the images are often recorded as a cine clip to allow later playback. Repeated injections of contrast are possible, if necessary, as the agents are of low toxicity.

The detection of subcentimeter liver metastases is improved when contrast media are used.[16] Contrast media can also be useful in differentiating benign from malignant tumors and characterizing the lesions.[17,18] It has been suggested that contrast agents should also be used in the assessment of abdominal trauma,[19] where it may be added to the FAST (focused assessment with sonography in trauma) protocol.[20]

The use of US contrast agents remains highly variable, despite some encouraging clinical results. This is due to many factors, including workflow issues, availability of suitable US machines, and remuneration. It is seems unlikely that they will become a method of choice for characterization of liver lesions, as some proponents suggest.[21]

ULTRASOUND ARTIFACTS

The ultrasonographer and radiologist should be familiar with common artifacts in order to minimize their effect on image quality and avoid confusion with significant pathology.[22] Some of the processes described as artifacts, however, can be helpful when interpreting images.

Several assumptions are made when forming a US image. It is assumed that the US beam travels in a straight line from the probe and in the body. The velocity of the sound wave is assumed to be constant on the path, and the received echoes are assumed to have traveled in a straight line back to the probe. If any of these assumptions are incorrect, then an artifact will be produced.

If the US wave is propagated through a substance with reduced attenuation compared with the surrounding tissues, then the region beyond it will appear brighter or more echogenic. This is due to the fact that a time-gain compensation function is applied to the image, whereby the received echoes are amplified proportional to the time interval between

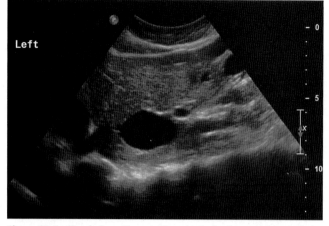

Figure 70-9. Simple hepatic cyst. Note the lack of perceptible wall, the anechoic contents, and the posterior acoustic enhancement.

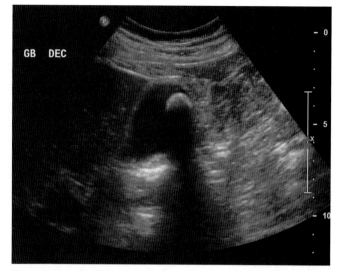

Figure 70-11. Single large gallstone. Note the bright anterior surface due to strong reflection and the posterior acoustic shadow.

pulse transmission and echo reception. The sound wave is attenuated as it passes through a structure, and the reflected echoes are also attenuated on their return to the transducer. If time-gain compensation were not applied, deeper structures would appear unacceptably dark. If a structure, for example, a fluid-filled cyst, transmits sound waves very effectively with little attenuation, then the tissue beyond the cyst will appear brighter than equivalent adjacent tissue (Fig. 70-9). This phenomenon is called "acoustic enhancement," and it is an important feature of fluid-filled lesions. Conversely, if a structure attenuates more than the surrounding tissue, then tissues beyond it will appear darker and lie within the "acoustic shadow." This is typical of solid lesions (Fig. 70-10). A very reflective surface such as bone or air will reflect the US beam and appear as a bright line with a very dark shadow beyond (Fig. 70-11). The ability to differentiate between solid and cystic lesions is a major diagnostic strength of US. Gas collections and gas within the bowel tend to produce "dirty" shadows, which are less clear than the shadows produced by a solid lesion such as a calculus.[23]

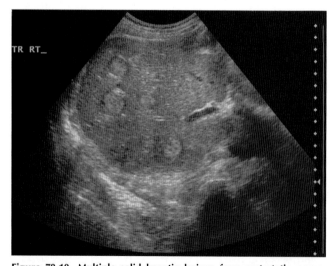

Figure 70-10. Multiple solid hepatic lesions from metastatic neuroendocrine tumor. Note the hypoechoic rims, echoes within the lesions, and the lack of posterior enhancement, differentiating them from cystic structures.

Reverberation artifacts are a common source of image degradation that may mask pathology. They occur when sound waves bounce back and forth between a strong interface and the transducer. As the reflections increase the length of the path, the artifact is seen deep to the interface. Such artifacts are commonly seen in the superficial aspect of the urinary bladder or in the near field of the liver.

Large specular reflectors such as the air–pleura interface at the diaphragm can produce artifactual structures to appear beyond them. As an example, the sound wave passes through the structure such as a lesion in the liver on the transmission path. Part of the sound wave is reflected back to the transducer and produces the appearance of the lesion in the correct location, but some passes through the lesion and is then reflected back toward the transducer by the right pleural–aerated lung interface acting as reflector. These sound waves will arrive at the transducer later than the "true" echoes from the liver lesion, and thus the artifactual structure will be placed deeper in the body on the display, beyond the reflecting surface. Common examples include liver lesions "reflected" posterior to the right hemidiaphragm (Fig. 70-12) and apparent pelvic masses reflected posterior to gas-containing loops of bowel in the pelvis.

If there are two or more reflectors close to each other, the sound waves may bounce back and forth between them and produce a "comet-tail" or "ring-down" artifact. "Ring-down" is a US artifact that appears as a solid streak or a series of parallel bands radiating away from the causative structure which appears as bands of bright lines posterior to the reflector, the lines becoming shorter and less intense as they become deeper. Rokitansky-Aschoff sinuses within the gallbladder wall (Fig. 70-13), gas in the biliary tract (Fig. 70-14), and surgical clips can produce these artifacts. Color Doppler will show a "twinkle artifact" analogous to a comet tail.

Refraction occurs when there is an oblique interface between tissues with different acoustic velocities. This is most commonly seen when the beam passes through the rectus muscles, and it can produce duplication of deeper structures. Movement of the probe eliminates the artifact.

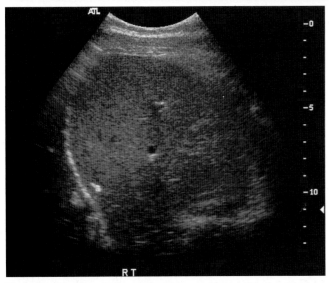

Figure 70-12. Mirror image artifact. Hemangioma within the right lobe of the liver reflected in the right pleura–lung interface (the bright line curving superior to the liver) to produce an apparent, artifactual lesion in the right lung base.

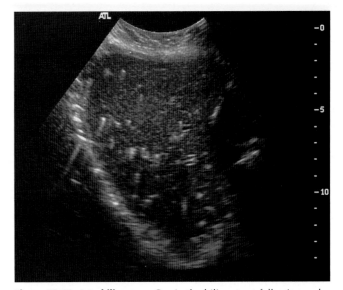

Figure 70-14. Intrabiliary gas. Gas in the biliary tract following endoscopic sphincterotomy producing bright linear shadows with posterior ring-down artifact.

LIVER

US of the liver is one of the most common examinations in a general US practice. Abnormalities of liver echotexture indicate diffuse liver disease, and focal liver lesions can be characterized as cystic or solid. US is frequently used to guide needle biopsy and drainage procedures as well.

The patient is initially positioned supine, although it may be necessary to rotate the patient onto their left side or into the left posterior oblique position during the examination. The patient is asked to take a deep breath in and hold it as inspiration will move the liver and spleen caudally, making them more amenable to examination from the subcostal position. A curved linear array probe (typically 2.5-5 MHz) is placed in the parasagittal plane in the subcostal region and angled cranially to include the superior segments of the liver. Sweeping the transducer medially and laterally in the para-sagittal plane in the right subcostal plane may be supplemented by scanning in the epigastric region to ensure adequate coverage of the entire liver, particularly the caudate and left lobes. The transducer is rotated to scan in the transverse plane. Scanning in the intercostal position is often necessary, which may necessitate an oblique transverse scan plane. This is best achieved with the patient in a left posterior oblique (LPO) or left lateral decubitus (left side down) position. A higher frequency linear probe may be used to examine the surface of the liver for nodularity or superficial lesions (Fig. 70-15). Fine surface nodularity in cirrhosis appears as a broken line on the surface of the liver.[24]

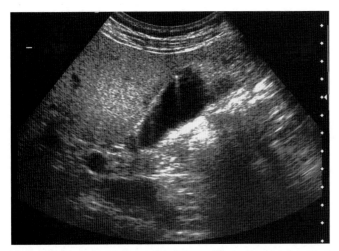

Figure 70-13. Comet-tail or ring-down artifact. Comet-tail artifact arising from strongly reflective small cholesterol crystals in Rokitansky-Aschoff sinuses in the anterior gallbladder wall.

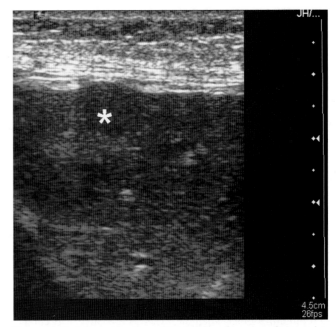

Figure 70-15. A linear transducer (7-12 MHz) probe was used to examine this cholangiocarcinoma metastasis (*) close to the surface of the liver. Linear transducers have better near-field resolution but are limited in their penetration. They are therefore suited to superficial lesions.

It is important to ensure that all segments of the liver are examined. Representative images are captured and recorded on film or a PACS system, but these only serve to demonstrate key anatomic structures or selected views of pathologic findings. The operator makes use of the dynamic nature of real-time US to differentiate between normal and pathologic liver. The person reporting static images must therefore be satisfied that the operator has covered the entire liver and has sufficient experience to recognize pathology. A cross section of a fluid-filled structure such as a hepatic vein may have very similar appearances to a cystic lesion on a static image, but in real-time it can be followed by sweeping the transducer from side to side or turning the transducer through 90 degrees and the tubular nature is appreciated in longitudinal section. A sweeping motion may also make subtle areas of altered echogenicity more apparent.

Appreciation of the anatomy of the liver is important for ensuring adequate coverage of the liver and for localizing lesions. The porta hepatis is the point at which the portal vein and hepatic artery enter the liver and the common hepatic duct leaves the liver. The plane of the porta lies approximately transversely. The portal vein divides into left and right branches before entering the liver itself; the anatomy of the hepatic artery is subject to much variation but always lies anterior to the portal vein. The artery lies medial to the common hepatic duct and in 90% it passes posterior to the duct but in 10% it passes anteriorly. The right portal vein passes laterally in the liver before dividing into anterior and posterior branches; the left passes anteriorly and superiorly in a C shape. The vascular structures of the liver are important in dividing the liver into the hepatic segments as defined by Couinaud,[25,26] which enables accurate localization and assessment of the resectability of lesions, although the system is based on the fetal rather than the adult pattern of circulation. Segment I is the caudate lobe, which receives blood from both the right and left portal veins; it also drains into the IVC via its own short veins (often not visible on US). It is often spared in early diffuse liver disease such as cirrhosis or in the Budd-Chiari syndrome. Segments II and III are supplied by the left portal vein and divided by the plane of the left hepatic vein. Segment IV corresponds to the quadrate lobe and is separated from segments II and III by the umbilical fissure. A plane between the IVC posteriorly and the gallbladder fossa anteriorly divides the left and right lobes of the liver and corresponds to the line of the middle hepatic vein. The plane of the right branch of the portal vein may be used to divide segment IV into IVA superiorly and IVB inferiorly. The right lobe of the liver consists of segments V through VIII. The plane of the anterior and posterior branches of the right portal vein divide the right lobe into superior (VIII anterior and VII posterior) and inferior (V anterior and VI posterior) segments. The right hepatic vein divides the anterior from the posterior segments. The use of segments to describe liver anatomy has become more important with increasing correlation between different cross-sectional modalities and the use of interventions such as segmental resection and radiofrequency ablation of focal hepatic lesions (Fig. 70-16).

The hepatic vasculature can also be interrogated with color and pulsed Doppler. The portal venous flow may be occluded by thrombus or reversed in advanced cases of portal hypertension. Color flow will give an indication of the direction of flow (which should be toward the liver), and thrombus may

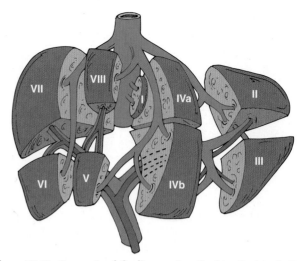

Figure 70-16. Segments of the liver as described by Couinaud. (From Meire H, Cosgrove D, Dewbury K, Farrant P: Clinical Ultrasound: A Comprehensive Text—Abdominal and General Ultrasound, vol 1, 2nd ed. London, Churchill Livingstone, 2001, p 167.)

be apparent as filling defects (Fig. 70-17). Pulsed Doppler allows examination of the waveform of flow in the portal vein and the branches. Normal portal venous flow is of low velocity toward the liver with a gentle respiratory variation (Fig. 70-18). In portal hypertension the flow may become "to and fro" then reversed (Fig. 70-19). Recanalization of the umbilical vein and other portosystemic shunts may occur (Fig. 70-20). The hepatic artery should normally not exceed 6 mm in diameter, but it may enlarge in cases of alcoholic hepatitis or cirrhosis.[27] The hepatic venous flow is normally triphasic, but the waveform may be altered by right heart failure (which may also cause dilation of the veins) or thrombosis may occur. The thrombus may be isoechoic with liver parenchyma and missed unless the hepatic veins are deliberately sought and color flow may help to visualize hypo/isoechoic thrombus. Occlusion of the veins may lead to Budd-Chiari syndrome with the development of congestive hepatopathy.

GALLBLADDER AND BILIARY TRACT

US has long been accepted as an excellent method of examining the gallbladder and the biliary tract.[28] It is often performed with examination of the liver and pancreas, but occasionally a focused study of the gallbladder and biliary tree is performed, for example, immediately prior to elective cholecystectomy to determine the need for bile duct exploration.

The patient should fast overnight (8-12 hours) to ensure adequate distention of the gallbladder. A 2.5- to 5-MHz curved linear array probe is sufficient for most examinations. THI may be useful to demonstrate the gallbladder and biliary tract.[29] The patient is placed supine initially, although the patient should be rolled into a right anterior oblique or left lateral decubitus position during the course of the examination. Erect positioning may also be necessary to demonstrate mobile gallstones or to visualize the distal common bile duct through a water-filled stomach and duodenum.

The transducer is placed in the right midclavicular line in a parasagittal orientation, and the long axis of the gallbladder is sought. Long-axis views are supplemented with

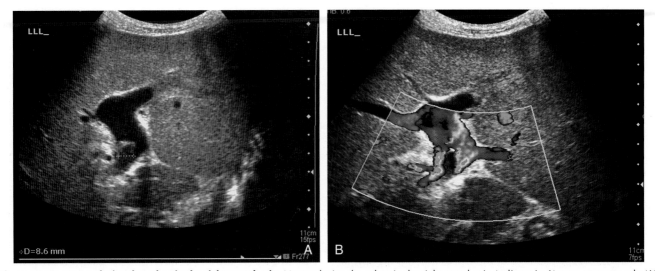

Figure 70-17. Nonocclusive thrombus in the right portal vein. Nonocclusive thrombus in the right portal vein (calipers in **A**) seen on gray-scale (**A**) and color Doppler (**B**) images.

short-axis views, and the entire gallbladder should be inspected. Suspended inspiration will help to move the gallbladder caudally, and intercostal views may be useful. The size, shape, and position of the gallbladder are highly variable, but a diameter of more than 5 cm is considered abnormal and indicates a distended gallbladder. It is commonly pear-shaped with the neck found near the porta hepatis and the fundus in a fossa on the undersurface of the right lobe of the liver, but it may be found in an intrahepatic position or on a mesentery and the fundus may reach the right iliac fossa, especially in the elderly. The fundus of the gallbladder may be folded (the "Phrygian cap"); maneuvers to unfold the fundus include further fasting to distend the gallbladder or placing the patient in the left lateral position. The wall is usually thin and uniform, and bile should appear hypoechoic. Particular attention should be paid to the neck of the gallbladder because stones may collect here in the supine position. Failure to demonstrate the gallbladder may be due to prior cholecystectomy, nonfasting state, calculous disease, shadowing, or reverberation from the near wall of the gallbladder or congenital absence of the gallbladder.[30]

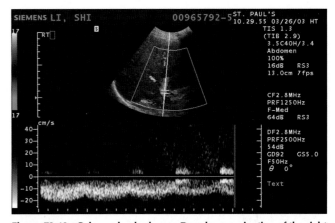

Figure 70-19. Color and pulsed-wave Doppler examination of the right portal vein showing reversed flow in a patient with cirrhosis and portal hypertension.

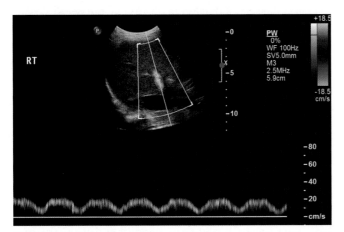

Figure 70-18. Color and pulsed-wave Doppler examination of the right portal vein showing normal flow.

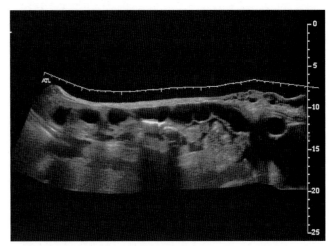

Figure 70-20. Dilated recanalized umbilical vein seen on an extended field of view image heading from the liver toward the umbilicus.

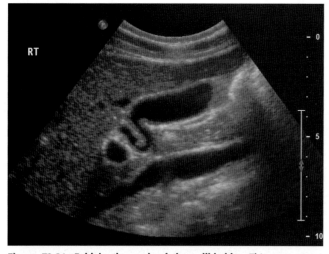

Figure 70-21. Fold in the neck of the gallbladder. This may cast a shadow and simulate calculi in the transverse plane.

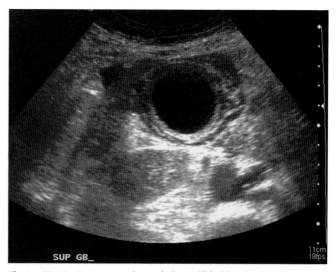

Figure 70-23. Transverse view of the gallbladder fundus showing a thickened edematous gallbladder wall.

Gallstones will appear as echogenic structures with distal acoustic shadowing. They are highly variable in size and shape and will usually move if the patient is rolled unless they are impacted in the neck of the gallbladder. A higher frequency probe may be used to look for small stones in a superficial gallbladder. False positives include folds in the wall of the gallbladder, which can be differentiated from stones be turning the transducer through 90 degrees (Fig. 70-21) or by repositioning the patient, and loops of echogenic bowel indenting the posterior wall of the gallbladder, which may peristalse and may cast a "dirty" shadow, unlike the clean shadow of a gallstone. A wall-echo-shadow (WES) pattern may be seen when a contracted gallbladder is full of calculi[31] (Fig. 70-22). Polyps are echogenic but less echogenic than stones; they do not cast distal acoustic shadows and are not mobile. They may be single or multiple, and most are benign. The probability of malignancy increases with the size of the polyp (most malignant polyps are greater than 10 mm in diameter), age, the presence of gallstones, and whether there are fewer than three polyps.[32-34]

The wall of the gallbladder may be generally thickened (greater than 2 mm) in acute cholecystitis, but this is not a specific sign.[35] It may also occur in the postprandial state and in other conditions including ascites, hypoalbuminemia, right-sided heart failure, pancreatitis, and hepatitis. Other signs of acute cholecystitis are gallbladder wall edema (Fig. 70-23), positive sonographic Murphy's sign, and pericholecystic fluid. Focal gallbladder wall thickening may be seen in adenomyomatosis, gallbladder carcinoma, and metastatic deposits. The gallbladder fills and drains via the cystic duct, which joins the common hepatic duct to form the common bile duct after a variable distance. The exact level at which this occurs is often not visible, and the extrahepatic bile duct may be referred to as the "common duct" when it is not clear where the cystic duct joins the common hepatic duct to form the common bile duct.

The biliary tract should be examined both within the liver and in its extrahepatic course. Normal intrahepatic bile ducts more peripheral than the left and right hepatic ducts are usually not visualized. When the intrahepatic bile ducts are dilated they can be recognized adjacent to the portal venous branches. Portal venous branches are visible even when of normal caliber and can be recognized by their echogenic borders due to the presence of adjacent fat. Visualization of dilated ducts and normal intrahepatic portal veins has been likened to a double-barreled shotgun.[36] The dilatation may be generalized if the obstruction is central at the porta or distally within the common duct, or it may be localized to a segment or lobe if there is a more proximal obstruction. A more patchy distribution of dilatation may be seen where a diffuse process affects the bile ducts such as diffuse cholangiocarcinoma. An attempt should be made to follow the extrahepatic common duct to the ampulla of Vater if possible. Shadowing from bowel gas may obscure the mid and distal duct, but changing the patient position, using the gallbladder as an acoustic window, or ingestion of water can improve visualization. This is particularly important when proximal dilatation of the biliary tract

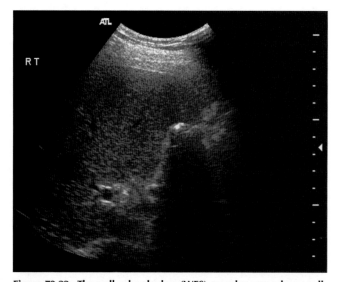

Figure 70-22. The wall-echo-shadow (WES) complex seen when a gallbladder that is full of calculi contracts. This may be confused for an echogenic gas-filled segment of bowel.

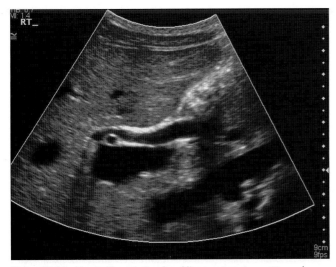

Figure 70-24. Normal hepatoduodenal ligament anatomy. Normal common duct showing the right hepatic artery crossing between the common hepatic duct (anterior) and the portal vein (posterior).

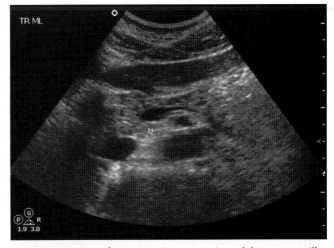

Figure 70-25. Normal pancreas. Transverse view of the pancreas illustrating the normal uncinate process (U) passing posterior to the superior mesenteric vein.

is encountered, and the level and cause of the obstruction are sought. Calculi within the distal duct and pancreatic head masses are common causes of distal common bile duct obstruction.

The common duct is measured close to the porta just distal to the point at which the right hepatic artery crosses between the portal vein and the duct (Fig. 70-24). The duct then continues in the free edge of the lesser omentum to the head of the pancreas and the sphincter of Oddi, and the diameter of the duct increases in the extrahepatic section before tapering in the head of the pancreas. The normal caliber varies with age but should be less than 5 mm in adults.[37] The duct does dilate with age, and the upper limit of normal should be increased to 8 mm in the elderly. If the patient has a dilated duct precholecystectomy, the duct may not return to a normal diameter postoperatively and a diameter of up to 10 mm can be seen in a nonobstructed, postcholecystectomy patient.[38,39]

PANCREAS

US evaluation of the pancreas can be limited by overlying bowel gas.[40] Visualization can be improved by displacing gas-filled loops of bowel by pressure, sitting the patient up, or administering gasless fluid and scanning the pancreas through the fluid-filled stomach. The pancreas has an oblique transverse lie and is divided into the head (including the uncinate process), neck, body, and tail. The head is situated to the right of the midline in the "C" of the duodenum. The uncinate process passes posteriorly and medially behind the superior mesenteric vein (Fig. 70-25). The neck of the pancreas connects the body to the tail anterior to the superior mesenteric artery and vein. The body then passes transversely and slightly cranially and the tail ends in the splenic hilum. Thus, for a transverse view of the pancreas, the transducer should be angled with the left edge more cranial than the right (Fig. 70-26). The tortuous splenic artery passes along the superior margin of the pancreas, whereas the splenic vein follows a straight course posterior to the gland and is a useful landmark. The splenic vein joins the superior mesenteric vein to form the portal vein posterior to the neck; the uncinate process may pass posterior

to this junction. The normal outline of the pancreas is slightly lobular. The pancreas is normally slightly more echogenic than the normal liver. The pancreas may become more echogenic with fatty infiltration. Due to differences in fatty infiltration of the dorsal and ventral pancreatic anlagen, the uncinate process and the posterior part of the head may be relatively hypoechoic (Fig. 70-27) to the body and tail, and this should not be confused with a tumor.[41]

The main pancreatic duct may be visualized in normal individuals, but the diameter in the head should not exceed 3 mm. Dilatation of the duct should prompt a search for an obstructing lesion.

Acute pancreatitis is a common condition often associated with gallstones or a history of alcohol use. There may be no abnormalities on US or CT for 24 to 48 hours. Areas of the gland then become swollen and edematous, manifested by hypoechoic areas on US. The duct can be obstructed by the swelling, leading to ductal dilatation. Fluid collections may be seen in the peripancreatic retroperitoneal space or in the

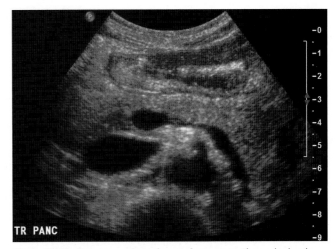

Figure 70-26. Transverse view of normal pancreas. The probe has been angled obliquely to include the tail of the pancreas, which passes laterally and cranially.

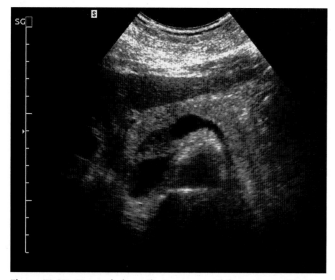

Figure 70-27. Hypoechoic uncinate process of the pancreas. This is a normal variant seen in up to 25% of patients.

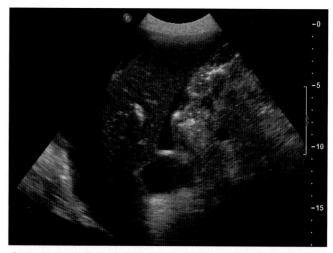

Figure 70-28. Left basal pleural effusion seen above the diaphragm. There is also some ascites adjacent to the spleen.

lesser sac. A search should always be made for gallstones as a treatable cause of pancreatitis, and elective cholecystectomy after the pancreatitis has resolved may prevent further episodes. Complications of pancreatitis include pseudocyst and pseudoaneurysm formation. Chronic pancreatitis may produce an enlarged gland in the early stages, but in the later stages, shrinkage, calcifications, and increased echogenicity are more common. Duct strictures and dilatation are seen, often with calculi, and are characteristic of the disease but are better demonstrated with pancreatography.

Pancreatic adenocarcinoma most commonly arises in the head and may cause dilation of the common bile duct and the pancreatic duct. The tumors are typically hypoechoic but attenuating. Endoscopic or intraoperative US may be used to improve lesion detection and characterization. The reduced need for penetration enables the use of higher frequencies and hence better resolution. Other tumors found in the pancreas include intraductal papillary mucinous tumors, and endocrine tumors (of which insulinoma is the most common).

SPLEEN

The spleen is well protected by the lower left ribs, and this can pose a challenge to the ultrasonographer. The patient is positioned in the right posterior oblique or right lateral decubitus position, and the spleen is scanned from the subcostal or intercostal approach. The spleen moves caudally on inspiration, and often this movement can be used to achieve a thorough examination of the entire spleen through a single intercostal space by a combination of breathing instructions to the patient and a sweeping movement of the transducer. The subphrenic space above the spleen should be examined for collections, and a left pleural effusion can often be seen above the diaphragm (Fig. 70-28). The spleen moves anterior to the left kidney on inspiration, a fact that should be borne in mind when attempting to establish the origin of a mass in the left upper quadrant.

The echotexture of the spleen is homogeneous and is normally slightly hyperechoic compared with the kidney and isoechoic or hyperechoic with the liver. The outer surface is

smooth and convex, whereas the visceral surface is concave and may show indentations for the adjacent organs. The splenic artery and vein enter and leave the spleen at the hilum, which is found on the visceral surface. Accessory spleens are common (10% of subjects in autopsy series) and are often seen in the region of the hilum or within the lienorenal ligament or the gastrosplenic ligament. They are rounded or oval, measuring 1 to 2 cm in diameter and isoechoic with spleen.[42] Vessels can often be traced from the splenic artery and vein to the accessory spleen.[43] It is important to differentiate accessory spleens from lymph nodes or masses, and in patients undergoing splenectomy for hematologic disease, the presence of accessory spleens should be carefully documented prior to surgery. Occasionally, the spleen may have a long vascular pedicle and is described as "wandering."[44] It may then be found in locations other than the left upper quadrant and is prone to torsion.

Assessment of splenic size by physical examination is inaccurate, and requests for evaluation with imaging are common. A single ultrasonic measurement of splenic length has been shown to be an accurate predictor of splenic volume,[45] and US is cheaper and more accessible than CT scanning without the risks of ionizing radiation. The longitudinal diameter of the spleen should measure less than 11 cm.[46] There are many causes of diffuse splenic enlargement, including infection, liver disease, portal hypertension (Fig. 70-29), lymphoma and other metastatic and primary neoplasms, hematopoietic disease, and splenic vein thrombosis.

US may be used to detect free fluid in an unstable trauma patient, and although large splenic lacerations may be visible, the sensitivity of US to splenic injuries (even with the use of contrast agents) is unacceptably low,[47] and CT is the investigation of choice in the acute setting. In the nontraumatic setting, focal splenic lesions are divided into cystic and solid lesions. Cystic lesions may be congenital, infectious (echinococcal), or secondary to trauma. Solid lesions may be benign or malignant. Splenic hemangiomas and hamartomas can be differentiated by the presence of vascular flow on Doppler imaging. Infarcts are typically peripheral, wedge-shaped, and hypoechoic in the acute stage but later may become hyperechoic. Common malignant solid lesions include primary lymphoma and metastases. These are typically hypoechoic.[48,49]

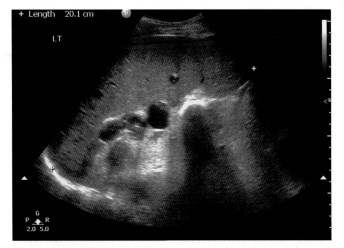

Figure 70-29. Splenomegaly in a patient with cirrhosis and portal hypertension. Note also the dilated splenic vein branches at the splenic hilum.

References

1. Sheafor DH, Paulson EK, Simmons CM, et al: Abdominal percutaneous interventional procedures: Comparison of CT and US guidance. Radiology 207:705-710, 1998.
2. Chatterton BE, Spyropoulos P: Colour Doppler induced streaming: An indicator of the liquid nature of lesions. Br J Radiol 71:1310-1312, 1998.
3. Lewin PA: Quo vadis medical ultrasound? Ultrasonics 42:1-7, 2004.
4. Oktar SO, Yucel C, Ozdemir H, et al: Comparison of conventional sonography, real-time compound sonography, tissue harmonic sonography, and tissue harmonic compound sonography of abdominal and pelvic lesions. AJR 181:1341-1347, 2003.
5. Shapiro RS, Wagreich J, Parsons RB, et al: Tissue harmonic imaging sonography: Evaluation of image quality compared with conventional sonography. AJR 171:1203-1206, 1998.
6. Choudhry S, Gorman B, Charboneau JW, et al: Comparison of tissue harmonic imaging with conventional US in abdominal disease. RadioGraphics 20:1127-1135, 2000.
7. Sodhi KS, Sidhu R, Gulati M, et al: Role of tissue harmonic imaging in focal hepatic lesions: Comparison with conventional sonography. J Gastroenterol Hepatol 20:1488-1493, 2005.
8. Rosenthal SJ, Jones PH, Wetzel LH: Phase inversion tissue harmonic sonographic imaging: A clinical utility study. AJR 176:1393-1398, 2001.
9. Hong HS, Han JK, Kim TK, et al: Ultrasonographic evaluation of the gallbladder: Comparison of fundamental, tissue harmonic, and pulse inversion harmonic imaging. J Ultrasound Med 20:35-41, 2001.
10. Timor-Tritsch IE, Platt LD: Three-dimensional ultrasound experience in obstetrics. Curr Opin Obstet Gynecol 14:569-575, 2002.
11. Yukisawa S, Ohto M, Masuya Y, et al: Contrast-enhanced three-dimensional fusion sonography of small liver metastases with pathologic correlation. J Clin Ultrasound 35:1-8, 2007.
12. Murphy KJ, Rubin JM: Power Doppler: It's a good thing. Semin Ultrasound CT MR 18:13-21, 1997.
13. Lunt MJ: The optimum frequency and angle of insonation for a Doppler ultrasonic flow velocity meter. Phys Med Biol 25:839-848, 1980.
14. Schneider M, Arditi M, Barrau MB, et al: BR1: A new ultrasonographic contrast agent based on sulfur hexafluoride-filled microbubbles. Invest Radiol 30:451-457, 1995.
15. Catalano O, Sandomenico F, Nunziata A, et al: Transient hepatic echogenicity difference on contrast-enhanced ultrasonography: Sonographic sign and pitfall. J Ultrasound Med 26:337-345, 2007.
16. Albrecht T, Hoffmann CW, Schmitz SA, et al: Phase-inversion sonography during the liver-specific late phase of contrast enhancement: Improved detection of liver metastases. AJR 176:1191-1198, 2001.
17. Bryant TH, Blomley MJ, Albrecht T, et al: Improved characterization of liver lesions with liver-phase uptake of liver-specific microbubbles: Prospective multicenter study. Radiology 232:799-809, 2004.
18. Migaleddu V, Virgilio G, Turilli D, et al: Characterization of focal liver lesions in real-time using harmonic imaging with high mechanical index and contrast agent levovist. AJR 182:1505-1512, 2004.
19. Catalano O, Lobianco R, Raso MM, Siani A: Blunt hepatic trauma: Evaluation with contrast-enhanced sonography: Sonographic findings and clinical application. J Ultrasound Med 24:299-310, 2005.
20. Blaivas M, Lyon M, Brannam L, et al: Feasibility of FAST examination performance with ultrasound contrast. J Emerg Med 29:307-311, 2005.
21. Catalano O, Nunziata A, Lobianco R, et al: Real-time harmonic contrast material-specific US of focal liver lesions. RadioGraphics 25:333-349, 2005.
22. Keogh CF, Cooperberg PL: Is it real or is it an artifact? Ultrasound Q 17:201-210, 2001.
23. Sommer FG, Taylor KJ: Differentiation of acoustic shadowing due to calculi and gas collections. Radiology 135:399-403, 1980.
24. Colli A, Fraquelli M, Andreoletti M, et al: Severe liver fibrosis or cirrhosis: Accuracy of US for detection—analysis of 300 cases. Radiology 227:89-94, 2003.
25. Couinaud C: Le Foie: Etudes Anatomiques et Chirurgicales. Paris, Masson, 1957.
26. Lafortune M, Madore F, Patriquin H, et al: Segmental anatomy of the liver: A sonographic approach to the Couinaud nomenclature. Radiology 181:443-448, 1991.
27. Wing VW, Laing FC, Jeffrey RB, et al: Sonographic differentiation of enlarged hepatic arteries from dilated intrahepatic bile ducts. AJR 145:57-61, 1985.
28. Cooperberg PL, Burhenne HJ: Real-time ultrasonography. Diagnostic technique of choice in calculous gallbladder disease. N Engl J Med 5;302:1277-1279, 1980.
29. Ortega D, Burns PN, Hope Simpson D, et al: Tissue harmonic imaging: Is it a benefit for bile duct sonography? AJR 176:653-659, 2001.
30. Hammond DI: Unusual causes of sonographic nonvisualization or nonrecognition of the gallbladder: A review. J Clin Ultrasound 16:77-85, 1988.
31. MacDonald FR, Cooperberg PL, Cohen MM: The WES triad—a specific sonographic sign of gallstones in the contracted gallbladder. Gastrointest Radiol 15;6:39-41, 1981.
32. Lee KF, Wong J, Li JC, et al: Polypoid lesions of the gallbladder. Am J Surg 188:186-190, 2004.
33. Persley KM: Gallbladder polyps. Curr Treat Options Gastroenterol 8:105-108, 2005.
34. Shinkai H, Kimura W, Muto T: Surgical indications for small polypoid lesions of the gallbladder. Am J Surg 175:114-117, 1998.
35. Sanders RC: The significance of sonographic gallbladder wall thickening. J Clin Ultrasound 8:143-146, 1980.
36. Weill F, Eisencher A, Zeltner F: Ultrasonic study of the normal and dilated biliary tree. The "shotgun" sign. Radiology 127:221-224, 1978.
37. Cooperberg PL, Li D, Wong P, et al: Accuracy of common hepatic duct size in the evaluation of extrahepatic biliary obstruction. Radiology 135:141-144, 1980
38. Graham MF, Cooperberg PL, Cohen MM, et al: The size of the normal common hepatic duct following cholecystectomy: An ultrasonographic study. Radiology 135:137-139, 1980.
39. Wedmann B, Borsch G, Coenen C, et al: Effect of cholecystectomy on common bile duct diameters: A longitudinal prospective ultrasonographic study. J Clin Ultrasound 16:619-624, 1988.
40. Walls WJ, Gonzalez G, Martin NL, et al: B-scan ultrasound evaluation of the pancreas. Advantages and accuracy compared to other diagnostic techniques. Radiology 114:127-134, 1975.
41. Donald JJ, Shorvon PJ, Lees WR: A hypoechoic area within the head of the pancreas—a normal variant. Clin Radiol 41:337-338, 1990.
42. Subramanyam BR, Balthazar EJ, Horii SC: Sonography of the accessory spleen. AJR 143:47-49, 1984.
43. Bertolotto M, Gioulis E, Ricci C, et al: Ultrasound and Doppler features of accessory spleens and splenic grafts. Br J Radiol 71:595-600, 1998.
44. Phillips GW, Hemingway AP: Wandering spleen. Br J Radiol 60:188-190, 1987.
45. Loftus WK, Chow LT, Metreweli C: Sonographic measurement of splenic length: Correlation with measurement at autopsy. J Clin Ultrasound 27:71-74, 1999.
46. Frank K, Linhart P, Kortsik C, et al: Sonographic determination of spleen size: Normal dimensions in adults with a healthy spleen. Ultraschall Med 7:134-137, 1986.
47. Poletti PA, Platon A, Becker CD, et al: Blunt abdominal trauma: Does the use of a second-generation sonographic contrast agent help to detect solid organ injuries? AJR 183:1293-1301, 2004.
48. Goerg C, Schwerk WB, Goerg K: Sonography of focal lesions of the spleen. AJR 156:949-953, 1991.
49. Gorg C, Graef C, Bert T: Contrast-enhanced sonography for differential diagnosis of an inhomogeneous spleen of unknown cause in patients with pain in the left upper quadrant. J Ultrasound Med 25:729-734, 2006.

Magnetic Resonance Imaging of Solid Parenchymal Organs

F. Scott Pereles, MD

INTRODUCTION

MR SPECTROSCOPY AND DIFFUSION

GENERAL IMAGING STRATEGIES

INTRODUCTION

MR of solid parenchymal organs has evolved significantly over the last decade. Due to the technological complexity and cost of high field MR machines (greater than 1-T field strength), CT remains the first line imaging modality for solid parenchymal organs. However, MR with its multiplanar and multiphasic capabilities offers several advantages over CT. MR does not rely on ionizing radiation to create images and its gadolinium-based contrast agents are less nephrotoxic and less allergenic than any iodinated CT contrast agents. At centers with up-to-date MR capabilities, MR is becoming a first-line imaging modality and remains the imaging modality of choice for complex problem solving cases.

The most important technological advances responsible for bringing body MR to the fore are the development of high-powered ultrafast gradients. "Ultrafast" gradient subsystems are capable of repetition times less than 4 msec and slew rates of 100 mT/m/msec and faster. These ultrafast gradients allow for multislice image acquisition in a comfortable breath-hold of 20 seconds or less. Breath-hold times are further decreased by the advent of parallel imaging algorithms such as GRAPPA (GeneRalized Autocalibrating Partially Parallel Acquisition) and SENSE (SENSitivity Encoding). Abdominal and pelvic MR of the 20th century relied on slower respiratory-gated imaging techniques and conventional spin-echo sequences. 21st-century MR is a combination of breath-hold rapid acquisition schemes such as fat-suppressed gradient-echo and motion-independent snapshot techniques such as half-Fourier acquisition single-shot turbo spin-echo (HASTE), single-shot fast spin-echo (SSFSE), true fast imaging with steady-state precession (FISP), fast imaging employing steady-state acquisition (FIESTA), and balanced fast field echo (FFE). Projectional 2D Rapid Acquisition Relaxation Enhancement (RARE) imaging of the pancreaticobiliary tree and 3D navigator

magnetic resonance cholangiopancreatography (MRCP) techniques round out the latest advances for solid organ imaging that now include depiction of ductal anatomy and pathology.

MR SPECTROSCOPY AND DIFFUSION

Magnetic resonance (MR) spectroscopy and diffusion-weighted abdominal imaging largely remain experimental at the time of this edition but may play an increasing clinical role in the future. Abdominal MR techniques discussed in this chapter will focus on imaging at 1.5 T. Body imaging at 3 T is not as widely available and has its own inherent set of technical intricacies related to greater sensitivity to field inhomogeneity, magnetohydrodynamic effects, and specific absorptive rate (SAR) limitations, as well as other problems, and therefore will not be discussed further in this chapter.

GENERAL IMAGING STRATEGIES

It is desirable to image not only the solid organ of interest but also the adjacent organs and any associated periparenchymal tissues. If the liver, spleen, or pancreas is the target organ of interest, complete MR will include all of these organs as well as their associated vasculature, biliary tract, surrounding support structures, and draining lymph nodes.

Dedicated surface coils placed on the patient's abdomen rather than the main magnet housing body coil are preferable for improved signal reception and higher signal-to-noise ratio. Although full T1 and T2 characterization imaging protocols have been replaced by an emphasis on dynamic contrast enhancement patterns demonstrated on fat-saturated gradient-recalled echo T1-weighted images, some type of balanced gradient-echo imaging or snapshot (often referred to as single-shot) fast spin-echo imaging (HASTE or SSFSE) is usually employed to give quick T2 information. Both two-dimensional (2D) and three-dimensional (3D) T2-weighted techniques are used depending on equipment vendor and capabilities. For 2D imaging, standard axial and coronal imaging planes are most frequently employed. The sagittal plane or in other obliquities are useful for niche applications such as MRCP.

MR angiography (MRA) with ultrafast contrast-enhanced 3D gradient-echo techniques may be included as part of general imaging protocols or may be performed as separate angiographic studies depending on institutional preferences and clinical situation. The use of gadolinium contrast-enhanced imaging is used in most general abdominal MR studies, with the exception of adrenal imaging or an isolated MRCP examination.

Contrast-enhanced imaging of solid abdominal organs can be performed using 2D or newer 3D techniques. Both are

effective, and it is a matter of personal preference whether one uses 2D fast low-angle shot (FLASH) (Siemens) or fast multiplanar spoiled gradient-echo (FMPSPGR) (General Electric) versus using 3D volume interpolated breath-hold examination (VIBE) (Siemens) or 3D fast acquisition with multiphase enhanced (FAME)/liver acquisition with volume acceleration (LAVA) (General Electric) or 3D (T1W High Resolution Isotropic Volume Examination (THRIVE) (Phillips). Proponents of 3D techniques argue that the acquired volume can then be interrogated in any plane with excellent spatial resolution and signal. In truth, few people interrogate these volumes on 3D workstations or even generate multiplanar reformat (MPR) images in planes other than those acquired. Actual results of 3D quality vary based on equipment capabilities. I find that in practice, even on high-end machines, the true partition thicknesses required for coverage from diaphragm to liver tip (often below the iliac crests) in a

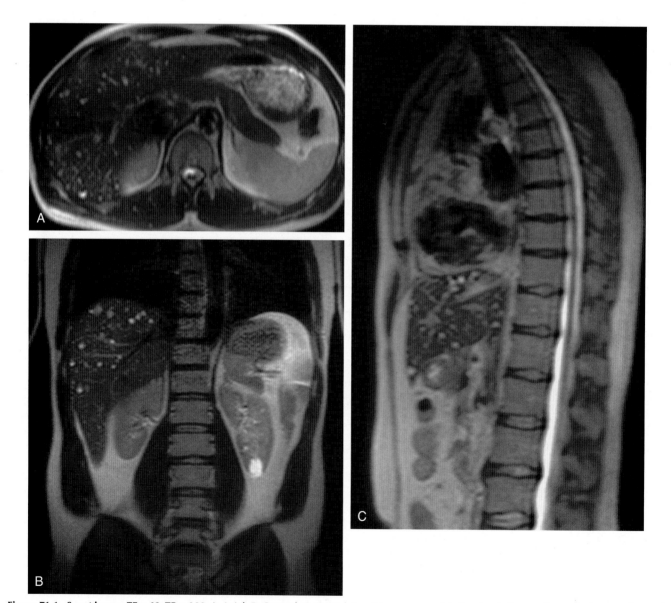

Figure 71-1. Scout images TE = 62, TR = 900. A. Axial. **B.** Coronal. **C.** Sagittal. Scout images are quick, low resolution gradient-echo images obtained in the axial, coronal, and sagittal planes to localize areas of interest and plan further sequences. The following features should be assessed: satisfactory surface coil position; homogeneity of signal across intensity in the image; artifacts such as eddy currents, susceptibility artifact from implants or foreign bodies. Additional scout images may be obtained to better localize the organ of interest and more accurately position individual pulse sequence acquisitions.

comfortable breath-hold are far greater than those published. In fact, to acquire the necessary dynamic 3D volumes, 3D parameters of partition thickness actually approach 2D slice thickness. Furthermore, the 3D slice profile is not as clean and therefore gives a slightly hazy patina to the images. I prefer to use 2D slices of 5- to 6-mm thickness with an acceptable gap of 1 or 2 mm but no greater. With these parameters, we keep breath-holds under 18 seconds and cover the entire abdomen from diaphragm to iliac crests or more. This discussion is included because clearly there are a number of rational ways to perform the same task and there has been much hype over the VIBE sequence and its analogs. For those imagers that have not been enamored with the use of 3D body sequences, I believe that a 2D approach is still defensible. This fact may change however; especially as MR machines continue to improve in speed when parallel imaging is used.

A general body MR protocol synopsis for abdominal solid organs follows. It is not all encompassing, but it is a relatively comprehensive base protocol serving to image the liver, spleen, pancreas, adrenals, and kidneys. All sequences are either breath-hold or breathing-independent snapshot-type acquisitions. Those mired in the past will wonder where all of the T2 imaging has gone. The simple answer is that on 1.5-T magnets built since 2000, adequate abdominal imaging of solid organs relies on the breath-held dynamic T1-weighted gradient-echo imaging with fat saturation. A mixed T1/T2 sequence such as HASTE or SSFSE is adequate to yield any necessary general T2 information. For pancreaticobiliary imaging such as MRCP, projectional T2 images such as RARE and thick-slab SSFSE and navigator 3D turbo spin-echo (TSE) or fast spin-echo (FSE) sequences are added.

1. Scout images (rapid three-plane gradient-echo or single-shot fast spin-echo) (Fig. 71-1)
2. Axial in- and opposed-phase T1-weighted gradient-echo images; useful for characterizing fatty liver infiltration or incidental adrenal nodules as adenomas or not (Fig. 71-2)
3. Axial T2 HASTE (SSFSE) images (Fig. 71-3)
4. Coronal T2 HASTE images (fat-saturated if desired for cholangiographic effect) (Fig. 71.4)
5. Axial fat-saturated T1-weighted gradient-echo images prior to contrast administration (Fig. 71-5)
6. Coronal fat-saturated T1-weighted gradient-echo images prior to contrast administration (Fig. 71-6)
7. Axial fat-saturated T1-weighted gradient-echo images after contrast administration during arterial liver phase (hepatic arteries and portal veins opacified but hepatic veins not opacified [about 25-30 seconds postcontrast]) (Fig. 71-7)
8. Axial fat-saturated T1-weighted gradient-echo images after contrast administration at portal hepatic phase (hepatic veins opacified [about 50-70 seconds postcontrast]) (Fig. 71-8)
9. Axial fat-saturated T1-weighted gradient-echo images after contrast administration at equilibrium phase (generally considered 90 to 120 seconds postcontrast) (Fig. 71-9)

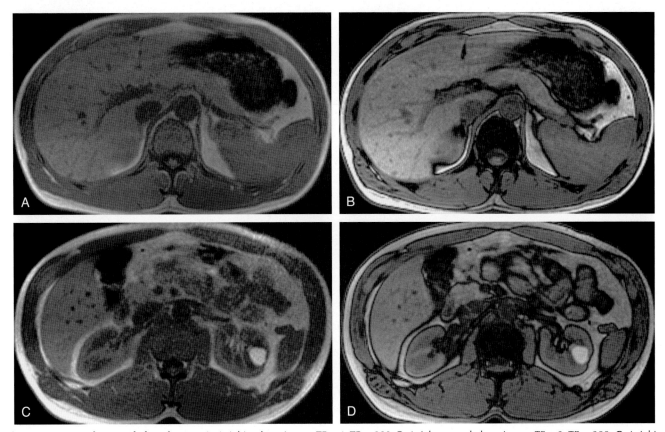

Figure 71-2. In and opposed phase images. A. Axial in phase image; TE = 4, TR = 200. **B.** Axial opposed phase image; TE = 2, TR = 200. **C.** Axial in phase image; TE = 4, TR = 200. **D.** Axial opposed phase image; TE = 2, TR = 200. In- and opposed-phase images are primarily employed to characterize adrenal lesions as lipid-rich adenomas, to detect hepatic steatosis and focal hepatic fat deposition, to identify fat-containing lesions, such as hepatic adenomas and hepatoma, renal angiomyolipomas, and adrenal myelolipomas. The processional frequencies of fat and water have resonance properties that can create constructive interference and form additive signal or make destructive interference patterns that cancel out signal depending upon the echo time chosen (TE).

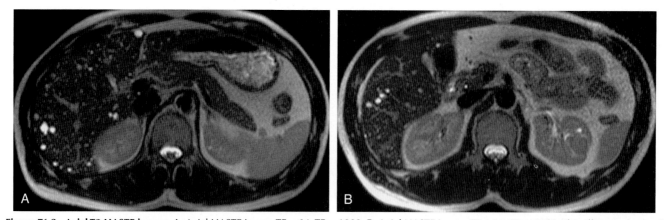

Figure 71-3. Axial T2 HASTE images. A. Axial HASTE image; TE = 64, TR = 1000. **B.** Axial HASTE image; TE = 64, TR = 1000. This all-purpose mixed T1- and T2-weighted sequence is sufficiently fast to be relatively motion resistant and therefore does not require a breath-hold. HASTE is a relatively signal starved sequence and as a result is not as sensitive for detecting solid lesions as T2 fast spin-echo imaging. It is however significantly faster and less motion sensitive and reliably detects fluid and fluid filled structures. It often does an adequate job of delineating bowel. Furthermore it is excellent for depicting cysts, hemangiomas, bile, and pancreatic ducts. It is not a stand alone sequence and is always performed as part of a larger exam that includes T1-weighted images prior to and following contrast administration.

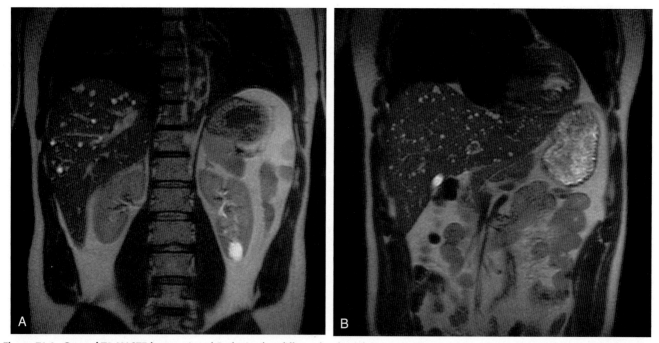

Figure 71-4. Coronal T2 HASTE images. A and **B** obtained at different levels in the same sequence. These images serve the same purpose as axial HASTE images but display anatomy in a more familiar way, similar to an abdominal radiograph or intravenous urogram. Fat saturation can be added to the coronal HASTE acquisition to render a cholangiographic appearance. The coronal HASTE images can show filling defects and stones in the bile ducts. Correlating coronal and axial images can help differentiate true stones from flow related and image-crosstalk artifacts that can simulate a stone. True stones are usually better defined and more eccentrically located within the ducts. Artifacts are usually centrally located within the duct and usually have mild to moderately centrally decreased signal intensity within the duct on one or two slices rather than the more discrete signal void produced by a stone.

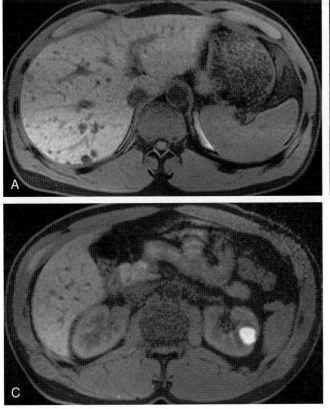

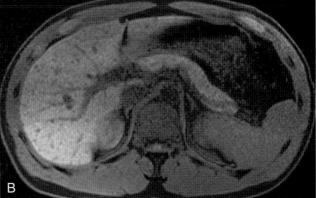

Figure 71-5. Axial fat-saturated T1 GRE images precontrast: TE = 1.94, TR = 2. A-C. Axial scans obtained at different levels in same series. These are the most sensitive images for detecting subtle pancreatic abnormalities. Edema, fibrosis, and carcinoma all decrease the nor-mal high T1 signal intensity of the pancreas. The pancreas is the T1 brightest organ in abdomen, having slightly greater intensity than the liver in normal patients. Precontrast images serve as a baseline reference to determine if any lesions show contrast enhancement. sub-acute hemorrhage, hematomas, endometriomas that contain T1 bright proteinatious debris as well as extracellular met-hemoglobin, and melanin in melanoma metastases.

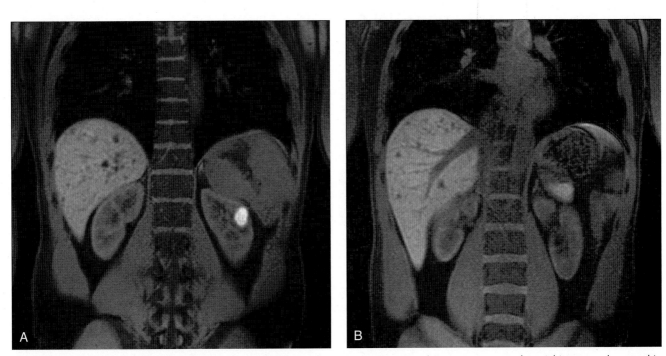

Figure 71-6. Coronal fat-saturated T1 GRE images precontrast. A and **B.** These images serve the same purpose as the axial images and are used in comparison with the postcontrast images of the coronal plane.

Continued

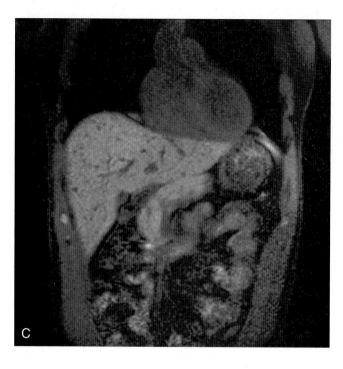

Figure 71-6, *cont'd.* **C. Coronal fat-saturated T1 GRE images precontrast.** These images serve the same purpose as the axial images and are used in comparison with the postcontrast images of the coronal plane.

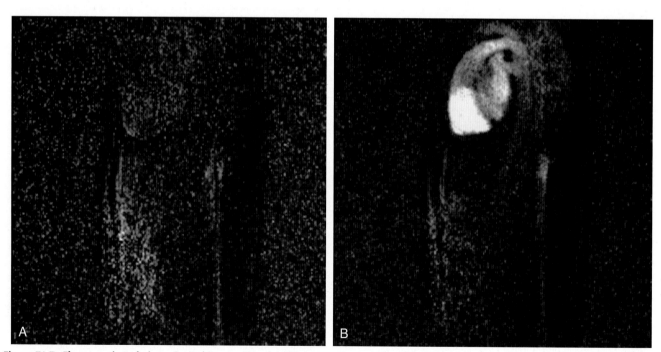

Figure 71-7. Fluoroscopic technique. Sagittal images; TE = 1.1, TR = 1000, TI = 500. **A** and **B.** A fluoroscopic technique for visualization of contrast arrival within the aorta can be used for timing abdominal MR examinations.

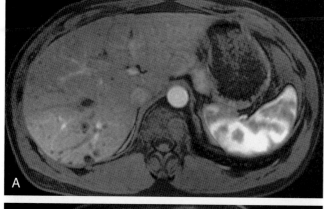

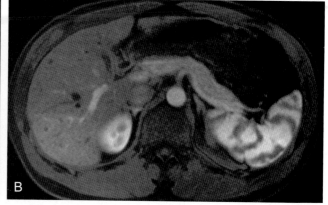

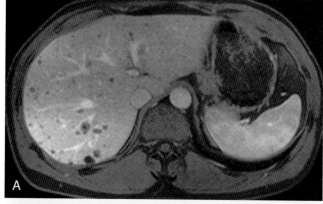

Figure 71-8. Axial fat-saturated T1 GRE images postcontrast (hepatic arterial phase approximately 30 seconds). A-C. Images obtained during hepatic arterial liver phase (hepatic arteries and portal veins opacified but hepatic veins not opacified (empirically about 30 seconds post-contrast infusion). Once contrast is seen in the abdominal aorta the acquisition is begun. This results in a very reliable scan during the arterial phase of liver enhancement. Arterial phase hypervascular lesions such as hepatocellular carcinoma, hepatic adenomas, focal nodular hyperplasia and some metastases (eg. renal cell, carcinoid) are often most apparent on this phase. This acquisition also serves as the corticomedullary phase for evaluation of the kidneys.

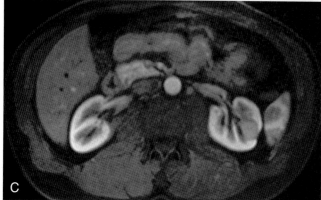

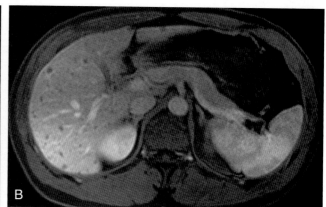

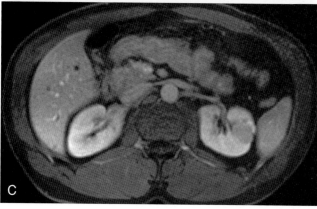

Figure 71-9. Axial fat-saturated T1 GRE images postcontrast (equilibrium phase approximately 90 seconds). A-C. This acquisition is important for characterizing solid organ lesions. It also serves as a nephrographic phase for renal evaluation.

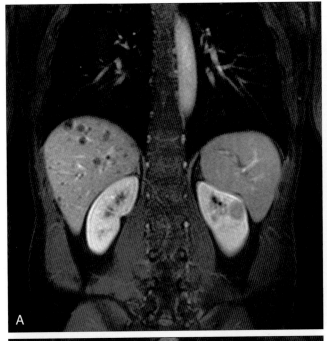

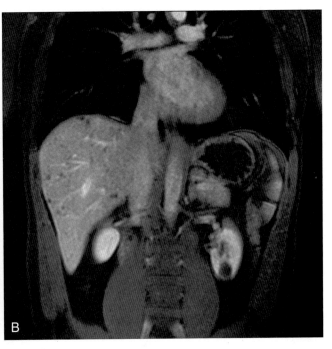

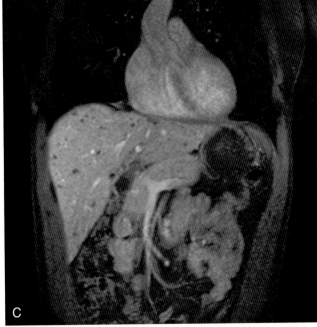

Figure 71-10. Coronal fat-saturated T1 GRE images postcontrast (early delayed phase approximately 120 seconds). A-C. This acquisition is employed for its multiplanar evaluation capabilities and is quite useful for defining surgical anatomy, the relationship of hepatic masses to the portal and hepatic veins as well as extent of organ and periorgan invasion. It also serves as a late nephrographic and early excretory phase for renal evaluation.

10. Coronal fat-saturated T1-weighted gradient-echo images after contrast administration at 2 to 3 minutes postcontrast (Fig. 71-10).
11. Axial fat-saturated T1-weighted gradient-echo images after contrast administration at approximately 5 minutes for delayed imaging (Fig. 71-11). This can be extended to 10 or even 20 minutes postcontrast in cases where cholangiocarcinoma is suspected for improved delayed imaging of such tumors.

In about one dozen short breath-holds, a complete abdominal examination can be obtained. The combined imaging time for such an examination is no more than 5 minutes including

a few repeat breath-holds if the patient is uncooperative in following directions. The actual length of the examination is typically no longer than 20 to 25 minutes including set-up time.

If software and hardware configurations are available on the equipment, parallel imaging techniques can be used for most of these sequences to decrease breath-hold times. Inherent in using parallel imaging algorithms with a typical acceleration factor of 2 is a loss of signal of about 15% to 20% depending on the exact implementation used in the MR unit, despite the fact that this is sometimes downplayed by equipment manufacturers and salespeople. Hence, if the image is starved for signal to begin with, using parallel imaging

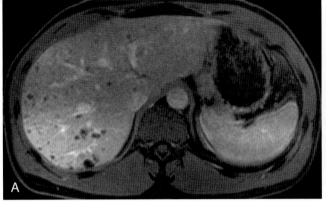

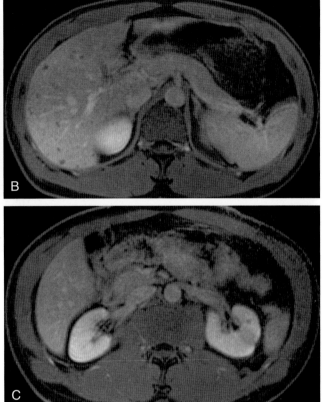

Figure 71-11. Axial fat-saturated T1 GRE images postcontrast (delayed phase approximately 180 seconds). A-C, this acquisition further characterizes most lesions and is especially helpful for depicting renal lesions.

is likely to be deleterious to diagnostic quality. But many imaging sequences, especially postcontrast, are not starved for signal, and therefore acceleration schemes are not detrimental to image quality. SENSE (SENSitivity Encoding) acceleration schemes like SENSE, modified SENSE (mSENSE), and array spatial sensitivity encoding technique (ASSET) typically require field of view to be increased so that there is no wrap in the imaged field of view. These algorithms manipulate data in the image domain after image reconstruction, and wrap can cause significant artifact to be propagated in the final image when using these parallel imaging schemes. Algorithms like SMASH (SiMultaneous Acquisition of Spatial Harmonics) with implementations such as GRAPPA (GeneRalized Autocalibrating Partially Parallel Acquisition) manipulate data before reconstruction and are slightly more forgiving regarding wrap and field of view issues.

Positron Emission Tomography/Computed Tomography of the Solid Parenchymal Organs

Karen A. Mourtzikos, MD

GALLBLADDER AND BILIARY TRACT

Minimal physiologic fluorine-18-deoxyglucose (FDG) activity is seen in the gallbladder or biliary tract, and these structures are usually indistinguishable from the liver. If the gallbladder, however, is distended, the lumen may appear photopenic on PET/CT images.

Cholangiocarcinoma

Studies demonstrate overall sensitivity and specificity of 61% and 80%, respectively, for cholangiocarcinoma. Further evaluation based upon morphology increased the sensitivity to 85% by analyzing only patients with the nodular type. Conversely, infiltrating cholangiocarcinoma showed a decreased sensitivity of only 18%.[1] In sclerosing cholangitis, the sensitivity was 100% and the specificity was 80%, with a false-positive secondary to acute cholangitis. Inflammation from biliary stents may present interpretation challenges, but use of the concomitant CT aids in appropriate diagnosis. Sensitivity for metastatic disease was 65%, with false-negatives related to intraperitoneal lesions of less than 1 cm.[1]

Gallbladder Carcinoma

Relative sensitivity and specificity for residual gallbladder carcinoma with FDG-PET were 78% and 80%, respectively.[1] Sensitivity for distant metastases was only 56%, and although PET detected laparoscopic port-site recurrence, it was limited, again, in its ability to identify carcinomatosis.

Because most patients are diagnosed with gallbladder carcinoma after cholecystectomy, the utility of PET/CT is primarily in the initial staging or in restaging when recurrence is suspected.

LIVER

The liver demonstrates diffusely increased FDG activity physiologically and is used as a qualitative comparison point for other foci of uptake in the body. Activity that is equal or greater than the liver raises concern for pathologic processes. Mild heterogeneity is usually present and is also physiologic. It is important to differentiate between small foci, which may represent early malignancy, and the heterogeneous nature of the liver parenchyma.

Metastases to the liver occur more frequently than primary hepatic malignancy, such as hepatocellular carcinoma, and typically arise from colorectal, gastric, pancreatic, lung, and breast carcinoma. FDG-PET imaging of hepatocellular carcinoma is somewhat limited due to the activity of glucose-6-phosphatase, which is found in varying degrees and even in higher amounts in this tumor.[2,3] Glucose-6-phosphatase dephosphorylates glucose, allowing for is transport out of the cell. In a similar manner, this enzyme acts upon FDG and can create the outflow of the radiopharmaceutical, thereby limiting accurate imaging and appropriate detection of tumor.

Hepatocellular carcinoma is more FDG avid than the liver in approximately 55% of cases; it is equal to or less avid in 30% and 15% of cases, respectively. PET detects only 50% to 70% of hepatocellular carcinomas[4,5] but is useful in detection of distant metastases as well as in evaluation of recurrence.

Initial Staging

In FDG avid hepatocellular carcinoma, PET/CT imaging is valuable to staging, especially in the assessment of distant metastatic disease. Studies have illustrated detection rate of 83% for extrahepatic metastases larger than 1 cm and 13% for lesions less than or equal to 1 cm.[6]

Monitoring of Therapy and Detection of Recurrence

Ablation of hepatocellular carcinomas is becoming an increasingly popular therapeutic means on treating unresectable tumors. Following treatment response with only anatomic imaging may limit assessment of residual viable tumor. FDG PET is useful in guidance of further therapy[7,8] by detecting metabolically active tissue. In order to limit confounding factors such as postablation inflammation, a delay of several weeks is recommended following therapy. Current research seeks to establish more definitive guidelines for the evaluation of post-therapy hepatocellular carcinoma using FDG-PET.

Similarly, in the detection of recurrence, PET plays a role in discovering metabolically active tumor prior to the development of anatomic evidence on conventional imaging. Evaluation of patients with elevated serum α-fetoprotein levels after the treatment of hepatocellular carcinoma and negative conventional imaging work-ups suggests a sensitivity, specificity, and accuracy of FDG-PET for detecting hepatocellular carcinoma recurrence of 73.3%, 100%, and 74.2%, respectively.[9]

Overall, most metastatic tumors are FDG avid and readily detectable using PET/CT. A fraction of hepatocellular carcinomas demonstrate increased radiopharmaceutical uptake and may be assessed using metabolic imaging. Approximately one third of hepatocellular carcinomas and most benign processes do not accumulate increased amounts of FDG and therefore cannot be reliably assessed on PET/CT scans. PET/CT is not indicated in the screening of patients who are at increased risk for hepatocellular carcinoma or in the evaluation of focal hepatic lesions in the setting of chronic hepatitis C virus infection, which can obscure minimal uptake in a malignant focus.

SPLEEN

Physiological activity in the spleen should be homogeneous and less than that of the liver. Focal abnormalities (Figs. 72-1 and 72-2) may indicate malignancy, such as metastasis or lymphoma, or infection, such as an abscess. Diffusely increased uptake to level of activity equal to or greater than the liver is

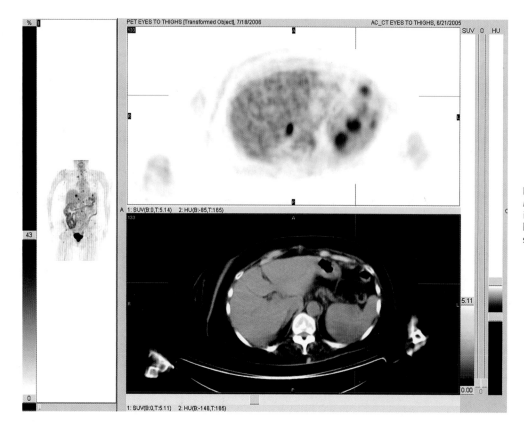
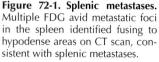

Figure 72-1. Splenic metastases. Multiple FDG avid metastatic foci in the spleen identified fusing to hypodense areas on CT scan, consistent with splenic metastases.

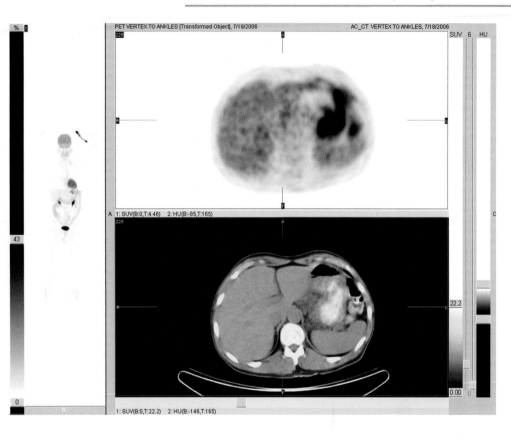

Figure 72-2. Diffuse splenic lymphoma. Diffusely increased radiopharmaceutical accumulation in the spleen, approximately equivalent to the level of activity in the liver, most suggestive of lymphomatous involvement of the spleen. The intensely increased activity in the stomach is consistent with gastric lymphoma.

concerning for lymphoma involvement. In the setting of growth colony stimulating factor administration, diffusely increased radiopharmaceutical uptake in the spleen is nonspecific, and although it is most likely secondary to effects of the drug, the possibility of underlying pathology cannot be completely excluded. Furthermore, varying degrees of diffuse splenic activity of uncertain significance have been identified in hematological conditions.

PANCREAS

Minimal physiological uptake is identified in pancreas on PET/CT scan. In cases of pancreatitis, the pattern of increased FDG activity may be diffuse or focal in nature and may be difficult to distinguish from malignancy.

Pancreatic Ductal Adenocarcinoma

CT and MRI are used primarily to image pancreatic ductal adenocarcinoma, but they may be limited in the setting of enlargement of the pancreatic head without discrete mass, in mass-forming pancreatitis, in diagnosis of small locoregional lymph nodes, or in the detection of distant metastases. Metabolic imaging may be applied to improve preoperative diagnostic accuracy and potentially limit adverse outcomes from inappropriate surgical interventions. Studies have demonstrated the relatively high sensitivity and specificity of PET in distinguishing benign and malignant lesions in the pancreas (Fig. 72-3)—92% and 85% in comparison to 65% and 62% for CT, respectively.[10] PET is also less dependent on lesion size for diagnostic accuracy.[11]

Staging

T staging is primarily determined by anatomic imaging techniques, as it depends upon the relationship among the tumor, vascular structure, and adjacent organs. FDG-PET is not clearly superior to CT for N staging, likely due to the proximity of lymph nodes to the primary mass, which may become obscured. However, in the case of anatomically small lymph nodes (less than 1 cm), with increased metabolic activity, PET/CT would have an advantage. PET/CT is more accurate than CT alone in the detection of distant metastatic disease. In studies, PET has demonstrated previously unsuspected metastases to the liver as well as in distant sites. In the instance where neither PET nor CT showed metastatic involvement, intraoperative findings demonstrated carcinomatosis.[10] Overall, PET/CT is a critical preoperative staging imaging modality for resection of pancreatic cancer, as it significantly improves patient selection and is ultimately cost-effective.[12]

Monitoring Response to Treatment and Detection of Recurrence

Although large-scale studies have not been completed, to date, preliminary work suggests the utility of PET/CT in determining response to neoadjuvant therapy and in predicting outcomes.[13] One such pilot study suggested that the absence of FDG activity 1 month following the completion of chemotherapy is an indicator of potentially improved survival in contradistinction to those with persistent uptake.[13] In terms of detection of recurrence, PET again demonstrates its ability to identify malignant foci before significant structural growth is detectable. Studies have shown up to 50% incremental

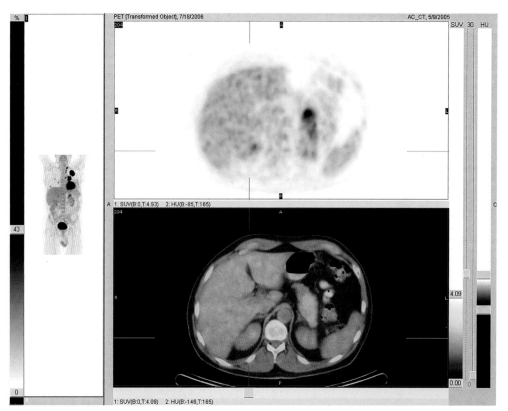

Figure 72-3. Pancreatic adenocarcinoma. Increased FDG activity is identified fusing to the distal portion of the pancreas, most consistent with pancreatic adenocarcinoma. This finding was made incidentally in a patient referred for lung cancer staging.

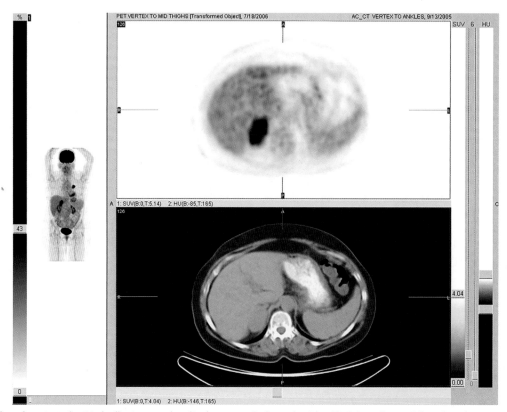

Figure 72-4. Adrenal metastasis. Markedly increased radiopharmaceutical uptake identified in a large right adrenal metastasis from primary adenocarcinoma of the lung.

information provided by PET, which resulted in alteration in the patient management plan.[14]

Limitations in Imaging

The primary challenge faced by PET/CT in the imaging of pancreatic cancer pertains to altered glucose metabolism created by glucose intolerance and diabetes seen in these patients. This setting may create false-negative findings in patients who are hyperglycemic or have inadequately controlled blood glucose levels. False-negatives may also result when the tumor is less than 1 cm, such as in small ampullary carcinomas. False-positives are mainly the result of inflammation secondary to pancreatitis, as discussed previously.

In summary, PET/CT is an important imaging adjunct to CT and may provide earlier detection of metastatic or recurrent disease, assisting in treatment planning as well as potentially improving outcome.

ADRENAL GLANDS

No increased FDG uptake is usually seen in the adrenal glands. At times, there may be unilateral or bilateral diffusely increased activity, which is physiological in nature and likely secondary to the functioning adrenal gland. Focally increased uptake may represent either adenoma or metastasis (Fig. 72-4). Overall, a comparison of adrenal gland uptake to liver activity in lung cancer patients demonstrated a sensitivity of 93% and a specificity of 90%.[15] In addition, with the use of a standard uptake valve (SUV) guideline of 3.1 in combination with concomitant CT data of Hounsfield units of less than 10, consistent with lipid-containing adenomas, the sensitivity and specificity were 100% and 98%, respectively.[16]

PET/CT is useful in the detection of adrenal uptake and in differentiating benign adenomas from potentially management altering adrenal metastases.[17]

References

1. Anderson CD, et al: Fluorodeoxyglucose PET imaging in the evaluation of gallbladder carcinoma and cholangiocarcinoma. J Gastrointest Surg 8:90-97, 2004.
2. Wong TZ, Paulson EK, Nelson RC, et al: Practical approach to diagnostic CT combined with PET. AJR Am J Roentgenol 188:622-629, 2007.
3. Blodgett TM, Meltzer CC, Townsend DW: PET/CT: Form and function. Radiology 242:360-385, 2007.
3. Weber G, Morris HP: Comparative biochemistry of hepatomas. III. Carbohydrate enzymes in liver tumors of different growth rates. Cancer Res 23:987-994, 1963.
4. Delbeke D, et al: Evaluation of benign vs malignant hepatic lesions with positron emission tomography. Arch Surg 133:510-515; discussion 515-516, 1998.
5. Khan MA, et al: Positron emission tomography scanning in the evaluation of hepatocellular carcinoma. J Hepatol 32:792-797, 2000.
6. Sugiyama M, et al: ^{18}F-FDG PET in the detection of extrahepatic metastases from hepatocellular carcinoma. J Gastroenterol 39:961-968, 2004.
7. Torizuka T, et al: Value of fluorine-18-FDG-PET to monitor hepatocellular carcinoma after interventional therapy. J Nucl Med 35:1965-1969, 1994.
8. Vitola JV, et al: Positron emission tomography with F-18-fluorodeoxyglucose to evaluate the results of hepatic chemoembolization. Cancer 78:2216-2222, 1996.
9. Chen YK, et al: Utility of FDG-PET for investigating unexplained serum AFP elevation in patients with suspected hepatocellular carcinoma recurrence. Anticancer Res 25:4719-4725, 2005.
10. Delbeke D, et al: Optimal interpretation of FDG PET in the diagnosis, staging and management of pancreatic carcinoma. J Nucl Med 40: 1784-1791, 1999.
11. Rose DM, et al: ^{18}Fluorodeoxyglucose-positron emission tomography in the management of patients with suspected pancreatic cancer. Ann Surg 229:729-737; discussion 737-738, 1999.
12. Heinrich S, et al: Positron emission tomography/computed tomography influences on the management of resectable pancreatic cancer and its cost-effectiveness. Ann Surg 242:235-243, 2005.
13. Maisey NR, et al: FDG-PET in the prediction of survival of patients with cancer of the pancreas: A pilot study. Br J Cancer 83:287-293, 2000.
14. Franke C, et al: 18-FDG positron emission tomography of the pancreas: Diagnostic benefit in the follow-up of pancreatic carcinoma. Anticancer Res 19:2437-2442, 1999.
15. Caoili EM, Korobkin M, Brown RK, et al: Differentiating adrenal adenomas from nonadenomas using (18)F-FDG PET/CT quantitative and qualitative evaluation. Acad Radiol 14:468-475, 2007.
16. Gross MD, Avram A, Fig LM, et al: Contemporary adrenal scintigraphy. Eur J Nucl Med Mol Imaging 34:547-557, 2007.
17. Weber WA, Figlin R: Monitoring cancer treatment with PET/CT: Does it make a difference? J Nucl Med 48 [Suppl 1]:36S-44S, 2007.

Techniques of Percutaneous Tissue Acquisition

Susan Delaney, MD • Erik K. Paulson, MD • Rendon C. Nelson, MD

PREPROCEDURE EVALUATION	Routes to Avoid
CHOICE OF MODALITY FOR IMAGE GUIDANCE	**SPECIFIC ORGAN-RELATED TECHNIQUES**
Fluoroscopy	Liver
Ultrasonography	Pancreas
Computed Tomography	Bowel
Magnetic Resonance Imaging	Lymph Nodes
CHOICE OF NEEDLES	Lymphoma
BIOPSY PLANNING	Spleen
Acceptable Routes	**COMPLICATIONS**

The acquisition of tissue from lesions that are neither visually apparent nor palpable has evolved from being performed in the operating room by surgeons to being performed percutaneously by radiologists using image guidance. Image-guided percutaneous biopsies have also evolved from being reserved for large and superficial lesions to include small, deep, and/or precariously positioned lesions. With these changes has come a trend toward more outpatient procedures, fewer complications, and lower cost. Because radiologists are willing to biopsy more challenging lesions, there has also been a trend toward imaging techniques with real-time guidance such as ultrasonography (US) or CT fluoroscopy. In the past, the success of image-guided biopsies has depended not only on the expertise of the radiologist but also on that of the cytopathologist. While a proficient cytopathologist is extremely advantageous, often enabling a sample consisting of only a minimal amount of tissue to be diagnostic, the increased utilization of core or cutting biopsy needles has diminished the overall impact of their contribution.[1]

The role of image-guided percutaneous biopsies is mainly to diagnose or exclude the presence of malignancy, to stage patients with a known malignancy, to monitor the response to tumor therapy, to confirm or exclude recurrent tumor, and to differentiate whether nodal enlargement is due to tumor or infection. Furthermore, biopsy techniques can be used to diagnose nonmalignant medical diseases in the liver and kidneys. For these "medical"-type biopsies, larger-bore needles are generally required to obtain specimens for histology.

The challenge facing radiologists is to provide a biopsy service where adequate tissue can be readily obtained from almost any lesion in the abdomen and pelvis, on almost any patient, with near real-time needle-tip visualization during both placement and sampling. This has numerous implications related to the coagulation status and patient condition, choice of imaging modality, choice of type and gauge of needles, and the transgression of normal structures. This chapter discusses the details of these techniques in a systematic fashion including the preprocedural evaluation, the choice of modality for image guidance, the choice of needles, biopsy planning, specific organ-related details, and complications.

PREPROCEDURE EVALUATION

A complete preprocedure evaluation is an important component of an efficient and effective biopsy service. This evaluation should consist of reviewing prior diagnostic imaging studies, obtaining a bleeding history and appropriate laboratory studies, and obtaining written informed consent.

Review of prior diagnostic imaging studies will confirm the presence of a lesion suitable for biopsy. Review of imaging also allows the radiologist to plan a specific approach, choose the appropriate guidance modality, and characterize the lesion to provide the pathologist with an appropriate differential diagnosis. The importance of reviewing prior imaging cannot be overstated. For example, a radiologist may be asked to biopsy a lesion that, on review, proves to be a benign hemangioma or cyst. In this scenario, confirmatory imaging or no further study at all, may be more appropriate than biopsy. Similarly, a deeply located retroperitoneal lymph node, easily detected by CT, may be difficult or even impossible to localize for a US-guided biopsy unless a diagnostic CT scan is readily available to serve as a reference.

The appropriate laboratory investigation of the patient before a biopsy remains the subject of debate. No single published guideline is widely accepted or used. This lack of consensus stems from the fact that no prospective evaluation of a large number of patients has been performed where various factors including patient history, specific type of procedure, and laboratory tests have been compared with outcome.[2,3]

Silverman and colleagues[2] proposed a strategy for screening laboratory tests for abdominal interventional procedures based primarily on the nature of the procedure itself and the medical history. The strategy involves placing procedures into two groups: those with a negligible bleeding risk and those with a significant bleeding risk. Procedures considered to be of negligible risk include fluid aspiration such as paracentesis. Procedures considered to be of significant risk include tissue biopsies and abscess drainage. The strategy also places patients into risk categories based on results of a detailed screening history focused on bleeding risk factors. The bleeding history is then combined with the procedure risk to determine whether laboratory tests are required. Silverman and colleagues' strategy suggests that all patients scheduled for a tissue biopsy, even those at low risk for bleeding, should undergo a screening prothrombin time (PT) and partial thromboplastin time (PTT) as well as a platelet count. The aim of such laboratory tests is to detect an unsuspected anticoagulant, thrombocytopenia, or occult disseminated intravascular coagulation. While the approach described

by Silverman and colleagues seems somewhat conservative and may not be cost effective, it may be justifiable in today's litigious medical climate. Indeed, as reviewed by Payne and colleagues,[4,5] surveys of the radiology community indicate widespread use of coagulation screening even though there is little data to support this practice. Similarly, recommendations from the American College of Radiology and Society of Interventional Radiology have been somewhat vague.[6]

An excellent method to assess a patient's bleeding risk is to simply obtain a focused bleeding history with queries directed toward bruising, prolonged bleeding, or oozing following tooth extraction or minor surgical procedures; general medical problems, including renal disease and hepatic disease; and medication use, including warfarin and aspirin.[4] It is particularly convenient to obtain such a history at the time a biopsy is scheduled by using a questionnaire administered by telephone. If the results of this interview fail to disclose a risk factor for bleeding, patients may be considered to be low risk.

If the bleeding history is positive or if it is not possible to obtain an accurate history or if the lesion for biopsy is particularly vascular, a PT/PTT and platelet count should be obtained. If the platelet count is greater than 100,000/mL, we proceed with the biopsy (Table 73-1). If the platelet count varies from 50,000 to 100,000/mL, patients are at increased risk of a bleeding complication but in the absence of concomitant diseases predisposing to bleeding, platelet transfusion is not required. If the platelet count is less than 50,000/mL, platelet transfusion should be performed before or during the biopsy. If either the PT or PTT is greater than 1.5 times the control value, our policy is to either administer fresh frozen plasma or to postpone the biopsy until the PT/PTT have been normalized (Table 73-2). An elevation of the PT induced by warfarin may be reversed by administering vitamin K intravenously. An elevation of PTT induced by heparin may be reversed with protamine, a heparin antagonist. As the half-life of heparin is only 60 minutes (in the absence of liver disease), one may discontinue heparin and perform the biopsy hours later, once the PTT has returned to normal.[4]

Table 73-1

Guideline for Transfusion of Fresh Frozen Plasma Before a Tissue Biopsy

Clotting Parameter	Value
Prothrombin time	>1.5 times normal (usually >18 seconds)
Activated partial thromboplastin time	>1.5 times normal (usually >55-60 seconds)

Adapted from Payne CS: A primer on patient management problems in interventional radiology. AJR Am J Roentgenol 170:1169-1176, 1998.

Table 73-2

Bleeding Risk From Tissue Biopsy in Thrombocytopenic Patients

Thrombocytopenia	Platelet Count (10³/mL)	Risk of Spontaneous Hemorrhage	Procedure Risk
Moderate	50-100	Low	Transfuse in the presence of other coagulation defects or comorbid diseases
Severe	20-50	Moderate	Reasonable likelihood of bleeding; transfuse to ≥50,000/mL
Profound	≤20	High	Bleeding extremely likely; transfuse to ≥50,000/mL

Adapted from Payne CS: A primer on patient management problems in interventional radiology. AJR Am J Roentgenol 170:1169-1176, 1998.

Although aspirin alters platelet function and likely places patients at risk for bleeding complications, it is controversial whether patients taking aspirin should have their procedure postponed; adoption of this practice, though, does seems prudent. To reduce the effect, patients should refrain from using aspirin for at least 1 week before the biopsy.

Written informed consent should be obtained from each patient. The biopsy procedure should be described to the patient thoughtfully using layman's terms. Patients should be informed of the risk of bleeding and infection and that biopsies of upper abdominal lesions may result in a pneumothorax and possibly chest tube placement. Patients should be informed that multiple needle passes may be required, the specimen may not be diagnostic, and additional work-up may be necessary. Patients with lesions near bowel are at risk of bowel injury and abscess though this complication, surprisingly, has only rarely been reported. It is our policy to obtain separate written informed consent for the use of conscious sedation. A detailed home care instruction form is reviewed with each patient before the biopsy that explains which symptoms are to be expected after the biopsy and which symptoms raise the question of a complication. This form provides a list of contact telephone numbers in case a complication occurs.

CHOICE OF MODALITY FOR IMAGE GUIDANCE

There are numerous modalities available for performing image-guided percutaneous biopsies: fluoroscopy, US, CT (with or without fluoroscopic capability), and MRI. Each of these techniques has strengths and weakness as well as specific indications, and they are discussed next.

Fluoroscopy

Fluoroscopy is used sparingly within the abdomen and pelvis and is reserved for lesions that are either large, palpable, superficial, and/or calcified. Fluoroscopy can also be used on occasion to perform a biopsy on obstructing lesions such as a cholangiocarcinoma located adjacent to or surrounding a surgically or endoscopically placed stent. US, however, can also accomplish this task. Preliminary cross-sectional imaging with CT, US, or MRI is important to determine which intervening structures the needle may transgress en route to the lesion.

Ultrasonography

The use of US for image-guided biopsies is common in Europe and Asia and is increasing in the United States. It has the major advantage of direct real-time visualization of the needle tip during both placement and sampling.[7] This advantage not only aids in avoiding blood vessels but also helps ensure that sampling is restricted to the lesion. Furthermore, the use of compression with the US transducer is a major advantage in that it not only reduces the distance between the skin surface and the lesion but also displaces bowel and other structures.

Careful sampling of the lesion alone is particularly important in certain scenarios such as differentiating a hepatocellular adenoma from focal nodular hyperplasia (FNH). The conspicuous absence of bile duct epithelium in adenomas is the key to differentiating these two hepatocyte-containing lesions. Therefore, if one is performing a biopsy of an adenoma and the needle tip ventures beyond the margins of the lesion into normal hepatic parenchyma, the bile duct constituents that are aspirated may cause the cytopathologist to inadvertently diagnose the lesion as an FNH. This could lead to an error in diagnosis, which is important to avoid; many adenomas are surgically resected because they are considered to be premalignant and can undergo spontaneous hemorrhage.

The disadvantages of US include the obscuration of some lesions by intervening lung, bone, or bowel and the difficulty that arises in needle-tip visualization with modern transducers that are narrowly collimated. This problem can often be circumvented by using an angled approach and/or transducer compression. The latter difficulty can be reduced by using an attached needle guide.

The two main techniques for US-guided biopsies are the freehand technique and the attached needle guide technique.[8,9] The freehand technique has the advantages of allowing many more degrees of freedom and the ability to separate the needle and the transducer, an approach that often results in better needle visualization. The main disadvantage is the steep learning curve, because needle-tip visualization can be difficult and time-consuming. The attached needle guide has the advantages of a shallow learning curve with easier and quicker needle-tip visualization. Disadvantages include a significant reduction in the degrees of freedom and the modest cost of the apparatus.

Computed Tomography

CT is widely used for image guidance in the United States primarily because of equipment availability and user preference. The latter is mainly related to the fact that previously most residency and fellowship training programs in this country emphasized the use of CT over US for image-guided biopsies. CT has the advantages of very high spatial resolution and lack of imaging "blind spots." Furthermore, the depiction of intervening structures is superb. Disadvantages include the exposure to ionizing radiation, the lack of direct real-time needle-tip visualization, the difficulty encountered in the biopsy of moving lesions, and the high cost. Although CT is limited to the axial plane, the ability to angle the gantry allows some limited flexibility in needle placement, particularly in the cephalocaudal direction.

CT fluoroscopy is capable of providing 6 to 8 lower-resolution and low milliampere images/s and near real-time needle-tip visualization.[10] This technique reduces the time advantages of US considerably and improves the targeting of moving lesions. It is particularly useful for procedures involving deep structures, such as retroperitoneal masses, or for procedures involving organs prone to respiratory motion, such as the liver. CT fluoroscopy may use a quick check technique, which is analogous to conventional CT and is used most frequently in our practice. This technique uses single-section CT fluoroscopic images to check needle location and to confirm appropriate alignment. Continuous CT fluoroscopic images may be obtained in the region of the needle when the needle tip is difficult to localize, such as when it is in an oblique or a transverse plane. This technique is analogous to conventional CT, except reconstruction times are faster and the radiologist may manually position the table. Continuous fluoroscopy denotes the use of continuous fluoroscopic exposure during needle advancement or manipulation. It is wise to use forceps as a needle holder to prevent primary beam irradiation of the radiologist's hands.

Radiation doses to the patient and radiologist are higher in CT fluoroscopy than in conventional CT; however, observed doses have fallen with the trend toward the quick check technique, short duration of CT fluoroscopy exposure, and low milliampere and kilovolt peak (kVP) technique.[11]

Magnetic Resonance Imaging

MRI has been used sparingly for guiding percutaneous biopsies, although the roadblocks to using this modality are diminishing. The advantages of MRI include high spatial resolution, very high inherent tissue contrast, lack of ionizing radiation, and virtually unlimited multiplanar capability. Disadvantages include the requirement for MR-compatible supplies and monitoring equipment, the lack of direct real-time needle-tip visualization, the considerable time commitment, and the high cost. Many of these disadvantages, however, are significantly reduced or eliminated with the open or dedicated interventional units, which allow placement of the needle while the patient is in the bore of the magnet and use fast imaging sequences that provide near real-time guidance.[12] The use of lower field strength in an open system decreases the signal-to-noise ratio and results in longer acquisition times, however, may still be sufficient for lesion visualization.[13] The high inherent tissue contrast attainable on noncontrast MRI can be a major advantage, and in most practices this modality is used selectively in patients with lesions that do not have *sustainable* contrast on US and CT. This imaging scenario, however, is quite infrequent in the abdomen.

CHOICE OF NEEDLES

There are many biopsy needles available. These can be broadly grouped into aspirating and cutting needles (Fig. 73-1). The aspirating needles are usually 20- to 22-gauge and are designed to yield individual cells or small clumps of cells that can be spread into a single cell layer for cytopathologic analysis. The tips of aspirating needles may have an angled bevel or a stylet with a sharp point. A drawback of the beveled needles is that they may deflect away from the intended target as they pass through tissue interfaces, which renders accurate needle placement somewhat more difficult. With beveled needles it is difficult to pierce the skin; therefore, a skin nick is required. Needles with a pointed stylet tend to track along

End-cutting needle (cytopathology)

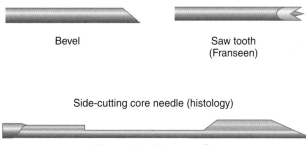

Bevel

Saw tooth
(Franseen)

Side-cutting core needle (histology)

Figure 73-1. Biopsy needles.

a straight line. The "skinny" 22- or 25-gauge needle, while in widespread use, is very flexible and particularly susceptible to bending and deflection. Compared with 22- or 25-gauge needles, 20-gauge needles are considerably stiffer and therefore may be easier to use.

Many radiologists attach a syringe and tube to the needle to apply suction during the actual biopsy. We have abandoned the use of this suction method in favor of simply removing the stylet and relying on natural capillary forces and mechanical agitation to draw tissue into the needle.[14] The main advantage of the nonsuction technique is that the specimens are usually free of blood. Fibrin clots form quickly within bloody aspirates rendering them difficult to smear onto a glass slide. Also, the presence of abundant erythrocytes obscures cellular detail.

The cutting needles, usually 14- to 20-gauge, are designed to obtain a core of tissue suitable for histologic analysis. Many surgeons still prefer to use the manual Tru-cut device (Travenol Laboratories, Baxter Healthcare), which has withstood the test of time, but most radiologists have adopted the use of automated cutting needles[15-17] (see Fig. 73-1). These automated needles have an inner slotted stylet for the specimen and an outer cutting stylet; they are much easier to use than the traditional manual Tru-cut needle. They consistently provide an excellent core of tissue. The prototype automated cutting needle, the Biopty gun (Bard Radiology, Covington, GA) was originally designed for prostate biopsies. Radiologists were quick to recognize the value of this new needle and adapted its use for biopsy in organs other than the prostate.[16] The Biopty device requires the needle to be mounted within a reusable spring loaded automated gun, which is heavy, cumbersome, and relatively expensive. Manufacturers have designed single use automated or semiautomated cutting needles that are so lightweight that they will maintain their position during the placement of patients into the CT gantry. Cutting needles with a short, long, or adjustable excursion are available. Many of these needles lend themselves to a coaxial technique, permitting several biopsy samples to be obtained from a single skin and organ puncture. In a blinded evaluation of 20 automated cutting biopsy devices, the best overall performance was obtained with 18-gauge needles with at least a 2-cm excursion.[17] A cutting needle (BioPince; MDTech, Gainesville, FL) is designed to obtain a full circular core of tissue rather than the traditional semicircular core. This needle may produce more tissue per pass than the traditional cutting.[18] Automated or semiautomated cutting vacuum needles are also available. These needles are designed with an airtight seal between the trocar and cannula that can be used to create a vacuum to hold tissue within the needle. Their main drawback is that occasionally they fail to aspirate any tissue at all. Also, the tissue architecture in the specimen may be distorted by the negative pressure.[19]

It has been suggested that radiologists should use the smallest gauge needle possible when performing biopsy procedures, based on the intuitive assumption that the risk of hemorrhage will increase with the use of larger-bore needles. However, few, if any, clinical studies have shown that the complication rate is higher when larger bore needles are used (unless the needles are cutting needles). Researchers have explored the effect of needle gauge on organ bleeding in the pig model.[20,21] This work shows that in general, large needles produce greater bleeding. The research also shows that large needles yield greater amounts of tissue. To the extent that each needle pass carries a certain risk, the maximum tissue yield can be obtained at minimum risk by performing fewer passes with a larger needle.

There are two caveats to consider, however. First, cyto-pathologists prefer to analyze a thin layer of single cells or clumps of cells. Samples obtained from thin needles (i.e., 20- to 25-gauge) may be easier to smear into a single cell layer than samples from larger needles (14- or 18-gauge). Second, use of cutting needles is riskier than use of aspirating needles. If the knifelike blade of the cutting needle encounters an artery or a vein, the vessel will be lacerated and bleed. In contrast, aspirating needles tend to displace rather than cut tissue.

Virtually all manufacturers now provide a needle tip customized for enhanced visualization with US. Such dedicated US needles may have tiny side holes or roughened surfaces or be coated with an echogenic polymer to enhance their specular reflectivity.[22] A manufacturer has gone so far as to devise an attachment that essentially converts the needle into a US transponder, which, when combined with the appropriate transducer, improves visualization.[23,24] An attachment that vibrates the needle at high frequency is also available. With use of color Doppler or power Doppler US, the oscillating needle shows as a shaft of color.[25] There is a personal computer–based guidance system in which attachments are placed on both the needle and the transducer.[9] This innovative device displays both the position of the needle tip and its anticipated path even when the needle is positioned outside the plane of the transducer. Whether this device will play a role in percutaneous tissue acquisition awaits clinical trials.

Over the next few years, MRI will be increasingly used to guide tissue biopsies particularly in the central nervous system and breast.[26,27] Dedicated MR-specific needles are now available.[28] These needles are readily visualized as a signal void and are safe to use in the magnetic field. The majority of conventional biopsy needles are ferromagnetic and cause considerable image distortion that may obscure the lesion of interest and hinder precise needle localization. Additionally, they may be torqued or deflected in the magnetic field, raising questions about their safety.

It is vital to coordinate needle selection with the pathologist who will interpret the case. If the pathologist is skilled in cytopathology, then small-bore (20 to 25 gauge) aspirating needles are recommended. If the pathologist prefers samples for histologic analysis, large-bore cutting needles are appropriate. Some groups perform a cytopathologic touch preparation for samples obtained using core needles. This technique allows a rapid preliminary diagnosis and preserves the core material for permanent fixation and sectioning.[29]

BIOPSY PLANNING

In planning the approach to a lesion, one must decide not only on the needle type but also on the needle route, the guidance modality, and the most efficient and comfortable patient position. The choice of needle route to a lesion will be based on the presence of intervening structures. Because needle passage through an organ creates both an entrance and exit wound, this is indeed an important consideration. While some organs tolerate this type of transgression, others do not, and henceforth these are referred to as acceptable and unacceptable transgressions.

Acceptable Routes

Organs through which needle transgression is acceptable include the liver, lungs, and gastrointestinal tract. The liver, because of its size and solid nature, provides not only a window for sonographic imaging of the upper abdomen but also an access route for the biopsy of deep masses. This includes masses involving the gallbladder, pancreatic head and body, porta hepatis, right adrenal (Fig. 73-2), and, on occasion, right kidney. Needles ranging up to 14 gauge in caliber and of all types are usually well tolerated as long as blood vessels are avoided.

The lungs can usually be avoided when using US for guidance because an off-axis approach allows one to angle the transducer cranially to avoid the pleural space. Even when the pleural space is violated, the lung parenchyma itself is often spared, reducing the risk of pneumothorax considerably. When using CT to biopsy subdiaphragmatic lesions, lung transgression is often unavoidable. This is usually well tolerated when needles of 20 gauge or smaller are used, and in the unlikely event of a pneumothorax, the volume is small so that chest tube placement is typically unnecessary. The exception, of course, would be in patients with emphysema.

The gastrointestinal tract can also tolerate needle transgression. The stomach, being thick-walled, can tolerate puncture with needles up to 18 gauge or even larger. Transgressing the stomach, however, can be challenging because the wall is resilient and the needle may induce a peristaltic contraction.

Some interventionalists hesitate to transgress the small bowel because of its thin wall and fear of perforation and abscess formation. However, in our experience using 20-gauge needles, such transgressions are well tolerated. Newer 20-gauge automated cutting needles are particularly useful for the biopsy of deep lesions or lymph nodes because transenteric excursion is virtually unavoidable. Transducer compression effectively reduces lesion depth by either displacing or flattening bowel and adipose tissue[30,31] (Fig. 73-3).

Transcolonic needle excursion is somewhat more controversial because of the fear of bacterial contamination within the peritoneal cavity. However, as with the small bowel, the

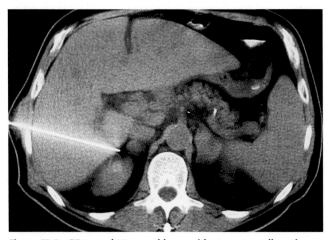

Figure 73-2. CT scan of 66-year-old man with squamous cell carcinoma of the lung. Axial noncontrast CT of the upper abdomen reveals bilateral adrenal masses. Although the right adrenal mass is smaller than the left, it is more easily accessed using a transhepatic approach. The liver tolerates needle transgression very well as long as blood vessels are avoided. Fine-needle aspiration revealed metastatic squamous cell carcinoma.

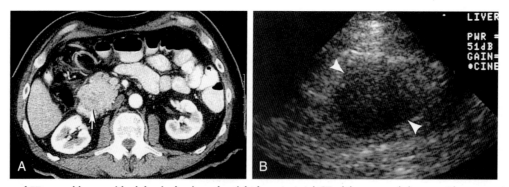

Figure 73-3. Images of 57-year-old man with abdominal pain and weight loss. A. Axial CT of the upper abdomen with contrast material reveals a rounded fullness in the pancreatic head with subtle hypoattenuation changes (*arrow*). Note numerous blood vessels anterolateral to the pancreatic head as well as colon and jejunum anteromedially. **B.** Gray-scale ultrasound in the transverse plane reveals a hypoechoic, rounded mass in the region of the pancreatic head (*arrowheads*). Note that with transducer compression, there has been considerable decrease in the distance from the skin to the mass as well as displacement of intervening bowel. Fine-needle aspiration revealed adenocarcinoma.

colon is undoubtedly violated at times during US-guided biopsies using transducer compression. Passing a needle through stool-filled bowel, which may be unavoidable with CT, may be another issue, at least empirically (Fig. 73-4). In this scenario it may be prudent to administer antibiotics (e.g., gentamicin 80 mg intramuscularly or 1.2 mg/kg intravenously) just before the biopsy and oral antibiotics (Cipro 250 to 500 mg twice daily) for 2 to 3 days after the biopsy. It is doubtful that transducer compression with US can flatten stool-filled colon, and this may explain the lack of infectious complications using this technique.[32] As with the small bowel, whenever colon transgression is anticipated, a needle on the order of 20 gauge or smaller is recommended.

Routes to Avoid

The following needle paths should be avoided if possible: through the pancreas, spleen, adrenals, kidneys, and major

blood vessels. When the normal pancreas is transgressed by a needle, the patient is at risk for acute pancreatitis.[33] This is true for both dedicated pancreatic biopsies and transpancreatic biopsies of deeper lesions (Fig. 73-5). The spleen is a solid but soft organ that, like the liver, can provide a window to the left upper quadrant, particularly when enlarged. However, because of its well-known susceptibility to blunt trauma, there is concern that a splenic biopsy might result in capsular rupture. Trans-splenic needle excursion is even more of a concern than splenic biopsies because the capsule is punctured twice. Although complications related to needles and the spleen may be overestimated, we recommend avoiding this organ when placing needles in the left upper quadrant.

The adrenals and kidneys are both associated with hemorrhagic complications when biopsied. Although retroperitoneal hemorrhage following these types of biopsies is often asymptomatic, even when substantial, transadrenal or transrenal needle excursion is not recommended.

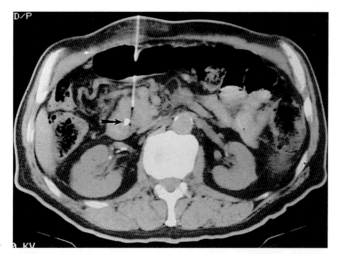

Figure 73-4. CT of 70-year-old woman with abdominal pain and jaundice. The patient underwent a preliminary endoscopic retrograde cholangiogram (not shown) suggesting a mass involving the distal common bile duct. A plastic biliary stent was inserted. Follow-up non-contrast axial CT scan of the upper abdomen reveals some rounded fullness of the pancreatic head but no obvious mass. Percutaneous biopsy was performed using an anterior transcolonic approach. Because no obvious mass was identified, biopsy samples were taken adjacent to the stent (*arrow*). Fine-needle aspiration revealed adenocarcinoma. There were no hemorrhagic or infectious complications.

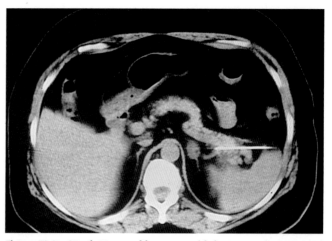

Figure 73-5. CT of 48-year-old woman with breast carcinoma. Axial CT of the upper abdomen with contrast material reveals a small nodule in the left adrenal gland. The right adrenal gland was normal. The left adrenal mass underwent biopsy percutaneously using an intercostal and transpancreatic approach. Because normal pancreatic parenchyma is prone to develop pancreatitis when transgressed, this technique is not recommended. Fine-needle aspiration revealed no evidence of malignancy.

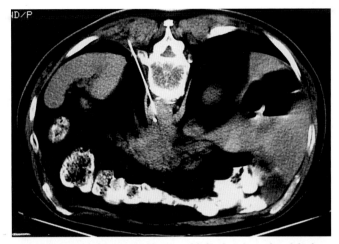

Figure 73-6. CT of 59-year-old man with back pain and weight loss. Preliminary CT revealed a mass in the pancreatic head and neck encasing the celiac axis and superior mesenteric artery. The mass subsequently underwent biopsy percutaneously in the prone position using a retroperitoneal approach. Initial needle placement revealed aortic violation. The needle was subsequently repositioned into the pancreatic mass, and fine-needle aspiration revealed adenocarcinoma. There were no hemorrhagic complications as a result of aortic transgression.

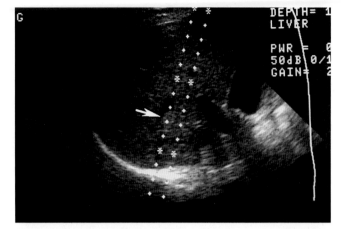

Figure 73-7. Ultrasonogram of 43-year-old woman with melanoma. Gray-scale ultrasound in the longitudinal plane reveals a small hyperechoic mass located deep in the right hepatic lobe (*arrow*). Using the attached needle guide, the mass underwent biopsy percutaneously using an intercostal approach. Note that the mass is aligned within the parallel dotted lines, which correspond to the proposed path of the needle when advanced through the attached guide. Fine-needle aspiration revealed a hemangioma.

Obviously, the transgression of blood vessels, particularly the aorta and inferior vena cava, is not advisable. However, in our experience hemorrhagic complications may also occur from transgression of much smaller arteries or veins. When performing a retroperitoneal biopsy, either from an anterior approach using US guidance or a posterior approach using CT guidance, the left side is generally preferred over the right to avoid transgressing the inferior vena cava. Although anecdotal, there is evidence to suggest that the aorta is more tolerant of needle transgression than the inferior vena cava, perhaps because the wall is thicker and more resilient (Fig. 73-6). Certainly the experience with translumbar aortography supports this contention.[34] The use of color Doppler US is very helpful for depicting blood flow in not only major vessels but also much smaller branches, as well. US machines that feature more flash-resistant color Doppler are advantageous because the color can be maintained during needle placement without obscuring the tip because of tissue motion.

SPECIFIC ORGAN-RELATED TECHNIQUES

Liver

The liver is a vascular but relatively resilient organ that tolerates needle placement quite well, whether to biopsy a focal liver abnormality, to biopsy hepatic parenchyma, or to traverse the liver en route to a deeper lesion. Needles up to a 14 gauge are commonly used without difficulty. The liver capsule is richly innervated; therefore, copious infiltration of the capsule with a local anesthetic, such as xylocaine, is necessary to achieve adequate pain control during needle placement. The liver can usually be accessed via a subcostal, subxiphoid, or intercostal approach. The latter approach is typically the most difficult, and care should be taken to avoid the intercostal neurovascular bundle, which courses along the inferior margin of each rib. Real-time guidance during needle placement is also helpful for avoiding major portal and hepatic

veins. It is advantageous to interpose a cuff of normal parenchyma between the liver capsule and the margin of a lesion, and this task is more easily accomplished with US using an off-axis approach (Fig. 73-7).

Fine needle aspiration of focal abnormalities for cytology is typically performed with a 20- to 22-gauge aspirating needle, either a Chiba or Franseen. Our particular preference is the Franseen-type needle because it has a diamond tip that readily perforates the skin without making an incision, experiences less tracking than the slant-tip Chiba, and is self-aspirating. Medical biopsy of hepatic parenchyma for histology is typically performed with a 14- to 18-gauge cutting needle, many of which have a spring-loaded rapid-fire mechanism. Routine assessment of the liver with color Doppler US after withdrawing one of these larger-gauge cutting needles often demonstrates a linear tract of blood flowing toward the capsule (Fig. 73-8). These tracts, however, typically resolve within 2 to 3 minutes without evidence of supcapsular accumulation of blood.

There has been considerable controversy over the biopsy of hepatic hemangiomas, whether inadvertent or intentional. Because these benign tumors consist of a tangle of thin-walled endothelium-lined blood vessels, there is presumed to be an increased risk for hemorrhagic complications. Several studies have shown, however, that hemangiomas can be biopsied safely with an acceptable complication rate[35-39] (Fig. 73-9). This includes the use of 18-gauge aspirating needles and 18-gauge cutting needles. These studies have also emphasized the importance of interposing a cuff of normal hepatic parenchyma between the capsule and the margin of the lesion. Although these results are encouraging, the number of patients included in each of these studies is relatively small, and it is presumed that a large-scale comparative trial of the biopsy of hemangiomas and metastases would reveal a slightly higher complication rate for the former lesion. While the noninvasive work-up of these common and, in most cases, inconsequential lesions cannot be overemphasized, it is

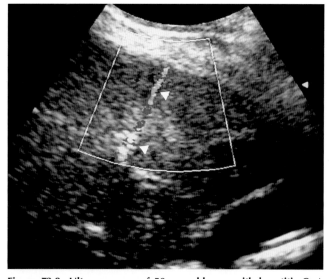

Figure 73-8. Ultrasonogram of 50-year-old man with hepatitis C. A medical-type liver biopsy under ultrasound guidance was requested. Following a percutaneous biopsy of hepatic parenchyma with an 18-gauge cutting needle, color Doppler ultrasound revealed a tract of blood flowing along the needle track toward the capsule (*arrowheads*). There was, however, no evidence of subcapsular accumulation of blood, and the tract resolved within 30 to 60 seconds.

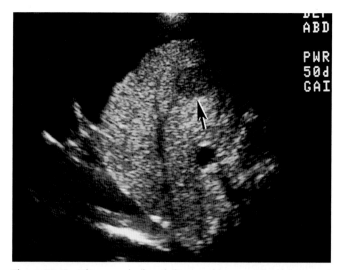

Figure 73-10. Ultrasonography of 42-year-old man with cirrhosis and portal hypertension. Gray-scale ultrasound of the liver in the longitudinal plane revealed a small, shrunken liver with heterogeneous echotexture consistent with cirrhosis. There is also a considerable amount of perihepatic ascites and a 2-cm hypoechoic nodule in the right hepatic lobe anteriorly (*arrow*). The mass underwent biopsy using ultrasound guidance via an intercostal space through the ascites. Fine-needle aspiration revealed hepatocellular carcinoma. There were no hemorrhagic complications.

comforting to know that if a hemangioma is biopsied, whether inadvertently or because of nonclassic imaging features, the complications rate is low.[38]

Another issue is the safety of performing a liver biopsy in the presence of ascites. It is presumed that direct contact with the diaphragm or abdominal wall functions to tamponade the capsular injury, thereby preventing significant subcapsular or intraperitoneal hemorrhage. Therefore, when the capsule is in contact with a layer of fluid, the risk of hemorrhagic complications is increased, particularly if patients have a tenuous coagulation status (Fig. 73-10). Two studies in

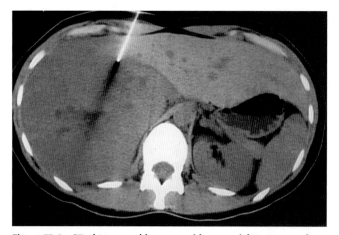

Figure 73-9. CT of 61-year-old woman with vague right upper quadrant pain. Axial noncontrast CT of the upper abdomen reveals a large hypoattenuating mass occupying most of the right hepatic lobe. A central hypoattenuating scar is noted within the mass. Although the mass is large and easily approached through an intercostal space, it underwent biopsy anteriorly, for a cuff of normal hepatic parenchyma to be interposed between the capsule and the mass. Fine-needle aspiration revealed a hemangioma.

particular have addressed the issue of ascites in patients with cirrhosis.[39,40] In both reports, the complication rate was low.

Hepatocellular carcinoma is a very locally invasive tumor that often infiltrates and obstructs portal veins, hepatic veins, and even bile ducts. The presence of underlying cirrhosis often excludes a patient from hepatic tumor resection, either because of inadequate residual function or because hepatomas in these patients are typically more aggressive. However, patients with little or no parenchymal dysfunction may be candidates for resection. In these patients, it is imperative to determine if portal or hepatic venous thrombosis is bland or malignant. There are noninvasive means of making this determination such as enhancement during the hepatic arterial dominant phase of a dynamic bolus CT with iodinated contrast material or MRI with a gadolinium chelate. However, these signs of unresectability are not often present. Biopsy of the intraluminal mass may be requested to both diagnose and stage this malignancy. It is useful to use a guidance technique with real-time capability, when biopsing an intraluminal mass, to ensure that the needle tip does not venture beyond the wall of the vein into an adjacent parenchymal tumor deposit.[41] This technique is considered safe because hemorrhagic complications are uncommon, similar to that experienced during transjugular liver biopsies.

In addition to biopsy of focal hepatic masses, US is increasingly used to guide random liver biopsies in medical liver disease such as hepatitis or hemochromatosis. End-stage liver disease associated with hepatitis C infection is already the leading indication for liver transplant in the United States. Furthermore, the incidence of hepatocellular carcinoma has approximately doubled over the past 3 decades with a concomitant shift in occurrence to relatively younger patients between the ages of 40 and 60. At least half of these cases have been attributed to the impact of hepatitis C.[18] In patients with mild clinical disease it has been recommended that they undergo random core biopsy of the liver parenchyma every 4 to 5 years to evaluate disease progression.[18] Comorbidities such as HIV, hepatic steatosis, alcoholism, and possibly diabetes are thought to accelerate disease progression and may prompt more frequent biopsy in these patient groups. Because of the nonuniform pattern of fibrosis the pathologist requires at least 15 to 20 portal triads for accurate evaluation.[18] To obtain sufficient material for pathologic diagnosis, we use a 14-gauge cutting needle.

Pancreas

The pancreas is a relatively soft unencapsulated organ located deep in the upper retroperitoneum that is prone to develop inflammation. Acute pancreatitis can occur not only following a needle biopsy but also following blunt trauma or the direct injection of contrast media into the pancreatic duct during an ERCP.[42] Pancreatic tumors, including both adenocarcinomas and islet cell tumors, are often difficult to visualize because there may not be a contour abnormality and/or there is little tissue contrast compared with adjacent nontumorous parenchyma. Furthermore, pancreatic adenocarcinomas are associated with a considerable amount of tissue desmoplasia, which can increase sampling error.[1]

We have seen a dramatic reduction in the number of requests for percutaneous pancreatic biopsy in our practice over the last 5 years. With the advent of endoscopic ultrasound (EUS), and EUS-guided biopsy, most lesions that were previously sampled percutaneously are now sampled endoscopically (see Chapter 13). Although CT remains superior in to EUS in assessing the N stage of pancreatic or ampullary cancer, EUS can often find small pancreatic or ampullary lesions that are not clearly visible with CT, MRI, or transabdominal US, thus providing a better guide for biopsy.[43,44] EUS-guided pancreatic biopsy through the duodenum provides a theoretical decreased risk of malignant seeding. The duodenum is removed during the Whipple procedure performed for carcinoma of the pancreatic head, thus removing any possible micrometastases deposited along the biopsy tract.

There are still occasions when percutaneous pancreatic biopsy is indicated, for example in when the lesion is within the body or tail. In general, small-caliber needles on the order of 20 to 22 gauge are used to biopsy the pancreas. Although there is concern about developing a fistula to the pancreatic duct with larger caliber needles, 18-gauge cutting needles can be used on occasion to biopsy large densely fibrotic masses. Currently, however, 20-gauge cutting needles are preferred in this scenario. Many of the needles used for fine needle aspiration are designed to be self-aspirating, although it may be advantageous to employ suction when performing a biopsy on pancreatic tumors that are desmoplastic.

Pancreatic masses are usually biopsied using an anterior approach, via either the left lobe of the liver or the gastrointestinal tract, typically the stomach or small bowel (see Fig. 73-4). Approaching a mass in the head of the pancreas via the right hepatic lobe, duodenum, gallbladder, and/or inferior vena cava is generally not recommended. Furthermore, approaching a mass in the tail of the pancreas via the spleen is not recommended.

In our practice, we use US for guidance in over 80% of pancreas cases but defer to CT on occasion when the mass is poorly visualized or when the initial US-guided biopsy was inadequate.[7] With US guidance it is generally easier than with CT to navigate a needle into the lesion without traversing the numerous peripancreatic blood vessels. Furthermore, perivascular tumor encasement can be biopsied directly and can serve to both diagnose and stage the tumor (Fig. 73-11). With an anterior approach, the use of compression with the US transducer not only reduces the depth of needle placement but also displaces many intervening structures, particularly the transverse colon and jejunum (see Fig. 73-3). In some cases, a discrete mass may not be appreciated yet diagnostic tissue can still be obtained by looking for indirect signs such as abrupt termination of a dilated duct or taking a biopsy sample adjacent to a biliary stent (see Fig. 73-4). The biopsy

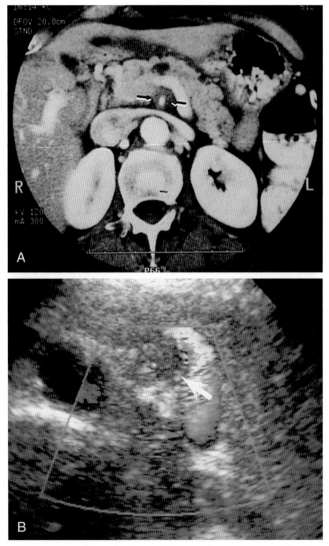

Figure 73-11. Images of 70-year-old man with vague upper abdominal pain and weight loss. A. Preliminary axial CT scan with contrast material did not reveal a definite pancreatic mass although there was evidence of circumferential soft tissue encasement of the superior mesenteric artery (*arrows*). **B.** This soft tissue encasement was subsequently biopsied percutaneously under ultrasound guidance using an anterior approach. Color Doppler ultrasound of the superior mesenteric artery in the transverse plane reveals hypoechoic soft tissue just lateral to the artery. An *arrow* demonstrates the needle tip placed directly in this soft tissue. Fine-needle aspiration revealed adenocarcinoma. There were no hemorrhagic complications and real-time guidance prevented transgression of the artery.

of peripancreatic lymph nodes or liver nodules in the setting of pancreatic carcinoma is often productive as well, especially for staging.

A concern about pancreatic biopsies is the potential for peritoneal tumor seeding.[45] This theory, however, is difficult to substantiate because the vast majority of patients are inoperable and do not have surgical confirmation and most do not survive long enough for the implants to reach a size detectable with cross-sectional imaging. It is doubtful that the biopsy of pancreatic adenocarcinoma negatively impacts outcome.

Bowel

Biopsies of the digestive tract almost always performed endoscopically and when not possible, usually open or laparoscopically. However, endoscopic biopsy may be impossible when the lesion or involved bowel segment lies between the ligament of Treitz and the ileocecal valve. In many of these cases there may be metastases elsewhere which are better suited to endoscopic biopsy. However, when an isolated bowel wall mass is not amenable to endoscopic biopsy, percutaneous sampling is appropriate.[46-48] For example, submucosal lesions such as gastrointestinal stromal tumors (GISTs) may not be easily identified endoscopically.

Percutaneous bowel wall biopsy may be performed with either US or CT guidance, depending on the lesion characteristics and the patient's body habitus. Our group prefers US guidance as compression with the US transducer may displace overlying bowel loops and anchor the targeted bowel segment, which may otherwise be displaced by the biopsy needle. Color Doppler US may also be used to identify and avoid adjacent mesenteric vessels.

Percutaneous bowel wall biopsy may be performed either with FNA or core needle biopsy. Although flow cytometery techniques have increase the diagnostic yield in FNA assessment of lymphoma, the preserved tissue architecture in core needle biopsies, may be a requirement in certain diagnoses such as lymphoma.[46]

Potential complications particular to biopsies of the digesive tract include bowel hematoma, bowel perforation and peritonitis. Choosing a biopsy route that does not traverse the bowel lumen may minimize the risk of bowel perforation. Even when the bowel lumen is traversed, the risk of perforation remains low. Santiago and associates' study included eight patients, whose histologic samples contained mucosa, indicating that the mucosa and lumen were perforated; however, none had an adverse outcome.[47]

Lymph Nodes

Lymph nodes represent the most common site of metastatic disease. With improvements in image guidance and needle design, radiologists are increasingly requested to biopsy lymph nodes in order to diagnose and stage a suspected malignancy or to obtain samples for culture. This increase in the number of requests for lymph node biopsy may be attributed to discovery of normal sized but hypermetabolic nodes on PET.

In the abdomen and retroperitoneum, lymph nodes are often small and deeply located or precariously positioned. Traditionally, North American radiologists have either de-

clined to attempt biopsies of small abdominal or retroperitoneal lymph nodes or have approached these biopsies solely with CT guidance.[49-53] However, as experience with US has increased, radiologists are beginning to use US guidance for the biopsy of small, deeply located lymph nodes.

We have found US guidance to be accurate and safe for biopsy of abdominal and retroperitoneal nodes with a success rate of 86%, similar to results from other institutions[30,31] (Fig. 73-13). With the use of a needle guide, the needle can be passed accurately into the lesion during real-time visualization and the procedure may be performed during one or two patient breath holds. Real-time needle-tip visualization helps ensure that sampling will be limited to the lesion; samples are far less likely to be contaminated with extraneous tissue or blood and thus may be easier to interpret by the cytopathologist. With real-time visualization, it is also possible to ensure that the needle excursions are short of adjacent critical structures such as blood vessels or the common bile duct. We have found that lymph node visualization is improved markedly by applying firm pressure with the transducer to compress and displace overlying fatty tissue and bowel loops, decreasing the necessary depth for sound penetration and length of needle excursion by approximately 50%. In order to biopsy lymph nodes, it is vital to review CT scans before the procedure to choose the optimal site and route.

Lymphoma

The role of image-guided biopsy in the work-up of patients with suspected lymphoma is controversial.[54-57] Some institutions perform excisional biopsy of all suspected lymphomatous masses with the goal of preserving tissue architecture for specific tumor classification. Others, however, excise only superficial or palpable lesions and perform percutaneous biopsy of deeply located masses to avoid the risks of surgical resection. At our institution the vast majority of both superficial and deep lesions are approached with image-guided biopsy.

Core biopsies are the "gold standard" for establishing the diagnosis of lymphoma. They provide sufficient material for histologic analysis and appropriate subclassification of lymphoma that guides therapeutic options. With the adoption of the new REAL (Revised European American Lymphoma) classification and the development of new immunocytochemical and flow cytometric techniques, material obtained using 20- to 22-gauge aspirating needles can now be used for the primary diagnosis and subclassification of lymphoma[57] (see Fig. 73-12). The new immunocytochemical techniques accurately separate the monoclonal non-Hodgkin's lymphoma cells from polyclonal benign or malignant lymphoproliferative disorder cells such as in Hodgkin's lymphoma. Flow cytometry techniques allow an evaluation of atypical lymphoid cells that are characterized for clonality and size using an automated system where individual cells are passed through a laser chamber. With the emergence of these new techniques, the role of fine needle aspiration may become increasingly important in the work-up of lymphoma. As these new cytopathologic techniques become more refined, it may be no longer necessary to use excisional biopsies or large bore cutting needles to accurately diagnose and subclassify lymphoma.

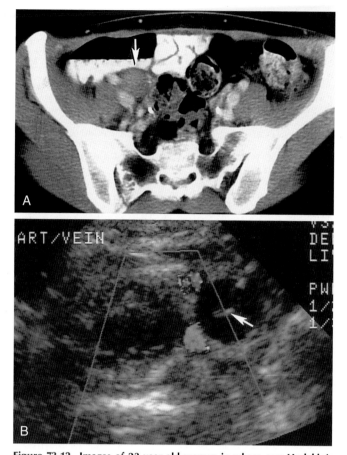

Figure 73-12. Images of 23-year-old woman in whom non-Hodgkin's lymphoma was suspected. A. Axial CT of the pelvis with contrast material shows an enlarged right external iliac lymph node (*arrow*). **B.** Color Doppler ultrasound in the transverse plane shows the echogenic tip of a 20-gauge needle within the lymph node (*arrow*). Real-time visualization of the needle tip during the biopsy ensures that the specimen will be obtained exclusively from the lymph node without contamination from adjacent normal tissue or transgression of the external iliac vein. Fine-needle aspiration revealed non-Hodgkin's lymphoma. (From Fisher AJ, Paulson EK, Sheafor DH, et al: Small lymph nodes of the abdomen, pelvis, and retroperitoneum: Usefulness of sonographically guided biopsy. Radiology 205:185-190, 1997.)

Spleen

Requests for percutaneous splenic biopsies are uncommon. This relates to the relative infrequency of isolated splenic pathology and the perceived risk of hemorrhagic complications in this soft, encapsulated organ. Several studies, however, describe the safe, successful biopsy of splenic lesions.[58-60] These studies recommend the use of small-caliber (20- to 22-gauge) needles. The advantages of interposing a cuff of normal splenic parenchyma between the capsule and the lesion are controversial (Fig. 73-13). Unless large, the spleen is approached via the intercostal space, and at times, pleural transgression is necessary. This is less of a problem with US than CT because an off-axis or angled approach can be employed.

COMPLICATIONS

In general, abdominal biopsies are safe. Minor complications include pain, vasovagal reactions, small hematomas, pneumothorax, bacteremia, and pancreatitis.[20,52] The most common minor complication is pain or vasovagal reaction, which occurs in approximately 1% to 5% of patients. Fortunately less than 1% of patients will have a hematoma large enough to require a transfusion. An additional minor complication of biopsies in the upper abdomen is pneumothorax.[52] While there is a theoretical risk of pneumothorax when the potential space of the pleura is transgressed, pneumothorax is extremely rare unless the aerated pulmonary parenchyma is transgressed as well. It is our impression that the risk of pneumothorax is decreased with the use of US compared with CT guidance. Postbiopsy pancreatitis is a well-described complication. Paradoxically, pancreatitis tends to only occur when the normal pancreatic parenchyma is transgressed; biopsies of the diseased pancreas (chronic pancreatitis or cancer) are usually well tolerated and rarely result in pancreatitis. While pancreatitis is often considered a minor complication, some patients with biopsy related pancreatitis may be critically ill requiring prolonged hospitalization.

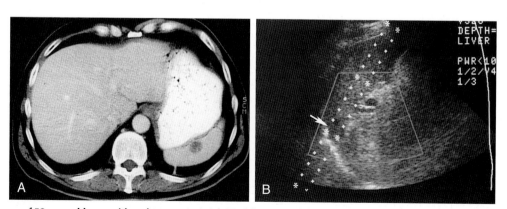

Figure 73-13. Images of 52-year-old man with melanoma. A. Axial CT of the upper abdomen with contrast material reveals a 1.5-cm hypoattenuating mass in the spleen. **B.** Gray-scale ultrasound of the spleen in the longitudinal plane reveals a hypoechoic mass located deep in the splenic parenchyma (*arrow*). With an intercostal approach, the mass underwent biopsy percutaneously using the attached needle guide. Note that the mass is aligned within the parallel dotted lines, which represent the proposed path of the needle when advanced via the attached guide. Fine-needle aspiration revealed metastatic melanoma.

When the bowel is transgressed there is a risk of microperforation and subsequent abscess formation. Theoretically, the risk of peritonitis is increased when the colon is transgressed compared with when the small bowel or stomach is transgressed due to the relatively sterile contents of the latter two structures. With the use of US guidance and abdominal wall compression, it is often not possible to differentiate collapsed loops of small bowel from mesenteric fatty tissues. There is no doubt that needle transgression of bowel occurs more frequently with US guidance than with CT guidance. Despite the recent increased use of US for guidance at our institution, we have not detected an increase in abscess formation or peritonitis. In support of this observation, Petit and associates[61] found that in pigs, transgressing the large and small bowel with 8 French catheters was not associated with peritonitis or abscess formation.

Fortunately, serious complications are quite rare.[54-64] The mortality rate from an image-guided percutaneous abdominal biopsy is widely considered to be 0.1%. However, a retrospective review of complications by Smith suggests that the mortality rate from abdominal fine needle aspirations may in fact be as low as 0.006% to 0.031%.[62] The majority of reported deaths from biopsies are from hemorrhage following a liver biopsy. Interestingly, most of the reported deaths from liver biopsies occurred using "skinny" needles of only 20 to 22 gauge. The second most frequent cause of death following an abdominal guided biopsy is pancreatitis due to transgression of normal pancreatic parenchyma.

Needle tract seeding is also a rare but major complication with a frequency ranging from 0.003% to 0.009%.[54] Most of the reported needle tract seedings are the result of biopsies of pancreatic cancer though virtually any tumor may spread along a needle tract.

References

1. Dodd LG, Mooney EE, Layfield LJ, et al: Fine-needle aspiration of the liver and pancreas: A cytology primer for radiologists. Radiology 203:1-9, 1997.
2. Silverman SG, Mueller PR, Pfister RC: Hemostatic evaluation before abdominal interventions: An overview and proposal. AJR 154:233-238, 1990.
3. Rapaport SI: Assessing hemostatic function before abdominal interventions. AJR 154:239-240, 1990.
4. Payne CS: A primer on patient management problems in interventional radiology. AJR 170:1169-1176, 1998.
5. Silverman SG, Coughlin BF, Seltzer SE, et al: Current use of screening laboratory tests before abdominal interventions: A survey of 603 radiologists. Radiology 181:669-673, 1991.
6. Spies JB, Bakal CW, Burke DR, et al: Practice guidelines in interventional radiology. J Vasc Interv Radiol 2:59-65, 1991.
7. Sheafor DH, Paulson EK, Simmons CM, et al: Abdominal percutaneous interventional procedures: Comparison of CT and US guidance. Radiology 207:705-710, 1998.
8. Paulson EK: Image guided percutaneous abdominal biopsies. Appl Radiol 24:11-15, 1995.
9. Nelson RC, Paulson EK, Kurylo LM, et al: Evaluation of a new electronic guidance system for ultrasound-guided needle placement. Radiology 209(P):219, 1998.
10. Katada K, Kato R, Anno H, et al: Guidance with real-time CT fluoroscopy: Early clinical experience. Radiology 200:851-856, 1996.
11. Paulson EK, Sheafor DH, Enterline DS, et al: CT fluoroscopy-guided interventional procedures: Techniques and radiation dose to radiologists. Radiology 220:161-167, 2001.
12. Silverman SG, Collick BD, Figueira MR, et al: Interactive MR-guided biopsy in an open-configuration MR imaging system. Radiology 197:175-181, 1995.
13. Kariniemi J, Blanco Sequeiros R, Ojala R, et al: MRI-guided abdominal biopsy in a 0.23-T open-configuration MRI system. Eur Radiol 15:1256-1262, 2005.
14. Hopper KD, Grenko RT, Fisher AI, et al: Capillary versus aspiration biopsy: Effect of needle size and length on the cytopathological specimen quality. J Cardiovasc Intervent Radiol 19:341-344, 1996.
15. Bernardino ME: Automated biopsy devices: Significance and safety. Radiology 176:615-616, 1996.
16. Parker SH, Hopper KD, Yakes WD, et al: Image directed percutaneous biopsies with a biopsy gun. Radiology 171:663-669, 1989.
17. Hopper KD, Ahendroth CS, Sturtz KW, et al: Automated biopsy devices: A blinded evaluation. Radiology 187:653-660, 1993.
18. Winter SR, Paulson EK: Ultrasound guided biopsy: What's new? Ultrasound Q 21:19-25, 2005.
19. Hopper KD, Abendroth CS, Sturtz KW, et al: CT percutaneous biopsy guns: Comparison of end-cut and side-notch devices in cadaveric specimens. AJR 164:195-199, 1995.
20. Gazelle GS, Haaga JR, Rowland DY: Effect of needle gauge, level of anticoagulation, and target organ on bleeding associated with aspiration biopsy. Radiology 183:509-513, 1992.
21. Plecha DM, Goodwin DW, Rowland DY, et al: Liver biopsy: Effects of biopsy needle caliber on bleeding and tissue recovery. Radiology 204:101-104, 1997.
22. Reading CC, Charboneau JW, FelmLee JR, et al: US-guided percutaneous biopsy: Use of a screw biopsy stylet to aid needle detection. Radiology 163:280-281, 1987.
23. Winsberg F, Mitty HA, Shapiro RS, et al: Use of an acoustic transponder for US visualization of biopsy needles. Radiology 180:877-878, 1991.
24. Perrella RR, Kimme-Smith C, Tessler FN, et al: A new electronically enhanced biopsy system: Value of improving needle tip visibility during sonographically guided interventional procedures. AJR 158:195-198, 1992.
25. Feld R, Needleman L, Goldberg BB: Use of a needle vibrating device and color Doppler imaging for sonographically guided invasive procedures. AJR 168:255-256, 1997.
26. Daniel BL, Birdwell RL, Ikeda DM, et al: Breast lesion location: A freehand, interactive MR imaging-guided technique. Radiology 207:455-463, 1998.
27. Kariniemi J, Blanco Sequeiros R, Ojala R, Tervonen O: MRI-guided abdominal biopsy in a 0.23-T open-configuration MRI system. Eur Radiol 15:1256-1262, 2005.
28. Moscatel MA, Shellock FG, Morisoli SM: Biopsy needles and devices: Assessment of ferromagnetism and artifacts during exposure to a 1.5-T MR system. J Magn Reson Imaging 5:369-372, 1995.
29. Diederich S, Padge B, Vossas U, et al: Application of a single needle type for all image-guided biopsies: Results of 100 consecutive core biopsies in various organs using a novel tri-axial, end-cut needle. Cancer Imaging 6:43-50, 2006.
30. Fisher AJ, Paulson EK, Shefor DS, et al: Small lymph nodes in the abdomen, pelvis, and retroperitoneum: Usefulness of sonographically guided biopsy. Radiology 205:185-190, 1997.
31. Memel DS, Dodd GD III, Esola CC: Efficacy of sonography as a guidance technique for biopsy of abdominal, pelvic and retroperitoneal lymph nodes. AJR 167:957-962, 1996.
32. McDermott VG, Schuster MG, Smith TP: Antibiotic prophylaxis in vascular and interventional radiology. AJR 169:31-38, 1997.
33. Mueller PR, Miketic LM, Simeone JF, et al: Severe acute pancreatitis after percutaneous biopsy of the pancreas. AJR 151:493-494, 1988.
34. van Schaik JPJ, Hawkins IF Jr: Redirection of translumbar catheters using a tip deflector technique. Radiology 155:744-746, 1985.
35. Solbiati L, Livraghi T, De Pra L, et al: Fine-needle biopsy of hepatic hemangioma with sonographic guidance. AJR 144:471-474, 1985.
36. Cronan JJ, Esparza AR, Dorfman GS, et al: Cavernous hemangioma of the liver: Role of percutaneous biopsy. Radiology 166:135-138, 1988.
37. Heilo A, Stenwig AE: Liver hemangioma: US-guided 18-gauge core-needle biopsy. Radiology 204:719-722, 1997.
38. Nelson RC, Chezmar JL: Diagnostic approach to hepatic hemangioma. Radiology 176:11-13, 1990.
39. Murphy FB, Barefield KP, Steinberg HV, et al: CT or sonography-guided biopsy of the liver in the presence of ascites: Frequency of complications. AJR 151:485-486, 1988.
40. Little AF, Ferris JV, Dodd GD III, et al: Image-guided percutaneous hepatic biopsy: Effect of ascites on the complication rate. Radiology 199:79-83, 1996.
41. Dodd GD III, Carr B: Percutaneous biopsy of portal vein thrombosis: A new staging technique for hepatocellular carcinoma. AJR 161:229-233, 1993.

42. Cohen SA, Siegel JH, Kasmin FE: Complications of diagnostic and therapeutic ERCP. Abdom Imaging 21:385-394, 1996.
43. Cannon ME, Carpenter SL, Elta GH, et al: EUS compared with CT, magnetic resonance imaging, and angiography and the influence of biliary stenting on staging accuracy of ampullary neoplasms. Gastrointest Endosc 50:27-33, 1999.
44. Agarwal B, Abu-Hamada E, Molke KL, et al. Endoscopic ultrasound-guided fine needle aspiration and multidetector spiral CT in the diagnosis of pancreatic cancer. Am J Gastroenterol 99:844-850, 2004.
45. Smith FP, MacDonald JS, Schein PS, et al: Cutaneous seeding of pancreatic cancer by skinny-needle aspiration biopsy. Arch Intern Med 140:855-856, 1980.
46. Farmer KD, Harries SR, Fox BM, et al: Core biopsy of the bowel wall: Efficacy and safety in the clinical setting. AJR 175:1627-1630, 2000.
47. Marco-Doménech SF, Gil-Sánchez S, Fernández-Garcia P, et al: Sonographically guided percutaneous biopsy of gastrointestinal tract lesions. AJR 176:147-151, 2000.
48. Tudor GR, Rodgers PM, West KP: Bowel lesions: Percutaneous US-guided 18-gauge needle biopsy—preliminary experience. Radiology 212:594-597, 1999.
49. Damgaard-Pedersen K, Von der Maase H: Ultrasound and ultrasound guided biopsy, CT and lymphography in the diagnosis of retroperitoneal metastases in testicular cancer. Scand J Urol Nephrol 137:139-144, 1991.
50. Matalon TAS, Silver B: US guidance of interventional procedures. Radiology 174:43-47, 1990.
51. Nagano T, Nakai Y, Taniguchi F, et al: Diagnosis of paraaortic and pelvic lymph node metastasis of gynecologic malignant tumors by ultrasound-guided percutaneous fine-needle aspiration biopsy. Cancer 68:2571-2574, 1991.
52. Nyman RS, Cappelen-Smith J, Brismar J, et al: Yield and complications in ultrasound-guided biopsy of abdominal lesions. Acta Radiol 36:485-490, 1995.
53. Tikkakoski T, Siniluoto T, Ollikainen A, et al: Ultrasound-guided aspiration cytology of enlarged lymph nodes. Acta Radiol 32:53-56, 1991.
54. Wittich GR, Nowels KW, Korn RL, et al: Coaxial transthoracic fine-needle biopsy in patients with a history of malignant lymphoma. Radiology 183:175-178, 1992.
55. Silverman SG, Lee BY, Mueller PR, et al: Impact of positive findings at image-guided biopsy of lymphoma on patient care: Evaluation of clinical history, needle size, and pathologic findings on biopsy performance. Radiology 190:759-764, 1994.
56. Quinn SF, Sheley RC, Nelson HA, et al: The role of percutaneous needle biopsies in the original diagnosis of lymphoma: A prospective evaluation. J Vasc Interv Radiol 6:947-952, 1995.
57. Liu K, Manu KP, Vitellas KM, et al: Fine needle aspiration with flow cytometric immunophentyping for primary diagnosis of intraabdominal lymphoma. Am J Clin Pathol 21: 98-104, 1999.
58. Kang M, Kalra N, Gulati M, et al: Image guided percutaneous splenic interventions. Eur J Radiol Mar 17, 2007. (Epub ahead of print)
59. Cavanna L, Lazzaro A, Vallisa D, et al: Role of image-guided fine-needle aspiration biopsy in the management of patients with splenic metastasis. World J Surg Oncol 5:13-18, 2007.
60. Keogan MT, Freed KS, Paulson EK, et al: Image-guided percutaneous biopsy of focal splenic lesions: Update on safety and effectiveness. AJR 172:933-937, 1999.
61. Petit P, Bret PM, Lough JO, et al: Risks associated with intestinal perforation during experimental percutaneous drainage. Invest Radiol 27:1012-1019, 1992.
62. Smith EH: Complications of percutaneous abdominal fine-needle biopsy. Radiology 178:253-258, 1991.
63. Nolsoe C, Nielsen L, Torp-Pedersen S, et al: Major complications and deaths due to interventional ultrasonography: A review of 8000 cases. J Clin Ultrasound 18:179-184, 1990.
64. Drinkovic I, Brkljacic B: Two cases of lethal complications following ultrasound-guided percutaneous fine-needle biopsy of the liver. J Cardiovasc Intervent Radiol 19:360-363, 1996.

Abdominal Abscess

Richard I. Chen, MD • Kent T. Sato, MD • Howard B. Chrisman, MD

Percutaneous abscess drainage (PAD) has become the standard first-line treatment for most intra-abdominal abscesses.[1] Left untreated, abdominal abscess is associated with a high mortality rate despite appropriate antibiotic coverage.[2,3] Fortunately, current imaging techniques allow for early detection of abscesses, which can provide an opportunity for timely treatment before serious septic complications arise.[4] A major benefit of PAD is that one does not have to wait for late manifestations of an abdominal abscess to present to justify intervention, due to the considerably lower relative risks of PAD compared with open surgical drainage.

Modern imaging techniques permit earlier, more accurate detection of abdominal fluid collections than ever before. The CT, ultrasound, MR, and nuclear medicine can promptly diagnose abdominal abscesses shortly after, and at times before, they are clinically suspected. CT and ultrasound are the primary means of diagnosing abdominal abscess, due to their availability and relative low cost. Consequently, these two modalities are used to guide PAD.

PAD has proved to be a safe and effective treatment method for a wide variety of abdominal abscesses in most every anatomic location. With success rates greater than 80%,[5-7] it has surpassed surgical drainage as the treatment of choice. Like most percutaneous therapies, PAD is less invasive than surgery and is associated with fewer complications, particularly related to respiratory issues (atelectasis/pneumonia), pain, and venous thrombosis.[8] PAD is becoming a mainstay in the management of intra-abdominal abscess because of its high success rate coupled with low complication rate.

PATHOPHYSIOLOGY OF PERCUTANEOUS ABSCESS DRAINAGE

The etiology of intra-abdominal abscesses is multifactorial, but the general pathophysiology is similar. Initially, either an existing intra-abdominal fluid collection becomes superinfected, or an abscess cavity forms de novo from an infectious nidus. A mature cavity then forms, which is encapsulated by a wall of fibrin, collagen, neovasculature, and leukocytes. This wall acts to confine the septic focus. As the contents of the abscess become more liquifactive under the influence of leukocyte action and enzymes, the pressure within the abscess increases, and the cavity assumes a spherical or ovoid configuration.[9] If the cavity becomes large enough, it can displace surrounding viscera sufficiently to facilitate a direct percutaneous approach.

Open surgical drainage was once regarded as the proper treatment for intra-abdominal abscesses because of approaches that allowed for extraperitoneal drainage (Ochsner's extraserous approach). Hesitance of surgeons in the past to accept PAD was in large part due to concerns of fascial transgression by the drainage catheter and expected risks of peritonitis. Due to this belief, early radiologic literature on PAD emphasized the importance of an extraperitoneal approach[10] to prevent peritoneal contamination. It is now known that the wall of the abscess is essentially preserved during PAD. This fact, combined with the wide safety margin of the procedure, allows PAD to be performed via a transperitoneal approach with minimal risk of peritoneal contamination or organ injury.

Another factor that historically led to delayed acceptance of PAD by surgeons was the skepticism that large cavities could be completely drained through relatively small-bore catheters.[11] Prior surgical experience with larger catheters and sump drains was checkered with difficulties; therefore, any effective treatment with smaller, percutaneously placed drains seemed unlikely. However, pus follows Poisseuille's law (as does any fluid with laminar flow through a tube), which states that the velocity of flow within a tube is related to the diameter of the tube and the viscosity of the fluid. This means that the main advantage large-bore catheters have over smaller-bore catheters is that they can drain pus more quickly, although not necessarily more effectively. This advantage is offset by the practical difficulty of inserting larger-bore catheters. Because smaller catheters are easier to place percutaneously, better tolerated by the patient, and are effective for draining pus, the practice of PAD has gravitated toward the use of smaller-bore catheters 8- to 16-French in diameter. We now know that with aggressive PAD catheter management, abscess cavity drainage can be rapid, further negating large-bore catheter advantages. The main therapeutic effect comes from initial decompression of the abscess cavity. In particular, when an abscess is mature and unilocular, the abscess fluid is usually of low viscosity and can be evacuated quickly. Clinical improvement, with defervescence and drop in leukocytosis, is usually evident within 12 to 24 hours.

PREPROCEDURAL PRINCIPLES OF ABSCESS DRAINAGE

Ideally, abscesses suitable for PAD should be mature with a well-defined wall. Patients generally present with signs and symptoms of infection, such as fever, abdominal pain, and leukocytosis. The size and location of the abscess should be evaluated on cross-sectional imaging to determine whether a safe route to the abscess is present, what intervening structures can be crossed, and whether or not a catheter can be placed within the collection. Multilocular collections may require more than one drainage catheter, and small collections may be more appropriate for aspiration without drain placement.

Once these issues have been appropriately addressed, the patient is then assessed for suitability for this procedure. Coagulation studies and CBC are typically obtained. Prothrombin time (PT) should be less than 3 seconds greater than control and/or the international normalized ratio (INR) should be less than or equal to 1.5. If abnormal, they should be corrected if possible. If the patient is on coumadin, it should be held if practical to allow for normalization of the PT/INR. If time allows, vitamin K supplements can be administered to correct the coagulopathy. Acutely, correction with transfusion of fresh frozen plasma (FFP) may be considered.

If the patient is on unfractionated heparin or a low-molecular-weight heparin such as Lovenox (enoxaparin sodium injection; Aventis Pharmaceuticals, Bridgewater, NJ), it should be discontinued and appropriate time elapsed to allow for normalization of coagulation parameters. Heparin should be discontinued at least 2 to 3 hours before the procedure to allow for approximately 2 half-lives to elapse. Lovenox has a longer half-life and should be held at least 12 hours before the procedure when practical. If the procedure is to be performed more urgently, both heparin and low-molecular-weight heparins can be reversed with protamine sulfate. Thrombocytopenia is another important consideration. To minimize bleeding complications, platelets should be greater than 50,000/μL when possible.[12] If appropriate, platelet transfusion before the procedure can be performed to raise the platelet count to an acceptable level. The patient should also be screened for use of platelet inhibitors such as aspirin or Plavix (clopidrogrel bisulfate, Bristol-Meyers Squibb, New York, NY). In an elective setting, these medications should be held for approximately 5 days before PAD. In a more urgent situation, thrombocytopenia can be overcome with platelet transfusion. Finally, if patients are not already on intravenous antibiotics, they should be started on appropriate broad-spectrum antibiotics before the procedure.

Ultimately, the global clinical picture must be considered. Extremely toxic patients in the intensive care unit with sepsis due to an abscess will require emergent treatment despite suboptimal laboratory values. Although every effort should be made to correct any related underlying abnormalities, this should not delay treating the patient. Both the benefits and risks must be weighed and the best plan of action taken. The various benefits, potential complications, and alternatives should be discussed with the patient and informed consent obtained.

IMAGING FINDINGS IN ABDOMINAL ABSCESS

Computed Tomography

Computed tomography is the imaging modality of choice for diagnosis of most intra-abdominal abscesses. Whenever possible, contrast-enhanced CT (CECT) should be performed to demonstrate an enhancing abscess wall if present. Wall enhancement is a sign that suggests that the abscess has matured and will respond well to PAD. Typically, an abscess appears as a well-circumscribed fluid collection, often spherical or ovoid in shape. Abscesses can also conform to the shape of the compartment in which they are located (e.g., lesser sac, pelvis). Within the peritoneum, abscesses can displace surrounding viscera. Oral contrast should be given to help distinguish bowel from extraluminal fluid collections. The measured density of the abscess will vary depending on the contents. It typically ranges from 0 to +30 HU depending on the degree of liquifaction within the abscess and the presence of gas.[13,14] Abscess contents do not typically enhance, and the presence of such enhancement should raise concern for the presence of necrotic tumor.

Gas is seen in about 50% of all intra-abdominal abscesses, which can be in the form of microbubbles or larger pockets of gas resulting in an air-fluid level. Due to the inflammation caused by the abscess, the surrounding mesenteric fat can show increased attenuation and is often associated with thickening of the adjacent fascial planes.[15]

CT offers exquisite anatomic detail regarding the extent of the cavity, its relationship to surrounding structures and the presence of unfavorable factors for PAD such as loculation.[16,17] Fistulization with bowel has been associated with poorer outcomes with PAD; however, it is no longer considered a contraindication for treatment. PAD has been shown to be effective even in the presence of an enteric fistula,[18,19] even if only as a temporizing measure to prevent a precipitous decline in the patient's clinical status.

Whenever possible, CT should be performed with oral contrast, as unopacified segments of bowel may mimic an abscess. When appropriate, rectal contrast may also help discern bowel loops from abscesses. When in doubt, a delayed scan or scanning in a different patient position can demonstrate changes in the appearance around a questionable structure. The configuration of bowel can change over time. If a definitive diagnosis is necessary, the collection can be accessed with a needle and aspirated. If the aspirated fluid appears grossly purulent, a drainage catheter can be inserted. Some have advocated placing a drain primarily and sending the fluid for Gram stain and culture with removal of the catheter if negative. It should be noted, however, cultures will only grow organisms approximately 60% to 70% of the time.[20,21] Because of this uncertainty, our practice has been to drain a collection as completely as possible and to empirically treat the collection as an abscess. This minimizes the need for repeat drainage in the event that the patient's clinical status does not improve.

Ultrasound

Ultrasound is a readily available modality that can be used to detect intra-abdominal abscesses. Due to its portability, ultrasound can be used to diagnose an abscess in intensive care unit patients who are too ill and unstable to safely leave the unit and obtain a CT scan. Sonographically, the appearance of an abscess varies from an anechoic, cystic structure to a complex, multiloculated, echogenic mass. They can assume the configuration of the compartment in which they are located or may displace surrounding structures. Gas within an abscess produces a highly echogenic, ill-defined area with "dirty" posterior acoustic shadowing. Unfortunately, its appearance is not specific and can resemble any number of intra-abdominal fluid collections. It is important to distinguish an abscess from a loop of bowel, which can usually be done based on the presence peristalsis or definite visualization of the bowel wall itself. Unlike CT or MRI, ultrasound is highly operator dependent, and patient body habitus, overlying bowel gas, wounds, drains, and dressings can all limit adequate visualization of abdominal structures. If possible, ultrasound should not be the primary imaging modality in diagnosing an abscess.

Magnetic Resonance Imaging

Magnetic resonance imaging is being used more frequently in the diagnosis of intra-abdominal abscesses because of its multiplanar imaging capabilities, as well as its ability to characterize the nature of a suspected abscess. Additionally, the use of intravascular gadolinium contrast provides information similar to CT, while avoiding nephrotoxic effects or allergies to iodinated CT contrast. Abscesses commonly demonstrate inhomogeneous areas of low T1-weighted signal intensity, which then show mural enhancement following intravenous contrast administration. T2-weighted images display intermediate to high signal intensities.

Nuclear Scintigraphy

Nuclear scintigraphy can be useful in septic patients without any localizing signs in whom CT, MRI, and/or ultrasound has failed to identify and abscess.[22,23] Gallium 67– and indium-111–labeled white cells are the standard isotopes used in abscess detection. ^{111}In-labeled white cells have a 73% to 86% sensitivity in abscess detection.[24] False-positive results can occur in patients with bowel infarction or hemorrhage and after repeated enemas.

Newer agents such as technetium (Tc) 99m–HMPAO-labeled white cells, ^{111}In-labeled polyclonal IgG, and ^{99m}Tc-labeled monoclonal antibodies are also being used with increasing frequency. Gallium scans are sensitive, although less specific, for detecting abscesses.[25] False-positive results can occur with tumors such as lymphoma, granulomatous lesions, wounds, and normal gut, which excretes approximately 10% of the administered dose. The major disadvantage of nuclear scintigraphy is the relatively poor anatomic detail provided. This may change with the increasing use of image fusion technology, which allows the user to combine images from a CT and a radionuclide examination.

Plain Films

Plain film radiography is an insensitive method for the detection of intra-abdominal abscesses and has little role in the primary diagnosis of abscesses. Abscesses can be incidentally diagnosed by the presence of an abnormal gas pattern, soft tissue mass, and loss of normal fat-soft tissue interfaces.

TECHNIQUE OF ABSCESS DRAINAGE

The specific techniques and equipment used for PAD will vary due to operator preference and/or available equipment. The two main variables in the technical aspect of percutaneous drain placement are (1) determining the type of image guidance to be used and (2) using either the Seldinger technique or the trocar technique for catheter insertion.

In our practice, the majority of PAD is performed in the interventional radiology department using ultrasound guidance for percutaneous needle access, and Seldinger technique under fluoroscopic guidance for wire and catheter manipulation. Given adequate preprocedural imaging (usually a CECT) as a reference, the majority of abdominal abscesses can be accessed using ultrasound guidance. We use an access needle with a highly echogenic stylet tip (Inrad Inc, Kentwood, MI) to aid in needle visualization. Ultrasound guidance for PAD access has numerous advantages. First, the ultrasound provides real-time imaging. This allows the operator to continually reevaluate the approach and visualize adjacent organs and vessels throughout the procedure, until the abscess has been reached. Second, ultrasound allows for more flexibility with regard to access routes due to the ability to easily change the orientation of the ultrasound probe and needle. Third, ultrasound is a mobile technology. If the patient is too unstable to travel to the radiology department, the machine can be taken to the bedside. Furthermore, ultrasound guidance can allow access to deeper collections through graded compression of movable structures (i.e., small bowel) to gain a direct pathway not obtainable with other methods. Avoiding ionizing radiation for access is an added benefit for both patient and operator. With experience, ultrasound guided abdominal interventions can often allow for faster, more accurate performance of procedures than CT guidance.[26]

Ultrasound certainly does have its limitations. Endomorphic body type and overlying bowel gas can degrade the ultrasound image. Deeper abscesses may not be clearly distinguishable from adjacent structures. Ultrasound is highly operator dependent; thus, some operators may not be as comfortable with the skill set required for this type of guided technique. In these circumstances, the anatomic detail provided by CT is clearly beneficial.

In many institutions, CT is the primary modality for PAD. CT guidance offers the operator high-resolution images for planning and performing PAD. The CT gantry angle may be adjusted to optimize the approach if the standard AP plane is not feasible. By using the same modality as the diagnostic study, one can be sure that the drainage catheter is actually treating the abscess in question. In other instances, one may require a portion of the procedure to be performed with CT guidance, while other parts may be done using fluoroscopic guidance.

Regardless of the guidance technique, the approach is essentially the same. The shortest and safest route to the collection should be chosen, while bowel and other vital organs should be avoided if possible. The catheter tip should ideally be positioned into the most dependent portion of the abscess. If the collection is oblong in shape, the catheter tip should be positioned in the location most distal to the catheter entry site. This is so as the cavity collapses, the catheter may be withdrawn to drain the remaining abscess without the need for another drain. Suction, irrigation, and thrombolytics are available, which can augment PAD. Percutaneous approaches through the flank, posterior abdominal wall, and gluteus muscles all achieve the objective of avoiding vital organs while providing dependent drainage.

In instances where an abscess is deep and central within the abdomen, a direct route may not be possible without transgressing some vital structure. In general, transhepatic placement of a drainage catheter can usually be performed with minimal sequelae. This route does incur the additional risk of bleeding from the liver; however, when necessary, it provides a viable window to access a difficult collection. The stomach is another organ that can be traversed with relative safety. Due to the multiple layers of smooth muscle within the stomach wall, placement of a transgastric drainage tube is also well tolerated with minimal complications.

There are two main techniques for catheter placement: the trocar method and the Seldinger method. Most commercially available drainage catheters have the ability to be placed using either technique. Although the Seldinger technique (Fig. 74-1) is the preferred method in our practice, operators should be comfortable with either technique.

The trocar method (Fig. 74-2) involves placing the catheter directly into the collection over a sharp metal trocar and stiffening cannula. The catheter is then advanced forward from the trocar and stiffener into the abscess. This method is ideal for large, superficial collections, which are relatively far from vital structures. The patient is sterilely prepped and draped and the superficial tissues are anesthetized. Moderate sedation is used when appropriate. A small skin nick is made with a scalpel, and the superficial tissues are bluntly dissected. If using CT for guidance, initial localization with a guiding needle within the collection can be performed and note is made of the trajectory and depth of the collection. The trocar is then inserted along the path of the guiding needle, and the catheter is coiled inside the abscess. CT for confirmation of appropriate drain location is performed. If real-time ultrasound is used, the guiding needle is not necessary. The trocar is directed into the collection using ultrasound, and the catheter is deployed. The catheter is then secured to the skin using a fixation device, and the contents are aspirated.

The Seldinger technique is our preferred method for abscess drainage. The basis for this technique is placement of a guidewire into the abscess through an access needle. Serial

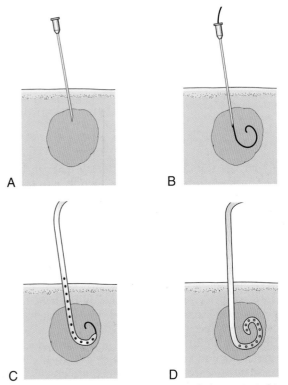

Figure 74-1. Seldinger technique for abscess drainage. A. A skin nick is made and dissected with a hemostat. An 18-gauge aspiration/biopsy needle is then placed into cavity under imaging guidance. **B.** A guidewire is passed through the needle and coiled within the cavity. **C.** Serial dilation performed over the guidewire using gradually increasing diameters of dilators and the catheter is advanced over the guidewire. **D.** The catheter is formed and the cavity is then aspirated completely.

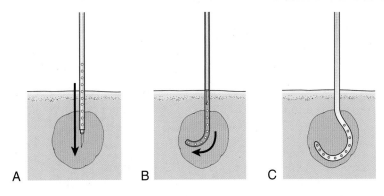

Figure 74-2. Trocar technique for catheter insertion. A. Once the proper location is chosen, a skin nick is made and dissected with a hemostat. The catheter with the trocar needle in place is inserted through the incision to the appropriate depth of the cavity. **B.** After confirming placement, the metal inner cannula is anchored in place and the catheter advanced over it. **C.** The cannula is removed and catheter formed. The cavity is then aspirated through the catheter.

dilations are then performed over the guidewire and until the catheter is advanced over the wire into the abscess. Using ultrasound guidance, an echogenic-tip needle is placed within the abscess. Through this needle, a 0.035- or 0.038-inch guidewire is coiled within the cavity. For deeper cavities, or patients with a large amount of subcutaneous adipose tissue, a stiffer wire may be required to prevent wire kinking as the dilators and catheters are advanced. The tract is dilated up to the size of the catheter to be placed. Routinely, we place either 8- or 10-French catheters for simple, liquefied collections. In the event that the fluid is unusually viscous or contains a significant amount of debris, a 12- or 14-French catheter is placed.

Once placed, the catheter position can be checked with ultrasound for collapse of the cavity and/or with fluoroscopy by injecting a small amount of radiopaque contrast. Care must be taken when injecting contrast into a distended cavity due to the risk of bacteremia; thus, the cavity should be aspirated before injecting contrast. Abcessograms through the catheter can help to guide optimal catheter positioning with the side holes of the catheter entirely within the abscess, thereby minimizing the risk of contamination of adjacent spaces. If the catheter placed under CT is not in an ideal position, it can be repositioned under fluoroscopy.

Once placed, catheters can be secured to the skin using a variety of fixation devices available on the market. We primarily use an adhesive ostomy ring to which the catheter is sutured using a silk suture. The catheter is then directly connected to a drainage bag and placed to gravity drainage. Some operators prefer to place a three-way stopcock between the catheter and drainage bag to facilitate drain irrigation. At the time of placement, the abscess is evacuated as completely as possible and gently irrigated. Once the cavity has been drained sufficiently, the drain is left in place and the patient returned to the floor for observation. Depending on the amount of output over the next several hours, a decision is made to either irrigate the drain with saline, or to augment drainage by instilling a fibrinolytic agent such as tissue plasminogen activator (tPA) or urokinase. Early experience with intracavitary urokinase showed that this was able to break down the fibrin within the abscess cavity and reduce the viscosity of the pus, facilitating drainage.[27] In 1999, urokinase was removed from the market due to concerns by the Food and Drug Administration about manufacturing processes. In that interval, tPA gained popularity for fibrinolysis and thrombolysis and has since become the drug of choice for this indication due to its efficacy and cost-effectiveness. In most

cases, the authors pursue a trial of gravity drainage because thick pus usually thins rapidly after catheter insertion. The pressure inside the abscess cavity plays a role in producing viscous pus, and catheter decompression usually results in an increased flow of pus.

Once placed, the patients and their catheters are followed daily by the interventional radiology service. Successful PAD requires active monitoring and maintenance of the catheter by the interventional radiology service.[5,28] The catheter is flushed with 5 to 10 mL of saline three times a day to prevent clogging. Catheter outputs are recorded every shift, and if a sudden drop in output is noted, the catheter is manually flushed to check for proper function. If unexpectedly high outputs are observed, some form of fistula to the cavity is likely. Clinical parameters such as drain output, patient temperature, hemodynamic status, leukocyte count, and culture results are followed daily as well to evaluate the patient's clinical progress. The catheter is visually inspected to check for any obvious migration, abnormal tension, or abnormal drainage. This type of close follow-up is required for successful PAD. By taking responsibility for the care of the patient, it enhances the quality of interaction with clinical colleagues, who now defer catheter management decisions to the radiologist.

Catheters can be placed to gravity drainage or suction drainage. The argument for passive drainage to gravity is that it minimizes the incidence of catheter occlusion due to aspirated debris. Conversely, drainage with low intermittent suction or with a suction bulb device can result in more rapid evacuation of an abscess. It can also oppose the walls of the abscess, possibly facilitating collapse of the cavity. For collections that may require aggressive suctioning due to viscous, complex fluid, a sump catheter with a separate venting lumen may be considered.

The decision to remove a catheter is based on a combination of clinical and radiographic criteria. Ideally, drainage should be less than 10 mL per day minus any catheter flush volume. Fever and leukocytosis attributed to the abscess should be resolved. Although a catheter can be removed based on clinical criteria alone, the conservative approach is to evaluate for residual cavity size and the presence of any fistula with an abscessogram or CT scan. If an abscessogram shows the cavity to be less than 10 mL in volume and no fistula to adjacent structures are seen, the catheter is removed. If a significant fistula is present, catheter drainage is continued until the fistula closes, or until PAD is considered a failure and a surgical therapy is considered (Fig. 74-3). Alternatively, a CT scan can be obtained to confirm resolution of the cavity.

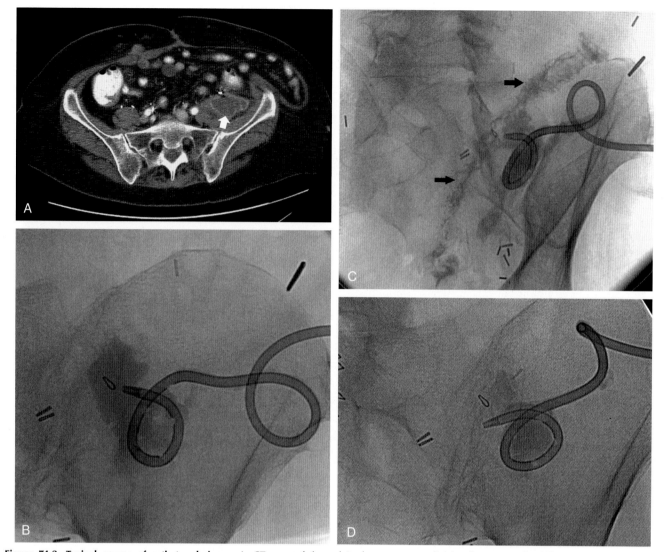

Figure 74-3. Typical course of catheter drainage. A. CT scan of the pelvis demonstrates a fluid collection in the left psoas muscle (*arrow*). **B.** Abscessogram at the time of drainage shows the catheter to be in good position within the cavity. **C.** Interval abscessogram demonstrating a fistula to the small bowel from the cavity (*arrows*). **D.** Final tube check demonstrates near complete resolution of the cavity and no enteric fistula. If the patient is clinically stable with minimal output from the drain, the catheter can be safely removed.

If the cavity is collapsed and the patient is clinically stable with minimal output from the cavity, the catheter can be removed. The disadvantage of using CT is that an occult fistula to bowel cannot be detected. If the criteria for removal are met, the catheter is removed in one step. The technique of gradually backing out the catheter was based on traditional surgical practices; however, is not necessary with the relatively small-bore catheters used today.

COMPLICATIONS OF PERCUTANEOUS ABSCESS DRAINAGE

Complications of PAD include sepsis, failure of drainage, catheter malposition, bowel injury, hemorrhage, pneumothorax, hemothorax, cardiorespiratory arrest, and peritonitis.[29] Careful preprocedure planning is key to avoiding many of these pitfalls. Once a catheter is placed, there should be minimal catheter manipulation. Vigorous irrigation of the cavity or high-volume abscessogram should also be avoided to pre-

vent episodes of bacteremia during the procedure. Bacteremic/septic patients may become symptomatic within 1 to 2 hours following the procedure, presenting with sudden onset of rigors, fevers, and/or hypotension. These patients should be treated with aggressive fluid resuscitation, antibiotics, and vasopressors in necessary to maintain an acceptable blood pressure. If persistent, they should be transferred to the intensive care unit for further support until the episode resolves.

Failure to drain an abscess is usually related to the characteristics of the collection rather than the technique. The abscess may be multilocular, poorly defined, or not mature and liquified enough to be drained effectively. Other causes of drainage failure include the presence of a necrotic tumor, fungal contamination, or Crohn's disease.

CATHETER SELECTION

There are two main types of catheters used in PAD: single-lumen and double-lumen sump catheters. The authors use single-lumen catheters almost exclusively. Catheters are available from 6- to 16-French in diameter. Most catheters are designed to be inserted using either the trocar technique or the Seldinger technique. The most commonly used catheters have a hydrophylic coating, which allows for easier insertion (Flexima catheter with Glidex hydrophylic coating; Boston Scientific, Natick, MA, or Ultrathane catheter with Slip-coat hydrophilic coating; Cook, Bloomington, IN). The hydrophilic coating absorbs and retains water and reduces the friction coefficient up to a factor of 20, greatly increasing the ease of catheter insertion. The two most common catheter configurations are a locking-pigtail design and a J-tip design.

Double-lumen sump catheters are designed to drain an abscess using suction. This is most often used when the material within the cavity is thick and viscous.[30,31] The mechanism of the sump catheter is a venting effect of the second lumen of the catheter. When the catheter is placed to suction, the walls of the cavity will naturally come into contact with the catheter side holes, thereby reducing the suction. The presence of a second venting lumen allows air to be sucked into the catheter, creating a vent effect. This prevents adherence of the catheter to the cavity walls and facilitates more effective drainage.

ASPIRATION OF ABSCESSES

Some cavities may not be amenable to catheter placement. The size of the abscess may be too small to accommodate a catheter, or the cavity may be in a location inaccessible to conventional catheter drainage. In these instances, the abscess may be treated with aspiration. Information obtained from the aspirated material may be of diagnostic benefit. Inaccessible cavities are commonly found in the lower abdomen and pelvis. Cavities may be deep within the bony pelvis, or between loops of bowel, which prevents safe catheter placement. If the clinical situation warrants, needle aspiration of the collection can be performed with a 20-gauge needle transgressing the intervening bowel loops. In these instances, aspiration alone may be sufficient to increase the efficacy of medical management.

USE OF THROMBOLYTICS AS ADJUNCTIVE THERAPY TO PERCUTANEOUS ABSCESS DRAINAGE

The utility of thrombolytic agents (streptokinase and urokinase) to assist in the treatment of empyema and abdominal fluid collections has been well described.[32-37] tPA has now become the preferred agent for thrombolysis and fibrinolysis.

In our practice, we routinely administer 4 to 6 mg of tPA reconstituted in 10 to 20 mL of normal saline. The volume can be adjusted based on the size of the cavity. Once the tPA has been instilled into the cavity, it is allowed to dwell for approximately 1 hour with the drainage catheter clamped. After the hour, the tube is opened to drainage and the output recorded. This is performed from once a day to up to three times a day and continued as long as effective. If the drain outputs continue to decline despite thrombolytic treatments, the patient is reimaged to evaluate the cavity

Although the dosing of urokinase is slightly different, it is administered in a similar fashion; 250,000 units are recon-stituted in 60 to 150 mL of sterile saline and divided into three equal aliquots. One aliquot containing 83,000 units is infused into the cavity and left to dwell for 30 minutes with the catheter closed. When the drain is reopened, the cavity is irrigated and returned to gravity drainage.

Thrombolytic therapy can be effective for the treatment of abscesses because of the presence of a fibrin matrix within the cavity. Fibrin deposition can cause loculation within the cavity, which can interfere with simple catheter drainage. tPA and urokinase activate plasminogen to plasmin. Plasmin, in turn, degrades fibrin and results in the breakdown of the loculations. It also acts to reduce the viscosity of the fluid within the collection, thus facilitating catheter drainage. Instillation of thrombolytics into abscesses has proved to be a safe therapy with only a minimal associated risk of bleeding.[27]

SPECIFIC APPLICATIONS OF PERCUTANEOUS ABSCESS DRAINAGE

Intraperitoneal Abscess

Intraperitoneal abscesses are generally the result of super-infection of existing intraperitoneal fluid collections, such as ascites, hematomas, bilomas, urinomas, and even peritoneal dialysate. Bile collections can result from trauma or iatrogenic bile duct injury or be postoperative in nature. Bilomas are prone to infection and following PAD, approximately 45% have a persistent biliary fistula.[13] The patient may require an additional procedure such as an ERCP with biliary stent placement or a percutaneous biliary drain to divert bile away from the site of injury.

Hematomas easily become infected. PAD can be effective if the hematoma has liquefied sufficiently. Fresh clot has the consistency of jelly and will not aspirate well through a catheter. In such instances, the use of tPA can assist in the evacuation of an infected hematoma.

Intraperitoneal abscesses tend to be large; therefore, successful percutaneous drainage may require the placement of more than one tube. Fortunately, larger collections make access less difficult. As always, the route of drainage should be carefully considered and superficial vessels such as the epigastric arteries should be avoided in order to prevent hemorrhagic complications.

Subphrenic Abscess

Most subphrenic abscesses are postoperative in origin. The location of these collections often necessitates an angulated approach to avoid the transgression of pleura. A subcostal approach is the most ideal method; however, depending on the anatomy, an intercostal approach may be necessary (Fig. 74-4). Whenever possible, the pleura should be avoided due to the risk of pneumothorax, hemothorax, or converting a pleural effusion into an empyema.

Ultrasound guidance is beneficial since the upper abdomen can be scanned in many different orientations to find the most appropriate route. When using CT guidance, the gantry can be tilted to achieve the same result. Patients occasionally demonstrate signs of diaphragmatic irritation from these abscesses, such as referred scapular/shoulder pain or intractable hiccups; however, these symptoms generally resolve when the abscess is drained.

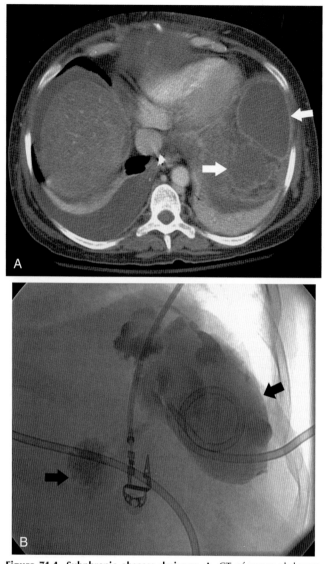

Figure 74-4. Subphrenic abscess drainage. A. CT of upper abdomen shows a bilobed fluid collection beneath the left hemidiaphragm (*arrows*). **B.** Drainage catheter placed through an intercostal route into the most peripheral collection. Abscessogram shows the same bilobed cavity (*arrows*). The catheter is in the main collection, and the cavity also communicates with the smaller collection seen on CT.

Diverticular Abscess

Some 10% to 20% of patients with diverticulosis present with diverticulitis.[1] The general mechanism of diverticular abscess formation starts with a microperforation causing a microabscess, which grows in size and becomes a macroabscess. Left untreated, the abscesses can rupture and result in gross fecal peritonitis.[38] Traditional therapy has been medical for early diverticulitis and surgical for advanced disease. When abscesses are involved, surgical resection involves a multistaged procedure, where the patient requires fecal diversion through an ileostomy or colostomy until the infection resolves and partial colectomy and colonic anastamosis can be performed.

For those patients who develop a well-defined pericolic abscess, percutaneous drainage has been very effective, with success rates of up to 90%.[1] These cavities respond well to catheter decompression and, combined with appropriate antibiotic therapy, can temporize the patient's disease until definitive therapy can be performed. By treating the abscess completely, surgery can be performed in one setting, sparing the patient the morbidity associated with multiple surgeries and the difficulties of living with a stoma for several weeks.[39,40]

The approach to diverticular abscesses is variable depending on the location of the abscess. Most commonly, an anterolateral approach or transgluteal approach is used. Imaging guidance can be provided with CT or ultrasound combined with fluoroscopy (Fig. 68-5). Catheter outputs are followed and the presence and extent of an enteric fistula are documented with an abscessogram several days following the procedure. Abscessograms can be performed every 1 to 2 weeks to document shrinkage of the cavity and resolution of the fistula. Once completed, the patient is reevaluated by the surgeon for definitive therapy.

Crohn's Disease

Patients with Crohn's disease are especially prone to form intra-abdominal abscesses. These can also be effectively treated with PAD without an untoward risk of enterocutaneous formation.[41,42] Abscesses most commonly occur in the right iliac fossa, the quadratus muscles, the iliopsoas muscle, or the pelvis. Percutaneous drainage may facilitate an existing enterocutaneous fistula to close, obviating surgery in some cases. If surgical resection is required, PAD may help convert a multiple to a single-stage surgery, similar to the treatment of diverticular abscesses.

Appendiceal Abscess

Appendicitis is a diagnosis that can be made using cross-sectional imaging with a high degree of accuracy.[43-45] The definitive therapy for uncomplicated appendicitis is surgical resection. In the setting of appendiceal rupture, the complication rates following surgery are high.[46] In these patients, PAD can temporize the situation and allow the acute inflammation to subside, resulting in a more straightforward surgery. In patients who are poor operative candidates, PAD can also be an alternative to surgery.[47] The approach to an appendiceal abscess can be challenging, as the abscess tends to be deep in the pelvis, or between bowel loops. Here proper planning and good preprocedural imaging will help identify the safest route to the abscess (Fig. 74-6).

Hepatic Abscess

Hepatic abscess can be pyogenic (bacterial), amebic, protozoan, or fungal in origin. Worldwide, amebic abscess is the most common cause of liver abscess. In the United States, pyogenic liver abscess (PLA) is the most common cause of hepatic abscesses.[48] PLA in North America has an incidence of two or three per 100,000.[49] Despite advances in antibiotic therapy, PLA continues to be associated with significant morbidity and mortality.

In the preantibiotic era, hepatic abscess formation most often occurred as a result of portal venous bacteremia from abdominal infections such as appendicitis, diverticulitis, or perforated colonic tumors. Liver abscess in this setting was nearly always fatal. Although liver abscesses from portal vein

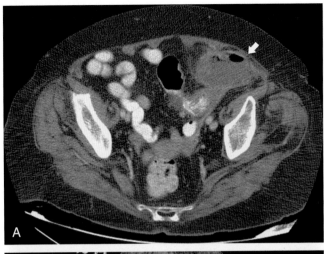

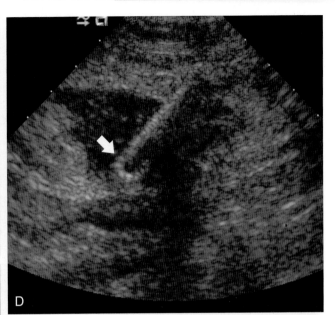

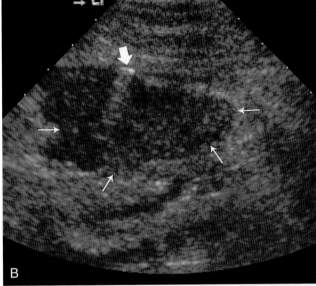

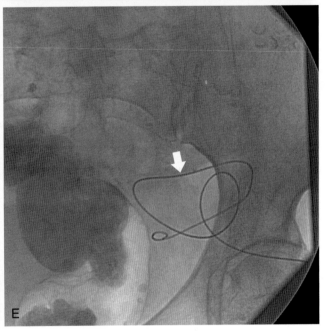

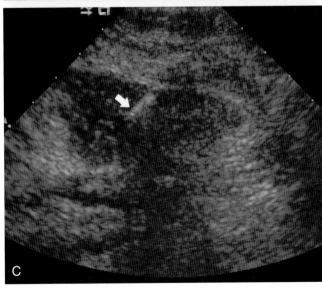

Figure 74-5. Diverticular abscess drainage. A. A 77-year-old patient with fevers and abdominal pain. CT scan shows an enhancing fluid collection with gas adjacent to the sigmoid colon, consistent with a diverticular abscess (*arrow*). **B.** Ultrasound shows the cavity (*thin arrows*) with a hyperechoic focus (*large arrow*) exhibiting ring-down artifact consistent with gas. **C.** Echogenic needle (*arrow*) placed into the cavity using ultrasound guidance. **D.** J-wire (*arrow*) placed through needle into cavity under ultrasound guidance. **E.** Fluoroscopic image of the J-wire coiled inside the cavity (*arrow*).

Continued

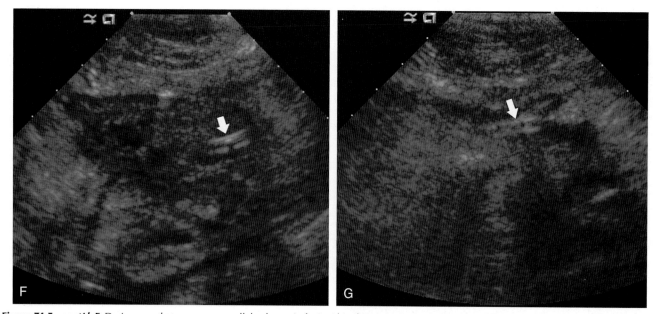

Figure 74-5. *cont'd,* **F.** Drainage catheter seen as parallel echogenic foci within the cavity (*arrow*). **G.** Catheter (*arrow*) seen within a collapsed cavity following aspiration.

bacteremia is much less common since the advent of antibiotics, the incidence of PLA has remained rather constant, as different modes of infection have evolved. PLA today is often seen in the setting of obstructive biliary disease, trauma, and iatrogenic causes. Prior hepatic surgeries involving biliary-enteric anastomosis or liver transplantation (especially with hepatic artery thrombosis) can also increase the risk for PLA. PLAs are also a complication of locoregional therapies for liver tumors such as transarterial chemoembolization and percutaneous tumor ablation. Other associated risk factors for PLA include diabetes, underlying biliary pathology (i.e., stones, strictures), malignancy, advancing age, and immunosupression. Common clinical and laboratory signs of PLA are generally nonspecific but can include abdominal pain, fever and chills, leukocytosis, elevated bilirubin, and alkaline phosphatase.[48]

On CECT, PLA typically appears as a low-attenuation, single or multifocal, rounded lesion. Most occur in the right lobe. Lesions that contain gas bubbles suggest a pyogenic etiology. An enhancing abscess wall with a halo of edema may be noted. Review of the patient history and imaging should be performed to rule out the possibility of a low-density tumor or tumor necrosis. Sonographically, abscesses may range from cystic to quite echogenic depending on the amount of debris or gas.

The majority of PLAs can be treated effectively with antibiotics in combination with catheter drainage and/or needle aspiration of lesions under ultrasound or CT guidance.[50] This therapy is effective in 70% to 94% of patients[51,52] (Fig. 74-7). The mortality of PLA, however, remains relatively high at approximately 10% despite current therapy.[49,52,53] This can be attributed in part to delayed diagnosis, sepsis, fungal superinfection, multiple and/or multiseptated abscesses, and underlying comorbidities.

Occasionally, large liver tumors can become necrotic and the liquefied material superinfected, and PAD may be performed as a palliative measure. Unless the tumor is resected, however, there may be persistent drainage even after the

initial infectious episode resolves. Patients should be informed that these drains may need to be in place for an extended period of time.

Amebic liver abscess should be suspected in patients with a history of travel to an area where *Entamoeba histolytica* is endemic or in immunocompromised patients with a corresponding liver lesion on imaging. Amebic abscess is usually a single, rounded, right lobe lesion, typically subcapsular in location. Echogenic debris within the lesion is often present. Serologic testing for confirmation should be performed, and the initial treatment of choice is metronidazole with or without the addition of a luminal antiamebic agent such as paromomycin.[54] Image-guided intervention should be reserved for cases where (1) the diagnosis remains in question and a wall biopsy or aspiration of the lesion is performed to isolate the organism or (2) an amebic abscess has not responded appropriately to drug therapy. Fluid from these lesions is often thick and classically described as resembling anchovy paste. Superinfection of an amebic abscess may be one cause for poor drug response.

Echinococcal liver cysts (hydatid cysts) are also lesions that should be suspected and diagnosed before surgical or percutaneous intervention whenever possible. This is due to the known potential for spilled contents of these lesions to cause anaphylaxis and/or rapid spread of daughter cysts. Although historically discouraged, many case reports and small series of successful percutaneous drainage of echinococcal liver cysts have been published.[55,56] PAD rather than surgical drainage remains controversial. If performed, injection of a scolecidal agent (e.g., hypertonic saline) and repeated aspiration have been described in combination with appropriate drug therapy (e.g., albendazole).[56-58]

The echinococcal liver abscess on imaging presents as a large cyst with calcified walls and multiple surrounding daughter cysts. The classic "water lily sign" on chest radiograph of a detached inner lining floating within the cyst may be present, with an analogous appearance on CT. The diagnosis can be confirmed with serologic and skin (Cansoni) tests.

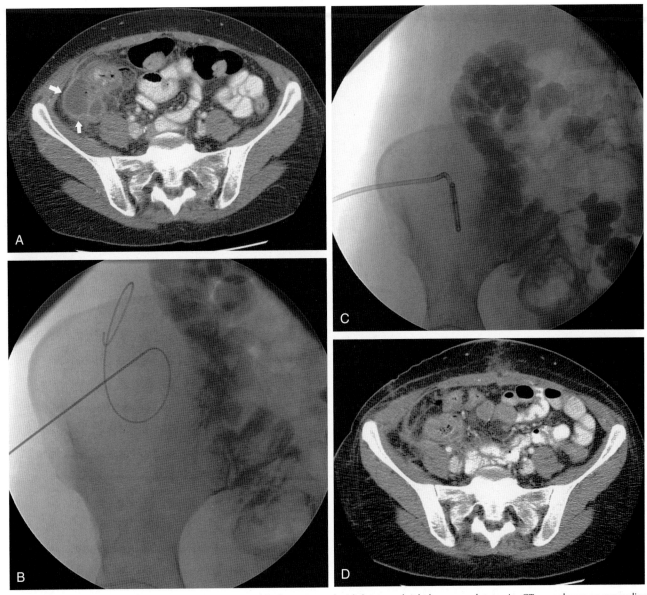

Figure 74-6. Appendiceal abscess drainage. A. A 19-year-old who presented with fevers and right lower quadrant pain. CT scan shows an appendiceal abscess (*arrows*). **B.** Following ultrasound guided needle placement, a guidewire is coiled in the cavity under fluoroscopy. **C.** An 8-Fr drain is placed under fluoroscopic guidance and the abscess is drained. **D.** Follow-up CT scan after catheter removal shows complete resolution of the abscess.

Splenic Abscess

Splenic abscess is relatively rare, but its incidence has increased over the past decade due to an increase in the immunocompromised patient population.[59] Untreated splenic abscess have a high mortality rate. Imaging with CECT or ultrasound should be performed to rule out splenic abscess in patients presenting with left upper quadrant pain, fever, and leukocytosis. Early detection can decrease the risks of sepsis and splenic rupture.[60]

Percutaneous drainage of splenic abscess along with antibiotic therapy has been shown to be an effective treatment, particularly when a single lesion is present (Fig. 74-8). Catheter drainage has the added advantage of preserving splenic function, as opposed to the surgical treatment of a total splenectomy.[61,62] When multiple abscesses are present, the risks and benefits of placing multiple drains versus splenectomy should

be weighed. In patients who are at high risk for surgery, PAD may be the best option. When placing a drain, a subcostal approach is generally preferred, but an intercostal approach is usually required due to the location of the spleen. In these instances, an angled, caudal-to-cranial approach for access can be used to avoid crossing the pleural space.

Pancreatic Collections

Manifestations of acute pancreatitis, such as pancreatic necrosis, pancreatic abscess, and pancreatic pseudocyst, are best diagnosed with contrast-enhanced MDCT.[63] It is important to differentiate pancreatic necrosis (devitalized pancreatic tissue with peripancreatic fat necrosis)[64] from a separate abscess or pseudocyst. Pancreatic necrosis has a higher morbidity and different treatment strategy than abscess or pseudocyst. When

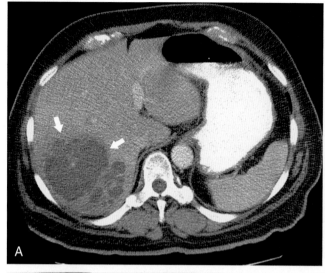

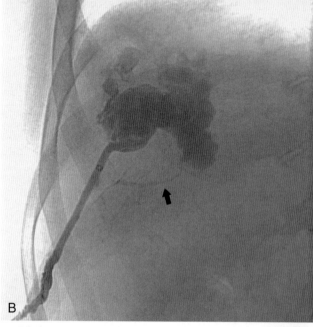

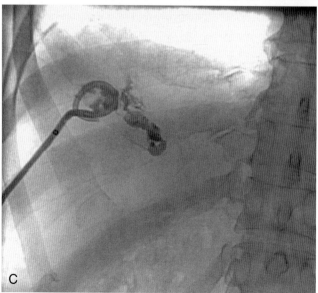

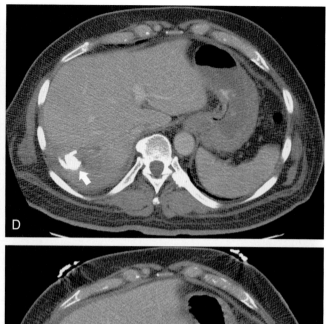

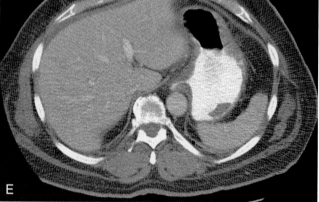

Figure 74-7. Liver abscess drainage. A. CT of the liver shows a multi-loculated abscess in the right lobe (*arrows*). **B.** Interval abscessogram shows a residual cavity with a biliary fistula (*arrow*). **C.** Follow-up abscessogram shows interval decrease in size of the cavity. **D.** CT obtained immediately after the abscessogram shows that the cavity (*arrow*) has significantly decreased in size. **E.** CT obtained several months after drain removal shows complete resolution of the abscess.

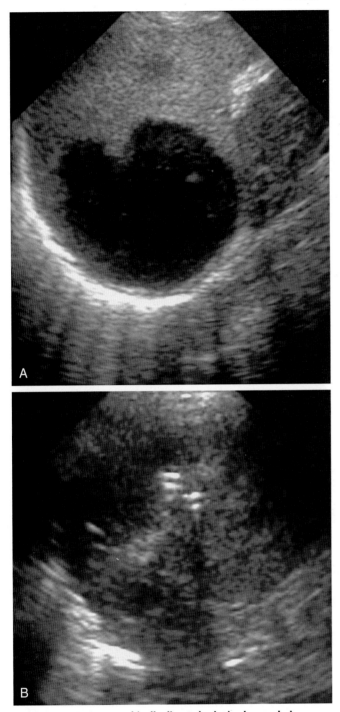

Figure 74-8. Sonographically directed splenic abscess drainage.

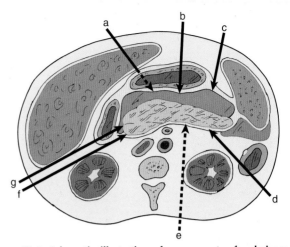

Figure 74-9. Schematic illustration of access routes for drainage of pancreatic and peripancreatic fluid collections. *a,* transhepatic; *b,* transgastric; *c,* transgastrosplenic ligament; *d,* pararenal; *e,* paravertebral; *f* and *g,* transduodenal.

drainage for a longer time period (weeks to months) may be required for pancreatic collections communicating with the pancreatic duct or with fistulas to the bowel to resolve.[68,69] Larger-bore catheters (12- to 14-French) may be used if significant debris is present or if the fluid is thick and viscous. In these cases, aggressive catheter management with irrigation and/or use of a sump catheter may be helpful.

Percutaneous approaches to retroperitoneal fluid collections are numerous and include transgastic, transhepatic, transgastrosplenic ligament, transgastocolic ligament, pararenal, paravertebral, and transduodenal routes (Fig. 74-9). Deep collections, or those immediately adjacent to the stomach, may be more amenable to endoscopic drainage. Similarly, larger collections may be treated surgically by creating a cystgastrostomy. These other approaches are still more invasive than percutaneous methods but should be considered when these collections are inaccessible percutaneously.

Pelvic Abscess

Common etiologies of pelvic abscesses include diverticulitis, appendicitis, Crohn's disease, postradiation, enteric fistulas, pelvic inflammatory disease, and infected postoperative fluid. Overlying bowel or bladder often precludes a direct anterior or anterolateral approach. Transgluteal, transvaginal, and transrectal approaches are commonly used routes for safe access to pelvic fluid collections. In our practice, the majority of pelvic drains are placed via a transgluteal approach. Ultrasound, CT, or fluoroscopic guidance is used to obtain access, preferably at the level of the sacrospinous ligament and as close to the sacrum as possible. This approach avoids the piriformis muscle, which, when traversed, can be associated with buttock pain. Access adjacent to the sacrum at this level also avoids the sciatic nerve. Overall, the transgluteal approach is very safe and effective for pelvic fluid drainage (Fig. 74-10).

In selected patients, transvaginal and transrectal approaches are also highly effective for aspiration, lavage (aspiration followed by saline irrigation until clear), or drainage catheter placement (Fig. 74-11). An endoluminal ultrasound probe with a guide is used for needle access or for trocar catheter insertion.[70-72]

infection of the necrotic pancreatic material is suspected, image-guided aspiration for Gram stain and culture is indicated to establish the diagnosis. When confirmed, open surgical debridement is the treatment of choice. Percutaneous drain placement in this scenario is reserved only as a temporizing measure for the most critically ill persons who cannot tolerate a surgery.[65,66]

If there is no evidence of pancreatic necrosis, percutaneous drainage of a pancreatic abscess or a mature pseudocyst can be an effective primary treatment.[67] Cure rates of 65% to 90% have been reported with catheter drainage, with surgical intervention reserved for unresponsive collections. Catheter

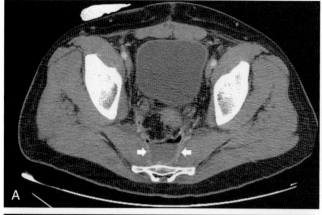

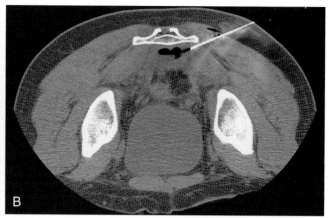

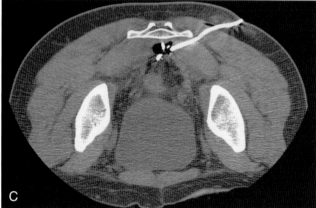

Figure 74-10. Transgluteal abscess drainage. A. CT scan demonstrates a small enhancing presacral cavity containing fluid and gas (*arrows*). **B.** The patient is placed prone for the CT-guided procedure. An 18-gauge needle is directed as close to the sacrum as possible to avoid the sciatic nerve and gluteal vessels. **C.** An 8-Fr catheter inserted using the Seldinger technique.

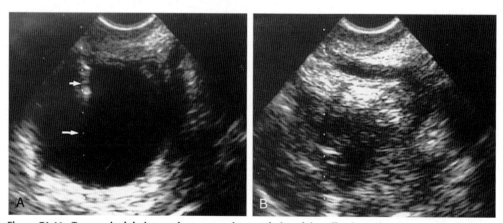

Figure 74-11. Transvaginal drainage of a noncomplex anechoic pelvic collection using sonographic guidance.

CONCLUSION

In conjunction with appropriate antibiotic therapy, image-guided PAD has become the preferred therapy for the management of abdominal abscess. PAD is highly effective and has a low complication rate, and it should be used over open surgical drainage whenever technically and clinically feasible.

References

1. Rypens F, Dubois J, Garel L, et al: Percutaneous drainage of abdominal abscesses in pediatric Crohn's disease. AJR 188:579-585, 2007.
2. Burke CT, Maura M, Molina PL: Interventional computed tomography. In Lee JKT, Sagel SS, Stanley RJ, et al (eds): Computed Body Tomography with MRI Correlation, 4th ed. Philadelphia, Lippincott Williams & Wilkins, 2006, pp 95-144.
3. Henry MC, Walker A, Silverman BL, et al: Risk factors for the development of abdominal abscess following operation for perforated appendicitis in children: A multicenter case-control study. Arch Surg 142:236-241, 2007.
4. Kumar RR, Kim JT, Haukoos JS, et al: Factors affecting the successful management of intra-abdominal abscesses with antibiotics and the need for percutaneous drainage. Dis Colon Rectum 49:183-189, 2006.
5. vanSonnenberg E, D'Agostino HB, Casola G, et al: US-guided transvaginal drainage of pelvic abscesses and fluid collections. Radiology 181:53-56, 1991.
6. vanSonnenberg E, Mueller PR, Ferrucci JT Jr: Percutaneous drainage of 250 abdominal abscesses and fluid collections. Part I: Results, failures, and complications. Radiology 151:337-341, 1984.
7. Mueller PR, vanSonnenberg E, Ferrucci JT Jr: Percutaneous drainage of 250 abdominal abscesses and fluid collections. Part II: Current procedural concepts. Radiology 151:343-347, 1984.

8. Dahnert W, Gunther RW, Borner N, et al: [Percutaneous drainage of abdominal abscesses. II. Value in comparison with septic surgery]. Chirurg 56:584-588, 1985.
9. Gerzof SG, Robbins AH, Birkett DH: Computed tomography in the diagnosis and management of abdominal abscesses. Gastrointest Radiol 3:287-294, 1978.
10. Kim YJ, Han JK, Lee JM, et al: Percutaneous drainage of postoperative abdominal abscess with limited accessibility: Preexisting surgical drains as alternative access route. Radiology 239:591-598, 2006.
11. Gobien RP, Stanley JH, Schabel SI, et al: The effect of drainage tube size on adequacy of percutaneous abscess drainage. Cardiovasc Intervent Radiol 8:100-102, 1985.
12. Payne CS: A primer on patient management problems in interventional radiology. AJR 170:1169-1176, 1998.
13. Mueller PR, Ferrucci JT Jr, Simeone JF, et al: Detection and drainage of bilomas: Special considerations. AJR 140:715-720, 1983.
14. Koehler PR, Moss AA: Diagnosis of intra-abdominal and pelvic abscesses by computerized tomography. JAMA 244:49-52, 1980.
15. Haaga JR, Weinstein AJ: CT-guided percutaneous aspiration and drainage of abscesses. AJR 135:1187-1194, 1980.
16. Gutierrez A, Lee H, Sands BE: Outcome of surgical versus percutaneous drainage of abdominal and pelvic abscesses in Crohn's disease. Am J Gastroenterol 101:2283-2289, 2006.
17. Buckley O, Geoghegan T, Ridgeway P, et al: The usefulness of CT guided drainage of abscesses caused by retained appendicoliths. Eur J Radiol 60:80-83, 2006.
18. Brusciano L, Maffettone V, Napolitano V, et al: Management of colorectal emergencies: Percutaneous abscess drainage. Ann Ital Chir 75:593-597, 2004.
19. Durmishi Y, Gervaz P, Brandt D, et al: Results from percutaneous drainage of Hinchey stage II diverticulitis guided by computed tomography scan. Surg Endosc 20:1129-1133, 2006.
20. Konig C, Simmen HP, Blaser J: Bacterial concentrations in pus and infected peritoneal fluid—Implications for bactericidal activity of antibiotics. J Antimicrob Chemother 42:227-232, 1998.
21. Durmaz B, Durmaz R, Tastekin N: Evaluation of culture results of specimens from patients with suspected anaerobic infection. New Microbiol 22:155-159, 1999.
22. Mettler FA, Guiberteau MJ: Essentials of Nuclear Medicine Imaging, 5th ed. Philadelphia, Saunders/Elsevier, 2006.
23. Levitt RG, Biello DR, Sagel SS, et al: Computed tomography and 67Ga citrate radionuclide imaging for evaluating suspected abdominal abscess. AJR 132:529-534, 1979.
24. Knochel JQ, Koehler PR, Lee TG, et al: Diagnosis of abdominal abscesses with computed tomography, ultrasound, and 111In leukocyte scans. Radiology 137:425-432, 1980.
25. Moir C, Robins RE: Role of ultrasonography, gallium scanning, and computed tomography in the diagnosis of intraabdominal abscess. Am J Surg 143:582-585, 1982.
26. Sheafor DH, Paulson EK, Simmons CM, et al: Abdominal percutaneous interventional procedures: Comparison of CT and US guidance. Radiology 207:705-710, 1998.
27. Lahorra JM, Haaga JR, Stellato T, et al: Safety of intracavitary urokinase with percutaneous abscess drainage. AJR 160:171-174, 1993.
28. Goldberg MA, Mueller PR, Saini S, et al: Importance of daily rounds by the radiologist after interventional procedures of the abdomen and chest. Radiology 180:767-770, 1991.
29. Lambiase RE, Deyoe L, Cronan JJ, et al: Percutaneous drainage of 335 consecutive abscesses: Results of primary drainage with 1-year follow-up. Radiology 184:167-179, 1992.
30. vanSonnenberg E, Ferrucci JT Jr, Mueller PR, et al: Percutaneous drainage of abscesses and fluid collections: Technique, results, and applications. Radiology 142:1-10, 1982.
31. Kerlan RK Jr, Ring EJ: A replaceable sump lumen catheter for abscess drainage. Gastrointest Radiol 11:112-113, 1986.
32. Sherry S, McCarty WR, Tillett WS: Rationale of therapeutic use of streptokinase-streptodornase in amebic abscess of liver. AMA Arch Intern Med 88:752-759, 1951.
33. Schiza S, Siafakas NM: Clinical presentation and management of empyema, lung abscess and pleural effusion. Curr Opin Pulm Med 12:205-211, 2006.
34. Moulton JS, Moore PT, Mencini RA: Treatment of loculated pleural effusions with transcatheter intracavitary urokinase. AJR 153:941-945, 1989.
35. Lee KS, Im JG, Kim YH, et al: Treatment of thoracic multiloculated

empyemas with intracavitary urokinase: A prospective study. Radiology 179:771-775, 1991.
36. Park JK, Kraus FC, Haaga JR: Fluid flow during percutaneous drainage procedures: An in vitro study of the effects of fluid viscosity, catheter size, and adjunctive urokinase. AJR 160:165-169, 1993.
37. Vogelzang RL, Tobin RS, Burstein S, et al: Transcatheter intracavitary fibrinolysis of infected extravascular hematomas. AJR 148:378-380, 1987.
38. Montgomery RS, Wilson SE: Intraabdominal abscesses: Image-guided diagnosis and therapy. Clin Infect Dis 23:28-36, 1996.
39. Brandt D, Gervaz P, Durmishi Y, et al: Percutaneous CT scan-guided drainage vs. antibiotherapy alone for Hinchey II diverticulitis: A case-control study. Dis Colon Rectum 49:1533-1538, 2006.
40. Siewert B, Tye G, Kruskal J, et al: Impact of CT-guided drainage in the treatment of diverticular abscesses: Size matters. AJR 186:680-686, 2006.
41. Lee H, Kim YH, Kim JH, et al: Nonsurgical treatment of abdominal or pelvic abscess in consecutive patients with Crohn's disease. Dig Liver Dis 38:659-664, 2006.
42. Casola G, vanSonnenberg E, Neff CC, et al: Abscesses in Crohn disease: Percutaneous drainage. Radiology 163:19-22, 1987.
43. Jeffrey RB Jr, Laing FC, Townsend RR: Acute appendicitis: Sonographic criteria based on 250 cases. Radiology 167:327-329, 1988.
44. Balthazar EJ, Megibow AJ, Siegel SE, et al: Appendicitis: Prospective evaluation with high-resolution CT. Radiology 180:21-24, 1991.
45. Rao PM, Rhea JT, Novelline RA, et al: Helical CT technique for the diagnosis of appendicitis: Prospective evaluation of a focused appendix CT examination. Radiology 202:139-144, 1997.
46. Teefey SA, Hildeboldt CC, Dehdashti F, et al: Detection of primary hepatic malignancy in liver transplant candidates: Prospective comparison of CT, MR imaging, US, and PET. Radiology 226:533-542, 2003.
47. Deakin DE, Ahmed I: Interval appendicectomy after resolution of adult inflammatory appendix mass—is it necessary? Surgeon 5:45-50, 2007.
48. Kim SB, Je BK, Lee KY: Computed tomographic differences of pyogenic liver abscesses caused by Klebsiella pneumoniae and non-Klebsiella pneumoniae. J Comput Assist Tomogr 31:59-65, 2007.
49. Kaplan GG, Gregson DB, Laupland KB: Population-based study of the epidemiology of and the risk factors for pyogenic liver abscess. Clin Gastroenterol Hepatol 2:1032-1038, 2004.
50. Yu SC, Ho SS, Lau WY, et al: Treatment of pyogenic liver abscess: Prospective randomized comparison of catheter drainage and needle aspiration. Hepatology 39:932-938, 2004.
51. Wong WM, Wong BC, Hui CK, et al: Pyogenic liver abscess: Retrospective analysis of 80 cases over a 10-year period. J Gastroenterol Hepatol 17:1001-1007, 2002.
52. Vogl TJ, Estifan F: [Pyogenic liver abscess: Interventional versus surgical therapy: technique, results and indications]. Rofo 173:663-667, 2001.
53. Nah BK, Kim YS, Moon HS, et al: [Recent changes of organism and treatment in pyogenic liver abscess]. Taehan Kan Hakhoe Chi 9:275-283, 2003.
54. Goessling W, Chung RT: Amebic liver abscess. Curr Treat Options Gastroenterol 5:443-449, 2002.
55. Mueller PR, Dawson SL, Ferrucci JT Jr, et al: Hepatic echinococcal cyst: Successful percutaneous drainage. Radiology 155:627-628, 1985.
56. Logeart D, Hatem SN, Rucker-Martin C, et al: Highly efficient adenovirus-mediated gene transfer to cardiac myocytes after single-pass coronary delivery. Hum Gene Therapy 11:1015-1022, 2000.
57. Crippa FG, Bruno R, Brunetti E, et al: Echinococcal liver cysts: Treatment with echo-guided percutaneous puncture PAIR for echinococcal liver cysts. Ital J Gastroenterol Hepatol 31:884-892, 1999.
58. Khuroo MS, Wani NA, Javid G, et al: Percutaneous drainage compared with surgery for hepatic hydatid cysts. N Engl J Med 337:881-887, 1997.
59. Farres H, Felsher J, Banbury M, et al: Management of splenic abscess in a critically ill patient. Surg Laparosc Endosc Percutan Tech 14:49-52, 2004.
60. Lieberman S, Libson E, Sella T, et al: Percutaneous image-guided splenic procedures: Update on indications, technique, complications, and outcomes. Semin Ultrasound CT MR 28:57-63, 2007.
61. Thanos L, Dailiana T, Papaioannou G, et al: Percutaneous CT-guided drainage of splenic abscess. AJR 179:629-632, 2002.
62. Tasar M, Ugurel MS, Kocaoglu M, et al: Computed tomography-guided percutaneous drainage of splenic abscesses. Clin Imaging 28:44-48, 2004.
63. Kumar P, Mukhopadhyay S, Sandhu M, et al: Ultrasonography, computed tomography and percutaneous intervention in acute pancreatitis: A serial study. Australas Radiol 39:145-152, 1995.
64. Bradley EL 3rd: A clinically based classification system for acute pancreatitis. Summary of the International Symposium on Acute Pancreatitis, Atlanta, GA, September 11 through 13, 1992. Arch Surg 128:586-590, 1993.

65. Mithofer K, Mueller PR, Warshaw AL: Interventional and surgical treatment of pancreatic abscess. World J Surg 21:162-168, 1997.

66. Szentkereszty Z, Kerekes L, Hallay J, et al: CT-guided percutaneous peripancreatic drainage: A possible therapy in acute necrotizing pancreatitis. Hepatogastroenterology 49:1696-1698, 2002.

67. Tsiotos GG, Sarr MG: Management of fluid collections and necrosis in acute pancreatitis. Curr Gastroenterol Rep 1:139-144, 1999.

68. Freeny PC, Lewis GP, Traverso LW, et al: Infected pancreatic fluid collections: Percutaneous catheter drainage. Radiology 167:435-441, 1988.

69. Torres WE, Evert MB, Baumgartner BR, et al: Percutaneous aspiration and drainage of pancreatic pseudocysts. AJR 147:1007-1009, 1986.

70. Sudakoff GS, Lundeen SJ, Otterson MF: Transrectal and transvaginal sonographic intervention of infected pelvic fluid collections: A complete approach. Ultrasound Q 21:175-185, 2005.

71. Maher MM, Gervais DA, Kalra MK, et al: The inaccessible or undrainable abscess: How to drain it. RadioGraphics 24:717-735, 2004.

72. Goharkhay N, Verma U, Maggiorotto F: Comparison of CT- or ultrasound-guided drainage with concomitant intravenous antibiotics vs. intravenous antibiotics alone in the management of tubo-ovarian abscesses. Ultrasound Obstet Gynecol 29:65-69, 2007.

IX

Gallbladder and Biliary Tract

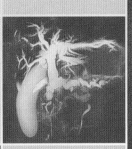
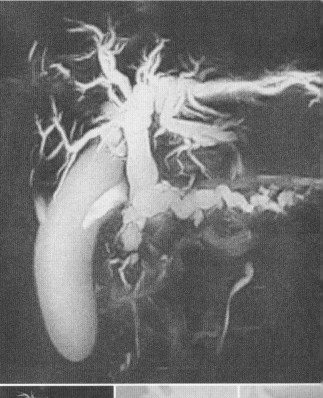
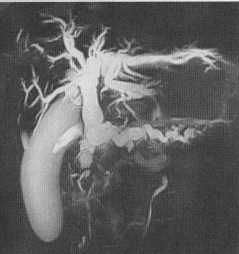

Gallbladder and Biliary Tract: Normal Anatomy and Examination Techniques

Mary Ann Turner, MD • Ann S. Fulcher, MD

Rapid advances in technology and refinements in both noninvasive and invasive techniques have improved the ability of imaging methods to make more precise diagnoses in disorders of the biliary tract. Ultrasound and CT, because of wide availability and ease of performance as well as high diagnostic accuracy, are the first-line imaging techniques. Magnetic resonance cholangiopancreatography (MRCP) is assuming a larger role as a rapid, accurate, and noninvasive method of evaluating the bile ducts and is replacing diagnostic endoscopic retrograde cholangiopancreatography (ERCP) in many instances. CT cholangiography, using oral or intravenous cholecystographic agents, has been widely used in Europe and has been used on a limited basis in some centers in the United States to evaluate ductal pathology. Percutaneous transhepatic cholangiography (PTC) and ERCP are methods of direct cholangiography used for evaluating biliary ductal disease. These techniques are invasive, but they are also safe and widely available. Improvements in the technical aspects of PTC and ERCP have led to the development of various interventional biliary procedures performed from both percutaneous and endoscopic routes. Plain radiographs play a minor role in imaging the gallbladder and bile ducts. The traditional indications for operative and postoperative cholangiography remain unchanged. Both techniques allow direct opacification of the biliary tree but require surgical access and have limited diagnostic use. Biliary scintigraphy has a limited role in biliary imaging, used mainly for confirming acute cholecystitis and identifying bile leaks. [1-17]

NORMAL ANATOMY

Gallbladder

The gallbladder is an elliptical organ located in a fossa on the undersurface of the liver between the right and the left lobes. Although size and shape vary, the relaxed gallbladder is approximately 10 cm long and 3 to 5 cm in diameter. Size may increase after vagotomy, in diabetes, or after cystic duct or common duct obstruction. Normal capacity is approximately 50 mL. The normal gallbladder wall is 2 to 3 mm thick, and the mucosa is composed of simple columnar epithelium. The gallbladder is usually apposed to the liver surface by parietal peritoneum. Rarely, the peritoneal reflection may be loose, forming a mesentery that allows the gallbladder enough mobility to extend into the pelvis or left abdomen, herniate into the lesser sac, or undergo torsion. The gallbladder is positioned partially or completely in an intrahepatic location in 10% of cases.

The gallbladder is divided into four parts—fundus, body, infundibulum, and neck (Fig. 75-1). The *fundus* is the rounded distal tip, which may project below the anterior inferior liver edge (Fig. 75-2). A characteristic deformity associated with septation and partial folding over of the gallbladder, the phrygian cap, may be found in the fundus. The *body* is the midportion of the gallbladder, which may be in contact with the duodenum and hepatic flexure. The *infundibulum* (Hartmann pouch) is the focally enlarged segment between the body and the neck. The *neck* of the gallbladder lies between the body and the cystic duct and points toward the porta hepatis. A mucosal fold, the junctional fold, is frequently seen near the gallbladder neck. The gallbladder neck bears a constant relationship to the major interlobar fissure and undivided right portal vein or main portal vein, an important anatomic relationship for imaging.[18-25]

Cystic Duct

The gallbladder is attached to the common bile duct (CBD) via the cystic duct, which is usually 2 to 4 cm long and contains tortuous folds, the spiral valves of Heister (see Fig. 75-1). The cystic duct usually joins the common hepatic duct (CHD)

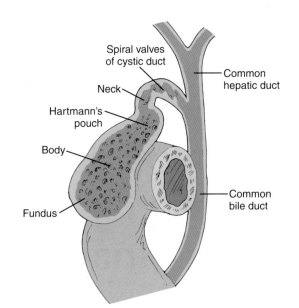

Figure 75-1. Normal anatomy of the gallbladder and cystic duct. (From Linder HH: Clinical Anatomy. East Norwalk, CT: Appleton & Lange, 1989, p 421.)

from the right lateral aspect approximately halfway between the porta hepatis and the ampulla of Vater to form the CBD. The point at which the cystic duct joins the CHD is variable, from high in the upper extrahepatic bile duct or one of the intrahepatic ducts (more often the right) to low at the

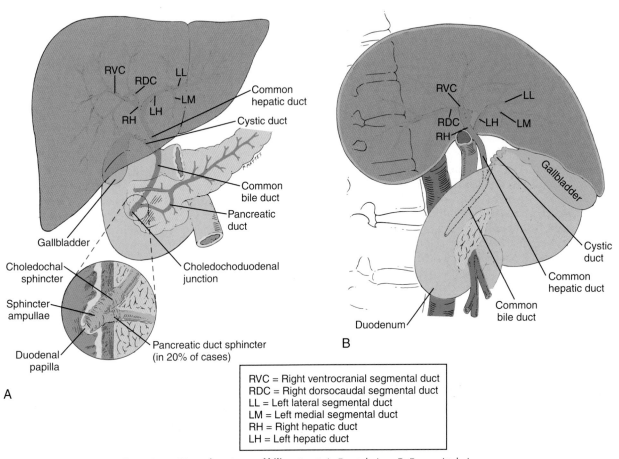

RVC = Right ventrocranial segmental duct
RDC = Right dorsocaudal segmental duct
LL = Left lateral segmental duct
LM = Left medial segmental duct
RH = Right hepatic duct
LH = Left hepatic duct

Figure 75-2. Normal anatomy of biliary tract. A. Frontal view. **B.** Parasagittal view.

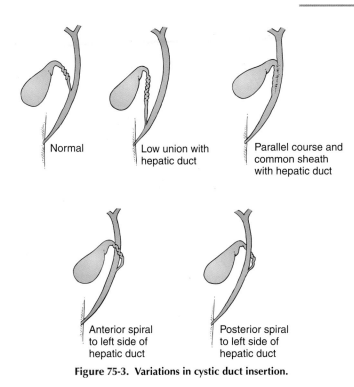

Figure 75-3. Variations in cystic duct insertion.

ampulla. The cystic duct usually runs parallel to the CHD at least for a short distance and may insert either anteriorly or posteriorly or spiral around to insert on the medial aspect. The two ducts may have a long parallel course and can be encircled in a common connective tissue sheath[20-23] (Fig. 75-3).

Bile Ducts

Intrahepatic Ducts

The liver is divided into right and left lobes on the basis of portal vein anatomy and biliary drainage. The right lobe is divided into anterior and posterior segments, and the left lobe is divided into medial and lateral segments by the fissure of the ligamentum teres. The bile ducts generally follow the internal hepatic segmental anatomy; however, marked variation in the branching pattern is common. Small branching interlobar bile ducts merge into larger ducts until the major left and right hepatic ducts are formed. A left medial segment duct and a left lateral segment duct normally join to form the main left hepatic duct. The right hepatic duct branches near its takeoff from the CHD. In approximately 60% of patients, the right hepatic duct has a dorsocaudal branch, with a characteristic

hooklike configuration proximally, draining the posterior segment of the right lobe, and a ventrocranial branch, draining the anterior segment of the right lobe. Variations in the anatomic arrangement of the bifurcation branches are common, however, and it may be impossible to differentiate the anterior and posterior segmental branches on frontal cholangiograms. Common bifurcation variations include drainage of either anterior or posterior right lobe segmental ducts into the left hepatic duct, or a trifurcation configuration may occur. The left hepatic duct is more anterior and is usually longer and wider than the right hepatic duct. The left hepatic duct has a longer extrahepatic course and tends to dilate more than the right hepatic duct with obstruction, presumably because there is less surrounding liver. Ductal drainage of the caudate lobe is variable and may be related to the left or right ductal system.[18-29]

Extrahepatic Ducts

The right and left hepatic ducts emerge from the liver and unite to form the 3- to 4-cm-long CHD, which then joins the cystic duct to form the CBD. The union of the right and left main hepatic ducts is usually just outside the liver but may be lower, resulting in a shorter CHD or CBD. The CHD courses ventrally and inferiorly from the porta hepatis in the hepatoduodenal ligament accompanied by the portal vein, which lies posteriorly, and the hepatic artery, which lies medially. As the CHD passes inferiorly, it angles anteriorly and then posteriorly, crossing over the right portal vein, and joins the cystic duct to form the CBD as it courses behind the postbulbar duodenum (see Fig. 75-1). The CBD averages 6 to 7 cm in length and is usually divided into suprapancreatic, intrapancreatic, and ampullary segments. In approximately 70% of patients, the CBD courses through the pancreatic head; in a smaller percentage, the CBD is located in a groove on the posterior surface of the pancreas. The CBD enters the posteriormedial aspect of the second portion of the duodenum through an oblique, 1- to 2-cm-long intramural tunnel terminating at the papilla of Vater.[18-24]

The exact union of the CBD and the pancreatic duct at the ampulla varies. Most commonly, the two ducts join in the duodenal wall and have a short common channel. Occasionally, separate orifices are present at the ampulla, or the ducts unite, forming a long common channel before entering the duodenal wall (Fig. 75-4). The sphincter of Oddi surrounds the common channel and the choledochal sphincter (sphincter of Boyden) surrounds the CBD from its entrance into the duodenal wall to its junction with the pancreatic duct.[30-32] The extrahepatic ducts are sparse in muscle fibers

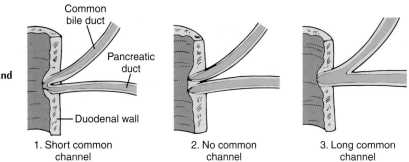

Figure 75-4. Types of union of common bile duct and pancreatic duct.

(except in the cystic duct and the sphincter areas) and are composed primarily of elastic fibers. This allows relatively rapid change in size in response to fluctuations in intraductal pressure. With age, loss of elasticity may occur, resulting in enlargement of the duct.[33-36]

Anatomic Variations

Anatomic variations and anomalies of bile duct anatomy are common (see Chapter 78). Although most are of no pathologic significance, an understanding of these variations is important for radiologic diagnosis. Anatomic variations have been reported in 23% to 46% of cholangiograms, with the most common sites of involvement at the hepatic bifurcation and in the insertion of the cystic duct.[37] An aberrant right hepatic duct (4.6%) entering at a variety of locations, including low along the CHD or into the cystic duct; an accessory right hepatic duct (1.9%); and high or low insertion of the cystic duct are congenital anomalies of significance because of the potential for injury at biliary surgery[20,22,24,25,37] (see Chapter 83).

EXAMINATION TECHNIQUES: GALLBLADDER

Modern gallbladder imaging involves primarily ultrasound and CT. Although the gallbladder is readily imaged by MR, this technique currently has a limited clinical role in gallbladder diagnosis because of the expense and lack of wide availability. MR and MRCP, however, may be used as the initial imaging study in patients with suspected gallbladder carcinoma. Real-time sonography is the dominant screening method for the detection of gallbladder disease. MDCT is commonly used to evaluate gallbladder disease, particularly neoplastic conditions and complicated cholecystitis, because of its ability to rapidly produce isotropic images of the upper abdomen.[1-6,10,16,17]

Plain Radiographs

Plain abdominal radiography is the simplest and least expensive gallbladder imaging method. It is frequently the first study obtained in patients with upper abdominal pain, however, its diagnostic utility in the diagnosis of gallbladder disease is limited. The normal gallbladder is not visible on plain radiographs. Only 10% to 15% of gallstones are sufficiently calcified to be visualized on the plain abdominal radiograph. "Porcelain" gallbladder, emphysematous cholecystitis, and milk of cal-cium bile (see Chapter 79) are other pathologic gallbladder conditions with characteristic findings that can be diagnosed on plain radiographs. A soft tissue mass in the right upper quadrant may be seen with hydrops of the gallbladder and gallbladder carcinoma.[38] Rarely, noncalcified cholesterol gallstones are visible on the abdominal radiograph as a result of nitrogen-containing clefts that produce a lucent, triradiate appearance, the "Mercedes-Benz" sign.[39]

Ultrasound

Real-time sonography is the most widely used diagnostic study for the gallbladder and is the primary screening examination for gallbladder disease. The gallbladder is visible on sonograms in virtually all fasting patients despite body habitus or clinical condition. Gallbladder sonography is noninvasive, quick, and easy to perform. The examination can be performed portably and, because no ionizing radiation is used, is safe in pregnant and pediatric patients. Adjacent upper abdominal organs can be imaged simultaneously. The success rate of obtaining a diagnostic study is greater than 95%.[4,5,40-43]

By far the most common indication for gallbladder sonography is the detection of gallstones. Overall, the sensitivity, specificity, and accuracy of ultrasound for detecting gallstones is 95% to 99% in most series.[4-6,10,40-43] The frequency of indeterminate studies with ultrasound is low.[40,41] False-positive ultrasound findings are uncommon and are due primarily to polyps, folds, or cholesterolosis of the gallbladder.[44] Although ultrasound is excellent for the demonstration of calculi, it does not provide direct information about gallbladder function or cystic duct patency. Sonography does have limitations in assessing the size and number of stones in cases of multiple stones. Sonography is useful to confirm the diagnosis of acute cholecystitis. Ultrasound has been shown to have a positive predictive value of 92% and a negative value of 95% for diagnosing cholecystitis in patients with gallstones and a positive sonographic Murphy sign.[45] Complications of cholecystitis, including gallbladder perforation, gangrenous cholecystitis, and emphysematous cholecystitis, are usually readily seen by ultrasound. Gallbladder carcinoma, polyps, metastatic nodules, and adenomyomatosis are uncommon conditions of the gallbladder with characteristic findings on sonography[4-6,42,43] (see Chapters 79 and 81).

Technique

The gallbladder is examined after the patient has fasted for at least 6 hours. This allows maximal distention of the gallbladder and enhances the detectability of stones. For most patients, real-time scanning is performed using a 3.5- or 4-MHz transducer. In thin patients or those with an anteriorly positioned gallbladder, a 5-MHz transducer provides superior resolution. A transducer of the highest possible frequency should be used because spatial resolution is improved when the transducer focal zone is the same depth as the gallbladder.[4,10,46] The examination is begun with the patient in the supine position. Scanning is performed in the right subcostal region or in one of the lower intercostal spaces, in approximately the anterior axillary line. The gallbladder is located in the longitudinal axis by identifying the major interlobar fissure of the liver (Fig. 75-5A). Views are obtained in the longitudinal and transverse planes to allow visualization of the entire gallbladder. Different degrees of inspiration may be necessary to move the gallbladder away from the overlying costal cartilage (Fig. 75-5B and C). Various scanning positions are used; decubitus positioning is often helpful in displaying the gallbladder, displacing bowel gas, unfolding kinks, and allowing small stones hidden in the neck to roll into the fundus and become detectable. The dependent portion of the gallbladder, particularly the neck, should be scrutinized for hidden stones (Fig. 75-5D). Suspended deep inspiration often serves to move the gallbladder into a more accessible position below the ribs. Magnified views, high-frequency transducers, and upright or Trendelenburg positioning are helpful adjuncts. Color Doppler sonography has been used in assessing cystic artery and wall flow in patients with acute cholecystitis or gangrenous cholecystitis and in evaluation of gallbladder carcinoma and metastatic disease to the gallbladder.[47-49] If the gallbladder is not readily identified in its

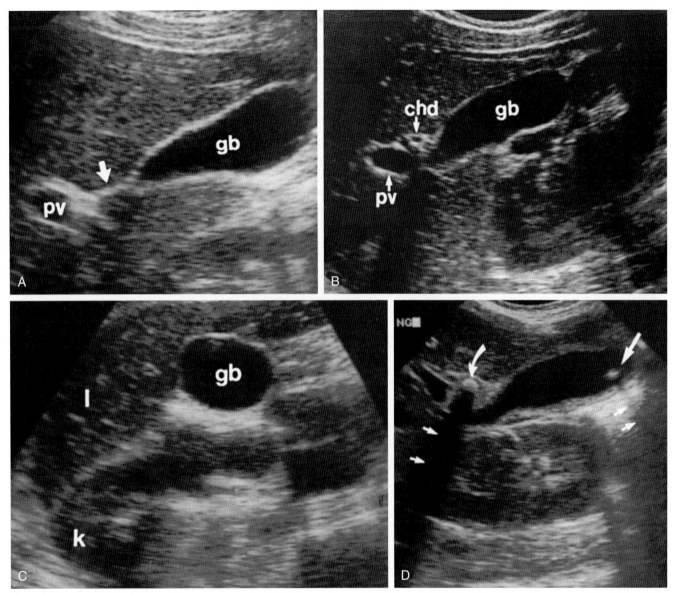

Figure 75-5. Normal gallbladder anatomy: sonography. A. The linear echogenic line (*arrow*) of the interlobar fissure bears a constant relationship to the gallbladder neck and aids in sonographic localization of the gallbladder (gb). Pv, portal vein. **B.** Longitudinal sonogram of the normal gallbladder (gb). Note the relationship of the gallbladder neck to the portal vein (pv, *arrow*) and common hepatic duct (chd, *arrow*). **C.** Transverse sonogram of the normal gallbladder (gb). Note the relationship to the liver (l) and the kidney (k). **D.** Sonogram shows a stone in a dependent position in the gallbladder (*large arrow*). A second stone behind the fold and impacted in the neck of the gallbladder (*curved arrow*) was seen only after careful evaluation of the neck in the erect position. Both stones cast characteristic acoustic shadows (*small arrows*).

usual subhepatic position, other locations must be evaluated to exclude a positional anomaly. Examination of the gallbladder is always accompanied by evaluation of the bile ducts.

Normal Anatomy

The normal gallbladder in the fasting patient appears as an oval sonolucent structure with a thin (2-3 mm), uniformly smooth wall (see Fig. 75-5B and C). It is located by identifying the major interlobar fissure of the liver, which is apparent as a highly reflective line (because of periportal fat extending into the fissure)[50] (see Fig. 75-5A). The interlobar fissure is an important sonographic landmark because of its constant relationship to the gallbladder neck. Although gallbladder shape and size vary, the sonographic upper limits of normal size are approximately 8 to 10 cm in length and 4 to 5 cm

in anterior-posterior diameter. Folds are commonly seen as echogenic foci adjacent to the wall. The junctional fold is a fold between the body and the infundibulum of the gallbladder, a common anatomic variant seen on sonography. If the gallbladder is not visualized by ultrasound, the most likely cause is a scarred contracted gallbladder containing calculi. Agenesis of the gallbladder, calcification of the gallbladder wall, and intramural or intraluminal gas are other causes of nonvisualization[51] (see Chapter 84).

Computed Tomography

The gallbladder in fasting patients is nearly always identified on CT scans of the upper abdomen. Although gallstones are frequently visible, CT is not used as a primary examination for detecting gallstones because of its lower sensitivity (80-85%) and higher cost compared with ultrasound.[2,41,42,52-55] Calcified gallstones present as high-density foci within the gallbladder lumen, and noncalcified stones are seen as low-attenuation filling defects within the surrounding bile. Although acute cholecystitis is accurately evaluated with sonography or scintigraphy, CT may show mural thickening, gallbladder dilatation, wall edema, septation, and increased bile density, which allow diagnosis. The main indication for CT in gallbladder disease is for the diagnosis and staging of gallbladder carcinoma (see Chapter 81) and evaluation of the complications of cholecystitis: perforation and pericholecystic abscess. Less common entities such as porcelain gallbladder, milk of calcium bile, and emphysematous cholecystitis are readily identified and have characteristic CT findings[2,40-42,53,56,57] (see Chapter 79).

Technique

The gallbladder is usually scanned as part of a routine upper abdominal examination. Helical or multislice CT scanning of the upper abdomen is performed during a single breathhold after rapid bolus intravenous infusion of contrast material. This permits visualization of the gallbladder and optimal delineation of the intrahepatic biliary ducts and extrahepatic bile duct by enhancing the contiguous liver and pancreatic parenchyma as well as blood vessels. Section thickness, gantry rotation time and table-top speed varies with the number of detector rows. Images of 3- to 5-mm slice thickness are used routinely for review. Postprocessing with reconstruction of axial images at 1.5 to 3 mm can be performed and may be helpful in clarifying suspicious areas and in maximizing stone detection. MDCT produce a volumetric data set which allows reconstruction of images in multiple planes, a feature helpful in some instances. Oral contrast material is routinely used in scanning the upper abdomen. However, when searching for smaller noncalcified stones, scans obtained without contrast material using thin sections filmed at narrow window settings optimize stone detection.[55,57]

Normal Anatomy

The normal gallbladder on CT scans is a low-density, fluid-filled, elliptical structure in the interlobar fissure of the liver (Fig. 75-6A). A thin (2-3 mm) wall is often seen in normal patients and may show contrast enhancement. The gallbladder neck is superior and medial to the fundus. The gallbladder neck is often folded, and a portion may be cut in cross section. More caudally, the fundus of the gallbladder projects anteriorly and laterally and may touch the anterior abdominal wall. The duodenal sweep, hepatic flexure, and gastric antrum are contiguous structures (Fig. 75-6B to D). Significant variations in gallbladder size, shape, and position may be seen; however, the gallbladder neck maintains a constant position relative to the major interlobar fissure. The collapsed gallbladder may be more difficult to identify on CT scans.[2,57]

Cholescintigraphy

Cholescintigraphy is used primarily for the diagnosis of acute cholecystitis. Three to 5 mCi of technetium 99m iminodiacetic acid (^{99m}Tc-IDA) compounds is injected intravenously and the tracer is taken up by the liver and rapidly excreted into bile without undergoing conjugation, allowing visualization

of the gallbladder and bile ducts (Fig. 75-7). Frequent anterior images are obtained up to 1 hour. Delayed imaging up to 4 hours and possibly 24 hours may be necessary in some instances. Nonfilling of the gallbladder on cholescintigraphy indicates functional obstruction of the cystic duct and is considered diagnostic of acute cholecystitis in the appropriate clinical setting. If the gallbladder fills, the cystic duct is deemed to be patent and acute cholecystitis is not present. This technique is highly sensitive and specific for the diagnosis of acute cholecystitis (95%-98%), and it is the procedure of choice for confirming the diagnosis.[58-61] Intravenous morphine sulfate and sincalide can assist gallbladder filling. Sincalide is a cholecystokinin analog that produces gallbladder contraction and empties the gallbladder before the study, allowing the gallbladder to more readily fill with the tracer.

Magnetic Resonance Imaging

The technology of MRI of the gallbladder and biliary ductal system has evolved since the early 1990s. The gallbladder is routinely imaged on conventional MR studies of the liver and upper abdomen using T1- and T2-weighted sequences. Techniques for imaging the gallbladder or bile ducts may be tailored to delineate either the wall of the gallbladder and bile ducts and the surrounding soft tissue or the biliary fluid within the lumen (see Chapter 77).

Imaging of the lumen requires optimal contrast between the biliary fluid and the surrounding tissues. Bright signal fluid techniques are generally employed using heavily T2-weighted sequences to produce an MR cholangiopancreatogram (MRCP). The development of MRCP has expanded the role of MRI as a noninvasive method to examine the biliary system. MRCP is performed with heavily T2-weighted sequences that depict fluid in the biliary ducts, pancreatic duct, and gallbladder as high signal intensity, whereas adjacent solid organs and flowing blood have little or no signal. The images produced resemble those of an ERCP (Fig. 75-8). Although the primary goal of MRCP is to delineate the biliary and pancreatic ducts, incidental and intentional imaging of the gallbladder are possible even in the nonfasting patient. In many cases, the cystic duct and its site of insertion into the bile duct are also visualized. Although MRCP results in high-resolution images of the gallbladder, its role relative to ultrasound and CT for evaluating gallbladder disease is still evolving. MR provides comprehensive imaging of the gallbladder and bile ducts as well as the surrounding structures, a feature most helpful in staging of tumors arising from or involving the gallbladder.[16,62-66]

Technique

Conventional MRI of the gallbladder and bile ducts frequently combines the use of T1- and T2-weighted sequences. T1-weighted fat-suppression sequences with and without intravenous gadolinium chelates may be helpful in demonstrating the lumen as well as the wall of the gallbladder and the bile ducts. T2-weighted sequences may be used in evaluating the surrounding soft tissues. Heavily T2-weighted MR sequences are used to perform MRCP. A number of sequences have been used since its introduction, including two-dimensional fast spin-echo and three-dimensional (3D) fast spin-echo. More recently, technical refinements provided by

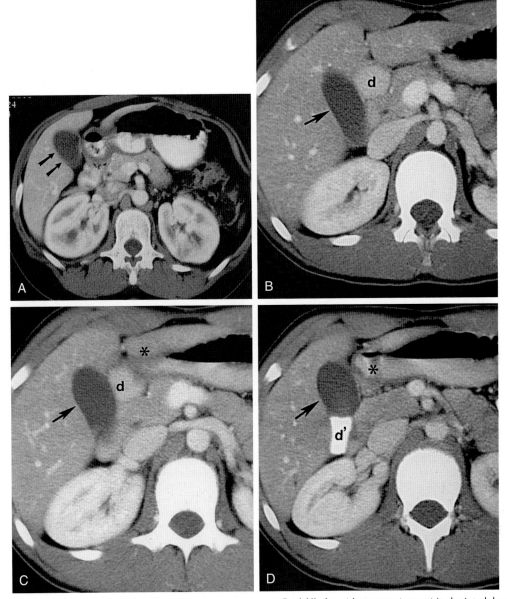

Figure 75-6. Normal gallbladder anatomy: CT. A. The gallbladder appears as a fluid-filled ovoid structure (*arrows*) in the interlobar fossa of the liver. **B–D.** Sequential CT scans show the normal position of the gallbladder *(arrows)* between the right and the left lobes of the liver and the relationship of the gallbladder to the antrum (*asterisk* in **C** and **D**), duodenal bulb (d in **B** and **C**), and c-sweep of the duodenum (d′).

the half-Fourier rapid acquisition with relaxation enhancement (RARE) sequence allow rapid imaging, such that the entire biliary tract can be imaged during an 18-second breath-hold.[65-67] A typical MRCP examination comprises multiple acquisitions obtained at variable angles that optimally delineate the biliary tract and gallbladder. The half-Fourier RARE sequence minimizes magnetic susceptibility artifacts such as those associated with surgical clips and bowel gas. Often a thin-slab, multislice technique is employed in both axial and coronal planes. From these source images, 3D reconstructions may be generated with a maximum-intensity projection (MIP) algorithm. No intravenous or oral contrast material is administered.

Normal Anatomy

On MR, the gallbladder lumen can have a high or low signal intensity depending on the chemical composition of bile and the pulse sequence used (Fig. 75-9). Concentrated bile is high signal intensity on T1- and T2-weighted images whereas dilute bile is low in signal intensity on T1-weighted images because of its higher water content. Because concentrated bile has a greater specific gravity than dilute bile, concentrated bile settles in the dependent portion of the gallbladder. On MRCP, gallbladder calculi, regardless of composition, appear as low signal intensity filling defects within the high signal intensity bile (Fig. 75-10). Calculi as small as 2 mm can be identified. In addition to calculi, MRCP can depict neoplastic disease of the

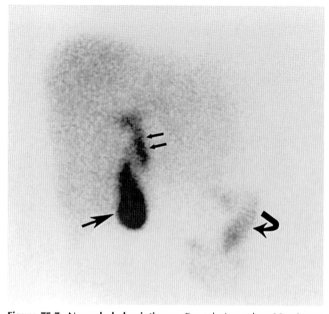

Figure 75-7. Normal cholescintigram. Frontal view taken 30 minutes after injection of radioisotope shows normal visualization of the gallbladder (*large arrow*), bile ducts (*small arrows*), and bowel (*curved arrow*).

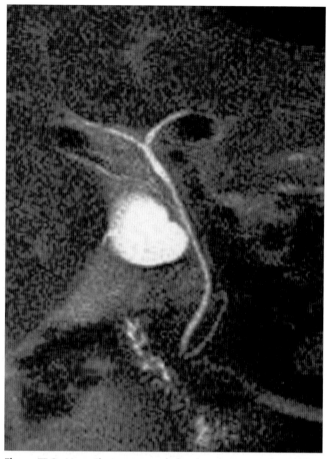

Figure 75-8. Magnetic resonance cholangiopancreatography (MRCP): normal gallbladder and bile duct. Heavily T2-weighted coronal image shows the gallbladder, hepatic confluence, and extrahepatic bile duct.

gallbladder and its extent. Adenomyosis of the gallbladder may be incidentally identified when the fluid-filled Rokitansky-Aschoff sinuses are seen within the gallbladder wall.[16,62,64,68-71]

EXAMINATION TECHNIQUES: BILIARY TRACT

A number of examination techniques are available for evaluating the biliary ducts. When selecting an imaging technique, several factors must be considered, including clinical presentation, diagnostic information desired, body habitus, and anatomic alterations from previous surgery. If direct cholangiography with PTC or ERCP is used, the potential for conversion to a therapeutic intervention must be considered as well as the skill of the participating radiologist and endoscopist.

Ultrasound and CT are the primary noninvasive methods for screening patients with suspected ductal pathology, although MRCP is assuming a larger role as the primary evaluation method of biliary ductal disease. MRCP is noninvasive and can be performed rapidly, depicting the intrahepatic and extrahepatic bile ducts as well as the pancreatic duct and surrounding structures. CT cholangiography has been widely used in Europe and on a limited basis in the US for ductal evaluation. CT cholangiography provides similar information as MRCP but requires oral or intravenous administration of a cholecystographic agent before the CT. The use of this technique has several limitations, including risk of reaction from the contrast agents, inconsistent opacification of the ducts from the oral agents which must be administered several hours before the study, and limited opacification of the ducts in patients with biliary obstruction.

Direct opacification of the bile ducts by PTC or ERCP can provide detailed information about ductal anatomy or

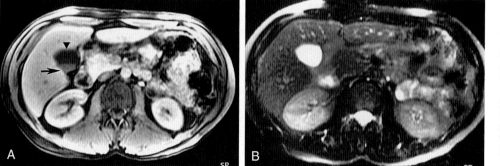

Figure 75-9. Normal gallbladder: MR. A. T1-weighted, fat-suppression image shows high signal intensity, concentrated bile in the dependent portion of the gallbladder (*arrow*) and low signal intensity, less-concentrated bile in the nondependent portion of the gallbladder (*arrowhead*). **B.** T2-weighted, fat-suppression image depicts bile in the gallbladder as high signal intensity.

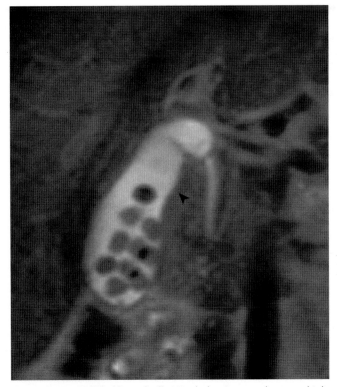

Figure 75-10. Gallbladder calculi. MR cholangiogram shows multiple gallbladder calculi as multiple filling defect in high signal intensity bile. The extrahepatic bile duct (*arrowhead*) is noted.

pathology. PTC or ERCP also serves as a preliminary step to nonsurgical therapeutic interventions such as biliary drainage, stent placement, stone removal, or stricture dilatation. Biliary scintigraphy is occasionally useful in detecting bile leaks, evaluating biliary enteric anastomoses, or diagnosing early or segmental biliary obstruction. Operative and postoperative cholangiography are standard methods for evaluating the bile ducts after surgical access to the ductal system. Plain radiographs have a very limited role and are rarely useful in defining bile duct pathology.

Plain Radiographs

The biliary ductal system is visible on plain radiographs only when it is outlined with air or calcification. Air in the biliary tree most commonly results from a surgically created biliary enteric anastomosis. Erosion of a gallstone into the gastrointestinal tract and erosion of a peptic ulcer or tumor into the biliary tree are other causes of biliary-enteric fistula that may result in biliary air. Rarely, calcified stones in the bile ducts are visible on plain film.[38]

Ultrasound

Evaluation of the bile ducts in search of stones, mass or obstruction is one of the main applications for ultrasound. Real-time ultrasound readily depicts dilated biliary ducts which, in most instances is indicative of biliary obstruction. The extrahepatic bile duct can be seen in most patients regardless of body habitus or clinical condition. Since the bile duct is oval in cross-section in the majority of patients, mea-

surement of the transverse diameter on axial images correlates more closely with ductal diameters measured on ERCP.[72] The CHD is the most easily visualized portion of the extrahepatic biliary system and can be rapidly visualized and measured in virtually all patients.[1,4-9,73] Intrahepatic ducts are rarely seen unless dilated. The distal CBD may be obscured by gas in the duodenum. The primary goal of biliary sonography is the detection of dilated ducts because the size of the extrahepatic duct is a fairly sensitive indicator of the presence of biliary obstruction. Early changes of intrahepatic and extrahepatic ductal dilatation are readily seen. Frequently, the lesion associated with biliary obstruction is identified as well.[4,5,73] Ultrasound is an accurate and reliable technique for assessing the intrahepatic and extrahepatic ducts as well as adjacent structures such as the pancreas.

Technique

The bile ducts are best evaluated with high-resolution real-time equipment using the highest-frequency transducer possible: 3.5 MHz in obese patients and 5 MHz in thin patients. Optimal imaging of the CHD and proximal CBD is obtained by parasagittal scanning with the patient in the supine left posterior oblique or left lateral decubitus position.[74] The CHD is identified as a tubular sonolucency anterior and lateral to the proximal main portal vein or the undivided right portal vein (Fig. 75-11A). The right hepatic artery passes between the posteriorly located portal vein and the anteriorly located CHD. In 10% to 15% of patients, the artery is anterior to the CHD. The standard measurement of the CHD is made at this level. The measurement is made from interior wall to interior wall perpendicular to the scan plane. Doppler sonography of the porta hepatis may be needed to distinguish the bile ducts from adjacent vascular structures.[75]

The distal CBD is more difficult and frequently impossible to image because of overlying gas in the duodenum and hepatic flexure. Visualization can be improved by scanning with the patient in the semierect (60 degrees to the vertical) right posterior oblique position in the transverse rather than the parasagittal plane[76] (Fig. 75-11B). This position minimizes antral and duodenal gas, allows fluid to enter the antrum and duodenum, and allows the left lobe of the liver to descend, creating an acoustic window. With this technique, the distal duct can be seen in up to 90% of cases.[77] The specific point of union of the CHD with the cystic duct is usually not seen.

After examination of the extrahepatic ductal system, the proximal ducts and intrahepatic ducts are examined with the patient in the supine or left posterior oblique position. The normal right and left main hepatic ducts can be visualized coursing anterior to the undivided right portal vein and the initial segment of the left portal vein, respectively.

Normal Anatomy

The normal intrahepatic ducts are less than 1 to 2 mm in diameter and are usually not visible. Although visualization of intrahepatic ducts generally implies biliary dilatation, larger central intrahepatic ducts can occasionally be visualized anterior to the portal veins in the right and left lobes near the porta hepatis in normal thin patients, using a 5-MHz transducer. Gross intrahepatic duct dilatation is easy to detect sonographically and results in the "too-many-tubes" sign, created by the increased number of radiolucent channels in the liver, or

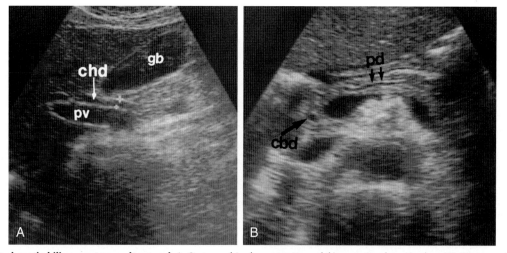

Figure 75-11. Extrahepatic biliary anatomy: ultrasound. A. Sonographic demonstration of the common hepatic duct (CHD) (*arrow*) located anterior to the portal vein (pv). Note the gallbladder (gb) anteriorly. **B.** Normal distal common bile duct (cbd, *arrow*) is seen in the head of the pancreas on a semierect transverse sonogram. Pancreatic duct (pd, *arrows*) is also seen.

the "parallel-channel" sign, formed by dilated intrahepatic ducts running anterior and parallel to the portal vein tributaries.[1,2,4-7] Dilated intrahepatic ducts tend to have acoustic enhancement posteriorly, which distinguishes them from veins. The use of color Doppler is very helpful to distinguish bile ducts from small hepatic vessels. This is especially so for the left lobe of the liver where parallel branching hepatic anterior and portal veins may mimic dilated left intrahepatic ducts.[75]

The normal CHD measures 4 to 5 mm or less on sonograms. The CBD measures 4 to 6 mm normally, with a 6- to 7-mm diameter considered equivocal. These measurements reflect the internal dimension of the duct. A diameter of more than 8 mm is indicative of ductal dilatation.[4-6,78-80] Sonographic measurements of duct size are smaller than those obtained by direct cholangiography because there is no radiographic magnification or distention resulting from injected contrast material.[81,82] Some variation in extrahepatic ductal diameter may be due to elastic properties of the bile ducts, which can expand and contract rapidly during normal physiologic filling and emptying, with Valsalva maneuver, or with deep inspiration. There is controversy about whether or not extrahepatic ductal diameter increases with aging. In a study by Wu, et al. of 256 normal patients, the CBD size was shown to increase roughly 1 mm per decade over the age of 50 years, indicating an apparently enlarged CBD may be seen in normal elderly patients. This study also suggested that the upper limit of normal may be up to 10 mm in the elderly population.[33] Two additional studies, one with a cohort of 350 patients[36] and another with a cohort of 45 patients,[35] support this data. These findings, however, were refuted in a more recent study by Horrow of 258 patients which did not confirm an association between age and size of the extrahepatic bile duct in an asymptomatic adult population.[34]

Ductal Diameter and Biliary Obstruction: Limitations

Sonography has an overall accuracy of more than 95% in detecting dilated ducts and diagnosing biliary obstruction.[73,78,80,83] Bile duct caliber does not always correlate with the presence or absence of biliary obstruction, however.

Biliary obstruction without dilatation may be seen in patients with low-grade or intermittent obstruction resulting from stricture or small stones and in patients with sclerosing cholangitis.[84,85] Alternatively, dilated ducts may be seen in the absence of obstruction in patients with prior biliary surgery or patients with resolved obstruction.[86,87] The decreased elasticity of a dilated duct may result in persistent dilatation despite relief of the obstruction. Intestinal hypomotility, recent laparotomy, hyperalimentation, and prolonged fasting can cause ductal dilatation presumably secondary to factors that inhibit relaxation of the sphincter of Oddi. An enlarged CBD may be seen in normal, unobstructed elderly patients.[33] Ultrasound is accurate in diagnosing the level of obstruction in 92% to 95% of cases and identifying the cause of obstruction in 70% to 88%.[5,6,73,77]

Postcholecystectomy Dilatation

Whether dilatation of the duct occurs after cholecystectomy has been debated in the literature for years. It has been proposed that in the absence of a gallbladder, the CBD dilates to function as a reservoir. Two studies, however, suggest that if the CBD is normal before surgery, it generally remains so after surgery unless disease intervenes.[78,88,89] A reassessment of the effect of cholecystectomy on duct size found that after cholecystectomy most patients did not have significant compensatory dilatation of the duct.[79,89] Once a duct dilates, it may lose elastic recoil and never return to normal. Accordingly, some postcholecystectomy patients have biliary "dilatation" but nonobstructed ducts. The maximal upper limit of the CBD allowed postcholecystectomy is 10 mm.[4] The general recommendation is that further studies are warranted if the CHD measures 6 mm or greater in symptomatic patients.

Fatty Meal Sonography

Administration of a fatty meal followed by sonography is an adjunctive maneuver that provides functional information, helps identify patients who require further evaluation with direct cholangiography, and increases the accuracy of ultrasound in detecting obstruction. This technique is helpful in postcholecystectomy patients with suspected obstruction in the absence of ductal dilatation, in patients with equivocal duct size, and in asymptomatic patients with abnormal liver function studies suggesting occult obstruction. Magnified views of the CHDs are obtained, and the internal diameter is measured at a fixed point. A fatty meal or intravenous cholecystokinin is administered, and another measurement of CHD caliber is obtained 30 to 45 minutes later if a fatty meal is used and 5 to 10 minutes later if cholecystokinin is used. A fatty meal and cholecystokinin cause gallbladder contraction, sphincter of Oddi relaxation, and increased bile flow. The normal, nonobstructed duct decreases in size or does not change in caliber. An increase in caliber—or if the duct is initially dilated, a failure to decrease in caliber—suggests some degree of ductal obstruction and the need for further evaluation with direct cholangiography. A true change in ductal diameter occurs only if the size changes by 2 mm or more.[90-92] Using these criteria, Simeone and colleagues reported 84% sensitivity for fatty meal sonography in predicting the presence or absence of CBD obstruction.[90]

Computed Tomography

The emergence of helical and multidetector scanning technology has enhanced the utility of CT for evaluating biliary duct disease. With the use of high-resolution scanners and fine collimation, minimally dilated intrahepatic and extrahepatic ducts are now easily visible. Visualization of the entire CBD is routine on CT scans of the upper abdomen.[2,93,94] Imaging is not inhibited by overlying gas. Although ultrasound continues to be used as the initial screening test for biliary disease, CT is as effective as sonography in determining the caliber of intrahepatic and extrahepatic ducts. In addition, because of more complete delineation of the total length of the CBD, CT may be more useful than sonography for precisely defining the site and cause of biliary obstruction. Also, if ultrasound results are equivocal, CT may be used to refine the data or confirm anatomy.[2,11,12,95]

CT has an accuracy of 96% to 100% in detecting the presence of biliary obstruction, 90% in determining the level of obstruction, and 70% in identifying the cause of obstruction.[2,94,96,97] In addition, CT can often differentiate benign from malignant causes of obstruction and can provide guidance for biopsy and staging of malignancies.[98]

Technique

Optimal CT scanning of the bile ducts requires rapid intravenous infusion of a bolus of contrast material combined with rapid helical scanning. With current MDCT technology, the entire abdomen, with complete depiction of the intrahepatic and extrahepatic biliary tree, can be imaged in 6 to 12 seconds. Section thickness, gantry rotation time, and table-top speed are selected depending on the scanner. Thin collimation (2.5-5 mm) is used. However, reconstruction at intervals of 1.25 to 3 mm can be performed to maximize detection of small lesions. MDCT scanners produces a volumetric data set that can be reconstructed on a dedicated three dimensional workstation for interpretation. High-quality multiplanar and 3D reconstructions of the biliary ductal system may be helpful in defining complex anatomy or to map the ducts for planning therapy. In cases of biliary obstruction, coronal reconstruction or 3D reformations of the dilated bile ducts from data obtained during routine scanning can be produced successfully by taking advantage of the "negative" contrast effect of low-attenuation bile in dilated ducts relative to the adjacent enhanced visceral organs and vessels.[2,73,93,94,99,100]

When searching for CBD stones, scanning may be performed initially without oral or intravenous contrast material. Although dense contrast medium in the bowel has the potential for causing streak artifacts across the CBD, obscuring detail, such artifacts are rarely a problem with MDCT scanners. Duodenal contrast medium may obscure an impacted stone in the ampulla, and contrast medium in a perivaterian duodenal diverticulum can simulate a stone. Contrast enhancement of the vasa vasorum of the CBD wall may also mimic choledocholithiasis. Scanning using a small field of view or target scanning in the region of the distal CBD aids in increasing spatial resolution and decreasing quantum mottle, which may allow better demonstration of calculi.[2,53,55,57,73,94,101,102] Proper selection of the correct window width and level is necessary to optimize visualization of the CBD throughout its entire course from the porta hepatis to the intrapancreatic portion.

Normal Anatomy

On MDCT scans of the liver and upper abdomen, the CHD and CBD are usually visualized throughout their entire course (Fig. 75-12A to D). Visualization of intrahepatic ducts on CT has been considered evidence of biliary dilatation and obstruction. However, with MDCT scanners, bolus contrast enhancement, and 3- to 5-mm-thick scans, visualization of normal intrahepatic ducts may be seen in 40% of normal individuals.[103] The average size of the normal intrahepatic ducts is 2 mm in the central liver and 1.8 mm in the periphery. Demonstration of intrahepatic bile ducts on CT scans does not necessarily indicate biliary obstruction; however, very few normal intrahepatic ducts should be seen. Truly dilated intrahepatic ducts are readily apparent and when present indicate biliary tract disease. Bile ducts appear as water-density tubular branching structures converging at the porta hepatis. The left and right hepatic bile ducts course through the porta hepatis and join to form the CHD lying anterior to the portal vein.[3,73]

The CHD and CBD are usually visible within the hepatoduodenal ligament[3,73,104,105] (see Fig. 75-12A). The proximal extrahepatic duct forms a fairly straight, thin-walled, low-density tube anterior-lateral to the portal vein, angling toward the midline. A more transverse orientation is present in approximately 6% of normal persons and 18% of those with dilated ducts.[105] The distal CBD appears on cross section as a circular, low-density structure in the pancreatic head or in a groove posterior-lateral to the pancreatic head (see Fig. 75-12B and D). Visibility of the normal CBD is increased by contrast enhancement of adjacent vascular structures, pancreas, and liver parenchyma. The normal CBD is seen on CT scans at least 50% of the time. However, this figure is higher with contrast enhanced MDCT, especially when thin slice thickness (3-5 mm) and smaller fields of reconstruction are used. In a study using optimal technique, the normal CHD and CBD were visualized in 66% and 82% of cases, respectively.[73,106] The duct wall may be discerned separately with a mean thickness of 1 mm and a maximal thickness of 1.5 mm. Contrast enhancement of the duct wall may occur in normal patients and should not be confused with peripheral calcification or stone. An isolated finding of duct wall enhancement should

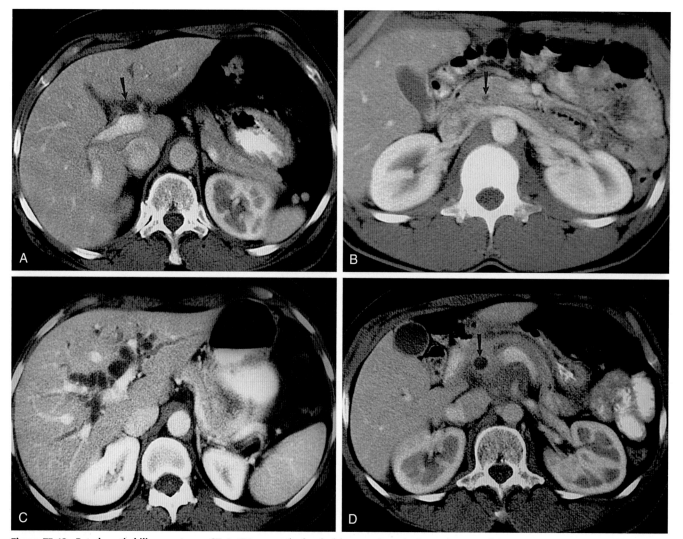

Figure 75-12. Extrahepatic biliary anatomy: CT. A. CT scan at the level of the porta hepatis shows the normal CHD (*arrow*). **B.** CT scan of the normal common bile duct (*arrow*) in cross section in the pancreatic head. **C.** Dilated intrahepatic bile ducts are seen as low-density branching structures adjacent to enhanced portal veins. **D.** CT scan of the dilated common bile duct (*arrow*) seen in the pancreatic head.

not be considered abnormal, although it can occur in pancreatitis, choledocholithiasis, sclerosing cholangitis, and cholangiocarcinoma.

The normal CHD on CT is 3 to 6 mm in diameter. A CBD diameter of 7 to 8 mm is generally considered upper limit of normal and 8 to 9 mm is considered dilated.[95,106] Anterior-posterior measurements are most accurate because the oblique segment of the CHD, when measured transversely, may give an artifactually large diameter. Axial CT images of the extrahepatic duct show sequential low-density circles that gradually taper as the duct courses through the head of the pancreas. The level of obstruction corresponds to the transition from dilated to nondilated duct.

Computed Tomography Cholangiography

CT cholangiography, obtained after intravenous or oral administration of a biliary contrast agent, displays biliary ductal anatomy and pathology similar to direct cholangiography. This technique has been used for the noninvasive detection of biliary anatomy and variations before laparoscopic cholecystectomy and in living donor candidates for right hepatic lobe transplantation.[107-110] CT cholangiography has also been used for noninvasive detection of bile leaks, bile duct stones, and evaluation of suspected biliary obstruction.[111-113] Most reported studies have reported using intravenous contrast material, meglumine iodipamide, which is the same agent used in the past for intravenous cholangiography. The agent is infused over 20 to 30 minutes and scanning is performed 15 minutes after the end of the infusion. Oral contrast material using iopanoic acid, the same agent used for oral cholecystography, has also been used in some studies for stone detection and evaluation of anatomy.[112,113]

After contrast administration, helical CT images are obtained in a single breath-hold with reconstruction using small field of view and intervals of 0.625 to 3 mm. Three-dimensional images are reconstructed using maximum intensity projection (MIP) and volume-rendered (VR) techniques (Fig. 75-13). CT cholangiography is not commonly used because of the increased reaction rate associated with intravenous biliary contrast agents, the increased study time necessitated by the contrast administration, the lack of effectiveness in patients with jaundice or elevated serum bilirubin, and the increased use of MRCP.[107-113]

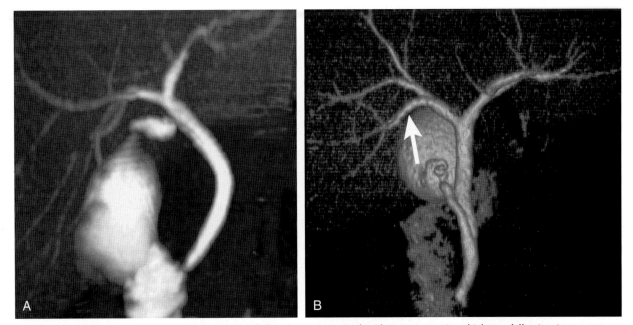

Figure 75-13. CT cholangiography. A. Coronal MIP CT cholangiogram acquired with 2.5-mm-section thickness following intravenous contrast administration. **B.** Reconstructed oblique coronal volume-rendered CT cholangiogram in a potential right hepatic lobe donor demonstrates normal branching anatomy of the bile ducts. (**A** From Wang ZJ, Yeh BM, Roberts JP, et al: Living donor candidates for right hepatic lobe transplantation: Evaluation at CT cholangiography—initial experience. Radiology 235:899-904, 2005. Reprinted with permission; **B** courtesy of Drs. Benjamin Yeh and Z. J. Wang.)

Magnetic Resonance Cholangiopancreatography

MRCP uses heavily T2-weighted sequences to generate bright signal from fluid in the bile and pancreatic ducts, allowing delineation of the ducts from surrounding tissues. An image of the ducts similar to those of ERCP is produced. Since its introduction in 1991, MRCP has undergone a number of technical refinements that now allow rapid imaging of the biliary system with consistent visualization of the entire extrahepatic ducts and most of the intrahepatic ducts in 90% to 100% of patients with normal-caliber ducts (see Fig. 75-8). Dilated ducts proximal to an obstruction are well visualized in virtually 100% of cases. The diagnostic accuracy of MRCP is comparable to that of ERCP in the evaluation of choledocholithiasis, malignant obstruction, and anatomic variants of the biliary tract. Simultaneous evaluation of the pancreatic duct is also obtained. The usefulness and accuracy of MRCP have been established in the evaluation of choledocholithiasis, malignant obstruction, congenital anomalies, and postsurgical alterations of the biliary tract[114-121] (Fig. 75-14). The improved spatial resolution afforded by recent refinements in MRCP permit visualization of calculi as small as 2 mm. In addition, MRCP depicts not only the dilated ducts proximal to a stricture but also the stricture itself. MRCP is particularly advantageous in the evaluation of patients who have experienced failed or incomplete ERCPs.[120] Although the role of MRCP in the evaluation of biliary diseases is expanding, the major disadvantage of MRCP is that it is purely diagnostic and does not provide an access for therapeutic intervention (see Chapter 77).

Technique

MRCP is performed with heavily T2-weighted sequences that depict the bile ducts as high signal intensity structures against the low signal intensity of the liver (see Fig. 75-8).

MRCP offers several advantages over direct cholangiography in general and ERCP in particular in that it avoids the administration of contrast material and exposure to ionizing radiation. The risks of pancreatitis, sepsis, and perforation associated with ERCP are avoided because the examination is performed without instrumentation. Because MRCP is entirely noninvasive, the high cost of sedation and postsedation recovery is eliminated.

MRCP may be performed with a variety of techniques. The multislice technique involves the acquisition of multiple, 3- to 5-mm-thick source images of the biliary tract, which may be obtained during breath-hold or shallow respiration.[16,114,115] With this technique, the biliary tract is first localized by obtaining a thick-slab image in the coronal plane (Fig. 75-15A). The middle third of the extrahepatic bile duct is localized, and a thick-slab axial image is obtained at this level (Fig. 75-15B). This axial image is used as a guide to prescribe the appropriate angles for optimally delineating the bile ducts with thin-slab (3- to 5-mm) images in the coronal oblique plane (Fig. 75-15C and D). Although imaging is most often conducted in the coronal plane, axial images may prove useful in confirming suspected CBD stones. From the thin-slab source images, 3D images may be generated with an MIP algorithm or with multiplanar reformatting techniques. An alternative MRCP technique is that of single-shot projection.[62] With the projection technique, a single thick (30- to 70-mm) image is generated during a 2-second acquisition.

Technical advances such as improvements in software and the use of phased-array surface coils have resulted in high-resolution images of the biliary tract that can be acquired during a single breath-hold. When rapid imaging is obtained during a breath-hold, artifacts resulting from respiratory excursion are eliminated. Although the breath-hold technique is recommended, high-quality MRCP images can be obtained in critically ill or ventilator-dependent patients who are not able to cooperate for a breath-hold.

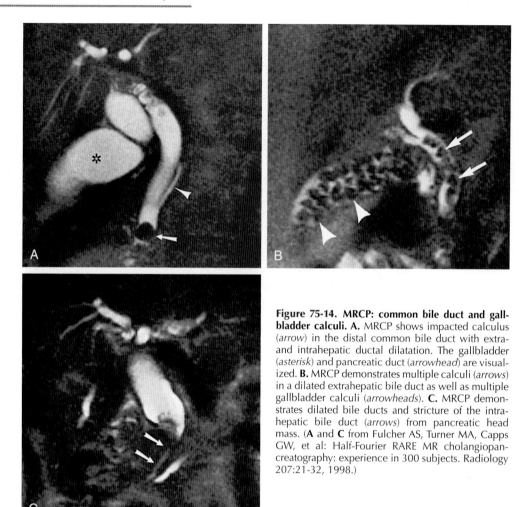

Figure 75-14. MRCP: common bile duct and gallbladder calculi. A. MRCP shows impacted calculus (*arrow*) in the distal common bile duct with extra- and intrahepatic ductal dilatation. The gallbladder (*asterisk*) and pancreatic duct (*arrowhead*) are visualized. **B.** MRCP demonstrates multiple calculi (*arrows*) in a dilated extrahepatic bile duct as well as multiple gallbladder calculi (*arrowheads*). **C.** MRCP demonstrates dilated bile ducts and stricture of the intrahepatic bile duct (*arrows*) from pancreatic head mass. (**A** and **C** from Fulcher AS, Turner MA, Capps GW, et al: Half-Fourier RARE MR cholangiopancreatography: experience in 300 subjects. Radiology 207:21-32, 1998.)

Whereas MRCP is a focused examination of the biliary tract, conventional MRI with T1- and T2-weighted sequences may show normal bile ducts as low signal intensity tubular structures on T1-weighted images and high signal intensity structures on T2-weighted images. Conventional MRI with T1- and T2-weighted sequences also provide complementary information about the adjacent hepatic and pancreatic parenchyma. The use of intravenous contrast agents to enhance ductal visualization continues to be investigated. Paramagnetic or T1 relaxation-enhancing agents, which are substantially excreted in the bile, may be used to obtain bright-signal delineation of the bile ducts. Mangofodipir trisodium and gadolinium-ethyl-benzyl-diethylene-triamine pentaacetic acid (Gd-EOB-DTBA) are two promising agents that result in contrast-enhanced high signal bile, permitting good visualization of the biliary tract. It is uncertain whether these agents have any advantage over the inherent contrast and clear ductal delineation provided by the heavily T2-weighted sequences of MRCP.[2,122-125]

Normal Anatomy

Normal-caliber proximal intrahepatic bile ducts and the entire extrahepatic bile duct are routinely visualized at MRCP. The intrahepatic bile ducts are depicted as high signal intensity branching, tubular structures against the low signal intensity background of the solid parenchymal organs. The intrahepatic

bile ducts can be distinguished from the low signal portal veins, which contain rapidly flowing blood. The high signal extrahepatic bile duct is seen throughout its course from the porta hepatis to the duodenum and is distinguished from the lower signal intensity solid organs.[16,62-64,66] On conventional MR, the normal extrahepatic duct is seen in approximately 50% of cases. The CBD is more readily depicted on axial projections in its intrapancreatic portion on conventional MR of the upper abdomen, whereas normal intrahepatic ducts are not usually seen.[122-124]

Direct Cholangiography

Despite the high accuracy of ultrasound, CT, and MRCP in biliary disease, direct cholangiography (PTC or ERCP) may be needed when findings on cross-sectional imaging are equivocal or discrepant or when a therapeutic intervention is needed. Direct cholangiography is used to verify the presence or absence of biliary obstruction and more precisely define the site and cause of an obstructive lesion. Direct cholangiography has a greater than 95% success rate in determining the site and a more than 90% success rate in determining the cause of biliary obstruction. Direct cholangiography should always be preceded by ultrasound, CT, or MRCP to reveal unusual anatomy, areas of segmental ductal obstruction, and intrahepatic or extrahepatic mass lesions that would alter

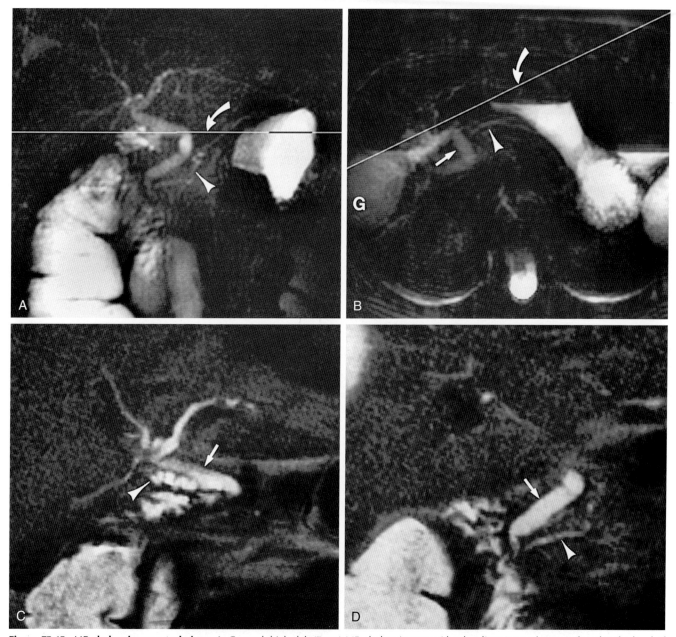

Figure 75-15. MR cholangiogram: technique. A. Coronal thick-slab (7-cm) MR cholangiogram with a localizer (*curved arrow*) placed at the level of the middle third of the extrahepatic bile duct demarcates the area through which an axial thick-slab image will be obtained. The pancreatic duct (*arrowhead*) is noted. **B.** Axial thick-slab (7-cm) MR cholangiogram obtained at the level of the middle third of the extrahepatic bile duct is used as a reference from which angles (*curved arrow*) are prescribed to obtain thin-slab images of the duct in the coronal oblique plane. The bile duct (*straight arrow*) and pancreatic duct (*arrowhead*) are shown. **C.** Coronal oblique, thin-slab (5-cm) MR cholangiogram demonstrates the proximal extrahepatic bile duct (*arrow*) and the cystic duct remnant (*arrowhead*). **D.** Coronal oblique thin-slab (5-cm) MR cholangiogram image obtained posterior to **C** shows the distal bile duct (*arrow*) and the pancreatic duct (*arrowhead*).

the manner in which cholangiography is performed and interpreted. Direct cholangiography clearly delineates biliary anatomy, an essential factor when planning surgical, radiologic, or endoscopic therapy. With the large variety of endoscopic and radiologic therapeutic interventions now available, direct cholangiography often serves as a prelude to nonsurgical biliary interventional procedures[7,15,126-130] (see Chapters 76 and 80). Direct cholangiography by PTC or ERCP for purely diagnostic purposes is being replaced more frequently in current clinical practice by noninvasive imaging, particularly MRCP.

Percutaneous Transhepatic Cholangiography Versus Endoscopic Retrograde Cholangiopancreatography

The choice of procedure for direct cholangiography depends on a number of factors: the clinical situation, the potential for therapeutic intervention, and the availability of a skilled endoscopist or radiologist.

Although there are many similarities in the information provided by antegrade (PTC) and retrograde (ERCP) cholangiography, the advantages and disadvantages of each procedure must be carefully weighed before making a decision. Both methods provide high-quality images of the ducts and are capable of evaluating intrahepatic and extrahepatic stenoses, ductal dilatation, filling defects, and leaks. Both procedures allow transformation of a diagnostic study to a variety of therapeutic maneuvers.

PTC is easier to perform, is less costly, and requires less operator skill. It has a high success rate; dilated ducts are opacified in virtually 100% and nondilated ducts in 80% to 85% of patients[127,129] (Fig. 75-16). The complication rate is low (3.4%), and the procedure is performed by the radiologist.[131,132] Therapeutic transhepatic options after PTC require a higher skill level and include biliary drainage; stone extraction, crushing, contact dissolution, laser fragmentation, and contact lithotripsy; stent placement; stricture dilatation; and biopsy. ERCP is more time-consuming, more expensive, and more dependent on the skill of the endoscopist. The suc-

cess rate for cannulating the bile duct varies from 80% to 95%, depending on the experience of the endoscopist.[14,130,133-137] ERCP offers the advantages of direct pancreatic duct visualization and inspection of the upper gastrointestinal tract and ampulla. The complication rate is comparable to that of PTC (3%-5%).[138-141] Therapeutic options at ERCP include sphincterotomy for stone extraction or ampullary stenosis, biliary stent placement, and balloon dilatation of strictures.[130,142,143] The procedure is performed by the endoscopist using fluoroscopic monitoring and usually in conjunction with the radiologist.

ERCP is preferred for evaluation of patients with nondilated ducts or more distal lesions. It is the procedure of choice if a primary pancreatic process is suspected and opacification of the pancreatic duct is desired (Fig. 75-17). ERCP is also recommended for patients with bleeding disorders, for

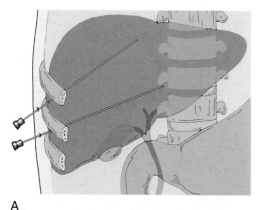

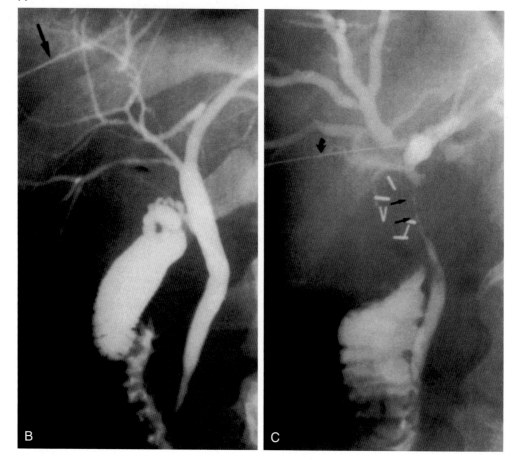

Figure 75-16. Percutaneous transhepatic cholangiogram (PTC). A. Diagram depicts the PTC technique. *Shaded area* between the needles is the preferred region for needle insertion. The *circular shaded area* should be avoided. **B.** PTC outlines the normal biliary ductal system. Note the needle (*arrow*) with the tip cannulating the small peripheral intrahepatic biliary radicle. **C.** PTC with the needle (*curved arrow*) in place shows the obstructive lesion (*straight arrows*) of the CHD and dilated intrahepatic ducts from metastatic periportal adenopathy. (**A** from Kadir S: Diagnostic Angiography. Philadelphia, WB Saunders, 1986.)

A

B

C

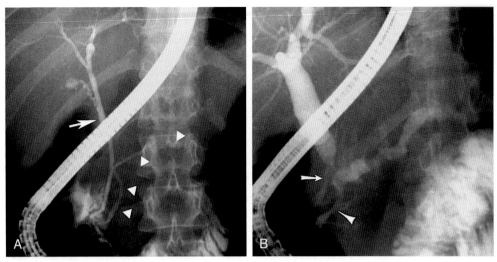

Figure 75-17. Endoscopic retrograde cholangiopancreatography. A. Filling of a normal nondilated bile duct (*arrow*) and normal pancreatic duct (*arrowheads*). **B.** The bile duct and pancreatic duct are dilated as a result of a distal common bile duct stricture (*arrow*) and pancreatic duct stricture (*arrowhead*) in a patient with chronic pancreatitis.

whom PTC may be risky. PTC is generally preferred when evaluating more proximal lesions involving the hepatic duct bifurcation, which may be difficult or impossible to delineate with a retrograde approach. PTC is recommended when endoscopy is not available or previous biliary enteric surgery has been performed. PTC is also used if ERCP fails, and vice versa.

The choice of diagnostic PTC or ERCP also depends on the therapeutic plan for the patient. If a CBD stone is suspected, ERCP should be used to perform a sphincterotomy and endoscopic stone extraction (see Chapters 76 and 80). If imaging studies indicate a lesion at the hepatic duct bifurcation, PTC is more likely to outline the extent of involvement, show the presence of segmental occlusions, and define drainage options.

Percutaneous Transhepatic Cholangiography

PTC is a widely used, successful, and safe method of directly opacifying the biliary ductal system. Its relative ease and safety are related to the use of a fine, 22-gauge, highly flexible Chiba or "skinny" needle, introduced by Okuda and associates in 1974.[144] The small caliber and flexibility of the needle decrease the likelihood of hepatic injury during respiratory motion and decrease procedure-related complications. The success of ductal opacification with PTC is virtually 100% for dilated ducts and 80% to 85% for nondilated ducts.[15,127,129] The success rate is improved with an increased number of needle passes. Failure to opacify the ducts during PTC should not be misinterpreted as absence of obstruction or dilated ducts; rather, it may indicate an inconclusive study.

The overall complication rate for PTC is 3.5%.[15,131,132] The most common serious complications include sepsis (1.4%), bile leak (1.45%), and intraperitoneal hemorrhage (0.35%). Rare complications include pneumothorax, hepatic arteriovenous fistula, reactions to contrast material, and death (0.2%).[15,129-132] There are no absolute contraindications to PTC except uncorrectable bleeding disorders. Ascites makes the procedure more difficult but is not an absolute contraindication.

Technique

Before the procedure, clotting studies are obtained, and any disorder should be corrected with fresh frozen plasma and platelets. Mild analgesia is provided. The patient should be well hydrated. Broad-spectrum antibiotics are routinely used; the data suggest that 80% of patients with biliary obstruction by CBD stones and 25% to 30% of patients with malignant obstruction may have infected bile, and sepsis is a potential risk.[15,128,129] Positive organisms are usually *Escherichia coli* and *Klebsiella pneumoniae*. The procedure is performed under fluoroscopic guidance. A percutaneous transhepatic puncture is made with the skinny needle using a right midaxillary approach (see Fig. 75-16A). Alternatively, a left-sided subxiphoid approach can be used if cannulation of the left hepatic duct is desired. The needle is inserted into the liver during suspended respiration, and contrast material is injected as the needle is slowly withdrawn until a duct is opacified. More than one puncture may be necessary, and there is no limit to the number of passes as long as the patient tolerates the procedure. After cannulation of an intrahepatic biliary radicle, contrast material is injected, outlining the biliary ductal system (see Fig. 75-16B). Images of the opacified biliary tree are obtained in the supine, both oblique, and if necessary, upright projections. In the presence of obstruction, it may be necessary to tilt the table upright or turn the patient to the left lateral decubitus position to allow contrast medium to fill the left hepatic ducts or flow to the site of a distal obstruction. Overdistention of the ductal system can cause sepsis and should be avoided. Contrast material is heavier than bile and may not mix readily with viscid bile in an obstructed system. In the supine patient, the posteriorly positioned right hepatic ducts are dependent and tend to fill preferentially, and the left ductal system may fail to opacify. Turning the patient to the left posterior oblique or left lateral decubitus position facilitates filling of the left duct. Failure to fill the right hepatic ducts in the supine position is abnormal and suggests a lesion obstructing the right hepatic duct. Erect views may be necessary for adequate filling of the CHD and distal CBD. Coned-down views of the ampulla region may be helpful in clarifying the cause of obstruction in this area. In cases of hepatic bifurcation obstruction or segmental occlusions, multiple passes may be necessary to map the extent of involvement and to determine operability and surgical approach to the lesion.

Transcholecystic Cholangiography

If the percutaneous transhepatic route is unsuccessful, transcholecystic cholangiography can be used to opacify the biliary tree when the gallbladder is present. The technique is simple and involves puncture of the gallbladder aided by ultrasonic guidance to place the needle directly into the gallbladder. Contrast material is then injected into the gallbladder to fill the bile ducts. This technique more easily opacifies the distal bile duct but gives inconsistent intrahepatic ductal opacification[129,145-147] (see Chapter 80).

Endoscopic Retrograde Cholangiopancreatography

Endoscopic cannulation of the papilla of Vater was first described in the United States by McCune and coworkers in 1968.[13,130] Advances in technique and improvement in design of the side-viewing endoscope since that time have made ERCP a reliable and safe procedure for evaluating both the pancreatic and the bile ducts. The primary indications for its use in the biliary tract are extrahepatic biliary obstruction, investigation of unexplained upper abdominal pain in patients with previous cholecystectomy, evaluation of cholangitis, suspected bile duct injury by previous surgery, and choledocholithiasis.[14,134,136] The performance, interpretation, and complications of this procedure are discussed in Chapter 76.

Normal Cholangiographic Anatomy

The main intrahepatic ducts, as well as the cystic duct, CHD, and CBD, are routinely opacified. Normal intrahepatic ducts measure 1 to 2 mm in diameter; however, the size is dependent on technical factors such as injection pressure, run-off into the gallbladder, and geometric magnification during filming. Second- and third-order branches are usually seen. The normal intrahepatic ducts branch regularly and smoothly. The extrahepatic bile duct is a smooth-walled, tubular structure extending from the porta hepatis to the duodenum. Distally, the intramural segment may be slightly narrowed and should not be confused with stricture. When partially relaxed, the choledochal sphincter (sphincter of Boyden) can create a wavy or narrowed appearance that may be mistaken for ampullary stenosis or neoplasm.[31] When contracted, its upper rounded border produces a pseudocalculous defect, mimicking an impacted stone.[148,149] This pseudocalculous defect disappears spontaneously after intravenous injection of glucagon, which relaxes the sphincter (Fig. 75-18). Contrast material should flow freely from the CBD into the duodenum during a normal cholangiogram. Normally, no splaying or crowding of ducts, caliber irregularity, strictures, or filling defects are seen.

The mean ductal diameter on direct cholangiography is less than 8 mm, with 10 mm considered the upper limit of normal. Magnification and injection pressure account for some of the discrepancy between cholangiographic and ultrasonic measurements. Studies have demonstrated a caliber increase of up to 5 to 6 mm simply as a result of the ERCP procedure.[150] Often, the normal common duct is quite small (<4 mm). The prepancreatic portion of the CBD tends to be the widest segment.

Operative and Postoperative Cholangiography

Operative Cholangiography

Operative cholangiography was first described by Mirizzi in 1932, and since that time, it has been an important adjunct to biliary tract surgery.[151] The procedure is done at the time of cholecystectomy to detect biliary stones and to determine the need for CBD exploration, a maneuver that substantially increases the time, morbidity, and mortality of gallbladder surgery.

TECHNIQUE

The bile duct is opacified during operative cholangiography by inserting a needle or cannula directly into the cystic duct or CBD and injecting contrast material. This technique can be used with open cholecystectomy or with laparoscopic cholecystectomy. However, the rate of successful cannulation and opacification of the ducts is lower with the laparoscopic approach. A small volume (5-7 mL) is injected initially, followed by the first radiograph. A second radiograph is taken after an additional 5 to 7 mL of contrast material is injected. Because air bubbles can simulate stones, the injection system should be cleared of air. Most operative cholangiography is performed using digital fluoroscopy. A portable radiographic unit with either a fixed or a movable table grid may also be used. The patient should be rotated slightly to the right to project the duct away from the spine. If common duct exploration is necessary, a T-tube (usually 12- to 16-Fr) is placed after the procedure and a completion cholangiogram is performed before closing. The cholangiogram should be free of motion, grid lines, and superimposed tubes or instruments. Adequate exposure factors and proper collimation should be used.[152,153] The study is considered suboptimal unless complete filling of the intrahepatic and extrahepatic ducts is accomplished (Fig. 75-19). Spasm of the sphincter occurs in as many as 25% of cases after CBD exploration.[154] This may be related to rapid or forceful contrast medium injection or surgical manipulation. Anesthetic agents such as morphine sulfate and fentanyl citrate are known to produce spasm.[155] If spasm is present, intravenous glucagon should be used to relax the sphincter.[156]

Postoperative Cholangiography

Following common duct exploration for stone disease or following liver transplantation with biliary ductal anastomosis, a surgically placed biliary catheter or T-tube is usually left in the extrahepatic bile duct to allow ductal decompression and provide access for postoperative cholangiography. Postoperative cholangiograms are obtained via the indwelling biliary tube. In the case of stone disease, a T-tube is usually left in place and the study is performed 5 to 10 days after surgery to check for retained stones or fragments. If none are identified, the T-tube is removed. If stones are present, they may be removed endoscopically or radiologically after maturation of the T-tube track (see Chapter 80). In the case of liver transplantation, a small-caliber biliary tube is left in place for a longer period of time, usually from 2 to 6 months, and cholangiography may be performed at any time to assess the status of the bile ducts and the anastomosis.

Contrast medium is administered by hand injection or by gravity drip infusion under fluoroscopic monitoring. Because of the risk of bacteremia, some authors recommend coverage

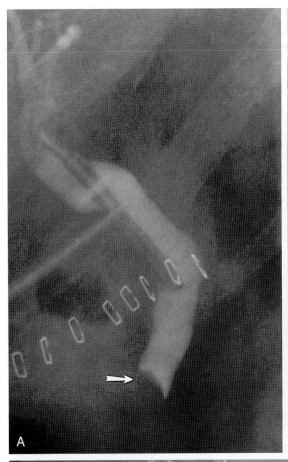

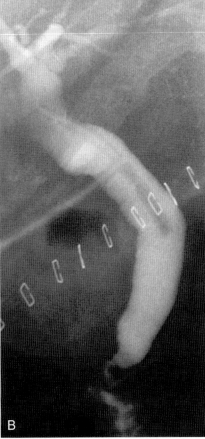

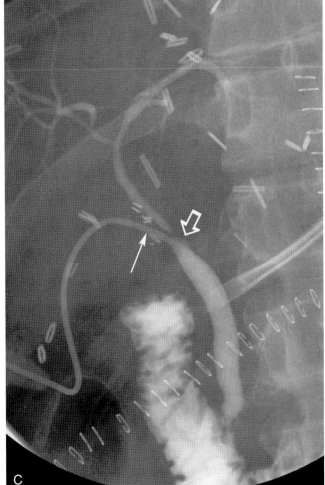

Figure 75-18. Postoperative cholangiogram. A. T-tube cholangiogram demonstrates pseudocalculous defect. Note meniscoid configuration (*arrow*) of the distal common bile duct from the contracted choledochal sphincter mimicking an impacted stone. **B.** Film taken during the same examination after intravenous glucagon shows disappearance of the pseudocalculous defect after relaxation of the choledochal sphincter. **C.** Biliary tube cholangiogram after liver transplantation with duct-to-duct anastomosis demonstrates straight, small-caliber tube entering the cystic duct remnant of the donor duct (*arrow*). Injected contrast material outlines the ductal system demonstrating mild narrowing at the duct-to-duct anastomosis (*open arrow*).

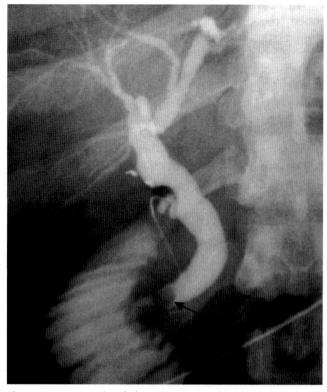

Figure 75-19. Operative cholangiogram. Note the cannula in the cystic duct remnant with filling of the bile duct. There is a retained distal common bile duct stone (*arrow*).

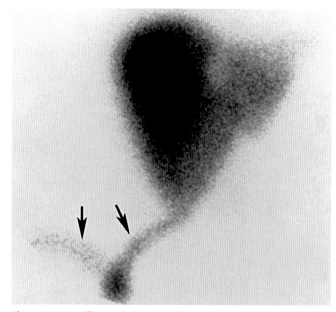

Figure 75-20. Biliary scintigraphy. This study demonstrates bile leak along the right upper quadrant drain (*arrows*) from a choledochojejunal anastomosis.

with antibiotics.[11,152,153] Antibiotics are routinely administered before postoperative cholangiography in patients following liver transplantation. During cholangiography, both the intrahepatic and the extrahepatic ducts should be opacified. Use of the upright position may be necessary to fill the distal CBD. Also, bubbles rise in the upright position, whereas stones gravitate into the distal duct. The Trendelenburg position facilitates intrahepatic ductal filling, and positioning the patient in the left posterior oblique or left lateral decubitus position helps opacify the left ducts. Oblique views minimize superimposition of intrahepatic branches. The optimal study is free of air bubbles, with adequate filling of the intrahepatic and extrahepatic biliary tree. Air bubbles may mimic stones but are usually differentiated by a smooth, round appearance and a tendency to cluster. Sphincter of Oddi spasm is relieved by increased injection pressure or the use of glucagon[152,153] (see Fig. 75-18).

The accepted radiographic technique for this examination includes low-kilovolts peak (70-75 kVp) exposures and dilute contrast material (10%-15% iodine). This technique frequently necessitates a long exposure time (2-4 seconds) to ensure good radiographic quality. The use of high-kilovolts peak (100-110 kVp) exposures and full-strength contrast material (30%-38% iodine) has been advocated to improve overall film quality with less motion, enhance stone detectability, and decrease radiation to the patient and personnel.[157]

Biliary Scintigraphy

Although used primarily to diagnose acute cholecystitis, biliary scintigraphy has several applications in evaluating biliary ductal disease. It is a noninvasive method of evaluating biliary drainage and segmental obstruction and can assess patency or bile leak after cholecystectomy or biliary enteric anastomoses[8,59,61] (Fig. 75-20). Biliary scintigraphy may also play a role in evaluating early biliary obstruction when ultrasound results are indeterminate and do not correspond to clinical or laboratory parameters.[158-160] Other uses for scintigraphic evaluation of the biliary tract include noninvasive evaluation of sphincter of Oddi dysfunction, assessment of bile duct injury and duodenogastric reflux and evaluation for congenital biliary anomalies.[59,161,162]

References

1. Watanabe Y, Nagayama M, Okumura A, et al: MR imaging of acute biliary disorders. RadioGraphics 27:477-495, 2007.
2. Shin SM, Kim S, Lee JW, et al: Biliary abnormalities associated with portal biliopathy: Evaluation on MR cholangiography. AJR 188:W341-347, 2007.
3. Friedman AC, Dachman AH (eds): Radiology of the Liver, Biliary Tract, and Pancreas. St. Louis, CV Mosby, 1994.
4. Inoue T, Kitano M, Kudo M, et al: Diagnosis of gallbladder diseases by contrast-enhanced phase-inversion harmonic ultrasonography. Ultrasound Med Biol 33:353-361, 2007.
5. Laing FC: The gallbladder and bile ducts. In Rumack CM, Wilson SR, Charboneau JW (eds): Diagnostic Ultrasound, 2nd ed. St. Louis, CV Mosby, 1998, pp 175-224.
6. Mittelstaedt CA: Ultrasound of the bile ducts. Semin Roentgenol 32: 161-171, 1997.
7. Yu J, Turner MA, Fulcher AS, et al: Congenital anomalies and normal variants of the pancreaticobiliary tract and the pancreas in adults: Part 1: Biliary tract. AJR 187:1536-1543, 2006.
8. Rubens DJ: Hepatobiliary imaging and its pitfalls. Radiol Clin North Am 24:257-278, 2004.
9. Burrell MI, Zeman RK, Simeone JF, et al: The biliary tract: Imaging for the 1990s. AJR 157:223-233, 1991.
10. Cooperberg PL, Gibney RG: Imaging of the gallbladder. Radiology 163:605-613, 1987.
11 Wyatt SH, Fishman EK: Biliary tract obstruction: The role of spiral CT in detection and definition of disease. Clin Imaging 21:27-34, 1997.
12. Karcaaltincaba M, Haliloglu M, Akpinar E, et al: Multidetector CT and MRI findings in periportal space pathologies. Eur J Radiol 61:3-10, 2007.

13. Jacobson IM (ed): ERCP and Its Applications. Philadelphia, Lippincott-Raven, 1997.

14. Silvis SE, Rohrmann CA Jr, Ansel HJ (eds): Text and Atlas of Endoscopic Retrograde Cholangiopancreatography. New York/Tokyo, Igaku-Shoin, 1995.

15. Yedlicka JW, Tadararthy SM, Letourneau JG, et al: Interventional techniques in the hepatobiliary system. In Castaneda-Zuniga WR (ed): Interventional Radiology, 3rd ed. Baltimore, Williams & Wilkins, 1997, pp 1439-1573.

16. Reinhold C, Bret PM: Current status of MR cholangiopancreatography. AJR 166:1285-1295, 1996.

17. Barish MA, Soto JA: MR cholangiopancreatography: Techniques and clinical applications. AJR 169:1295-1303, 1997.

18. Friedman AC, Sachs L: Embryology, anatomy, histology and radiologic anatomy. In Friedman AC (ed): Radiology of the Liver, Biliary Tract, Pancreas and Spleen. Baltimore, Williams & Wilkins, 1987, pp 305-332.

19. Netter FH: The Ciba Collection of Medical Illustrations, Volume III, Digestive System, Part III, Liver, Biliary Tract and Pancreas. Summit, NJ, Ciba Pharmaceutical Products, 1957, pp 22-24.

20. Schulte SJ: Anatomy and anomalies of the biliary tract. In Radiology of the Liver, Biliary Tract, and Pancreas. Categorical Course Syllabus. American Roentgen Ray Society 96th Annual Meeting, 1996, pp 107-117.

21. Balfe DM, Molmenti EP, Bennett HF: Normal abdominal and pelvic anatomy. In Lee JKT, Sagel SS, Stanley RJ, et al (eds): Computed Body Tomography With MRI Correlation, 3rd ed. Philadelphia, Lippincott-Raven, 1998, pp 573-635.

22. Schulte SJ: Embryologic and congenital anomalies of the biliary and pancreatic ducts. In Silvis SE, Rohrmann CA, Ansel HJ (eds): Technique and Interpretation of Endoscopic Retrograde Cholangiopancreatography with Endoscopic Intervention. New York, Igaku-Shoin, 1995, pp 114-115.

23. Turner MA, Fulcher: The cystic duct: Normal anatomy and disease processes. RadioGraphics 21:3-22, 2001.

24. Linder HH, Green RB: Embryology and surgical anatomy of the extrahepatic biliary tree. Surg Clin North Am 44:1273-1285, 1964.

25. Hatfield PM, Wise RE: Anatomy variation in the gallbladder and the bile ducts. Semin Roentgenol 11:157-164, 1976.

26. Healey JE Jr, Schnoy PC: Anatomy of the biliary ducts within the liver: Analysis of prevailing patterns of branchings and the major variations of the biliary ducts. Arch Surg 66:599-616, 1953.

27. Schein CJ, Stern WZ, Jacobsen HG: The hepatic ductal system: A correlation of endoscopic and roentgenographic findings. Surgery 51:718-723, 1962.

28. Silvis SE: The normal bile duct. In Silvis SE, Rohrmann CA Jr, Ansel HJ (eds): Text and Atlas of Endoscopic Retrograde Cholangiopancreatography. New York/Tokyo, Igaku-Shoin, 1995, pp 168-192.

29. Bret PM, de Stempel JV, Atri M, et al: Intrahepatic bile duct and portal vein anatomy revisited. Radiology 169:405-407, 1988.

30. Sterling JA: The common channel for bile and pancreatic ducts. Surg Gynecol Obstet 98:420-424, 1954.

31. Boyden EA: The anatomy of the choledochoduodenal junction. Surg Gynecol Obstet 104:641-652, 1957.

32. Hand BH: An anatomical study of the choledochoduodenal junction. Br J Surg 50:486-494, 1963.

33. Wu CC, Ho VH, Chen CY: Effect of aging on common bile duct diameter: A real-time ultrasonographic study. J Clin Ultrasound 12:473-478, 1984.

34. Horrow MM, Horrow JC, Niakosari A, et al: Is age associated with size of adult extrahepatic bile duct? Sonographic study. Radiology 221:411-414, 2001.

35. Kaim A, Steinke K, Frank M, et al: Diameter of the common bile duct in the elderly patient: Measurement by ultrasound. Eur J Radiol 8: 1413-1415, 1983.

36. Kaude JV: The width of the common bile duct in relation to age and stone disease: An ultrasonographic study. Eur J Radiol 3:115-117, 1983.

37. Puente SG, Bannuraga C: Radiological anatomy of the biliary tract: Variations and congenital abnormalities. World J Surg 7:261-266, 1983.

38. Berk RN: The plain abdominal radiograph. In Berk RN, Ferrucci JT Jr, Leopold GR (eds): Radiology of the Gallbladder and Bile Ducts: Diagnosis and Intervention. Philadelphia, WB Saunders, 1983, pp 1-29.

39. Meyers MA, O'Donahue N: The Mercedes-Benz sign: Insight into the dynamics of formation and disappearance of gallstones. AJR 119:63-70, 1973.

40. Cooperberg PL: Sonography of the gallbladder and biliary tract. In Radiology Of the Liver, Biliary Tract, and Pancreas. Categorical Course Syllabus. American Roentgen Ray Society 96th Annual Meeting 1996, pp 95-105.

41. Zeman RK: Cholelithiasis and cholecystitis. In Gore RM, Levine MS (eds): Textbook of Gastrointestinal Radiology, 2nd ed. Philadelphia, WB Saunders; 2000, pp 1321-1345.

42. Gore RM, Vaghmai V, Newmark G, et al: Imaging benign and malignant disease of the gallbladder. Radiol Clin N Am 40:1307-1328, 2002.

43. Bortoff GA, Chen MY, Ott DJ, et al: Gallbladder stones: Imaging and intervention. RadioGraphics 20:751-766, 2000.

44. Rosenthal SJ, Cox GG, Wetzel LH, et al: Pitfalls and differential diagnosis in biliary sonography. RadioGraphics 10:285-311, 1990.

45. Rall PW, Colletti PM, Lapin SA, et al: Real-time sonography in suspected acute cholecystitis. Radiology 155:767-771, 1985.

46. Colhoun EN, Fitzgerald EJ, McKnight L: The importance of appropriate frequency selection in sonographic gallstone detection. Br J Radiol 60:645-648, 1987.

47. Lee FJ, Delone DR, Bean DW: Acute cholecystitis in an animal model: Findings on color Doppler sonography. AJR 165:85-90, 1995.

48. Jeffrey RB, Nino MM, Ralls PW, et al: Color Doppler sonography of the cystic artery: Comparison of normal controls and patients with acute cholecystitis. J Ultrasound Med 14:33-36, 1995.

49. Wilbur AC, Sagireddy PB, Aizenstein RI: Carcinoma of the gallbladder: Color Doppler US and CT findings. Abdom Imaging 22:187-190, 1997.

50. Callen PW, Filly RA: Ultrasonic localization of the gallbladder. Radiology 133:687-691, 1979.

51. Hammond DI: Unusual causes of sonographic nonvisualization of the gallbladder: A review. J Clin Ultrasound 16:77-85, 1988.

52. Barakos JA, Ralls PW, Lapin SA, et al: Cholelithiasis: Evaluation with CT. Radiology 162:415-418, 1987.

53. Van Beers BE, Pringot JH: Imaging of cholelithiasis: Helical CT. Abdom Imaging 26:15-20, 2001.

54. Baron RL. Diagnosing choledocholithiasis: How far can we push helical CT? Radiology 203:601-603, 1997.

55. Neitlich JD, Topazian M, Smith RC, et al: Detection of choledocholithiasis: Comparison of unenhanced helical CT and endoscopic retrograde cholangiopancreatography. Radiology 203:753-757, 1997.

56. Gale ME, Robbins AH: CT of the gallbladder: Unusual diseases. J Comput Assist Tomogr 9:439-443, 1985.

57. Brink JA, Semin MD: Biliary stone disease. In Gazelle GS, Saini S, Mueller PR (eds): Hepatobiliary and Pancreatic Radiology: Imaging and Intervention. New York, Thieme, 1998, pp 590-629.

58. Samuels BI, Freitas JE, Bree RL, et al: Comparison of radionuclide hepatobiliary imaging and real-time ultrasound for the detection of acute cholecystitis. Radiology 147:207-210, 1983.

59. Thrall JH, Zeissmn HA: Hepatobiliary system. In Gay S (ed): Nuclear Medicine. St. Louis, Mosby-Year Book, 1995, pp 199-204.

60. Rosenthal L: Nuclear medicine. In Margulis AR, Burhenne HJ (eds): Alimentary Tract Radiology. St. Louis, CV Mosby, 1989, pp 1341-1365.

61. Kim EE, Moon TY, Delpassend ES, et al: Nuclear hepatobiliary imaging. Radiol Clin North Am 31:923-933, 1993.

62. Reinhold C, Bret PM, Guiband L, et al: MR cholangiopancreatography: Potential clinical application. RadioGraphics 16:309-320, 1996.

63. Reinhold C, Bret C: MR cholangiopancreatography. Abdom Imaging 21:105-116, 1996.

64. Coakley FV, Schwartz LH: Magnetic resonance cholangiopancreatography. J Magn Reson Imag 9:157-162, 1999.

65. Barish MA, Yucel EK, Soto JA, et al: MR cholangiopancreatography: Efficacy of three-dimensional turbo spin-echo technique. AJR 165: 295-300, 1995.

66. Fulcher AS, Turner MA, Capps GW, et al: Half-Fourier RARE MR cholangiopancreatography: Experience in 300 subjects. Radiology 207:21-32, 1998.

67. Glockner JF: Hepatobiliary MRI: Current concepts and controversies. J Magn Reson Imaging 25:681-695, 2007.

68. Moon KL, Hricak H, Margulis AR, et al: Nuclear magnetic resonance imaging characteristics of gallstones in vitro. Radiology 148:753-756, 1983.

69. Sagoh T, Itoh K, Togashi K, et al: Gallbladder carcinoma: Evaluation with MR imaging. Radiology 174:131-136, 1990.

70. Rossman MD, Friedman AC, Radecki PD, et al: MR imaging of gallbladder carcinoma. AJR 148:143-145, 1987.

71. Fulcher AS, Turner MA: MR cholangiopancreatography. Radiol Clin N Am 40:1363-1370, 2002.

72. Wachsberg RH, Kim KH, Sundaram W: Sonographic versus endoscopic retrograde cholangiographic measurements of the bile duct revisited: Importance of the transverse diameter. AJR 170:669-674, 1998.

73. Baron RL, Tublin ME, Peterson MS: Imaging the spectrum of biliary tract disease. Radiol Clin N Amer 40:1325-1354, 2002.

74. Behan M, Kazam E: Sonography of the common bile duct: Value of the right anterior oblique view. AJR 130:701-709, 1978.

75. Berland LL, Lawson TL, Foley WP: Porta hepatis: Sonographic discrimination of bile ducts from arteries with pulsed Doppler with new anatomic criteria. AJR 138:833-840, 1982.

76. Laing FC, Jeffrey RB, Wing VW: Improved visualization of choledocholithiasis by sonography. AJR 143:949-952, 1984.

77. Laing FC, Jeffrey RB, Wing VW, et al: Biliary dilatation: Defining the level and cause by real-time US. Radiology 160:39-42, 1986.

78. Niederau C, Muller J, Sonnenberg A, et al: Extrahepatic bile ducts in healthy subjects, in patients with cholelithiasis and post-cholecystectomy patients: A prospective ultrasonic study. J Clin Ultrasound 11:23-27, 1983.

79. Majeed AW, Ross B, Johnson AG: The preoperatively normal bile duct does not dilate after cholecystectomy: Results of a five year study. Gut 45:741-743, 1999.

80. Reinus WR, Shady K, Lind M, et al: Ultrasound evaluation of the common duct in symptomatic and asymptomatic patients. Am J Gastroenterol 87:489-492, 1992.

81. Sauerbrei E, Cooperberg P, Gordon P, et al: The discrepancy between radiographic and sonographic bile duct measurements. Radiology 137: 751, 1980.

82. Davies RP, Downey PR, Moore WR, et al: Contrast cholangiography versus ultrasonographic measurement of the "extrahepatic" bile duct: A two-fold discrepancy revisited. J Ultrasound Med 10:653-657, 1991.

83. Cooperberg P, Li D, Wong P, et al: Accuracy of common hepatic duct size in the evaluation of extrahepatic biliary obstruction. Radiology 135:141, 1980.

84. Muhletaler CA, Gerlock AJ Jr, Fleischer AC, et al: Diagnosis of obstructive jaundice with non-dilated bile ducts. AJR 134:1149-1152, 1980.

85. Beinart C, Efremidis S, Cohen B, et al: Obstruction without dilatation. JAMA 245:353-356, 1981.

86. Weinstein BJ, Weinstein DP: Biliary tract dilatation in the non-jaundiced patient. AJR 134:899-901, 1980.

87. Zeman RK, Taylor KJW, Burrell MI, et al: Ultrasound demonstration of anicteric dilatation of the biliary tree. Radiology 134:689, 1980.

88. Graham MF, Cooperberg PL, Cohen MM, et al: The size of the normal common hepatic duct following cholecystectomy: An ultrasonographic study. Radiology 135:137-139, 1980.

89. Feng B, Song Q: Does the common bile duct dilate after cholecystectomy? Sonographic evaluation in 234 patients. AJR 165:859-861, 1995.

90. Simeone JF, Butch RJ, Mueller PR, et al: The bile ducts after a fatty meal: Further sonographic observations. Radiology 154:763-768, 1985.

91. Wilson SA, Gosink BB, van Sonnenberg E: Unchanged size of dilated common duct after fatty meal: Results and significance. Radiology 160:29-31, 1986.

92. Darweesh RMA, Dodds WJ, Hogan WJ: Fatty-meal sonography for evaluating patients with suspected partial common duct obstruction. AJR 151:63-68, 1988.

93. Zeman RK, Silverman PM, Ascher SM, et al: Helical (spiral) CT of the pancreas and biliary tract. Radiol Clin North Am 33:887-890, 1995.

94. Baron RL. Computed tomography of the bile ducts. Semin Roentgenol 32:172-187, 1997.

95. Co CS, Shea WJ, Goldberg H: Evaluation of common duct diameter using high resolution computed tomography. J Comput Assist Tomogr 10:424-427, 1986.

96. Pedrosa CS, Casanova R, Rodriguez R, et al: Computed tomography in obstructive jaundice. Part I. The level of obstruction. Radiology 139: 627-634, 1981.

97. Pedrosa CS, Casanova R, Lezana AH, et al: Computed tomography in obstructive jaundice. Part II. The cause of obstruction. Radiology 139:635-645, 1981.

98. Gibson RN, Young E, Thompson JN, et al: Bile duct obstruction: Radiologic evaluation of level, cause and tumor resectability. Radiology 160:43-47, 1986.

99. Zeman RK, Berman PM, Silverman PM, et al: Biliary tract: Three-dimensional helical CT without cholangiographic contrast material. Radiology 196:865-867, 1995.

100. Fleishmann D, Ringle H, Schofl R, et al: Three-dimensional spiral CT cholangiography in patients with suspected obstructive biliary disease: Comparison with endoscopic retrograde cholangiography. Radiology 198:861-868, 1996.

101. Baron RL: Common bile duct stones: Re-assessment of criteria for CT diagnosis. Radiology 162:419-424, 1987.

102. Stockberger SM, Sherman S, Kopecky KK: Helical CT cholangiography. Abdom Imaging 21:98-104, 1996.

103. Liddell RM, Baron RL, Ekston JE, et al: Normal intrahepatic bile ducts: CT depiction. Radiology 176:633-635, 1990.

104. Weinstein JB, Heiken JP, Lee JKT, et al: High resolution CT of the porta hepatis and hepatoduodenal ligament. RadioGraphics 6:55-74, 1986.

105. Foley WD, Wilson CR, Quiroz FA: Demonstration of the normal extrahepatic biliary tree with computed tomography. J Comput Assist Tomogr 4:48-52, 1980.

106. Shulte SJ, Baron RL, Teefey SA, et al: CT of the extrahepatic bile ducts: Wall thickness and contrast enhancement in normal and abnormal ducts. AJR 154:79-85, 1990.

107. Kim HJ, Park DI, Park JH, et al: Multidetector computed tomography cholangiography with multiplanar reformation for the assessment of patients with biliary obstruction. J Gastroenterol Hepatol 22:400-405, 2007.

108. Van Beers BE, Lacrosse M, Trigaux JP, et al: Noninvasive imaging of the biliary tree before or after laparoscopic cholecystectomy: Use of three-dimensional spiral CT cholangiography. AJR 162:1331-1335, 1994.

109. Yeh BM, Breiman RS, Taouli B, et al: Biliary tract depiction in living potential liver donors: Comparison of conventional MR, mangafodipir trisodium-enhanced excretory MR, and multi-detector row CT cholangiography-Initial experience. Radiology 230:645-651, 2004.

110. Wang ZJ, Yeh BM, Roberts JP, et al: Living donor candidates for right hepatic lobe transplantation: Evaluation at CT cholangiography-Initial experience. Radiology 235:899-904, 2005.

111. Dinkel HP, Moll R, Gassel HJ, et al: Helical CT cholangiography for the detection and localization of bile duct leakage. Am J Roentgen 173:613-617, 1999.

112. Soto JA, Velez SM, Guzman J: Choledocholithiasis: Diagnosis with oral contrast-enhanced CT cholangiography. AJR 172:943-948, 1999.

113. Caoli EM, Paulson EK, Heyneman L, et al: Helical CT cholangiography with three-dimensional volume rendering using an oral biliary contrast agent: Feasibility of a novel technique. AJR 174:487-492, 2000.

114. Soto JA, Barish MA, Yacel EK, et al: Pancreatic duct: MR cholangiopancreatography with a three-dimensional fast spin echo technique. Radiology 196:459-464, 1995.

115. Guibaud L, Bret PM, Reinhold C, et al: Bile duct obstruction and choledocholithiasis: Diagnosis with MR cholangiography. Radiology 197:109-115, 1995.

116. Miller JC, Harisinghani M, Richter JM, et al: Magnetic resonance cholangiopancreatography. J Am Coll Radiol 4:133-136, 2007.

117. Wielopolski PA, Gaa J, Wielopolski DR, et al: Breath-hold MR cholangiopancreatography with three-dimensional, segmented, echo-planar imaging and volume rendering. Radiology 210:247-252, 1999.

118. Taourel P, Bret PM, Reinhold C, et al: Anatomic variants of the biliary tree: Diagnosis with MR cholangiopancreatography. Radiology 199: 521-527, 1996.

119. Fulcher AS, Turner MA, Capps GW: MR cholangiography: Technical advances and clinical applications. RadioGraphics 19:25-41, 1999.

120. Soto JA, Yucel EK, Barish MA, et al: MR cholangiopancreatography after unsuccessful or incomplete ERCP. Radiology 199:91-98, 1996.

121. Schmidt S, Chevallier P, Novellas S, et al: Choledocholithiasis: Repetitive thick-slab single-shot projection magnetic resonance cholangiopancreaticography versus endoscopic ultrasonography. Eur Radiol 17:241-250, 2007.

122. Semelka RC, Ascher SM, Reinhold C: MRI of the Abdomen and Pelvis. New York, Wiley-Liss, 1997, pp 138-148.

123. Spritzer C, Kressel HY, Mitchell D, et al: MR imaging of normal extrahepatic bile duct. J Comput Assist Tomogr 11:248-252, 1987.

124. Dooms GC, Fisher MR, Higgins CG, et al: MR imaging of the dilated biliary tract. Radiology 158:337-341, 1986.

125. Gandhi SN, Brown MA, Wong JG, et al: MR contrast agents for liver imaging: what, when, how. RadioGraphics 26:1621-1636, 2006.

126. Matzen P, Hanberg A, Holst-Christensen J, et al: Accuracy of direct cholangiography by endoscopic or transhepatic route in jaundice: A prospective study. Gastroenterology 81:237-241, 1981.

127. Mueller PR, Harbin WP, Ferrucci JT Jr, et al: Fine needle transhepatic cholangiography: Reflections after 450 cases. AJR 136:85-90, 1981.

128. Tobin RS, Vogelzang RL, Gore RM, et al: A comparative study of computed tomography and ERCP in pancreatobiliary disease. J Comput Assist Tomogr 11:1-3, 1987.

129. Wall SD, Yee J: Diagnostic ERCP and PTC. In Gazelle GS, Saini S, Mueller PR (eds): Hepatobiliary and Pancreatic Radiology: Imaging and Intervention. New York, Thieme, 1998, pp 154-170.

130. Ahmad NA, Shah JN, Kochman ML: Endoscopic ultrasonography and endoscopic retrograde cholangiopancreatography imaging for pancreatobiliary pathology: The gastroenterologist's perspective. Radiol Clin N Am 40:1377-1395, 2002.

131. McNichols MMJ, Lee MJ, Dawson SL, et al: Complications of percutaneous biliary drainage and stricture dilatation. Semin Interv Radiol 11:242-253, 1994.

132. Harbin WP, Mueller PR, Ferrucci JT Jr: Transhepatic cholangiography: Complications and use patterns of the fine needle technique. A multi-institutional survey. Radiology 135:15-22, 1980.

133. Birns MT: Endoscopic retrograde cholangiopancreatography: General considerations and the role of the radiologist. In Friedman AC (ed): Radiology of the Liver, Biliary Tract, Pancreas and Spleen. Baltimore, Williams & Wilkins, 1987, pp 333-350.

134. Shapiro RH: ERCP in the diagnosis of pancreatic and biliary disease. In Jacobson IM (ed): ERCP: Diagnostic and Therapeutic Implications. New York, Elsevier Science, 1989, pp 9-39.

135. Conners PJ, Carr-Locke DL: Biliary endoscopy. Curr Opin Gastroenterol 6:697-707, 1990.

136. Stewart ET: Radiographic technique for endoscopic retrograde cholangiopancreatography and endoscopic retrograde sphincterotomy. In Silvis SE, Rohrmann CA Jr, Ansel HJ (eds): Text and Atlas of Endoscopic Retrograde Cholangiopancreatography. New York/Tokyo, Igaku-Shoin, 1995, pp 51-77.

137. Silvis SE, Meier PB: Technique for endoscopic retrograde cholangiopancreatography. In Silvis SE, Rohrmann CA Jr, Ansel HJ (eds): Text and Atlas of Endoscopic Retrograde Cholangiopancreatography. New York/Tokyo, Igaku-Shoin, 1995, pp 22-35.

138. Cohen SA, Siegel JH, Kasmin FE: Complications of diagnostic and therapeutic ERCP. Abdom Imaging 21:385-394, 1996.

139. Rochester JS, Jaffe DL: Minimizing complications in endoscopic retrograde cholangiopancreatography and sphincterotomy. Gastrointest Endosc Clin N Am 17:105-127, 2007.

140. Vandervoort J, Soetikno RM, Tham TC, et al: Risk factors for complications after performance of ERCP. Gastrointest Endosc 56:652-656, 2002.

141. Anacker H, Weiss HD, Kramann B: Indications, contraindications and complications. In Anacker H, Weiss HD, Kramann B (eds): Endoscopic Retrograde Pancreaticocholangiography. New York, Springer-Verlag, 1977, pp 25-30.

142. Ott DJ, Gillian JH, Zagoria RJ, et al: Interventional endoscopy of the biliary and pancreatic ducts: Current indications and methods. AJR 158:243-250, 1992.

143. Kozarek R: Biliary ERCP. Endoscopy 39:11-16, 2007.

144. Okuda K, Tanikawa K, Emura T, et al: Nonsurgical percutaneous transhepatic cholangiography: Diagnostic significance in medical problems of the liver. Am J Dig Dis 19:21-36, 1974.

145. Teplick SK, Haskin PH, Sammon JK, et al: Common bile duct obstruction. Assessment by transcholecystic cholangiography. Radiology 161:135-138, 1986.

146. Vogelzang RL, Nemcek AA Jr: Percutaneous cholecystostomy: Diagnostic and therapeutic efficacy. Radiology 168:29-34, 1988.

147. vanSonnenberg E, Wittich GR, Casola G, et al: Diagnostic and therapeutic percutaneous gallbladder procedures. Radiology 160:23-26, 1986.

148. Beneventano TC, Schein CJ: The pseudocalculus sign in cholangiography. Arch Surg 98:731-733, 1969.

149. Mujahed Z, Evans JA: Pseudocalculous defect in cholangiography. AJR 116:337-341, 1972.

150. Chang VH, Cunningham JJ, Frankes JJ: Sonographic measurement of the extrahepatic bile duct before and after retrograde cholangiography. AJR 144:753-755, 1985.

151. Mirizzi PL: La cholangiographia durante las operaciones de las vias biliares. Bol Soc Cir Buenos Aires 16:1133-1136, 1932.

152. Thompson WM: The optimal radiographic technique for operative and T-tube cholangiography. Crit Rev Diagn Imaging 26:107-176, 1986.

153. Letourneau JG, Thompson WM: Intraoperative and postoperative cholangiography. Semin Ultrasound CT MR 8:126-133, 1987.

154. Chessick KC, Black S, Hoy SJ: Spasm and operative cholangiography. Arch Surg 110:53-57, 1975.

155. Chisholm RJ, Davis FM, Billings JD, et al: Narcotics and spasm of the sphincter of Oddi: A retrospective study of operative cholangiograms. Anesthesia 38:689-691, 1986.

156. Jones RM, Coultras JR, Pollard BJ, et al: Reversal of biliary sphincter spasm with low dose glucagon during operative cholangiography. Anaesth Intensive Care 11:175-177, 1983.

157. Thompson WM, Halvorsen RA, Gedgaudis RK, et al: High KVP vs low KVP for T-tube and operative cholangiography. Radiology 146:635-642, 1983.

158. Kaplan L, Weismann HS, Rosenblatt R: The early diagnosis of common bile duct obstruction using cholescintigraphy. JAMA 254:2431-2434, 1985.

159. Zeman RK, Lee C, Jaffe MH, et al: Hepatobiliary scintigraphy and sonography in early biliary obstruction. Radiology 153:793-798, 1984.

160. Noel AW, Velchik MG, Alava A: The "liver scan" appearance in cholescintigraphy, a sign of complete bile duct obstruction. Clin Nucl Med 10:264-269, 1985.

161. Negrin JA, Zanzi I, Margouleff D: Hepatobiliary scintigraphy after biliary tract surgery. Semin Nucl Med 25:28-35, 1995.

162. Sevilla A, Howman-Giles R, Saleh H, et al: Hepatobiliary scintigraphy with SPECT in infancy. Clin Nucl Med 32:16-23, 2007.

Endoscopic Retrograde Cholangiopancreatography

Andrew J. Taylor, MD

The role of endoscopic retrograde cholangiopancreatography (ERCP) in the evaluation and treatment of pancreatocobiliary tract disease continues to change. At its inception in the 1960s, ERCP was purely diagnostic. The development and subsequent improvement of CT and ultrasound began to replace some of ERCP's diagnostic uses with noninvasive ductal display. MR cholangiopancreatography (MRCP) provides a two- and three-dimensional display of the pancreatic and bile ducts as well as visualization of periductal anatomy. Although the role of purely diagnostic ERCP has diminished, advances in therapeutic endoscopic methods make ERCP critical in the management of biliary tract and pancreatic duct disorders.

Various authors and formal proceedings have tried to define the present use of ERCP.[1] However, local expertise and practice patterns will also play a part in what role ERCP may play in a particular case.

Keeping the above transition in mind, ERCP is still an important examination for a radiologist's interpretation. This chapter will focus on the following: ERCP technique, anatomy of the pancreaticobiliary tree, inflammation and neoplastic disease related to these duct networks, and endoscopic interventional procedures.

TECHNIQUE

Cooperation between the radiologist and gastroenterologist is important in obtaining the highest quality ERCP examination and interpretation. A dedicated technologist acting as a knowledgeable surrogate for the radiologist, in addition to a closed circuit TV system available for a radiologist to view, can help in the examination quality and communication between these services.

Imaging should begin with an appropriately positioned plain radiograph centered to include the upper right abdomen. This film allows detection of any abnormal calcifications and permits visualization of any material that might obscure the biliary tree or pancreatic duct prior to examination. Even obvious calcifications on plain radiographs can be lost if obscured with injected contrast material.

Filming usually occurs quickly after successful cannulation of the duct systems. The radiographic technique of 80 kVp for fluoroscopy and for image capture is generally used with an increase to 90 kVp or even 100 kVp for the larger patient. A 60% equivalent of contrast medium is used for opacification of both duct systems.

Obtaining images early in the injection of either duct system can be critical. Similarly, adequate distention of the injected duct is important. Using gravity for contrast medium flow into the ducts can be helpful, as is keeping in mind that change in patient position may also be needed for optimal duct opacification and display. Assessing drainage of either duct system can also be very helpful in trying to establish obstruction. The pancreatic duct should be drained of most of its contrast within 10 minutes from the end of injection. In a biliary tree without a gallbladder, duct drainage can take up to 45 minutes and still be normal.[2]

ANATOMY

Biliary Tract

The biliary tract can be divided into the intrahepatic and extrahepatic systems. The intrahepatic biliary tract follows the arterial blood supply of the liver draining the eight hepatic segments (see Chapter 75). It is important to remember which ERCP examination is performed in the prone position as opposed to the supine position that radiologists use when examining the biliary tract. In the prone position, the left intrahepatic ducts should fill first, as opposed to the right system seen in the supine patient. And although most images are obtained with the patient prone or in the left anterior oblique (LAO) position on the fluoroscopic table, other projections, such as a true left lateral or right anterior oblique position (RAO), can be critical in defining normal anatomy or pathologic change.

An attempt should be made to identify all of the central intrahepatic bile ducts. Lateral positioning of the patient can be very helpful in distinguishing right versus left ducts. In this position, the more anterior ducts belong to the left system (Fig. 76-1). There is moderate variability in the intrahepatic duct network. The duct draining the right posterior segment is frequently aberrant (Fig. 76-2). The intrahepatic ducts should appear smooth and gently taper as they course peripherally. The angles formed by these branches should be acute. Changes resulting in pruning of peripheral ducts, stiffening of the duct system, or deviation of the "flowing" appearance of this duct network should raise concern.

The extrahepatic biliary tract (EHBT) begins with the caudal most portion of the right and left hepatic ducts that exit the liver. The union of these two ducts forms the common hepatic duct (CHD), which is 2 to 4 cm in length. The cystic duct unites with the CHD, usually at acute angles on the CHD's right side. Again, normal anatomic variants are common and need be recognized. The cystic duct may insert high in the extrahepatic biliary tract or may even course into the right posterior duct (see Fig. 76-2). Conversely, it may insert very distally or medially (Fig. 76-3). These variations need to be noted because of potential complications that may occur during surgical or interventional procedures.

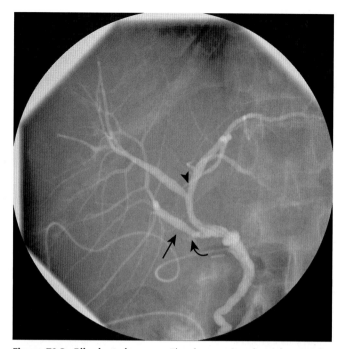

Figure 76-2. Bile duct aberrancy. The duct serving the right posterior hepatic segment is the most common anomalous intrahepatic biliary tree duct segment. A post–liver transplant T-tube cholangiogram shows the right posterior duct (*arrow*) exiting below the bifurcation (*arrowhead*), in this case consisting of the right anterior segment and the left hepatic duct. Also note that the transplant's cystic duct (*curved arrow*) originates from this aberrant duct.

The common bile duct (CBD) is approximately 10 cm in length. It courses caudally in a gentle posterior to anterior tilt with the patient in the prone position (see Fig. 76-1). The combined CHD and CBD segments may be referred to as "common duct" or extrahepatic biliary tract.

The distal CBD usually joins the main pancreatic duct to be wrapped together in a muscular envelope, the sphincter of Oddi (Fig. 76-4). This complex then courses intramurally within the duodenum to exit the papilla in the duodenal lumen. These ducts blend into a "common channel" 80% to 90% of the time. This channel may be long or short. In 10% to 20% of cases, each duct will separately exit into the papilla but will still reside within the muscular wrap. The distal most segment of the CBD is usually smooth but may be finely pleated or may contain small diverticular outpouchings. The common channel formed by the CBD and pancreatic duct varies from 2 to 10 mm and up to 15 mm in length although it averages approximately 5 mm.[3,4] The sphincteric wrap measures 5 to 15 mm in length.[5]

The sphincter segment has a constant, mild muscular tone but has superimposed contractions of approximately four to six times per minute. During these contractions, this duct segment may appear narrowed or even completely collapsed and thus simulate an obstructing distal duct stone resulting in the "pseudocalculus" sign (Fig. 76-5). With sphincter relaxation, the duct will revert to its normal appearance.

By convention, the diameter of the extrahepatic biliary tract is measured in the CBD. This duct measurement at ERCP will differ from that described for ultrasound, CT, or MRI. The CBD diameter is probably affected both by ductal relaxation produced by conscious sedation as well as by the active

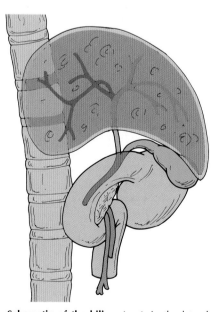

Figure 76-1. Schematic of the biliary tract. In the lateral projection, with the patient prone, the left intrahepatic biliary tract (*dark gray*) will fill before the right intrahepatic duct system (*light gray*). Also in the prone position, injected contrast medium will flow away from the sphincteric segment because of the gentle downhill course of the extrahepatic biliary tract.

Pancreatic Duct

The main pancreatic duct (PD) measures from 10 to 25 cm in length[6,7] but averages approximately 16 to 17 cm.[8] There is also great variability in the course of the main PD at the papilla to the splenic hilum. The main PD is divided into segments by parenchymal landmarks. The main PD usually has an "S-shaped" configuration. The "toe" of the "S" emanates horizontally from the sphincteric segment and flows into an ascending segment. This segment is related to the pancreatic head. Next comes the "shoulder" of the "S" with the main PD coursing over the superior mesenteric artery and vein. This segment is referred to as the "neck." The upstream duct continues as the "body." The distinction between the body and tail divisions is poorly defined. Some authors consider the duct to the left of the spine as the tail.

At the neck of the main PD, there can be a subtle circumferential narrowing without upstream dilatation, which is thought to be the site of the embryologic union of the dorsal and ventral ductal systems. The PD frequently bifurcates to demarcate the termination of the upstream segment. When describing main PD anatomy, the tail is anatomically proximal while the portion at the sphincteric segment is distal. Many clinicians use "upstream" (toward the tail) and "downstream" (toward the head).

The portion of the main PD, which courses into the minor papilla (minor papilla being approximately 2 cm proximal to the major papilla in the second portion of duodenum), is called the accessory duct or the duct of Santorini. In a common variant, this duct does not empty into the minor papilla, in which case it is considered just another major side branch of the PD.

Embryologically, the ventral duct is the duct of Wirsung. However, when the dorsal and ventral ducts fuse, the original dorsal duct (except for that which becomes the duct of Santorini) becomes part of the duct of Wirsung. This is frequently called the main PD. The main PD has a smooth, gentle narrowing from the head to the tail. With age the main PD may develop a mild "stiffness." The duct may also develop mild irregularity as a normal senescent change.

The side branch system of the PD can vary from patient to patient in its diameter. Some will be only threadlike in appearance while other systems will have slightly larger channels coursing from the main PD with a gentle taper as these ducts extend into the parenchyma. However, within a given patient all side branches should be similar, alternating as they exit either side of the main duct. Care must be given when trying to fill the side branch system. Side branches need to be filled adequately when trying to diagnose chronic pancreatitis, but over injection will cause acinarization, which puts the patient at risk for pancreatitis.

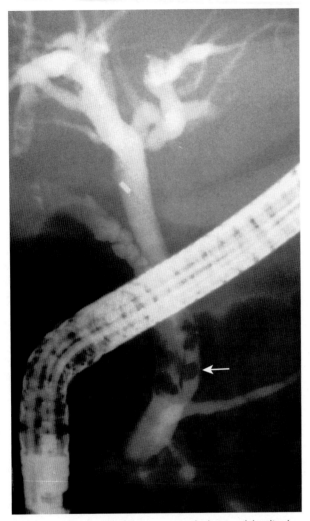

Figure 76-3. Aberrant cystic duct. A magnified view of the distal common duct shows the cystic duct (*arrow*) originating medially from the intrapancreatic portion of the extrahepatic biliary tree. This anatomy is important to identify, alerting the surgeon prior to laparoscopic cholecystectomy. Numerous faceted gallstones are present in both the cystic and common duct.

injection of contrast to distend the duct. Most authors suggest that the CBD diameter has an upper limit of normal of 10 mm. With age, there is a degeneration of the elastic tissue that makes up this duct system, developing the "floppy duct." Thus, this diameter may normally be larger in the elderly population. An exact measurement of the duct diameter can be obtained by setting up a ratio to account for the image magnification. The therapeutic endoscope is 12 mm in diameter.

Figure 76-4. Ductal unions at the papilla. The "Y"-type junction has a relatively long common channel compared with the short "V" type. In a minority of cases each duct exits the papilla separately in a "U" configuration.

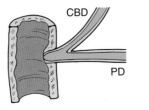

Y-Type junction

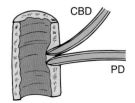

V-Type junction

U-Type junction

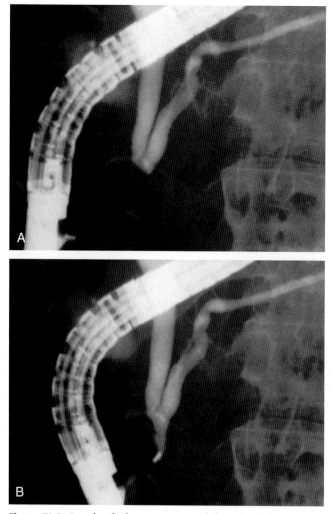

Figure 76-5. Pseudocalculus appearance of the sphincteric segment.
The initial image (**A**) is taken with the sphincter contracted. The flattened
terminus could simulate a stone. A few seconds later (**B**) the sphincter
relaxes showing the normal, patent ductal segment.

BILIARY TRACT NEOPLASIA

The biliary tract may be involved by benign and malignant
primary tumors as well as metastatic disease. These tumors as
well as infections and inflammatory disease can lead to ductal
narrowing. When attempting to determine the cause of a bile
duct stricture, the endoscopic retrograde cholangiography
(ERC) appearance must be correlated with CT, MRI, and
ultrasound exams when available, as well as the patient's
clinical course. Bile duct neoplasms are discussed further in
Chapter 81, and biliary infectious and inflammatory diseases,
in Chapter 82.

In differentiating cholangiographic benign from malignant
biliary strictures, malignant disease tends to produce a longer
segment of narrowing that is irregular or asymmetric in
appearance. The edges of malignant disease usually have an
abrupt (<1 cm) transition with a nodular or rounded shoulder.
Benign strictures have a longer transition zone with the narrowing itself having a smooth, concentric morphology. It is
important to remember that this latter appearance can also
be caused by an extrinsic process such as metastatic disease
to the peribiliary or peripancreatic lymph nodes or hepatic
parenchyma. Thus, a "benign" appearance may have a malig-

nant etiology. Various studies have shown the relative lack
of specificity of cholangiography and MRCP in differentiating
benign versus malignant strictures.[9,10]

The most common primary biliary tract neoplasm is the
cholangiocarcinoma. This malignant tumor has one of three
patterns. The most frequent type is the sclerosing variety,
which leads to a variable length of irregular ductal narrowing
(Fig. 76-6A). However, this stricture may be relatively focal or
smooth in appearance as well. When this type of cholangiocarcinoma occurs at the biliary hilum, it is called a Klatskin
tumor (Fig. 76-6B). The cholangiographic appearance can

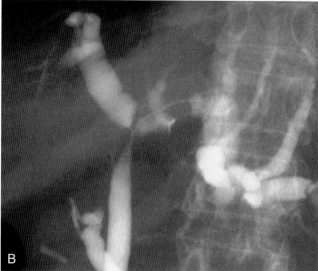

Figure 76-6. Cholangiocarcinoma. A. This cholangiocarcinoma presents
as a fairly long segment in the CHD. The irregularity and narrowing
extends to the bifurcation. **B.** In another patient with a Klatskin tumor,
the malignant stricture is unusual in its smooth appearance as it narrows
the proximal CHD continuing proximally to involve both the right and
left hepatic ducts.

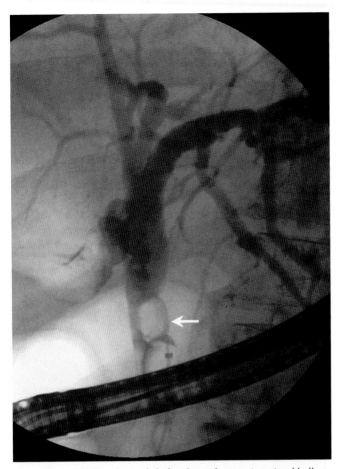

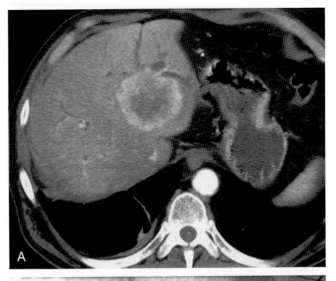

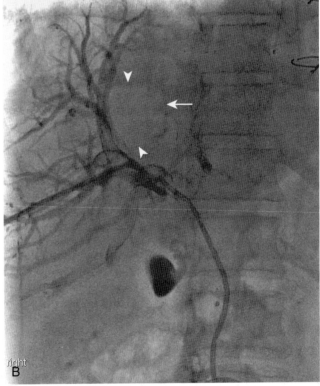

Figure 76-7. Papillary form of cholangiocarcinoma. A retrieval balloon is inflated just below the common bile duct spherical mass (*arrow*) that was confirmed to be a papillary cholangiocarcinoma at surgery.

help define the potential resectability of the tumor. The presence of right and left hepatic duct involvement that extends within the hepatic parenchyma will make curative resection of the underlying tumor impossible.

The papillary form of cholangiocarcinoma, occurring in the EHBT, has the best prognosis (Fig. 76-7). Some believe it is related to the early symptoms caused by the rounded mass obstructing the CBD. Others suggest that the histology of this morphologic type is less aggressive.[11]

The third type of cholangiocarcinoma is the intrahepatic form. This variety is typically seen as a large, intrahepatic mass on cross sectional imaging studies (Fig. 76-8). The mass is made up of malignant cells originating from the intrahepatic biliary tree, which elicits a fibrotic reaction. Cholangiography is rarely obtained, but when imaged radiographically, the ducts have a distorted course and an irregular in appearance, reflecting its sclerosing nature.

Other primary biliary tract neoplasms are rare and tend to be less aggressive. The biliary cystadenoma is an unusual, typically intrahepatic, tumor. It has a bile duct origin but usually has ovarian stromal tissue present. The patient is almost exclusively female in the fifth to sixth decade. Cholangiographic appearance typically has the intrahepatic biliary tree being smoothly splayed by a large mass. Occasionally, there may be an intraluminal component as well.

Another set of uncommon primary tumors are the biliary adenoma and papilloma. The adenoma tends to be a single

Figure 76-8. Intrahepatic cholangiocarcinoma. A. A late arterial phase CT shows the peripherally enhancing mass in the left lobe of the liver, typical for the intrahepatic cholangiocarcinoma that was subsequently pathologically proven. **B.** At cholangiography there is mass effect with splaying of the right anterior duct system (*arrowheads*). The left duct system that can be seen is narrowed and attenuated (*arrow*).

filling defect within the extrahepatic biliary tree while the papilloma tends to be multiple creating a papillomatosis (Fig. 76-9). This latter tumor tends to appear in the sixth to seventh decade without gender predisposition. This tumor tends to recur after resection and has a malignant potential. While the adenoma is usually found as an incidental finding, biliary papillomatosis can cause obstruction from the multiple polyps or as a result of mucus that some tumors produce.

Biliary tract mucin can also be secreted by a malignant biliary tumor, which is itself usually not identified. This

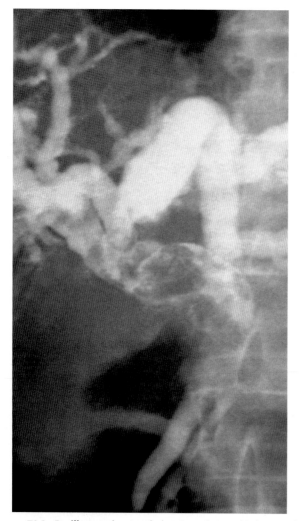

Figure 76-9. Papillomatosis. At cholangiography, multiple rounded filling defects are seen in the extrahepatic duct system. Malignant cells were retrieved at brushing.

tumor is usually more peripheral in the duct system with its presence manifest only by its obstructive mucus (Fig. 76-10). Some authors call this tumor the mucin hypersecretory biliary neoplasm[12] while more recent literature labels this entity as an intraductal papillary mucinous tumor of the bile ducts.[13,14]

Another rare primary tumor that is distinguished by its specific demographic is the granular cell tumor. This submucosal growth of neurogenic origin tends to occur almost exclusively in young to middle-aged women, usually of African American origin. The bile duct is obstructed by a relatively short, smooth, annular appearing stricture (Fig. 76-11).

The bile duct may also be obstructed by a group of tumors of varied histologies occurring at the papilla. There are four possible origins of this neoplastic process, which may be difficult to differentiate at imaging, with surgery, or even at pathologic examination. Because of this difficulty, a general term, a "periampullary" tumor is used to describe this entity. Pancreatic carcinoma and distal cholangiocarcinoma have the worst prognosis of this group. An ampullary carcinoma has a better prognosis. The fourth obstructive process can

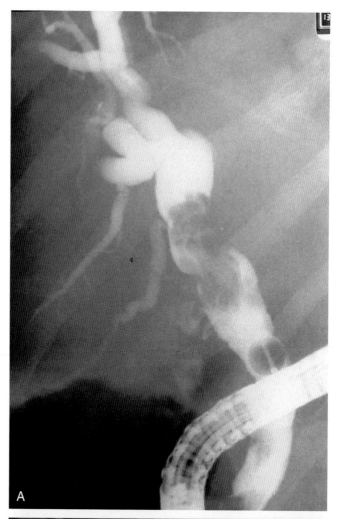

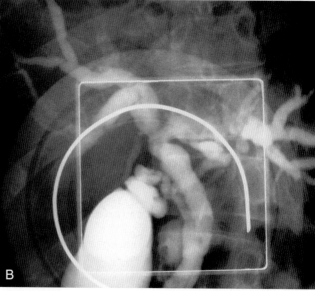

Figure 76-10. Intraductal papillary mucinous tumor of the bile duct. A. At ERC, a dilated biliary tract with a filling defect in the proximal extrahepatic biliary tree is seen. The left hepatic duct is not filled. **B.** After removal of the mucus, which was causing the filling defect, the dilated left intrahepatic system is visualized. There is, however, no visualization of the abnormal cells producing the mucus.

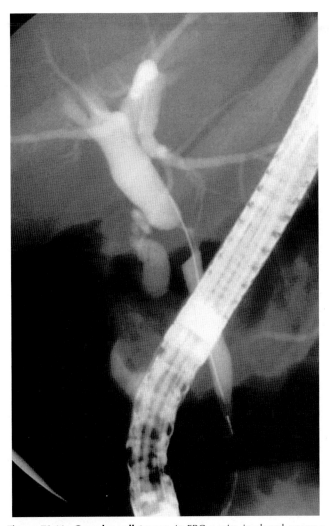

Figure 76-11. Granular cell tumor. At ERC a wire is placed across a smooth, submucosal/extrinic appearing common bile duct narrowing in this young woman with elevated liver functions. A granular cell tumor was found at surgery.

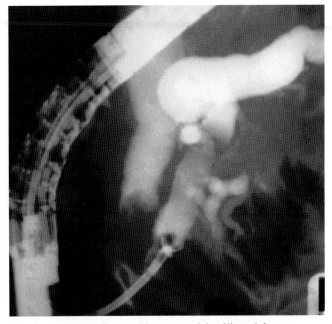

Figure 76-12. Ampullary carcinoma. Nodular filling defects are seen both in the common bile duct and main pancreatic ducts. A forceps biopsy confirmed the diagnosis of ampullary carcinoma.

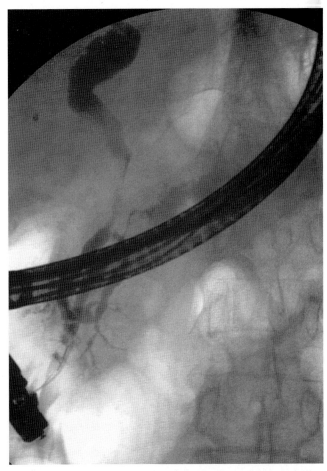

Figure 76-13. The double duct sign of pancreatic carcinoma. Adjacent irregular strictures are present in the common duct and pancreatic duct. The common duct stricture is somewhat high, demonstrating that a primary malignancy of the pancreatic neck can involve the biliary tract.

originate from the duodenum. The periampullary tumor can grow into either or both ducts as a nodular filling defect (Fig. 76-12) or present as a stricture.

The biliary tract is at great risk for metastatic disease because of its location within the liver, porta hepatic, hepatoduodenal ligament, and pancreas. Pancreatic carcinoma is the most common secondary malignancy of the biliary tract. The distal CBD runs either within the pancreatic parenchyma or immediately dorsal to it, placing this segment in harms way from a pancreatic head carcinoma. Involvement of the bile duct can be smooth or irregular at ERC. The CBD is obstructed in approximately 60% of cases of cases of cancer of the pancreatic head. The PD is obstructed with upstream dilatation resulting in the "double duct sign" (Fig. 76-13).

Although less common, pancreatic carcinoma can affect the remainder of the biliary tract as well. A lesion in the pancreatic neck can locally invade the mid extrahepatic biliary tract. A body or tail lesion can metastasize to the peribiliary lymph nodes of the proximal extrahepatic biliary tree or hilum (Fig. 76-14). With hepatic metastases, the intrahepatic biliary tract can be displaced or invaded.

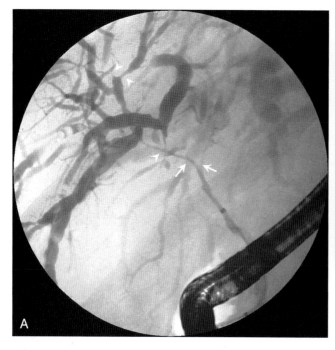

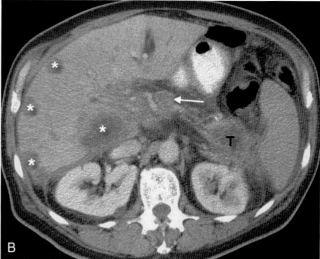

Figure 76-14. Pancreatic carcinoma with proximal biliary tract compromise. A. ERC demonstrates stricturing in the hila (*arrows*) as well as the extrahepatic biliary tract (*arrowhead*). **B.** CT shows the pancreatic tail primary (T), metastatic hilar lymph nodes (*arrow*), and hepatic metastases (*asterisks*).

The biliary tract can also be locally invaded by gallbladder carcinoma. Local spread occurs by direct extension down the cystic duct, lymphatic spread, or peribiliary lymph node involvement. There is also a tendency for this cancer to grow directly into the adjacent liver. Thus both intrahepatic and especially extrahepatic involvement may be present. The extrahepatic involvement is manifest by a medial splaying of the mid and proximal extrahepatic duct system (Fig. 76-15). This segment of duct may be draped by the mass effect or obstructed by local invasion. These findings are nonspecific,

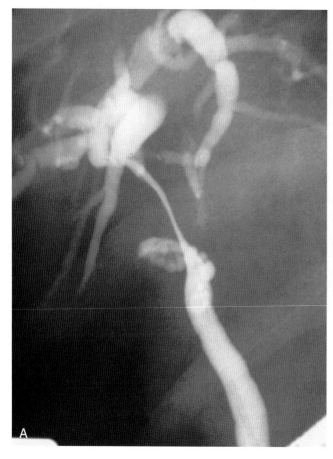

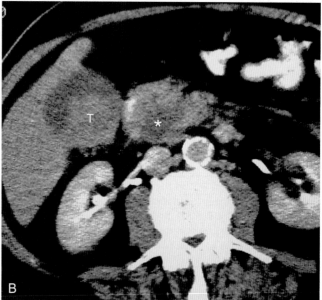

Figure 76-15. Gallbladder carcinoma. A. A diffuse, smooth narrowing of the CHD with mild bowing is present. Partial filling of the cystic duct is also seen. **B.** The corresponding CT shows the soft tissue mass in the gallbladder (T) with the adjacent necrotic lymph node metastases (*asterisk*) responsible for the CHD effacement.

also being seen in the Mirizzi's syndrome, pseudocyst mass effect, cholangiocarcinoma, or other metastatic disease to the adjacent lymph nodes.

Hepatocellular carcinoma is another local malignancy that can affect the biliary tract. A large hepatic mass or multifocal disease will cause intrahepatic distortion and even invasion. The duct distortion can be difficult to separate from cirrhotic changes that are usually present in this patient population. Hepatocellular carcinoma can extend into the bile duct lumen (Fig. 76-16). Metastases to the hilar lymph nodes can compress or invade the biliary tract at the hilum.

Metastatic disease from distant malignancies and lymphoma can also involve the bile duct. Extensive lymphatic network from the hepatic hilum to the duct's duodenal insertion can receive drainage from the liver, much of the alimentary tract, and retroperitoneum. Breast cancer and lung cancer can also metastasize to this area. Rarely, metastases will be

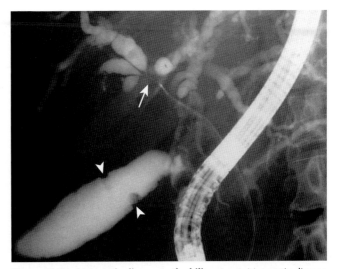

Figure 76-17. Metastatic disease to the biliary tract. Metastatic disease from cervical cancer not only obstructs the hilum by lymph node involvement (*arrow*) but also has metastatic deposits directly to the gallbladder wall (*arrowheads*).

deposited directly into the ductal wall itself (Fig. 76-17). Usually, metastases are to the lymph nodes of the subperitoneal portion of the hepatoduodenal ligament.

Lymphoma can cause narrowing or displacement of either the CBD or the intrahepatic duct system. Bulky extrahepatic lymph nodes displace but tend not to completely obstruct the extrahepatic bile ducts (Fig. 76-18). Hepatic lymphoma can similarly efface the intrahepatic biliary tree.

BILIARY TRACT INFLAMMATION

Ascending cholangitis is a biliary bacterial infection that develops above an obstruction. The obstruction is usually caused by stone disease or an inflammatory stricture. Charcot's clinical triad of abdominal pain, fever, and jaundice is frequently present. A patient with right upper quadrant pain, fever, and a dilated bile duct is considered to have ascending cholangitis until proven otherwise. Ascending cholangitis may take a benign course requiring only antibiotic therapy. Alternatively, the patient may present with sepsis and need rapid duct decompression in addition to antibiotic coverage.

ERC is an appropriate first step to define and relieve the obstruction in ascending cholangitis. It is important to relieve obstruction without significantly adding to the upstream pressure with excess injection of contrast. Thus the potential cholangiographic changes ranging from mild wall irregularity and pleating to total loss of duct integrity should rarely be seen.

Primary sclerosing cholangitis (PSC) tends to be an indolent process of chronic cholestasis typically seen in the young to middle-aged male. It may present only as an incidental elevation of alkaline phosphatase on a routine checkup or nonspecific signs and symptoms of abdominal pain, pruritis, jaundice, or even with stigmata of portal hypertension.

ERCP has, until recently, been the standard for duct definition in PSC. Early stricture disease is seen by mild ductal irregularity without upstream dilatation (Fig. 76-19). The peripheral intrahepatic duct network is still visualized. With

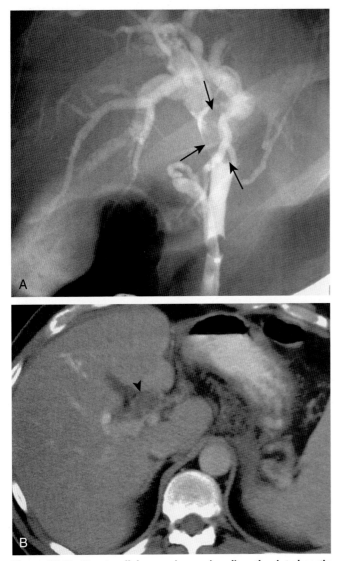

Figure 76-16. Hepatocellular carcinoma invading the intrahepatic biliary tract to cause an intraductal filling defect. A. Balloon occlusion injection at ERC shows the spherical intraductal mass (*arrows*) at the bile duct bifurcation. **B.** CT from the same patient also shows the mass distending the biliary tract (*arrowhead*) just anterior to the portal vein bifurcation.

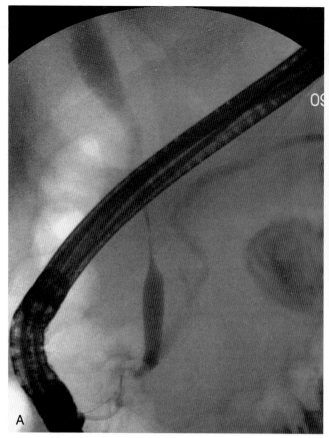

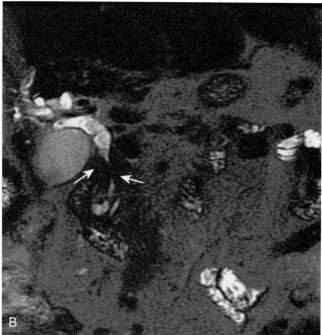

Figure 76-18. Lymphoma affecting the biliary tract. A. ERC demonstrates a long, smooth common duct narrowing with some upstream dilatation. **B.** A coronal T2-weighted MRI shows the extent of lymphadenopathy extending from the retroperitoneum into the peribiliary chain of lymph nodes (*arrows*).

disease progression, prominent strictures develop with mild upstream dilatation associated with pruning of the peripheral duct system. Eventually, with severe narrowing, none of the peripheral duct system will opacify.

A similar process is present in the extrahepatic biliary tract with early duct irregularity progressing to worsening strictures that can lead to weblike narrowings with beading and diverticular change (see Fig. 76-19C).

Occasionally, a large pool of bile will be seen in an ectatic intrahepatic segment forming the "bile lake." Finally, many PSC patients will have associated small intraluminal concretions, which should not be mistaken for secondary sclerosing cholangitis from biliary tract stone disease.

ERCP can be used to endoscopically dilate central strictures in an attempt to preserve hepatic function. Brushings of strictures and collections of bile for cytology should also be done at this time in an attempt to identify the complication of cholangiocarcinoma. The signs of cholangiocarcinoma, related to either a polypoid mass greater than 1 cm, rapidly progressing stricture, or rapid upstream dilatation from the stricture, are poor cholangiographic predictors of cholangiocarcinoma.

MRCP can display moderate to severe ductal changes in PSC[15,16] (see Fig. 76-19B). MRCP can be used to show the status of ducts proximal to obstructions.

There are two other autoimmune processes that can affect the biliary tract and may have a cholangiographic appearance similar to PSC. One is autoimmune hepatitis. This disease may develop, or may overlap the characteristics of PSC both in imaging and clinical manifestations.[17] In one study,[18] 40%

of patients who had the diagnosis of autoimmune hepatitis as well as ulcerative colitis had an abnormal biliary tract similar to PSC at cholangiography (Fig. 76-20).

Another autoimmune process, autoimmune pancreatitis can also be associated with an abnormal biliary tract. Autoimmune pancreatitis may cause biliary strictures that differ from PSC (see Fig. 76-20). The former disease causes longer strictures that result more frequently in upstream dilatation as opposed to the shorter, bandlike strictures with PSC, which has relatively minor upstream dilatation.[19] Differentiating autoimmune pancreatitis from PSC can lead to the use of corticosteroids, which has a greater positive impact in autoimmune pancreatitis compared with the negligible effect for PSC.[20]

As mentioned, the biliary tract can develop both intrahepatic and extrahepatic strictures from a variety of sources. The causes of "secondary" sclerosing cholangitis need to be ruled out prior to the diagnosis of primary sclerosing cholangitis. One of the more common causes of scarring is biliary stone disease associated with bacterial infection (Fig. 76-21). Both the intrahepatic and extrahepatic bile ducts can be involved. Usually, a history of chronic biliary tract stone disease is present to help establish this diagnosis.

Cirrhosis can also be a cause of distorted intrahepatic biliary tract changes. The ducts demonstrate a crowded appearance because of parenchymal loss. The ducts themselves will appear to be splayed, angulated, or "corkscrew" in appearance secondary to the regenerative nodules and fibrosis that surround the bile ducts in cirrhosis. There is also a decrease in peripheral ductal opacification.[21]

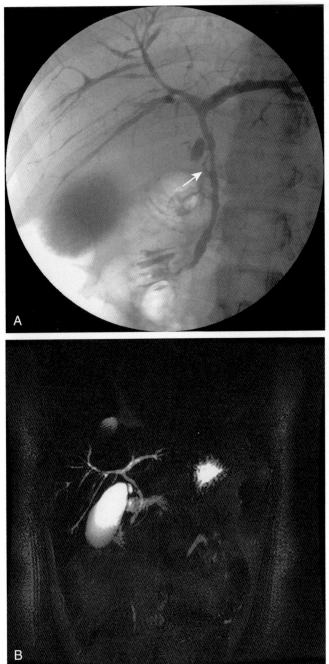

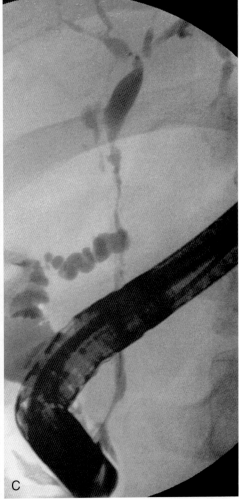

Figure 76-19.   Primary sclerosing cholangitis. A. Mild changes of PSC with diffuse irregularity of both the intrahepatic and extrahepatic biliary tract are present. Even with multiple strictures, there is no significant upstream dilatation. Note the aberrant low insertion of the right posterior segment (*arrow*). **B.** MRCP of the same patient demonstrates similar changes, but the fine detail of the diffuse biliary tract strictures are better displayed at ERC. **C.** ERC in a different patient shows more severe PSC changes. There is marked stricture disease with some dilatation of the proximal CHD.

Ischemic cholangiopathy is usually associated with ortho-topic liver transplantation, because the biliary tract has only a single blood supply, the hepatic artery. In this setting, severe hepatic artery stenosis or occlusion can cause diffuse intrahepatic biliary stricture formation or even loss of duct integrity (Fig. 76-22).

Both intra-arterial hepatic chemotherapy and radiation therapy can cause biliary tract strictures. These strictures can effect either the intrahepatic or extrahepatic system. In radiation therapy, the involved site is dependent on the radia-tion field (Fig. 76-23). Strictures associated with intra-arterial chemotherapy, which is usually done for colonic hepatic metastases, will diffusely affect both the intrahepatic and extrahepatic ductal systems (Fig. 76-24).

A rare but important consideration of inflammatory change in the biliary tract is a benign fibrotic process that has a tendency to involve the biliary hilum.[22] This inflammatory process can simulate a Klatskin tumor.

Diffuse metastatic disease, however, can simulate a sclerotic biliary tract process. Metastases, multifocal hepatoma, or even lymphoma can produce diffuse stricture disease in an intra-hepatic location, while deposits in the peribiliary or peri-pancreatic lymph nodes can cause extrahepatic strictures. This is one of the many cases in which correlation with cross sectional imaging studies along with the patient history is vital.

Another inflammatory process that ERCP can help diag-nose and is recurrent pyogenic cholangitis, also known as

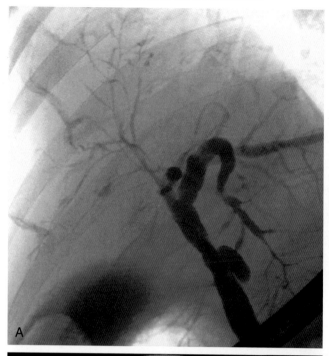

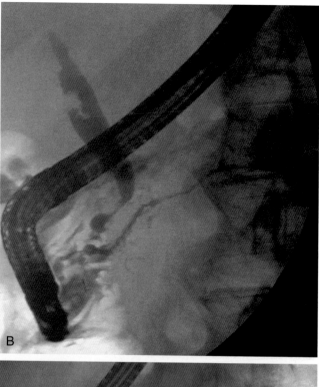

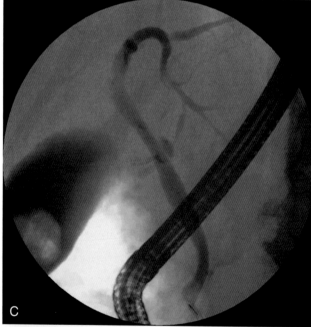

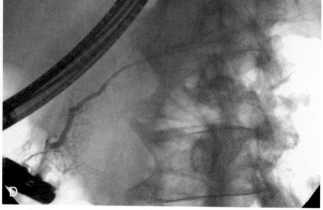

Figure 76-20. Autoimmune pancreatitis. A. There is severe intrahepatic biliary tract stricturing of the right intrahepatic duct system with mild irregularity of the extrahepatic biliary tract that simulates PSC. **B.** The distal extrahepatic biliary tract is strictured along with the diffusely irregular and narrowed pancreatic duct. **C.** Following steroids, there has been a marked improvement of the biliary tract. **D.** The pancreatic duct is now nearly normal after steroid treatment.

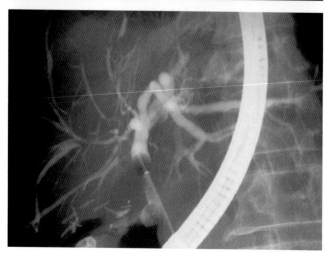

Figure 76-21. Secondary sclerosing cholangitis. ERC in this patient with past history of numerous bouts of ascending cholangitis from stone disease demonstrates strictures greater on the right than left of the intrahepatic biliary tract. These changes could be mistaken for PSC.

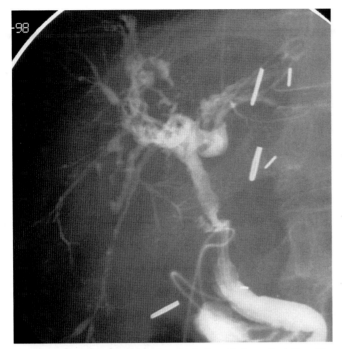

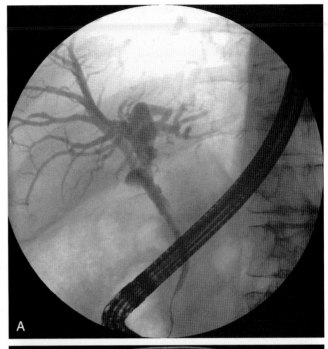

Figure 76-22. Ischemic cholangiopathy in hepatic transplantation. The T-tube cholangiogram in this patient, status post–orthotopic liver transplant with hepatic artery thrombosis, shows diffuse stricturing of the transplant biliary tract. There are areas of ill-defined duct borders compatible with the beginning of loss of ductal integrity.

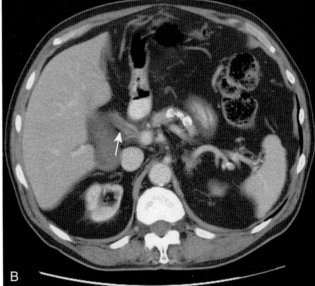

Figure 76-23. Radiation therapy of the biliary tract. A. ERC in a patient with prior radiation therapy for gastric carcinoma shows diffuse extrahepatic biliary tract narrowing, worse distally. **B.** A CT of the same patient shows diffuse thickening of the mid extrahepatic biliary tract (*arrow*).

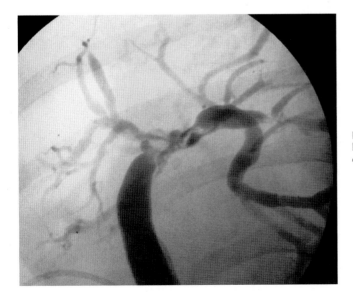

Figure 76-24. Biliary tract changes from intra-arterial chemotherapy. A hilar stricture is seen in this patient undergoing intra-arterial hepatic chemotherapy for colon cancer.

oriental cholangiohepatitis. Most patients will present with ascending cholangitis, some with abdominal pain without the cholangitis and less frequently with only pancreatitis.

Although ultrasound or CT may be the first imaging examination, ERCP can help confirm the disease, define the extent of disease, and help in relief of obstruction. Ductal changes relate to moderate dilatation of the extrahepatic biliary tree coursing back to the central intrahepatic ducts, which quickly taper (forming the "arrowhead" sign) to obstruction. The downstream dilatation is probably a manifestation of sphincteric segment stenosis related to inflammation caused by stone passage. The intrahepatic duct obstruction can be related to the periportal inflammation or to obstructing pigmented, "mud" stones. The majority of cholangiograms will also show intraluminal filling defects consisting of sludge and/or stones (Fig. 76-25). Use of a retrieval balloon can help clear central duct debris.

Another inflammatory process of the bile ducts, AIDS cholangiopathy, has significantly decreased in conjunction with the very successful antiretroviral therapy.[23] The now rare presence of this cholangiopathy will usually only occur with a low CD4 lymphocyte count. The cholangiographic appearance is variable, but it is usually a combination of primary sclerosing cholangitis changes combined with that of papillary stenosis.

Papillary stenosis, also known as sphincter of Oddi dysfunction (SOD), is another intrinsic biliary tract problem with a component of inflammation. There are three types of SOD that can affect either the biliary tract or the PD. Type I in the biliary tract is thought to be related to an inflammatory stenosis at the papilla. There is a mild to moderate dilatation of the biliary tree down to the sphincteric segment in a patient with abdominal pain and elevated liver enzymes (Fig. 76-26). A delay in complete drainage of the biliary tract of over 45

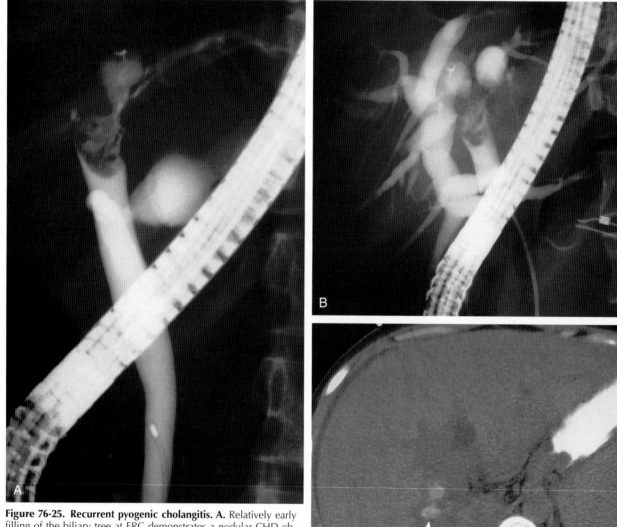

Figure 76-25. Recurrent pyogenic cholangitis. A. Relatively early filling of the biliary tree at ERC demonstrates a nodular CHD obstruction. **B.** With further injection, contrast is injected beyond this partially obstructing sludge. The central hepatic ducts are dilated but quickly taper to form the "*arrowhead*" appearance. **C.** A nonconstrast CT scan of the same patient shows the increased attenuation sludge/stones in the right intrahepatic duct system (*arrow*). There is also intrahepatic biliary tract dilatation, which is better appreciated with contrast enhancement.

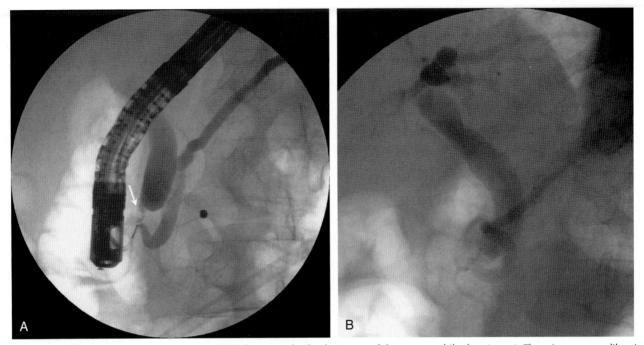

Figure 76-26. Sphincter of Oddi dysfunction. A. ERC shows a tight distal stricture of the common bile duct (*arrow*). There is upstream dilatation. **B.** An image 45 minutes after examination termination reveals contrast remaining in both the biliary tree and pancreatic duct to confirm obstruction of either system.

minutes in a patient without a gallbladder is also evidence for biliary tract obstruction in this entity. One of the most important imaging goals in this patient population is to make sure there is not another cause for ductal obstruction such as stone disease or possibly a small periampullary tumor to cause signs or symptoms of SOD. Brushings or biopsy of the sphincterotomy site, done for treatment of type 1 SOD, can help in differentiation if this is any question of underlying malignancy.

Type II SOD has only either elevated liver function tests or dilated biliary tree with abdominal pain, but not both. There will also be a delay in drainage post ERC. Sphincter of Oddi manometry can be helpful to provide confirmation in this case.[24] Type III SOD is much more nebulous possibly being an "irritable bowel equivalent" at the sphincter segment.

Postsurgical complication resulting in a biliary tract stricture is also a frequent intrinsic inflammatory process that usually affects the extrahepatic biliary tree. These strictures may occur months or years following surgery, almost always post cholecystectomy. Duct disruption at the time of surgery will define itself immediately with symptoms of bile leak. This acute duct damage should be surgically repaired at this time. However, surgical manipulation at the cystic duct may compromise the microvasculature to the adjacent extrahepatic biliary tree with the resultant stricture taking years to become symptomatic. This stricture is typically located in the mid to proximal extrahepatic biliary tree. A short, concentric narrowing is usually present (Fig. 76-27). But as in other strictures of the biliary tract, a variable appearance from a long segment to a bandlike narrowing may develop.

Endoscopic retrograde cholangiography will help define the appearance but, also importantly, the site of this stricture. Because surgery is the treatment of choice, it is important to display the narrowing in relationship to the hilum according

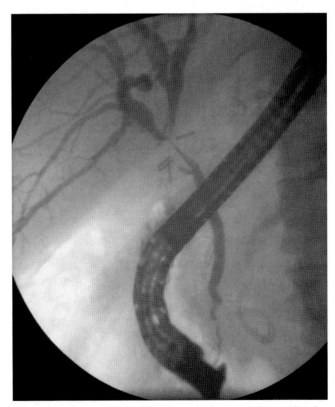

Figure 76-27. Postoperative biliary tract stricture. ERC 6 weeks after laparoscopic cholecystectomy demonstrates a smooth narrowing of the proximal CHD extending into the right and left common duct.

to the Bismuth classification (Fig. 76-28). If the stricture is completely obstructing to retrograde flow, MRCP is now the first option to display the upstream duct system in contemplation of treatment options.

The biliary tract can also be involved in adjacent inflammatory processes. Depending on the patient population, extrahepatic biliary tree narrowing from pancreatitis can be very common. The distal common duct is intimately associated with the pancreas, coursing either within the parenchyma, or immediately posterior to the pancreatic head. Thus, this segment is at risk for repeated bouts of pancreatitis, which can cause an acute edematous impingement or chronic fibrotic change to narrow this duct segment. An acute bout of pancreatitis can lead to a superimposed edematous component on the chronic underlying fibrotic change.

The typical appearance of bile duct compromise in chronic pancreatitis is a long, smooth, gentle tapering of the intrapancreatic portion of the CBD as it courses to the sphincteric segment (Fig. 76-29). Frequently, the distal most duct segment will widen back toward normal forming the so-called "hour glass" appearance of pancreatitis. However, in one study,[25] one third of common duct strictures were atypical. Abrupt narrowing, shouldering, or complete obstruction with upstream dilatation could be present to simulate a more aggressive stricture etiology (Fig. 76-30). This is one more example of the nonspecificity of cholangiographic findings. Correla-

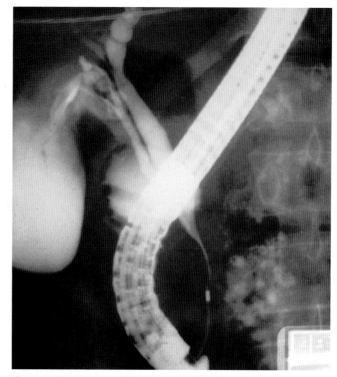

Figure 76-29. Common bile duct narrowing from chronic pancreatitis. A long, smooth narrowing of the intrapancreatic common bile duct is adjacent to the calcified concretions seen in the pancreas.

tion with endoscopic retrograde pancreatography (ERP) findings, axial imaging, and lab values may be needed to try to resolve the stricture's true cause.

The biliary tract can also be narrowed and displaced by another adjacent inflammatory reaction involving the gall-

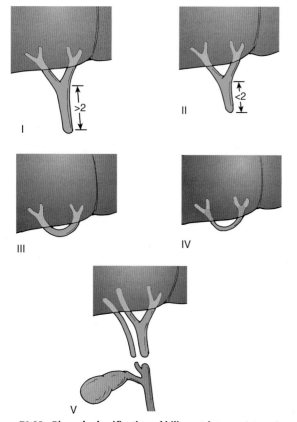

Figure 76-28. Bismuth classification of biliary strictures. A type I configuration represents the stricture occurring 2 cm or more from the CHD bifurcation. A type II configuration has <2 cm of normal duct prior to the bifurcation. The type III configuration leaves only the bifurcation intact. Type IV has narrowing of the bifurcation. Type V refers to injury of aberrant branches of the biliary tree. (From Taylor AJ, Bohorfoush AG III: Interpretation of ERCP. Philadelphia, Lippincott-Raven, 1997.)

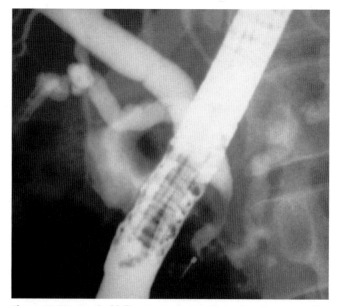

Figure 76-30. Atypical biliary tract changes from chronic pancreatitis. This chronic pancreatitis biliary tract stricture is a variation of the "hourglass" stricture. ERC demonstrates a rapid transition, simulating a more aggressive appearing stricture. The abnormal adjacent main pancreatic duct, without a double duct appearance, helps identify the stricture in the common bile duct as inflammatory.

bladder containing a gallstone, resulting in the Mirizzi syndrome. This syndrome may result from the mass affect generated from a gallstone impacted against the gallbladder neck occurring after numerous bouts of prior cholecystitis. Some authors suggest that the anatomy of the terminal cystic duct that parallels the CBD also helps facilitate the development of this obstructive process. This impacted gallstone impresses and displaces the adjacent CHD, causing the draping and narrowing of this duct segment (Fig. 76-31). If this combination of impaction and inflammation continues, the gallstone can erode through the gallbladder wall, common duct wall, and communicate with the extrahepatic biliary tree. With this fistula present, the gallstone can course into the extrahepatic biliary tree causing the Mirizzi type II syndrome.

The extrahepatic biliary tree can also be splayed or draped by an adjacent abscess, pseudocyst, or inflamed gallbladder causing variable degrees of obstruction. Also inflammation of hilar or peribiliary lymph nodes can cause their enlargement with secondary impingement upon the adjacent extrahepatic biliary tree. Enlarged hyperplastic lymph nodes can result from viral hepatitis, PSC, or primary biliary cirrhosis. A systemic process such as sarcoidosis[26] can enlarge these lymph nodes to cause biliary compromise.

The intrahepatic biliary tree can also be involved in a suppurative process. Hematogenous hepatic abscesses may cause mass effect on intact intrahepatic ducts. This will be different from a hepatic abscess resulting from ascending cholangitis, and subsequent duct disruption (Fig. 76-32).

PANCREATIC NEOPLASIA

Pancreatic carcinoma can be diagnosed and staged with multidetector CT (MDCT), MRCP, transabdominal ultrasound, and endoscopic ultrasound (EUS). ERCP has now been relegated to a secondary role in this diagnosis. The active injection of contrast into the main PD can uncover subtle strictures and opacification of side branches can confirm questioned parenchymal textural abnormalities.

The term "pancreatic carcinoma" refers to a primary ductal adenocarcinoma. As the name implies, the PD is the origin of this malignancy. The main PD will be involved in the vast majority of cases, but the malignancy may begin in the ductal epithelium of the side branch system. A small tumor in the side branch system can be difficult to appreciate at ERCP. However, if the main duct is not involved, close inspection of the side branch system is critical (Fig. 76-33). The side branches can be distorted or amputated and may be the only evidence of ductal abnormality related to the carcinoma.

Since pancreatic carcinoma most frequently involves the pancreatic head, the common duct is also usually involved leading to the "double duct" sign (see Fig. 76-13). As described earlier the double duct sign can also be caused by metastatic disease to the peribiliary lymph nodes from a cancer occurring upstream from the head. It should be kept in mind that the double duct sign can also occur with chronic pancreatitis. Correlation with ERP findings, axial imaging, and laboratory values may be needed to try to resolve the strictures true cause.

The most common malignant findings at ERP are ductal stricture and obstruction. But similar to ERC, the PD assessment for differentiating malignant from inflammatory processes is inexact.

Strictures of a primary ductal carcinoma tend to be longer, 1 to 3.5 cm, than the typically short, less than 1 cm, stricture of chronic pancreatitis. Malignant strictures also tend to occur on the background of an otherwise normal main PD with this exception of resultant upstream dilatation. The malignant stricture itself will usually appear irregular and have an abrupt or shouldered transition. The side branches in the strictured segment will be distorted or amputated if they opacify at all.

PD obstruction is as common as stricture formation in pancreatic carcinoma. There are multiple terminus appearances: a relatively long transition to eventual obstruction, which results in a "rat tail" configuration; an abrupt transition to complete obstruction with a flat, rounded, or nodular appearance; there may also be extravasation into the pancreatic substance associated with obstruction.

Another pancreatic malignancy that will have intrinsic ductal involvement is the intraductal papillary mucinous neoplasm (IPMN). Symptoms relate to recurrent acute pancreatitis, abdominal pain, weight loss, endocrine/exocrine dysfunction or possibly jaundice.[27]

The abnormal epithelial cells of this neoplasm produce mucus, which will distend the local side branch system and/or main PD depending on their location (Fig. 76-34). When this mucus enlarges the ampulla of Vater, it creates the "fish eye" appearance at endoscopy.

If found initially on CT or ultrasound, an IPMN may be difficult to differentiate from other cystic pancreatic lesions. ERCP has a potential role in diagnosis in these patients. Early on in the examination, the fish eye appearance of the abnormal papilla can be seen endoscopically. PD injection may then show ductal ectasia from mucinous distention. At this time, a retrieval balloon can be used to strip away the mucus from the main duct to allow injected contrast into an abnormal side branch system or possibly show an underlying mass effect in the main duct IPMN. This mucus can also be retrieved and be examined at cytology, looking for abnormal epithelium suspended in the gel. Removal of this mucus can temporarily relieve obstruction and improve some of the patient's symptoms.

Another cystic/mucinous tumor is the mucinous cystic neoplasm (MCN). This also is a potentially malignant tumor that typically presents in the elderly woman, being much more common in women than men. The pancreatic mass is usually found incidentally at physical examination or during an imaging study done for some other reason. Occasionally, there will be a specific complaint relating to mass effect in the upper abdomen.

On CT, ultrasound, or MRI, the large mass is usually located in the body or tail of the pancreas with a varied internal architecture from cystic to complex cystic to a compilation of large (>2 cm) cysts.

At ERP, there should not be communication of the PD with this cystic structure as opposed to the 50% to 70% of communication seen with a pseudocyst. The PD may be effaced by the MCN, but it is only rarely invaded by the malignant MCN.

There are numerous other pancreatic tumors that can efface the main PD but should not invade it: serous cystadenoma (microcystic cystadenoma), solid and pseudopapillary epithelial neoplasm and neuroendocrine tumor (formerly islet cell tumor).

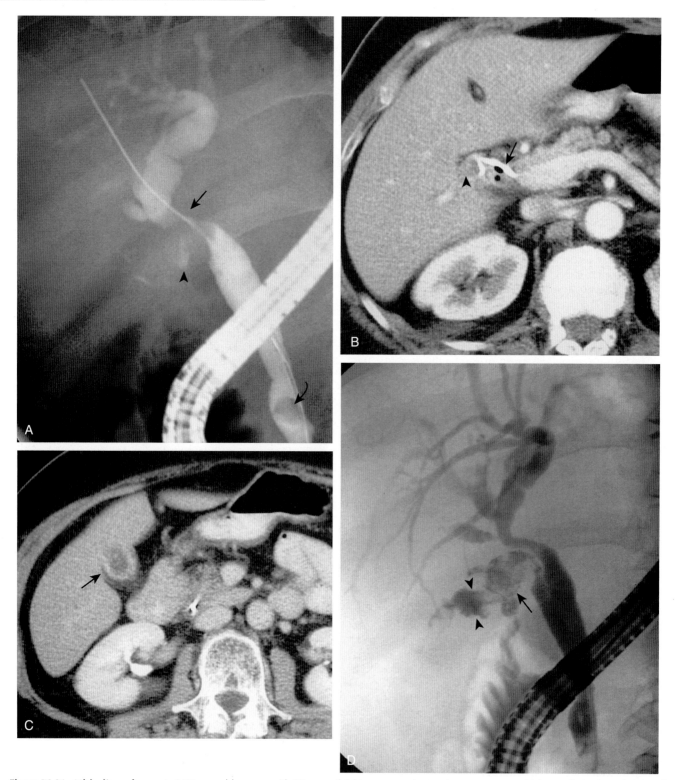

Figure 76-31. Mirizzi's syndrome. A. A 54-year-old woman with 10 years of right upper quadrant pain now presents with increasing pain and elevated liver function tests. The initial ERC shows proximal CHD obstruction (*arrow*) with adjacent curvilinear calcification (*arrowhead*). A wire has been advanced through the narrowing. Also note the distal common bile duct stone (*curved arrow*). **B.** Three days following this, a CT was obtained. This shows the biliary stent (*arrow*) coursing adjacent to the duodenum (seen by air bubbles) and also by a calcification at the gallbladder neck (*arrowhead*). **C.** CT section slightly more caudad than **B** demonstrates a thickened, contracted gallbladder (*arrow*). **D.** ERC 1 month later demonstrates the contracted gallbladder (*arrowheads*) with a moderate-sized stone at the gallbladder neck (*arrow*). The CHD is now patent but is still indented by the adjacent inflammatory process.

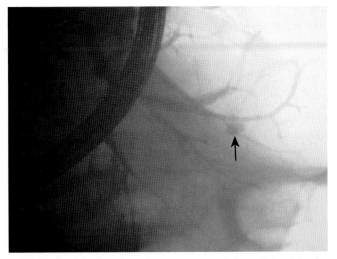

Figure 76-32. Small hepatic abscess from ascending cholangitis. The intrahepatic biliary tract during ERC shows a small cavity (*arrow*) from an abscess following a bout of ascending cholangitis.

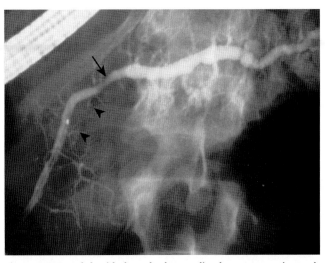

Figure 76-33. Subtle side branch abnormality from pancreatic carcinoma. In this 38-year-old woman with a presenting complaint of pancreatitis, the side branch system of the downstream body shows subtle distortion or amputation (*arrowheads*). Also note the subtle main pancreatic duct narrowing in the same area (*arrow*) with upstream ductal dilatation.

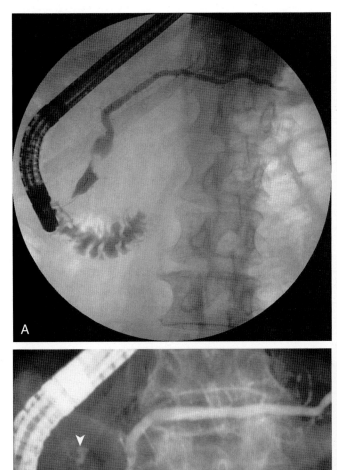

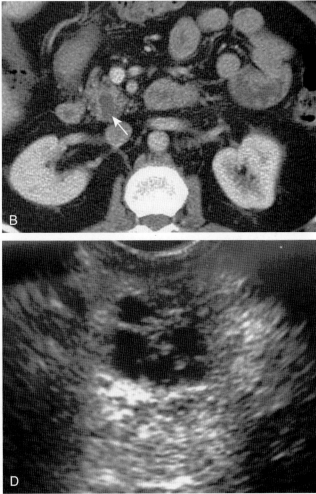

Figure 76-34. Intraductal papillary mucinous neoplasm. A. The first patient has a filling defect partially filling the main pancreatic duct at ERP. The associated side branches containing the mucin-producing cells are not visualized because of the obstructing mucus. **B.** However, the corresponding CT shows the ectatic uncinate side branches (*arrow*) seen as bilobed low attenuation areas. **C.** In another patient the multiple, ectatic side branches forming cystic dilatations (*arrowheads*) are visualized with only a small amount of mucin seen as a filling defect. **D.** This second patient underwent EUS, which shows the numerous cystic areas representing the ectatic side branches. At EUS, biopsies were taken returning mucin and abnormal cells.

Lymphoma and metastatic disease to the peripancreatic lymph nodes will usually displace the main PD and only rarely can cause ductal compromise. Occasionally, metastatic disease to peripancreatic lymph nodes or the pancreatic parenchyma, can invade the main duct and simulate a pancreatic ductal primary neoplasm.

PANCREATIC INFLAMMATION

Inflammation of the pancreas can be divided into three major categories: acute, chronic, and acute relapsing pancreatitis. Acute pancreatic is most frequently seen with alcohol ingestion or gallstone disease with numerous other, but rarer, causes. In general, ERCP should be deferred in a patient with acute pancreatitis. Main PD injection will not help diagnostically or therapeutically but may result in worsening of pancreatitis and can cause sepsis. Some authors suggest that common duct stone removal may help decrease the severity of acute pancreatitis.[28,29] In this case judicious contrast injection, only into the common duct, should be obtained to assure entry into the correct duct for stone removal.

Acute relapsing pancreatitis is an entity with recurrent bouts of pancreatitis without an obvious cause. ERCP can be of help in this patient population. Bile can be aspirated to assess for microlithiasis. There is some question as to the pancreatic divisum's role in recurrent bouts of pancreatitis. Finally, SOD can be a cause, possibly leading to manometry for diagnosis or sphincterotomy for treatment.

Chronic pancreatitis is the result of pancreatic inflammation that leads to permanent parenchymal/ductal damage. In a majority of cases, up to 70%, alcohol is thought to be the cause.

The diagnosis is suggested by symptoms related to abdominal pain and/or pancreatic insufficiency. Imaging can be a critical component in making the diagnosis. This imaging may be easily accomplished by finding calcified pancreatic concretions on a plain film of the abdomen. If not, ERCP may be the next step. MRCP, possibly with the addition of secretin, is improving and may replace ERCP as the next step in the work-up. Endoscopic ultrasound has also shown to be effective in diagnosis.[30]

There is a spectrum of ERP findings for chronic pancreatitis (Fig. 76-35) that are categorized in the Cambridge classification.[31] The earliest changes occur in the side branches: ectasia, ostial narrowing, filling defects, and cystic change being present singly or in combination. The main duct changes will follow. Early on, the main duct will appear "stiff" or have mild irregularity. In a slightly more advanced stage the irregularities within the main duct begin to deepen with diffuse irregularity present. This irregularity can form focal strictures intermingled with ectatic duct segments creating the "chain of lakes" appearance in the late stage of chronic pancreatitis.

ERCP can also be used for presurgical roadmap in chronic pancreatitis. The severity of stricture disease, amount of ductal concretions present, the presence of pseudocysts, and, finally, the degree of main duct dilatation and/or extent of CBD compromise can all potentially impact on the decision to do surgery or the type of surgery.[32,33]

Autoimmune pancreatitis is an increasingly recognized disorder of the pancreas related to other autoimmune diseases. It is important to recognize this entity because it can mimic pancreatic carcinoma and will benefit from corticosteroid therapy.[20] This disease tends to affect the elderly male but can be seen in the young and in the female population as well.[34,35]

Both the biliary tract and pancreatic ducts can be involved (see Fig. 76-20). The pancreas is diffusely or focally infiltrated by a lymphoplasmacytic inflammatory process that can progress to a fibrotic infiltrate.[34] The pancreatogram shows irregularity and narrowing of the main PD, which can be reversed by steroids. As discussed in the biliary tract inflammation segment, the fibroinflammatory process can lead to intrahepatic and extrahepatic ductal changes resembling primary sclerosis and cholangitis but will again potentially improve with steroids.[34,36]

Finally, pancreatic ductal changes can be seen in a minority of patients with PSC. AIDS can also affect the main PD and papilla.

INTERVENTIONAL PROCEDURES

Interventional applications of ERCP include treatment of biliary stone disease, cell/tissue sample for histologic diagnosis, relief of ductal obstruction, treatment of biliary leak, management of biliary tract problems in the orthotopic liver transplant patient and manometry for the diagnosis of SOD.

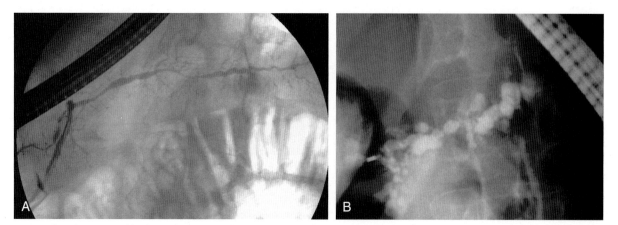

Figure 76-35. Chronic pancreatitis changes at ERP. A. The irregular side branches with narrowings at the ductal origins as well as a series of main pancreatic duct narrowings lead to the diagnosis of chronic pancreatitis. **B.** In a second patient, severe chronic pancreatitis changes are seen with the so-called "chain of lakes" series of main duct strictures along with ectatic and truncated side branches.

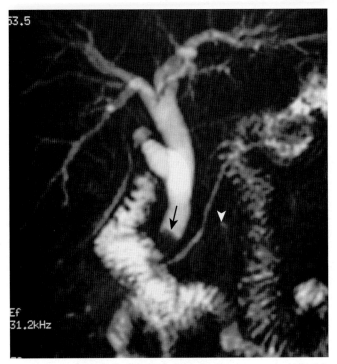

Figure 76-36. MRCP of choledocholithiasis. A two-second, thick-slab coronal MRCP shows the typical low signal stone (*arrow*) obstructing distally. The normal main pancreatic duct (*arrowhead*) is also seen.

In a patient with a high index of suspicion for choledocholithiasis, ERCP can still serve as the primary diagnostic and therapeutic procedure. In more equivocal cases, MRCP can reliably and noninvasively diagnose choledocholithiasis (Fig. 76-36). When using ERC as the initial examination for biliary tract stone disease, having the cannula at the sphincteric segment and obtaining images early during injection are critical (Fig. 76-37). Otherwise, smaller stones, at the sphincteric segment, can be lost in the contrast or be pushed back to be hidden behind the scope. Conversely, a large stone can be impacted at the sphincteric segment to make differentiation of stone versus tumor difficult. The differential diagnosis of biliary tract stone includes the pseudocalculus sign of sphincteric contraction, admixture artifact, air bubbles, blood clots, and tumor fragments.

Once the diagnosis of choledocholithiasis is made, the stone can usually be removed with a combination of sphincterotomy and endoscopic retrieval. However, there is a limit as to how large of a stone can be delivered intact through a sphincterotomy. Intact stones up to 10 to 12 mm can usually be delivered endoscopically. Greater than 90% of common duct stones can be removed via an endoscopic approach.[37] Larger stones can be fragmented by endoscopic mechanical lithotripsy with subsequent removal by retrieval balloon (Fig. 76-38). Stone fragmentation can also be done with electrohydraulic or laser lithotripsy but this equipment is less readily available. If stone removal must be delayed, a plastic stent can be placed along side the stone to keep the stone from impacting and obstructing the duct.

Tissue retrieval via endoscopic brushing is often necessary in patients with indeterminate structures or filling defects. Duct brushings, fine-needle aspiration, forceps biopsy, bile cytology, and washings from a removed stents are all tech-

niques available for cell acquisition. Some studies report that brushings or biopsies return malignant cells in only up to 46% of cases.[38,39] The combination of tissue sampling techniques results in a higher yield but is still relatively poor 77%.[40] The use of a forceps biopsy (see Fig. 76-12) provided a diagnosis of malignancy with a sensitivity of 52% and specificity of 100% in one study.[41]

While there is controversy concerning the use of internal biliary stents for operable pancreaticobiliary malignancy, endoscopic stenting is the treatment of choice in patients with inoperable malignant strictures in the mid to low extrahepatic biliary tract. With these more distal obstructions successful endoscopic decompression is achieved on over 90% of cases.[42] Metal stents provide longer patency rates with fewer bouts of obstructive ascending cholangitis than plastic stents.[37,43,44] If a metallic stent does become obstructed, a plastic stent can be advanced through the lumen of the metal stent to reestablish patency.

Although surgery is the gold standard therapy for benign biliary tract strictures, endoscopic stent placement is a important option in certain circumstances as well such as biliary tract strictures in chronic pancreatitis.[45,46]

Endoscopy sphincterotomy and/or plastic stent placement can also be effective in the treatment of postcholecystectomy bile leaks. Approximately 2% of patients develop a bile leak after laparoscopic cholecystectomy.[47] This leak usually occurs at the cystic duct where the clip placed at surgery may fall off or necrosis at the end of the duct stump leads to leak (Fig. 76-39). Another source of leak is due to aberrant right hepatic ducts (the ducts of Luschka), which are a developmental ductal communications between the gallbladder and the right hepatic duct. These communications are severed with removal of the gallbladder.

Endoscopic treatment is effective in approximately 90% of cases.[47] With a larger leak, sphincterotomy and temporary stent is necessary. A smaller leak may only require sphincterotomy for successful treatment.

An endoscopic approach is appropriate for many of the biliary tract complications associated with orthotopic liver transplant. Bile duct complications after liver transplant vary widely from 11% to 34%.[37,48] Most of these complications relate to bile leak or obstruction. Obstruction can be related to an anastomotic or nonanastomotic stricture. Intraluminal obstruction from a stone or biliary cast formation can also occur. Balloon dilatation is an appropriate first step for bile duct strictures (Fig. 76-40). Stones or biliary casts can be extracted via sphincterotomy and retrieval balloon. Biliary leaks that are associated with anastomotic or T-tube insertion sites can be treated with endoscopic sphincterotomy and/or plastic stent placement.

A complex, and at times controversial, area of ERCP intervention is SOD.[49] Manometry of the sphincter of Oddi and associated ductal changes can be assessed during ERCP. Sphincterotomy may be an appropriate treatment for patients with sphincter dysfunction.

New advances into endoscopic treatment related to the PD are also being developed. Endoscopic maneuvers for treatment of PD disruption and pain are being reported.[50-53]

Endoscopic pancreatic stenting across duct disruption is advocated by some for pancreatic trauma. Although pancreatic trauma is rare, defining the presence or absence of PD disruption is important for subsequent morbidity and for

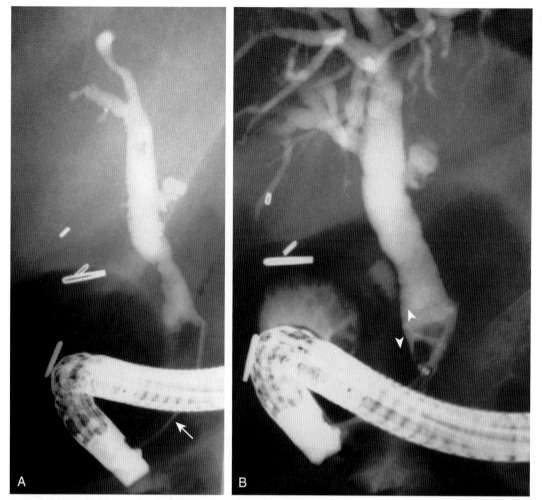

Figure 76-37. ERC and choledocholithiasis. A. During the initial common duct injection, the cannula (*arrow*) has been advanced too far up the duct. **B.** Filling the duct further with the catheter now placed more inferiorly demonstrates two large stones (*arrowheads*).

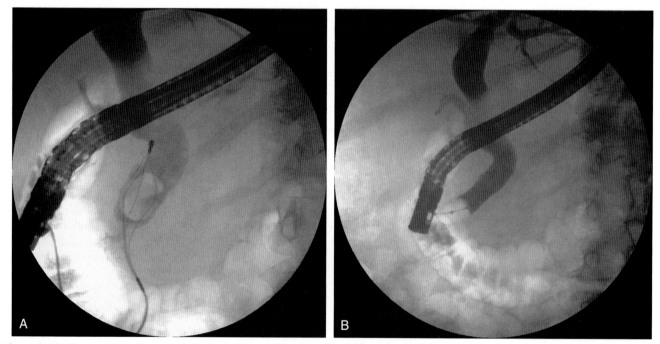

Figure 76-38. Common duct stone manipulation. A. This large common duct stone cannot be delivered through even a large sphincterotomy. Thus a mechanical lithotripter is used to slice and crush this stone into smaller fragments. **B.** The smaller fragments can now be pulled out through the papilla with a retrieval balloon.

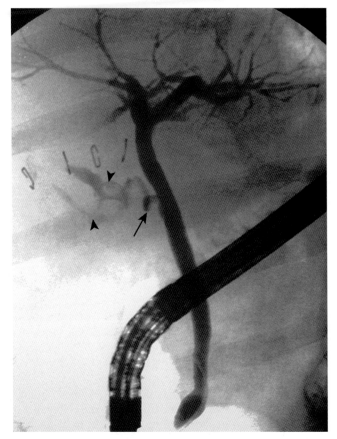

Figure 76-39. Cystic duct leak following laparoscopic cholecystectomy. At ERC, the remnant cystic duct (*arrow*) is seen just prior to the extravasated contrast (*arrowheads*). This small leak was successfully treated with a small-bore biliary stent only.

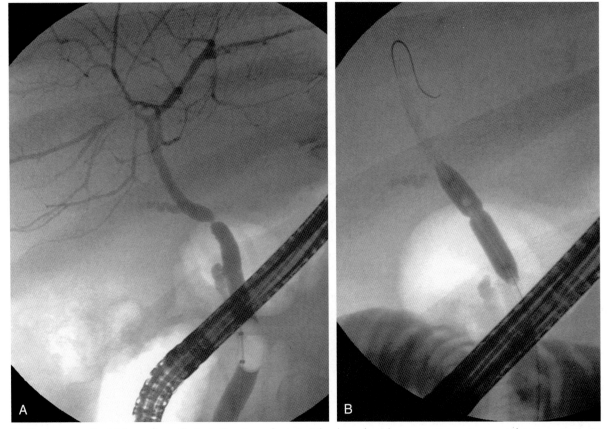

Figure 76-40. Anastomotic stricture after orthotopic liver transplant. A. A focal, moderately severe stricture is seen at the anastomotic site during ERC. **B.** A vascular-type balloon dilator is used to dilate this stricture. The balloon's "waist" gives way as the stricture is successfully dilated.

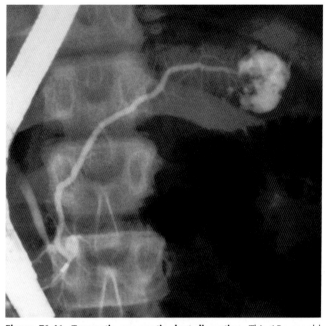

Figure 76-41. Traumatic pancreatic duct disruption. This 15-year-old boy was kicked in the left upper quadrant. Extravasation at the pancreatic tail is found at ERP.

management (Fig. 76-41).[54] Even though CT is the examination of choice to assess post-traumatic, intra-abdominal changes, ERP with possible stenting is thought to be the best method for detecting and treating duct disruption.[55]

COMPLICATIONS OF ENDOSCOPIC RETROGRADE CHOLANGIO-PANCREATOGRAPHY

Complications of ERCP include pancreatitis, infection, bleeding, and perforation. Pancreatitis may result from papillary manipulation and/or the effect of contrast on the pancreatic acini. Infection of the biliary tract may develop particularly in an obstructed system. The incidence of perforation increases when a therapeutic procedure is performed. It has been reported to be as low as 0.35%.[56] The majority of these perforations are retroperitoneal and can usually be managed conservatively. Endoscopic sphincterotomy can also result in significant bleeding, but the incidence is less than 5%. The presence of coagulopathy, cirrhosis, and the length of endoscopic sphincterotomy all increase this risk. Here again, conservative treatment usually suffices with only local therapy such as cauterization being necessary.

References

1. Wamsteker EJ: Updates in biliary endoscopy 2007. Curr Opin Gastroenterol 23:324-328, 2007.
2. Belsito AA, Marta JB, Cramer GG, et al: Measurements of biliary tract size and drainage time. Composition of endoscopic and intravenous cholangiography. Radiology 122:65, 1977.
3. Kim OH, Chung HJ, Choi BG: Imaging of the choledochal cyst. RadioGraphics 15:69-88, 1995.
4. Wiedmeyer DA, Stewart ET, Geenen JE, et al: Choledochal cyst: Findings on cholangiopancreatography with emphasis on ectasia of the common channel. AJR 153:969-972, 1989.
5. Dodds WJ: Biliary tract motility and its relationship to clinical disorders. AJR 155:247-258, 1990.
6. Classen M, Hellwig H, Rosch W: Anatomy of the pancreatic duct, a duodenoscopic-radiological study. Endoscopy 5:14-17, 1973.
7. Cotton PB: The normal endoscopic pancreatogram. Endoscopy 6:65-70, 1974.
8. Kasugai T, Kuno N. Kobayashi S, et al: Endoscopic pancreatocholangiography. Gastroenterology 63:217-226, 1972.
9. Rosch T, Meining A, Fruhmorgen S, et al: A prospective comparison of the diagnostic accuracy of ERCP, MRCP, CT, and EUS in biliary strictures. Gastrointest Endosc 55:870-876, 2002.
10. Park MS, Kim TK, Kim KW, et al: Differentiation of extrahepatic bile duct cholangiocarcinoma from benign stricture: Findings at MRCP versus ERCP. Radiology 33:234-240, 2004.
11. Patel T, Singh P: Cholangiocarcinoma: Emerging approaches to a challenging cancer. Curr Opin Gastroenterol 23:317-323, 2007.
12. Kokubo T, Itai Y, Ohtomo K, et al: Mucin-hypersecreting intrahepatic biliary neoplasms. Radiology 168:609-614, 1988.
13. Lim JH, Yoon KH, Kim SH, et al: Intraductal papillary mucinous tumor of the bile ducts. RadioGraphics 24:53-66, 2004.
14. Levy AD: Invited commentary. RadioGraphics 24:66-67, 2004.
15. Fulcher AS, Turner MA, Franklin KJ, et al: Primary sclerosing cholangitis: Evaluation with MR cholangiography—a case-control study. Radiology 215:71-80, 2000.
16. Vitellas KM, El-Dieb A, Vaswani KK, et al: MRCP in patients with primary sclerosing cholangitis: Interobserver variability and comparison with endoscopic ERCP. AJR 179:399-407, 2002.
17. Abdo AA, Bain VG, Kichian K, Lee SS. Evolution of autoimmune hepatitis to primary sclerosing cholangitis: A sequential syndrome. Hepatology 36:1393-1399, 2002.
18. Perdigoto R, Carpenter HA, Czaja AJ. Frequency and significance of chronic ulcerative colitis in severe corticosteroid-treated autoimmune hepatitis. J Hepatol 14:325-331, 1992.
19. Nakazawa T, Ohara H, Sano H, et al: Cholangiography can discriminate sclerosing cholangitis with autoimmune pancreatitis from primary sclerosing cholangitis. Gastrointest Endosc 60:937-944, 2004.
20. Kloppel G, Luttges J, Lohr M, et al: Autoimmune pancreatitis: Pathological, clinical, and immunological features. Pancreas 27:14-19, 2003.
21. Altman C, Fabre M, Adrien C, et al: Cholangiographic features in fibrosis and cirrhosis of the liver. Dig Dis Sci 40:2128-2133, 1995.
22. Verbeek PC, van Leeuwen DJ, de Wit LT, et al: Benign fibrosing disease at the hepatic confluence mimicking Klatskin tumors. Surgery 112:866-872, 1992.
23. Enns R: AIDS cholangiopathy: "An endangered disease." Am J Gastroenterol 98:2111-2112, 2003.
24. Petersen BT: An evidence-based review of sphincter of Oddi dysfunction: Part I, presentations with "objective" biliary findings (types I and II). Gastrointest Endosc 59:525-534, 2004.
25. Petrozza JA, Dutta SK: The variable appearance of distal common bile duct stenosis in chronic pancreatitis. J Clin Radiol 7:447-450, 1985.
26. Bloom R, Sybert A, Mascatello VJ: Granulomatous biliary tract obstruction due to sarcoidosis. Report of a case and review of the literature. Am Rev Respir Dis 117:783-787, 1978.
27. Fujii T, Ishikawa T, Kanazumi N, et al: Analysis of clinicopathological features and predictors of malignancy in intraductal papillary mucinous neoplasms of the pancreas. Hepatogastroenterology 54:272-277, 2007.
28. Fan S-T, Lai ECS, Mok FPT, et al: Early treatment of acute biliary pancreatitis by endoscopic papillotomy. N Engl J Med 328:228-232, 1993.
29. Folsch UR, Nitsche R, Ludtke R, et al: German study group on acute biliary pancreatitis. Early ERCP and papillotomy compared with conservative treatment for acute biliary pancreatitis. N Engl J Med 336:237-242, 1997.
30. Lehman GA: Role of ERCP and other endoscopic modalities in chronic pancreatitis. Gastrointest Endosc 56:S237-S240, 2002.
31. Axon ATR: Endoscopic retrograde cholangiopancreatography in chronic pancreatitis. Cambridge classification. Radiol Clin North Am 27:39-50, 1989.
32. Nealon WH, Townsend CM Jr, Thompson JC: Preoperative endoscopic retrograde cholangiopancreatography (ERCP) in patients with pancreatic pseudocyst. Ann Surg 209:532-538, 1989.
33. O'Connor M, Kolars J, Ansel H, et al: Preoperative endoscopic retrograde cholangiopancreatography in the surgical management of pancreatic pseudocysts. Am J Surg 151:18-24, 1986.
34. Sahani DV, Kalva SP, Farrell J, et al: Autoimmune pancreatitis: Imaging features. Radiology 233:345-352, 2004.

35. Wakabayashi T, Kawaura Y, Satomura Y, et al: Clinical study of chronic pancreatitis with focal irregular narrowing of the main pancreatic duct and mass formation: Comparison with chronic pancreatitis showing diffuse irregular narrowing of the main pancreatic duct. Pancreas 25:283-289, 2002.

36. Kwon S, Kim MH, Choi EK: The diagnostic criteria for autoimmune chronic pancreatitis: It is time to make a consensus. Pancreas 34:279-286, 2007.

37. Shah JN, Kochman ML: Endoscopic management of biliary tract disease. Curr Opin Gastroenterol 17:468-473, 2001.

38. Brugge WR: Endoscopic techniques to diagnose and manage biliary tumors. J Clin Oncol 23:4561-4565, 2005.

39. de Bellis M, Fogel EL, Sherman S, et al: Influence of stricture dilation and repeat brushing on the cancer detection rate of brush cytology in the evaluation of malignant biliary obstruction. Gastrointest Endosc 58:176-182, 2003.

40. Ponchon T, Pilleul F: Diagnostic ERCP. Endoscopy 34:29-42, 2002.

41. Domagk D, Poremba C, Dietl KH, et al: Endoscopic transpapillary biopsies and intraductal ultrasonography in the diagnostics of bile duct strictures: A prospective study. Gut 51:240-244, 2002.

42. Soehendra N: Common areas of interest between interventional biliary radiology and endoscopy. AJR 164:547-551, 1995.

43. Martin RC II, Vitale GC, Reed DN, et al: Cost comparison of endoscopic stenting vs surgical treatment for unresectable cholangiocarcinoma. Surg Endosc 16:667-670, 2002.

44. Flamm CR, Mark DH, Aronson N: Evidence-based assessment of ERCP approaches to managing pancreaticobiliary malignancies. Gastrointest Endosc 56(6 Suppl):S218-S225, 2002.

45. Costamagna G, Pandolfi M, Mutignani M, et al: Long-term results of endoscopic management of postoperative bile duct strictures with increasing numbers of stents. Gastrointest Endosc 54:162-168, 2001.

46. Kahl S, Zimmermann S, Glasbrenner B, et al: Treatment of benign biliary strictures in chronic pancreatitis by self-expandable metal stents. Dig Dis 20:199-203, 2002.

47. Sandha GS, Bourke MJ, Haber GB: Endoscopic therapy for bile leak based on a new classification: Results in 207 patients. Gastrointest Endosc 60:567-574, 2004.

48. Lew RJ, Kochman ML: Endoscopic management of biliary disease. Curr Opin Gastroenterol 16:454-460, 2000.

49. Baillie J: Sphincter of Oddi dysfunction: Overdue for an overhaul. Am J Gastroenterol 100:1217-1220, 2005.

50. Nealon WH, Walser E: Duct drainage alone is sufficient in the operative management of pancreatic pseudocyst in patients with chronic pancreatitis. Ann Surg 237:614-620, 2003.

51. Varadarajulu S, Noone TC, Tutuian R, et al: Predictors of outcome in pancreatic duct disruption managed by endoscopic transpapillary stent placement. Gastrointest Endosc 61:568-575, 2005.

52. Gabbrielli A, Pandolfi M, Mutignani M, et al: Efficacy of main pancreatic-duct endoscopic drainage in patients with chronic pancreatitis, continuous pain, and dilated duct. Gastrointest Endosc 61:576-581, 2005.

53. Gleeson FC, Topazian M: Endoscopic retrograde cholangiopancreatography and endoscopic ultrasound for diagnosis of chronic pancreatitis. Curr Gastroenterol Rep 9:123-129, 2007.

54. Teh SH, Sheppard BC, Mullins RJ, et al: Diagnosis and management of blunt pancreatic ductal injury in the era of high-resolution computed axial tomography. Am J Surg 193:641-643, 2007.

55. Canty TG Sr., Weinman D: Treatment of pancreatic duct disruption in children by an endoscopically placed stent. J Pediatr Surg 36:345-348, 2001.

56. Enns R, Eloubeidi MA, Mergener K, et al: ERCP-related perforations: Risk factors and management. Endoscopy 34:293-298, 2002.

57. Rochester JS, Jaffe DL: Minimizing complications in endoscopic retrograde cholangiopancreatography and sphincterotomy. Gastrointest Endosc Clin N Am 17:105-127, 2007.

Magnetic Resonance Cholangiopancreatography

Ann S. Fulcher, MD • Mary Ann Turner, MD

Since the first clinical application of magnetic resonance cholangiopancreatography (MRCP) in the early 1990s, MRCP has evolved from a technique with questionable potential for imaging the biliary tract and pancreatic duct to one that is now recognized as a pivotal tool for diagnosing pancreaticobiliary disease. In fact, the evolution of MRCP has been such that at many centers MRCP has replaced diagnostic endoscopic retrograde cholangiopancreatography (ERCP) in a number of clinical scenarios.

For many years, ERCP has been considered the standard of reference for imaging the biliary tract and pancreatic duct due to its ability to render high-quality images of the ducts. However, ERCP is an invasive examination associated with complications that occur in up to 5% of all attempts and that range from subclinical to life threatening.[1] Those complications include pancreatitis, hemorrhage, cholangitis, and gastrointestinal tract perforation.

The relatively rapid acceptance of MRCP is related, in large part, to its ability to provide images of the ducts similar to ERCP. These images can be obtained without the associated complications of ERCP while offering comparable sensitivity, specificity, and accuracy. In addition, MRCP is readily performed in the outpatient setting and does not expose patients to ionizing radiation. In most instances, performance of MRCP does not require administration of sedation. In contrast to ERCP, MRCP readily depicts ducts proximal to a high-grade obstruction as well as ducts in patients with surgical alterations of the biliary tract and gastrointestinal tract such

as biliary-enteric anastomoses. Although ERCP yields exquisite images of the ductal systems, it provides no direct information about the solid organs and vessels of the abdomen. However, when MRCP is performed in conjunction with conventional MR and, when necessary, MR angiography (MRA), a comprehensive examination is achieved. This information assists in determining resectability of neoplasms such as pancreatic carcinoma and in detecting complications of primary sclerosing cholangitis such as cirrhosis and cholangiocarcinoma.

TECHNIQUE

Before the acquisition of the MRCP, many advocate the use of heavily T2-weighted, non–fat-suppressed sequences such as the half-Fourier acquisition single-shot turbo spin-echo (HASTE) sequence in order to provide an overview of the entire abdomen (Fig. 77-1A). These comprehensive images allows for visualization of the solid organs as well as the pancreaticobiliary tract and gallbladder. The MRCP is then acquired. This can be achieved by using a two-dimensional (2D), heavily T2-weighted, fat-suppressed, breath-hold sequence. This sequence can provide single thick slab images with slice thicknesses ranging from 10 to 70 mm and in multiple thin slab images with slice thicknesses ranging from 2 to 5 mm[2,3] (Fig. 77-1B–D). The images depict the biliary tract, pancreatic duct, and gallbladder as high signal intensity structures. Multiple acquisitions are conducted in the coronal and

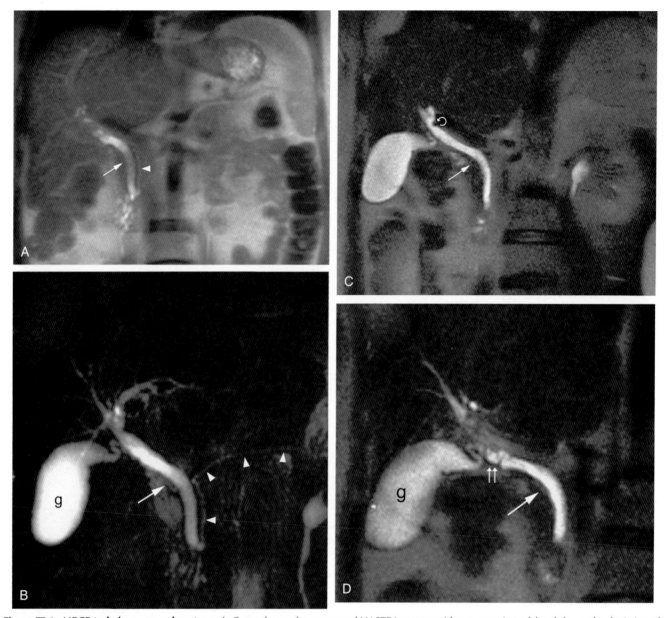

Figure 77-1. MRCP technique: normal anatomy. A. Coronal, non–fat-suppressed HASTE image provides an overview of the abdomen by depicting of the liver and spleen as well as the distal half of the bile duct (*arrow*) and pancreatic duct (*arrowhead*) in the head of the pancreas. **B.** Coronal, fat-suppressed, thick-slab (40 mm) MRCP shows the intrahepatic bile ducts, extrahepatic bile duct (*arrow*), pancreatic duct (*arrowheads*), and gallbladder (g) in a single image. **C.** Coronal-oblique, fat-suppressed, thin-slab (5 mm) MRCP demonstrates the finer details of the extrahepatic bile duct (*arrow*) compared with the thick-slab MRCP. Extrinsic compression (*curved arrow*) of the proximal extrahepatic bile duct by the crossing hepatic artery is noted. **D.** Coronal-oblique, fat-suppressed, thin-slab (5 mm) MRCP reveals the gallbladder (g), cystic duct (*double arrow*) and a portion of the extrahepatic bile duct (*arrow*).

coronal-oblique planes in order to optimally image the ducts. In addition, the axial plane is useful in distinguishing stones, which layer in the dependent portion of the duct, from pneumobilia, which is nondependent. In general, the thin slab images allow for improved delineation of the finer details of the ductal systems, while the thick slab images provide comprehensive views of the ducts that assist in the depiction of diffuse ductal diseases such as primary sclerosing cholangitis. Although the thin slab images may be manipulated with a maximum intensity projection algorithm (MIP), most diagnostic decisions are made directly from the 2D images. When interpreting MIP images, it should be remembered that at times the high signal intensity that is characteristic of MIPs

may obscure subtle intraductal filling defects such as small stones.

More recently, three-dimensional (3D) sequences used in conjunction with respiratory triggering, thin sections (1-2 mm), and high matrices have been used to generate MRCPs. With this technique, the source images can be viewed as individual images much like MRCPs acquired with 2D sequences. The advantage of 3D imaging is that it yields isotropic images that can be reformatted in any plane, thereby obviating the need to acquire images in multiple planes.

Some investigators advocate the performance of contrast-enhanced MRCP with 3D T1-weighted sequences and hepatocyte-specific, manganese-based contrast agents that are excreted into the biliary tract. This technique has been shown useful in the detection of biliary complications following laparoscopic cholecystectomy and in depicting the intrahepatic bile ducts in living liver transplant donor candidates.[4,5] Another development is the use of gadobenate dimeglumine, which offers the combined advantages of an extracellular agent such as gadolinium and an intrabiliary agent. Preliminary data suggest that gadobenate dimeglumine may be able to provide a comprehensive preoperative evaluation of the liver, bile ducts, and vessels in living donor–related liver transplantation candidates.[6]

CLINICAL APPLICATIONS

Bile Duct Calculi

Historically, many patients with suspected choledocholithiasis and a negative sonogram or CT underwent diagnostic ERCP to determine the presence or absence of stones. The introduction of MRCP provided a long-awaited, noninvasive alternative to diagnostic ERCP for the detection and exclusion of common bile duct stones. However, in order for MRCP to gain widespread acceptance, it had to compare favorably with ERCP. In an analysis of 72 patients studied with intraoperative cholangiography and ERCP, Frey and associates[7] found a sensitivity of 90% and a specificity of 98% for ERCP in the setting of suspected choledocholithiasis.

Initial reports of MRCP in the detection of common bile duct stones noted sensitivities as low as 81%.[8] However, technical advances in MR hardware and the introduction of sequences that allowed for breath-hold imaging and that suppressed artifacts arising from surgical clips and bowel gas improved MRCP image quality substantially and, in turn, enhanced the MRCP diagnosis of common bile duct stones. Subsequent studies performed with state-of-the-art scanners and sequences demonstrated sensitivities of 90% to 100%, specificities of 92% to 100%, and positive predictive value of 96% to 100% matching and in most cases exceeding those of ERCP.[2,9-13] Although many physicians focus on the sensitivity offered by a technique, it is equally important to consider the negative predictive value. The negative predictive values of MRCP are high, ranging from 96% to 100%.[2,11,14] Therefore, if an MRCP is interpreted as negative for common duct stones, then one can be confident that stones are not present in most cases and ERCP can be avoided.[2,14] In fact, one of the major benefits of MRCP in the setting of suspected biliary calculi is the reduction of unnecessary ERCPs.[13]

In the setting of symptomatic gallstones, MRCP has been shown to be highly accurate in the detection of coexistent choledocholithiasis in patients with high, moderate, and low risks for harboring common bile duct stones based on clinical, laboratory, and sonographic findings.[9] Kim and colleagues[9] recommend that MRCP be performed prior to cholecystectomy in patients with a moderate or high risk of common bile duct stones in an effort to reduce morbidity associated with undetected choledocholithiasis and to decrease the performance of purely diagnostic ERCPs.

In addition to the detection of common bile duct stones, MRCP performs well in the detection of intrahepatic stones. One study revealed that the sensitivity and specificity of MRCP for detecting intrahepatic stones was 97% and 93%, respectively, while those of ERCP were 59% and 97%, respectively.[15]

Both extrahepatic or intrahepatic bile duct stones are seen as well-defined, low signal intensity fillings defects in the high signal intensity bile (Fig. 77-2). MRCP has been shown to detect stones as small as 2 mm even in normal-caliber ducts.[2] Although the coronal and coronal oblique planes demonstrate stones in most instances, at times acquiring MRCPs in the axial plane is helpful in detecting small stones and in differentiating stones that lie in the dependent portion of the duct from pneumoblia that lies in the nondependent portion of the duct (Fig. 77-3).

Although MRCP performs well in the detection of stones, one must be aware of mimickers of stones that may result in false-positive diagnoses. These include pneumobilia, en face visualization of the cystic duct inserting into the bile duct, and compression of the duct by an adjacent vessel.[16,17]

Neoplasms

MRCP is very useful in the evaluation of suspected malignancies of the pancreaticobiliary tract. Multiple studies have demonstrated the ability of MRCP to determine the presence, level, and type of malignancy with a high degree of accuracy.[2,18-21] In a study of 62 patients with biliary obstruction, Kim and associates[22] demonstrated that the addition of conventional MRI to MRCP significantly improves the accuracy in the diagnosis of pancreaticobiliary disease and aids in the differentiation of benign from malignant causes of biliary dilatation. When MRCP is supplemented by conventional MR and MRA, a comprehensive examination results that allows for depiction of the pancreaticobiliary tract, solid organs, and vasculature and, in turn, permits determination of resectability of neoplastic disease. This comprehensive examination is most beneficial for patient care. Specifically, if a neoplasm is deemed resectable, then the patient should be spared an unnecessary ERCP and stent placement as there is no established role for preoperative biliary drainage by ERCP in these patients.[23] On the other hand, if a neoplasm is deemed unresectable, the patient may be spared an unnecessary laparotomy. An additional advantage of MRCP offered in the setting of pancreaticobiliary tract malignancies is that MRCP depicts the entire biliary and pancreatic duct even in the presence of high-grade strictures and allows for planning of surgical and percutaneous interventions.

Pancreatic Carcinoma

With the use of newer scanners and sequences that afford high-resolution imaging, MRCP readily not only identifies the ductal dilatation that occurs as the result of pancreatic carcinoma but also depicts the malignant ductal strictures themselves and localizes the neoplastic process to the pancreas. MRCP depicts bile duct involvement by pancreatic carcinoma as an abrupt transition between the dilated suprapancreatic duct and the markedly narrowed intrapancreatic duct, often referred to as a rat-tail configuration (Fig. 77-4A and B). In the case of pancreatic head carcinoma obstructing the bile and pancreatic ducts, MRCP shows dilatation of both ducts, known as the *double duct sign*. While the double duct sign is often seen in association with pancreatic head carcinoma, it is a nonspecific sign that may occur due to a benign or malignant process involving the pancreatic head.[24] In the setting of carcinoma involving the body or tail of the pancreas, the ductal

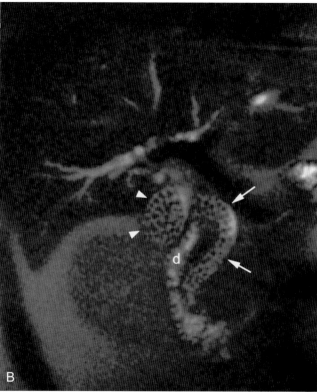

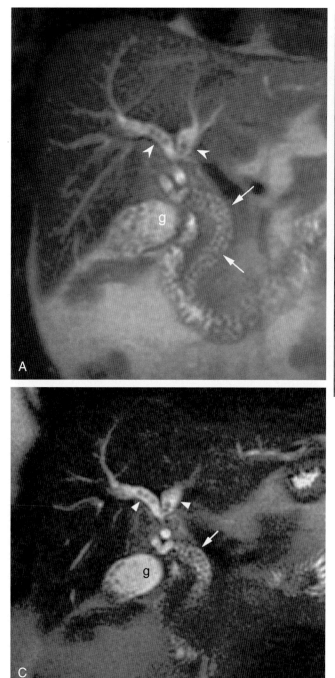

Figure 77-2. Multiple extrahepatic and intrahepatic bile duct calculi.
A. Coronal HASTE MRCP provides a comprehensive image of the abdomen by showing multiple, low signal intensity calculi in the dilated extrahepatic bile duct (*arrows*), central intrahepatic ducts (*arrowheads*), and gallbladder (g). **B.** Thin-slab MRCP focusing on the distal bile duct (*arrows*) shows multiple, intraductal calculi as well as gallbladder calculi (*arrowheads*). The fluid-filled duodenum (d) is noted. C. Thin-slab MRCP shows stones in the proximal extrahepatic bile duct (*arrow*), central intrahepatic ducts (*arrowheads*), and gallbladder (g).

dilatation is limited to the pancreatic duct proximal to the obstruction. Because the entire pancreatic duct is rarely depicted on a single 2D MRCP image, axial MRCPs are often useful in demonstrating the obstructing tumor and the transition between the dilated and nondilated pancreatic duct.

The performance of conventional MR and MR angiography in conjunction with MRCP allows for determination of resectability (Fig. 77-4C and D). T1-weighted, fat-suppressed, unenhanced sequences are particularly helpful in depicting even small tumors in the pancreas. Pancreatic adenocarcinomas present as areas of low signal intensity against the high signal intensity of the normal pancreatic parenchyma. In addition to detecting the primary tumor, conventional MR

is useful in detecting liver metastases, nodal enlargement, and peritoneal carcinomatosis. The MRA plays an important role in detecting neoplastic involvement of the celiac axis, hepatic artery, superior mesenteric artery and vein, and portal vein. In patients with unresectable pancreatic carcinoma, MRCP yields information important in planning palliative and endoscopic drainage procedures.

In a prospective study of 124 patients with clinical and sonographic findings strongly suggestive of pancreatic neoplasia, Adamek and associates[20] showed that the sensitivity and specificity of MRCP in diagnosing pancreatic carcinoma (84% and 97%) exceeded those of ERCP (70% and 94%). Unfortunately, the distinction between pancreatic carcinoma

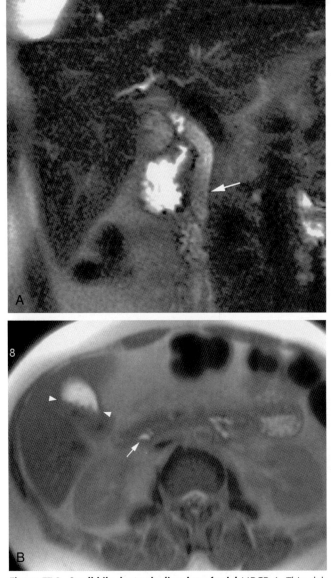

Figure 77-3. Small bile duct calculi: value of axial MRCP. A. Thin-slab MRCP reveals small, low signal intensity foci in the distal bile duct (*arrow*) later removed during therapeutic ERCP. **B.** Axial MRCP shows the small, low signal intensity stones layering in the dependent portion of the intrapancreatic bile duct (*arrow*) with high signal intensity bile seen anteriorly in the duct. A similar stone-bile level (*arrowheads*) is noted in the gallbladder.

and focal chronic pancreatitis will likely remain problematic in some instances despite technical improvements in MR, MRA, and MRCP.[25]

Cholangiocarcinoma—Hilar and Distal Duct

Hilar cholangiocarcinoma is the most common manifestation of cholangiocarcinoma and is depicted as a high-grade stricture of the confluence of the right and left hepatic ducts. In the past, much emphasis was placed on palliative procedures such as percutaneous biliary drainages and endoscopic stent placement due to the poor prognosis associated with this neoplasm. However, with the advent of improved surgical and radiation therapy techniques, greater attention is directed

toward imaging examinations that assist in determining disease extent and resectability.

Over the past decade, MRCP has become an important tool in the evaluation of cholangiocarcinoma in general and hilar cholangiocarcinoma in particular. As with direct cholangiography, MRCP demonstrates marked narrowing of the proximal extrahepatic bile duct, the often-present extension to the central right and left hepatic ducts, and dilatation proximal to the obstruction[26,27] (Fig. 77-5A and B). Because MRCP readily depicts ducts proximal to high-grade obstructions that are often not opacified at ERCP, MRCP typically is superior in determining disease extent and resectability.[26,27] As with other pancreaticobiliary tract neoplasms, MR performed in association with MRCP offers the added advantage of demonstrating disease that has extended from the ducts into the liver and adjacent structures (Fig. 77-5C). These factors have allowed MRCP to assume an important role in the noninvasive evaluation of hilar cholangiocarcinoma and to facilitate planning of surgical, percutaneous and radiation therapy procedures.

Cholangiocarcinomas that involve the extrahepatic duct distal to the confluence are often referred to as the distal duct type. Distal duct cholangiocarcinomas are seen as strictures or intraductal, polypoid masses resulting in biliary obstruction on both MRCP and ERCP. In a retrospective study of 50 patients with extrahepatic bile duct cholangiocarcinoma and 23 patients with benign strictures, MRCP was shown to have an accuracy comparable to ERCP in making the distinction between cholangiocarcinoma and benign strictures.[28] Distal duct cholangiocarcinoma confined to the intrapancreatic bile duct is difficult to distinguish from pancreatic head carcinoma with either MRCP or ERCP (Fig. 77-6). However, the clinical impact of this deficiency is of no consequence, as the treatment of both tumors is identical and is predicated upon resectablity.

Intraductal Papillary Mucinous Neoplasm of the Pancreas

Intraductal papillary mucinous neoplasms (IPMNs) are categorized as main duct type and branch duct type depending on the duct of origin and may be benign or malignant. IPMNs are well demonstrated on MRCP because they produce mucin, which appears as high signal intensity within the ducts.[29-31] MRCP can reveal the entire spectrum of IPMNs—main duct dilatation, cystic dilatation of the side branches, nodules, septa, and intraductal filling defects—and is able to show communication between the tumor and the pancreatic duct (Fig. 77-7). A study of 34 IPMNs in 31 patients examined with MRCP and correlated with surgical and pathologic findings revealed that intraductal filling defects are indicative of malignancy and that diffuse dilatation of the main pancreatic duct greater than 15 mm in main duct–type tumors is strongly associated with malignancy.[29] In branch duct–type tumors, the absence of main pancreatic duct dilatation suggests a benign tumor.

Congenital Anomalies

Choledochal/Bile Duct Cysts

MRCP reliably detects choledochal or bile duct cysts in adults and children and provides diagnostic information equivalent

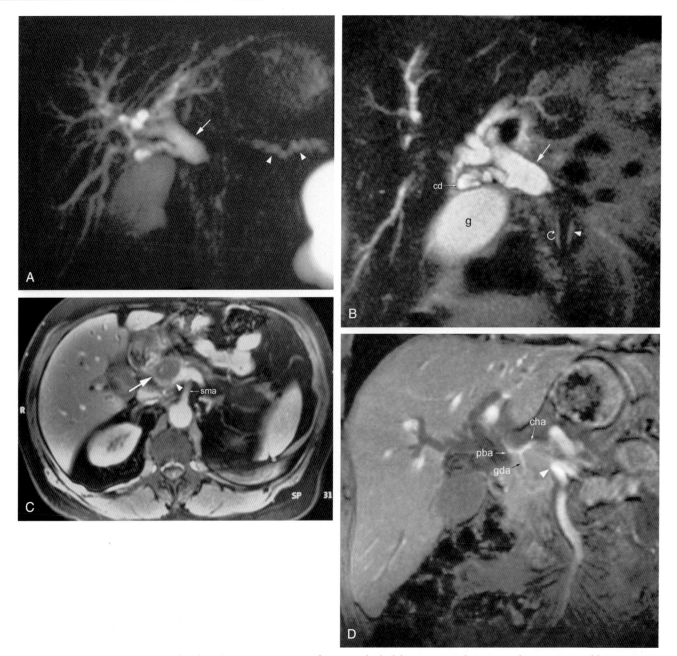

Figure 77-4.   Unresectable pancreatic head carcinoma: MRCP, MR, and MRA. A. Thick-slab MRCP provides a comprehensive image of the pancreatico-biliary tract that demonstrates high-grade obstruction of the extrahepatic bile duct (*arrow*) and minor dilatation of the pancreatic duct (*arrowheads*) in the body and tail of the pancreas. **B.** Thin-slab MRCP reveals the finer details of the ductal systems and shows that the extrahepatic bile duct (*arrow*) is obstructed at the pancreatic head. The intrapancreatic portion of the bile duct (*curved arrow*) and the pancreatic duct (*arrowhead*) in the head of the pancreas are narrowed. The distended gallbladder (g) and cystic duct (cd) are shown. **C.** Transverse, T1-weighted, enhanced abdominal MR shows that the cause of the obstruction is a low signal intensity pancreatic head carcinoma (*arrow*) that has occluded the distal superior mesenteric vein (*arrowhead*). There is no evidence of tumor surrounding the superior mesenteric artery (sma). **D.** Coronal, 2D time-of-flight MR angiogram shows that the pancreatic head mass has occluded the distal superior mesenteric vein (*arrowhead*) and is inseparable from the common hepatic artery (cha), proximal proper hepatic artery (pha), and gastroduodenal artery (gda). (From Fulcher AS, Turner MA: MR cholangiopancreatography. Radiol Clin N Am 40:1367, 2002, with permission.)

to that of ERCP without the risk of complications[32-34] (Fig. 77-8). MRCP nicely delineates the extent of the cyst, and detects anomalous pancreaticobiliary junctions (APBJs), critical factors in planning cyst excision and bile duct reconstruction.[35] Matos[32] and Yu[36] and their colleagues note that the accuracy of MRCP in the detection of APBJ is comparable to that of ERCP. For these reasons, MRCP has been proposed as the imaging modality of choice in evaluation of choledochal cysts.[33,34]

Anatomic Variants of the Biliary Tract

Anatomic variations of the biliary tract occur in up to 37% of individuals and include crossover anomalies such as the

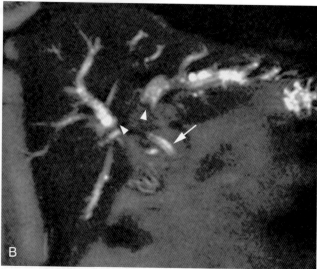

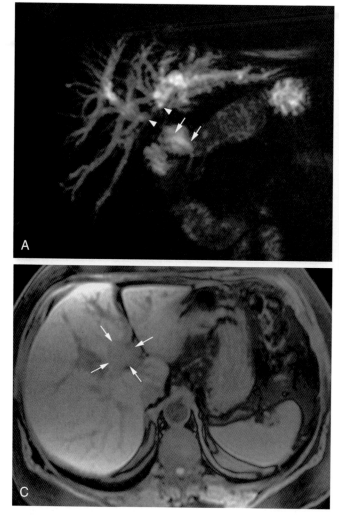

Figure 77-5. Hilar cholangiocarcinoma. A. Coronal thick-slab MRCP reveals high-grade, isolated obstructions of the central right and left hepatic ducts (*arrowheads*) due to hilar cholangiocarcinoma. The extrahepatic bile duct distal to the obstruction (*arrows*) is seen adjacent to the fluid-filled duodenal bulb. **B.** Thin-slab MRCP reveals in greater detail the points of obstruction of the central right and left hepatic ducts (*arrowheads*) due to cephalad extension of the hilar cholangio-carcinoma. The normal-caliber extrahepatic bile duct (*arrow*) located just distal to the tumor is noted. **C.** T1-weighted, fat-suppressed, unenhanced abdominal MR reveals low signal intensity tumor (*arrows*) that has extended beyond the confines of biliary tract to invade the hepatic parenchyma.

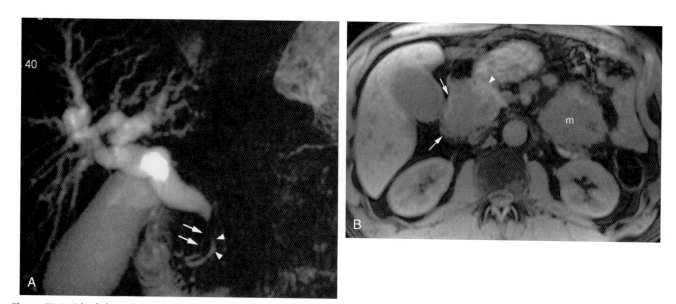

Figure 77-6. Distal duct cholangiocarcinoma. A. Coronal thick-slab MRCP shows a high-grade stricture of the intrapancreatic bile duct (*arrows*) resulting in proximal biliary ductal dilatation. The pancreatic duct (*arrowheads*) is normal in caliber. **B.** T1-weighted, fat-suppressed, unenhanced abdominal MR shows a mass (*arrows*) involving the pancreatic head that is low in signal intensity relative to the adjacent normal pancreatic parenchyma (*arrowhead*). Pathologic analysis revealed cholangiocarcinoma. A large, mesenteric metastasis (m) was present at the time of diagnosis.

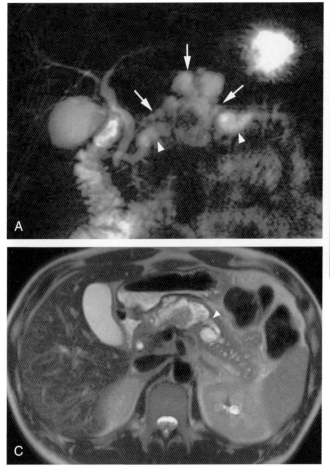

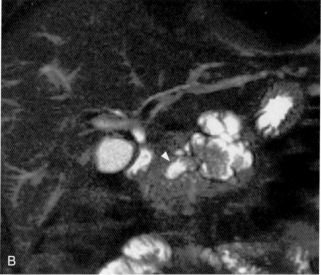

Figure 77-7. Malignant intraductal papillary mucinous neoplasm of the pancreas (IPMN)—main duct type. A. Coronal thick-slab MRCP reveals a large cystic lesion (*arrows*) that contains nodular filling defects and that communicates with the main pancreatic duct in the pancreatic body (*arrowheads*). Incidental note is made of pancreas divisum as evidenced by the horizontal orientation of the main pancreatic duct in the pancreatic head. **B–D.** Coronal-oblique thin-slab MRCP, axial HASTE image, and axial T1-weighted, fat-suppressed, contrast-enhanced abdominal MR show in detail the lobulated cystic mass and the nodular filling defects as well as the dilated pancreatic duct (*arrowhead*) from which the mass arises.

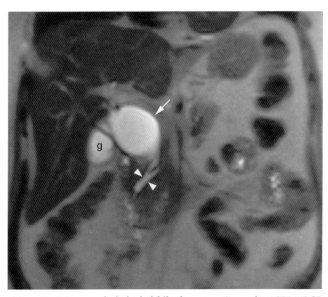

Figure 77-8. Type 1 choledochal/bile duct cyst. Coronal HASTE MRCP shows fusiform dilatation of the majority of the extrahepatic bile duct (*arrow*) indicative of a type 1 choledochal/bile duct cyst. An anomalous pancreaticobiliary junction (*arrowhead*) is present. The gallbladder (g) is noted.

dorsocaudal branch of the right hepatic duct entering the central left hepatic duct, trifurcations, accessory or aberrant ducts that enter the extrahepatic duct or cystic duct, and cystic duct variants.[37] MRCP has been shown to accurately detect these variants.[38,39] Although ductal variants are usually of no consequence in the general population, they are of great importance in patients undergoing cholecystectomy because some variants predispose to ductal injury.[40] Ductal variants posed less risk in the era of open cholecystecomy because the biliary tract was directly visualized. Because most cholecystectomies are now performed laparoscopically, which does not provide the same degree of direct visualization of the biliary tract, the preoperative recognition of these anomalies is paramount. The increasing use of right lobe living donor liver transplantations has heightened the awareness of radiologists and surgeons alike to the importance of ductal variants such as crossover anomalies (Fig. 77-9). While these variants do not preclude transplantation in most cases, preoperative identification assists in avoiding inadvertent surgical ligations. Awareness of ductal variants is also important in the planning of complex percutaneous and endoscopic biliary interventions.

Pancreas Divisum

Pancreas divisum occurs in up to 5.5% to 7.5% of the general population.[41,42] While most individuals with pancreas divisum

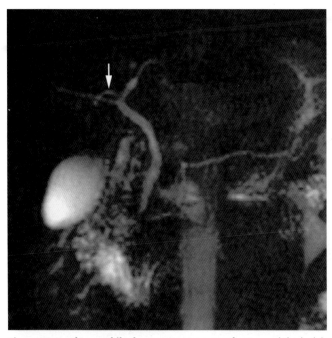

Figure 77-9. Aberrant bile duct: crossover anomaly. Coronal thick-slab MRCP depicts the dorsocaudal branch of the right hepatic duct (*arrow*) entering the central left hepatic duct.

readily achieved by reviewing the images at a workstation rather than on film.

POSTOPERATIVE ALTERATIONS OF THE PANCREATICOBIILIARY TRACT AND GASTROINTESTINAL TRACT

Multiple studies have demonstrated the utility and accuracy of MRCP in depicting normal anatomy and pathology of the ducts in patients with postsurgical alterations of the pancreaticobiliary tract and gastrointestinal tract.[44-49] Specifically, MRCP readily depicts anastomotic strictures, intraductal stones, bile plugs, and, in some cases, injuries of the ducts following cholecystectomy with sensitivities up to 100%.[45,47]

MRCP has been used successfully in imaging patients following cadaveric and living donor liver transplantations, hepatic resection, pancreatoduodenectomym and creation of a biliary-enteric anastomosis (Fig. 77-11). MRCP is particularly well suited to the evaluation of patients with biliary-enteric anastomoses. The performance of ERCP is very difficult, if not impossible, in these patients due to the surgical alteration of the gastrointestinal tract. Before the advent of MRCP, depiction of the ducts in patients with biliary-enteric anastomoses could be achieved only by performing percutaneous transhepatic cholangiography (PTC), which is an invasive procedure associated with complications such as bleeding and infection.

MRCP is often used to evaluate the biliary tract following liver transplantation for complications such as strictures and stones. ERCP and PTC may lead to serious complications in this seriously ill patient group. If complications are detected with MRCP, patients can then be referred for therapeutic ERCP or PTC. If complications are excluded with MRCP, then the patient will be spared an unnecessary invasive procedure and its attendant complications.

Although MRCP is highly accurate in imaging the postoperative pancreaticobiliary tract, it is associated with a number of pitfalls and limitations. In patients with biliary enteric anastomoses, pneumobilia may mimic intraductal stones as both appear as filling defects in the high signal intensity bile. In most instances, the distinction can be made by observing that pneumobilia is located in the nondependent portion of the duct and stones are located in the dependent portion of the duct on coronal and axial images.[44,45] A limitation of MRCP in the assessment of biliary strictures was noted by Ward and associates,[44] who found a tendency of MRCP to overestimate the grade of strictures. Finally, despite studies reporting the utility of MRCP performed in conjunction with agents excreted into the biliary tract for detecting bile duct leaks,[50] it is likely that diagnostic ERCP will remain the primary means of detecting leaks as ERCP also provides access for stent placement in the same setting as the diagnostic ERCP. Nevertheless, MRCP has emerged as an accurate, noninvasive means of evaluating the ductal systems in patients with postsurgical alterations of the pancreaticobiliary tract and gastrointestinal tract.

PRIMARY SCLEROSING CHOLANGITIS

For many years, direct cholangiography (ERCP and, to a lesser extent, PTC) has been considered the imaging examination

demonstrate no symptoms referable to the pancreas, others present with recurrent bouts of unexplained pancreatitis. In fact, pancreas divisum has been shown to occur with significantly greater frequency in patients with acute idiopathic pancreatitis than in the general population.[41] MRCP has gained an increasingly prominent role in the evaluation of patients with idiopathic pancreatitis because this technique can detect pancreas divisum and other ductal anomalies with a high degree of accuracy. Unlike diagnostic ERCP, MRCP does not carry the risk of inducing pancreatitis in this group of patients who are predisposed to its development.[34] Manfredi and associates[43] note that secretin-enhanced MRCP assists in identifying pancreas divisum and sometimes the associated cystic dilatation of the distal dorsal duct often referred to as a "santorinicele." MRCP is also useful in delineating the ductal changes of chronic pancreatitis: dilatation of the main pancreatic duct, side branch ectasia, strictures, and intraductal stones. In addition, T1-weighted, fat-suppressed, unenhanced sequences performed in conjunction with MRCP assist in detecting associated pancreatic atrophy and fibrosis. With these sequences, fibrosis is seen as decreased signal intensity of the pancreas compared with that of the liver secondary to replacement of aqueous protein in the pancreatic parenchyma.

At MRCP, pancreas divisum is usually depicted as two separate drainage systems of the pancreas (Fig. 77-10). The larger dorsal duct drains the majority of the pancreas and enters the duodenum at the minor papilla cephalad to and separate from the ventral duct. The smaller ventral duct drains the inferior pancreatic head and uncinate process and enters the duodenum at the major ampulla with the distal bile duct. In order to establish the diagnosis of pancreas divisum at MRCP, care must be taken to ensure that there is no communication between the dorsal and ventral ducts. This is most

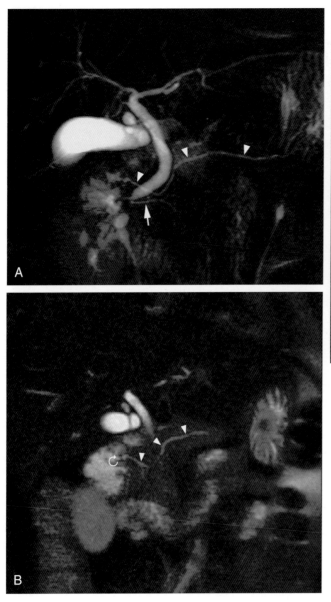

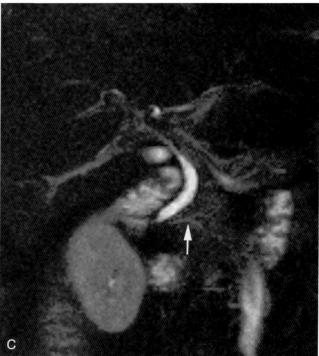

Figure 77-10. Pancreas divisum. A. Coronal thick-slab MRCP demonstrates two separate ducts draining the pancreas—the larger dorsal duct (*arrowheads*) and the smaller ventral duct (*arrow*). **B.** Coronal-oblique thin-slab MRCP shows in greater detail the dorsal duct (*arrowheads*) with a horizontal orientation in the pancreatic head entering the duodenum at the minor ampulla (*curved arrow*). **C.** Coronal-oblique thin-slab MRCP 5 mm posterior to **B** depicts the smaller ventral duct (*arrow*) joining with the distal bile duct to enter the duodenum at the major ampulla distal to and separate from the dorsal duct (*arrow*).

of choice for diagnosing primary sclerosing cholangitis (PSC) and following its progression. Although both ERCP and PTC yield exquisite images of the ducts and provide access for interventions, these invasive examinations place patients at risk of complications such as cholangitis, pancreatitis, hemorrhage, and infection. MRCP provides a noninvasive diagnostic alternative for evaluating patients with known or suspected PSC.

Direct cholangiographic findings of PSC include multifocal, annular strictures of the intrahepatic and/or extrahepatic bile ducts that alternate with normal or slightly dilated segments resulting in a "beaded" appearance of the ducts; diverticulum-like outpouchings; mural irregularities; and pruning of the peripheral intrahepatic bile ducts.[51] Due to technical advances, MRCP is able to depict the fine details of the ducts and to demonstrate the typical ductal abnormalities of PSC with a high degree of accuracy[52-55] (Figs. 77-12 and 77-13). Vitellas and associates[54,55] showed that MRCP is superior to ERCP for depicting intrahepatic ducts and intra-

hepatic ductal strictures in part due to the ability of MRCP to demonstrate ducts proximal to a high-grade obstruction. MRCP also is useful in detecting recurrent PSC following liver transplantation as MRCP readily depicts the intrahepatic and extrahepatic bile ducts in these patients with a biliary enteric anastomosis who would otherwise require PTC to visualize the biliary tract.[52] Despite the utility and accuracy of MRCP in the diagnosis of PSC, the distinction between a benign stricture due to PSC and a malignant stricture related to cholangiocarcinoma will likely remain problematic.

A prospective case-control study in which 102 patients (34 with PSC and 68 age-matched controls with hepatobiliary diseases other than PSC) underwent MRCP revealed that MRCP was accurate in detecting and localizing PSC.[52] In the detection of PSC, the sensitivities were 85% and 88%; specificities, 92% and 97%; positive predictive value, 85% and 94%; and negative predictive value, 93% and 94%, for two independent readers. Interobserver agreement was excellent. All false-positive diagnoses were related to distortion of the ducts

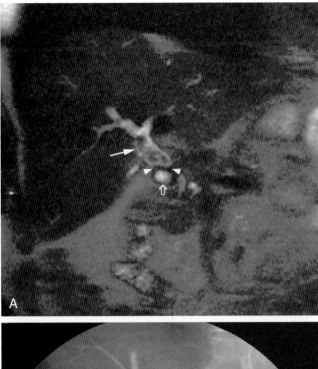

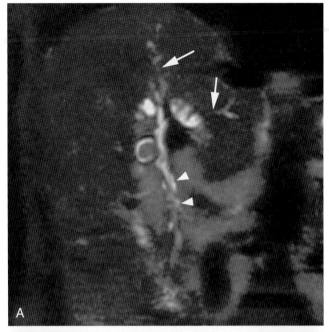

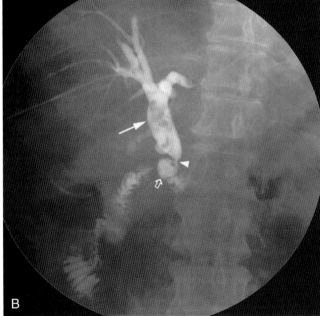

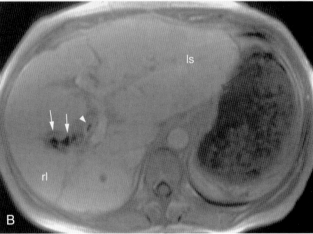

Figure 77-12. Intrahepatic and extrahepatic primary sclerosing cholangitis. A. Coronal-oblique thin-slab MRCP depicts strictures (*arrows*) and dilatation of the intrahepatic bile ducts and marked mural irregularity and diverticulum-like outpouchings of the extrahepatic bile duct (*arrowheads*). **B.** Axial, T1-weighted, fat-suppressed, enhanced image of the abdomen reveals cirrhosis complicating PSC as evidenced by lateral segment (ls) hypertrophy and right lobe (rl) atrophy. Thickening and enhancement of the wall of the proximal extrahepatic bile duct (*arrowhead*) is noted as well as intrahepatic ductal dilatation (*arrows*).

Figure 77-11. Biliary enteric anastomotic stricture and intraductal stones. A. Coronal-oblique thin-slab MRCP shows dilatation of the residual proximal extrahepatic bile duct (*arrow*) indicative of a stricture of the biliary enteric anastomosis (*arrowheads*). Intraductal filling defects represent stones that have formed secondary to stasis. The rounded, fluid-filled structure (*open arrow*) represents the proximal aspect of the jejunal limb. **B.** Direct cholangiogram performed during a percutaneous biliary drainage procedure confirms the biliary enteric anastomotic stricture (*arrowhead*), ductal dilatation (*arrow*), intraductal stones, and the proximal jejunal limb (*curved arrow*). Slow passage of contrast material occurred from the duct to the jejunal limb.

by underlying cirrhosis. Five false-negative diagnoses occurred and were related to marked cirrhosis that obscured the intrahepatic ducts in two patients and early changes of PSC that were limited to the peripheral intrahepatic ducts in the remaining three patients.

Talwalkar and colleagues[53] proposed to determine the average cost per correct diagnosis using MRCP or ERCP as the initial means for the diagnosis of PSC. Seventy-three patients with clinically suspected PSC formed the basis of the study; the prevalence of PSC in the study cohort was 32%. The sensitivity and specificity of MRCP for the diagnosis of PSC were 82% and 98%, respectively. Talwalkar and colleagues[53] found that the accuracy of MRCP was comparable to that of ERCP and that MRCP resulted in cost savings when used as the initial test for diagnosing PSC in their study population. The value of MRCP in the patient with PSC is enhanced when it is performed in association with conventional MR, which can demonstrate cirrhosis, portal hypertension, cholangiocarcinoma, and hepatic parenchymal changes related to

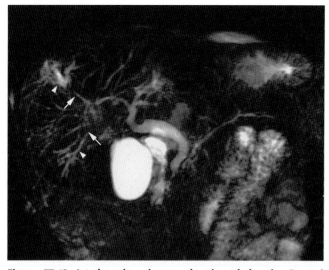

Figure 77-13. Intrahepatic primary sclerosing cholangtis. Coronal thick-slab MRCP shows dilatation (*arrowheads*) and multiple strictures (*arrows*) of the intrahepatic bile ducts. The slightly dilated extrahepatic bile duct shows no evidence of PSC.

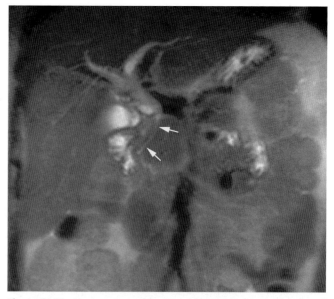

Figure 77-14. Acute pancreatitis. Coronal HASTE reveals dilatation of the intrahepatic and suprapancreatic bile ducts and smooth, narrowing of the intrapancreatic bile duct (*arrows*) due to compression by the edematous pancreas. MRCP performed after resolution of acute pancreatitis showed that the duct returned to a normal caliber (not shown).

altered perfusion and inflammation of the bile ducts[56] (see Fig. 77-12B).

MRCP has emerged as a viable alternative to ERCP in the diagnosis of PSC. The utility of MRCP in this setting is related to its accuracy and noninvasive nature and its ability to depict ducts proximal to a high-grade obstruction. As a result, at some centers ERCP is now used primarily as a means of gaining access for interventions such as stent placements instead of a diagnostic tool. Nevertheless, ERCP, and at times PTC, may prove useful in detecting PSC in problematic cases such as in patients with minor changes of PSC limited to the peripheral intrahepatic ducts.

PANCREATITIS

Acute Pancreatitis

The primary role of MRCP in the setting of acute pancreatitis is the identification of structural abnormalities that predispose to its development such as common bile duct stones, pancreas divisum, and tumors obstructing the pancreatic duct. Depending on the severity of acute pancreatitis, edema of the pancreatic parenchyma may result in smooth narrowing of the intrapancreatic bile duct and/or pancreatic duct (Fig. 77-14). When these findings are confined to the pancreatic head, the ductal narrowing and the pancreatic parenchymal enlargement may mimic pancreatic neoplasia. However, as the edema resolves, the ducts and parenchyma return to normal.

In the setting of acute pancreatitis, the combined MR and MRCP examinations assist in detecting the cause, extent and complications of this inflammatory process. Pancreatic enlargement, simple and infected fluid collections, necrosis, thoracopancreatic fistulas, vascular thrombosis, and pseudo-aneurysms are well depicted. In fact, MR has been shown to perform well compared with CT in the evaluation of inflammation and necrosis and in the calculation of the severity index.[57] In one study, MR was superior to CT and ultra-

sonography for detecting debris in subacute pancreatic fluid collections an important factor when assessing drainability.[58]

Therefore, an examination including both MRCP and MR, and at times MRA, yields information about the pancreaticobiliary tract, pancreatic parenchyma, surrounding tissues, and vessels in a single, noninvasive examination that does not expose the patient to radiation or iodinated contrast material. The disadvantages of MR in the setting of severe acute pancreatitis include the fact that MR cannot be performed as rapidly as CT and that CT must be used for critically ill patients on ventilators.

Chronic Pancreatitis

MRCP and MR have emerged as useful tools in demonstrating the ductal and parenchymal manifestations of chronic pancreatitis.[2,59] The ductal features include dilatation of the main pancreatic duct and its sidebranches, mural irregularity, intraductal stones, and strictures of the pancreatic duct and the intrapancreatic bile duct (Fig. 77-15). A study comparing ERCP with MRCP revealed very good correlation between MRCP and ERCP findings but showed that both modalities failed to depict some abnormalities depicted by the other technique.[59] In another study including 36 patients with chronic pancreatitis, MRCP identified biliary strictures in 16 and correctly classified all as benign.[2] MRCP provides accurate delineation of the ductal manifestations of chronic pancreatitis, which is of utmost importance in determining disease extent and in planning surgical drainage procedures. In some instances, MRCP demonstrates the ductal disease more completely than ERCP because MRCP readily demonstrates ducts proximal to a high-grade stricture.

MR is helpful in showing parenchymal manifestations of chronic pancreatitis such as atrophy and fibrosis, as well as

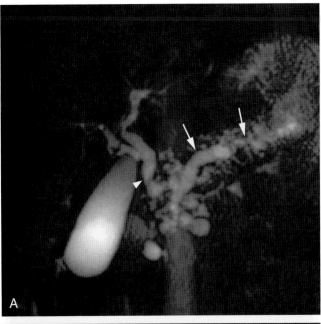

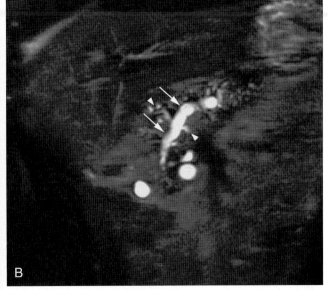

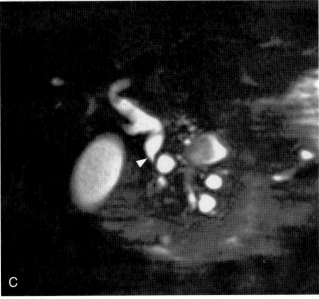

Figure 77-15. Chronic pancreatitis. A. Coronal thick-slab MRCP provides a comprehensive image of the pancreaticobiliary tract by demonstrating marked dilatation of the main pancreatic duct (*arrows*) and its side branches and a tapered stricture of the intrapancreatic bile duct (*arrowhead*). **B.** Coronal-oblique thin-slab MRCP focusing on the pancreatic body depicts the dilatation of the main pancreatic duct (*arrow*), its dilated side branches (*arrowheads*) and rounded, intrapancreatic pseudocysts. **C.** Coronal-oblique thin-slab MRCP focusing on the pancreatic head demonstrates the smooth, tapered stricture of the intrapancreatic bile duct (*arrowhead*) that results in dilatation of the suprapancreatic bile duct. Again noted are the intrapancreatic pseudocysts and the dilated pancreatic duct and its side branches.

peripancreatic findings such as pseudocysts. T1-weighted, fat-suppressed, unenhanced sequences are particularly useful in delineating fibrosis and atrophy that result in diminished signal intensity of the pancreas relative to the liver owing to the replacement of aqueous protein in the pancreatic parenchyma.[60,61] Pancreatic enhancement is reduced in patients with chronic calcific pancreatitis compared with glands without calcifications.[60] This is presumably due to more severe disease.

Secretin-enhanced MRCP improves visualization of the morphologic features of chronic pancreatitis and can assist in determining function of the exocrine pancreas by assessing fluid output.[62-64]

GALLBLADDER DISEASES

Sonography is the initial modality used to evaluate the gallbladder as it is accurate, relatively inexpensive, readily available, rapidly performed, and portable. MRCP is quite useful in detecting abnormalities including gallstones, acute cholecystitis (Fig. 77-16), gangrenous cholecystitis, gallbladder perforation, Mirizzi syndrome, carcinoma, and adenomyomatosis (Fig. 77-17).[2,65-67] In the setting of acute cholecystitis, MRCP coupled with MR is useful in detecting bile duct stones and in demonstrating extension of infection from the gallbladder to the adjacent hepatic parenchyma. When gallbladder carcinoma is suspected, MR used in conjunction with MRCP assists in staging.[66-68]

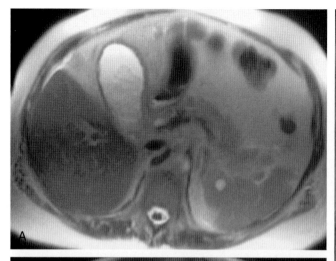

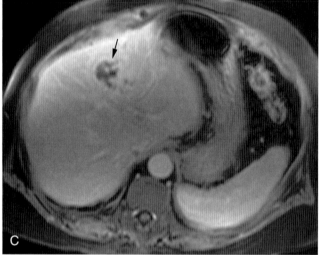

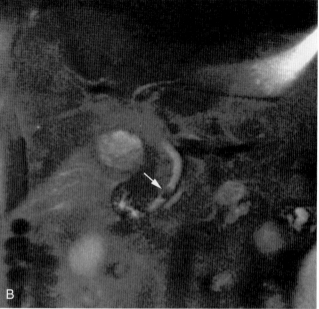

Figure 77-16. Acute cholecystitis complicated by a bile duct stone and hepatic abscess. A. Axial HASTE image shows a distended gallbladder with a thick, irregular wall indicative of acute cholecystitis in this patient with right upper quadrant pain and leukocytosis. **B.** Coronal-oblique thin-slab MRCP shows a distal common bile duct stone (*arrow*). **C.** Axial, T1-weighted, fat-suppressed, enhanced MR reveals an abscess (*arrow*) in the medial segment of the left hepatic lobe due to contiguous extension from the gallbladder.

Figure 77-17. Adenomyomatosis. MIP image shows the "pearl necklace" sign of adenomyomatosis that represents dilated Rokitansky-Aschoff sinuses (*arrows*). Artifactual narrowing of the proximal extrahepatic bile duct (*arrowhead*) is noted.

References

1. Masci E, Toti G, Mariani A, et al: Complications of diagnostic and therapeutic ERCP: A prospective multicenter study. Am J Gastroenterol 96:417-423, 2001.

2. Fulcher AS, Turner MA, Capps GW, et al: Half-Fourier RARE MR cholangiopancreatography: Experience in 300 subjects. Radiology 207:21-32, 1998.

3. Irie H, Honda H, Tajima T, et al: Optimal MR cholangiopancreatographic sequence and its clinical application. Radiology 206:379-387, 1998.

4. Park MS, Kim KW, Yu JS, et al: Early biliary complications of laparoscopic cholecystectomy: Evaluation on T2-weighted MR cholangiography in conjunction with mangafodipir trisodium-enhanced 3D T1-weighted MR cholangiography. AJR 183:1559-1566, 2004.

5. Lee VS, Krinsky GA, Nazzaro CA, et al: Defining intrahepatic biliary anatomy in living liver transplant donor candidates at mangafodipir trisodium-enhanced MR cholangiography versus conventional T2-weighted MR cholangiography. Radiology 233:659-666, 2004.

6. Lim JS, Kim MJ, Kim JH, et al: Preoperative MRI of potential living-donor-related liver transplantation using a single dose of gadobenate dimeglumine. AJR 185:424-431, 2005.

7. Frey CF, Burbige EJ, Meinke WB, et al: Endoscopic retrograde cholangio-pancreatography. Am J Surg 144:109-114, 1982.

8. Guibaud L, Bret PM, Reinhold C, et al: Bile duct obstruction and choledocholithiasis: Diagnosis with MR cholangiography. Radiology 197;109-115, 1995.

9. Kim JH, Kim MJ, Park SI, et al: MR cholangiography in symptomatic gallstones: Diagnostic accuracy according to clinical risk group. Radiology 224:410-416, 2002.

10. Soto JA, Barish MA, Alvarez O, et al: Detection of choledocholithiasis with MR cholangiography: Comparison of three-dimensional fast spin-echo and single- and multisection half-Fourier rapid acquisition with relaxation enhancement sequences. Radiology 215:737-745, 2000.

11. Reinhold C, Taourel P, Bret PM, et al: Choledocholithiasis: Evaluation of MR cholangiography for diagnosis. Radiology 209:435-442, 1998.

12. Becker CD, Grossholz M, Becker M, et al: Choledocholithiasis and bile duct stenosis: Diagnostic accuracy of MR cholangiopancreatography. Radiology 205:523-530, 1997.

13. Demartines N, Eisner L, Schnabel K, et al: Evaluation of magnetic resonance cholangiography in the management of bile duct stones. Arch Surg 135:148-152, 2000.

14. Hallal AH, Amortegui JD, Jeroukhimov IM, et al: Magnetic resonance cholangiopancreatography accurately detects common bile duct stones in resolving gallstone pancreatitis. J Am Coll Surg 200:869-875, 2005.

15. Kim TK, Kim BS, Kim JH, et al: Diagnosis of intrahepatic stones: Superiority of MR cholangiography over endoscopic retrograde cholangio-pancreatography. AJR 179:429-434, 2002.

16. Fulcher AS, Turner MA: Pitfalls of magnetic resonance cholangio-pancreatography (MRCP). J Comput Assist Tomogr 22:845-850, 1998.

17. Watanabe Y, Dohke M, Ishimori T, et al: Pseudo-obstruction of the extrahepatic bile duct due to artifact from arterial pulsatile compression: A diagnostic pitfall of MR cholangiography. Radiology 214:856-860, 2000.

18. Soto JA, Alvarez O, Lopera JE, et al: Biliary obstruction: findings at MR cholangiography and cross-sectional MR imaging. RadioGraphics 20:353-366, 2000.

19. Schwartz LH, Coakley FV, Sun Y, et al: Neoplastic pancreaticobiliary duct obstruction: Evaluation with breath-hold MR cholangiography. AJR 170:1491-1495, 1998.

20. Adamek HE, Albert J, Breer H, et al: Pancreatic cancer detection with magnetic resonance cholangiopancreatography and endoscopic retrograde cholangiopancreatography: A prospective controlled study. Lancet 356:190-193, 2000.

21. Magnuson TH, Bender JS, Duncan MD, et al: Utility of magnetic resonance imaging in the evaluation of biliary obstruction. J Am Coll Surg 189:63-71, 1999.

22. Kim MJ, Mitchell DG, Ito K, et al: Biliary dilatation: Differentiation of benign from malignant causes—Value of adding conventional MR imaging to MR cholangiopancreatography. Radiology 214:173-181, 2000.

23. NIH state-of-the-science statement on endoscopic retrograde cholangio-pancreatography (ERCP) for diagnosis and therapy. NIH Consens State Sci Statements 19:1-26, 2002.

24. Plumley TF, Rohrmann CA, Freeny PC, et al: Double duct sign: Reassessed significance in ERCP. AJR 138:31-35, 1982.

25. Johnson PT, Outwater EK: Pancreatic carcinoma versus chronic pancreatitis: Dynamic MR imaging. Radiology 212:213-218, 1999.

26. Fulcher AS, Turner MA: HASTE MR cholangiography in the evaluation of hilar cholangiocarcinoma. AJR 169:1501-1505, 1997.

27. Lopera JE, Soto JA, Múnera F: Malignant hilar and perihilar biliary obstruction: Use of MR cholangiography to define the extent of biliary ductal involvement and plan percutaneous interventions. Radiology 220:90-96, 2001.

28. Park MS, Kim TK, Kim KW, et al: Differentiation of extrahepatic bile duct cholangiocarcinoma from benign stricture: Findings at MRCP versus ERCP. Radiology 233:234-240, 2004.

29. Irie H, Honda H, Aibe H, et al: MR cholangiopancreatographic differentiation of benign and malignant intraductal mucin-producing tumors of the pancreas. AJR 174:1403-1408, 2000.

30. Koito K, Namieno T, Ichimura T, et al: Mucin-producing pancreatic tumors: Comparison of MR cholangiopancreatography with endoscopic retrograde cholangiopancreatography. Radiology 208:231-237, 1998.

31. Onaya H, Itai Y, Niitsu M, et al. Ductectatic mucinous cystic neoplasms of the pancreas: Evaluation with MR cholangiopancreatography. AJR 171:171-177, 1998.

32. Matos C, Nicaise N, Devière J, et al: Cholecohal cysts: Comparison of findings at MR cholangiopancreatography and endoscopic retrograde cholangiopancreatography in eight patients. Radiology 209:443-448, 1998.

33. Lam WWM, Lam TPW, Saing H, et al: MR cholangiography and CT cholangiography of pediatric patients with choledochal cysts. AJR 173:401-405, 1999.

34. Yu J, Turner MA, Fulcher AS, et al: Congenital anomalies and normal variants of the pancreaticobiliary tract and the pancreas in adults. Part 2: Pancreatic duct and pancreas. AJR 187:1544-1553, 2006.

35. Okada A, Oguchi Y, Kamata S, et al: Common channel syndrome-diagnosis with endoscopic retrograde cholangiopancreatography and surgical management. Surgery 93:634-642, 1983.

36. Yu ZL, Zhang LJ, Fu JZ, et al: Anomalous pancreaticobiliary junction: Image analysis and treatment principles. Hepatobiliary Pancreat Dis Int 3:136-139, 2004.

37. Huang TL, Cheng YF, Chen CL, et al: Variants of the bile ducts: Clinical application in the potential donor of living-related hepatic transplantation. Transplant Proc 28:1669-1670, 1996.

38. Taourel P, Bret PM, Reinhold C, et al: Anatomic variants of the biliary tree: Diagnosis with MR cholangiopancreatography. Radiology 199:521-527, 1996.

39. Fulcher AS, Szucs RA, Bassignani MJ, et al: Right lobe living donor liver transplantation: Preoperative evaluation of the donor with MR imaging. AJR 176:1483-1491, 2001.

40. Suhocki PV, Meyers WC: Injury to aberrant bile ducts during cholecystectomy: A common cause of diagnostic error and treatment delay. AJR 172:955-959, 1999.

41. Bernard JP, Sahel J, Giovannini M, et al: Pancreas divisum is a probable cause of acute pancreatitis: A report of 137 cases. Pancreas 5:248-254, 1990.

42. Millbourn E: On the excretory ducts of the pancreas in man, with special reference to their relations to each other, to the common bile duct and to the duodenum. Acta Anat 9:1-34, 1950.

43. Manfredi R, Costamagna G, Brizi MG, et al: Pancreas divisum and "santorinicele": Diagnosis with dynamic MR cholangiopancreatography with secretin stimulation. Radiology 217:403-408, 2000.

44. Ward J, Sheridan MB, Guthrie JA, et al: Bile duct strictures after hepatobiliary surgery: Assessment with MR cholangiography. Radiology 231:101-108, 2004.

45. Fulcher AS, Turner MA: Orthotopic liver transplantation: Evaluation with MR cholangiography. Radiology 211:715-722, 1999.

46. Valls C, Alba E, Cruz M, et al: Biliary complications after liver transplantation: Diagnosis with MR cholangiopancreatography. AJR 184:812-820, 2005.

47. Tang Y, Yamashita Y, Arakawa A, et al: Pancreaticobiliary ductal system: Value of half-Fourier rapid acquisition with relaxation enhancement MR cholangiopancreatography for postoperative evaluation. Radiology 215:81-88, 2000.

48. Ragozzino A, De Ritis R, Mosca A, et al: Value of MR cholangiography in patients with iatrogenic bile duct injury after cholecystectomy. AJR 183:1567-1572, 2004.

49. Monill J, Pernas J, Clavero J, et al: Pancreatic duct after pancreato-duodenectomy: Morphologic and functional evaluation with secretin-stimulated MR pancreatography. AJR 183:1267-1274, 2004.

50. Vitellas KM, El-Dieb A, Vaswani KK, et al: Using contrast-enhanced MR cholangiography with IV mangafodipir trisodium (Teslascan) to evaluate bile duct leaks after cholecystectomy: A prospective study of 11 patients. AJR 179:409-416, 2002.

51. MacCarty RL, LaRusso NF, Wiesner RH, Ludwig J: Primary sclerosing cholangitis: Findings on cholangiography and pancreatography. Radiology 149:39-44, 1983.

52. Fulcher AS, Turner MA, Franklin KJ, et al: Primary sclerosing cholangitis: Evaluation with MR cholangiography—a case-control study. Radiology 215:71-80, 2000.

53. Talwalkar JA, Angulo P, Johnson CD, et al: Cost-minimization analysis of MRC versus ERCP for the diagnosis of primary sclerosing cholangitis. Hepatology 40:39-45, 2004.

54. Vitellas KM, El-Dieb A, Vaswani KK, et al: MR cholangiopancreatography in patients with primary sclerosing cholangitis: Interobserver variability and comparison with endoscopic retrograde cholangiopancreatography. AJR 179:399-407, 2002.

55. Vitellas KM, Enns RA, Keogan MT, et al: Comparison of MR cholangiopancreatographic techniques with contrast-enhanced cholangiography in the evaluation of sclerosing cholangitis. AJR 178:327-334, 2002.

56. Elsayes KM, Oliveira EP, Narra VR, et al: MR and MRCP in the evaluation of primary sclerosing cholangitis: Current applications and imaging findings. J Comput Assist Tomogr 30:398-404, 2006.

57. Lecesne R, Taourel P, Bret PM, et al: Acute pancreatitis: Interobserver agreement and correlation of CT and MR cholangiopancreatography with outcome. Radiology 211:727-735, 1999.

58. Morgan DE, Baron TH, Smith JK, et al: Pancreatic fluid collections prior to intervention: evaluation with MR imaging compared with CT and US. Radiology 203:773-778, 1997.

59. Sugiyama M, Haradome H, Atomi Y: Magnetic resonance imaging for diagnosing chronic pancreatitis. J Gastroenterol 42 (Suppl 17):108-112, 2007.

60. Czako L: Diagnosis of early-stage chronic pancreatitis by secretin-enhanced magnetic resonance cholangiopancreatography. J Gastroenterol 42 (Suppl 17):113-117, 2007.

61. Gallix BP, Bret PM, Atri M, et al: Comparison of qualitative and quantitative measurements on unenhanced T1-weighted fat saturation MR images in predicting pancreatic pathology. J Magn Reson Imaging 21:583-589, 2005.

62. Kinney TP, Punjabi G, Freeman M: Technology insight: Applications of MRI for the evaluation of benign disease of the pancreas. Nat Clin Pract Gastroenterol Hepatol 4:148-159, 2007.

63. Heverhagen JT, Müller D, Battmann A, et al: MR hydrometry to assess exocrine function of the pancreas: Initial results of noninvasive quantification of secretion. Radiology 218:61-67, 2001.

64. Manfredi R, Costamagna G, Brizi MG, et al: Severe chronic pancreatitis versus suspected pancreatic disease: Dynamic MR cholangiopancreatography after secretin stimulation. Radiology 214:849-855, 2000.

65. Choi BW, Kim MJ, Chung JJ, et al: Radiologic findings of Mirizzi syndrome with emphasis on MRI. Yonsei Med J 41:144-146, 2000.

66. Schwartz LH, Black J, Fong Y, et al: Gallbladder carcinoma: Findings at MR imaging with MR cholangiopancreatography. J Comput Assist Tomogr 26:405-410, 2002.

67. Haradome H, Ichikawa T, Sou H, et al: The pearl necklace sign: An imaging sign of adenomyomatosis of the gallbladder at MR cholangiopancreatography. Radiology 227:80-88, 2003.

68. Hellund JC, Skattum J, Buanes T, Geitung JT. Secretin-stimulated magnetic resonance cholangiopancreatography of patients with unclear disease in the pancreaticobiliary tract. Acta Radiol 48:135-141, 2007.

Anomalies and Anatomic Variants of the Gallbladder and Biliary Tract

Richard M. Gore, MD • Ann S. Fulcher, MD •
Andrew J. Taylor, MD • Gary G. Ghahremani, MD

There are many congenital abnormalities of the gallbladder and bile ducts (Fig. 78-1), which, excluding biliary atresia and choledochal cysts, are usually of no clinical or functional significance.[1] These anomalies are usually found in the course of evaluating biliary disease in an adult patient and are of interest primarily to the surgeon, who must deal with the anatomic variation during the course of surgery.[2,3]

EMBRYOLOGY

When the human embryo is 2.5 mm in size (Fig. 78-2A), a bifid bud forms along the anterior margin of the primitive foregut and proliferates laterally into the septum transversum. The more cephalad of these two diverticula is responsible for the formation of the liver and intrahepatic bile ducts, whereas the caudal diverticulum develops into the gallbladder and extrahepatic biliary tree. At the 5-mm stage of development (Fig. 78-2B), the originally hollow primordium of the gallbladder and common bile duct becomes occluded with endodermal cells but is soon revacuolated. If recanalization is incomplete, a compartmentalized multiseptate gallbladder results. A single, transversely oriented septum results in the

phrygian cap deformity, whereas longitudinal septa produce a bifid or triple gallbladder. The lumen of the common bile duct is reestablished at the 7.5-mm stage and the gallbladder and duodenal lumen somewhat later. Bile is secreted by the 12th week.[4,5]

At the 10- to 15-mm stage (6-7 weeks), the gallbladder has formed and is connected to the duodenum by a canalized choledochocystic duct. This duct originates from the lateral aspect of the primitive foregut and eventually terminates on the medial or posteromedial aspect of the descending portion of the duodenum after the foregut completes its 270-degree rotation (Fig. 78-2C and D).[4-6]

The formation of the intrahepatic ducts is preceded by the development of the portal and hepatic veins and the formation of the hepatocytes and Kupffer cells. The intrahepatic ducts by the 18-mm stage consist only of a blindly ending solid core of cells that extends from the junction of the cystic and common ducts toward the liver hilum. At the point of contact between this blindly ending ductal anlage and the hepatocytes, the intrahepatic ducts develop along the framework of the previously formed portal vein branches similar to vines on a trellis. Significant variation in the configuration

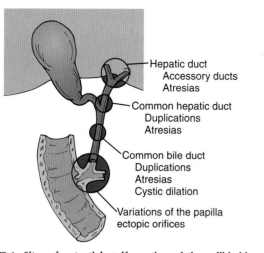

Figure 78-1. Sites of potential malformation of the gallbladder and biliary tract. (From Gray SW, Skandalakis JR: Embryology for Surgeons. Philadelphia, WB Saunders, 1972.)

Hepatic duct
Accessory ducts
Atresias

Common hepatic duct
Duplications
Atresias

Common bile duct
Duplications
Atresias
Cystic dilation

Variations of the papilla
ectopic orifices

of the intrahepatic ducts can be accounted for by the unpredictable manner in which they wind around preexisting portal veins.[4-6]

AGENESIS OF THE GALLBLADDER

Agenesis of the gallbladder is caused by failure of development of the caudal division of the primitive hepatic diverticulum or failure of vacuolization after the solid phase of embryonic development. Atresia or hypoplasia of the gallbladder also represents aborted development of the organ.[7-9] Other congenital anomalies are present in two thirds of these patients, including congenital heart lesions, polysplenia, imperforate anus, absence of one or more bones, and rectovaginal fistula.[10] There appears to be a genetic input as well, because several families with multiple individuals having agenesis have been identified.[10] This malformation is reported in 0.013% to 0.155% of autopsy series, but many of these cases are in stillborn and young infants. The surgical incidence of

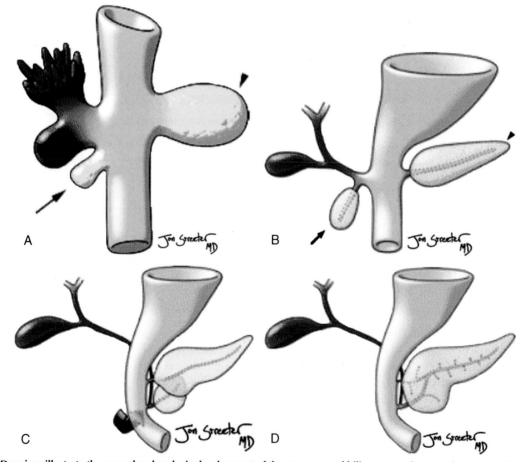

Figure 78-2. Drawings illustrate the normal embryologic development of the pancreas and biliary tract. The ventral pancreatic bud (*arrow* in **A** and **B**) and biliary system arise from the hepatic diverticulum, and the dorsal pancreatic bud (*arrowhead* in **A** and **B**) arises from the dorsal mesogastrium. **C.** After clockwise rotation of the ventral bud around the caudal part of the foregut, there is fusion of the dorsal pancreas (located anterior) and ventral pancreas (located posterior). **D.** Finally, the ventral and dorsal pancreatic ducts fuse, and the pancreas is predominantly drained through the ventral duct, which joins the common bile duct (CBD) at the level of the major papilla. The dorsal duct empties at the level of the minor papilla. (From Mortele KR, Rochar TC, Streeter JL, et al: Multimodality imaging of pancreatic and biliary congenital anomalies. RadioGraphics 26:715-731, 2006.)

gallbladder agenesis is approximately 0.02%.[10,11] Nearly two thirds of adult patients with agenesis of the gallbladder have biliary tract symptoms, and extrahepatic biliary calculi are reported in 25% to 50% of these patients.[12-14]

Preoperative diagnosis of gallbladder agenesis is difficult, and the absence of the gallbladder is often an intraoperative finding.[2,8,14] Ultrasound or CT may suggest the diagnosis, but this disorder is usually diagnosed at surgery when the gallbladder is not found at cholangiography.[15] Intraoperative ultrasound may be helpful in establishing the diagnosis and excluding a completely intrahepatic gallbladder.[16] Agenesis of the gallbladder is a rare cause of false-positive hepatobiliary scintiscans.[17]

DUPLICATION OF THE GALLBLADDER

Gallbladder duplication occurs in about 1 in 4000 people and 4.8% of domestic animals.[18-20] This anomaly is caused by incomplete revacuolization of the primitive gallbladder, resulting in a persistent longitudinal septum that divides the gallbladder lengthwise. Another possible mechanism is the occurrence of separate cystic buds. To establish the diagnosis, two separate gallbladder cavities, each with its own cystic duct, must be present. These duplicated cystic ducts may enter the common duct separately or form a Y configuration before a common entrance.[21]

Most reported cases of gallbladder duplication have a clinical picture of cholecystitis with cholelithiasis in at least one of the gallbladders. Sometimes one of the gallbladders appears normal on oral cholecystography, while the second, diseased, nonvisualized, and unsuspected gallbladder produces symptoms.[22-24]

A number of entities can mimic the double gallbladder at sonography: a folded gallbladder, bilobed gallbladder, choledochal cyst, pericholecystic fluid, gallbladder diverticulum, vascular band across the gallbladder, and focal adenomyomatosis.[25-28] Complications associated with double gallbladder include torsion and the development of papilloma, carcinoma, common duct obstruction, and secondary biliary cirrhosis.[27] Treatment of this disorder consists of removal of both gallbladders.

Triple and quadruple gallbladders have also been reported.[28] Diverticular gallbladders without cystic ducts are classified as accessory gallbladders.

ANOMALIES OF GALLBLADDER SHAPE

Phrygian Cap

Phrygian cap is the most common abnormality of gallbladder shape, occurring in 1% to 6% of the population.[29] It is named after the headgear worn by ancient Greek slaves as a sign of liberation. This deformity is characterized by a fold or septum of the gallbladder between the body and fundus. Two variations of this anomaly have been described. In the retroserosal or concealed type, the gallbladder is smoothly invested by peritoneum, and the mucosal fold that projects into the lumen may not be visible externally. In the serosal or visible type, the peritoneum follows the bend in the fundus, then reflects on itself as the fundus overlies the body. This anomaly is of no clinical significance unless it is mistaken for a layer of stones or hyperplastic cholecystosis.[3,15,24-29]

Multiseptate Gallbladder

The multiseptate gallbladder is a solitary gallbladder characterized by multiple septa of various sizes internally and a faintly bosselated surface externally.[28-30] The gallbladder is usually normal in size and position, and the chambers communicate with one another by one or more orifices from fundus to cystic duct. These septations lead to stasis of bile and gallstone formation.[31] On ultrasound studies, multiple communicating septations and locules are seen bridging the gallbladder lumen.[32] Oral cholecystography reveals the "honeycomb" multicystic character of the gallbladder. The sonographic differential diagnoses are desquamated gallbladder mucosa and hyperplastic cholecystoses.

Diverticula

Gallbladder diverticula are rare and usually clinically silent. They can occur anywhere in the gallbladder and are usually single and vary greatly in size. Congenital diverticula are true diverticula and contain all the mural layers, as opposed to the pseudodiverticula of adenomyomatosis, which have little or no smooth muscle in their walls. Acquired traction diverticula from adjacent adhesions or duodenal disease must be also be excluded.[7,8,15]

ABNORMALITIES OF GALLBLADDER POSITION

Wandering Gallbladder

When the gallbladder has an unusually long mesentery, it can "wander" or "float."[33-37] The gallbladder may "disappear" into the pelvis on upright radiographs or wander in front of the spine or to the left of the abdomen. Rarely, the gallbladder can herniate through the foramen of Winslow into the lesser sac. In these cases, cholecystography reveals an unusual angulation of the gallbladder, which lies parallel and adjacent to the duodenal bulb with its fundus pointing to the left upper quadrant. The herniation can be intermittent and may be responsible for abdominal pain. It is best seen using a barium meal in conjunction with an oral cholecystogram. Cross-sectional imaging may not be specific, showing only a cystic structure in the lesser sac.

Gallbladder Torsion

Three unusual anatomic situations give rise to torsion of the gallbladder, and they all produce twisting of an unusually mobile gallbladder on a pedicle: (1) a gallbladder that is completely free of mesenteric or peritoneal investments except for its cystic duct and artery, (2) a long gallbladder mesentery sufficient to allow twisting, and (3) the presence of large stones in the gallbladder fundus that cause lengthening and torsion of the gallbladder mesentery. Kyphosis, vigorous gallbladder peristalsis, and atherosclerosis have also been implicated as other predisposing or contributing factors.[38] The mesentery is sufficiently long to permit torsion in 4.5% of the population. Most cases of gallbladder torsion occur in women (female/male ratio of 3:1).[39] The usual preoperative diagnosis is acute cholecystitis. The presence of fever is variable, leukocytosis is common, and one third of patients have a right upper quadrant mass. Gangrene develops in more than 50% of cases and is extremely common when the pain has been present for more than 48 hours. On cross-sectional imaging, the gallbladder is distended and may have an unusual location and show mural thickening. The diagnosis is seldom made preoperatively, however.[40,41]

Ectopic Gallbladder

The gallbladder can be located in a variety of anomalous positions (Fig. 78-3). In patients with an intrahepatic gallbladder, the gallbladder is completely surrounded by hepatic parenchyma. The intrahepatic gallbladder usually presents little difficulty in imaging, but it may complicate the clinical diagnosis of acute cholecystitis because of a paucity of peritoneal signs resulting from the long distance between the gallbladder and peritoneum. This anomaly also makes cholecystectomy more difficult. On sulfur colloid scans, the intrahepatic gallbladder presents as a cold hepatic defect.

The gallbladder has also been reported in the following positions: suprahepatic, retrohepatic (Fig. 78-4), supradiaphragmatic, and retroperitoneal. In patients with cirrhosis, small or absent right lobes, or chronic obstructive pulmonary disease, the gallbladder together with the colon is often interposed between the liver and the diaphragm.[42] Left-sided gallbladders may occur in situs inversus or as an isolated finding. They can also lie in the falciform ligament, transverse mesocolon, and anterior abdominal wall.

ABNORMALITIES IN GALLBLADDER SIZE

Cholecystomegaly

Enlargement of the gallbladder has been reported in a number of disorders including diabetes (because of an autonomic neuropathy) and after truncal and selective vagotomy. The gallbladder also becomes larger than normal during pregnancy, in patients with sickle hemoglobinopathy, and in extremely obese people.[43-46]

Microgallbladder

In patients with cystic fibrosis, the gallbladder is typically small, trabeculated, contracted, and poorly functioning. It often contains echogenic bile, sludge, and cholesterol gallstones. These changes are presumably due to the thick, tenacious bile that is characteristic of this disease.[47,48]

BILIARY TRACT ANOMALIES

Anomalies of the biliary system are found in 2.4% of autopsies, 28% of surgical dissections, and 5% to 13% of operative cholangiograms.[6] The most common anomaly is an aberrant intrahepatic duct draining a circumscribed portion of the liver, such as an anterior or posterior segment right lobe duct that drains into the left main rather than the right main hepatic duct. The aberrant duct can join the common hepatic duct, common bile duct, or cystic duct or insert into a low

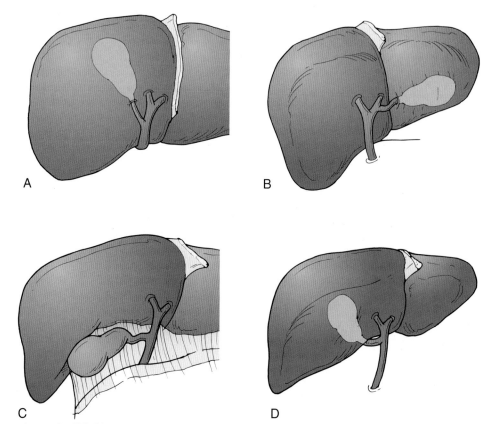

Figure 78-3. Common forms of gallbladder ectopia. A. Intrahepatic. **B.** Left sided. **C.** Transverse. **D.** Retrodisplaced. (**A** to **D** from Knight M: Anomalies of the gallbladder, bile ducts and arteries. In Smith R, Sherlock S [eds]: Surgery of the Gallbladder and Bile Ducts. London, Butterworth, 1981, pp 97-106.)

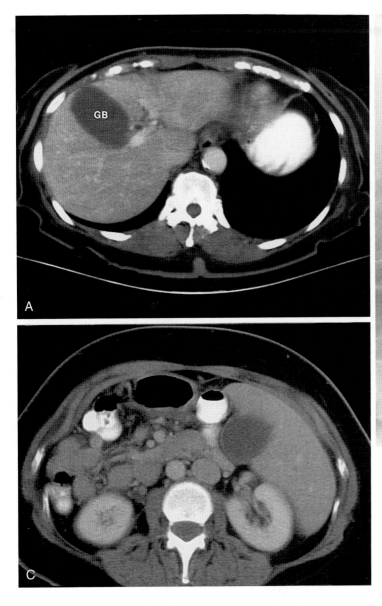

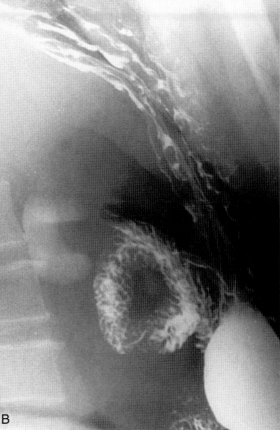

Figure 78-4. Gallbladder ectopia. A. Intrahepatic gallbladder (GB) demonstrated on CT scan. **B.** Retrohepatic gallbladder shown on an oral cholecystogram. **C.** Situs inversus with left-sided gallbladder.

right hepatic duct. Rarely, it may run through the gallbladder fossa or into the gallbladder, predisposing it to injury at cholecystectomy.

The hepatic ducts may join either higher or lower than normal. Surgical difficulties may arise when the cystic duct enters into a low inserting right hepatic duct or when the right hepatic duct enters into the cystic duct before joining the left hepatic duct. Duplications of the cystic duct and common bile duct are rare. Anomalies of cystic duct insertion (Fig. 78-5) occur as well.

Congenital tracheobiliary fistula is a rare disorder that presents with respiratory distress and cough with bilious sputum. The fistula begins near the carina, traverses the diaphragm, and usually communicates with the left hepatic duct. Pneumobilia may be seen on plain radiograph, and the diagnosis is confirmed with biliary scintigraphy.

Choledochal cysts, choledochoceles, and Caroli's disease are a part of a spectrum of biliary anomalies that produce dilatation of the biliary tree. They are discussed individually in the following section, and their relationship is illustrated in Figure 78-6.

Choledochal Cysts

Choledochal cysts are congenital cystic dilatations of any portion of the extrahepatic bile ducts, most commonly the main portion of the common bile duct.[49-55] It is postulated that this condition begins with an anomalous junction of the common bile duct and pancreatic duct proximal to the duodenal papilla (Fig. 78-7). Higher pressure in the pancreatic duct combined with an absent ductal sphincter allows free reflux of enzymes into the biliary tree, weakening the wall of the common bile duct. There is a 3:1 female predominance, and 60% of patients present before age 10, although choledochal cysts can present from birth to old age. This anomaly is associated with an increased incidence of gallbladder anomalies, other biliary anomalies (e.g., biliary stenosis or atresia), and congenital hepatic fibrosis. Complications of choledochal cysts in adults include rupture with bile peritonitis, secondary infection (cholangitis), biliary cirrhosis and portal hypertension, calculus formation, portal vein thrombosis, liver abscess, hemorrhage, and malignant transformation into cholangiocarcinoma.[55-57]

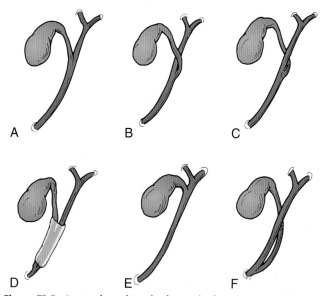

Figure 78-5. Anatomic variants in the cystic duct. Drawings illustrate how the cystic duct may insert into the extrahepatic bile duct with a shows right lateral insertion (A), anterior spiral insertion (B), posterior spiral insertion (C), low lateral insertion with a common sheath (D), proximal insertion (E), or low medial insertion (F). (From Turner MA, Fulcher AS: The cystic duct: Normal anatomy and disease processes. RadioGraphics 21:3-22, 2001.)

Newborns and infants present with obstructive jaundice.[54,55] Older children and adults may have the classic triad of right upper quadrant pain, intermittent jaundice, and a palpable right upper quadrant mass. In adult patients, a choledochal cyst is often first diagnosed on cross-sectional imaging. CT (Fig. 78-8) and ultrasound demonstrate a fluid-filled structure beneath the porta hepatis separate from the gallbladder that communicates with the hepatic ducts. An abrupt change in the caliber of the ducts occurs at the site of the cysts. Intrahepatic ductal dilatation may be present as well.

Cholangiography is necessary to confirm the diagnosis. It demonstrates a cystic structure 2 to 15 cm in diameter that communicates with the hepatic ducts. An abrupt change in ductal caliber occurs at the site of the cyst. Mild intrahepatic ductal dilatation, stones, or sludge may be present as well. Cholangiography is useful for fully defining ductal anatomy.

Upper gastrointestinal series may show a soft tissue mass in the right upper quadrant that causes anterior displacement of the second portion of the duodenum and antrum or inferior displacement of the duodenum or widening of the duodenal sweep.[54-56]

Ultrasound findings reflect the specific type of choledochal cyst, although a cystic extrahepatic mass is typically present. Often a portion of the proximal bile duct can be seen extending into the choledochal cyst. Hepatobiliary scans show late filling and stasis of the isotope within the choledochal cyst.[53] They are useful in excluding hepatic cyst, pancreatic pseudocyst, and enteric duplication.

Direct coronal MR imaging demonstrates a dilated tubular structure that follows the expected course of the common bile duct. MR cholangiopancreatography (MRCP) can also demonstrate these dilated biliary structures because the luminal contents of the bile appear hyperdense in contrast to the portal vein. MR cholangiopancreatography can also diagnose biliary

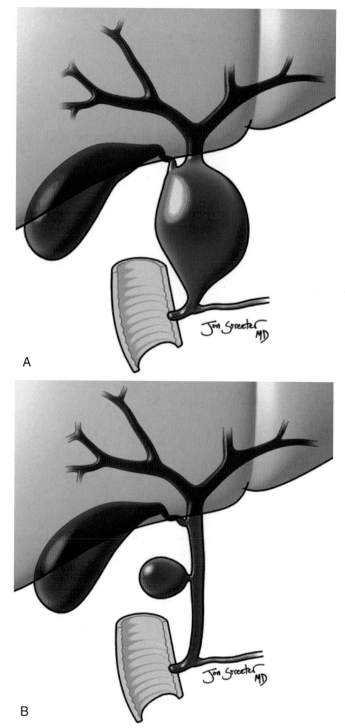

Figure 78-6. Choledochal cysts. A. Type I choledochal cyst. **B.** Type II choledochal cyst.

calculi and stricture formation that frequently complicate cystic disease of the bile ducts. Two studies showed that MR cholangiopancreatography offered equivalent information to endoscopic retrograde cholangiopancreatography (ERCP), without the potential complications inherent in the latter procedure. In patients with choledochal cysts who are reluctant to undergo surgical resection, periodic follow-up ultrasound and MR cholangiopancreatography may help achieve early detection of malignant change.[52] The management of choledochal cysts is surgical, with excision of all cyst tissue

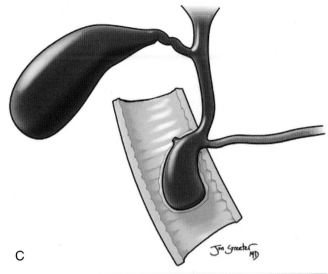

C

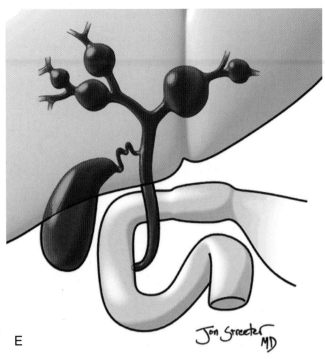

E

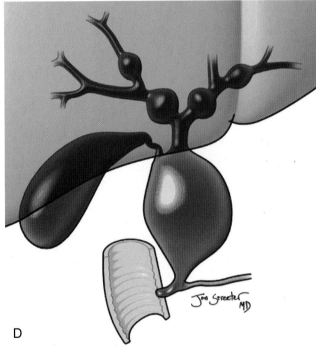

D

Figure 78-6, *cont'd*. C. Choledochocele or type III choledochal cyst. **D.** Type IV choledochal cysts. **E.** Type V choledochal cyst (Caroli disease). (From Mortele KR, Rochar TC, Streeter JL, et al: Multimodality imaging of pancreatic and biliary congential anomalies. RadioGraphics 26:715-731, 2006.)

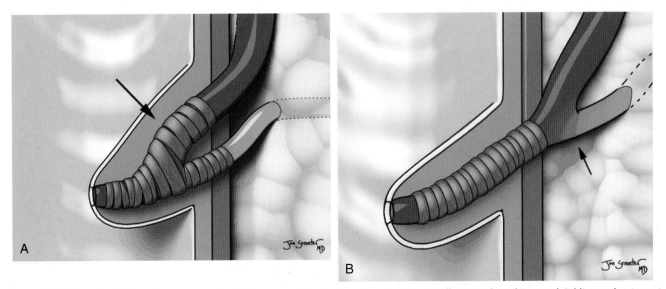

Figure 78-7. Normal and anomalous pancreatic duct–common bile duct anatomy. A. Drawing illustrates the sphincter of Oddi complex (*arrow*) encompassing the distal CBD and pancreatic duct. **B.** Drawing illustrates a long common channel (>15 mm). Note that the sphincter of Oddi does not reach the confluence (*arrow*) of the ducts. (From Mortele KR, Rochar TC, Streeter JL, et al: Multimodality imaging of pancreatic and biliary congenital anomalies. RadioGraphics 26:715-731, 2006.)

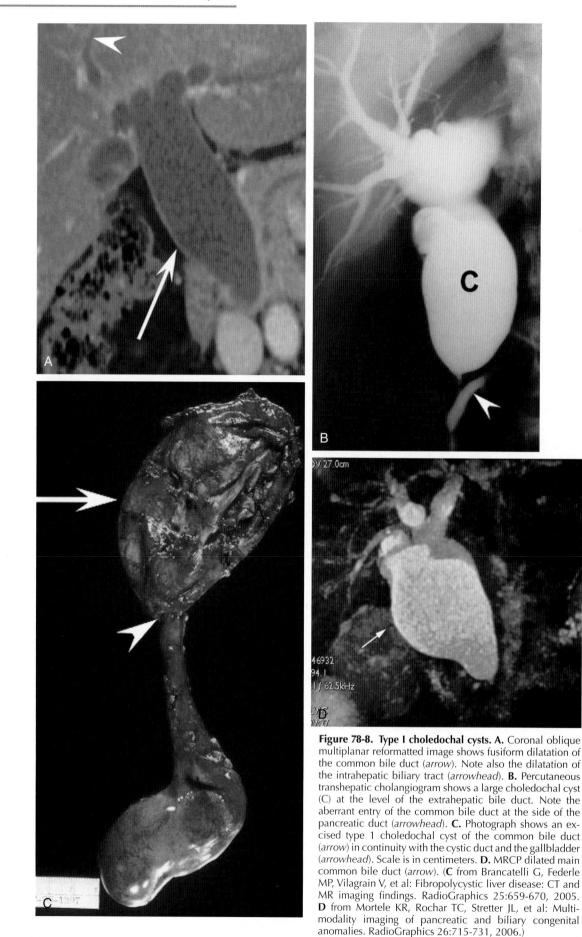

Figure 78-8. Type I choledochal cysts. A. Coronal oblique multiplanar reformatted image shows fusiform dilatation of the common bile duct (*arrow*). Note also the dilatation of the intrahepatic biliary tract (*arrowhead*). **B.** Percutaneous transhepatic cholangiogram shows a large choledochal cyst (C) at the level of the extrahepatic bile duct. Note the aberrant entry of the common bile duct at the side of the pancreatic duct (*arrowhead*). **C.** Photograph shows an excised type 1 choledochal cyst of the common bile duct (*arrow*) in continuity with the cystic duct and the gallbladder (*arrowhead*). Scale is in centimeters. **D.** MRCP dilated main common bile duct (*arrow*). (**C** from Brancatelli G, Federle MP, Vilagrain V, et al: Fibropolycystic liver disease: CT and MR imaging findings. RadioGraphics 25:659-670, 2005. **D** from Mortele KR, Rochar TC, Stretter JL, et al: Multimodality imaging of pancreatic and biliary congenital anomalies. RadioGraphics 26:715-731, 2006.)

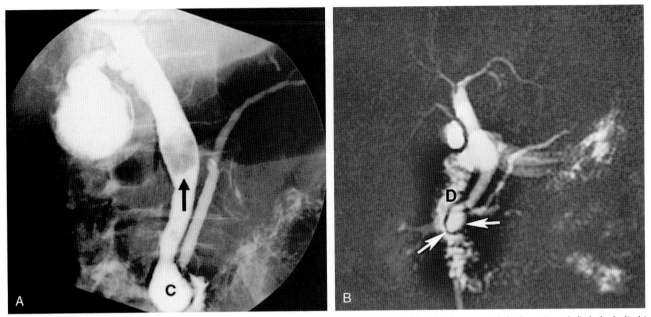

Figure 78-9.   Type III Choledochocysts: choledochocele. A. ERCP shows saccular dilatation of the distal common bile duct (C) and choledocholiathias (*arrow*). **B.** Coronal MRCP image demonstrates bulbous dilatation of the intramural segment of the distal common bile duct (*arrows*), which protrudes into the duodenum (D).

and reconstruction of continuity between the liver and gut by a Roux-en-Y hepaticojejunostomy.[57]

Choledochoceles

A choledochocele is a rare, easily overlooked anomaly of unknown cause. This anomaly has been called variously an intraduodenal choledochal cyst, duodenal duplication cyst, diverticulum of the common bile duct, and enterogenous cyst of the duodenum. It is a protrusion of a dilated intramural segment of common bile duct into the duodenum, analogous to a ureterocele.[58-60] It is often seen on cholangiograms in patients who have had a cholecystectomy, so that the lesion may be partly acquired.

Choledochoceles usually manifest in adulthood with long-standing nausea, vomiting, and episodic abdominal pain. Stones and sludge are often present, and patients often have episodes of biliary colic, intermittent jaundice, and pancreatitis as well.[54,55]

Cholangiography shows smooth clublike or saclike dilatation of the intramural segment of the common bile duct (Fig. 78-9A). Barium studies demonstrate a smooth, well-defined intraluminal duodenal filling defect in this region of the papilla that changes in shape with compression and peristalsis. In contrast to intraluminal diverticula, choledochoceles do not fill with barium.[58-60] On MR cholangiopancreatography images, they have a high signal intensity, "cobra-head" appearance bulging into the duodenum (Fig. 78-9B).

Caroli's Disease

Caroli's disease, also known as communicating cavernous ectasia, is characterized by multifocal segmental saccular dilatation of the intrahepatic bile ducts, a predisposition to biliary calculi and cholangitis, and an association with various forms of cystic renal disease. Caroli's disease usually manifests

in adulthood; however, it can be seen in newborns and infants. Adult patients present with recurrent attacks of cholangitis and crampy right upper quadrant pain with occasional fever and mild jaundice. Infants and children may present with hematemesis caused by portal hypertension from hepatic fibrosis.[54,55,61-63] This disease appears to be autosomal recessively inherited in most cases. Complications of Caroli's disease include stone formation (95%) within the dilated intrahepatic ducts, recurrent cholangitis, and liver abscess. There is also a 100-fold increase in the incidence of bile duct carcinoma, occurring in 7% of patients.

Caroli's disease is best demonstrated by cholangiography (Fig. 78-10), which shows saccular dilatations of the intra-

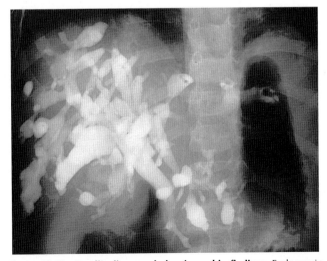

Figure 78-10. Caroli's disease: cholangiographic findings. Endoscopic retrograde cholangiopancreatography demonstrates bulbous dilatations of the peripheral intrahepatic biliary radicals characteristic of Caroli's disease. (From Taylor AJ, Bohorfoush AG: Interpretation of ERCP with Associated Digital Imaging. Philadelphia, Lippincott-Raven, 1997, p 52, with permission.)

hepatic ducts, stones, strictures, and communicating hepatic abscesses. CT can also demonstrate tiny dots with strong contrast enhancement within dilated intrahepatic bile ducts (the "central dot" sign). These intraluminal dots correspond to intraluminal portal veins.[64-68] CT and ultrasound demonstrate multiple cystic areas within the liver[69-71] (Fig. 78-11). Technetium Tc 99m sulfur colloid scans show multiple cold defects, and hepatobiliary scans show an unusual pattern of retained activity throughout the liver.[54,55]

MRCP with three-dimensional display is an accurate method for demonstrating Caroli's disease because the luminal contents of the bile ducts appear hyperintense in contrast to the portal vein, which usually appears as signal void. Cystic expansions of the intrahepatic biliary tract are depicted as oval-shaped structures in continuity with the biliary tract (Fig. 78-12). They are nearly signal void on black bile techniques and have a high signal intensity on bright bile or MR cholangiopancreatography sequences.[72]

Treatment depends on the clinical features and location of the biliary abnormality. When the disease is localized to one hepatic lobe, hepatectomy relieves symptoms and appears to remove the risk of malignancy. In diffuse Caroli's disease, treatment options include conservative or endoscopic therapy, internal biliary bypass procedures, and liver transplantation in carefully selected cases.

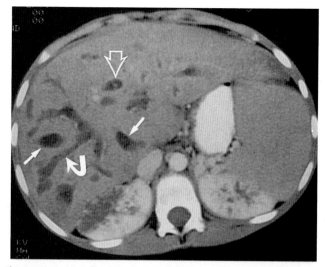

Figure 78-11. Caroli's disease: CT findings. The dilated segments of the intrahepatic biliary tract may be visualized as "cysts" (*straight arrows*), which are occasionally attached to more proximal ectatic segments of the biliary radicles (*curved arrow*). The defining CT feature of Caroli's disease is the central dot sign (*open arrow*). There is ectasia of the distal nephrons in the kidneys. (From Taylor AJ, Bohorfoush AG: Interpretation of ERCP with Associated Digital Imaging. Philadelphia, Lippincott-Raven, 1997, p 52, with permission.)

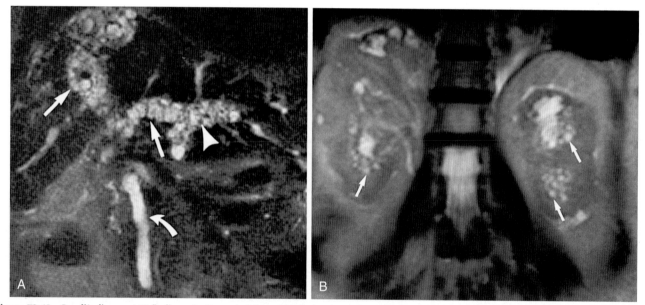

Figure 78-12. Caroli's disease: MR findings. A. Coronal oblique MR cholangiopancreatography demonstrates multiple segmental saccular dilatations of the intrahepatic bile ducts (*arrows*). *Curved arrow,* common bile duct. **B.** Coronal half-Fourier rapid acquisition with relaxation enhancement (RARE) image of the kidneys shows multiple fluid-containing foci (*arrows*) in the papillae indicating renal tubular ectasia (medullary sponge kidney).

References

1. Fitoz S, Erden A, Boruban S: Magnetic resonance cholangiopancreatography of biliary system abnormalities in children. Clin Imaging 31:93-101, 2007.
2. Savader SJ, Venbrux AC, Faerber AC, et al: Biliary tract anomalies, congenital and neonatal disorders, and hepatobiliary cystic malformations. In Friedman AC, Dachman AH (eds): Radiology of the Liver, Biliary Tract, and Pancreas. St. Louis, CV Mosby, 1994, pp 397-444.
3. Kamath BM, Piccoli DA: Heritable disorders of the bile ducts. Gastroenterol Clin North Am 32:857-875, 2003.
4. Taylor AJ, Bohorfoush AG: Interpretation of ERCP with Associated Digital Imaging Correlation. Philadelphia, Lippincott-Raven, 1997, pp 41-58.
5. Bader TR, Semelka RC, Reinhold C: Gallbladder and biliary system. In Semelka RC (ed): Abdominal-Pelvic MRI. New York, Wiley-Liss, 2002, pp 319-372.
6. Lack EE: Pathology of the Pancreas, Gallbladder, Extrahepatic Biliary Tract, and Ampullary Region. Oxford, Oxford University Press, 2003, pp 395-413.
7. Haller JO, Slovis TL: Pediatric gallbladder and biliary tract: Sonographic evaluation. Ultrasound Q 9:271-311, 1992.

8. Kamath BM, Piccoli DA: Heritable disorders of the bile ducts. Gastroenterol Clin North Am. 32:857-875, 2003.
9. Coughlin JP, Rector FE, Klein MD: Agenesis of the gallbladder in duodenal atresia: Two case reports. J Pediatr Surg 27:1304, 1992.
10. Bani-Hani KE: Agenesis of the gallbladder: Difficulties in management. J Gastroenterol Hepatol 20:671-675, 2005.
11. Senecail B, Nonent M, Kergastel I, et al: Ultrasonic features of congenital anomalies of the gallbladder. J Radiol 81:1591-1594, 2000.
12. Vijay KT, Kocher HH, Koti RS, et al: Agenesis of gallbladder: A diagnostic dilemma. J Postgrad Med 42:80-82, 1996.
13. Bartone NF, Grieco RV: Absent gallbladder and cystic duct. AJR 110:252-255, 1970.
14. Fisichella PM, Di Stefano A, Di Carlo I: Isolated agenesis of the gallbladder: Report of a case. Surg Today 32:78-80, 2002.
15. Berk RN: Oral cholecystography. In Berk RN, Ferrucci JT, Leopold GR (eds): Radiology of the Gallbladder and Bile Ducts. Philadelphia, WB Saunders, 1983, pp 83-162.
16. Bayraktar Y, Balaban HY, Arslan S, et al: Agenesis of gallbladder and multiple anomalies of the biliary tree in a patient with portal thrombosis: A case report. Turk J Gastroenterol 17:212-215, 2006.
17. Warshauer DM, Sulzer JL: Agenesis of the gallbladder: A rare cause for a false-positive hepatobiliary image. Clin Nucl Med 13:468, 1988.
18. Meilstrup JW, Hopper KD, Thieme GA: Imaging of gallbladder variants. AJR 157:1205-1208, 1991.
19. Paciorek ML, Lackner D, Daley C, et al: A unique presentation of multiseptate gallbladder. Dig Dis Sci 42:2519-2523, 1997.
20. Yamamoto T, Matsumoto J, Hashiguchi S, et al: Multiseptate gallbladder with anomalous pancreaticobiliary ductal union: A case report. World J Gastroenterol 11:6066-6068, 2005.
21. Udelsman R, Sugerbaker PH: Congenital duplication of the gallbladder associated with an anomalous right hepatic artery. Am J Surg 149:812-815, 1985.
22. Horaths MC: Gallbladder duplication and laparoscopic management. J Laparoendosc Adv Surg Tech 8:231-235, 1998.
23. Ozgen A, Akata D, Arat A, et al: Gallbladder duplication: Imaging findings and differential considerations. Abdom Imaging 24:285-288, 1999.
24. Chawla Y, Makharia G, Gupta S, et al: Bilobed gallbladder with gallstones and choledocholithiasis. Trop Gastroenterol 19:64-66, 1998.
25. Chiba T, Shinozaki M, Kato S, et al: Caroli's disease: central dot sign re-examined by CT arteriography and CT during arterial portography. Eur Radiol 12:701-702, 2002.
26. Takayashiki T, Miyazaki M, Kato A, et al: Double cancer of gallbladder and bile duct associated with anomalous junction of the pancreaticobiliary ductal system. Hepatogastroenterology 49:109-112, 2002.
27. Oyar O, Yesildag A, Gulsoy U, et al: Bilobed gallbladder diagnosed by oral cholecysto-CT. Comput Med Imaging Graph 27:315-319, 2003.
28. Foster DR: Triple gallbladder. Br J Radiol 54:817-818, 1981.
29. Boyden EA: The "phrygian cap" in cholecystography. AJR 33:589-596, 1935.
30. Paciorek ML, Lackner D, Daly G, et al: A unique presentation of multiseptate gallbladder. Dig Dis Sci 42:2519-2523, 1997.
31. Saddik D: Multiseptate gallbladder: Incidental diagnosis on ultrasound. Australas Radiol 42:374-376, 1998.
32. Lev-Toaff AS, Friedman AC, Rindsberg SN, et al: Multiseptate gallbladder: Incidental diagnosis on sonography. AJR 14:1119-1120, 1987.
33. Blanton DE, Bream CA, Mandel SR: Gallbladder ectopia: A review of anomalies of position. AJR 121:296-300, 1974.
34. Van Gansbeke D, de Toeuf J, Engelholm L, et al: Suprahepatic gallbladder: A rare congenital anomaly. Gastrointest Radiol 9:941-943, 1984.
35. Senecail B, Texier F, Kergastel I, et al: Anatomic variability and congenital anomalies of the gallbladder: Ultrasonographic study of 1823 patients. Morphologie 84:35-39, 2000.
36. Naganuma S, Ishida H, Konno K, et al: Sonographic findings of anomalous position of the gallbladder. Abdom Imaging 23:67-72, 1998.
37. Banzo I, Carril JM, Arnal C, et al: Left-sided gallbladder: An incidental finding on hepatobiliary scintigraphy. Clin Nucl Med 15:358, 1990.
38. Yeh HC, Weiss MF, Gerson CD: Torsion of the gallbladder: The ultrasonographic features. J Clin Ultrasound 17:123-125, 1989.
39. Quinn SF, Fazzio F, Jones E: Torsion of the gallbladder: Findings on CT and sonography and role of percutaneous cholecystostomy. AJR 148:881-882, 1987.
40. Matsuhashi N, Satake S, Yawata K, et al: Volvulus of the gall bladder diagnosed by ultrasonography, computed tomography, coronal magnetic resonance imaging and magnetic resonance cholangio-pancreatography. World J Gastroenterol 12:4599-4601, 2006.
41. Wellstad M, Kam L, Funstom MR: Radiological pointers to preoperative diagnosis of torsion of the gallbladder in patients with cirrhosis: CT findings and clinical implications. Radiology 171:739-742, 1989.
42. Gore RM, Ghahremani GG, Joseph AE, et al: Acquired malposition of the colon and gallbladder in patients with cirrhosis: CT findings and clinical implications. Radiology 171:739-742, 1989.
43. Bartoli E, Calonaci N, Nenci R: Ultrasonography of the gallbladder in pregnancy. Gastrointest Radiol 9:35-38, 1984.
44. Everson GT, Nemeth A, Kourourian S, et al: Gallbladder function is altered in sickle hemoglobinopathy. Gastroenterology 96:1307-1316, 1989.
45. Mitsukawa T, Takemura J, Ohgo S: Gallbladder function and plasma cholecystokinin levels in diabetes mellitus. Am J Gastroenterol 85:981-984, 1990.
46. Vezina WC, Paradis RL, Grace DM, et al: Increased volume and decreased emptying of the gallbladder in large (morbidly obese, tall normal and muscular normal) people. Gastroenterology 98:1000-1007, 1990.
47. McHugo JM, McKeown C, Brown MT, et al: Ultrasound findings in children with cystic fibrosis. Br J Radiol 60:137-141, 1987.
48. Willi UV, Reddish JM, Teele RL: Cystic fibrosis: Its characteristic appearance on abdominal sonography. AJR 131:1005-1010, 1980.
49. Kim WS, Kim IO, Yeon KM, et al: Choledochal cyst with or without biliary atresia in neonates and young infants: US differentiation. Radiology 209:465-469, 1998.
50. Lam WW, Lam TP, Saing H, et al: MR cholangiography and CT cholangiography of pediatric patients with choledochal cysts. AJR 173:401-405, 1999.
51. Krause D, Cercueil JP, Dranssart M, et al: MRI for evaluating congenital bile duct abnormalities. J Comput Assist Tomogr 26:541-552, 2002.
52. Trinidad-Hernandez M, Rivera-Perez VS, Hermosillo-Sandoval JM: Adult choledochal cyst. Am J Surg 193:221-222, 2007.
53. Arshanskiy Y, Vyas PK: Type IV choledochal cyst presenting with obstructive jaundice: role of MR cholangiopancreatography. AJR 171:457-459, 1998.
54. Matos C, Nicaise N, Deviere J, et al: Choledochal cysts comparison of findings at MR cholangiopancreatography and endoscopic retrograde cholangiopancreatography in eight patients. Radiology 209:443-448, 1998.
55. Brancatelli G, Federle MP, Vilgrain V, et al: Fibropolycystic liver disease: CT and MR imaging findings. RadioGraphics 25:659-670, 2005.
56. Irie H, Honda H, Jimi M, et al: Value of MR cholangiopancreatography in evaluating choledochal cysts. AJR 171:1381-1385, 1998.
57. Wang HP, Wums, Lin CC, et al: Pancreaticobiliary diseases associated with anomalous pancreaticobiliary ductal union. Gastrointest Endosc 48:184-189, 1998.
58. Scholz FJ, Carrera GF, Larsen CR: The choledochocele: Correlation of radiological, clinical and pathological findings. Radiology 118:28, 1976.
59. Catalano O: Conventional x-ray and CT findings in a case of intraluminal choledochocele. Rofo 169:210-212, 1998.
60. Woon CY, Tan YM, Oei CL, et al: Adult choledochal cysts: An audit of surgical management. ANZ J Surg 76:981-986, 2006.
61. Krepel HP, Siersema PD, Tilanus HW, et al: Choledochocele presenting with anaemia. Eur J Gastroenterol Hepatol 9:641-643, 1997.
62. Bockhorn M, Malago M, Lang H, et al: The role of surgery in Caroli's disease. J Am Coll Surg 202:928-932, 2006.
63. Madjov R, Chervenkov P, Madjova V, et al: Caroli's disease. Report of 5 cases and review of literature. Hepatogastroenterology 52:606-609, 2005.
64. Levy AD, Rohrmann CA Jr, Murakata LA, et al: Caroli's disease: Radiologic spectrum with pathologic correlation. AJR 179:1053-1057, 2002.
65. Sood GK, Mahapatra JR, Khurana A, et al: Caroli disease: Computed tomographic diagnosis. Gastrointest Radiol 16:243-244, 1991.
66. Chiba T, Shinozaki M, Kato S, et al: Caroli's disease: Central dot sign re-examined by CT arteriography and CT during arterial portography. Eur Radiol 12:701-702, 2002.
67. Seth AK, Chawla Y, Dhiman RK, et al: Caroli's disease: A central dot means a lot. Trop Gastroenterol 18:165-166, 1997.
68. Ahmadi T, Itai Y, Minami M: Central dot sign in entities other than Caroli's disease. J Clin Ultrasound 26:283-287, 1998.
69. Breysam L, Opdenakker G, Smet M, et al: Caroli's syndrome. J Belge Radiol 81:1-2, 1998.
70. Gorka W, Lewall DB: Value of Doppler sonography in the assessment of patients with Caroli's disease. J Clin Ultrasound 26:283-287, 1998.
71. Guy F, Cognet F, Dranssart M, et al: Caroli's disease: Magnetic resonance imaging features. Eur Radiol 12:2730-2736, 2002.
72. Ananthakrishnan AN, Saeian K: Caroli's disease: Identification and treatment strategy. Curr Gastroenterol Rep 9:151-155, 2007.

Cholelithiasis, Cholecystitis, Choledocholithiasis, and Hyperplastic Cholecystoses

Genevieve L. Bennett, MD

This chapter provides a review of the imaging assessment of gallbladder and biliary calculi. Cholecystitis, both acute and chronic, and associated complications will be discussed. Other disorders related to gallstones, including spilled gallstones after laparoscopic surgery, Mirizzi syndrome, and gallstone ileus will also be reviewed. The chapter will conclude with a discussion of the spectrum of noninflammatory gallbladder conditions referred to as the hyperplastic cholecystoses.

The imaging evaluation of cholelithiasis and associated complications has evolved significantly in the past decade. Cholescintigraphy and sonography continue to serve as the primary imaging modalities for the initial assessment of most suspected gallbladder disorders. Computed tomography (CT) and magnetic resonance imaging (MRI), however, have proved to be of considerable value in certain circumstances. These may be performed for initial evaluation or serve as an important adjunct to these other imaging modalities when further information is required. The role of CT and MRI in the evaluation of cholecystitis, choledocholithiasis, and the hyperplastic cholecystoses will be discussed.

CHOLELITHIASIS

Pathogenesis and Epidemiology

The prevalence of gallstones varies with age and gender. Gallstones are present in an estimated 10% to 15% of men and 20% to 40% of women over the age of 60 years.[1] In general, the risk for stones increases with history of childbearing, estrogen replacement therapy, oral contraceptive use, and obesity. Stones are also associated with hypertriglyceridemia, Crohn's disease, and parenteral hyperalimentation. Gallstones are symptomatic in 20% to 30% of patients, with biliary pain or colic the most common symptom. This is most often related to impaction of a stone in the cystic duct. The most common acute complications of gallstones include acute cholecystitis, acute pancreatitis, and ascending cholangitis. Chronic complications include chronic cholecystitis, Mirizzi syndrome, cholecystoenteric fistula, and gallstone ileus.

Gallstones are composed mainly of cholesterol, bilirubin and calcium salts with smaller amounts of protein and other materials, including bile acids, fatty acids, and inorganic salts.[2] Stones form when there is supersaturation of various bile components. Lithogenic bile usually results from increased biliary cholesterol output, but decreased bile acid synthesis or a combination defect may play a role in stone development.[1] Biliary dysmotility and prolonged intestinal transit may also be contributing factors.[3]

In Western countries, cholesterol is the principal constituent of more than 75% of gallstones. Many stones are greater than 80% cholesterol with smaller amounts of calcium bilirubinate. Pure cholesterol stones contain over 90% cholesterol and are relatively uncommon, accounting for less than 10% of biliary calculi.[2] Pigment stones contain less than 25% cholesterol and are relatively uncommon, comprising up 10% to 25% of gallstones in North America.[4] These stones consist of calcium salts of bilirubin and are categorized as black or brown pigment stones. Black pigment stones consist of polymers of bilirubin with large amounts of mucin glycoproteins. These are more common in patients with cirrhosis or chronic hemolytic anemias in whom biliary excretion is increased. Brown pigment stones are made up of calcium salts of unconjugated bilirubin, with variable amounts of protein and cholesterol, and are more commonly associated with bacterial infection. The deconjugation of bile by bacterial enzymes is also considered an etiologic factor.

Imaging

Abdominal Radiography

Only about 15% to 20% of gallstones are calcified enough to be visualized on conventional abdominal radiographs[5] (Fig. 79-1). Therefore, abdominal radiographs have a limited role in the detection of gallstones. Oral cholecystography was introduced in the 1920s and for many years was the primary modality for evaluation of gallbladder pathology, including stones. However, this technique has largely been replaced by sonography.

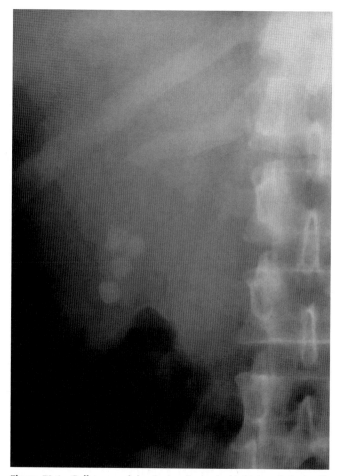

Figure 79-1. Gallstones: abdominal radiograph. Multiple calcified gallstones are identified.

Ultrasound

Sonography is now considered the imaging tool of choice for the detection of gallstones, with a reported accuracy of 96%.[5-7] However, recent advances in sonographic technology resulting in improved spatial resolution may allow for even higher diagnostic accuracy. Other advantages of sonography include the ability to perform studies at the bedside and lack of ionizing radiation. Sonography can also evaluate other structures in the right upper quadrant when alternative diagnoses are under consideration.

At sonography, a gallstone appears as a highly reflective echo that is generally mobile and associated with posterior acoustic shadowing (Fig. 79-2). Both mobility and acoustic shadowing are important features that help to differentiate gallstones from other echogenic foci in the gallbladder lumen, such as sludge or solid masses. An aggregate of sludge or sludge ball (also referred to as tumefactive sludge) may be mobile but will not cast an acoustic shadow (Fig. 79-3). A solid mass will not be mobile and will not shadow and may exhibit vascularity upon color Doppler interrogation.

Very small stones may not always cast a shadow. Ex vivo studies have demonstrated that calculi larger than 3 mm produce acoustic shadowing regardless of composition.[8,9] The demonstration of a posterior acoustic shadow, however, is also dependent upon transducer frequency and beam width. In a study by Grossman and colleagues,[10] when a 5-MHz

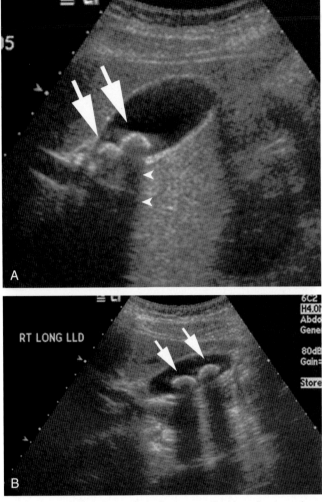

Figure 79-2. Gallstones: sonography. A. Two highly reflective echoes (*arrows*) are located in the dependent portion of the gallbladder lumen with posterior acoustic shadowing (*arrowheads*). **B.** When the patient is imaged in the left lateral decubitus position (LLD), the gallstones (*arrows*) change location, indicating mobility.

transducer was used, 0.2- to 0.3-cm stones were associated with shadowing, whereas when a 2.25-MHz transducer was used, only stones measuring at least 0.4 cm in size cast a shadow. Using a tissue phantom, Filly and associates[9] found that acoustic shadowing was present when the stone was at or near the center of the beam but not at the periphery. These studies demonstrate that in order to maximize detection, the highest frequency transducer possible should be employed with the focal zone placed at the level of the stone. In recent years, the use of tissue harmonic imaging has been shown to improve the detection rate of gallbladder calculi[11,12] (Fig. 79-4).

Gallstones may not be detected at sonography if they are small in size, hidden behind a gallbladder fold or the cystic duct, if intraluminal sludge is present, or if the exam is technically suboptimal related to patient body habitus or operator inexperience. Chintapalli and colleagues[13] studied 946 patients with surgically proved gallstones. In 98.7%, preoperative sonography showed single or multiple echogenic foci with or without acoustic shadowing in the gallbladder for a false negative rate of 1.3%. In the patients with false negative exams, sonographic findings were consistent with polyps (five cases), sludge,[5] or both[1] and the ultrasound was normal in one patient. Missed stones were 5 mm or smaller in 10 patients and less than 1.0 cm in all 12 patients. Stones located in the gallbladder neck or trapped behind a fold may be overlooked when the patient is evaluated only in the supine position. Also, small stones may become more conspicuous when the patient is evaluated in the decubitus or upright position, as they produce a shadow only when imaged in aggregate (Fig. 79-5). Therefore, it is always important to evaluate the patient in more than one position when assessing for the presence of gallstones. A follow-up study may be suggested if the clinical index of suspicion is high and the initial examination is negative.

If the gallbladder is contracted and the lumen is filled with shadowing stones, a high amplitude echo results which is usually linear or curvilinear in configuration and associated posterior acoustic shadowing. Careful observation will

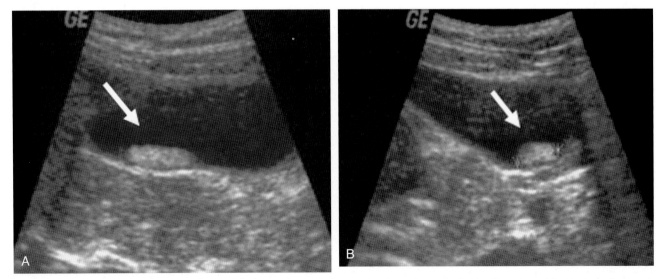

Figure 79-3. Tumefactive sludge: sonography. A. In the supine position, there is an echogenic nonshadowing focus (*arrow*) in the dependent portion of the gallbladder lumen. There is no posterior acoustic shadowing. **B.** In the upright position, the sludge ball moved into the gallbladder fundus (*arrow*).

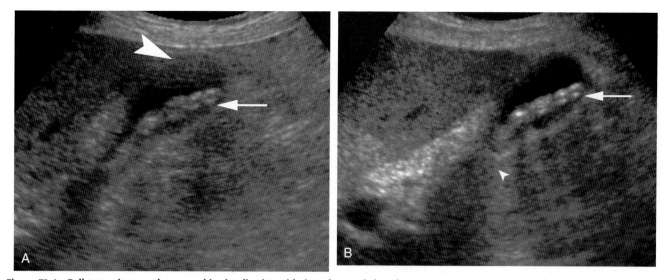

Figure 79-4. Gallstones: improved sonographic visualization with tissue harmonic imaging. A. Image obtained with 4-MHz transducer demonstrates gallstones (*arrows*). Nearfield echoes (*arrowhead*) correspond to reverberation artifact. **B.** Image obtained with tissue harmonic imaging eliminates reverberation artifact. Gallstones are better delineated (*arrow*) and posterior acoustic shadowing is more evident (*arrowhead*).

demonstrate a perceivable gallbladder wall separate from the intraluminal stones, sometimes facilitated by the use of a high resolution linear transducer (Fig. 79-6). This appearance has been called the wall-echo-shadow sign or WES.[14] The main differential diagnostic considerations are a porcelain gallbladder, with calcification in the gallbladder wall, or air in the gallbladder, such as in emphysematous cholecystitis. Correlation with abdominal radiograph or CT can be helpful as a problem solving tool (Fig. 79-7).

Computed Tomography

The ability to detect stones at CT depends on differing density of the stone with respect to bile.[15,16] The reported sensitivity of CT for detection of gallstones is approximately 75%.[17] Calcified stones are readily identified as they are denser than bile (Fig. 79-8A). Stones with high concentration of cholesterol may also be readily identified as these stones are less dense than bile (Fig. 79-8B). When stones degenerate, nitrogen gas may collect in central fissures and create the "Mercedes-Benz "sign. This may be the only visualized evidence of a gallstone and appear as a focal collection of gas located in the non-dependent gallbladder lumen (Fig. 79-8C). Noncalcified pigment stones are soft tissue attenuation density (Fig. 79-8D). Many stones are composed of a mixture of calcium, bile pigments, and cholesterol and may be similar in density to bile and therefore not visible at CT (Fig. 79-9). The size of the stone is also an important factor determining if a stone is visible at CT. Small stones are frequently missed unless the density differs markedly from bile. In one series, only 78.9% of patients with stones demonstrated at sonography were found to have stones at CT.[18] Most stones missed prospectively were faintly calcified and were retrospectively detected only as subtle defects within the gallbladder.

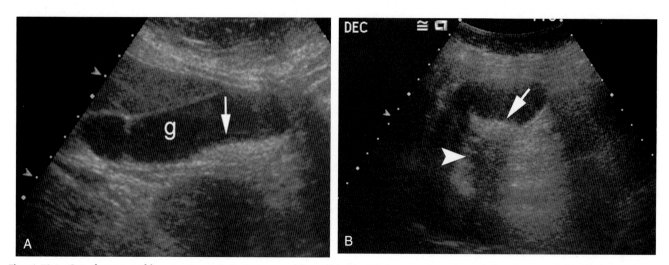

Figure 79-5. Gravel: sonographic appearance. A. Supine scan of the gallbladder (g) demonstrates echogenic layering material in the lumen (*arrow*) with no posterior acoustic shadowing. **B.** In the decubitus position, the material pools in the fundus of the gallbladder (*arrow*) and a shadow is now demonstrated (*arrowhead*) consistent with small stones or gravel.

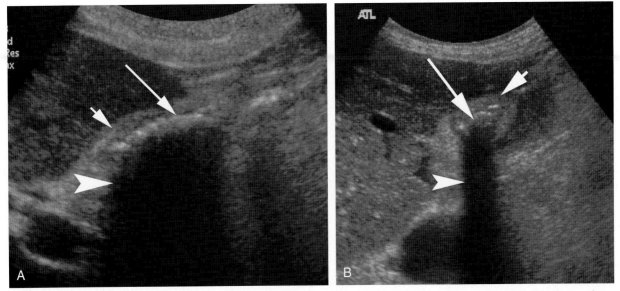

Figure 79-6. Wall-echo-shadow sign (WES) on ultrasound. Multiple gallstones are present within a contracted gallbladder. Sagittal (**A**) and transverse (**B**) views. Short *arrows* points to gallbladder wall that appears as an echogenic arc. Long *arrows* points to gallstones that appear as bright echoes. The *arrowhead* points to posterior acoustic shadowing.

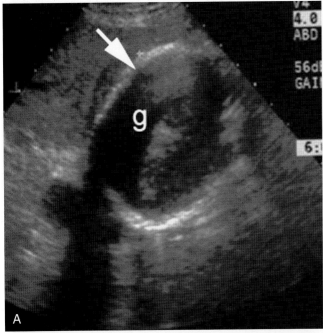

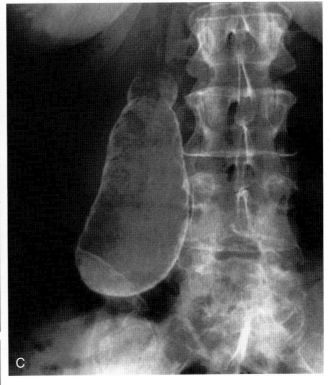

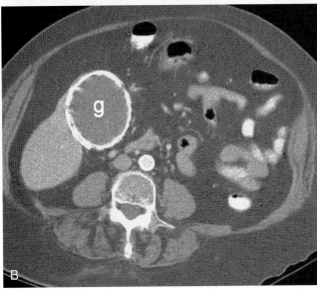

Figure 79-7. Porcelain gallbladder: imaging features. A. Ultrasound demonstrates increased echogenicity of the wall (*arrow*) of the gallbladder (g). **B.** CT scan shows concentric mural calcification of the gallbladder (g) confirming porcelain gallbladder. **C.** Abdominal radiograph shows concentric mural calcification.

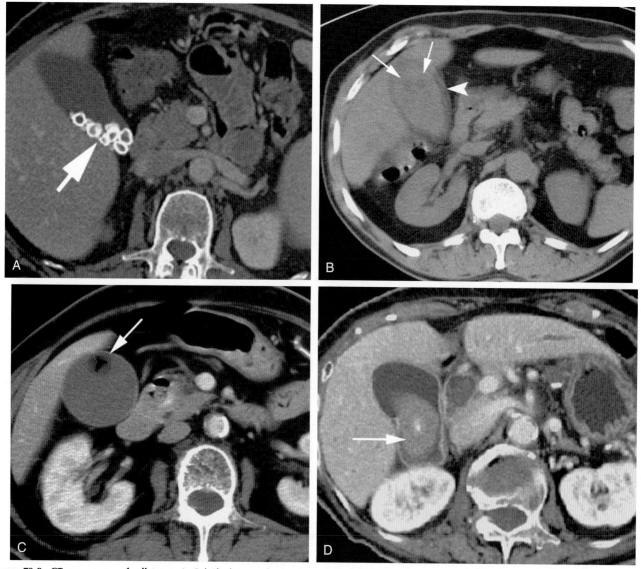

Figure 79-8. CT appearance of gallstones. A. Calcified stones depicted as calcified dependent densities in gallbladder lumen (*arrow*). **B.** Noncalcified stones may be visible if less dense than bile (*arrows*). This patient also had acute cholecystitis. Note thickened gallbladder wall (*arrowhead*). **C.** Mercedes-Benz sign. Gas-containing stone floating in bile (*arrow*). **D.** Pigment stone (*arrow*) is soft tissue density with only small central nidus of calcification.

Magnetic Resonance Imaging

On T2-weighted MR image, gallstones manifest as signal voids in the high signal intensity bile (Fig. 79-10). Cholesterol stones are generally isointense or hypointense on T1-weighted images, whereas pigment stones have been shown to have high signal intensity on T1-weighted images. This signal hyperintensity is caused by the presence of metal ions in the pigment stones, shortening the T1 relaxation time.[19,20] Another recent study of gallstone appearance at MR imaging also correlated signal intensity with chemical composition.[21] T2-weighted central high signal intensity corresponded to fluid-filled clefts in the stones, whereas central and peripheral high signal areas on T1-weighted images corresponded to fluid-clefts as well as regions high in copper content. Other intraluminal filling defects that may mimic gallstones on T2-weighted images include tumor, blood clot or gas bubbles.

BILIARY SLUDGE

Pathogenesis

Biliary sludge, also referred to as microlithiasis, biliary sand or sediment, pseudolithiasis, and microcrystalline disease, is a suspension of bile and particulate material in the gallbladder.[22] The chemical composition consists of various proportions of calcium bilirubinate and cholesterol monohydrate crystals and gallbladder mucus. The proposed pathogenesis is similar to that of gallstones. A combination of impaired gallbladder motility and alteration in nucleation factors leads to the formation of sludge with additional precipitate aggregation resulting in gallstone formation.[23] Clinical conditions that increase sludge formation include fasting, pregnancy, total parenteral nutrition, and critical illness. Sludge may resolve, have a cyclical pattern of appearance and disappearance,

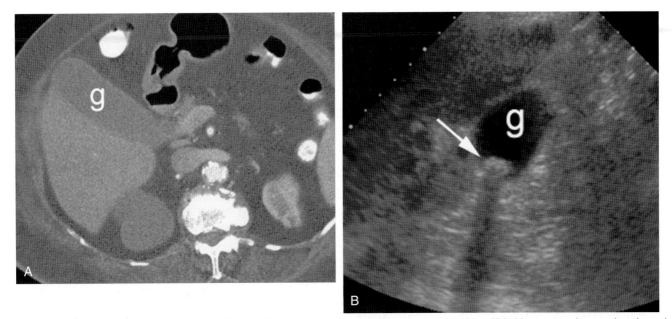

Figure 79-9. Noncalcified gallstones not visualized at CT. A. CT scan demonstrates no stones in the gallbladder (g). **B.** Ultrasound performed immediately after CT demonstrates shadowing stone (*arrow*) in gallbladder (g) lumen.

or progress to stone formation.[24] Although patients may generally be asymptomatic, symptoms can include biliary pain, cholecystitis, cholangitis, or pancreatitis. Treatment is symptom directed.

Imaging

At sonography, sludge typically appears as low level echoes that layer dependently within the gallbladder lumen (Fig. 79-11). When the gallbladder lumen is entirely filled with sludge, this yields an appearance referred to as "hepatization" of the gallbladder. In this situation, the gallbladder assumes the

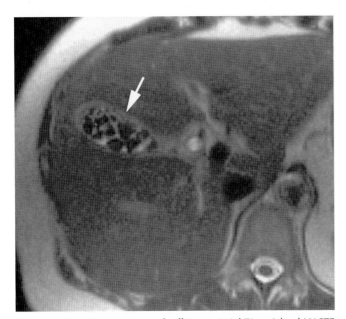

Figure 79-10. MR appearance of gallstones. Axial T2-weighted HASTE image demonstrates multiple low signal intensity filling defects in gallbladder lumen (*arrow*).

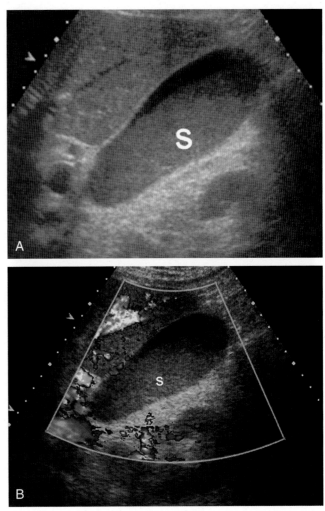

Figure 79-11. Sludge: sonographic findings. A. Ultrasound shows low-level, nonshadowing intraluminal echoes (s). **B.** Color Doppler shows no vascularity in sludge (s) helping to exclude a solid, intraluminal mass.

same echotexture as the liver parenchyma (Fig. 79-12A and B). The use of color Doppler imaging is important to exclude other more significant pathology such as intraluminal soft tissue masses. If findings are equivocal and there is suspicion for a possible intraluminal mass, MRI with contrast and subtraction images can be helpful (Fig. 79-12C and D). An aggregate of intraluminal sludge can also mimic a soft tissue density mass (tumefactive sludge). As discussed, gravity dependence should be demonstrated to differentiate sludge from a gallbladder polyp or mass (Fig. 79-13). Doppler demonstration of vascularity within the abnormality confirms the presence of a soft tissue mass. However, absence of demonstrable vascularity is less helpful, and short interval follow-up exam or assessment with precontrast and postcontrast CT or MRI may be indicated.

ACUTE CHOLECYSTITIS

Pathogenesis and Epidemiology

Acute cholecystitis occurs in approximately one third of patients with gallstones and results from persistent obstruction of the cystic duct or gallbladder neck with resulting distention of the gallbladder and increased intraluminal pressure.[25-26] Inflammation of the gallbladder mucosa may result from chemical injury caused by bile salts and/or superimposed infection. If untreated, the inflammation eventually progresses to involve all layers of the gallbladder wall and may lead to necrosis, gangrene and gallbladder perforation. In most patients, acute cholecystitis is associated with gallstones.

Acute cholecystitis is the most common cause of right upper quadrant pain and the primary mode of treatment

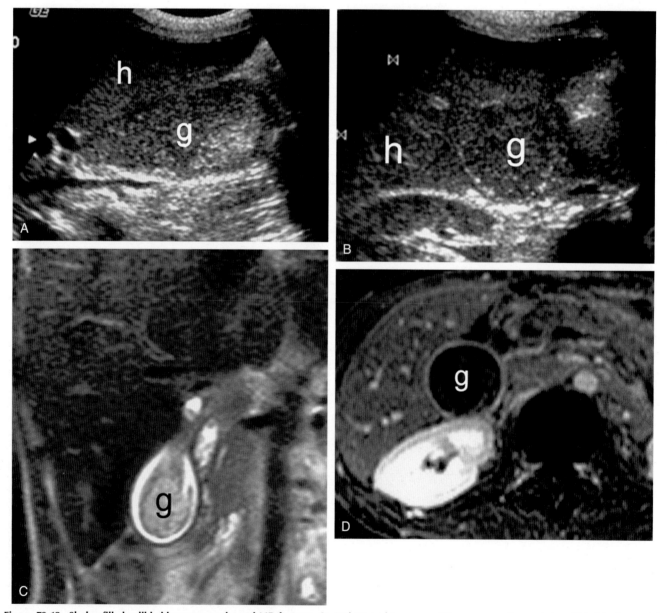

Figure 79-12. Sludge-filled gallbladder: sonography and MR features. Sagittal (**A**) and transverse (**B**) sonograms demonstrate gallbladder lumen (g) filled with echogenic material. The echotexture is similar to that of the adjacent liver parenchyma (h). This appearance is referred to as "hepatization" of the gallbladder. **C.** Coronal T2-weighted HASTE MR image demonstrates intermediate signal intensity material in the gallbladder lumen (g). **D.** Axial contrast-enhanced T1-weighted fat suppressed MR image with subtraction shows no enhancement of gallbladder lumen (g), excluding an intraluminal mass.

imaging evaluation is critical to provide prompt diagnosis and appropriate intervention.

Imaging

The relative roles of ultrasonography versus cholescintigraphy using technetium-tagged iminodiacetic acid (IDA) and IDA-like agents for the diagnosis of acute cholecystitis has been extensively addressed in the literature. In a study published in 1982, the accuracy of scintigraphy with IDA compared with sonography showed similar excellent results in 91 patients with suspected acute cholecystitis, with accuracy of ultrasound of 88% and of scintigraphy of 85%.[29] A study in 1983 of 194 patients showed that sensitivity of both modalities was high but the specificity of ultrasound was lower at 64% with a positive predictive value of 40%.[30] The sonographic Murphy sign, however, was not evaluated in this study and there was no correlation with clinical data. A more recent study comparing cholescintigraphy and sonography in surgically proven cases of acute cholecystitis, showed an accuracy of scintigraphy of 91% versus 77% for sonography.[31] Sensitivity of IDA scanning for acute cholecystitis (90.9%) was also higher than that of ultrasound (62%) in a second recent study.[32]

Although possibly somewhat less sensitive and specific for the diagnosis of acute cholecystitis compared to cholescintigraphy, ultrasound does have the advantages of being readily available, rapidly performed, involving no radiation and allowing for detection of cholecystitis related complications as well as alternative diagnoses. Ultrasound can confirm the diagnosis of acute cholecystitis and distinguish from chronic cholecystitis with an accuracy of 95% to 99%.[25] The disadvantages of radionuclide scintigraphy include the time to perform the examination (up to 4 hours) and inability to evaluate for nonbiliary conditions. Furthermore, false positive results can occur in patients with high bilirubin levels and severe intercurrent illnesses. False negative results, however, are rare.

Depending on the clinical circumstances, a combination of both cholescintigraphy and sonography may be required to make a definitive diagnosis of acute cholecystitis. The American College of Radiology (ACR) appropriateness criteria[27] score ultrasound slightly higher than cholescintigraphy for evaluation of the patient with right upper quadrant pain, fever, elevated white blood cell count (WBC), and positive Murphy sign but state that either modality may be utilized. With this clinical spectrum and a normal gallbladder at sonography, cholescintigraphy is given the highest score. If there is pain but no fever or leukocytosis, ultrasound is given the highest score and if there are only gallstones and pain, cholescintigraphy is considered the test of choice. CT and MRI can also play an important role when ultrasound findings are equivocal or further evaluation is required, such as when complications are suspected (discussed further below).

Cholescintigraphy

Normally, the hepatic parenchyma is observed within 1 minute with peak activity at 10 to 15 minutes.[33] The bile ducts are usually visible within 10 minutes and the gallbladder should appear within one hour if the cystic duct is patent (Fig. 79-14A). If the gallbladder has not been defined, imaging should be carried out further, up to 4 hours. Prompt biliary excretion

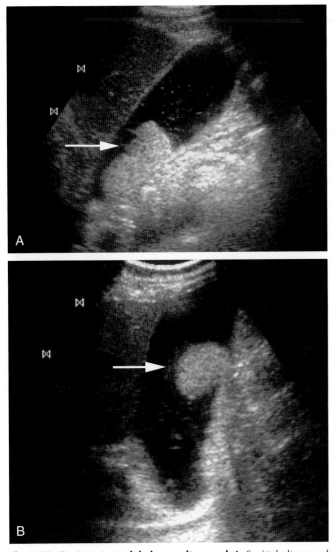

Figure 79-13. Aggregate of sludge on ultrasound. A. Sagittal ultrasound image of the gallbladder demonstrates an echogenic nonshadowing abnormality located dependently within the gallbladder lumen (*arrow*). **B.** When the patient is imaged in the upright position, this abnormality changes location and configuration (*arrow*), confirming aggregate of sludge rather than soft tissue mass.

is laparoscopic cholecystectomy. Clinical findings include fever, right upper quadrant pain, and elevated white blood cell count. Approximately one third of patients have a clinically positive Murphy's sign, which refers to focal tenderness over the gallbladder upon inspiration. However, the clinical manifestations may overlap considerably with other intra-abdominal processes not related to the biliary tract, such as acute hepatitis, primary liver pathology including abscess or neoplasm, peptic ulcer disease, and pancreatitis. Also, clinical findings in the elderly or critically ill patient may be more subtle. Approximately one third of patients with the presumptive diagnosis of acute cholecystitis will not have acute cholecystitis on follow-up, and 20% to 25% of patients who have surgery for acute cholecystitis will ultimately have a different diagnosis.[27] In a series of 52 patients with right upper quadrant pain suspected of having acute cholecystitis, acute cholecysitis was confirmed in 34.6%, chronic cholecystitis in 32.7%, and 32.7% had normal gallbladders.[28] Therefore,

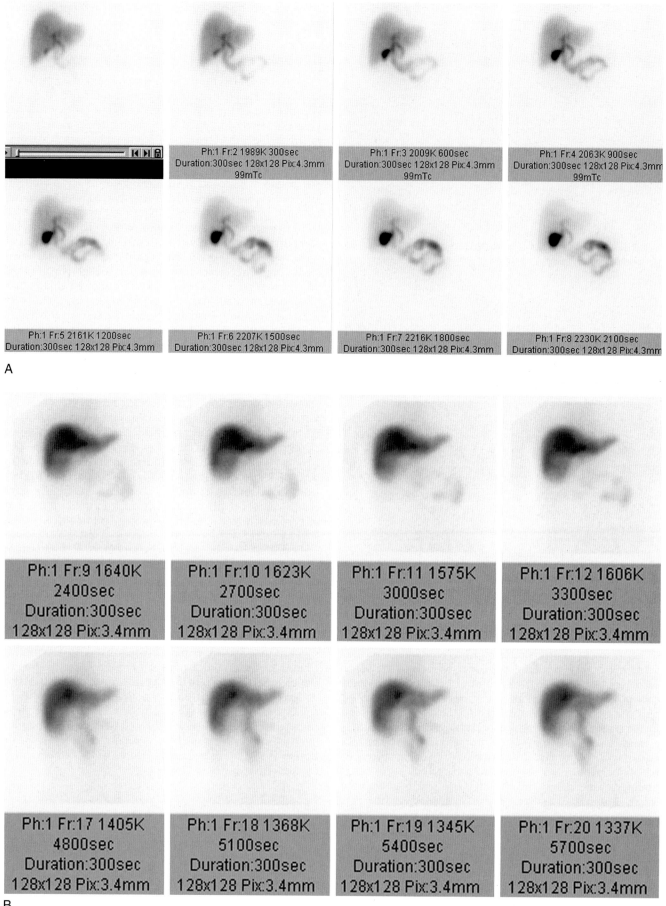

A

B

Figure 79-14. Cholescintigraphy. A. Negative hydroxy iminodiacetic acid scintiscan (HIDA) shows prompt filling of the gallbladder lumen with tracer, confirming patency of the cystic duct. **B.** Positive HIDA scan. There is no filling of the gallbladder, confirming obstruction of the cystic duct and the presence of acute cholecystitis. (Images courtesy of Dr. Elissa Kramer, Department of Nuclear Medicine, New York University Medical Center.)

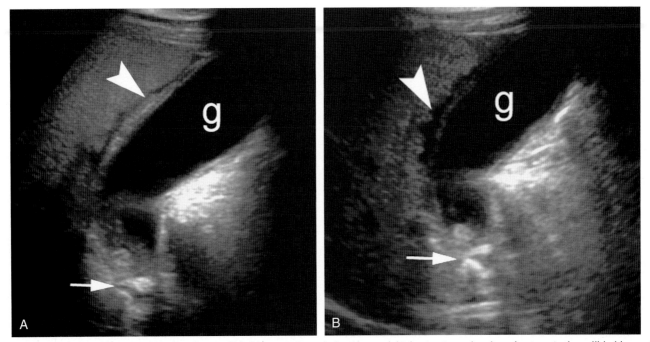

Figure 79-15. Acute cholecystits: ultrasound. A. Gallbladder (g) is distended, with mural thickening (*arrowhead*), and a stone in the gallbladder neck (*arrow*). Positive sonographic Murphy sign was present. **B.** In the upright position, the gallbladder (g) is distended, and pericholecystic fluid is evident (*arrowhead*). Stone (*arrow*) does not change location, confirming impaction in gallbladder neck.

of tracer without demonstration of the gallbladder is the hallmark of acute cholecystitis (Fig. 79-14B). As noted above, false positive results may occur in patients with abnormal bile flow because of liver disease or a prolonged fast with distended sludge-filled gallbladder. Also, delayed gallbladder filling can occur in the setting of chronic cholecystitis. If the gallbladder is not visualized after 1 hour and there is visualization of the biliary tree and duodenum, intravenous (IV) morphine may be administered, which causes spasm of the sphincter of Oddi, raising pressure within the bile ducts and increasing the likelihood of bile flow into the gallbladder. If the patient has been fasting for more than 24 hours, an oral fatty meal or IV cholecystokinin may be administered, resulting in gallbladder contraction so that the gallbladder can empty and then refill.

Ultrasound

The ultrasound findings in acute uncomplicated cholecystitis are well-described and include gallstones, a positive sonographic Murphy sign, gallbladder distention, wall thickening and pericholecystic fluid[25,26,34-36] (Figs. 79-15 and 79-16). The sonographic Murphy sign refers to maximum tenderness during compression with the ultrasound transducer placed directly over the gallbladder. Of these findings, the first two are considered the most specific. In a study by Ralls et al,[37] a positive sonographic Murphy sign and the presence of gallstones had a positive predictive value of 92% for the diagnosis of acute cholecystitis. It is cautioned that the sonographic Murphy sign may be blunted if the patient has received pain medication prior to ultrasound evaluation. Furthermore,

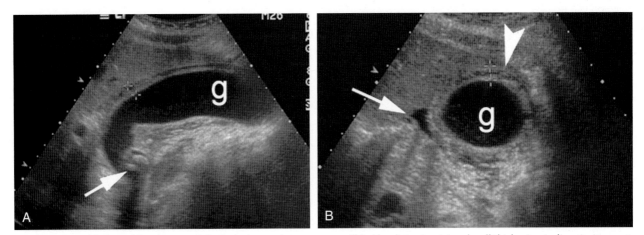

Figure 79-16. Acute cholecystitis: ultrasound. A. Sagittal scan demonstrates gallbladder distension (g) and wall thickening (calipers). *Arrow*, stones in gallbladder neck. **B.** Transverse scan of gallbladder (g) demonstrates wall thickening (*arrowhead*) and pericholecystic fluid (*arrow*). A positive sonographic Murphy sign was demonstrated.

1422 SECTION IX Gallbladder and Biliary Tract

impaired mental status may preclude evaluation of this sign. Last, the sonographic Murphy sign may be negative in the setting of gangrenous cholecystitis (see later). If it can be demonstrated that a stone is impacted in the gallbladder neck or cystic duct, this is also an important finding that increases the likelihood of acute cholecystitis (see Fig. 79-15B). To determine that a stone is impacted in the gallbladder neck or cystic duct requires evaluating the patient in the left lateral decubitus or upright position to assess for mobility of the stone.

Less specific ultrasound findings of acute cholecystitis include gallbladder distention, wall thickening, pericholecystic fluid, or the presence of other intraluminal material such as sludge. In most cases of acute cholecystitis, the gallbladder will be distended. An exception to this occurs when acute cholecystitis complicates chronic cholecystitis when there may be mural fibrosis impeding distention. Also, if there has been free perforation of the gallbladder, it may appear completely collapsed (discussed further later). Diffuse gallbladder wall thickening, measuring greater than 3 mm, is present in 50% to 75% of patients with acute cholecystitis but may also be associated with chronic inflammation.[25] Furthermore, gallbladder wall thickening may be associated with many other conditions including liver disease, such as acute hepatitis, ascites, hypoalbuminemia, alcoholism, as well as congestive heart failure, acquired immunodeficiency syndrome (AIDS), and sepsis (Fig. 79-17). In patients with AIDS, cholangiopathy may be related to infection with such organisms as *Cryptosporidium*. Other causes include adenomyomatosis and gallbladder neoplasm. In acute cholecystitis, wall thickening is generally diffuse, and if more focal, a complication such as gangrenous change or other etiology, such as neoplasm, should be considered. Pericholecystic fluid is generally associated with more severe cholecystitis and may be associated with perforation or abscess formation. However, this may also be nonspecific, especially in the setting of generalized ascites. Other entities that clinically can mimic acute cholecystitis,

such as peptic ulcer disease and pancreatitis, may also be associated with pericholecystic fluid. Sludge, related to bile stasis, can develop in patients with acute cholecystitis due to gallbladder obstruction.

The role of color and power Doppler evaluation as an adjunct to gray-scale imaging in the diagnosis of acute cholecystitis is somewhat controversial. Although there may be overlap between findings in acute and chronic cholecystitis,[38] there may be a potential role for Doppler evaluation of the inflamed gallbladder[39] (Fig. 79-18).

Computed Tomography

Although not the first-line imaging modality for the evaluation of suspected acute gallbladder pathology, the role of CT in the evaluation of the patient with acute abdominal pain continues to expand. The etiology of patient symptoms may initially be unclear due to nonspecific clinical findings. CT may be the initial study performed as it allows for more comprehensive evaluation of the abdomen and pelvis and can identify other acute inflammatory processes that may simulate acute cholecystitis. Therefore, it is important to become familiar with the spectrum of CT findings in acute cholecystitis. CT is also a useful adjunct to ultrasound when ultrasound findings are equivocal or complications are suspected (see later). In a recent retrospective study at the author's institution,[40] the overall sensitivity, specificity and accuracy of CT for the diagnosis of acute cholecystitis were 91.7%, 99.1%, and 94.3%, respectively.

The CT findings of acute cholecystitis include gallstones, gallbladder distention, thickening of the gallbladder wall, pericholecystic inflammation, and fluid[17,36,41-44] (Fig. 79-19). CT is limited with respect to detection of gallstones as up to only 75% are visualized.[17] Of these signs, the presence of pericholecystic inflammatory change is believed to be the most specific.[17,42] The presence of gallbladder wall thickening on CT is a very nonspecific finding and may be secondary to a broad

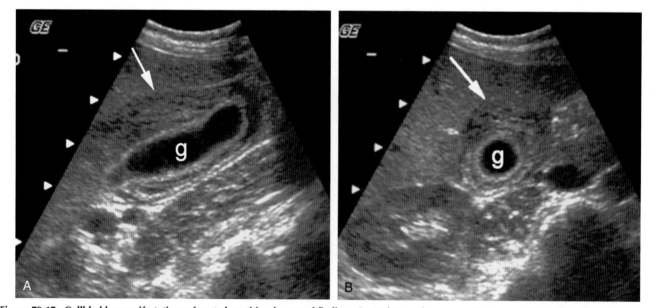

Figure 79-17. Gallbladder manifestations of acute hepatitis: ultrasound findings. Sagittal (**A**) and transverse (**B**) images of the gallbladder demonstrate that the gallbladder lumen (g) is not significantly distended. The wall is markedly thickened (*arrows*) and has a striated appearance indicating mural edema.

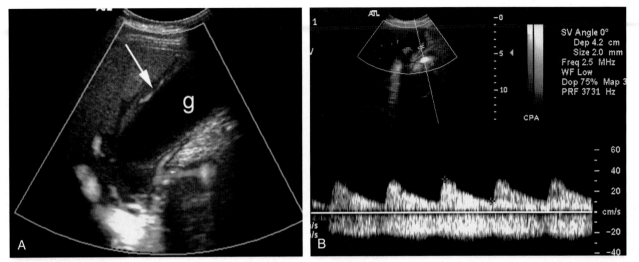

Figure 79-18. Acute cholecystitis: Doppler ultrasound. A. Sagittal scan of the gallbladder (g) demonstrates distention and wall thickening. Increased mural vascularity is demonstrated (*arrow*) with power Doppler. **B.** Spectral Doppler tracing confirms arterial waveform.

spectrum of both inflammatory and neoplastic disorders.[45] Gallbladder carcinoma tends to cause greater mural thickening than benign disorders.[46]

Occasionally, it may be difficult to differentiate gallbladder wall thickening from pericholecystic fluid. Pericholecystic fluid tends to be more focal and irregularly marginated, whereas mural thickening is concentric. Punctuate foci of contrast enhancement may be observed corresponding to enhancing vessels within the gallbladder wall. A target appearance corresponds to an inner layer of enhancing mucosa, an outer layer of enhancing serosa with hypoattenuating submucosal edema between the two.

An ancillary CT finding of gallbladder inflammation is increased contrast enhancement in the liver parenchyma adjacent to the gallbladder[44,47,48] (Fig. 79-20). This finding results from hepatic arterial hyperemia secondary to gallbladder inflammation. Recently, increased density of the gallbladder wall has been described as a finding on unenhanced CT, found in approximately 51% of patients.[49] This is found in

patients with mucosal hemorrhage and necrosis and may be a predictor of gangrenous change.

Magnetic Resonance Imaging

Like CT, MRI is usually employed in the setting of suspected acute cholecystitis when other imaging findings are equivocal or the clinical setting is ambiguous.[50-52] MRCP is very sensitive in the diagnosis of choledocholithiasis, which is particularly important if laparoscopic cholecystectomy is performed. In addition to gallstones, MR readily demonstrates gallbladder wall edema,[52,53] which manifests as high signal intensity on T2-weighted images.[52,53] In one series, pericholecystic high signal intensity on single-shot fast spin-echo (SSFSE) images had an overall accuracy of 89%, specificity of 79%, positive predictive value of 87%, and negative predictive value of 85% for the diagnosis of acute cholecystitis.[54] Loud and associates[51] found contrast-enhanced T1-weighted images useful for the diagnosis of acute cholecystitis. Patients with surgically proved

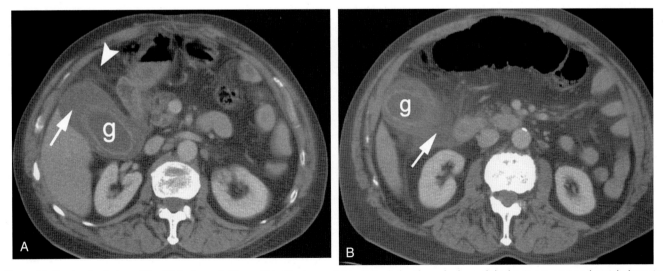

Figure 79-19. Acute cholecystitis: CT features. A. The gallbladder lumen (g) is distended with marked mural thickening (*arrow*) and pericholecystic inflammatory changes (*arrowhead*). **B.** Slightly more inferior image demonstrate pericholecystic fluid (*arrow*).

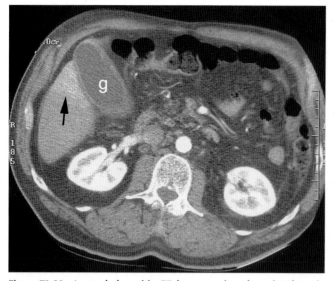

Figure 79-20. Acute cholecystitis: CT demonstration of transient hepatic attenuation difference (THAD). Gallbladder (g) is distended with mural thickening. There is focal increase in contrast enhancement of the liver parenchyma adjacent to the gallbladder (*arrow*) representing hyperemia related to adjacent gallbladder inflammation.

acute cholecystitis had greater than 80% contrast enhancement of the wall, which helped to differentiate acute from chronic cholecystitis. A transient increase in hepatic enhancement may be seen around the gallbladder in 70% of cases during the arterial phase of enhancement and, as with CT, may be an important indicator of acute gallbladder inflammation[51,52] (Fig. 79-21). MR has been shown to be superior to ultrasound for detection of obstructing calculi in the gallbladder neck and the cystic duct (see Fig. 79-21C and D).[55] MRI may also be helpful to identify complications of acute cholecystitis. Magnetic resonance cholangiopancreatography (MRCP) is more completely discussed in Chapter 77.

ACUTE ACALCULOUS CHOLECYSTITIS

Epidemiology and Pathophysiology

The reported incidence of acute cholecystitis in the absence of gallstones ranges from approximately 5% to 10%.[25] In one large surgical series,[56] acute acalculous cholecystitis (AAC) represented 14% of cases of acute cholecystitis and was responsible for 2% of all cholecystectomies. Bile stasis, gallbladder ischemia, cystic duct obstruction, and systemic infection are considered to be the most important factors in pathogenesis of acute acalculous cholecystitis (AAC).[57,58] Histologic features include gallbladder wall inflammation, with necrosis of blood vessels in the muscularis and serosa of the gallbladder.[59] AAC occurs with increased incidence in patients who are critically ill or with prolonged illness, such as in the setting of trauma or after prolonged stay in the intensive care unit. Other risk factors include major cardiovascular disorders, cardiopulmonary bypass, diabetes, autoimmune disease, bacterial and fungal sepsis, hyperalimentation, and AIDS. Although much less common, the disease can occur de novo in the absence of these other risk factors in otherwise apparently healthy individuals.[60,61]

AAC is a more fulminant form of acute cholecystitis with higher morbidity and mortality and rapid progression to gangrene and perforation. Mortality is reported to be as high as 65%[62]; therefore, early diagnosis is important. The diagnosis of AAC, however, often presents a challenge, particularly if there are no apparent risk factors. Clinical findings, such as fever and leukocytosis, are nonspecific. The diagnosis should be suspected in critically ill or injured patients who have fever or infection with no other apparent source.

Imaging

Ultrasound

The reported sensitivity of ultrasound in AAC varies widely from 36% to 92%[56] (Fig. 79-22). Gallstones are not present and afflicted patients are often insensitive to pain due to altered mental status or medications, thus making the sonographic Murphy sign unreliable.[63] These patients may also have hypoalbuminemia, congestive heart failure, and longstanding parenteral nutrition, all of which are associated with gallbladder wall thickening, distention, and sludge. There is a great degree of overlap in ultrasound findings of intensive care unit patients with AAC and those without. In one study evaluating the ultrasound findings in ICU patients, the majority of patients had some abnormality of the gallbladder.[64] Nevertheless, ultrasound has the advantage of being performed portably at the bedside and remains a reasonable first study for the diagnosis of AAC.

Cholescintigraphy is also of limited value in the diagnosis of AAC with a significant false positive rate (nonvisualization of the gallbladder) of up to 40% in patients with hepatocellular dysfunction, prolonged fasting, or severe illness.[63,65] A negative study is useful for excluding acalculous cholecystitis; however, a positive study must be interpreted with caution. The specificity can be improved to 88% with the use of morphine.[66] A prospective study comparing ultrasound and morphine scintigraphy (MC) in the diagnosis of AAC found that the sensitivity of ultrasound and MC was 50% and 67%, specificity was 94% and 100%, positive predictive value was 86% and 100%, negative predictive value was 71% and 80%, and accuracy was 75% and 86%, respectively.[67] Combining the two modalities may lead to greater diagnostic accuracy.

CT/MRI

CT or MRI may be helpful in the diagnosis of AAC in the patient who is stable enough to undergo imaging. With the exception of the absence of gallstones, the CT and MRI findings of AAC are similar to those of calculous cholecystitis. The advantage of these modalities is that they may demonstrate pericholecystic inflammatory change and fluid and abnormalities of the gallbladder wall or adjacent hepatic parenchyma, which may not be appreciated at sonography, allowing for a more specific diagnosis[50,52,68-70] (Fig. 79-23).

Many times, these patients are too ill for additional cross-sectional imaging evaluation. If there is no other source of sepsis discovered, it may be prudent to proceed with percutaneous cholecystostomy, which can be performed at the bedside. This has been shown to be a safe and effective procedure in the patient with acute cholecystitis who is not a surgical candidate.[71] This can be helpful, for both diagnosis

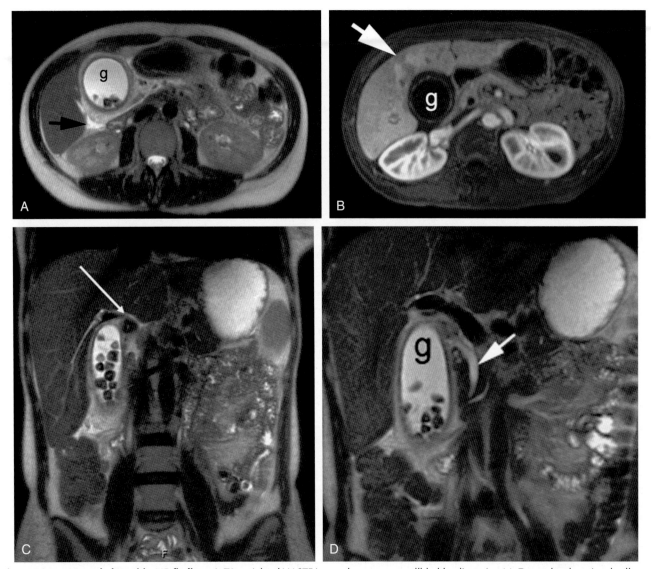

Figure 79-21. Acute cholecystitis: MR findings. A. T2-weighted HASTE image demonstrates gallbladder distension (g). Dependent low signal gallstones are evident. Gallbladder wall is thickened and there is pericholecystic fluid (*arrow*). **B.** Contrast-enhanced T1-weighted gradient echo fat suppressed image demonstrates gallbladder distension (g) with wall thickening. Increased enhancement is present in adjacent liver parenchyma (*arrow*). **C.** Coronal HASTE image demonstrates distended gallbladder with multiple stones. *Arrow*, stone in gallbladder neck. **D.** Coronal HASTE image demonstrates normal common bile duct (CBD) (*arrow*).

and treatment, in patients with sepsis of unknown cause and equivocal imaging findings of AAC.[72,73] A study showed that percutaneous cholecystostomy was superior to gallbladder aspiration in terms of clinical effectiveness and was associated with the same complications.[74]

COMPLICATIONS OF ACUTE CHOLECYSTITIS

Gangrenous Cholecystitis

Gangrenous cholecystitis is a severe form of acute cholecystitis associated with vascular compromise and intramural hemorrhage, necrosis, and intramural abscess formation. This is usually caused by a stone impacting the cystic duct, with progressive distension of the gallbladder and ultimately ischemic necrosis of the wall.[75] The incidence ranges from

2% to approximately 30% in various surgical series.[76-78] The incidence is increased in men, patients of advanced age, and those with cardiovascular disease. Once diagnosed, treatment is generally emergency cholecystectomy to avoid life-threatening complications such as perforation. There is a higher rate of conversion to open cholecystectomy than in uncomplicated acute cholecystitis.[79-81]

At sonography, the features of gangrenous cholecystitis include the presence of heterogeneous, striated thickening and irregularity of the gallbladder wall, and intraluminal membranes resulting from desquamation of the gallbladder mucosa[82,83] (Figs. 79-24 and 79-25). The irregular or asymmetric thickening of the gallbladder wall likely results from ulceration, hemorrhage, necrosis, or microabscess formation. In a series by Jeffrey and colleagues,[83] these findings were present in 50% of patients. A striated appearance of the gallbladder wall was found in 40% of patients in the series by Teefey and

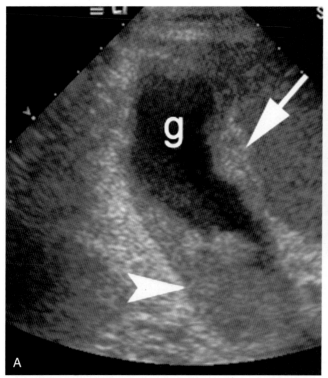

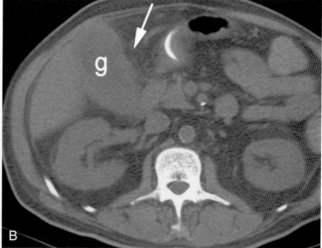

Figure 79-22. Acute acalculous cholecystitis: ultrasound and CT findings. A. Gallbladder (g) is distended, with mural thickening (*arrow*), and contains dependent echoes indicating sludge (*arrowhead*). These are common ultrasound findings in acutely ill patients. **B.** Noncontrast CT scan demonstrates gallbladder distension (g) with inflammatory changes in pericholecystic fat (*arrow*), confirming presence of gallbladder inflammation.

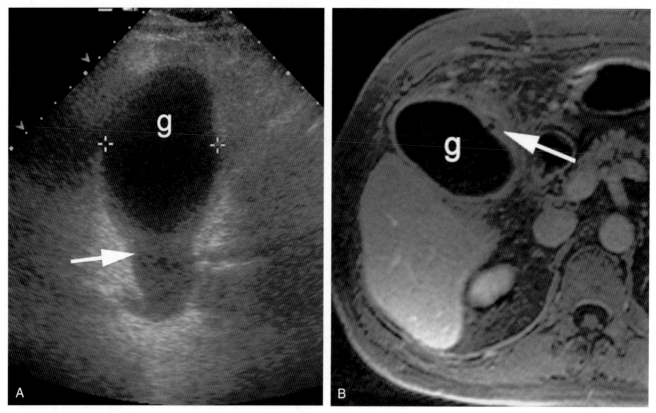

Figure 79-23. Acute acalculous cholecystitis: ultrasound and MR features. A. Ultrasound demonstrates markedly distended gallbladder (g) with layering sludge (*arrow*). **B.** Axial T1-weighted fat suppressed gradient-echo image with gadolinium enhancement demonstrates distended gallbladder (g), wall thickening, and pericholecystic inflammatory change. *Arrow* points to small intramural abscess not suspected clinically.

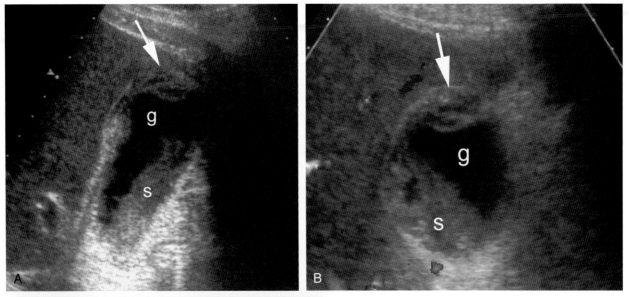

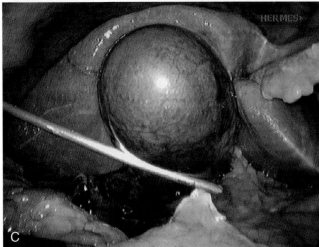

Figure 79-24. Acute gangrenous cholecystitis: ultrasound findings. Sagittal (**A**) and transverse (**B**) ultrasound images demonstrate distended gallbladder (g) containing intraluminal sludge (s). Gallbladder wall is irregular in contour with asymmetric thickening (*arrow*). **C.** Laparoscopic cholecystectomy image show edematous, ischemic gallbladder wall.

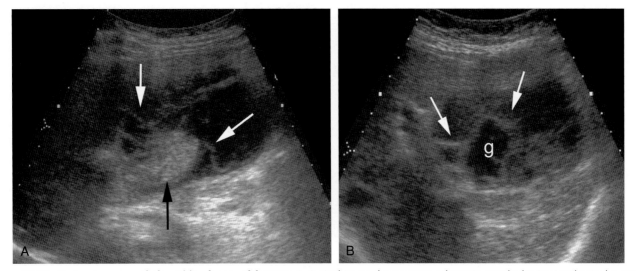

Figure 79-25. Acute gangrenous cholecystitis: ultrasound features. A. Sagittal image demonstrates echogenic, nonshadowing intraluminal material indicating aggregates of sludge (*black arrow*). Curvilinear intraluminal echogenic regions (*white arrows*) represent intraluminal membranes secondary to sloughed mucosa. **B.** Transverse image demonstrates intraluminal membranes (*arrows*) in gallbladder (g) lumen.

associates[82] However, this finding can be found in other conditions that cause gallbladder wall edema, such as hepatitis; therefore, this is not specific for gangrenous cholecystitis. The presence of intraluminal membranes is considered a more specific finding (see Fig. 79-25). It is important to remember that the sonographic Murphy sign may be not be present due to associated dennervation of the gallbladder wall. In a series by Simeone and colleagues,[84] the sonographic Murphy sign was positive in only 33% of patients with gangrenous cholecystitis. Additional findings include intramural abscess formation and/or pericholecystic fluid collection or abscess formation caused by perforation of the gallbladder.

CT findings of gangrenous cholecystitis parallel findings at sonography and include intraluminal membranes, intraluminal hemorrhage, and irregularity or disruption of the gallbladder wall[17,40,42,85-87] (Fig. 79-26). An additional finding detectable at CT is irregular or lack of gallbladder wall enhancement[40,87] (Fig. 79-27). A study by the author evaluated the sensitivity and specificity of CT for the diagnosis of gangrenous cholecystitis.[40] CT was highly specific for identifying acute gangrenous cholecystitis (96%) but had low sensitivity (29.3%). The most specific findings at CT for the presence of gangrenous cholecystitis were gas in the gallbladder wall or lumen, intraluminal membranes, irregularity or absence of the gallbladder wall, pericholecystic abscess, and lack of gallbladder wall enhancement. In this study, the presence of pericholecystic fluid, degree of gallbladder distention in the short axis, and degree of mural thickening were also predictive of the severity of gallbladder inflammation. When CT is performed to evaluate for cholecystitis, intravenous contrast should be administered if possible since this improves delineation of the wall and identification of lack of enhancement, intramural abscess or focal disruption which are all important features of gangrenous cholecystitis.

Hemorrhagic Cholecystitis

Hemorrhagic cholecystitis is an uncommon complication of acute cholecystitis and usually occurs in the setting of cholelithiasis and gangrenous cholecystitis. Transmural inflamma-

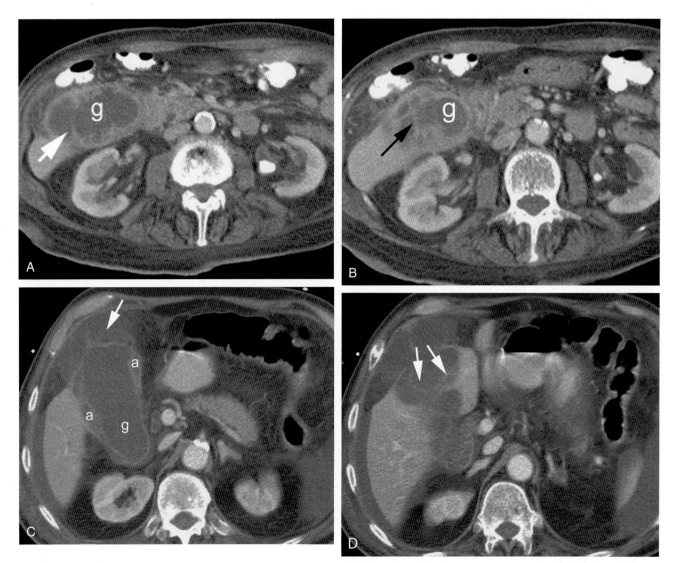

Figure 79-26. Acute gangrenous cholecystitis: CT findings. A and **B.** Gallbladder (g) is distended with thickened, irregularly enhancing wall. *Arrows* —intraluminal membranes. **C.** Scan obtained in a different patient shows distended gallbladder (g) with thickened wall, which demonstrates heterogeneous contrast enhancement. Low attenuation areas correspond to intramural abscesses (a). *Arrows*—loculated pericholecystic fluid collection secondary to contained gallbladder perforation. **D.** Slightly more inferior image demonstrates intraluminal membranes (*arrows*).

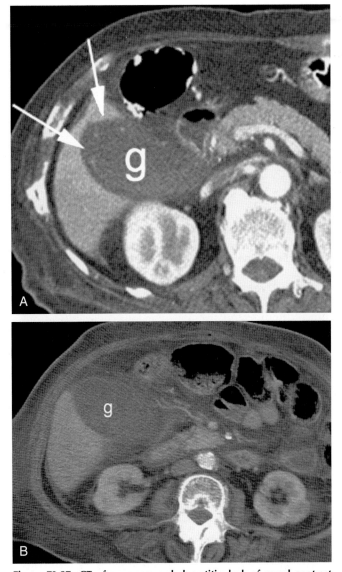

Figure 79-27. CT of gangrenous cholecystitis: lack of mural contrast enhancement. A. There is apparent discontinuity of the gallbladder wall (*arrows*) where no mucosal enhancement is noted. g, distended gallbladder. **B.** Contrast-enhanced CT scan in a second patient demonstrates distended gallbladder (g) with extensive pericholecystic inflammatory change. There is no contrast enhancement of gallbladder wall.

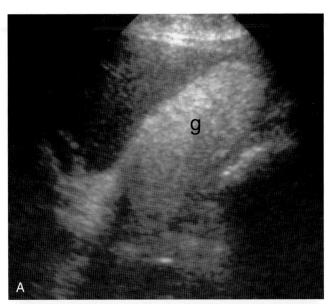

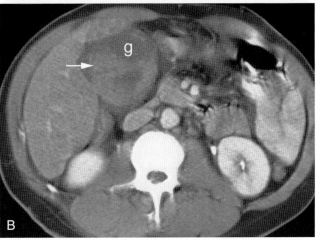

Figure 79-28. Hemorrhagic cholecystitis: ultrasound and CT findings. A. Sagittal ultrasound scan demonstrates distended gallbladder (g) with lumen completely filled with echogenic material corresponding to hemorrhagic bile. **B.** CT scan demonstrates distended gallbladder (g) with fluid/fluid level (*arrow*) with high attenuation dependent component. These findings represent intraluminal blood clot.

tion causes mural necrosis and ulceration and results in hemorrhage into the gallbladder lumen.[88-90] Atherosclerotic change in the gallbladder wall may be a predisposing factor.[90] Blood clots in the lumen may become impacted in the cystic duct or common bile duct or pass into the small bowel. The clinical presentation may be identical to uncomplicated acute cholecystitis with fever, right upper quadrant pain but may also include biliary colic, jaundice, hematemesis, and melena.[91] Massive upper gastrointestinal bleeding and hemoperitoneun rarely occur.[92] Prompt diagnosis is essential due to associated high mortality rate.

At sonography, blood in the gallbladder lumen can be recognized as hyperechoic material that demonstrates greater echogenicity than sludge (Fig. 79-28). This may form a dependent layer; however, clotted blood may appear as a clump or mass adherent to the gallbladder wall or heterogeneous echogenic material.[88,91,93] An organized clot may simulate a polypoid, intraluminal mass.[94] As the hemorrhage evolves, the clot may become more cystic in appearance.[95] In addition to other findings of cholecystitis, CT shows increased density of bile[88] (see Fig. 79-28B). A fluid-fluid level may be observed with a high attenuation dependent component simulating the hemtocrit effect observed in acute hemorrhage[91] (Fig. 79-29A). Other causes of high density bile include biliary excretion of iodinated contrast material or milk of calcium; these do not generally appear as echogenic at sonography nor is a fluid-fluid level observed. If there is associated perforation of the gallbladder, hemoperitoneum will also be observed (Fig. 79-29B). On MRI, blood products appear as high signal intensity within the gallbladder lumen on T1-weighted images and moderate to high heterogeneous signal intensity on T2-weighted images.[52] The multiplanar capability of MRI may

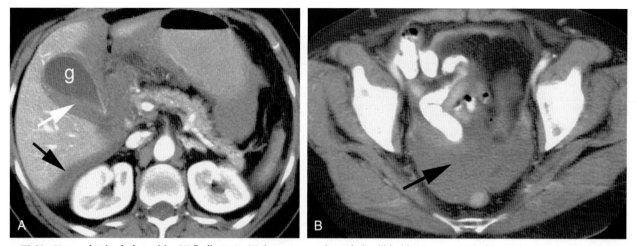

Figure 79-29. Hemorrhagic cholecystitis: CT findings. A. CT demonstrates distended gallbladder (g) containing layering material of high attenuation corresponding to intraluminal blood (*white arrow*). There has been perforation of the gallbladder resulting in hemoperitoneum (*black arrow*). **B.** Additional blood is demonstrated in the pelvis (*arrow*).

help to differentiate intraluminal blood from hemorrhage in the wall. MR angiography (MRA) may supplement conventional imaging if vascular pathology is suspected.

Emphysematous Cholecystitis

Emphysematous cholecystitis is a rare life-threatening and rapidly progressive complication of acute cholecystitis. Cystic artery compromise is thought to promote the proliferation of gas-producing organisms in an anaerobic environment and penetration of gas into the gallbladder wall.[96,97] The organisms most commonly isolated are *Clostridium welchii* and *Escherichia coli*.[97] At pathology, gallbladders with emphysematous cholecystitis have a higher incidence of endarteritis obliterans supporting vascular insufficiency as a causative factor. This complication occurs with higher frequency in patients with diabetes (up to 50%) and male patients (up to 71%).[98] Gallstones may be absent in up to one third of patients, and there is a high risk of gangrene and a perforation rate five times higher than in acute uncomplicated cholecystitis.[98,99]

The mortality rate for emphysematous cholecystitis is 15% versus 4% in uncomplicated acute cholecystitis.[98] Therefore, prompt diagnosis is critical. The clinical presentation is often indistinguishable from uncomplicated acute cholecystitis. In the diabetic patient, in particular, severe symptoms may be absent and there needs to be a high clinical index of suspicion. Prior to cross sectional imaging, emphysematous cholecystitis was diagnosed on the abdominal radiograph and classically described in three stages. Stage 1 includes gas in the gallbladder lumen, stage 2 includes gas in the gallbladder wall, and stage 3 includes gas in the pericholecystic soft tissues. Ultrasound and CT are now considered more sensitive in the detection of smaller amounts of gas. Ultrasound findings vary depending on the amount and location of gas.[25,26,100,101] A small amount of gas in the wall may appear as an echogenic focus with associated ring down or comet-tail artifact. Larger amounts of gas and intraluminal gas may appear as a curvilinear arc of increased echogenicity with associated "dirty" posterior acoustic shadowing[25] (Fig. 79-30A). In this setting, the gallbladder may be difficult to visualize due to associated acoustic shadowing. Sonographically it may be

difficult to differentiate emphysematous cholecystitis from a contracted gallbladder with stones or a porcelain gallbladder with calcified wall.[100]

CT has a higher sensitivity than sonography for the identification of emphysematous cholecystitis.[102] If emphysematous cholecystitis is suspected at sonography or there is a high clinical index of suspicion and ultrasound findings are equivocal, CT should be performed. CT is also indicated when the gallbladder cannot be adequately visualized at sonography. CT findings include gas within the gallbladder wall or nondependent portion of the lumen[103-105] (Fig. 79-31).

There may be extension into the pericholecystic soft tissues.[105] CT may also demonstrate other complications such as abscess formation and perforation (Fig. 79-30C and D; see Fig. 79-31B and C). Free intraperitoneal gas indicates associated free gallbladder perforation and constitutes a surgical emergency.

The MRI features of emphysematous cholecystitis have not yet been well described. A recent report describing MR imaging features in a case of emphysematous cholecystitis included (1) a signal void in the nondependent portion of the gallbladder and intermediate signal intensity fluid in the dependent portion of the gallbladder, representing a gas-fluid level, (2) low signal intensity rim surrounding the gallbladder, indicating gas in the gallbladder wall, and (3) regions of very low signal intensity in the pericholecystic soft tissues, indicating extraluminal gas due to perforation.[106] Gas can be recognized as blooming artifact on gradient echo and echo-planar sequences.

Gallbladder Perforation

Gallbladder perforation can occur in the setting of cholelithiasis, cholecystitis, trauma, neoplasm, steroid use, or vascular compromise. Perforation is most often a complication of severe acute cholecystitis, occurring in approximately 8% to 12% of cases.[107,108] In one series, associated mortality was 24.1%.[107] In acute cholecystitis, progressive gallbladder distention and inflammation is followed by vascular compromise, gangrene, necrosis, and ultimately perforation.[108,109] The fundus is the most frequent site of perforation due to the

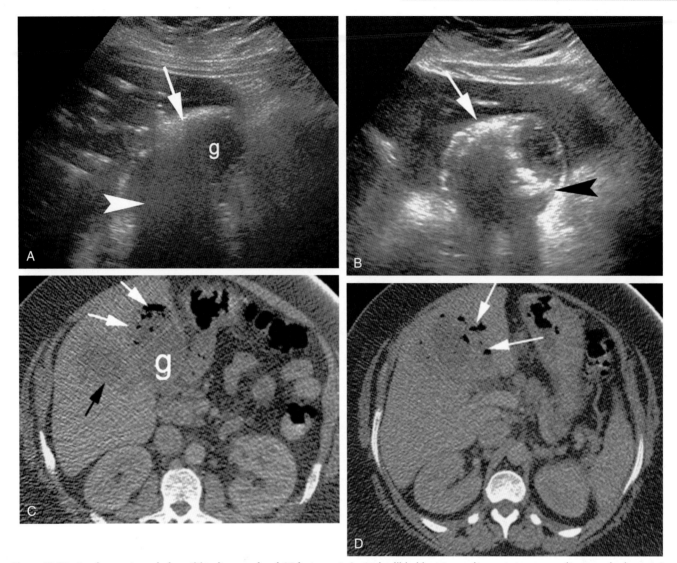

Figure 79-30. Emphysematous cholecystitis: ultrasound and CT features. A. Sagittal gallbladder (g) scan demonstrates an arc of increased echogenicity (*arrow*) in expected location of the gallbladder wall. This is associated with "dirty" posterior acoustic shadowing (*arrowhead*), suggesting intramural gas. **B.** Transverse image demonstrates intramural gas (*white arrow*) and intraluminal echogenic foci with posterior acoustic shadowing (*arrowhead*) indicating gallstones. **C.** Noncontrast CT demonstrates gas (*white arrows*) within lumen and wall of gallbladder (g). Low attenuation area in the adjacent liver is due to an abscess (*black arrow*). **D.** Gas (*arrows*) is present in the pericholecystic soft tissues.

relatively poor blood supply in this area. Associated complications include bacteremia, septic shock, bile peritonitis, and abscess formation with mortality rates ranging from 6% to 70%.[107,110-113]

Gallbladder perforation has been classified into three types[110]: (1) acute free perforation into the peritoneal cavity, (2) subacute perforation with pericholecystic abscess, and (3) chronic perforation with cholecystoenteric fistula formation. Subacute perforation with pericholecystic abscess formation is the most common type.[111] Abscess formation may be confined to the gallbladder fossa or spread into the peritoneal cavity or involve the liver.[114,115] Type 1 free perforation is associated with the highest mortality rate.[111] Type 3 perforation is associated with gallstone ileus, discussed later in this chapter.

Prompt diagnosis of gallbladder perforation is imperative. Emergent cholecystectomy is the treatment of choice. Clinical signs and symptoms may be nonspecific and may

be indistinguishable from uncomplicated cholecystitis, particularly in the diabetic patient, so that imaging plays an important diagnostic role.[116] At sonography, the gallbladder wall is irregular or ill-defined, there is a large amount of pericholecystic fluid or a loculated pericholecystic collection[109] (Fig. 79-32A). A focal defect in the wall of the gallbladder is a more specific finding but may not always be visualized[117] (Fig. 79-33A and B).

CT plays an important role in the evaluation of suspected gallbladder perforation when ultrasound findings are equivocal.[114,118,119] Interruption of the gallbladder wall or a focal mural defect may be more readily identified at CT (Fig. 79-33C) Associated findings include pericholecystic or intrahepatic abscess and spilled stones (Fig. 79-32B). Free gallbladder perforation is identified when there is free intraperitoneal fluid corresponding to bile (Fig. 79-34). In this setting, the gallbladder may be collapsed which may provide an additional diagnostic challenge as the diagnosis of acute cholecystitis

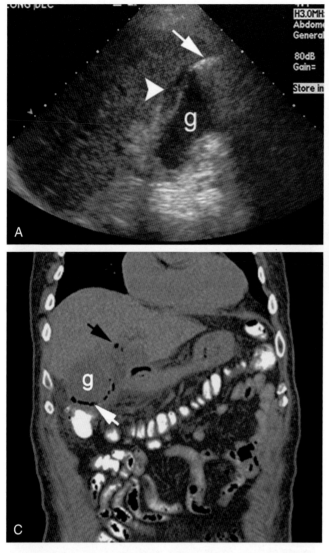

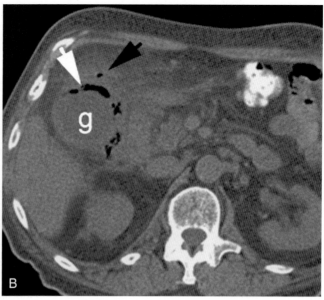

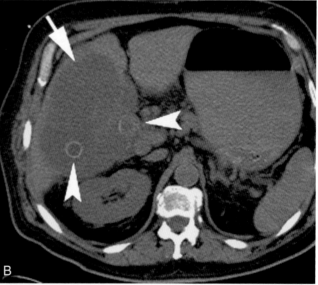

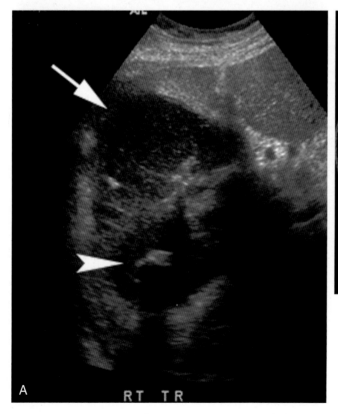

Figure 79-31. Emphysematous cholecystitis: ultrasound and CT features. A. Sagittal ultrasound demonstrates distended gallbladder (g) with thickened wall (*arrowhead*). Anterior wall (*arrow*) demonstrates increased echogenicity with dirty posterior acoustic shadowing, consistent with gas. **B.** Noncontrast CT demonstrates crescent of gas (*white arrow*) in gallbladder (g) wall. Extraluminal gas (*black arrow*) indicates perforation. **C.** Coronal reformatted CT image demonstrates gas in a dependent location (*arrow*) confirming intramural location. Gas in pericholecystic soft tissues (*black arrow*) indicates perforation. G, gallbladder.

Figure 79-32. Gallbladder perforation. A. Ultrasound demonstrates complex fluid collection in gallbladder fossa (*arrow*). Gallbladder wall is not delineated and perforated gallbladder with abscess was suspected. *Arrowhead*, gallstones. **B.** Noncontrast CT image demonstrates a large complex fluid collection in gallbladder fossa (*arrow*). There are spilled gallstones (*arrowheads*) due to gallbladder perforation.

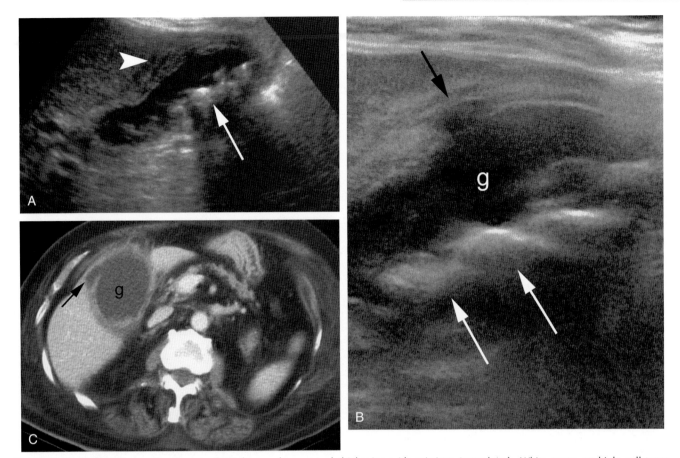

Figure 79-33. Gallbladder perforation. A. Sagittal scan shows mural thickening with striations (*arrowhead*). *White arrow*, multiple gallstones. **B.** Sagittal scan obtained with a linear transducer (8 MHz), produces higher resolution image. Focal defect in gallbladder wall (*black arrow*) is now evident. This indicates a focal intramural abscess or contained perforation. *White arrows*, gallstones. **C.** Contrast-enhanced CT confirms focal defect (*arrow*) in gallbladder (g) wall. Mural thickening and pericholecystic inflammatory changes are present, consistent with acute cholecystitis.

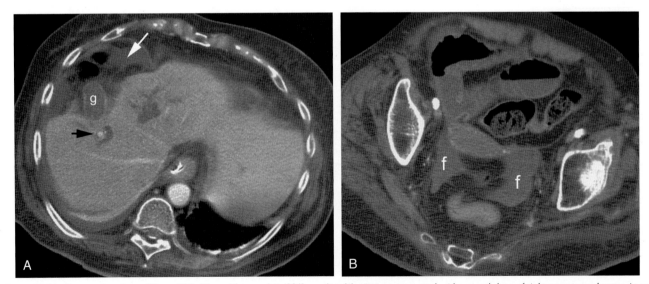

Figure 79-34. Free perforation of the gallbladder with associated bile peritonitis. Patient presented with several days of right upper quadrant pain and fever. **A.** Contrast enhanced CT demonstrates that gallbladder (g) is not distended. Calcified stone (*black arrow*) appears to be outside of gallbladder lumen. *White arrow*, perihepatic free fluid. **B.** Image of the pelvis demonstrates moderate free fluid (f) corresponding to bile.

may not be readily apparent. In these instances, presence of localized pericholecystic inflammatory change offers a diagnostic clue as to the etiology of free fluid and peritoneal inflammatory changes.

In a study comparing ultrasound with CT in 13 patients with surgically proven gallbladder perforation, a mural defect was visualized in 7 patients (53.8%) at CT but in no patient on ultrasound.[119] Ultrasound and CT were similar in demonstrating pericholecystic fluid collections, gallbladder wall thickening and cholelithiasis. Bulging or irregular contour of the gallbladder was demonstrated on ultrasound in five cases and on CT in two cases. In all cases, the site of the gallbladder wall defect or bulging on ultrasound or CT corresponded to the site of perforation. These authors concluded that CT was superior to ultrasound for the diagnosis of gallbladder perforation because of improved ability to demonstrate a focal wall defect. A more recent study by Sood and associates,[120] however, found that there was no statistically significant difference in the ability of ultrasound or CT to detect a focal wall defect in 18 patients evaluated with both modalities. This may be due to recent improvements in ultrasound technology allowing for better resolution and definition of the gallbladder wall. MR because of its superior soft tissue resolution and multiplanar imaging capability, may also be a useful adjunct if ultrasound and CT findings remain equivocal.

CHRONIC CHOLECYSTITIS

Pathogenesis and Epidemiology

Chronic cholecystitis is associated with cholelithiasis in 95% of cases and may occur after a single bout or multiple recurrent episodes of acute cholecystitis. Etiology is related to intermittent obstruction of the cystic duct or neck as well as gallbladder dysmotility.[2] Chronic inflammatory changes cause the gallbladder wall to become thickened and fibrotic and with increasing fibrosis, the gallbladder eventually becomes shrunken and distorted. If there are coexisting acute and chronic inflammatory changes at pathology, the term *chronic active cholecsytitis* may be used.[121]

Imaging

A diagnosis of chronic cholecystitis is difficult to establish with imaging and clinical correlation is required. Ultrasound findings include gallstones and thickened gallbladder wall with contraction of the gallbladder that persists in the fasting state (Fig. 79-35). On CT, pericholecystic inflammatory change may be absent.[44] On MR, gallbladder wall thickening related to chronic inflammation will demonstrate low signal intensity whereas acute cholecystitis is associated with edema in the wall, which demonstrates increased signal intensity on T2-

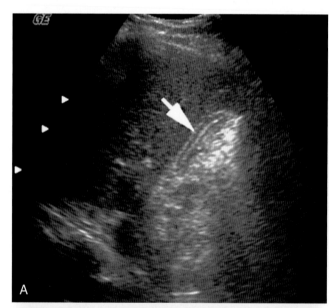

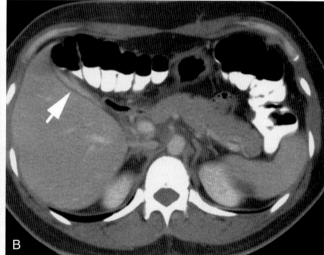

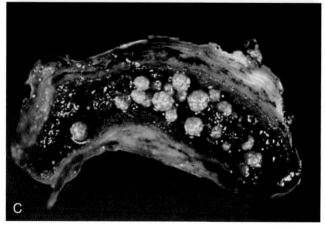

Figure 79-35. Chronic cholecystitis. A. Ultrasound demonstrates contracted gallbladder (*arrow*) in patient with repeated episodes of right upper quadrant pain. Patient was fasting at time of exam. **B.** The finding was confirmed at CT, with completely contracted gallbladder (*arrow*). Cholecystectomy was performed and chronic cholecystitis was confirmed at pathology. **C.** Specimen radiograph in a different patient shows multiple stones and a thick gallbladder wall.

weighted images.[52] Also, the increased perihepatic contrast enhancement observed with acute cholecystitis can be helpful in differentiating acute from chronic inflammation.[51,52]

Chronic Acaculous Cholesystitis

Chronic acalculous cholecystitis, a disorder characterized by recurrent biliary colic in a patient without radiographic evidence of gallstones, often creates a diagnostic dilemma for clinicians. In the absence of gallstones, it is often difficult to attribute patient symptoms to gallbladder inflammation. However, these patients may benefit from cholecystectomy for relief of symptoms.[122] A specific diagnosis may require nuclear medicine evaluation, including evaluation of the gallbladder ejection fraction. A decrease in gallbladder ejection fraction is a common feature of both calculus and acalculous chronic cholecystitis.[123] Cholecystokinin cholescintigraphy with calculation of gallbladder ejection fraction has been shown to be a predictor of pathology as well as subsequent symptom relief after cholecystectomy.[124]

Xanthogranulomatous Cholecystitis

Xanthogranulomatous cholecystitis (XGC) is a rare chronic inflammatory condition of the gallbladder, representing a form of chronic cholecystitis. Goodman and Ishak[125] reported the first series of cases at the Armed Forces Institute of Pathology in 1981. The estimated incidence is 1% to 2% of all cases of cholecystitis[126] and most patients present in the sixth or seventh decade.[127] In one recent surgical review, this disorder was found in 1.46% of all cholecystectomy specimens and was associated with gallstones in 85%, with average age of presentation of 52 years.[128] The proposed etiology of this disorder involves chronic gallbladder infection, usually in the setting of cholelithiasis, with mural microabscesses that involve Rokitansky-Aschoff sinuses. This may result from obstruction of gallbladder outflow, extravasation of bile into the gallbladder wall, and mucosal ulceration. Histiocytes accumulate in the gallbladder wall as a reaction to the extravasated bile and ultimately xanthogranulomatous nodules form in addition to extensive fibrous reaction.[129] On gross examination, the wall is thickened and irregular with yellow or brown nodules of varying sizes. Microscopically, the xanthogranulomatous nodules are composed of histiocytes, giant cells, and other chronic inflammatory cells such as lymphocytes and plasma cells. Hemosiderin and extravasated bile along with cholesterol clefts are present in the gallbladder wall. There may be associated biliary obstruction secondary to extrinsic compression of the bile duct and associated Mirizzi syndrome. The gallbladder often becomes adherent to adjacent organs and may be associated with fistula formation. There are no specific clinical or laboratory features and presentation may be similar to acute or chronic cholecystitis from any cause. Clinical symptoms may include right upper quadrant pain, nausea, vomiting, fever, anorexia, and weight loss.[129]

Both the ultrasound and CT features of xanthogranulomatous cholecystitis have been described[129-134] and overlap with findings of acute and chronic cholecystitis. On both modalities, the gallbladder wall is often markedly thickened and irregular with loss of normal planes with adjacent structures. An infiltrating mass may be apparent. More recent studies have described the presence of intramural nodules visualized

on both sonography and CT (Fig. 79-36A and B). In their series, Chun and colleagues[133] found low-density nodules in 11 cases of XGC, compared with only 7 of 17 cases of carcinoma. Intramural nodules are also a prominent finding of XGC described in other series[130-134] as well as a hypoechoic band around the gallbladder.[130,131] By performing ultrasound on pathologic specimens, Parra and associates[130] showed that the intramural hypoehocic nodules correspond to xanthogranulomatous nodules and the hypoechoic band may correspond to more generalized involvement. However, these nodules may also be confused with intramural abscesses in gangrenous cholecystitis and large Rokitansky-Aschoff sinuses in adenomyomatosis.

It can be very difficult to prospectively distinguish between XGC and gallbladder carcinoma on cross-sectional imaging studies due to many overlapping features, such as marked gallbladder wall thickening, irregularity, nodularity, and infiltration of the pericholecystic soft tissues. There is a 10% incidence of carcinoma in XCG[127] and fine-needle aspiration

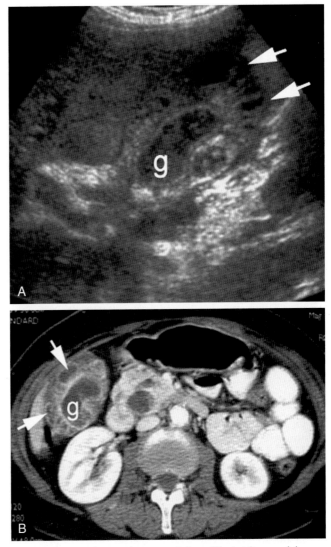

Figure 79-36. Xanthogranulomatous cholecystitis. A. Ultrasound demonstrates intralumenal echogenic material due to sludge. Gallbladder (g) wall is markedly thickened and contains hypoechoic nodules (*arrows*). **B.** Contrast-enhanced CT demonstrates marked gallbladder (g) wall thickening and hypoattenuating mural nodes (*arrows*).

biopsy has been successful in establishing the diagnosis.[135] Surgery is often difficult in these patients with a high conversion rate to open cholecystectomy.

CHOLEDOCHOLITHIASIS

Pathogenesis and Epidemiology

Biliary stones that form de novo within the biliary tract are referred to as primary stones whereas those that migrate from the gallbladder through the cystic duct or a cholecystocholedochal fistula are referred to as secondary stones.[136] The majority of stones within the bile ducts are secondary stones and pathogenesis is similar to that of gallstones. Migration of gallstones among asymptomatic patients is estimated to occur in 3% to 5% of patients per year, with 1% to 2% of patients per year developing symptoms, including biliary colic or acute pancreatitis.[137,138] Between 7% and 20% of patients undergoing cholecystectomy are found to have one or more stones in the common bile duct and these may be clinically silent.[139] Twenty percent to 30% of patients with gallstone pancreatitis have persistent common bile duct stones that fail to traverse the ampulla.[140] If a stone remains lodged in the common bile duct this can also lead to a potentially life-threatening emergency because of associated cholangitis.

Primary stones are classified according to their location within the biliary tract: intrahepatic, extrahepatic or ampullary. These develop in the setting of bile stasis and colonization of the bile with enteric organisms. Obstruction of bile may be related to inflammatory or iatrogenic strictures, congenital strictures or periampullary diverticula.[136] These stones are frequently associated with parasitic infections of the biliary tree, such as *Ascaris lumbricoides*. These worms become the nidus for stone and inflammatory stricture formation.

Imaging

ERCP

Endoscopic retrograde cholangiopancreatography (ERCP) and percutaneous transhepatic cholangiography (PTC) are highly accurate for the detection of choledocholithiasis and also provide access for therapeutic intervention. However, these are invasive procedures with associated risks including pancreatitis, sepsis, and hemorrhage. The reported complication rate of ERCP ranges from 3.0% to 5.5% and mortality rate from 0.2% to 1.0%.[141,142] Therefore, ERCP is generally reserved for patients who require therapy, such as secondary to an impacted stone, or with a high probability of stones and negative prior exams. Stones within the biliary tract may be readily detected with MRCP as less accurately with ultrasound and CT.

Ultrasound

Ultrasound is the primary imaging modality for evaluation of right upper quadrant pain and is considered superior to CT in the initial imaging evaluation of biliary disease.[36,143] The reported sensitivity of ultrasound ranges from 22% to 75% for common bile duct stones.[3,144-146] Limited sensitivity results in part from inability to completely visualize the duct,

particularly distally, due to interposed bowel gas, and distal stones are most commonly overlooked. In a study by Laing and colleagues,[147] 8 of 9 (89%) and 16 of 23 (70%) of distal CBD stones were visualized at sonography. Scanning the patient in the erect right posterior oblique (RPO) or right lateral decubitus position minimizes gas in the gastric antrum and duodenum and improves visualization of the distal duct. Water may also be administered orally to provide an acoustic window in the gastric antrum or duodenum.[26] Improved contrast enhancement and reduction of side lobe artifacts afforded by tissue harmonic imaging improves the sonographic detection of choledocholithiasis.[148] CBD stones appear as echogenic foci, which may or may not cause posterior acoustic shadowing depending upon size and composition (Figs. 79-37 and 79-38). As with cholelithiasis, nonshadowing stones may be difficult to differentiate from aggregates of sludge or soft tissue masses. Improved accuracy can be accomplished with the use of endoscopic ultrasound,[149] but this is more invasive and operator dependent (see Chapter 15).

Computed Tomography

Unenhanced conventional CT has a sensitivity of 75% in the detection of choledocholithiasis.[150-152] Indirect signs such as ductal dilatation or abrupt termination of the duct may be useful but are not conclusive. MDCT has a higher sensitivity, ranging from 65% to 88%.[153-156] MPR coronal images through the CBD may be useful in depicting stones (Fig. 79-39; see Fig. 79-37C). When specifically evaluating for choledocholithiasis, water should be used to opacify the bowel since positive oral contrast material may obscure visualization of distal CBD stones and fill perivaterian duodenal diverticulae. In a study comparing MDCT and ERCP for the detection of CBD calculi, CT had a sensitivity of 88%, specificity of 97%, and accuracy of 94%.[153] Bile window settings (adjusting the window level setting to the mean attenuation of the common bile duct and the window width to 150 HU) improves visualization of noncalcified stones, by creating better contrast between bile and soft tissues.

The CT appearance of CBD stones is variable. Depending on their composition, stones may be calcified, soft tissue or low density with respect to bile. Calcified stones are the most readily identified (Fig. 79-40A). Unenhanced images are better for detection as most stones are slightly hyperdense. Four CT criteria for detection of CBD stones have been: (1) a target sign refers to a central density, corresponding to the stone, surrounded by hypoattenuating bile or ampullary soft tissue; (2) the rim sign corresponds to a faint rim of increased density along the margin of a low density area (Fig. 79-40B); (3) the crescent sign refers to a calculus with increased density surrounded by a crescent of hypoattenuating bile (Fig. 79-40C); and (4) indirect signs include abrupt termination of a dilated distal common bile duct without visible surrounding mass or biliary dilatation.[150] Using these criteria, 76% of stones were detected in this series.[150] These authors found that abrupt termination of the CBD without soft tissue mass was most often associated with pancreatic carcinoma; CBD stones manifested either as a densely calcified object or as a target sign.

CT cholangiography is redefining the role of CT as a technique for visualizing the biliary tract and choledocholithiasis.

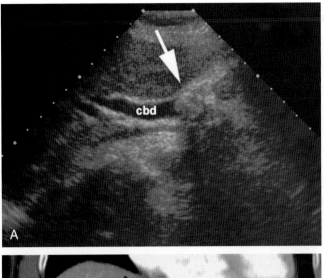

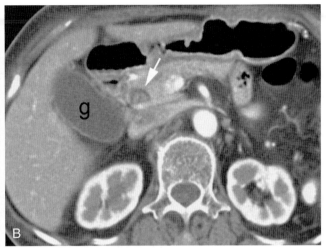

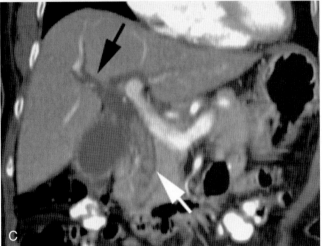

Figure 79-37. Choledocholithiasis: ultrasound and CT features. A. Sagittal image demonstrates common bile duct (CBD) dilation. There is an intraductal echogenic shadowing focus (*arrow*), consistent with a large stone. **B.** Axial contrast enhanced CT demonstrates increased density in dilated common bile duct (*arrow*) consistent with stones. G, gallbladder. **C.** CT image reformatted in coronal plane. Multiple stones in the dilated duct (*white arrow*). *Black arrow,* intrahepatic biliary dilation.

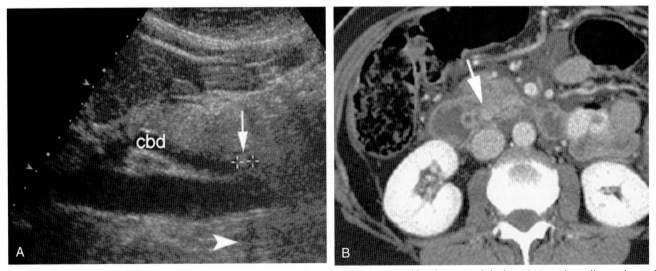

Figure 79-38. Choledocholithiasis: ultrasound and CT findings. A. Ultrasound demonstrates dilated common bile duct (CBD) with small stone located distally (*arrow*). Note posterior acoustic shadowing (*arrowhead*). **B.** Contrast-enhanced CT demonstrates small distal stone (*arrow*) which was not identified prospectively.

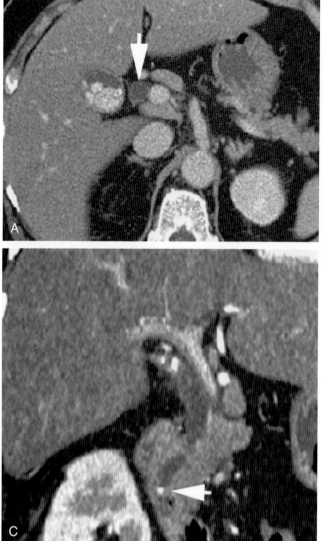

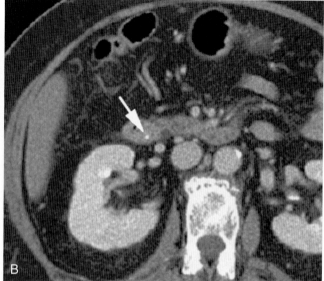

Figure 79-39. Choledocholithiasis: CT appearance. A. There are multiple small stones in gallbladder with dilation of CBD (*arrow*). **B.** More caudal image demonstrates small stone at level of ampulla (*arrow*). **C.** Coronal reformatted image shows CBD stone (*arrow*).

MDCT is performed after indirect opacification of the biliary tract with oral or intravenous iodinated cholangiographic agents.[157,158] Improved *z*-axis resolution is achieved with multidetector array scanners and high resolution reconstructions of the biliary tract.[159] In one series, CT cholangiography was shown to provide excellent visualization of biliary anatomy and filling defects, with 95% sensitivity for choledocholithiasis.[160] Other more recent series also show promise of these techniques in evaluation of choledocholithiasis.[161-164] A major drawback of this technique is associated risks of contrast induced allergic reactions.[165] At the author's institution, this technique is currently utilized primarily to define donor biliary anatomy prior to liver transplantation and does not play a role in evaluation of the choledocholithiasis.

Magnetic Resonance Imaging

Magnetic resonance cholangiopancreatography (MRCP) was introduced in the 1990s as a noninvasive and low-risk technique to evaluate the biliary system and is an excellent modality for the detection of CBD stones.[166,167] Reported sensitivity, specificity, and accuracy of MRCP for choledocholithiasis range from 85% to 100%, 90% to 90%, and 89% to 97%, respectively.[168,169] MRCP has been shown to be more sensitive for the detection of common bile duct stones than ultrasound and CT[20] and is highly accurate for the detection of common bile duct stones in patients with symptomatic gallstones.[169] The MRCP technique is discussed more fully in Chapter 77.

Thin-slice (3-4 mm) half-Fourier acquisition single-shot TSE (HASTE) images, also referred to as half-Fourier rapid acquisition relaxation enhancement (RARE) images, allow for rapid acquisition, with imaging of the biliary tract in a single breath-hold, decreasing motion artifact.[168,170-172] Conventional unenhanced T1- and T2-weighted MR images are also usually performed. Gadolinium-enhanced images are helpful if neoplasm or inflammatory disease is suspected.[172] High resolution fat-suppressed T1-weighted three-dimensional (3D) gradient-echo images allow for high-resolution images of the biliary tree that can be reconstructed in any plane. Additional techniques include the use of contrast agents that are taken up by hepatocytes and excreted through the biliary system, such as manganese dipyridoxyl diphosphate, and the use of oral contrast agents, such as ferumoxsil (Gastromark, Mallinckrodt, Maryland Heights, MO) or diluted IV contrast, gadopentate

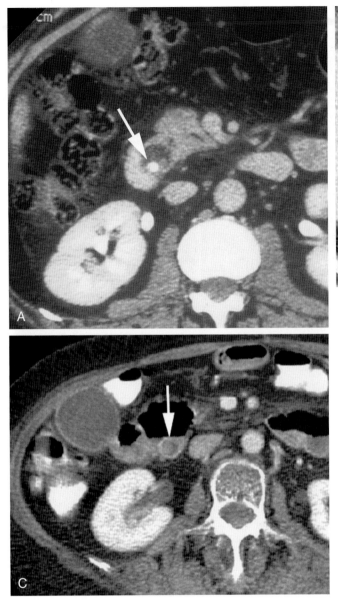

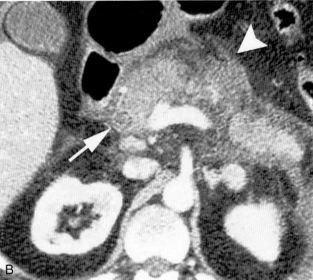

Figure 79-40. Choledocholithiasis: various appearances at CT. A. Calcified stone (*arrow*) in CBD. **B.** Rim calcified stone (*arrow*) in CBD. There is peripancreatic inflammatory change (*arrowhead*) due to acute pancreatitis. **C.** Soft tissue density noncalcified stone (*arrow*) in CBD with low density crescent of bile.

dimeglumine (Magnevist, Berlex Laboratories, Wayne, NJ). Pineapple juice, which has a high manganese content, can also be used to decrease signal from hyperintense bowel fluid.[168] Recently, 3D T2-weighted TSE is also promising and offers improved anatomic accuracy, higher signal-to-noise ratio, and thinner sections without gaps.[173-175] When combined with new techniques such as parallel acquisition technique (PAT), data acquisition time is shortened while retaining spatial resolution and contrast.[176] Faster gradients and navigator-based respiratory triggering also allow for improved image quality.[168]

AT MRCP, stones will generally appear as well-circumscribed low signal intensity filling defects in the biliary tract (Fig. 79-41). MRCP can detect stones as small as 2 mm[20] and may be a helpful adjunct to ultrasound and CT when biliary calculi are suspected but not definitively visualized (Fig. 79-42). MRCP may also be helpful if a noncalcified stone is difficult to differentiate from a soft tissue mass. Diagnostic pitfalls include gas, blood, or other abnormality within the duct simulating stones as well as signal loss due to surgical clips after cholecystectomy. High signal from adjacent fluid collections, ascites or edema may also interfere with biliary signal. Pseudo-obstruction of the extrahepatic bile duct may be caused by arterial pulsatile compression most commonly at the common hepatic duct due to the right hepatic artery,[177] and flow artifacts may mimic filling defects.[178] It is important to review coronal source and transverse T2-weighted images to avoid these pitfalls.

INTRAHEPATIC BILIARY CALCULI

Recurrent Pyogenic Cholangitis

The presence of calculi within the intrahepatic bile ducts is uncommon in patients with gallstones. This can occur in the setting of biliary strictures with longstanding obstruction, such as after biliary surgery or in the setting of Caroli's disease.[179] In the Asian population, the most common entity

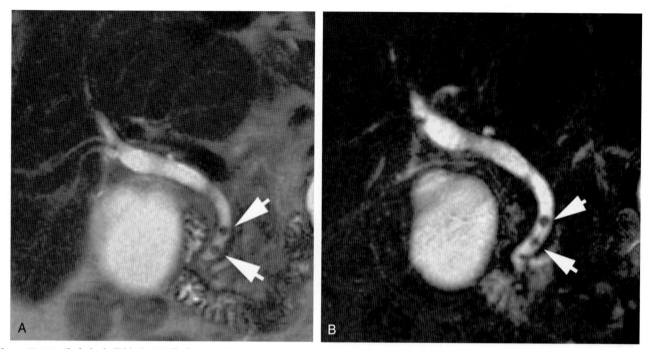

Figure 79-41. Choledocholithiasis: MR findings. A. T2-weighted coronal HASTE image shows low signal intensity CBD stones (*arrows*). G, gallbladder. **B.** Two-dimensional thick slab image demonstrates stones (*arrows*).

associated with the formation of primary intrahepatic stones is recurrent pyogenic cholangitis (RPC), also referred to as oriental cholangiohepatitis. This is an endemic disease in Southeast Asia that is more frequently encountered in the United States due to increased immigration from Asia.[180,181] The hallmark features of this disorder include pigment stone formation within the intrahepatic and extrahepatic bile ducts, stricture development, and biliary dilatation. Clinically, this disorder is characterized by recurrent attacks of fever, chills, jaundice, and abdominal pain. The cause of this disorder is not entirely clear, although it is postulated that infection of the biliary tract with parasitic organisms such as *Clonorchis senensis* results in biliary stasis and stone formation. Ultimately, there is progression to stricture formation, biliary obstruction, and hepatic cirrhosis with an increased risk of cholangiocarcinoma.

Imaging

Although traditionally imaging of this disorder has been performed with invasive cholangiographic methods, noninvasive cross-sectional imaging techniques, including CT, ultrasound, and MRI, now play a more important role.[182-186] Ultrasonography is usually the initial imaging modality and demonstrates intrahepatic and extrahepatic biliary dilatation, with intrahepatic stones which may or may not shadow (Fig. 79-43A). A nonshadowing stone may mimic an echogenic soft tissue mass. CT provides for more complete evaluation of the full extent of disease and associated complications such as liver abscess and pancreatitis (Fig. 79-43B). CT can be particularly helpful if the patient has already undergone biliary enteric bypass surgery in which case associated pneumobilia may obscure findings at sonography. Noncontrast images may be helpful to identified noncalcified pigment stones which

are soft tissue density[182] (Fig. 79-44). The use of intravenous contrast allows for better detection of complications such as cholangitis with improved visualization of ductal wall and periductal enhancement indicating active infection/inflammation[184] as well as abscess formation (Fig. 79-45). The left hepatic lobe, particularly the lateral segment, most often shows biliary dilatation and stone disease. This is an important distinguishing feature of this disorder. Chronic findings include segmental lobe atrophy involving the lateral left lobe, portal vein thrombosis and ultimately changes of cirrhosis. Hepatic atrophy has been shown to correlate with portal vein occlusion and is usually most prominent in the lateral segment of the left lobe.[187] MR and MRCP methods have also proved useful in the identification of intrahepatic biliary calculi and associated parenchymal abnormalities.[183]

OTHER CONDITIONS RELATED TO GALLSTONES

Spilled Gallstones after Laparoscopic Cholecystectomy

Gallbladder perforation during laparoscopic cholecystectomy is reported to occur in 10% to 40% of cases with spillage of gallstones occurring less frequently, approximately 6% to 8% of the time.[188] This complication occurs more frequently during surgery for an acutely inflamed gallbladder and may occur during dissection of the gallbladder from the hepatic bed or removal through the umbilical incision. Late abscess formation due to spilled stones is rare with an incidence of less than 1%,[189-191] occurring more frequently when both bile and calculus spillage occur. Infectious complications are more likely to occur with bilirubinate stones since they contain viable bacteria. The spilled stones may remain in the perito-

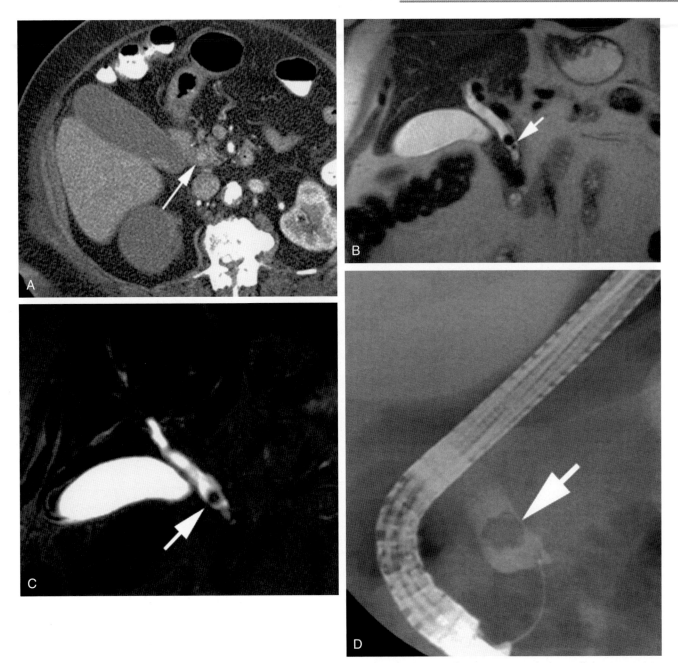

Figure 79-42. Choledocholithiasis: imaging features. An 80-year-old woman with right upper quadrant pain. **A.** CT shows small density suspicious for stone in distal CBD (*arrow*). **B.** Coronal T2-weighted HASTE MR image confirms the presence of stones in the distal duct (*arrow*). G, gallbladder. **C.** Stones (*arrow*) demonstrated on 2D thick slab MR image. **D.** ERCP confirms stone (*arrow*). Sphincterotomy and stone retrieval were performed.

neal cavity adjacent to the liver and cause a subhepatic abscess or abscess in the retroperitoneum below the subhepatic space. However, due to pneumoperitoneum and peritoneal irrigation at the time of laparoscopy, stones may also migrate to distant sites. More unusual locations for abscess formation include the pleural space, abdominal wall at the trocar site and within an incisional hernia. Due to the indolent nature of the infection, the time interval for presentation after surgery is variable, ranging from 1 month to 10 years with a reported peak incidence around 4 months.[188] The patient usually presents with vague constitutional symptoms such as nausea, anorexia and low-grade fever.

Ultrasound, CT, and MRI are effective in identifying the abscess and associated dropped gallstones. The abscess appears as a thick walled fluid collection, most commonly located posterior to the right lobe of the liver (Fig. 79-46A and B). On ultrasound, stones appear as echogenic foci and at CT as calcified densities. At MRI, stones may be identified as low signal intensity foci on T2 weighted images. In a series of 5 patients by Morrin and associates,[192] in only two of five patients the diagnosis of abscess formation secondary to dropped stones was made prospectively using a combination of imaging modalities. In retrospect, however, the diagnosis could be made in all patients. Recognizing the history of prior

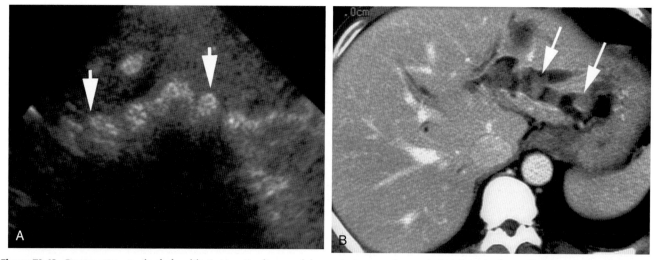

Figure 79-43. Recurrent pyogenic cholangitis. A. Hepatic ultrasound demonstrates cast of stones in intrahepatic ducts of left lateral segment (*arrows*). These appear as echogenic material with posterior acoustic shadowing. **B.** Contrast enhanced CT demonstrates soft tissue density material in dilated ducts (*arrows*) corresponding to pigment stones. The lateral segment is primarily involved, a typical feature of recurrent pyogenic cholangitis.

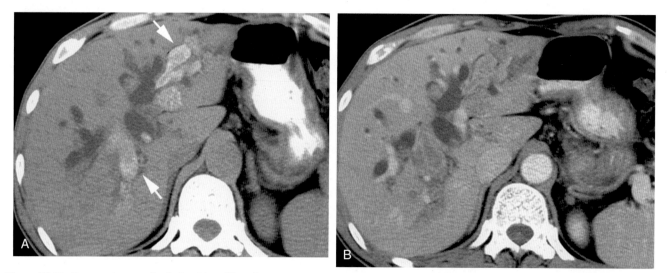

Figure 79-44. Recurrent pyogenic cholangitis: utility of noncontrast CT. A. Precontrast CT scan shows cast of stones in dilated intrahepatic ducts (*arrows*). **B.** After IV contrast, stones are less conspicuous.

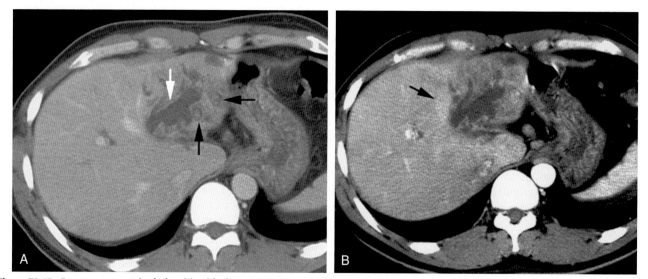

Figure 79-45. Recurrent pyogenic cholangitis with abscess. A. CT scan obtained during portal venous phase demonstrates stones in dilated intrahepatic ducts of left lateral segment (*black arrows*). There is an abscess with fluid attenuation in the liver parenchyma (*white arrow*). **B.** Scan obtained during the arterial phase demonstrates increased contrast enhancement around the abscess (*arrow*) related to hyperemia (THAD).

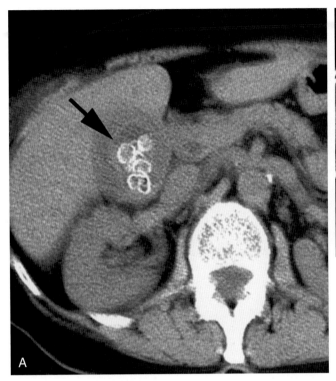

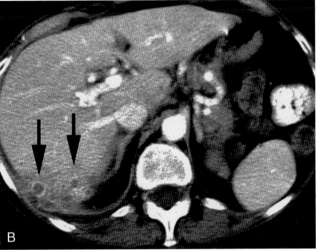

Figure 79-46. Spilled gallstones after laparoscopic cholecystectomy. **A.** Contrast-enhanced CT obtained prior to surgery demonstrates multiple calcified stones in thick-walled gallbladder (*arrow*) with pericholecystic fluid, indicating acute cholecystitis. **B.** CT obtained 1 year after cholecystectomy when the patient returned with right upper quadrant pain demonstrates abscess posterior to the right hepatic lobe containing spilled stones (*arrows*).

laparoscopic cholecystectomy and careful search for spilled stones, particularly when an abscess is identified in the subhepatic space, is important in making the diagnosis. The abscess may be misdiagnosed as tumor or abscess from another cause if the stones are not radioopaque or not recognized or located in an atypical location (Fig. 79-47). Surgical or percutaneous removal of the stones is necessary for complete cure as infected stones cannot be sterilized with antibiotic therapy.[193,194]

Mirizzi Syndrome

Mirizzi syndrome refers to common hepatic or CBD obstruction due to extrinsic compression from an impacted gallstone in the gallbladder neck or cystic duct or from associated inflammatory changes. This may be complicated by a cholecystocholedochal fistula.[195-197] Mirizzi syndrome is an uncommon complication of longstanding cholelithiasis and recurrent episodes of jaundice and cholangitis the usual clinical presentation. This syndrome is reported in up to 2% of patients operated on for symptomatic gallbladder disease.[198] Preoperative diagnosis is important since standard cholecystectomy technique is associated with an increased risk of extrahepatic bile duct injury secondary to dense fibrosis and edema around the hepatoduodenal ligament.[199]

Mirizzi syndrome may be diagnosed with ultrasound, CT, or MRI.[200,201] The hallmark is intrahepatic biliary dilatation and dilatation of the common hepatic duct to the level of the porta hepatis with normal caliber of the more distal CBD. A stone may be identified in the gallbladder neck or cystic duct (Fig. 79-48). MPR imaging with either CT or MR can be particularly helpful to identify the extrinsic nature of the obstruction. MRI has been proposed as most useful for demonstrating dilatation of the intrahepatic ducts, the level of obstruction and location of gallstones.[201]

Gallstone Ileus

Gallstone ileus is mechanical obstruction of the bowel by an impacted gallstone and results from perforation of the gallbladder and fistula formation between the gallbladder and an adjacent viscus. Fistula formation most commonly occurs between the gallbladder and duodenum, followed by the colon and stomach.[3,202] Obstruction usually occurs in the small intestine when a gallstone larger than 2.5 cm in size lodges in the lumen. The most common sites of gallstone impaction are: the ileum (54%-65%), the jejunum (27%), and the duodenum (1-3%).[203] The term "Bouveret's syndrome" refers to proximal gallstone impaction resulting in duodenal or pyloric obstruction. Gallstone ileus accounts for approximately 1% to 5% of all cases of nonmalignant small bowel obstruction, increasing up to 25% in patients over the age of 65.[203]

Less than half of patients presenting with gallstone ileus have a known history of preexisting gallbladder disease. Patients usually present with clinical symptoms of bowel obstruction and an abdominal radiograph may be the initial imaging study performed. The classic triad of findings, referred to as Rigler's triad,[204] includes presence of bowel obstruction, pneumobilia, and the obstructing gallstone. However, this is visualized in only 30% to 35% of patients[205] (Fig. 79-49). CT is frequently employed to evaluate patients with bowel obstruction to confirm diagnosis and determine etiology of obstruction and evaluate for complications. CT is superior to the plain abdominal radiograph for visualization of the obstructing gallstone and detection of small amounts of gas in the gallbladder and biliary tree[203,206-208] (Fig. 79-50). The cholecystoenteric fistula may also be demonstrated. Cholecystoenteric fistula may develop in the absence of gallstone ileus, usually resulting from chronic gallbladder inflammation. CT findings include a contracted gallbladder containing air and visualization of a fistulous tract (Fig. 79-51).

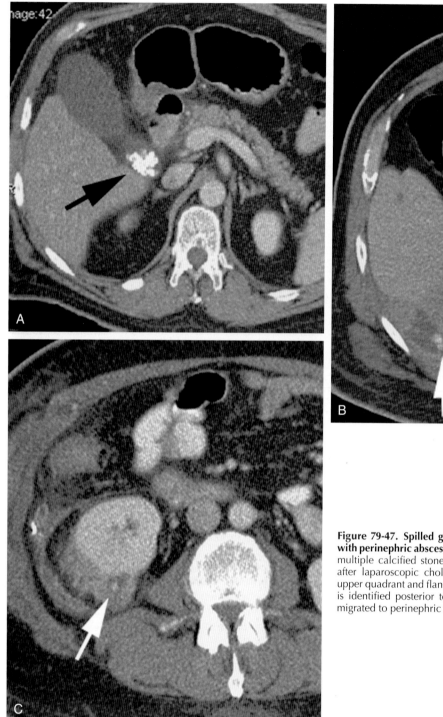
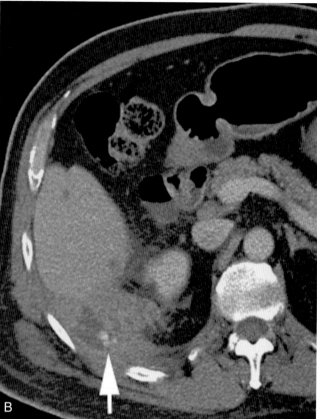

Figure 79-47. Spilled gallstones after laparoscopic cholecystectomy with perinephric abscess. A. Initial contrast-enhanced CT demonstrates multiple calcified stones in gallbladder neck (*arrow*). **B.** Six months after laparoscopic cholecystectomy, the patient returned with right upper quadrant and flank pain. An abscess with retained stones (*arrow*) is identified posterior to the right hepatic lobe. **C.** Stones had also migrated to perinephric space (*arrow*) causing a perinephric abscess.

HYPERPLASTIC CHOLECYSTOSES

The term hyperplastic cholecystoses was introduced in 1960 by Jutras[209] in order to designate a spectrum of gallbladder abnormalities separate from inflammatory disease. Hyperplastic refers to a benign proliferation of normal tissue elements and cholecystoses refers to a pathologic process distinct from inflammation.[210] The two major conditions within this spectrum of disorders are cholesterolosis and adenomyomatosis.

Cholesterolosis

Pathogenesis and Epidemiology

Cholesterolosis results from the accumulation of neutral lipid, in particular cholesterol esters and triglyceride, within macrophages in the lamina propria of the gallbladder.[2] The cholesterol is likely deposited in the epithelium initially, accumulates in the lamina propria and subsequently is taken up by the macrophages.[210] The accumulation of lipid creates

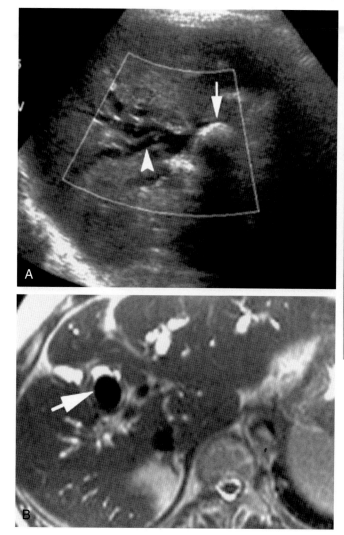

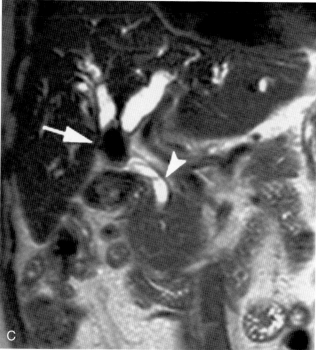

Figure 79-48. Mirizzi syndrome: imaging features. A. Ultrasound demonstrates large gallstone in gallbladder neck (*arrow*) associated with intrahepatic biliary dilatation (*arrowhead*). **B.** Axial T2-weighted HASTE MR image demonstrates the large stone in the gallbladder neck (*arrow*) as well as the intrahepatic biliary dilatation. **C.** Coronal T2-weighted HASTE MR image demonstrates stone (*arrows*) which is located outside of the CB.

yellow excrescences on the surface of the mucosa that can be seen by the naked eye. Associated hyperemia of the mucosa gives the appearance of a strawberry, and the term "strawberry gallbladder" has been used to describe the appearance of the gallbladder in this disorder.[211] The pathogenesis of this disorder is not completely understood. Altered hepatic cholesterol synthesis may play an etiologic role leading to increased cholesterol levels in the bile.[212] Impaired cholesterol transport out of the mucosa may also play a role. This disorder is not associated with cholesterol gallstones, hyperlipidemia, or atherosclerosis. There may be an increased incidence of gallstones, present in 50% in one surgical series.[213] In an autopsy study involving 1,319 cases, there were 165 cases of cholesterolosis for an incidence of 12.5%.[214] There are no specific clinical findings and presentation is usually the result of a complicating disorder such as cholelithiasis or cholecystitis.

Pathologically, cholesterolosis is defined by the deposition of lipid within the gallbladder mucosa in one of four patterns: (1) diffuse involvement (80%); (2) cholesterol polyps resulting from focal excrescences of lipid-containing epithelium projecting into the gallbladder lumen, usually measuring 2 to 10 mm in size; (3) combined diffuse and polypoid form (10%); and (4) focal cholesterolosis with only a portion of the gallbladder affected.[215] Cholesterol polyps account for 60% to 90% of gallbladder polyps and are not true neoplasms.[2] They may be solitary but are most commonly multiple. At histology, the polyp has a vascular connective tissue stalk and a branching villous or complex papillary pattern; however, foamy macrophages within the lamina propria are the dominant cellular component.[2]

Imaging

The diffuse form of cholesterolosis cannot be diagnosed at imaging. Traditionally, oral cholecystography (OCG) was utilized to diagnose the polypoid variety, which appears as numerous fixed filling defects in the lumen of the gallbladder. As this technique is no longer widely performed, findings are now apparent primarily at sonography. Cholesterol polyps may appear as single or multiple nonshadowing foci adherent to the gallbladder wall and projecting into the gallbladder lumen (Fig. 79-52). Gallbladder polyps may also be visible at CT (Fig. 79-53). When polypoid lesions in the gallbladder are identified at either ultrasound or CT, small (less than 1 cm in size) and multiple, the diagnosis of benign cholesterol polyps is most likely.[216] Initial 3- to 6-month ultrasound

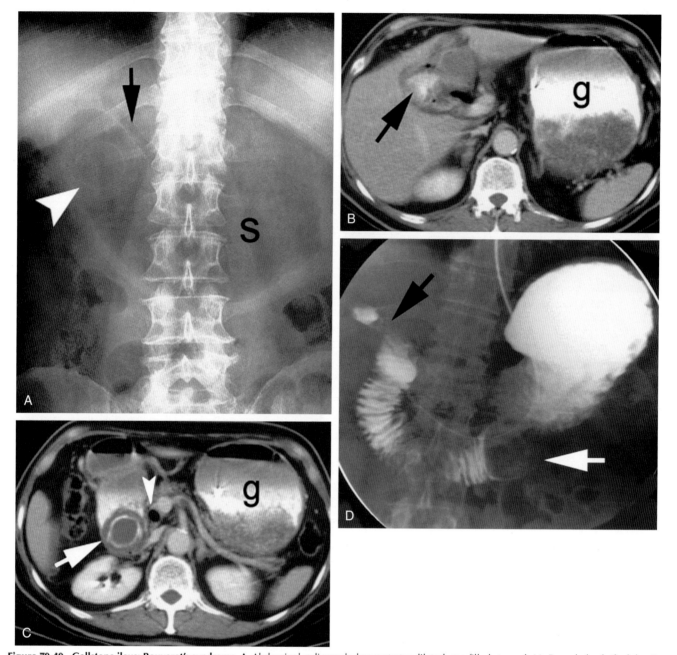

Figure 79-49. Gallstone ileus: Bouveret's syndrome. A. Abdominal radiograph demonstrates dilated, gas-filled stomach (s). Rounded calcified density (*arrowhead*) represents a large stone in the region of the gastric antrum. There is pneumobilia (*arrow*). The presence of bowel obstruction, pneumobilia, and obstructing gallstone constitutes Rigler's triad. **B.** Oral and IV contrast enhanced CT demonstrates distended, contrast-filled stomach (g) consistent with gastric outlet obstruction. There is oral contrast and bubbles of air in gallbladder fossa (*arrow*) consistent with cholecystoenteric fistula. **C.** Slightly more inferior CT image demonstrates large obstructing gallstone (*arrow*) in the region of the proximal duodenum. Air is also present in the CBD (*arrowhead*). **D.** Upper gastrointestinal series demonstrates stone as large filling defect which has migrated to duodenal/jejunal junction (*white arrow*). Fistula between the gallbladder and proximal duodenum is also demonstrated (*black arrow*).

follow-up can be performed for 1 to 2 years to ensure stability. When polyps are single, greater than 10 mm in size, sessile, or occurring in individuals over age 50, differentiation from other polypoid masses such as adenomas or primary or metastatic neoplasm is not possible and surgical evaluation may be required.[217] In a surgical series of gallbladder polypoid lesions, using size greater than 10 mm, a 100% sensitivity, and 86.95% specificity in the diagnosis of malignancy was achieved.[218]

Adenomyomatosis

Pathogenesis and Epidemiology

Adenomyomatosis of the gallbladder, also referred to as adenomyomatous hyperplasia and intramural diverticulosis, is an acquired, hyperplastic lesion of the gallbladder characterized by excessive proliferation of surface epithelium with invaginations into the thickened, hypertrophied muscularis propria.[215] The intramural diverticula formed by epithelial

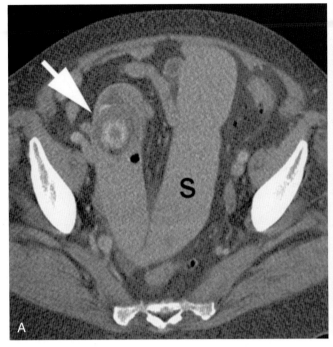

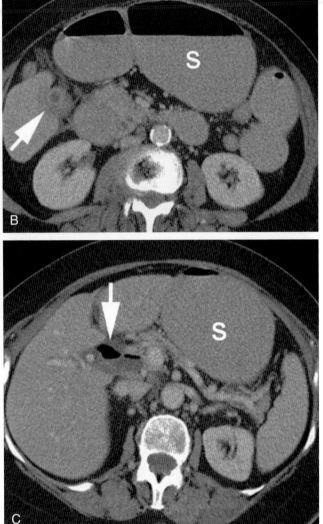

Figure 79-50. Gallstone ileus. A. CT demonstrates dilated fluid-filled small bowel (s). There is a partially calcified gallstone at the point of transition in the right lower quadrant (*white arrow*). **B.** CT image of upper abdomen demonstrates collapsed gallbladder (*arrow*). The stomach (s) is dilated and fluid-filled. **C.** Slightly more inferior image demonstrates air in the CBD (*arrow*).

invaginations into the muscularis are referred to as Rokitansky-Aschoff sinuses (RAS) and dilated RAS are a prominent feature of this disorder. The pathophysiology of this disorder is not entirely certain. This is not usually associated with cholesterolosis, indicating a separate pathophysiology. Pathogenesis has been postulated to result from mechanical obstruction of the gallbladder (from stones, cystic duct kinking or congenital septum), chronic inflammation and anomalous pancreaticobiliary ductal union.[215] The functional obstruction to bile outflow causes increased pressure within the gallbladder lumen and results in invagination of the mucosa through the muscularis, forming the dilated RAS. The reported incidence of adenomyomatosis in cholecystectomy specimens is up to 8%.[219] The association of this disorder with clinical findings is controversial The disorder may be asymptomatic or associated with symptoms of chronic cholecystitis. Over 90% of cases are associated with gallstones which may be responsible for biliary symptoms.[2] Adenocarcinoma of the gallbladder has been found in association with adenomyomatosis, however, a causal link has not been established.[215] In a surgical series of 3,000 resected gallbladders, there was a higher frequency of gallbladder carcinoma (6.4%) in gallbladders with segmental adenomyomatosis than those without.[219]

Adenomyomatosis may be generalized, segmental or focal and the focal form is most common.[220] Diffuse adenomyomatosis causes thickening and irregularity of the mucosa and muscular layer with associated RAS, which on gross inspection appear as collections of bile in the gallbladder wall. In the segmental or annular form, a focal circumferential stricture divides the gallbladder lumen into separate compartments. The focal form, which causes a focal mass or nodule, usually is fundal in location, frequently referred to as an adenomyoma.

Imaging

In the past, OCG played an important role in the diagnosis of adenomyomatosis.[210] The hallmark of this disorder is the filling of intramural diverticula with contrast material which manifest as radiopaque dots that parallel the gallbladder lumen. In the fundal form, findings may mimic a polyp or other mass. The segmental form may present as circumferential narrowing of the lumen.

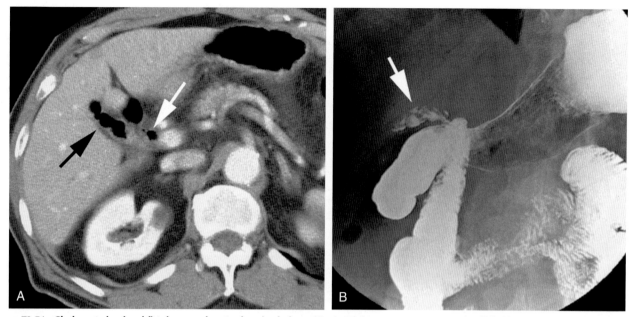

Figure 79-51. Cholecystoduodenal fistula secondary to chronic cholecystitis. A. CT demonstrates contracted gallbladder containing air (*black arrow*). There is also air in the CBD (*white arrow*). **B.** Upper gastrointestinal series demonstrates fistula between gallbladder and proximal duodenum (*arrow*).

Ultrasound

The ultrasound findings in adenomyomatosis have been well-described and include diffuse or segmental thickening of the gallbladder wall, and anechoic intramural diverticula.[221-223] Biliary sludge or gallstones within the diverticula may appear as echogenic foci.[221] A V-shaped reverberation or comet-tail artifact may emanate from small cholesterol stones that are lodged in the RAS (Fig. 79-54). This artifact occurs as a result of sound reverberating within or between cholesterol crystals[26] and helps to differentiate gallbladder wall thickening related to adenomyomatosis from other abnormalities (Fig. 79-55A). There may be nonspecific thickening of the gallbladder wall if the diverticula and associated reverberation artifact are not resolved. This mural thickening may be indistinguishable from acute or chronic cholecystitis and gallbladder carcinoma on the basis of imaging; therefore, knowledge of the clinical setting is essential. The segmental form of adenomyomatosis results in annular narrowing, usually of the body of the gallbladder, with resulting compartmentalization or segmentation of the gallbladder lumen. In this setting, the fundal compartment may be overlooked. Stones are often trapped within this fundal compartment and are not readily visualized. Again, if the reverberation artifact is not observed, this focal mural thickening may be indistinguishable from gallbladder

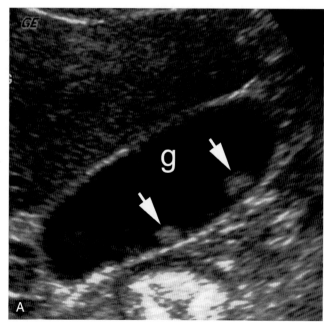

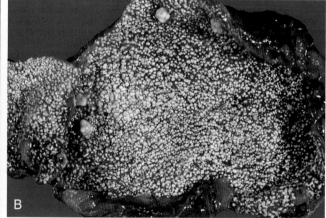

Figure 79-52. Cholesterol polyps: ultrasound and pathology findings. A. Sagittal ultrasound image demonstrate two echogenic nonshadowing foci (*arrows*) adherent to the posterior wall of the gallbladder (g) consistent with cholesterol polyps. **B.** Specimen image in a different patient demonstrates a diffuse granular pattern of cholesterolosis with several cholesterol polyps.

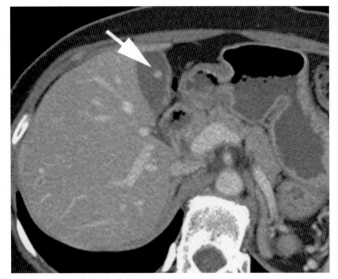

Figure 79-53. Cholesterol polyp: CT. CT demonstrates polypoid excrescence arising from the gallbladder wall (*arrow*).

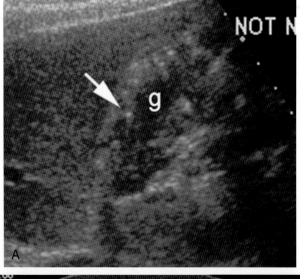

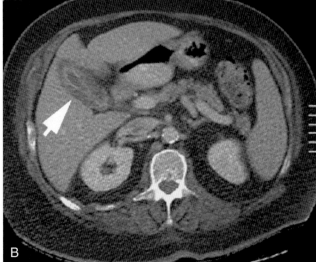

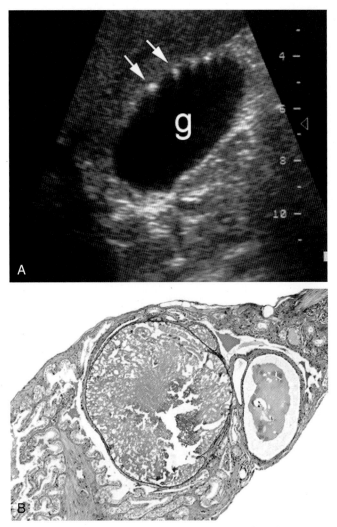

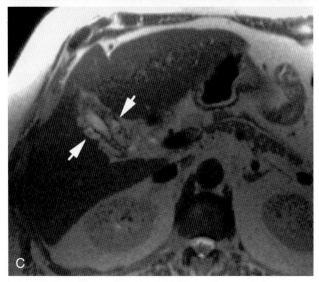

Figure 79-54. Adenomyomatosis: ultrasound and pathologic features. **A.** Ultrasound demonstrates multiple comet tail artifacts (*arrows*) arising from the wall of the gallbladder (g). **B.** Histologic specimen in a different patient demonstrates debris in a Rokitansky-Aschoff sinus.

Figure 79-55. Diffuse adenomyomatosis. A. Ultrasound demonstrates diffuse thickening of gallbladder (g). There are echogenic foci in the wall (*arrow*) with associated comet-tail artifact. **B.** Contrast-enhanced CT demonstrates thickening gallbladder wall (*arrow*) with intramural regions of low attenuation. **C.** Axial T2-weighted HASTE image demonstrates thickened gallbladder wall with multiple high signal intensity areas (*arrows*) corresponding to the dilated Rokitansky-Aschoff sinuses (RAS).

carcinoma (Fig. 79-56A). The focal form of adenomyomatosis most commonly appears as a sessile, polypoid mass in the region of the fundus, protruding into the gallbladder lumen (Fig. 79-57A). This may mimic other gallbladder masses, including neoplasm. Coexisting gallstones are a frequent finding, with increased incidence in patients with the segmental form.[224]

Computed Tomography

On CT, the diffuse form of gallbladder adenomyomatosis manifests with visualization of intramural diverticula[222,225] (Fig. 79-55B). The segmental and focal forms can be particularly difficult to differentiate from carcinoma since they appear as focal thickening of the gallbladder wall or a fundal intraluminal mass (Figs. 79-56B and 79-57B). The findings

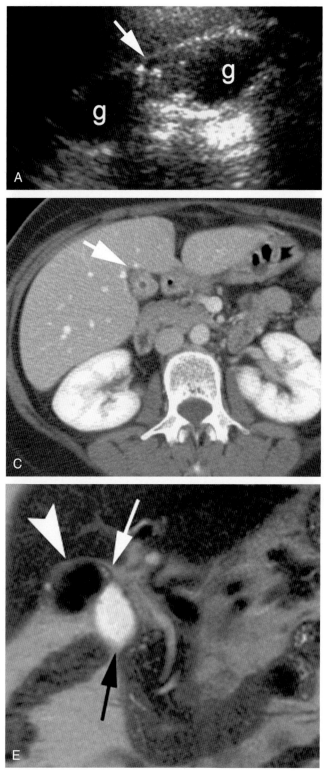

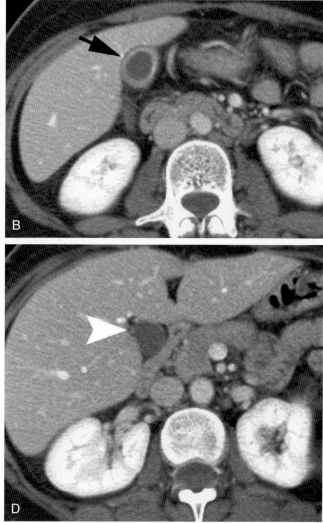

Figure 79-56. Annular/segmental adenomyomatosis. A. Sagittal image of the gallbladder (g) demonstrates focal thickening in the mid portion of the gallbladder (*arrow*) resulting in compartmentalization. Echogenic foci with ring down artifact are noted at this location which helps exclude other causes of focal gallbladder wall thickening such as carcinoma. **B** to **D.** Sequential CT images in a second patient from the level of the gallbladder fundus to neck demonstrate focal mural thickening at the midportion of the gallbladder in the area of focal adenomyomatosis (*white arrow*). There are two compartments of the gallbladder: one in the region of the fundus (*black arrow*) and one in the region of the neck (*arrowhead*). **E.** Coronal T2-weighted HASTE image in a third patient demonstrates compartmentalization of the gallbladder with annular narrowing at midportion resulting in two compartments (*arrowhead* and *black arrow*). Low signal intensity filling defect in the fundal compartment (*arrowhead*) corresponds to a trapped stone in fundal compartment. At point of narrowing, there are high signal intensity foci (*white arrow*) corresponding to the dilated RAS.

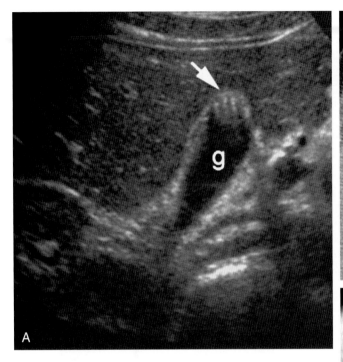

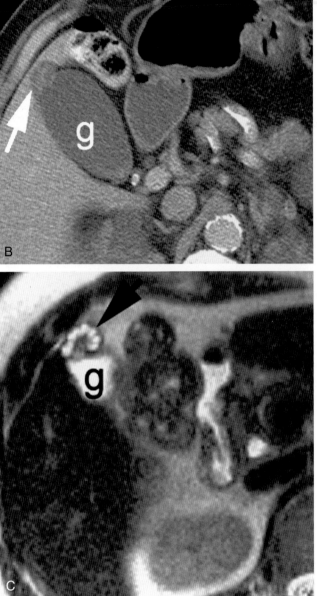

Figure 79-57. Focal fundal adenomyomatosis. A. Sagittal ultrasound image of the gallbladder (g) demonstrates focal fundal thickening (*arrow*) with multiple comet-tail artifacts. **B.** CT in a different patient demonstrates a nodule (*arrow*) in the region of the fundus of the gallbladder (g). There is a low attenuation area centrally corresponding to dilated RAS. **C.** Coronal T2-weighted HASTE MR image in a third patient demonstrated multiple high signal intensity foci (*arrow*) in the region of the fundus of the gallbladder (g) corresponding to the dilated RAS. This has been referred to as the "string of pearls" sign.

at CT may not be diagnostic and follow-up with ultrasound may be necessary. The advantage of ultrasound is that the reverberation artifact related to the RAS may be demonstrated. This finding is not seen with adenocarcinomas. Small RAS may be overlooked.[225]

Magnetic Resonance Imaging

MR has been shown to serve as a very helpful problem-solving tool in patients with gallbladder adenomyomatosis. The demonstration of RAS on T2-weighted images is critical in diagnosing this disorder.[226] These appear as high signal intensity foci in the gallbladder wall (Figs. 79-55C, 79-56D, and 79-57C). In a study comparing ultrasound, CT, and MRI,[227] MRI using a half-Fourier RARE sequence was superior to helical CT and transabdominal ultrasound in establishing the diagnosis of adenomyomatosis. Helical CT showed most lesions as a thickened wall or mass, with limited ability to delineate the RAS. MRI was found to have an accuracy of

93% versus 75% for CT and 66% for ultrasound. MRI offers more complete visualization of the gallbladder and more definitive identification RAS. Yoshimitsu and colleagues[226] also found a higher sensitivity of MRI for detection of the RAS in the thickened gallbladder wall and referred to this finding as the "string of pearls" sign (see Fig. 79-57C). The specificity of this sign for adenomyomatosis is 92%, helpful in the differentiation from gallbladder carcinoma, where this sign is never observed. If findings on ultrasound are equivocal, MR with MRCP is the next best test. There is an increased incidence of gallbladder carcinoma reported in patients with segmental adenomyomatosis[219]; therefore, these patients should be closely followed.

MILK OF CALCIUM BILE

When the cystic duct is obstructed by a gallstone, the gallbladder may become chronically inflamed filling with a putty-

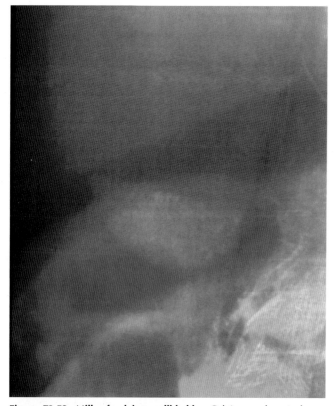

Figure 79-58. Milk of calcium gallbladder. Calcium carbonate layers dependently on this upright radiograph.

like material consisting of calcium carbonate. This dense material can be visualized on abdominal plain films (Fig. 79-58) and CT.

GALLBLADDER HYDROPS

Massive enlargement of the gallbladder can develop proximal to an obstructing stone in the gallbladder neck or cystic duct. If there is no supervening infection, the gallbladder lumen becomes progressively distended due to the accumulation of sterile mucus secreted by the epithelial cells (Fig. 79-59). The patient usually has few symptoms but may have chronic right-upper-quadrant discomfort. A right upper quadrant mass may be palpable.

Plain radiographs may show a right upper quadrant mass indenting the lateral border of the duodenum. Sonography shows a distended gallbladder (>5 cm) with a biconvex shape and normal wall thickness. Sludge may be present. CT shows lumen distention and normal mural thickness.

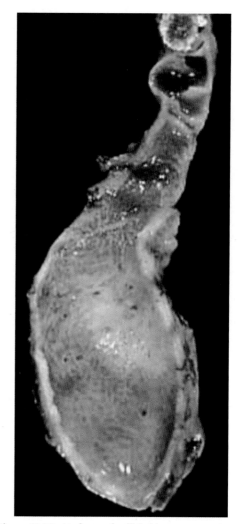

Figure 79-59. Hydrops of gallbladder: gross specimen.

References

1. Tazuma S: Gallstone disease: Epidemiology, pathogenesis, and classification of biliary stones (common bile duct and intrahepatic). Best Pract Res Clin Gastroenterol 20:1075-1083, 2006.
2. Lack EE. Cholecystitis, cholelithiasis and unusual infections of the gallbladder. In: Pathology of the pancreas, gallbladder, extrahepatic biliary tract, and ampullary region. Oxford, University Press, Oxford, 2003, pp 414-452.
3. Bortoff GA, Chen MYM, Ott DJ, et al: Gallbladder stones: Imaging and intervention. RadioGraphics 20:751-766, 2000.
4. Trotman BW: Pigment gallstone disease. Gastroenterol Clin North Am 20:111-126, 1991.
5. Weltman DI, Zeman RK: Acute diseases of the gallbladder and biliary ducts. Radiol Clin N Am 32:933-950, 1994.
6. Cooperberg P: Imaging of the gallbladder. Radiology 163:605, 1987.
7. McIntosh DM, Penney HF: Gray-scale ultrasonography as a screening procedure in the detection of gallbladder disease. Radiology 136:725-727, 1980.
8. Carroll BA: Gallstones: In vitro comparison of physical, radiographic and ultrasonic characteristics. AJR 131:223, 1978.
9. Filly RA, Moss AA, Way LW: In vitro investigation of gallstone shadowing with ultrasound tomography. J Clin Ultrasound 7:255-262, 1979.
10. Grossman M: Cholelithiasis and acoustic shadowing. J Clin Ultrasound 6:182, 1978.
11. Desser TS, Jeffrey RB Jr, Lane MJ, et al: Tissue harmonic imaging: Utility in abdominal and pelvic sonography. J Clin Ultrasound 27:135-142, 1999.
12. Oktar SO, Yucel C, Ozdemer H, et al: Comparison of conventional sonography, real-time compound sonography, tissue harmonic sonography, and tissue harmonic compound sonography of abdominal and pelvic lesions. AJR 181:1341-1347, 2003.
13. Chintapalli KN, Ghiatas AA, Chopra, S, et al: Sonographic findings in cases of missed gallstones. J Clin Ultrasound 27:117-121, 1999.
14. MacDonald FR, Cooperberg PL, Cohen MM: The WES triad: A specific sonographic sign of gallstones in the contracted gallbladder. Gastrointestinal Radiol 1981.6:39-41.
15. Baron RL, Rohrmann CA, Lee SP, et al: CT Evaluation of gallstones in vitro: Correlation with chemical analysis. AJR 151:1123-1128, 1988.
16. Brakel, K, Lameris JS, Nijs HG, et al: Predicting gallstone composition with CT: In vivo and in vitro analysis. Radiology 174:337-341, 1990.

17. Paulson EK: Acute cholecystitis: CT findings. Semin Ultrasound CT MR 21:56-63, 2000.

18. Barakos JA, Ralls PW, Lapin SA, et al: Cholelithiasis: Evaluation with CT. Radiology 162:415-418, 1987.

19. Tsai HM, Lin XZ, Chen CY, et al: MRI of gallstones with different compositions. AJR 182:1513-1519, 2004.

20. Hartman EM, Barish MA: MR cholangiography. Magn Reson Imaging Clin N Am 4:841-855, 2001.

21. Ukayi M, Ebara M, Tsuchiya Y, et al: Diagnosis of gallstone composition in magnetic resonance imaging: In vitro analysis. Eur J Radiol 41:49-56, 2002.

22. Ko CW, Sekijima JH, Lee SP: Biliary sludge. Ann Intern Med 130:301-311, 1999.

23. Lee SP: Pathogenesis of biliary sludge. Hepatology 12:2005-2035, 1990.

24. Jain R: Biliary sludge: When should it not be ignored? Curr Treat Options Gastroenterol 7:105-109, 2004.

25. Laing FC: Ultrasonography of the acute abdomen. Radiol Clin N Am 30:389-404, 1992.

26. Laing FC: The gallbladder and bile ducts. In Rumack CM, Wilson SR, Charboneau JW (eds): Diagnostic Ultrasound, 2nd ed. St. Louis, Mosby, 1998, pp 187-193.

27. American College of Radiology (ACR): Acute right upper quadrant pain, ACR Appropriateness Criteria TM, 1999. Available at http://www.acr.org.

28. Laing FL, Federle MP, Jeffrey RB, et al: Ultrasonic evaluation of patients with acute right upper quadrant pain. Radiology 140:449-455, 1981.

29. Ralls PW, Colletti PM, Halls JM, et al: Prospective evaluation of 99mTc-IDA cholescintigraphy and gray-scale ultrasound in the diagnosis of acute cholecystitis. Radiology 144:369-371, 1982.

30. Samuels BI, Freitas JE, Bree RL, et al: Comparison of radionuclide hepatobiliary imaging and real-time ultrasound for the detection of acute cholecystitis. Radiology 147:207-210, 1983.

31. Chatziioannou SN, Moire WH, Ford PV, et al: Hepatobiliary scintigraphy is superior to abdominal ultrasonography in suspected acute cholecystitis. Surgery 127:609-613, 2000.

32. Alobaidi M, Gupta R, Jafri SZ, et al: Current trends in imaging evaluation of acute cholecystitis. Emerg Radiol 10:256-258, 2004.

33. Palmer EL, Scott JA, Strauss HW: Abdominal imaging. In Practical Nuclear Medicine. Philadelphia, WB Saunders, 1992, pp 275-285.

34. Sherman M, Ralls PW, Quinn M, et al: Intravenous cholangiography and sonography in acute cholecystitis: Prospective evaluation. AJR 135:311-313, 1980.

35. Laing FC, Federle MP, Jeffrey RB Jr, et al. Ultrasonic evaluation of patients with acute right upper quadrant pain. Radiology 140:449-455, 1981.

36. Hanbidge A, Buckler PM, O'Malley ME, et al: Imaging evaluation for acute pain in the right upper quadrant. RadioGraphics 24:1117-1135, 2004.

37. Ralls PW, Colleti PM, Lapin SA, et al. Real-time sonography in suspected acute cholecystitis. Radiology 155:767-771, 1985.

38. Paulson EK, Kliewer MA, Hertzberg BS, et al: Diagnosis of acute chole-cystitis with color Doppler sonography: Significance of arterial flow in thickened gallbladder wall. AJR 162:1105-1108, 1994.

39. Schiller VL, Turner RR, Sarti DA: Color Doppler imaging of the gall-bladder wall in acute cholecystitis: Sonographic-pathologic correlation. Abdom Imaging 21:233-237, 1996.

40. Bennett GL, Rusinek H, Lisi V, et al: CT findings of acute gangrenous cholecystitis. AJR 178:275-281, 2002.

41. Kane RA, Costello, P, Duszlak E: Computed tomography in acute cholecystitis: New observations. AJR 141:697-701, 1983.

42. Fidler J, Paulson EK, Layfield L: CT evaluation of acute cholecystitis: Findings and usefulness in diagnosis. AJR 166:1085-1088, 1996.

43. Gore RM, Yaghmai, V, Newmark GM, et al: Imaging benign and malig-nant disease of the gallbladder. Radiol Clin N Am 40:1307-1323, 2002.

44. Grand D, Horton KM, Fishman E: CT of the gallbladder: Spectrum of disease. AJR 183:163-170, 2004.

45. Zissin R, Osadchy A, Shapiro-Feinberg M, Gayer G: CT of thickened-wall gall bladder. Br J Radiol 76:137-143, 2003.

46. Rooholamini SA, Tehrani NS, Razavi MK, et al: Imaging of gallbladder carcinoma. RadioGraphics 14:291-306, 1994.

47. Yamashita K, Jin MJ, Hirose Y, et al: CT findings of transient focal increased attenuation of the liver adjacent to the gallbladder in acute cholecystitis. AJR 164:343-346, 1995.

48. Ito K, Awaya H, Mitchell DG, et al. Gallbladder disease: Appearance of associated transient increased attenuation in the liver at biphasic, contrast-enhanced dynamic CT. Radiology 204:723-728, 1997.

49. Cheng SM, Ng SP, Shih SL: Hyperdense gallbladder sign: An overlooked sign of acute cholecystitis on unenhanced CT examination. Clin Imaging 28, 128-131, 2004.

50. Adusumilli S, Siegelman ES: MR imaging of the gallbladder. MRI Clin N Am 10:165-184, 2002.

51. Loud PA, Semelka RC, Kettriz U, et al: Magn Reson Imaging 14:349-355, 1996.

52. Pedrosa I, Rofsky NM: MR imaging in abdominal emergencies. Magn Reson Imaging Clin N Am 12:603-635, 2004.

53. Hakansson K, Leander P, Ekberg O, et al: MR imaging in clinically suspected acute cholecystitis. A comparison with ultrasonography. Acta Radiol 41:322-328, 2000.

54. Regan F, Schaefer DC, Smith DP, et al: The diagnostic utility of HASTE MRI in the evaluation of acute cholecystitis. Half-Fourier acquisition single-shot turbo SE. J Comput Assist Tomogr 22:638-642, 1998.

55. Park MS, Yu JS, Kim YH, et al: Acute cholecystitis: Comparison of MR cholangiography and US. Radiology 209:781-785, 1998.

56. Kalliafas S, Ziegler DW, Flancbaum L, et al: Acute acalculous cholecystitis: Incidence, risk factors, diagnosis, and outcome. Am Surg 64:471-475, 1998.

57. Barie PS, Fischer E: Acute acalculous cholecystitis. J Am Coll Surg 180:232-244, 1995.

58. Kang JY, Williamson RC: Cholecystitis without gallstones. HPB Surg 2:83-103, 1990.

59. Glenn, F, Becker CG: Acute acalculous cholecystitis. An increasing entity. Ann Surg 195:131-136, 1982.

60. Parithivel,V.S, Gerst PH, Banerjee, S, et al: Acute acalculous cholecystitis in young patients without predisposing factors. Am Surg 65:366-368, 1999.

61. Savoca PE, Longo WE, Zucker KA, et al. The increasing prevalence of acalculous cholecystitis in outpatients. Ann Surg 211:433-437, 1990.

62. Flancbaum L, Choban PS: Use of morphine cholescintigraphy in the diagnosis of acute cholecystitis in critically ill patients. Intensive Care Med 21:120-124, 1995.

63. Shuman WP, Rogers JV, Rudd TG, et al. Low sensitivity of sonography and cholescintigraphy in acalculous cholecystitis. AJR 142:531-534, 1984.

64. Boland GWL, Slater G, Lu DSK, et al: Prevalence and significance of gallbladder abnormalities seen on sonography in intensive care unit patients. AJR 174:973-977, 2000.

65. Kalff V, Froelich JW, Lloyd R, et al: Predictive value of an abnormal hepatobiliary scan in patients with severe intercurrent illness. Radiology 146:191-194, 1983.

66. Flancbaum L, Alden SM: Morphine cholescintigraphy. Surg Gynecol Obstet 171:227-232, 1990.

67. Mariat G, Mahul P, Prevot N, et al: Contribution of ultrasonography and cholescintigraphy to the diagnosis of acute acalculous cholecystitis in intensive care patients. Intensive Care Med 26:1658-1663, 2000.

68. Mirvis SE, Vainright JR, Nelson AW, et al: The diagnosis of acute acalculous cholecystitis: A comparison of sonography, scintigraphy and CT. AJR 147:117-115, 1986.

69. Mirvis SE, Whitley NO, Miller JW: CT diagnosis of acalculous cholecysitits. J Comput Assist Tomogr 11:83-87, 1987.

70. Blankenberg F, Wirth R, Jeffrey RB, et al: Computed tomography as an adjunct to ultrasound in the diagnosis of acute acalculous chole-cystitis. Gastrointest Radiol 16:149-153, 1991.

71. McGahan JP, Lindfors KK: Percutaneous cholecystostomy: An alter-native to surgical cholecystectomy for acute cholecystitis? Radiology 173:481-485, 1989.

72. Boland GW, Lee MJ, Mueller PR, et al: Gallstones in critically ill patients with acute calculous cholecystitis treated by percutaneous cholecyst-ostomy: Nonsurgical therapeutic options. AJR 162:1101-1103, 1994.

73. Lo LD, Vogelzang RL, Braun MA, et al: Percutaneous cholecystostomy for the diagnosis and treatment of acute calculous and acalculous cholecystitis. Vasc Interv Radiol 6:629-634, 1995.

74. Ito K, Fujita N, Noda Y, et al: Percutaneous cholecystostomy versus gallbladder aspiration for acute cholecystitis: A prospective randomized controlled trial. AJR 183:193-196, 2004.

75. Cotran RS, Kumar V, Robbins SL: Pathologic Basis of Disease, 4th ed. Philadelphia, WB Saunders, 1989.

76. Morfin E, Ponka J, Brush B: Gangrenous cholecystitis. Arch Surg 96:567-572, 1968.

77. Wilson AK, Kozol RA, Salwen WA, et al: Gangrenous cholecystitis in an urban VA hospital. J Surg Res 56:402-404, 1994.

78. Ahmad MM, Macon WL: Gangrene of the gallbladder. Am Surg 49:155-158, 1983.

79. Merriam LT, Kanaan SA, Dawes LG, et al: Gangrenous cholecystitis: Analysis of risk factors and experience with laparoscopic cholecystectomy. Surgery 126:680-686, 1999.

80. Jacobs M, Verdeja J, Goldstein HS: Laparoscopic cholecystectomy in acute cholecystitis. J Laparoendosc Surg 1:175-177, 1991.

81. Singer JA, McKeen RV: Laparoscopic cholecystectomy for acute or gangrenous cholecystitis. Am Surg 60:326-328, 1994.

82. Teefey SA, Baron RL, Radke HM, et al: Gangrenous cholecystitis: New observations on sonography. J Ultrasound Med 134:191-4, 1991.

83. Jeffrey RB, Laing FC, Wong, W, et al: Gangrenous cholecystitis: Diagnosis by ultrasound. Radiology 148:219-221, 1983.

84. Simeone J, Brink J, Mueller P, et al: The sonographic diagnosis of acute gangrenous cholecystitis: Importance of the Murphy sign. AJR 152:209-290, 1989.

85. Lamki N, Raval B, St. Ville E: Computed tomography of complicated cholecystitis. J Comput Assist Tomogr 10:319-324, 1986.

86. Varma DGK, Faust JM: Computed tomography of gangrenous acute postoperative acalculous cholecystitis. CT J Comput Tomogr 12:29-31, 1988.

87. Bridges MD, Jones BC, Morgan DE, et al: Acute cholecystitis and gallbladder necrosis: Value of contrast enhanced CT [abstract]. AJR 172: 34-35, 1999.

88. Jenkins M, Golding RH, Cooperberg PL: Sonography and computed tomography of hemorrhagic cholecystitis. AJR 140:1197-1198, 1983.

89. Shah VR, Clegg JF: Haemorrhagic cholecystitis. Br J Surg 66:404-405, 1979.

90. Hudson PB, Johnson PP: Hemorrhage from the gallbladder. N Engl J Med 234:438-441, 1946.

91. Moskos MM, Eschelman DJ: Hemorrhagic cholecystitis. AJR 156: 1304-1305, 1991.

92. Polse S, Stoney RJ, Baldwin JN: Hemorrhage from the gallbladder. Calif Med 107:51-53, 1967.

93. Chinn DH, Miller EI, Piper N: Hemorrhagic cholecystitis. Sonographic appearance and clinical presentation. J Ultrasound Med 6:313-317, 1987.

94. Gremmels JM, Kruskal JB, Parangi S, et al: Hemorrhagic cholecystitis simulating gallbladder carcinoma. J Ultrasound Med 23:993-995, 2004.

95. Yiu-Chiu VS, Chiu LC, Wedel VJ: Current Cases and Concepts: Acalculous hemorrhagic cholecystitis. CT J Comput Tomogr 4:201-206, 1980.

96. Jacob H, Appelman R, Stein HD: Emphysematous cholecystitis. Am J Gastroenterol 71:325-330, 1979.

97. May RE, Strong R: Acute emphysematous cholecystitis. Br J Surg 58: 453-458, 1971.

98. Mentzer RM Jr, Golden GT, Chandler JG, et al: A comparative appraisal of emphysematous cholecystitis. Am J Surg 129:10-15, 1975.

99. Garcio-Sancho Tellez L, Rodriguez-Montes JA, Fernandez de Lis S, et al: Acute emphysematous cholecystitis: Report of twenty cases. Hepatogastroenterology 46:2144-2148, 1999.

100. Konno K, Ishida H, Naganuma H, et al: Emphysematous cholecystitis: Sonographic findings. Abdom Imaging 27:191-195, 2002.

101. Bloom RA, Libson E, Lebensart PD. et al: The ultrasound spectrum of emphysematous cholecystitis. J Clin Ultrasound 17:251-256, 1989.

102. Gill KS, Chapman AH, Weston MJ. The changing face of emphysematous cholecystitis. Br J Radiol 70:986-991, 1997.

103. McMillin K: Computed tomography of emphysematous cholecystitis. J Comput Assist. Tomogr 9:330-332, 1985.

104. Chiu HH, Chen CM, Mo LR: Emphysematous cholecystitis. Am J Surg 188:325-326, 2004.

105. Watanabe Y, Nagayama M, Okumura A, et al: MR imaging of acute biliary disorders. RadioGraphics 27:477-495, 2007.

106. Koenig T, Tamm EP, Kawashima A: Magnetic resonance imaging findings in emphysematous cholecystitis. Clin Radiol 59:455-458, 2004.

107. Diffenbaugh WG: Gangrenous perforation of the gallbladder. Arch Surg 59:743-749, 1949.

108. Strohl EL, Digffenbaugh WG, Baker JH, et al: Collective reviews: Gangrene, and perforation of the gallbladder. Int Abst Surg 114:1-7, 1962.

109. Madrazo BL, Francis I, Hricak H, et al: Sonographic findings in perforation of the gallbladder. AJR 139:491-496, 1982.

110. Niemeier OW: Acute free perforation of the gallbladder. Am Surg 99:922-924, 1934.

111. Fletcher AG, Ravdin IS: Perforation of the gallbladder. Am J Surg 81:178-185, 1951.

112. Heuer GJ: The factors leading to death in operations upon the gallbladder and bile ducts. Ann. Surg 99:881-892, 1934.

113. Cowley LL, Harkins HN: Perforation of the gallbladder. Surg Gynecol Obstet 77:661-668, 1943.

114. Peer A, Witz E, Manor H, et al: Intrahepatic abscess due to gallbladder perforation. Abdom Imaging 20:452-455, 1995.

115. Chen JJ, Lin HH, Chiu CT, et al: Gallbladder perforation with intrahepatic abscess formation. J Clin Ultrasound 18:43-45, 1990.

116. Ikard RW: Gallstones, cholelithiasis and diabetes surgery. Gynecol Obstet 171:528-532, 1990.

117. Chau WK, Na WT, Feng TT, et al: Ultrasound diagnosis of perforation of the gallbladder: Real time application and the demonstration of a new sonographic sign. J Clin Ultrasound 16:358-360, 1988.

118. Fitoz S, Erden A, Karagulle T, et al: Interruption of gallbladder wall with pericholecystic fluid: A CT finding of perforation. Emerg Radiol 7:253-255, 2000.

119. Kim PN, Lee KS, Kim IY, et al: Gallbladder perforation: Comparison of US findings with CT. Abdom Imaging 19:239-242, 1994.

120. Sood BP, Kalra N, Gupta S, et al: Role of sonography in the diagnosis of gallbladder perforation. J Clin Ultrasound 30:270-274, 2002.

121. Saul SH: Gallbladder and extrahepatic biliary tree. In Steinberg SS (ed): Diagnostic Surgical Pathology, 3rd ed. Philadelphia, Lippincott, 1999, pp 1629-1670.

122. Jagannath SB, Singh V, Cruz-Correa M, et al: A long-term cohort study of outcome after cholecystectomy for chronic acalculous cholecystitis. Am J Surg 185:91-95, 2003.

123. Krishnamurthy GT, Krishnamurthy S, Brown PH: Constancy and variability of gallbladder ejection fraction: Impact on diagnosis and therapy. J Nucl Med 45:1872-1877, 2004.

124. Poynter MT, Saba AK, Evans RA, et al: Chronic acalculous biliary tract disease: Cholecystokinin cholescintigraphy is useful in formulating treatment strategy and predicting success after cholecystectomy. Am Surg 68:382-384, 2002.

125. Goodman ZD, Ishak KG: Xanthogranulomatous cholecystitis. Am J Surg Pathol 5:653-659, 1981.

126. Ros PR, Goodman ZD: Xanthogranulomatous cholecystitis versus gallbladder carcinoma. Radiology 203:10-12, 1997.

127. Reed A, Ryan C, Schwartz SI: Xanthogranulomatous cholecystitis. J Am Coll Surg 179:249-252, 1994.

128. Guzman-Valdivia G: Xanthogranulomatous cholecystitis: 15 Years' experience. World J Surg 28:254-257, 2004.

129. Hsu CH, Hurwitz JL, Schuss A, et al: Radiology-Pathology Conference: Xanthogranulomatous cholecystitis. J Clin Imaging 27:421-425, 2003.

130. Parra JA, Acinas O, Bueno J, et al: Xanthogranulomatous cholecystitis: Clinical, sonographic, and CT findings in 26 patients. AJR 174:979-983, 2000.

131. Casas D, Perez-Andres R, Jimenez JA, et al: Xanthogranulomatous cholecystitis: A radiological study of 12 cases and a review of the literature. Abdom Imaging 21:456-460, 1996.

132. Kim PN, Lee SH, Gong GY, et al: Xanthogranulomatous cholecystitis: Radiologic findings with histologic correlation that focuses on intramural nodules. AJR 172:949-953, 1999.

133. Chun KA, Ha HK, Yu ES, et al: Xanthogranulomatous cholecystitis: CT features with emphasis on differentiation from gallbladder carcinoma. Radiology 203:93-97, 1997.

134. Lichtman JB, Varma VA: Ultrasound demonstration of xanthogranulomatous cholecystitis. J Clin Ultrasound 15:342-345, 1987.

135. Shukla S, Krishnani N, Jain M, et al: Xanthogranulomatous cholecystitis. Fine needle aspiration cytology in 17 cases. Acta Cytol 41:413-418, 1997.

136. Liu TH, Moody FG: Pathogenesis and presentation of common bile duct stones. Semin Laparosc Surg 7:224-231, 2000.

137. Lamont JT, Afdhal NH: Cholesterol gallstone disease: From pancreatitis to prevention. Curr Opin Gastroenterol 10:523-525, 1994.

138. Hermann RE: The spectrum of biliary stone disease. Am J Surg 158: 171-173, 1989.

139. Raraty MG, Finch M, Neoptolemos JP: Acute cholangitis and pancreatitis secondary to common duct stones: Management update. World J Surg 22:1155-1161, 1998.

140. Makary MA, Duncan MD, Harmon JW, et al: The role of magnetic resonance cholangiography in the management of patients with gallstone pancreatitis. Ann Surg 241:119-124, 2005.

141. Bilbao MK, Dotter CT, Lee TG, et al: Complications of endoscopic retrograde cholangiopancreatography. A study of 10,000 cases. Gastroenterology 70:314-320, 1976.

142. Lo SK, Chen J: The role of ERCP in choledocholithiasis. Abdom Imaging 21:120-132, 1996.

143. Harvey RT, Miller WT Jr: Acute biliary disease: Initial CT and follow-up US versus initial US and follow-up CT. Radiology 213:831-836, 1999.
144. Pasanen P, Partanen K, Pikkarainen P, et al: Ultrasonography, CT and ERCP in the diagnosis of choledochal stones. Acta Radiol 33:53-56, 1992.
145. Stott MA, Farrands PA, Guyer PB, et al: Ultrasound of the common bile duct in patients undergoing cholecystectomy. J Clin Ultrasound 19:73-76, 1991.
146. Dong B, Chen M: Improved sonographic visualization of choledocholithiasis. J Clin Ultrasound 15:185-190, 1987.
147. Laing FC, Jeffrey RB, Wing VW: Improved visualization of choledocholithiasis by sonography. AJR 143:949-952, 1984.
148. Ortega D, Burns PN, Simpson DH, et al: Tissue harmonic imaging: Is it a benefit for bile duct sonography? AJR 176:653-665, 2001.
149. Amouyal P, Amouyal G, Levy P, et al: Diagnosis of choledocholithiasis by endoscopic ultrasonography. Gastroenterology 106:1062-1067, 1994.
150. Baron RL: Common bile duct stones: Reassessment of criteria for CT diagnosis. Radiology 162:419-424, 1987.
151. Baron RL: Diagnosing choledocolithiasis: How far can we push helical CT? Radiology 203:601-603, 1997.
152. Pickuth D: Radiologic diagnosis of common bile duct stones. Abdom Imaging 25:618-621, 2000.
153. Neitlich JD, Topazian M, Smith RC, et al: Detection of choledocholithiasis: Comparison of unenhanced helical CT and endoscopic retrograde cholangiopancreatography. Radiology 203:753-757, 1997.
154. Soto JA, Alvarez O, Munera F, et al: Diagnosing bile duct stones: Comparison of unenhanced helical CT, oral contrast-enhanced CT cholangiography, and MR cholangiography. AJR 175:1127-1134, 2000.
155. Jimenez Cuenca I, del Olmo Martinez L, Perez Horns M: Helical CT without contrast in choledocholithiasis diagnosis. Eur Radiol 11:197-201, 2001.
156. Van Beers BE, Pringot JH: Imaging of cholelithiasis: Helical CT. Abdom Imaging 26:15-20, 2001.
157. Klein HM, Wein B, Truong S, et al: Computed tomographic cholangiography using spiral scanning and 3D imaging processing. Br J Radiol 66:762-767, 1993.
158. Breen DJ, Nicholson AA: The clinical utility of spiral CT cholangiography. Clin Radiol 55:733-739, 2000.
159. Xu AM, Cheng HY, Jiang WB, et al: Multislice three-dimensional spiral CT cholangiography: A new technique for diagnosing biliary disease. Hepatobiliary Pancreat Dis Int 1:595-603, 2002.
160. Cabada Giadas T, Sarria Octavio de Toledo L, Martinez-Berganza Asensio MT, et al: Helical CT cholangiography in the evaluation of the biliary tract: Application to the diagnosis of choledocholithiasis. Abdom Imaging 27:61-70, 2002.
161. Okada M, Fukada JI, Toya K, et al: The value of drip infusion cholangiography using multidetector-row helical CT in patients with choledocholithiasis. Eur Radiol 15:2140-2145, 2005.
162. Zandrino F, Curone P, Benzi L, et al: MR versus multislice CT cholangiography in evaluating patients with obstruction of the biliary tract. Abdom Imaging 30:77-85, 2005.
163. Gibson RN, Vincent JM, Spur T, et al: Accuracy of computed tomographic intravenous cholangiography (CT-IVC) with iotrexate in the detection of choledocholithiasis. Eur Radiol 15:1634-1642, 2005.
164. Ahmetoglu A, Kosucu P, Kul S, et al: MDCT cholangiography with volume rendering for the assessment of patients with biliary obstruction. AJR 183:1327-1332, 2004.
165. Baille J, Paulson EK, Vitellas KM: Biliary imaging: A review. Gastroenterol Clin N Am 124:1686-1699, 2003.
166. Fulcher AS, Turner MA: Benign disease of the biliary tract: Evaluation with MR cholangiography. Semin Ultrasound CT MR 20:294-303, 1999.
167. Reinhold C, Taourel P, Bret PM, et al: Choledocholithiasis: Evaluation of MR cholangiography for diagnosis. Radiology 209:435-442, 1998.
168. Heller SL, Lee VS: MR imaging of the gallbladder and biliary system. Magn Reson Imaging Clin N Am 13:295-311, 2005.
169. Kim JH, Kim MJ, Park S, et al: MR cholangiography in symptomatic gallstones: Diagnostic accuracy according to clinical risk group. Radiology 224:410-416, 2002.
170. Schmidt S, Chevallier P, Novellas S, et al: Choledocholithiasis: Repetitive thick-slab single-shot projection magnetic resonance cholangiopancreaticography versus endoscopic ultrasonography. Eur Radiol 17:241-250, 2007.
171. Regan F, Smith D, Khazan R, et al: MR cholangiography in biliary obstruction using half-Fourier acquisition. J Comput Assist Tomogr 20:627-632, 1996.
172. Kim M-J, Mitchell DG, Ito K, et al: Biliary dilatation: Differentiation of benign from malignant causes- value of adding conventional MR imaging to MR cholangiography. Radiology 214:173-181, 2000.
173. Wieloplski PA, Gaa J, Wielopolski DR, et al: Breath-hold MR cholangiopancreatography with three-dimensional, segmented, echo-planar imaging and volume rendering. Radiology 210:247-252, 1999.
174. Soto JA, Barish MA, Yucel E, et al: Pancreatic duct: MR cholangiopancreatography with a three-dimensional fast spin-echo technique. Radiology 196:459-464, 1995.
175. Barish M, Yucel E, Soto J, et al: MR cholangiopancreatography: Efficacy of three-dimensional turbo spin-echo technique. AJR 196:459-464, 1995.
176. McKenzie CA, Lim D, Ransil BJ, et al: Shortening MR image acquisition time for volumetric interpolated breath-hold examination with a recently developed parallel imaging reconstruction technique: Clinical feasibility. Radiology 230:589-594, 2003.
177. Watanabe Y, Dohke M, Ishimori T, et al: Pseudo-obstruction of the extrahepatic bile duct due to artifact from arterial pulsatile compression: A diagnostic pitfall of MR cholangiopancreatography. Radiology 214:856-860, 2000.
178. Sugita R, Sugimura E, Itoh M, et al: Pseudolesion of the bile duct caused by flow effect: A diagnostic pitfall of MR cholangiopancreatography. AJR 180:467-471, 2003.
179. Menu Y, Lorphelin JM, Scherrer A, et al: Sonographic and computed tomographic evaluation of intrahepatic calculi. AJR 145:579-583, 1985.
180. Carmona RH, Crass RA, Lim RC Jr, et al: Oriental cholangitis. Am J Surg 148:117-124, 1984.
181. Sperling RM, Koch J, Sandhu JS, et al: Recurrent pyogenic cholangitis in Asian immigrants to the United States. Natural history and role of therapeutic ERCP. Dig Dis Sci 42:865-871, 1997.
182. Yassa NA, Stain S, Ralls PW: Recurrent pyogenic cholangitis. Ultrasound Q 14:41-47, 1998.
183. Kim M-J, Cha S-W, Mitchell DG, et al: MR imaging findings in recurrent pyogenic cholangitis. AJR 173:1545-1549, 1999.
184. Chan F-L, Man S-W, Leong LLY, et al: Evaluation of recurrent pyogenic cholangitis with CT: Analysis of 50 patients. Radiology 170:165-169, 1989.
185. Federle MP, Cello JP, Laing FC, et al: Recurrent pyogenic cholangitis in Asian immigrants. Use of ultrasonography, computed tomography and cholangiography. Radiology 143:151-156, 1982.
186. Lim JH, Ko YT, Lee DH, et al: Oriental cholangiohepatitis: Sonographic findings in 48 cases. AJR 155:511-514, 1990.
187. Kusano S, Okada Y, Endo T, et al: Oriental cholangiohepatitis: Correlation between portal vein occlusion and hepatic atrophy. AJR 158:1011-1014, 1992.
188. Sathesh-Kumar T, Saklani AP, Vinayagam R, et al: Spilled gallstones during laparoscopic cholecystectomy: A review of the literature. Postgrad Med J 80:77-79, 2004.
189. Litwin DEM, Girotti MJ, Poulin EC, et al: Laparoscopic cholecystectomy: Trans-Canada experience with 2201 cases. Can J Surg 35:291-296, 1992.
190. Larson GM, Vitale GC, Casey J, et al: Multipractice analysis of laparoscopic cholecystectomy in 1,983 patients. Am J Surg 163:221-226, 1992.
191. Cuschieri A, Dubois F, Mouiel J, et al: The European experience with laparoscopic cholecystectomy. Am J Surg 161:385-387, 1991.
192. Morrin MM, Kruskal JB, Hochman MG, et al: Radiologic features of complications arising from dropped gallstones in laparoscopic cholecystectomy patients. AJR 174:1441-1445, 2000.
193. Trerotola SO, Lillemoe KD, Malloy PC, et al: Percutaneous removal of "dropped" gallstones after laparoscopic cholecystectomy. Radiology 188:419-421, 1993.
194. Campbell WB, McGarity WC: An unusual complication of laparoscopic cholecystectomy. Am Surg 184:195-200, 1992.
195. Mirizzi PC: Sindrome del conducto hepatico. J Int Chir 8:731-777, 1948.
196. McSherry C, Ferstenberg H, Virshup M: The Mirizzi syndrome: Suggested classification and surgical therapy. Surg Gastroenterol 1:219-225, 1982.
197. Abou-Saif A, Al-Kawas FH: Complications of gallstone disease: Mirizzi syndrome, cholecystocholedochal fistula and gallstone ileus. Am J Gastroenterol 97:249, 2002.
198. Sharma AK, Rangan HK, Choubey RP, et al: Pitfalls in the management of Mirizzi's syndrome. Trop Gastroenterol 19:72-74, 1998.
199. Karademir S, Astarioglu H, Sokmen S, et al: Mirizzi's syndrome: Diagnostic and surgical considerations in 25 patients. J Hepatobiliary Pancreat Surg 7:72-77, 2000.

200. Berland LL, Lawson TL, Stanley RJ: CT appearance of Mirizzi syndrome. J Comput Assist Tomogr 8:165-166, 1984.

201. Kim PN, Outwater EK, Mitchell DG: Mirizzi syndrome: Evaluation by MR imaging. Am J Gastroenterol 94:2546-2550, 1999.

202. Wakefield EG, Vickers PM, Walters W: Intestinal obstruction caused by gallstones. Surgery 5:670-673, 1939.

203. Chen MYM: Gallstone ileus: CT findings. Appl Radiol 20:37-38, 1991.

204. Rigler LG, Borman CN, Noble JF: Gallstone obstruction: Pathogenesis and roentgen manifestations. JAMA 117:1753-1759, 1941.

205. Balthazar EJ, Schechter LS: Air in gallbladder: A frequent finding in gallstone ileus. AJR 131:219-222, 1978.

206. Delabrousse E, Bartholomot B, Sohm O, et al: Gallstone ileus: CT findings. Eur Radiol 10:938-940, 2000.

207. Loren I, Lasson A, Nilsson A, et al: Gallstone ileus demonstrated by CT. J Comput Assist Tomogr 18:262-265, 1994.

208. Swift SE, Spencer JA: Gallstone ileus: CT findings. Clin Radiol 53:451-456, 1998.

209. Jutras JA: Hyperplastic cholecystosis. AJR 83:795-827, 1960.

210. Berk RN, van der Vegt JH, Lichtenstein JE: The hyperplastic cholecystoses: Cholesterolosis and adenomyomatosis. AJR 146:593-601, 1983.

211. Kopp JG: The strawberry gallbladder. Arch Klin Chir 151:411-429, 1928.

212. Tilvis RS, Aro J, Strandberg TE, et al: Lipid composition of bile and gallbladder mucosa in patients with acalculous cholesterolosis. Gastroenterology 82:607-615, 1982.

213. Judd ES, Mentzer SH: Cholesterolosis of the gallbladder. I. A clinical study. Collected papers. Mayo Clin Proc 19:310-316, 1927.

214. Feldman M, Feldman M Jr: Cholesterolosis of the gallbladder. An autopsy study of 165 cases. Gastroenterology 27:641-648, 1954.

215. Owen CC, Bilhartz LE: Gallbladder polyps, cholesterolosis, adenomyomatosis and acute acalculous cholecystitis. Semin Gastrointest Dis 14:178-188, 2003.

216. Lee KF, Wong J, Li JCM, et al: Polypoid lesions of the gallbladder. Am J Surg 188:186-190, 2004.

217. Terzi C, Sokmen S, Seckin S, et al: Polypoid lesions of the gallbladder: Report of 100 cases with special reference to operative indications. Surgery 127:622-627, 2000.

218. Chattopadhyay D, Lochan R, Balupuri S, et al: Outcome of gallbladder polypodal lesions detected by transabdominal ultrasound scanning: A nine year experience. World J Gastroenterol 11:2171-2173, 2005.

219. Ootani T, Shirai Y, Muto T, et al: Relationship between gallbladder carcinoma and the segmental type of adenomyomatosis. Cancer 69:2647-2652, 1992.

220. Colquhoun J: Adenomyomatosis of the gall-bladder (intramural diverticulosis). Br J Radiol 34:101-112, 1961.

221. Raghavendra BN, Subramanyam BR, Balthazar EJ, et al: Sonography of adenomyomatosis of the gallbladder: Radiologic-pathologic correlation. Radiology 146:747-752, 1983.

222. Hwang JI, Chou SH, Tsay SH, et al: Radiologic and pathologic correlation of adenomyomatosis of the gallbladder. Abdom Imaging 23:73-77, 1998.

223. Halpert RD, Bedi DG, Tirman PJ, et al: Segmental adenomyomatosis of the gallbladder. A radiologic, sonographic and pathologic correlation. Am Surg 55:570-572, 1989.

224. Nishimura A, Shirai Y, Hatakeyama K: Segmental adenomyomatosis of the gallbladder predisposes to cholecystolithiasis. J Hepatobiliary Pancreat Surg 11:342-347, 2004.

225. Gerard PS, Berman D, Zafaranloo S: CT and ultrasound of gallbladder adenomyomatosis mimicking carcinoma. J Comput Assist Tomogr 14:490-491, 1990.

226. Yoshimitsu K, Honda H, Jimi M, et al: MR diagnosis of adenomyomatosis of the gallbladder and differentiation from gallbladder carcinoma: Importance of showing Rokitansky-Aschoff sinuses. AJR 172:1535-1540, 1999.

227. Yoshimitsu K, Honda H, Aibe H, et al: Radiologic diagnosis of adenomyomatosis of the gallbladder: Comparative study among MRI, helical CT and transabdominal US. J Comput Assist Tomogr 25:843-850, 2001.

228. Boscak AR, Al-Hawary M, Ramsburgh SR: Best cases from the AFIP: Adenomyomatosis of the gallbladder. RadioGraphics 26:941-946, 2006.

229. Yoon JH, Cha SS, Han SS, et al: Gallbladder adenomyomatosis: Imaging findings. Abdom Imaging 31:555-563, 2006.

230. Whittle C, Hepp J, Soto E, et al: Pseudotumoral adenomyomatosis of the gallbladder diagnosed by ultrasound: Report of one case. Rev Med Chil 135:212-215, 2007.

Interventional Radiology of the Gallbladder and Biliary Tract

David Hahn, MD

The role of percutaneous therapy in the management of gallbladder and biliary disease continues to evolve. The technique of puncturing the abdomen with needles for diagnostic and therapeutic purposes was initially thought by our medical and surgical colleagues to be too dangerous for common practice.[1] However, the indications for percutaneous intervention and resultant outcomes began to gain acceptance in the late 1970s with published outcomes of abdominal abscess management.[2] Today, interventional radiologists are further defining the role of these minimally invasive procedures as adjuncts, alternatives, and bridges to surgical therapy in critically ill and high surgical risk patients. This chapter focuses on the current indications, techniques, and outcomes of percutaneous gallbladder and biliary interventions and their roles in medical and surgical decision-making.

PREPROCEDURAL MANAGEMENT

The initial encounter with a patient requiring biliary intervention starts with a thorough and up-to-date history and physical. The radiologist should review the relevant laboratory data which should include complete blood count, coagulation profile, blood urea nitrogen and creatinine, electrolytes, liver enzymes including total bilirubin, direct and indirect, and a metabolic profile. The patient's complete list of allergies should be reviewed with particular attention to antibiotic allergies and prophylaxis against iodinated contrast allergies when appropriate. All relevant imaging findings should be reviewed, including recent CT scans, ultrasound, MR studies, plain radiographs and nuclear scintigraphy.

At our institution, as a general rule, we require a patient's platelet count to be above 50,000 prior to a biliary or gallbladder intervention. If below 50,000, the patient should receive a transfusion of platelets either the night before or during the procedure. In patients on warfarin therapy, we require the international normalized ratio (INR) to be 1.5 or less, with fresh frozen plasma and/or vitamin K given as appropriate by the medical service. For heparinized patients, those on heparin drips have their heparin held 2 to 4 hours prior to their procedure; those on subcutaneous heparin have their injections held the day of the procedure. Antiplatelet agents such as aspirin and clopidrogel are held 3 to 5 days prior to the procedure when possible as additional precautions against bleeding complications.

Antibiotic prophylaxis remains one of the most important considerations prior to planning a biliary or gallbladder intervention. While postprocedural infection rates remain low in interventional procedures as compared to conventional surgery, infection continues to be the Achilles' heel of biliary intervention. The need for adequate antibiotic prophylaxis is underscored by the increasing numbers of elderly and immunocompromised patients that comprise our growing patient population. In 1998, a survey conducted by the Society of Interventional Radiology (SIR) uncovered wide variations among interventionalists in both their perception of the need for antibiotic prophylaxis and the role of antibiotics during their daily practice.[3] The bulk of our guidelines for prophylactic antibiotic use in interventional procedures is extrapolated from surgical data and common surgical practice. However, despite this lack of substantial evidence-based data, general guidelines and recommendations in the literature for biliary intervention include (1) 1 g of ceftriaxone intravenously; (2) 1.5 to 3 g of ampicillin/sulbactam intravenously; (3) 1 g of cefotetan intravenously plus 4 g of mezlocillin intravenously; and (4) 1 g of ceftazidine intravenously.[4] Note should be made of the patient's antibiotic hypersensitivities and consultation with the institution's pharmacy should be made when appropriate.

THE GALLBLADDER

Traditionally, the surgical management of the patient with acute cholecystitis has been intravenous antibiotic therapy followed by early cholecystectomy.[5] However, while laparoscopic techniques continue to improve, the mortality rates following cholecystectomy for acute cholecystitis can be high, especially in the elderly and in patients with significant comorbidities, with mortality ranging from 14% to 33% and complication rates as high as 33% to 66%.[6-9] In recent years, many general surgeons have changed their approach from early surgery to stabilization of the acute infection or inflammation by image-guided gallbladder drainage, followed by elective laparoscopic cholecystectomy.[10-14] This section focuses on the role of gallbladder intervention as a surgical adjunct to the management of acute cholecystitis in the high risk patient.

Cholecystography and Percutaneous Cholecystostomy

The role of diagnostic cholecystography in the setting of acute right upper quadrant syndrome and a high-risk patient is to obtain pertinent information useful in determining whether emergent and potentially risky surgery is indicated. Other indications for gallbladder aspiration include (1) as a diagnostic tool in the stable patient who has failed endoscopic retrograde cholangiopancreatography (ERCP) in order to exclude a common duct stone before laparoscopic cholecystectomy; (2) as a means to opacify the intrahepatic biliary tract for establishment of endobiliary drainage; (3) for decompression of the biliary tract when there is a common bile duct obstruction, if the cystic duct is patent; and (4) in the intubated patient with an unexplained leukocytosis, fever, or poor oxygenation.[15,16] Percutaneous cholecystography is easily and safely performed using a small-bore needle, usually 18 or 22 gauge, and best done under ultrasound guidance. Whether the intent for percutaneous gallbladder access is for aspiration purposes only or for possible conversion to a cholecystostomy tube using the Seldinger technique, the access should be performed in the same manner in order to avoid multiple punctures to the gallbladder. Therefore, percutaneous access should always be done in a manner safe for conversion to cholecystostomy drain placement if necessary.

Technique

Using ultrasound, CT, or occasionally fluoroscopic guidance, an 18- or 22-gauge needle is passed into the gallbladder. The author's preferred approach is through a portion of lower liver tissue, avoiding the hepatic flexure of the colon and the pleural space. A subcostal approach is performed when possible although an intercostal approach is performed just as easily, keeping the needle adjacent to the superior margin of the rib in order to avoid the more inferior neurovascular bundle. At one point, it was believed that the gallbladder puncture should traverse the bare area of the liver to avoid significant peritoneal bile leak. Several studies, however, have document the safety of a lower transhepatic approach to the gallbladder, and some authors consider a transperitoneal approach to be safe, with or without the placement of retention anchors.[17,18]

Once the gallbladder is cannulated, bile is aspirated and sent for Gram stain and aerobic and anaerobic cultures. In the setting of acute cholecystitis, one should avoid injecting contrast material into an already distended gallbladder in order to avoid causing or worsening sepsis by backflow of bacteria into systemic circulation. If the intended procedure is cholecystostomy drain placement, a guidewire is inserted under fluoroscopic guidance with adequate purchase of wire into the gallbladder lumen to avoid loss of access. After passing dilators over the guidewire, a locking pigtail drainage catheter is placed over the wire, usually an 8- or 10-French catheter. The catheter may then be connected to either a gravity drainage bag or a Jackson-Pratt bulb.

Once the drain is placed, it should be maintained for 2 to 4 weeks in order to allow time for an epithelial tract to form around the catheter to the skin before catheter removal. This tract provides a route for bile to escape out the skin rather than into the peritoneum, causing a chemical peritonitis. During this period, after the clinical signs of infection have subsided, the drain may be injected with contrast in order to study the patency of the cystic and common bile duct and to evaluate for the presence of stones anywhere along the drainage pathway of the gallbladder (Fig. 80-1).

Complications

The risk of serious complications following percutaneous cholecystostomy are low, less than 2%.[19] The main risks are hemorrhage, either subcapsular or hemobilia, bile leak, puncture of the pleural space or colon, and sepsis. Minor complications include tube dislodgment, tube occlusion, and minor bleeding around the entry site.

Gallbladder Aspiration versus Percutaneous Cholecystostomy

There are advocates for both gallbladder aspiration only and for primary percutaneous cholecystostomy in the setting of

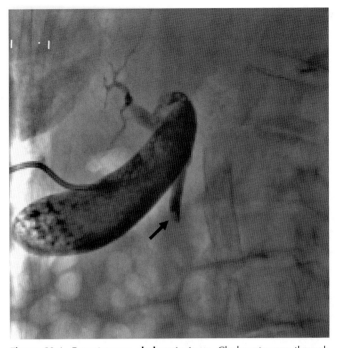

Figure 80-1. Percutaneous cholecystostomy. Cholecystogram through existing percutaneous cholecystostomy drain placed 2 weeks prior demonstrating innumerable small gallstones with an obstructing stone in the distal common bile duct. Patient went on to successful ERCP with sphincteromtomy and stone retrieval.

THE BILIARY TRACT

As noninvasive imaging techniques of the biliary tree continue to improve, the more invasive technique of percutaneous transhepatic cholangiography (PTC) as a diagnostic tool has been largely replaced by magnetic resonance cholangio-pancreaticography (MRCP) and higher resolution CT and ultrasound imaging. PTC is reserved for an intent-to-treat situation, usually followed by percutaneous transhepatic biliary drainage (PTBD). PTBD remains the basis for most biliary interventions, allowing the necessary access to perform biliary drainage and stenting, lithotripsy or choledocholithotomy, and management of biliary strictures and leaks.

Patients presenting with jaundice or chronic right upper quadrant syndrome are initially studied with ultrasound, CT or MRI. ERCP is often the next diagnostic step, demonstrating excellent biliary and pancreatic ductal detail and providing a route for treatment such as biliary decompression via sphincterotomy, stone removal and biliary or pancreatic stent placement. When ERCP fails, PTBD is indicated. Reasons for failed ERCP include: difficult anatomy, complex post-operative anatomy such as a Roux-en-Y diversion, tight strictures technically unfeasible to cross from a retrograde approach, and in diffuse biliary disease such as in primary sclerosing cholangitis or in cholangiocarcinoma.[28] Other indications for ERCP are (1) palliation of unresectable malignant disease causing obstructive jaundice; (2) postsurgical or traumatic biliary leak; (3) cholangitis in an obstructed biliary system in which the gallbladder cannot be accessed; and (4) preoperative improvement of hepatorenal function before a biliary-enteric anastamosis.[29-34]

Percutaneous Transhepatic Cholangiography and Percutaneous Transhepatic Biliary Drainage

Technique

PTC and PTBD (Fig. 80-2) can be accomplished from either a subcostal approach into the left lobe of the liver or an intercostal or subcostal approach into the right lobe. When the left lobe is anatomically accessible, a left subcostal approach to PTBD is usually favored at centers that routinely use ultrasound guidance.[35] Dilated left bile ducts are more easily seen during ultrasonography from an infrasternal view, and there is usually a shorter distance to traverse from the subcostal skin to a peripheral left duct. Other advantages include less catheter pain in some patients, an increased likelihood of success with a single-stick method, and in those patients with ascites, less leakage around the catheter.[36]

The traditional biliary drainage technique, which dates from preultrasound and rotating image intensifier days, is via the right lobe of the liver using fluoroscopy alone and bony anatomic landmarks as guides for needle puncture. This technique is still widely used and effective. A 22-gauge needle is advanced into the liver from roughly the midcoronal plane, at a level just above the 10th rib or more caudal. More cephalad approaches may be necessary in some patients, but there is progressive risk of traversing the pleural space. Some centers approach from below the costal margin.[37] Fluoroscopy is used to avoid crossing bowel or pleura.

an elderly or high-risk patient with acute right upper quadrant syndrome. While both procedures carry a high rate of technical success, some advocates of gallbladder aspiration argue that percutaneous cholecystostomy carries a significantly higher complication rate than aspiration alone while producing comparable clinical outcomes in both groups, therefore suggesting that aspiration alone should be the initial approach in this patient subtype.[20] However, proponents of percutaneous cholecystostomy claim greater clinical effectiveness with tube drainage while maintaining an acceptably low complication rate as compared to aspiration alone. One recent prospective randomized controlled series found a good clinical response in 90% of the percutaneous cholecystostomy group compared to 61% in the aspiration only group ($p < 0.05$), and technical success rates of 100% and 82%, respectively.[21]

At our institution, percutaneous cholecystostomy is favored to gallbladder aspiration in the setting of acute cholecystitis as tube drainage provides a more rapid and thorough drainage of the infected bile contents than can be achieved through needle aspiration alone. Clinical response is rapid, with 90% reaching a good response in the first 72 hours after tube placement.[20] While percutaneous cholecystostomy may be used as the primary therapy in the critically ill patient unfit for surgery, there is a rapidly growing body of literature that advocates cholecystostomy as the initial treatment of choice for high risk patients, serving as a bridge to elective laparoscopic cholecystectomy and significantly lower rates of morbidity and mortality as compared to emergent open or laparoscopic cholecystectomy.[22-27] In addition, percutaneous cholecystostomy provides a suitable route for alternate treatment options such as endoscopic assisted gallbladder stenting and percutaneous cholecystolithotomy.

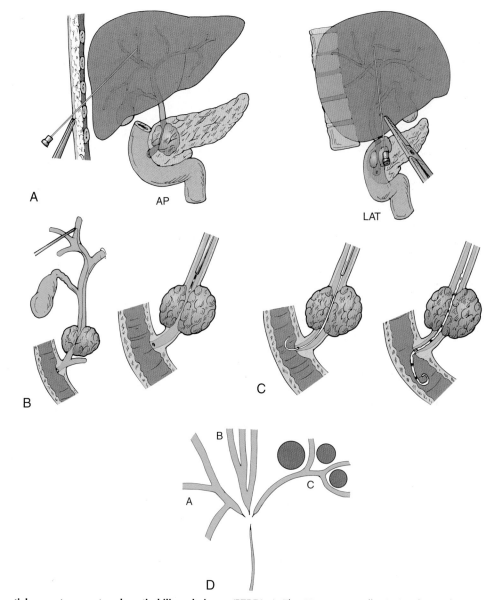

Figure 80-2. One-stick percutaneous transhepatic biliary drainage (PTBD). A. The 22-gauge needle tip is advanced into an appropriate duct for conversion. AP, anteroposterior view; LAT, lateral view. **B.** After removal of the stylet, an 0.018-inch guidewire is inserted and advanced into the common bile duct. The 22-gauge needle is removed, and coaxial dilators are inserted. **C.** The inner dilator is removed, which permits placement of larger guidewires that negotiate the obstruction into the duodenum. Subsequently, a PTBD catheter is inserted. **D.** Choosing an appropriate duct for PTBD. Segment A should be selected for drainage. Segment B should not be used because it shows crowding of dilated ducts, which indicates parenchymal atrophy. Segment C shows metastases and also should not be chosen. (**A-C** from Kadir S: Percutaneous transhepatic cholangiography and biliary drainage. In Kadir S [ed]: Current Practice of Interventional Radiology. Philadelphia, BC Decker, 1991, pp 497-510; **D.** From Chapman AH: Radiological stenting of malignant biliary obstruction. In Bennett JR, Hunt RH [eds]: Therapeutic Endoscopy and Radiology of the Gut, 2nd ed. Baltimore, Williams & Wilkins, 1990, pp 309-326, © 1990, the Williams & Wilkins Co., Baltimore.)

In a patient with biliary dilatation, one to five passes are usually needed to successfully cannulate a bile duct. Contrast material is then gently injected under fluoroscopic guidance while slowly withdrawing the needle to opacify the biliary system. Nondilated ducts are much more difficult to access. Ultrasound is useful for positioning the needle just anterior to the right portal vein to improve the chances of finding a diagnostic duct. If the cannulated duct is suitably peripheral and the angle of approach favorable, biliary drainage can be performed from a diagnostic needle using a variety of kits designed for this purpose. If the initial duct cannulated is too central, then it is safer to place a second needle in a more peripheral duct using fluoroscopic guidance to diminish the risk of hemorrhage.

It is technically easier to cross a biliary stricture from the antegrade approach in contrast to the retrograde technique during ERCP. Therefore, it is useful to establish biliary-enteric access during the initial PTBD. Hydrophilic-coated wires and catheters greatly facilitate the crossing of tight strictures. If a stricture cannot be traversed, a small locking pigtail catheter can be left above the level of obstruction for biliary decompression. The patient can then be brought back after the inflammation of the biliary ducts subsides for easier crossing of the stricture.

The goal in acute management of endobiliary drainage is the establishment of internal/external drainage. Various catheters have been designed that have multiple sideholes and some form of distal locking mechanism, usually a Cope loop. One to three catheters may be necessary to affect endobiliary drainage, depending on the number or isolated, dilated biliary segments. These internal/external drains may form the basis of long-term care, as in the setting of cholangiocarcinoma, or they may be internalized using a variety of temporary or permanent stents.

Complications

ERCP is usually attempted before percutaneous techniques because the risk of major complications, principally bleeding and sepsis, is thought to be lower. In the setting of acute cholangitis, ERCP should be the initial treatment of choice with PTC and PTBD indicated when ERCP fails and surgery reserved for definitive treatment of the underlying cause.[38] The risk of serious complications associated with PTBD is about 5%, versus 1% for ERCP.[37] Complications associated with PTC and PTBD include intraparenchymal and subcapsular bleeding, infection and sepsis, hemobilia, and death. Patient selection is the key to favorable outcomes, and the overall risks should be quite low in experienced centers.

Management of Iatrogenic Complications: Bile Leak and Biliary Strictures

Historically, iatrogenic bile duct injuries were by and large, comprised of mainly complications arising from hepatobiliary surgery. The arrival of new surgical techniques in both hepatobiliary and liver transplant surgery has increased the incidence of vascular and biliary complications in recent years.[39,40] However, while surgical complications are the most common cause of iatrogenic bile duct injury, a growing acceptance in liver directed oncologic therapies as well as newer liver transplantation techniques is giving rise to new etiologies of bile leak and benign biliary strictures.

Bile duct injuries are more common and more complex with laparoscopic cholecystectomy than with open cholecystectomy. The incidence of bile duct injury during laparoscopic cholecystectomy ranges from 0.5% to 1.4%.[41] Anatomic variants are a common cause of these injuries, particularly aberrant, low insertion of a right hepatic duct into the common bile duct or the cystic duct. If the amount of liver drained by the injured aberrant duct is small, the transaction may be asymptomatic. If the amount drained is significant, then the patient can develop a chronic biloma or cholangitis.[42] The types of injury range from minor to complex, from small leaks to those requiring surgical bilioenteric reconstruction. It is unclear whether or not these leaks should be managed early or late.[43] Regardless of the type of injury, however, it is clear that they should be managed at experienced centers that can offer a multidisciplinary approach.

The goal of interventional radiology in this situation is to (1) document the nature of bile duct injury; (2) to drain a biloma; (3) to divert bile if there is obstruction or leak when ERCP is not successful; and (4) to provide a percutaneous

alternative in the treatment of biliary strictures when surgery or ERCP is not feasible.

Long-term Treatment for Biliary Obstruction

It is critical to customize the correct long-term drainage plan for each patient. Therapeutic options include balloon dilatation of certain benign strictures, surgery, or the placement of various indwelling endoprostheses, either via ERCP or through a percutaneous approach.[44] Internal endoprostheses fall into two main categories, plastic devices that are removable or metal stents that are permanent.[45] The plastic devices may be further divided into those that extent to the skin, which provide internal/external drainage, and those that are entirely internal. Although the selection of the method of long-term biliary drainage depends in part on regional variation and personal preference, proper management is usually dictated by the clinical setting.

Focal, Benign, Reversible Disease

Iatrogenic injuries are the most common cause of benign biliary strictures. Although the incidence of postlaparoscopic cholecystectomy stricture in experienced centers is less than 1%, there has nevertheless been a 5- to 10-fold increase in the incidence of strictures when compared with the open cholecystectomy era.[46,47] New advances and techniques in liver directed therapies for benign and malignant liver pathology also comprise a growing number of causes for iatrogenic bile duct injury. This includes hepatic artery embolization (HAE), radiofrequency ablation (RFA) if there is a tumor, and cryoablation and chemical ablation of hepatic hemangiomas.[48] The stricture may either manifest itself several weeks after RFA or several years after surgery.

Surgical complications causing bile duct strictures are usually categorized by the level of obstruction, using the Bismuth classifications.[49] The higher the obstruction, the poorer is the prognosis. ERCP is usually performed initially to characterize the level of obstruction and, if possible, to decompress the biliary tree through use of plastic, removable endoprostheses. When decompression cannot be achieved via ERCP, a percutaneous drainage is performed. Prompt drainage of an obstructed system is critical to patient management, since cholangitis in an obstructed system increases the risk of poor outcome during balloon dilatation or surgical repair.

Diffuse Disease, Benign or Malignant

In the setting of diffuse biliary disease, such as sclerosing cholangitis, cholangiocarcinoma, and metastatic liver disease, internal/external drainage with a catheter may be advantageous for long-term drainage over the placement of metal stents (Fig. 80-3). The internal/external drainage catheters consist typically of hydrophilic-coated plastic locking pigtail drains, ranging in size from 8 to 12 French. The catheters may be placed from the right or left biliary tracts or bilaterally if there is a need to decompress a noncommunicating biliary system. These stents can be easily exchanged or repositioned as the natural history of the disease progresses. With careful maintenance, patients can have endobiliary patency for years.

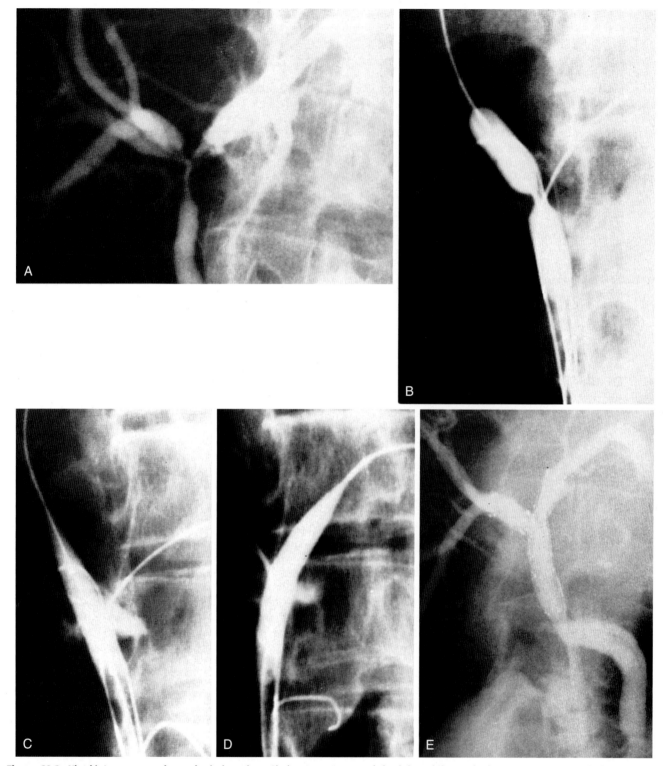

Figure 80-3. Klatskin's tumor: endoprosthesis insertion. Cholangiocarcinoma of the biliary hilum (Klatskin's tumor). **A.** Initial cholangiogram demonstrates obstruction of the right, left, and proximal common hepatic ducts. For insertion of a biliary endoprosthesis, each ductal system required balloon dilatation. The right ductal system is shown during (**B**) and after (**C**) balloon dilatation. **D.** The left ductal system was also dilated. **E.** Gianturco stents were then inserted.

Technique

Our method of PCCL is similar to that described by Cope and coworkers.[62] If there is no direct access to the gallbladder, cholecystostomy is performed. Some authors favor the use of retrievable anchoring devices during cholecystostomy to prevent bile leakage.[63] Our experience and that of others is that anchoring devices are not usually necessary, especially if a transhepatic route to the gallbladder is used. Ultrasound is used to perform safe needle puncture, with an angle and level of approach designed to permit access to the cystic duct. The placement of a second cholecystostomy access adjacent to the first can be performed to maintain access and provide irrigation during PCCL. The initial cholecystostomy catheters are 8 French. The catheter should remain in place for 2 to 4 weeks to establish a mature cutaneous tract.

During the second visit, at least 2 weeks after initial cholecystostomy, the integrity of the tract is tested to exclude bile leak. This is done by exchanging the catheter over a guidewire for a vascular sheath and performing pullback injection over the wire, opacifying the tract. If the tract is mature, then it is dilated to 16 French with a catheter left in place for several days until the inflammation from dilatation subsides.

The patient is admitted to the hospital for PCCL. Epidural anesthesia during the procedure allows for more aggressive stone extraction than typically tolerated by conscious sedation alone. The mature tract allows for passage of a choledochoscope without the need for a sheath. Stone extraction can then be accomplished with a flexible endoscope and contact lithotripsy used to break the stones into small fragments that are easily removed through the dilated cholecystostomy. The second small gallbladder access is used for irrigation in order to facilitate gravel and fragment removal.[64]

If there are stones in the cystic duct, this structure should be selected and an 8-French endobiliary drainage catheter used to maintain patency. Stone extraction may be formed through basketing or lithotripsy, either extracorporeal or contact.

Complete stone extraction may require several sessions. After the stones are removed, a new catheter is inserted to maintain the tract. For this purpose, a Foley catheter is preferred as it is softer and more comfortable than a conventional drainage catheter. The patient may be discharged with gravity drainage bag. The cholecystostomies may be removed the following week as an outpatient, after cholangiography demonstrates the gallbladder to be clear and the cystic duct patent.

Outcomes

The reported rates of technical success are high, between 80% to 100%.[65] The patient and referring physician should be warned that stones recur, approximately 40% at 5 years.[65] The incidence of recurrence appears to be diminished if the patient is placed on chenodeoxycholic acid therapy.

Choledocholithotomy

When a large stone is lodged in the common bile duct, ERCP extraction may be unsuccessful due to either the inability to enter the duct or the inability to pull out the stone using balloon techniques. These patients can benefit from percutaneous endobiliary drainage, followed by endoscopic lithotripsy.

The protocol and technique is similar to PCCL. The stone fragments can be removed percutaneously through the dilated, mature tract or pushed into the duodenum with a compliant balloon[66] (Fig. 80-4). Alternative methods include sweeping the stones into the duodenum from above using a 10- or 12-French balloon over a guidewire, or a combined interventional/endoscopic procedure in which a guidewire is placed percutaneously into the bowel in difficult or postsurgical anatomy to facilitate the access to the stone via ERCP.[67]

References

1. Cope C: Percutaneous nonvascular abdominal interventions: Reflections on the past and ideas for the future. J Vasc Interv Radiol 14:861-864, 2003.
2. Gerzof SG, Robbins AH, Johnson WC, et al: Percutaneous catheter drainage of abdominal abscesses: A five-year experience. N Engl J Med 305:653-657, 1981.
3. Dravid VS, Gupta A, Zegel HG, et al: Investigation of antibiotic prophylaxis usage for vascular and nonvascular interventional procedures. J Vasc Interv Radiol 9:401-406, 1998.
4. Ryan JM, Ryan, BM, Smith TP: Antibiotic prophylaxis in interventional radiology. J Vasc Interv Radiol 15:547-556, 2004.
5. Nahrwold DL: Acute cholecystitis. In Sabiston D Jr (ed): Textbook of Surgery, 15th ed. Philadelphia, WB Saunders, 1997, pp 1126-1131.
6. Huber DF, Edward W, Cooperman M: Cholecystectomy in elderly patients. Am J Surg 146:719-722, 1983.
7. Escarce JJ, Shea JA, Chen W, et al: Outcomes of open cholecystectomy in the elderly: A longitudinal analysis of 21,000 cases in the prelaparoscopic era. Surgery 117:156-164, 1995.
8. Houghton PW, Jenkinson LR, Donaldson LA: Cholecystectomy in the elderly: A prospective study. Br J Surg 72:220-222, 1985.
9. Kimura Y, Takada T, Kawarada Y, et al: Definitions, pathophysiology, and epidemiology of acute cholangitis and cholecystitis: Tokyo Guidelines. J Hepatobiliary Pancreat Surg 14:15-26, 2007.
10. Kuster GG, Domagk D: Laparoscopic cholecystectomy with delayed cholecystectomy as an alternative to conversion to open procedure. Surg Endosc 10:426-428, 1996.
11. Patterson EJ, Mclaughlin RF, Mathieson JR, et al: An alternative approach to acute cholecystitis: Percutaneous cholecystostomy and interval laparoscopic cholecystectomy. Surg Endosc 10:1185-1188, 1996.
12. Borzellino G, Manzoni G, Ricci F, et al: Emergency cholecystostomy and subsequent cholecystectomy for acute gallstone cholecystitis in the elderly. Br J Surg 86:1521-1525, 1999.
13. Berber E, Engle KL, String A, et al: Selective use of tube cholecystostomy with interval laparoscopic cholecystectomy in acute cholecystitis. Arch Surg 135:341-346, 2000.
14. Spira RM, Nissan A, Zamir O, et al. Percutaneous transhepatic cholecystostomy and delayed laparoscopic cholecystectomy in critically ill patients with acute calculus cholecystitis. Am J Surg 183:62-66, 2002.
15. England RE, McDermott VG, Smith TP, et al: Percutaneous cholecystostomy: Who responds? AJR 168:1247-1251, 1997.
16. Gervais DA, Mueller PR: Percutaneous cholecystostomy. Semin Interv Radiol 13:35-50, 1996.
17. Caridi JG, Hawkins IF, Akins EW, et al: Button self-retaining drainage catheter. Cardiovasc Interv Radiol 20:317-321, 1997.
18. Hatjdakis AA, Karampekios S, Prassopoulous P, et al: Maturation of the tract after percutaneous cholecystostomy with regard to the access route. Cardiovasc Interv Radiol 21:36-41, 1998.
19. Goodwin SC, Bansal V, Greaser LE, et al: Prevention of hemobilia during percutaneous biliary drainage: Long-term followup. J Vasc Interv Radiol 8:881-885, 1997.
20. Chopra S, Dodd GD III, Mumbower AL, et al: Treatment of acute cholecystitis in non-critically ill patients at high surgical risk: Comparison of clinical outcomes after gallbladder aspiration and after percutaneous cholecystostomy. AJR 176:1025-1031, 2001.
21. Ito K, Fujita N, Noda Y, et al: Percutaneous cholecystostomy versus gallbladder aspiration for acute cholecystitis: A prospective randomized controlled trial. AJR 183:193-196, 2004.
22. Byrne MF, Suhocki P, Mitchell RM, et al: Percutaneous cholecystostomy in patients with acute cholecystitis: Experience of 45 patients at a US referral center. J Am Coll Surg 197:206-211, 2003.

23. Macri A, Scuder G, Saladino E, et al: Acute gallstone cholecystitis in the elderly: Treatment with emergency ultrasonographic percutaneous cholecystostomy and interval laparoscopic cholecystectomy. Surg Endosc 20:88-91, 2006.

24. Welschbillig-Meunier K, Pessaux P, Lebigot J, et al: Percutaneous cholecystostomy for high-risk patients with acute cholecystitis. Surg Endosc 19:1256-1259, 2005.

25. Teoh WM, Cade RJ, Banting SW, et al: Percutaneous cholecystostomy in the management of acute cholecystitis. ANZ J Surg 75:396-398, 2005.

26. Li JC, Lee DW, Lai CW, et al: Percutaneous cholecystostomy for the treatment of acute cholecystitis in the critically ill and elderly. Hong Kong Med J 10:389-393, 2004.

27. Tsumura H, Ichikawa T, Hiyama E, et al: An evaluation of laparoscopic cholecystectomy after selective percutaneous transhepatic gallbladder drainage for acute cholecystitis. Gastrointest Endosc 59:839-844, 2004.

28. Lo SK, Chen J: Role of ERCP in choledocholithiasis. Abdom Imaging 21:120-124, 1996.

29. Ferrucci JT, Mueller PR, Harbin WP: Percutaneous transhepatic biliary drainage. Radiology 135:1-13, 1980.

30. Hoevels J: Percutaneous transhepatic cholangiography and percutaneous biliary drainage. In Dondelinger RF, Rossi P, Kurdziel JC, et al (eds): Interventional Radiology. Stuttgart, Georg Thieme Verlag, 1990, pp 187-208.

31. Gunther RW, Schild H, Thelens M: Percutaneous transhepatic biliary drainage: Experience with 311 procedures. Cardiovasc Interv Radiol 11:65-71, 1988.

32. Bonnel D, Ferrucci JT, Mueller PR, et al: Surgical and radiological decompression in malignant biliary obstruction: A retrospective study using multivariate risk factor analysis. Radiology 152:347-351, 1984.

33. Venbrux AC: Interventional radiology of the biliary tract. Curr Opin Radiol 4:83-92, 1992.

34. Yee ACN, Ho C-S: Percutaneous transhepatic biliary drainage: A review. Crit Rev Diagn Radiol 30:247-279, 1990.

35. Hayashi N, Sakai T, Kitagawa M, et al: US-guided left-sided biliary drainage: Nine-year experience. Radiology 204:119-123, 1997.

36. Koito K, Namieno T, Nagakawa T, et al: Percutaneous transhepatic biliary drainage using color Doppler ultrasonography. J Ultrasound Med 15:203-208, 1996.

37. Wu DM, Marchant LK, Haskal ZJ: Percutaneous interventions in the biliary tree. Semin Roentgenol 32:228-242, 1997.

38. Bornman PC, van Beljon JI, Krige JE: Management of cholangitis. J Hepatobiliary Pancreat Surg 10:406-414, 2003.

39. Huang ZQ, Huang XQ: Changing patterns of traumatic bile duct injuries: A review of forty years experience. World J Gastroenterol 8:5-12, 2002.

40. Denys A, Chevallier P, Doenz F, et al: Interventional radiology in the management of complications after liver transplantation. Eur Radiol 14:431-439, 2004.

41. de Reuver PR, Grossman I, Busch OR, et al: Referral pattern and timing of repair are risk factors for complications after reconstructive surgery for bile duct injury. Ann Surg 245:763-770, 2007.

42. Slanetz PJ, Boland GW, Mueller PR: Imaging and interventional radiology in laparoscopic injuries to the gallbladder and biliary system. Radiology 201:595-599, 1996.

43. Mercado MA: Early versus late repair of bile duct injuries. Surg Endosc 20:1644-1647, 2006.

44. England RE, Martin DF: Endoscopic and percutaneous intervention in malignant obstructive jaundice. Cardiovasc Intervent Radiol 19:381-386, 1996.

45. Lammer J, Hausegger KA, Fluckiger F, et al: Common bile duct obstruction due to malignancy: Treatment with plastic versus metal stents. Radiology 201:167-172, 1996.

46. Bonnell DH, Liguory CL, Lefebvre JF, et al: Placement of metallic stents for treatment of postoperative biliary strictures: Long-term outcome in 25 patients. AJR 169:1517-1521, 1998.

47. Yoon H-K, Sung K-B, Song H-Y, et al: Benign biliary strictures associated with recurrent pyogenic cholangitis: Treatment with expandable metallic stents. AJR 169:1523-1525, 1997.

48. Stippel DL, Tox U, Gossmann A, et al: Successful treatment of radiofrequency-induced biliary lesions by interventional endoscopic retrograde cholangiography (ERC). Surg Endosc 17:1965-1970, 2003.

49. Lillemoe KD, Winick AB, Kalloo AN: Benign strictures. In Pitt HA, Carr-Locke DL, Ferrucci JT (eds): Hepatobiliary and Pancreatic Disease. Boston, Little, Brown, 1995, pp 259-272.

50. Lubienski A, Duex M, Lubienski K, et al: [Interventions for benign biliary strictures.] Radiologe 45:1012-1019, 2005.

51. Alfke H, Alfke B, Froelich JJ, et al: [Treatment for malignant biliary occlusion by means of transhepatic percutaneous biliary drainage with insertion of metal stents: Results of an 8-year follow-up and analysis of the prognostic parameters.] Rofo 175:1125-1129, 2003.

52. Hii MW, Gibson RN: Role of radiology in the treatment of malignant hilar biliary strictures 1: Review of the literature. Austras Radiol 48:3-13, 2004.

53. Ikeda S, Maeshiro K: [Interventional treatment of biliary stricture.] Nippon Geka Gakkai Zasshi 105:374-379, 2004.

54. Morgan RA, Adam AN: Malignant biliary disease: percutaneous interventions. Tech Vasc Interv Radiol 4:147-152, 2001.

55. Lammer J, Klein GE, Kleinert R, et al: Obstructive jaundice: Use of expandable metal endoprostheses for biliary drainage. Radiology 177:789-792, 1990.

56. Boguth L, Tatalovic S, Antonucci F, et al: Malignant biliary obstruction: Clinical and histopathologic correlation after treatment with self-expanding metal prostheses. Radiology 192:669-674, 1994.

57. Schoder M, Rossi P, Uflacker R, et al: Malignant biliary obstruction: Treatment with e-PTFE-FEP-covered endoprostheses- initial technical and clinical experiences in a multicenter trial. Radiology 225:35-42, 2002.

58. Baron TH, Poterucha JJ: Insertion and removal of covered expandable metal stents for closure of complex biliary leaks. Clin Gastroenterol Hepatol 4:381-386, 2006.

59. Bezzi M, Zolovkins A, Cantisani V, et al: New ePTFE/FEP-covered stent in the palliative treatment of malignant biliary obstruction. J Vasc Interv Radiol 13:581-589, 2002.

60. Burhenne HJ: Percutaneous extraction of retained biliary tract stones: 661 Patients. AJR 134:889-898, 1980.

61. Courtois CS, Picus D, Hicks ME, et al: Percutaneous gallstone removal: long-term follow-up. J Vasc Interv Radiol 7:229-235, 1996.

62. Cope C, Burke DR, Meranze SG: Percutaneous extraction of gallstones in 20 patients. Radiology 176:19-24, 1990.

63. Picus D, Hicks ME, Darcy MD, et al: Percutaneous cholecystolithotomy: Analysis of results and complications in 58 consecutive patients. Radiology 183:779-784, 1992.

64. Gilliams A, Curtis SC, Donald J, et al: Technical considerations in 113 percutaneous cholecystolithotomies. Radiology 183:163-166, 1992.

65. McDermott CG, Arger P, Cope C: Gallstone recurrence and gallbladder function following percutaneous cholecystolithotomy. J Vasc Interv Radiol 5:473-478, 1994.

66. Rossi P, Bezzi M, Fiocca F, et al: Percutaneous cholangioscopy. Semin Interv Radiol 13:185-193, 1996.

67. Li ZF, Chen XP: Recurrent lithiasis after surgical treatment of elderly patients with choledocholithiasis. Hepatobiliary Pancreas Dis Int 6:67-71, 2007.

chapter 81

Neoplasms of the Gallbladder and Biliary Tract

Byung Ihn Choi, MD • Jeong Min Lee, MD

Most neoplasms that arise from the gallbladder and bile ducts are malignant. Although infrequent, gallbladder and bile duct carcinomas are not rare. Gallbladder carcinoma is the seventh most common malignancy of the gastrointestinal tract and is the most common biliary malignancy; bile duct carcinoma occurs less often.[1] Familiarity with the imaging characteristics of gallbladder and bile duct neoplasms is important to expedite diagnosis and appropriate treatment of patients, who often present with nonspecific symptoms of right upper quadrant pain, jaundice, and weight loss.

GALLBLADDER CARCINOMA

Epidemiology

Carcinoma of the gallbladder is responsible for at least 3000 deaths per year in the United States.[1] Carcinoma of the gallbladder is two to three times more common in women than in men, and its incidence steadily increases with age, although it varies greatly in different parts of the world.[2-6] More than 90% of patients are older than 50 years; the peak incidence is 70 to 75 years. Some geographic areas have a high incidence of gallbladder cancer, including South America and India.[5] Certain groups, such as Israelis, Native Americans, Spanish Americans in the southwest United States, and Eskimos in Alaska, have a significantly higher incidence of gallbladder carcinoma and cholelithiasis than do populations.[7,8]

Etiology

Several factors have been associated with an increased risk of developing gallbladder carcinoma. The presence of gallstones is considered to be an important risk factor for gallbladder carcinoma. Of patients with gallbladder carcinoma, 65% to 90% have gallstones, an incidence considerably higher than that for age- and sex-matched control groups.[6,9] Diffuse mural calcification, the "porcelain" gallbladder, is another predisposing factor.[10,11] Other risk factors include the presence of gallbladder adenomas, an anomalous pancreaticobiliary duct junction, and exposure to carcinogenic chemicals.[6,12,13]

Pathologic Findings

Most carcinomas of the gallbladder are adenocarcinomas (85% to 90%) and can be papillary, tubular, mucinous, or signet cell type. The remainder are anaplastic, squamous cell, or adenosquamous carcinomas.[14,15] Macroscopically, carcinomas of the gallbladder can appear as poorly defined areas of diffuse gallbladder wall thickening (infiltrating) or as a cauliflower mass (fungating) that grows into the gallbladder lumen. The infiltrating type invades the gallbladder wall and ultimately replaces the lumen with a tumor mass. The papillary form grows into and eventually fills the lumen.[16] Some tumors may show a combination of the infiltrating and fungating patterns. Approximately 60% of carcinomas originate in the fundus, 30% in the body, and 10% in the neck.[17] In some cases, the tumor may diffusely infiltrate the entire gallbladder, making its organ of origin impossible to identify.

The gallbladder has a unique anatomic features: the wall consists of a mucosa, a lamina propria, a smooth muscle layer, perimuscular connective tissue, and serosa without a submucosa. Furthermore, no serosa exists at the attachment to the liver and along the hepatic surface. The connective tissue is continuous with the interlobular connective tissue of the liver.[17] Gallbladder carcinoma is staged surgically by the depth of invasion, extension of disease into adjacent structures, involvement of lymph nodes, and presence of metastases using the American Joint Committee on Cancer TNM staging system[2,18] (Table 81-1). Invasion of the muscularis mucosa distinguishes T1 from T2 cancers.

Clinical Findings

Gallbladder carcinoma most often presents with right upper quadrant abdominal pain simulating more common biliary and nonbiliary disorders.[19] Weight loss, jaundice, and an abdominal mass are less common presenting symptoms. Patients may have longstanding symptoms of chronic cholecystitis with a recent change in the quality or frequency of the painful episodes. Other common presentations are similar to either acute cholecystitis or symptoms of biliary malignancy. Gallbladder carcinoma is occasionally an incidental finding on abdominal imaging studies. Elevated serum levels of α-fetoprotein and carcinoembryonic antigen have been reported in association with gallbladder carcinoma.[17,20]

Radiographic Findings

Traditional plain oral cholecystography, and barium studies of the gastrointestinal tract have a limited role in the imaging of gallbladder carcinoma. Abdominal radiographs may show calcified gallstones, porcelain gallbladder, or, rarely, punctate calcifications from mucinous carcinomas.[21] Biliary gas from malignant gallbladder–enteric fistula is another rare finding.[22] The gallbladder fails to opacify in at least two thirds of patients with carcinoma of the gallbladder, usually because of cystic duct obstruction.[16] Barium studies are abnormal in limited cases, showing displacement or direct invasion of the duodenum or anterior limb of the hepatic flexure.

Ultrasound, CT, and MRI are the most valuable imaging modalities for evaluating patients with gallbladder carcinoma. Patients with right upper quadrant pain should initially be examined with ultrasound. The diagnostic accuracy of ultra-

Table 81-1
TNM Classification System for Staging Gallbladder Carcinoma

Primary tumor (T)	
TX	Primary tumor cannot be assessed
TO	No evidence of primary tumor
Tis	Carcinoma in situ
T1	Tumor invades mucosa or muscle layer
T1 a	Tumor invades the mucosa
T1 b	Tumor invades the muscle layer
T2	Tumor invades the perimuscular connective tissue; no extension beyond the serosa or into the liver
T3	Tumor perforates the serosa (visceral peritoneum) or directly invades into one adjacent organ, or both (extension ≤2 cm into the liver)
T4	Tumor extends >2 cm into the liver and/or into two or more adjacent organs (stomach, duodenum, colon, pancreas, omentum, extrahepatic bile ducts, any involvement of liver)
Regional lymph nodes (N)	
NX	Regional lymph nodes cannot be assessed
NO	No regional lymph node metastasis
N1	Metastasis in cystic duct, pericholedochal, and/or hilar lymph nodes (i.e., in the hepatoduodenal ligament)
N2	Metastasis in peripancreatic (head only), periduodenal, periportal, celiac, and/or superior mesenteric lymph nodes
Distant metastasis (M)	
MX	Presence of distant metastasis cannot be assessed
MO	No distant metastasis
Mi	Distant metastasis

Stage grouping			
Stage 0	Tis	NO	MO
Stage I	T1	NO	MO
Stage II	T2	NO	MO
Stage III	T1	N1	MO
	T2	N1	MO
	T3	NO	MO
	T3	N1	MO
Stage IVA	T4	NO	MO
	T4	N1	MO
Stage IVB	Any T	N2	MO
	Any T	Any N	M1

From Greene FL, Page DL, Fleming ID, et al (eds). AJCC Cancer Staging Handbook, 6th ed. New York, Springer, 2002, pp 139-144.

sound in gallbladder cancer is over 80%, but it has limitations in tumor staging.[23] Endoscopic ultrasound is useful in depicting the depth of tumor invasion and for characterizing polypoid lesions.[24,25] CT is superior to ultrasound in assessing lymphadenopathy and spread of the disease into the liver, porta hepatis, or adjacent structures and is useful in predicting which patients will benefit from surgical therapy.[26,27] Although MRI can be useful in assessing the cause of focal or diffuse mural thickening and helps differentiate gallbladder cancer from adenomyomatosis and chronic cholecystitis,[28,29] magnetic resonance cholangiopancreatography (MRCP) provides more detailed information regarding biliary involvement of the tumor than ultrasound or CT.

Although direct cholangiographic techniques such as endoscopic retrograde cholangiopancreatography (ERCP) or percutaneous transhepatic cholangiography are of little value in detecting the presence of gallbladder carcinoma, they are helpful in planning surgical procedure because they can show tumor growth into adjacent intrahepatic ducts or into the common bile duct.[6] The cholangiographic differential diagnosis includes cholangiocarcinoma, metastases, Mirizzi's syndrome, and pancreatic carcinoma.

Radiologic Evaluation of the Primary Tumor

Gallbladder carcinomas have three major histologic and imaging presentations: (1) focal or diffuse thickening and/or irregularity of the gallbladder wall; (2) polypoid mass originating in the gallbladder wall and projecting into the lumen; and (3) most commonly, a mass obscuring or replacing the gallbladder, often invading the adjacent liver.[26,27]

Carcinoma Manifesting as Mural Thickening

Focal or diffuse thickening of the gallbladder wall is the least common presentation of gallbladder carcinoma and is the most difficult to diagnose, particularly in the early stages. Gallbladder carcinoma may cause mild to marked mural thickening in a focal or diffuse pattern. This thickening is best appreciated sonographically; the gallbladder wall is normally 3 mm or less in thickness.[30] Carcinomas confined to the gallbladder mucosa may present as flat or slightly raised lesions with mucosal irregularity that are difficult to appreciate sonographically. In one sonographic series, half the patients

with these early carcinomas had no protruding lesions, and fewer than one third were identified preoperatively.[31] More advanced gallbladder carcinomas can cause marked mural thickening, often with irregular and mixed echogenicity (Fig. 81-1). The gallbladder may be contracted, normal sized, or distended, and gallstones are usually present.

Four factors interfere with the sonographic recognition of carcinoma as the cause of gallbladder wall thickening. (1) Changes of early gallbladder carcinoma may be only subtle mucosal irregularity or mural thickening. (2) Gallbladder wall thickening is a nonspecific finding that can also be caused by acute or chronic cholecystitis, hyperalimentation, portal hypertension, adenomyomatosis, inadequate gallbladder distention, hypoalbuminemia, hepatitis, or hepatic, cardiac, or renal failure. Sometimes the echo architecture of the wall can help narrow the differential diagnosis.[32,33] In acute cholecystitis, the wall often has irregular, discontinuous hypoechoic and echogenic bands. Chronic cholecystitis often results in a uniformly echodense band surrounding the mucosa, and hypoproteinemia may have a hypoechoic central band. Pronounced wall thickening (>1.0 cm) demonstrated by ultrasonography with associated mucosal irregularity or marked asymmetry should raise concerns for malignancy or complicated cholecystitis.[27] (3) Chronic cholecystitis is often present in patients with gallbladder carcinoma. (4) Shadowing stones or gallbladder wall calcification may obscure the carcinoma.

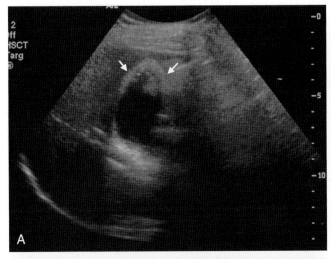

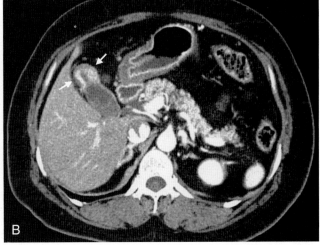

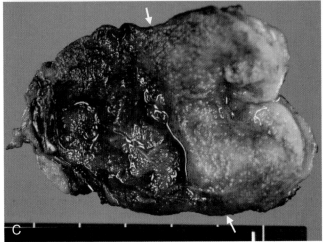

Figure 81-1. Gallbladder carcinoma: mural thickening. A. Subcostal sonogram shows a markedly thickened, in homogeneous gallbladder wall (*arrows*). **B.** CT shows an enhancing, thick gallbladder wall (*white arrows*) with lumen narrowing. **C.** Photograph of the opened resected specimen shows a thickening of the gallbladder wall (*arrows*).

Although CT is inferior to ultrasound for evaluating the gallbladder wall for mucosal irregularity, mural thickening, and cholelithiasis, it is superior for evaluating the thickness of portions of the gallbladder wall that are obscured by interposed gallstones or mural calcifications on ultrasound. On CT, focal malignant wall thickening shows enhancement after administration of intravenous contrast material.[27,34] When focal or irregular thickening of the gallbladder wall is encountered on CT, the images should be carefully inspected for bile duct dilatation, local invasion, metastasis, or adenopathy.[35]

Carcinoma Manifesting as a Polypoid Mass

About one fourth of gallbladder carcinomas manifest as a polypoid mass projecting into the gallbladder lumen. Identification of these neoplasms is particularly important because they are well differentiated and are more likely to be confined to the gallbladder mucosa or muscularis when discovered.[36]

Polypoid carcinomas on ultrasound usually have a homogeneous tissue texture, are fixed to the gallbladder wall at their base, and do not cast an acoustic shadow (Fig. 81-2). Most are broad based with smooth borders, although occasional tumors have a narrow stalk or villous fronds. The polyp may be hyperechoic, hypoechoic, or isoechoic relative to the liver. Gallstones are usually present, and the gallbladder is either normal sized or expanded by the mass.

A small polypoid carcinoma can be indistinguishable from a cholesterol polyp, adenoma, or adherent stone. Most benign polyps are small, measuring less than 1 cm. If a gallbladder polyp is larger than 1 cm in diameter and is not clearly benign, cholecystectomy should be considered. Tumefactive sludge or blood clot can simulate a polypoid carcinoma. Positional maneuvers usually differentiate these entities; clots and sludge move, albeit slowly, whereas cancers do not.

When polypoid carcinomas are sufficiently large, they manifest as soft tissue masses that are denser than surround-

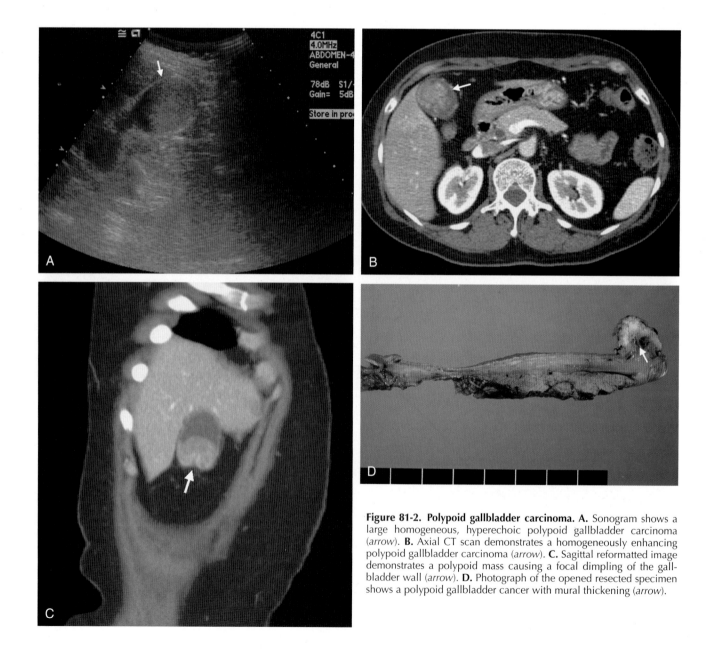

Figure 81-2. Polypoid gallbladder carcinoma. A. Sonogram shows a large homogeneous, hyperechoic polypoid gallbladder carcinoma (*arrow*). **B.** Axial CT scan demonstrates a homogeneously enhancing polypoid gallbladder carcinoma (*arrow*). **C.** Sagittal reformatted image demonstrates a polypoid mass causing a focal dimpling of the gallbladder wall (*arrow*). **D.** Photograph of the opened resected specimen shows a polypoid gallbladder cancer with mural thickening (*arrow*).

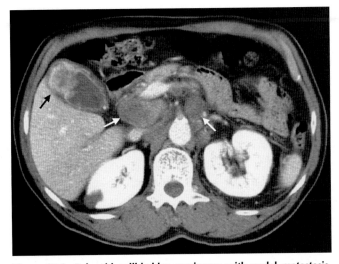

Figure 81-3. Polypoid gallbladder carcinoma with nodal metastasis. CT scan demonstrates a polypoid gallbladder carcinoma (*black arrow*) and a low-density portocaval and para-aortic lymph nodes containing metastases (*white arrows*).

ing bile on CT scans (Fig. 81-3). The polypoid cancer usually enhances homogeneously after administration of contrast medium, and the adjacent gallbladder wall may be thickened (see Figs. 81-2 and 81-3). Necrosis or calcification is uncommon.

Carcinoma Manifesting as a Gallbladder Fossa Mass

A large mass obscuring or replacing the gallbladder is the most common (42% to 70%) presentation of gallbladder carcinoma.[26,27] Sonographically, the mass is often complex, with regions of necrosis, and small amounts of pericholecystic fluid are often present. Gallstones are commonly seen within the ill-defined mass, which typically invades hepatic parenchyma.

On CT scans, infiltrating carcinomas that replace the gallbladder often show irregular contrast enhancement with scattered regions of internal necrosis (Fig. 81-4). Unless the associated gallstones are densely calcified, they may be diffi-

cult to identify. Invasion of the liver or hepatoduodenal ligament, satellite lesions, hepatic or nodal metastases, and bile duct dilatation are also common.

MRI findings in gallbladder carcinoma are similar to those reported with CT. MRI demonstrates prolongation of the T1 and T2 relaxation time in gallbladder carcinoma. These lesions are heterogeneously hyperintense on T2-weighted images and hypointense on T1-weighted images compared with liver parenchyma.[37] Ill-defined early enhancement is a typical appearance of gallbladder carcinoma on dynamic gadolinium-enhanced MRI[29] (Fig. 81-5). MRI with MRCP offers the potential of evaluating parenchymal, vascular, biliary, and nodal involvement with a single noninvasive examination (Fig. 81-6). On the basis of MRI alone, it may be difficult to distinguish carcinoma of the gallbladder from inflammatory and metastatic disease.

Differential Diagnosis

The differential diagnosis of infiltrating gallbladder carcinomas includes more common inflammatory and noninflammatory causes of wall thickening. These include heart failure, cirrhosis, hepatitis, renal failure, complicated cholecystitis, xanthogranulomatous cholecystitis, and adenomyomatosis.[27,32] Clinically and radiologically, gallbladder carcinoma can be difficult to differentiate from cholecystitis with pericholecystic fluid and abscess. A low-attenuation intrahepatic halo surrounding the gallbladder wall on CT scans is fairly specific for complicated cholecystitis.[38,39] Gallbladder carcinoma should be suspected when there are features of a focal mass, lymphadenopathy, hepatic metastases, and biliary obstruction at the level of the porta hepatis. Diffuse gallbladder wall thickening and streaky densities in the pericholecystic fat are seen with both inflammation and carcinoma. Xantho-granulomatous cholecystitis is a pseudotumoral inflammatory condition of the gallbladder that radiologically simulates gallbladder carcinoma.[40] In the few cases in which it is impossible to distinguish complicated cholecystitis from neoplasm, ultrasound-directed or CT-directed needle biopsy can provide a tissue diagnosis. Adenomyomatosis, which is

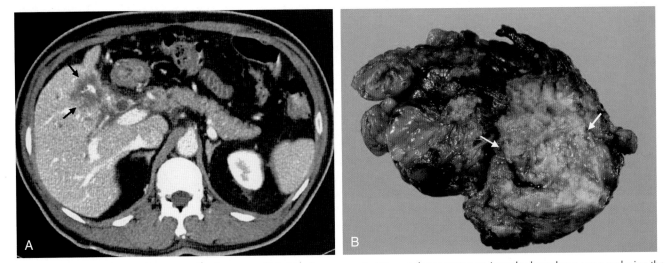

Figure 81-4. Gallbladder carcinoma manifesting as a gallbladder fossa mass. A. CT scan demonstrates an irregular hypodense mass replacing the gallbladder extending into the hepatic parenchyma (*arrows*). Note dilated common duct with wall thickening, suggesting spreading to the extrahepatic bile duct. **B.** Photograph of the resected specimen shows a large mass replacing the gallbladder (*arrows*).

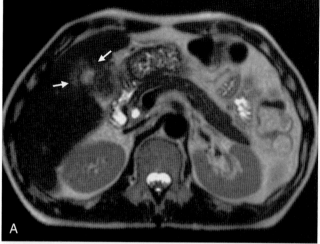

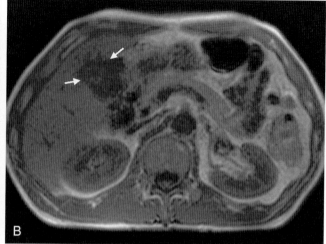

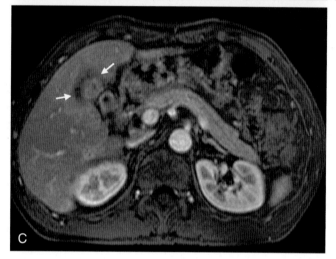

Figure 81-5. Gallbladder carcinoma: MR features. A. T2-weighted MR image shows a thickened moderately hyperintense gallbladder wall (*arrows*). **B.** T1-weighted MR image demonstrates a thickened hypointense gall-bladder wall (*arrows*). **C.** Postgadolinium fat-suppressed T1-weighted image reveals slightly heterogeneous enhancement of the thickened gallbladder wall (*arrows*).

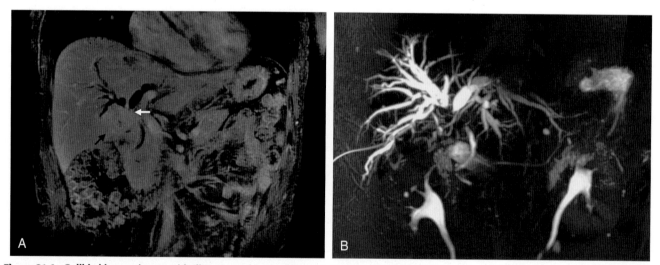

Figure 81-6. Gallbladder carcinoma with direct spread to the bile duct. A. Coronal MR image demonstrates an enhancing gallbladder carcinoma (*black arrow*) with involvement of adjacent bile duct (*white arrow*). **B.** MRCP maximum intensity projection (MIP) image demonstrates an obstruction at the confluence of the right and left hepatic ducts with dilation of the intrahepatic bile ducts.

characterized by focal or diffuse gallbladder wall thickening with dilated Rokitansky-Aschoff sinuses, may simulate gallbladder carcinoma on CT. MRI can be useful for distinguishing this entity from gallbladder carcinoma.[28]

The differential diagnosis of those tumors that present as an intraluminal polypoid mass includes adenomatous, hyperplastic, and cholesterol polyps; carcinoid tumor; metastatic melanoma; and hematoma.[27] The differential diagnosis for a mass replacing the gallbladder fossa includes hepatocellular carcinoma, cholangiocarcinoma, and metastatic disease to the gallbladder fossa. Hepatomas occurring near the gallbladder fossa may be confused with gallbladder cancer radiographically, but they usually occur in cirrhotic livers and do not typically invade the gallbladder. Patients with liver metastases to the gallbladder fossa usually have a known primary neoplasm.

Pathways of Tumor Spread

Gallbladder carcinoma spreads beyond the wall by several routes: (1) direct invasion of the liver, hepatoduodenal ligament, duodenum, or colon; (2) lymphatic spread to regional lymph nodes; (3) hematogenous spread to the liver; (4) intraductal tumor extension; and (5) metastasis to the peritoneum.[41,42] Distant metastases are unusual.

Gallbladder carcinoma spreads most commonly via direct invasion of the liver.[42,43] Liver invasion is facilitated by its proximity and the thin gallbladder wall, which lacks a submucosa and has only a single muscular layer. Invasion of the gastrohepatic ligament is also common and may cause biliary obstruction at the porta hepatis. Invasion into the duodenum or colon is less common. On ultrasound images, the gallbladder wall becomes ill defined as an inhomogeneous mass extends into the liver parenchyma. On CT scans, portions of the invading tumor show enhancement after administration of contrast medium. The gallbladder wall is poorly defined adjacent to the carcinoma invading liver parenchyma. Detection of subtle hepatic invasion is improved by using narrow collimation to avoid partial volume averaging, and coronal or sagittal reformations. On MRI, direct hepatic invasion or distant liver metastases are well shown on T2-weighted or gadolinium-enhanced images. The tumor has the same signal intensity as the primary tumor in most cases.

The prevalence of lymphatic spread is high in gallbladder carcinoma[27] (see Fig. 81-3B). Lymphatic metastases progress from the gallbladder fossa through the hepatoduodenal ligament to nodal stations near the head of the pancreas. The cystic and pericholedochal lymph nodes are the most commonly involved at surgery and are a critical pathway to involvement of the celiac, superior mesenteric, and para-aortic lymph nodes.[44-46] Because the gallbladder drains into these more distal nodes, hepatic hilar nodes are usually not involved. Positive lymph nodes are more likely to be greater than 10 mm in anteroposterior diameter and have heterogeneous contrast material enhancement.[44]

Dilated bile ducts are present in about half the patients at the time of presentation.[47] Biliary obstruction may develop in patients with gallbladder cancer for a variety of reasons: (1) lymphadenopathy, usually surrounding the common bile duct; (2) tumor invasion into the hepatoduodenal ligament, often at the porta hepatis (see Fig. 81-6); (3) intraductal tumor growth; or (4) rarely, choledocholithiasis. Adenopathy and invasion into the hepatoduodenal ligament are the most common causes of obstruction; intraductal spread is infrequent but may be seen as a polypoid mass extending into the common bile duct. Ultrasound, CT, and MRI reveal biliary dilatation and can usually show the level of obstruction. Invasion of the hepatoduodenal ligament is often better demonstrated with coronal reformatted CT or MRI than with axial CT.[48,49]

Treatment and Prognosis

Survival in patients with gallbladder carcinoma is strongly influenced by the pathologic stage at presentation.[16,50] Patients with cancer limited to the gallbladder mucosa have an excellent prognosis, but most patients with gallbladder carcinoma have advanced, unresectable disease at the time of presentation. As a result, fewer than 15% of all patients with gallbladder carcinoma are alive after 5 years. Surgical management of gallbladder carcinoma is based on the local extension of the tumor. If there is direct extension of disease to the muscularis propria, a radical cholecystectomy is necessary. When disease extends through the serosa, more radical procedures including extended cholecystectomy, pancreatoduodenectomy, and major hepatic resection can be performed. However, radical tumor resection in this setting is associated with a high operative mortality and few long-term survivors.

OTHER MALIGNANT GALLBLADDER NEOPLASMS

A number of malignant diseases can metastasize to the gallbladder. Among the most common primary malignancies are melanoma, breast carcinoma, hepatocellular carcinoma, and lymphoma.[48,51-53] On cross-sectional images, metastases show focal wall thickening, one or more polypoid masses, or replacement of the gallbladder by neoplasm (Fig. 81-7). Metastatic neoplasms of the gallbladder may be indistinguishable from primary gallbladder carcinoma except that gallstones are less frequently seen in patients with metastases.

Primary carcinoid tumors, lymphomas, and sarcomas of the gallbladder have also been reported.[16,54] Carcinoids and lymphomas manifest as polypoid masses that sometimes obstruct the cystic duct.[54] Sarcomas are bulky polypoid masses that are indistinguishable from primary gallbladder carcinoma.

BENIGN GALLBLADDER NEOPLASMS

A diverse spectrum of benign tumors arises from the gallbladder. Benign neoplasms are derived from the epithelial and nonepithelial structures that compose the normal gallbladder.[55] Although these lesions are relatively uncommon, their importance lies in their ability to mimic malignant lesions of the gallbladder. Most benign neoplasms of the gallbladder are adenomas. At gross examination, gallbladder adenomas appear as polypoid structures and may be sessile or pedunculated. They are generally less than 2 cm in size. Tubular adenomas are typically lobular in contour, whereas papillary adenomas have a cauliflower-like appearance.[55]

On ultrasound, adenomas appear as small, broad-based, nonshadowing, sessile or pedunculated polypoid filling defects that do not move with gravitational maneuvers. The

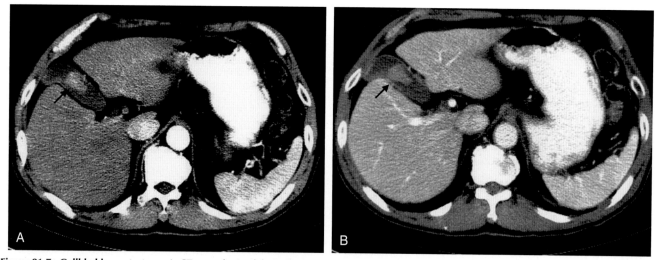

Figure 81-7. Gallbladder metastases. A. CT scan obtained during hepatic arterial phase shows an enhancing polypoid mass (*arrow*) of the gallbladder. **B.** CT scan obtained during portal venous phase shows early contrast washout of the gallbladder carcinoma (*arrow*).

echotexture of adenomas is typically homogeneous and hyperechoic. Adenomas tend to be less echogenic and more heterogeneous as they increase in size[55] (Fig. 81-8). Focal gallbladder wall thickening adjacent to a polypoid mass should raise concern for malignancy. These polyps manifest as enhancing intraluminal soft tissue masses. They are difficult to distinguish from the more common cholesterol polyp. Cholesterol polyps are more often smaller and multiple. Other rare benign neoplasms of the gallbladder include cystadenoma, granular cell tumors, hemangioma, lipoma, and leiomyoma.[56,57]

CHOLANGIOCARCINOMA

Epidemiology

Cholangiocarcinoma is a malignant tumor arising from the epithelium of the bile ducts. Cholangiocarcinomas is an uncommon tumor; between 2500 and 3000 new cases of cholangiocarcnoma are diagnosed annually in the United States.[4,18,19] This tumor is more prevalent in the Far East and Southeast Asia, where liver fluke infection and choledochalithiasis are common. Cholangiocarcinomas occur slightly more often in men, with a male/female ratio of 1.3:1; the average age at diagnosis is between 50 and 70 years.[58] Risk factors for this neoplasm include primary sclerosing cholangitis, choledochal cyst, familial polyposis, congenital hepatic fibrosis, bile duct stone disease, prior biliary-enteric anastomosis, infection with the Chinese liver fluke *Clonorchis sinensis*, and history of exposure to thorium dioxide (Thorotrast).[59,60]

Pathologic Findings

More than 95% of cholangiocarcinomas are adenocarcinomas originating from bile duct epithelium. Cholangiocarcinomas is classified anatomically into three groups: (1) intrahepatic and peripheral to the liver hilus, (2) hilar, or (3) extrahepatic. These three types of cholangiocarcinomas are regarded as distinct disease entities therapeutically. Intrahepatic tumors are treated with hepatectomy, when possible, and hilar tumors are managed with resection of the bile

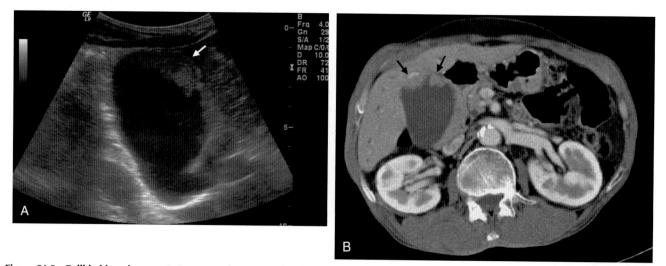

Figure 81-8. Gallbladder adenoma. A. Sonogram shows a sessile polypoid mass (*arrow*). **B.** CT scan demonstrates on enhancing polypoid gallbladder adenoma (*arrows*).

duct preferably with hepatectomy. Extrahepatic tumors are treated in a fashion similar to other periampullary malignancies with pancreatoduodenectomy. Although their precise definitions are controversial, a tumor that arises peripheral to the secondary bifurcation of the left or right hepatic duct is considered an intrahepatic cholangiocarcinoma. A tumor that arises from one of the hepatic ducts or from the bifurcation of the common hepatic duct is classified as a hilar cholangiocarcinoma.[61] Peripheral intrahepatic cholangiocarcinoma accounts for 10% of all cholangiocarcionomas, hilar cholangiocarcinomas for 25%, and extrahepatic cholangiocarcinoma for 65%.[62]

Cholangiocarcinomas are also divided into three types on the basis of their morphology: (1) mass forming, (2) periductal infiltrating, causing stricture, and (3) intraductal growing.[63,64] Mass-forming intrahepatic cholangiocarcinoma is a gray-white mass often accompanied by satellite nodules (Fig. 81-9). Fibrosis and necrosis are frequently seen centrally. The periductal-infiltrating type of cholangiocarcinoma grows along the bile duct wall, resulting in concentric mural thickening and proximal dilation.[65] A dense fibroblastic reaction may encase the adjacent hepatic artery or portal vein, complicating surgical resection. Intraductal-growing papillary cholangiocarcionoma is characterized by the presence of

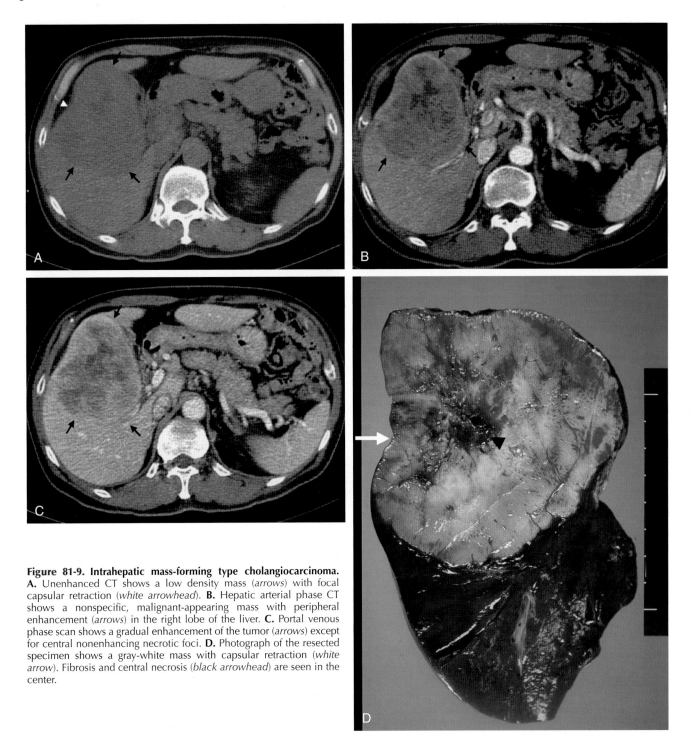

Figure 81-9. Intrahepatic mass-forming type cholangiocarcinoma. A. Unenhanced CT shows a low density mass (*arrows*) with focal capsular retraction (*white arrowhead*). **B.** Hepatic arterial phase CT shows a nonspecific, malignant-appearing mass with peripheral enhancement (*arrows*) in the right lobe of the liver. **C.** Portal venous phase scan shows a gradual enhancement of the tumor (*arrows*) except for central nonenhancing necrotic foci. **D.** Photograph of the resected specimen shows a gray-white mass with capsular retraction (*white arrow*). Fibrosis and central necrosis (*black arrowhead*) are seen in the center.

intraluminal papillary tumors of the intrahepatic and/or extrahepatic bile ducts with partial obstruction and dilation of the bile ducts.[64] The tumors are usually small but often spread superficially along the mucosal surface, resulting in multiple tumors along the adjacent segments of the bile ducts or a tumor cast. Some papillary tumors of the bile ducts produce a large amount of mucin and may impede the flow of bile.[66] Ducts both proximal and distal to the tumor can be dilated, because mucin may obstruct the papilla of Vater.

Clinical Findings

Patients with hilar or extrahepatic cholangiocarcinomas usually present with painless jaundice. Anorexia, weight loss, vague gastrointestinal symptoms, ill-defined upper abdominal discomfort, and elevated serum alkaline phosphatase and bilirubin levels also can be seen. Cholangitis is unusual as a presenting symptom but most commonly develops after biliary manipulation. Patients with intrahepatic cholangiocarcinoma are usually asymptomatic and are rarely jaundiced until late in the course of disease.

Radiographic Findings

The radiologic evaluation of patients with cholangiocarcinoma should delineate the overall extent of the tumor, including involvement of the bile ducts, liver, portal vessels, and distant metastases.[19] Various imaging tests are available to assess patients with cholangiocarcinoma, and the initial radiographic studies consist of either ultrasound or CT. Ultrasound can quickly establish the level of biliary obstruction. Contrast-enhanced multidetector CT provides more staging information. In most centers, ERCP or percutaneous transhepatic cholangiography is used to evaluate the extent of biliary involvement and provide palliation for jaundice. MRI with MRCP offers the potential of evaluating parenchymal, vascular, biliary, and nodal involvement with a single non-invasive examination[67] (see Chapter 83). The imaging features of cholangiocarcinoma depend on tumor location and type.

Intrahepatic Type

The most common appearance of a mass-forming cholangiocarcinoma on sonography, CT, and MRI is a well-defined, predominantly homogeneous mass with irregular borders.[68] Sonographically, these masses may have mixed echogenicity or may be predominantly hypoechoic or hyperechoic. Because of the peripheral location of the mass, bile duct obstruction is uncommon. Unenhanced CT scans show a hypoattenuating mass, either solitary or with satellite lesions (see Fig. 81-9). After the administration of contrast medium, there is irregular peripheral and patchy enhancement in the tumor. The dense fibrotic nature of the tumor often produces capsular retraction. Small necrotic regions and focal intrahepatic bile ductal dilation around the mass are common.[69] A higher incidence of cholangiocarcinoma is associated with clonorchiasis infestation (Fig. 81-10). The CT appearance of clonorchiasis is diffuse, mild dilation of the intrahepatic biliary ducts, especially the peripheral portions, without any evidence of obstruction.

The typical appearance of cholangiocarcinoma on MRI is a nonencapsulated mass that is hypointense on T1-weighted

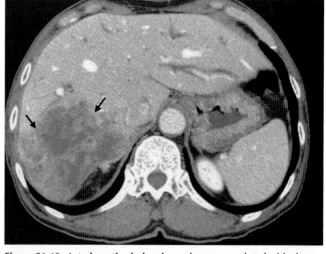

Figure 81-10. Intrahepatic cholangiocarcinoma associated with clonorchiasis. Contrast-enhanced CT scan shows an irregular low density cholangiocarcinoma (*arrows*) in the right lobe of the liver, and mild, diffuse dilation of intrahepatic bile ducts, suggesting clonorchiasis.

images and hyperintense on T2-weighted images[70] (Fig. 81-11). Central hypointensity corresponding to fibrosis may be seen on T2-weighted images. Capsular retraction is found in 21% of mass forming cholangiocarcinomas and seems to be related to the dense fibrotic nature of the tumor.[69,70] In addition, in patients with associated clonorchiasis, dilation of the peripheral portion of the intrahepatic bile ducts is occasionally seen. Cholangiography demonstrates displacement of bile ducts away from the intrahepatic cholangiocarcinoma, obstruction of an intrahepatic duct, or a polypoid mass in the intrahepatic ducts.

Exophytic, intrahepatic cholangiocarcinomas simulate other hepatic malignancies, particularly hepatocellular carcinoma, on cross-sectional imaging. Most cholangiocarcinomas, however, occur in noncirrhotic livers. In addition, on dynamic CT or MRI, typical mass-forming cholangiocarcinoma shows thin rim-like or thick band-like enhancement around the tumor during the hepatic arterial and portal venous phases. On delayed (10 to 15 minutes) scans, there is progressive and concentric filling of the contrast material[68-70] (see Fig. 81-11). The enhancement pattern of cholangiocarcinoma is explained by slow diffusion of contrast material into the interstitial spaces of the tumor.[71] This pattern differs from that of hepatocellular carcinomas, which typically shows robust enhancement in the hepatic arterial phase and iso- or low attenuation on the portal venous phase.[72] Hypovascular metastases, especially from adenocarcinoma of the gastrointestinal tract, may show an enhancment pattern similar to that of peripheral cholangiocarcinomas. Absence of a known primary malignancy, relatively large tumor size, and bile duct dilation favor mass-forming cholangiocarcinomas over metastases.[68]

Intrahepatic cholangiocarcinomas (Fig. 81-12) may also be polypoid or focally stenotic. If exophytic intrahepatic cholangiocarcinomas are excluded, about three fourths of cholangiocarcinomas manifest as a focal stricture, and one fourth are polypoid or diffusely stenotic.[73]

Focally stenotic or papillary cholangiocarcinomas often cause segmental bile duct dilatation and may induce lobar

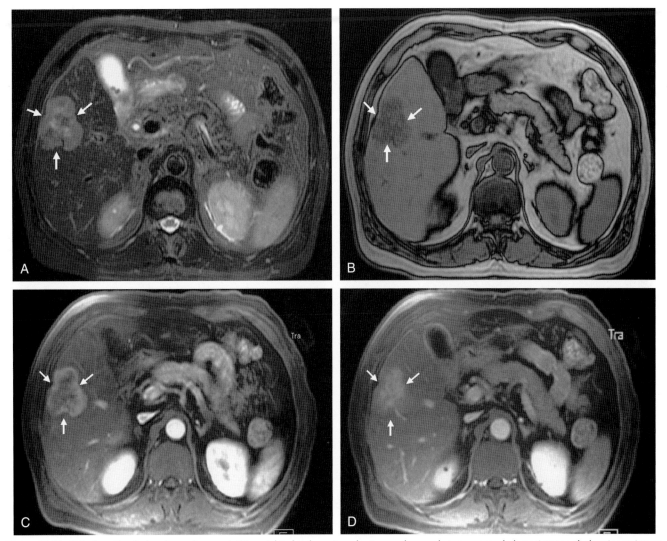

Figure 81-11. Intrahepatic cholangiocarcinoma. A. T2-weighted turbo spin-echo image shows a heterogeneously hyperintense cholangiocarcinoma (*arrows*) in the right lobe of the liver. **B.** Opposed phase MR image demonstrates a hypointense mass (*arrows*). **C** and **D.** Dynamic gadolinium-enhanced T1-weighted gradient-echo images at 1 and 5 minutes after contrast injection reveal progressive centripetal enhancement of the tumor (*arrows*).

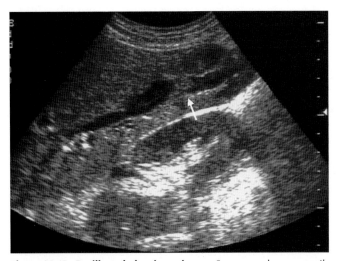

Figure 81-12. Papillary cholangiocarcinoma. Sonogram shows a papillary cholangiocarcinoma filling the dilated right intrahepatic bile duct (*arrow*).

atrophy if the tumor is central in location. Papillary intrahepatic cholangiocarcinoma occasionally produce abundant mucin, resulting in a well-marginated cystic mass that resembles biliary cystadenocarcinoma (Fig. 81-13). A correct diagnosis of intraductal cholangiocarcinoma can be made by demonstrating direct continuity of the peripheral bile ducts with the tumor and incorporated hepatic parenchyma between cysts.[74] Mucin may result in tumor calcification and can also obstruct the duct lumen distal to the carcinoma (Fig. 81-14).

Hilar Type

Cholangiocarcinomas most often occur at the confluence of the right and left bile ducts and the proximal common hepatic duct. These so-called Klatskin's tumors are usually periductal infiltrating types.[75] The sonographic features of Klatskin's tumors include duct dilatation, isolation of the right and left bile duct segments, mass or bile duct wall thickening at the hilum, and lobar atrophy with crowded, dilated bile ducts. Klatskin's tumors almost invariably cause biliary

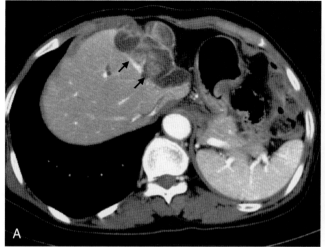

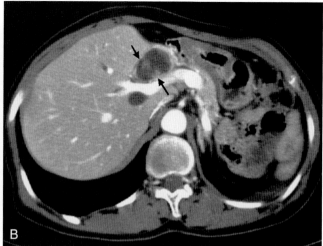

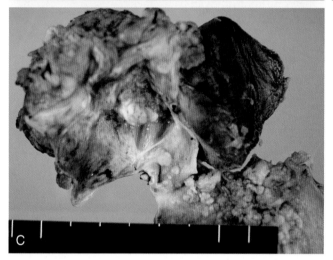

Figure 81-13. Multiple papillary cholangiocarcinomas. A. CT shows multiple enhancing papillary cholangiocarcinomas (*arrows*) in the dilated left intrahepatic bile duct. **B.** CT scan caudal to **A** demonstrates multiple polypoid tumors (*arrows*) in the dilated common bile duct. **C.** Photograph of the resected specimen shows multiple polypoid tumors in left hepatic duct and common bile duct.

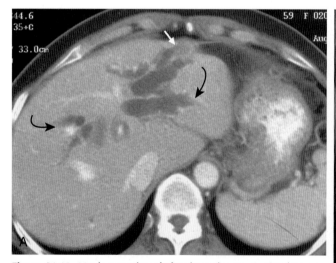

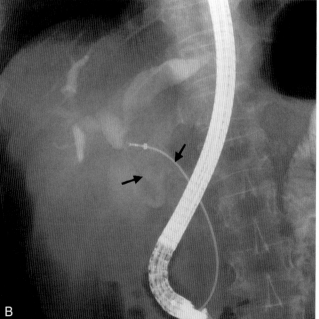

Figure 81-14. Mucin-secreting cholangiocarcinoma. A. CT shows a polypoid mass (arrow) in the left hepatic lobe and dilated left and right intrahepatic bile ducts (*curved arrows*), and dilated left and common hepatic bile ducts. **B.** ERCP demonstrates mucin expanding the extra-hepatic bile ducts (*arrows*). At endoscopy, mucin was seen coming from the common bile duct.

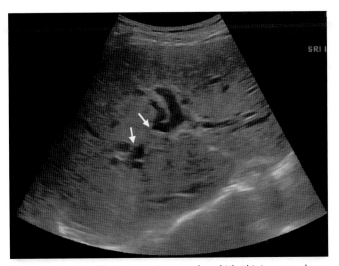

Figure 81-15. Klatskin's tumor. Sonography of Klatskin's tumor shows dilation of intrahepatic bile ducts and nonunion of right and left intrahepatic bile ducts (*arrows*).

dilatation. Although the tumor can appear as mural thickening or an encircling mass along the bile duct wall, a definite mass is rarely seen on ultrasound[76-80] (Fig. 81-15). Less often, a polypoid mass can cause hilar obstruction.

CT is more sensitive than ultrasound in detecting obstructing ductal masses, which are usually small (Fig. 81-16). Multidetector CT allows more accurate evaluation of these small lesions and better demonstrates the status of the hepatic arterial or portal venous circulation. The mass is hypodense to liver on most scans before and after administration of contrast material.[68] On contrast-enhanced CT, infiltrating tumors are seen as a focal thickened of the duct wall, obliterating the lumen. About 80% of these tumors are hyperattenuating relative to the liver on arterial or portal phase or both.[64,79] Due to their sclerotic nature, most lesions show tumor enhancement 8 to 15 minutes after contrast medium injection[80,81] (see Fig. 81-12A and B).

Cholangiocarcinomas are either isointense or low in signal intensity relative to the liver on T1-weighted images. On T2-weighted images, the tumor signal intensity ranges from markedly increased to mildly increased relative to liver. Tumors with high fibrous content tend to have lower signal intensity on T2-weighted images[82] (Fig. 81-17). Cholangiocarcinomas enhance to a moderate degree on gadolinium-enhanced T1-weighted MR images (see Fig. 81-17). As with CT, contrast enhancement is better appreciated on delayed images because of the nature of the tumor (Fig. 81-18).

Lobar hepatic atrophy with marked dilatation and crowding of bile ducts is seen on CT and MRI in approximately one fourth of patients with hilar cholangiocarcinomas.[80] There is dominant involvement of the duct supplying the atrophied segment. Lobar hepatic atrophy with biliary dilatation strongly suggests cholangiocarcinoma, although long-standing biliary obstruction from surgical trauma or focal biliary obstruction can cause similar findings.[49,82] The liver parenchyma and hepatoduodenal ligaments are commonly invaded by Klatskin tumors. Lymphatic metastases most commonly involve the portocaval, superior pancreaticoduodenal, and posterior pancreaticoduodenal lymph nodes.[45] Retroperitoneal lymphadenopathy, peritoneal spread, and proximal intestinal obstruction occur in advanced stages of hilar cholangiocarcinoma.

In patients with hilar cholangiocarcinoma, accurate evaluation of tumor extent is necessary for proper treatment and assessment of resectability.[19] Nonresectability of hilar cholangiocarcinoma is suggested by (a) cholangiographic evidence of severe bilateral involvement of the secondary confluence, (b) involvement of the main trunk of the portal vein, (c) involvement of both branches of the portal vein or bilateral involvement of the hepatic artery and portal vein, or (d) vascular involvement on one side of the liver and extensive bile duct involvement on the other side. Unilateral involvement of the hepatic artery or portal vein or both vessels is compatible with resection.[18,19,83] Precise preoperative evaluation of tumor extent often requires several imaging studies.[68]

Direct cholangiography (Fig. 81-19) is used to evaluate the extent of hilar cholangiocarcinomas. There is characteristic stenosis of the central, right, and left common hepatic ducts, with smooth shoulders or irregular tapering of ducts. These

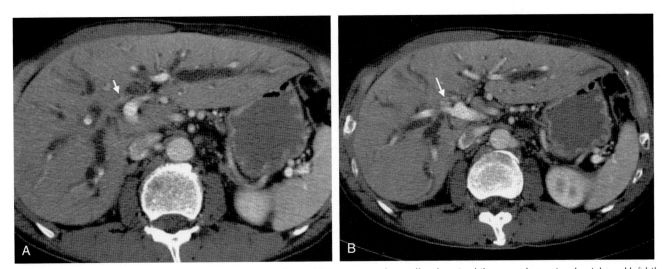

Figure 81-16. Hilar cholangiocarcinoma. A and **B.** Contrast-enhanced CT scans reveal a small, enhancing hilar mass obstructing the right and left bile ducts (*arrow*).

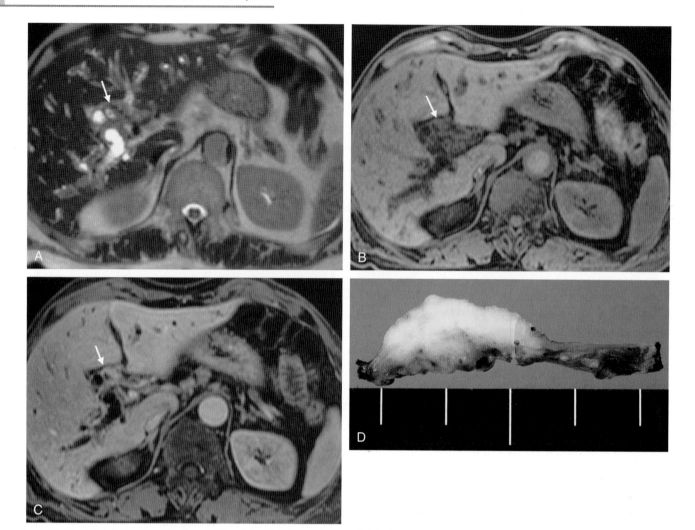

Figure 81-17. Hilar cholangiocarcinoma. A. T2-weighed MR image shows a slightly hyperintense hilar cholangiocarcinoma (*arrow*). **B.** T1-weighted MR image reveals a hypointense hilar cholangiocarcinoma (*arrow*). **C.** Gadolinium-enhanced T1-weighted images demonstrate an enhancing mass (*arrow*) in left main hepatic duct. **D.** Photograph of the resected specimen shows an infiltrating cholangiocarcinoma involving the left main hepatic duct and proximal common duct.

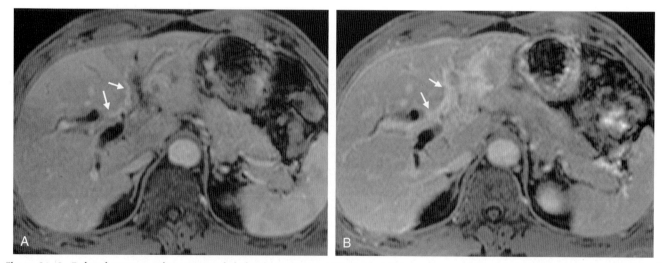

Figure 81-18. Delayed contrast enhancement of cholangiocarcinoma: MRI. A. Gadolinium-enhanced T1-weighted image obtained during portal venous phase shows an infiltrating hilar cholangiocarcinoma involving ductal bifurcation area and both main hepatic ducts (*arrows*). **B.** A 10-minute delayed T1-weighted MR image shows delayed enhancement of the mass (*arrows*). Tumor involves periportal fat with encased left portal vein.

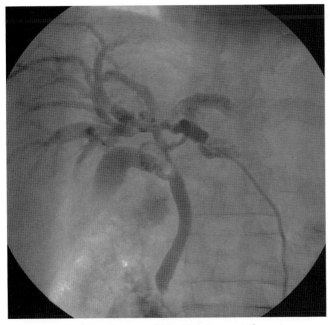

Figure 81-19. Cholangiogram of Klatskin's tumor. Hilar strictures are associated with proximal bile duct dilatation.

neoplastic strictures tend to branch and may extend into second-order biliary radicles. Direct cholangiography is of limited value in assessing submucosal tumor spread and in lesions that extend beyond the porta hepatis because of incomplete filling of bile ducts proximal to the tumor. In addition, CT is ineffective in detecting superficially spreading tumors that extend above the level of biliary obstruction because tumor with a superficial spreading pattern shows enhancement of the inner wall of the bile duct with a preserved lumen. Therefore, combined assessment with CT and state-of-the-art cholangiography or choledochoscopy (through the percutaneous transhepatic biliary drainage tract) and biopsy are needed to evaluate tumor extent.[68] Along these lines, a combination of MRCP and conventional MRI can provide complete tumor staging that assesses liver, portal node, and portal vein involvement[84] (Fig. 81-20).

Hilar cholangiocarcinomas can usually be differentiated cholangiographically from hilar lymphadenopathy or benign stricture. Lymphadenopathy compresses and displaces rather than invades the extrahepatic ducts. Benign strictures complicating cholecystectomy or distal gastric surgery are typically short and cause symmetric narrowing of the common hepatic bile duct. Rarely, lymphoma or sarcoidosis of the bile ducts may be indistinguishable from cholangiocarcinoma.[85]

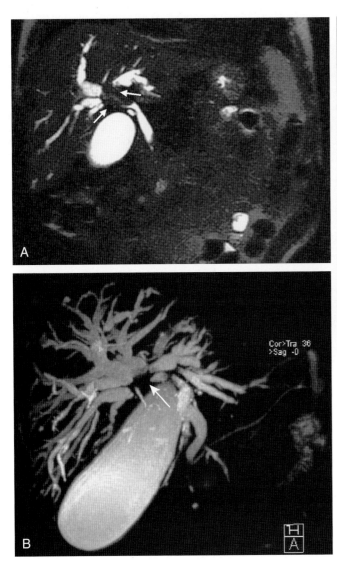

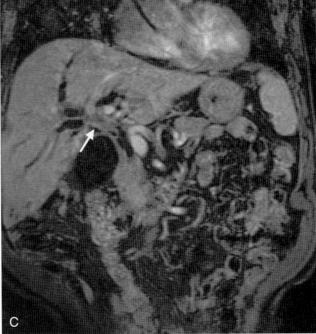

Figure 81-20. Hilar cholangiocarcinoma: MRI and MRCP. A. Oblique coronal T2-weighted image reveals hilar obstruction indicative of cholangiocarcinoma. Extension into right and left hepatic ducts (*arrows*) causes dilatation of intrahepatic bile ducts. **B.** MRCP demonstrates hilar obstruction (*arrow*) and proximal extent of disease. **C.** Gadolinium-enhanced coronal T1-weighted gradient-echo image obtained during portal venous phase, shows an infiltrative, enhancing mass (*arrow*) indicating hepatic tumor extension.

Extrahepatic Type

Carcinomas of the distal common hepatic or common bile duct are usually small and have a better prognosis than the more central Klatskin's tumor.[18,19] Fifty percent to 75% of extrahepatic cholangiocarcinomas occur in the upper third, 10% to 30% in the middle third, and 10% to 20% in the lower third of extrahepatic duct.[86] Cholangiography demonstrates a short stricture or, less often, a polypoid mass, which almost always causes biliary obstruction. CT and MRI can depict an obstructing nodular mass or a concentric or asymmetric thickening of the bile duct wall with enhancement at the transition zone or intraductal polypoid tumors as well as biliary ductal dilation[87] (Fig. 81-21). Adjacent periductal fat may be infiltrated by direct invasion, and lymph node metastasis is relatively frequent. Cholangiocarcinomas that arise in the intrapancreatic portion of the common bile duct are well depicted as low signal intensity masses against the background of the high signal intensity head of the pancreas on T1-weighted fat-suppressed images.

For patients with advanced primary sclerosing cholangitis, the risk of developing cholangiocarcinoma is significant. In

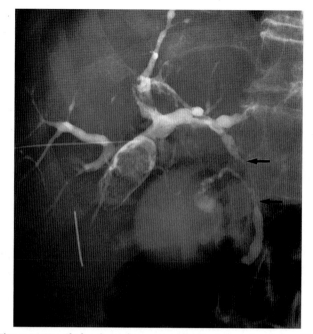

Figure 81-22. Cholangiocarcinoma complicating sclerosing cholangitis. Cholangiocarcinoma is causing a stricture (*arrows*) in the common hepatic duct in a patient with primary sclerosing cholangitis. Despite the dominant stricture with some biliary dilatation proximally, this narrowing could be inflammatory or neoplastic. Calculi are present in the right intrahepatic bile ducts.

one study, careful pathologic examination of the native liver removed for transplantation showed that 10% of patients with primary sclerosing cholangitis had coexisting cholangiocarcinoma.[88] It is often difficult to appreciate malignant degeneration in sclerosing cholangitis. Features that suggest malignancy include progression of strictures on serial cholangiograms, marked biliary dilatation above a dominant stricture, and a polypoid ductal mass of 1 cm in diameter or greater[89] (Fig. 81-22).

Adults with fusiform extrahepatic choledochal cysts also are at increased risk for developing cholangiocarcinoma (Fig. 81-23). These neoplasms develop within the cyst itself in only about 50% of cases and elsewhere in the biliary system in the remainder. In fact, the cancer can occur after resection of the cyst.[90] Most manifest as polypoid masses that may be large enough to be visible on cross-sectional imaging.

Treatment

Treatment of cholangiocarcinoma includes surgical resection, radiation, laser therapy, biliary stenting, and liver transplantation.[18,19] There are some long-term survivors after resection, and radiation and bile duct stenting may palliate symptoms for months to years.

PERIAMPULLARY CARCINOMA

Periampullary carcinomas are those tumors arising from or within 1 cm of the papilla of Vater and include ampullary, pancreatic, bile duct, and duodenal cancers.[91] It is often impossible by histologic examination to be certain of the origin of the tumor. There is a high incidence of these tumors in patients with familial adenomatous polyposis, and cancer is

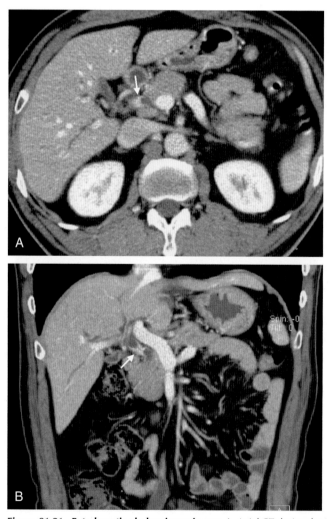

Figure 81-21. Extrahepatic cholangiocarcinoma. A. Axial CT during the portal venous phase shows an enhancing mass (*arrow*) in common bile duct. **B.** Coronal MR image demonstrates focal mural thickening and enhancement (*arrow*) of common bile duct.

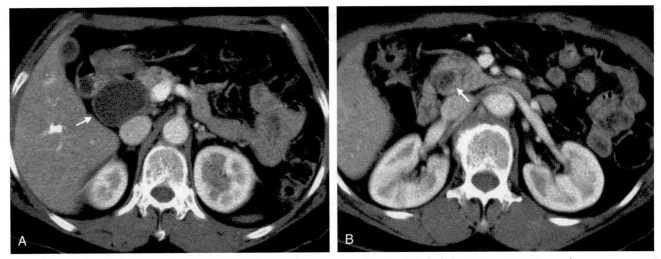

Figure 81-23. Cholangiocarcinoma complicating choledochal cyst. A. CT scan shows a choledochal cyst (*arrow*). **B.** CT scan shows an asymmetric thickening (*arrow*) of intrapancreatic common bile duct with enhancement.

often preceded by ampullary or duodenal adeomas.[91] Peri-ampullary neoplasms tend to be polypoid and lower in grade than more proximal biliary neoplasms.

Biliary dilatation to the level of the ampulla of Vater is seen in 75% of cases, and pancreatic ductal dilatation is seen in 67%.[92] These masses tend to be small and may not be seen on CT scans, in which case abrupt termination of a dilated bile duct in the head of the pancreas is demonstrated. A polypoid mass at the ampulla or abrupt termination of the common bile duct without mass may be seen cholangio-graphically. Occasionally, a villous polypoid lesion may be seen in the distal common bile duct and duodenum. Liver metastases or lymphadenopathy is present at the time of diagnosis in only a small percentage of cases.

On T1-weighted fat-suppressed images, periampullary tumors appear as a low signal intensity mass in the region of the ampulla. On immediate postgadolinium T1-weighted images, these lesions are often visualized as areas of low signal intensity, reflecting their hypovascular character compared to background pancreatic tissue. On 2-minute post-gadolinium fat-suppressed images, a thin rim of enhancement is commonly observed along the periphery of the tumor[49] (Fig. 81-24). MRCP and sectional MRI can be useful in determining the origins of periampullary carcinomas.

CYSTIC BILE DUCT NEOPLASMS: CYSTADENOMA AND CYSTADENOCARCINOMA

Biliary cystadenoma and cystadenocarcinoma are rare cystic neoplasms lined by mucin-secreting columnar epithelium.[55] Histologically, they are similar to cystadenomas and cystadeno-carcinomas of the ovary and pancreas. They are usually seen in middle-aged women, who present with abdominal pain, distention, and occasionally jaundice.

Most cystadenomas and cystadenocarcinomas manifest as intrahepatic masses that are hypoechoic on ultrasound and have a low-attenuation, uniloculated or multiloculated, cystic appearance on CT.[55] The CT attenuation of the fluid

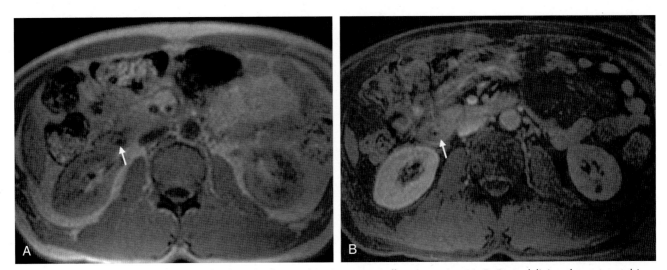

Figure 81-24. Ampullary cancer. A. T1-weighted image shows a hypointense ampullary tumor (*arrow*). **B.** Postgadolinium fat suppressed image demonstrates a thin rim of enhancement (*arrow*) along the periphery of the tumor.

component in a biliary cystadenoma depends on the fluid content. While CT is usually superior in demonstrating the size and extent of these tumors, sonography is superior to CT in depicting internal morphology[93] (Fig. 81-25). Irregular, papillary growths and mural nodules along the internal septa and wall are seen in cystadenoma and cystadenocarcinoma, although papillary excrescences and solid portions are more common in latter[93-95] (Fig. 81-26). Cystadenomas occasionally have fine septal calcifications; cystadenocarcinomas may have thick, coarse, mural, and septal calcifications.[93,95] Communication of these tumors with large intrahepatic ducts is rare. Several case reports have suggested malignant transformation of cystadenomas to cystadenocarcinomas based on several years of follow-up after resection.[96,97] The differential diagnosis of biliary cystadenoma and cystadenocarcinoma includes hepatic cysts, hydatid cysts, liver abscesses, cystic metastases, hematoma, cystic sarcomas, and choledochal cysts.[93]

OTHER MALIGNANT NEOPLASMS OF THE BILE DUCTS

In adults, cholangiocarcinoma and biliary cystadenocarcinomas account for most malignant bile duct neoplasms. Lymphomas, leiomyosarcomas, carcinoid tumors, and metastases rarely occur in the bile ducts (Fig. 81-27). Non-Hodgkin's lymphoma of the bile ducts can rarely mimic cholangio-

carcinoma or primary sclerosing cholangitis.[85] In a patient with known lymphoma, cholangiographic findings of smooth, tapered strictures combined with the absence of a portal mass on CT should suggest the diagnosis. Sarcomas and metastases present as masses projecting into the bile duct lumen, causing biliary obstruction.[98,99]

After choledochal cyst, embryonal rhabdomyosarcoma is the second most common cause of jaundice in the pediatric population. After infancy, it usually occurs between ages 4 and 6 years but has been reported in children aged 1 to 11 years. Sonography and CT will show intrahepatic duct dilation and a soft tissue mass in the region of the common bile duct and/or porta hepatis. The radiologic appearance of the lesion is similar to that of congenital choledochal cyst if there is no local invasion to adjacent tissues.[100]

BENIGN BILE DUCT NEOPLASMS

Benign neoplasms of the bile ducts are quite rare.[55] Adenomas are the most common type; others include granular cell tumors, hamartomas, fibromas, neuromas, lipomas, and heterotopic gastric or pancreatic mucosal rests.

Most adenomas manifest as small asymptomatic polyps in the extrahepatic bile ducts that are found incidentally at surgery (Fig. 81-28). Occasionally, they become large and cause biliary obstruction. Multiple papillary adenomas have

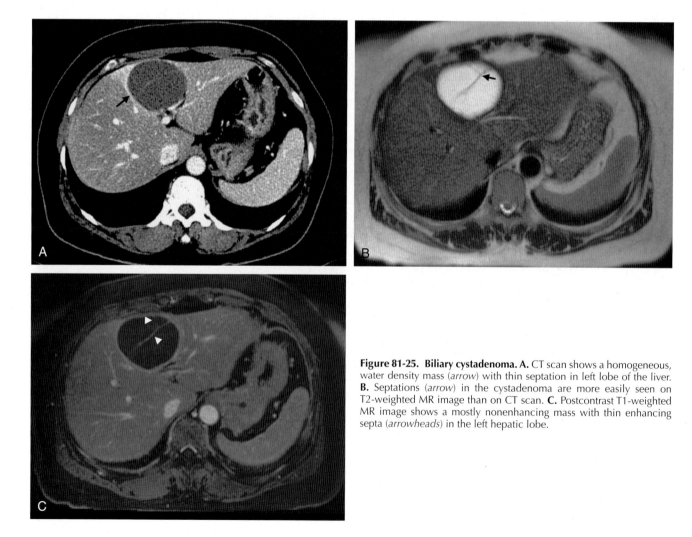

Figure 81-25. Biliary cystadenoma. A. CT scan shows a homogeneous, water density mass (*arrow*) with thin septation in left lobe of the liver. **B.** Septations (*arrow*) in the cystadenoma are more easily seen on T2-weighted MR image than on CT scan. **C.** Postcontrast T1-weighted MR image shows a mostly nonenhancing mass with thin enhancing septa (*arrowheads*) in the left hepatic lobe.

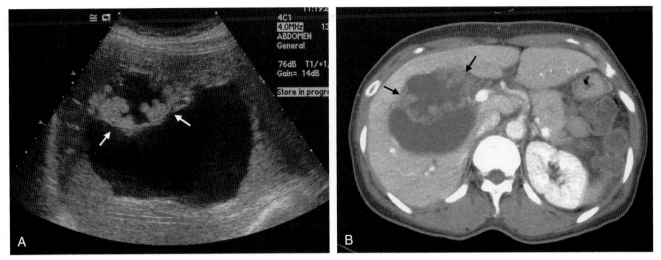

Figure 81-26. Biliary cystadenocarcinoma. A. Transverse sonogram shows a large, lobulated cystic mass with thick septation and multiple mural nodules (*arrows*). **B.** CT scan shows a lobulated cystic mass with thick septation and enhancing mural nodules (*arrows*).

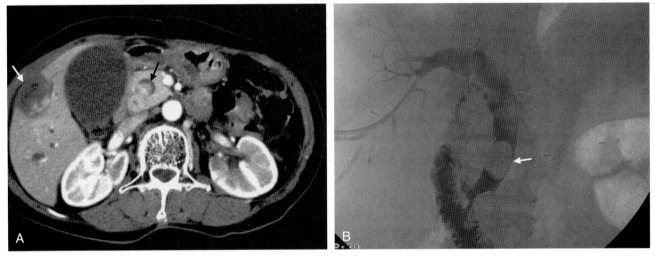

Figure 81-27. Leiomyosarcoma metastatic to the common hepatic duct. A. CT scan shows an enhancing polypoid tumor (*black arrow*) in dilated common bile duct. *White arrow* indicates liver metastasis. **B.** Cholangiography shows an intraluminal mass (*arrow*) of the common bile duct.

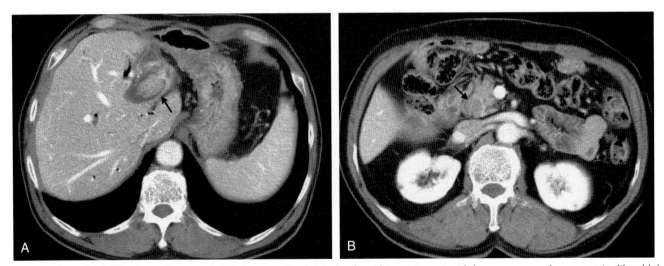

Figure 81-28. Multiple bile duct adenomas. A. CT shows an intraluminal polypoid tumor (*arrow*) with homogeneous enhancement in dilated left intrahepatic bile duct. **B.** CT scan demonstrates similar intraductal mass (*arrow*) in common bile duct.

been reported in association with obstructive biliary villous adenoma and ampullary carcinoma.[55,101-103]

Granular cell tumors of the bile ducts occur most often in young African American women and cause abdominal pain and jaundice.[57] Most granular cell tumors are extrahepatic masses and are less than 3 cm in great dimension, and as the cell infiltrate the wall of the bile duct, the lumen is obliterated. CT and ultrasound usually show bile duct obstruction without identifying the mass. Cholangiograms demonstrate either the extrahepatic bile ducts or a small polypoid mass.[57] Surgical resection is curative.

References

1. Jemal A, Siegel R, Ward E, et al: Cancer statistics, 2007. CA Cancer J Clin 57:43-66, 2007.
2. American Joint Committee on Cancer: Gallbladder and extrahepatic bile ducts. In Greene F, Page D, Fleming I, et al (eds): American Joint Committee on Cancer Staging Manual, 6th ed. New York, Springer-Verlag, 2002, pp 139-150.
3. Meyers MA: Carcinoma of the gallbladder: Imaging, staging, and management. In Meyers MA (ed): Neoplasms of the Digestive Tract. Philadelphia, Lippincott-Raven, 1998, pp 479-484.
4. Carriaga MT, Henson DE: Liver, gallbladder, extrahepatic bile ducts, and pancreas. Cancer 75:171-190, 1995.
5. Kiran RP, Pokala N, Dudrick SJ: Incidence pattern and survival for gallbladder cancer over three decades—an analysis of 10301 patients. Ann Surg Oncol 14:827-832, 2007.
6. Misra S, Chaturvedi A, Misra NC, Sharma ID: Carcinoma of the gallbladder. Lancet Oncol 4:167-176, 2003.
7. Foster JM, Hoshi H, Gibbs JF, et al: Gallbladder cancer: Defining the indications for primary radical resection and radical re-resection. Ann Surg Oncol 14:833-840, 2007.
8. Roa I, Araya JC, Villaseca M, et al: Gallbladder cancer in a high risk area: Morphologic features and spread patterns. Hepatogastroenterology 46:1540-1546, 1999.
9. Maringhini A, Moreau JA, Melton J, et al: Gallstones, gallbladder cancer, and other gastrointestinal malignancies. Ann Intern Med 107:30-35, 1987.
10. Berk RN, Armbuster TG, Saltzstein SL: Carcinoma in the porcelain gallbladder. Radiology 106:29-31, 1973.
11. Stephen AE, Berger DL: Carcinoma in the porcelain gallbladder: A relationship revisited. Surgery 129:699-703, 2001.
12. Aldridge MC, Bismuth H: Gallbladder cancer: The polyp cancer sequence. Br J Surg 77:363-364, 1990.
13. Chijiiwa K, Kimura H, Tanaka M: Malignant potential of the gallbladder in patients with anomalous pancreaticobiliary ductal junction. Int Surg 80:61-64, 1995.
14. Albores-Saavedra J, Henson DE, Sobin LH: The WHO histological classification of tumours of the gallbladder and extrahepatic bile duct. A commentary on the second edition. Cancer 70:410-414, 1992.
15. Henson DE, Albores-Saavedra J, Corle D: Carcinoma of the gallbladder. Histologic types, stage of disease, grade and survival rates. Cancer 70:1493-1497, 1992.
16. Dachman AH: Benign and malignant tumors of the gallbladder. In Friedman AC, Dachman AH (eds): Radiology of the Liver, Biliary Tract, and Pancreas. St Louis, Mosby–Year Book, 1994, pp 155-576.
17. Albores-Saavedra J, Henson DE: Tumors of the Gallbladder and Extrahepatic Bile Ducts: Atlas of Tumor Pathology, fascicle 22, 2nd series. Washington, DC, Armed Forced Institute of Pathology, 1986.
18. Weber S, O'Reily EM, Abou-Alfa GK, Blumgart L: Liver and bile duct cancer. In Abeloff MD, Armitage JO, Niederhuber et al (eds): Clincal Oncology, 3rd ed. Edinburgh, Churchill Livingstone, 2005, pp 1981-2007.
19. Ahrendt SA, Pitt HA: Biliary tract. In Townsend CM, Beauchamp RD, Evers BM, Mattox KL (eds): Sabiston Texbook of Surgery, 17th ed. Philadelphia, Elsevier Saunders, 2004, pp 1112-1143.
20. Brown JA, Roberts CS: Elevated serum alpha-fetoprotein levels in primary gallbladder carcinoma without hepatic involvement. Cancer 70:1838-1840, 1992.
21. Cho KC: Plain films of the liver, bile ducts and spleen. In Baker SR, Choi KC (eds): The Abdominal Plain Film with Correlative Imaging, 2nd ed. Stamford, CT, Appleton & Lange, 1999.
22. Berk RN, Ferrucci JT, Leopold GR: Radiology of the Gallbladder and Bile Ducts. Philadelphia, WB Saunders, 1983, p 54.
23. Bach AM, Loring LA, Hann LE, et al: Gallbladder cancer: Can ultrasonography evaluate extent of disease? J Ultrasound Med 17:303-309, 1998.
24. Soyer P, Gouhiri M, Boudiaf M, et al: Carcinoma of the gallbladder: Imaging features with surgical correlation. AJR 169:781-784, 1997.
25. Sadamoto Y, Kubo H, Harada N, et al: Preoperative diagnosis and staging of gallbladder carcinoma by EUS. Gastrointest Endosc 58:536-541, 2003.
26. Azuma T, Yoshikawa T, Araida T, Takasaki K: Differential diagnosis of polypoid lesions of the gallbladder by endoscopic ultrasonography. Am J Surg 181:65-70, 2001
27. Wilbur AC, Sagireddy PB, Aizenstein RI: Carcinoma of the gallbladder: Color Doppler ultrasound and CT findings. Abdom Imaging 22:187-190, 1997.
28. Levy AD, Murakata LA, Rohrmann CA Jr: Gallbladder carcinoma: Radiologic-pathologic correlation. RadioGraphics 21:295-314, 2001.
29. Yoshimitsu K, Honda H, Jimi M, et al: MR diagnosis of adenomyomatosis of the gallbladder and differentiation from gallbladder carcinoma: Importance of showing Rokitansky-Aschoff sinuses. AJR 172:1535-1540, 1999.
30. Demach H, Matsui O, Hoshiba K, et al: Dynamic MRI using a surface coil in chronic cholecystitis and gallbladder carcinoma: Radiologic and histopathologic correlation. J Comput Assist Tomogr 21:643-651, 1997.
31. Onoyama H: Diagnostic imaging of early gallbladder cancer: Retrospective study of 53 cases. World J Surg 23:708-712, 1999.
32. Tsuchiya Y: Early carcinoma of the gallbladder: Macroscopic features and ultrasonography findings. Radiology 179:171-175, 1991.
33. Mizuguchi M, Kudo S, Fukahori T, et al: Endoscopic ultrasonography for demonstrating loss of multiple-layer pattern of the thickened gallbladder wall in preoperative diagnosis of gallbladder cancer. Eur Radiol 7:1323-1328, 1997.
34. Teefey SA, Baron RL, Bigler SA. Sonography of the gallbladder: Significance of striated (layered) thickening of the gallbladder wall. AJR 156:945-947, 1991.
35. Lee HY, Kim SH, Lee JM, et al: Preoperative assessment of resectability of hepatic hilar cholangiocarcinoma: Combined CT and cholangiography with revised criteria. Radiology 239:113-121, 2006.
36. Kim HJ, Kim AY, Hong SS, et al: Biliary ductal evaluation of hilar cholangiocarcinoma: Three-dimensional direct multi-detector row CT cholangiographic findings versus surgical and pathologic results—feasibility study. Radiology 238:300-308, 2006.
37. Ouchi K, Owada Y, Matsuno S, et al: Prognostic factors in the surgical treatment of gallbladder carcinoma. Surgery 101:731-737, 1987.
38. Schwartz LH, Black J, Fong Y, et al: Gallbladder carcinoma: Findings at MR imaging with MR cholangiopancreatography. J Comput Assist Tomogr 26:405-410, 2002.
39. Yamashita K, Jin MJ, Hirose Y, et al: CT finding of transient focal increased attenuation of the liver adjacent to the gallbladder in acute cholecystitis. AJR 164:343-346, 1995.
40. Choi SH, Lee JM, Lee KH, et al: Relationship between various patterns of transient increased hepatic attenuation on CT and portal vein thrombosis related to acute cholecystitis. AJR 183:437-442, 2004.
41. Ros PR, Goodman ZD: Xanthogranulomatous cholecystitis versus gallbladder carcinoma [editorial]. Radiology 203:10-12, 1997.
42. Ogura Y, Mizumoto R, Isaji S, et al: Radical operations for carcinoma of the gallbladder: Present status in Japan. World J Surg 15:337-343, 1991.
43. Kondo S, Nimura Y, Kamiya J, et al: Mode of tumor spread and surgical strategy in gallbladder carcinoma. Langenbecks Arch Surg 387:222-228, 2002.
44. Ohtsuki M, Miyazaki M, Itoh H, et al: Routes of hepatic metastasis of gallbladder carcinoma. Am J Clin Pathol 109:62-68, 1998.
45. Ohtani T, Shirai Y, Tsukada K, et al: Spread of the gallbladder carcinoma: CT evaluation with pathologic correlation. Abdom Imaging 21:195-199, 1996.
46. Engels JT, Balfe DM, Lee JKT: Biliary carcinoma: CT evaluation of extrahepatic spread. Radiology 172:35-40, 1989.
47. Tsukada K, Kurosaki I, Uchida K, et al: Lymph node spread from carcinoma of the gallbladder. Cancer 80:661-667, 1997.
48. Thorsen MK, Quiroz F, Lawson TL, et al: Primary biliary carcinoma: CT evaluation. Radiology 152:479-483, 1984.
49. Yoshimitsu K, Honda H, Kaneko K, et al: Dynamic MRI of the gallbladder lesions: Differentiation of benign from malignant. J Magn Reson Imaging 7:696-703, 1997.

50. Bader TR, Semelka RC, Reinhold C. Gallbladder and biliary system. In Semelka RC, Reinhold C (eds): Abdominal-Pelvic MRI. New York, Wiley-Liss, 2002, pp 319-371.

51. Fong Y, Jarnagin W, Blumgart LH. Gallbladder cancer: Comparison of patients presenting initially for definitive operation with those presenting after prior noncurative intervention. Ann Surg 232:557-569, 2000.

52. Terasaki S, Nakanuma Y, Terada T, Unoura M. Metastasis of hepatocellular carcinoma to the gallbladder presenting massive intraluminal growth: Report of an autopsy case. J Clin Gastroenterol. 12:714-715, 1990.

53. Holloway BJ, King DM: Ultrasound diagnosis of metastatic melanoma of the gallbladder. Br J Radiol 70:1122-1126, 1997.

54. Inoue T, Kitano M, Kudo M, et al: Diagnosis of gallbladder diseases by contrast-enhanced phase-inversion harmonic ultrasonography. Ultrasound Med Biol 33:353-361, 2007.

55. Anjaneyulu V, Shankar-Swarnalatha G, Rao SC: Carcinoid tumor of the gall bladder. Ann Diagn Pathol 11:113-116, 2007.

56. Levy AD, Murakata LA, Abbott RM, Rohrmann CA. Benign tumors and tumorlike lesions of the gallbladder and extrahepatic bile ducts: Radiologic-pathologic correlation. RadioGraphics 22:387-413, 2002.

57. Simmons TC, Miller C, Pesigan AM, et al: Cystadenoma of the gallbladder. Am J Gastroenterol 84:1427-1430, 1989.

58. Butterly LF, Schapiro RH, LaMuraglia GM, et al: Biliary granular cell tumor: A little-known curable bile duct neoplasm of young people. Surgery 103:328-334, 1988.

59. Henson DE, Albores-Saavedra J, Corle D: Carcinoma of the extrahepatic bile ducts: Histologic types, stage of disease, grade, and survival rates. Cancer 70:1498-1501, 1992.

60. de Groen PC, Gores GJ, LaRusso NF, et al: Biliary tract cancers. N Engl J Med 341:1368-1378, 1999.

61. Khan ZR, Neugut AI, Ahsan H, et al: Risk factors for biliary tract cancers. Am J Gastroenterol 94:149-152, 1999.

62. Han JK, Choi BI, Kim AY, et al: Cholangiocarcinoma: Pictorial essay of CT and cholangiographic findings. RadioGraphics 22:173-187, 2002.

63. Nakanuma Y, Minato H, Kida T, Terada T: Pathology of cholangiocarcinoma. In Tobe T, Kameda H, Okudaira M, Ohto M (eds): Primary Liver Cancer in Japan. Tokyo, Springer -Verlag, 1994, pp 39-50.

64. Liver Cancer Study Group of Japan: The General Rules for the Clinical and Pathological Study of Primary Liver Cancer, 4th ed. Tokyo, Kanehara, 2000.

65. Lim JH: Cholangiocarcinoma: Morphologic classification according to growth pattern and imaging findings. AJR 181:819-827, 2003.

66. Anthony PP: Tumors and tumor-like lesions of the liver and biliary tract: Aetiology, epidemiology and pathology. In MacSween RNM, Burt AD, Portmann BC, et al (eds): Pathology of the Liver, 4th ed. Edinburgh, Churchill Livingstone, 2002, pp 743-747.

67. Lim JH, Yoon KH, Kim SH: Intraductal papillary mucinous tumor of the bile ducts. RadioGraphics 24:53-67, 2004.

68. Heller SL, Lee VS: MR imaging of the gallbladder and biliary system. Magn Reson Imaging Clin N Am 13:295-311, 2005.

69. Choi BI, Lee JM, Han JK: Imaging of intrahepatic and hilar cholangiocarcinoma. Abdom Imaging 29:548-557, 2004.

70. Kim TK, Choi BI, Han JK, et al: Peripheral cholangiocarcinoma of the liver: Two phase spiral CT findings. Radiology 204:539-543, 1997.

71. Choi BI, Kim TK, Han JK, et al: MRI of clonorchiasis and cholangiocarcinoma. J Magn Reson Imaging 8:359-353, 1998.

72. Honda H, Onitsuka H, Yasumori K, et al: Intrahepatic peripheral cholangiocarcinoma: Two-phased dynamic incremental CT and pathological correlation. J Comput Assist Tomogr 17:397-402, 1993.

73. Choi BI, Han JK, Cho JM, et al: Characterization of focal hepatic tumors: Value of two-phase scanning with spiral computed tomography. Cancer 76:2434-2442, 1995.

74. Kokubo T, Itai Y, Ohtomo K, et al: Mucin-hypersecreting intrahepatic biliary neoplasms. Radiology 168:609-614, 1988.

75. Han JK, Lee JM: Intrahepatic intraductal cholangiocarcinoma. Abdom Imaging 29:558-564, 2004.

76. Klatskin G: Adenocarcinoma of the hepatic duct at its bifurcation with the porta hepatis. Am J Med 38:241-256, 1965.

77. Tillich M, Mischinger H-J, Preisengger K-H, et al: Multiphasic helical CT in diagnosis and staging of hilar cholangiocarcinoma. AJR 171:651-656, 1998.

78. Soyer P, Bluemke DA, Reichle R, et al: Imaging of intrahepatic cholangiocarcinoma. 2. Hilar cholangiocarcionoma. AJR 165:1433-1436, 1995.

79. Garber SJ, Donald JJ, Lees WR: Cholangiocarcinoma: Ultrasound features and correlation with survival. Abdom Imaging 18:66-69, 1993.

80. Hamer OW, Schlottmann K, Sirlin CB, et al: Technology insight: Advances in liver imaging. Nat Clin Pract Gastroenterol Hepatol 4:215-228, 2007.

81. Lacomis JM, Baron RL, Oliver JH, et al: Cholangiocarcinoma: Delayed CT contrast enhancement patterns. Radiology 203:98-102, 1997.

82. Keogan MT, Seabourn JT, Paulson EK, et al: Contrast-enhanced CT of intrahepatic and hilar cholangiocarcinoma: Delay time for optimal imaging. AJR 169:1491-1496, 1997.

83. Manfredi R, Masselli G, Maresca G et al: MR imaging and MRCP of hilar cholangiocarcinoma. Abdom Imaging 28:319-325, 2003.

84. Stain SC, Baer HU, Dennison AR, Blumgart LH: Current management of hilar cholangiocarcinoma. Surg Gynecol Obstet 175:579-588, 1992.

85. Hanninen EL, Jonas PS, Ricke JJ, et al: Magnetic resonance imaging including magnetic resonance cholangiopancreatography for tumor localization and therapy planning in malignant hilar obstructions. Acta Radiol 46:461-470, 2005.

86. Tartar VM, Balfe DM: Lymphoma in the wall of the bile ducts: radiologic imaging. Gastrointest Radiol 15:53-57, 1990.

87. Alexander F, Rossil RL, O'Bryan M, et al: Biliary carcinoma. A review of 109 cases. Am J Surg 147:503-509, 1984.

88. Lim JH, Lee WJ, Takehara Y, Lim HK: Imaging of extrahepatic cholangiocarcinoma. Abdom Imaging 29:565-571, 2004.

89. Herbener T, Zajko AB, Koneru B, et al: Recurrent cholangiocarcinoma in the biliary tree after liver transplantation. Radiology 169:641-642, 1988.

90. Campbell WL, Ferris JV, Holbert BL, et al: Biliary tract carcinoma complicating sclerosing cholangitis: Evaluation with CT, cholangiography, ultrasonography, and MR imaging. Radiology 207:41-45, 1998.

91. Visser BD, Suh I, Way LW. Kang SM: Congenital choledochal cysts in adults. Arch Surg 139:855-862, 2004.

92. Dittrick GW, Mallat DB, Lamont JP: Management of ampullary lesions. Curr Treat Options Gastroenterol 9:371-376, 2006.

93. Qiao QL, Zhao YG, Ye ML, et al: Carcinoma of the ampulla of Vater: Factors influencing long-term survival of 127 patients with resection. World J Surg 31:137-143, 2007.

94. Choid BI, Lim JH, Han MC, et al: Biliary cystadenoma and cystadenocarcinoma: CT and sonographic findings. Radiology 171:57-61, 1989.

95. Meyer X, Henry L, Garcia P, et al: Microcystic variant of biliary mucinous cystadema: Ultrasonography, CT, and MR findings. J Comput Assist Tomogr 21:1015-1019, 1997.

96. Korobkin M, Stephens DH, Lee JKT, et al: Biliary cystadenoma and cystadenocarcinoma: CT and sonographic findings. AJR 153:507-511, 1989.

97. Coulter GN, Baxter JN: Cystadenoma of the common bile duct with malignant transformation. Aust N Z J Surg 59:291-294, 1989.

98. O'Shea JS, Shah D, Cooperman AM: Biliary cystadenocarcinoma of extrahepatic duct origin arising in previously benign cystadenoma. Am J Gastroenterol 82:1306-1310, 1987.

99. Whitcomb FF, Corley GJ, Babigian DN, et al: Leiomyosarcoma of the bile ducts. Gastroenterology 52:94-97, 1967.

100. Jutte DL, Bell RH, Penn I, et al: Carcinoid tumor of the biliary system. Dig Dis Sci 32:763-769, 1986.

101. Tireli GA, Sander S, Dervisoglu S, et al: Embryonal rhabdomyosarcoma of the common bile duct mimicking choledochal cyst. J Hepatobiliary Pancreat Surg 12:263-265, 2005.

102. Kawakatsu M, Vilgrain V, Zins M, et al: Radiologic features of papillary adenoma and papillomatosis of the biliary tract. Abdom Imaging 22:87-93, 1997.

103. Gulluoglu MG, Ozden I, Poyanli A, et al: Intraductal growth-type mucin-producing peripheral cholangiocarcinoma associated with biliary papillomatosis. Ann Diagn Pathol 11:34-38, 2007.

Inflammatory Disorders of the Biliary Tract

Vikram A. Rao, MD • Uday K. Mehta, MD • Robert L. MacCarty, MD

PRIMARY SCLEROSING CHOLANGITIS

Epidemiology and Clinical Findings

Primary sclerosing cholangitis (PSC) is a chronic cholestatic liver disease of unknown cause. Approximately 70% of patients are male, and the median age of onset is 40 years.[1] PSC is commonly associated with inflammatory bowel disease, particularly ulcerative colitis (UC), but also, to a much lesser extent, Crohn's disease. Approximately 70% of patients with PSC have UC. In patients with UC, 3% to 7.5% have or will develop PSC.[2] The term "primary" is used even when there is associated UC because there is no convincing evidence that PSC is caused by or is secondary to inflammatory bowel disease. In fact, the hepatobiliary disease precedes the clinical onset of the bowel disease in some patients. Other associated conditions include sicca complex, Riedel's struma, retroperitoneal fibrosis, and mediastinal fibrosis, but none of these has been reported consistently.[3,4]

Approximately 25% of patients with PSC are asymptomatic at presentation.[2] Clinical features of PSC include fatigue, pruritus, jaundice, right upper quadrant pain, and hepatosplenomegaly. Elevations of serum bilirubin and serum aspartate transaminase values are usually not as marked or as consistent as are elevations of serum alkaline phosphatase values. There is strong evidence that genetic and immunologic factors are important in the pathogenesis of PSC, but there is no specific serologic marker for PSC.[5,6]

The natural history of PSC is variable but usually progressively downhill, with a 5-year survival of 88% and a median survival of 11.9 years from the time of diagnosis.[3] No known therapy, short of liver transplantation, has been proved effective.

Pathology

PSC is characterized by fibrosing inflammation of the biliary tree (Fig. 82-1). Inflammatory cells are scanty on microscopic examinations, however, and ductal fibrosis is nonspecific and difficult to quantitate pathologically. The diagnosis therefore cannot be made solely on the basis of an extrahepatic duct biopsy specimen.[7] In fact, biopsy specimens of the extrahepatic ducts should not be obtained unless cholangiocarcinoma must be ruled out.

Tissue samples from the liver may rarely show specific findings of PSC: cholangiectasis in combination with fibrous obliteration of large intrahepatic bile ducts.[7-9] These tissue samples are generally available only at autopsy or transplantation and not during routine clinical work-up of the patient. Histologic changes found on conventional needle liver biopsy, although not diagnostic, may strongly support the diagnosis

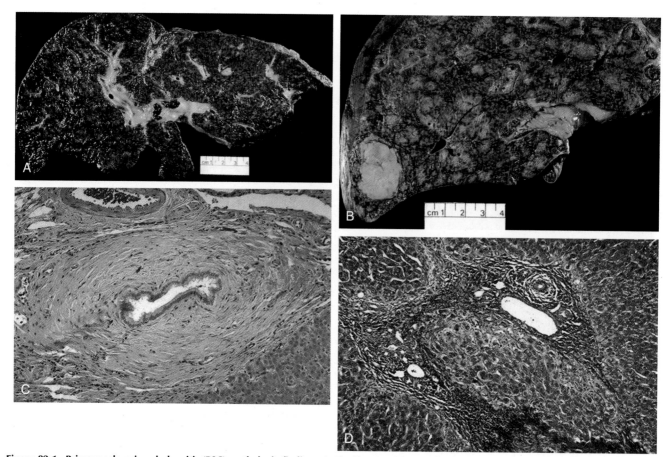

Figure 82-1. Primary sclerosing cholangitis (PSC): pathologic findings. A. The liver in PSC typically is green and becomes progressively darker green with advancing stage; cirrhosis is illustrated here. **B.** In this advanced case, a cholangitis abscess is present and a peripheral cholangiocarcinoma is present. **C.** Early phases of ductal fibrous cholangitis show concentric periductal fibrosis and mild epithelial atrophy. **D.** Trichrome stain shows dense fibrosis in this liver.

of PSC (nonsuppurative, nongranulomatous destruction of septal or interlobular bile ducts in some portal tracts). Other portal tracts in the same patient may demonstrate ductal proliferation and periportal edema secondary to large duct obstruction.[10] The histologic stages of PSC are as follows: portal hepatitis or cholangitis (stage 1); periportal hepatitis or fibrosis (stage 2); septal fibrosis or bridging necrosis, or both (stage 3); and cirrhosis (stage 4). The injury to the liver in PSC is the result of both a chronic hepatitis and bile duct obstruction, and the staging system applies to the liver disease, not the bile duct lesions per se.

The term "pericholangitis" has been used when features of stage 1 and stage 2 disease are seen. These changes are now considered to be part of the spectrum of PSC, and patients are classified as having small duct PSC (visible microscopically) or large duct PSC (visible cholangiographically), or both.

Large duct PSC virtually always involves the intrahepatic ducts and almost always the extrahepatic ducts. The common bile duct, the common hepatic duct, and the first 1 cm of the left and right hepatic ducts (which are truly anatomically extrahepatic in most patients) are spared cholangiographically in only 1% to 2% of patients. In 20% of patients, the disease is confined cholangiographically to the intrahepatic and hilar ducts.

In the absence of complicating cholangiocarcinoma, large duct PSC progresses slowly. In one series, 80% of patients with uncomplicated PSC showed no change on serial cholangiograms during a period of 6 months to 6.5 years.[11]

Gallbladder abnormalities occur in 40% of patients with PSC; the most common abnormality is gallstones (26%). Direct involvement of the gallbladder wall by PSC occurs in about 15% of patients, and approximately 4% of patients have gallbladder neoplasms, such as adenoma and adenocarcinoma.[12]

Radiographic Findings

While findings from liver biopsy may be compatible with PSC, they alone are not diagnostic. The diagnosis of PSC must take into account clinical findings, laboratory tests, and, importantly, radiographic studies.

Cholangiography

Although features of PSC can be demonstrated on a variety of imaging modalities, the most important and most characteristic radiographic findings are seen at cholangiography[13] (Fig. 82-2). Cholangiography is usually accomplished by endoscopic retrograde cholangiopancreatography (ERCP). If certain segments of the biliary tract are unable to be visualized by ERCP, then percutaneous transhepatic cholangiography (PTC) may be performed.

Multiple segmental strictures involving both the intrahepatic and the extrahepatic bile ducts are the hallmark of PSC. They attest to the nonuniform involvement of the biliary tree by inflammatory fibrosis. Normal or less-involved duct

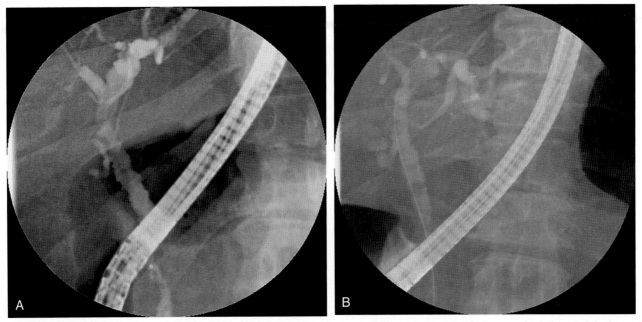

Figure 82-2. PSC: ERCP findings. A and **B.** There are multifocal, irregular strictures and dilatations involving the intra- and extrahepatic bile ducts with a predilection for bifucations. The strictures are usually short and annular, alternating with normal or slightly dilated segments, producing a beaded appearance. Coarse nodular mural irregularities are often seen as well as small eccentric outpouchings and webs.

segments alternating with segmental strictures produce the classic beaded appearance. Stricture length can vary from 1 to 2 mm (so-called band strictures) to several centimeters in length, with the most common length being 1 to 1.5 cm. When peripheral ducts are obliterated, the bile ducts take on a "pruned tree" appearance.

Diverticular outpouchings, varying in size from 1 to 2 mm to 1 cm, are seen in about 25% of patients on high-quality cholangiograms and are a characteristic feature of PSC. Some diverticula appear to develop as herniations adjacent to strictures, whereas others arise in the absence of strictures, apparently as mucosal extensions into the thickened duct wall.

Almost half of patients with PSC have some degree of mural irregularity varying from a fine, brush-border appearance to a coarse, shaggy, or frankly nodular appearance. The combined findings of short strictures, beading, pruning, diverticula, and mural irregularities often result in a composite cholangiographic appearance that is nearly pathognomonic for PSC.

Ultrasound, CT, and MR Imaging

Cross-sectional imaging is frequently used early in the evaluation of abnormal liver function tests. Ultrasound, CT, and MRI are modalities that can effectively assess for the presence of biliary tract abnormalities. Cross-sectional imaging allows for evaluation of not only the bile duct but also the bile duct wall and the surrounding liver parenchyma. In patients with PSC, cross-sectional imaging allows for detection of complications such as cirrhosis and malignancy.

Because ultrasound (Fig. 82-3) is relatively inexpensive and can effectively evaluate the biliary system, it is commonly the initial imaging modality used in the evaluation of cholestatic liver disease. Findings of PSC by ultrasound include duct dilatation and wall thickening of the common bile duct or the intrahepatic ducts in a smooth or irregular manner.

The normal intrahepatic bile ducts have a wall thickness of less than 1 mm and appear sonographically as a thin echogenic line. Thickened bile ducts appear as two parallel echogenic lines with a central hypoechoic stripe.[14] Bile duct wall thickening in PSC usually measures 2 to 5 mm. Common bile duct wall thickening, when present, can be easily seen by ultrasound. Detecting intrahepatic bile duct wall thickening, on the other hand, is difficult as this modality is operator dependent and this is a subtle finding not always readily apparent.

With ever improving technology, CT scanning continues to serve as one of the primary imaging modalities for the evaluation of abdominal pathology. Current-generation multidetector CT scanners allow for rapid acquisition of data

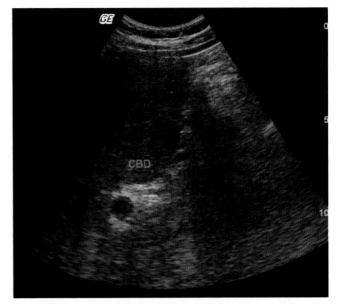

Figure 82-3. PSC: sonographic findings. Mural thickening of the common bile duct (CBD) is identified on this transverse sonogram.

and the creation of high-resolution reformatted images for the evaluation of the biliary system, a technique known as CT cholangiography (CTC). CTC uses axial CT data, which are then reconstructed into two-dimensional and three-dimensional images to evaluate the biliary tree, particularly the extrahepatic bile ducts. Oral or intravenous cholangiographic contrast material is used to opacify the bile ducts prior to scanning. CTC allows for cross-sectional imaging of the biliary tree in patients who do not qualify for MRI, such as patients who have aneurysm clips or a pacemaker, who are claustrophobic, or who have too many surgical clips within the porta hepatis from prior surgery.[15]

CT findings of PSC are similar to ERCP findings and include segmental intrahepatic biliary duct dilatation with focal constrictions (Fig. 82-4). The common hepatic duct and common bile duct can also demonstrate alternating narrowing and dilatation. Mural contrast enhancement of the extrahepatic bile ducts can be seen, although this is a nonspecific finding that can be seen with other causes of cholangitis (see Fig. 82-15). Intrahepatic bile duct calculi are present in approximately 8% of patients with PSC. These calculi appear as foci of faint high attenuation or as coarse calcifications and are best seen on noncontrast images.[16] Upper abdominal lymphadenopathy is frequently seen in patients with PSC, although this is nonspecific. The presence of lymphadenopathy does not necessarily indicate the development of cholangiocarcinoma and should not be regarded as an exclusion criterion for liver transplantation.[17]

There are unique hepatic morphologic changes associated with PSC-induced cirrhosis that can be seen with CT. The liver is markedly deformed with severe contour lobulations, creating a rounded-appearing organ. This is due to atrophy of both the posterior segment of the right hepatic lobe and the lateral segment of the left lobe and marked hypertrophy of the caudate lobe. Additionally, the atrophied right hepatic lobe may be hypodense (due to fibrosis) relative to the hypertrophied caudate lobe, creating the effect of a pseudotumor. When these morphologic changes are seen in conjunction with scattered, dilated intrahepatic bile ducts and intrahepatic bile duct stones, PSC can be suggested as the cause of the cirrhosis.[18] There is substantial overlap in the appearance of livers affected by cirrhosis due to PSC and by those affected by end stage cirrhosis caused by the usual factors (alcohol and hepatitis). The typical findings cirrhosis due to any cause include a nodular liver surface caused by variably sized regenerative nodules, areas of confluent fibrosis, atrophy of the right hepatic lobe, and hypertrophy of the caudate lobe.

Introduced in 1991, MRCP (magnetic resonance cholangiopancreatography) is a technique that uses heavily T2-weighted pulse sequences to depict the bile and pancreatic ducts. MRCP is noninvasive and does not require the use of iodinated contrast material or ionizing radiation.[19] Studies have shown good correlation between MRCP and ERCP in the diagnosis of PSC.[20-23] MRCP findings of PSC are similar to ERCP findings and include multifocal segmental strictures alternating with normal or slightly dilated bile duct segments (Fig. 82-5). The strictures are usually out of proportion to the degree of upstream ductal dilatation. Periductal inflammation and fibrosis prevent the ducts from dilating; therefore, high-grade strictures can be present with only minimal proximal dilatation. With progressive fibrosis, the peripheral bile ducts obliterate resulting in a "pruned tree" appearance.

Other findings include mural irregularities, webs, diverticula, and stones.[24]

Hepatic parenchymal changes associated with PSC can be observed by MRI. Extension of the ductal inflammation into the hepatic parenchyma, retention of bile salts, and the accumulation of copper in hepatocytes are thought to be responsible for the parenchymal changes seen on MRI.[25] The extrahepatic bile duct demonstrates wall thickening (1.5 mm or greater) and enhancement. On T1-weighted images, randomly distributed areas of high signal intensity can be seen in a minority of patients. This abnormal signal is assumed to be due to cholestasis and lipofucin deposits in atrophic liver cells.[26] T2-weighted images may demonstrate increased signal intensity in a peripheral wedge-shaped or fine reticular pattern. Extension of periductal inflammation to involve the vascular and lymphatic channels is considered to be the reason for the signal abnormality. Inflammatory changes of the hilar bile ducts results in a high T2 signal along the porta hepatis.[25] Postcontrast images can demonstrate peripheral areas of enhancement possibly due to alterations in blood flow in response to regional inflammation.[26]

The morphologic changes of the liver affected by cirrhosis from chronic PSC have been previously discussed with respect to CT. These similar changes and others can be observed by MRI. A macronodular pattern of cirrhosis can be demonstrated in patients with PSC. These large nodules (usually greater than 3 cm) can be found predominantly within the central portion of the liver. The nodules are typically isointense on T1-weighted images and hypointense on T2-weighted images. Following the administration of contrast, the nodules are hypointense immediately after the injection and 2 minutes afterward, eventually becoming isointense.[27] The peripheral wedge-shaped areas of parenchymal atrophy seen with PSC-induced cirrhosis is typically hypointense on T1-weighted images and hyperintense on T2-weighted images. Corresponding areas demonstrate hypoenhancement on images obtained immediately after contrast administration and hyperenhancement on images obtained 2 minutes afterward.[27]

Differential Diagnosis

Cholangiocarcinoma

In 90% of cases, cholangiocarcinoma presents cholangiographically either as a focal stricture or, less often, as a polypoid mass, neither of which should be confused with PSC. In about 10% of cases, however, there is metastatic spread or multicentricity, or both, such that the tumor involves the biliary tree diffusely and simulates PSC. When diffuse band strictures and multiple diverticula are identified by cholangiography, PSC may be confidently diagnosed because these findings do not occur in cholangiocarcinoma. Only one fourth of patients with PSC demonstrate these findings, leaving a large percentage of PSC patients in whom cholangiocarcinoma cannot be excluded. Even more problematic is the fact that cholangiocarcinoma complicates PSC in about 15% of patients, and when the two diseases coexist, the duct alterations from the underlying PSC can easily mask the presence of the carcinoma.[11] Because of the segmental nature of PSC, some portions of the biliary tree remain relatively free of fibrosis and retain the ability to dilate in response

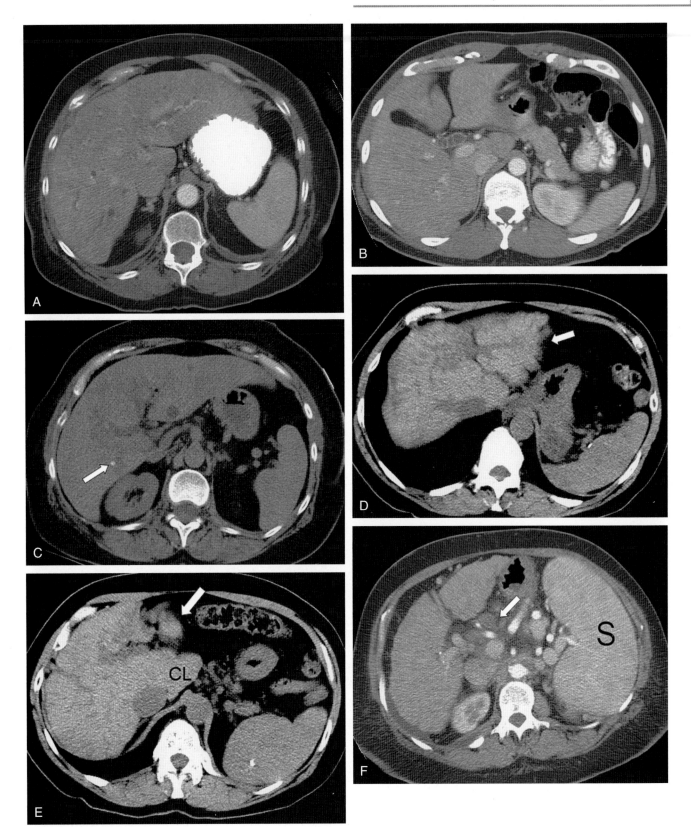

Figure 82-4.   PSC: CT findings. A. There is abnormal enhancement of the walls of the irregular intrahepatic bile ducts. **B.** Abnormal mural thickening and enhancement are identified in the common bile duct. **C.** Noncontrast scan shows an intrahepatic bile duct stone (*arrow*). **D** and **E.** Noncontrast scans demonstrate a nodular liver with marked atrophy of the lateral segment of the left lobe (*arrow*) and enlargement of the caudate lobe (CL). **F.** Contrast-enhanced scan in a different patient shows cirrhosis of the liver, splenomegaly (S), and adenopathy in the porta hepatis (*arrow*), a common finding in patients with PSC.

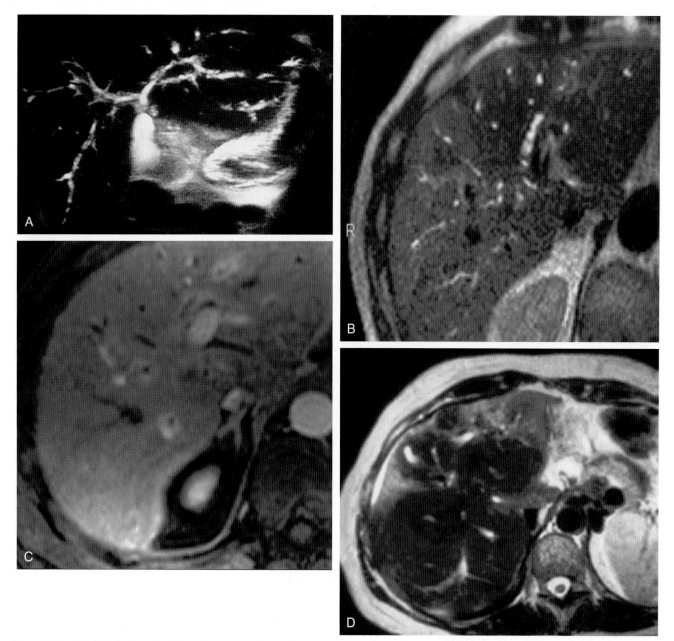

Figure 82-5. PSC: MR findings. A. MR cholangiogram shows characteristic irregular strictures and segmental dilatations involving intrahepatic and extrahepatic ducts. **B** and **C.** Abnormal periductal enhancement is identified on these axial images. **D.** MR image of patient with secondary biliary cirrhosis due to sclerosing cholangitis. **E.** MR image of a different patient showing marked nodularity of the hepatic contour and atrophy of the lateral segment of the left lobe and hypertrophy of the caudate lobe.

to obstruction. Cholangiocarcinomas usually obstruct more completely than the fibrous strictures of PSC. Therefore, more markedly dilated ducts should be viewed as a worrisome sign of complicating carcinoma.

Because PSC is usually a slowly progressive disease, interval stricture formation and biliary dilatation on serial cholangiograms favor the presence of superimposed malignant disease, especially in association with clinical deterioration.[11,28] Intraluminal filling defects occur in 5% to 10% of PSC patients but are usually small, measuring 2 to 5 mm in diameter.

Filling defects of 1 cm or larger occur in about 50% of patients with PSC complicated by cholangiocarcinoma, and when they are present, a presumptive diagnosis of malignant disease should be made if choledocholithiasis can be excluded.

On cholangiographic examination, about 25% of patients with PSC show a *dominant stricture*, in which a segment of the biliary tree, often near the hilum, appears more severely strictured than the remainder of the ducts. Although the concept of the dominant stricture was originally proposed to justify aggressive surgical approaches for management of benign strictures of PSC, some dominant strictures actually represent cholangiocarcinomas.[29,30] If cholangiography or clinical course suggests the possibility of complicating cholangiocarcinoma, CT, ultrasound, or MRI should be performed. Cross-sectional imaging can confirm the presence of neoplasm in 50% to 80% of cases,[31,32] particularly those arising from intrahepatic ducts, where cholangiocarcinomas often form bulky, exophytic masses. Mural thickening of the extrahepatic bile ducts of 5 mm or greater is presumptive evidence of cholangiocarcinoma.[33] Periportal soft tissue of 1.5 cm or greater in thickness is also suspicious for malignant tumor.[34] Contrast-enhanced CT and MRI with thin sections and delayed images are superior to 10-mm-thick, unenhanced images and increase the sensitivity for detecting malignant tumors in patients with PSC.

Benign Ductal Diseases

Primary biliary cirrhosis (PBC), secondary sclerosing cholangitis (from a variety of known causes), and some parasitic infestations all share some pathologic, clinical, and imaging features with PSC. The differential diagnostic considerations for these disorders are discussed under their separate headings.

Thiabendazole (Mintezol), an anthelmintic medication, has been reported to cause a cholestatic disorder characterized histologically by destruction of interlobular bile ducts, possibly with an autoimmune basis.[35] Although the microscopic findings can be confused with small duct PSC, the large ducts are normal on cholangiograms, and the history of thiabendazole treatment is diagnostic.

Hepatic sarcoidosis can lead to a granulomatous cholangitis, which on liver biopsy resembles PSC or PBC in some cases.[36] In addition, strictures of the extrahepatic bile ducts have been reported in sarcoidosis. The diagnosis is usually known because clinical evidence of sarcoidosis has preceded the onset of cholestasis in reported cases.

Eosinophilic cholangitis is another rare cause of extrahepatic biliary obstruction. Marked wall thickening of the extrahepatic ducts can be seen on CT and sonography.[37]

Arteriohepatic dysplasia (Alagille's syndrome) is a rare familial cholestatic syndrome characterized by abnormalities of the heart, skeleton, and eyes; a characteristic physiognomy including a broad forehead, flattened malar eminence, and pointed mandible; and loss of interlobular bile ducts as seen on liver biopsy.[38] Cholangiograms show segmental strictures of both the intrahepatic and the extrahepatic bile ducts, resembling PSC. These ductal changes, however, appear to be due to a defect in duct development, leading to segmental hypoplasia or atresia, rather than secondary to fibrosis or ductal destruction as found in PSC. The familial inheritance, onset during infancy, absence of associated UC, and characteristic facies should allow easy distinction from PSC (see Chapter 123).

Allograft rejection after liver transplantation can lead to loss of interlobular bile ducts and strictures of the intrahepatic and extrahepatic bile ducts, closely resembling PSC.[39] Similar changes in the large bile ducts can result from ischemia if there is a delay in reestablishing hepatic arterial circulation or if hepatic artery thrombosis occurs after transplantation.[39] Other causes of biliary ischemia may also result in biliary strictures resembling PSC.[40] In transplantation for PSC, recurrent disease should be considered in patients in whom strictures occur in the absence of rejection, infection, or ischemia. A complete discussion of biliary complications of liver transplantation can be found in Chapter 94.

A spontaneous stricture of the biliary tree, usually a major duct, occasionally causes diagnostic confusion. In most cases, focal biliary strictures have a malignant cause. Some cholangiocarcinomas induce so much fibrosis that biopsy results are falsely negative, leading to an erroneous diagnosis of benign stricture. Nevertheless, benign, focal biliary strictures do occur rarely in the absence of previous surgery, known infection, or other injury. These are sometimes labeled PSC but probably represent a different disease process or at most represent a forme fruste of PSC.

PRIMARY BILIARY CIRRHOSIS

Epidemiology and Clinical Findings

Although the term *primary biliary cirrhosis* was first used in 1950, the condition was originally described nearly 100 years earlier.[41,42] Similar to PSC, PBC is a chronic cholestatic syndrome of unknown cause characterized by destruction of small bile ducts with four histologic stages seen on liver biopsy.[43,44] Chronic cholestasis leads to hepatic copper overload in both PBC and PSC, but the role of copper in duct injury remains unclear (Fig. 82-6).

The clinical presentation of PBC is often dominated by the insidious onset of diffuse pruritus owing to cutaneous accumulation of bile salts. Itching generally precedes the onset of cutaneous jaundice by 6 months to 2 years. In later stages of the disease, osteomalacia, liver failure, and portal hypertension are seen.

Alterations of cell-based immunity are an important feature of PBC. Sensitized T lymphocytes and possibly B lymphocytes may mediate the duct injury.[45] Associated autoimmune and collagen-vascular diseases include rheumatoid arthritis, Sjögren's syndrome, Hashimoto's thyroiditis, dermatomyositis, scleroderma, CRST (calcinosis cutis, Raynaud's phenomenon, sclerodactyly, and telangiectasia) syndrome, and systemic lupus erythematosus.

As in PSC, serum alkaline phosphatase levels are reliably elevated, whereas serum bilirubin values are more likely to fluctuate and are seldom significantly elevated at presentation. Serum bilirubin is an important prognostic indicator; elevated levels are inversely related to life expectancy.

Despite some similarities to patients with PSC, patients with PBC exhibit important differences clinically and pathologically. About 90% of patients with PBC are female; the ratio of males to females in PSC is greater than 2:1. UC is common in PSC but is not associated with PBC. Serologic markers, especially antimitochondrial antibody, are frequently present in PBC, often in high titers, whereas they are not consistently present in PSC. On pathologic examination, small duct destruction in PBC is accompanied by inflammatory cellular infiltrate, including lymphocytes, plasma cells, histiocytes, and eosinophils, and by granuloma formation. In contrast, the destructive cholangitis in PSC is relatively hypocellular and lacks granuloma formation. The conspicuous fibrous thickening of bile duct walls seen in PSC is absent in PBC. The natural history of PBC is variable but usually inexorably downhill; the mean survival in symptomatic patients is 5.5 to 6 years with a range of 3 to 11 years.[46,47]

Radiographic Findings

Imaging typically plays a minor role in the diagnosis of PBC. The diagnosis is usually based on clinical features and laboratory evaluation. Cross-sectional imaging has traditionally been used to stage liver disease by demonstrating portal hypertension

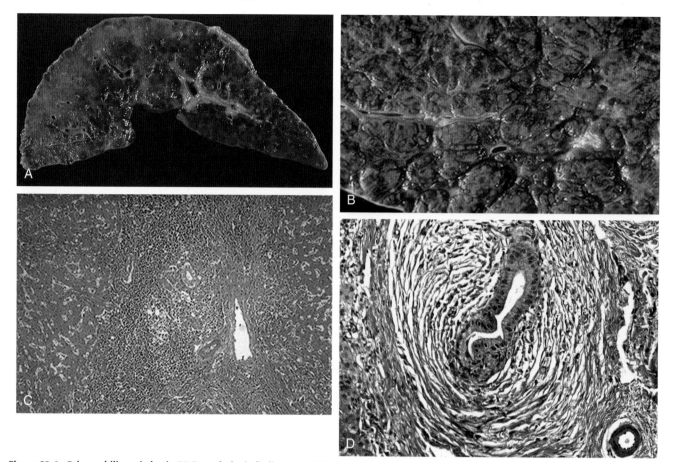

Figure 82-6. Primary biliary cirrhosis (PBC): pathologic findings. A and **B.** Gross appearance of stage IV disease; a mixture of tan and green regenerative nodules is typical. **C.** Histologic specimen showing periportal inflammation with lymphocytes and plasma cells. **D.** Periductal lymphocytic infiltration is present.

and cirrhosis. Imaging is useful to detect the development of hepatic malignancies.

In most patients with PBC, cholangiograms are normal, especially during the early stages of the disease. With disease progression, the intrahepatic bile ducts can become tortuous and attenuated in response to the surrounding cirrhosis (Fig. 82-7). In areas of parenchymal atrophy, the ducts become crowded and tortuous; in areas of compensatory hypertrophy or nodular regeneration, the ducts become splayed or displaced. There can be extrinsic compression of the common bile duct due to lymphadenopathy within the porta hepatis.[48]

CT and ultrasound scans performed at the time of diagnosis usually demonstrate hepatomegaly (Fig. 82-8). Over time, with progression of PBC, the liver volume decreases with atrophy of the right hepatic lobe and relative hypertrophy of the caudate and left hepatic lobes. Several different patterns of fibrosis can be demonstrated in patients with PBC, but the one that seems characteristic is the lacelike pattern of thin or thick bands of low attenuation that surround regenerating nodules. Regenerating nodules are seen as small rounded hyperdense foci on unenhanced scans. Fibrosis is best demonstrated on noncontrast examinations. Lymphadenopathy is seen 80% to 90% of patients with PBC and is typically present within the porta hepatis and portacaval locations.[49] Ascites, splenomegaly, and varices are findings indicative of portal hypertension. These findings can sometimes

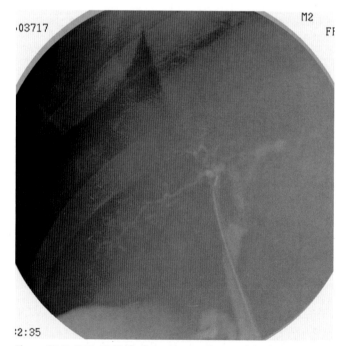

Figure 82-7. PBC: ERCP findings. The intrahepatic bile ducts are small and attenuated, giving the "pruned tree" appearance. The extrahepatic ducts are normal. In PSC, the intrahepatic and extrahepatic ductal systems are usually involved together.

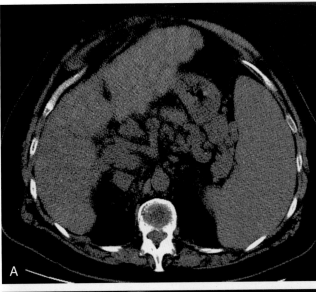

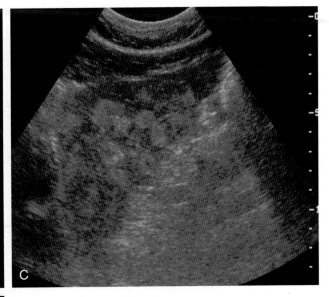

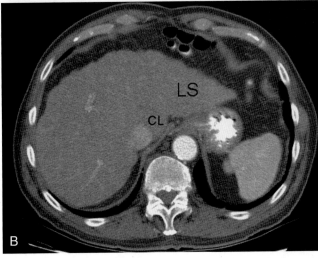

Figure 82-8. PBC: CT and ultrasound findings: A. Transverse non-enhanced CT scan (narrow window setting) shows a small liver with a nodular contour, heterogeneous parenchyma, hypertrophy of the lateral segment, and splenomegaly. Enlarged lymph nodes are present in the lesser omentum. **B.** Contrast-enhanced CT scan shows a nodular hepatic contour, hypertrophy of the lateral segment (LS) of the left lobe, and a relatively normal-sized caudate lobe. End-stage PSC is almost always associated with caudate lobe hypertrophy and left lobe atrophy. **C.** Longitudinal scan of the left lobe shows multiple regenerating nodules producing multiple echogenic masses. (Case courtesy of Dr. Peter Cooperberg.)

be observed before clinical and CT findings of cirrhosis develop.

MRI findings are similar to CT scan findings in patients with PBC, demonstrating morphologic changes associated with cirrhosis and lymphadenopathy. An MRI sign that has been described as the "periportal halo sign" can aid in the diagnosis of end-stage PBC (Fig. 82-9). The periportal halo sign is considered present when a small (5-mm to 1-cm) rounded lesion of decreased T1 and T2 signal intensity is seen surrounding a portal venous branch. Typically, the lesions are numerous, involve all hepatic segments, and fail to exert mass effect.[50] The lesions must be differentiated from re-generating nodules, which are usually variable in size and signal intensity and may exhibit mass effect. The sign should also not be confused with periportal edema, which is seen as high signal intensity on T2-weighted images in a periportal distribution. Histologic examination reveals that the periportal halo sign correlates with periportal hepatocellular parenchymal extinction, which is encircled by regenerating nodules.[50]

Cholangiography can be helpful in differentiating PSC from PBC. Strictures are the hallmark of PSC by cholangiography. With PBC, the bile duct deformities are less severe and mainly confined to the intrahepatic bile ducts.[13] The diverticular outpouchings and mural irregularities that are classic in PSC are not seen with PBC.

OBSTRUCTIVE CHOLANGITIS

Biliary obstruction induces bile stasis and predisposes to bacterial infection. Although bacterial cholangitis is nearly always associated with biliary obstruction, benign causes (choledocholithiasis, surgical anastomotic stricture, papillary stenosis) are much more likely to lead to clinical infection than are malignant causes (cholangiocarcinoma, pancreatic carcinoma, malignant hilar lymphadenopathy).[51,52]

Patients present clinically with right upper quadrant abdominal pain, chills, fever, and jaundice. *Escherichia coli* is the most common infecting organism,[51] but most infections are polymicrobial.[52] In acute ascending cholangitis, purulent bile may be identified as intraluminal echogenic material within involved ducts by ultrasound or as high-density intra-ductal material by CT. Cholangiography may demonstrate irregular tubular filling defects in dilated ducts above the obstruction. Hepatic abscesses not uncommonly complicate the bacterial cholangitis. They are readily demonstrated by

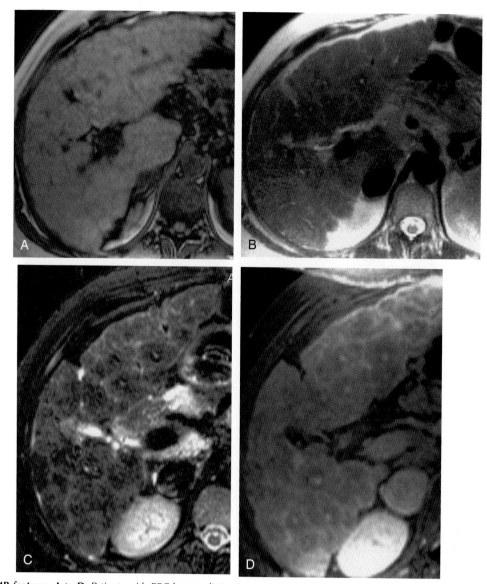

Figure 82-9. PBC: MR features. A to D. Patients with PBC have a distinctive conspicuous low signal intensity abnormality centered around portal venous branches on T1- and T2-weighted MR images, the "periportal halo sign." This abnormality consists of a rounded lesion centered on a portal venous branch, 5 mm to 1 cm in size. These are numerous lesions involving all hepatic segments with low signal intensity on T1- and T2-weighted images and no mass effect. These criteria allow differentiation of this finding from regenerating nodules, which are usually of various sizes and signal intensity, may exert mass effect, and are not centered on portal venous branches. (Case courtesy of Glenn Krinsky, MD.)

ultrasound and CT, and communication with the biliary tree can be documented on cholangiography[51] (Fig. 82-10).

Although all of the aforementioned are important radiologic signs in obstructive cholangitis, the most important diagnostic objective is to identify the nature and level of the obstruction and to decide the best means of relieving the obstruction. Injection of contrast medium under pressure above an obstruction may exacerbate an existing infection or introduce an infection into a previously sterile biliary tree. If intraductal pressure exceeds portal venous pressure or if communication to the hepatic venous system becomes established, life-threatening septicemia may ensue. Thus, prompt biliary drainage and broad-spectrum antibiotic coverage are mandatory whenever an obstructed infected biliary system is identified on direct cholangiography.[52]

Chronic obstructive cholangitis with repeated episodes of infection may lead to duct strictures, peripheral attenuation of the intrahepatic bile ducts, and biliary cirrhosis. The appearances may resemble PSC, but the cause of obstruction, such as choledocholithiasis or postoperative stricture, is usually clinically or radiologically obvious.

Bacterial infection, usually accompanied by stone formation, may complicate a preexisting biliary tract disease. Congenital cystic disease, including Caroli's disease, is frequently complicated by choledocholithiasis, infection, and stricture formation, which may potentially mask the underlying disease. Similarly, patients with PSC often form pigment stones within poorly draining portions of the biliary tree, which makes it difficult to establish a primary diagnosis. If clinical and radiologic evidence of an underlying disease is compelling, however, pigmented duct stones and clinical infection should be considered secondary phenomena.[53,54] Intrahepatic duct stones in PSC patients may be quite subtle and are often overlooked on contrast-enhanced CT.

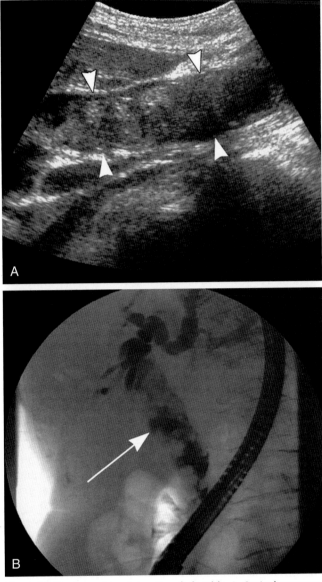

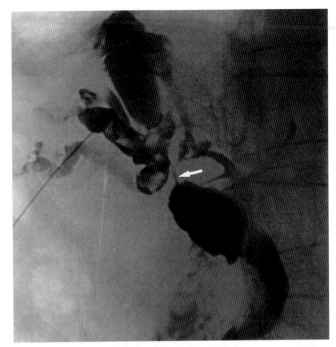

Figure 82-11. Oriental cholangiohepatitis. PTC shows severe stricture (*arrow*), with dilated ducts, multiple filling defects, and abrupt tapering in the right anterior segment. (From Mi-Suk Park M-S, Yu J-S, Kim KW, et al: Recurrent pyogenic cholangitis: Comparison between MR cholangiography and direct cholangiography. Radiology 220:677-681, 2001.)

Figure 82-10. Ascending obstructive cholangitis. A. Sagittal sonogram shows a markedly dilated common bile duct (*arrowheads*) filled with sludge and stones. **B.** ERCP shows a dilated intrahepatic and extrahepatic biliary system with multiple filling defects (*arrow*). The patient recovered after urgent papillotomy and administration of antibiotics and intravenous fluids. (From Hanbidge AE, Buckler PM, O'Malley ME, et al: Imaging evaluation for acute pain in the upper abdomen. RadioGraphics 24:1117-1135, 2004.)

RECURRENT PYOGENIC CHOLANGITIS (ORIENTAL CHOLANGIOHEPATITIS)

Certain Asian populations have a propensity to form pigmented stones in the intrahepatic and extrahepatic bile ducts that are commonly accompanied by recurrent gram-negative bacterial infections.[52,55-59] This condition has been variously termed Oriental cholangiohepatitis, Oriental cholangitis, Hong Kong disease, and biliary obstruction of the Chinese. A more inclusive name, recognizing the sporadic occurrence in non-Asians, is recurrent pyogenic cholangitis (RPC). The pattern of stone disease in RPC differs from that in typical Western populations, in which the ductal stones are primarily

extrahepatic, are predominantly composed of cholesterol, and most often originate in the gallbladder.[59] Parasitic infestation (*Clonorchis sinensis, Ascaris lumbricoides*), malnutrition, and portal bacteremia have been etiologically implicated in RPC, but the cause and pathogenesis remain unproved.

Right upper quadrant pain, chills, fever, and jaundice are the common clinical features of RPC; the natural history is characterized by exacerbations and remissions of cholangitis, with duct injury and cholestasis leading to biliary cirrhosis. During the acute phases, sepsis may be life threatening.

Dilated ducts containing stones and sludge are usually identifiable by CT and ultrasound, although large amounts of nonshadowing, isodense material may mask duct dilatation. All segments of the biliary tree may be involved, but the lateral segment of the left lobe is most often and extensively involved. Additional cross-sectional imaging findings of RPC include parenchymal atrophy, fatty metamorphosis, duct wall enhancement, segmental parenchymal enhancement, hepatic abscess, biloma, and pneumobilia.[56,57] Strictures are suggested by the presence of abruptly tapered ducts. Cholangiography provides the best detail on the status of the ducts (Fig. 82-11) and is a necessary component of the radiologic interventional management of stones and strictures.[55,60]

CHOLANGITIS RELATED TO ACQUIRED IMMUNODEFICIENCY SYNDROME

A secondary cholangitis resembling PSC is an uncommon but well-recognized component of AIDS. The condition is thought to be secondary to opportunistic infection by *Cryptosporidium*, cytomegalovirus, or both.[61-63] In addition to biliary tract signs and symptoms, patients with AIDS-related

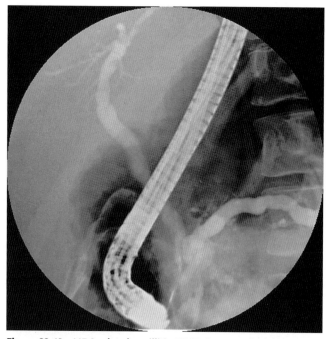

Figure 82-12. AIDS-related papillitis. ERCP shows marked dilatation of the common bile duct and pancreatic duct, a finding indicating low obstruction.

cholangitis may have abdominal pain and diarrhea from cryptosporidial enteritis.

Cholangiograms typically show irregularities and strictures of the intrahepatic and extrahepatic bile ducts with associated ductal dilatation. Papillary stenosis can occur as an isolated phenomenon or in conjunction with more proximal ductal strictures (Fig. 82-12). Polypoid intraluminal filling defects resulting from granulation tissue have been reported in one fourth of patients on ERCP.[64] CT and ultrasound may demonstrate mural thickening of the gallbladder and bile ducts as well as other extraductal manifestations of AIDS. A hyperechoic nodule at the distal end of the common duct, attributed to inflammation and edema of the papilla of Vater, has been reported in one series of patients.[65]

FLOXURIDINE CHOLANGITIS

Intra-arterial infusion of chemotherapeutic agents for the treatment of liver metastasis has been shown to cause bile duct strictures.[40,66-69] In one series, 15% of patients receiving intra-arterial therapy showed abnormalities on cholangiograms in the absence of tumor progression.[69] Floxuridine (5-fluorodeoxyuridine) has been the offending agent in almost all cases. Ductal damage is believed to be due to chemical toxic effects of the drug on the ducts or drug-induced intravascular thrombosis of hilar vessels.[40] Histologic examination of strictured areas shows dense fibrosis of involved bile ducts and surrounding liver parenchyma. Nevertheless, cholangiograms obtained after cessation of chemotherapy have shown reversibility of some strictures.

In patients with chemotherapy-related cholangitis, direct cholangiography shows segmental strictures of variable length, similar to those seen in PSC. Floxuridine-associated strictures have a marked propensity to involve the hilar area and

to spare the lower common duct and the peripheral intrahepatic ducts.[69] The gallbladder and cystic duct are also usually more severely involved in floxuridine cholangitis than in PSC. The clinical setting leaves no doubt about the diagnosis if tumor progression can be excluded by CT, MRI, ultrasound, or other means.

PARASITIC INFESTATION

Ascariasis

Ascaris lumbricoides is the most prevalent human helminth worldwide (Fig. 82-13). Infestation results from ingestion of ova, with adult worms becoming established in the small bowel after larval migration through the liver and lungs. Clinical symptoms depend on the magnitude of infestation and are generally more frequent and severe in children. The most common clinical presentation is intestinal obstruction secondary to obturation of the small bowel lumen by a mass of entangled worms. Acute appendicitis and pancreatitis also occur. Biliary colic develops when worms occupy and obstruct the common duct.[52] Surgical removal is curative, but if worms become trapped in the biliary tree and are not removed, thousands of eggs may be released as the worms disintegrate, leading to acute and chronic suppurative cholangitis.[70] In mild cases, ascaridic cholangitis resolves with granuloma formation and scarring. In more severe cases, life-threatening complications may ensue. Extension into the portal or hepatic veins may lead to inflammation and thrombosis (pyelephlebitis). Liver abscesses can potentially perforate into the peritoneal cavity and extend into the pleural space.

Worms may be seen as longitudinal filling defects up to several inches in length on direct or intravenous cholangiograms or as thin, long, or coiled echogenic intraluminal structures on ultrasound scans.[70-72] On sonograms, an echogenic focus within a duct results in a "bull's-eye" appearance.[73] A central anechoic component, probably representing the worm's digestive tract, has also been described. Worms may occupy any portion of the biliary tree, including the gallbladder. Real-time ultrasound confirms the diagnosis by demonstrating the worm's motility.[73,74]

Clonorchiasis

The most important liver fluke is *Clonorchis sinensis*, for which humans are the definitive host (Fig. 82-14). The eggs of *C. sinensis* are passed in human feces, and infestation occurs by ingestion of raw fish after an initial intermediate phase hosted by one of several types of freshwater snails. Clonorchiasis is endemic in Asia but may be seen in Western countries as a result of travel and immigration.

Within the biliary tree, the worms obstruct the flow of bile and incite an inflammatory cell infiltrate. In later stages, periductal fibrosis, ductal epithelial hyperplasia, and cholangiocarcinoma are seen.[52] Clinical symptoms depend on the number of flukes, the duration of infestation, and the presence of complications. With mild infection, patients may be asymptomatic. Early symptoms associated with moderate disease are nonspecific and include anorexia, dyspepsia, abdominal fullness, and right upper quadrant discomfort. Severe disease induces more significant systemic symptoms, including palpitations, weight loss, and diarrhea. Jaundice

Figure 82-13. Ascariasis. A. Life cycle: Adult worms (1) live in the lumen of the small intestine. A female may produce approximately 200,000 eggs per day, which are passed with the feces (2). Unfertilized eggs may be ingested but are not infective. Fertile eggs embryonate and become infective after 18 days to several weeks (3), depending on the environmental conditions (optimum: moist, warm, shaded soil). After infective eggs are swallowed (4), the larvae hatch (5), invade the intestinal mucosa, and are carried via the portal, then systemic circulation to the lungs (6). The larvae mature further in the lungs (10 to 14 days), penetrate the alveolar walls, ascend the bronchial tree to the throat, and are swallowed (7). Upon reaching the small intestine, they develop into adult worms (1). Between 2 and 3 months are required from ingestion of the infective eggs to oviposition by the adult female. Adult worms can live 1 to 2 years. (Source: CDC; available at http://www.dpd.cdc.gov.) **B.** ERCP shows a linear filling defect in the common bile duct, which is the ascaris worm. **C.** Worm extracted with biopsy forceps from the papilla of Vater during an ERCP.

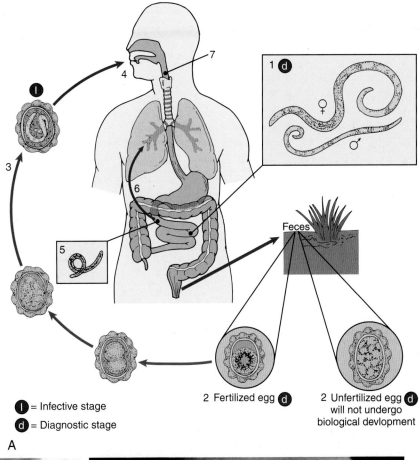

I = Infective stage

d = Diagnostic stage

2 Fertilized egg d

2 Unfertilized egg d will not undergo biological devlopment

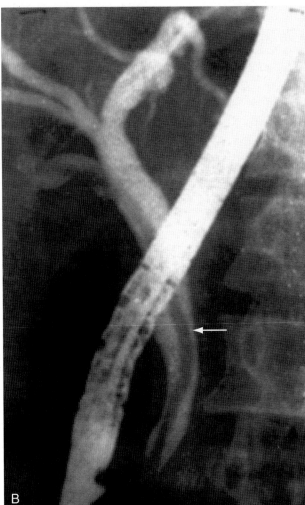

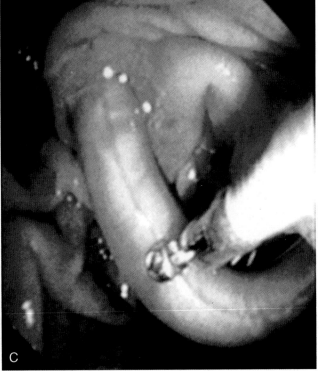

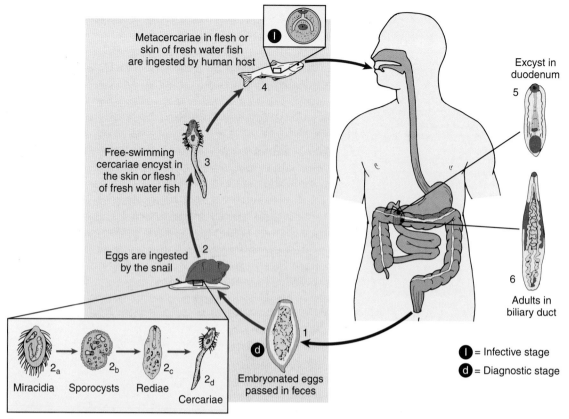

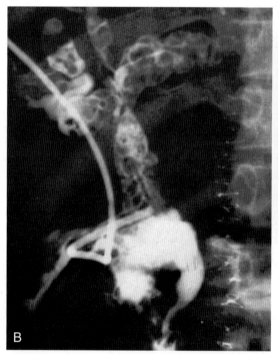

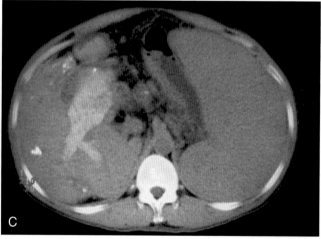

Figure 82-14. Clonorchiasis. A. Life cycle. Embryonated eggs are discharged in the biliary ducts and in the stool (1). Eggs are ingested by a suitable snail intermediate host; there are more than 100 species of snails that can serve as intermediate hosts. Each egg releases a miracidia (2$_a$), which go through several developmental stages [sporocysts (2$_b$), rediae (2$_c$), and cercariae (2$_d$)]. The cercariae are released from the snail, and after a short period of free-swimming time in water, they come in contact and penetrate the flesh of freshwater fish, where they encyst as metacercariae (3). Infection of humans occurs by ingestion of undercooked, salted, pickled, or smoked freshwater fish (4). After ingestion, the metacercariae excyst in the duodenum (5) and ascend the biliary tract through the ampulla of Vater (6). Maturation takes approximately 1 month. The adult flukes (measuring 10 to 25 mm × 3 to 5 mm) reside in small and medium sized biliary ducts. In addition to humans, carnivorous animals can serve as reservoir hosts. (Source: CDC; available at http://www.dpd.cdc.gov.) **B.** T-tube cholangiogram shows innumerable 1- to 2-cm filling defects within the dilated bile ducts. The flukes can be identified by their typical comma-shaped or crescentic outlines; other filling defects may represent associated stones and biliary sludge. Short strictures and gross dilatations of the ducts are present as the result of chronic obstruction and cholangitis. **C.** Nonenhanced CT scan in the same patient shows hyperdense material within grossly distended major intrahepatic bile ducts, which on pathological examination was proven to be a combination of pigmented biliary stones and sludge and *Clonorchis* flukes. Several calcified stones can be seen in peripheral ducts. The spleen is enlarged. (B and C courtesy of Dr. Joan Kendall.)

results from obstruction of the biliary tree by the worms, periductal tissue reaction, or cholangiocarcinoma.

The normal habitat of *C. sinensis* is the intrahepatic bile ducts, where on cholangiograms, they appear as ellipsoid, leaflike filling defects measuring 2 to 10 mm in length.[75] Contrast opacification of the peripheral intrahepatic ducts is impeded by the worms and periductal tissue reaction.

CT and ultrasound show characteristic dilatation of the small intrahepatic ducts with accompanying thickening of the duct wall and periductal tissues. The extrahepatic ducts are typically spared.[76] Flukes and fluke aggregates are more easily identified within the ducts by ultrasound than by CT. Unenhanced CT scans demonstrate branching low-density structures representing a combination of dilated ducts and periductal inflammatory fibrosis With contrast enhancement, the apparent diameter of these structures diminishes as the periductal tissue component increases in density and blends in with the surrounding parenchyma.

The association of *C. sinensis* and cholangiocarcinoma is well known.[75,77] Carcinomas in this setting tend to occur peripherally, where the flukes are most concentrated. Therefore, jaundice is often absent, and the tumors may reach considerable size before detection). Stippled or powder-like areas of high attenuation, corresponding to mucin on pathologic examination, have been reported within cholangiocarcinomas associated with clonorchiasis but not in cholangiocarcinomas without clonorchiasis.[77] Additional complications of clonorchiasis include intraductal calculus formation, suppurative cholangitis, cholangiohepatitis, and liver abscess, all of which may yield positive findings on cross-sectional imaging and cholangiography.[78]

Infestation with Other Liver Flukes

Other liver flukes known to infest humans share many features with *C. sinensis*, including similar life cycles and morphologic features, mode of infestation, and pathologic alterations in the liver and biliary tree with the exception of cholangiocarcinoma. *Opisthorchis felineus* and *Opisthorchis viverrini* gain access to the biliary tree via the ampulla of Vater; *Fasciola hepatica* gains access transperitoneally, by penetrating the liver capsule.[52,79,80]

Echinococcal Cholangitis

Echinococcus granulosus and *Echinococcus multilocularis* are small tapeworms whose larvae may lodge in human livers.[52] *E. granulosus* produces hydatid cysts in the liver, whereas *E. multilocularis* produces "alveolar" echinococcosis. The latter is a more aggressive, invasive form with much tissue destruction. Either form may compress the biliary tree or rupture into it, producing obstruction, inflammation, and secondary bacterial infection.[81] A more complete discussion of hepatobiliary echinococcosis can be found in Chapter 90.

References

1. Talwalkar JA, Lindor KD: Sclerosing cholangitis. Curr Opin Gastroenterol 18:372-377, 2002.
2. Zein CO, Lindor KD: Primary sclerosing cholangitis. Semin Gastrointest Dis 12:103-112, 2001.
3. Wiesner RH: Current concepts in primary sclerosing cholangitis. Mayo Clin Proc 69:969-982, 1994.
4. Lee YM, Kaplan MM: Primary sclerosing cholangitis. N Engl J Med 332:924-933, 1995.
5. Charatcharoenwitthaya P, Lindor KD: Primary sclerosing cholangitis: Patients with a rising alkaline phosphatase at annual follow-up. Clin Gastroenterol Hepatol 5:32-36, 2007.
6. Abdalian R, Heathcote EJ: Sclerosing cholangitis: A focus on secondary causes. Hepatology 44:1063-1074, 2006.
7. Larusso NF: Sclerosing cholangitis: Pathogenesis, pathology, and practice. Proc R Health Sci J 18:11-17, 1999.
8. Ludwig J, MacCarty RL, LaRusso NF, et al: Intrahepatic cholangiectases and large-duct obliteration in primary sclerosing cholangitis. Hepatology 6:560-568, 1986.
9. Fleming KA: The hepatobiliary pathology of primary sclerosing cholangitis. Eur J Gastroenterol Hepatol 4:266-271, 1992.
10. Ludwig J, Barham SS, LaRusso NF, et al: Morphologic features of chronic hepatitis associated with primary sclerosing cholangitis and chronic ulcerative colitis. Hepatology 1:632-640, 1981.
11. MacCarty RL, LaRusso NF, May GR, et al: Cholangiocarcinoma complicating primary sclerosing cholangitis: Cholangiographic appearances. Radiology 156:43-46, 1985.
12. Brandt DJ, MacCarty RL, Charboneau JW, et al: Gallbladder disease in patients with primary sclerosing cholangitis. AJR 150:571-574, 1988.
13. MacCarty RL, LaRusso NF, Wiesner RH, et al: Primary sclerosing cholangitis: Findings on cholangiography and pancreatography. Radiology 149:39-44, 1983.
14. Parulekar S: Transabdominal sonography of bile ducts. Ultrasound Q 18:187-202, 2002.
15. Caoili EM, Paulson EK, Heyneman LE, et al: Helical CT cholangiography with three-dimensional volume rendering using an oral biliary contrast agent: Feasibility of a novel technique. AJR 174:487-492, 2000.
16. Dodd GD, Niedzwiecki GA, Campbell WL, et al: Bile duct calculi in patients with primary sclerosing cholangitis. Radiology 203:443-447, 1997.
17. Johnson KS, Olliff JF, Olliff SP: The presence and significance of lymphadenopathy detected by CT in primary sclerosing cholangitis. Br J Radiol 71:1279-1282, 1998.
18. Dodd GD, Baron RL, Oliver JH, et al: End-stage primary sclerosing cholangitis: CT findings of hepatic morphology in 36 patients. Radiology 211:357-362, 1999.
19. Silva AC, Friese JL, Hara AK, et al: MR cholangiopancreatography: Improved ductal distention with intravenous morphine administration. RadioGraphics 24:677-687, 2004.
20. Ernst O, Asselah T, Sergent G, et al: MR cholangiography in primary sclerosing cholangitis. AJR 171:1027-1030, 1998.
21. Fulcher AS, Turner MA, Franklin KJ, et al: Primary sclerosing cholangitis: Evaluation with MR cholangiography: A case-controlled study. Radiology 215:71-80, 2000.
22. Vitellas KM, Enns RA, Keogan MT, et al: Comparison of MR cholangiopancreatographic techniques with contrast-enhanced cholangiography in the evaluation of sclerosing cholangitis. AJR 178:327-334, 2002.
23. Vitellas KM, El-Dieb A, Vaswani KK, et al: MR cholangiopancreatography in patients with primary sclerosing cholangitis: Interobserver variability and comparison with endoscopic retrograde cholangiopancreatography. AJR 179:339-407, 202.
24. Vitellas KM, Keogan MT, Freed KS, et al: Radiologic manifestations of sclerosing cholangitis with emphasis on MR cholangiopancreatography. RadioGraphics 20:959-975, 2000.
25. Meagher S, Yusoff I, Kennedy W, et al: The roles of magnetic resonance and endoscopic retrograde cholangiopancreatography (MRCP and ERCP) in the diagnosis of patients with suspected sclerosing cholangitis: A cost-effectiveness analysis. Endoscopy 39:222-228, 2007.
26. Ito K, Mitchell DG, Outwater EK, et al: Primary sclerosing cholangitis: MR imaging features. AJR 172:1527-1533, 1999.
27. Bader TR, Beavers KL, Semelka RC: MR imaging features of primary sclerosing cholangitis: Patterns of cirrhosis in relationship to clinical severity of disease. Radiology 226:675-685, 2003.
28. Hultcranz R, Olsson R, Danielsson A, et al: A 3-year prospective study on serum tumor markers used for detecting cholangiocarcinoma in patients with primary sclerosing cholangitis. J Hepatol 30:669-673, 1999.
29. Alexander SG, Howard TJ, Kopecky KK, et al: Sclerosing cholangitis. In Pitt HA, Carr-Locke DL, Ferrucci JT (eds): Hepatobiliary and Pancreatic Disease: The Team Approach to Management. Boston, Little, Brown, 1995, pp 247-258.
30. Cameron JL, Pitt HA, Zinner MJ, et al: Resection of hepatic duct bifurcation and transhepatic stenting for sclerosing cholangitis. Ann Surg 207:614-622, 1988.

31. Nesbit GM, Johnson CD, James EM, et al: Cholangiocarcinoma: Diagnosis and evaluation of resectability by CT and sonography as procedures complementary to cholangiography. AJR 151:933-938, 1988.

32. Campbell WL, Ferris JV, Holbert BL, et al: Biliary tract carcinoma complicating primary sclerosing cholangitis: Evaluation with CT, cholangiography, US, and MR imaging. Radiology 207:41-50, 1998.

33. Schulte SJ, Baron RL, Teefey SA, et al: CT of the extrahepatic bile ducts: Wall thickness and contrast enhancement in normal and abnormal ducts. AJR 154:79-85, 1990.

34. Matsui HO, Kadoya M, Takashima T, et al: Intrahepatic periportal abnormal intensity on MR images: An indication of various hepatobiliary disease. Radiology 171:335-338, 1989.

35. Manivel JC, Bloomer JR, Snover DC: Progressive bile duct injury after thiabendazole administration. Gastroenterology 93:245-249, 1987.

36. Ishak KG: Sarcoidosis of the liver and bile ducts. Mayo Clin Proc 73:467-472, 1998.

37. Song HH, Byn JY, Jung SE, et al: Eosinophilic cholangitis: US, CT, and cholangiography findings. J Comput Assist Tomogr 21:251-253, 1997.

38. Gorelick FS, Dobbins JW, Burrell M, et al: Biliary tract abnormalities in patients with arteriohepatic dysplasia. Dig Dis Sci 27:815-820, 1982.

39. Ward EM, Kiely MJ, Maus TP, et al: Hilar biliary strictures after liver transplantation: Cholangiography and percutaneous treatment. Radiology 177:259-263, 1990.

40. Batts KP: Ischemic cholangitis. Mayo Clin Proc 73:380-385, 1998.

41. Ahrens EH Jr, Payne MA, Kunkel HG, et al: Primary biliary cirrhosis. Medicine (Baltimore) 29:299, 1950.

42. Hiramatsu K, Aoyama H, Zen Y, et al: Proposal of a new staging and grading system of the liver for primary biliary cirrhosis. Histopathology 49:466-478, 2006.

43. Lindor KD: Primary biliary cirrhosis. In Feldman M, Scharschmidt BF, Sleisenger MH (eds): Sleisenger and Fordtran's Gastrointestinal and Liver Disease, 6th ed. Philadelphia, WB Saunders, 1998, pp 1275-1283.

44. Scheuer PJ: Pathologic features and evolution of primary biliary cirrhosis and primary sclerosing cholangitis. Mayo Clin Proc 73:179-183, 1998.

45. Nakanuma Y: Distribution of B lymphocytes in nonsuppurative cholangitis in primary biliary cirrhosis. Hepatology 18:570-575, 1993.

46. Poupon R, Poupon RE: Primary biliary cirrhosis. In Zakim D, Boyer TD (eds): Hepatology: A Textbook of Liver Disease, 3rd ed. Philadelphia, WB Saunders, 1996, pp 1329-1365.

47. van Dam GM, Gips CH, Reisman Y, et al: Major clinical events, signs, and severity assessment scores related to actual survival in patients who died from primary biliary cirrhosis. A long-term historical cohort study. Hepatogastroenterology 46:108-115, 1999.

48. Summerfield JA, Elias E, Hungerford GD, et al: The biliary system in primary biliary cirrhosis: A study by endoscopic retrograde cholangiopancreatography. Gastroenterology 70:240-243, 1976.

49. Blachar A, Federle MP, Brancatelli G: Primary biliary cirrhosis: Clinical, pathologic, and helical CT findings in 53 patients. Radiology 220:329-336, 2001.

50. Wenzel JS, Donohoe A, Ford KL, et al: Primary biliary cirrhosis: MR imaging findings and description of MR imaging periportal halo sign. AJR 176:885-889, 2001.

51. Bass NM: Sclerosing cholangitis and recurrent pyogenic cholangitis. In Feldman M, Scharschmidt BF, Sleisenger MH (eds): Sleisenger and Fordtran's Gastrointestinal and Liver Disease, 6th ed. Philadelphia, WB Saunders, 1998, pp 1275-1283.

52. Carpenter HA: Bacterial and parasitic cholangitis. Mayo Clin Proc 73:473-478, 1998.

53. Pokorny CS, McCaughan GW, Gallagher ND, et al: Sclerosing cholangitis and biliary tract calculi: Primary or secondary? Gut 33:1376-1380, 1992.

54. Dodd GD 3rd, Niedzwiecki GA, Campbell WL, Baron RL: Bile duct calculi in patients with primary sclerosing cholangitis. Radiology 203:443-447, 1997.

55. vanSonnenberg E, Casola G, Cubberley DA, et al: Oriental cholangiohepatitis: Diagnostic imaging and interventional management. AJR 146:327-331, 1986.

56. Chan FL, Man SW, Leong LLY, et al: Evaluation of recurrent pyogenic cholangitis with CT: Analysis of 50 patients. Radiology 170:165-169, 1989.

57. Lim JH, Ko YT, Lee DH, et al: Oriental cholangiohepatitis: Sonographic findings in 48 cases. AJR 155:511-514, 1990.

58. Kusano S, Okada Y, Endo T, et al: Oriental cholangiohepatitis: Correlation between portal vein occlusion and hepatic atrophy. AJR 158:1011-1014, 1992.

59. Schulman A: Non-Western patterns of biliary stones and the role of ascariasis. Radiology 162:425-430, 1987.

60. Kerlan RK Jr, Pogany AC, Goldberg HI, et al: Radiologic intervention in Oriental cholangiohepatitis. AJR 145:809-813, 1985.

61. Dolmatch BL, Laing FC, Federle MP, et al: AIDS-related cholangitis: Radiographic findings in nine patients. Radiology 163:313-316, 1987.

62. Cockerill FR, Hurley DV, Malagelada JR, et al: Polymicrobial cholangitis and Kaposi's sarcoma in blood product transfusion-related acquired immune deficiency syndrome. Am J Med 80:1237-1241, 1986.

63. McCarty M, Choudhri AH, Helbert M, et al: Radiological features of AIDS-related cholangitis. Clin Radiol 40:582-585, 1989.

64. Collins CE, Forbes A, Harcourt-Webster JN, et al: Radiological and pathological features of AIDS-related polypoid cholangitis. Clin Radiol 48:307-310, 1993.

65. Da Silva F, Boudghene F, Lecomte I, et al: Sonography in AIDS-related cholangitis: Prevalence and cause of an echogenic nodule in the distal end of the common bile duct. AJR 160:1205-1207, 1993.

66. Pien EH, Zeman RK, Benjamin SB, et al: Iatrogenic sclerosing cholangitis following hepatic arterial chemotherapy infusion. Radiology 156:329-330, 1985.

67. Andrews JC, Kuntsen C, Terio P, et al: Hepatobiliary toxicity of 5-fluoro-2-deoxyuridine: intra-arterial versus portal venous routes of infusion. Invest Radiol 26:461-464, 1991.

68. Botet JF, Watson RC, Kemeny N, et al: Cholangitis complicating intra-arterial chemotherapy in liver metastasis. Radiology 156:335-337, 1985.

69. Shea WJ Jr, Demas BD, Goldberg HI, et al: Sclerosing cholangitis associated with hepatic arterial FUDR chemotherapy: Radiographic-histologic correlation. AJR 146:717-721, 1986.

70. Cevallos AM, Farthing MJG: Parasitic infections of the gastrointestinal tract. Curr Opin Gastroenterol 9:96-102, 1993.

71. Schulman A: Ultrasound appearances of intra- and extrahepatic biliary ascariasis. Abdom Imaging 23:60-66, 1998.

72. Larrubia JR, Ladero JM, Mendoza JL, et al: The role of sonography in the early diagnosis of biliopancreatic Ascaris infestation. J Clin Gastroenterol 22:48-50, 1996.

73. Cremin BJ: Ultrasonic diagnosis of biliary ascariasis: "A bull's eye in the triple O." Br J Radiol 55:683-684, 1982.

74. Cerri GG, Leite GJ, Simoes JB, et al: Ultrasonic evaluation of ascaris in the biliary tract. Radiology 146:753-754, 1983.

75. Lim JH: Radiologic findings of clonorchiasis. AJR 155:1001-1008, 1990.

76. Choi BI, Kim HJ, Han MC, et al: CT findings of clonorchiasis. AJR 152:281-284, 1989.

77. Choi BI, Park JH, Kim YI, et al: Peripheral cholangiocarcinoma and clonorchiasis: CT findings. Radiology 169:149-153, 1988.

78. Choi BI, Kim TK, Han JK: MRI of clonorchiasis and cholangiocarcinoma. J Magn Reson Imaging 8:359-366, 1998.

79. Van Beers B, Pringot J, Geubel A, et al: Hepatobiliary fascioliasis: Noninvasive imaging findings. Radiology 174:809-810, 1990.

80. Ooms HWA, Puylaert JBCM, van der Werf SDJ: Biliary fascioliasis: US and endoscopic retrograde cholangiopancreatography findings. Eur Radiol 2:1-4, 1994.

81. Mergen H, Genc H, Tavusbay C: Assessment of liver hydatid cyst cases—10 years' experience in Turkey. Trop Doct 37:54-56, 2007.

82. Delis SG, Bakoyiannis A, Exintabelones T, et al: Rare localizations of the hydatid disease: Experience from a single center. J Gastrointest Surg 11:195-198, 2007.

Postsurgical and Traumatic Lesions of the Biliary Tract

Gabriela Gayer, MD • Daphna Weinstein, MD • Marjorie Hertz, MD • Rivka Zissin, MD

Gallstone disease is a very common disorder, and more cholecystectomies are performed each year in the United States than any other elective abdominal operation.[1,2] In the United States alone, an estimated 700,000 people undergo cholecystectomy for gallstones each year.[2] Most cholecystectomies are currently performed laparoscopically; this approach is now considered the standard therapeutic option for cholelithiasis.[3]

This chapter focuses on the complications of laparoscopic cholecystectomy (LC) and on the role of imaging in diagnosis and in nonsurgical management.

Biliary tract injury from blunt and penetrating trauma is also discussed. These injuries are rare and difficult to detect, and are associated with a high morbidity and mortality if left untreated.[4-6]

CHOLECYSTECTOMY—NORMAL AND ABNORMAL POSTSURGICAL FINDINGS

LC has replaced open cholecystectomy (OC) as the accepted therapy for symptomatic gallbladder (GB) disease, because it entails less postoperative pain, shorter hospital stay, improved cosmetic results, and earlier return to work.[7]

Technical Considerations of Laparoscopic Cholecystectomy

The most common indications for LC are symptomatic cholelithiasis, acalculous cholecystitis, symptomatic GB polyps, and GB dyskinesia.[8-10] Contraindications include inability to undergo general anesthesia, intractable coagulopathy, and end-stage liver disease.[7]

Conversion of LC to OC occurs in 5% to 10%, most often due to adhesions.[3,11] LC is performed with the aid of four trocars placed through the abdominal wall (Fig. 83-1A). The first trocar is inserted at the umbilicus after a pneumoperitoneum of 15 mm Hg has been created by insufflating carbon dioxide through a Veress needle inserted in this location. A laparoscope is then introduced and three other trocars are inserted under direct vision, enabled by the laparoscope. The placement sites of these trocars are referred to as ports and their location is fairly standardized in the epigastrium and right abdomen (Fig. 83-1B). Then specialized surgical instruments are placed through the trocar barrels. Under laparoscopic visualization, blunt dissection is used to identify and isolate the cystic duct and artery. Clips are placed on these structures (Fig. 83-1C), and they are then divided. The GB is dissected off the liver bed and the GB fossa is coagulated

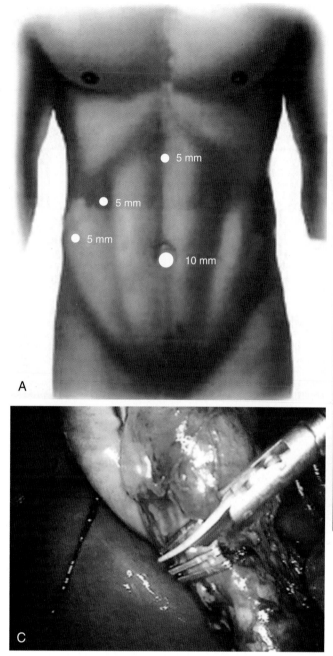

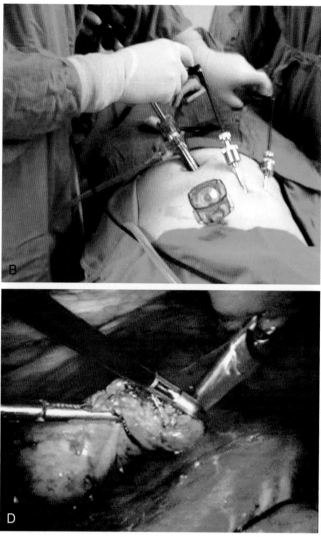

Figure 83-1. Laparoscopic surgery. A. The four trocar insertion sites during laparoscopic cholecytectomy. **B.** Trocars in place during surgery. **C.** Clips are applied to cystic duct. **D.** Gallbladder is prepared for removal.

as necessary. The GB is removed (Fig. 83-1D) through the periumbilical port. With a successful laparoscopic procedure, the patient can be discharged the next day.[7,9]

Normal Imaging Findings after Uncomplicated Laparoscopic Cholecystectomy

Imaging findings in the early postoperative period are minimal and include the following:

- *A small amount of pneumoperitoneum*[12,13]—the volume of free air after laparoscopic procedures is generally smaller and lasts for a shorter time compared to open surgery, because of the very small incisions in the abdominal wall and the use of carbon dioxide, which is rapidly absorbed.[14-16]

- *Subcutaneous emphysema* results from dissection of insufflated carbon dioxide around the trocars into the soft tissues. This finding is quite common in the first 24 to 48 hours after surgery[13,17] (Fig. 83-2).

- Trocar insertion causes *small densities in the subcutaneous fat of the anterior abdominal wall*.[17] Small postoperative fluid collections are often identified in the GB fossa and may be accompanied by a small amount of fluid in the pelvis.[17-20] These fluid collections are usually asymptomatic and resolve spontaneously.[18]

- *Permanent surgical materials* such as surgical clips are a common finding at the GB fossa. Absorbable hemostatic sponges, occasionally used intraoperatively to control bleeding, may cause diagnostic confusion. The most commonly used of these materials is gelatin sponge

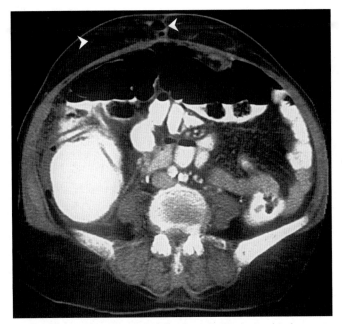

Figure 83-2. Subcutaneous air following LC. CT obtained 2 days post-LC shows gas bubbles in the abdominal wall in the area of the umbilicus, a normal postoperative findings (*arrowheads*).

(Gelfoam; Pharmacia and Upjohn, Kalamazoo, MI) or oxidized reabsorbable cellulose (Surgicel; Ethicon, Somerville, NJ). These are gradually absorbed over time. On CT, these absorbable materials appear as masses with a mixed or low attenuation and with central and occasionally peripheral gas collections (Fig. 83-3). This can be confused with a postoperative abscess or fluid collection, and a discussion with the surgeon may help make this differentiation.[21] If not, serial CT examinations can be performed, as the absorbable material should disappear over a period of weeks.

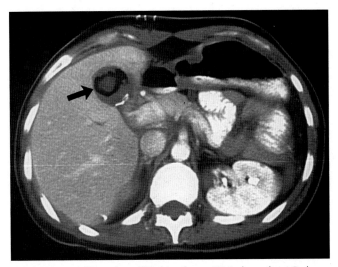

Figure 83-3. Gelfoam in gallbladder fossa. CT 3 days after LC shows heterogeneous density consisting of fluid and air (*arrow*), in gallbladder fossa adjacent to surgical clips. Gelfoam, used in this patient for hemostasis, accounts for this finding.

POSTSURGICAL COMPLICATIONS

The postoperative complication rate for LC is less than that for OC.[8,22,23] Risk factors for complications include previous and current attacks of cholecystitis, male gender, advanced age, and previous abdominal surgery.[7]

Complications of LC include those associated with the laparoscopic procedure itself, as well as those occurring after cholecystectomy.[9] The former include abdominal wall or omental bleeding, intraperitoneal or retroperitoneal vessel injury, gastrointestinal perforation, and solid visceral injury.[9] The latter include GB fossa bleeding, bile duct injury, bile leakage, GB perforation, retained biliary stones, "dropped" stones, and biliary strictures.[9] The majority of complications present in the early postoperative period, but others may appear weeks and even months after the procedure.[18,24]

A postoperative complication should be suspected if the patient develops symptoms such as fever, persistent abdominal or shoulder tip pain, jaundice, leukocytosis, tachycardia, vomiting, or bile leakage from a drain or wound site.

Biliary tract injuries are the most serious complication of cholecystectomy and include bile leak from the cystic duct stump or small aberrant bile ducts, retained stones, bile duct strictures, and spilled stones in the peritoneal cavity.[18,25] These injuries are often not recognized at the time of surgery, and there is a delay in diagnosis.[22,23,25,26]

Bile Duct Injury and Bile Leak

Bile duct injuries include tear, transection, and ligation.[27] The reported incidence of bile duct injuries from LC is 0.1% to 1.3%,[25,28-32] higher than that after OC (0.1% to 0.2%).[7,29,30] They seem also to be more severe.[22,33-35] Risk factors include acute or chronic inflammation, inadequate exposure, patient obesity, and congenital anatomic anomalies of the bile ducts.[36] The typical injury is a defect lesion of the common bile duct (CBD). This is due to a part of the CBD having been mistaken for the cystic duct and been partially or completely transected.[31]

Bile leaks usually derive from the cystic duct stump or the GB bed. Leaks from the cystic duct stump are due to clip displacement or necrosis of the cystic duct after clipping.[31] Leaks most often occur when dissection of the cystic duct and common hepatic duct is difficult due to adhesions and less often from interrupted aberrant ducts.[17,31]

Bile leaks are usually detected during the early postoperative period. Patients most often present within days to weeks after surgery with obstructive jaundice, progressive elevation of liver function tests, or leakage of bile from a drain.[37,38]

Bile can leak freely into the peritoneal cavity, resulting in sterile or infected biliary ascites (Figs. 83-4 through 83-7). Alternatively, bile can accumulate into a loculated fluid collection, resulting in a sterile biloma or an infected subhepatic or subdiaphragmatic abscess[36,39] (Figs. 83-4A, 83-8, and 83-9).

The definitive treatment of bile duct injuries remains controversial. A bile leak from the cystic duct stump can be managed successfully by endoscopic stenting; endoscopic sphincterotomy alone usually is insufficient to stop the leak.[26] A bile leak from the CBD may require a different approach: some groups support the use of endoscopic biliary stents,[40] while others suggest that this merely delays satisfactory surgical treatment.[41]

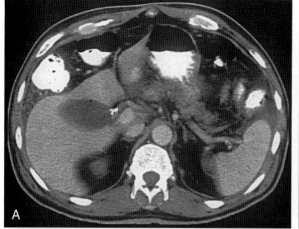

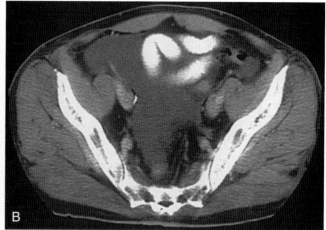

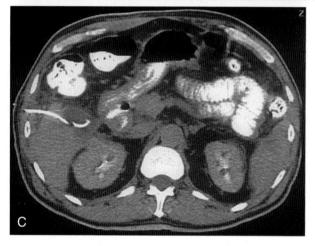

Figure 83-4. Bile leak resulting in a biloma and biliary ascites. A. CT several days after LC shows a biloma in the gallbladder fossa adjacent to surgical clips. Free fluid surrounds the spleen. **B.** Pelvis shows a large amount of clear fluid, its density compatible with bile. **C.** Scan following percutaneous drainage.

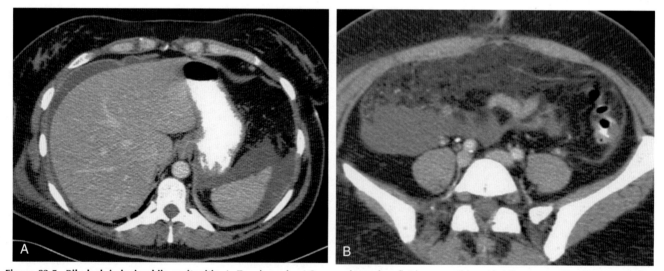

Figure 83-5. Bile leak inducing bile peritonitis. A. Ten days after LC, scan shows free fluid, compatible with bile, surrounding liver, and spleen. **B.** Pelvic CT scan shows a large amount of free fluid and infiltration of mesentery and omentum, indicating infected bile.

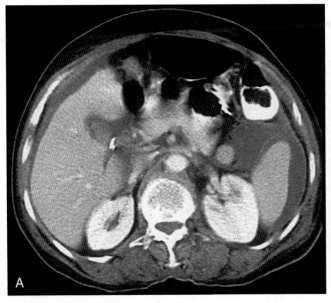

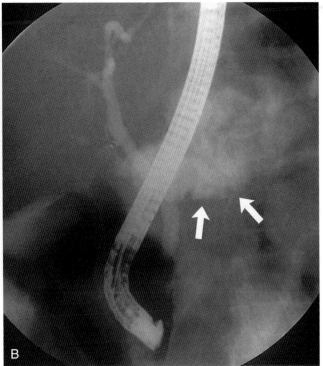

Figure 83-6. Postoperative bile leak. A. CT obtained 5 days after LC shows free fluid in the upper abdomen mainly around the spleen and the liver and some fluid also in the gallbladder fossa, adjacent to a surgical clip. **B.** ERCP after the CT study shows extensive extravasation, probably from the cystic duct remnant (*arrows*).

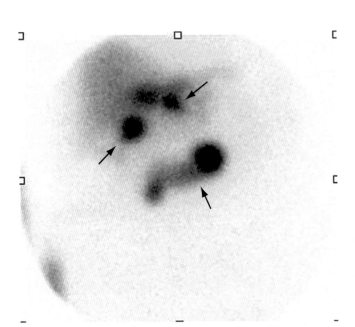

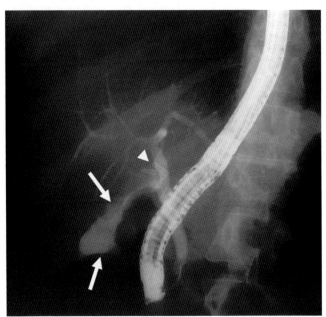

Figure 83-7. Bile leakage from choledochoduodenostomy. Four days after LC, which was converted to OC with subsequent choledochoduo-denostomy due to impacted stones in CBD. Tc 99m-iminodiacetic acid scintigraphy 50-minute image shows extravasated tracer activity in the gallbladder fossa and porta hepatis (*upper two arrows*). Tracer activity is also present in the duodenum (*inferior arrow*), indicating bile leak but not complete transection. (Courtesy of M. Cohenpour, MD.)

Figure 83-8. Bile leak from cystic duct stump. ERC 9 days after LC shows leak of contrast originating adjacent to surgical clips (*arrowhead*) at the cystic duct stump. The leaking contrast material assumes a pear-shaped configuration, a biloma, resembling the gallbladder (*arrows*).

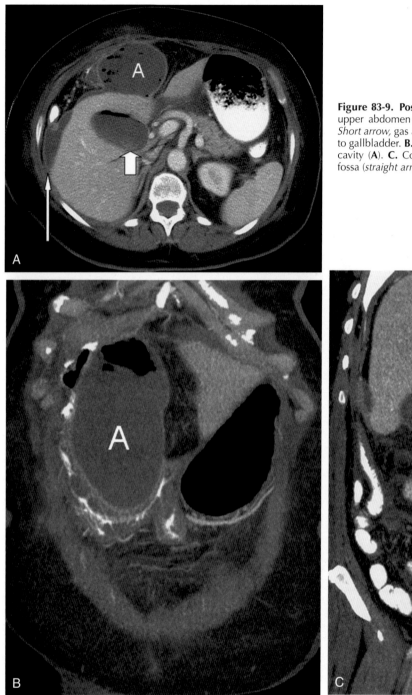

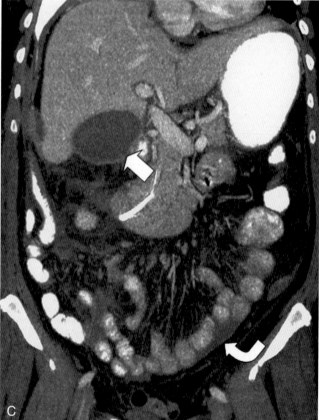

Figure 83-9. Postoperative abscess following LC. A. Axial image of upper abdomen shows gas containing abscess (**A**) anterior to liver. *Short arrow,* gas and fluid in gallbladder fossa; *long arrow,* fluid lateral to gallbladder. **B.** Coronal reformatted image shows full extent abscess cavity (**A**). **C.** Coronal reformatted image shows fluid in gallbladder fossa (*straight arrow*) and pelvis (*curved arrow*).

Retained Biliary Stones

Small biliary stones may be present within the cystic duct remnant or intrahepatic or extrahepatic biliary tree.[8] These stones can migrate distally into the CBD, resulting in biliary obstruction. The incidence of retained stones after LC is 0.5%. The diagnosis is usually made in the first 2 postoperative months.[23]

Symptoms of retained CBD stones include jaundice and right upper quadrant pain.[29] On occasion, retained CBD stones may secondarily give rise to biliary leakage from the cystic duct remnant by causing increased biliary pressure that dis-

places the cystic duct clips. This phenomenon is referred to as "cystic duct blowout."[8] Retained stones can usually be extracted at endoscopic retrograde cholangiography (ERC) and sphincterotomy (Fig. 83-10). Open or laparoscopic CBD exploration is only rarely necessary.[23,29]

Bile Duct Strictures

Postoperative bile duct strictures are seen more often since the introduction of LC.[38] The formation of such strictures is attributed to ischemia of the bile duct that may occur during dissection or to an intense connective tissue response with

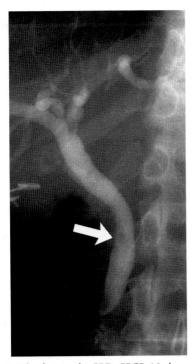

Figure 83-10. Retained stone in CBD. ERCP 16 days after LC shows small calculus (arrow), in distal CBD. Sphincterotomy was performed and the stone was removed.

fibrosis and scarring that can develop after bile duct injury.[36] These strictures are sometimes recognized months to years after surgery, with cholangitis being the most common presenting symptom. Less commonly, patients present with painless jaundice and no evidence of sepsis. Patients may ultimately present with advanced biliary cirrhosis and its complications.[36]

Endoscopic placement of plastic stents can resolve most strictures with permanent dilatation.[42] The most often employed surgical procedure with the best overall results for the treatment of bile duct stricture is a Roux-en-Y hepaticojejunostomy.[38]

Imaging of Postoperative Bile Duct Injuries

Ultrasonography and Computed Tomography

Ultrasonography (US) and contrast-enhanced CT are the initial imaging studies performed in patients with suspected bile leak or biliary sepsis in the early postoperative period. Both studies are useful in detecting intra-abdominal fluid collections, but both are unable to differentiate between a lymphocele, hematoma, seroma, or biloma. The nature of free and loculated fluid can be determined by percutaneous puncture and aspiration under imaging guidance.[39] US can be unreliable in detecting bile leaks, because bile can disperse widely throughout the peritoneal cavity, without collecting in the GB bed or subhepatic space.[25,26,37]

Neither US nor CT can accurately define the source of the leak, and cholangiography is necessary to differentiate a cystic duct versus common bile duct leak.

On US, retained biliary stones may demonstrate highly echogenic foci with posterior acoustic shadowing within a cystic duct remnant, although, in the majority of cases, US fails to demonstrate any abnormality in the absence of CBD dilatation.[8]

US and CT are important in the initial evaluation of a suspected bile duct stricture by demonstrating a dilated biliary tract.[36] The absence of bile duct dilatation, however, does not exclude bile duct injury,[25,37] and further investigations will often be necessary. The choice lies between hepatobiliary scintigraphy, percutaneous transhepatic cholangiography (PTC), endoscopic retrograde cholangiopancreatography (ERCP), and magnetic resonance cholangiopancreatography (MRCP).

Hepatobiliary Scintigraphy

In a stable, nonjaundiced patient, hepatobiliary scintigraphy is a good method for diagnosing bile leaks after cholecystectomy, with an accuracy of about 85%.[24,43] However, the anatomical site of the leak and level of injury cannot be determined by this study[25] (see Fig. 83-7).

Interpretation of scintigraphy alone without ERC may lead to underestimation of the severity of the complication. This might occur in case of ductal transection, when scintigraphy may demonstrate merely bile leakage and not the extent of the injury.[24]

Percutaneous Transhepatic Cholangiography

PTC is a superb method for evaluating patients with bile duct strictures. PTC is superior to ERCP by virtue of its ability to clearly demonstrate the proximal biliary tree, which will be used in surgical reconstruction. Furthermore, PTC can be followed by placement of percutaneous transhepatic catheters, which are useful in decompressing the biliary system, to either treat or prevent cholangitis. These catheters can also assist in surgical reconstruction and provide access to the biliary tract for nonoperative dilatation.[18,26,29]

Endoscopic Retrograde Cholangiopancreatography

ERCP is an excellent test for the diagnosis and management of biliary complications of LC (Fig. 83-11; see Figs. 83-6B, 83-8, 83-10) and may be the only study necessary when the injury is in the distal CBD.

With high ductal injuries or when complete obstruction is demonstrated on ERCP, PTC is necessary to determine the proximal level of bile duct injury.[26,29] When both studies are performed, a gap of several centimeters may be present between a blind-ending distal duct demonstrated on ERCP and the proximal bile ducts opacified on PTC, precluding percutaneous transhepatic stricture dilatation.[29] ERCP also has an important role in the treatment of bile leaks, as this complication can be managed endoscopically in 80% of patients.[37] In case of retained biliary stones, ERCP offers both diagnostic and therapeutic options.[8] ERCP is, however, an invasive technique, requires patient sedation, and carries a significant risk of postprocedural complications.[8]

Magnetic Resonance Cholangiopancreatography

MRCP is a noninvasive technique that provides excellent delineation of the biliary anatomy. This technique is rapidly

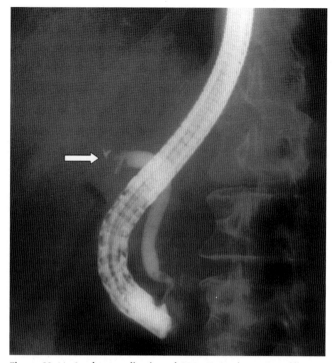

Figure 83-11. Inadvertent ligation of CBD. ERCP shows CBD filling to level of surgical clips (*arrow*), indicating the site where the cystic duct had originated. No contrast is identified proximally in the bile duct.

evolving and may become the initial step in the evaluation of patients with suspected bile duct injuries.[8,36] It can accurately diagnose postoperative bile duct injuries, retained biliary stones, and biliary strictures and can characterize and anatomically classify these injuries for planning corrective surgery, thus obviating the need for ERCP in some patients.[44-47] The main limitations of MRCP are that the quality of images depends heavily on the patient's ability to adequately breath-hold and its relatively high cost.[8] MRCP is discussed in detail in Chapter 77.

Spilled Gallstones

GB perforation and intrapertioneal spillage of gallstones occurring during dissection and GB removal are estimated to occur in up to one third of patients undergoing LC.[48,49] In contrast, this complication is rarely encountered with OC, because the entire intra-abdominal field remains well visualized during the surgery, so that any spillage can be immediately addressed intraoperatively.[50]

Despite the high incidence of spillage, complications resulting from "spilled" gallstones (also often referred to as "dropped" gallstones) are rare.[48,49] The most frequent complication is the formation of an intra-abdominal abscess, most of them in or around the liver.[49,51,52] Other complications include abdominal wall abscess and fistula.[31,48,49] Clinically, patients may present with abdominal pain, abdominal swelling,

fever and/or chills, nausea and/or vomiting, weight loss, and other symptoms.[49] The delay between LC and abscess presentation can be considerable (mean, 5.5 months; range, 0-36 months) because of a combination of the indolent nature of the inflammatory process and the sometimes unusual site of the abscess.[49,50]

Transdiaphragmatic migration of stones can occur either from gallstone erosion through the diaphragm into the thorax or from formation of a subphrenic abscess, which subsequently connects supradiaphragmatically into the pleural space, the lung, or the bronchial tree.[53] This results in cholelithoptysis (expectoration of gallstones) or pleurolithiasis.[31,49,54]

US and CT may demonstrate spilled stones lying free in the abdomen, mainly around the liver, or as a nidus of an abscess[50] (Fig. 83-12). The majority of these abscesses are confined to the subhepatic space or the retroperitoneum below the subhepatic space.[50] Unusual locations have, however, been described, including the right thorax, the subphrenic space, the abdominal wall at trocar sites, and the sites of incisional hernias.[50] These abscesses appear on CT as one or more fluid collections containing small opacities, ranging in density from hypodense to that of partially or completely calcified nodules, compatible with the dropped gallstones.[48,50,53] On US, echogenic shadowing foci within a fluid collection are typical of dropped stones.[50] The presence of calculi within a collection is virtually diagnostic of spilled stones complicated by an abscess formation.[50] Dropped gallstone–associated abscesses often require surgical removal as opposed to imaging-guided percutaneous drainage.[50]

IMAGING OF POST-TRAUMATIC LESIONS

Extrahepatic biliary tract and GB injuries are rare but may occur after both blunt and penetrating abdominal trauma.[4,5] These injuries may be difficult to detect and are associated with high morbidity and mortality.[6] The most common location of biliary injury is the GB,[4,6] found in up to 3% of patients undergoing laparotomy after blunt trauma.[55,56] It is often associated with injuries to other abdominal organs, most often the liver.[4,6,57] Blunt GB injuries may be classified into different degrees of severity: contusion, laceration/perforation, and complete avulsion.[6,55] Initial symptoms may be minimal with gradual clinical deterioration related to spillage of bile into the peritoneal cavity.[58]

GB injuries can be detected with CT, US, hepatobiliary scintigraphy, or MRCP. CT is the most widely used modality in the evaluation of abdominal trauma. CT findings of GB injury are largely nonspecific and are often overlooked because of injuries to adjacent organs. Pericholecystic fluid is often present. It may, however, originate from injuries to the liver or right kidney and not necessarily from the GB.[6,55] Dense layering fluid within the GB lumen may be an indication of intraluminal hemorrhage (Fig. 83-13), although milk of calcium or vicarious excretion of intravenous contrast media from prior imaging studies may cause similar findings and present a diagnostic dilemma. A collapsed GB, particularly in a fasting patient, or thickening or poor definition of its wall should raise the possibility of GB perforation or avulsion.[6,55]

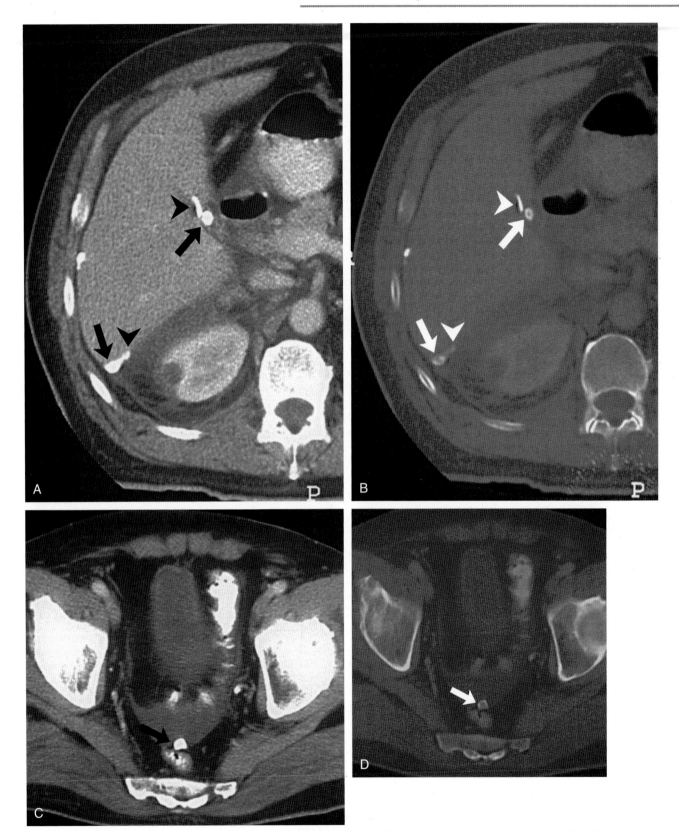

Figure 83-12. Spilled gallstones. A and **B.** CT at the level of the midabdomen in different window settings (**A,** soft tissue; **B,** bone) in a patient with jaundice 3 months after LC shows two small calcified foci (*arrows*), one in the gallbladder fossa and the other posterior to the liver, both adjacent to surgical clips (*arrowheads*). The calcified rim, typical of a gallstone, is more clearly seen on the bone window (**B**). **C** and **D.** Pelvic CT in different window settings (**C,** soft tissue; **D,** bone) shows a small amount of free fluid with a small calcified focus in the dependent part of fluid (*arrow*) (**C**). More densely calcified rim, typical of a gallstone (*arrow*), is better seen on corresponding bone window setting (**D**).

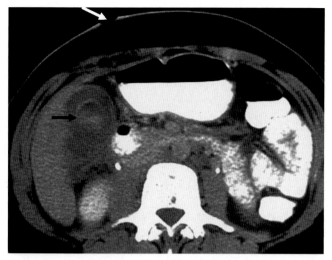

Figure 83-13. Gallbladder trauma. CT 2 days after stab wound to the right upper quadrant shows gallbladder wall thickening with an intra-luminal bile-blood level and infiltration of the pericholecystic tissue (*black arrow*). A subcutaneous RUQ (*white arrow*) defect indicates the location of the penetrating knife. At surgery two lacerations were found in the anterior and posterior aspect of the gallbladder with mild biliary peritonitis. (From Zissin R, Osadchy A, Shapiro-Feinberg M, et al: CT of a thickened-wall gall bladder. Br J Radiol 76:137-143, 2003.)

References

1. Speets AM, Van der Graaf Y, Hoes AW, et al: Expected and unexpected gallstones in primary care. Scand J Gastroenterol 42:351-355, 2007.
2. Mulvihill SJ: Surgical management of gallstone disease and postoperative complications. Semin Gastrointest Dis 14:237-244, 2003.
3. Livingston EH, Rege RV: A nationwide study of conversion from laparoscopic to open cholecystectomy. Am J Surg 188:205-211, 2004.
4. Burgess P, Fulton RL: Gallbladder and extrahepatic biliary duct injury following abdominal trauma. Injury 23:413-414, 1992.
5. Carrillo EH, Lottenberg L, Saridakis A: Blunt traumatic injury of the gallbladder. J Trauma 57:408-409, 2004.
6. Gupta A, Stuhlfaut JW, Fleming KW, et al: Blunt trauma of the pancreas and biliary tract: A multimodality imaging approach to diagnosis. RadioGraphics 24:1381-1395, 2004.
7. Strasberg S, Drebin J: Calculous biliary disease. In Greenfield LJ (ed): Surgery, Scientific Principles and Practice. Philadelphia, Lippincott Williams & Wilkins, 2001, pp 1011-1033.
8. Lohan D, Walsh S, McLoughlin R, Murphy J: Imaging of the complications of laparoscopic cholecystectomy. Eur Radiol 97:261-262, 2005.
9. Wright TB, Bertino RB, Bishop AF, et al: Complications of laparoscopic cholecystectomy and their interventional radiologic management. RadioGraphics 13:119-128, 1993.
10. Bittner R: The standard of laparoscopic cholecystectomy. Langenbecks Arch Surg 389:157-163, 2004.
11. Fathy O, Zeid MA, Abdallah T, et al: Laparoscopic cholecystectomy: A report on 2000 cases. Hepatogastroenterology 50:967-971, 2003.
12. McAllister JD, D'Altorio RA, Rao V: CT findings after uncomplicated and complicated laparoscopic cholecystectomy. Semin Ultrasound CT MR 14:356-367, 1993.
13. McAllister JD, D'Altorio RA, Snyder A: CT findings after uncomplicated percutaneous laparoscopic cholecystectomy. J Comput Assist Tomogr 15:770-772, 1991.
14. Schauer PR, Page CP, Ghiatas AA, et al: Incidence and significance of subdiaphragmatic air following laparoscopic cholecystectomy. Am Surg 63:132-136, 1997.
15. Millitz K, Moote DJ, Sparrow RK, et al: Pneumoperitoneum after laparoscopic cholecystectomy: Frequency and duration as seen on upright chest radiographs. AJR Am J Roentgenol 163:837-839, 1994.
16. Gayer G, Jonas T, Apter S, et al: Postoperative pneumoperitoneum as detected by CT: Prevalence, duration, and relevant factors affecting its possible significance. Abdom Imaging 25:301-305, 2000.
17. Moran J, Del Grosso E, Wills J, et al: Laparoscopic cholecystectomy: Imaging of complications and normal postoperative CT appearance. Abdom Imaging 19:143-146, 1994.
18. McGahan JP, Stein M: Complications of laparoscopic cholecystectomy: Imaging and intervention. AJR Am J Roentgenol 165:1089-1097, 1995.
19. Choi JY, Kim MJ, Park MS, et al: Imaging findings of biliary and nonbiliary complications following laparoscopic surgery. Eur Radiol 16:1906-1914, 2006.
20. Hakansson K, Leander P, Ekberg O, Hakansson HO: MR imaging of upper abdomen following cholecystectomy. Normal and abnormal findings. Acta Radiol 42:181-186, 2001.
21. O'Connor AR, Coakley FV: Retained surgical materials in the postoperative abdomen and pelvis. Semin Ultrasound CT MR 25:290-302, 2004.
22. Deziel DJ, Millikan KW, Economou SG, et al: Complications of laparoscopic cholecystectomy: A national survey of 4,292 hospitals and an analysis of 77,604 cases. Am J Surg 165:9-14, 1993.
23. Konstadoulakis MM, Antonakis PT, Karatzikos G, et al: Intraoperative findings and postoperative complications in laparoscopic cholecystectomy: The Greek experience with 5,539 patients in a single center. J Laparoendosc Adv Surg Tech A 14:31-36, 2004.
24. Trerotola SO, Savader SJ, Lund GB, et al: Biliary tract complications following laparoscopic cholecystectomy: Imaging and intervention. Radiology 84:195-200, 1992.
25. Thomson BN, Cullinan MJ, Banting SW, Collier NA; Universities of Melbourne Hepatobiliary Group: Recognition and management of biliary complications after laparoscopic cholecystectomy. Aust N Z J Surg 73:183-188, 2003.
26. de Reuver PR, Grossmann I, Busch OR, et al: Referral pattern and timing of repair are risk factors for complications after reconstructive surgery for bile duct injury. Ann Surg 245:763-770, 2007.
27. Seeliger H, Furst A, Zulke C, Jauch KW: Surgical management of bile duct injuries following laparoscopic cholecystectomy: Analysis and follow-up of 28 cases. Langenbecks Arch Surg 387:286-293, 2002.
28. Ahmad F, Saunders RN, Lloyd GM, et al: An algorithm for the management of bile leak following laparoscopic cholecystectomy. Ann R Coll Surg Engl 89:51-56, 2007.
29. Ward EM, LeRoy AJ, Bender CE, et al: Imaging of complications of laparoscopic cholecystectomy. Abdom Imaging 18:150-155, 1993.
30. MacFadyen BV Jr, Vecchio R, Ricardo AE, Mathis CR. Bile duct injury after laparoscopic cholecystectomy. The United States experience. Surg Endosc 12:315-321, 1998.
31. Shamiyeh A, Wayand W. Laparoscopic cholecystectomy: Early and late complications and their treatment. Langenbecks Arch Surg 389:164-171, 2004.
32. Z'graggen K, Wehrli H, Metzger A, et al: Complications of laparoscopic cholecystectomy in Switzerland. A prospective 3-year study of 10,174 patients. Swiss Association of Laparoscopic and Thoracoscopic Surgery. Surg Endosc 12:1303-1310, 1998.
33. Deziel DJ. Complications of cholecystectomy. Incidence, clinical manifestations, and diagnosis. Surg Clin North Am 74:809-823, 1994.
34. Walsh RM, Henderson JM, Vogt DP, et al: Trends in bile duct injuries from laparoscopic cholecystectomy. J Gastrointest Surg 2:458-462, 1998
35. Slater K, Strong RW, Wall DR, Lynch SV: Iatrogenic bile duct injury: The scourge of laparoscopic cholecystectomy. Aust N Z J Surg 72:83-88, 2002
36. Lillemoe KD: Biliary strictures and sclerosing cholangitis. In Greenfield LJ (ed): Surgery, Scientific Principles and Practice. Philadelphia, Lippincott Williams & Wilkins, 2001, pp 1046-1061.
37. Dexter SP, Miller GV, Davides D, et al: Relaparoscopy for the detection and treatment of complications of laparoscopic cholecystectomy. Am J Surg 179:316-319, 2000.
38. Lillemoe KD: Benign post-operative bile duct strictures. Baillieres Clin Gastroenterol 11:749-779, 1997.
39. Braithwaite BM, Cabanilla LT, Lilly M: Hepatic subcapsular biloma: A rare complication of laparoscopic cholecystectomy and common bile duct exploration. Curr Surg 60:196-198, 2003.
40. Barton JR, Russell RC, Hatfield AR: Management of bile leaks after laparoscopic cholecystectomy. Br J Surg 82:980-984, 1995
41. Stewart L, Way LW. Bile duct injuries during laparoscopic cholecystectomy. Factors that influence the results of treatment. Arch Surg 130:1123-1128; 1995.
42. Costamagna G, Shah SK, Tringali A: Current management of postoperative complications and benign biliary strictures. Gastrointest Endosc Clin N Am 13:635-648, ix, 2003.
43. Ray CE Jr, Hibbeln JF, Wilbur AC: Complications after laparoscopic cholecystectomy: Imaging findings. AJR 160:1029-1032, 1993.
44. Khalid TR, Casillas VJ, Montalvo BM, et al: Using MR cholangio-pancreatography to evaluate iatrogenic bile duct injury. AJR 177:1347-1352, 2001.

45. Ward J, Sheridan MB, Guthrie JA, et al: Bile duct strictures after hepatobiliary surgery: Assessment with MR cholangiography. Radiology 231:101-108, 2004.
46. Ragozzino A, De Ritis R, Mosca A, et al: Value of MR cholangiography in patients with iatrogenic bile duct injury after cholecystectomy. AJR 183:1567-1572, 2004.
47. Park MS, Kim KW, Yu JS, et al: Early biliary complications of laparoscopic cholecystectomy: Evaluation on T2-weighted MR cholangiography in conjunction with mangafodipir trisodium-enhanced T1-weighted MR cholangiography. AJR 183:1559-1566, 2004.
48. Bennett AA, Gilkeson RC, Haaga JR, et al: Complications of "dropped" gallstones after laparoscopic cholecystectomy: Technical considerations and imaging findings. Abdom Imaging 25:190-193, 2000.
49. Brockmann JG, Kocher T, Senninger NJ, Schurmann GM. Complications due to gallstones lost during laparoscopic cholecystectomy. Surg Endosc 16:1226-1232, 2002.
50. Morrin MM, Kruskal JB, Hochman MG, et al: Radiologic features of complications arising from dropped gallstones in laparoscopic cholecystectomy patients. AJR 174:1441-1445, 2000.
51. Viera FT, Armellini E, Rosa L, Ravetta V, et al: Abdominal spilled stones: Ultrasound findings. Abdom Imaging 31:564-567, 2006.
52. Zamir G, Lyass S, Pertsemlidis D, Katz B: The fate of the dropped gallstones during laparoscopic cholecystectomy. Surg Endosc 13:68-70, 1999.
53. Koc E, Suher M, Oztugut SU, et al: Retroperitoneal abscess as a late complication following laparoscopic cholecystectomy. Med Sci Monit 10:CS27-29, 2004.
54. Hanna SJ, Barakat O, Watkin S. Cholelithoptysis: an unusual delayed complication of laparoscopic cholecystectomy. J Hepatobiliary Pancreat Surg 11:190-192, 2004
55. Erb RE, Mirvis SE, Shanmuganathan K: Gallbladder injury secondary to blunt trauma: CT findings. J Comput Assist Tomogr 18:778-784, 1994.
56. Chen X, Talner LB, Jurkovich GJ: Gallbladder avulsion due to blunt trauma. AJR Am J Roentgenol 177:822, 2001.
57. Sharma O: Blunt gallbladder injuries: presentation of twenty-two cases with review of the literature. J Trauma 39:576-580, 1995.
58. Zissin R, Osadchy A, Shapiro-Feinberg M, et al: CT of a thickened-wall gall bladder. Br J Radiol 76:137-143, 2003.

chapter

84

Gallbladder and Biliary Tract: Differential Diagnosis

Richard M. Gore, MD

GALLBLADDER IMAGING

Table 84-1
Gallbladder Filling Defects

Common
Gallstones
Sludge
Mucosal folds
Partial volume artifact (ultrasound, CT)
Adenomyomatosis
Cholesterolosis
Pseudomass-duodenal impression (ultrasound)
Air volume averaging with adjacent bowel (CT, MR)

Uncommon
Carcinoma
Metastases, especially melanoma, lung, kidney, esophagus
Adenoma
Papilloma
Villous hyperplasia
Epithelial cyst
Mucus retention cyst
Worms and parasites: *Ascaris, Paragonimus, Clonorchis, Filaria, Schistosoma, Fasciola*
Fibrinous debris
Desquamated mucosa
Metachromatic leukodystrophy
Ectopic pancreatic, gastric, hepatic, intestinal, prostatic tissue
Varices
Inflammatory polyp
Food via enterobiliary fistula
Fibroadenoma
Neurinoma
Hemangioma

Table 84-2
Enlarged Gallbladder

Common
Cystic duct or common bile duct obstruction
Hyperalimentation
Postsurgery
Prolonged fasting
Vagotomy
Diabetes mellitus
AIDS
Mucocele
Empyema
Hydrops
Hepatitis
Pancreatitis
Alcoholism
Narcotic analgesia
Anticholinergics

Uncommon
Kawasaki's syndrome
Leptospirosis
Scarlet fever
Acromegaly

Table 84-3
Small Gallbladder

Chronic cholecystitis
Congenital multiseptate gallbladder
Postprandial study
Chronic cholecystitis
Cystic fibrosis
Congenital hypoplasia
Congenital multiseptate gallbladder
Hypoplastic gallbladder

Table 84-4
Gallbladder Wall Thickening

Common
Acute cholecystitis
Chronic cholecystitis
Hyperplastic cholecystosis
Hepatitis
Portal hypertension
Right-sided heart failure
Hypoproteinemia or hypoalbuminema
Gallbladder carcinoma
Renal failure
Total parenteral nutrition
Cirrhosis
Sepsis
Infectious mononucleosis
Acute pancreatitis
AIDS
Postprandial study
Pyelonephritis of right kidney

Uncommon
Sclerosing cholangitis
Schistosomiasis
Xanthogranulomatous cholecystitis
Extrahepatic portal vein obstruction
Lymphatic obstruction
Gallbladder wall varices
Multiple myeloma
Lymphoma
Obstructed gallbladder lymphatics
Acute myelogenous leukemia
Brucellosis
Graft-versus-host disease

Table 84-5
Pericholecystic Fluid

Pericholecystic abscess
Pancreatitis
Acute cholecystitis
Pericholecystic abscess
Ascites
Pancreatitis
AIDS
Peritonitis

Table 84-6
Multiseptate Gallbladder

Desquamated gallbladder mucosa
Congenital malformation
Normal folded gallbladder
Desquamated gallbladder mucosa
Cholesterolosis
Adenomyomatosis

Table 84-7
Gas in the Gallbladder or Biliary Tract

Common
Postoperative (e.g., status post sphincterotomy or Whipple's procedure)
Biliary-enteric fistula (see Table 84-8)
Pancreatitis
Emphysematous cholecystitis

Uncommon
Common duct entry into duodenal diverticulum
Crohn's disease
Incompetent sphincter
Carcinoma of the gallbladder, ampulla, duodenum, bile ducts, stomach, colon
Metastases
Lymphoma
Trauma
Status postintubation or ERCP
Parasites: *Strongyloides, Clonorchis, Ascaris*, ruptured amebic abscess of liver

Table 84-8
Cholecystoenteric and Biliary-Enteric Fistula

Common
Gallstone fistula from gallbladder or bile ducts
Postoperative (e.g., Whipple's procedure)

Uncommon
Carcinoma of the gallbladder, bile ducts, duodenum, colon, stomach
Peptic ulcer perforation into biliary tract
Crohn's disease
Diverticulitis of the duodenum or hepatic flexure
Actinomycosis
Tuberculosis
Trauma
Lymphoma
Perforating cholecystitis

ULTRASOUND

Table 84-9
Focal, Mobile, Shadowing Gallbladder Reflectors

Gallstones
Intraluminal gas
Calcified parasites: *Ascaris, Clonorchis, Fasciola*

Table 84-10
Focal, Mobile, Nonshadowing Gallbladder Reflectors

Small stones not in transducer focal zone
Blood clots
Pus
Sludge balls
Parasites: *Ascaris, Clonorchis, Fasciola*
Precipitated contrast material from ERCP
Fibrinous debris
Desquamated mucosa

Table 84-11
Focal, Nonmobile, Shadowing Gallbladder Reflectors

Stone or crystal in Rokitansky-Aschoff sinus
Impacted gallstone
Spiral valve folds
Polyp-containing cholesterol
Adherent gallstone

Table 84-12
Hyperechoic Foci in Gallbladder Wall

Polyps
Adherent stones
Intramural gas in emphysematous cholecystitis
Intramural microabscesses
Rokitansky-Aschoff sinuses

Table 84-13
Nonvisualization of the Gallbladder by Ultrasound

Common
Postprandial contraction
Postcholecystomy
Chronic cholecystitis
Technical factors: obese patient or thin patient with superficial gallbladder
Ectopic gallbladder
Gallbladder obscured by gas

Uncommon
Carcinoma of the gallbladder
"Porcelain" gallbladder
Gangrenous cholecystitis
Emphysematous cholecystitis
Metastases to the gallbladder
Acute hepatic dysfunction (e.g., hepatitis)
Congenital absence (0.03% of population)

Table 84-14
Artifacts That Mimic Gallstones

Partial volume artifact with duodenal impression
Refraction from folds in gallbladder neck
Inspissated sludge
Any cause of intraluminal defect

Table 84-15
Structures That Sonographically Mimic the Gallbladder

Fluid-filled duodenal bulb
Dilated cystic duct remnant
Hepatic cyst
Renal cyst
Omental cyst
Ligamentum teres abscess
Choledochal cyst

COMPUTED TOMOGRAPHY

Table 84-16
Increased Attenuation of Gallbladder Lumen

Gallstones
Sludge
Debris
Vicarious excretion of contrast medium
Hemobilia
Milk of calcium bile
Mucinous adenocarcinoma of the gallbladder
Volume averaging with adjacent structures
Hydrops
Hemorrhagic cholecystitis
Prior ERCP or oral cholecystography

NUCLEAR MEDICINE

Table 84-17
Nonvisualization of the Gallbladder by Scintigraphy

Common
Acute cholecystitis

Uncommon
Prolonged fasting
Carcinoma of the gallbladder
Chronic cholecystitis
Severe hepatocellular disease
Complete common bile duct obstruction
Acute pancreatitis
Nonfasting patient
Gallbladder hydrops
Postcholecystectomy
Hyperalimentation

Rare
Alcoholism
Choledochal cyst
Dubin-Johnson syndrome
Kawasaki's syndrome
Mirizzi's syndrome

Table 84-18
Delayed Visualization of the Gallbladder

Common
Chronic cholecystitis

Uncommon
Acalculous cholecystitis
Pancreatitis
Hepatocellular disease
Total parenteral nutrition
Carcinoma of the gallbladder
Dubin-Johnson syndrome

Table 84-19
Nonvisualization of the Isotope in Bowel

Common
Choledocholithiasis

Uncommon
Obstructive pancreatic carcinoma
Drug-induced cholestasis
Sphincter of Oddi spasm secondary to morphine
Severe hepatocellular disease
Biliary atresia

Rare
Pancreatitis
Cholangiocarcinoma
Sepsis
Choledochal cyst with complete obstruction
Portal vein thrombosis
Surgical ligation of common bile duct

Table 84-20
Delayed Bowel Activity

Common
Choledocholithiasis with incomplete obstruction
Severe hepatocellular disease

Uncommon
Acute and chronic cholecystitis
Sphincter of Oddi spasm, stricture, or tumor
Ascending cholangitis
Choledochal cyst with incomplete obstruction

Table 84-21
"Rim" Sign

Common
Acute cholecystitis
Gangrenous cholecystitis
Emphysema of the gallbladder
Gallbladder perforation

Uncommon
Chronic cholecystitis
Adjacent hepatic inflammatory process
Hepatic amebic abscess

BILIARY TRACT IMAGING

Table 84-22
Filling Defects or Segmental Lesions of Bile Ducts

Common
Gallstone
Air bubble
Blood clot
Sphincter of Oddi or Boyden spasm (pseudocalculus)
Ampullary edema
Sludge or debris
Cholangiocarcinoma
Carcinoma of the ampulla, duodenum, or pancreas
Stricture
Postoperative defect
Dilated crossing vessel
Mirizzi's syndrome

Uncommon
Metastases
Neoplasms: adenoma, papilloma, spindle cell, hamartoma, polyp, sarcoma
Parasites: *Ascaris lumbricoides, Clonorchis sinensis, Fasciola hepatica, Echinococcus granulosus*
Enlarged lymph node
Hydatid cyst eroding into biliary tree

Table 84-24
Biliary Dilatation

Common
Calculus
Advanced age
Carcinoma of pancreas, bile duct, ampulla
Cholangitis
Pancreatitis
Distal ductal stricture: postoperative, inflammatory
Sclerosing cholangitis
Adenopathy with extrinsic compression

Uncommon
Papillitis or fibrosis of ampulla
Caroli's disease
Choledochal cyst, choledochocele
Mirizzi's syndrome
Parasites: *Ascaris, Clonorchis, Fasciola, Echinococcus, Opisthorchis*
Liver abscess
Extrinsic compression from duodenal or ductal diverticulum
Liver infarcts after transcatheter embolization of hepatic artery
Metastasis
Penetrating duodenal ulcer
Biliary diaphragm or web
Extrinsic compression from aneurysm of the hepatic artery or aorta
Extrahepatic biliary atresia
Hepatic fibrosis with ductal ectasia
Retroperitoneal fibrosis

Table 84-23
Bile Duct Narrowing or Obstruction

Malignant Strictures
Cholangiocarcinoma
Hepatoma
Ampullary carcinoma
Lymphoma
Metastasis from neoplasms of pancreas, gallbladder, stomach, lymph nodes, hepatic parenchyma, hepatoduodenal ligament

Benign Strictures
Acquired
Cholangitis
Choledocholithiasis
Papillary stenosis
Sclerosing cholangitis
Cholangiolytic hepatitis
Mirizzi's syndrome
Duodenal diverticulum

Iatrogenic or Traumatic
Surgical injury
Hepatic artery chemotherapy
Trauma
Radiation therapy
Hepatic artery embolization

Infectious
AIDS
Clonorchis sinensis
Fasciola hepatica
Ascaris lumbricoides
Echinococcus
Tuberculous adenitis
Cytomegalovirus

Extrinsic
Acute pancreatitis
Chronic pancreatitis
Tuberculous lymphadenitis
Sarcoid lymphadenitis
Cirrhosis
Hepatitis
Perforated duodenal ulcer
Abscess

Congenital
Biliary atresia
Membranous diaphragm
Congenital hepatic fibrosis
Complicated Caroli's disease

Table 84-25
Biliary Dilatation without Jaundice

Postcholecystectomy
Sequelae of common duct exploration
Early obstruction
Postobstruction
Postcholecystectomy
Advanced age
Worms or parasites
Nonobstructive gallstone
Normal variant
Sequelae of common duct exploration
Intestinal hypomotility

Table 84-26
Biliary Obstruction without Dilatation

Acute severe biliary obstruction (first 3 days)
Cholangiocarcinoma with tumor
Cholangitis
Sclerosing cholangitis
Ascending cholangitis
Debris-filled ducts
Pancreatitis
Hemobilia
Cholangiocarcinoma with tumor encasement

Table 84-27
Cystic Dilatation of the Bile Ducts

Oriental cholangiohepatitis
Papillomatosis of intrahepatic bile ducts
Choledochal cyst
Choledochocele
Caroli's disease
Oriental cholangiohepatitis
Congenital hepatic fibrosis
Papillomatosis of intrahepatic bile ducts

IMAGING FINDINGS IN SPECIFIC GALLBLADDER AND BILIARY DISEASES

Table 84-28
Acute Cholecystitis

Sonographic Findings
Gallbladder wall thickening >3 mm
Gallbladder wall lucency ("halo" sign): three-layer configuration with sonolucent middle layer
Striated wall thickening: alternating echogenic and hypodense mural bands
Gallbladder distention > 5 cm in anteroposterior diameter
Sonographic Murphy sign
Pericholecystic fluid
Pseudomembrane formation
Gallstones

Nuclear Scintigraphy
Nonvisualization of the gallbladder despite the presence of isotope in the bile ducts and duodenum
Rim sign: increased activity in the gallbladder fossa conforming to the inferior hepatic edge

CT
Gallstones, mural thickening, pericholecystic fluid
Increased gallbladder wall enhancement
Focal or nonuniform contrast-enhanced thickening
Mural nodularity, loss of crisp demarcation between gallbladder and liver, mild infiltration of pericholecystic fat
Elevated attenuation of gallbladder bile because of hemorrhage or empyema
Low-density edema in the hepatocholecystic space
Transient hepatic attenuation difference in adjacent liver

MRI
Gallstones, mural thickening, pericholecystic fluid
Gallbladder wall and adjacent tissues demonstrate increased enhancement on gadolinium-enhanced, fat-suppressed images
Transient hepatic intensity difference in adjacent liver

Table 84-29
Chronic Cholecystitis

Sonographic Findings
Gallstones
Smooth irregular gallbladder wall thickening >3 mm
Noncontractility or decreased response after cholecystokinin injection

Nuclear Scintigraphy
Normal, delayed, or absent gallbladder visualization
Visualization of bowel before gallbladder
Noncontractility or decreased response after cholecystokinin injection

CT
Mural thickening and gallstones
Lack of contrast enhancement of gallbladder bile
Small, contracted gallbladder

MRI
Small, irregularly shaped gallbladder with a thickened, mildly enhancing wall on gadolinium-enhanced, fat-suppressed images

Table 84-30
Sclerosing Cholangitis

Location
Intrahepatic and extrahepatic ducts involved (90%)
Intrahepatic ducts only (1-5%)
Extrahepatic ducts only (5-10%)
Cystic duct involved (18%)

Cholangiography
Multifocal strictures with predilection for bifurcations
Small saccular outpouchings
Beaded appearance with alternating segments of dilatation and stenosis
"Pruned tree" appearance with opacification of central ducts and nonfilling of more peripheral ducts
Intrahepatic ductal dilatation
Coarse, nodular mural irregularities
Gallbladder irregularities

CT
Skip dilatation, stenosis, pruning, beading of intrahepatic bile ducts
Dilatation, stenosis, enhancing mural nodularity, thickening, and contrast enhancement of the bile ducts
Mural thickening of the gallbladder
Periportal adenopathy
Caudate lobe hypertrophy
Atrophy lateral segment left lobe liver

Ultrasound
Brightly echogenic portal triads
Mural thickening of the gallbladder and extrahepatic bile ducts
Focal areas of intrahepatic biliary dilatation
Periportal adenopathy
Caudate lobe hypertrophy
Atrophy lateral segment left lobe liver

MRI
Mild duct wall thickening, beading, skip dilatations
Periportal inflammation with mural and periportal enhancement on gadolinium-enhanced T1-weighted imaging
Peripheral, wedge-shaped zones of hyperintense signal on T2-weighted imaging
Increased signal intensity in liver on T1-weighted imaging not corresponding to fat

Table 84-30
Sclerosing Cholangitis (*cont'd*)

Patchy, segmental, peripheral parenchymal enhancement on immediate postgadolinium injection images
Periportal adenopathy
Caudate lobe hypertrophy
Atrophy lateral segment left lobe liver

Hepatobiliary Scintigraphy
Multiple focal areas of isotope retention in the intrahepatic biliary tree
Prolongation of hepatic clearance
Gallbladder visualized in only 70% of cases

Table 84-31
Primary Biliary Cirrhosis

Cholangiography
Only intrahepatic ducts are involved
Tortuous intrahepatic ducts with narrowing, caliber variation, decreased arborization—the "tree in winter" appearance

Hepatobiliary Scintigraphy
Marked prolongation of hepatic isotope clearance
Uniform hepatic isotope retention
Normal visualization of the gallbladder and bile ducts

CT and Ultrasound
Gallstones (40%)
Hepatomegaly (50%)
Periportal adenopathy
Caudate lobe hypertrophy

MRI
Periportal halo sign due to periportal fibrosis
Periportal adenopathy
Caudate lobe hypertrophy

Table 84-32
Cholangiocarcinoma

Location
Distal common bile duct (30%-50%)
Proximal common bile duct (15%-30%)
Common hepatic duct (14%-37%)
Confluence of hepatic ducts (10%-26%)
Left or right hepatic duct (8%-13%)
Cystic duct (6%)

Cholangiography
Long, or rarely short, concentric focal stricture with wall irregularities
Exophytic intraductal tumor mass, 2 to 4 mm in diameter
Prestenotic diffuse focal biliary dilatation
Progression of ductal strictures

Ultrasound
Biliary dilatation
Hyperechoic (75%), hypoechoic (14%), or isoechoic mass (14%)

CT
Predominantly homogeneous, hypodense mass with irregular borders
No enhancement or mild ring enhancement on portal venous phase
Diffuse contrast enhancement seen on delayed (10-15 min) image because of the nature of the vascularity of this tumor
Ancillary findings: hepatic lobar atrophy associated with crowding of ducts, asymmetric, intrahepatic bile duct dilatation, segmental or lobar attenuation abnormalities

MRI
High-grade biliary obstruction and bile duct wall thickness >5 mm
Tumor is isointense or low signal relative to liver on T1-weighted images
Tumor signal intensity on T2-weighted images ranges from markedly increased to mildly increased relative to liver
Tumor enhances moderately on gadolinium-enhanced T1-weighted images
Ductal tumors arising in intrapancreatic portion of common bile duct are well delineated as low signal intensity masses highlighted by the high signal intensity of the pancreatic head on fat-suppressed T1-weighted images

Scintigraphy
Biliary obstruction on hepatobiliary scan
Intrahepatic tumors are cold on sulfur colloid and hepatobiliary scans
Mass may show focal uptake on gallium scan

Angiography
Hypervascular tumor with neovascularity (50%)
Poor or absent tumor stain
Arterioarterial collaterals along the course of the bile ducts associated with arterial obstruction
Displacement, encasement, or occlusion of the hepatic artery and portal vein

Table 84-33

Gallbladder Carcinoma

Replacement of gallbladder by tumor (40%-65%)
Focal or diffuse, asymmetric, irregular thickening of the gallbladder wall (20%-30%)
Bulky tumor involving the gallbladder fossa, adjacent liver, and hepatoduodenal ligament
Granular punctate calcifications with mucinous adenocarcinoma
Liver metastases, enlarged regional lymph nodes, intraperitoneal seeding, invasion of adjacent duodenum, colon, right kidney, stomach
Mass has increased signal intensity on T2-weighted MR sequences

Table 84-34

Cystic Biliary Disease: Caroli's Disease, Choledochal Cyst, Choledochocele

Caroli's Disease

Multiple cystic structures that converge toward the porta hepatis as either localized or diffusely scattered cysts communicating with bile ducts
Segmental saccular or beaded appearance of the intrahepatic ducts
Extrahepatic ducts frequently ectatic
Sludge and calculi often present in these dilated ducts

Choledochal Cyst

Location
Intrahepatic and extrahepatic ducts (73%)
Extrahepatic ducts alone (27%)
Dilated left and right main intrahepatic ducts (45%); bilateral (58%); unilateral (42%) left lobe only

Cholangiography
Dilated duct diameter (2-15 cm)
Abrupt change in ductal caliber at site of cyst

CT and Ultrasound
Large, fluid-filled structure beneath the porta hepatis separate from the gallbladder, which communicates with the hepatic ducts
Abrupt caliber change at junction of dilated segment and normal ducts
Intrahepatic biliary dilatation

Hepatobiliary Scintigraphy
Late filling and stasis of isotope within cyst
Dilatation of intrahepatic biliary system

Upper Gastrointestinal Tract Series
Soft tissue mass in right upper quadrant
Anterior displacement of the second portion of the duodenum and distal stomach
Widening of the duodenal sweep
Inferior displacement of the duodenum
Extrinsic compression of the proximal duodenum

Choledochocele

Smooth clublike or saclike dilatation of the intramural segment of the common bile duct
Smooth, well-defined intraluminal duodenal filling defect in the region of the papilla on barium studies that changes shape with compression and peristalsis

References

1. Dähnert W: Radiology Review Manual, 5th ed. Baltimore: Williams & Wilkins, 2003.
2. Reeder MM: Reeder and Felson's Gamuts in Radiology, 4th ed. New York, Springer-Verlag, 2003.
3. Eisenberg RL: Gastrointestinal Radiology—A Pattern Approach, 4th ed. New York, Lippincott-Raven, 2004.
4. Chapman S, Nakielny R: Aids to Radiological Differential Diagnosis. London, Bailliere Tindall, 1990.
5. Baker SR: The Abdominal Plain Film. East Norwalk, CT, Appleton & Lange, 1990.
6. Lee JKT, Sagel SS, Stanley RJ, Heiken J (eds): Computed Body Tomography with MRI Correlation. New York, Raven, 2006.
7. Rumack CM, Nilson SR, Charboneau JW (eds): Diagnostic Ultrasound, 3rd ed. St. Louis, CV Mosby, 2006.
8. Semelka RC: Abdominal-Pelvic MRI. New York, Wiley-Liss, 2002.
9. Datz FL: Gamuts in Nuclear Medicine, 3rd ed. St. Louis, CV Mosby, 1995.

X

Liver

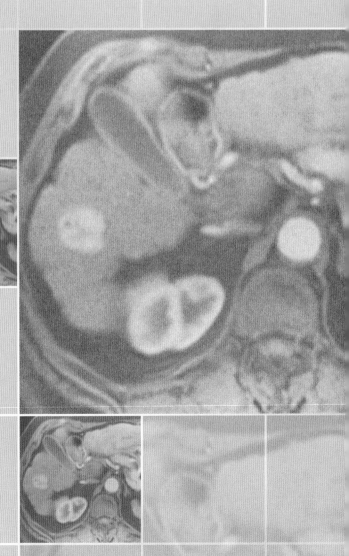

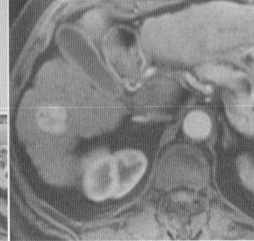

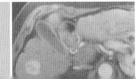

Liver: Normal Anatomy and Examination Techniques

Saravanan Namasivayam, MD, DNB, DHA • Mannudeep K. Kalra, MD •
William C. Small, MD, PhD • Sanjay Saini, MD, MBA

NORMAL ANATOMY

The liver is the largest abdominal organ, occupying the right upper abdominal quadrant. The diaphragm borders the liver superiorly, laterally, and anteriorly. The stomach, duodenum, and transverse colon border the liver medially, hepatic flexure inferiorly, and right kidney and adrenal gland, posteriorly. The liver is encapsulated by a dense layer of connective tissue-Glisson's capsule. Peritoneum covers the liver, except in the regions of gallbladder fossa, fossa for inferior vena cava (IVC), and the bare area. The surface morphology of the liver features a convex diaphragmatic surface and a concave visceral surface. The bare area abuts the diaphragmatic surface posteriorly and is demarcated by the coronary ligament. The coronary ligament is formed by folds of parietal and visceral peritoneum. The superior and inferior limbs of the coronary ligament fuse to form the right and left triangular ligaments laterally (Fig. 85-1). The right and left limbs of the coronary ligament fuse ventrally and extend as the falciform ligament that contains the ligamentum teres, which extends from the umbilicus to the superior surface of the liver.[1]

The porta hepatis is a transverse slit in the hilum of the liver that is perforated by the right and left hepatic ducts, hepatic artery, and portal vein. The common bile duct, hepatic artery, portal vein, nerves of liver, and lymphatics lie enclosed within the layers of the hepatoduodenal ligament (free edge of lesser omentum). The gastrohepatic ligament, the superior portion of the lesser omentum, attaches the liver to lesser curvature of stomach.

Hepatic Blood Supply

The liver has a dual blood supply from the hepatic artery, which provides systemic arterial circulation, and the portal vein, which returns blood from the gastrointestinal tract and spleen.[2] Hepatic arterial flow provides about 25% of the hepatic blood supply. The major blood supply of the liver is from the mesenteric portal drainage, which is a consequence of gastrointestinal functional activity.[3] Factors that influence the relative contribution of arterial and portal venous blood flow include hormones, autonomic neural stimulation, nutritional state, and presence of hepatic parenchymal disease.[1,4]

Portal Vein

The portal vein arises from the confluence of superior mesenteric and splenic veins, located posterior to the neck of pancreas (Figs. 85-2 and 85-3). The portal vein courses superiorly and to the right, posterior to common bile duct and hepatic artery within the hepatoduodenal ligament. At the porta hepatis, the portal vein divides into right and left branches. The right branch courses horizontally and bifurcates into anterior and posterior branches. The left branch is horizontal initially, then it turns cranially and terminates into ascending and descending branches. The left portal vein joins the obliterated umbilical vein within the fissure for ligamentum teres.[2,3,5,6] In embryonic life, blood in the umbilical vein empties into the left portal vein, and much of it is shunted to the IVC and systemic circulation through the ductus venosus.

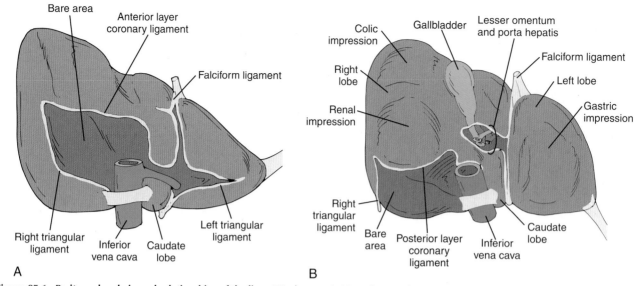

Figure 85-1. Peritoneal and visceral relationships of the liver. Diaphragmatic (**A**) and visceral (**B**) surfaces of the liver from a radiologic perspective.

The anatomic variations of the portal vein include absence of the right portal vein with anomalous branches from the main portal vein, and the left portal vein, and, rarely, absence of the horizontal segment of the left portal vein.

Hepatic Artery

The celiac axis divides into the common hepatic, splenic, and left gastric arteries at the level of T12-L1. The common hepatic artery courses along the upper border of the pancreatic head, anteriorly and to the right, behind the posterior layer of peritoneum of the lesser sac. After giving off the gastroduodenal artery, the common hepatic artery becomes the proper hepatic artery (see Fig. 85-3). The proper hepatic artery enters the subperitoneal space of the hepatoduodenal

ligament at the upper margin of the duodenum.[4] The proper hepatic artery ascends to the liver, anterior to the portal vein, and medial to the common bile duct. After entering the porta hepatis, the proper hepatic artery divides into a right, a left, and occasionally a middle hepatic artery. The right and left hepatic arteries supply the right and left lobes of the liver, respectively. The middle hepatic artery, if present, supplies the medial segment of the left lobe, augmented by branches of the left hepatic artery. Branches of the right hepatic artery supply the caudate lobe, but in some individuals the left or even middle hepatic artery contributes.[2,5] The right hepatic artery also gives off the cystic artery to the gallbladder.

This classic arrangement of the hepatic arterial anatomy is seen in only 55% of patients[2] (Figs. 85-4 and 85-5). Common variants include the right hepatic artery partially (18%) or

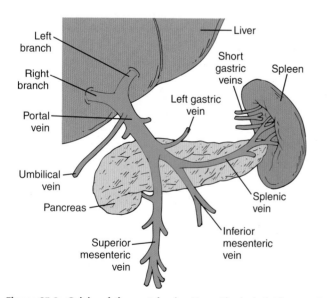

Figure 85-2. Origin of the portal vein. (From Sherlock S: The portal venous system and portal hypertension. In Sherlock S [ed]: Diseases of the Liver and Biliary System. Oxford, Blackwell Scientific, 1985, pp 134-181.)

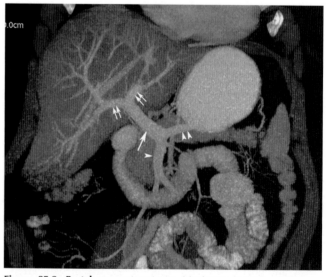

Figure 85-3. Portal venous anatomy. Maximum intensity projection image of CT of upper abdomen demonstrates confluence of superior mesenteric vein (*single arrowhead*) and splenic vein (*double arrowheads*) forming main portal vein (*arrow*). Main portal vein divides into right and left branches (*double arrows*) at porta.

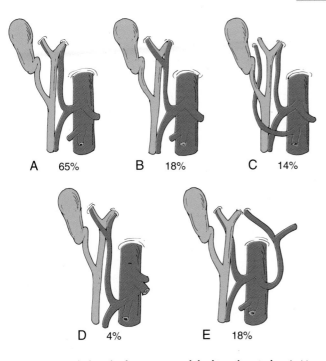

Figure 85-4. Variations in the anatomy of the hepatic arteries. A. Normal pattern. Right hepatic artery (RHA) posterior to common hepatic duct (CHD). **B.** RHA anterior to CHD. **C.** RHA from superior mesenteric artery (SMA) (sole or accessory). **D.** Common hepatic artery from SMA. **E.** Left hepatic artery from left gastric artery.

completely (14%) replaced by a branch from the superior mesenteric artery, entire hepatic artery arising from the superior mesenteric artery (2%-4%), partially or completely replaced origin of the left hepatic artery from the left gastric artery (18%-25%), and the left hepatic artery giving rise to the middle hepatic artery (45%).[4,5]

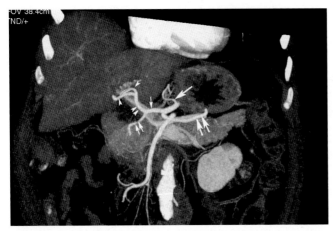

Figure 85-5. Hepatic arterial anatomy. Maximum intensity projection image of CT of upper abdomen demonstrates left gastric artery (*arrow*), splenic artery (*double arrows*), and common hepatic artery (CHA) (*small arrow*) arising from celiac axis. CHA continues as proper hepatic artery (PHA) (*double arrowheads*) after giving off gastroduodenal artery (*double small arrows*). PHA divides into right and left branches (*arrowheads*) at porta.

Hepatic Veins

The right, middle, and left hepatic veins lie within the posterosuperior aspect of liver. These veins course through the liver superiorly and obliquely, and drain into the IVC. Several small emissary hepatic veins drain the caudate lobe independently into the IVC. The diameter of hepatic veins is variable and may increase transiently with the Valsalva maneuver. Persistent dilatation of the IVC is seen with right-sided heart failure.

Duplication of the right, middle, and left hepatic veins is seen in 20%, 5%, and 15% of subjects, respectively.[7] Absence of the main hepatic veins occurs in 8% of subjects.[8] Accessory hepatic veins may also be seen in the liver. The most common accessory hepatic vein drains the antero-superior segment of the right hepatic lobe in one third of the population, which empties into the middle hepatic vein or occasionally into the right hepatic vein. Rarely, a separate inferior right hepatic vein drains directly into the IVC.[7]

Lobar and Segmental Anatomy of Liver

The liver can be divided into the right, left, and caudate lobes. The interlobar fissure separating the right and left lobes is oriented along a line passing through the gallbladder fossa inferiorly and the middle hepatic vein superiorly. Although this fissure is well formed in some patients, it may be incomplete in others. The fissure for ligamentum teres forms the left intersegmental fissure, which divides the left lobe into medial and lateral segments. The fissure for ligamentum venosum separates the left lateral hepatic segment from the caudate lobe.

Advances in surgical techniques of liver lesion resection have made the conventional hepatic lobar anatomy obsolete. The surgeons need precise localization of liver lesions in the functional segments, rather than lobes, for planning resection. The functional segmentation of the liver is based on surgical definition of feasible intrahepatic boundaries for resection. The segmental anatomy of liver is primarily based on vascular anatomy that can be illustrated on cross-sectional imaging[9-13] (Fig. 85-6). Each segment has its independent vascular supply and biliary drainage. The portal venous, hepatic arterial, and bile duct branches course through the segments (intrasegmental). The main hepatic veins course in between the segments (intersegmental).[9-13] The Bismuth-Couinaud system is the most common segmental nomenclature now used[14,15] (Fig. 85-7).

The Bismuth-Couinaud system serves as the anatomic basis for localizing focal hepatic lesions. In this system, the liver is divided into one segment and eight subsegments. The vertical divisions along planes of the main hepatic veins are maintained and are further divided by a horizontal plane passing through the right and left portal veins. The plane through middle hepatic vein separates right lobe from left lobe. Using these vascular landmarks, segmental localization of liver lesion can be performed with cross-sectional imaging.[16,17] Segment I is the caudate lobe. The caudate lobe is a pedunculated portion of liver extending medially from the right lobe between the portal vein and the IVC (Fig. 85-8). It has some unique features.[18,19] Functionally, the caudate lobe is an autonomous part of the liver, which has separate blood supply, bile drainage, and venous drainage. The right border of the caudate lobe is continuous with parenchyma of the

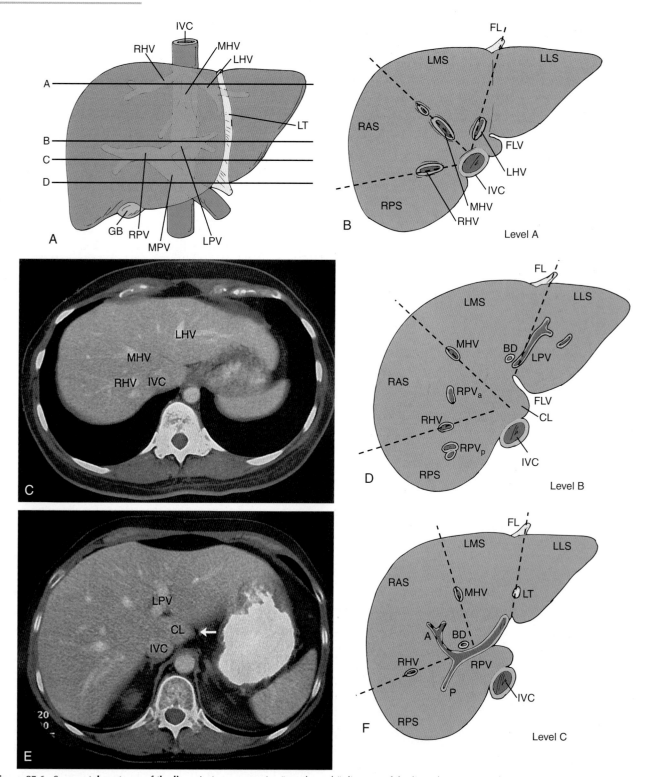

Figure 85-6. Segmental anatomy of the liver. A. Anteroposterior "see-through" diagram of the liver demonstrates the major venous anatomy and the levels of multiple axial sections used to depict segmental hepatic anatomy. **B.** Axial anatomy, level A. The right, middle, and left hepatic veins (RHV, MHV, and LHV) drain into the inferior vena cava (IVC). The RHV separates the anterior segment right lobe (RAS) from the posterior segment right lobe (RPS). The MHV separates the medial segment left lobe (LMS) from the RAS. The LHV acts as a boundary between the LMS and the lateral segment left lobe (LLS) and lies in the same plane as the falciform ligament (FL). FLV, fissure for the ligamentum venosum. **C.** Axial anatomy, level A. Axial CT. **D.** Axial anatomy, level B. At this level, the ascending portion of the left portal vein (LPV) courses between the LLS and LMS of the left lobe. The anterior and posterior segments of the right portal vein (RPV$_a$, RPV$_p$) are bisected by the RHV. **E.** Corresponding CT scan. **F.** Axial anatomy, level C. This is at the level of the horizontal portion of the RPV and its bifurcation into anterior (A) and posterior (P) branches. The RHV lies midway between the portal venous branches. The LT and FL serve as a border between the LLS and LMS.

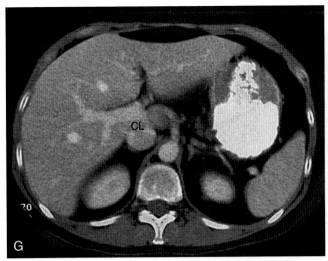

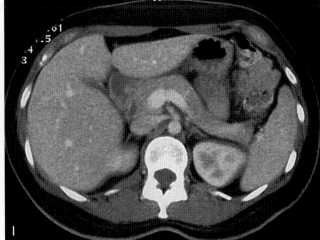

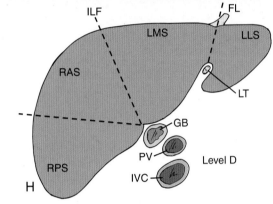

Figure 85-6, cont'd. **G.** Corresponding CT section. **H.** Axial anatomy, level D. The right and left hepatic lobes are separated by a line drawn through the IVC and the gallbladder fossa-interlobar fissure. This fissure extends superiorly from the neck of the gallbladder and is often incompletely visualized on CT. The LLS and LMS are separated by the LT. **I.** Corresponding CT scan. FLV, fissure of the ligamentum venosum; ILF, interlobar fissure; MPV, main portal vein; GB, gallbladder; CL, caudate lobe; dashed lines, segmental hepatic boundaries; D, diaphragm; R, right; L, left.

right hepatic lobe via an isthmus. Posteriorly, the IVC borders the caudate lobe. Inferiorly, the caudate lobe forms the superior margin of the foramen of Winslow, and it divides into a left-sided anterior prominence called the papillary process and a transverse caudate process that protrudes laterally to join the right hepatic lobe. The papillary process can be promi-

nent and penetrate the lesser sac behind the gastric antrum in proximity to the hepatic artery and the portal vein.[18,19] In some cases, it may simulate an enlarged lymph node or pancreatic mass on cross-sectional images.[20]

The next consecutive segment numbers are given to segments of the left lobe, followed by the right lobe, in a clockwise fashion as seen in the frontal projection, except for the segment IVa. The lateral segments II and III of the left lobe lie lateral and to the left of the left hepatic vein. Segment II lies above and segment III lies below the plane of the portal vein. Segment IV lies between the middle and left hepatic veins. Segment IVa and segment IVb lie above and below the plane of the portal vein, respectively. In the right lobe, the right hepatic vein separates the anterior segments (V and VIII) from the posterior segments (VI and VII). The superior segments (VII and VIII) and the inferior segments (V and VI) lie above and below the plane of the portal vein, respectively. However, segmental localization is difficult in patients with variant hepatic vascular anatomy. Hepatic vein landmarks may be unreliable in patients with duplication of hepatic veins. The dorsal portion of the segment IV is supplied by a branch from the right hepatic artery in 8% of subjects. Accessory portal segments with independent blood supply from the main portal vein or its right branch may be seen in 30% of subjects. The Riedel's lobe is an inferiorly positioned portion of the right hepatic lobe extending below the expected confines of the liver. Following segmental hepatic resection, the remaining segments hypertrophy and distort the segmental anatomy by displacing the vessels.

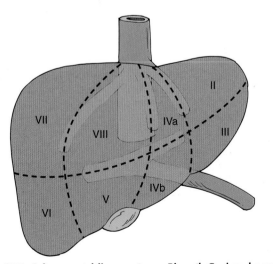

Figure 85-7. Subsegmental liver anatomy: Bismuth-Couinaud nomenclature. Frontal projection. Segments II and III compose the lateral segment of the left lobe and segments IVa and IVb the medial segment. Segments V and VI compose the anterior segment of the right lobe and VI and VII the posterior. Segment I (the caudate lobe) is not shown.

SECTION X Liver

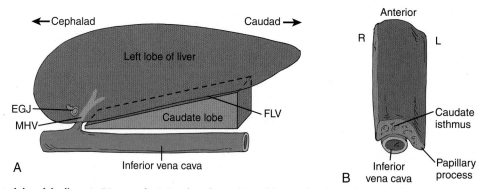

Figure 85-8. Caudate lobe of the liver. A. Diagram depicting the relationships of the caudate lobe of the liver. The caudate lobe is wedge shaped, and its posterior border abuts the inferior vena cava (IVC). The anterior border of the caudate lobe is separated from the left lobe (L) of the liver by the fissure for the ligamentum venosum (FLV). The inferior margin of the caudate lobe forms the superior margin of the foramen of Winslow, which leads to the lesser sac. The superior margin of the caudate lobe is the cephalic portion of the right hepatic lobe, where the middle hepatic vein (MHV) enters the IVC. This corresponds to the level of the esophagogastric junction (EGJ). **B.** Schematic representation of the caudate lobe view frontally. The right margin of the caudate lobe connects to the right hepatic lobe by an isthmus. Its anterior border (Ant.) is formed by the fissure of the ligament venosum. The papillary process projects from the caudal margin of the caudate lobe. R, right; L, left. (**A** and **B** from Dodds WJ, Erickson SJ, Taylor AJ, et al: Caudate lobe of the liver: anatomy, embryology, and pathology. AJR 154:87-93, 1990 © by American Roentgen Ray Society.)

Porta Hepatis

The porta hepatis is the hilum of liver through which the portal vein, hepatic artery, common hepatic duct, nerves, and lymphatics enter the liver (Fig. 85-9). The portal vein is the most consistent anatomic landmark. The common hepatic duct is a 3- to 5-mm thin-walled structure that lies anterior to the portal vein and lateral to the common hepatic artery.[21-23] The right hepatic artery lies posterior to the common hepatic duct in 75% of subjects and anterior in 25% of subjects.

Bile Ducts

The segmental distribution of bile ducts closely follows the course of hepatic arterial branches (Fig. 85-10A). The ducts draining the right and left lobes communicate only at the porta hepatis. There is no communication between the bile ducts of anterior and posterior segments of right lobe.[24]

Hepatic Lymphatics

Superficial lymphatics originate from subperitoneal tissue of liver surface. The visceral surface drains into lymph nodes at the porta hepatis. The diaphragmatic surface drains toward the IVC, aortic nodes near the celiac axis (Fig. 85-10B). Some lymphatics penetrate the diaphragm to enter retrosternal, cardiohepatic nodes that ascend to the neck with the right thoracic artery.[2] The deep lymphatics of liver form a major and a smaller trunk. Major trunk passes through porta hepatic nodes and cisterna chyli and, finally, into thoracic duct. The smaller trunk courses along with hepatic veins and terminate

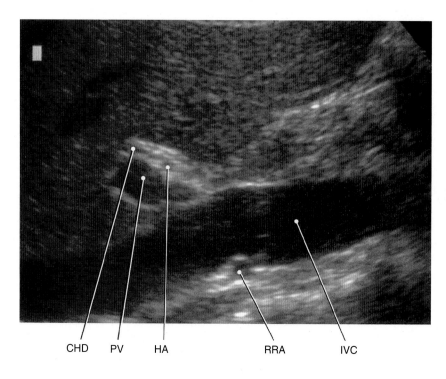

Figure 85-9. Porta hepatis. Oblique sagittal sonogram demonstrates a branch of the portal vein (PV), common hepatic duct (CHD), hepatic artery (HA), inferior vena cava (IVC), and right renal artery (RRA).

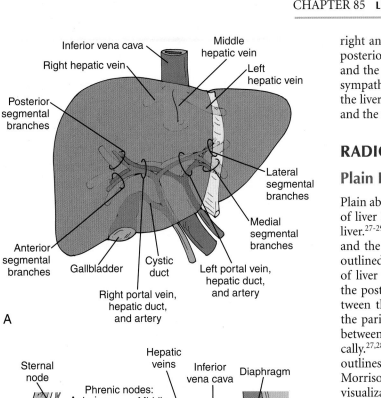

A

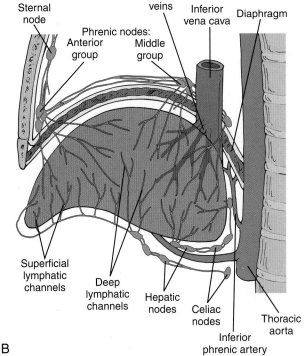

B

Figure 85-10. Hepatic bile ducts and lymphatics. A. Usual branching pattern of bile ducts (*green*), hepatic artery (*red*), and portal vein (*blue*). **B.** Diagram depicting the lymphatic drainage of the liver. (**B** from Woodburne RT, Burkell WE: Essentials of Human Anatomy. New York, Oxford University Press, 1988, pp 461 and 466.)

in lymph nodes near the IVC. Lymphatics of liver dilate due to cirrhosis, portal hypertension, veno-occlusive disease, right-sided heart failure, pericardial effusion, low serum protein levels, liver transplant rejection, and glycogenesis.[2]

Nerve Supply

The anterior hepatic plexus surrounds the hepatic artery. It consists primarily of branches of the left celiac plexus, the right and left vagus nerves, and the right phrenic nerve. The posterior hepatic plexus is located around the portal vein and the bile ducts. The hepatic arteries are innervated by the sympathetic nervous system. Pain from the gallbladder and the liver capsule is referred to the right shoulder via the third and the fourth cervical nerves.[2,25,26]

RADIOLOGIC TECHNIQUES

Plain Radiography

Plain abdominal radiographs have a limited role in evaluation of liver lesion due to the homogeneous soft tissue density of liver.[27-29] The superior border of liver is outlined by the lung and the diaphragm. Other borders are seen only if they are outlined by fat or gas-filled bowel loops. The lateral border of liver is outlined by extraperitoneal fat continuous within the posterior pararenal space. This fat is also interposed between the inferior surface of the right hemidiaphragm and the parietal peritoneum. It may appear as a thick black line between the diaphragm and the liver dome radiographically.[27,28,30] Retroperitoneal fat in the anterior pararenal space outlines the posteroinferior margin of the liver. Fluid in Morrison's pouch obscures this interface resulting in non-visualization of the edge of the liver. The anteroinferior liver edge is less commonly seen because the amount of omental and pericolic fat that outlines the margin is more variable.[31] The left lobe of liver extends to the left of midline ventral to the stomach and superior to the transverse colon. Radiographic estimation of liver size is unreliable due to inconsistent visualization of borders, although it is more accurate than clinical palpation.[32] Plain abdominal radiographs can aid in detection of portal or hepatic venous gas and biliary tract air and calcified liver lesions.[30,33]

Ultrasound

The liver has a broad area of contact with abdominal wall, making it an ideal organ for evaluation with real-time sonography. Sonography is a safe, noninvasive, quick, and inexpensive means of evaluation of liver. It can be performed at the bedside, needing little patient cooperation.

Examination Techniques

The liver is ideally examined following a 6-hour fast so that gallbladder is not contracted. The highest possible transducer frequency should be chosen that maintains sound penetration to the posterior aspect of the liver. Near and far gain settings should be adjusted for uniform representation of the echo texture of the liver parenchyma.[34] A small footprint transducer may improve visualization of liver by an intercostal approach. Both supine and right anterior oblique views should be obtained. Breath-hold following deep inspiration causes caudal displacement of liver and improves the visualization of dome of the liver. Sagittal, transverse, coronal, and subcostal oblique views complete the examination. Focal lesions are easily identified on the real-time study and may be less well appreciated on the hard copy films.[35-39]

Sonography is an excellent modality for evaluation of the course of the hepatic and portal veins. The portal vein divides at the porta hepatis into the right and left main branches.

The portal veins are anechoic structures with echogenic walls. The bile ducts run with the portal veins and are too small to be seen except at the hilum, unless they are dilated.[40] Contrary to common belief, there is no constant anteroposterior relationship between the intrahepatic bile ducts and their corresponding portal veins. The hepatic arteries also run with these structures but are usually too small to be seen except with the aid of color flow Doppler imaging.[41-45]

The hepatic veins course posteriorly and superiorly through the liver to the IVC. They are intersegmental, whereas portal veins are intrasegmental with the exception of the ascending segment of the left portal vein. The walls of hepatic veins are usually less echogenic than those of the portal veins.

Size and Architecture

Although ultrasound of liver is commonly used for evaluating hepatic size, no single measurement of the liver reflects the true volume due to its variable shape.[46,47] On longitudinal scans obtained through the midhepatic line, if the liver measures less than or equal to 13 cm, it is normal in 93% of individuals. If this measurement is 15.5 cm or above, liver is enlarged in 75% of cases.[48] Liver size should be evaluated in at least two planes to compensate for variable hepatic configuration. In the midclavicular line, the normal liver measures 10.5 ± 1.5 cm in longitudinal diameter and 8.1 ± 1.9 cm in the anteroposterior projection, with 12.6 cm and 11.3 cm being

the 95th percentile. In the midline, normal liver measures 8.3 ± 1.7 cm (95th percentile, 10.9 cm) and 5.7 ± 1.5 cm (95th percentile, 8.2 cm) in longitudinal and anteroposterior dimensions.[49] Subjective evaluation of configuration of the inferior border of liver can be used to predict liver enlargement.[39] A caudal margin of more than 45 degrees in the left lobe and more than 90 degrees in the right lobe indicates hepatomegaly. When the liver is enlarged, its area of contact with the anterior border of right kidney extends below the superior two thirds of right kidney.

The normal tissue texture of the liver is homogenous, with fine echoes that appear as moderately short dots or lines.[50,51] The normal liver has a uniform brightness and texture interrupted only by the hepatic veins, portal vein, and fissures. The echogenicity of liver parenchyma depends on the equipment, transducer, and gain settings. Hence, hepatic parenchymal echogenicity is judged by comparing it with internal references: the right renal cortex, the body of pancreas, portal vein walls, and spleen. The liver is either minimally hyperechoic or isoechoic compared with the adjacent normal right renal cortex in parasagittal or lateral coronal scans (Fig. 85-11A). When compared with the liver, the pancreas is hypoechoic in young, isoechoic in adults and hyperechoic in the elderly due to increasing fatty infiltration of the pancreas with age (Fig. 85-11B). The liver is hypoechoic to the spleen. Lateral segment of the left lobe of liver may extend to the left and abut the spleen, mimicking a subphrenic or

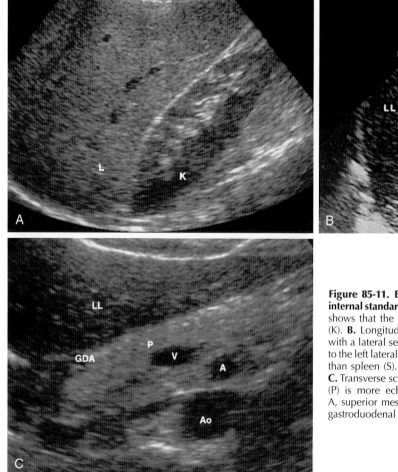

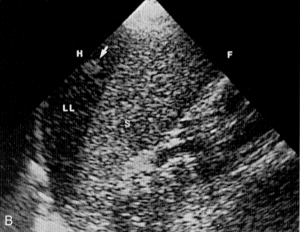

Figure 85-11. Echogenicity of the normal liver compared with internal standards. A. Longitudinal scan of the right upper quadrant shows that the liver (L) is more echogenic than the right kidney (K). **B.** Longitudinal scan of the left upper quadrant in a patient with a lateral segment of the left lobe of the liver (LL) that extends to the left lateral abdominal wall shows normal liver less echogenic than spleen (S). The liver contains a small hemangioma *(arrow).* **C.** Transverse scan of the epigastrium shows that normal pancreas (P) is more echogenic than liver (LL). H, superior; F, inferior; A, superior mesenteric artery; V, superior mesenteric vein; GDA, gastroduodenal artery; Ao, aorta.

a subcapsular splenic fluid collection[52] (Fig. 85-11C). The portal vein wall is quite echogenic in the normal liver. All these architectural comparisons assume that the kidney and pancreas are normal. When these structures are diseased, internal sonographic references are less useful. In acute hepatitis, the parenchyma is hypoechoic to right renal cortex and the portal vein walls appear exceptionally bright.[53] Conversely, in fatty infiltration and cirrhosis, the liver is markedly hyperechoic to right renal cortex and the portal vein walls are "silhouetted out" by the echogenic hepatic parenchyma.[54]

Artifacts

Sonographic artifacts observed in the liver can mimic pathology.[55-60] Focal fatty infiltration and focal fat sparing of liver can appear as a hyperechoic and hypoechoic pseudolesions, respectively. These lesions commonly involve the periportal region of the medial segment of the left lobe. Focal subcapsular fat infiltration may occur in diabetic patients treated with insulin in peritoneal dialysate.[61] The caudate lobe may appear as a hypoechoic mass due to attenuation of the sound beam by the fissure for the ligamentum venosum. The ligamentum teres surrounded by the collagen combined with the fat of falciform ligament can simulate an echogenic mass. However, this can be recognized by its typical location. Ascites can increase sound transmission to a nodular portion of the liver, simulating an echogenic mass. Accessory fissures and folding of diaphragm into the liver can also cause echogenic pseudolesions.[55-60]

Intraoperative Ultrasound

Transabdominal ultrasound of liver is limited by scattering and acoustic attenuation by subcutaneous fat and bowel gas. These problems are avoided by intraoperative ultrasound in which a high-frequency probe is directly placed on the liver surface, producing high-resolution images. This examination should be tailored to the specific needs of the surgeon to avoid undue prolongation of total duration of the surgical procedure. Intraoperative ultrasound can be performed during open laparotomy as well as laparoscopy. Small, superficially focused, high-frequency, linear array transducers are used for ultrasound during laparotomy. These transducers have a wide field of view in the near-field with improved near-field resolution. Intraoperative ultrasound can also provide imaging guidance for intraoperative ablation of focal hepatic masses[62-70] (Fig. 85-12).

The most common application of intraoperative ultrasound is during surgery in patients undergoing segmental resection for hepatic metastases from colorectal carcinoma. Intraoperative ultrasound can provide information about the relationship of normal vascular anatomy to pathologic masses, vascular invasion or thrombosis caused by tumors and small, nonpalpable lesions that are difficult to detect on preoperative imaging studies.[63,70] Intraoperative ultrasound can accurately detect cysts as small as 1 to 3 mm and solid focal lesions of 3 to 5 mm. Brower and associates[71] reported that the sensitivity, specificity, and accuracy of intraoperative ultrasound (78%, 100%, and 84%, respectively) are superior to those of arteriography, CT, preoperative ultrasound, and palpation for detection of liver lesions. Intraoperative ultrasound can detect additional liver lesions and modify the surgical management of patients with liver metastases from colorectal carcinoma.[72,73] The sensitivity of intraoperative ultrasound was reported to be superior to superparamagnetic iron oxide–enhanced MRI for detection of liver metastases.[74] In a recent study, intraoperative ultrasound provided additional information compared with triphasic CT in 13 of 26 patients who underwent resection for liver lesion.[61] The accuracy of intraoperative ultrasound is comparable with that

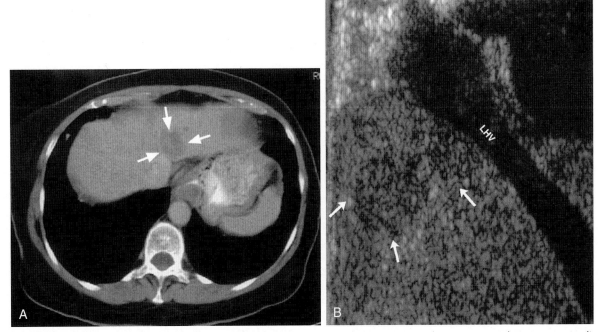

Figure 85-12. Hepatocellular carcinoma: intraoperative ultrasound and CT. A. CT demonstrates a low attenuation lesion (*arrows*) adjacent to combined confluence of left and middle hepatic veins. **B.** Sagittal ultrasound image during laparotomy confirms that the lesion (*arrows*) cannot be resected free of the left hepatic vein (LHV). (Courtesy of Helena Gabriel, MD, Chicago, IL.)

of contrast-enhanced MRI for detection of liver lesions. Intra-operative ultrasound can also be used to guide interstitial radiotherapy, thermal ablation, and cryotherapy for the treatment of liver metastases.[76-78]

During laparoscopic ultrasound, the transducer is introduced through the laparoscopic port, usually periumbilical or right lower quadrant. A multifrequency 5-, 6.5-, and 7.5-MHz curvilinear laparoscopic ultrasound probe with a flexible tip is used. A substantial pitfall during laparoscopic ultrasound has been poor near-field visualization. Laparoscopic ultrasound can demonstrate more liver lesions compared with CT[79] and CT portography.[80] Laparoscopic ultrasound identified liver tumors not seen at laparoscopy in 33% and provided additional staging information to laparoscopy alone in 42% in a study of patients with potentially resectable liver lesions as judged by preoperative imaging.[81]

Doppler Ultrasound

Duplex and color flow Doppler imaging improve the diagnostic capabilities of ultrasound by enabling the evaluation of complex circulatory dynamics of liver.[33,82-87] Thrombosis, reverse flow, aneurysms, and fistulas are better demonstrated with duplex and color flow Doppler sonography than with gray-scale ultrasound.[33,83,87,88] Doppler settings need to be optimized to achieve the greatest sensitivity to allow the detection of low flow. Color gain must be increased to a level just below the level which would create artifacts. In addition, Doppler can be used for detection of tumor vascularity and vascular invasion by focal hepatic lesions. Color and spectral Doppler studies are unable to detect the vascularity of the majority of focal lesions of liver due to low intensity of the signals. Tumor vascularity is better evaluated with power Doppler and intravascular ultrasound contrast agents.

The normal Doppler tracing of the hepatic artery demonstrates a high diastolic flow that indicates low impedance (Fig. 85-13A). Doppler sonography is most often used to differentiate the hepatic artery from a bile duct in the porta hepatis. Color flow images may be needed to localize the hepatic artery.[89] The intrahepatic branches of the hepatic artery are usually not visualized on gray-scale ultrasound. When there is compensatory dilatation of intrahepatic branches of hepatic artery in cirrhosis, Doppler ultrasound can differentiate this from dilatation of intrahepatic biliary radicals.

In liver transplant recipients, survival of the allograft depends on patency of the hepatic artery. Changes in the normal hepatic artery waveform may suggest stenosis or thrombosis in these patients.[90,91] These changes include slow rise to peak systole, diminished amplitude, and prominent diastolic flow, which are referred to as a tardus-parvus waveform. The normal marked increase in postprandial hepatic artery resistive index seen in normal individuals is generally not seen with severe liver disease.[92]

The flow pattern of the hepatic veins (Fig. 85-13B) is similar to that of the IVC and other large systemic veins, undulating with cardiac and respiratory motion. Normal hepatic venous flow is directed toward the vena cava. With tricuspid regurgitation, there is a pronounced systolic reversal of hepatic venous blood flow.[93] The triphasic pattern is lost in cirrhosis where the encased hepatic veins become less compliant.[94]

The portal vein has a characteristic continuous flow pattern (Fig. 85-13C) modulated by respiratory variations. This normal respiratory variation is either attenuated or lost in portal hypertension.[95-97] Portal vein pulsatility is increased in patients with right-sided heart failure, as cardiac pulsations are transmitted to the portal vein.

Tissue Harmonic Imaging

Conventional gray-scale ultrasound transmits and receives sound beam at the same frequency. In tissue harmonic imaging (THI), the second harmonic signal is received by filtering out the fundamental echoes from the tissue being evaluated. Body wall artifacts, side lobes, and scatter are minimized, and signal-to-noise ratio is improved with THI, as the harmonic signals are generated in the tissues.[98] The shorter wavelength of the sound beam used in THI results in improved axial resolution. THI can detect additional liver lesions and alter the clinical management compared with conventional ultrasound.[99]

Ultrasound Contrast Agents

Ultrasound contrast agents are exogenous substances that can be administered, either in the blood pool or in a cavity to enhance sonographic signals. Contrast agents increase the backscattered signal intensity, which results in improved gray-scale echogenicity on harmonic imaging and pulse inversion sequences, as well as increased color and spectral Doppler signal strength. Agents are injected intravenously, and imaging proceeds immediately thereafter. One major drawback of these agents has been the narrow window available for scanning after contrast administration. There are two major types of ultrasound contrast agents: blood pool agents and agents that act by selective uptake into tissues.

The most commonly used type of ultrasound contrast agent is inert microbubble. Microbubbles can be either non-encapsulated or encapsulated.[100] Nonencapsulated microbubbles are unstable and can be used for evaluation of right heart only. Encapsulated microbubble agent SHU 508A (Levovist; Schering AG, Berlin, Germany) uses stabilized microbubbles, which are adsorbed on galactose particles and palmitic acid. SHU 508A enhances small vessels and improves Doppler signal in the portal vein and has been found to improve the visualization of tumor vessels in hepatocellular carcinoma.[101,102] SHU 508A is useful in helping differentiate between benign hyperechoic lesions and hepatocellular carcinoma. It is also useful in identifying slow portal vein flow in cirrhotics and in patients who have undergone transjugular intrahepatic portosystemic shunt procedure.[103] It can also help identify hepatic artery flow after liver transplantation. The imaging window of SHU 508A is less than 7 minutes. More recently, developed agents use low-solubility gases. Perfluorocarbons are inert gases that are not metabolized, so they tend to enhance for a longer duration.[104,105]

Some ultrasound contrast agents have a late liver-specific phase where the bubbles accumulate in normal liver parenchyma 2 to 5 minutes after injection when the vascular enhancement has faded. This late phase is useful for the detection and characterization of hepatic lesions.[98] Microbubbles known to exhibit liver-specific behavior are SHU 508A, SHU 563A

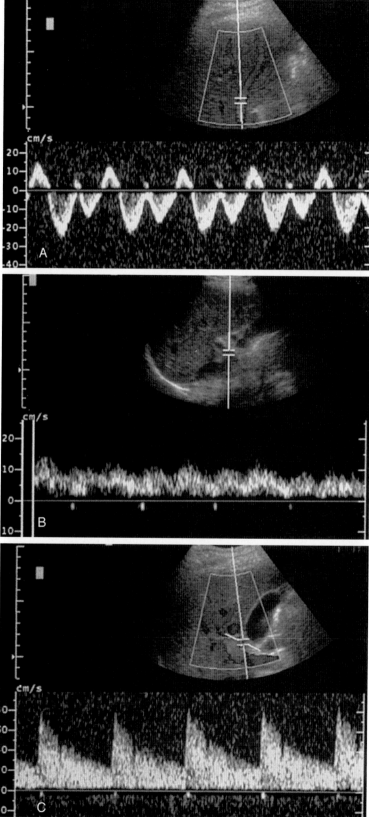

Figure 85-13. Normal duplex Doppler sonography of the hepatic vessels. A. The normal hepatic vein has a complex triphasic waveform because of the combination of regurgitation of blood from the right atrium associated with atrial systole and variations of intra-abdominal pressure associated with respiration. **B.** The normal portal vein has a characteristic continuous flow pattern that is modulated by respiratory variation. **C.** The normal hepatic artery demonstrates forward flow throughout diastole. The amount of diastolic flow varies with fasting status.

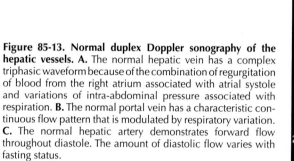

(Sonavist; Schering AG), NC100 100 (Sonazoid; General Electric Healthcare Technologies, Oslo, Norway), and BR14 (Bracco Diagnostics, Milan, Italy).[98] Perfluoro-octylbromide has been shown to produce an echogenic rim around liver tumors.[106] Iodipamide ethyl ester has been shown to enhance the echogenicity of normal hepatic parenchyma containing Kupffer cells and not non–Kupffer cell–containing tumors in animal models.[107]

Harmonic imaging detects microbubbles as they resonate at their characteristic frequencies.[101] Microbubble contrast agents are better demonstrated and detected longer in various organs as well as tumor vessels with harmonic imaging than with color Doppler.[108] Quaia and colleagues[106] reported that pulse inversion harmonic imaging with SHU 508A detected additional liver metastases in 47% of patients compared with conventional gray-scale ultrasound. Liver metastases as small as 2 mm can be detected by pulse inversion harmonic imaging with SHU 508A.[109,110]

Computed Tomography

Advances in multidetector row CT (MDCT) technology have revolutionized liver imaging. MDCT enables fast scan coverage and improved resolution due to isotropic image acquisition. Faster image acquisition enables multiphasic CT acquisition through the liver with a single bolus of contrast injection. Isotropic image dataset improves the quality of three-dimensional reformations.[111] The multiplanar reformations can better demonstrate the anatomic relationship of hepatic focal lesions with the blood vessels, which can help the surgeons to plan segmental resection of the liver. The three-dimensional reformations enable illustration of the liver vascular anatomy for evaluation of liver donors.

Unenhanced Computed Tomography

Noncontrast CT scans of the liver are inferior to contrast-enhanced studies for lesion detection and thus are not routinely performed except in certain specific situations.[112-114] Liver disorders that diffusely alter hepatic attenuation, such as fatty change, hemochromatosis, glycogen storage diseases, chemotherapy, amiodarone administration, and gold therapy, should be evaluated with noncontrast CT. Patients with cirrhosis should also undergo noncontrast scans to search for iron in dysplastic and siderotic nodules. Noncontrast liver CT may be indicated for evaluation of lesion calcification, hemorrhage (in lesions like hepatocellular adenomas) (Fig. 85-14) and metastases from hypervascular tumors like carcinoid, renal, thyroid, insulinoma, pheochromocytoma, and breast.[115-118] These hypervascular metastases may become isodense after contrast enhancement.[119,120]

Contrast-Enhanced Computed Tomography

Iodinated Contrast Dynamics

The goal of contrast enhancement is to improve lesion visibility by increasing the relative attenuation difference between the lesion and normal hepatic parenchyma. This difference is a fundamental factor in lesion conspicuity and characterization.[117] Many factors affect the timing and degree of hepatic

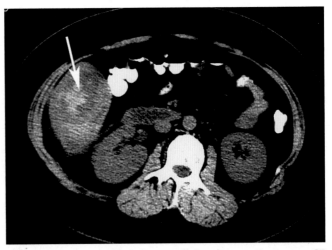

Figure 85-14. Hemorrhage in hepatocellular adenoma. Noncontrast CT of upper abdomen of a 28-year-old woman with hepatocellular adenoma reveals a central hyperdense area (*arrow*) within the hypodense mass suggestive of hemorrhage.

enhancement and, thus, the contrast difference between normal hepatic parenchyma and lesions. Hepatic enhancement is most dependent on the phase of the contrast delivery during which scanning occurs. These phases can be divided into vascular, redistribution, and equilibrium.[121] During the vascular phase, there is a rapid increase in aortic enhancement and a slow increase in hepatic enhancement. This phase is short because iodinated contrast material diffuses rapidly from the vascular blood pool to the extravascular or interstitial space of the liver, thus beginning the redistribution phase. During this time, there is a rapid decrease in aortic enhancement and increase in hepatic enhancement. This represents the ideal time for detecting most lesions (Fig. 85-15). In the equilibrium phase, there is decline in aortic and hepatic enhancement. Hence lesions may become isoattenuating to hepatic parenchyma.

Helical CT technology allows multiphase CT acquisition with a single bolus of contrast administration. An initial acquisition can be obtained during the hepatic arterial phase, so that highly vascular lesions are highlighted against a background of nonenhanced normal liver parenchyma. These lesions may become isodense with remaining liver if scanning is performed later. A later, portal venous (redistribution) phase scan is obtained when most of the contrast bolus enhances the normal hepatic parenchyma. Because metastases receive primarily arterial blood supply, most metastases are hypodense compared with normal liver (see Fig. 85-15). These phases are further discussed in the section on biphasic scanning.

The timing of these different phases and peak enhancement is directly affected by the way in which contrast material is delivered. The volume, type, concentration, and rate of injection of contrast material used affect the time to peak enhancement. Several studies suggest that the time to peak contrast enhancement is dependent on the duration of contrast injection.[122-124] Higher injection rate or lower contrast volume injections produce an earlier peak enhancement due to short injection duration.

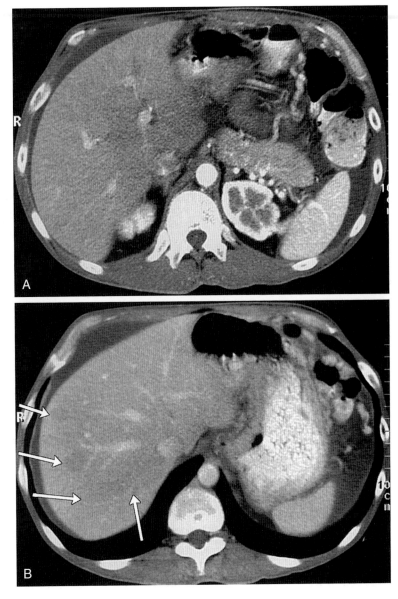

Figure 85-15. Importance of contrast bolus timing in liver lesion detection on CT. To evaluate a possible pancreatic mass, a thin-collimation spiral was obtained from the inferior pancreas upward, with a second spiral covering the craniad portion of the liver. Although present on subsequent ultrasound, no metastases were detected on the lower image (**A**) because scanning occurred during the arterial phase. The more craniad portal venous phase image (**B**) demonstrates multiple metastases (*arrows*) from a nonhypervascular carcinoid tumor.

The amount of hepatic enhancement is determined by technical and patient-related factors. Technical factors include the contrast concentration, volume, and injection rate. These factors have interdependent effects.[122] Hepatic enhancement increases with higher contrast volume, injection rate, and concentration of the contrast material.[125-131] Increasing the injection rate from 2 to 3 mL/s results in 16% increase in peak hepatic enhancement.[132] However, increasing the injection rate above 4 to 5 mL/s does not result in substantial increase in peak hepatic enhancement.[133]

Patient-related factors that affect enhancement include weight and cardiac output. There is decreasing hepatic enhancement with increasing patient weight.[123] In thin patients undergoing spiral CT, contrast dose may be reduced by up to 40%.[129] Megibow and associates[130] reported that a weight-based dose of 1.5 mL/kg of 300 mg/mL iodine contrast material can provide acceptable contrast enhancement in most patients, with a significant cost savings. Although faster image acquisition with MDCT has enabled considerable contrast dose re-duction for CT angiography studies,[134] enthusiastic contrast dose reduction for CT evaluation of liver is limited by the minimum iodine dose required for optimum liver enhancement. The iodine dose required to achieve a hepatic enhancement of 50 Hounsfield Units (HU) has been reported to be 521 mg/mL iodine.[135,136] Decreased cardiac output delays hepatic enhancement.

Faster image acquisition with MDCT mandates high iodine influx rate for optimum enhancement. High concentration contrast material is a valuable option for this due to limited range of possible fast injection rates. Increased enhancement of hepatocellular carcinoma in arterial phase CT and improved lesion conspicuity with high concentration contrast material (370 mg/mL iodine) have been reported.[137] This improved enhancement with high concentration contrast material is visually significant in patients weighing more than 65 kg.[138] The use of a 20 mL of saline chaser bolus has been reported to increase the enhancement of liver, portal vein, and aorta.[139]

Automated methods of timing contrast delivery have been advocated to achieve a greater and more consistent level of hepatic enhancement from patient to patient than the use of a conventional fixed delay time.[140,141] These methods make use of a region of interest placed on the aorta, portal vein, or liver parenchyma. During contrast delivery, multiple images are obtained at a fixed level at 3- to 5-second intervals. When a preselected threshold of 50 HU is reached, the scan is initiated.[142] Automated bolus tracking can increase the mean liver parenchymal enhancement substantially, compared with empirical time-delay scanning.[143-145] In addition, automated bolus tracking can improve the liver-to-lesion conspicuity.[146]

Helical Portal-Venous Phase Scan (Single-Phase Scan)

This is the preferred CT technique for routine hepatic evaluation. With helical CT, the entire liver can be scanned during peak parenchymal enhancement, further improving diagnostic accuracy.[147] This is accomplished by imaging the liver beginning at about 55 to 70 seconds after the start of the contrast bolus, depending on injection rate. Reduced cardiac output can delay the peak hepatic enhancement. Most centers use 100 to 150 mL of 300 to 370 mg/mL iodine contrast material injected at a rate of 3 mL/s or more.

Biphasic Helical Scan

Biphasic CT using a hepatic artery dominant phase technique and a portal venous phase technique is more efficacious than conventional CT using a single portal venous phase technique to detect hypervascular lesions, including hepatocellular carcinoma and metastases from renal, breast, carcinoid, and pancreatic islet cell tumors. Attenuation differences between an intensely enhancing hypervascular metastasis supplied by hepatic arterial flow and remainder of the liver are maximized during the arterial phase scan (Fig. 85-16A). Portal vein flow would render the hypervascular metastases isoattenuating (Fig. 85-16B). Arterial phase images are acquired by scanning 20 to 30 seconds after the start of contrast injection. The time of onset of arterial phase is dependent on contrast injection rate.[148] With a fixed injection rate, small changes in contrast

volume do not affect the duration of the arterial phase.[149] Faster injection rates increase the amount of arterial enhancement, as well as the length of time between peak aortic enhancement and the end of the arterial phase, which might increase detection of hypervascular tumors.[148] A second acquisition is then obtained during the portal venous phase, after a delay of 55 to 65 seconds from the beginning of contrast injection. Contrast material is delivered at a faster rate of 4 to 5 mL/s for biphasic CT study, instead of 3 mL/s, which is used for single-phase CT study.

Biphasic helical scanning has been found especially helpful in hepatocellular carcinoma, in which the addition of arterial phase scan improves lesion detection compared with portal phase scans alone or CT arterial portography.[150-152] In addition, arterial phase data enable vascular road mapping for oncologic liver surgery planning.[153] Detection of a hypervascular hepatic lesion in a patient with cirrhosis is suggestive of hepatocellular carcinoma. Biphasic technique for the detection of hypervascular metastases has had more mixed results. Several studies have found that 21% to 37% of lesions 2 cm or smaller in size are either visible only or are more conspicuous on arterial phase images.[154,155] Another study, however, found that nonenhanced and portal venous phase images detected significantly more hypervascular metastases than did hepatic arterial phase and portal venous phase or portal venous phase images alone.[156] Hepatic arterial phase scanning need not be performed for evaluation of hypovascular hepatic lesions, as they do not show enhancement during the hepatic arterial phase.[157] Although multiphase liver imaging with MDCT improves sensitivity and specificity of liver imaging, the risk of radiation exposure increases with this.[158] Application of automatic exposure control may result in substantial reduction of radiation dose to the patient, while maintaining acceptable image quality.[159,160]

Delayed Iodine Scanning

Delayed scanning has been employed to improve detection of intrahepatic cholangiocarcinoma (Fig. 85-17) and metastases.[161-166] Cholangiocarcinoma appears hyperdense on de-

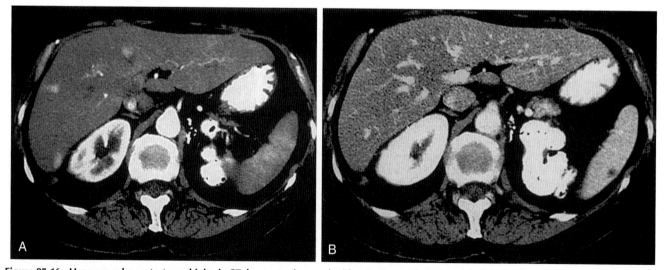

Figure 85-16. Hypervascular metastases: biphasic CT demonstrating carcinoid metastases only on arterial phase images. Arterial phase CT image (**A**) demonstrates multiple brightly enhancing metastases that are invisible on portal venous phase (**B**) scan. Images are displayed at narrow (liver) windows.

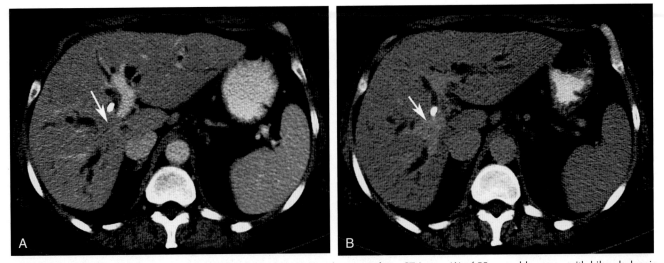

Figure 85-17. Delayed enhancement of hilar cholangiocarcinoma. Portal venous phase CT image (**A**) of 55-year-old woman with hilar cholangio-carcinoma causing biliary obstruction, demonstrates isodense mass (*arrow*) at porta hepatis with intrahepatic biliary dilatation. Delayed image (**B**) obtained after 10 minutes reveals enhancement of this mass (*arrow*). Images are displayed at narrow (liver) windows

layed scans in 74% of patients.[161] Studies assessing whether delayed scanning is helpful in detecting hepatocellular carcinoma have produced conflicting results.[150,152] In a recent study, the sensitivity of detection of hepatocellular carcinoma increased by 4% by addition of delayed phase scanning (180 seconds) to the hepatic arterial and portal venous phase scanning.[167] In addition, the filling in of hemangioma with contrast can be demonstrated on delay phase scans.

Computed Tomographic Angiography and Portography

In this technique, an arterial catheter is placed selectively in the hepatic, splenic, or superior mesenteric artery in the angiography suite and contrast is injected through this catheter.[117,168,169] Hence, during CT arterial portography (CTAP), there is dense enhancement of liver parenchyma receiving portal venous blood.[170-172] Liver lesions that receive primarily arterial rather than portal venous blood supply appear as hypodense defects on CTAP.[169,170,173]

Perfusion defects and other artifacts diminish the specificity of CTAP.[174,175] CTAP has a false-positive rate of 15% to 17%.[176] An additional delayed phase acquisition can improve the specificity of CTAP.[177] CTAP is seldom performed now due to its invasive nature and increasing use of noncatheter CT angiography intraoperative ultrasound.

Computed Tomography Perfusion Imaging

CT perfusion imaging provides the ability to detect regional and global alterations in organ blood flow. It enables resolution of arterial and portal venous components of blood flow on a global and regional basis.[178] This technique is thought to improve the sensitivity and specificity of liver imaging as most hepatic pathology affects blood flow regionally, globally, or both. Earlier detection of primary and metastatic liver lesions and cirrhosis may be possible based on the relative increase in hepatic arterial blood flow associated with these conditions.[178] Beers and associates[176] reported an increased fractional arterial perfusion of liver in patients with cirrhosis

compared with healthy controls. MDCT perfusion technique can provide high spatial and temporal resolution for entire liver perfusion studies. However, the risk of radiation exposure due to CT perfusion study raises serious concern, as it is three to six times greater than that of a routine abdominal CT study.[178,179]

Size, Shape, and Density

On noncontrast CT scans, the liver parenchyma is usually homogeneous with attenuation values ranging between 40 and 70 HU. The attenuation of the liver is variable from person to person and may be different from time to time in the same individual.[180,181] It usually has an attenuation of 10 HU greater than that of spleen on noncontrast images, due the glycogen content of liver. After contrast administration, differential liver-spleen attenuation depends on scan delay and injection protocol.[182] Glycogen depletion and concomitant deposition of fat lower the density of the liver. In patients with anemia, a false appearance of increased hepatic density may occur because of the decreased attenuation of the blood pool.

On CT, the liver has the shape of an irregular hemisphere with a smooth convex superior, lateral, and anterior surface and a concave inferior, posterior, and medial surface that has a number of impressions. Accessory fissures of the liver formed by invagination of the diaphragm may cause deformities on the parietal surface of the liver that should not be confused with intrahepatic masses or peritoneal implants along the hepatic surface[183] (Fig. 85-18). When multiple clefts are present on the liver surface, the appearance may simulate that of cirrhosis.[56,184]

Intrahepatic bile ducts are generally not visible on CT studies. With 5-mm-thick sections, ducts can be seen in 40% of patients with an average size of 2 mm in the central part of the liver and 1.8 mm in the periphery. Ducts are visualized more commonly in the right than in the left lobe. Dilated lymphatics or perivascular fat may simulate dilated bile ducts.[185]

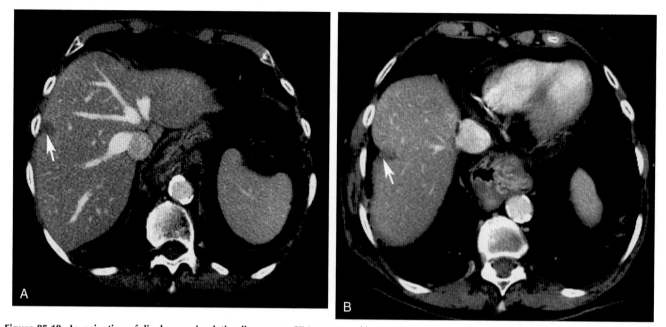

Figure 85-18. Invagination of diaphragm simulating liver mass. CT image (**A**) of liver at the level of hepatic veins reveals a hypodense focal lesion (*arrow*). A section at higher level (**B**) indicates that invagination of diaphragm (*arrow*) simulates a focal lesion in liver.

Magnetic Resonance Imaging

The recent development of rapid acquisition techniques with excellent image quality and tissue-specific contrast agents has made MRI the most accurate imaging modality for the evaluation of liver disease.[186] In many instances, with the appropriate combination of sequences, MRI can diagnose and characterize diffuse liver disease accurately and obviate the need for invasive procedures.[187] MRI plays an important role in the evaluation of complications and follow-up of diffuse hepatic disease and may have prognostic as well as therapeutic implications.

Many different pulse sequences can be used in hepatic MRI. Sequence performance depends on field strength, software, and gradients. In general, T1- and T2-weighted sequences are performed. Generally, contrast agents are added in most situations. Torso phased-array surface coils are an alternative to body coils and have the advantage of increasing the signal-to-noise ratio by at least a factor of 2.[188] They have been shown to increase lesion-to-liver contrast, lesion detection, and image definition.[189] Structures near the surface coils, such as subcutaneous fat, have markedly increased signal.[188] Phase ghost artifact is also propagated through the entire image.[188] These limitations can occasionally cause significant image degradation.

T1-Weighted Sequences

The sequences most frequently used for T1 weighting include spin echo or gradient echo (such as fast low-angle shot [FLASH] or fast multiplanar spoiled gradient-echo [FMPSPGR]). Short TR and TE and high flip angle for gradient echo are required to achieve T1 weighting. Several techniques to minimize artifact have been used, including obtaining multiple signal averages, respiratory compensation, fat suppression, and saturation pulses for abdominal wall fat.

Spoiled gradient-echo sequences have become a common method to obtain T1-weighted images (Fig. 85-19). The images are obtained during a single 15- to 25-second breath-hold. Imaging of the entire liver during a single breath-hold is useful for dynamic gadolinium administration when images are acquired at multiple time points after contrast administration.[190-199] Relative disadvantages of gradient-echo images include less signal-to-noise ratio than with spin-echo images, more artifacts and signal inhomogeneity, and the need for a cooperative patient capable of suspending respiration.[200,201]

On T1-weighted images, the signal intensity of normal liver (see Fig. 85-19) is greater than that of spleen, muscle, and kidney and less than that of surrounding fat. Bile, ascites, and fluid-filled gut have the lowest signal intensities.[202] Bile within the gallbladder may have a layering of signal intensities related to the state of fasting and relative lipid, aqueous, proteinaceous, and calcified contents.[203] Most hepatic tumors and abscesses have a long T1 and thus appear as hypointense lesions on T1-weighted images. Most blood vessels appear as dark structures because of flow void phenomena.[12,204] Portions of the hepatic or portal venous system and IVC may appear hyperintense or isointense with the liver because of inflow phenomena and even-echo rephasing.[205]

T2-Weighted Sequences

Spin-echo, segmented spin-echo (such as fast or turbo spin-echo), and short tau inversion recovery (STIR) sequences can be used to obtain T2-like information (Fig. 85-20). When spin-echo techniques with a long TR (>2000 msec) and long TE (80-120 msec) are used, T2 differences predominate[206,207] (see Fig. 85-20). Signal intensity increases with increasing T2 values and structures with long T2 values, such as gallbladder, fluid-filled bowel, ascites, spleen, and kidney, become bright. Fat is somewhat less bright and liver and muscle are relatively hypointense. The lung and air-filled bowel are black.

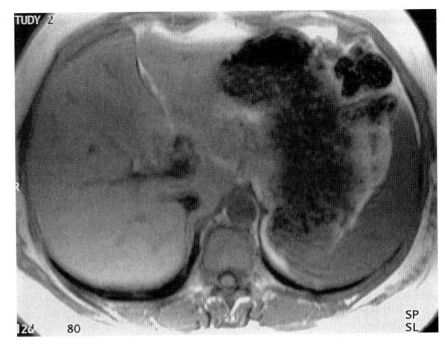

Figure 85-19. Liver MR: T1-weighted gradient-echo image. This axial T1-weighted gradient-echo image (142/4.4/80 degrees) has excellent anatomic detail. The signal intensity of the liver is greater than that of spleen and muscle. Note the peripheral bright signal intensity from the torso phased-array coil.

Segmented (fast) spin-echo sequences are commonly used in place of conventional spin-echo images to achieve T2-weighted images (see Fig. 85-19). In these sequences, a series of seven or more spin echoes is typically acquired after an initial 90-degree excitation. This enables substantial scan time reduction.[198,208,209] Fast spin-echo techniques have shown consistently sharper anatomic detail with less respiratory and cardiac motion artifacts than conventional spin-echo sequences.[210] Segmented spin-echo sequences can also be performed as a breath-hold technique to reduce motion and aortic pulsation artifacts further.[211] These sequences are thought to be at least equivalent to conventional spin-echo sequences.[212] Half-Fourier acquisition single-shot turbo spin-echo (HASTE) is a modification of turbo spin echo allowing for a further reduction in scan time, by using a slab acquisition mode.[213]

STIR imaging can be performed to acquire T2-like information. These sequences suppress fat signal, relying on its short T1 relaxation time. When the TI of inversion recovery sequences is reduced to 80 to 120 msec, the signal from fat is suppressed because it is near the null point (inversion point) of magnetization recovery. Because fat in the body wall and mesentery is a major source of motion artifact, this sequence increases signal-to-noise and contrast-to-noise ratios.[214-217] The sequence yields excellent lesion-to-liver contrast, which helps to confirm the presence of a lesion or increases confidence in its absence. It also has a high sensitivity for fatty infiltration, periportal changes, and biliary dilatation but suffers from relatively low signal-to-noise ratio. A short TI makes the image both T1 and T2 dependent, so that structures with long T1 and T2 values, such as tumors, are conspicuously bright. The STIR sequence is usually not used by

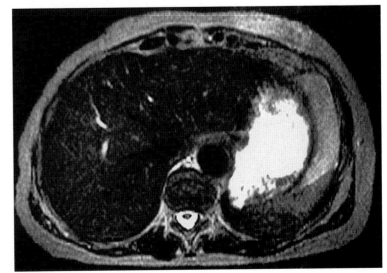

Figure 85-20. Liver MR: Rapid T2-weighted image. This axial T2-weighted turbo spin-echo image (2118/80 degrees) exploits differences in T2 relaxation between normal liver and masses. Spleen, kidneys, gallbladder, and bile become brightest. Liver and muscle become relatively hypointense. This image was obtained in a body coil.

itself but is useful in confirming the presence of a lesion or increasing confidence in its absence.

Fat-Suppression Techniques

Fat suppression is most typically achieved on T1-weighted gradient-echo images by using chemical shift gradient-echo imaging.[218-220] Fat protons resonate at a slightly lower frequency than water protons, such that the two constantly fall in and out of phase with each other. When fat and water exist in the same voxel (as in fatty metamorphosis), choosing a TE when their signals are out of phase results in signal loss.[221] Normal liver and most cancers do not contain an observable amount of triglyceride, so that the image intensity remains the same on inphase and opposed-phase images. In the presence of fatty change, the signal intensity of the liver decreases on opposed-phase images compared with inphase images. Likewise, fat within lesions can be detected, improving lesion characterization.[222] Using opposed-phase sequences for postgadolinium imaging can lead to a paradoxical decrease in signal intensity in tissues with predominantly fat content.[223]

Frequency-selective fat suppression is based on presaturation of the fat by using a narrow-band excitation pulse, centered at the resonant frequency of fat, which does not affect water protons. Frequency-selective fat suppression can be used to produce fat suppression with both gradient-echo and spin-echo techniques. It is especially useful on fast spin-echo T2 images in which fat is relatively bright because of the application of the multiple 180-degree pulses. Fatty liver may diminish conspicuity of focal high signal intensity lesions. Fat suppression can help minimize this effect. In the presence of magnetic field or radiofrequency inhomogeneities and imperfect radiofrequency profiles, the homogeneity of the frequency-selective fat saturation is appreciably compromised. As discussed previously, STIR can be used in both spin-echo and gradient-echo sequences to achieve a more uniform fat suppression.

Magnetic Resonance Contrast Agents

MR contrast agents can improve liver lesion detection and characterization.[224,225] They can be categorized based on their mode of altering liver signal intensity.

Extracellular Fluid Agents

This class of agents includes the gadolinium chelates: gadopentetate dimeglumine (Gd-DTPA) and gadoterate meglumine (Gd-DOTA). These paramagnetic agents act by shortening T1 relaxation times.[226,227] These agents function in a manner analogous to iodinated CT contrast agents by rapidly diffusing from the intravascular space to the extracellular space. Thus, they require rapid imaging to exploit differences between liver lesions and normal hepatic parenchyma. Rapid imaging is most frequently accomplished with a multislice spoiled gradient-echo technique, allowing the entire liver to be imaged in a single breath-hold (15-25 seconds). Although the signal-to-noise ratio is less than that of higher-resolution sequences, such as spin-echo sequences, this technique allows faster imaging in multiple phases of contrast enhancement, analogous to multiphasic spiral CT. Images are obtained before contrast administration, in the arterial-predominant phase, in the portal-predominant phase (Fig. 85-21), and then during equilibrium.

Dynamic contrast enhancement has proved useful in characterizing hemangiomas, detecting hypervascular metastases or small hepatocellular lesions, and detecting enhancement in the central scar of focal nodular hyperplasia.[228-230] It has been shown not only to improve the distinction between benign and malignant lesions but also to achieve a specific diagnosis in many focal lesions.[231] Gadolinium chelate–enhanced three-dimensional rapid gradient-echo images have been found superior to T2-weighted fast spin-echo images (with or without fat suppression and breath holding) for the detection of focal liver masses.[232]

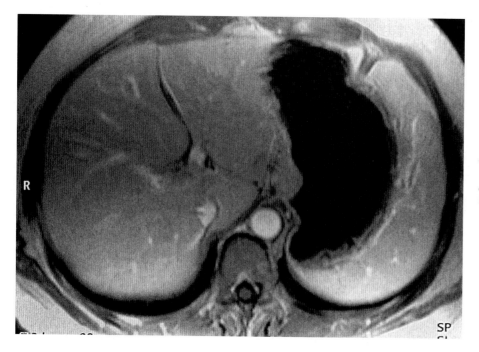

Figure 85-21. Liver MR: Postgadolinium T1-weighted gradient echo image. The aorta, IVC, and hepatic parenchyma are brightly enhanced. Gadolinium enhancement affords improved characterization of focal lesions.

Reticuloendothelial (Macrophage-Monocytic Phagocytic System) Agents

Uptake of reticuloendothelial system agents occurs in endothelial and Kupffer cells of the liver. This class of agents includes superparamagnetic iron oxide particles coated with dextran, ferumoxide (AMI-25), and ultrasmall superparamagnetic iron oxide agents like SHU-555A and AMI-227.[233-235] They function as T2 relaxation promoters and lower the normal signal of reticuloendothelial system containing tissue. Reticuloendothelial system agents are used primarily for lesion detection. Their effect depends on the strength of the applied magnetic field.[236] These agents characterize a lesion by determining the absence of Kupffer cells within the mass.

Ferumoxides is most often used to optimize lesion detection in patients in whom the resection of a metastasis is contemplated or when there is a high suspicion for metastatic disease and the CT scan is negative[237-239] (Fig. 85-22). Ferumoxide-enhanced MR can detect 27% more lesions than nonenhanced MRI and 40% more than CT.[237]

Hepatobiliary Agents

Hepatobiliary agents mangafodipir trisodium (Mn-DPDP), gadoxetate (Gd-EOB-DTPA), and gadobenate dimeglumine (Gd-BOPTA) promote T1 relaxation, thus increasing the signal intensity of normal liver and hepatocyte-containing lesions on T1-weighted images. This increased signal intensity improves the contrast difference between liver parenchyma and lesions. Mn-DPDP is primarily used in the detection of lesions, but it does provide some lesion characterization ability.[240] Usually, intrahepatic cholangiocarcinomas, lymphomas, and most metastases do not show uptake of these agents. However, some lesions that show uptake reveal peripheral, rim enhancement. Hepatocellular carcinoma, focal nodular hyperplasia, regenerating nodules, and dysplastic nodules show uptake due to the presence of functional hepatocytes.[241] Uptake is diminished in cirrhosis.[242] Mn-DPDP does not suffer from the time constraints that extra-cellular fluid agents (Gd-DTPA and Gd-DOTA) do because enhancement persists for several hours.[243] Mn-DPDP and Gd-BOPTA (0.1 mmol/kg) can provide equal liver enhancement and lesion conspicuity.[244] Liver MRI after Gd-BOPTA can increase the detection of liver lesions in patients with primary malignant hepatic neoplasm, especially for lesions less than 1 cm.[245]

Gd-EOB-DTPA and Gd-BOPTA cause prominent and prolonged enhancement of normal hepatic parenchyma (Fig. 85-23). These agents can be delivered as a bolus and thus has the added benefit of assessing the vascularity of a lesion, like an extracellular agent.[246,247] Studies have shown a 60% increase in tumor-liver contrast and contrast-to-noise ratio[248] and 56% increased detection of liver metastases with the use of these contrast agents.[246-248] Decreased hepatic blood flow and liver dysfunction diminish hepatic enhancement.[249] After the hepatic parenchymal phase, these agents are secreted in the biliary tract (see Fig. 85-23), which may enable diagnostic imaging of the bile ducts. Gd-BOPTA produces sustained enhancement of normal liver parenchyma as well as the biliary tree.[250] The contrast-to-noise ratio on postcontrast gradient-echo images increases by five times for metastases when a dose of 100 µmol/kg is used.[243]

Magnetic Resonance Perfusion Imaging

Perfusion MRI represents an useful alternative to CT perfusion imaging for surveillance of hepatocellular carcinoma. Jackson and associates[251] reported a three-dimensional dynamic contrast-enhanced perfusion MRI in humans for lesion-specific permeability mapping. Perfusion characteristics of lesions with dual blood supply were unreliable, as they used only the hepatic arterial supply as input function.[178] Annet and colleagues[247] reported increased fractional arterial perfusion and decreased mean transit time when they evaluated humans with cirrhosis by dual-input, single-compartment perfusion MRI with a standard low-molecular-weight contrast material. Further technical improvements are required.

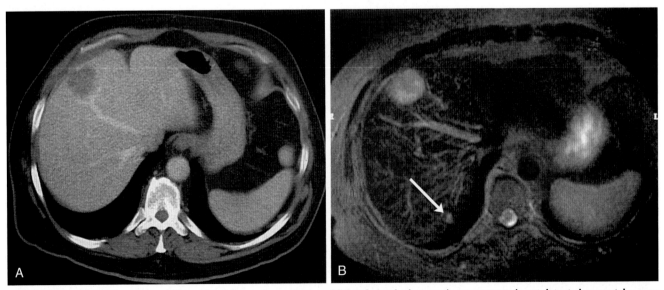

Figure 85-22. Ferumoxide-enhanced T1-weighted image demonstrates additional rectal adenocarcinoma metastasis not detected on portal venous phase CT. A. CT demonstrates large metastasis straddling the medial segment of left lobe and anterior segment of right lobe. **B.** Additional subcentimeter metastasis is detected after ferumoxide on T2-weighted MRI (*arrow*), not seen on CT or nonenhanced MR.

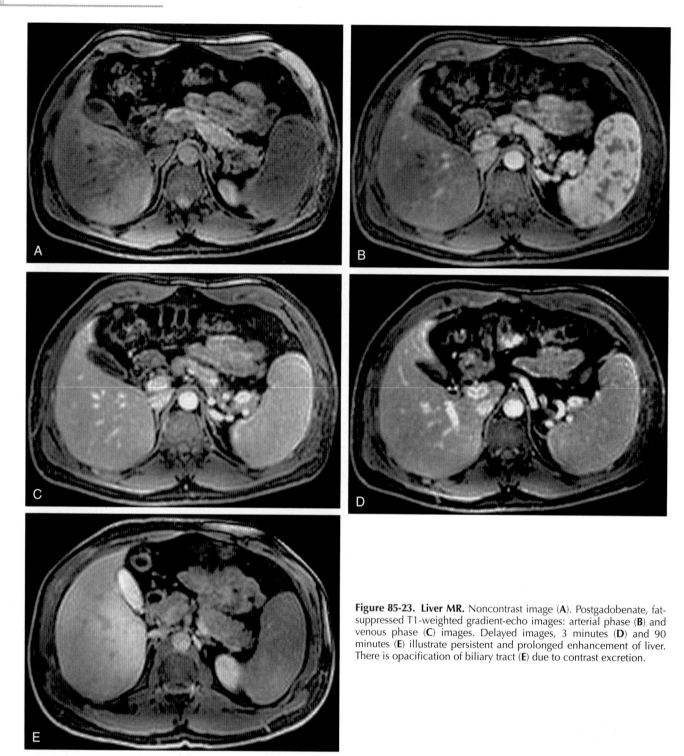

Figure 85-23. Liver MR. Noncontrast image (**A**). Postgadobenate, fat-suppressed T1-weighted gradient-echo images: arterial phase (**B**) and venous phase (**C**) images. Delayed images, 3 minutes (**D**) and 90 minutes (**E**) illustrate persistent and prolonged enhancement of liver. There is opacification of biliary tract (**E**) due to contrast excretion.

Diffusion-Weighted Magnetic Resonance Imaging

The advent of echoplanar imaging techniques enabled diffusion-weighted MRI of abdomen.[252-254] Diffusion-weighted MRI can help differentiate benign from malignant hepatic lesions. Malignant lesions like hepatocellular carcinoma and metastases have low apparent diffusion coefficient. Benign lesions, including hemangioma and cysts, have high apparent diffusion coefficients.[255] Diffusion-weighted MRI has also been used to differentiate liver abscess from cystic or necrotic tumor. Liver abscess is markedly hyperintense, whereas cystic or necrotic liver tumors are hypointense on diffusion-weighted MRI.[253]

Selecting an Appropriate Imaging Technique

Technological advances in radiology offers several imaging tools for evaluation of focal liver lesions; these include ultrasound, CT, and MRI. Choosing the most appropriate imaging modality for evaluating the liver lesion under question depends on the information required from imaging for clinical management decisions. Although ultrasound might be an appropriate examination for a patient with no prior medical history and increased alkaline phosphatase and bilirubin levels, ultrasound is not an adequate screening test for hepatocellular carcinoma in a patient with cirrhosis and increased α-fetoprotein. Although MDCT serves as the first-line imaging modality for evaluation of liver, MRI offers an attractive alternative to radiation-based CT examination. The clinical applications of MRI for evaluation of liver is rapidly expanding, due to availability of faster sequences and newer contrast agents. Indeed, in some centers, MRI is being used as the imaging modality of choice for evaluation of liver disease.[256,257] However, in most centers, MRI is still reserved for certain clinical situations, such as further characterization of liver lesions detected on CT, patients with iodinated contrast allergy, and work-up for hepatic resection.[186] Intraoperative ultrasound has become a standard liver imaging tool for resection of liver metastases from colorectal carcinoma. The choice of appropriate imaging modality should be made on an individual case basis depending on the lesion under question, availability of imaging facilities, and cost issues.

Acknowledgment

We would like to thank Dr. Diego Martin, Department of Radiology, Emory University Hospital, Atlanta, for contributing some of the MR images for this chapter.

References

1. Jones AL: Anatomy of the normal liver. In Zakim D, Boyer TD (eds): Hepatology. Philadelphia, WB Saunders, 1996, pp 3-31.
2. Schneck CD: Embryology, histology, gross anatomy, and normal imaging anatomy of the liver. In Friedman A, Dachman A (eds): Radiology of the Liver, Biliary Tract, and Pancreas. St. Louis, Mosby, 1994, pp 1-24.
3. Raytch RE, Smith GW: Anatomy and physiology of the liver. In Zuidema GD (ed): Shackelford's Surgery of the Alimentary Tract, vol IV. Philadelphia, WB Saunders, 1996, pp 257-273.
4. Reuter SR, Redman HC, Cho KJ: Gastrointestinal Angiography, 3rd ed. Philadelphia, WB Saunders, 1986.
5. Wanless IR: Anatomy and developmental anomalies of the liver. In Feldman M, Scharschmidt BF, Sleisenger MH (eds): Sleisenger and Fordtran's Gastrointestinal and Liver Disease. Philadelphia, WB Saunders, 1998, pp 1055-1060.
6. Cohen EI, Wilck EJ, Shapiro RS: Hepatic imaging in the 21st century. Semin Liver Dis 26:363-372, 2006.
7. Makuuchi M, Hasegawa H, Yamazuki S, et al: The inferior right hepatic vein: Ultrasonic demonstration. Radiology 148:213-217, 1983.
8. Oshima K, Kaneko T, Kawase Y: Quantitative analysis of doppler waveform of hepatic veins for assessment of hepatic functional reserve. Hepatogastroenterology 54:180-185, 2007.
9. Mukai JK, Stack CM, Turner DA, et al: Imaging of surgically relevant hepatic vascular and segmental anatomy: Part 2. Extent and resectability of hepatic neoplasms. AJR 149:293-297, 1987.
10. Mukai JK, Stack CM, Turner DA, et al: Imaging of surgically relevant hepatic vascular and segmental anatomy: Part 1. Normal anatomy. AJR 149:287-292, 1987.
11. Gazelle GS, Haaga J: Hepatic neoplasms: Surgically relevant segmental anatomy and imaging techniques. AJR 158:1015-1018, 1992.
12. Waggenspack GA, Tabb DR, Tiruchelvam V, et al: Three-dimensional localization of hepatic neoplasms with computer-generated scissurae recreated from axial CT and MR images. AJR 160:307-309, 1993.
13. Silverman PM, Zeman RK: Normal anatomy of the liver and biliary system. In Silverman PM, Zeman RK (eds): CT and MRI of the Liver and Biliary System. New York, Churchill Livingstone, 1990, pp 1-20.
14. Couinaud C: Le Foie: Études Anatomiques et Chirurgicales. Paris: Masson, 1957.
15. Bismuth H, Houssin D, Castaing D: Major and minor segmentecomies "réglées" in liver surgery. World J Surg 6:10-24, 1982.
16. Soyer P, Bluemke DA, Bliss DF, et al: Surgical segmental anatomy of the liver: Demonstration with spiral CT during arterial portography and multiplanar reconstruction. AJR 163:99-103, 1994.
17. Lafortune M, Madore F, Patriquin H, et al: Segmental anatomy of the liver: A sonographic approach to the Couinaud nomenclature. Radiology 181:443-448, 1991.
18. Dodds WJ, Erickson SJ, Taylor AJ, et al: Caudate lobe of the liver: Anatomy, embryology, and pathology. AJR 154:87-93, 1990.
19. Auh YH, Rosen A, Rubenstein WA, et al: CT of the papillary process of the caudate lobe of the liver. AJR 142:535-538, 1984.
20. Donoso L, Martinez-Noguera A, Zidan A, et al: Papillary process of the caudate lobe of the liver: Sonographic appearance. Radiology 173:631-633, 1989.
21. Balfe DM, Mauro MA, Koehler RE, et al: Gastrohepatic ligament: Normal and pathologic CT anatomy. Radiology 150:485-490, 1984.
22. Zirinsky K, Auh YH, Rubenstein WA, et al: The portacaval space: CT with MR correlation. Radiology 156:453-458, 1985.
23. Weinstein JB, Heiken JP, Lee JKT, et al: High resolution CT of the porta hepatis and hepatoduodenal ligament. RadioGraphics 6:1-37, 1986.
24. Russell E, Yrizzary JM, Montalvo BM, et al: Left hepatic duct anatomy: Implications. Radiology 174:353-356, 1990.
25. Meyers WC, Jones RS: Textbook of Liver and Biliary Surgery. Philadelphia, JB Lippincott, 1990.
26. Taylor HM, Ros PR: Hepatic imaging. Radiol Clin North Am 36:237-246, 1998.
27. Gelfand DW: The liver: plain film diagnosis. Semin Roentgenol 10:177-187, 1975.
28. Gore RM, Goldberg HI: Plain film and cholangiographic findings in liver tumors. Semin Roentgenol 12:87-93, 1983.
29. Rogers JV, Torres WE, Clements J, et al: Plain film diagnosis of the liver. In Bernardino ME, Sones PJ (eds): Hepatic Radiography. New York, Macmillan, 1984, pp 1-49.
30. Baker SR: The Abdominal Plain Film. East Norwalk, CT, Appleton & Lange, 1990.
31. Love L, Demos TC, Reynes CJ, et al: Visualization of the lateral edge of the liver in ascites. Radiology 122:619-622, 1977.
32. Fleischner FG, Sayegh V: Assessment of the size of the liver. N Engl J Med 259:271-274, 1985.
33. Darlak JJ, Moskowitz M, Kattan K: Calcifications in the liver. Radiol Clin North Am 18:209-220, 1980.
34. Cooperberg PL, Rowley VA: Abdominal sonographic examination technique. In Taveras J, Ferrucci J (eds): Radiology: Diagnosis, Imaging, Intervention. Philadelphia, JB Lippincott, 1990, pp 1-11.
35. Parulekar SG, Bree RL: Liver. In McGahan JP, Goldberg BB (eds): Diagnostic Ultrasound: A Logical Approach. Philadelphia, Lippincott-Raven, 1998, pp 599-692.
36. Withers CE, Wilson SR: The Liver. In Rumack CM, Wilson SR, Charboneau JW (eds): Diagnostic Ultrasound, 2nd ed. St. Louis, Mosby, 1998, pp 87-154.
37. Shkolnik ML: Guide to the Ultrasound Examination of the Abdomen. New York, Springer-Verlag, 1986.
38. Chan V, Hanbidge A, Wilson S, et al: Case for active physician involvement in US practice. Radiology 199:555-560, 1996.
39. Grant EG: Liver. In Mittelstaedt C (ed): General Ultrasound. New York, Churchill Livingstone, 1992, pp 173-249.
40. Wing VW, Laing FC, Jeffrey RB, et al: Sonographic differentiation of enlarged hepatic arteries from dilated intrahepatic bile ducts. AJR 145:57-61, 1985.
41. Berland LL, Lawson TL, Foley WD: Porta hepatis: Sonographic discrimination of bile ducts from arteries with pulsed Doppler with new anatomic detail. AJR 138:833-840, 1987.
42. Bret P, de Stempel JV, Atri M, et al: Intrahepatic bile duct and portal vein anatomy revisited. Radiology 169:405-407, 1988.
43. Fraser-Hill MA, Atri M, Bret PM, et al: Intrahepatic portal venous system: Variations demonstrated with duplex and color Doppler US. Radiology 177:523-526, 1990.
44. Lim JH, Ryuk N, Ko YT, et al: Anatomic relationship of intrahepatic bile ducts to portal veins. J Ultrasound Med 9:137-143, 1990.
45. Lautt WW, Greenway CV: Conceptual review of the hepatic vascular bed. Hepatology 7:952-963, 1987.

46. Skrainka B, Stahlut J, Fulbeck CL, et al: Measuring liver span: Bedside examination versus ultrasound and scintiscan. J Clin Gastroenterol 8:267-270, 1990.

47. Meire HB: Ultrasound of the liver. In Wilkins R, Nunnerley H (eds): Imaging of the Liver, Pancreas and Spleen. Oxford, Blackwell Scientific, 1990, pp 10-24.

48. Gosink BB, Leymaster CE: Ultrasonic determination of hepatosplenomegaly. J Clin Ultrasound 9:37-41, 1981.

49. Niederau C, Sonnenberg AM, Muller JE, et al: Sonographic measurements of the normal liver, spleen, pancreas, and portal vein. Radiology 149:537-540, 1983.

50. Iijima H, Sasaki S, Moriyasu F, et al: Dynamic US contrast study of the liver: Vascular and delayed parenchymal phase. Hepatol Res 37:27-34, 2007.

51. Leung NWY, Farrant P, Peters TJ: Liver volume measurement by ultrasonography in normal subjects and alcoholic patients. J Hepatol 2:157-164, 1986.

52. Aube C, Oberti F, Korali N, et al: Ultrasonographic diagnosis of hepatic fibrosis or cirrhosis. J Hepatol 30:472-478, 1999.

53. Simonousky V: The diagnosis of cirrhosis by high resolution ultrasound of the liver surface. Br J Radiol 72:29-34, 1999.

54. Arita J, Kokudo N, Zhang K, et al: Three-dimensional visualization of liver segments on contrast-enhanced intraoperative sonography. AJR 188(5):W464-466, 2007.

55. Tochio H, Kudo M, Okabe Y, et al: Association between a focal spared area in the fatty liver and intrahepatic efferent blood flow from the gallbladder wall: Evaluation with color Doppler sonography. AJR 172:1249-1253, 1999.

56. Auh YH, Rubenstein WA, Zirinsky K, et al: Accessory fissures of the liver: CT and sonographic appearance. AJR 143:565-572, 1984.

57. Hillman BJ, D'Orsi CJ, Smith EH, et al: Ultrasonic appearance of the falciform ligament. AJR 132:205-206, 1979.

58. Sones PJ Jr, Torres WE: Normal ultrasonic appearance of the ligamentum teres and falciform ligament. J Clin Ultrasound 6:392-394, 1978.

59. Parulelekar SG: Ligaments and fissures of the liver: Sonographic anatomy. Radiology 130:409-411, 1979.

60. Taylor KJW, Carpenter DA: The anatomy and pathology of the porta hepatis demonstrated by gray scale ultrasonography. J Clin Ultrasound 3:117-119, 1975.

61. Kallio T, Nevalainen PI, Lahtela JT, et al: Hepatic subcapsular steatosis in diabetic CAPD patients treated with intraperitoneal insulin: Description of a typical pattern. Acta Radiol 42:323-325, 2001.

62. Kulig J, Popiela T, Klek S, et al: Intraoperative ultrasonography in detecting and assessment of colorectal liver metastases. Scand J Surg 96:51-55, 2007.

63. Castainy D, Edmond J, Bismuth H, et al: Utility of operative ultrasound in the surgical management of liver tumors. Ann Surg 204:600-605, 1986.

64. Gozzetti G, Angelini L: The use of intraoperative ultrasonography in hepatic surgery. In Kurtz A, Goldberg B (eds): Gastrointestinal Ultrasonography. New York, Churchill Livingstone, 1988, pp 237-251.

65. Parker GA, Lawrence W, Horsley JS, et al: Intraoperative ultrasound of the liver affects operative decision making. Ann Surg 209:569-577, 1989.

66. Igawa S, Sakai K, Kihoshita H, et al: Intraoperative sonography: Clinical usefulness in liver surgery. Radiology 156:473-478, 1985.

67. Glen PM, Noseworthy J, Babcock DS: Use of the intraoperative ultrasonography to localize a hepatic abscess. Arch Surg 119:347-348, 1984.

68. el Mouaaouy A, Naruhn M, Becker HD: Diagnosis of liver metastases from malignant gastrointestinal neoplasms: Results of preoperative and intraoperative ultrasound examinations. Surg Endosc 5:209-213, 1991.

69. Simeone JF: Intraoperative ultrasonography of liver. In Ferrucci J, Stark D (eds): Liver Imaging. Boston, Andover Medical, 1990, pp 247-255.

70. Rappeport ED, Loft A, Berthelsen AK, et al: Contrast-enhanced FDG-PET/CT vs. SPIO-enhanced MRI vs. FDG-PET vs. CT in patients with liver metastases from colorectal cancer: A prospective study with intraoperative confirmation. Acta Radiol 48:369-378, 2007.

71. Hagspiel KD, Neidl KF, Eichenberger AC, et al: Detection of liver metastases: Comparison of superparamagnetic iron oxide-enhanced and unenhanced MR imaging at 1.5 T with dynamic CT, intraoperative US, and percutaneous US. Radiology 196:471-478, 1995.

72. Sahani DV, Kalva SP, Tanabe KK, et al: Intraoperative US in patients undergoing surgery for liver neoplasms: Comparison with MR imaging. Radiology 232:810-814, 2004.

73. Ravikumar TS, Kane R, Cady B, et al: Hepatic cryosurgery with intraoperative ultrasound monitoring for metastatic colon carcinoma. Arch Surg 122:403-404, 1987.

74. Onik G, Kane R, Steele G, et al: Monitoring hepatic cryosurgery with sonography. AJR 147:665-669, 1986.

75. Dritschio A, Grant EG, Harter KW, et al: Interstitial radiation therapy for hepatic metastases: Sonographic guidance for applicator placement. AJR 146:275-278, 1986.

76. Marchesa P, Milsom JW, Hale JC, et al: Intraoperative laparoscopic liver ultrasonography for staging of colorectal cancer: Initial experience. Dis Colon Rectum 39(10 suppl):S73-S78, 1996.

77. Feld RI, Liu JB, Nazarian L, et al: Laparoscopic liver sonography: Preliminary experience in liver metastases compared with CT portography. J Ultrasound Med 15:288-295, 1996.

78. John TG, Greig JD, Crosbie JL, et al: Superior staging of liver tumors with laparoscopy and laparoscopic ultrasound. Ann Surg 220:711-719, 1994.

79. Koslin DB, Mulligan SA, Berland LL: Duplex assessment of the portal venous system. Semin Ultrasound CT MR 13:22-33, 1992.

80. Grant EG, Tessler FN, Perrella RR: Clinical Doppler imaging. AJR 152:707-717, 1989.

81. Foley WD, Erickson SJ: Color Doppler flow imaging. AJR 156:3-13, 1991.

82. Zweibel WJ, Fruechte D: Basics of abdominal and pelvic duplex: Instrumentation, anatomy and vascular Doppler signatures. Semin Ultrasound CT MR 13:3-21, 1992.

83. Carlisle KM, Halliwell M, Read AE, et al: Estimation of total hepatic blood flow by duplex ultrasound. Gut 3:92-97, 1992.

84. Parvey HR, Eisenberg RL, Giyanani V, et al: Duplex sonography of the portal venous system: Pitfalls and limitations. AJR 152:765-770, 1989.

85. Foley WD: Abdominal color-flow ultrasound imaging. Ultrasound Q 7:271-291, 1989.

86. Ralls PW: Color Doppler sonography of the hepatic artery and portal venous system. AJR 155:517-525, 1990.

87. Dodd GD 3rd, Memel DS, Zajko AB, et al: Hepatic artery stenosis and thrombosis in transplant recipients: Doppler diagnosis with resistive index and systolic acceleration time. Radiology 192:657-661, 1994.

88. Platt JF, Yutzy GG, Bude RO, et al: Use of Doppler sonography for revealing hepatic artery stenosis in liver transplant recipients. AJR 168:473-476, 1997.

89. Joynt LK, Platt JF, Rubin JM, et al: Hepatic artery resistance before and after standard meal in subjects with diseased and healthy livers. Radiology 196:489-492, 1995.

90. Lafortune M, Patriquin H: Doppler sonography of the liver and splanchnic veins. Semin Interv Radiol 7:27-38, 1990.

91. Koslin DB, Mulligan SA, Berland LL: Duplex assessment of splanchnic vasculature. Semin Ultrasound CT MR 13:34-39, 1992.

92. Madrazo BL, Jafri SZ, Shirkhoda A, et al: Portosystemic collaterals: Evaluation with color Doppler imaging and correlation with CT and MRI. Semin Interv Radiol 7:169-184, 1990.

93. Buonamico P, Sabba C: Echo Doppler duplex scanner and color in the study of portal hypertension. J Clin Gastroenterol 13:342-347, 1991.

94. Van Leeuwen MS: Doppler ultrasound in the evaluation of portal hypertension. In Taylor K, Strandness D (eds): Duplex Doppler Ultrasound. New York, Churchill Livingstone, pp 53-76, 1990.

95. Harvey CJ, Albrecht T: Ultrasound of focal liver lesions. Eur Radiol 11:1578-1593, 2001.

96. Hann LE, Bach AM, Cramer LD, et al: Hepatic sonography: Comparison of tissue harmonic and standard sonography techniques. AJR 173:201-206, 1999.

97. Robbin ML: Ultrasound contrast agents: A promising future. Radiol Clin North Am 39:399-414, 2001.

98. von Herbay A, Haeussinger D, Gregor M, et al: Characterization and detection of hepatocellular carcinoma (HCC): Comparison of the ultrasound contrast agents SonoVue (BR 1) and Levovist (SH U 508A). Ultraschall Med 28:168-175, 2007.

99. Li R, Guo Y, Hua X, et al: Characterization of focal liver lesions: Comparison of pulse-inversion harmonic contrast-enhanced sonography with contrast-enhanced CT. J Clin Ultrasound 35:109-117, 2007.

100. Tano S, Ueno N, Tomiyama T, et al: Possibility of differentiating small hyperechoic liver tumours using contrast-enhanced colour Doppler ultrasonography: A preliminary study. Clin Radiol 52:41-45, 1997.

101. Burns PN, Wilson SR: Focal liver masses: enhancement patterns on contrast-enhanced images—concordance of US scans with CT scans and MR images. Radiology 242:162-174, 2007.

102. Mattrey RF, Wrigley R, Steinbach GC, et al: Gas emulsions as ultrasound contrast agents: Preliminary results in rabbits and dogs. Inv Radiol 29(suppl 2):S139-S141, 1994.

103. Blomley MJ, Albrecht T, Cosgrove DO, et al: Improved imaging of liver metastases with stimulated acoustic emission in the late phase of enhancement with US contrast agent SHU508A: Early experience. Radiology 210:409-416, 1999.

104. Parker KJ, Baggs RB, Lerner RM, et al: Ultrasound contrast for hepatic tumors using IDE particles. Invest Radiol 25:1135-1139, 1990.

105. Rawool NM, Forsberg F, Liu J, et al: US contrast enhancement in conventional and harmonic imaging modes. Radiology 201:514, 1996.

106. Quaia E, Bertolotto M, Forgacs B, et al: Detection of liver metastases by pulse inversion harmonic imaging during Levovist late phase: Comparison with conventional ultrasound and helical CT in 160 patients. Eur Radiol 13:475-483, 2003.

107. Esteban JM, Molla MA, Tomas C, Maldonado L: Improved detection of liver metastases with contrast-enhanced wideband harmonic imaging: Comparison with CT findings. Eur J Ultrasound 15:119-126, 2002.

108. Maher MM, Kalra MK, Sahani DV, et al: Techniques, clinical applications and limitations of 3D reconstruction in CT of the abdomen. Korean J Radiol 5:55-67, 2004.

109. Paushter DM, Zeman RK, Scheibler ML, et al: CT evaluation of suspected hepatic metastases: Comparison of techniques for i.v. contrast enhancement. AJR 152:267-271, 1989.

110. Mayo-Smith WW, Gupta H, Ridler MS, et al: Detecting hepatic lesions: The added utility of CT liver window settings. Radiology 210:601-604, 1999.

111. Zeman RK, Clements LA, Silverman PM, et al: CT of the liver: A survey of prevailing methods for administration of contrast material. AJR 150:107-109, 1988.

112. Mathieu D, Runeton JN, Drouillard J, et al: Hepatic adenomas and focal nodular hyperplasia: Dynamic CT study. Radiology 160:53-57, 1986.

113. Berland LL, Lawson TL, Foley WD, et al: Comparison of pre- and postcontrast CT in hepatic masses. AJR 138:853-858, 1982.

114. Dodd GD III, Baron RL: Investigation of contrast enhancement in CT of the liver: The need for improved methods. AJR 160:643-646, 1993.

115. Dubrow RA, David CL, Libshitz HI, et al: Detection of hepatic metastases in breast cancer: The role of nonenhanced and enhanced CT scanning. J Comput Assist Tomogr 14:366-369, 1990.

116. Bressler EL, Alpern MB, Glazer GM, et al: Hypervascular hepatic metastases: CT evaluation. Radiology 162:49-54, 1987.

117. Patten RM, Byun JY, Freeny PC: CT of hypervascular hepatic tumors: Are unenhanced scans necessary for diagnosis? AJR 161:979-984, 1993.

118. Uchida M, Ishibashi M, Abe T, et al: Three-dimensional imaging of liver tumors using helical CT during intravenous injection of contrast material. J Comput Assist Tomogr 23:435-440, 1999.

119. Chambers TP, Baron RL, Lush RM: Hepatic CT enhancement: Part I. Alterations in the volume of contrast material within the same patients. Radiology 193:513-517, 1994.

120. Heiken JP, Brink JA, McClennan BL, et al: Dynamic incremental CT: Effect of volume and concentration of contrast material and patient weight on hepatic enhancement. Radiology 195:353-357, 1995.

121. Garcia PA, Bonaldi VM, Bret PM, et al: Effect of rate of contrast medium injection on hepatic enhancement at CT. Radiology 199:185-189, 1996.

122. Irie T, Kusano S: Contrast-enhanced spiral CT of the liver: Effect of injection time on time to peak hepatic enhancement. J Comput Assist Tomogr 20:633-637, 1996.

123. Freeny PC, Gardner JC, vonIngersleben G, et al: Hepatic helical CT: Effect of reduction of iodine dose of intravenous contrast material on hepatic contrast enhancement. Radiology 197:89-93, 1995.

124. Baker ME, Beam C, Leder R, et al: Contrast material for combined abdominal and pelvic CT: Can cost be reduced by increasing the concentration and decreasing the volume? AJR 160:637-641, 1993.

125. Heiken JP: Liver. In Lee J, Sagel S, Stanely R, et al (eds): Computed Body Tomography With MRI Correlation, 3rd ed. Philadelphia, Lippincott-Raven; 1998, pp 701-777.

126. Brink JA, Heiken JP, Forman HP, et al: Hepatic spiral CT: Reduction of dose of intravenous contrast material. Radiology 197:83-88, 1995.

127. Megibow AJ, Jacob G, Heiken JP, et al: Quantitative and qualitative evaluation of volume of low osmolality contrast medium needed for routine helical abdominal CT. AJR 176:583-589, 2001.

128. Birnbaum BA, Jacobs JE, Yin D: Hepatic enhancement during helical CT: A comparison of moderate rate uniphasic and biphasic contrast injection protocols. AJR 165:853-858, 1995.

129. Foley WD, Hoffmann RG, Quiroz FA, et al: Hepatic helical CT: Contrast material injection protocol. Radiology 192:367-371, 1994.

130. Chambers TP, Baron RL, Lush RM: Hepatic CT enhancement: Part II. Alterations in contrast material volume and rate of injection within the same patients. Radiology 193:518-522, 1994.

131. Heiken JP: Liver. In Lee JKT, Sagel SS, Stanley RJ, Heiken JP (eds): Computed Body Tomography with MRI Correlation. Philadelphia, Lippincott-Raven, 1998, pp 701-778.

132. Foley WD, Karcaaltincaba M. Computed tomography angiography: Principles and clinical applications. J Comput Assist Tomogr 27: S23-S30, 2003.

133. Yagyu Y, Awai K, Inoue M, et al: MDCT of hypervascular hepatocellular carcinomas: A prospective study using contrast materials with different iodine concentrations. AJR 184:1535-1540, 2005.

134. Hannienen EL, Vogl TJ, Relfe R, et al: Detection of focal liver lesions at biphasic spiral CT: Randomized double-blind study of the effect of iodine concentration in contrast materials. Radiology 216:403-409, 2000.

135. Sultana S, Morishita S, Awai K, et al: Evaluation of hypervascular hepatocellular carcinoma in cirrhotic liver by means of helical CT: Comparison of different contrast medium concentrations within the same patient. Radiat Med 21:239-245, 2003.

136. Schoellnast H, Tillich M, Deutschmann HA, et al: Improvement of parenchymal and vascular enhancement using saline flush and power injection for multiple-detector-row abdominal CT. Eur Radiol 14: 659-664, 2004.

137. Silverman PM, Roberts S, Tefft MC, et al: Helical CT of the liver: Clinical application of an automated computer technique, SmartPrep, for obtaining images with optical contrast enhancement. AJR 165:73-78, 1995.

138. Kopka L, Funke M, Fischer U, et al: Parenchymal liver enhancement with bolus-triggered helical CT: Preliminary clinical results. Radiology 195:282-284, 1995.

139. Paulson EK, Fisher AJ, DeLong DM, Parker DD, Nelson RC: Helical liver CT with computer-assisted bolus-tracking technology: Is it possible to predict which patients will not achieve a threshold of enhancement? Radiology 209:787-792, 1998.

140. Silverman PM, Roberts SC, Ducic I, et al: Assessment of technology that permits individualized scan delays on helical hepatic CT: A technique to improve efficiency in use of contrast material. AJR 167:79-84, 1996.

141. Dinkel HP, Fieger M, Knupffer J, Moll R, Schindler G. Optimizing liver contrast in helical liver CT: Value of a real-time bolus-triggering technique. Eur Radiol 8:1608-1612, 1998.

142. Kopka L, Funke M, Fischer U, et al: Parenchymal liver enhancement with bolus-triggered helical CT: Preliminary clinical results. Radiology 195:282-284, 1995.

143. Mehnert F, Pereira PL, Trubenbach J, Kopp AF, Claussen CD: Automatic bolus tracking in monophasic spiral CT of the liver: Liver-to-lesion conspicuity. Eur Radiol 11:580-584, 2001.

144. Nelson RC, Moyers JH, Chezmar JL, et al: Hepatic dynamic sequential CT: Section enhancement profiles with a bolus of ionic and nonionic contrast agents. Radiology 178:499-502, 1991.

145. Kim T, Murakami T, Tsuda K, et al: Effects of injection rates of contrast material on arterial phase hepatic CT. AJR 171:429-432, 1998.

146. Kopka L, Rodenwaldt J, Fischer U, et al: Dual-phase helical CT of the liver: Effects of bolus tracking and different volumes of contrast material. Radiology 201:321-326, 1996.

147. Choi BI, Lee HJ, Han JK, et al: Detection of hypervascular nodular hepatocellular carcinomas: Value of triphasic helical CT compared with iodized-oil CT. AJR 168:219-224, 1997.

148. Kanematsu M, Oliver JH 3rd, Carr B, et al: Hepatocellular carcinoma: The role of helical biphasic contrast-enhanced CT versus CT during arterial portography. Radiology 205:75-80, 1997.

149. Hwang GJ, Kim MJ, Yoo HS, et al: Nodular hepatocellular carcinomas: Detection with arterial-, portal-, and delayed-phase images at spiral CT. Radiology 202:383-388, 1997.

150. Sahani D, Mehta A, Blake M, et al: Preoperative hepatic vascular evaluation with CT and MR angiography: Implications for surgery. RadioGraphics 24:1367-1380, 2004.

151. Hollett MD, Jeffrey RB Jr, Nino-Murcia M, et al: Dual-phase helical CT of the liver: value of arterial phase scans in the detection of small (≤1.5 cm) malignant hepatic neoplasms. AJR 164:879-884, 1995.

152. Miller FH, Butler RS, Hoff FL, et al: Using triphasic helical CT to detect focal hepatic lesions in patients with neoplasms. AJR 171:643-649, 1998.

153. Oliver JH 3rd, Baron RL, Federle MP, et al: Hypervascular liver metastases: Do unenhanced and hepatic arterial phase CT images affect tumor detection? Radiology 205:709-715, 1997.

154. Federle MP, Blachar A: CT evaluation of the liver: Principles and techniques. Semin Liver Dis 21:135-146, 2001.

155. Kalra MK, Maher MM, Rizzo S, Saini S: Radiation exposure and projected risks with multidetector row computed tomography scanning: Clinical strategies and technologic developments for dose reduction. J Comput Assist Tomogr 28:S46-S49, 2004.

156. Kalra MK, Maher MM, Toth TL, et al: Comparison of z-axis automatic tube current modulation technique with fixed tube current CT scanning of abdomen and pelvis. Radiology 232:347-353, 2004.

157. Kalra MK, Prasad S, Saini S, et al: Clinical comparison of standard-dose and 50% reduced-dose abdominal CT: Effect on image quality. AJR 179:1101-1106, 2002.

158. Lacomis JM, Baron RL, Oliver JH 3rd, et al: Cholangiocarcinoma: Delayed CT contrast enhancement patterns. Radiology 203:98-104, 1997.

159. Keogan MT, Seabourn JT, Paulson EK, et al: Contrast-enhanced CT of intrahepatic and hilar cholangiocarcinoma: Delay time for optimal imaging. AJR 169:1493-1499, 1997.

160. Bernardino ME, Erwin BC, Steiberg HV, et al: Delayed hepatic CT scanning: Increased confidence and improved detection of hepatic metastases. Radiology 159:71-74, 1986.

161. Miller DL, Simmons JT, Chang R, et al: Hepatic metastasis detection: Comparison of three CT contrast enhancement methods. Radiology 165:785-790, 1987.

162. Perkerson RB, Erwin BC, Baumgartner BR, et al: CT densities in delayed iodine hepatic scanning. Radiology 155:445-446, 1985.

163. Phillips VM, Erwin BC, Bernardino ME: Delayed iodine scanning of the liver: A promising CT technique. J Comput Assist Tomogr 9:415-419, 1985.

164. Iannaccone R, Laghi A, Catalano C, et al: Hepatocellular carcinoma: Role of unenhanced and delayed phase multi-detector row helical CT in patients with cirrhosis. Radiology 234:460-467, 2005.

165. Nelson RC, Moyers JH, Chezmar JL, et al: Hepatic dynamic sequential CT: Section enhancement profiles with a bolus on ionic and nonionic contrast agents. Radiology 178:499-502, 1991.

166. Heiken JP, Weyman PJ, Lee JKT, et al: Detection of focal hepatic masses: Prospective evaluation with CT, delayed CT, CT during arterial portography, and MR imaging. Radiology 171:47-51, 1989.

167. Bluemke DA, Soyer PA, Chan BW, et al: Spiral CT during arterial portography: Technique and applications. RadioGraphics 15:623-637, 1995.

168. Nghiem HV, Dimas CT, McVicar JP, et al: Impact of double helical CT and three-dimensional CT arteriography on surgical planning for hepatic transplantation. Abdom Imaging 24:278-284, 1999.

169. Freeny PC, Nghiem HV, Winter TC: Helical CT during arterial portography: Optimization of contrast enhancement and scanning parameters. Radiology 194:83-90, 1995.

170. Soyer P, Roche A, Gad M, et al: Preoperative segmental localization of hepatic metastases: utility of three-dimensional CT during arterial portography. Radiology 180:653-658, 1991.

171. Freeny PC, Marks WM: Hepatic perfusion abnormalities during CT angiography: Detection and interpretation. Radiology 159:685-691, 1986.

172. Fernandez MDP, Bernardino ME: Hepatic pseudolesion: Appearance of focal low attenuation in the medial segment of the left lobe at CT arterial portography. Radiology 181:809-812, 1992.

173. DeSanctis JT, Gazelle GS, Saini S: CT techniques. In Gazelle GS, Saini S, Mueller PR (eds): Hepatobiliary and Pancreatic Radiology Imaging and Intervention. New York, Thieme, 1998, pp 38-61.

174. Li L, Liu LZ, Xie ZM, et al: Multi-phasic CT arterial portography and CT hepatic arteriography improving the accuracy of liver cancer detection. World J Gastroenterol 10:3118-3121, 2004.

175. Pandharipande PV, Krinsky GA, Rusinek H, et al: Perfusion imaging of the liver: Current challenges and future goals. Radiology 234:661-673, 2005.

176. Van Beers BE, Leconte I, Materne R, et al: Hepatic perfusion parameters in chronic liver disease: Dynamic CT measurements correlated with disease severity. AJR 176:667-673, 2001.

180. Kemmerer SR, Mortele KS, Ros PR: CT scan of the liver. Radiol Clin North Am 36:247-262, 1998.

177. Piekarski J, Goldberg AI, Royal SA, et al: Differences between liver and spleen CT numbers in normal adults: Its usefulness in predicting the presence of diffuse liver disease. Radiology 137:727-729, 1980.

178. Jacobs JE, Birnbaum BA, Shapiro MA, et al: Diagnostic criteria for fatty infiltration of the liver on contrast-enhanced helical CT. AJR 171:659-664, 1998.

179. Nishikawa J, Itai Y, Tasaka: Lobar attenuation differences of the liver on computed tomography. Radiology 141:725-728, 1981.

180. Fried AM, Kreel L, Cosgrove DO: The hepatic interlobar fissure: Combined in vitro and in vivo study. AJR 143:561-564, 1984.

181. Liddell RM, Baron RL, Ekstrom JE, et al: Normal intrahepatic bile ducts: CT depiction. Radiology 176:633-635, 1990.

182. Danet IM, Semelka RC, Braga L: MR imaging of diffuse liver disease. Radiol Clin North Am 41:67-87, 2003.

183. Saini S, Nelson RC: Technique for MR imaging of the liver. Radiology 197:575-577, 1995.

184. Smith RC, Lange RC: Multicoils. In Smith R, Lange R (eds): Understanding Magnetic Resonance Imaging. Boca Raton, FL, CRC, 1998, pp 179-181.

185. Yu JS, Park JG, Jeong EK, et al: Hepatic MRI using the double-echo chemical shift phase-selective gradient-echo technique. AJR 88:W49-56, 2007.

186. Urhahn R, Drobnitzky M, Klose K-C, et al: Incremental flip angle snapshot FLASH MRI of hepatic lesions: Improvement of signal-to-noise and contrast. J Comput Assist Tomogr 16:219-225, 1992.

187. Taupitz M, Hamm B, Speidel A, et al: Multisection FLASH: Method for breath-hold MR imaging of the entire liver. Radiology 183:73-79, 1992.

188. Gehl H-B, Bohndorf K-C, Klose KC, et al: Two-dimensional MR angiography in the evaluation of abdominal veins with gradient refocused sequences. J Comput Assist Tomogr 14:619-624, 1990.

189. Raval B, Mehta S, Narayana P, et al: Feasibility of fast MR imaging of the liver at 1.5 T. Magn Reson Imaging 7:203-210, 1989.

190. Semelka RC, Hricak H, Bis KG: Liver lesion detection: Comparison between excitation-spoiling fat suppression and regular spin-echo at 1.5T. Abdom Imaging 18:56-60, 1993.

191. Vassiliades VCG, Bernardino ME: Magnetic resonance imaging of the liver. Top Magn Reson Imaging 2:1-16, 1990.

192. Semelka RC, Simm FC, Recht M, et al: T1-weighted sequences for MR imaging of the liver: Comparison of three techniques for single-breath whole-volume acquisition at 1.0 and 1.5 T. Radiology 180:629-635, 1991.

193. Meyer CA, Colon E, Provost T, et al: Delineation of surgical segmental anatomy: Value of PRISE, and MR fast-scanning technique. AJR 158:299-301, 1992.

194. Nghiem HV, Herfkens RJ, Francis IR, et al: T2-weighted fast spin echo MR imaging of the abdomen and pelvis. Radiology 185:213-217, 1992.

195. Chien D, Atkinson DJ, Edelman RR: Strategies to improve contrast in turbo FLASH imaging: Reordered phase encoding and K-space segmentation. J Magn Reson Imaging 1:63-70, 1991.

196. Haacke EM, Tkach JA: Fast MR imaging: Techniques and clinical applications. AJR 155:951-964, 1990.

197. Low RN, Francis IR, Herfkens RJ, et al: Fast multiplanar spoiled gradient-recalled imaging of the liver: Pulse sequence optimization and comparison with spin-echo imaging. AJR 160:501-509, 1993.

198. Kanematsu M, Hoshi H, Itoh K, et al: Focal hepatic lesion detection: Comparison of four fat-suppressed T2-weighted MR imaging pulse sequences. Radiology 211:363-371, 1999.

199. McCarthy S, Hricak H, Cohen M, et al: Cholecystitis: Detection with MR imaging. Radiology 158:333-336, 1986.

200. Spritzer CE: Vascular diseases and MR angiography of the liver. Magn Reson Imaging Clin North Am 5:377-396, 1997.

201. Mitchell DG, Nazarian LN: Hepatic vascular disease: CT and MRI. Semin Ultrasound CT MRI 16:49-68, 1995.

202. Foley WD, Kneeland JB, Cates JD, et al: Contrast optimization for the detection of focal hepatic lesions by MR imaging at 1.5 T. AJR 149:1155-1160, 1987.

203. Henkelman RM, Hardy P, Poon PY, et al: Optimal pulse sequence for imaging hepatic metastases. Radiology 161:727-730, 1986.

204. Jolesz FA, Higuchi N, Oshio K, et al: Clinical implementation of fast spin-echo imaging. Radiology 181:164-165, 1991.

205. Melki PS, Mulkern RV, Panych LS, et al: Comparing the FAISE method with conventional dual-echo sequences. J Magn Reson Imaging 1:319-326, 1991.

206. Low RN, Francis IR, Sigeti JS, et al: Abdominal MR imaging: Comparison of T2-weighted fast and conventional spin-echo, and contrast enhanced fast multiplanar spoiled gradient-recalled imaging. Radiology 186:803-811, 1993.

207. Soyer P, Le Normand S, Clement de Givry S, et al: T2-weighted spin-echo MR imaging of the liver: Comparison of breath-hold fast spin-echo with non-breathhold fast spin-echo with and without fat supression. AJR 166:593, 1996.

208. Siegelman ES, Outwater EK: MR imaging techniques of the liver. Radiol Clin North Am 36:263-284, 1998.

209. Semelka RC, Kelekis NL, Thomasson D, et al: HASTE MR imaging: Description of technique and preliminary results in the abdomen. J Magn Reson Imaging 6:698-699, 1996.

210. Bydder GM, Steiner RE, Blumgart CH, et al: MR imaging of the liver using short T1 inversion recovery sequences. J Comput Assist Tomogr 9:1084-1089, 1985.

211. Bydder GM, Young IR: MRI: Clinical uses of the inversion recovery sequence. J Comput Assist Tomogr 9:659-675, 1985.

212. Dousset M, Weissleder R, Hendrick RE, et al: Short T1 inversion recovery imaging of the liver: pulse sequence optimization and comparison spin echo imaging. Radiology 171:327-333, 1989.

213. Shuman WP, Baron RL, Peters MJ, et al: Comparison of STIR and spin echo MR imaging at 1.5 T in 90 lesions of the chest, liver, and pelvis. AJR 152:853-859, 1989.

214. Schertz D, Lee JKT, Heiken JP, et al: Proton spectroscopic imaging (Dixon method) of the liver: Clinical utility. Radiology 173:401-406, 1989.

215. Lee JKT, Dixon NT, Ling D, et al: Fatty infiltration of the liver: Demonstration by proton spectroscopic imaging: preliminary observations. Radiology 153:195-199, 1984.

216. Brateman L: Chemical shift imaging: A review. AJR 146:971-980, 1986.

217. Wehrli FW, Perkins TG, Shimakawa A, et al: Chemical shift-induced amplitude modulations in images obtained with gradient refocusing. Magn Reson Imaging 5:157-158, 1987.

218. Martin J, Sentis M, Zidan A, et al: Fatty metamorphosis of hepatocellular carcinoma: Detection with chemical shift gradient-echo MR imaging. Radiology 195:125, 1995.

219. Karcaaltincaba M, Akhan O: Imaging of hepatic steatosis and fatty sparing. Eur J Radiol 61:33-43, 2007.

220. Semelka RC, Helmberger TKG: Contrast agents for MR imaging of the liver. Radiology 218:27-38, 2001.

221. Harisinghani MG, Jhaveri KS, Weissleder R, et al. MRI contrast agents for evaluating focal hepatic lesions. Clin Radiol 56:714-725, 2001.

222. Edelman RR, Siegel JB, Singer A, et al: Dynamic MR imaging of the liver with Gd-DTPA: Initial clinical results. AJR 153:1213-1219, 1989.

223. Saini S: Should Gd chelates be used routinely for liver MR imaging? AJR 164:1550, 1995.

224. Brancatelli G, Federle MP, Baron RL, et al: Arterially enhancing liver lesions: Significance of sustained enhancement on hepatic venous and delayed phase with magnetic resonance imaging. J Comput Assist Tomogr 31:116-122, 2007.

225. Kelekis NL, Semelka RC, Worawattanakul S, et al: Hepatocellular carcinoma in North America: A multiinstitutional study of appearance on T1-weighted, T2-weighted, and serial gadolinium-enhanced gradient-echo images. AJR 170:1005-1013, 1998.

226. Mahfouz A-E, Hamm B: Contrast agents. Magn Reson Imaging Clin North Am 5:223-240, 1997.

227. Soyer P, de Givry SC, Gueye C, et al: Detection of focal hepatic lesions with MR imaging: Prospective comparison of T2-weighted fast spin-echo with and without fat suppression, T2-weighted breath-hold fast spin-echo, and gadolinium chelate-enhanced 3D gradient-recalled imaging. AJR 166:1115-1121, 1996.

228. Namkung S, Zech CJ, Helmberger T, et al: Superparamagnetic iron oxide (SPIO)-enhanced liver MRI with ferucarbotran: Efficacy for characterization of focal liver lesions. J Magn Reson Imaging 25:755-765, 2007.

229. Saini S, Edelman RR, Sharma P, et al: Blood-pool MR contrast material for detection and characterization of focal hepatic lesions: Initial clinical experience with ultrasmall superparamagnetic iron oxide (AMI-227). AJR 164:1147-1152, 1995.

230. Saini S, Sharma R, Baron RL, et al: Multicenter dose-ranging study on the efficacy of USPIO ferumoxtran-10 for liver MR imaging. Clin Radiol 55:690-695, 2000.

231. Ward J, Naik KS, Guthrie JA, et al: Hepatic lesion detection: Comparison of MR imaging after the administration of superparamagnetic iron oxide with dual-phase CT by using alternative-free response receiver operating characteristic analysis. Radiology 210:459-466, 1999.

232. Savranoglu P, Obuz F, Karasu S, et al: The role of SPIO-enhanced MRI in the detection of malignant liver lesions. Clin Imaging 30:377-381, 2006.

233. Poeckler-Schoeniger C, Koepke J, Gueckel F, et al: MRI with superparamagnetic iron oxide: Efficacy in the detection and characterization of focal hepatic lesions. Magn Reson Imaging 17:383-392, 1999.

234. Yamashita Y, Yamamoto H, Hirai A, et al: MR imaging enhancement with superparamagnetic iron oxide in chronic liver disease: Influence of liver dysfunction and parenchymal pathology. Abdom Imaging 21:318-323, 1996.

235. Sahani DV, O'Malley ME, Bhat S, et al: Contrast-enhanced MRI of the liver with mangafodipir trisodium: Imaging technique and results. J Comput Assist Tomogr 26:216-222, 2002.

236. Murakami T, Baron RL, Peterson MS, et al: Hepatocellular carcinoma: MR imaging with mangafodipir trisodium (Mn-DPDP). Radiology 200:69-77, 1996.

237. Murakami TM, Baron RL, Federle MP, et al: Cirrhosis of the liver: MR imaging with mangafodipir trisodium (Mn-DPDP). Radiology 198:567-572, 1996.

238. Hahn PF, Saini S: Liver-specific MR imaging contrast agents. Radiol Clin North Am 36:287-297, 1998.

239. Schima W, Petersein J, Hahn PF, et al: Contrast-enhanced MR imaging of the liver: Comparison between Gd-BOPTA and Mangafodipir. J Magn Reson Imaging 7:130-135, 1997.

240. Pena CS, Saini S, Baron RL, et al: Detection of malignant primary hepatic neoplasms with gadobenate dimeglumine (Gd-BOPTA) enhanced T1-weighted hepatocyte phase MR imaging: Results of off-site blinded review in a phase-II multicenter trial. Korean J Radiol 2:210-215, 2001.

241. Hamm B, Staks T, Taupitz M: Phase I clinical evaluation of Gd-EOB-DTPA as a hepatobiliary MR contrast agent: Safety, pharmacokinetics, and MR imaging. Radiology 195:785-792, 1995.

242. Vogl TJ, Kummel S, Hammerstingl R, et al: Liver tumors: Comparison of MR imaging with Gd-EOB-DTPA and Gd-DTPA. Radiology 200:59-67, 1996.

243. Reimer P, Rummeny EJ, Daldrup HE, et al: Enhancement characteristics of liver metastases, hepatocellular carcinomas, and hemangiomas with Gd-EOB-DTPA: Preliminary results with dynamic MR imaging. Eur Radiol 7:275-280, 1997.

244. Giovagnoni A, Paci E: Liver, III: Gadolinium-based hepatobiliary contrast agents (Gd-EOB-DTPA and Gd-BOPTA/Dimeg). Magn Reson Imaging Clin North Am 4:61-72, 1996.

245. Vogl TJ, Pegios W, McMahon C, et al: Gadobenate dimeglumine, a new contrast agent for MR imaging: Preliminary evaluation in healthy volunteers. AJR 158:887-892, 1992.

246. Jackson A, Haroon H, Zhu XP, et al: Breath-hold perfusion and permeability mapping of hepatic malignancies using magnetic resonance imaging and a first-pass leakage profile model. NMR Biomed 15:164-173, 2002.

247. Annet L, Materne R, Danse E, et al: Hepatic flow parameters measured with MR imaging and Doppler US: Correlations with degree of cirrhosis and portal hypertension. Radiology 229:409-414, 2003.

248. Chan JHM, Tsui EYK, Luk SH, et al: Diffusion-weighted MR imaging of the liver: Distinguishing hepatic abscess from cystic or necrotic tumor. Abdom Imaging 26:161-165, 2001.

249. Saini S, Reimer P, Hahn PF, Cohen MS: Echoplanar MR imaging of the liver in patients with focal hepatic lesions: Quantitative analysis of images made with various pulse sequences. AJR 163:1389-1393, 1994.

250. Taouli B, Vilgrain V, Dumont E, et al: Evaluation of liver diffusion isotropy and characterization of focal hepatic lesions with two single-shot echo-planar MR imaging sequences: Prospective study in 66 patients. Radiology 226:71-78, 2003.

251. Namasivayam S, Martin DR, Saini S: Imaging of liver metastases: MRI. Cancer Imaging 7:2-9, 2007.

252. Vauthey JN: Liver imaging: A surgeon's perspective. Radiol Clin North Am 36:445-458, 1998.

253. Wallis F, Gilbert FJ: Magnetic resonance imaging in oncology: An overview. J R Coll Surg Edinb 44:117-125, 1999.

254. Glockner JF: Hepatobiliary MRI: Current concepts and controversies. J Magn Reson Imaging 25:681-695, 2007.

255. Girometti R, Furlan A, Bazzocchi M, et al: Diffusion-weighted MRI in evaluating liver fibrosis: A feasibility study in cirrhotic patients. Radiol Med (Torino) 112:394-408, 2007.

256. Hamer OW, Schlottmann K, Sirlin CB, et al: Technology insight: Advances in liver imaging. Nat Clin Pract Gastroenterol Hepatol 4:215-228, 2007.

257. Kanematsu M, Goshima S, Kondo H, et al: Gadolinium-enhanced multiphasic 3D MRI of the liver with prospective navigator correction: Phantom study and preliminary clinical evaluation. AJR 188:W309-316, 2007.

258. Zizka J, Klzo L, Ferda J, et al: Dynamic and delayed contrast enhancement in upper abdominal MRI studies: Comparison of gadoxetic acid and gadobutrol. Eur J Radiol 62:186-191, 2007.

Interventional Radiology in the Cirrhotic Liver

Rajeev Suri, MD • Gerald D. Dodd III, MD

NONONCOLOGIC INTERVENTIONS IN THE CIRRHOTIC LIVER

Image-Guided Random Liver Biopsy

Transjugular Intrahepatic Portosystemic Shunt

Interventional Radiological Management of Ascites

Preoperative Portal Vein Embolization

Splenic Arterial Embolization

ONCOLOGIC INTERVENTIONS IN THE CIRRHOTIC LIVER

Image-Guided Percutaneous Liver Mass Biopsy

Image-Guided Interstitial Treatment of Hepatocellular Carcinoma

Endovascular Management of Hepatocellular Carcinomas

Combined Endovascular and Interstitial Management

Liver cirrhosis is caused most frequently by hepatitis or alcoholism and was the 12th leading cause of death in the United States in 2003 accounting for 27,000 deaths.[1] Most of the morbidity associated with cirrhosis is due to the sequelae of portal hypertension—variceal hemorrhage, ascites, and hydrothorax. The cirrhosis predisposes to the development of hepatocellular carcinoma (HCC) which represents 5% of all cancers worldwide and currently represents one of the most common causes of death in the cirrhotic patient.[2] In recent years important advances have been made in the management of cirrhosis and its complications. This chapter presents an overview of the pivotal role that interventional radiology has played in the diagnosis and treatment of the nononcologic and oncologic aspects of cirrhosis.

NONONCOLOGIC INTERVENTIONS IN THE CIRRHOTIC LIVER

Image-Guided Random Liver Biopsy

Percutaneous Liver Biopsy

Percutaneous liver biopsy has been performed routinely in patients with cirrhosis for diagnosis, staging and prognosis and for monitoring response to therapy. The procedure was first described in 1945,[3] and was widely accepted after Menghini's landmark publication in 1958.[4]

Percutaneous liver biopsy is a safe procedure that can be performed as an outpatient procedure with or without imaging guidance. Imaging guidance has the advantage of decreasing the incidence of complications such as adjacent organ injury and providing a superior diagnostic yield, when compared with non–image-guided techniques,[5] especially in the small cirrhotic liver. The choice of CT or ultrasound guidance is dependant on a physician's familiarity and skills and the availability of the imaging technique. Sonography carries the advantage of real time guidance, multidirectional imaging, portability, and visualization and avoidance of major blood vessels during the needle pass.[6] Ultrasound-guided random liver biopsies are safer, more comfortable, and only marginally more expensive than a blind biopsy.[7]

Preprocedural evaluation includes checking for a coagulopathy disorder and withholding medications that inhibit coagulation factors. Corrective therapy should be applied in patients with a prothrombin time greater than 15 seconds, a partial thromboplastin time greater than 45 seconds, an INR greater than 1.5, and/or a platelet count less than 50,000/mm.[3] The presence of ascites is not a contraindication to liver biopsy, since no significant difference has been demonstrated in postbiopsy complications in the presence or absence of ascites.[8,9]

Imaging-guided biopsies can be performed via a subcostal or intercostal approach, however, an intercostal approach carries the added risk of creating a pneumothorax or injuring

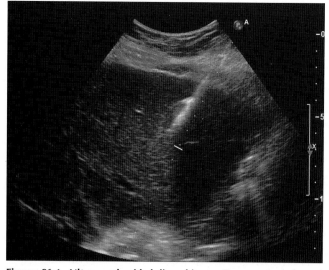

Figure 86-1. Ultrasound-guided liver biopsy. Transverse ultrasound scan of liver shows an echogenic biopsy needle traversing the left lobe.

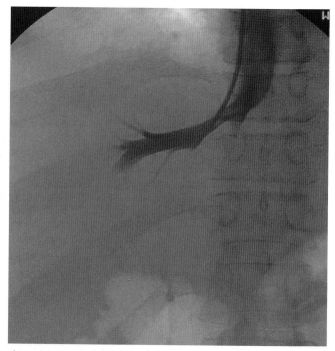

Figure 86-2. Transjugular liver biopsy. Hepatic venogram demonstrates adequate location of the catheter in the right hepatic vein before introducing the biopsy needle.

an intercostal artery. Sonographically guided interventions can be performed by the free-hand technique or with an attached guide (Fig. 86-1). The freehand technique allows greater freedom in needle placement, whereas the attached-guide technique provides greater accuracy, especially for the less-experienced radiologist. The size of the biopsy needle and its impact on the diagnostic yield of the sample is controversial. The sonographic visualization of the needle tip varies with needle design, some needles being much more visible than others. Needles are most easily visualized while they are moving within the plane of the ultrasound beam.

Complications are uncommon and can be minor (pain, transient hypotension, and bleeding not requiring blood transfusion) or major (bleeding requiring further management, damage to adjacent organs, pneumothorax, hemothorax, peritonitis, or death). Major nonfatal complications occur in less than 1% of procedures with a reported mortality rate of 0.02% to 0.1%.[10,11] The number of needle passes, age of the patient, presence of malignancy, and prebiopsy hemoglobin have been identified as individual variables associated with increased hemorrhagic complications.[12]

Transjugular Liver Biopsy

The major risk associated with percutaneous liver biopsy is intraperitoneal hemorrhage with a reported incidence for fatal and nonfatal hemorrhages ranging between 0.11% and 0.24%, respectively.[12] The likelihood of hemorrhagic complications increases with the presence of coagulopathy.[13] Transjugular liver biopsy is an alternative technique for obtaining tissue samples, and is preferred in patients with uncorrectable coagulopathy.[14] The usual indications for transjugular liver biopsy are (a) coagulopathy, with platelet counts less than 60,000/cm and/or prothrombin times more than 3 seconds above normal, (b) massive ascites and (c) desire to perform adjunctive procedures such as measurement of venous pressures or anatomic delineation of hepatic veins and inferior vena cava. Less common indications for transjugular liver

biopsy include failed percutaneous biopsy, massive obesity, small cirrhotic livers, and suspected peliosis hepatitis.[15]

When performing this procedure, the right internal jugular vein is accessed and the hepatic vein is cannulated via the inferior vena cava (Fig. 86-2). Liver biopsy performed from the endovascular approach has a decreased risk of hypotension and life threatening hemorrhage, as puncture of the liver capsule is avoided, and any bleeding occurs along the biopsy track into the systemic venous system thus avoiding intraperitoneal blood loss.

Results from several centers indicate that adequate diagnostic liver tissue is obtained in 81% to 97% of cases.[15] Causes for failed transjugular liver biopsy include Budd-Chiari syndrome and hepatic vein occlusion or unsuitable hepatic venous anatomy.[16] Minor complications may occur in 1% to 15% and major complications (perforation of the hepatic capsule, cholangitis, and intraperitoneal bleeding) are observed in 1% to 3% of cases. The most common complication is perforation of the liver capsule (Fig. 86-3), which if deemed clinically significant can be plugged with microcoils. Mortality related to the procedure varies from 0.2% to 0.3%.[15,16]

Transjugular Intrahepatic Portosystemic Shunt

A transjugular intrahepatic portosystemic shunt (TIPS) is a minimally invasive technique for decreasing portal venous hypertension by creating a communication between the portal and systemic circulation. Though first described in the animal model by Rösch in 1969,[17] the first TIPS in a human was created in Germany in 1988.[18] Multiple studies have since confirmed the efficacy of TIPS in the management of the sequelae of portal hypertension not responding to medical therapy.

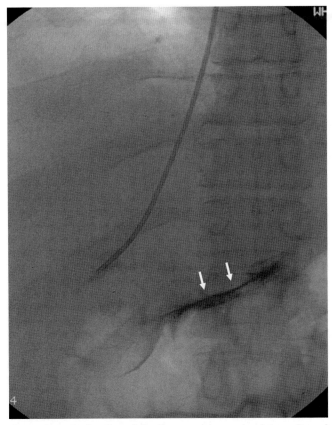

Figure 86-3. Perforation of the liver capsule causing intraperitoneal extravasation (*arrows*) and bleeding after a transjugular liver biopsy.

Patient Selection Criteria

TIPS creation is indicated for uncontrollable or recurrent variceal hemorrhage (despite endoscopic therapy), portal hypertensive gastropathy, refractory ascites, hepatic hydrothorax and Budd-Chiari syndrome.[19] Patency of the portal, splenic and hepatic veins and the hepatic artery needs to be confirmed prior to the study by imaging studies (multiphasic MDCT scan, MR imaging, or Doppler US).

There are no absolute contraindications to TIPS, though the following relative contraindications can increase the risk of procedural and postprocedural complications—elevated right/left heart pressures, heart failure/valvular insufficiency, rapidly progressive hepatic failure, severe or uncontrolled hepatic encephalopathy, uncontrolled sepsis, unrelieved biliary obstruction or Caroli's disease, polycystic liver disease, extensive primary/metastatic malignancy (especially infiltrating the porta hepatis), hepatic artery thrombosis, portal venous thrombosis, or severe uncorrectable coagulopathy.[19]

Post-TIPS morbidity is based on physiological and health variables including the patient's liver function, renal function, and the need for emergent TIPS. Increased risk of early death after TIPS has been well documented with Child-Pugh class C disease (score >12), high Acute Physiology and Chronic Health Evaluation (APACHE) II score (>18), and high Model for End-Stage Liver Disease (MELD) score (>18).[20,21]

Mechanism

TIPS is a percutaneous transjugular method of reducing portal vein pressure, in which a decompressive portosystemic channel is created between a hepatic vein and an intrahepatic branch of the portal vein. The shunt has been created historically with bare metal stents (initially balloon expandable and later self-expanding stents). Bare stents have been associated with a high rate of shunt dysfunction due to acute thrombosis, pseudointimal hyperplasia (secondary to bile leaks into the shunt lumen), and intimal hyperplasia of the hepatic venous outflow. Recent multicenter trials have confirmed the efficacy of polytetrafluoroethylene (PTFE)-covered stent-grafts for TIPS with improved stent patency rates.[22,23] Improved endothelialization of the stent due to avoidance of bile leakage into the stent lumen is related to decreased abluminal porosity of the PTFE coating.

Equipment

The required equipment includes a needle access set (for accessing the internal jugular vein); a hepatic vein to portal vein needle access set—Colapinto-Ring hepatic access set (Cook, Bloomington, IN), Rösch-Uchida set (Cook, Bloomington, IN) or the Hawkins set (Angiodynamics, Queensbury, NY); and stents—self-expanding metallic stent (Wallstent, Boston Scientific, Natick, MA) or PTFE stent-graft (Viatorr, W.L. Gore and Associates, Flagstaff, AZ).

Technique

TIPS can be performed with sedation (with midazolam and fentanyl or propofol) or general anesthesia. The right internal jugular vein is accessed and the hepatic vein is catheterized via the inferior vena cava. Wedge hepatic vein pressures are measured to indirectly assess the portal venous pressure, and free/wedged hepatic venography is performed. Understanding the intrahepatic vascular anatomy of the liver is essential—the right hepatic vein (RHV) is the hepatic vein of choice, lying posterior to the right portal vein (RPV)/main portal vein (MPV) bifurcation. The intrahepatic portal vein branch is catheterized close to the portal bifurcation with the transparenchymal passage of a long curved needle from the chosen hepatic vein. After direct measurement of the systemic and portal venous pressures, the hepatic parenchymal tract is balloon dilated and the stent is deployed to keep the tract open (Fig. 86-4). Angiographic and hemodynamic measurements for pressure reductions are performed, aiming for a portosystemic pressure gradient of ≤12 mm Hg. Variceal embolization is performed when indicated, especially if varices persist despite an adequate portosystemic pressure gradient.

Follow-up

Since shunt dysfunction (stent thrombosis, stent stenosis, and stenosis of the hepatic venous outflow) develops in more than 50%[24] of patients with TIPS, regular surveillance is mandatory to detect and allow correction of shunt dysfunction prior to recurrent variceal bleeding. Though angiography is the gold standard for diagnosing these complications, its invasive nature limits its use as a screening technique. Doppler sonography is the current modality of choice for noninvasive imaging follow-up of TIPS and has proved to be 100% sensitive and 96% specific for stent thrombosis,[25] highly sensitive and 70% to 80% specific for stent stenosis, and highly sensitive and specific for hepatic vein stenosis.[26] The first post-TIPS sonogram is obtained within 24 hours of TIPS creation to assess for acute stent thrombosis and to assess baseline

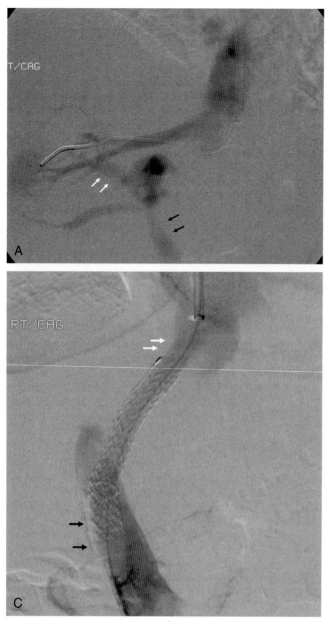

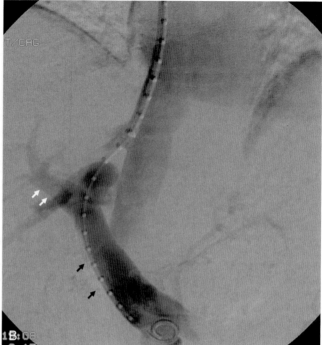

Figure 86-4. Transjugular intrahepatic portosystemic shunt. A. Carbon dioxide wedge hepatic venogram demonstrating patent right portal vein (*white arrows*) and main portal vein (*black arrows*). **B.** Prestent deployment portal venogram and hepatic/inferior vena cavogram with a marker catheter within, confirms entry of the needle into the patent right portal vein (*white arrows*) and main portal vein (*black arrows*). Portal to right atrial pressure gradient was measured at 25 mm Hg. **C.** PTFE-covered stent-graft extending from the main portal vein (*black arrows*) to the hepatic vein (*white arrows*) with reduction of portal to right atrial pressure gradient to 6 mm Hg.

velocities. PTFE-covered TIPS prevent visualization of flow through the stent in the early postprocedural period. However, hepatopetal flow in the main portal vein and flow in the hepatic vein confirms the patency of the shunt. Follow-up sonograms are obtained at 3- to 6-month intervals to assess for antegrade shunt flow with normal velocities being 50 to 200 cm/second. Temporal or spatial changes in the peak velocity through the stent greater than 50 cm/second, or velocities greater than 200 cm/second or less than 50 cm/second are highly suggestive of shunt dysfunction and should prompt a shunt venogram.[26] Helical CT has been demonstrated to have 92% sensitivity and 77% specificity for hemodynamically significant abnormalities[27] but has not had a significant role in TIPS follow-up.

Results

Success can be classified as technical, hemodynamic and clinical. Technical success describing successful creation of a shunt

between the hepatic vein and intrahepatic branch of the portal vein is seen in greater than 95%.[19] Hemodynamic success refers to reduction of the portosystemic gradient to ≤12 mm Hg with nonfilling of varices, and is seen also in approximately 95%.[19] Clinical success for the treatment of variceal bleeding or refractory ascites is measured by the postprocedural improvement and by the event-free survival interval, and varies among studies due to different inclusion and evaluation criteria.

Randomized trials comparing TIPS and endoscopic variceal therapy (sclerotherapy or variceal banding) for variceal bleeding have demonstrated less frequent bleeding after TIPS (10%-25%) versus after endoscopic therapy (35%-50%), though higher rates of hepatic encephalopathy (30% versus 15%, respectively) are associated with TIPS.[28,29] Medical treatment failure of acute bleeding is associated with up to 80% mortality;[30] emergent TIPS in such patients stops active bleeding and has an early clinical success in 90% to 100%.[19] However, a significant difference in long-term survival or decrease in overall mortality has not been demonstrated after TIPS.[31]

Transjugular intravascular embolization of varices using microcoils, tissue adhesives, or absolute alcohol appears to prevent early rebleeding after TIPS, however, its benefit has not been confirmed by randomized trials.

TIPS is superior to medical treatment for patients with refractory ascites. However, there is an increased incidence of encephalopathy with TIPS. Russo and colleagues[32] reported a complete cumulative response rate of 45% at 6 months, with at least some improvement in ascites seen in 63% of patients.

As shunt dysfunction after bare metal stents can occur in more than 50% of patients during the first year, the use of PTFE-covered stents was proposed in the swine model in 1995,[33] and several clinical series have since proven their role. Primary and secondary patency rates of 81% and 100% have been reported at 1 year, with less than 5% incidence of restenosis after PTFE-coated TIPS.[34] Overall technical and hemodynamic success and mortality rates are similar to bare stents, though with markedly reduced stent malfunction rates requiring less frequent interventions.[23]

Complications

Major complications result in of TIPS procedures including hemoperitoneum, hemobilia, stent malposition, and death, hospital admission for therapy, or prolonged hospitalization in 3% of patients.[19] Minor complications may require nominal therapy and include fever, transient pulmonary edema, and contrast-induced renal failure. Complication rates with bare or covered stents are similar.[19]

The incidence of severe uncontrolled encephalopathy (requiring hospitalization) after portosystemic diversion increases with a worsening Child-Pugh stage of liver disease and can occur in 30% to 40% of cases with refractory/severe ascites. Severe encephalopathy is associated with a very high mortality rate. The predictors of post-TIPS encephalopathy include the presence of pre-TIPS encephalopathy, advanced age (>60 years) and advanced liver disease. Encephalopathy controlled by medical therapy can occur in 15% to 25% of patients after TIPS.[19]

Accelerated liver failure from hepatic ischemia (due to decreased portal inflow) and death after TIPS are highly dependent on patient selection and comorbid factors such as preexisting multiorgan system failure, elevated APACHE II scores, and high Child-Pugh and MELD scores.[20]

Interventional Radiological Management of Ascites

Development of ascites is the most common complication of cirrhosis, seen in more than 50% of cirrhotic patients within 10 years.[35] The prognosis is poor for patients with refractory ascites and is associated with a diminished quality of life and an increased risk of infections and renal failure. Refractory ascites is defined by the "International Ascites Club" as diuretic-resistant or diuretic-intractable ascites, and approximately 5% to 10% of patients with ascites fall in this category.[36] The probability of death in the cirrhotic patient hospitalized with refractory ascites is approximately 40% at 2 years.[37,38]

TIPS creates a portosystemic diversion that improves renal function and sodium excretion causing the resolution of ascites and has largely replaced surgically placed shunts. In appropriately selected patients based on the MELD scores and Child-Pugh classification, TIPS is an effective treatment for ascites. TIPS has proved to be clearly superior to large volume paracentesis in the control of ascites with a similar frequency of adverse events.[39]

Preoperative Portal Vein Embolization

Recent advances in surgical techniques have improved outcomes after hepatic resection, though there is a risk of perioperative liver failure related to the volume of the remnant liver.[40] Resection of the functional liver mass of more than 60% in cirrhotic livers and more than 75% to 80% in the normal liver increases the risk of complications.[40,41] To improve the safety of major hepatectomy, preoperative portal vein embolization (PVE) is considered the standard of care to increase the future liver remnant (FLR) volume. PVE redirects portal flow to the FLR, thus initiating its hypertrophy, and reducing postoperative morbidity especially in patients with marginal FLR. Experimental observation of PVE/ligation causing hypertrophy of the spared liver segments was first reported in 1920,[42] though it was first used clinically for this purpose in 1990 to induce preoperative left liver hypertrophy in a patient with hilar cholangiocarcinoma.[43]

Mechanism

Regenerative response in the liver following resection or PVE is mediated by hepatocyte growth factors, transforming growth factor-α, and epidermal growth factors, which induce cytokine production and subsequent hepatocyte regeneration. Hepatocyte replication may be delayed by a few days after apoptosis (due to PVE) compared to hepatocyte removal (due to resection), with replication rates being slower in cirrhotic livers and in those patients with diabetes.[44] Preoperative PVE minimizes abrupt portal pressure increases in the FLR and decreases postresection liver dysfunction, the mild elevation of liver enzymes post PVE resolving within 7 to 10 days.

Patient Selection

PVE should be performed when the estimated FLR is less than 40% in patients with cirrhosis, chronic liver disease (e.g., steatosis) or severe fibrosis. Patients with overt portal hypertension are not considered candidates for hepatic resection. Relative contraindications include tumor extension into the FLR, extrahepatic metastases, uncorrectable coagulopathy, tumor invading the portal veins precluding safe access, renal failure, and biliary dilatation in the FLR.

Technique

PVE maybe performed percutaneously (transhepatic ipsilateral or contralateral approach) or intraoperatively (transileocolic venous approach). The transhepatic contralateral approach developed by Kinoshita and colleagues[45] is the most commonly used technique. For a right portal vein embolization, a branch of the contralateral left portal vein is accessed and a 6-Fr balloon occlusion catheter is advanced to the right portal vein for embolization. The procedure is technically easier though there is a concomitant risk of injury to the FLR and left portal vein. Injury to the FLR is avoided with the transhepatic ipsilateral approach first described by Nagino and colleagues.[46] Embolization agents include fibrin glue, *n*-BCA (*n*-butyl cyanoacrylate) and ethiodized oil, microparticles, microcoils, and absolute alcohol. These embolization agents carry the risk of nontarget embolization and periportal inflammation especially with *n*-BCA and alcohol, which could affect subsequent interventions.

Results

In patients with chronic liver disease, 28% to 46% increases in volume are seen in the nonembolized FLR 4 weeks after the procedure.[44] The parenchymal fibrosis present in these patients may limit regeneration.[47] Compared with hepatectomy without PVE, preoperative PVE is associated with decreased liver failure and fewer postresection complications, though the overall and disease free survival rates are similar with or without PVE.[48] Significantly higher cumulative survival rates have been seen with PVE versus without PVE in patients with cirrhosis and HCC.[49]

Complications

In a retrospective analysis of 188 patients, procedure related complications occurred in 12.8% and included hemoperitoneum, hemobilia, vascular complications (arteriovenous and arterioportal fistula/shunt, pseudoaneurysm, and portal vein thrombosis), pneumothorax, and sepsis.[50]

Splenic Arterial Embolization

Partial splenic arterial embolization to treat variceal hemorrhage and control portal hypertension may be performed either alone or in combination with endoscopic variceal ligation.[51] The rationale is that reduced splenic volume results in decreased venous drainage and hence reduction of portal venous blood flow and pressure.

Technique

Partial splenic embolization maybe performed by either selectively catheterizing the distal splenic arterial branches or nonselectively by placing the catheter in the main splenic artery (beyond the origin of the pancreatic branches). The embolic agents used include gelatin sponge pledgets and PVA (polyvinyl alcohol). Due to associated risk of splenic abscesses, patients are pretreated with antibiotics, and adequate analgesics are also given to decrease the pain associated with splenic infarction. Reduced extent of initial splenic embolization (30%-40%) is associated with lower morbidity,[52] and hence in patients with advanced liver disease graded partial splenic embolization should be considered.

Results

Partial splenic embolization has been reported to improve the mean hemoglobin values and platelet count with a significant decrease in the variceal bleeding and improvement of clinical status.[53] By combining partial splenic arterial embolization with endoscopic variceal ligation, esophageal varices are well controlled without recurrent hemorrhage because there is significant reduction in the flow rate and maximum flow velocity in the main portal vein.[54]

Complications

Complications include fever, abdominal pain, hepatic insufficiency, complete splenic infarction, and portal venous thrombosis.

ONCOLOGIC INTERVENTIONS IN THE CIRRHOTIC LIVER

There is an approximately 10% to 16% risk of developing hepatocellular carcinoma (HCC) in the cirrhotic liver,[2,55] with the annual incidence ranging from 2% to 8%.[56-58] Overall, HCC is one of the most common causes of death in a cirrhotic patient. The prognosis in patients with HCC depends on the severity of liver cirrhosis, the general health of the patient, and the stage, aggressiveness, and growth rate of the tumor at the time of diagnosis. Survival is positively impacted by the early detection and treatment of HCC.

Image-Guided Percutaneous Liver Mass Biopsy

Indications for Biopsy of a Liver Mass and Associated Findings

Surveillance for HCC is routinely performed in patients with Child-Pugh A and B cirrhosis.[57] Sonography and serum α-fetoprotein (AFP) performed every 6 to 12 months are the primary screening techniques for the detection of HCC worldwide. If a tumor nodule is detected that measures more than 1 cm in size, further evaluation is performed with contrast-enhanced CT or MR imaging. Although the CT and MR imaging characteristics of HCC are diagnostic for larger lesions, lesion characterization may be difficult.[59,60] As per the conclusions of the Barcelona-2000 European Association for the Study of the Liver (EASL) conference, if a nodule in the cirrhotic liver measures less than 1 cm in diameter, biopsy is not recommended.[61] If the nodule is 1 to 2 cm in size, biopsy is recommended as imaging techniques are not sufficiently reliable at this size to allow a definitive diagnosis. If the nodule is greater than 2 cm, HCC can be diagnosed by two coincident imaging techniques (US, CT, MR, or angiography) that demonstrate arterial hypervascularity, or one positive imaging technique with a serum AFP level greater than 400 ng/mL, thus avoiding biopsy. Thus, biopsy is necessary for suspicious lesions between 1 and 2 cm, and for tumors greater than 2 cm that are hypovascular on contrast-enhanced imaging studies.[61]

Thrombosis of the portal vein in a cirrhotic liver can be due to benign causes (portal hypertension or stasis) or malignant causes (due to HCC). Establishing the etiology of portal venous thrombosis is essential for the management of HCC as portal venous invasion from a HCC indicates a dismal prognosis with a limited role for invasive therapy. Although imaging characteristics of benign and malignant thrombi have been described,[62] these imaging characteristics can be ambiguous thus necessitating a biopsy and pathologic examination of the thrombus for staging.[63-65]

Technique

The preprocedural evaluation and technique for biopsy of liver lesions, portal vein thrombus, and portal lymph nodes are similar to that described for image-guided random liver biopsies with the exception that the biopsy specimen must

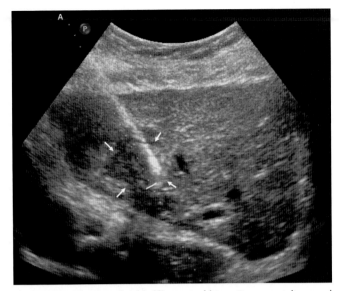

Figure 86-5. Ultrasound-guided liver mass biopsy. Transverse ultrasound scan of liver shows 1-cm heterogeneous nodule (*white arrows*) with an echogenic needle traversing most of its diameter.

come from the tissue in question. When attempting to biopsy a liver mass, every effort should be made to perform the biopsy through a mantle of normal liver parenchyma (Fig. 86-5) to decrease the risk of bleeding and tumor seeding along the needle track. A mantle of normal liver tissue is less likely to bleed than is tumor and the thicker the mantle the less the risk of spilling tumor cells into the peritoneum or dragging them through the perihepatic and subcutaneous tissues.

Liver masses can be biopsied using fine needles (22-25 gauge) with cytological evaluation, or 16- to 20-gauge core biopsy needles with traditional histological evaluation. When using a biopsy gun to obtain the specimen, the tip of the biopsy needle should be positioned such that the specimen is obtained across the transitional zone from normal liver to tumor. Obtaining specimens from the transitional zone of a tumor will decrease the rate of inadequate specimens when compared to biopsies obtained from the center of a tumor as it is often necrotic. The diagnostic accuracy of image-guided biopsy of liver masses is approximately 93%.[66]

Portal vein thrombus biopsy is more demanding than standard hepatic mass biopsy. The specimen obtained from the thrombus must not be contaminated with tissue from the adjacent liver or most importantly an adjacent tumor, as the inclusion of extraneous tissue could lead to a false positive diagnosis of a malignant thrombus. Either an end-cutting needle with a tightly occluding stylette or a biopsy gun can be used to biopsy a portal vein thrombus. Sonography is the best guidance method to use for this procedure as it gives the best real-time visualization of the process.[63,64]

The procedure used to biopsy perihepatic lymph nodes is similar to that used to biopsy a portal vein thrombus. If the node is smaller than the excursion of a biopsy gun, then the use of an end-cutting needle is indicated.[67]

Complications

Major and minor complications are similar to those with random liver biopsies. Additionally, tumor seeding along the

intrahepatic and extrahepatic tract after needle biopsy is documented though rare, with incidences ranging from 0.5% to 2%.[66,68,69]

Image-Guided Interstitial Treatment of Hepatocellular Carcinoma

The prognosis for patients with HCC and compensated cirrhosis is diminished relative to patients with compensated cirrhosis alone. In patients with advanced HCC, the prognosis is dismal with most patients dying within 6 months following diagnosis. For patients with small asymptomatic HCC and compensated cirrhosis, the 1-, 2-, and 3-year survival rates are 81%, 56%, and 21%, respectively.[70] While little can be done for the patients with advanced tumors, the survival of patients with small HCC can be improved with effective therapy. Systemic chemotherapy has little impact on HCC and is hence reserved for advanced or otherwise untreatable HCC, with median survival of 8.9 months being reported with combination chemotherapy.[71,72] Surgical resection of HCC in patients with compensated cirrhosis improves survival with five-year survival rates of 50% to 83%.[73-75] Zhou and colleagues demonstrated that the survival rate for these patients is related to the size of a tumor at the time of resection with the five-year survival rates for patients with tumors less than 2.1 cm being 82.5%, with tumors between 2.1 and 3 cm being 66.3%, and with tumors between 3.1 and 5 cm being 61.2%.[75] However, surgical resection is an imperfect treatment for HCC for multiple reasons. Postoperative morbidity is significant and recovery can be prolonged. Despite a successful resection, the risk of recurrent intrahepatic tumor is substantial and can exceeding 50% at 3 years and 70% at 5 years.[73,76] Lastly, many patients are not surgical candidates because their tumors are in unresectable locations, they have advanced liver cirrhosis with insufficient hepatic reserve to allow resection, or they have comorbid diseases that make them a poor surgical risk.

Due to the high risk of recurrent HCC in the native cirrhotic liver, hepatic transplantation is considered to be the only truly curative therapy for patients with HCC and cirrhosis. However, like hepatic resection, it is not a viable therapy for patients with advanced HCC. Hepatic transplantation is currently restricted to patients who meet the Milan criteria (up to three tumors less than or equal to 3 cm, or a single tumor less than 5 cm) for tumor burden.[77,78] Last, an international shortage of liver donors combined with the high cost of hepatic transplantation limits its usefulness as therapeutic option for most people.

The limited usefulness and applicability of conventional therapies for the treatment of HCC has driven the development of alternative minimally invasive therapies. Many of these therapies embrace the following attributes—the ability to eradicate targeted tumors, minimal invasiveness, low morbidity, low cost, and the ability to be repeated as necessary to treat recurrent disease. To date, these therapies consist of several image-guided techniques including interstitial ablative technologies such as chemical, radiofrequency, microwave, laser, or cryoablation, and endovascular therapeutic techniques.[79]

Chemical Ablation

Percutaneous chemical ablation is probably the most established minimally invasive technique for treating HCC. It is inexpensive and effective for the treatment of small hepatic tumors.[80] Ethanol is the most ubiquitous agent used for chemical ablation, although, acetic acid has also been used since 1994 with similar results.

Ethanol Ablation (PEI)

MECHANISM

Ethanol causes cytoplasmic dehydration and cellular protein denaturation with subsequent coagulative necrosis in the tumor cells. Additionally, it induces endothelial necrosis and platelet aggregation in neoplastic vessels, which in turn causes small vessel thrombosis and ischemia.

The size and shape of necrosis induced by injected ethanol is not reproducible as the distribution of ethanol varies depending on tissue consistency. More uniform distribution is seen with soft small (≤3 cm) HCC, than in tumors with hard fibrous tissue, septations, or daughter nodules. Ethanol ablation does not work well in most metastases as they are often hard and fibrous. The distribution of ethanol can be improved by increasing the amount and concentration of the injected agent and by using either a multiple side hole needle or by injecting in multiple different sites within a tumor.

EQUIPMENT

The required equipment is inexpensive and includes sterile 95% ethanol, a syringe, connecting tubing, and a 20- to 22-gauge conical tip needle with multiple side holes.

PATIENT SELECTION CRITERIA

Patients considered eligible for percutaneous ethanol injection (PEI) therapy should have a total tumor volume less than 30% of the total volume of the liver, individual HCC ≤3 cm, and no extrahepatic or vascular tumor invasion. Patients with solitary tumors are better candidates than those with multiple tumors. Contraindications to PEI include Child-Pugh class C cirrhosis, extrahepatic disease and malignant portal vein thrombosis. Coagulopathy if present should be corrected to a target INR less than 1.5 and a platelet count more than 50,000/mm.[3]

TECHNIQUE

Worldwide, PEI is performed predominantly with ultrasound guidance. PEI may be performed with conscious sedation in an outpatient multisession setting or as an inpatient one-shot technique with general anesthesia. In either situation one or more 20- to 22-gauge needles are inserted into a tumor with 0.1- to 0.2-mL aliquots of ethanol infused as the needles are systematically withdrawn until the entire tumor is infused. Ultrasound is particularly effective for monitoring the infusion process as the injected ethanol causes an echogenic "cloud" in the permeated tissue that is easily identified. Care should be taken to avoid filling of the bile ducts, portal veins, hepatic veins or hepatic artery and gallbladder because of risk of hemobilia, thrombosis, or necrosis. Once the tumor is rendered completely echogenic, the needle is left in situ for 1 to 2 minutes and withdrawn with aspiration to prevent intraperitoneal spillage. 1 to 8 mL of ethanol may be injected per session, with up to two sessions performed per week, for a total of 4 to12 sessions.

The total ethanol volume required for ablation of the tumor volume with a surgical margin of 1 cm is calculated by the following formula: $V = 4/3p\ (r + 0.5)$,[3] where V is the target volume of ethanol, r the radius of the lesion (in centimeters), and *0.5* the correction for the additional surgical margin (as microscopic disease may extend beyond the visualized tumor margin). This equation is problematic as it assumes constant radial diffusion of the ethanol, and as previously described multiple factors can affect perfusion uniformity.

The one-shot technique, initially described by Livraghi and colleagues in 1993, though not widely practiced in the United States, is used for the treatment of tumors ≤3 cm in size. The procedure is performed with general anesthesia using larger volumes of ethanol along with intravenous fructose 1,6-diphosphate (FDP) and glutathione to prevent systemic ethanol toxicity or intoxication.[81]

RESULTS

Survival after PEI depends on the histologic grade of the tumor, the size and number of lesions and the Child-Pugh score. Complete ablation is seen 70% to 75% of HCC less than 5 cm in size, compared with about 60% for lesions measuring 5 to 8 cm.[82,83] In patients with Child-Pugh A cirrhosis, the three- and five-year survival rates after PEI are 60% to 70% and 30% to 50%, respectively, for a solitary lesion 3 cm or less in diameter.[84,85] In patients with Child-Pugh A cirrhosis the 1- and 3-year survival rates after PEI are 94% and 68%, respectively, for multiple hepatocellular carcinomas (maximum three nodules, maximum size 3 cm), 72% and 57% for 5- to 8.5-cm encapsulated hepatocellular carcinomas, and 73% and 42% for 5- to 10-cm infiltrating HCC.[82,83] Similar 5-year survival rates of 59% for PEI and 61% for surgical resection have been reported for patients with three or fewer HCC, all of which are ≤3 cm in diameter.[86] Risk factors for local recurrence include tumor size >3 cm, multiple hepatocellular carcinomas and an elevated baseline AFP level.

COMPLICATIONS

PEI is usually well tolerated. Di Stasi and colleagues[87] conducted a multicenter survey of 1066 patients with PEI demonstrating overall major and minor complication rate of 3.2%. Major complications included hemoperitoneum, hemobilia and liver abscess. Tract seeding was observed in 0.7% cases. The one-shot PEI technique for larger lesions is associated with a higher major complication rate of 4.6%[81] and a 0.7% to 1.9% mortality rate due to an increased risk of hemoperitoneum and variceal hemorrhage.[88]

Thermal Ablation

The aim of thermal ablation in liver tumors is to destroy malignant cells using heat (radiofrequency, microwave, and laser ablation) or freezing (cryoablation), with minimal damage to the adjacent liver and without damaging adjacent organs.[79,89] Each of the thermal ablative techniques requires placement of a needle-like thermal applicator directly into the tumor, the tip of which produces concentrated thermal energy causing hyperthermic or hypothermic injury. Similar to the chemical ablation techniques, thermal ablative techniques also aim to destroy a 5- to 10-mm circumferential cuff of hepatic parenchyma adjacent to the tumor margin. Though originally proposed as an alternative technique for the treatment of tumors in patients who were not surgical candidates, thermal ablation has developed into a first-line therapy for the treatment of HCC. The indications and advantages of these thermal techniques relative to one another is not well defined and the decision regarding which ablation technique or imaging modality to use is typically decided on the basis of physician preference and available resources.

PATIENT SELECTION CRITERIA FOR THERMAL TECHNIQUES

The patient selection criteria for the heating and cryoablative techniques are similar. Patient selection is based on tumor number (fewer than 5), size (each less than 5 cm), location (remote to hollow viscera and major portal vessels), and absence of extrahepatic spread of tumor. The ideal tumor is less than 3 cm in diameter, 1 cm or more deep to the liver capsule, and 2 cm or more away from major hepatic vessels.

Larger tumors may be treated with thermal ablation alone depending on individual circumstances or in combination with chemical or endovascular techniques. Juxtadiaphragmatic lesions and subcapsular lesions adjacent to the bowel or gallbladder can be thermally ablated,[90] although they should be approached with caution due to the risk of diaphragmatic injury and gallbladder/bowel perforation. These lesions can be treated by interposing percutaneously instilled glucose to tamponade against bowel/diaphragmatic thermal injury, or treated in combination with percutaneous chemical and endovascular treatment options.

Tumors adjacent to large blood vessels are difficult to ablate completely due to the "heat sink effect" of blood flow causing perfusion-mediated cooling of the adjacent tumor. Thermal ablation of tumors adjacent to the portal triads poses a risk of damage to bile ducts. Contraindications to treatment include excessive tumor burden (large tumor size and extrahepatic spread), markedly deranged liver function (Child Class C cirrhosis and uncorrectable coagulopathy) and severe debilitation.

HEATING ABLATIVE TECHNIQUES

The current ablative techniques that use hyperthermia to induce tissue necrosis include radiofrequency ablation (RFA), microwave ablation and laser ablation.

Radiofrequency Ablation

McGahan and colleagues[91] and Rossi and colleagues[92] in 1990 reported the first use of RFA to create deep-seated thermal lesions in porcine liver tissue. The first clinical report of the use of RFA to treat HCC was published in 1993.[93] Since then, multiple clinical studies have confirmed its safety and efficacy in the management of HCC.[94-96]

MECHANISM

Alternating electric current in the radiofrequency range (460-500 kHz) is used in a circuit established between the tip of an interstitial electrode and multiple large adhesive dispersive electrodes (ground pads) to produce local ionic agitation and subsequent frictional heat in the tissues surrounding the interstitial electrode. Temperatures above 51° C are lethal and above 60° C produce intracellular protein denaturation, destruction of RNA and DNA, and coagulative necrosis of the tissue.[97,98]

EQUIPMENT

Existing RFA devices differ in their design and ablation algorithms. Each design strives to maximize the size, uniformity, and reliability of the ablation zone.[99] Three devices currently dominate the U.S. market. These devices utilize one of two probe designs, a multi-tined expandable electrode (Radiotherapeutics, Sunnyvale, CA; and RITA Medical Systems Inc., Mountain View, CA) or an internally cooled electrode (Valley Lab, Boulder, CO) (Fig. 86-6). All of the devices are driven by an alternating electric current generator (460-500 kHz at 150-250 W) and utilize two or more dispersive electrodes.

The multitined expandable electrodes have an outer needle cannula that deploys an array of electrode tines from its tip into the adjacent tissue. The Radiotherapeutics probe consists of a 14-gauge needle with 10 retractable curved prongs and is operated using a tissue impedance algorithm. The RITA device consists of a 15-gauge needle with four to eight retractable prongs and is operated using a tissue temperature algorithm. The internally cooled Valley Lab probe consists of a 17-gauge straight needle electrode (single or in a triangular three-needle cluster) that is continuously cooled by a chilled perfusate throughout the ablation cycle. The generator algorithm is pulsed with the objective of maintaining maximal power without a significant rise in impedance.

TECHNIQUE

RFA can be performed percutaneously under ultrasound, CT, or MR imaging guidance or intraoperatively (laparoscopically or via laparotomy). The choice of the RFA device, the imaging guidance technique, the approach (percutaneous or intraoperative) and the type of sedation (conscious or general anesthesia) depends on the physician and institutional preference. The percutaneous approach can be used for tumors less than 5 cm in size, fewer than 5 in number, visible on an imaging technique, and with a safe percutaneous access route. An intraoperative approach may be needed for tumors larger than 5 cm, tumors either inadequately visualized or inaccessible by a percutaneous approach, or positioned adjacent to bowel. Laparotomy and laparoscopy allow direct visualization of the peritoneal cavity, and the added ability to perform a Pringle maneuver (temporary occlusion of the portal vein and hepatic artery) to increase the ablation zone.[100]

Irrespective of the device used, the needle electrodes are positioned such that the active elements are positioned symmetrically across each tumor. The length of an ablation cycle varies with the device and can run 8 to 20 minutes per ablation cycle. The size of the thermal injury produced with each device can vary from 2 to 7 cm depending on the size of the tumor being ablated as well as the vascularity of the tumor and surrounding hepatic parenchyma. The extent of the induced coagulative necrosis is well delineated by MR thermal mapping or sonographically by visualizing the acute echogenic reaction caused by the vaporization of the water in the ablated tissue[101] (Fig. 86-7). An ablation session may consist of one or more ablations performed on one or more tumors. Small tumors (≤2 cm) can be destroyed by a single ablation, while larger tumors require multiple overlapping ablations to destroy the entire tumor.[102] Each of the probes can be used to cauterize the needle track at the conclusion of the ablation to decrease the risk of hemorrhage and tumor seeding along the needle tract.

Microwave Ablation

Percutaneous microwave ablation was first used in 1986 in Japan by Tabuse and colleagues to ablate deep liver tissue[103] and was subsequently adapted in the early 1990s for liver

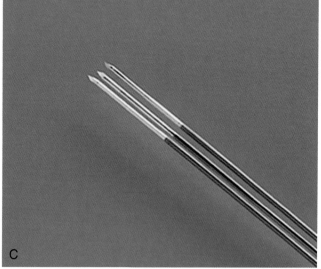

Figure 86-6. Photographs showing radiofrequency needles. A. A 15-gauge needle electrode with retractable prongs (RITA Medical Systems, Freemont, CA). **B.** A 14-gauge needle electrode with 10 retractable prongs (Radiotherapeutics). **C.** A 17-gauge internally cooled tip three needle cluster (Radionics, Burlington, MA).

tumor ablation. It is used clinically in Japan and China and is undergoing clinical trials in the United States.

MECHANISM

The alternating electric component of ultra-high-speed microwaves emitted from a bipolar antenna needle tip causes vibration and rotation of molecular dipoles (water molecules) thus heating the tissue surrounding the antenna and causing coagulative necrosis.

EQUIPMENT

The equipment consists of a microwave generator and needle electrodes (antenna). Two main types of microwave delivery systems have been used—the first type in clinical use in Japan and China (Microtaze, Nippon Shoji, Osaka, Japan; and UMC-1, Institute 207 of the Aerospace Industry Company and PLA General Hospital, Beijing, China), and the second system (Valley Lab, Boulder, CO) used in the United States. The latter device consists of the microwave generator emitting 915-MHz microwaves, and either a 13-gauge unified needle antenna with a 3.7-cm exposed active dipole element tip, or a 14-gauge cannula that deploys three circular antenna

(Fig. 86-8). Thermal ablation performed at 40 W for 10 minutes with the straight electrode results in an ablation zone similar to an RFA device, while larger ablation zones can be created with the circular antenna and higher wattage.[104]

TECHNIQUE

Like RFA, microwave ablation can be performed by the percutaneous or intraoperative approach, with similar criteria for selecting either of these approaches. The positioning and operation of the microwave electrode is similar to the techniques used for RFA. The progress of the ablation can be monitored by either MR thermal mapping or by the echogenic reaction produced in the ablated tissue. Treatments can be repeated as necessary to treat residual or recurrent tumor.

Laser Ablation

The first interstitial laser thermal ablation of a tumor was reported by Bown in 1983,[105] with subsequent experimental and clinical studies demonstrating reproducible thermal injury with the neodymium yttrium aluminum garnet (Nd:YAG) lasers.[106,107]

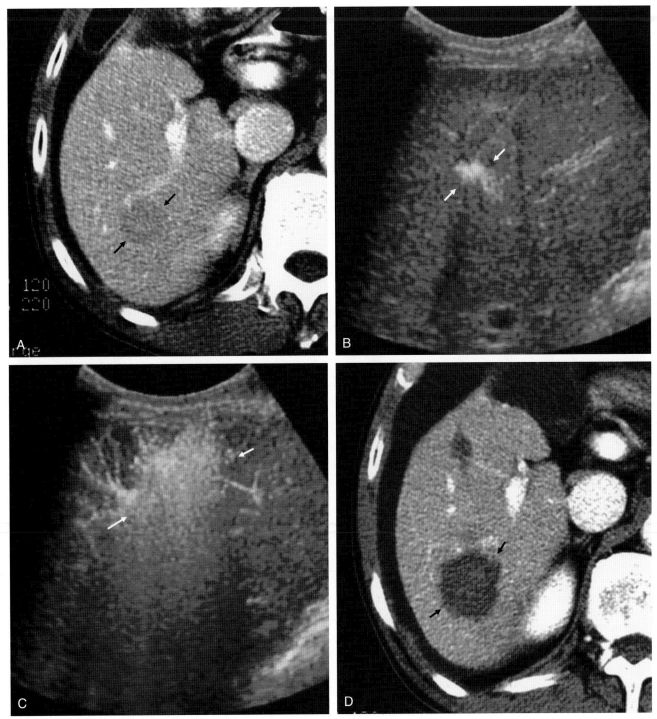

Figure 86-7. Ablation of a hepatocellular carcinoma. A. A 2-cm hepatocellular carcinoma (*black arrows*) in posterior right lobe of liver in segment 6.
B and **C.** Expanding hyperechoic zone (*arrows*) formed from production of microbubbles by the ablation that coalesces into a rough sphere. **D.** CT scan after RFA shows a low attenuation ablation zone (*black arrow*), larger than the index tumor.

MECHANISM

Light emitted at optical or near-infrared wavelengths from a single bare 400-μm laser fiber is converted into heat within the tissue. Light energy of 2 to 2.5 W produces a 2-cm size spherical zone of coagulative necrosis; however, higher power results in charring of the tissue and a decreased zone of coagulative necrosis. Larger volumes of necrosis can be produced either by simultaneously firing multiple bare fibers within the tumor or by using cooled tip diffuser probes to deposit 30 W over a larger surface area.

EQUIPMENT

Nd:YAG lasers (Dornier MedTech GmbH, Wessling, Germany; and Deka Mela, Florence, Italy) deliver concentrated light at 1064-nm wavelength through 10-m-long fibers, which are compatible with MR imaging.

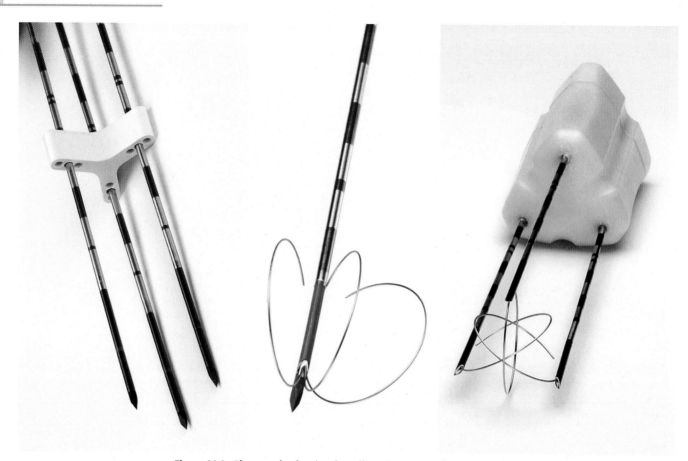

Figure 86-8. Photographs showing the Valley Lab Vivant microwave needles.

TECHNIQUE

The laser fibers are placed into tumors through small needles positioned using ultrasound, CT, or MR. The ablation process can be monitored by MR thermal mapping. Up to eight optical fibers at 2-cm intervals can be inserted into the tumor to deposit a large amount of energy to create large areas of coagulation. Ablation times of 60 to 90 minutes can yield confluent 6- to 7-cm ablations with the size of the ablations depending on tumor vascularity and vasodilatory response of the adjacent liver parenchyma.[79]

Freezing Ablative Techniques: Cryoablation

Cryoablation is the oldest thermal ablation modality, with its role in liver tumor treatment first described in 1963.[105] Since then multiple clinical reports have confirmed its efficacy in liver tumor ablation. While the earlier reports used large applicators that required a surgical approach; more recent reports describe miniaturized probes that can be used percutaneously.

Supercooled gas or liquid circulating through a penetrating/surface cryoprobe causes subfreezing temperatures (−20° C to −30° C) adjacent to the exposed probe tip, thus causing denaturation of cellular proteins, cell membrane rupture, ischemic hypoxia, cellular dehydration, and subsequent irreversible tissue destruction.

Cryoprobes use either argon gas or nitrogen (liquid/gas). Argon gas cryoprobe manufacturers include Cryohit (Galil Medical, Yokneam, Israel) and Cryocare (Endocare, Irvine, CA) (Fig. 86-9), while liquid nitrogen system manufacturers include Liquid Cryo (Spembly Medical, Andover, UK) and Accuprobe (Cryomedical Sciences, Inc., Rockville, MD).[108] Cryoprobes are available for intraoperative and percutaneous use. Simultaneous activation of multiple probes allows ablation sizes of ≤5 cm.

Cryoablation is performed predominantly intraoperatively and more recently via a percutaneous approach. Depending on tumor size, one or more probes are positioned in the lesion and cryogenic material at −196° C is circulated through the probes. The ice ball produced can be monitored by ultrasound or CT/MR imaging, with the goal of achieving a 5- to 10-mm ablation margin. The first freeze takes 5 to 15 minutes followed by a spontaneous thaw and a second freeze cycle to reach and exceed the previously achieved ablation margin. The probe is subsequently thawed and removed.

Assessment of Treatment Response to Thermal Ablation

The assessment of interstitial treatment of HCC can be performed by either CT or MR imaging. Postprocedure dynamic contrast-enhanced CT scans or contrast-enhanced MR scans performed immediately after or within 4 weeks of the ablation procedure are used to assess the adequacy of an ablation procedure and to serve as a baseline imaging study for subsequent imaging follow-up. Nonenhancing tumor tissue signifies tissue necrosis after treatment, while viable tumor is recognized as enhancing tissue. If imaging is performed shortly after the procedure it is common to visualize a peripheral smooth halo of enhancing tissue surrounding the

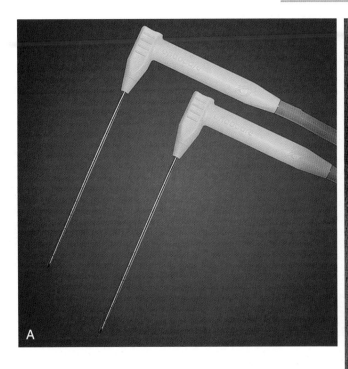

Figure 86-9. Cryoablation therapy. A. Photograph showing the Cryo-care cryoablation single needle. **B.** Ice ball formed as a part of the freeze-thaw cycle.

treated lesion. This halo is termed postablation hyperemia and is best seen in the arterial phase (Fig. 86-10). It represents an inflammatory reaction to the ablation and is usually distinguishable from the nodular enhancement seen with residual viable tissue. Postablation peritumoral hyperemia usually resolves within 3 to 6 months after the procedure.

A standard imaging protocol for follow-up of treated patients should include either CT or MR contrast-enhanced scans every 3 months to assess for recurrent tumor. Color Doppler ultrasound, even when using contrast agents, is not as accurate as either CT or MR imaging for the detection of recurrent tumor. Serum AFP levels are only useful as a follow-up mechanism if the AFP was elevated prior to treatment. In those patients, a complete response should be associated with a decrease in the AFP levels.

Results of Thermal Ablation Techniques

Multiple clinical series of thermal ablation over the last 10 years have confirmed its efficacy for the treatment of HCC. Among the heating ablative techniques, the interest in RFA has far exceeded that for microwave, laser, or cryoablative techniques.

Multiple clinical studies have confirmed RFA as an effective technique for tumor ablation.[95,109,110] High complete ablation rates of up to 98% with a low local recurrence rate at 1-year

have been reported for RFA of HCC.[95] However, the success of RFA is clearly tied to tumor size; with complete ablation rates in the 90-plus percent range for tumors less than 3 cm, while the complete ablation rate for tumors greater than 3 cm have been reported as low as 47.6%.[94] Comparing radio-frequency ablation with PEI for HCC ≤3 cm, Livraghi and colleagues[109] reported a higher rate of complete ablation with RFA (90% for RFA versus 80% for PEI) with fewer required treatment sessions (1.2 for RFA versus 4.8 sessions per tumor for PEI) to produce a complete ablation. The 2-year local recurrence free survival rates for RFA (96%) were superior to PEI (62%) in another prospective randomized trial of the two techniques.[110]

Studies have also confirmed the efficacy of microwave ablation of small HCC, although the literature is still limited. Complete ablation rates of 89% to 92% have been described with 1-, 2-, and 5-year survival rates 92% to 96%, 81% to 83%, and 56%, respectively, for smaller lesions. Complete ablation rates were lower and tumor progression rates were higher for microwave ablation of tumors ≤4 cm in size.[111-113]

Laser ablation has been shown to induce complete ablation in small HCC. Complete ablation rates of 82% to 97% have been described for HCC ≤3 cm, with local recurrence rates of 1.6% to 6% over 1 to 5 years and cancer-free survival rates of 73% to 24% over 1 to 4 years.[114,115]

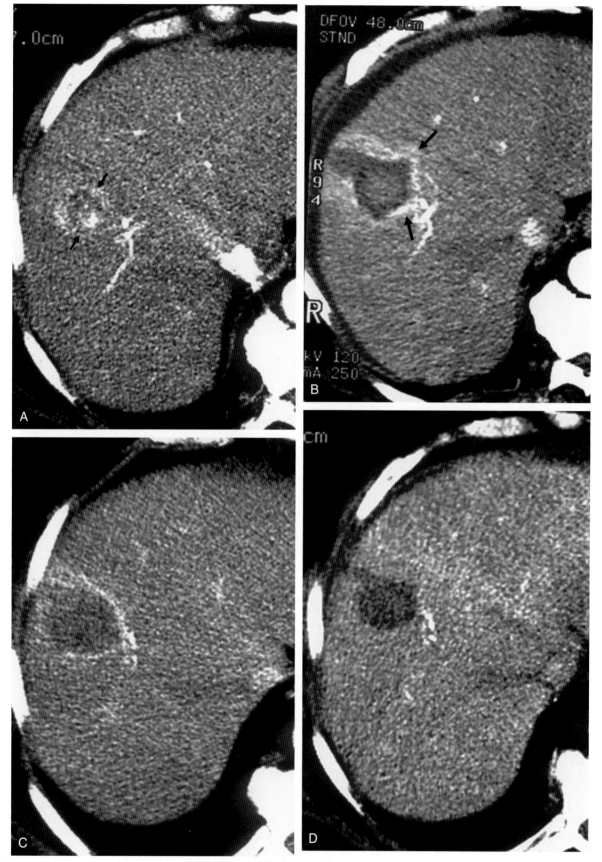

Figure 86-10. CT appearances of the ablations produced by all of the thermal ablation techniques are very similar. A 63-year-old man with a 2.4-cm HCC. **A.** CT scan before RFA shows tumor (*arrows*) in liver segment VIII. **B.** CT scan immediately after solitary RF ablation shows a low attenuation ablation zone with peripheral arterially enhancing halo (*arrows*). The ablation zone is larger than the index tumor. Follow-up CT scans at 1 month (**C**) and 3 months (**D**) reveal resolution of this hyperemic zone.

Literature for cryoablation for the treatment of HCC is limited. One-, 3-, and 5-year survival rates of 63.9%, 40.3% and 26.9%, respectively, have been reported.[116] The overall results are significantly better for patients with HCC than for patients with nonhepatic primary tumors.[117]

Complications of Thermal Ablative Techniques

Pain is the most common side effect of thermal ablations, especially for subcapsular lesions. After hyperthermic ablation techniques, a postablation syndrome characterized by low-grade fever, malaise, nausea, and delayed pain lasting up to 3 weeks and occurring in approximately one third of treated patients has been described.[118] This transient flu-like syndrome is treated conservatively and is directly related to the volume of tissue ablated.

Major complications have been reported in 6% of patients undergoing RFA and include peritoneal or intrahepatic hemorrhage (requiring embolization or surgical management), tumor seeding of the needle tract, intrahepatic abscesses (especially with history of prior surgical interventions to the biliary system) (Fig. 86-11), thermal injury to adjacent organs (diaphragmatic, gallbladder, and bowel), and pneumothorax.[119,120] Death due to RFA is rare and has been encountered in 0.2% of patients in a large multicenter study of 2320 patients.[121] Minor complications can be seen in up to 36%[119] of cases.

Reported complications after microwave ablation are similar to RFA and include pain, fever, mild liver dysfunction, pleural complications, subcapsular hemorrhage, skin burns, and hepatic abscesses.

Complications after laser ablation are similar to those with other ablation techniques as demonstrated in a large series of 899 patients.[122] Major complications included three deaths, pleural effusion, hepatic abscesses, bile duct injury, and hemorrhage.

Complication rates after cryoablation may be higher than for thermal ablations, with some complications being unique to cryoablation. Cryoshock refers to postprocedural pulmonary, renal, and coagulation abnormalities, which can occur in different combinations with varying severity and can lead to death.[123] Hypothermia with intraoperative cryoablation occurs more often than with percutaneous cryoablation. Major complications develop in fewer than 20% of patients and include biliary stenosis, enterobiliary fistulas, abscesses, and septicemia.[124] Tumor recurrence has been reported in 13% of patients.[124]

Combined Thermal and Chemical Ablation

Combination of two interstitial techniques for tumor ablation can be useful for treating residual/recurrent tumors, larger lesions, or lesions too difficult to ablate completely due to anatomic considerations (i.e., lesions adjacent to blood vessels or bowel). Chemical ablation can be performed either as the initial therapy in combination with thermal ablation, or as an adjunctive procedure during follow-up if there is residual HCC. For anatomically difficult to treat lesions, 99.5% ethanol can be injected into the portion of the HCC located in the regions where RFA would be contraindicated, with RFA used to treat the remaining tumor.[125] Alternatively, it has been reported that ethanol and RFA may be used in combination for the treatment of any tumor to achieve a larger ablation in fewer sessions compared with RFA alone.[126,127] However, the true utility of this combinational therapy remains unproven.

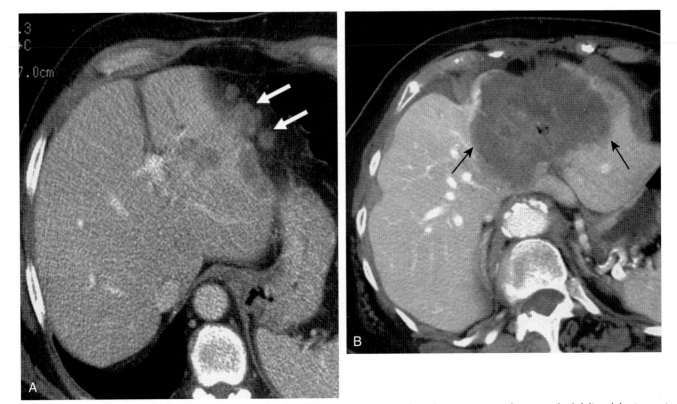

Figure 86-11. Complications of RFA. A. CT scan 5 months after RFA shows nodularity along the access tract adjacent to the left liver lobe (*arrows*) indicating tumor seeding. **B.** Hepatic abscess (*arrows*) in the left lobe post RFA.

Endovascular Management of Hepatocellular Carcinomas

Endovascular treatment is one of the most common techniques used to treat unresectable HCC. The rationale for endovascular treatment of liver tumors stems from the observation that normal liver receives approximately 75% of its blood supply from the portal vein, whereas liver tumors receive most (90%-100%) of their blood supply from the hepatic artery. The most common hepatic arterial directed therapies can be divided into those that are embolic (transarterial chemoembolization [TACE], transarterial embolization [TAE], and intra-arterial brachytherapy) or infusional (pump based—hepatic arterial chemoinfusion).

Patient Selection Criteria

Indications and contraindications for endovascular therapy for HCC remain controversial, as the response to treatment is affected by the grade of HCC and underlying liver disease. As liver tumor characterization is not encompassed in the Child-Pugh classification, other classifications that include variables of tumor morphology, AFP levels and portal vein thrombus like the CLIP (Cancer of the Liver Italian Program) have been demonstrated to better assess the prognostic value for patients with HCC.[128]

Tumoral characteristics associated with poor outcomes include diameter greater than 10 cm, tumor replacing more than 50% of the liver, and diffuse infiltrating tumors; positive prognostic indicators include tumors that retain a higher degree of oil during TACE, and tumor diam-eter less than 8 cm, replacing less than 50% of the liver.[129,130] The risk of acute liver failure increases with lactate dehydrogenase levels greater than 425 IU/L, aspartate aminotrans-ferase level greater than 100 IU/L, total bilirubin level greater than 2 mg/dl (34 μmol/L), and albumin levels less than 35 g/L, with a questionable role of TACE in patients with hepatic encephalopathy, extrahepatic metastases and other comorbidities.[130] Though biliary obstruction or prior biliary reconstructive surgery are not absolute contraindications, the risk of biliary necrosis and abscess formation warrants prophylactic antibiotics, preprocedure biliary decompression for obstruction, and adjusting the amount of chemoembolization agents to reduce bile duct injury.[131] Similarly, portal vein thrombosis is not a contraindication to endovascular therapy but does require superselective/segmental catheterization and a reduced degree of embolization.[132,133]

Preprocedurally, the patient undergoes clinical evaluation to assess comorbid conditions, the quality of life, and to assess the severity of underlying cirrhosis; radiologic evaluation with CT or MR imaging to assess the tumor morphology, extrahepatic spread, and liver vascularity; and laboratory evaluation to assess liver and renal function and coagulation parameters.

Angiographic Considerations

An assessment of the hepatic arterial anatomy is essential for planning regional endovascular therapy for HCC and to avoid nontarget embolization. Preprocedural CT and MR imaging have proven effective for assessing portal venous patency and variant anatomy of the large vessels. Variant vessel anatomy includes replaced/accessory right hepatic artery (from the superior mesenteric artery [SMA]), replaced/accessory left hepatic artery (from the left gastric), double hepatic and middle hepatic arteries. Angiography is essential to delineate smaller vessels to avoid complications in undesirable arterial beds such as the cystic artery (cholecystitis), right gastric artery (gastric ulceration), pancreaticoduodenal/supraduodenal/retrouodenal arcade (pancreatitis and duodenal ulceration), falciform artery (supraumbilical rash and pain), and suprarenal arteries (adrenal hemorrhage).[134] The initial angiographic study should therefore include an abdominal aortogram and selective superior mesenteric, celiac, right hepatic, left hepatic, and gastroduodenal artery (GDA) arteriograms. Angiography also evaluates the degree of arteriovenous shunting, the stenosis/tortuosity of the feeding vessels and other factors that could alter regional blood flow to the tumor and potentially lower the response to TACE or radioembolization. With extracapsular invasion of HCC, parasitization of extrahepatic arteries is common and delineation of the feeders from the inferior phrenic, superior mesenteric, left gastric, and celiac arteries is essential.

Transcatheter Arterial Chemoembolization

The term "chemoembolization" implies localized intra-arterial delivery of chemotherapeutic agents combined with embolic material. TACE has been used the longest of the several minimally invasive techniques that are available to treat HCC.

Mechanism

The aim of chemoembolization is to minimize systemic toxicity, deliver highly concentrated chemotherapeutic agents to tumor cells, and prolong the contact time between the drug and the cancer cells, thus synergistically achieving tumor necrosis. Ischemia induced failure of transmembrane pumps in tumor cells allows increased absorption and decreased washout of the chemotherapeutic agent, thus prolonging contact time.

Chemotherapeutic Agents

The combination chemotherapy drug regimen most commonly used comprises cisplatin 100 mg (Bristol Myers Squibb, Princeton, NJ), doxorubicin 50 mg (Adriamycin; Pharmacia-Upjohn, Kalamazoo, MI) and mitomycin C 10 mg (Bedford Laboratories, Bedford, Ohio) mixed in 10 mL of water-soluble contrast material, and emulsified in an equivalent volume of ethiodized oil. The most common independently used agent is doxorubicin, though a recent study has shown cisplatin to be more effective than doxorubicin as a single agent against HCC.[135] The suspension agent ethiodol preferentially accumulates in HCC and is a key component due to its liver tumor seeking and embolic properties. Embolization can be performed with either gelatin sponge powder or pledgets for temporary occlusion, or polyvinyl alcohol (150-250 μm particles) or trisacryl gelatin microspheres for permanent occlusion.

Technique

After overnight fasting, patients are vigorously hydrated (with normal saline at 200-300 mL/hour), and premedicated with prophylactic antibiotics (cefazolin 1 g, metronidazole 500 mg) and antiemetics (ondansetron hydrochloride 24 mg). Diagnostic visceral angiography determines the normal and variant hepatic arterial supply and patency of the portal vein.

The catheter is subsequently advanced into the right or left hepatic artery, and either lobar TACE for multiple/diffuse lesions or selective TACE for unifocal lesions is performed to preserve functional liver tissue. For selective catheterization of the second or third order branches a 3-Fr microcatheter preferably with a 0.027-inch inner lumen is recommended (Fig. 86-12). Although multiple regimens of chemoembolization delivery techniques are described (chemotherapy agents, embolic material and oil delivered as a mixed slurry or injected separately), delivering the embolic material after injecting the entire dose of the chemotherapeutic agent increases the injected volume of the agents and maintains long-term arterial patency, thus allowing TACE to be repeated multiple times and achieving maximal effect of tumor ablation. TACE is performed under conscious sedation with intravenous fentanyl and morphine along with intra-arterial lidocaine for pain relief.

Postprocedurally, most patients are discharged from the hospital within 2 days. Oral antibiotics maybe continued for 5 days with antiemetics or oral narcotic analgesics if required.

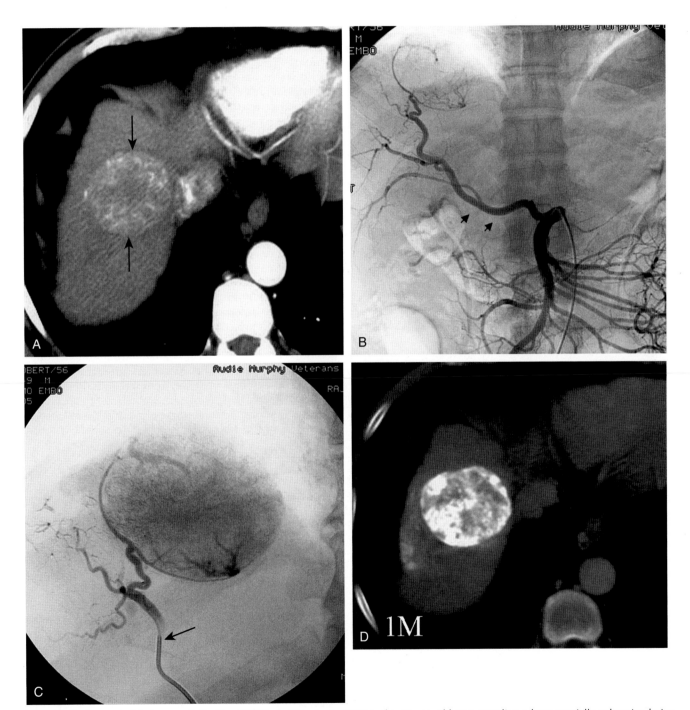

Figure 86-12. Transarterial chemoembolization (TACE). A. CT prior to TACE in this 56-year-old man revealing a large arterially enhancing lesion (*arrows*) in the right lobe. **B.** Superior mesenteric angiogram reveals a replaced right hepatic artery (*arrows*) supplying the right hepatic lobe mass via tertiary branches. **C.** Selective catheterization of the tertiary right hepatic arterial branch with a microcatheter (*arrow*) and intra-arterial injection of the chemotherapy drugs mixed with ethiodol. **D.** Post-TACE CT revealing adequate ethiodol uptake in the right hepatic lobe HCC.

Transcatheter Arterial Embolization

The term "transarterial embolization" implies embolization of the artery feeding the tumor. The concept of treating liver neoplasms by interrupting the arterial blood supply was introduced by Markovitz in 1952,[136] and is based on the observation that obstruction of the hepatic artery supplying an HCC will cause extensive tumor necrosis. The main reason for bland embolization is to decrease side effects and patient discomfort related to chemotherapeutic agents.

Mechanism

Embolization of the artery feeding the tumor results in tumor ischemia and hypoxia with subsequent tumor necrosis. The true mechanism of TAE-induced tumor necrosis is not yet clear. Hypoxia is a potent stimulator of angiogenesis and *p53* mutations and a promoter of glucose consumption by cancer cells.[130] However, despite the premise that TAE-induced hypoxia could inadvertently promote tumorigenesis, few clinical studies have shown TAE to be less effective than TACE.

Embolic Agents

Ethiodol is an effective embolic agent due to its preferential and prolonged uptake in tumoral cells and its metabolism by Kupffer cells. Particles used for embolization include gelfoam, polyvinyl alcohol (PVA), or trisacryl gelatin microspheres.[137] Gelatin microspheres have the advantage of deeper penetration and embolization of smaller and peripheral vessels due to their lack of aggregation and their smooth hydrophilic surface and deformability.

Technique

Like TACE, transcatheter arterial embolization involves similar premedication (with antibiotics, analgesics, and antiemetics) and angiographic evaluation (to assess variant anatomy). Lobar or selective TAE is performed according to the size and extent of the tumor, with the volume of embolic agent injected being aimed at decreasing arterial inflow to the tumor. Stasis or stagnant flow may not correlate with the true distribution of the embolic agent, because reversal of flow and subsequent nontarget embolic effects may continue even after completion of regional therapy. In patients with tumor involving both lobes, only one lobe is embolized during one treatment session. Care is taken to avoid embolizing undesirable arterial beds thus preventing nontarget embolization.

Transcatheter Arterial Radioembolization

Traditionally, whole liver external beam radiation therapy has had a limited role in the treatment of unresectable HCC due to the relative radiosensitivity of liver parenchyma at radiation doses that are tumoricidal for the relatively radiation resistant HCC. Intra-arterial brachytherapy (radioembolization) is a relatively new treatment modality that involves administration of yttrium 90 microspheres such as Theraspheres (MDS Nordion, Ottawa, ON, Canada) or SIR-spheres (Sirtex Medical Inc., North Ryde, Australia) selectively into the hepatic artery branch delivering internal β-radiation therapy to HCC, sparing the liver parenchyma.

Mechanism

Radioembolization concentrates internal β-radiation to the tumor causing localized generation of oxygen-free radicals thus triggering and promoting apoptosis and direct radiation necrosis. The preservation of blood flow and hence oxygenation to the target tumor enhances the response to therapeutic radiation. Relative low concentration of superoxide dismutase in tumor cells limits their ability to compensate in a free radical rich environment.[138] Yttrium 90 is a pure β emitter with a half-life of 64.1 hours with an average energy of 0.9367 MeV per β particle. The mean tissue penetration of yttrium 90 is 2.5 mm with a maximum penetration of 10 mm.[139]

Radioembolization Agents

Theraspheres consist of nonbiodegradable glass microspheres ranging from 15 to 35 μm in diameter and SIR spheres are similar sized biocompatible microspheres, both having yttrium 90 as an integral constituent. These radioactive microspheres are administered intra-arterially to achieve tumoricidal radiation doses (50-150 Gy) at the segmental or lobar level or to the whole liver depending on the extent of tumor. The volume of the injected agent depends on the target tumor volume. Due to their small size, the embolic effect of the microspheres, especially of Theraspheres is negligible, with the particles lodging mainly in the tumor microcirculation, thereafter causing direct radiation necrosis.

Technique

Similar to other endovascular interventional techniques, the initial angiographic evaluation is a must to assess for variant vessel anatomy and delineate enteric and nonhepatic arterial beds to prevent complications. Infusion of radioactive microspheres into unrecognized collateral vessels could result in undesirable clinical toxicities which might include cholecystitis, gastrointestinal ulceration, pancreatitis, and skin irritation. Aggressive prophylactic embolization is therefore recommended for the cystic, gastroduodenal, right gastric, esophageal, accessory phrenic, falciform, supraduodenal and retroduodenal arteries, and other hepaticoenteric arterial communications to prevent these nontarget complications. Reflux of the embolic material and nontarget embolization can be controlled with proper dosimetry, embolization of collaterals, and dose fractionation (injecting as small doses especially for SIR spheres).

Hepatic Arterial Chemoinfusion

The side effects of systemic chemotherapy are reduced by the localized intra-arterial delivery of the chemotherapeutic agent. Hepatic arterial chemoinfusion began with surgical placement of the catheters in the gastroduodenal artery (GDA), the surgical technique involving cholecystectomy and ligation of the gastroduodenal/right gastric arteries prior to catheter placement. However, despite meticulous surgical technique, misperfusion, or inadequate perfusion was seen in up to 45% of cases.[140] The development of intra-arterial chemoinfusion for unresectable hepatic tumors has significantly evolved during the last four decades from an intraoperative technique into image-guided endovascular hepatic arterial chemoinfusion.

Mechanism

The rationale for the use of hepatic arterial chemoinfusion is to deliver a higher therapeutic concentration of anticancer agent, to maximize tumor uptake (based on the premise of high extraction by the target organ) and to reduce systemic toxicity. The antitumor effect of cisplatin and 5-fluorouracil (5-FU) is enhanced by the synergistic role of cisplatin as a modulator of 5-FU, inhibiting the transport of neutral amino acids into tumor cells, with enhancement of its antitumor effects thus allowing lower dose administration and reduced adverse reactions.

Intra-arterial Chemotherapy Agents

The agents used include cisplatin and 5-FU, which can be infused at differing protocols using a mechanical infusion pump connected to the subcutaneous port.

Technique

Similar to TAE, the initial angiographic evaluation identifies variant vessel anatomy, and prophylactic embolization is performed for the cystic artery and enterohepatic collateral vessels (especially the GDA) to prevent complications. The catheter tip is placed in the proper hepatic artery and the other end connected to an injection port implanted subcutaneously in the right lower abdominal quadrant (with femoral artery access) or in the infraclavicular chest wall (with subclavian artery access).

Assessment of Treatment Response to Endovascular Techniques

The treatment response to endovascular techniques requires assessment by imaging techniques and laboratory evaluation. Contrast-enhanced CT or MR imaging is performed within 4 weeks of the endovascular procedure to determine treatment response and extent of ethiodol uptake, and to assess for residual tumor. Tissue necrosis appears as nonenhanced tumoral tissue and viable tumor shows contrast enhancement. To assess questionable areas of enhancement, MR is especially advantageous. Dense ethiodol can mask the detection of residual enhancing tumor on CT scan, but does not present a similar problem for MR. The imaging protocol for follow-up consists of repeat scans every three/four months to assess for recurrent tumor or new lesions. Laboratory evaluation is performed within 3 weeks to assess for liver toxicity along with AFP levels to assess for treatment response.

Results

Several studies have assessed the efficacy of endovascular treatment options for HCC citing multiple factors including patient survival, imaging response, biologic response, quality of life, and symptomatic improvement.

Llovet and colleagues compared TACE (with doxorubicin), TAE and conservative treatment for localized HCC in patients with preserved liver function, confirming reduction of mortality by 53% in patients treated with TACE compared to conservative management.[141] Improved 2-year survival rates were seen with TACE (63%) versus TAE (50%) and only 27% for conservative therapy.[141] Similarly, other retrospective studies have also demonstrated improved patient survival, with survival rates of 64%, 38%, 27%, and 27% at 1, 2, 3, and 4 years, respectively, after TACE versus 18%, 6%, and 5% at 1, 2, and 3 years, respectively, with supportive care.[142] One prospective randomized trial comparing TACE (cisplatin with lipiodol and gelatin sponge particles) versus symptomatic treatment in unresectable HCC in 80 patients demonstrated

significantly better survival in the TACE group (1 year, 57%; 2 years, 31%; 3 years, 26%) versus the supportive care group (1 year, 32%; 2 years, 11%; 3 years, 3%).[143] However, randomized control trials and a recent meta-analysis have failed to show any effect of TACE on patient survival,[144] though procedural variability and flaws in trial design limit evaluation. Clearly, additional well-executed randomized trials are needed to accurately evaluate the survival rates after TACE.

Bland arterial embolization is described in literature, though few randomized trials are available to support its effect on patient survival.[141] Using lipiodol and cyanoacrylate cumulative survival rates of 71% to 77%, 59% to 64%, and 47% to 55% have been reported at 6, 12, and 24 months, respectively, with better survival rates at 6 months in patients with Okuda I stage disease.[137,145] Yttrium-90 TheraSphere treatment for unresectable HCC is well tolerated and appears to extend survival with studies showing a median survival of 11 months and 7 months in Okuda stage II and III patients, respectively.[146]

Intra-arterial chemotherapy may aid in downstaging of advanced HCC prior to resection or ablation. Median survival for unresectable and untreated HCC has been only a few months while a median survival of 10 months has been reported with hepatic arterial chemoinfusion.[147] Unresectable HCC with portal vein thrombosis has a poorer prognosis if untreated, though recent studies with hepatic arterial chemoinfusion have demonstrated response rates of 48% and median survival of 10.2 months in these patients.[148]

Complications

Transcatheter arterial interventions are generally well tolerated with major complications in 4% to 7% of procedures (most commonly liver abscesses especially in patients with biliary obstruction or surgery) and a 30-day mortality of 1%.[149,150] Patients should also be informed about the "postembolization syndrome" which can occur in 80% to 90% of patients after TACE and manifests as fever, nausea, and vomiting and can last from a few hours to few days.[130,149]

Combined Endovascular and Interstitial Management

For larger lesions the effect of ablation can be potentiated after TACE and vice versa. The combination of TACE and PEI was proposed by Tanaka and colleagues in 1991,[151] and has been evaluated subsequently by several series and two randomized trials. The premise of this therapeutic approach is that tissue changes induced in the tumor after TACE augment the diffusion of ethanol through the tumor thus producing a more effective ablation. The results of a randomized study showed that survival rate after a single session of combined TACE and PEI for large (3-8 cm) HCC was similar to that with two to five sessions of TACE alone.[152] Another randomized trail comparing PEI alone and TACE with PEI for the treatment of three or fewer HCC each measuring ≤3 cm demonstrated that TACE with PEI was better than PEI alone. Fewer treatment sessions (3.8 versus 5.3), decreased 2-year tumor recurrence rates (35% versus 65%), and better 3-year survival rates (100% versus 62%) were seen with TACE with PEI versus PEI alone, respectively.[153] The combination of TACE and thermal ablation has also been studied for large lesions (3.5-9.6 cm) with a reported 90% complete ablation rate and a local recurrence rate of 7% at 3 years.[154,155]

References

1. Heron MP, Smith BL: Deaths: Leading causes for 2003. Natl Vital Stat Rep 15:1-92, 2007.
2. Parikh S, Hyman D: Hepatocellular cancer: A guide for the internist. Am J Med 120:194-202, 2007.
3. Sherlock S: Aspiration liver biopsy: Technique and diagnostic application. Lancet II:397-401, 1945.
4. Menghini G: One-second needle biopsy of the liver. Gastroenterology 35:190-199, 1958.
5. Gilmore IT, Burroughs A, Murray-Lyon IM, et al: Indications, methods, and outcomes of percutaneous liver biopsy in England and Wales: An audit by the British Society of Gastroenterology and the Royal College of Physicians of London. Gut 36:437-441, 1995.
6. Dodd GD 3rd, Esola CC, Memel DS, et al: Sonography: The undiscovered jewel of interventional radiology. RadioGraphics 16:1271-1288, 1996.
7. Farrell RJ, Smiddy PF, Pilkington RM, et al: Guided versus blind liver biopsy for chronic hepatitis C: Clinical benefits and costs. J Hepatol 30:580-587, 1999.
8. Murphy FB, Barefield KP, Steinberg HV, Bernardino ME: CT- or sonography-guided biopsy of the liver in the presence of ascites: Frequency of complications. AJR 151:485-486, 1988.
9. Little AF, Ferris JV, Dodd GD 3rd, Baron RL: Image-guided percutaneous hepatic biopsy: Effect of ascites on the complication rate. Radiology 199:79-83, 1996.
10. Younossi ZM, Teran JC, Ganiats TG, Carey WD: Ultrasound-guided liver biopsy for parenchymal liver disease: An economic analysis. Dig Dis Sci 43:46-50, 1998.
11. Piccinino F, Sagnelli E, Pasquale G, Giusti G: Complications following percutaneous liver biopsy. A multicentre retrospective study on 68,276 biopsies. J Hepatol 2:165-173, 1986.
12. McGill DB, Rakela J, Zinsmeister AR, Ott BJ: A 21-year experience with major hemorrhage after percutaneous liver biopsy. Gastroenterology 99:1396-1400, 1990.
13. Tobkes AI, Nord HJ: Liver biopsy: Review of methodology and complications. Dig Dis 13:267-274, 1995.
14. Hanafee W, Weiner M: Transjugular percutaneous cholangiography. Radiology 88:35-39, 1967.
15. McAfee JH, Keeffe EB, Lee RG, Rosch J: Transjugular liver biopsy. Hepatology 15:726-732, 1992.
16. Garcia-Compean D, Cortes C: Transjugular liver biopsy. An update. Ann Hepatol 3:100-103, 2004.
17. Rosch J, Hanafee WN, Snow H: Transjugular portal venography and radiologic portacaval shunt: An experimental study. Radiology 92:1112-1114, 1969.
18. Richter GM, Noeldge G, Palmaz JC, et al: Transjugular intrahepatic portacaval stent shunt: Preliminary clinical results. Radiology 174(3 Pt 2):1027-1030, 1990.
19. Haskal ZJ, Martin L, Cardella JF, et al: Quality improvement guidelines for transjugular intrahepatic portosystemic shunts. J Vasc Interv Radiol 14(9 Pt 2):S265-S270, 2003.
20. Ferral H, Patel NH: Selection criteria for patients undergoing transjugular intrahepatic portosystemic shunt procedures: Current status. J Vasc Interv Radiol 16:449-455, 2005.
21. Montgomery A, Ferral H, Vasan R, Postoak DW: MELD score as a predictor of early death in patients undergoing elective transjugular intrahepatic portosystemic shunt (TIPS) procedures. Cardiovasc Intervent Radiol 28:307-312, 2005.
22. Charon JP, Alaeddin FH, Pimpalwar SA, et al: Results of a retrospective multicenter trial of the Viatorr expanded polytetrafluoroethylene-covered stent-graft for transjugular intrahepatic portosystemic shunt creation. J Vasc Interv Radiol 15:1219-1230, 2004.
23. Saxon RR: A new era for transjugular intrahepatic portosystemic shunts? J Vasc Interv Radiol 15:217-219, 2004.
24. Sanyal AJ, Freedman AM, Luketic VA, et al: The natural history of portal hypertension after transjugular intrahepatic portosystemic shunts. Gastroenterology 112:889-898, 1997.
25. Chong WK, Malisch TA, Mazer MJ, et al: Transjugular intrahepatic portosystemic shunt: US assessment with maximum flow velocity. Radiology 189:789-793, 1993.
26. Dodd GD 3rd, Zajko AB, Orons PD, et al: Detection of transjugular intrahepatic portosystemic shunt dysfunction: Value of duplex Doppler sonography. AJR 164:1119-1124, 1995.
27. Chopra S, Dodd GD 3rd, Chintapalli KN, et al: Transjugular intrahepatic portosystemic shunt: Accuracy of helical CT angiography in the detection of shunt abnormalities. Radiology 215:115-122, 2000.
28. Jalan R, Forrest EH, Stanley AJ, et al: A randomized trial comparing transjugular intrahepatic portosystemic stent-shunt with variceal band ligation in the prevention of rebleeding from esophageal varices. Hepatology 26:1115-1122, 1997.
29. Merli M, Salerno F, Riggio O, et al: Transjugular intrahepatic portosystemic shunt versus endoscopic sclerotherapy for the prevention of variceal bleeding in cirrhosis: A randomized multicenter trial. Gruppo Italiano Studio TIPS (G.I.S.T.). Hepatology 27:48-53, 1998.
30. Burroughs AK, Patch D: Transjugular intrahepatic portosystemic shunt. Semin Liver Dis 19:457-473, 1999.
31. Sorbi D, Gostout CJ, Peura D, et al: An assessment of the management of acute bleeding varices: A multicenter prospective member-based study. Am J Gastroenterol 98:2424-2434, 2003.
32. Russo MW, Sood A, Jacobson IM, Brown RS Jr: Transjugular intrahepatic portosystemic shunt for refractory ascites: An analysis of the literature on efficacy, morbidity, and mortality. Am J Gastroenterol 98:2521-2527, 2003.
33. Nishimine K, Saxon RR, Kichikawa K, et al: Improved transjugular intrahepatic portosystemic shunt patency with PTFE-covered stent-grafts: Experimental results in swine. Radiology 196:341-347, 1995.
34. Hausegger KA, Karnel F, Georgieva B, et al: Transjugular intrahepatic portosystemic shunt creation with the Viatorr expanded polytetrafluoroethylene-covered stent-graft. J Vasc Interv Radiol 15:239-248, 2004.
35. Reynolds TB: Ascites. Clin Liver Dis 4:151-168, vii, 2000.
36. Arroyo V, Gines P, Gerbes AL, et al: Definition and diagnostic criteria of refractory ascites and hepatorenal syndrome in cirrhosis. International Ascites Club. Hepatology 23:164-176, 1996.
37. Salerno F, Borroni G, Moser P, et al: Survival and prognostic factors of cirrhotic patients with ascites: A study of 134 outpatients. Am J Gastroenterol 88:514-519, 1993.
38. Runyon BA: Management of adult patients with ascites caused by cirrhosis. Hepatology 27:264-272, 1998.
39. Sanyal AJ, Genning C, Reddy KR, et al: The North American Study for the Treatment of Refractory Ascites. Gastroenterology 124:634-641, 2003.
40. Shirabe K, Shimada M, Gion T, et al: Postoperative liver failure after major hepatic resection for hepatocellular carcinoma in the modern era with special reference to remnant liver volume. J Am Coll Surg 188:304-309, 1999.
41. Shoup M, Gonen M, D'Angelica M, et al: Volumetric analysis predicts hepatic dysfunction in patients undergoing major liver resection. J Gastrointest Surg 7:325-330, 2003.
42. Rous P, Larimore LD: Relation of the portal blood flow to liver maintenance: A demonstration of liver atrophy conditional on compensation. J Exp Med 31: 609-632, 1920.
43. Makuuchi M, Thai BL, Takayasu K, et al: Preoperative portal embolization to increase safety of major hepatectomy for hilar bile duct carcinoma: A preliminary report. Surgery 107:521-527, 1990.
44. Madoff DC, Abdalla EK, Vauthey JN: Portal vein embolization in preparation for major hepatic resection: Evolution of a new standard of care. J Vasc Interv Radiol 16:779-790, 2005.
45. Kinoshita H, Sakai K, Hirohashi K, et al: Preoperative portal vein embolization for hepatocellular carcinoma. World J Surg 10:803-808, 1986.
46. Nagino M, Nimura Y, Kamiya J, et al: Selective percutaneous transhepatic embolization of the portal vein in preparation for extensive liver resection: The ipsilateral approach. Radiology 200:559-563, 1996.
47. Nagino M, Nimura Y, Kamiya J, et al: Changes in hepatic lobe volume in biliary tract cancer patients after right portal vein embolization. Hepatology 21:434-439, 1995.
48. Farges O, Belghiti J, Kianmanesh R, et al: Portal vein embolization before right hepatectomy: Prospective clinical trial. Ann Surg 237:208-217, 2003.
49. Tanaka H, Hirohashi K, Kubo S, et al: Preoperative portal vein embolization improves prognosis after right hepatectomy for hepatocellular carcinoma in patients with impaired hepatic function. Br J Surg 87: 879-882, 2000.
50. Di Stefano DR, de Baere T, Denys A, et al: Preoperative percutaneous portal vein embolization: Evaluation of adverse events in 188 patients. Radiology 234:625-630, 2005.
51. Romano M, Giojelli A, Capuano G, et al: Partial splenic embolization in patients with idiopathic portal hypertension. Eur J Radiol 49:268-273, 2004.
52. Harned RK 2nd, Thompson HR, Kumpe DA, et al: Partial splenic embolization in five children with hypersplenism: Effects of reduced-volume embolization on efficacy and morbidity. Radiology 209:803-806, 1998.

53. Palsson B, Hallen M, Forsberg AM, Alwmark A: Partial splenic embolization: Long-term outcome. Langenbecks Arch Surg 387(11-12): 421-426, 2003.

54. Xu RY, Liu B, Lin N: Therapeutic effects of endoscopic variceal ligation combined with partial splenic embolization for portal hypertension. World J Gastroenterol 10:1072-1074, 2004.

55. Peterson MS, Baron RL, Marsh JW Jr, et al: Pretransplantation surveillance for possible hepatocellular carcinoma in patients with cirrhosis: Epidemiology and CT-based tumor detection rate in 430 cases with surgical pathologic correlation. Radiology 217:743-749, 2000.

56. El-Serag HB, Mason AC: Rising incidence of hepatocellular carcinoma in the United States. N Engl J Med 340:745-750, 1999.

57. Bolondi L, Sofia S, Siringo S, et al: Surveillance programme of cirrhotic patients for early diagnosis and treatment of hepatocellular carcinoma: A cost effectiveness analysis. Gut 48:251-259, 2001.

58. Fattovich G, Giustina G, Schalm SW, et al: Occurrence of hepatocellular carcinoma and decompensation in western European patients with cirrhosis type B. The EUROHEP Study Group on Hepatitis B Virus and Cirrhosis. Hepatology 21:77-82, 1995.

59. Dodd GD 3rd, Baron RL, Oliver JH 3rd, Federle MP. Spectrum of imaging findings of the liver in end-stage cirrhosis: Part II, Focal Abnormalities. AJR 173:1185-1192, 1999.

60. Baron RL, Oliver JH 3rd, Dodd GD 3rd, et al: Hepatocellular carcinoma: Evaluation with biphasic, contrast-enhanced, helical CT. Radiology 199:505-511, 1996.

61. Bruix J, Sherman M, Llovet JM, et al: Clinical management of hepatocellular carcinoma. Conclusions of the Barcelona-2000 EASL conference. European Association for the Study of the Liver. J Hepatol 35:421-30, 2001.

62. Tublin ME, Dodd GD 3rd, Baron RL: Benign and malignant portal vein thrombosis: Differentiation by CT characteristics. AJR 168:719-23, 1997.

63. Dodd GD 3rd, Carr BI: Percutaneous biopsy of portal vein thrombus: A new staging technique for hepatocellular carcinoma. AJR 161:229-233, 1993.

64. de Sio I, Castellano L, Calandra M, et al: Diagnosis of hepatocellular carcinoma by fine needle biopsy of portal vein thrombosis. Ital J Gastroenterol 24:75-76, 1992.

65. Dodd GD 3rd, Baron RL, Oliver JH 3rd, et al: Enlarged abdominal lymph nodes in end-stage cirrhosis: CT-histopathologic correlation in 507 patients. Radiology 203:127-130, 1997.

66. Herszenyi L, Farinati F, Cecchetto A, et al: Fine-needle biopsy in focal liver lesions: The usefulness of a screening programme and the role of cytology and microhistology. Ital J Gastroenterol 27:473-478, 1995.

67. Memel DS, Dodd GD 3rd, Esola CC: Efficacy of sonography as a guidance technique for biopsy of abdominal, pelvic, and retroperitoneal lymph nodes. AJR 167:957-962, 1996.

68. Durand F, Regimbeau JM, Belghiti J, et al: Assessment of the benefits and risks of percutaneous biopsy before surgical resection of hepatocellular carcinoma. J Hepatol 35:254-258, 2001.

69. Chang S, Kim SH, Lim HK, et al: Needle tract implantation after sonographically guided percutaneous biopsy of hepatocellular carcinoma: Evaluation of doubling time, frequency, and features on CT. AJR 185:400-405, 2005.

70. Barbara L, Benzi G, Gaiani S, et al: Natural history of small untreated hepatocellular carcinoma in cirrhosis: A multivariate analysis of prognostic factors of tumor growth rate and patient survival. Hepatology 16:132-137, 1992.

71. Leung TW, Patt YZ, Lau WY, et al: Complete pathological remission is possible with systemic combination chemotherapy for inoperable hepatocellular carcinoma. Clin Cancer Res 5:1676-1681, 1999.

72. Cance WG, Stewart AK, Menck HR: The National Cancer Data Base Report on treatment patterns for hepatocellular carcinomas: Improved survival of surgically resected patients, 1985-1996. Cancer 88:912-920, 2000.

73. Arii S, Yamaoka Y, Futagawa S, et al: Results of surgical and nonsurgical treatment for small-sized hepatocellular carcinomas: A retrospective and nationwide survey in Japan. The Liver Cancer Study Group of Japan. Hepatology 32:1224-1229, 2000.

74. Llovet JM, Fuster J, Bruix J: Intention-to-treat analysis of surgical treatment for early hepatocellular carcinoma: Resection versus transplantation. Hepatology 30:1434-1440, 1999.

75. Zhou XD, Tang ZY, Yang BH, et al: Experience of 1000 patients who underwent hepatectomy for small hepatocellular carcinoma. Cancer 91:1479-1486, 2001.

76. Poon RT, Fan ST, Lo CM, et al: Intrahepatic recurrence after curative resection of hepatocellular carcinoma: Long-term results of treatment and prognostic factors. Ann Surg 229:216-222, 1999.

77. Mazzaferro V, Regalia E, Doci R, et al: Liver transplantation for the treatment of small hepatocellular carcinomas in patients with cirrhosis. N Engl J Med 334:693-699, 1996.

78. Sauer P, Kraus TW, Schemmer P, et al: Liver transplantation for hepatocellular carcinoma: Is there evidence for expanding the selection criteria? Transplantation 80(1 Suppl):S105-S108, 2005.

79. Dodd GD 3rd, Soulen MC, Kane RA, et al: Minimally invasive treatment of malignant hepatic tumors: At the threshold of a major breakthrough. RadioGraphics 20:9-27, 2000.

80. Clark TW, Soulen MC: Chemical ablation of hepatocellular carcinoma. J Vasc Interv Radiol 13(9 Pt 2):S245-S2452, 2002.

81. Livraghi T, Lazzaroni S, Pellicano S, et al: Percutaneous ethanol injection of hepatic tumors: Single-session therapy with general anesthesia. AJR 161:1065-1069, 1993.

82. Livraghi T, Benedini V, Lazzaroni S, et al: Long term results of single session percutaneous ethanol injection in patients with large hepatocellular carcinoma. Cancer 83:48-57, 1998.

83. Livraghi T, Giorgio A, Marin G, et al: Hepatocellular carcinoma and cirrhosis in 746 patients: Long-term results of percutaneous ethanol injection. Radiology 197:101-108, 1995.

84. Kotoh K, Sakai H, Sakamoto S, et al: The effect of percutaneous ethanol injection therapy on small solitary hepatocellular carcinoma is comparable to that of hepatectomy. Am J Gastroenterol 89:194-198, 1994.

85. Lencioni R, Pinto F, Armillotta N, et al: Long-term results of percutaneous ethanol injection therapy for hepatocellular carcinoma in cirrhosis: A European experience. Eur Radiol 7:514-9, 1997.

86. Yamamoto J, Okada S, Shimada K, et al: Treatment strategy for small hepatocellular carcinoma: Comparison of long-term results after percutaneous ethanol injection therapy and surgical resection. Hepatology 34(4 Pt 1):707-713, 2001.

87. Di Stasi M, Buscarini L, Livraghi T, et al: Percutaneous ethanol injection in the treatment of hepatocellular carcinoma. A multicenter survey of evaluation practices and complication rates. Scand J Gastroenterol 32:1168-1173, 1997.

88. Giorgio A, Tarantino L, de Stefano G, et al: Ultrasound-guided percutaneous ethanol injection under general anesthesia for the treatment of hepatocellular carcinoma on cirrhosis: Long-term results in 268 patients. Eur J Ultrasound 12:145-154, 2000.

89. LeVeen R: Laser hyperthermia and radiofrequency ablation of hepatic lesions. Semin Interv Radiol 14: 313-324, 1997.

90. Chopra S, Dodd GD 3rd, Chanin MP, Chintapalli KN: Radiofrequency ablation of hepatic tumors adjacent to the gallbladder: Feasibility and safety. AJR 180:697-701, 2003.

91. McGahan JP, Browning PD, Brock JM, Tesluk H: Hepatic ablation using radiofrequency electrocautery. Invest Radiol 25:267-270, 1990.

92. Rossi S, Fornari F, Pathies C, Buscarini L: Thermal lesions induced by 480 KHz localized current field in guinea pig and pig liver. Tumori 76:54-57, 1990.

93. Rossi S, Fornari F, Buscarini L: Percutaneous ultrasound-guided radiofrequency electrocautery for the treatment of small hepatocellular carcinoma. J Interv Radiol 8: 97-103, 1993.

94. Livraghi T, Goldberg SN, Lazzaroni S, et al: Hepatocellular carcinoma: Radio-frequency ablation of medium and large lesions. Radiology 214:761-768, 2000.

95. Curley SA, Izzo F, Delrio P, et al: Radiofrequency ablation of unresectable primary and metastatic hepatic malignancies: Results in 123 patients. Ann Surg 230:1-8, 1999.

96. Tanabe KK, Curley SA, Dodd GD, et al: Radiofrequency ablation: The experts weigh in. Cancer 100:641-650, 2004.

97. Curley SA: Radiofrequency ablation of malignant liver tumors. Ann Surg Oncol 10:338-347, 2003.

98. McGahan JP, Brock JM, Tesluk H, et al: Hepatic ablation with use of radio-frequency electrocautery in the animal model. J Vasc Interv Radiol 3:291-297, 1992.

99. Goldberg SN, Charboneau JW, Dodd GD 3rd, et al: Image-guided tumor ablation: Proposal for standardization of terms and reporting criteria. Radiology 228:335-345, 2003.

100. Washburn WK, Dodd GD 3rd, Kohlmeier RE, et al: Radiofrequency tissue ablation: Effect of hepatic blood flow occlusion on thermal injuries produced in cirrhotic livers. Ann Surg Oncol 10:773-737, 2003.

101. Leyendecker JR, Dodd GD 3rd, Halff GA, et al: Sonographically observed echogenic response during intraoperative radiofrequency ablation of cirrhotic livers: Pathologic correlation. AJR 178:1147-1151, 2002.

102. Dodd GD 3rd, Frank MS, Aribandi M, et al: Radiofrequency thermal ablation: Computer analysis of the size of the thermal injury created by overlapping ablations. AJR 177:777-782, 2001.

103. Tabuse Y, Tabuse K, Mori K, et al: Percutaneous microwave tissue coagulation in liver biopsy: Experimental and clinical studies. Nippon Geka Hokan 55:381-392, 1986.

104. Shock SA, Meredith K, Warner TF, et al: Microwave ablation with loop antenna: In vivo porcine liver model. Radiology 231:143-149, 2004.

105. Bown SG: Phototherapy in tumors. World J Surg 7:700-709, 1983.

106. Matthewson K, Coleridge-Smith P, O'Sullivan JP, et al: Biological effects of intrahepatic neodymium:yttrium-aluminum-garnet laser photocoagulation in rats. Gastroenterology 93:550-557, 1987.

107. Steger AC, Lees WR, Walmsley K, Bown SG: Interstitial laser hyperthermia: A new approach to local destruction of tumours. BMJ 299(6695):362-365, 1989.

108. Head HW, Dodd GD 3rd: Thermal ablation for hepatocellular carcinoma. Gastroenterology 127(5 Suppl 1):S167-S178, 2004.

109. Livraghi T, Goldberg SN, Lazzaroni S, et al: Small hepatocellular carcinoma: Treatment with radio-frequency ablation versus ethanol injection. Radiology 210:655-661, 1999.

110. Lencioni RA, Allgaier HP, Cioni D, et al: Small hepatocellular carcinoma in cirrhosis: Randomized comparison of radio-frequency thermal ablation versus percutaneous ethanol injection. Radiology 228:235-240, 2003.

111. Dong B, Liang P, Yu X, et al: Percutaneous sonographically guided microwave coagulation therapy for hepatocellular carcinoma: Results in 234 patients. AJR 180:1547-1555, 2003.

112. Xu HX, Xie XY, Lu MD, et al: Ultrasound-guided percutaneous thermal ablation of hepatocellular carcinoma using microwave and radiofrequency ablation. Clin Radiol 59:53-61, 2004.

113. Lu MD, Chen JW, Xie XY, et al: Hepatocellular carcinoma: US-guided percutaneous microwave coagulation therapy. Radiology 221:167-172, 2001.

114. Giorgio A, Tarantino L, de Stefano G, et al: Interstitial laser photocoagulation under ultrasound guidance of liver tumors: Results in 104 treated patients. Eur J Ultrasound 11:181-188, 2000.

115. Pacella CM, Bizzarri G, Magnolfi F, et al: Laser thermal ablation in the treatment of small hepatocellular carcinoma: Results in 74 patients. Radiology 221:712-720, 2001.

116. Zhou XD, Tang ZY: Cryotherapy for primary liver cancer. Semin Surg Oncol 14:171-174, 1998.

117. Silverman SG, Tuncali K, Adams DF, et al: MR imaging-guided percutaneous cryotherapy of liver tumors: Initial experience. Radiology 217:657-664, 2000.

118. Dodd GD 3rd, Napier D, Schoolfield JD, Hubbard L: Percutaneous radiofrequency ablation of hepatic tumors: Postablation syndrome. AJR 185:51-57, 2005.

119. Rhim H, Dodd GD 3rd, Chintapalli KN, et al: Radiofrequency thermal ablation of abdominal tumors: Lessons learned from complications. RadioGraphics 24:41-52, 2004.

120. Llovet JM, Vilana R, Bru C, et al: Increased risk of tumor seeding after percutaneous radiofrequency ablation for single hepatocellular carcinoma. Hepatology 33:1124-1129, 2001.

121. Livraghi T, Solbiati L, Meloni MF, et al: Treatment of focal liver tumors with percutaneous radio-frequency ablation: Complications encountered in a multicenter study. Radiology 226:441-451, 2003.

122. Vogl TJ, Straub R, Eichler K, et al: Malignant liver tumors treated with MR imaging-guided laser-induced thermotherapy: Experience with complications in 899 patients (2,520 lesions). Radiology 225:367-377, 2002.

123. Littlewood K: Anesthetic considerations for hepatic cryotherapy. Semin Surg Oncol 14:116-121, 1998.

124. McPhee MD, Kane RA: Cryosurgery for hepatic tumor ablation. Sem Interv Radiol 14: 285-293, 1997.

125. Kurokohchi K, Watanabe S, Masaki T, et al: Combination therapy of percutaneous ethanol injection and radiofrequency ablation against hepatocellular carcinomas difficult to treat. Int J Oncol 21:611-615, 2002.

126. Kurokohchi K, Watanabe S, Masaki T, et al: Combined use of percutaneous ethanol injection and radiofrequency ablation for the effective treatment of hepatocelluar carcinoma. Int J Oncol 21:841-846, 2002.

127. Sakr AA, Saleh AA, Moeaty AA, Moeaty AA: The combined effect of radiofrequency and ethanol ablation in the management of large hepatocellular carcinoma. Eur J Radiol 54:418-425, 2005.

128. Cancer of the Liver Italian Program (CLIP) Investigators: A new prognostic system for hepatocellular carcinoma: A retrospective study of 435 patients. Hepatology 28:751-755, 1998.

129. Vogl TJ, Trapp M, Schroeder H, et al: Transarterial chemoembolization for hepatocellular carcinoma: Volumetric and morphologic CT criteria for assessment of prognosis and therapeutic success-results from a liver transplantation center. Radiology 214:349-357, 2000.

130. Ramsey DE, Kernagis LY, Soulen MC, Geschwind JF: Chemoembolization of hepatocellular carcinoma. J Vasc Interv Radiol 13(9 Pt 2): S211-S221, 2002.

131. Kim W, Clark TW, Baum RA, Soulen MC: Risk factors for liver abscess formation after hepatic chemoembolization. J Vasc Interv Radiol 12:965-968, 2001.

132. Uraki J, Yamakado K, Nakatsuka A, Takeda K: Transcatheter hepatic arterial chemoembolization for hepatocellular carcinoma invading the portal veins: Therapeutic effects and prognostic factors. Eur J Radiol 51:12-18, 2004.

133. Salem R, Lewandowski R, Roberts C, et al: Use of yttrium-90 glass microspheres (TheraSphere) for the treatment of unresectable hepatocellular carcinoma in patients with portal vein thrombosis. J Vasc Interv Radiol 15:335-345, 2004.

134. Liu DM, Salem R, Bui JT, et al: Angiographic considerations in patients undergoing liver-directed therapy. J Vasc Interv Radiol 16:911-935, 2005.

135. Ono Y, Yoshimasu T, Ashikaga R, et al: Long-term results of lipiodol-transcatheter arterial embolization with cisplatin or doxorubicin for unresectable hepatocellular carcinoma. Am J Clin Oncol 23:564-568, 2000.

136. Markovitz J: The hepatic artery. Surg Gynecol Obstet 95:644-646, 1952.

137. Rand T, Loewe C, Schoder M, et al: Arterial embolization of unresectable hepatocellular carcinoma with use of microspheres, lipiodol, and cyanoacrylate. Cardiovasc Intervent Radiol 28:313-318, 2005.

138. Das U: A radical approach to cancer. Med Sci Monit 8:RA79-92, 2002.

139. Goin JE, Salem R, Carr BI, et al: Treatment of unresectable hepatocellular carcinoma with intrahepatic yttrium 90 microspheres: Factors associated with liver toxicities. J Vasc Interv Radiol 16(2 Pt 1):205-213, 2005.

140. Allen PJ, Stojadinovic A, Ben-Porat L, et al: The management of variant arterial anatomy during hepatic arterial infusion pump placement. Ann Surg Oncol 9:875-880, 2002.

141. Llovet JM, Real MI, Montana X, et al: Arterial embolisation or chemoembolisation versus symptomatic treatment in patients with unresectable hepatocellular carcinoma: A randomised controlled trial. Lancet 359(9319):1734-1739, 2002.

142. Bronowicki JP, Vetter D, Dumas F, et al: Transcatheter oily chemoembolization for hepatocellular carcinoma. A 4-year study of 127 French patients. Cancer 74:16-24, 1994.

143. Lo CM, Ngan H, Tso WK, et al: Randomized controlled trial of transarterial lipiodol chemoembolization for unresectable hepatocellular carcinoma. Hepatology 35:1164-1171, 2002.

144. Geschwind JF, Ramsey DE, Choti MA, et al: Chemoembolization of hepatocellular carcinoma: Results of a metaanalysis. Am J Clin Oncol 26:344-349, 2003.

145. Loewe C, Cejna M, Schoder M, et al: Arterial embolization of unresectable hepatocellular carcinoma with use of cyanoacrylate and lipiodol. J Vasc Interv Radiol 13:61-69, 2002.

146. Liu MD, Uaje MB, Al-Ghazi MS, et al: Use of yttrium-90 TheraSphere for the treatment of unresectable hepatocellular carcinoma. Am Surg 70:947-953, 2004.

147. Sangro B, Rios R, Bilbao I, et al: Efficacy and toxicity of intra-arterial cisplatin and etoposide for advanced hepatocellular carcinoma. Oncology 62:293-298, 2002.

148. Ando E, Tanaka M, Yamashita F, et al: Hepatic arterial infusion chemotherapy for advanced hepatocellular carcinoma with portal vein tumor thrombosis: Analysis of 48 cases. Cancer 95:588-595, 2002.

149. Sakamoto I, Aso N, Nagaoki K, et al: Complications associated with transcatheter arterial embolization for hepatic tumors. RadioGraphics 18:605-619, 1998.

150. Chung JW, Park JH, Han JK, et al: Hepatic tumors: Predisposing factors for complications of transcatheter oily chemoembolization. Radiology 198:33-40, 1996.

151. Tanaka K, Okazaki H, Nakamura S, et al: Hepatocellular carcinoma: treatment with a combination therapy of transcatheter arterial embolization and percutaneous ethanol injection. Radiology 179:713-717, 1991.

152. Bartolozzi C, Lencioni R, Caramella D, et al: Treatment of large HCC: Transcatheter arterial chemoembolization combined with percutaneous ethanol injection versus repeated transcatheter arterial chemoembolization. Radiology 197:812-818, 1995.

153. Koda M, Murawaki Y, Mitsuda A, et al: Combination therapy with transcatheter arterial chemoembolization and percutaneous ethanol injection compared with percutaneous ethanol injection alone for patients with small hepatocellular carcinoma: A randomized control study. Cancer 92:1516-1524, 2001.

154. Pacella CM, Bizzarri G, Cecconi P, et al: Hepatocellular carcinoma: Long-term results of combined treatment with laser thermal ablation and transcatheter arterial chemoembolization. Radiology 219:669-678, 2001.

155. Kim SH, Lee WJ, Lim HK, et al: Prediction of viable tumor in hepatocellular carcinoma treated with transcatheter arterial chemoembolization: Usefulness of attenuation value measurement at quadruple phase helical computed tomography. J Comput Assist Tomogr 31:198-203, 2007.

Anomalies and Anatomic Variants of the Liver

Ali Shirkhoda, MD

The diagnostic pitfalls in cross-sectional imaging studies of the liver include variants of normal anatomy, developmental anomalies, and postsurgical changes. Others are often related to intravenous contrast and scanning at various hepatic phases. This chapter focuses on anatomic variants and anomalies and describes how they can be recognized, because they may simulate pathologic processes.

While congenital abnormalities of human liver are rare, hepatic anatomic variants are relatively common and represent normal interindividual variation of liver morphology. Such variants include diaphragmatic slips, "sliver of liver" (a left-ward extension of the lateral segment of the left lobe), and the variants related to papillary process of the caudate lobe.

There are many kinds of congenital hepatic abnormalities that result from disturbed development of the liver. There are many anatomic variations of the hepatic vascular anatomy that may affect liver morphology.[1,2] The anomalies that result from excessive development of hepatic tissue occur as a lobar anomaly and include Riedel's lobe as well as other accessory lobes. Those resulting from defective development of the liver include agenesis, hypoplasia, and aplasia of the right or left hepatic lobes. Agenesis refers to complete absence of a lobe, whereas hypoplasia represents a small hepatic lobe that is diminutive but otherwise normal. Aplasia is defined as a small lobe that is structurally abnormal and contains abundant connective tissue, scattered hepatic parenchyma, numerous bile ducts, and abnormal blood vessels.[3,4]

The position and orientation of the liver may also be altered during embryologic development, resulting in situs inversus, situs ambiguous, and liver herniation. Bipartite liver is extremely rare and occurs when the right and left hepatic lobes are in their respective upper quadrants and are connected by a bridge of tissue.

HEPATIC EMBRYOLOGY

During the third week of fetal life, the liver primordium appears as an outgrowth endodermal epithelium at the distal end of the foregut. This outgrowth, known as the hepatic diverticulum or liver bud, consists of rapidly proliferating cell strands that penetrate the septum transversum, which is the mesodermal plate between the primitive heart and the stalk of the yolk sac. While the hepatic cell strands continue to penetrate into the septum transversum, the connection between the hepatic diverticulum and the distal foregut narrows, thus forming the bile duct.

With further development, the epithelial liver cords intermingle with the vitelline and umbilical veins, forming the hepatic sinusoids (Fig. 87-1). The liver cords differentiate in the hepatocytes and form the lining of the biliary ducts. The Kupffer cells and connective tissue cells of the liver are derived from the mesoderm of the septum transversum.[5]

NORMAL ANATOMIC VARIANTS

Accessory Fissures and Diaphragmatic Slips

The two main fissures of the liver are fissures for falciform ligament and ligamentum venosum. However, the liver may also contain accessory and pseudoaccessory fissures. True accessory fissures are rare and are the result of an inward folding of the peritoneum, usually involving the undersurface

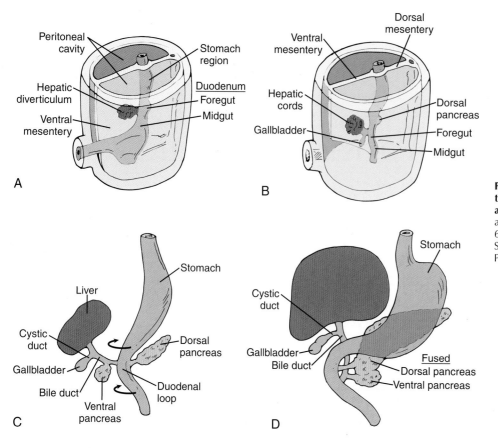

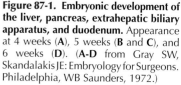

Figure 87-1. Embryonic development of the liver, pancreas, extrahepatic biliary apparatus, and duodenum. Appearance at 4 weeks (**A**), 5 weeks (**B** and **C**), and 6 weeks (**D**). (**A-D** from Gray SW, Skandalakis JE: Embryology for Surgeons. Philadelphia, WB Saunders, 1972.)

of the liver. The most common one is the inferior accessory fissure (Fig. 87-2), which divides the posterior segment of the right hepatic lobe into lateral and medial portions.[6-9]

Pseudoaccessory fissures are common anatomic variants that result from invaginations of diaphragmatic muscle fibers, usually along the superior surface of the liver (Fig. 87-3). They are more frequently seen involving the right hepatic lobe, but they can occur on the left as well.[5] These infoldings of the

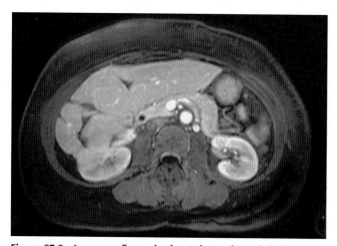

Figure 87-2. Accessory fissure in the under surface of the liver. The accessory fissure in the right lobe clearly seen in this patient's contrast-enhanced T1-weighted fat-suppression image of the liver. This fissure divides the posterior segment of the right hepatic lobe into lateral and medial subsegments.

diaphragm often seen in elderly patients can give the liver a scalloped or a lobular appearance and should not be mistaken for macronodular liver in cirrhosis. They can also be a cause for hypodense peripheral pseudomasses on CT (Fig. 87-4). On ultrasound, they may appear occasionally as echogenic focus in one plane; however when scanning in the orthogonal plane, the true linear morphology of a fissure is revealed.

Sliver of Liver

Leftward extension of the lateral segment of the left hepatic lobe is referred to as "sliver of the liver." It is a common anatomic variant and appears as a crescentic density that wraps around the spleen (Fig. 87-5) and may lie lateral, medial, and even posterior to the spleen. It is important not to confuse this variant with either perisplenic or perigastric pathology. On ultrasound, this variant can mimic perisplenic hypoechoic collections, and the correct diagnosis is achieved by using color Doppler and documenting continuity with the remainder of the left hepatic lobe.[6,10]

Papillary Process of the Caudate Lobe

The caudate lobe is a portion of the liver that extends medially from the right lobe between the inferior vena cava and the fissure for ligamentum venosum. Occasionally, it is divided into two processes. The anterior-medial extension of the caudate lobe is known as the papillary process, which extends anteriorly and to the left in the region of the lesser sac. The posterior extension is referred to as caudate process. Below

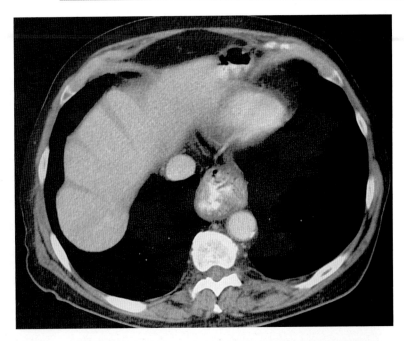

Figure 87-3. Diaphragmatic invagination in the liver. As a result of invagination of the diaphragmatic slips along the superior aspect of the liver, pseudoaccessory fissures are formed.

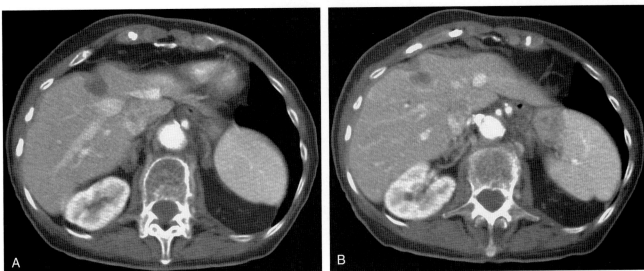

Figure 87-4. Diaphragmatic invagination mimicking hepatic nodule. A and **B.** As a result of diaphragmatic invagination, occasionally a small, round, low-density mass may be suspected in the right hepatic lobe.

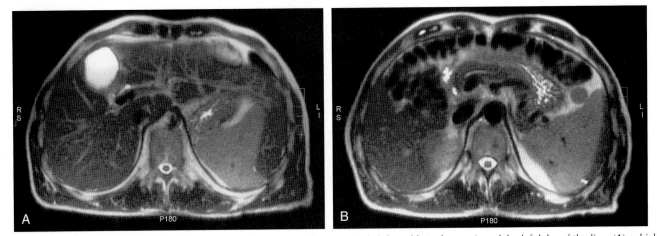

Figure 87-5. Sliver of liver. The T2-weighted image of the upper abdomen reveals leftward lateral extension of the left lobe of the liver (**A**), which appears as a crescentic low-intensity structure wrapping around the lateral aspect of the spleen. **B.** Where the communication is not seen, it can mimic abnormal structure lateral to the spleen. This occasionally is the case in abdominal ultrasound.

the porta hepatis, this papillary process can appear separate from the caudate process, by a cleft in its inferior margin and can mimic periportal node (Fig. 87-6) or a mass near the head of the pancreas or near the inferior vena cava[5,6] (Fig. 87-7). However, on multidetector CT and by using multiplanar reformation, this anatomic variant is easily recognizable.

ANATOMIC ANOMALIES

Riedel's Lobe

Described by Bernhard Moritz Carl Ludwig Riedel, a German surgeon (1846-1916), Riedel's lobe is the most common accessory lobe of the liver, and it is seen most frequently in asthenic women. It is a tonguelike projection from the anterior aspect of the right lobe of the liver that can extend quite inferiorly in some patients. It usually extends along the right paracolic gutter into the iliac fossa (Fig. 87-8) and can be 20 cm or more in length. On physical examination, this anomaly can be mistaken for an enlarged liver or a right renal mass. Riedel's lobe may be connected to the liver by pedicle

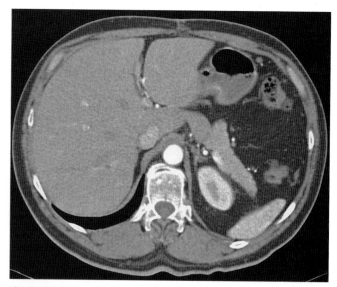

Figure 87-6. Papillary process of the caudate lobe. The contrast-enhanced CT scan shows medial and posterior extension of the papillary process near the head of the pancreas mimicking a mass lesion.

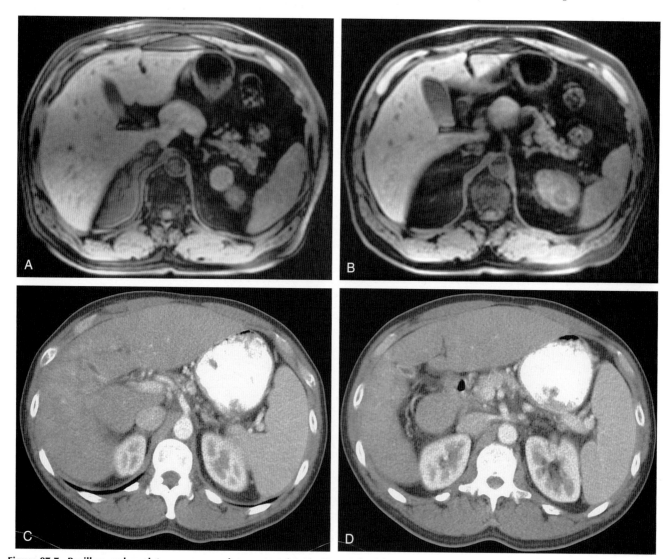

Figure 87-7. Papillary and caudate process pseudomass. A and **B.** The T1-weighted fat-suppression images reveal medial extension of the papillary process near the head of the pancreas. Notice the signal characteristics of this mass being similar to the remainder of the liver and not of the pancreas. **C** and **D.** Contrast-enhanced CT scan of the upper abdomen in a different patient reveals inferior extension of an enlarged caudate process mimicking a mass anterior and lateral to the inferior vena cava.

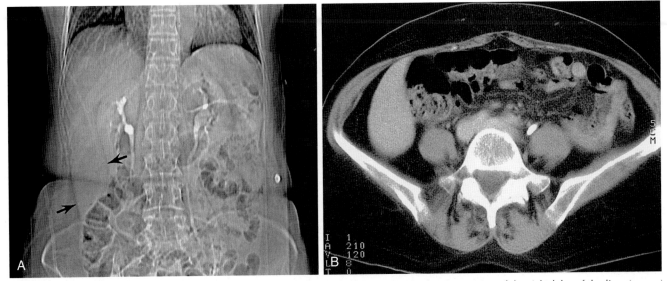

Figure 87-8. Riedel's lobe. A. Topogram from the patient's CT scan displays an elongated inferior extension of the right lobe of the liver (*arrows*) characteristic of a Reidel lobe. **B.** Axial CT image reveals inferior extension of the right lobe of the liver below the iliac crest.

consisting of hepatic parenchyma or fibrous tissue. It is usually asymptomatic and is discovered incidentally; however, it may be complicated by torsion with gangrenous changes.[4] Occasionally, the left lobe can behave as a Riedel lobe and extend inferiorly in the abdomen.[6]

Pedunculated Accessory Hepatic Lobes

Accessory lobe of the liver is an uncommon anatomical variation that is usually asymptomatic. In this condition, the liver tissue is in communication with the main liver (Fig. 87-9), while in ectopic liver, the liver tissue lies in the vicinity of the liver without communication with the liver. When an accessory lobe loses its continuity with the liver, it becomes an ectopic liver nodule, which may be attached to the gallbladder, umbilical cord, or pancreas or may lie within the gastrohepatic ligament or thoracic cavity. Ectopic liver has higher incidence of malignancy.[11] Sato et al.,[12] in a series of 1800 laproscopic studies, found congenital anomalies of the liver in 19% of the cases with the incidence of ectopic liver lobe and accessory liver lobe being 0.7%. Other anomalies that were found in this study included fissure formation with anomalous lobation in 4.3%, lobar fusion in 0.5%, left deviation of the round ligament in 3.6%, and high insertion of the round ligament in 2.8%. The accessory lobe is composed of normal hepatic tissue and contains its own hepatic blood vessels and bile ducts. It is connected to the rest of the liver by either normal hepatic parenchyma or a mesentery[12,13] (Fig. 87-10). Most accessory lobes are attached to the inferior surface of the liver and have been found in the vicinity of several anatomic sites, including the gallbladder fossa, gastrohepatic ligament, umbilicus, adrenal gland, pancreas, esophagus, and rarely the thoracic cavity. These accessory lobes, particularly when the liver is infiltrated by fat, may be spared and therefore can occasionally mimic masses or adenopathy in these regions[14] (Fig. 87-11). Multiplanar reconstruction and review of continuous thin slice images are often the key to their diagnosis.

Although most accessory lobes of the liver are asymptomatic, some are pedunculated and suspended from a mesentery that may undergo torsion,[15-17] causing both acute and recurrent abdominal pain (Fig. 87-12). There is an increased incidence of accessory lobes in patients with abdominal wall defects, such as omphalocele.

Agenesis and Hypoplasia of the Right Hepatic Lobe

Agenesis and hypoplasia of the right lobe of the liver are rare entities that is diagnosed by noting absence or hypoplasia of liver tissue to the right of the main interlobar fissure.[18-20] This disorder is thought to be a developmental abnormality that results from either failure of the right portal vein to develop or an error in the mutual induction between the septum transversum (primitive liver).[20,21] This entity is usually seen in asymptomatic individuals and is discovered incidentally when imaging studies are being performed for unrelated reasons (Fig. 87-13). Occasionally, a segment such as anterior segment of the right lobe may be absent. Postnecrotic cirrhosis, biliary obstruction, and venous occlusive disease have been associated with atrophy or hypoplasia of a hepatic lobe or segment and should be differentiated from congenital absence or hypoplasia.[18]

Agenesis of the right lobe of the liver alters the normal anatomy of the upper abdomen. This is in part due to absence of the right lobe as well as compensatory hypertrophy of the left lobe. Colonic interposition, high position of the right kidney, ectopy of the gallbladder (which can be suprahepatic subdiaphragmatic, or infrahepatic in location), and a U- or hammock-shaped stomach can all be seen in individuals with agenesis of the right lobe. The caudate lobe may be absent, normal, or hypertrophied.[21-23] This entity may also be associated with partial or complete absence of the right hemidiaphragm, intestinal malrotation, choledochal cysts, and agenesis of the gallbladder. Other, more common conditions can mimic agenesis of the right lobe of the liver, including cirrhosis, atrophy secondary to biliary obstruction, hepatic surgery (Fig. 87-14), and trauma.[24] A careful clinical history as well as any associated imaging findings will help to arrive at the correct diagnosis.[21,25]

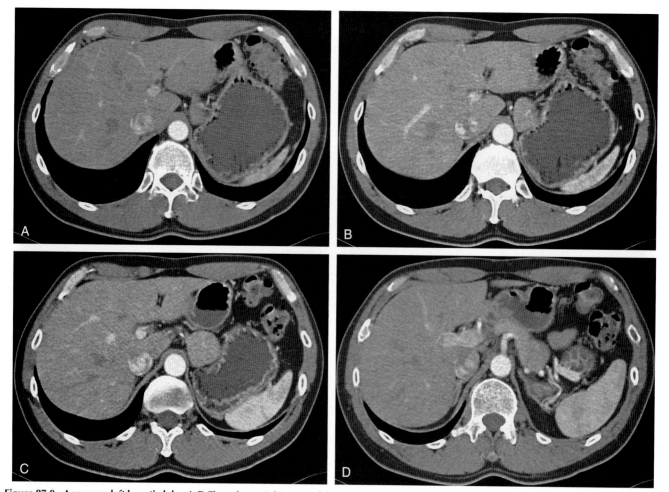

Figure 87-9. Accessory left hepatic lobe. A-D. These four axial images of the contrast-enhanced CT scan reveal a pedunculated accessory hepatic lobe that extends inferiorly mimicking a mass in the gastrohepatic ligament. The communication of this accessory lobe with the remainder of the liver is best seen on image **A.** It mimics a pancreatic mass on image **D.**

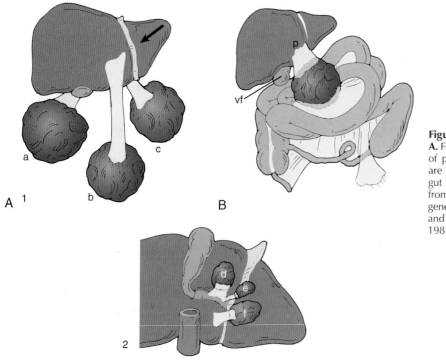

Figure 87-10. Pedunculated accessory hepatic lobes. A. Frontal (1) and caudal (2) diagrams depict a variety of pedunculated hepatic lobulations (a-f). **B.** They are usually asymptomatic unless they obstruct the gut with their pedicle (p). vf, gallbladder. (**A** and **B** from Champetier J, Yver R, Letoublon C, et al: A general review of anomalies of hepatic morphology and their clinical implications. Anat Clin 7:285-299, 1985.)

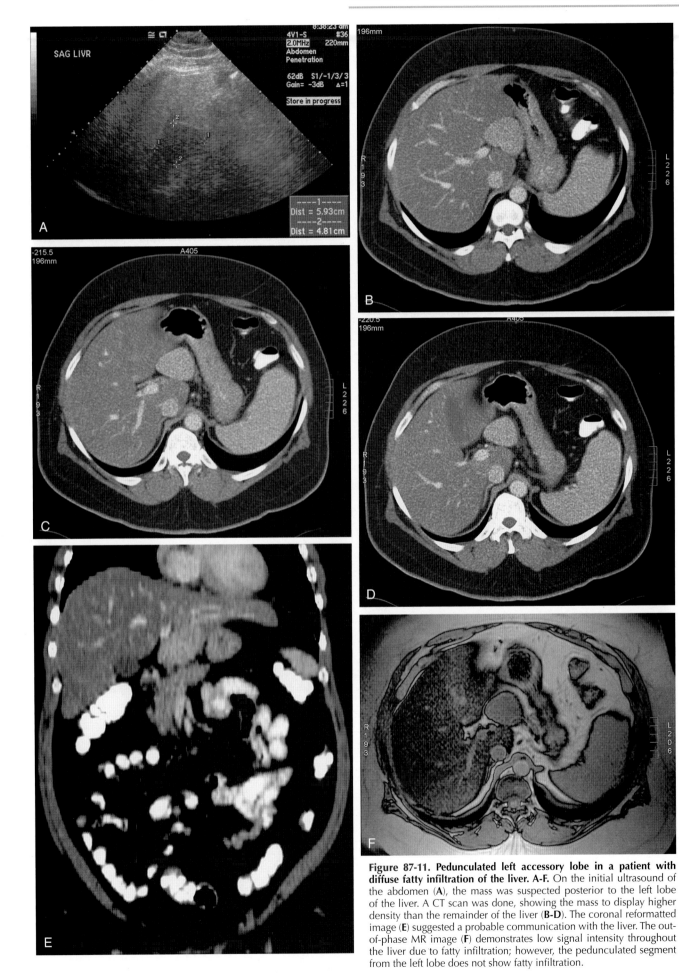

Figure 87-11. Pedunculated left accessory lobe in a patient with diffuse fatty infiltration of the liver. A-F. On the initial ultrasound of the abdomen (**A**), the mass was suspected posterior to the left lobe of the liver. A CT scan was done, showing the mass to display higher density than the remainder of the liver (**B-D**). The coronal reformatted image (**E**) suggested a probable communication with the liver. The out-of-phase MR image (**F**) demonstrates low signal intensity throughout the liver due to fatty infiltration; however, the pedunculated segment from the left lobe does not show fatty infiltration.

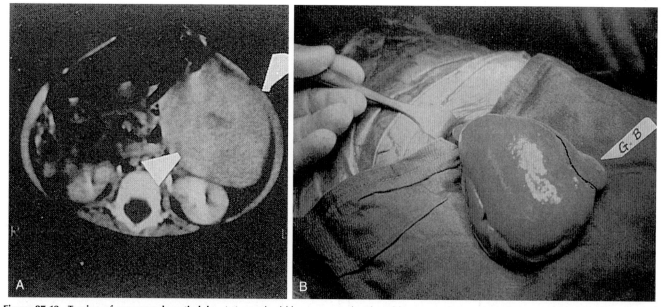

Figure 87-12. Torsion of accessory hepatic lobe. A 6-month-old boy presented with sudden onset of cyanosis, lethargy, and hematochezia. **A.** Mid-abdominal CT shows a mass (*arrowheads*) in the left side of the abdomen. **B.** Exploration of the abdomen revealed torsion of an accessory lobe of the liver with the gallbladder (G.B) embedded therein. (**A** and **B** from Elmasalme F, Aljudaibi A, Matbouly S, et al: Torsion of an accessory lobe of the liver in an infant. J Pediatr Surg 30:1348-1350, 1995.)

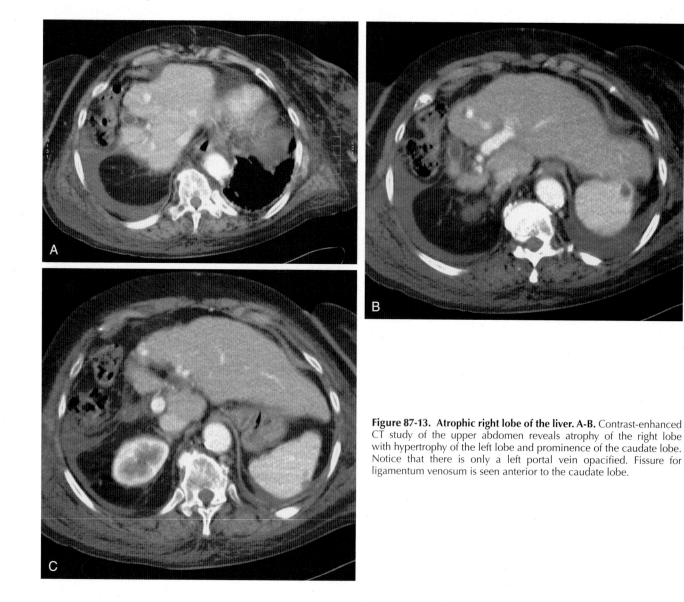

Figure 87-13. Atrophic right lobe of the liver. A-B. Contrast-enhanced CT study of the upper abdomen reveals atrophy of the right lobe with hypertrophy of the left lobe and prominence of the caudate lobe. Notice that there is only a left portal vein opacified. Fissure for ligamentum venosum is seen anterior to the caudate lobe.

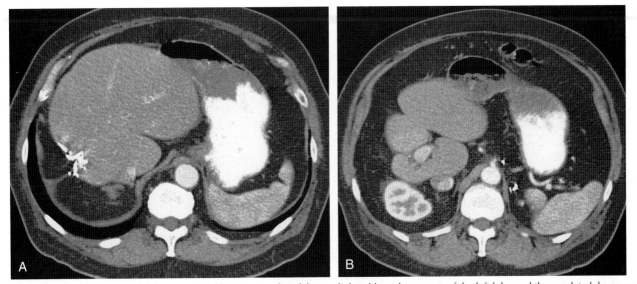

Figure 87-14. Post right hepatic lobectomy. A and **B.** Hypertrophy of the medial and lateral segments of the left lobe and the caudate lobe are seen in this patient who has total right hepatic lobectomy for metastatic colon carcinoma. Notice marked deviation of the left hepatic lobe to the right upper quadrant.

Even though a retrohepatic gallbladder and a severely distorted hepatic morphology due to compensatory hypertrophy of the left and caudate lobes may raise a suspicion for agenesis of the right lobe of the liver (Fig. 87-15), absence of visualization of all of the right hepatic vein, right portal vein and its branches, and occasionally dilated left intrahepatic ducts is a prerequisite for the diagnosis of agenesis of the right hepatic lobe on CT. In severe lobar atrophy, at least one of these structures is recognizable.[25]

Agenesis and Hypoplasia of the Left Hepatic Lobe

Agenesis and hypoplasia of the left hepatic lobe are rare but slightly more common than the right-sided anomalies; however, these are still rare occurrences.[26] The diagnosis is made by noting absence or hypoplasia of liver tissue to the left of the main interlobar fissure. Failure to visualize the falciform ligament or ligamentum teres is supportive evidence of agenesis (Fig. 87-16). This disorder is believed to result from the extension of the obliterative process that closes the ductus venosus to the left branch of the portal vein (Fig. 87-17). Hann et al.[27] described 13 cases of hepatic lobar atrophy that were evaluated for vascular patency and bile duct obstruction. Hepatic lobar atrophy usually occurs in the setting of combined biliary and portal vein obstruction. A correlation exists between lobar atrophy and ipsilateral portal vein obstruction. Ishida et al.[28] reported six cases of lobar atrophy and investigated the relationship between lobar atrophy and portal flow disturbance. In their report, atrophy of the right lobe was always associated with marked enlargement of the left lobe, but obstruction of flow to the left lobe did not universally result in hypertrophy of the right lobe. As in agenesis of the right lobe of the liver, left lobe agenesis is usually asymptomatic and is discovered incidentally when imaging studies are being performed for other unrelated reasons.[21,26]

Agenesis of the left lobe of the liver also alters the normal topography of the upper abdomen.[26] The stomach and splenic flexure of the colon migrate superiorly and medially to fill the area normally occupied by the left hepatic lobe (Fig. 87-18). Associated findings include a high position of the duodenal bulb, a U-shaped stomach (Fig. 87-19), and a low-lying hepatic flexure of the colon secondary to compensatory hypertrophy of the right lobe of the liver.[21,29] This anomaly may also be associated with partial or complete absence of the left hemidiaphragm and gastric volvulus.

Before making a diagnosis of agenesis of the left lobe of the liver, it is important to exclude others causes of acquired atrophy of the left hepatic lobe, caused by cirrhosis, malignancy, malnutrition or rarely vascular compromise.[30,31] In these disorders, at least some liver tissue is found left of the main lobar fissure.

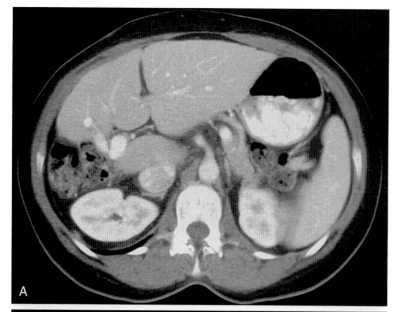

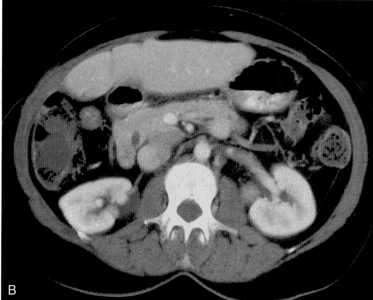

Figure 87-15. Agenesis of the right hepatic lobe. A. CT reveals agenesis of the right lobe of the liver with compensatory hypertrophy of the left lobe. **B.** On a more inferior image, only the left lobe of the liver is identified. The colon occupies the bed of the right hepatic lobe.

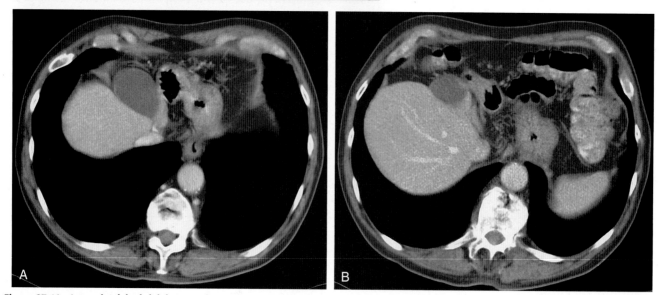

Figure 87-16. Agenesis of the left lobe. A and **B.** In this contrast-enhanced CT of the upper abdomen, there is total agenesis of the left lobe with the gallbladder being seen anterior and medial to the right lobe. The gastric fundus is displaced medially. **B.** Notice absence of the left hepatic vein, while the middle and right hepatic veins are opacified.

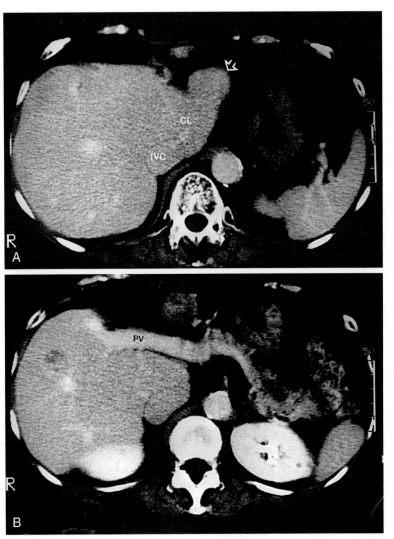

Figure 87-17. Agenesis of the left hepatic lobe. This anomaly was found incidentally in a 68-year-old woman who presented with congestive heart failure. **A.** CT shows a tonguelike projection (*arrow*) of the caudate lobe (CL). IVC, inferior vena cava. **B.** Scan at the level of the portal vein (PV) shows failure to visualize the left lobe and the left branch of the portal vein. There is an incidental hemangioma. (**A** and **B** from Kakitsubata Y, Nakamora R, Mitsuo H, et al: Absence of the left lobe of the liver: US and CT appearance. Gastrointest Radiol 16:323-325, 1991. With kind permission from Springer Science and Business Media.)

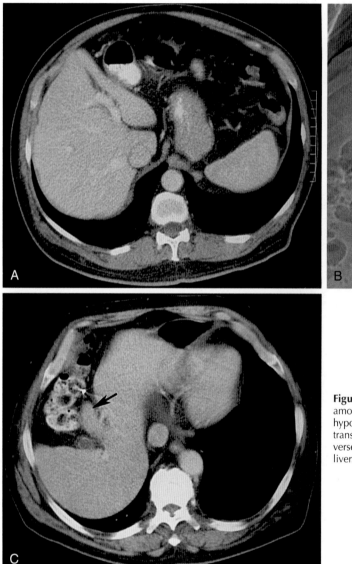

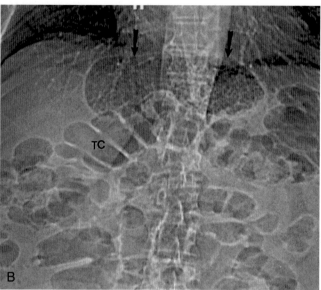

Figure 87-18. Hypoplastic left hepatic lobe. A. CT reveals a small amount of liver tissue to the left of the left portal vein, consistent with hypoplasia of the lateral segment of the left lobe. **B.** Topogram shows a transverse, high-riding stomach (*arrows*) as well as a high-riding transverse colon (TC) due to the underdevelopment of the left lobe of the liver. **C.** Hypoplastic medial segment of the left lobe (*arrow*).

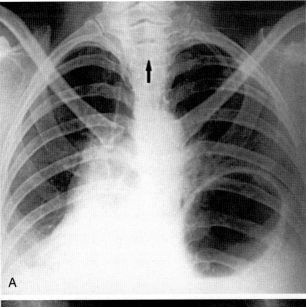

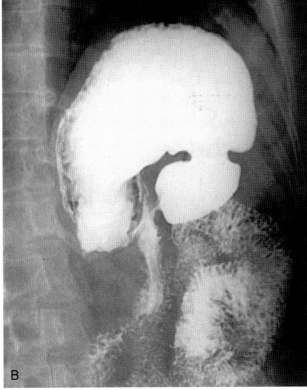

Figure 87-19. Hypoplasia of the left hepatic lobe. Hypoplasia of the cupula of the diaphragm associated with hypoplasia of the left lobe of the liver. **A.** Expiratory anteroposterior radiograph shows the left diaphragmatic hernia. **B.** The upper gastrointestinal series shows an associated organomesenteric rotation and gastric malposition. (**A** and **B** from Champetier J, Yver R, Letoublon C, et al: A general review of anomalies of hepatic morphology and their clinical implications. Anat Clin 7:285-299, 1985.)

References

1. Dirisamer A, Friedrich K, Schima W: Anatomy and variants of hepatic segments, vessels, and bile ducts. Radiologie 45:8-14, 2005.
2. Koops A, Wojciechowski B, Broering DC, et al: Anatomic variations of the hepatic arteries in 604 selective celiac and superior mesenteric angiographies. Surg Radiol Anat 26:239-244, 2004.
3. Champetier J, Yuer R, Letoublon C, et al: A general review of anomalies of hepatic morphology and their clinical implications. Anat Clin 7:285-299, 1985.
4. White M: Hepatic anatomic variations and developmental anomalies. In Ferrucci J (ed): Radiology. Philadelphia, Lippincott-Raven, 1997.
5. Sadler T: Medical Embryology, 5th ed. Baltimore, Williams & Wilkins, 1985, pp 230-232.
6. Kasales CJ, Patel S, Hopper KD: Imaging variants of the liver, pancreas, and spleen. Crit Rev Diagn Imaging 35:485-543, 1994.
7. Farah M, Shirkhoda A: The diaphragm in variants and pitfalls in body imaging. Philadelphia, Lippincott, Williams and Wilkins, 2000, pp 133-151.
8. Krebs C, Giyanani V, Eisenberg R: Ultrasound Atlas of Disease Processes. Norwalk, CT, Appleton & Lange, 1993, p 19.
9. Martinoli C, Cittadini G, Conzi R: Sonographic characterization of an accessory fissure of the left hepatic lobe determined by omental infolding. J Ultrasound Med 11:103-107, 1992.
10. Dunlop D, Evans R: Congenital abnormality of the liver initially misdiagnosed as splenic haematoma. J R Soc Med 89:702-704, 1996.
11. Caygill CP, Gatenby PA: Ectopic liver and hepatocarcinogenesis. Eur J Gastroenterol Hepatol 16:727-729, 2004.
12. Sato N, Kawakami K, Matsumoto S, et al: Agenesis of the right lobe of the liver. Surg Today 18:643-646, 1998.
13. Bedda S, Bataille N, Montariol T, Zareski E: Accessory liver lobe torsion mimicking a pancreatic tumor. Ann Chir 128:53-54, 2003.
14. Hashimoto M, Oomachi K, Watarai J: Accessory lobe of the liver mimicking a mass in the left adrenal gland. A case report. Acta Radiol 38:309-310, 1997.
15. Sanguesa C, Esteban M, Gomez J, et al: Liver accessory lobe torsion in the infant. Pediatr Radiol 25:153-154, 1995.
16. Koumandidou C, Nasi E, Koutrouveli E, et al: Torsion of an accessory hepatic lobe in a child: Ultrasound, computed tomographic, and magnetic resonance imaging findings. Pediatr Surg Int 13:526-527, 1998.
17. Ladurner R, Brandacher G, Mark W, et al: Complete hepatic Ischemia due to torsion of a large accessory liver lobe: First case to require transplantation. Transpl Int 18:467, 2005.
18. Chou CK, Mak CW, Lin MB, et al: CT of agenesis and atrophy of the right hepatic lobe, Abdom Imaging 23:603-607, 1998.
19. Makanjuola D, al-Smayer S, al-Orainy I, et al: Radiographic features of lobar agenesis of the liver. Acta Radiol 37:255-258, 1996.
20. Cesani F, Walser E, Goodacre B, et al: Agenesis of the right lobe of the liver. Clin Nucl Med 21:1001-1002, 1996.
21. Kakitsubata Y, Kakitsubata S, Asada K, et al: MR imaging of anomalous lobes of the liver. Acta Radiol 34:417-419, 1993.
22. Karamen C, Ozek T, Urhan M, et al: Agenesis of the right lobe of the liver. Case report. Acta Radiol 38:428-430, 1997.
23. Kakitsubata Y, Kakitsubata S, Asada K, et al: Anomalous right lobe of the liver. CT appearance. Gastrointest Radiol 16:326-328, 1991.
24. Couanet D, Shirkhoda A, Wallace S: Computed tomography after partial hepatectomy, J Comput Assist Tomogr 8:453-457, 1984.
25. Kakitsu Y, Kakitsubata S, Watanabe K: Hypoplasia of the right hepatic lobe with ectopy of the gallbladder. Clin Imaging 19:85-87, 1995.
26. Sener R, Yorulmaz I, Oyar O, et al: Hypoplasia of the left lobe of the liver. AJR 158:213-214, 1992.
27. Hann IE, Getrajdman GI, Brown KT, et al: Hepatic lobar atrophy: Association with ipsilateral portal vein obstruction. AJR 167: 1017-1021, 1996.
28. Ishida H, Naganuma H, Konno K, et al: Lobar atrophy of the liver. Abdom Imaging 23:150-153, 1998.
29. Ozgun B, Warshauer D: Absent medial segment of the left hepatic lobe. CT appearance. J Comput Assist Tomogr 16:666-668, 1992.
30. Hiroshi Y, Masahiko O, Takashi T, et al: Extreme left hepatic lobar atrophy in a case with hilar cholangiocarcinoma. J Nippon Med Sch 69(3), 2002.
31. Lupescu IG, Grasu M, Capsa R, et al: Hepatic perfusion disorders: Computer-tomographic and magnetic resonance imaging. Gastrointest Liver Dis 15:273-279, 2006.

Benign Tumors of the Liver

Pablo R. Ros, MD • Sukru Mehmet Erturk, MD

Each of the cellular components of the liver can give rise to both benign and malignant tumors. Hepatocytes can give rise to both hepatocellular adenoma and hepatocellular carcinoma; biliary epithelium can degenerate into cystadenomas and cholangiocarcinoma; and mesenchymal tissue may produce hemangiomas or angiosarcomas. In this chapter, the benign primary hepatic neoplasms are discussed (Table 88-1).

IMAGING EVALUATION OF FOCAL LIVER LESIONS

The liver is a large and homogeneous organ and therefore is well suited for evaluation by many imaging techniques. The study of liver neoplasms is particularly challenging. In many cases, a preoperative diagnosis may be achieved with the appropriate combination of imaging techniques in a purely noninvasive fashion. This is important because many adults have benign, nonsurgical hepatic lesions, such as hemangioma or simple cyst. For many tumors, each imaging technique provides a piece of information that, like a puzzle, must be combined with findings from other imaging techniques as well as clinical information to achieve a diagnosis.

The study of focal liver lesions by imaging can be likened to a game in which different "players" (imaging techniques) must be used appropriately to achieve the diagnosis.[1] In evaluating focal liver diseases, the following imaging techniques are available: (1) plain abdominal radiographs, (2) nuclear medicine (positron emission tomography [PET], red blood cells [RBCs] tagged with technetium 99m), (3) ultrasonography (gray-scale and color Doppler sonograms, contrast-enhanced examinations), (4) multidetector row computed tomography (MDCT; nonenhanced scans and contrast-enhanced dynamic scans including arterial, portal venous, and delayed phases), (5) angiography, and (6) magnetic resonance imaging (MRI) (nonenhanced, vascular enhanced with gadolinium, reticuloendothelial enhanced with small and ultrasmall superparamagnetic iron oxide particles [SPIOs and USPIOs], hepatocyte enhanced with gadolinium benzyloxypropionictetraacetate [Gd-BOPTA], and gadolinium ethoxybenzyl diethylenetriaminepentaacetic acid [gadoxetate; Gd-EOB-DTPA]). The "plays" that the foregoing players can offer are listed in Table 88-2.

With the widespread use of new cross-sectional imaging techniques such as MDCT and the development of reticuloendothelial and hepatocyte-specific MRI contrast agents, the

---

Table 88-1
Benign Liver Tumors and Tumor-like Conditions

HEPATOCELLULAR ORIGIN
Hepatocellular adenoma
Hepatocellular hyperplasia
    Focal nodular hyperplasia
    Nodular regenerative hyperplasia
    Macroregenerative nodule (adenomatous hyperplasia)
CHOLANGIOCELLULAR ORIGIN
Hepatic cysts
    Simple hepatic cysts
    Congenital hepatic fibrosis or polycystic liver disease
Biliary cystadenoma
Bile duct adenoma
MESENCHYMAL ORIGIN
Mesenchymal hamartoma
Hemangioma
Infantile hemangioendothelioma
Lymphangioma
Lipoma, angiomyolipoma, myelolipoma
Leiomyoma
Fibroma
Heterotopic tissue
    Adrenal rests
    Pancreatic rests
    Primary hepatic carcinoma

Table 88-2
Imaging Techniques in Liver Neoplasms

TO ASSESS VASCULARITY
Contrast-enhanced CT
Gadolinium-enhanced MR
Contrast-enhanced US
Angiograms
Blood pool studies (^{99m}Tc-labeled red blood cells)
TO ASSESS HEPATOCYTE FUNCTION OR BILIARY EXCRETION
MR imaging enhanced with hepatocyte specific contrast agents
TO ASSESS METABOLIC ACTIVITY OF NEOPLASMS
^{18}F-FDG PET imaging
TO ASSESS KUPFFER CELL ACTIVITY
MR imaging enhanced with intravenous superparamagnetic iron oxide
TO ASSESS TUMORAL CALCIFICATION
CT
US
Plain radiographs
TO ASSESS CAPSULE PRESENCE
CT (enhanced/nonenhanced)
Ultrasound (enhanced/nonenhanced)
MR (enhanced/nonenhanced)
TO ASSESS INTERNAL NATURE OF NEOPLASMS (e.g., SOLID VERSUS CYSTIC, HEMORRHAGE, FIBROSIS)
CT
MR
Ultrasound

role of older techniques such as angiography and nuclear scintigraphy has become more limited. The majority of liver lesions can now be detected and characterized noninvasively, and angiography is required only in exceptional circumstances. Although conventional scintigraphic techniques are only exceptionally used for the evaluation of focal liver lesions, PET and PET-CT are effective techniques, especially for detection of hepatic metastatic disease. Today, most focal liver lesions are diagnosed using ultrasound (US), CT, and MRI.

HEMANGIOMA

Pathologic Findings

A *hemangioma* is defined microscopically as a tumor composed of multiple vascular channels lined by a single layer of endothelial cells supported by a thin, fibrous stroma[2] (Fig. 88-1). The channels are separated by thin fibrous septa, which may form fingerlike protrusions into the channels. Grossly, it is frequently solitary, well circumscribed, and blood filled and ranges in size from a few millimeters to more than 20 cm.[2] Hemangiomas may be multiple in up to 50% of cases.

Hemangiomas larger than 10 cm are defined as giant hemangiomas. On cut sections, hemangiomas are almost always heterogeneous with areas of fibrosis, necrosis, and cystic change.[3,4] The radiologic-pathologic correlates of hemangioma are listed in Table 88-3.

Incidence and Clinical Presentation

Hemangioma is the most common benign tumor of the liver, with a reported incidence ranging from 1% to 20%.[5] The latter figure is the result of a prospective autopsy study in which a dedicated search for this lesion was performed.[4]

Hemangiomas occur primarily in women (female/male ratio of 5:1). Although hemangiomas may be present at all ages, they are seen more commonly in postmenopausal women. The worldwide prevalence of this tumor is fairly uniform. In a study of Vilgrain and associates,[6] it was reported that there was a significant association between focal nodular hyperplasia (FNH) and hemangioma in the liver. While each of these lesions is found commonly as an isolated hepatic mass, in 20% of patients in the study group of Vilgrain and associates, both lesions were present together.

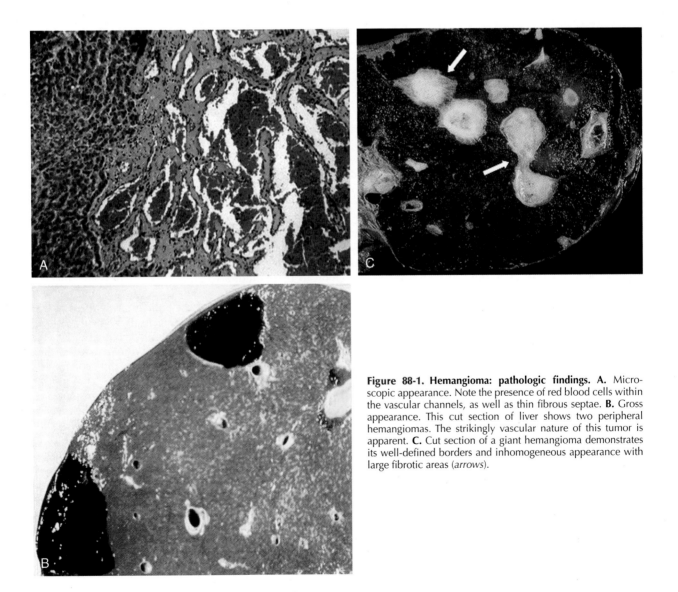

Figure 88-1. Hemangioma: pathologic findings. A. Microscopic appearance. Note the presence of red blood cells within the vascular channels, as well as thin fibrous septae. **B.** Gross appearance. This cut section of liver shows two peripheral hemangiomas. The strikingly vascular nature of this tumor is apparent. **C.** Cut section of a giant hemangioma demonstrates its well-defined borders and inhomogeneous appearance with large fibrotic areas (*arrows*).

Table 88-3
Hemangioma*

Pathologic Features	Radiologic Features
Vascular channels	Echogenic mass: ultrasound
Blood-filled cavity	Hyperintense mass: T2-weighted image (MR)
No arteriovenous shunting	Early globular peripheral enhancement on contrast-enhanced helical CT, dynamic Gd-DTPA–enhanced T1-weighted MR and USPIO-enhanced T1-weighted MR
	Delayed-persistent filling on red blood cell scan, enhanced conventional CT, Gd-DTPA–enhanced MR, angiogram
Fibrosis	Hypodense region: CT
	Hypointense region: MR
	Hypoechoic region: ultrasound
Calcification	Dense region: plain films, CT
	Absent signal: MR
	Hyperechoic shadowing region: ultrasound

*See text for full names of imaging agents.

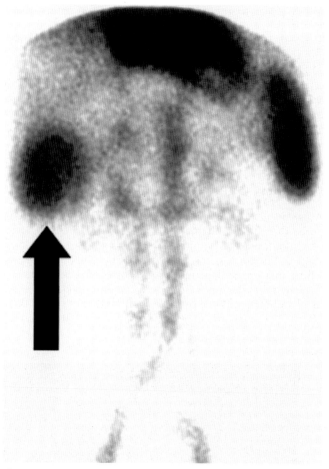

Figure 88-2. Hemangioma: Tc 99m–labeled red blood cell scintiscan. Two-hour delayed scintiscan show persistent uptake of the isotope within the tumor (*arrow*).

Plain Radiographic Findings

Calcification is rare in this tumor; less than 10% of hemangiomas have calcification detectable by plain radiographs.[7] Calcification can be either large and coarse (amorphous calcification within zones of fibrosis) or phlebolith-like thrombi within the vascular channels of hemangioma.

Nuclear Scintigraphy

Radionuclide scintigraphy for identification of hemangiomas is not performed routinely in all centers, especially outside the United States.[6] With tagged RBC pool scans, there is a defect in the early phases that shows prolonged and persistent "filling in" on delayed scans[8,9] (Fig. 88-2). Many vascular tumors, such as hepatocellular carcinoma, adenoma, and FNH, may have persistent uptake, but all exhibit early uptake rather than a defect. Rarely, angiosarcomas can demonstrate the hemangioma pattern of early defect and late isotope uptake.[10] In this context, new hybrid SPECT/CT systems may further aid diagnosis of hemangiomas by means of a more accurate anatomic localization of the lesions. In a study, SPECT/CT increased the accuracy of RBC scintigraphy, in classifying the hepatic lesions as hemangiomas and nonhemangiomas, from 70.8% to 87.5%.[11]

Ultrasound

Sonographically, hemangiomas are typically hyperechoic and well demarcated and exhibit faint acoustic enhancement[12,13] (Fig. 88-3). The echogenicity may vary because these tumors may contain cystic and fibrotic regions. Color Doppler ultrasound demonstrates filling vessels in the periphery of the tumor but no significant color Doppler flow deep within the hemangioma itself. Power Doppler, however, may detect minimal flow within hemangiomas, but the pattern is nonspecific and may be seen in hepatocellular carcinomas and metastases.[14]

Hemangiomas, like other focal lesions of the liver, are detected and characterized with ultrasound not only by an analysis of echogenicity and vascularity but also by the changes occurring in inflow kinetics of ultrasound contrast agents.[15] In general, ultrasound contrast agents consist of microbubbles of air or perfluorocarbon gas stabilized by a protein, lipid, or polymer shell.[16] The small size (approximately the same as RBCs) and stability of the bubbles allow them to traverse the pulmonary and cardiac circulations following intravenous injection. The bubbles cannot move through the vascular endothelium into the interstitium and remain within the vessel until they disappear due to the diffusion of the gas through their thin shell. Therefore, they are true blood pool agents and have a typical half-life of a few minutes in the circulation. Bubbles respond to sound emitted by the imaging transducer by oscillating and returning detectable echoes to the transducer.

On contrast-enhanced ultrasonography, hemangiomas demonstrate a typical specific peripheral nodular contrast enhancement and centripetal fill in. While the "filling in" of the lesion can take several minutes using CT and iodinated contrast material, the kinetics of ultrasound contrast agents are different, and using them, the process can last even less than a minute.[15,16] Therefore, imaging in the first 60 seconds is critical in characterizing hemangiomas at ultrasound.

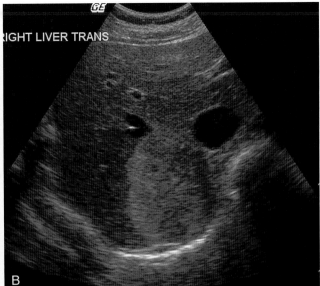

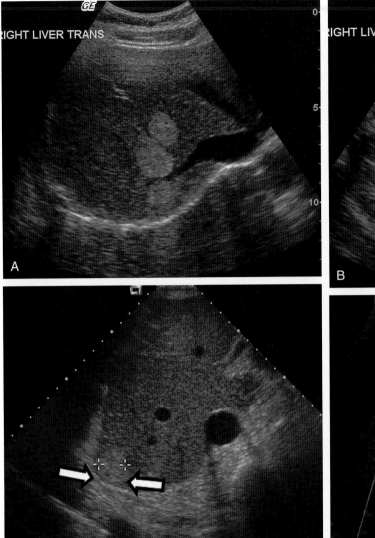

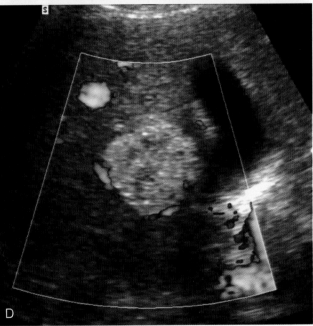

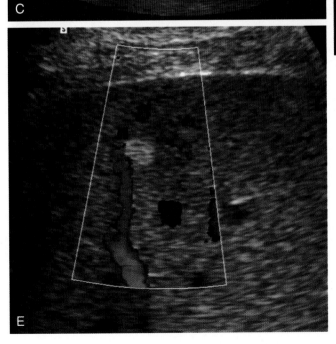

Figure 88-3. Hemangioma: sonographic findings. A. Transverse sono-gram demonstrates three small, well-marginated, uniformly hyper-echoic hemangiomas adjacent to the right hepatic vein. **B.** Larger hemangiomas tend to be inhomogeneous due to hemorrhagic necrosis, scarring, and myxomatous change centrally. **C.** Acoustic enhancement (*arrows*) is often seen due to the primarily fluid (blood) component of this echogenic lesion. **D** and **E.** Despite the vascular nature of this tumor, the blood flow is very slow so no significant flow is identified on these color Doppler images.

Computed Tomography

Hemangiomas appear as low-density masses with well-defined, lobulated borders on nonenhanced CT scans. Calcification is observed in 10% to 20% of cases.[5] After intravenous administration of contrast material, both arterial phase and portal venous phase CT scans show early, peripheral, globular enhancement of the lesion. The attenuation of the peripheric nodules is equal to that of aorta.[17,18] In a study of Leslie and colleagues,[19] the presence of globular enhancement isodense with the aorta was found to be 67% sensitive and 100% specific in differentiating hemangioms from hepatic metastases. Therefore, if this pattern is visualized, no further evaluation is required. If obtained, venous phase CT shows centripetal enhancement that progresses to uniform filling that persists on delayed phase images (Fig. 88-4). Although small lesions often fill in completely, large tumors may not show central nonenhancing zones during venous and delayed phases, corresponding to scar tissue or cystic cavities.[20] On the other hand, approximately 16% of all hemangiomas and 42% of small ones (<1 cm in diameter) show immediate homogeneous enhancement at arterial phase CT imaging.[17,21] This feature is relatively challenging for the differential diagnosis because other hypervascular tumors, including hepatocellular carcinoma, also may enhance rapidly during this phase of imaging. In such cases, accurate diagnosis can be made with delayed phase CT imaging because hemangiomas remain hyperatenuating, whereas hypervascular metastases do not.[17]

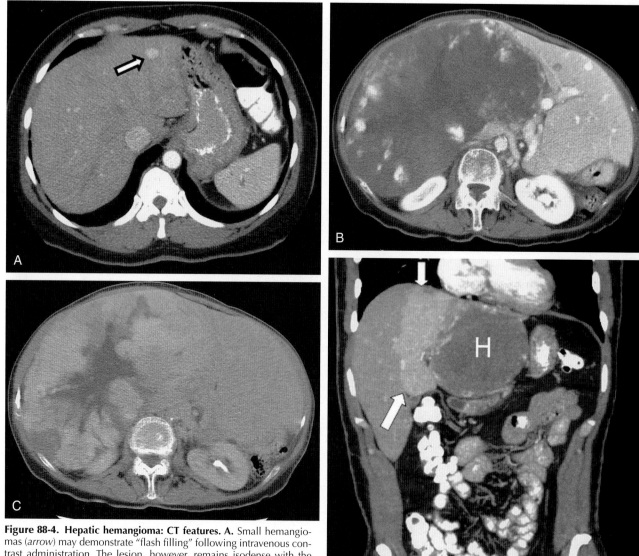

Figure 88-4. Hepatic hemangioma: CT features. A. Small hemangiomas (*arrow*) may demonstrate "flash filling" following intravenous contrast administration. The lesion, however, remains isodense with the blood pool, unlike focal nodular hyperplasia, adenoma, hepatoma, and hypervascular metastases, which may also show "flash filling." **B** and **C.** Giant hemangioma, which replaces the right lobe, shows peripheral nodular enhancement, which progresses in a centripetal fashion. The attenuation of the enhanced portions of the mass is isodense with the blood pool. The central portion of the lesion is a low attenuation region of central fibrosis. **D.** This hemangioma (H) in the lateral segment of the left lobe is causing a transient hepatic attenuation difference (THAD) in the medial segment of the left hepatic lobe (*arrows*).

Another important and helpful imaging finding in diagnosis of this type of hemangiomas is that their attenuation is equal to that of the aorta during all phases of dynamic CT imaging.[22] Hemangiomas may also be a cause of transient hepatic attenuation differences (THADs).

Angiography

Although angiography is not routinely used in the diagnostic evaluation of hepatic hemangiomas, knowledge of the characteristic appearances is important because hemangiomas may coexist with metastases. In this scenario, correct identification of the lesions is vital because therapeutic options such as hepatic resection depend on the number and distribution of metastases. Angiographically, there is pooling of contrast medium within the hemangioma, producing a characteristic "cotton wool" appearance, without evidence of arteriovenous shunting or tumor neovascularity.[23] Hemangiomas typically retain contrast medium well beyond the venous phase.

Magnetic Resonance Imaging

The study of hemangiomas of the liver is one of the major applications of abdominal MRI (Figs. 88-5, 88-6, and 88-7). Hemangiomas generally have moderately low signal intensity on T1-weighted images and characteristically demonstrate marked hyperintensity on T2-weighted images, which may contain low-intensity areas correlating with zones of fibrosis.[3,24-29] They maintain high signal intensity on longer TE (>120 milliseconds) T2-weighted sequences.[30] Nevertheless, the signal characteristics of other masses and neoplasms may overlap with those of hemangioma due to their similar T2 values, and because of this overlap, characteristics at contrast-enhanced MRI are used for further evaluation.[31] Suspected hemangiomas

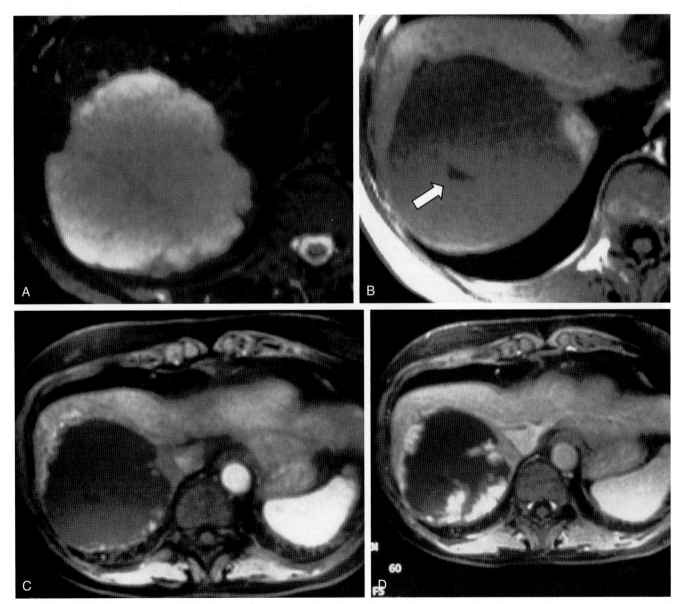

Figure 88-5. Hepatic hemangioma: MRI findings. A. Nonenhanced T2-weighted MR image shows a large hyperintense hepatic mass. **B.** Nonenhanced T1-weighted image shows low signal intensity. There is a central scar (*arrow*) that is often seen in large hemangiomas. **C** and **D.** Gadolinium enhancement demonstrates the characteristic peripheral nodular enhancement pattern that shows centripetal progression.

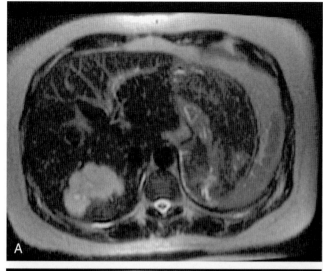

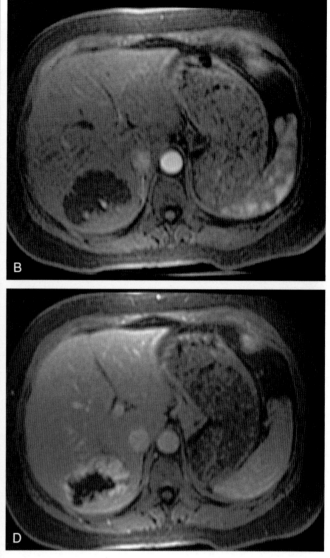

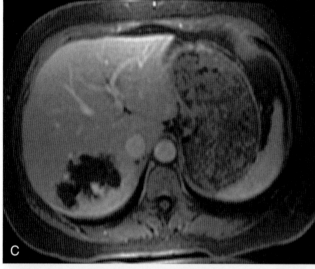

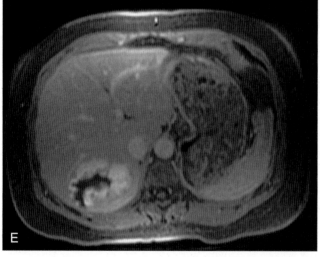

Figure 88-6. Hepatic hemangioma: MRI features. Hemangioma in the posterior aspect of the right hepatic lobe. The lesion is hyperintense on T2-weighted MR image (**A**) and shows gradual peripheral filling on dynamic MRI after intravenous administration of gadolinium (**B-E**).

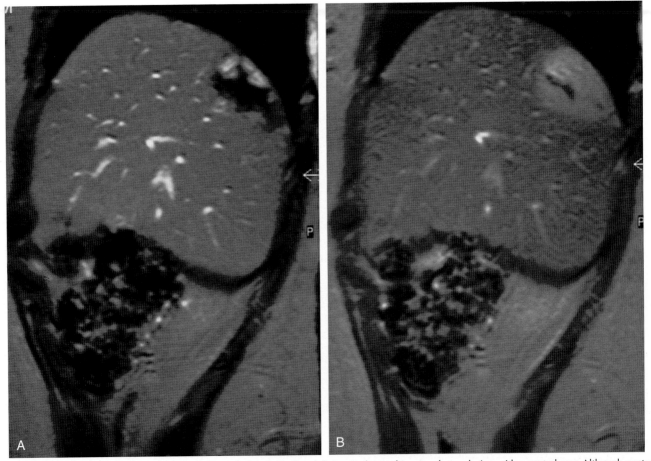

Figure 88-7. Hepatic hemangioma: MRI features. A and **B.** Sagittal gadolinium-enhanced images show a lesion with a central scar. Although central scars are generally associated with focal nodular hyperplasia, the contrast retention in this lesion establishes the diagnosis of a hemangioma.

should be evaluated using a dynamic breath-hold sequence, in a manner similar to contrast-enhanced dynamic CT protocol. After intravenous contrast agent administration, a fast gradient-echo (GRE) T1-weighted sequence (20-30 seconds) is repeatedly acquired once per minute, until the lesion has filled in completely or nearly completely. In fact, three patterns of enhancement may be seen, depending on the size of the lesion.[32] The majority of small (<1.5 cm) lesions show uniform early enhancement or peripheral nodular enhancement progressing centripetally to uniform enhancement. This second pattern is commonly seen in medium sized lesions (1.5-5 cm) and in a few large (>5 cm) lesions.[32] Most large hemangiomas exhibit peripheral nodular enhancement while the center of the lesion remains hypointense.[32] Peripheral nodular enhancement is a useful discriminating feature in the differential diagnosis between hemangiomas and metastases.[33] However, small lesions can be a diagnostic problem because a uniform pattern of enhancement is seen in both hemangiomas and vascular metastases.[32] In the majority of cases, the combination of T2-weighted image (T2WI) and serial dynamic postgadolinium images allows a confident diagnosis of hemangioma to be made.[34] The role of USPIOs has been also evaluated in the characterization of hemangiomas.[35] This agent is ultimately cleared by the reticuloendothelial system but resides in the intravascular compartment ("blood pool") immediately after injection.[35] On T1-weighted images, hemangiomas enhance immediately due to their vascularity

and become isointense with normal liver. On T2-weighted scans, hemangiomas demonstrate decreased signal intensity and may become isointense to the liver at higher doses of USPIOs.[35] Hemangiomas do not demonstrate uptake of superparamagnetic iron oxide particles or manganese-DPDP because they do not contain Kupffer cells or normal hepatocytes.[1]

Diagnostic Work-up

Differentiating hepatic hemangiomas from other benign and malignant focal liver lesions is one of the most common problems in abdominal imaging.[36] Most authorities believe that if a focal liver lesion has the classic appearance of a hemangioma on ultrasound, CT, or MRI examinations, it should be left alone. We believe that in patients with known malignancy or abnormal liver function tests, one of the tests with high accuracy should be performed, such as multiphasic MDCT or gadolinium-enhanced dynamic MRI, for confirmation. In atypical cases, biopsy should be considered.[37]

FOCAL NODULAR HYPERPLASIA

Pathologic Findings

Focal nodular hyperplasia (FNH) is defined microscopically as a tumorlike condition characterized by a central fibrous

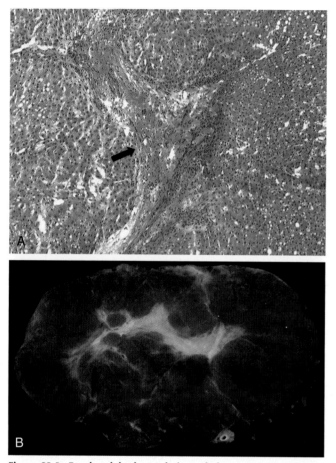

Figure 88-8. Focal nodular hyperplasia: pathology. A. Normal hepatocytes are arranged in incomplete nodules that are partially separated by fibrous tissue (*arrow*). **B.** This lesion is usually lighter brown than the adjacent liver. It has a central fibrous scar that consists of fibrovascular tissue, which explains its enhancement pattern following the administration of intravenous contrast medium.

scar with surrounding nodules of hyperplastic hepatocytes and small bile ductules.[2] The nodules seen in focal nodular hyperplasia lack normal central veins and portal tracts. The bile ductules seen in the central scar do not connect to the biliary tree. Vessels course through the tumor and are most abundant in the fibrous scar[38] (Fig. 88-8A).

Grossly, FNH is a well-circumscribed, solitary mass (95%) that is often located on the surface of the liver or pedunculated.[2] On cut section, the majority of these tumors have an obvious central fibrous scar, and although the margin is sharp, there is no capsule (Fig. 88-8B). Hemorrhage and necrosis are rare because this tumor has excellent vascularity. The majority of FNHs are smaller than 5 cm and have a mean diameter of 3 cm at the time of diagnosis. Occasionally, FNH replaces an entire lobe of the liver (lobar FNH).[2] The consistency is firm to rubbery, and the color is always paler than that of the surrounding liver. When an FNH is sectioned, it bulges from the cut surface with the stellate scar depressed and forming stellate fibrous septa that course through the tumor. Multiple FNHs have been reported in association with vascular malformations of various organs and neoplasia of the brain.[39] FNH is believed to be a hyperplastic response to an underlying "spider-like" arterial malformation.[40] It has to be emphasized that microscopically, particularly by needle

Table 88-4
Focal Nodular Hyperplasia*

Hyperplasia of normal liver	
Uptake of SPIO results in loss of signal	

Pathologic Features	Radiologic Features
Central scar with vessels and bile ducts	Hyperintense region: T2-weighted images (MR) Spoke-wheel pattern: angiography Calcification rare Sulfur colloid uptake (80%)
Hyperplasia of normal liver (Kupffer cells, portal spaces, bile ductules)	Iminodiacetic acid uptake and excretion Homogeneous mass: CT, ultrasound, MR, angiography Hyperdense relative to liver on arterial phase of contrast-enhanced helical CT, becoming isodense during portal venous phase of enhancement Uptake of SPIO results in loss of signal on T2-weighted MR Uptake of hepatobiliary contrast agents (e.g., Mn-DPDP, Gd-EOB-DTPA) results in hyperintensity relative to liver on T1-weighted images

*See text for full names of imaging agents.

biopsy, the appearance of FNH resembles that of a cirrhotic process; however, acinar landmarks are not present.[41]

Radiologic-pathologic correlates of this tumor are listed in Table 88-4.

Incidence and Clinical Presentation

FNH is the second most common benign hepatic tumor, constituting 8% of primary hepatic tumors in autopsy series.[2] FNH is more common in women, predominating in the third to fifth decades of life. Oral contraceptives have a trophic effect on FNH, but there is debate as to whether these agents actually cause this tumor.

Clinically, FNH is usually an incidental finding at autopsy, elective surgery, or cross-sectional imaging. Fewer than one third of cases are discovered because of clinical symptoms, usually right upper quadrant or epigastric pain.

Plain Radiographic Findings

Plain radiograph calcification is almost never present. Occasionally, a pedunculated FNH lesion may project to the margin of the liver and compress the adjacent stomach or hepatic flexure.[42]

Nuclear Scintigraphy

In the past, sulfur colloid scintigraphy was the preferred imaging technique in the diagnosis of FNH due to the presence of Kupffer cells within the tumor. Sulfur colloid scintigraphy demonstrates normal tracer uptake in approximately 50% and a defect is seen in 40% of FNH cases. "Hot spots," present in 10% of lesions, indicate an increased number of Kupffer cells.[43] Hepatobiliary scans show tracer uptake in the majority of cases, and isotope excretion can be observed in 50% of delayed scans.[44] Tagged RBC pool studies show early

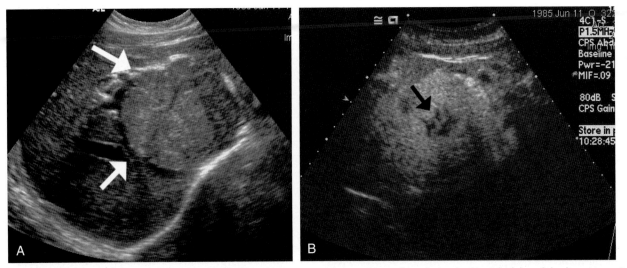

Figure 88-9. Focal nodular hyperplasia: ultrasound findings. A. Sonogram demonstrates a large lesion in the right lobe of the liver (*arrows*). **B.** Contrast-enhanced sonogram demonstrates early arterial enhancement of FNH; note that central scar shows no enhancement (*arrow*).

isotope uptake and late defect. There is no gallium uptake in FNH.

There are only a few studies about PET imaging of FNH. In one study, it was reported that in contrast to liver metastases, there is no increased glucose metabolism in FNH in vivo. Also, the imaging features of FNH on ^{18}F-fluorodeoxyglucose (FDG)-PET imaging are not specific.[45]

Today, CT and MRI are used in the diagnostic work-up of FNH, and nuclear medicine studies are reserved for exceptional circumstances.

Ultrasound

On gray-scale ultrasound studies, FNH typically appears as a well-demarcated, hypoechoic mass that is homogeneous in tissue texture except for a central scar[44,46] (Fig. 88-9). Rarely (1.4%), calcifications may be seen within FNH, and the lesion may resemble fibrolamellar hepatocellular carcinoma.[47] On color Doppler sonography (Fig. 88-10), FNH shows increased blood flow, and a pattern of blood vessels radiating peripherally from a central feeding artery may be seen, similar to the findings at conventional angiography.[48] In a contrast-enhanced examination, like hepatocellular carcinoma, FNH in the early arterial phase appears typically as a hyperperfused structure relative to the adjacent liver tissue. However, the specific morphologic features of these two entities are different. FNH typically enhances uniformly without the necrosis and heterogeneity often seen in hepatocellular carcinoma. The stellate lesion vascularity, a central nonenhancing scar, and a tortuous feeding artery are the other typical features of FNH.

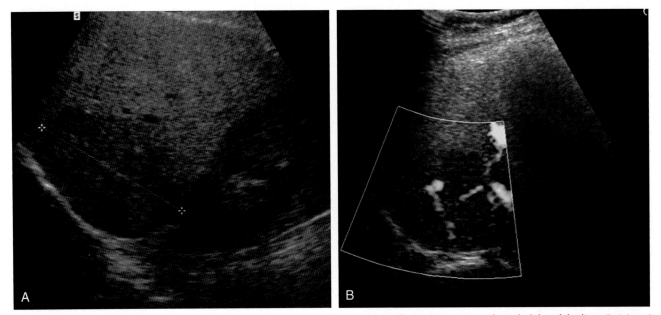

Figure 88-10. Focal nodular hyperplasia: color Doppler ultrasound. A. There is a large hypoechoic mass in the right lobe of the liver. **B.** It is quite vascular on color Doppler imaging.

Nevertheless, portal venous phase imaging is critical to reach an accurate diagnosis. During this phase, as opposed to hepatocellular carcinoma, in which washout is generally seen, FNH remains isoechogenic with the portal vein and later with the liver parenchyma.[15,16]

Computed Tomography

On nonenhanced scans, FNH usually appears as a homogeneous, hypodense mass (Fig. 88-11). In a third of cases, a low-density central area is seen, corresponding to the scar.[49,50] During the arterial phase of contrast-enhanced CT, FNH enhances rapidly and becomes hyperdense relative to normal liver[51] (Fig. 88-12). The low-attenuation scar appears conspicuous against the hyperdense tissue, and foci of enhancement may be seen within the scar representing arteries[51] (see Fig. 88-11B). In the portal venous phase and later phases of enhancement, the difference in attenuation between FNH and normal liver decreases and the FNH may become isodense with normal liver.[51-53] Ten-minute delayed images can show increased contrast uptake in the scar relative to surrounding liver.[18]

Angiography

Angiographically, FNH is a hypervascular tumor with a centrifugal blood supply creating a "spoke-wheel" pattern[54] in 70% of cases. The scar is usually hypovascular. During the capillary phase, an intense and inhomogeneous stain without avascular zones is characteristic. During the venous phase, large veins draining the hypervascular FNH are noted. Angiography is no longer primarily used to diagnose FNH.

Magnetic Resonance Imaging

MRI has higher sensitivity (70%) and specificity (98%) for FNH than CT and ultrasound.[50] On nonenhanced MRI studies, FNH is an isointense tumor on T1-weighted images that becomes slightly hyperintense to isointense on T2-weighted images (Figs. 88-13 and 14). The central scar is hypointense on T1-weighted images and hyperintense on T2-weighted images.[55,56] However, there is overlap in the appearance of FNH and malignant lesions on nonenhanced T1-weighted and T2-weighted images, and further characterization using contrast-enhanced dynamic studies may be necessary.

FNH, which is a hypervascular tumor, enhances robustly and homogeneously in the arterial phase, with the exception of late enhancing central scar (see Figs. 88-13 and 14).[30,52,55] Hepatocellular adenomas show less intense enhancement and lack a central scar.

Although other focal liver lesions such as giant hemangiomas and hepatocellular carcinomas may also have a central scar, MRI findings can help establish a specific diagnosis. The central scar in giant hemangiomas is typically larger and

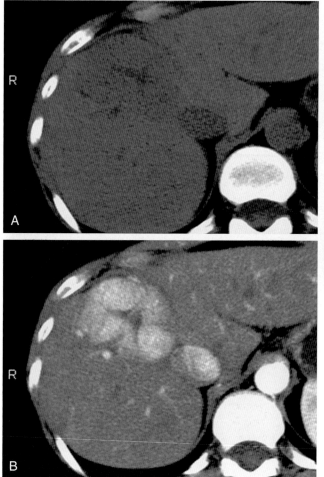

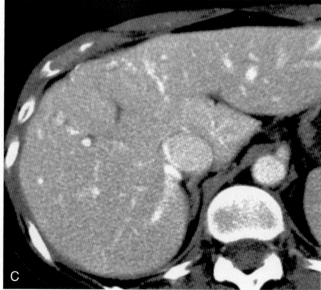

Figure 88-11. Focal nodular hyperplasia: CT features. A. On non-contrast scans, FNH is usually isodense with normal liver. Note the central scar. **B.** This lesion shows striking enhancement during the arterial phase with the exception of the scar. **C.** The lesion rapidly becomes isodense with normal liver.

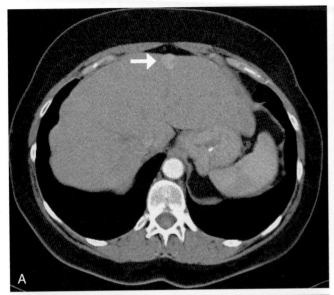

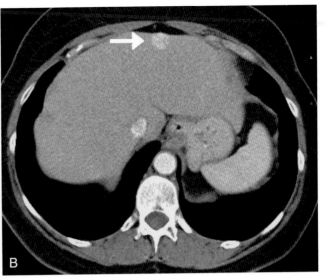

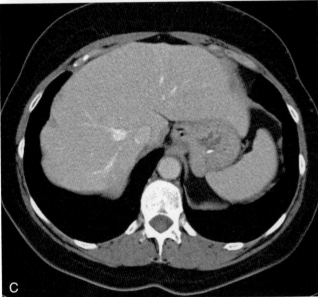

Figure 88-12. Focal nodular hyperplasia: CT findings. Early arterial (**A**) and late arterial (**B**) phase CT scans show an FNH as an enhancing lesion (*arrows*). FNH becomes isodense with the normal liver in the portal venous phase (**C**). (Courtesy of Dr. N. Cem Balci, Saint Louis University, Saint Louis, MO.)

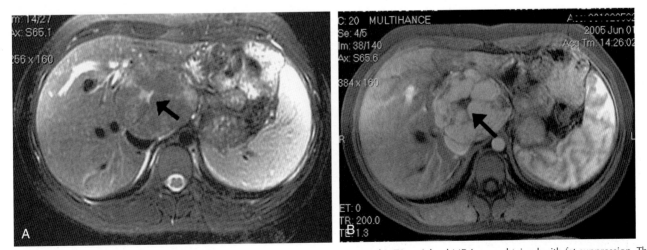

Figure 88-13. Focal nodular hyperplasia: MRI features. A. A large lesion is seen on this T2-weighted MR image obtained with fat suppression. The lesion is isointense to the normal liver, and the central scar is hyperintense (*arrow*). **B.** Gadolinium-enhanced early arterial phase demonstrates homogeneous enhancement of the lesion. The central scar (*arrow*) does not enhance early.

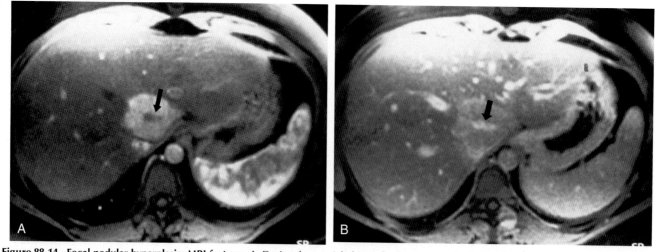

Figure 88-14. Focal nodular hyperplasia: MRI features. A. During the arterial phase of enhancement, the lesion shows robust enhancement with the exception of the central scar (*arrow*). **B.** The mass rapidly de-enhances, and there is enhancement of the central scar (*arrow*).

brighter on T2-weighted images. Due to the presence of scar tissue, calcifications, or necrosis, the central scar in hepatocellular carcinoma tends to show low signal intensity on T2- and T1-weighted images and does typically not enhance that much on contrast-enhanced images. Nevertheless, in some cases, FNH may show atypical features such as very high signal intensity on T2-weighted images and a central scar with a low signal intensity imaging that causes difficulty in differential diagnosis. In such cases, application of more sophisticated contrast media such as SPIOs or hepatobiliary agents including Gd-EOB-DTPA may be necessary to demonstrate the hepatocellular origin of the lesion. On T2-weighted images with superparamagnetic iron oxide administration, FNH shows loss of signal due to uptake of iron oxide particles by Kupffer cells within the lesion.[55] The degree of signal loss seen in FNH using SPIOs is significantly greater than in other focal liver lesions such as metastases and hepatocellular adenoma.[56] Hepatobiliary agents can also helpful in characterization of FNH. FNH contains hepatocytes which take up these agents, resulting in hyperintensity of the lesion relative to the liver on T1-weighted images.[57-59]

FNH does not have a true tumor capsule. A pseudocapsule may be present due to compression of the adjacent liver parenchyma and surrounding inflammation. The pseudocapsule is typically a few millimeters thick and hyperintense on T2-weighted images. It may also show some enhancement on delayed postcontrast images.[52]

Fatty change in the liver parenchyma is not uncommon in patients with FNH, the lesion may tend to show mildly low signal intensity on inphase gradient-echo T1-weighted images and high signal intensity on out-of-phase images.

Telengiectatic Focal Nodular Hyperplasia

The uncommon telengiectatic subtype of FNH is characterized by the presence of centrally located, multiple dilated blood-filled spaces and is commonly associated with multiple FNH syndrome. In telengiectatic FNH, arteries have hypertrophied muscular media but no intimal proliferation in contrast to the classic form. Furthermore, these abnormal vessels drain directly into the adjacent sinusoids, while in classic

FNH, connections to the sinusoids are almost never seen.[60,61] Besides this histological differences, there are also reported imaging differences of telengiectatic FNH. Telengiectatic subtype of FNH may be hyperintense on T1-weighted images and strongly hyperintense on T2-weighted images and show persistent lesion enhancement on delayed phase images. All of these features are extremely rare in classic FNH and relatively common in telengiectatic subtype. Furthermore, absence of a central scar is not an uncommon finding in this subentity.[62]

HEPATOCELLULAR ADENOMA

Pathologic Findings

Hepatocellular adenoma (HCA) should be considered as a spectrum of lesions that are associated with a number of diseases and etiologic factors and that demonstrate a variety of histologic appearances. Accordingly, a new classification of adenomas (Table 88-5) has been proposed in which, in addition to the typical adenoma, anabolic steroid–associated HCA is described separately.[2] This is due to its distinctive histologic appearance, which often resembles that of hepatocellular carcinoma. In addition, multiple hepatocellular adenomatosis should be considered separately from typical HCA.

Typical HCA is defined as a tumor composed of hepatocytes arranged in cords that occasionally form bile[2] (Fig. 88-15). The tumor lacks portal tracts and terminal hepatic veins;

Table 88-5
Hepatocellular Adenoma: Classification

1. Typical hepatocellular adenoma	
Type I	Estrogen-associated hepatocellular adenoma
Type II	Spontaneous hepatocellular adenoma in women
Type III	Spontaneous hepatocellular adenoma in men
Type IV	Spontaneous hepatocellular adenoma in children
Type V	Metabolic disease-associated hepatocellular adenoma
2. Anabolic steroid–associated hepatocellular adenoma	
3. Multiple hepatocellular adenomas (adenomatosis)	

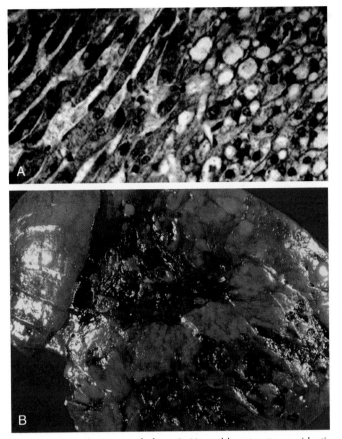

Figure 88-15. Adenoma: pathology. A. Normal hepatocytes are identified on the left side of this histologic image. On the right, fat-containing hepatocytes are present. **B.** Gross section shows hemorrhage within a large adenoma.

consequently, necrosis, hemorrhage, and rupture commonly occur in large tumors.[28]

Grossly, a typical HCA is a large tumor (usually 8-10 cm in diameter at discovery), readily seen from the external surface of the liver.[38] Pedunculation is seen in approximately 10% of cases. On cut section, its surface is tan and irregular and frequently has large areas of hemorrhage or infarction. However, homogeneous adenomas without rupture can be seen with numerous blood vessels throughout the tumor and occasionally fibrous septa. Large vessels run through the surface of adenomas.[38] Most adenomas are solitary.[41]

Microscopically, the tumor is composed of neoplastic cells that are separated by compressed sinusoidal spaces, resulting in a sheetlike pattern.[2] The sinusoids are lined by endothelial cells, and enzymatically active Kupffer cells have been demonstrated in adenomas.[63] Fatty hepatocytes are frequently present as well. Adenomas rarely undergo malignant transformation to hepatocellular carcinoma, even after years of maintaining a stable appearance.[64]

Radiologic-pathologic correlates of HCA are given in Table 88-6.

Incidence and Clinical Presentation

The majority of HCAs are related to the use of oral contraceptives, with an overall estimated incidence of four adenomas per 100,000 users.[65,66] Withdrawal of estrogen compounds

Table 88-6
Hepatocellular Adenoma*

Pathologic Features	Radiologic Features
Rich in fat	Hyperechoic mass: ultrasound Hypodense mass: CT Hyperintense mass: MR
No stroma, internal hemorrhage	Anechoic, potentially cystic mass: ultrasound Hyperdense area: CT Hyperintense area: T1-weighted images (MR) Avascular areas: angiography
Peripheral "feeders"	Peripheral enhancement: angiography, contrast-enhanced MDCT, and MR
Kupffer cells	Sulfur colloid uptake (20%), SPIO uptake resulting in reduced signal on T2-weighted MR images
Hepatocytes, no ductules	IDA uptake, no excretion

*See text for full names of imaging agents.

may result in regression of the HCA, which can require a period of several months.[67]

Plain Radiographic Findings

When sufficiently large, HCAs can cause a right upper quadrant mass on plain radiographs.[7] When these lesions rupture, free intraperitoneal hemorrhage can occur, producing the typical "ground glass" appearance of free intraperitoneal fluid.

Nuclear Scintigraphy

As in hemangioma and FNH, nuclear scintigraphy is no longer routinely used in the diagnostic work-up of hepatocellular adenoma. There are also no studies reporting usefulness of PET imaging in this context. Sulfur colloid scintigraphy demonstrates a defect in 80% of cases, although tracer uptake can be present in up to 20% of tumors.[43] Uptake is found in adenomas with a vascular supply sufficient to deliver the isotope to the prominent sinusoids.

Hepatobiliary scans show tracer uptake in the majority of cases; however, no excretion is seen on delayed scans because of lack of bile ductules.[44] Tagged RBC scintigraphy demonstrates early uptake and a delayed defect, indicating the vascular nature of this tumor.

Ultrasound

Sonography typically demonstrates a large hyperechoic lesion with central anechoic areas, corresponding to zones of internal hemorrhage if present[46] (Fig. 88-16). These findings are nonspecific. Occasionally, adenomas may undergo massive necrosis and hemorrhage, and the ultrasound appearance is that of a complex mass with large cystic components. Color Doppler ultrasound demonstrates peripheral arteries and veins, correlating well with both gross and angiographic findings. In addition, color Doppler may identify intratumoral veins.[68] This finding is absent in FNH and may be a useful discriminating feature for HCA.[68] Contrast-enhanced phase inversion ultrasonography demonstrates pronounced arterial and portal venous enhancement in the majority of the

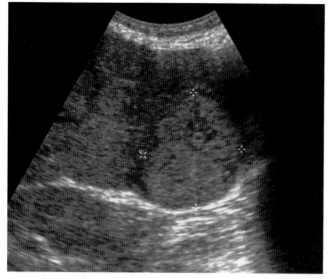

Figure 88-16. Adenoma: ultrasound findings. There is a large, solid echogenic mass in the right lobe of the liver. Note the fairly well-defined hypoechoic rim.

patients with FNH and no enhancement during hepatic portal venous phase in patients with HCA.[69]

Computed Tomography

Nonenhanced CT usually demonstrates a hypodense mass due to the presence of fat and glycogen within the tumor[49] (Fig. 88-17). However, hyperdense areas corresponding to fresh hemorrhage can be noted (Fig. 88-18).

On MDCT, small HCAs enhance rapidly after administration of intravenous contrast medium.[70] The enhancement does not persist in adenomas because of arteriovenous shunting,[5] and the lesions become nearly isodense to normal liver on portal venous and delayed scans. A peripheral and centripetal enhancement pattern, reflecting the presence of the large subcapsular feeding vessels, may also be seen.[64] Larger HCAs may be more heterogeneous than smaller lesions and the CT appearance is nonspecific.[70]

Angiography

Angiographically, HCA presents as a hypervascular mass with centripetal flow and large peripheral vessels.[71,72] Frequently, avascular areas resulting from internal hemorrhage are seen.[7]

Magnetic Resonance Imaging

On MRI, adenomas are heterogeneous in appearance (Fig. 88-19). They contain areas of increased signal intensity on T1-weighted images resulting from the presence of fat and hemorrhage and low signal areas corresponding to necrosis[73] (Fig. 88-20). Hepatocellular adenomas are predominantly hyperintense relative to liver on T2-weighted images. As on T1-weighted images, they contain areas of heterogeneous signal intensity reflecting the presence of hemorrhage and necrosis. One third of HCAs have a peripheral rim corresponding to a fibrous capsule.[74] In most cases, this rim has a low signal intensity on both T1 and T2-weighted images.[74] Hepatic adenomas typically demonstrate decreased signal intensity on

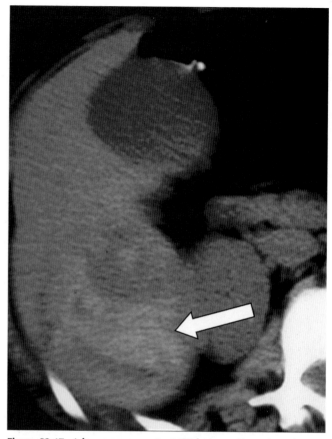

Figure 88-17. Adenoma: noncontrast CT features. Hyperdense hemorrhage is present within the right lobe of the liver.

out-of-phase T1-weighted gradient-echo images or fat-suppressed T1-weighted images because of their fat content.[30]

On contrast-enhanced dynamic studies, the adenomas show early enhancement during the arterial phase and a rapid washout. Hepatic adenomas show a more uniform and moderate enhancement on arterial phase images compared to intense homogeneous and peripheral nodular enhancement patterns of focal nodular hyperplasias and hemangiomas, respectively. Adenomas usually do not show uptake of SPIOs.[64] However, hepatocyte-specific contrast agents, such as Gd-EOB-DTPA, will show uptake in adenomas due to the presence of hepatocytes.

Multiple Hepatocellular Adenomatosis

Multiple hepatocellular adenomatosis is a rare entity is characterized by the presence of multiple (more than four) HCAs, usually present in both hepatic lobes.[75,76] This entity should not be confused with other hyperplastic hepatocellular conditions, such as nodular regenerative hyperplasia (NRH), macroregenerative nodules of cirrhosis, or adenomatous hyperplastic nodules (Table 88-7).

NODULAR REGENERATIVE HYPERPLASIA

Pathologic Findings

NRH is defined as diffuse nodularity of the liver produced by many regenerative nodules that are not associated with

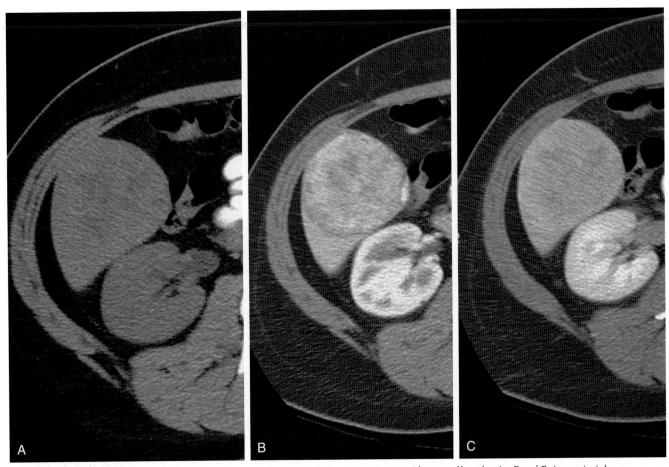

Figure 88-18. Adenoma: CT features. A. Noncontrast scan shows an inhomogeneous mass with areas of low density. **B** and **C.** A mosaic, inhomogeneous enhancement pattern is seen following intravenous contrast administration.

fibrosis.[77] Grossly, NRH is characterized by the presence of multiple bulging nodules in the external surface of the liver that on cut surface appear as discrete, round, flat nodules that resemble diffuse involvement with metastatic carcinoma (Fig. 88-21A). The nodules vary in size from a few millimeters to several centimeters and are diffusely scattered.

Microscopically, the nodules are composed of cells resembling normal hepatocytes and no fibrosis is noted.[78] This is an important difference between NRH and regenerating nodules of cirrhosis.

Incidence and Clinical Presentation

NRH is known by numerous synonyms, including nodular transformation of the liver, partial nodular transformation, miliary hepatocellular adenomatosis, adenomatous hyperplasia, diffuse nodular hyperplasia, and noncirrhotic nodulation.[2] NRH is rare, although autopsy series have shown a prevalence as high as 0.6%.[79] Approximately one third of cases were initially considered cases of FNH. Clinically, NRH is discovered either incidentally on autopsy or in the work-up of portal hypertension and its complications.

Table 88-7
Comparison of Hyperplastic Hepatocellular Conditions

Criteria	Focal Nodular Hyperplasia	Hepatocellular Adenoma	Nodular Regenerative Hyperplasia	Multiple Hepatocellular Adenoma	Macroregenerative Nodule
Gross	Scar	Hemorrhage, necrosis	Bulging nodules	Bulging nodules	Bulging nodules
Number of lesions	1 (90%)	1 (90%)	Many	Many	Many or few
Size (average range)	1-6 cm	4-12 cm	>1.5 cm	2-9 cm	1-6 cm
Key feature	Pseudoductules	Neohepatocytes	Small nodules	Normal cords	Portal tracts
Prior liver disease	None	None	None	None	Submassive hepatic necrosis or cirrhosis
Associated etiology	None	Estrogen, anabolic steroids	Vascular disease	None	None

Modified from Craig GR, Peters RL, Edmonson HA: Tumors of the liver and intrahepatic bile ducts. In Atlas of Tumor Pathology (2nd series). Washington, DC: Armed Forces Institute of Pathology, 1989.

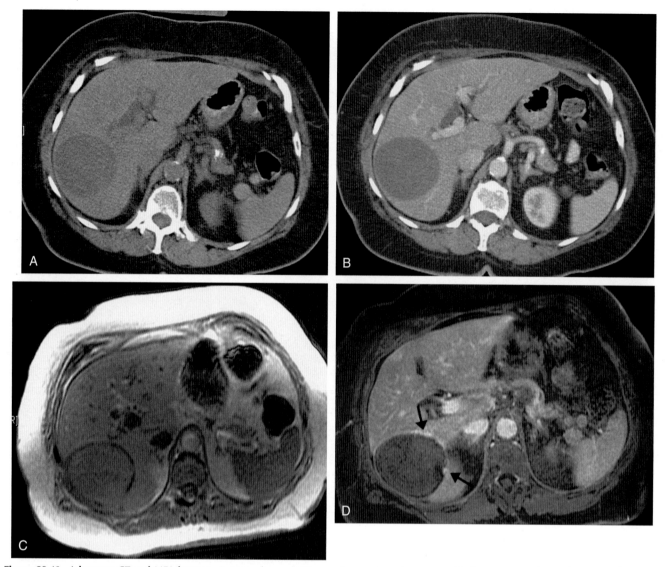

Figure 88-19. Adenoma: CT and MRI features. A. Nonenhanced CT scan shows a hypodense mass. **B.** On contrast-enhanced CT scan, the lesion shows no enhancement. **C.** On T1-weighted MR image, adenoma is slightly hypointense in comparison with the normal liver, and the fibrous capsule is isointense. **D.** Contrast-enhanced T1-weighted image demonstrates the subcapsular feeding vessels (*arrows*).

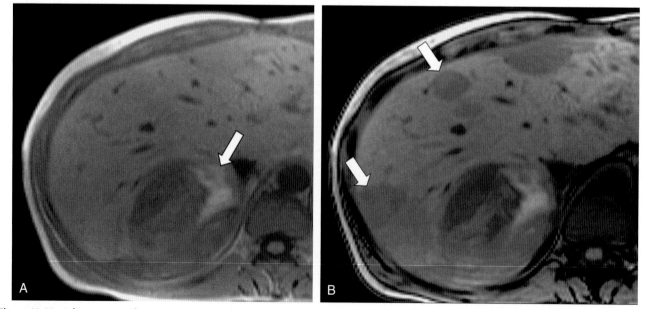

Figure 88-20. Adenoma: MRI features. A. Inphase image shows high signal intensity hemorrhage (*arrow*) within this mass. **B.** Opposed-phase image shows loss of signal intensity of the mass indicating fat. There are multiple areas of focal fatty infiltration (*arrows*).

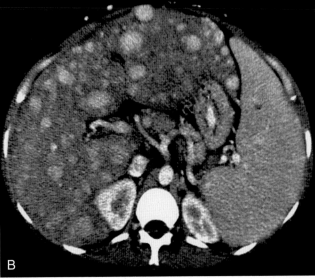

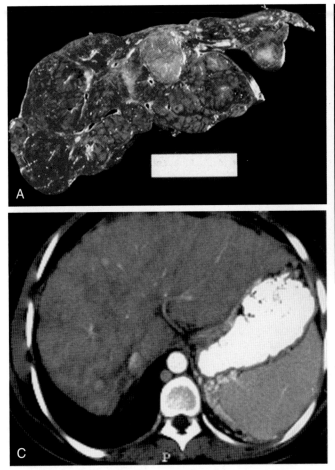

Figure 88-21. Nodular regenerative hyperplasia. A. This rare condition is characterized by small regenerative nodules composed of hepatocytes that compress the surrounding parenchyma and are not surrounded by fibrous tissue. This lack of fibrosis differentiates nodular regenerative hyperplasia from cirrhosis. **B** and **C.** Multiple robustly enhancing hepatic masses are identified on these contrast-enhanced CT scans in these two patients with the Budd-Chiari syndrome. (**A** and **B** courtesy of Michael P. Federle, MD, Pittsburgh, PA.)

Various systemic diseases and drugs are often associated with NRH[80-82]: myeloproliferative syndromes (polycythemia vera, chronic myelogenous leukemia, and myeloid metaplasia), lymphoproliferative syndromes (Hodgkin's and non-Hodgkin's lymphoma, chronic lymphocytic leukemia, and plasma cell dysplasias), chronic vascular disorders (rheumatoid arthritis), Felty's syndrome, polyarteritis nodosa, scleroderma, calcinosis cutis, Raynaud's phenomenon, sclerodactyly and telangiectasia, lupus erythematosus, steroids, and antineoplastic medication.[78]

As described earlier, the appearance grossly and, therefore at laparotomy, is that of a cirrhotic liver with diffuse nodularity.[83]

Plain Radiographic Findings

Plain abdominal radiographs may demonstrate splenomegaly, ascites, and other signs of portal hypertension.

Nuclear Scintigraphy

Because NRH nodules are composed of abnormal hepatocytes with Kupffer cells, they take up technetium Tc 99m sulfur colloid. The appearance of the liver may be normal if the nodules are small. Large nodules, measuring up to several centimeters, take up sulfur colloid as well.[82] There are no studies reporting the usefulness of PET imaging in this context.

Ultrasound

The sonographic appearance of NRH ranges from that of a normal liver to that of a liver with focal nodules that vary in echogenicity. Central hemorrhage within a large nodule may occur and produce a complex mass.

Computed Tomography

On CT scans, the appearance of NRH ranges from that of a normal liver to that of a liver with focal nodules of varying attenuation that are primarily hypodense.[82] Central hemorrhage within a large nodule may produce a complex mass with variable density. On contrast-enhanced MDCT scans, arterial phase imaging shows hypervascular lesions (Fig. 88-21B and C) that may become almost imperceptible on portal venous examination.[18]

Angiography

Angiographically, the typical findings of portal hypertension with esophageal varices, portal collaterals, and splenomegaly are demonstrated.[82] Occasionally, individual nodules of NRH can be distinguished; they are vascular and fill from the periphery.

Magnetic Resonance Imaging

Lesions are isointense to normal liver on T2-weighted images and contain foci of high signal on T1-weighted scans.[84]

These lesions may show robust enhancement following the intravenous administration of Gd-DTPA.

Summary

NRH is an underdiagnosed disease, frequently related to chronic illnesses and/or prolonged therapy. NRH can present as tiny nodules diffusely involving the liver or as focal larger nodules producing a spectrum of radiologic findings ranging from a normal-appearing liver with associated portal hypertension to multiple hepatic masses.

NRH must be differentiated from other hepatocellular hyperplasias.

Currently, hepatocellular hyperplasia is divided into several categories and some groups overlap with prior concepts of these conditions. FNH, HCA, NRH, multiple HCAs (hepatocellular adenomatosis), and microregenerative nodules are considered separate entities, and their differences are included in Table 88-7.

LIPOMATOUS TUMORS

Pathologic Findings

Benign hepatic tumors composed of fat cells include lipoma, hibernoma, and combined tumors such as angiomyolipoma (fat and blood vessels), myelolipoma (fat and hematopoietic tissue), and angiomyelolipoma.[38]

Grossly, lipomatous tumors are usually solitary, well circumscribed, and round and usually occur in a noncirrhotic liver.[85] The microscopic features are similar to those of lipomatous tumors of soft tissues. There is no sex predilection and they have been reported in a broad age range (24-70 years).[2] Approximately 10% of patients with tuberous sclerosis and renal angiolipomas have hepatic fatty tumors, either lipoma (Fig. 88-22) or angiomyolipoma (Fig. 88-23).[86] Most lipomatous tumors of the liver are asymptomatic and are incidental findings. These tumors occasionally bleed, causing abdominal pain.

Radiologic Findings

Angiomyolipomas are highly echogenic on sonography and indistinguishable from hemangiomas.[86] On CT scans, these tumors appear as well-defined masses with attenuation values in the range of those of fat.[86,87] Angiographically, angiomyolipomas are hypervascular and may show large aneurysms, as in angiomyolipomas of the kidneys.[88] On MRI scans, the fatty component of angiomyolipomas is of high signal on T1- and T2-weighted images.[89] However, hepatocellular carcinomas containing fat deposits may have a similar appearance. The early phase of contrast-enhanced dynamic CT or MRI may be useful in discriminating between angiomyolipomas and hepatocellular carcinomas with fat, since the fatty areas of angiomyolipomas are well vascularized and enhance early.[89] Conversely, the areas of fatty change in hepatocellular carcinoma are relatively avascular and enhancement is less obvious.[89] MRI using fat suppression is a useful technique in the characterization of hepatic angiomyolipomas.[90] The lesions have high signal intensity on T1- and T2-weighted images and appear hypointense to liver on images obtained with fat

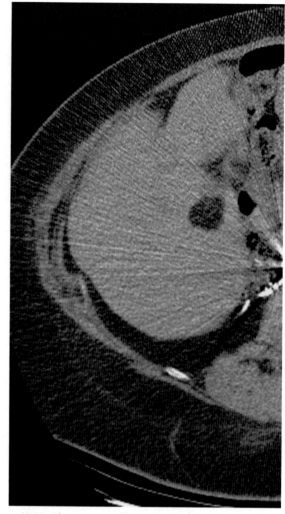

Figure 88-22. Lipoma. A well-marginated homogeneous fat density mass is present within the left lobe of the liver.

suppression.[90] The presence of large intratumoral vessels ("macroaneurysms") is a classic feature of large angiomyolipomas. Color Doppler ultrasound, CT, and MRI are useful techniques in the detection of macroaneurysms.[91]

Other focal fatty lesions of the liver include pseudolipoma and focal fatty change.

Pseudolipoma

Pseudolipoma is usually due to fat ectopia within Glisson's capsule. It represents epiploic appendices that become attached to or embedded in the liver parenchyma.[92]

CYSTS AND CYSTIC TUMORS

The classification of hepatic cysts is somewhat confusing because of varying criteria and incomplete histologic evaluation. Hepatic cysts should be distinguished from other cystic masses of the liver determined by radiologic as well as gross characteristics.[93] The following is a discussion of the "true" cyst of the liver, or bile duct cyst, defined by the presence of an epithelial lining.

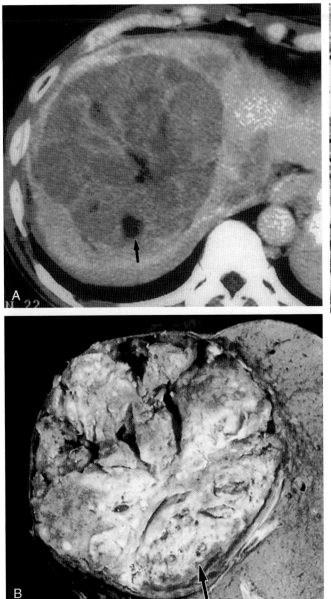

Figure 88-23. Angiomyolipoma. A. Contrast-enhanced CT scan shows a well-circumscribed, heterogeneous tumor of the right lobe with foci of fat (*arrow*). **B.** Photograph of the gross specimen shows that the tumor is large and lobulated with areas containing fat (*arrow*). **C.** Photomicrograph (hematoxylin-eosin stain; original magnification, 200) shows proliferating smooth muscle (*arrow*), vessels, and adipose tissue (*arrowheads*). (From Prasad SR, Wang H, Rosas H, et al: Fat-containing lesions of the liver: Radiologic-pathologic correlation. RadioGraphics 25:321-331, 2005.)

Simple Cyst

Pathologic Findings

A simple hepatic (bile duct) cyst (Fig. 88-24A and B) is defined as a single, unilocular cyst lined by a single layer of cuboidal, bile duct epithelium. The wall is a thin layer of fibrous tissue and the adjacent liver is normal. Grossly, the wall is 1 mm or less in thickness and typically occurs just beneath the surface of the liver, although some may occur deeper. The simple hepatic cyst is considered to be of congenital, developmental origin, although it is usually discovered in the fifth through seventh decades of life.[94]

Incidence and Clinical Presentation

Simple hepatic (bile duct) cysts range in incidence from 1% to 14% in autopsy series and appear to occur more commonly in women than in men (5:1).[2] Simple cysts are usually found incidentally, although up to 20% have been reported in surgical series of patients who presented with symptoms caused by a mass effect (abdominal pain, jaundice, intra-abdominal mass).[95] Asymptomatic cysts are not usually treated unless complicated by hemorrhage or infection. The treatment for symptomatic cysts is wide incision and drainage.

Radiologic Findings

Simple cysts cause a nonspecific photopenic defect on hepatobiliary scans with sulfur colloid and iminodiacetic acid derivatives. Sonographically (Fig. 88-24C), uncomplicated simple (bile duct) cysts present as anechoic masses, with smooth borders, lateral shadowing, posterior echo enhancement nondetectable walls, no septations, and no mural calcification.

The CT features (Fig. 88-24D) of an uncomplicated hepatic cyst are (1) a well-defined intrahepatic mass; (2) water attenuation; (3) round or oval shape; (4) smooth, thin walls;

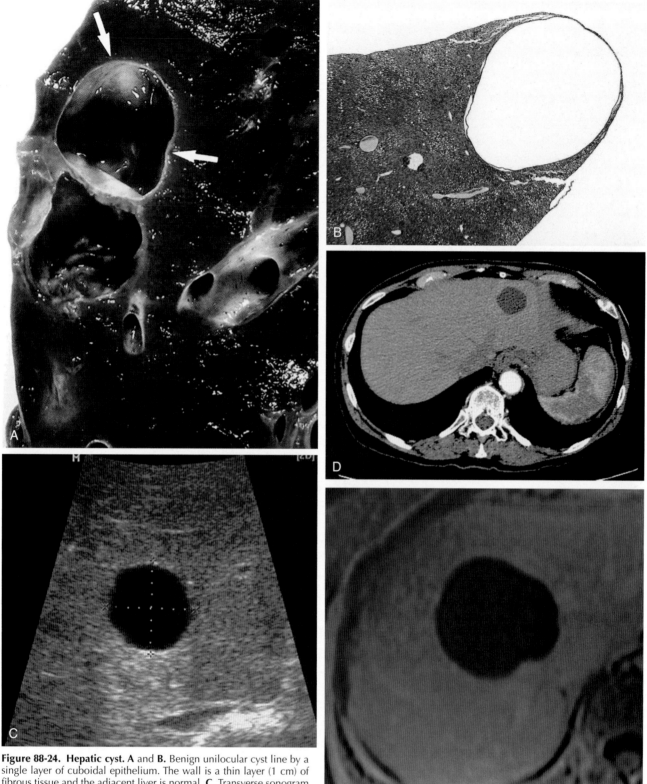

Figure 88-24. Hepatic cyst. A and **B.** Benign unilocular cyst line by a single layer of cuboidal epithelium. The wall is a thin layer (1 cm) of fibrous tissue and the adjacent liver is normal. **C.** Transverse sonogram shows an anechoic, well-marginated, simple cyst with a thin wall and posterior acoustic enhancement. **D.** Contrast-enhanced CT shows a homogeneous, low-attenuation (8 HU) cyst in the left lobe of the liver. There is no mural enhancement.

Continued

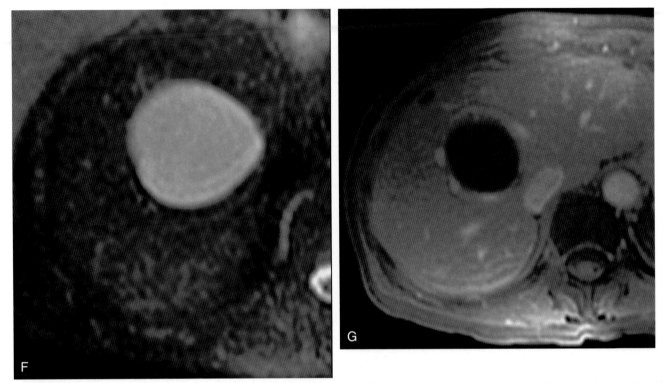

Figure 88-24, *cont'd* On MRI, cysts show low signal intensity on the T1-weighted image (**E**), high signal intensity on the T2-weighted image (**F**), and no enhancement following the intravenous administration of contrast (**G**).

(5) absence of internal structures; and (6) no enhancement after administration of contrast material.[93]

As implied in the definition, simple cysts of the liver are usually solitary but can number fewer than 10. When more than 10 cysts are seen, one of the fibropolycystic diseases should be considered.[96]

On MRI studies (Fig. 88-24E-G), simple cysts are extremely hyperintense on T2-weighted images and hypointense on T1-weighted images. They usually have a homogeneous, well-defined, oval-shaped appearance.[30] Cysts with intracystic hemorrhage may show high signal intensity on both T1-weighted and T2-weighted images.[97] No enhancement is seen after administration of gadolinium chelates.

Summary

Ultrasound is the best way to confirm the cystic nature of a hepatic mass. Cysts complicated by infection or hemorrhage may have septations and/or internal debris, as well as enhancement of the wall. Percutaneous aspiration and sclerotherapy with alcohol are useful for treating symptomatic hepatic cysts.[98,99]

Bile Duct Hamartomas (von Meyenberg Complexes)

Bile duct hamartomas (BDHs) are a focal disorderly collection of bile ducts that is due to failure of involution of embryonic bile ducts. With extreme dilatation these ducts become visible on imaging. These lesions are 1 to 5 mm in size (Fig. 88-25). There can be 50,000 to 100,000 BDHs in a normal-sized liver.

Nearly all individuals with adult polycystic liver disease (APLD) have multiple BDHs and 11% of patients with multiple BDHs have APLD. It is postulated that the larger cysts of APLD result from gradual dilatation of the hamartomas. BDHs have a 0.69% to 5.6% incidence at autopsy.

On CT, innumerable cystic lesions less than 5 mm in diameter are present. They show no contrast enhancement. On MRI, BDH have low signal intensity on T2-weighted images and high signal intensity on T2-weighted images.

Congenital Hepatic Fibrosis and Polycystic Liver Disease

Pathologic Findings

Congenital hepatic fibrosis is part of the spectrum of hepatic cystic diseases. Congenital hepatic fibrosis is characterized by aberrant bile duct proliferation and periductal fibrosis.[2] In typical congenital hepatic fibrosis, cysts are not visible without a hand lens. However, in the polycystic liver disease variant, numerous large and small cysts coexist with fibrosis (Fig. 88-26A). In cases of polycystic liver and/or kidney disease, the liver surrounding the cysts is not normal, frequently containing von Meyenburg complexes and increased fibrous tissue.[2] In patients with adult polycystic kidney disease, there is hepatic involvement in approximately 30% to 40%.[98] Occasionally, hepatic cysts occur without radiographically identifiable renal involvement.[96]

Incidence and Clinical Presentation

The incidence of congenital hepatic fibrosis and polycystic liver disease is difficult to determine because of the various

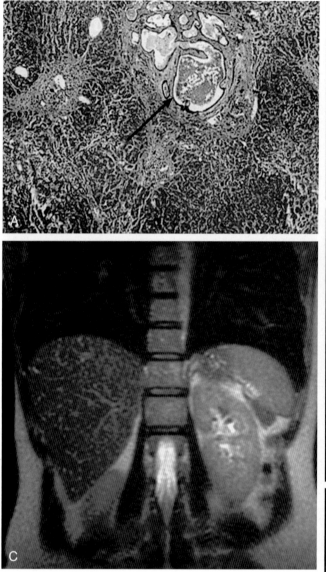

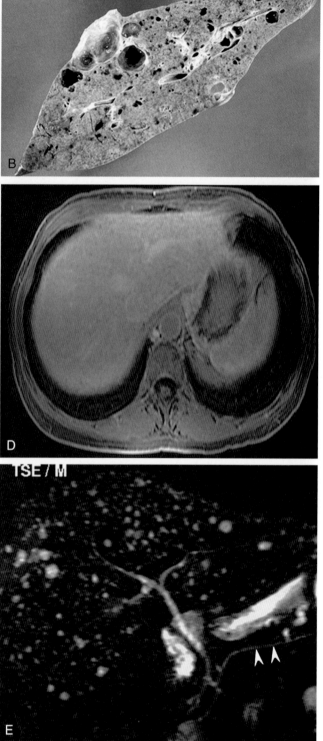

Figure 88-25. Multiple bile duct hamartomas (von Meyenberg complexes). A. These are small bile ductules embedded in a fibrous, sometimes hyalinized stroma. Each lumen may contain inspissated bile (*arrow*) concretements, and the lumina may interconnect. These are usually incidental findings at autopsy and cross-sectional imaging. **B.** They are usually small and multiple, located in the subcapsular region and distributed in both lobes. **C.** Coronal, T2-weighted MRI scan shows multiple, tiny hyperintense lesions in the liver. **D.** MRCP images show these hyperintense lesions. They have fluid (bile) signal intensity. **E.** MRCP image demonstrates innumerable tiny hyperintense cysts typical of this disorder. Arrows point to pancreatic duct.

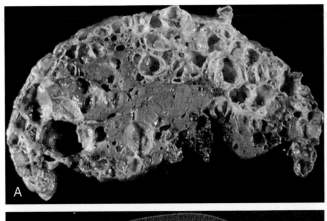

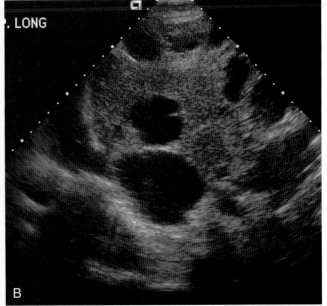

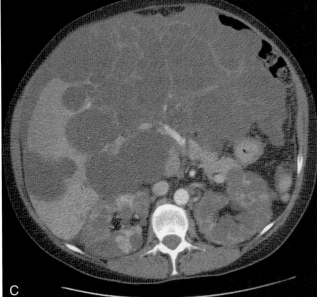

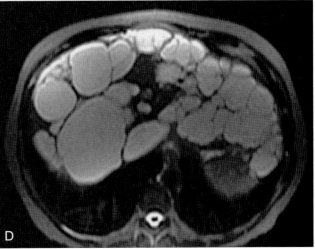

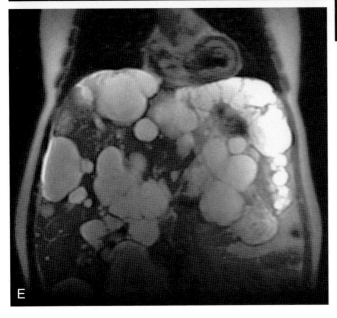

Figure 88-26. Polycystic liver disease. A. Pathologic specimen shows multiple cysts replacing the liver. **B.** Sonogram demonstrates multiple sepatated and simple cysts. **C.** CT scan shows multiple cysts replacing the liver and kidney. Several of the hepatic cysts have mural calcification. **D.** Axial T2-weighted MR image shows multiple hyperintense hepatic cysts. **E.** Coronal T2-weighted MR image demonstrates multiple hyperintense hepatic and renal cysts.

degrees of expression.[100] Clinically, the majority of patients present in childhood, when congenital hepatic fibrosis predominates, with bleeding varices and other manifestations of portal hypertension.[101]

In patients with polycystic liver disease predominance, the lesions are usually identified incidentally at radiologic examination. Approximately 70% of patients with polycystic liver disease also have adult polycystic kidney disease. Congenital hepatic fibrosis is also related to Caroli's disease, which is discussed in Chapter 87.

Radiologic Findings

Cross-sectional imaging shows multiple cysts in the liver (Fig. 88-26B), frequently associated with multiple renal cysts.[96] Hypoattenuating cystic lesions demonstrate regular outlines on nonenhanced CT scans and no wall or content enhancement on contrast-enhanced images (Fig. 88-26C). At MRI, cysts show a very low signal intensity on T1-weighted images and do not enhance after administration of gadolinium. Due to their fluid content, on T2-weighted MR images, they show high signal intensity (Fig. 88-26D and E). Signal intensity alterations indicating intracystic hemorrhage are commonly seen.[97] Calcification in the cyst wall is occasionally seen and the cysts may contain blood and fluid levels.[93] These hepatic cysts are pathologically identical to simple or bile duct cysts.

Cystadenoma

Biliary cystadenoma is a cystic tumor of the liver with a recognized propensity to develop malignancy. It is considered a premalignant lesion and is discussed with cystadenocarcinoma in Chapter 89.

INFANTILE HEMANGIOENDOTHELIOMA

Pathologic Findings

Infantile hemangioendothelioma (IHE) is a vascular tumor derived from endothelial cells that proliferate and form vascular channels. Grossly, IHEs are usually multiple and diffuse; a solitary lesion is an uncommon variant.[102] The nodules of IHEs vary from a few millimeters to 15 cm or more in size. Lesions are usually multiple, nodular, round, red-brown, and spongy to white-yellow with fibrotic predominance in mature cases.[7] Calcification may be present.

Microscopically, IHEs are composed of a proliferation of small vascular channels lined by endothelial cells. Cavernous areas, as well as zones of hemorrhage, thrombosis, fibrosis, and calcification, are common. The cavernous areas noted in some lesions correspond to the areas of puddling of contrast material seen angiographically. The multinodular type may involve other organs and the skin, where angiomas are also present. The solitary variant has no associated skin hemangiomas.[2]

Incidence and Clinical Presentation

IHE is the most common benign vascular tumor of infancy and accounts for 12% of all childhood hepatic tumors.[103,104] Eighty-five percent of patients with IHE present as young infants between 1 and 6 months of age, with less than 5% of cases detected beyond 1 year of age and females affected more

often than males. Clinical findings include hepatomegaly, congestive heart failure (present in up to 25% of cases), thrombocytopenia caused by trapping of platelets by the tumor, and occasional rupture with hemoperitoneum.[105,106] Most tumors continue to grow during the first year of life and then spontaneously regress, probably due to thrombosis and scar formation.[107] Cutaneous hemangiomas, as described earlier, are more commonly present in the multinodular form of IHE, occurring in up to 40% of patients.

Plain Radiographic Findings

On plain radiographs of the abdomen, IHE appears as an upper abdominal mass or as hepatomegaly if the liver is diffusely involved. Speckled calcifications may be present.[108] Chest radiographs may show signs of congestive heart failure in 30% of cases.[108]

Ultrasound

Ultrasonographic features of IHE are varied. Typically there is a complex liver mass with large draining hepatic veins.[109] Single or multiple lesions may be seen, and the lesions may range from hypochoic to hyperechoic. During a period of months, these lesions tend to involute slowly and develop increased echogenicity.[108,110] Dilated hepatic vasculature with prominent blood flow is typical at Doppler US, if significant arteriovenous shunting is present.

Computed Tomography

On precontrast CT scans, IHE appears as a single or multiple hypodense masses with or without calcifications[111] (Fig. 88-27A). At contrast-enhanced CT shows an enhancement pattern that may resemble an adult giant hemangioma, with "nodular" peripheral early enhancement and delayed progression to the center of the lesion (Fig. 88-27B). In larger tumors, the central portion of the tumor remains hypodense due to fibrosis, hemorrhage, or necrosis.[107,112]

Angiography

Angiographically, enlarged tortuous feeding arteries are seen, as well as draining vessels and large vascular lakes with prolonged pooling of contrast agent. The aorta typically has a decreased caliber distal to the origin of the hepatic mass, indicating the large blood supply to the tumor.[113,114]

Magnetic Resonance Imaging

On MRI, IHE has a nonspecific appearance and is predominantly hypointense on T1-weighted images and hyperintense on T2-weighted images.[111] Foci of hyperintense or hypointense signal on T1-weighted scans correspond to areas of hemorrhage and fibrosis.[111,115] In tumors with arteriovenous shunting and high blood flow, flow voids may be seen on T2-weighted images. On contrast-enhanced dynamic MRI (Fig. 88-27C), the lesions usually demonstrate an enhancement pattern similar to that of MDCT. In some cases, however, the lesion may show a complete "rimlike" enhancement at dynamic imaging, which may simulate other childhood tumors.[104]

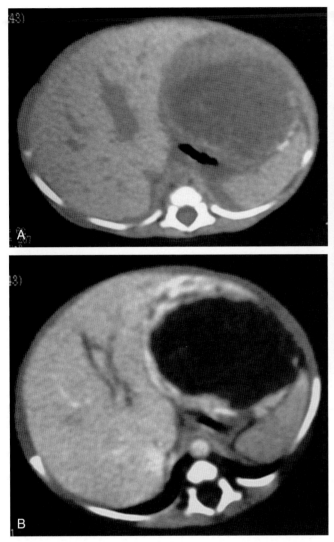

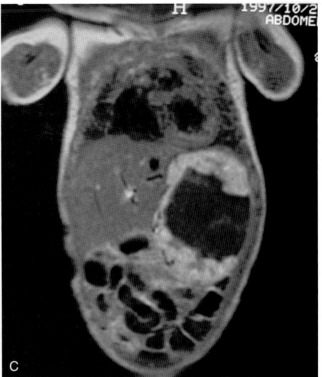

Figure 88-27. Infantile hemangioendothelioma: CT and MRI appearance. A. On the nonenhanced CT, there is a large hypodense lesion in the left lobe of the liver with some peripheral calcification. **B.** After contrast administration, there is peripheral enhancement, similar to that of a hemangioma identified on the axial MR image. **C.** Coronal MR image demonstrates peripheral enhancement.

Summary

IHE is the most common liver tumor during the first 6 months of life. These lesions are usually multiple and markedly hypervascular and may be associated with cutaneous angiomas. Although IHE may grow to a large size, producing cardiac failure, it involutes spontaneously with time. The radiologic findings for IHE are similar to those for multiple hemangiomas of the liver in the adult.

MESENCHYMAL HAMARTOMA

Pathologic Findings

Mesenchymal hamartoma is a benign cystic developmental lesion and is not considered a true neoplasm. It is composed of gelatinous mesenchymal tissue with cyst formation, as well as remnants of normal hepatic parenchyma.[116,117] Grossly, mesenchymal hamartoma is a large, soft, predominantly cystic mass measuring 15 cm or more in largest diameter at the time of diagnosis.[118] These tumors are well defined and encapsulated or pedunculated.[119] Cysts are present grossly in 80% of cases. On cut section, mesenchymal harmartomas can have

either mesenchymal predominance (a solid appearance) or cystic predominance (the bulk of the tumor appears as multiloculate cystic masses). Histologically, the tumor consists of cysts, remnants of portal triads, hepatocytes, and fluid-filled mesenchyme.

Incidence and Clinical Presentation

Mesenchymal hamartoma is an uncommon lesion, accounting for 8% of all childhood liver tumors.[118] The majority of cases occur during the first 3 years of life, and there is a slight male predominance.[117] Clinically, slow, progressive, painless abdominal enlargement is seen. Sometimes rapid enlargement may occur because of rapid accumulation of fluid in the cyst. This enlargement may occasionally cause respiratory distress and edema of the lower extremities.[120]

Plain Radiographic Findings

This large tumor manifests as a noncalcified right upper quadrant soft tissue mass on radiographs.

Ultrasound

Sonography demonstrates either large cysts within internal septa (cystic predominance) or, less commonly, smaller cysts with thick septa (mesenchymal predominance).[119]

Computed Tomography

On CT, these tumors appear as well-defined masses with central hypodense areas and internal septa (Fig. 88-28A). Both solid and cystic components may be distinguished.[119,121] Following the administration of contrast media, enhancement of the solid areas may be detectable.[112]

Angiography

Angiography shows a hypovascular or avascular mass causing displacement of vessels. Hypervascularity has been described in the solid portions.[121,122]

Magnetic Resonance Imaging

The MRI appearance of mesenchymal hamartoma depends on whether an individual lesion is predominantly stromal or cystic. For lesions with stromal predominance, the intensity on T1-weighted images is lower than that of the normal liver because of increased fibrosis. Conversely, if there is cystic predominance, the mesenchymal hamartoma is predominantly hypointense on T1-weighted images and markedly hyperintense on T2-weighted images (Fig. 88-28B). On T2-weighted images, multiple septa can be seen transversing the tumor, indicating that the mass is not a simple cyst.[115] The stromal components may enhance after the administration of gadolinium-chelate agents.[123]

Summary

Mesenchymal hamartoma is a rare liver tumor that occurs in the first 2 years of life. Hepatoblastoma and IHE have a similar age presentation but are solid, whereas mesenchymal hamartomas are predominantly cystic.

Mesenchymal hamartoma is not a neoplasm but a failure of normal development. Therefore, it does not require extensive surgery; single excision, marsupialization, or incisional drainage may be sufficient therapy.

Mesenchymal hamartoma should not be confused with other cystic-appearing masses that may occur in the liver of toddlers, such as abscesses or hematomas.

MISCELLANEOUS BENIGN TUMORS

Bile Duct Adenoma

This benign, solitary, small (<1 cm) mass is composed of small bile ducts and is discovered incidentally at autopsy.[2]

Lymphangiomatosis

Hepatic lymphangiomatosis is defined by the presence of multiple masses composed of prominent lymphatic channels that compress the normal hepatic architecture.[2] Usually, it is part of a systemic syndrome in which other organs, including the spleen, skeleton, soft tissues, lung, and/or brain, are also involved.

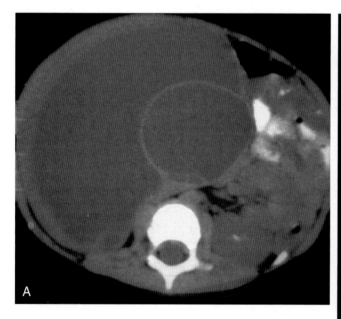

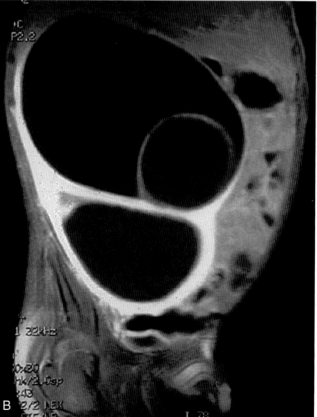

Figure 88-28. Mesenchymal hamartoma: CT (**A**) and MRI appearance (**B**). The lesion is markedly cystic and has septae.

Leiomyoma

This extremely rare lesion is a well-circumscribed smooth muscle tumor arising in the liver with nonspecific radiologic characteristics.[124] Several cases of leiomyoma have recently been reported in adults and children infected with HIV, sug- gesting that there may be a clinical association between these two entities.[125-127] On ultrasound examination, the lesion may appear solid or hypoechoic with internal echoes.[126,127] Leio- myomas are of low attenuation relative to the liver on non- contrast CT scans and display two distinct enhancement patterns: peripheral rim enhancement similar to abscesses or

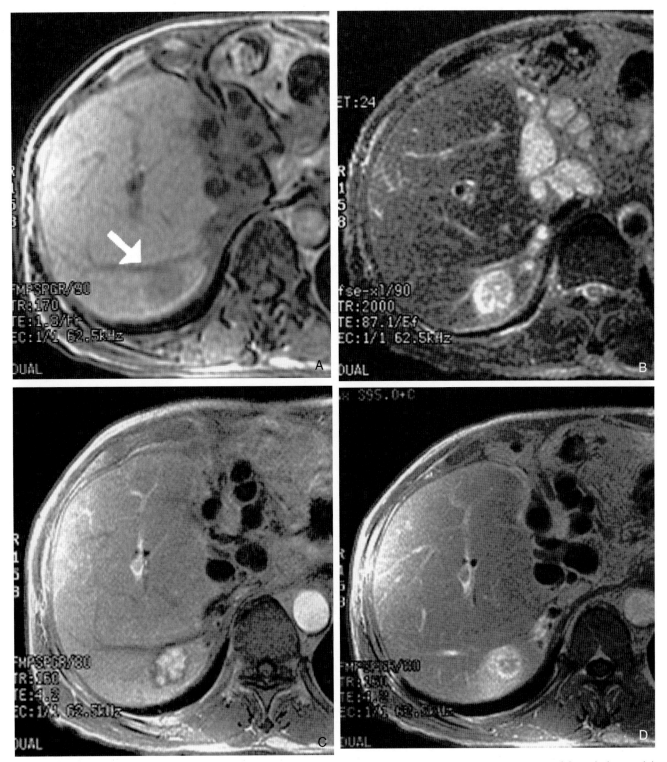

Figure 88-29. Inflammatory pseudotumor. A. T1-weighted MR image shows a hypointense lesion in the posterior aspect of the right hepatic lobe (*arrow*). **B.** The lesion is hyperintense on T2-weighted images. Note the dilated biliary ducts due to cholangitis. **C.** Gadolinium-enhanced arterial phase T1-weighted MR image shows enhancing inflammatory pseudotumor. **D.** On the delayed phase images, the enhancement of the liver parenchyma surrounding the tumor indicates inflammation. (Courtesy of Dr. Tomoaki Ichikawa, Yamanashi University, Yamanashi, Japan.)

homogeneous enhancement resembling hemangioma.[125-127] On MRI, leiomyomas are hypointense relative to the liver on T1-weighted images and hyperintense on T2-weighted images.[126,127]

Fibroma (Fibrous Mesothelioma)

Fibrous mesotheliomas are rare tumors that localize on the surface of the liver.[41,128] They are usually large and consist histologically of spindle cells and collagen.

Adrenal Rest Tumor

Adrenal rest tumors are derived from ectopic adrenal tissue that is histologically identical to that in adrenocortical tumors. They are extremely rare.[129]

Pancreatic Heterotopia

Ectopic pancreas in the liver has been rarely described.[130,131]

Inflammatory Pseudotumor

Inflammatory pseudotumor is a rare uncommon space-occupying lesion. It is characterized by proliferating fibrovascular tissue mixed with inflammatory cells. The exact etiology of this entity is uncertain, but it has been stated that inflammatory pseudotumors have been associated with lymphoma or inflammatory processes, including inflammatory bowel disease and primary sclerosing cholangitis. Interestingly, they appear to be more common in non-European populations such as southeast Asians.[132] Inflammatory pseudotumors do not require surgical resection and typically resolve completely.[18] On the other hand, it may be challenging to differentiate them from malignant liver neoplasms or abscesses.

Inflammatory pseudotumor is usually large (>3 cm) at presentation. The ultrasound appearance may be hypoechoic, isoechoic, or hyperechoic. On nonenhanced CT images, the lesion is hypodense or isodense with the liver. At contrast-enhanced dynamic CT imaging, pseudotumors show early arterial enhancement and they are almost isodense or slightly hyperdense in portal venous phase.[18] Delayed phase images may show increased contrast retention within the lesion relatively to normal liver parenchyma. The signal intensity on both precontrast T1- and T2-weighted images varies from hypointense to hyperintense. The most common, although nonspecific, precontrast MRI finding is hyperintensity on T2-weighted images[133] (Fig. 88-29). Contrast enhancement patterns on MRI are similar to those observed on CT. Because of the nonspecific imaging characteristics of this entity, a core biopsy is usually required for accurate diagnosis.

References

1. Burns PN, Wilson SR: Focal liver masses: Enhancement patterns on contrast-enhanced images—concordance of US scans with CT scans and MR images. Radiology 242:162-174, 2007.
2. Terkivatan T, Hussain SM, De Man RA, Ijzermans JN: Diagnosis and treatment of benign focal liver lesions. Scand J Gastroenterol Suppl 243:102-115, 2006.
3. Ros PR, Lubbers PR, Olmsted WW, et al: Hemangioma of the liver: Magnetic resonance-gross morphologic correlation. AJR 149:1167-1170, 1987.
4. Karhunen PJ: Benign hepatic tumors and tumor-like conditions in men. J Clin Pathol 39:183-188, 1986.
5. Ros PR: Computed tomography: Pathologic correlations in hepatic tumors. In Ferrucci JT, Mathieu DG (eds): Advances in Hepatobiliary Radiology. St. Louis, CV Mosby, 1990, pp 75-108.
6. Vilgrain V, Uzan F, Brancatelli G, et al: Prevalence of hepatic hemangioma in patients with focal nodular hyperplasia: MR imaging analysis. Radiology 229:75-79, 2003.
7. Ros PR, Rasmussen JF, Li KCP: Radiology of malignant and benign liver tumors. Curr Probl Diagn Radiol 18:95-155, 1989.
8. Moihuddin M, Allison JR, Montgomery JH, et al: Scintigraphic diagnosis of hepatic hemangioma: Its role in the management of hepatic mass lesions. AJR 145:223-228, 1985.
9. Schillaci O, Filippi L, Danieli R, et al: Single-photon emission computed tomography/computed tomography in abdominal diseases. Semin Nucl Med 37:48-61, 2007.
10. Buetow PR, Buck JL, Ros PR, et al: Malignant vascular tumors of the liver: Radiologic-pathologic correlation. RadioGraphics 14:153-166, 1994.
11. Schillaci O, Danieli R, Manni C, et al: Technetium-99m-labelled red blood cell imaging in the diagnosis of hepatic haemangiomas: The role of SPECT/CT with a hybrid camera. Eur J Nucl Med Mol Imaging 31:1011-1015, 2004.
12. Heiken JP: Liver. In Lee JKT, Sagel SS, Stanley RJ, et al (eds): Computed Body Tomography with MRI Correlation, 3rd ed. Philadelphia, Lippincott-Raven, 1998, pp 701-778.
13. Celli N, Gaiani S, Piscaglia F, et al: Characterization of liver lesions by real-time contrast-enhanced ultrasonography. Eur J Gastroenterol Hepatol 19:3-14, 2007.
14. Kim SH, Lee JM, Kim KG, et al: Comparison of fundamental sonography, tissue-harmonic sonography, fundamental compound sonography, and tissue-harmonic compound sonography for focal hepatic lesions. Eur Radiol 16:2444-2453, 2006.
15. Dietrich CF: Characterisation of focal liver lesions with contrast enhanced ultrasonography. Eur J Radiol 51(suppl):S9-S17, 2004.
16. Brannigan M, Burns PN, Wilson SR: Blood flow patterns in focal liver lesions at microbubble-enhanced US. RadioGraphics 24:921-935, 2004.
17. Vilgrain V, Boulos L, Vullierme MP, et al: Imaging of atypical hemangiomas of the liver with pathologic correlation. RadioGraphics 20:379-397, 2000.
18. Ibrahim S, Chen CL, Wang SH, et al: Liver resection for benign liver tumors: Indications and outcome. Am J Surg 93:5-9, 2007.
19. Leslie DF, Johnson CD, Johnson CM, et al: Distinction between cavernous hemangiomas of the liver and hepatic metastases on CT: Value of contrast enhancement patterns. AJR 164:625-629, 1995.
20. Yamashita Y, Ogata I, Urata J, et al: Cavernous hemangioma of the liver: Pathologic correlation with dynamic CT findings. Radiology 203:121-125, 1997.
21. Kim T, Federle MP, Baron RL, et al: Discrimination of small hepatic hemangiomas from hypervascular malignant tumors smaller than 3 cm with three-phase helical CT. Radiology 219:699-706, 2001.
22. Quinn SF, Benjamin GG: Hepatic cavernous hemangiomas: Simple diagnostic sign with dynamic bolus CT. Radiology 182:545-548, 1992.
23. Mergo PJ, Ros PR: Benign lesions of the liver. Radiol Clin North Am 36:319-332, 1998.
24. Semelka RC: Liver. In Semelka RC, Ascher SM, Reinhold C (eds): MRI of the Abdomen and Pelvis. New York, Wiley-Liss, 1997, pp 19-136.
25. Siegelman ES, Outwater EK: MR imaging techniques of the liver. Radiol Clin North Am 36:263-287, 1998.
26. Schima W, Saini S, Echeverri JA, et al: Focal liver lesions: Characterization with conventional spin-echo T2-weighted MR imaging. Radiology 202:389-394, 1997.
27. Soyer P, Bluemke DA, Rymer R: MR imaging of the liver: Technique. Magn Reson Imaging Clin North Am 5:205-222, 1997.
28. Yoshida H, Itai Y, Ohtomo K, et al: Small hepatocellular carcinoma and cavernous hemangioma: Differentiation with dynamic FLASH MR imaging with Gd-DTPA. Radiology 171:339-342, 1989.
29. Ohtomo K, Itai Y, Yoshikawa K, et al: Hepatic tumors: Dynamic MR imaging. Radiology 163:27-31, 1987.
30. Motohara T, Semelka RC, Nagase L: MR imaging of benign hepatic tumors. Magn Reson Imaging Clin N Am 10:1-14, 2002.
31. Kamel IR, Bluemke DA: MR imaging of liver tumors. Radiol Clin North Am 41:51-65, 2003.
32. Semelka RC, Brown ED, Ascher SM, et al: Hepatic hemangiomas: A multi-institutional study of appearance on T2-weighted and serial gadolinium-enhanced gradient-echo MR images. Radiology 192:401-406, 1994.

33. Whitney WS, Herfkens RJ, Jeffrey RB, et al: Dynamic breath-hold multi-planar spoiled gradient-recalled MR imaging with gadolinium enhancement for differentiating hepatic hemangiomas from malignancies at 1.5T. Radiology 189:863-870, 1993.

34. Caseiro-Alves F, Brito J, Araujo AE, et al: Liver haemangioma: Common and uncommon findings and how to improve the differential diagnosis. Eur Radiol [Epub ahead of print], 2007.

35. Saini S, Edelman RR, Sharma P, et al: Blood-pool MR contrast material for detection and characterization of focal hepatic lesions: Initial clinical experience with ultrasmall superparamagnetic iron oxide (AMI-227). AJR 164:1147-1152, 1995.

36. Kim MJ, Kim JH, Chung JJ, et al: Focal hepatic lesions: Detection and characterization with combination gadolinium- and superparamagnetic iron oxide-enhanced MR imaging. Radiology 228:719-26, 2003.

37. Nelson RC, Chezmar JL: Diagnostic approach to hepatic hemangiomas. Radiology 176:11-13, 1990.

38. Goodman ZD: Benign tumors of the liver. In Okuda K, Ishak KG (eds): Neoplasms of the Liver. Tokyo, Springer-Verlag, 1987, pp 105-125.

39. Wanless IR, Albrecht S, Bilbow J, et al: Multiple focal nodular hyperplasia associated with vascular malformation of various organs and neoplasia of the brain: A new syndrome. Mod Pathol 2:456-462, 1989.

40. Wanless IR, Mawdsley C, Adams R: On the pathogenesis of focal nodular hyperplasia of the liver. Hepatology 5:1194-1200, 1985.

41. Ishak KG: Benign tumors and pseudotumors of the liver. Appl Pathol 6:82-104, 1988.

42. Bioulac-Sage P, Balabaud C, Bedossa P, et al: Pathological diagnosis of liver cell adenoma and focal nodular hyperplasia: Bordeaux update. J Hepatol 46:521-527, 2007.

43. Welch TJ, Sheedy PF II, Johnson CM, et al: Focal nodular hyperplasia and hepatic adenoma: Comparison of angiography, CT, US and scintigraphy. Radiology 156:593-595, 1985.

44. Shen YH, Fan J, Wu ZQ, et al: Focal nodular hyperplasia of the liver in 86 patients. Hepatobiliary Pancreat Dis Int 6:52-57, 2007.

45. Kurtaran A, Becherer A, Pfeffel F, et al: 18F-fluorodeoxyglucose (FDG)-PET features of focal nodular hyperplasia (FNH) of the liver. Liver 20:487-490, 2000.

46. Kamel IR, Liapi E, Fishman EK: Focal nodular hyperplasia: Lesion evaluation using 16-MDCT and 3D CT angiography. AJR Am J Roentgenol 186:1587-1596, 2006.

47. Caseiro-Alves F, Zins M, Mahfouz A-E, et al: Calcification in focal nodular hyperplasia: A new problem for differentiation from fibrolamellar hepatocellular carcinoma. Radiology 198:889-892, 1996.

48. Huang-Wei C, Bleuzen A, Bourlier P, et al: Differential diagnosis of focal nodular hyperplasia with quantitative parametric analysis in contrast-enhanced sonography. Invest Radiol 41:363-368, 2006.

49. Huang-Wei C, Bleuzen A, Olar M, et al: Role of parametric imaging in contrast-enhanced sonography of hepatic focal nodular hyperplasia. J Clin Ultrasound 34:367-373, 2006.

50. Mortele KJ, Praet M, Van Vlierberghe H, et al: CT and MR imaging findings in focal nodular hyperplasia of the liver: Radiologic-pathologic correlation. AJR 175:687-692, 2000.

51. Buetow PC, Pantongrag-Brown L, Buck JL, et al: Focal nodular hyperplasia of the liver: Radiologic-pathologic correlation. RadioGraphics 16:369-388, 1996.

52. Hussain SM, Terkivatan T, Zondervan PE, et al: Focal nodular hyperplasia: Findings at state-of-the-art MR imaging, US, CT, and pathologic analysis. RadioGraphics 24:3-17, 2004.

53. Brancatelli G, Federle MP, Grazioli L, et al: Focal nodular hyperplasia: CT findings with emphasis on multiphasic helical CT in 78 patients. Radiology 219:61-68, 2001.

54. Lizardi-Cervera J, Cuellar-Gamboa L, Motola-Kuba D: Focal nodular hyperplasia and hepatic adenoma: A review. Ann Hepatol 5:206-211, 2006.

55. Mahfouz A-E, Hamm B, Taupitz M, et al: Hypervascular liver lesions: Differentiation of focal nodular hyperplasia from malignant tumors with dynamic gadolinium-enhanced MR imaging. Radiology 186:133-138, 1993.

56. Terkivatan T, van den Bos IC, Hussain SM, et al: Focal nodular hyperplasia: Lesion characteristics on state-of-the-art MRI including dynamic gadolinium-enhanced and superparamagnetic iron-oxide-uptake sequences in a prospective study. J Magn Reson Imaging 24:864-872, 2006.

57. Marin D, Iannaccone R, Laghi A, et al: Focal nodular hyperplasia: Intraindividual comparison of dynamic gadobenate dimeglumine- and ferucarbotran-enhanced magnetic resonance imaging. J Magn Reson Imaging 25:775-782, 2007.

58. Paley MR, Mergo PJ, Ros PR: Characterization of focal liver lesions with SPIO-enhanced T2WI: Patterns of signal intensity and liver lesion contrast change. Radiology 205:455-456, 1997.

59. Mathieu D, Vilgrain V, Mahfouz A-E, et al: Benign liver tumors. MRI Clin North Am 5:255-258, 1997.

60. Wanless IR, Albrecht S, Bilbao J, et al: Multiple focal nodular hyperplasia of the liver associated with vascular malformations of various organs and neoplasia of the brain: A new syndrome. Mod Pathol 2:456-462, 1989.

61. Nguyen BN, Flejou JF, Terris B, et al: Focal nodular hyperplasia of the liver: A comprehensive pathologic study of 305 lesions and recognition of new histologic forms. Am J Surg Pathol 23:1441-1454, 1999.

62. Attal P, Vilgrain V, Brancatelli G, et al: Telangiectatic focal nodular hyperplasia: US, CT, and MR imaging findings with histopathologic correlation in 13 cases. Radiology 228:465-472, 2003.

63. Brancatelli G, Federle MP, Vullierme MP, et al: CT and MR imaging evaluation of hepatic adenoma. J Comput Assist Tomogr 30:745-750, 2006.

64. Grazioli L, Federle MP, Brancatelli G, et al: Hepatic adenomas: Imaging and pathologic findings. RadioGraphics 21:877-892, 2001.

65. Rooks JB, Ory HW, Ishak KG, et al: Epidemiology of hepatocellular adenoma: The role of contraceptive steroid use. JAMA 242:644-648, 1979.

66. Christopherson WM, Mays ET, Barrows G: A clinicopathologic study of steroid-related tumors. Am J Surg Pathol 1:31-41, 1977.

67. Anderson PH, Packer JT: Hepatic adenoma: Observations after estrogen withdrawal. Arch Surg 111:898-900, 1976.

68. Golli M, Nhieu JTV, Mathieu D, et al: Hepatocellular adenoma: Color Doppler US and pathologic correlations. Radiology 190:741-744, 1994.

69. Dietrich CF, Ignee A, Trojan J, et al: Improved characterisation of histologically proven liver tumours by contrast enhanced ultrasonography during the portal venous and specific late phase of SHU 508A. Gut 53:401-405, 2004.

70. Bluemke DA, Soyer P, Fishman EK: Helical (spiral) CT of the liver. Radiol Clin North Am 33:863-886, 1995.

71. Goldstein HM, Neiman HL, Mena E, et al: Angiographic findings in benign liver cell tumors. Radiology 110:339-343, 1974.

72. Freeny PC: Angiography of hepatic neoplasms. Semin Roentgenol 18:114-122, 1983.

73. Hussain SM, van den Bos IC, Dwarkasing RS, et al: Hepatocellular adenoma: Findings at state-of-the-art magnetic resonance imaging, ultrasound, computed tomography and pathologic analysis. Eur Radiol 16:1873-1886, 2006.

74. Arrive L, Flejou J-F, Vilgrain V, et al: Hepatic adenoma: MR findings in 51 pathologically proved lesions. Radiology 193:507-512, 1994.

75. Chen KT, Bocian JJ: Multiple hepatic adenomas. Arch Pathol Lab Med 107:274-275, 1983.

76. Lewin M, Handra-Luca A, Arrive L, et al: Liver adenomatosis: Classification of MR imaging features and comparison with pathologic findings. Radiology 241:433-440, 2006.

77. Steiner PE: Nodular regenerative hyperplasia of the liver. Am J Pathol 49:943-953, 1959.

78. Stromeyer FW, Ishak KG: Nodular transformation (nodular "regenerative" hyperplasia) of the liver. A clinicopathological study of 30 cases. Hum Pathol 12:60-71, 1981.

79. Wanless IR, Todwin TA, Allen F, et al: Nodular regenerative hyperplasia of the liver in hematologic disorders, a possible response to obliterative portal venopathy: A morphometric study of nine cases with an hypothesis on the pathogenesis. Medicine (Baltimore) 49:367-379, 1980.

80. Wanless IR, Solt LC, Kortan P, et al: Nodular regenerative hyperplasia of the liver associated with macroglubulinemia. Am J Med 170:1203-1209, 1981.

81. Nakanuma Y, Ohta G, Sasaki K: Nodular regenerative hyperplasia of the liver associated with polyarteritis nodosa. Arch Pathol Lab Med 108:133-135, 1984.

82. Dachman AH, Ros PR, Goodman ZD, et al: Nodular regenerative hyperplasia of the liver: Clinical and radiologic observations. AJR 148:717-722, 1987.

83. Mones JM, Saldana MJ: Nodular regenerative hyperplasia of the liver in a 4-month-old infant. Am J Dis Child 138:79-81, 1984.

84. Siegelman ES, Outwater EK, Furth EE, et al: MR imaging of hepatic nodular regenerative hyperplasia. JMRI 5:730-732, 1995.

85. Goodman ZD, Ishak KG: Angiomyolipomas of the liver. Am J Surg Pathol 8:745-750, 1984.

86. Roberts JL, Fishman EK, Hartman DS, et al: Lipomatous tumors of the liver: Evaluation with CT and US. Radiology 158:613-617, 1986.

87. Prayer LM, Schurawitzki HJ, Wimberger DM: Case report: Lipoma of the liver: Ultrasound, CT and MR imaging. Clin Radiol 45:353-354, 1992.

88. Bret PM, Bretagnolle M, Gaillard D: Small asymptomatic angiomyolipomas of the kidney. Radiology 154:7-10, 1985.

89. Murakami T, Nakamura H, Hori S, et al: Angiomyolipoma of the liver. Ultrasound, CT, MR imaging and angiography. Acta Radiol 34:392-394, 1993.

90. Hooper LD, Mergo PJ, Ros PR: Multiple hepatorenal angiomyolipomas: Diagnosis with fat suppression, gadolinium-enhanced MRI. Abdom Imaging 19:549-551, 1994.

91. Ros PR: Hepatic angiomyolipoma: Is fat in the liver friend or foe? Abdom Imaging 19:552-553, 1994.

92. Valls C, Iannacconne R, Alba E, et al: Fat in the liver: Diagnosis and characterization. Eur Radiol 16:2292-2308, 2006.

93. Murphy BJ, Casillas J, Ros PR, et al: The CT appearance of cystic masses of the liver. RadioGraphics 9:307-322, 1989.

94. Litwin DE, Taylor BR, Langer B, et al: Nonparasitic cysts of the liver: The case for conservative surgical management. Ann Surg 205:405-408, 1991.

95. Sanfelippo PM, Beahrs OH, Weiland LK: Cystic diseases of the liver. Ann Surg 179:922-925, 1974.

96. Bosniak MA, Ambos MA: Polycystic kidney disease. Semin Roentgenol 10:133-143, 1975.

97. Mortele KJ, Ros PR. Cystic focal liver lesions in the adult: Differential CT and MR imaging features. RadioGraphics 21:895-910, 2001.

98. Kairaluoma M, Leinonen A, Stahlberg MM, et al: Percutaneous aspiration and alcohol sclerotherapy for symptomatic hepatic cysts. Ann Surg 210:208-215, 1989.

99. Bean WJ, Rodan BA: Hepatic cysts: Treatment with alcohol. AJR 144:237-241, 1985.

100. Levine E, Cook LT, Grantham JJ: Liver cysts in autosomal-dominant polycystic kidney disease: Clinical and computed tomographic study. AJR 145:229-233, 1985.

101. Kerr DN, Harrison CV, Sherlock S, et al: Congenital hepatic fibrosis. Q J Med 30:91-133, 1961.

102. McLean RH, Moller JH, Warwick WJ: Multinodular hemangiomatosis of the liver in infancy. Pediatrics 49:563-573, 1972.

103. Dehner LP: Hepatic tumors in the pediatric age group: A distinctive clinicopathologic spectrum. Perspect Pediatr Pathol 4:217-268, 1978.

104. Mortele KJ, Vanzieleghem B, Mortele B, et al: Solitary hepatic infantile hemangioendothelioma: Dynamic gadolinium-enhanced MR imaging findings. Eur Radiol 12:862-5, 2002.

105. Earnest F 4th, Johnson CD: Hepatic epithelioid hemangioendothelioma. Radiology 240:295-298, 2006.

106. Braun P, Ducharme JC, Riopelle JL, et al: Hemangiomatosis of the liver in infants. J Pediatr Surg 10:121-126, 1975.

107. Roos JE, Pfiffner R, Stallmach T, et al: Infantile hemangioendothelioma. RadioGraphics 23:1649-1655, 2003.

108. Alomari AI: The lollipop sign: A new cross-sectional sign of hepatic epithelioid hemangioendothelioma. Eur J Radiol 59:460-464, 2006.

109. Weiner SN, Parulekar SG: Scintigraphy and ultrasonography of hepatic hemangioma. Radiology 132:149-153, 1979.

110. Pardes JG, Bryan PJ, Gauderer MWL: Spontaneous regression of infantile hemangioendotheliomatosis of the liver. J Ultrasound Med 1:349-353, 1982.

111. Pobiel RS, Bisset GS III: Pictorial essay: Imaging of liver tumors in the infant and child. Pediatr Radiol 25:495-506, 1995.

112. Helmberger TK, Ros PR, Mergo PJ, et al: Pediatric liver neoplasms: A radiologic-pathologic correlation. Eur Radiol. 9:1339-1347, 1999.

113. Slovis TL, Berdon WE, Haller JO, et al: Hemangiomas of the liver in infants. AJR 123:791-801, 1975.

114. Moss AA, Clark RE, Palubinskas AJ, et al: Angiographic appearance of benign and malignant hepatic tumors in infants and children. AJR 113:61-69, 1971.

115. O'Neil J, Ros PR: Knowing hepatic pathology aids MRI of liver tumors. Diagn Imaging 19:58-67, 1989.

116. Dehner LP, Ewing SL, Sumner HW: Infantile mesenchymal hamartoma of the liver. Histologic and ultrastructural observations. Arch Pathol Lab Med 99:379-382, 1975.

117. Stocker JT, Ishak KG: Mesenchymal hamartoma of the liver: Report of 30 cases and review of the literature. Pediatr Pathol 1:245-267, 1983.

118. Molina EG, Schiff ER: Benign solid lesions of the liver. In Schiff ER, Sorrell MF, Maddrey WC (eds): Diseases of the Liver, 8th ed. Philadelphia, Lippincott Williams & Wilkins, 1999, pp 1245-1268.

119. Ros PR, Goodman ZD, Ishak KG, et al: Mesenchymal hamartoma of the liver: Radiologic-pathologic correlation. Radiology 158:619-624, 1986.

120. Stringer MD: The role of liver transplantation in the management of paediatric liver tumours. Ann R Coll Surg Engl 89:12-21, 2007.

121. Stanley P, Hall TR, Woolley MM, et al: Mesenchymal hamartomas of the liver in childhood: Sonographic and CT findings. AJR 147:1035-1039, 1986.

122. Kaude JV, Felman AH, Hawkins IF: Ultrasonography in primary hepatic tumors in early childhood. Pediatr Radiol 9:77-83, 1980.

123. Siegel MJ, Hoffer FA. Magnetic resonance imaging of nongynecologic pelvic masses in children. Magn Reson Imaging Clin N Am.10:325-344, 2002

124. Hawkins EP, Jordan GL, McGavran MH: Primary leiomyoma of the liver. Successful treatment by lobectomy and presentation of criteria for diagnosis. Am J Surg Pathol 4:301-304, 1980.

125. Mueller BU, Butler KM, Higham MC, et al: Smooth muscle tumors in children with human immunodeficiency virus infection. Pediatrics 90:460-463, 1992.

126. Reinertson TE, Fortune JB, Peters JC, et al: Primary leiomyoma of the liver: A case report and review of the literature. Dig Dis Sci 37:622-627, 1992.

127. Wachsberg RH, Cho KC, Adekosan A: Two leiomyomas of the liver in an adult with AIDS: CT and MR appearance. J Comput Assist Tomogr 18:156-157, 1994.

128. Saul SH: Masses of the liver. In Sternberg SS (ed): Diagnostic Surgical Pathology, 3rd ed. Philadelphia, Lippincott Williams & Wilkins, 1999, pp 1553-1628.

129. Wilkins L, Ravich MM: Adrenocortical tumor arising in the liver of a three-year-old boy with signs of virilism and Cushing's syndrome. Report of a case with cure after partial resection of the right lobe of the liver. Pediatrics 9:671-680, 1952.

130. Mobini J, Krouse TB, Cooper DR: Intrahepatic pancreatic heterotopia. Review and report of a case presenting as an abdominal mass. Am J Dig Dis 19:64-70, 1974.

131. Wanless IR: Anatomy and developmental anomalies of the liver. In Feldman M, Scharschmidt BF, Sleisinger MH (eds): Sleisinger and Fordtran's Gastrointestinal and Liver Disease, 6th ed. Philadelphia, WB Saunders, 1998, pp 1055-1060.

132. Koea JB, Broadhurst GW, Rodgers MS, McCall JL. Inflammatory pseudotumor of the liver: Demographics, diagnosis, and the case for nonoperative management. J Am Coll Surg 196:226-235, 2003.

133. Mortele KJ, Wiesner W, de Hemptinne B, et al: Multifocal inflammatory pseudotumor of the liver: Dynamic gadolinium enhanced, ferumoxides-enhanced, and mangafodipir trisodium-enhanced MR imaging findings. Eur Radiol 12:304-308, 2002.

Malignant Tumors of the Liver

Pablo R. Ros, MD • Sukru Mehmet Erturk, MD

Primary malignant neoplasms of the liver are classified by the cell of origin (Table 89-1). Secondary malignant liver tumors are metastases and lymphomas. Overall, metastases are the most frequent malignant tumors of the liver, except in patients with preexisting cirrhosis, in whom primary malignancies are more frequent.[1]

In this chapter, primary malignant liver tumors of hepatocyte origin are discussed first: hepatocellular carcinoma (HCC),

Table 89-1
Malignant Liver Tumors

Hepatocellular Origin
Hepatocellular carcinoma
Atypical hepatocellular carcinoma
Clear cell carcinoma
Giant cell carcinoma
Childhood hepatocellular carcinoma
Carcinosarcoma
Fibrolamellar carcinoma
Hepatoblastoma
Sclerosing hepatic carcinoma

Cholangiocellular Origin
Cholangiocarcinoma
Cystadenocarcinoma

Mesenchymal Origin
Angiosarcoma
Epithelioid hemangioendothelioma
Leiomyosarcoma
Fibrosarcoma
Malignant fibrous histiocytoma
Primary lymphoma
Primary hepatic osteosarcoma

fibrolamellar carcinoma (FLC), and hepatoblastoma. Intrahepatic carcinoma and cystadenocarcinoma that arise from biliary cells are then considered. Angiosarcoma, undifferentiated (embryonal) sarcoma (UES), epithelial hemangioendothelioma (EHE), and other mesenchymal sarcomas that originate in the mesenchymal tissue are reviewed. Finally, the secondary liver tumors, lymphomas and metastases, are discussed.

HEPATOCELLULAR CARCINOMA

Pathologic Findings

Hepatocellular carcinoma (HCC) is the most common primary hepatic tumor and one of the most common visceral malignancies worldwide.[2] Terms such as hepatoma and primary liver cancer are often used synonymously with HCC, but they should be avoided in the interest of clarity and the term *hepatocellular carcinoma* should be encouraged.[3]

HCC is a malignant lesion composed of cells that attempt to differentiate into normal liver, mimicking hepatocyte cords. However, their abnormal growth prevents the malignant hepatocytes from forming normal hepatic acini. Several clinical and histologic patterns occur, and the prognosis differs according to the associated condition (e.g., cirrhosis) and the extent of the tumor at diagnosis.[2]

Grossly, there are three major patterns of growth (Fig. 89-1): (1) single or massive HCC characterized by the presence of a solitary, often large, mass; (2) nodular or multifocal HCC, in which multiple well-separated nodules are seen throughout the liver, mimicking the appearance of metastases; and (3) diffuse or cirrhotomimetic HCC, in which multiple small foci are seen throughout the liver in a diffuse manner.

A gross variant, encapsulated HCC, has a better prognosis because of its greater resectability[4,5] (Fig. 89-2).

Regardless of its gross appearance, HCC is a soft tumor that frequently undergoes necroses and hemorrhages because of lack of stroma. Vascular invasion of perihepatic vessels is common.[6] Conversely, biliary invasion is uncommon.[6]

Microscopically, the cells of HCC resemble normal liver cells and it is often difficult to distinguish normal hepatocytes from cells of HCC and/or hepatocellular adenoma.[7] This is

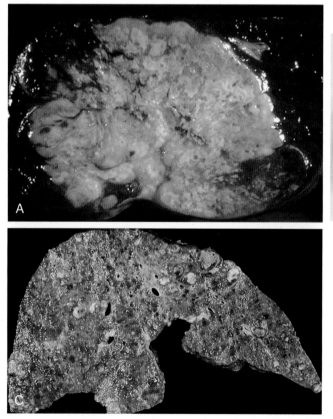

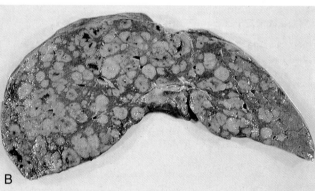

Figure 89-1. Hepatocellular carcinoma (HCC): gross forms. A. Single or massive form. Large mass occupies the right lobe of the liver. **B.** Multifocal or nodular HCC in a cirrhotic liver. Multiple independent tumor nodules are identified. This appearance resembles metastases. **C.** Diffuse or cirrhotomimetic HCC. This cut section shows innumerable nodules of HCC, ranging from several centimeters to subcentimeter in size, replacing the normal liver. In these cases, HCC may be indistinguishable from cirrhosis with macroregenerating nodule on imaging.

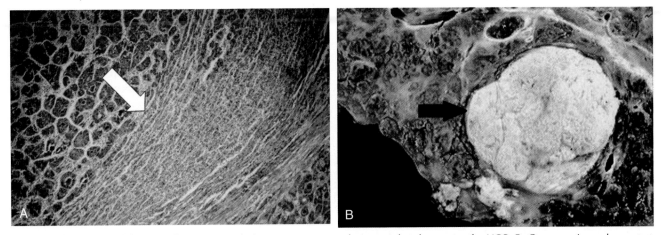

Figure 89-2. Encapsulated HCC. A. Photomicrograph demonstrates a capsule (*arrow*) that demarcates the HCC. **B.** Gross specimen demonstrates bands of fibrous tissue (*arrow*) that surrounds this HCC.

of considerable importance when planning an aspiration biopsy of a focal liver lesion. In some cases, the malignant hepatocytes are so well differentiated that they even produce bile, which is seen in tumor cells and in biliary canaliculi. A variety of products can be produced by the abnormal hepatocytes of HCC: Mallory bodies, α-fetoprotein, α_1-antitrypsin, and other serum proteins. Fat and glycogen are often present in the cytoplasm of HCC hepatocytes. If there are large amounts of fat, the tumor is called clear cell carcinoma of the liver.

The most frequent HCC histologic growth pattern is trabecular, in which the tumor cells attempt to recapitulate the cords seen in normal liver.[8] The trabeculae are separated by vascular spaces with no stroma or supportive connective tissue. Occasionally, the center of the trabeculae contains tumor secretions, giving the tumor a pseudoglandular or acinar pattern. In other cases, the trabeculae grow together, producing a solid pattern (Fig. 89-3).

These microscopic variations are important for the radiologist to appreciate because cellular HCCs may appear similar to normal liver, so that only subtle changes in density and/or echogenicity may be present. However, if there is fat deposition

or pseudogland formation, the HCC may appear hyperechoic on ultrasound studies, hypodense on computed tomography (CT) scans, and hyperintense on magnetic resonance (MR) imaging.[9]

The radiologic correlates of the pathology of HCCs are listed in Table 89-2.

An important challenge for radiologists and pathologists lies in the early diagnosis of HCC particularly within a cirrhotic liver. Successful treatment of HCCs using any of the available therapies such as surgical resection, liver transplantation, percutaneous ethanol injection, and transcatheter embolization is most likely if the lesion is small, so early detection is critical.[10] With this aim, an attempt has been made to standardize the terminology of nodular liver lesions thereby clarifying the pathogenesis of HCC in the cirrhotic liver and enhancing the early diagnosis of premalignant nodules and small HCCs.[11] A cirrhotic nodule is defined as a regenerative nodule composed of hepatocytes and is largely or completely surrounded by fibrous septa. A "dysplastic" nodule, which is an intermediate stage between a cirrhotic nodule and HCC, is at least 1mm in diameter and contains areas of dysplasia but no histologic evidence of malignancy.[11,12] Synonyms for

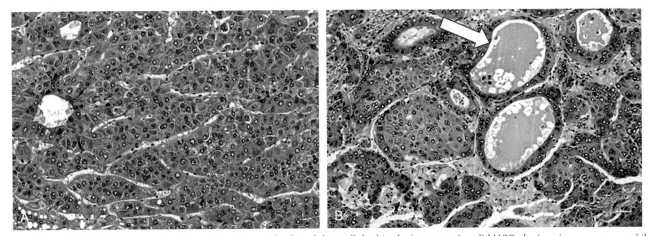

Figure 89-3. HCC: histologic appearance. A. Photomicrograph of a solid or cellular histologic pattern. In solid HCC, the imaging appearance of the tumor is similar to that of normal liver because of its marked cellularity. **B.** Photomicrograph of a well-differentiated HCC with an acinar pattern. Large amounts of tumor secretions are seen within HCC cells (*arrow*). HCCs with large intratumoral secretions have a lower CT density than normal liver. The spectrum of microscopic finds explains the spectrum of radiologic appearances in HCC.

Table 89-2
Imaging Techniques in Liver Neoplasms

To Assess Vascularity
Contrast-enhanced CT
Gadolinium-enhanced MRI
Contrast-enhanced US
Angiograms
Blood pool studies (^{99m}Tc-labeled red blood cells)

To Assess Hepatocyte Function or Biliary Excretion
MRI enhanced with hepatocyte-specific contrast agents

To Assess Metabolic Activity of Neoplasms
^{18}F-FDG-PET imaging

To Assess Kupffer Cell Activity
MRI enhanced with intravenous superparamagnetic iron oxide

To Assess Tumoral Calcification
CT
US
Plain radiographs

To Assess Capsule Presence
CT (enhanced/unenhanced)
US (enhanced/unenhanced)
MRI (enhanced/unenhanced)

To Assess Internal Nature of Neoplasms (e.g., Solid Versus Cystic, Hemorrhage, Fibrosis)
CT
MRI
US

"dysplastic nodule" include "adenomatous hyperplasia" and "macroregenerative nodule."[11] Dysplastic nodules are subdivided into low-grade and high-grade types on the basis of findings at light microscopy.[11] It is widely accepted that dysplastic nodules are premalignant, although the exact mechanisms of transformation of cirrhotic nodule to dysplastic nodule to HCC have yet to be defined.[13]

Incidence and Clinical Presentation

Although histologically HCC has a similar appearance worldwide, it has a bimodal geographic distribution in terms of incidence and clinical presentation. It is rare in the Western hemisphere (low-incidence areas) and relative frequent in sub-Saharan Africa and Asia (high-incidence areas).[14]

Even in the United States, the incidence varies. According to the World Health Organization, the incidence ranges from 0.9 per 100,000 in women in New York to 30.9 per 100,000 in men of Chinese origin in San Francisco.[2] Worldwide, the highest incidence is in Japan, where it is reported to be as high as 4.8%.[15]

Clinically, in the low-incidence areas, symptoms are insidious in onset and include malaise, fever, and abdominal pain.[2,6] Jaundice is rare. Liver function tests are normal and indistinguishable from those in cirrhosis, except for elevation of the α-fetoprotein level. Other proteins produced by HCC may give rise to numerous paraneoplastic syndromes such as erythrocytosis, hypercalcemia, hypoglycemia, hypercholesterolemia, and hirsutism. The usual age of presentation in the low-incidence areas is 70 to 80 years and the male/female ratio is 2.5:1.[2,14] Most patients have a long history of alcoholic cirrhosis, hemochromatosis, or steroid use.

In the high-incidence areas, the age at presentation is younger (30 to 45 years) and men are affected eight times more frequently than women.[14] The primary etiologic factors in high-incidence areas are hepatitis B and C viruses and exposure to aflatoxins. In these areas HCC is aggressive and may present with hepatic rupture and massive hemoperitoneum.[16]

Radiologic Findings

Plain Radiographs

When sufficiently large, HCC may appear as a nonspecific upper abdominal mass on plain abdominal radiographs. Calcification is rare in the typical HCC but more common in other hepatocellular neoplasms such as fibrolamellar carcinoma. In patients with hemochromatosis, plain radiographs of the extremities demonstrate degenerative changes with calcium pyrophosphate deposition disease in cartilages.

Nuclear Scintigraphy

Nuclear scintigraphy is only occasionally used for the detection of HCC. On sulfur colloid studies of Western patients, HCC manifests as a defect in a cirrhotic liver. Hepatomegaly with heterogeneous uptake of the radionuclide and colloid shift to the spleen and bone marrow are frequently noted.[16] It is reported that 30% to 50% of HCC are not ^{18}F-fluorodeoxyglucose (FDG) avid or are only mildly avid[17,18] due to the abundant amount of the enzyme glucose-6-phosphatase in the certain types of HCC. Glucose-6-phosphatase dephosphorylates FDG-6-phosphatase and a result of this, FDG "leaks back" to the circulation. However, the use of ^{11}C acetate as a PET tracer for detection of kinetics and uptake characteristics of fatty acid synthesis in HCC, has shown promising results. Well-differentiated HCC tends to show negative uptake for FDG because of the glucose-6-phosphatase, has uptake of ^{11}C. Unfortunately, ^{11}C has a short half-life of 20 minutes, which leads to the need for an on-site cyclotron. Therefore, routine situations, there is little role of PET or PET/CT in the diagnosis or staging of HCC.

Ultrasound

The sonographic appearance of HCC is varied (Fig. 89-4). These lesions are frequently hyperechoic, particularly if there is fatty change or marked sinusoidal dilatation.[19-21] Ultrasonography can detect extremely small tumors and, when combined with serum α-fetoprotein assays, serves as an excellent screening method for high-risk patients with long-standing cirrhosis.[22,23] This approach to patients has been very successful in Asia but has found to be far less accurate in the United States because of differences in patient body habitus and sonography expertise.

Some authors explain the varied sonographic appearance of HCC on the basis of size. Small HCCs (<3 cm) often appear hypoechoic and are associated with posterior acoustic enhancement, and tumors larger than 3 cm more often have a mosaic or mixed pattern.[24,25,26] Ultrasound is also capable of demonstrating the capsule in encapsulated HCC, which appears as a thin, hypoechoic band.[4]

Sonography, in conjunction with color and duplex Doppler, can diagnose tumor thrombus in the portal and hepatic veins as well as the inferior vena cava.[27,28]

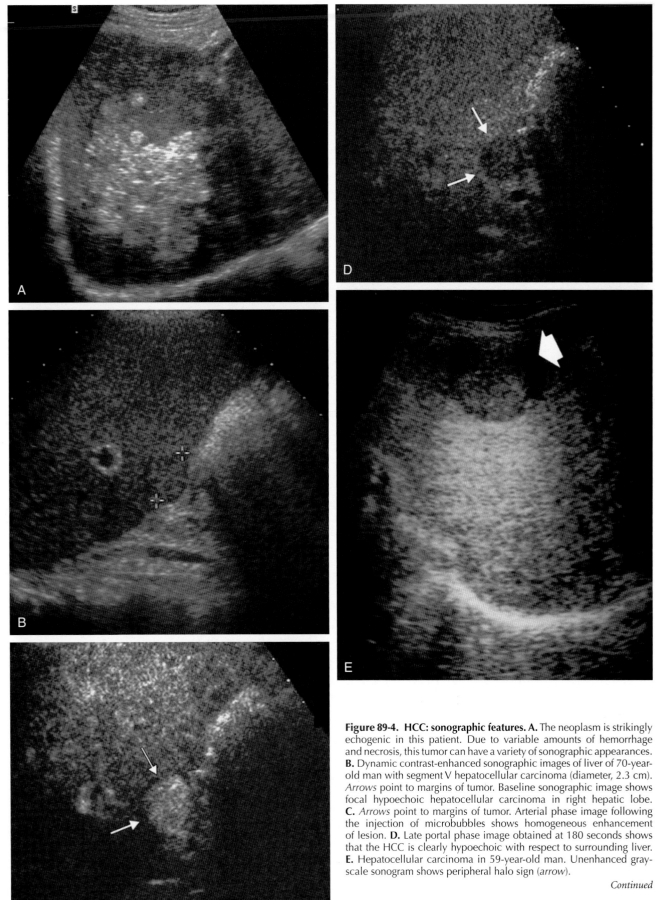

Figure 89-4.   HCC: sonographic features. A. The neoplasm is strikingly echogenic in this patient. Due to variable amounts of hemorrhage and necrosis, this tumor can have a variety of sonographic appearances. **B.** Dynamic contrast-enhanced sonographic images of liver of 70-year-old man with segment V hepatocellular carcinoma (diameter, 2.3 cm). *Arrows* point to margins of tumor. Baseline sonographic image shows focal hypoechoic hepatocellular carcinoma in right hepatic lobe. **C.** *Arrows* point to margins of tumor. Arterial phase image following the injection of microbubbles shows homogeneous enhancement of lesion. **D.** Late portal phase image obtained at 180 seconds shows that the HCC is clearly hypoechoic with respect to surrounding liver. **E.** Hepatocellular carcinoma in 59-year-old man. Unenhanced gray-scale sonogram shows peripheral halo sign (*arrow*).

Continued

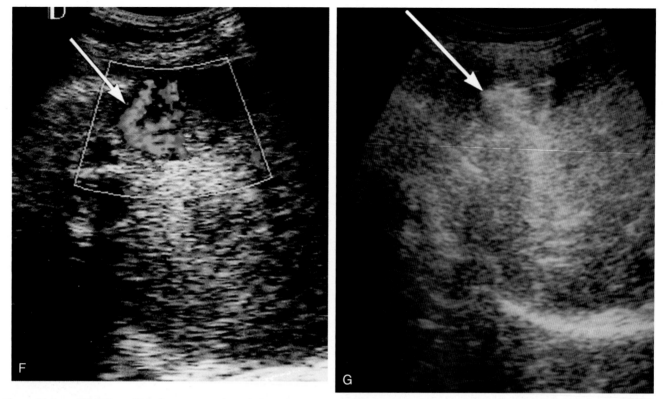

Figure 89-4, cont'd F. Power Doppler sonogram shows heterogeneous vascularity (*arrow*). **G.** Early phase CO_2-enhanced sonogram shows vascularity (*arrow*) similar to that seen in **F.** (**B-D** from Nicolau V, Vilana R, Catalá V, et al: Importance of evaluating all vascular phases on contrast-enhanced sonography in the differentiation of benign from malignant focal liver lesions. AJR 186:158-167, 2006. **E-G** from Chen R-C, Chen W-T, Tu H-Y, et al: Assessment of vascularity in hepatic tumors: Comparison of power Doppler sonography and intraarterial CO_2-enhanced sonography. AJR 178:67-73, 2002. Reprinted with permission from the American Journal of Roentgenology.)

Color Doppler ultrasound has been used to assess the vascularity of HCC.[29] These data, plus the resistive index of tumor vessels, have been used to differentiate HCC from other tumors.[30,31] Color Doppler ultrasound demonstrates an intralesional tangle of vessels, the "basket" pattern, in up to 15% of cases, indicating hypervascularity and tumor shunting.[32,33] Power Doppler has also been assessed in the characterization of HCCs. Although most HCCs show a central pattern of vascularity, so do some hemangiomas and metastases and the clinical usefulness of this technique is therefore limited.[34]

The introduction of intravascular contrast agents has improved the ability of ultrasound to diagnose HCC. An HCC typically demonstrates an early hyperperfusion compared with the adjacent normal liver tissue. A chaotic vessel dysmorphology and washout during the portal venous phase are the other characteristics of the tumor.[35,36]

Computed Tomography

Unenhanced CT scans demonstrate a large, hypodense mass with central areas of lower attenuation that correspond to the tumor necrosis frequently seen in HCC (Figs. 89-5 and 89-6). In North American and European patients, the remainder of the liver shows cirrhosis (60%) or hemochromatosis (20%)[3,5] (Fig. 89-7).

Multiphasic multidetector computed tomography (MDCT) including nonenhanced, hepatic arterial, portal venous, and delayed phase images is an efficient technique for determination of HCC and preoperative staging of HCC.[37,38] Since

HCC derives most of its blood supply from the hepatic artery, the tumor demonstrates early enhancement during arterial phase and is relatively hypodense on the delayed phase images due to the early washout of contrast medium by arterial blood (see Figs. 89-5 and 89-6). The tumor has a very variable appearance on the portal phase images.[39] Small tumors may appear as lesions of different attenuation while larger ones almost always demonstrate central necrosis (see Fig. 89-7). The capsule appears isodense or hypodense relative to the liver during the hepatic arterial phase, and enhances on delayed CT images (see Fig. 89-7).

HCC has a tendency to invade the portal and hepatic veins so that an enlarged venous segment that exhibits intraluminal low attenuation is highly suggestive of tumor thrombus. Differential diagnosis of tumor thrombus can be made through demonstration of the expansion of the main portal vein diameter (≥ 23 mm) and intrathrombus neovascularity on arterial phase images.[40] It should be also noted that hepatic venous tumor thrombus may extend into the inferior vena cava and even to the right atrium in some cases. CT can also depict complications of HCC such as hemoperitoneum associated with rupture of HCC and vascular invasion.[5,41] Ruptured tumors tend to be located in the periphery of the liver and have a protruding contour.[42] On arterial phase images, a ruptured tumor appears as a nonenhancing hypodense lesion with focal discontinuity and peripheral rim enhancement. This finding is termed as "enucleation sign" because of its similarity to an enucleated orbital globe with the remaining intact sclera.[39]

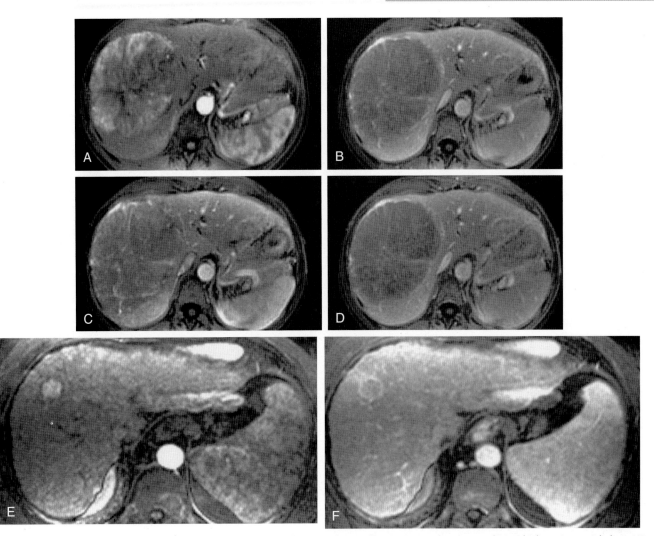

Figure 89-9. HCC: MR contrast enhancement patterns. Hypervascular HCC shows robust contrast enhancement during the hepatic arterial phase (**A**), which rapidly becomes isointense during the portal venous phase (**B**). This tumor rapidly becomes hypointense relative to the normal liver on delayed phase imaging. **C** and **D**. In a different patient with cirrhosis, this small HCC shows uniform enhancement during the hepatic arterial phase (**E**) and washout with ring enhancement on the portal venous phase image (**F**).

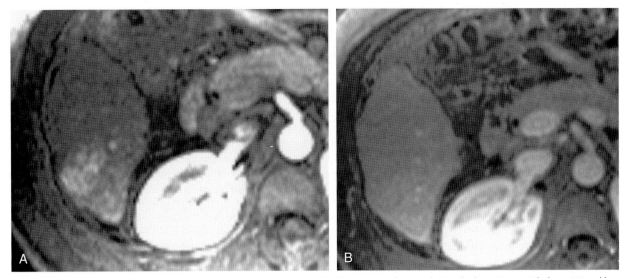

Figure 89-10. HCC: the importance of hepatic arterial phase imaging on MR. The tumor enhances during the hepatic arterial phase (**A**) and becomes isodense with the adjacent parenchyma during the portal venous phase (**B**). Thus this lesion would not be detected if scans were only obtained during the portal venous phase.

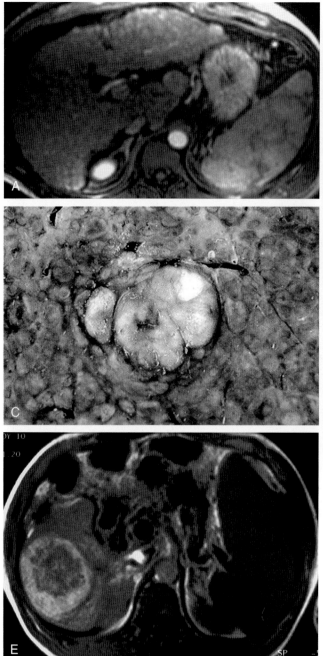

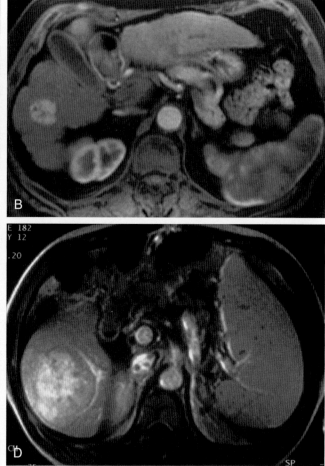

Figure 89-11. HCC: MR appearances. A. Miliary pattern in which innumerable nodules mimic regenerating nodules of cirrhosis. **B** and **C.** A unifocal tumor that is encapsulated is seen in this patient with cirrhosis. **D** and **E.** This large HCC in the right lobe is inhomogeneous on both pulse sequences.

and consequently, cirrhotic nodules appear relatively hypo-intense.[52] In contrast, HCCs are often hyperintense on T2-weighted images and can be distinguished from hypointense nodules.[52] However, some well-differentiated HCCs have similar signal characteristics to cirrhotic nodules and diagnosis is less straightforward.[52] HCC arising within a siderotic nodule has a characteristic "nodule within a nodule" appearance on MR imaging. The HCC appears as a small focus of high signal intensity within the low signal intensity nodule.[52] These lesions are often demonstrated only at MR imaging and MR-guided biopsy is now being performed at many centers.[53] However, biopsy may be technically difficult because the lesions are small and direct referral for surgery may be a better option if the patient is a good surgical candidate.[52,53]

As with CT, HCC during dynamic gadolinium-enhanced MR imaging (see Fig. 89-9) shows early enhancement in the hepatic arterial phase. In the portal venous phase, the tumor is usually isointense and in delayed phase, it becomes hypo-intense due to the contrast medium washout. However, it should be also noted that some tumors may show progressive enhancement in the dynamic imaging.[39] HCCs larger than 1.5 cm tend to have a fibrous capsule that may be demonstrated as a hypointense band on delayed-phase images.[54] MR depicts vascular invasion, which is seen in 30% to 50% of patients, as a lack of signal void on multislice T1-weighted GRE and flow-compensated T2-weighted fast spin-echo images.[55] On gadolinium-enhanced images, the tumor thrombus shows a typical early arterial enhancement.

Intravenous administration of superparamagnetic iron oxide (SPIO) also increases the detection sensitivity of MR.[56] MR imaging with SPIO is especially helpful in the detection of small HCCs in cirrhotic livers. In a study more HCCs were detected on images acquired with SPIO-enhanced FLASH and long TR sequences (2000/70 and 2000/28) than on unenhanced scans.[57] A potential limitation of this technique is that early HCCs may accumulate iron due to the presence of reticuloendothelial cells and will therefore mimic normal liver parenchyma on SPIO-enhanced sequences.[57] In these cases, unenhanced MR images may provide valuable information concerning the internal morphology of these lesions enabling the correct diagnosis of HCCs.[57] Hepatobiliary contrast agents such as gadoxetate (Gd-EOB-DTPA) may be useful in the characterization of questionable lesions. Use of hepatobiliary contrast agents may allow differentiation of hepatocellular tumors such as HCC from nonhepatocellular tumors.[58]

Regenerative nodules and dysplastic nodules are the two key cirrhotic nodular lesions that are important to identify and differentiate from HCC. Regenerative nodules have primarily portal venous blood supply with mild contribution from hepatic artery blood.[54] Therefore, they typically do not show early enhancement during the arterial phase of dynamic MR imaging, while enhancing with the rest of the liver in the portal phase. Regenerative nodules are usually isointense on both T1- and T2-weighted images with the exception of some "siderotic" nodules that contain iron and have, therefore, a low signal intensity on T1- and T2-weighted MRI.[54] Although the blood supply to the dysplastic nodules is also mainly from the portal venous system, some are supplied primarily by the hepatic artery.[54,58,59] Their usual MR appearance is that of homogeneous hyperintensity on T1-weighted images and hypointensity on T2-weighted images. A high signal intensity focus within a low signal intensity nodule on T2-weighted images, is the "nodule within a nodule appearance" of a dysplastic nodule with a focus of HCC.[54,60]

HCC has been treated with chemotherapeutic embolization and/or direct intratumoral injection of alcohol.[61-70] In general, the results have been good, reducing tumor size sufficiently to allow surgical resection in some cases. This therapy can also be useful in patients who are poor surgical risks. Occasionally, liver atrophy may occur after percutaneous ethanol injection and/or transcatheter arterial embolization.[70]

FIBROLAMELLAR CARCINOMA

Pathologic Findings

Fibrolamellar carcinoma (FLC) is a slow-growing tumor that arises in normal liver. It is composed of neoplastic hepatocytes separated into cords by lamellar fibrous strands.[2] These lesions have a distinctive microscopic pattern with eosinophilic, malignant hepatocytes containing prominent nuclei[71] (Fig. 89-12). Some of the markers usually present in typical HCC, such as inclusions of α-fetoprotein bodies, are not present. The fibrous component accounts for one half of the tumor distributed in multilamellate strands, except in larger tumors containing large central scars.[2]

Grossly, FLC usually arises in a normal liver, with only 20% of patients having underlying cirrhosis.[71] Satellite nodules are often present. The appearance of FLC is somewhat similar to that of focal nodular hyperplasia (FNH) in that both tumors

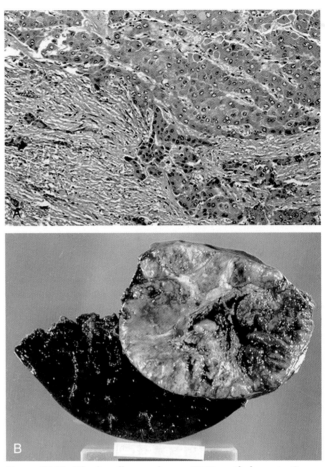

Figure 89-12. Fibrolamellar carcinoma (FLC): pathology. A. Coarse lamellar fibrosis is characteristic of FLC. **B.** Cut section demonstrates a central scar with radiating septae.

have a central scar and multiple fibrous septa (see Fig. 89-19). Hemorrhage and necrosis are rare. Radiologic-pathologic correlates are given in Table 89-3.

Incidence and Clinical Presentation

There is some confusion in the literature about the incidence and clinical presentation of FLC because it was not recognized as a biologic entity until the 1980s.[72] FLC usually occurs in adolescents and adults younger than 40 years of age and without underlying cirrhosis or other predisposing risk factors.[71] There is no sex predominance, and the mean survival is

Table 89-3
Fibrolamellar Carcinoma

Pathologic Features	Radiologic Features
Lamellar fibrosis (septa) "true scar"	Hypovascular: CT, angiography
	Hypointense: T2-weighted MR images
	Calcification: CT, plain radiographs, ultrasound
No necrosis or hemorrhage	Homogeneous mass: CT, ultrasound, MRI
No underlying cirrhosis	Normal hepatic morphology except for mass: CT, ultrasound, MRI

considerably better than that for other types of HCC (45-60 months versus 6 months), with a high likelihood of cure (40%) if the tumor is surgically respectable.[73,74]

Clinically, patients with HCC usually present with pain, malaise, and weight loss; jaundice occurs only occasionally, when FLC invades the biliary tree. A palpable mass is seen in two thirds of patients.[75] Alpha-fetoprotein levels are usually normal.

Radiologic Findings

Plain Radiographs

On plain abdominal radiographs, FLC frequently appears as a partially calcified upper abdominal mass.

Nuclear Scintigraphy

Nuclear scintigraphy is no longer routinely used in the detection of FLC. Sulfur colloid scintiscans usually demonstrate a defect in a liver that has no evidence of underlying cirrhosis. Multiple defects can be seen in cases of multifocal FLC.

Ultrasound

Sonography typically demonstrates a large, well-defined, lobulated mass (Fig. 89-13) with variable echotexture. Fibro-lamellar carcinoma usually is of mixed echogenicity (60% of cases) and predominantly contains hyperechoic or isoechoic

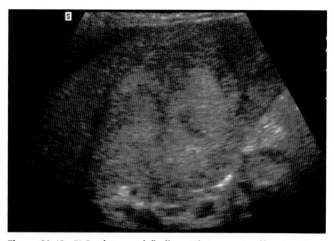

Figure 89-13. FLC: ultrasound findings. The extensive fibrosis present within this neoplasm accounts for the echogenic appearance of this mass.

components.[76] If present, the central scar may be visualized as a central area of hyperechogenicity.

Computed Tomography

On unenhanced CT scans, FLC appears as a hypodense mass with a well-defined contour (Figs. 89-14 and 89-15). Areas of decreased density within the tumor correspond to the central scar or necrosis and hemorrhage.[77] Stellate calci-

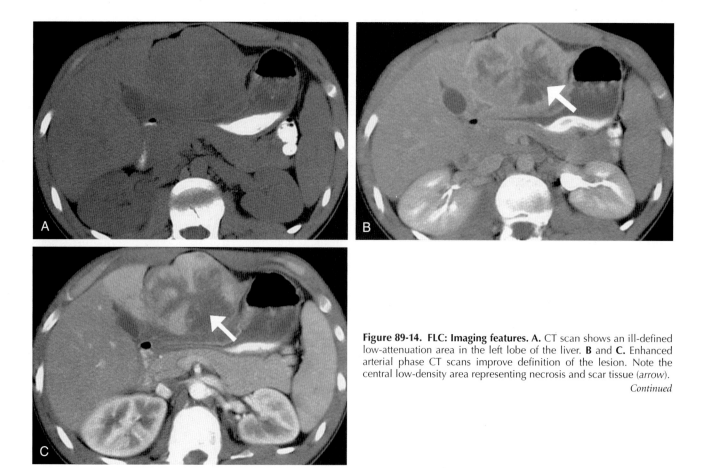

Figure 89-14. FLC: Imaging features. A. CT scan shows an ill-defined low-attenuation area in the left lobe of the liver. **B** and **C.** Enhanced arterial phase CT scans improve definition of the lesion. Note the central low-density area representing necrosis and scar tissue (*arrow*).

Continued

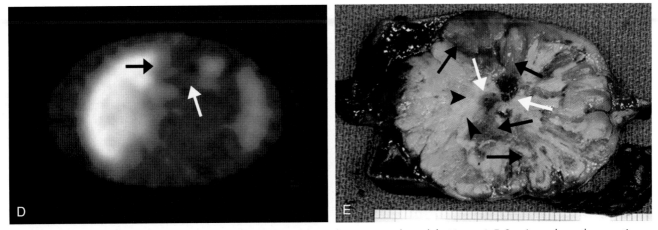

Figure 89-14, cont'd. D. Single photon emission CT (SPECT) image shows the tumor as a large defect (*arrows*). **E.** Specimen shows the necrotic areas (*black arrows*), central scar (*arrowheads*), and intratumoral hemorrhage (*white arrows*).

fication within the central scar can also occur.[75,77] During the arterial and portal phases of dynamic enhanced CT, the "nonscar" portion of fibrolamellar carcinoma enhances heterogeneously. This heterogeneous enhancement pattern during the arterial and portal phases likely corresponds to the more vascular, cellular portions of the tumor in comparison with the fibrous (lamellae and scar) and necrotic portions.[76] On the other hand, the relative delayed-phase homogeneity of the tumor, probably reflects the washout of the contrast material from its more vascular portions together with delayed enhancement of the fibrous lamellae. In some cases, central scar may also demonstrate delayed enhancement and the appearance of the tumor, on delayed images, may closely simulate that of FNH. Although FLC is a tumor not characteristically encapsulated, the compressed liver tissue adjacent to it, may demonstrate delayed enhancement.[76] Features that determine the resectability of FLCs such as portal vein invasion and lymphadenopathy are well seen on CT scans.[77-79]

Angiography

Angiographically, FLC is a hypervascular tumor with compartmentalization in the capillary phase resulting from multiple fibrous septa.[75] Daughter nodules or secondary lesions may be noted in the capillary phase of arteriograms.

Magnetic Resonance Imaging

FLC is hypointense or isointense with normal liver on T1-weighted images and isointense or slightly hyperintense on T2-weighted images.[80,81] Because of its purely fibrous nature, the scar is hypointense on both T1- and T2-weighted images (Fig. 89-16). However hyperintensity of the central scar on T2-weighted images has been described in a biopsy-proved FLC that was initially diagnosed as FNH on the basis of imaging findings alone.[82] The enhancement pattern of FLC seen with gadolinium-enhanced dynamic MR imaging parallels the enhancement seen with dynamic contrast-enhanced CT. The tumor demonstrates heterogeneous enhancement in the arterial and portal phases and progressively becomes more homogeneous on delayed images.[81] In "atypical" cases of FNH, when the MR features are consistent with FNH, but no uptake of sulfur colloid is seen at scintigraphy; then biopsy of the lesion is recommended to confirm or exclude a diagnosis of FLC.[82] Whereas FNH is treated conservatively, surgery is appropriate for most FLCs.[82]

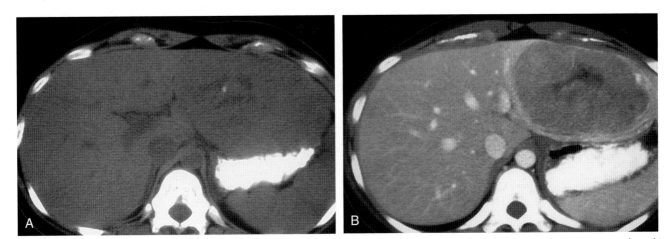

Figure 89-15. FLC: CT findings. A. This noncontrast scan shows calcification of the central scar. **B.** The central scar is better appreciated on this contrast-enhanced scan.

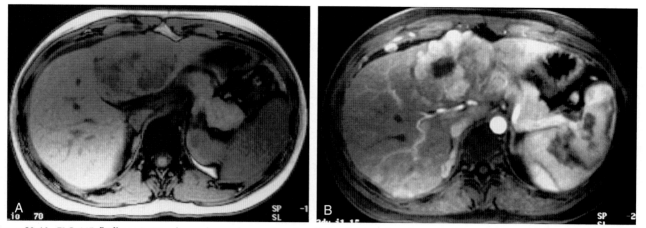

Figure 89-16. FLC: MR findings. A. Unenhanced scan shows a low signal intensity mass that showed striking enhancement (**B**) with the exception of the central scar on the contrast-enhanced images.

Differential Diagnosis

The major differential diagnosis with FLC is FNH. FNH can be differentiated from FLC in the majority of cases because (1) the central scar of FNH is hyperintense on T2-weighted images; (2) FNH rarely has calcification within the scar (<1.5% of cases compared to up to 55% of FLCs)[77,83]; (3) FNH is usually asymptomatic, while patients with FLC usually presents with some symptoms; and (4) biopsy demonstrates malignant, eosinophilic hepatocytes in FLC and normal hepatocytes with bile ductules in FNH (Table 89-4).

HEPATOBLASTOMA

Pathologic Findings

Hepatoblastoma is a malignant tumor of hepatocyte origin that often contains mesenchymal elements.[84] Microscopically, it can be classified as epithelial or mixed (epithelial-mesenchymal).[2]

Epithelial hepatoblastoma consists of fetal and/or embryonal malignant hepatocytes. Mixed hepatoblastoma has both an epithelial (hepatocyte) component and a mesenchymal component consisting of primitive mesenchymal tissue and osteoid material and/or cartilage[85] (Fig. 89-17). This histologic classification has prognostic implications: the epithelial type, particularly if it has fetal hepatocyte predominance, has a better prognosis than the other forms. Embryonal epithelial cells are more primitive than fetal epithelial and mesenchymal cells, and tumors with the former histologic type have a worse prognosis.[85,86] A rare anaplastic form of hepatoblastoma has an even poorer prognosis than the mixed form of hepatoblastoma.[2]

Grossly, hepatoblastoma is usually a large, well-circumscribed solitary mass that has a nodular or lobulated surface; 20% are multifocal.[2] On cut section, the appearance varies according to the histologic type. Epithelial hepatoblastomas are more homogeneous; mixed hepatoblastomas with osteoid and cartilage have large calcifications, fibrotic bands, and overall a more heterogeneous appearance.[87]

Incidence and Clinical Presentation

Hepatoblastoma is the most common primary liver neoplasm in childhood. It usually develops in the first 3 years of life. Although it may be present at birth or develop in adolescents and young adults,[88] this tumor has a peak incidence between 18 and 24 months of age. Hepatoblastoma is more frequent in males than in females.

Clinically, children with hepatoblastoma present with abdominal swelling that may be accompanied by anorexia or weight loss. More rarely children may present with precocious puberty due to secretion of gonadotrophins or testosterone by the tumor.[89] The serum α-fetoprotein level is markedly elevated in most patients. This tumor is aggressive and lung metastases are frequently encountered at the time of diagnosis.[90] Conditions associated with hepatoblastoma include

Table 89-4
Focal Nodular Hyperplasia Versus Fibrolamellar Carcinoma

Features	Focal Nodular Hyperplasia	Fibrolamellar Carcinoma
Scar	Hyperintense on T2-weighted images	Hypointense on T2-weighted images
	High signal intensity (flow) on GRE images	No signal on GRE images
Calcification	No	Frequent
Symptoms	No (usually incidental finding)	Symptomatic
Biopsy	Normal hepatocytes	Malignant eosinophilic hepatocytes
	Portal branches	No portal branches
	Biliary ductules	No biliary ductules

GRE, gradient-recalled echo.

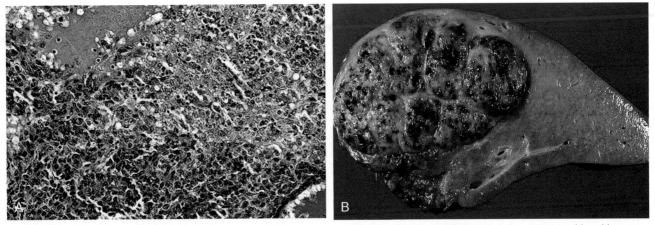

Figure 89-17. Hepatoblastoma: pathologic findings. A. Small tumor cells with fairly round to oval nuclei form tubular, acinar, or ribbon-like arrangements. **B.** This tumor typically is a large, solitary mass that is often multinodular due to foci of hemorrhage and necrosis.

Beckwith-Wiedemann syndrome, hemihypertrophy, familial polyposis coli, and Wilm's tumor.[89]

Radiologic Findings

Plain Radiographs

Because hepatoblastoma is usually a large solitary tumor, a large right upper quadrant mass may be detected on plain abdominal radiographs. Extensive coarse, dense calcification is often present due to osteoid formation.[90]

Nuclear Scintigraphy

Hepatoblastoma appears as a large defect on sulfur colloid scans. It may take up gallium and FDG and excrete iminodiacetic acid derivative agents.

Ultrasound

Sonographically, hepatoblastoma appears as an echogenic mass that may have shadowing echogenic foci corresponding to intratumor calcification.[90] Hyperechoic and/or cystic areas, corresponding to hemorrhage within the tumor, and/or necrotic areas may be present as well.[91,92] Hepatoblastoma is associated with high Doppler frequency shifts that correlate with the neovascularity typical of this tumor.[93]

Computed Tomography

On unenhanced CT scans, hepatoblastoma appears as a solid hypodense mass, with or without calcification, that may occupy large portions of the liver. Frequently, a lobulated pattern caused by bands of fibrosis can be seen.[90] Calcification and a heterogeneous appearance are particularly extensive in mixed hepatoblastoma. After IV contrast agent administration, the tumor appears hyperdense, in keeping with its hypervascular nature. In the early arterial phase, enhancement of a thick peripheral rim, corresponding to the viable portion of the tumor, may be seen.[94] Invasion of perihepatic vessels or other structures can be demonstrated.[90] Three-dimensional reconstruction of helical CT data provides important information in the preoperative assessment of

patients with hepatoblastoma[95] (Fig. 89-18). For example, when tumor impinges on the portal vein, the initial treatment is chemotherapy in order to reduce the size of the lesion. If shrinkage of the tumor away from the vessel is seen on follow-up 3D CT, then surgery is indicated.[95]

Angiography

Angiographically, hepatoblastoma is hypervascular and occasionally has a "spoke-wheel" pattern, reminiscent of FNH, that is due to the presence of multiple fibrous septa and bands. Arteriovenous shunting is uncommon and invasion of the vessels is rare.[96] Hypovascular or avascular zones resulting from hemorrhage can occur within the tumor.

Magnetic Resonance Imaging

Hepatoblastoma is hyperintense on T2-weighted images and hypointense on T1-weighted images. Foci of high signal may be seen on T1-weighted images due to hemorrhage.[97] On T2-weighted images, internal septa corresponding to fibrosis within the tumor appear as hypointense bands.[98] The mixed type, may demonstrate a more heterogeneous appearance on T1- and T2-weighted images due to the necrosis, hemorrhage, fibrosis, calcification, cartilage and fibrous septa contents. After intravenous gadolinium administration, hepatoblastoma show immediate diffuse (homogeneous or heterogeneous) enhancement followed by a rapid washout. MR also demonstrates the presence of perihepatic vascular invasion. MR can be more accurate than conventional CT in both assessing preoperative tumor extension and detecting postoperative tumor recurrence.[99] However, CT has an important advantage over MR imaging in the evaluation of the pediatric abdomen—shorter scanning times, which result in less motion artifact, obviating the need for sedation.[95]

INTRAHEPATIC CHOLANGIOCARCINOMA

Pathologic Findings

Intrahepatic cholangiocarcinoma (ICAC), or adenocarcinoma of biliary duct origin, originates in the small intrahepatic ducts and represents only 10% of all cholangiocarcinomas.[2]

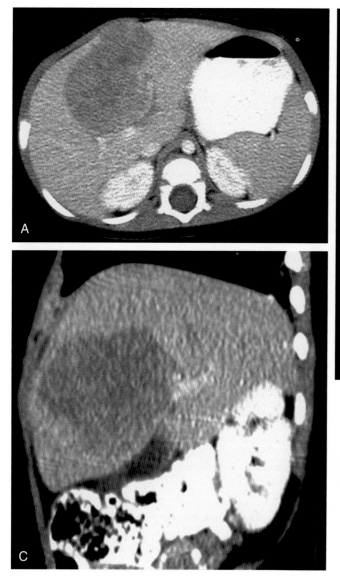

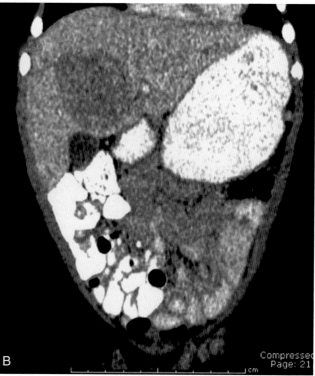

Figure 89-18. Hepatoblastoma: imaging features. Axial (**A**), coronal (**B**), and sagittal (**C**) CT images demonstrate a large hypodense mass in the right hepatic lobe.

Hilar (Klatskin's) and bile duct cholangiocarcinomas account for the remaining 90%.[2,100] Grossly, these neoplasms are large, firm masses (Fig. 89-19). On cut section, they are characterized by the presence of large amounts of whitish, fibrous tissue. They rarely have internal areas of necrosis and hemorrhage.[101]

Microscopically, the tumor is an adenocarcinoma with a glandular appearance and cells resembling biliary epithelium.[102] Mucin and calcification can often be demonstrated. A large amount of desmoplastic reaction is typical of cholangiocarcinoma.

Pathologic-radiologic correlates of this lesion are given in Table 89-5.

Incidence and Clinical Presentation

Intrahepatic cholangiocarcinoma (ICAC) is the second most common primary hepatic malignancy in adults. It is usually seen in the seventh decade of life and there is a slight male predominance.[2]

Clinical signs and symptoms are related to the site of origin of the tumor. Symptoms are vague until the tumor is far advanced, and patients present with abdominal pain and a palpable mass in the upper abdomen. Jaundice is rarely a presenting symptom in ICAC, whereas it is common with hilar or ductal cholangiocarcinoma.

Table 89-5
Intrahepatic Cholangiocarcinoma

Pathologic Features	Radiologic Features
Fibrosis	Calcification: CT, ultrasound
	Hypodense areas: CT
	Hypointense areas: MRI
	Hyperechoic areas: ultrasound
No necrosis or hemorrhage	Homogeneous mass: CT, ultrasound, MRI
Vascular encasement	Hypovascular mass: angiography, contrast CT, MRI
	Encasement: angiography, Doppler, contrast CT, MRI

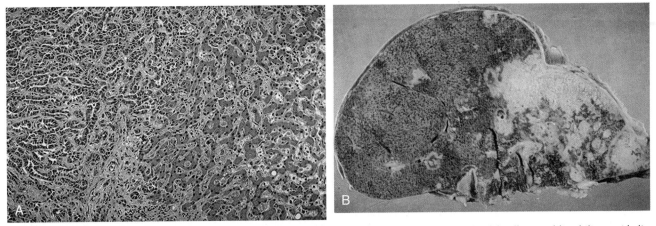

Figure 89-19. Intrahepatic cholangiocarcinoma (ICAC): pathology. A. Photomicrograph demonstrates cuboidal cells resembling biliary epithelium with pseudogland formation. **B.** The gross specimen shows a large, whitish, homogeneous lesion within a cirrhotic liver. The tumor extends to the liver capsule. The whitish, homogeneous nature is indicative of the large amount of fibrosis and relative hypovascularity of these neoplasms.

Radiologic Findings

Plain Radiographs

On plain radiographs, ICAC may appear as a large upper abdominal mass. Calcification is frequently seen and results from mucous secretions or amorphous calcification in sclerotic areas.[101]

Nuclear Scintigraphy

Sulfur colloid and hepatobiliary scans demonstrate a large defect; signs of cirrhosis are present in 20% of patients with ICAC.[101] There is no accumulation of gallium in ICAC. Red blood cell scans demonstrate a defect without late filling, reflecting the markedly hypovascular nature of this tumor.

Ultrasound

On sonograms, ICAC appears as a homogeneous mass that is usually hypoechoic.[103] Satellite nodules may be seen.

Calcified foci can be seen as high-level echoes with acoustic shadowing. Although the majority of the tumors appear as slightly hyperperfused in color Doppler US studies, Doppler imaging findings vary widely.[36] In the arterial phase of contrast-enhanced sonography, the perfusion picture of ICAC is variable, but mainly hyperperfused. In the late portal venous phase, the tumor is contrasted as punched-out defects.

Computed Tomography

On unenhanced CT, this lesion usually manifests as a homogeneous, hypodense mass. After contrast injection there is early peripheral enhancement with delayed, persistent central enhancement that may take 5 to 15 minutes to manifest[101-106] (Fig. 89-20). Retraction of the overlying liver capsule is a feature suggestive of ICAC.[103] A central scar may be seen in 30% of cases.[99] Small areas of necrosis, hemorrhage, mucin, and calcification can also be present within the tumor. Biliary dilatation adjacent to the tumor is another finding which is seen in 20% of the cases.

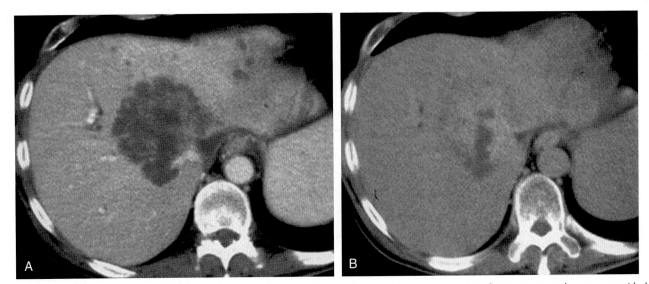

Figure 89-20. ICAC: CT features. A. This lesion does not enhance on the portal venous phase image. **B.** Significant contrast enhancement, with the exception of the central scar is present on the 10-minute delayed scan.

Extension through the hepatic capsule and invasion of organs adjacent to the liver are common in ICAC but rare in HCC. Invasion of vascular structures around the liver is uncommon but may be seen with ICAC.

Angiography

Angiographically, ICAC is predominantly hypovascular with small, thin vessels corresponding to the fibrous nature of this tumor.[107] Encasement of hepatic arteries and other major vessels is associated with the degree of sclerosis resulting from the tumor.

Magnetic Resonance Imaging

On MR, ICAC appears as a large mass of decreased signal intensity on T1-weighted images and increased signal on T2-weighted images.[108,109] A central area of hypointensity is seen in some cases on T2-weighted images and corresponds to the central scar. The pattern of enhancement on gadolinium-DTPA–enhanced scans depends on the size of the lesion.[109] Whereas larger ICACs (>4 cm) show peripheral enhancement which progresses centipetally and spares the central scar (Fig. 89-21). Smaller lesions (2-4 cm) enhance homo-

geneously.[109] These patterns of enhancement may also be seen in hemangiomas. However the degree of enhancement of hemangiomas is greater.[108,109] In addition ICACs may have other features such as satellite nodules, invasion of the portal vein and dilatation of intrahepatic bile ducts distal to the lesion which are not associated with hemangiomas.[108] Radiologic-pathologic correlates of ICAC are shown in Table 89-5.

CYSTADENOMA AND CYSTADENOCARCINOMA

Pathologic Findings

Biliary cystadenoma and cystadenocarcinoma are currently considered forms of the same disease, with cystadenocarcinoma being overtly malignant and cystadenoma having malignant potential. Transformation of cystadenoma to cystadenocarcinoma is a recognized complication.[110,111]

Microscopically (Fig. 89-22), cystadenomas and cystadenocarcinomas are commonly mucinous, but a serous variety is also recognized. The locules of these tumors are lined by columnar, cuboidal, or even flattened epithelium.[2] Polypoid projections and papillary areas are frequently present. There

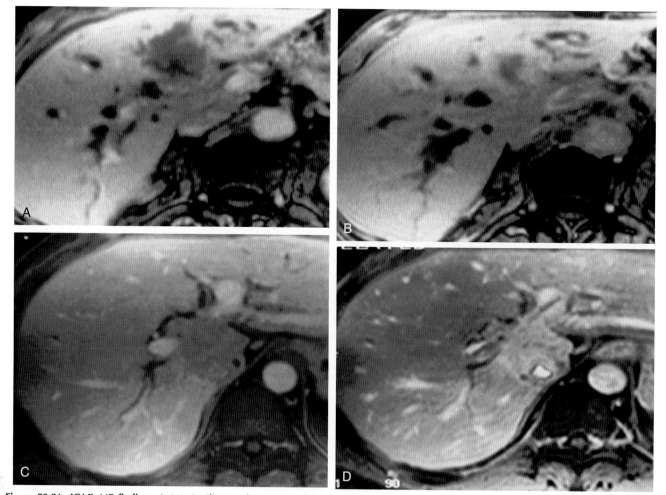

Figure 89-21. ICAC: MR findings. A. No significant enhancement of the tumor is noted on the early phase scan, but on the 10-minute delayed scan (**B**), there is enhancement with the exception of the central scar. In a different patient, the lesion in the caudate lobe does not enhance early on (**C**) but does on delayed scans (**D**).

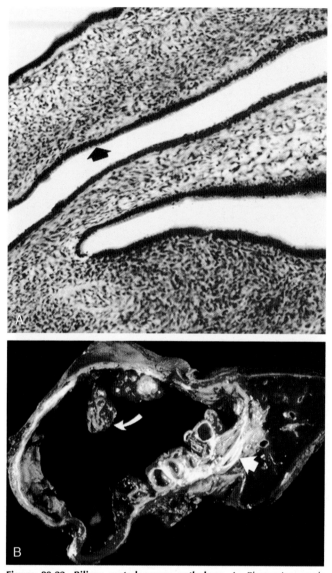

Figure 89-22. Biliary cystadenoma: pathology. A. Photomicrograph shows the cyst wall lined by benign cuboidal epithelium (*arrow*) with a subepithelial mesenchymal "ovarian-like" stroma. **B.** Photograph of the cut resected left lobe shows the fibrous wall of the tumor, multiple tumor nodules (*curved arrow*), and loculi. The mass arises from the compressed bile duct (*straight arrow*). (From Levy AD, Murukata LA, Abbott RM, Rohrmann CA Jr: Benign tumors and tumorlike lesions of the gall-bladder and extrahepatic bile ducts: Radiologic-pathologic correlation. RadioGraphics 22:387-413, 2002.)

is a well-formed wall, and focal calcification within the wall is rare. Biliary-type epithelium lines the cysts. In cystadenocarcinoma, malignant epithelial cells line the cysts. Pathologists have categorized biliary cystadenocarcinoma depending on whether ovarian stroma is present or absent.[112] Cystadenocarcinoma with ovarian stroma is found in women and has an indolent course and a good prognosis, whereas tumors without ovarian stroma are found in both sexes and have an aggressive clinical course and a poor prognosis.[112]

Grossly, these tumors are usually solitary and may become up to 30 cm in size.[2] The surface is shiny, smooth, or bosselated. On cut section, multiple communicating locules of variable size have a smooth and glistening lining. Papillary excrescences or mural nodules are seen in the tumor wall.

Incidence and Clinical Presentation

Cystadenomas and cystadenocarcinomas are rare and represent only 5% of all intrahepatic cysts of bile duct origin.[113] They are probably congenital in origin because of the presence of aberrant bile ducts. There are no associated pathogenic factors, and these tumors usually occur in middle-aged women.[2]

A "microcystic" cystadenoma variant is composed of multiple small cysts lined by a single layer of cuboidal epithelial cells that are rich in glycogen.[114] The papillary features and the cellular mesenchymal stroma typical of the mucinous variety of cystadenoma or cystadenocarcinoma are not seen in microcystic, glycogen-rich cystadenoma. No radiologic descriptions of microcystic cystadenoma of the liver have been published.

Radiologic Findings

Endoscopic retrograde cholangiography (ERCP) studies can show communication of the tumor with the bile duct (Fig. 89-23). Cystadenoma or cystadenocarcinoma of the liver usually appears as a large, unilocular or multilocular mass on cross-sectional imaging. Ultrasound nicely demonstrates the septa, as well as the mural nodules in the wall of these tumors (Fig. 89-24). Good correlation is seen between the nodularity and septation seen on US scans and gross specimens.[112]

On CT scans, these tumors are large, unilocular or multilocular low-attenuation intrahepatic masses[112] with well-defined thick fibrous capsules, mural nodules, and internal septa[115] (Fig. 89-25). Calcification may be seen within the wall and septa in a minority of cases.[112]

Angiographically most cystadenomas and cystadenocarcinomas are avascular although a small peripheral vascular blush may be seen in a few cases.[112]

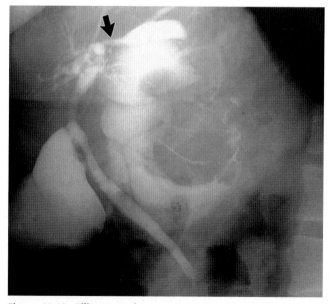

Figure 89-23. Biliary cystadenoma: ERCP. Lateral radiograph of the abdomen obtained after ERCP shows communication of the tumor (*arrow*) with the biliary system. The gallbladder has an anterior location. (From Levy AD, Murukata LA, Abbott RM, Rohrmann CA Jr: Benign tumors and tumorlike lesions of the gallbladder and extrahepatic bile ducts: Radiologic-pathologic correlation. RadioGraphics 22:387-413, 2002.)

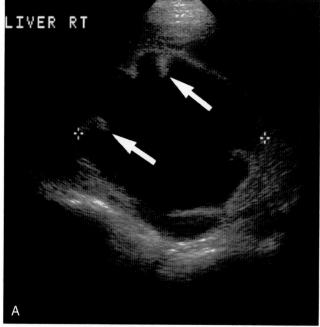

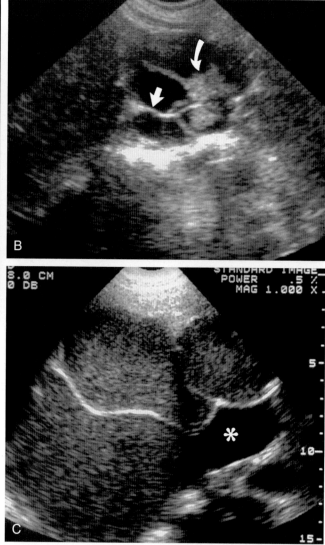

Figure 89-24. Biliary cystadenoma: sonographic findings. A. Transverse image of the liver shows a well-defined anechoic cystic structure with enhanced through-transmission. There are multiple echogenic tumor excrescences extending into the cyst lumen (*arrows*). **B.** Transverse image of the left hepatic lobe in a different patient reveals a complex anechoic cyst containing echogenic septa (*straight arrow*) and tumor nodules (*curved arrow*). **C.** Transverse image of the liver in a different patient shows a biliary cystadenoma composed of complex fluid containing diffuse low-level internal echoes. Echogenic septa course through the complex fluid. A portion of the tumor (*) contains simple anechoic fluid. (From Levy AD, Murukata LA, Abbott RM, Rohrmann CA Jr: Benign tumors and tumorlike lesions of the gallbladder and extrahepatic bile ducts: Radiologic-pathologic correlation. RadioGraphics 22:387-413, 2002.)

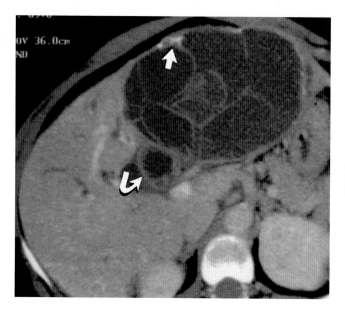

Figure 89-25. Biliary cystadenoma: CT. Contrast-enhanced scans shows a multilocular cyst with septations and mural calcifications (*straight arrow*) in the left hepatic lobe. There is duct dilatation and extension of the cyst into the left hepatic and common bile ducts (*curved arrow*). (From Levy AD, Murukata LA, Abbott RM, Rohrmann CA Jr: Benign tumors and tumorlike lesions of the gallbladder and extrahepatic bile ducts: Radiologic-pathologic correlation. RadioGraphics 22:387-413, 2002.)

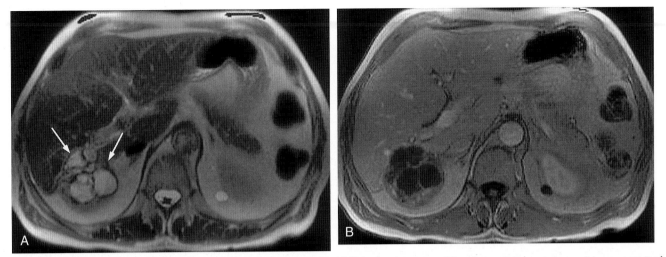

Figure 89-26. Biliary cystadenoma on MRI. A. Fast spin-echo T2-weighted MR image shows a multilocular, septated mass (*arrows*) in segment 7 of the liver, with high signal intensity within the tumor. **B.** Corresponding portal-venous-phase gadolinium-enhanced T1-weighted MR image shows enhancement of the capsule and septa. (From Mortele KJ, Ros PR: Cystic focal liver lesions in the adult: Differential CT and MR imaging features. RadioGraphics 2001; 21:895-910.)

On MR, the tumors are multiseptated and have predominantly high signal on T1-weighted images and mixed or low signal on T1-weighted images (Fig. 89-26). The areas of high signal on T1-weighted images represent hemorrhagic fluid components.[112] A low signal rim on T2-weighted images may be due to hemorrhage in the wall of the lesion.[112] Variable signal intensity within the locules of biliary cystadenoma and cystadenocarcinoma on both T1- and T2-weighted images was reported as a new sign[116] (see Fig. 89-37C). This feature may prove extremely useful in the characterization of a multiseptate hepatic lesion as cystadenoma or cystadenocarcinoma.

Radiologically, it is impossible to distinguish cystadenomas from cystadenocarcinomas. However, the combination of septation and nodularity is suggestive of cystadenocarcinoma (Fig. 89-27) while septation without nodularity is seen only in cystadenoma.[112] In addition, the presence of distant metastases, adenopathy or other signs of widespread malignancy are consistent with cystadenocarcinoma.[112] It is also difficult to distinguish between cystadenoma or cystadenocarcinoma, hydatid disease, and abscess on cross-sectional imaging.[112,117] However, use of clinical and laboratory findings should enable identification of an infectious cause.[112]

ANGIOSARCOMA

Pathologic Findings

Angiosarcoma of the liver is a malignant tumor derived from endothelial lining cells that occurs primarily in adults with exposure to a variety of chemical agents and radiation (thorium oxide administration).[2,118,119]

Microscopically, angiosarcomas are composed of malignant endothelial cells lining vascular channels of variable size from cavernous to capillary. These vascular channels try to form sinusoids. Thorotrast particles can be found within the malignant endothelial cells in cases of Thorotrast-induced angiosarcoma.

Grossly, the majority of angiosarcomas are multiple and have areas of internal hemorrhage.[118] When angiosarcoma appears as a single, large mass, it does not have a capsule and frequently contains large cystic areas filled with bloody debris.

The radiologic correlates of the pathology of angiosarcoma are given in Table 89-6.

Incidence and Clinical Presentation

Angiosarcoma is a rare neoplasm that occurs most frequently in males (2:1 to 4:1 more often than in females) in the seventh decade of life. It is 30 times less common than HCC.[120] Angiosarcoma is associated with previous exposure to toxins such as Thorotrast, vinyl chloride, arsenicals, and steroids. It has also been found in association with hemochromatosis.

Clinically, patients with angiosarcoma frequently present with generalized weakness, weight loss, abdominal pain, hepatomegaly, and ascites. Thrombocytopenia caused by platelet sequestration within a large angiosarcoma may be present. Rupture and acute hemoperitoneum are rare.[121,122]

Table 89-6
Angiosarcoma

Thorium oxide (Thorotrast)	
Persistence of contrast medium: red blood cell scan	
Pathologic Features	**Radiologic Features**
Multiple nodules	Hyperechoic nodules: ultrasound
	Hypodense nodule (central): CT
	Hypointense nodule: MRI
Thorium oxide (Thorotrast) deposition	Metallic density: CT
Areas of hemorrhage	Heterogeneous mass: CT, ultrasound
	Hyperdense regions: CT
	Hyperechoic regions: ultrasound
	Hyperintense regions: T1-weighted MR images
Vascular channels	Persistence of contrast medium: red blood cell scintigraphy, contrast-enhanced CT and MRI

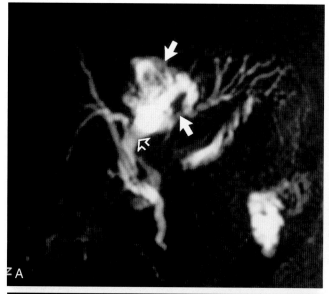
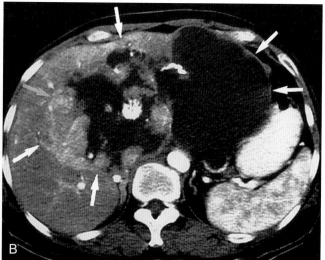
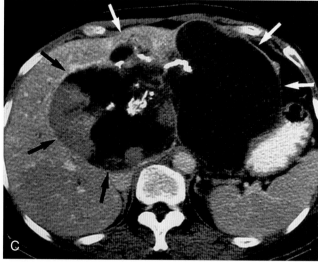

Figure 89-27. Biliary cystadenocarcinoma: Imaging features. A. MRCP. Biliary cystadenocarcinoma in a 65-year-old woman with abdominal pain. Single-shot fast spin-echo MRCP image shows a large, fluid-filled mass in the left hepatic lobe (*solid arrows*), with proximal dilatation of the left intrahepatic bile ducts. The low-signal-intensity filling defects in the mass are related to polypoid masses of the wall, and the low-signal-intensity filling defect in the common hepatic duct (*open arrow*) is related to mucin secreted by the mass. In a different patient, arterial- (**B**) and equilibrium-phase CT scans (**C**) show a large, bilobular, cystic mass with internal septation and calcification (*arrows*) that involves the left hepatic lobe. Papillary excrescences and mural nodules along the cyst wall enhance well during the arterial phase. (**A** from Vitellas KM, Keogan MT, Spritzer CE, et al: MR cholangiopancreatography of bile and pancreatic duct abnormalities with emphasis on the single-shot fast spin-echo technique. RadioGraphics 20:939-957, 2000; **B** and **C** from Lee WJ, Lim HK, Jangy KM, et al: Radiologic spectrum of cholangiocarcinoma: Emphasis on unusual manifestations and differential diagnoses. RadioGraphics 21:S97-S116, 2001.)

Radiologic Findings

Plain Radiographs

The plain abdominal radiographic findings depend on the presence or absence of prior Thorotrast exposure. If there is no history of Thorotrast exposure, the findings of angio-sarcoma are nonspecific: a soft tissue density mass in the upper abdomen may be detected if there is a large predominant angiosarcoma nodule.

If there is a history of Thorotrast exposure, localized areas of increased density, in a network fashion, are visualized in the liver and spleen as well as in the mesenteric and celiac lymph nodes. Circumferential displacement of the Thoro-trast by nodules of angiosarcoma can be identified on plain films.[123]

Nuclear Scintigraphy

Sulfur colloid scans demonstrate either solitary or multiple filling defects in an often diffusely abnormal liver. A defect is also noted on hepatobiliary and gallium scans. Tagged red blood cell pool studies may show early as well as late uptake.

Angiosarcoma, therefore, can mimic the appearance of hemangiomas on red blood cell studies, with persistent uptake of the tracer.[124] The retention of the tagged red blood cells by this tumor is not as prolonged as that by hemangiomas, however.

Ultrasound

On ultrasound studies, angiosarcomas appear as either single or multiple hyperechoic masses. The echo architecture is heterogeneous because of hemorrhage of various ages.

Computed Tomography

Computed tomography (CT) scans show the reticular pattern of deposition of Thorotrast extremely well in both the liver and the spleen. Circumferential displacement of Thorotrast in the periphery of a nodule has been described as a characteristic finding of angiosarcoma.[124]

When there is no evidence of Thorotrast deposition, angio-sarcomas present with single or multiple masses that are hypo-dense on unenhanced CT scans except for hyperdense areas of fresh hemorrhage. In case of rupture of the hepatic angiosarcoma, the diagnosis is maid by demonstrating free intraperitoneal fluid and focal high density area adjacent to the tumor representing acute blood clot.[125] Centripetal enhancement with contrast material can be seen mimicking the hemangioma pattern.[126] However, in most cases, angiosarcomas have additional imaging features that are atypical for hemangiomas such as focal areas of enhancement that show less attenuation than the aorta or peripheral ring-shaped enhancement.

Angiography

Angiographically, these moderately hypervascular tumors show diffuse puddling of contrast medium that persists into the venous phase.[127] Angiosarcomas are fed by large peripheral vessels and centripetal flow can be recorded angiographically. Avascular areas corresponding to central hemorrhage can be seen within the tumors. Occasionally, angiosarcomas may rupture, and angiography and CT can demonstrate the bleeding as well as the presence of hemoperitoneum.[122]

Magnetic Resonance Imaging

Angiosarcoma (Fig. 89-28) is of low signal intensity on T1-weighted images and is of predominantly high signal on T2-weighted images with central areas of low signal.[97,128] Imaging features that have been described on T2-weighted images include fluid-fluid levels reflecting the hemorrhagic nature of the tumor and marked heterogeneity with focal areas of high intensity along with septum-like or rounded areas of low intensily. On T1-weighted imaging, areas of hyperintensity are related to hemorrhage. During dynamic scanning following intravenous gadolinium-DTPA administration peripheral nodular enhancement is seen, which progresses centripetally.[128] On delayed postcontrast images, the peripheral enhancement persists while the center of the lesion remains unenhanced and may represent fibrous tissue or deoxyhemoglobin.[97,128] Although the pattern of enhancement mimics hemangiomas, the inhomogeneity of angiosarcomas

on T2-weighted images is not seen in hemangiomas.[97,128] Because Thorotrast does not produce a recognizable MR signal, it, like the presence of calcification, may easily be missed.

UNDIFFERENTIATED (EMBRYONAL) SARCOMA

Pathologic Findings

Undifferentiated (embryonal) sarcoma (UES), or mesenchymal sarcoma, is a malignant tumor occurring primarily in children. It is composed of primitive, undifferentiated spindle cells, with frequent mitoses and myxoid stroma, that resemble primitive (embryonal) cells.[129] Grossly, UES is a large, usually solitary, spheric mass with well-defined margins (Fig. 89-29). Occasionally, a pseudocapsule is present. On cut surface, it has a variegated, glistening appearance with cystic areas of variable size that contain necrotic debris, hemorrhagic fluid, blood, and/or gelatinous material.[129,130] Cystic tumors are seen more frequently than solid ones.

Incidence and Clinical Presentation

UES is the fourth most common hepatic neoplasm in children, after hepatoblastoma, infantile hemangioendothelioma, and HCC.[129] It usually occurs in older children, 6 to 10 years of age, and 90% of patients are younger than 15 years.[131]

The incidence is almost the same in males and females. The usual presenting symptoms are pain and abdominal mass, with fever, jaundice, weight loss, and gastrointestinal complaints found less commonly. Alpha-fetoprotein levels are usually not elevated.

Radiologic Findings

Plain Radiographs

Abdominal radiographs demonstrate a large, usually noncalcified mass in the upper abdomen associated with displacement of adjacent structures and elevation of right diaphragm.

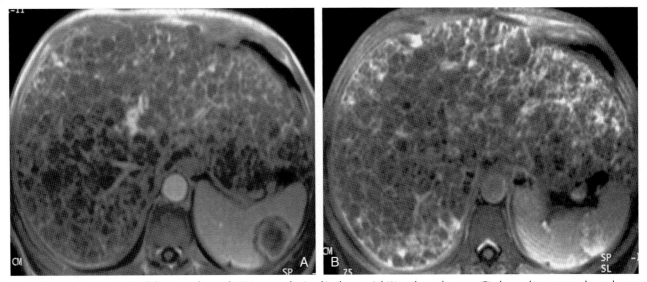

Figure 89-28. Angiosarcoma. Gadolinium-enhanced MR images obtained in the arterial (**A**) and portal venous (**B**) phases demonstrate the replacement of the liver parenchyma with numerous nodules. There is also an angiosarcoma in the spleen.

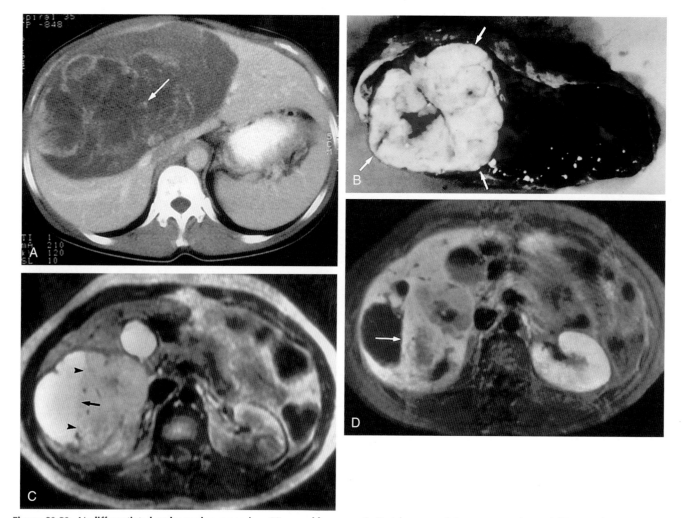

Figure 89-29. Undifferentiated embryonal sarcoma in a 22-year-old woman. A. Portal-venous phase contrast-enhanced CT scan shows a 10-cm-diameter cystic lesion with septa in the right lobe of the liver. Note the calcifications (*arrow*) within the mass. **B.** Specimen photograph shows that the mass has predominantly solid components (*arrows*) with coexisting hemorrhagic areas. Undifferentiated embryonal sarcoma in a 36-year-old woman. **C.** T2-weighted MR image shows a mass in the right lobe of the liver. The solid portions of the mass (*arrowheads*) are hyperintense relative to normal liver tissue, and the cystic portions (*arrow*) have signal intensity similar to that of water. **D.** Delayed-phase gadolinium-enhanced T1-weighted MR image shows heterogeneous enhancement of the solid portions of the lesion (*arrow*). (From Koenraad J, Mortele KJ, Ros PR: Cystic focal liver lesions in the adult: Differential CT and MR imaging features. RadioGraphics 21: 895-910, 2001.)

Calcification, although rare, may occur, with small, punctate chunks of calcium seen within the solid portions of this tumor.[131]

Nuclear Scintigraphy

On liver sulfur colloid scans, UES is usually a well-defined intrahepatic defect. Blood pool studies demonstrate no early uptake or delayed filling, corresponding to the hypovascular nature of this tumor.[131] Bone scintigraphy and gallium scans demonstrate no uptake by UES.[131]

Ultrasound

On sonograms, the appearance of UES ranges from a multiseptate cystic mass to an inhomogeneous, predominantly echogenic solid mass. The cysts range in size from a few millimeters to several centimeters, corresponding to the cystic changes seen grossly.[131] In a recent review of 28 cases of UES, all tumors were predominantly solid.[132]

Computed Tomography

On CT scans, UES appears as a hypodense mass resembling old intrahepatic hemorrhage and/or a biloma[133] (see Fig. 89-29A). Calcification is a rare feature.[132] Septa are seen as dense bands within the cystic tumor, corresponding to solid portions. If there is a pseudocapsule, a thin rim of dense tissue may surround the predominantly cystic tumor. On contrast-enhanced CT images, heterogeneous enhancement is present in the solid, usually peripheral portions of the mass, especially on delayed images.[94,115]

Angiography

Angiographic studies demonstrate a large hypovascular to avascular mass. Abnormal vessels, as well as hypervascular portions, can be seen in the solid component of UES. Intratumoral aneurysms, arteriovenous shunting, pooling of contrast medium, and arterial encasement can be found in tumors with a sizable solid component.

Magnetic Resonance Imaging

On MRI, UES has similar signal characteristics to cerebrospinal fluid (CSF) with high signal on T2-weighted images and low signal on T1-weighted images.[132] In addition foci of high signal intensity are seen on T1-weighted images corresponding to hemorrhage[132] (see Fig. 89-29C). If present, the pseudocapsule and septations are of low signal intensity on both T1- and T2-weighted images. The enhancement pattern of UES on postcontrast MR images is parallel to that on CT images (see Fig. 89-29D).

EPITHELIAL HEMANGIOENDOTHELIOMA

Pathologic Findings

Epithelial hemangioendothelioma (EHE) is a rare malignant hepatic neoplasm of vascular origin that develops in adults. It should not be confused with infantile hemangioendothelioma, which occurs predominantly in young children.

Incidence and Clinical Presentation

EHE is usually discovered incidentally, although jaundice, liver failure, and occasionally rupture with hemoperitoneum may be present.[134] It is more common in women than in men.

Grossly, the tumors are often multiple and are composed of neoplastic cells that infiltrate the sinusoids and intrahepatic veins. The prognosis of EHE is much more favorable than that of angiosarcoma; extrahepatic metastases occur in only one third of the reported cases.[134] It appears that the biologic behavior of this tumor is related to its matrix, including inflammation, sclerosis, and calcification.

Radiologic Findings

EHEs appear as multiple nodules that grow and coalescese, forming large confluent masses. This lesion usually develops in the periphery of the liver and commonly shows calcifications corresponding to the fibrotic nature of this tumor.[135] The calcifications are visible on plain radiographs in 15% of cases.[124]

Sonographically, EHE is primarily hypoechoic.[124,136] On CT scans, the full spectrum of growth may be seen from multiple nodules to large confluent masses.[124] On unenhanced CT scans, EHE is of low attenuation, corresponding to myxoid stroma.[124] Portions of these large, low-attenuation masses become isodense after administration of contrast material, so it is often easier to identify the extent of the disease on unenhanced scans. With extensive involvement, compensatory enlargement of the uninvolved portions of the liver is seen.[124] On angiographic examination, the tumor may be hypervascular, hypovascular, or avascular depending on the extent of hyalinization and sclerosis within the tumor.[124,136]

Invasion of hepatic veins may be seen.[124]

The MRI features of EHEs are similar to the CT appearances and either peripheral nodules or larger confluent lesions are seen.[137,138] The tumors are hypointense on T1- and hyperintense on T2-weighted images although a hypointense center may be seen on both sequences corresponding to calcification, necrosis and hemorrhage.[138] After intravenous administration of gadolinium-DTPA moderate peripheral enhancement and delayed central enhancement is seen.[138] MRI also demonstrates invasion of the portal veins by the tumor.[138] With the exception of calcification, MRI demonstrates the internal architecture of EHE better than CT.[138]

OTHER MESENCHYMAL SARCOMAS (LEIOMYOSARCOMA, MALIGNANT FIBROUS HISTIOCYTOMA)

Pathologic Findings

Primary tumors arising in mesenchymal elements of the adult liver are extremely rare. They include angiomyosarcoma, fibrous sarcoma, rhabdomyosarcoma, leiomyosarcoma, and malignant fibrous histiocytoma.[139-141] These sarcomas of the liver are usually large, solid, smoothly lobulated tumors and on cut surface show fibrous septa and/or central necrosis and hemorrhage.

Incidence and Clinical Presentation

Primary leiomyosarcoma of the liver is rare, with few cases reported in the literature.[139] The majority of patients are adults with an average age at discovery of 57 years. Leiomyosarcomas grow slowly with slowly evolving clinical abnormalities present for several months. Survival ranges from several months to years.

Radiologic Findings

On CT scans, both leiomyosarcoma and malignant fibrous histiocytoma have a similar appearance: a large, noncalcified, hypodense, homogeneous mass that exhibits inhomogeneous peripheral enhancement after contrast agent administration.[142,143] Ultrasound demonstrates a variable appearance from hyperechoic to isoechoic and hypoechoic patterns.

LYMPHOMA

Pathologic Findings

Hepatic lymphoma can be either primary or secondary and can occur in both Hodgkin's disease (HD) and non-Hodgkin's lymphoma (NHL). The majority of lymphomas of the liver are secondary; primary lymphoma is rare.[144] However, secondary lymphoma of the liver is found in more than 50% of patients with HD or NHL.[145,146]

Grossly, nodular and diffuse forms of hepatic lymphoma are seen. HD occurs more often as miliary lesions than as masses. Early in the disease, liver involvement is microscopic, but with time, small nodules from a few millimeters to several centimeters in size develop.[147] HD of the liver is almost invariably associated with splenic involvement, and the likelihood of hepatic disease is greater if there is extensive splenic disease.[148,149]

In patients with HD, a Reed-Sternberg variant type of cell is accepted as evidence for liver involvement. Typical Reed-Sternberg cells are rarely identified, particularly in biopsy specimens. In NHL, the lymphocytic form tends to be miliary whether the large cell or histiocytic varieties are nodular or tumoral.[150] In both HD and NHL, initial involvement is seen in the portal areas, because this is where the majority of the scant lymphatic tissue of the liver is found.

Incidence and Clinical Presentation

Primary hepatic lymphoma occurs most commonly in middle-aged white men.[151] Organ transplant recipients and patients with acquired immunodeficiency syndrome are at high risk for developing hepatic lymphoma. Patients usually present with right upper quadrant pain, hepatomegaly, or a tender upper abdominal mass. Hepatomegaly may be present in an uninvolved liver, and a diffusely infiltrated liver can be of normal size.[152]

Radiologic Findings

Plain Abdominal Radiographs

Plain abdominal radiographs may demonstrate hepatomegaly in cases in which the liver is markedly enlarged. Calcifications are not detected in untreated hepatic lymphoma. Barium studies may demonstrate other involved areas in the gut.

Nuclear Scintigraphy

Lymphomas may present as focal defects on technetium 99m sulfur colloid scans or with diffusely inhomogeneous hepatic uptake. Gallium citrate is taken up by normal liver tissue and lymphoma and the usefulness of the technique in the diagnosis of hepatic lymphoma is therefore questionable. However, it may help to confirm areas of liver involvement seen by other imaging techniques and may have a role in assessing response to therapy.[151,153] Occasionally, areas of increased uptake in relation to normal liver can be identified.

Ultrasound

On ultrasound studies, hepatic lymphoma appears as a hypoechoic mass or masses in the tumoral form of the disease. In the diffuse form, the echogenicity of the hepatic parenchyma may be normal or the overall architecture of the liver may be altered.[151] If there is bleeding within the lymphoma deposit, true cystic ultrasonographic characteristics may be detected.[154]

Computed Tomography

CT is currently the preferred imaging method for evaluating lymphoma of the liver, with a specificity of almost 90% and a sensitivity of almost 60%.[155,156]

Secondary hepatic lymphoma most commonly manifests as multiple well-defined, large, homogeneous low-density masses (Fig. 89-30). Areas of diffuse infiltration by lymphoma causing hepatomegaly may not be distinguishable from normal liver tissue by CT. Frequently, additional areas of involvement in the spleen; para-aortic, celiac, and periportal lymph nodes; and kidneys may be noted.[156]

Angiography

Angiographically, primary and secondary lymphomatous liver masses are usually hypovascular or avascular. There may

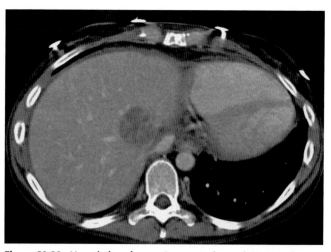

Figure 89-30. Hepatic lymphoma. Contrast-enhanced CT scan shows a lesion with heterogeneous low attenuation in the right hepatic lobe.

be arterial displacement; however, encasement is not noted. In the capillary phase, the tumor mass is relatively hypolucent.

Magnetic Resonance Imaging

Hepatic lymphoma is hypointense compared with normal liver on T1-weighted images and hyperintense on T2-weighted images. After intravenous contrast administration transient perilesional enhancement of focal hepatic lymphoma deposits has been reported. However, these tumors generally remain hypointense during the dynamic study as a result of their poor vascularity.[54,157] Although it is easy to distinguish normal liver, the difference in relaxation times of lymphoma and metastases is not significant. Diffuse hepatic lymphoma is more readily detectable by CT than by MR. Although some authors indicate that MR may be slightly more sensitive than CT for all forms of hepatic involvement, this has not been completely proved.[158]

METASTASES

Pathologic Findings

Gross Pathology

Metastases vary in size, consistency, uniformity of growth, stromal response, and vascularity (Fig. 89-31). They can be infiltrative or expansive. All these factors depend on the primary source and mode of metastasis. The gross morphologic patterns of the major liver metastases are described in Table 89-7.[159,160]

Metastatic adenocarcinomas from the gallbladder and colon often have a slimy cut surface because of mucin production. Tumors that are expanding and massive, such as colon cancer metastases, often have central liquefactive necrosis. Metastases that have significant necrosis and/or fibrosis can umbilicate the surface of the liver capsule, which is a helpful diagnostic feature because HCCs rarely cause umbilication.[159,160]

Poorly differentiated tumors such as seminomas, oat cell carcinomas, NHLs, and undifferentiated sarcomas tend to have a uniformly soft, "fish flesh-like" consistency. Squamous

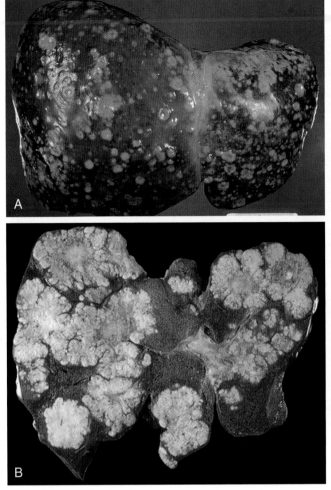

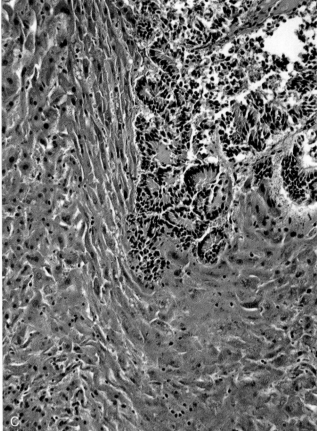

Figure 89-31. Hepatic metastases: pathology. A. Multiple metastases from breast cancer are present in both lobes of the liver. **B.** Cut section shows multiple large metastases from lung cancer. **C.** Photomicrograph shows normal liver on left and gastric cancer metastases on the right side of the image.

cell carcinomas have a granular and caseous central portion that lacks the shiny appearance of most adenocarcinomas.[159,160]

Individual metastases in the same liver can vary greatly in appearance because of differences in blood supply, hemorrhage, cellular differentiation, fibrosis, and necrosis. This variable pattern is particularly common in the vascular metastases: carcinoid, renal cell carcinoma, choriocarcinoma, and bronchogenic carcinoma.[159,160]

An unusual zone of venous stasis up to 1 cm in size is observed in approximately 25% of affected livers. This zone is uniformly circumferential, and either all or none of the metastatic foci has this finding. This phenomenon is seen most commonly with bronchogenic cancer and least commonly with colon cancer and has important implications for imaging and enhancement with contrast material.[159,160]

Microscopic Pathology

Most metastases maintain the microscopic features of the primary tumor, including the degree of stromal growth. Metastatic carcinomas of the pancreas and breast incite an intense fibrous or sclerosing reaction around the tumor acini, leading to fibrous scar formation. Oat cell carcinoma intermingles with the liver plates, blending in with the hepatocytes. In fact, some tumors with no organoid pattern at the primary site (e.g., bronchogenic carcinoma, bladder carcinoma) may retain the pattern of the sinusoidal bed and simulate a ductal liver neoplasm. In colon cancer metastases, a thin collagenous pseudocapsule is often situated between the tumor margin and compressed liver but does not surround individual tumor glands.[159,160]

Table 89-7
Morphologic Patterns of Metastatic Tumors to Liver

Pattern	Site
Expanding massive (solitary with satellites or multiple foci)	Colon, gallbladder, testis
Uniformly nodular	Lung, melanoma, pancreas
Infiltrative massive	Lung, breast, pancreas, bladder, melanoma
Uniformly multifocal	Breast, pancreas, lung, melanoma
Diffuse	Breast, pancreas, lymphomas
Surface spreading	Colon, ovary, occasionally stomach
Miliary	Prostate, occasionally any
Mixed or indeterminate	Any

Modified from Edmondson HA, Craig JR: Neoplasms of the liver. In Schiff L, Schiff ER (eds): Diseases of the Liver, 8th ed. Philadelphia, JB Lippincott, 1987, pp 1109-1158.

Approximately 7% to 15% of patients with metastatic liver disease have tumor thrombi that occlude the portal and/or hepatic veins. Metastases that penetrate the large portal veins disseminate throughout peripheral portal branches. When the hepatic veins are penetrated, pulmonary metastases can develop.[159,160]

In the presence of mucin, necrosis, and phosphatase activity, metastases can develop calcification that is detectable radiographically.[161,162] This is particularly common in metastases from mucinous adenocarcinomas of the colon, pancreas, and stomach.

Incidence and Clinical Presentation

Metastases (Table 89-8) are by far the most common cause of malignant focal liver lesions, outnumbering primary malignant tumors by a factor of 18:1. The liver is second only to regional lymph nodes as a site of metastatic disease, and approximately 25% to 50% of all patients who die of cancer have liver metastases at autopsy. Colon (42%), stomach (23%), pancreas (21%), breast (14%), and lung (13%) are the most common primary neoplasms. A silent primary with hepatic metastasis most often occurs in carcinoma of the pancreas, stomach, and lung. The highest percentage of liver metastases occurs in primary carcinoma of the gallbladder, pancreas, colon, and breast and the lowest in prostate cancer.

Approximately 50% of patients who die with metastatic carcinoma of the liver have some hepatic signs or symptoms. Hepatomegaly (31%) is the most common finding, followed by ascites (18%), jaundice (14.5%), and varices (1%). Liver function tests are notoriously unreliable for detecting metastases; they are normal in 25% to 50% of patients with metastases and can be abnormal in any number of conditions, such as parenchymal tumor replacement, tumor obstructing the intra- and/or extrahepatic bile ducts, or chemotherapy hepatotoxicity. For this reason, imaging is the key to both the diagnosis and serial follow-up of liver metastases.[161,163] In addition, cross-sectional imaging techniques now have a

unique and important role in the management of patients with hepatic metastases from colorectal cancer. Many of these patients have good survival rates of 20% to 40% at 5 years if resection of liver metastases is performed. However, the preoperative evaluation of these patients is vital in selecting those who will benefit from surgery. Accurate assessment of the presence, extent and number of liver metastases as well as the delineation of extrahepatic disease are requirements of any imaging technique.[164]

Radiologic Findings

Plain Radiographs

Plain abdominal radiographs in patients with metastatic disease are most commonly normal. Nonspecific findings include hepatomegaly, ascites, and splenomegaly, which may be due to humoral factors, tumor, or portal hypertension.[165,166]

Calcification (Table 89-9) is a more specific sign but is insensitive (<1%) except in small children with metastatic neuroblastoma, in whom the sensitivity approaches 25%. Colloid carcinomas of the colon or stomach most commonly cause calcification that has been described as stippled, amorphous, flaky, punctate, granular, or poppyseed-like. The pattern of calcification, however, seldom indicates whether the tumor is primary or metastatic, and even differentiation from benign disease may be difficult. When there is a progressive increase in the size and number of calcifications accompanied by hepatomegaly, the diagnosis of neoplasm is nearly certain. Calcification may also occur in focal areas of metastasis after radiation or chemotherapy.

Nuclear Scintigraphy

Metastases typically present as focal defects on both sulfur colloid and hepatobiliary scintiscans.[167-170] They are, in fact, the most common cause of focal "cold" liver lesions. Most often, multiple round focal defects of relatively uniform size are seen. The scintigraphic pattern, however, depends on the primary tumor type, stage of disease, and presence of underlying hepatic disease such as cirrhosis, acute or chronic hepatitis, or steatosis. When only a single defect is seen, it must be differentiated from a normal variant, cyst, abscess, or intrahepatic gallbladder. Multiple defects make the diagnosis of metastases likely, but occasionally multiple cysts, hemangiomas, or abscesses may have the appearance.[171,172]

Some tumors (leukemia, lymphoma) may infiltrate the liver diffusely whereas others (breast and oat cell carcinoma)

Table 89-8
Most Common Nonlymphoma Hepatic Metastases

Tumor	No. of Primary Tumors	No. With Metastases	Percentage With Metastases
Lung	682	285	41.8
Colon	323	181	56.0
Pancreas	179	126	70.4
Breast	218	116	53.2
Stomach	159	70	44.0
Unknown primary	102	59	57.0
Ovary	97	47	48.0
Prostate	333	42	12.6
Gallbladder	49	38	77.6
Cervix	107	34	31.7
Kidney	142	34	23.9
Melanoma	50	25	50.0
Bladder and ureter	66	25	37.9
Esophagus	66	20	30.3
Testis	45	20	44.4
Endometrium	54	17	31.5
Thyroid	70	12	17.1

Modified from Edmondson HA, Craig JR: Neoplasms of the liver. In Schiff L, Schiff ER (eds): Diseases of the Liver, 8th ed. Philadelphia, JB Lippincott, 1987, pp 1109-1158.

Table 89-9
Metastatic Liver Tumors That May Calcify

Mucinous carcinoma of the colon, stomach, and pancreas
Islet cell pancreatic tumor
Leiomyosarcoma, osteogenic sarcoma, rhabdomyosarcoma, chondrosarcoma
Papillary serous ovarian cystadenocarcinoma
Malignant melanoma
Pleural mesothelioma
Neuroblastoma
Embryonal tumor of the testis
Bronchogenic carcinoma
Breast cancer

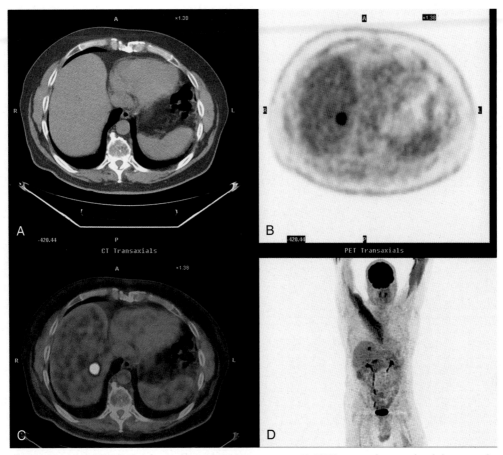

Figure 89-32. Hepatic metastases: PET/CT. A. Axial, unenhanced CT shows no mass. **B.** PET image at the same level shows uptake of FDG in the right lobe. **C.** Fused image provides precise localization of the colon cancer metastasis. **D.** Whole body PET image shows the solitary hepatic metastasis.

cause numerous small focal nodules. In both of these circumstances, hepatomegaly or diffuse heterogeneity of uptake or both may be seen. Colon cancers commonly produce large, often solitary defects.[171,172]

While nuclear scintigraphy is no longer routinely used for the detection of hepatic metastatic lesions, positron emission tomography (PET) using ^{18}F-fluorodeoxyglucose (^{18}F-FDG) recently emerged as a sensitive tool for the detection of liver metastases from colorectal primaries (Fig. 89-32).[173] ^{18}F-FDG is a glucose analog which is metabolized more rapidly in tumor cells than normal cells resulting in increased uptake in malignant lesions.[173] However, PET has important limitations. The spatial resolution is poor so complementary anatomic information from cross-sectional imaging techniques such as CT is necessary for evaluation of PET findings.[164] PET/CT is a very efficient tool to solve this problem by means of combining the metabolic imaging and spatial localization advantages of PET and CT. A second limitation is the ^{18}F-FDG uptake by inflammation which makes clinical correlation necessary to assess the significance of PET findings.[174] A possible role for PET scanning lies in assessing the response of liver metastases to therapies such as radiotherapy and chemotherapy.[175,176]

Ultrasound

Ultrasound has a diagnostic sensitivity of over 90% in the detection of metastases.[177] In the absence of complications, such as hemorrhage, infection, or necrosis, focal metastatic liver disease presents with five basic sonographic patterns (Fig. 89-33): hypoechoic, "bull's-eye" or "target" pattern, calcified, cystic, and diffuse. Although there is no consistent correlation between sonographic appearance and primary tumor type, certain generalities can be made (Table 89-10).[177-183]

Hyperechoic Metastases

These usually arise from colon cancers and other gastrointestinal neoplasms. Vascular metastases from islet cell tumors, carcinoid, choriocarcinoma, and renal cell carcinoma tend to be echogenic as well.[178] They are echogenic because of numerous interfaces arising from the abnormal vessels.

Bull's-Eye or Target Pattern

The anechoic, thin, poorly defined halo that often surrounds solid liver metastases is most often a result of peritumoral compression of normal parenchyma and less often a result of tumor infiltrating into the surrounding parenchyma. Its presence usually indicates an aggressive tumor.[184,185] This is frequently seen in metastases from bronchogenic carcinoma.

Hypoechoic Metastases

These lesions tend to be hypovascular and highly cellular with few internal interfaces. Lymphoma, particularly when associated with acquired immunodeficiency syndrome, can manifest with multiple hypoechoic deposits. More commonly, lymphoma is diffusely infiltrating.[178,179]

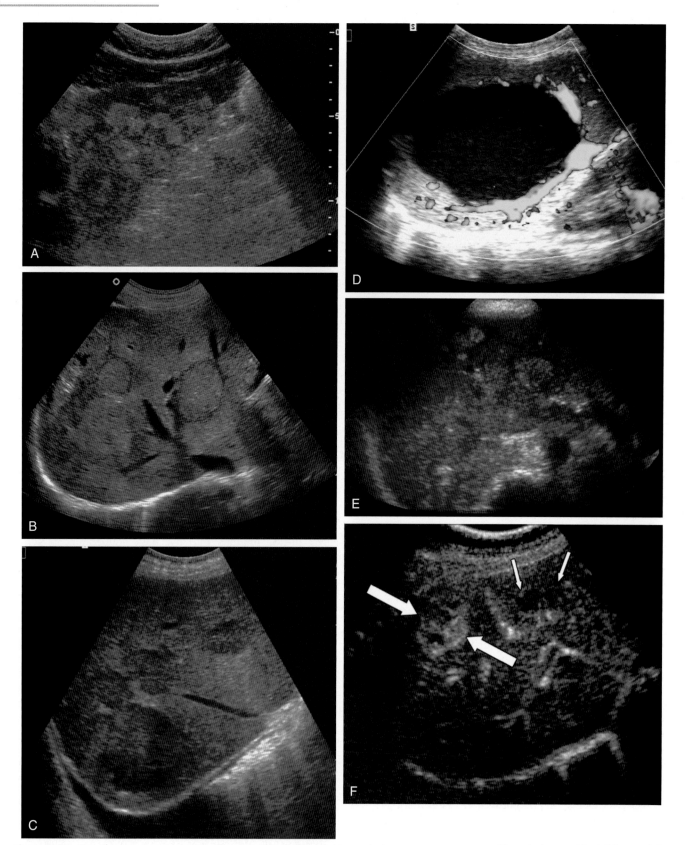

Figure 89-33.   Hepatic metastases: spectrum of sonographic findings. A. Hyperechoic metastases are seen on this sagittal scan of the left hepatic lobe in a patient with carcinoid tumor. **B.** Bull's eye lesions are present on this axial scan in a patient with metastatic lung cancer. **C.** Hypoechoic metastases are demonstrated in this patient with pancreatic cancer. There is a pleural effusion as well. **D.** Cystic metastasis with multiple fine internal echoes is present in this patient with mucinous ovarian carcinoma. **E.** Calcified metastases are seen in this patient with mucinous colon carcinoma. Hypervascular liver metastases in a 60-year-old man with previously resected retroperitoneal sarcoma. **F.** Early arterial phase US image obtained 20 seconds after contrast material injection shows a large lesion with heterogeneous and mostly peripheral (nonglobular) enhancement (*large arrows*). Two small lesions remain hypoechoic (*small arrows*).

Continued

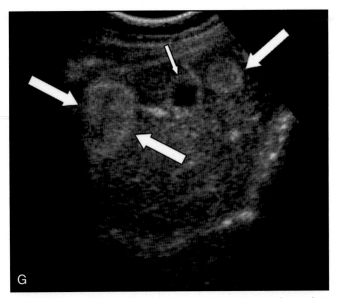

Figure 89-33, *cont'd.* **G.** Delayed arterial phase US image obtained 34 seconds after injection shows homogeneous enhancement of the large lesion and one of the small lesions (*large arrows*) and rim enhancement of the other small lesion (*small arrow*). Note that, in this case, lesion enhancement is variable and asynchronous. (**F** and **G** from Catalano O, Nunziata A, Lobianco R, et al: Real-time harmonic contrast material-specific US of focal liver lesions. RadioGraphics 25:333-349, 2005.)

Cystic Metastases

Cystic metastases usually develop in patients with primary neoplasms that have a cystic component: cystadenocarcinoma of the pancreas and ovary and mucinous carcinoma of the colon.[185] Indeed, these lesions may resemble benign cysts on CT scans. Ultrasound, however, can usually reveal

Table 89-10
Sonographic Patterns of Liver Metastases

Hypoechoic
Lymphoma
Pancreas
Cervical carcinoma
Adenocarcinoma of the lung
Nasopharyngeal cancer

Mixed Echogenicity
Breast cancer
Lung cancer
Stomach cancer
Anaplastic cancer
Cervical cancer
Carcinoid

Hyperechoic
Colon cancer
Hepatoma
Treated breast cancer

Cystic
Mucinous ovarian carcinoma
Colorectal carcinoma
Sarcoma
Melanoma
Lung cancer
Carcinoid

certain differentiating features: septa, mural nodules, debris, fluid-fluid levels, and mural thickening. When the central portion of a liver metastasis undergoes extensive necrosis, sonolucent metastases with low-level echoes and an irregularly thickened wall may be seen.[186]

Calcified Metastases

These metastases are relatively distinctive because of their marked echogenity and acoustic shadowing (see Table 89-9). Mucinous adenocarcinoma of the colon is the most common primary neoplasm associated with calcified liver metastases.[187,188]

Diffuse Infiltration

This diffuse permeative infiltration is the most difficult sonographic pattern to appreciate because the tissue texture is diffusely inhomogeneous, without the presence of well-defined masses. Diagnosis is further compromised in the presence of cirrhosis and fatty infiltration.[178,189]

Contrast-enhanced US shows lesion blood flow in metastases as a reflection of the vascularity of the primary tumor.[35] Because of this, considerable variation is seen during the arterial phase enhancement. Hypervascular metastases may reveal enhancement feature that overlap with HCC. Hypovascular metastases mostly show a slight signal enhancement with a marginal emphasis ("halo sign," "rim sign").[36] Fortunately, regardless of their appearance during the arterial phase, metastases have consistently shown less enhancement than the liver during the portal venous phase of contrast-enhanced US.

Computed Tomography

On CT scans, metastases can be hyperdense, isodense, hypodense, hypodense with peripheral enhancement, cystic, complex, calcified, or diffusely infiltrating (Figs. 89-34 through 89-37). The CT appearance depends on tumor size and vascularity, the degree of hemorrhage and necrosis, and the quality of the intravenous contrast bolus. Thus, individual metastatic lesions within the liver can have different CT findings and metastases from different cell types can appear identical.[190-194]

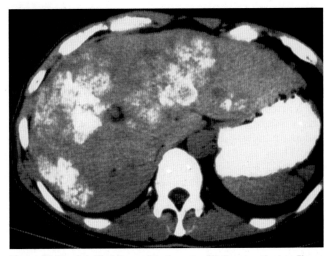

Figure 89-34. Calcified liver metastases on CT. Same patient as Figure 89-33E with mucinous adenocarcinoma of the colon.

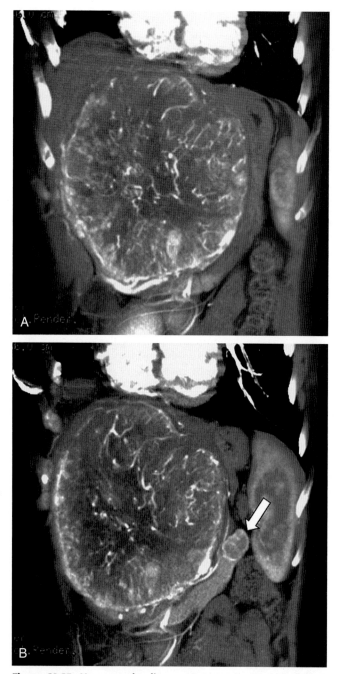

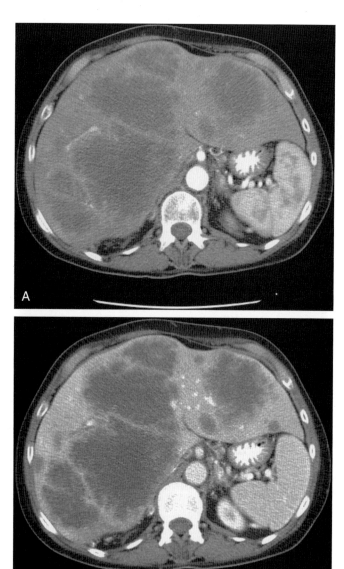

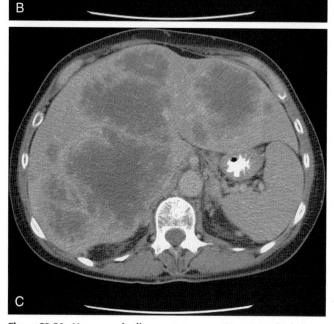

Figure 89-35. Hypervascular liver metastases on CT. A and **B.** A dominant strikingly hypervascular mass from metastatic from metastatic leptomeningeal hemangiopericytoma is demonstrated on these two coronal volume rendered images. *Arrow,* pancreatic tail metastasis.

Hyperdense metastases (see Fig. 89-35) are uncommon. These lesions are usually hypervascular (Table 89-11) and enhance rapidly and diffusely becoming isodense with normal liver. These lesions may be difficult to visualize on contrast-enhanced CT scans obtained during the portal venous phase of enhancement. Hypervascular lesions may occasionally be also seen as hypoattenuating lesions on portal venous phase (PVP) images.[195]

Islet cell tumors are among the most common of the very hypervascular metastases, with breast carcinoma, carcinoid, melanoma, thyroid carcinoma, and renal cell carcinoma also resulting in hypervascular metastases.[196]

Figure 89-36. Hypovascular liver metastases on CT. A-C. Multiple large, hypodense masses are present in both lobes of the liver. These lesions do show uniform rim enhancement.

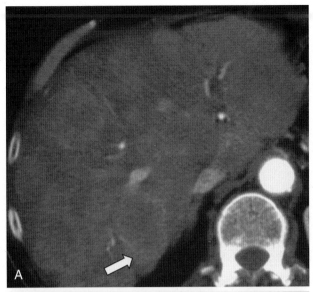

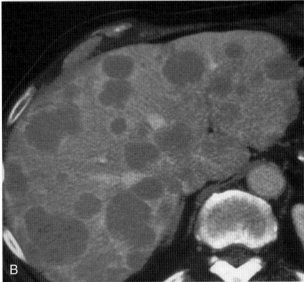

Figure 89-37. Ring enhancement of liver metastases on CT. Arterial (**A**) and portal venous (**B**) phase images show a hypervascular ring of enhancement. This complete ring of enhancement is typical of metastases but can also be seen in hepatic abscesses.

The majority of metastases are hypodense (see Fig. 89-36) with an attenuation between that of water and that of normal liver. These lesions are usually hypovascular, and intravenous contrast medium increases their conspicuity by increasing the density of normal liver. These lesions are best depicted during the portal phase of enhancement (60 seconds after

Table 89-11
Hypervascular Liver Metastases

Melanoma
Carcinoid
Pancreatic islet cell tumor
Choriocarcinoma
Pheochromocytoma
Breast cancer
Thyroid carcinoma
Renal cell carcinoma

intravenous contrast).[195,197] Colon, lung, prostate, gastric, and transitional-cell carcinoma are the most common tumors that appear as hypovascular liver metastases.[198]

On the delayed phase images, metastases are often iso-attenuating but on a 4- to 6-hour delayed phase contrast-enhanced CT scan may again appear to be of low attenuation. Some metastases will show hypoattenuating peripheral areas surrounding an enhanced center on delayed images. This appearance is thought to represent contrast material washing out of the viable tumor periphery while remaining in the extracellular space of the center.[199]

Certain metastases may be cystic, having an attenuation less than 20 Hounsfield units. Ultrasound may be needed to differentiate these lesions from simple cysts. Calcifications are also well demonstrated on CT scans.

Rim enhancement (see Fig. 89-37) of a hypodense metastasis represents a vascularized viable tumor periphery contrasted with a hypovascular or necrotic center.[190,193]

Unless the size or contour of the liver is altered, diffusely infiltrating metastases can be difficult to appreciate. Diagnosis is also difficult in patients with cirrhosis and hepatic steatosis. In these cases MR can be useful in appreciating the tumor nodules.

The borders of hepatic metastases can be sharp, ill-defined, or nodular and their shape may be ovoid, round, or irregular.

Magnetic Resonance Imaging

The T1 and T2 relaxation times of liver metastases vary considerably, depending on the primary tumor, the degree of necrosis, hemorrhage, and vascularity. Nevertheless, the T1 and T2 relaxation times of most liver metastases (Fig. 89-38) are longer than those of normal liver and shorter than those of simple cysts or hemangiomas.[200-208] Six major morphologic patterns have been described for metastases on MR images.[209]

"Doughnut"

On T1-weighted images, metastases, because of their long T1 relaxation time, present as a low signal intensity mass containing a distinct central region of even lower signal intensity. This pattern is usually seen with larger lesions and those that are prone to undergo necrosis. Metastases that contain considerable mucin, fat, subacute hemorrhage, or melanin, however, may have a relatively high signal intensity on T1-weighted images. High signal intensity has also been observed in carcinoids with hemorrhage.[209]

Target

On T2-weighted images, some metastases present with a central smooth or irregularly rounded area of high signal intensity surrounded by a rind of tissue with a somewhat weaker signal intensity. This pattern is also seen in lesions that are large and tend to undergo necrosis.[209-211]

Amorphous

These metastases have variable increased signal intensity with inhomogeneous and featureless contents. The outer margins tend to be round and indistinct.

"Halo"

These masses have a distinct but not necessarily smooth circumferential rim of high signal intensity. The rim varies

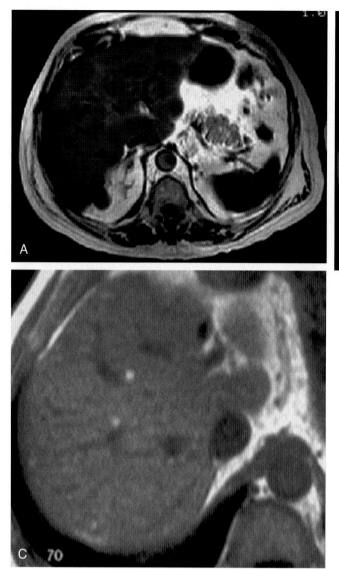

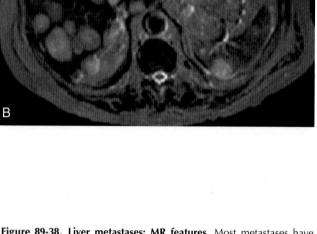

Figure 89-38. Liver metastases: MR features. Most metastases have prolonged T1 and T2 relaxation times compared with normal liver. Thus, these lesions have low signal intensity on T1-weighted images (**A**) and high signal intensity (**B**) on T2-weighted images. There are exceptions such as metastatic melanoma (**C**), in which the lesions have high signal intensity on T1-weighted images due to the presence of hemorrhage, mucin, or paramagnetic contents such as melanin. (**C** courtesy of Jay P. Heiken, MD, St. Louis, MO.)

in thickness from 2 to 10 mm and encircles a lesion of somewhat lower signal intensity. The lower signal intensity may reflect the presence of fibrosis, coagulative necrosis, and mucin. This halo is probably a manifestation of greater water content than in adjacent normal liver parenchyma, perhaps reflecting an edematous reaction incited by tumor cell infiltration. Alternatively, it may reflect a viable tumor. Therefore, the peripheral zone of hyperintensity should be assumed to represent tumor for the purposes of surgical planning and estimating tumor volume. Some 50% of colon cancer metastases have some central hypointensity.[209-211]

"Light Bulb"

These lesions are smooth, sharply defined, and round or elliptic. The contents have high signal intensity, similar to that of gallbladder, cerebrospinal fluid, cysts, and hemangiomas. In these cases the high signal intensity on T2-weighted images is attributed to either fluid contents or considerable blood flow. In metastases, this may be due to complete tumor necrosis and liquefaction or a hypervascular mass. The light bulb sign has been described in cystic neoplastic metastases, pheochromocytoma, carcinoid, and islet cell tumor.[209-212]

Role of MR Imaging

The introduction of hepatic resection as a potentially curative treatment for patients with liver metastases from colorectal primaries has created major challenges for MR imaging. The preoperative assessment of these patients requires accurate delineation of the precise number and location of metastases and their relationship to adjacent vascular structures. Also, because benign liver lesions such as cysts and hemangiomas are relatively common, imaging techniques must be able to distinguish between benign and malignant lesions with a high degree of specificity.[213] In order to improve the performance of MRI in this clinical context, numerous different sequences and contrast agents have been evaluated. The use of gadolinium-DTPA in the detection of liver metastases has been disappointing and no clear benefit of using dynamic gadolinium-enhanced sequences over unenhanced T1-weighted images has been demonstrated at 1.5 T.[214] After the administration of IV contrast material with dynamic imaging (Fig. 89-39), enhancement patterns of the hepatic metastases are similar to those on CT. Hypervascular metastases show marked early enhancement as a continuous ring that

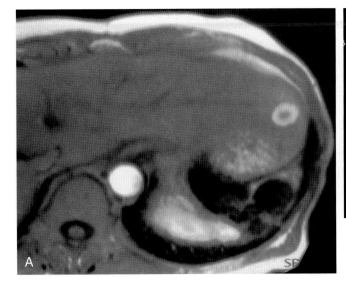

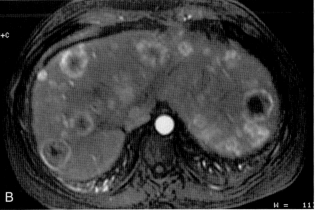

Figure 89-39. Liver metastases: ring enhancement on MR. There are complete rings of lesion enhancement seen in this patient with breast cancer and a solitary metastasis in the left lobe (**A**) and in a different patient with multiple carcinoid metastases (**B**).

on later images fill in centrally, or they may show early uniform enhancement. During the portal venous phase, hypervascular metastases may become isointense or hypointense. Hypovascular metastases are seen as hypointense masses that may have an enhancing peripheral rim best seen during the arterial phase. Progressive centripetal fill-in may occur on delayed phases.

Several recent studies have evaluated the accuracy of SPIO-enhanced MRI in the detection of liver metastases using findings at intraoperative US and pathologic examination as the gold standard.[215-217] Using SPIO, metastatic lesions should appear unenhanced against a negatively enhanced liver.[199] SPIO-enhanced MR images detected more lesions than unenhanced MRI, percutaneous US, and contrast-enhanced CT and was comparable to CTAP.[215,216] Important advantages of SPIO-enhanced MRI are its lack of invasiveness compared to CTAP and the availability of an extended imaging window allowing greater flexibility in scanning times (Fig. 89-40).[218] Gadobentate dimeglumine (Gd-BOPTA) and

gadoxetate (Gd-EOB-DTPA) are hepatobiliary positive contrast agents that show their enhancement effect on T1-weighted sequences. Using them, metastatic lesions should appear unenhanced against a positively enhanced liver. Although they have shown promising results in the detection of focal liver lesions, their exact role in the evaluation of patients with hepatic metastases and in differentiation of metastatic disease from primary disease has yet to be defined.[219-221]

Angiography

Angiography is no longer used to diagnose liver metastases but is performed to provide a vascular "road map" for the surgeon and to guide intra-arterial therapy.[222] Because metastases are almost completely supplied by the hepatic artery, injection of the celiac or superior mesenteric artery may show hypervascular tumor circulation early and hypovascularity during the venous phase as portal blood containing contrast medium perfuses the surrounding normal hepatic parenchyma.[222-224]

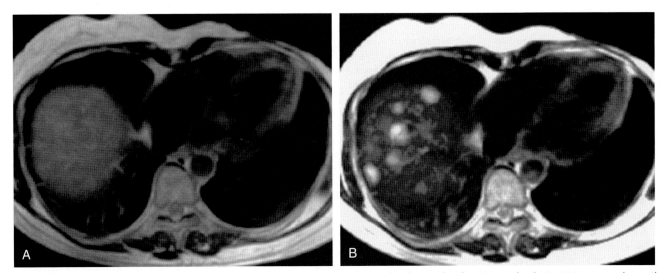

Figure 89-40. MR of liver metastases with SPIO-enhanced scan. Metastases that are barely visualized on T2-weighted (**A**) MR image can be easily detected after the administration of SPIO (**B**). (Courtesy of Dr. Tomoaki Ichikawa, Yamanashi University, Yamanashi, Japan.)

DIFFERENTIAL DIAGNOSIS—INCIDENTAL MASS

Improvements in cross-sectional imaging have led to the detection of more and smaller hepatic lesions. Detection of lesions smaller than 15 mm can be problematic because of their uncertain clinical significance. In one study using CT, a single small (<1.5 cm) lesion was benign in 65% of patients and two to four tiny lesions were benign in 59% of cases. When the number of lesions increases or an additional large lesion is present, the likelihood of malignancy increases. Even in the presence of extrahepatic malignancy, 51% of these small lesions are benign. This has important implications for patients with dominant metastases who are being considered for hepatic resection. The possibility that the other lesions are benign should be considered.[225]

Metastases are not the only causes of multiple hepatic masses. Abscess, cyst, extramedullary hematopoiesis, multifocal or diffuse HCC, ICAC, angiosarcoma, nodular regenerative hyperplasia, and hemangioma can all be multiple.

PRACTICAL APPROACH TO LIVER MASSES

The evaluation of focal liver masses should be systematic and include both radiologic appearance and clinical information to help narrow the differential diagnosis. The three most important pieces of clinical information in evaluating liver neoplasms are the age and sex of the patient and the presence of extrahepatic malignancy. In adults, metastases, FLC, FNH, and hepatocellular adenoma are seen in patients younger than 40 years of age. Metastases, typical HCC, ICAC, angiosarcoma, and hemangioma are most frequently seen in patients older than 50 years of age. In pediatric patients, the vascular tumors infantile hemangioendothelioma and hemangioma are seen in the first 6 months of life. Hepatoblastoma usually presents in the first 3 years of life, and although it may be present at birth, the peak incidence is at 18 months. Benign mesenchymal hamartoma has an incidence similar to that of hepatoblastoma. Tumors that occur in older children and adolescents include HCC and UES. With regard to sex, malignant primary liver tumors are generally more frequent in men and benign primary tumors in women. Metastases are overwhelmingly more frequent than primary liver neoplasms in both the pediatric and the adult population.

Other significant clinical data include a history of chronic steroid and contraceptive use. Neoplasms related to steroid use include hepatocellular adenoma and to a lesser degree FNH, nodular regenerative hyperplasia, hemangioma, and HCC.

Multiple imaging tests are available for evaluating hepatic neoplasms. Contrast-enhanced dynamic MR and CT imaging and sonography provide important diagnostic clues that can help establish a final diagnosis. When interpreting a hepatic imaging study, the parameters to consider are the presence of single versus multiple masses; calcification; sharpness of contour; presence, absence, or persistence of enhancement; patency of vessels; and extrahepatic extension.

After all these considerations, the radiologist must determine whether a hepatic mass is a nonsurgical lesion. In the adult, the two most common nonsurgical primary tumors are hemangioma and FNH. All other primary neoplasms of the liver are surgical lesions if they are resectable. Therefore, the two most important determinations the radiologist must make are whether the mass in the liver is either hemangioma or FNH and, if it is not, whether the mass is resectable for cure. Metastases, HCC, FLC, ICAC, angiosarcoma, and hepatocellular adenoma are all potentially resectable in the adult. In children, hepatoblastoma, UES, HCC, and mesenchymal hamartoma are all surgical lesions. Infantile hemangioendothelioma does not require surgery if the patient can survive with supportive therapy or embolization until the tumor regresses spontaneously.

Hemangioma has a highly suggestive appearance on ultrasound, CT, MR, and scintigraphic studies. However, the optimal imaging techniques are dynamic MRI with gadolinium enhancement and contrast-enhanced CT (see Chapter 84). The appearance of FNH on US, CT, and unenhanced MRI is nonspecific, unless a central scar is present, and overlaps with FLC and HCA. However, gadolinium-enhanced dynamic MR imaging and T2-weighted MR images enhanced with SPIO may demonstrate imaging features of FNH which aid in narrowing differential diagnosis. FNH shows characteristically dramatic signal loss. The degree of signal loss is greater than in other focal liver lesions such as HCA and metastases and is a useful diagnostic feature for FNH.[226]

Finally, the use of percutaneous needle biopsies should be considered for exceptional cases, when noninvasive imaging studies have yielded atypical or inconclusive findings. In general, liver biopsies are devoid of significant risk when performed with CT or ultrasound guidance.[227] Sometimes, the material obtained by percutaneous biopsy is not sufficient for a diagnosis and an open biopsy should be done.

In summary, the differential diagnosis of a liver neoplasm can be narrowed significantly by using different imaging and clinical features.[228] In addition, percutaneous biopsy may be useful in further defining tumors without a characteristic imaging appearance.

References

1. Burns PN, Wilson SR: Focal liver masses: Enhancement patterns on contrast-enhanced images—concordance of US scans with CT scans and MR images. Radiology 242:162-174, 2007.
2. Ros PR, Rasmussen JF, Li KCP: Radiology of malignant and benign liver tumors. Curr Probl Diagn Radiol 11:95-99, 1989.
3. Lim JH, Choi D, Park CK, et al: Encapsulated hepatocellular carcinoma: CT-pathologic correlations. Eur Radiol 16:2326-2333, 2006.
4. Freeny PC, Baron RL, Teefey SA: Hepatocellular carcinoma: Reduced frequency of typical findings with dynamic contrast-enhanced CT in a non-Asian population. Radiology 182:143-148, 1992.
5. Catala V, Nicolau C, Vilana R, et al: Characterization of focal liver lesions: Comparative study of contrast-enhanced ultrasound versus spiral computed tomography. Eur Radiol 17:1066-1073, 2007.
6. Noguchi S, Yamamoto R, Tatsuta M, et al: Cell features and patterns in fine-needle aspirates of hepatocellular carcinoma. Cancer 58:321-328, 1986.
7. Nakashima T, Kojiro M: Hepatocellular Carcinoma: An Atlas of Its Pathology. Tokyo, Springer-Verlag, 1987.
8. Ros PR: Focal liver masses other than metastases. In Gore RM (ed): Syllabus for Categorical Course on Gastrointestinal Radiology. Reston, VA, American College of Radiology, 1991, pp 159-169.
9. Sadek AG, Mitchell DG, Siegelman ES, et al: Early hepatocellular carcinoma that develops within macroregenerative nodules: Growth depicted at serial MR imaging. Radiology 195:753-756, 1995.
10. International Working Party: Terminology of nodular hepatocellular lesions. Hepatology 22:983-993, 1995.
11. Hecht EM, Holland AE, Israel GM, et al: Hepatocellular carcinoma in the cirrhotic liver: Gadolinium-enhanced 3D T1-weighted MR imaging as a stand-alone sequence for diagnosis. Radiology 239:438-447, 2006.

12. Wu T-T, Boitnott J: Dysplastic nodules: A new term for premalignant hepatic nodular lesions. Radiology 201:21-22, 1996.
13. Kew MC: Hepatic tumors and cysts. In Feldman M, Scharschmidt BF, Sleisinger MH (eds): Sleisinger & Fordtran's Gastrointestinal and Liver Disease, 6th ed. Philadelphia, WB Saunders, 1998, pp 1364-1387.
14. Nakashima T, Okuda K, Kojiro M, et al: Pathology of HCC in Japan: 232 Consecutive cases autopsied in ten years. Cancer 51:863-877, 1983.
15. Kanematsu M, Imaeda T, Yamawaki Y, et al: Rupture of hepatocellular carcinoma: Predictive value of CT findings. AJR 158:1247-1250, 1992.
16. Kudo M, Hirasa M, Takakuwa H, et al: Small hepatocellular carcinomas in chronic liver disease: Detection with SPECT. Radiology 159:697-703, 1986.
17. Ho CL: Clinical PET imaging—an Asian perspective. Ann Acad Med Singapore 33:155-65, 2004.
18. Cottone M, Mareceno MP, Maringhini A, et al: Ultrasound in the diagnosis of hepatocellular carcinoma associated with cirrhosis. Radiology 147:517-519, 1983.
19. Tanaka S, Kitamura T, Imaoka S, et al: Hepatocellular carcinoma: Sonographic and histologic correlation. AJR 140:701-707, 1983.
20. Kudo M, Ikekubo K, Yamamoto K, et al: Distinction between hemangioma of the liver and hepatocellular carcinoma: Value of labeled RBC-SPECT scanning. AJR 152:977-983, 1989.
21. Shapiro RS, Katz R, Mendelson DS et al: Detection of hepatocellular carcinoma in cirrhotic patients: Sensitivity of CT and ultrasonography. J Ultrasound Med 15:497-502, 1996.
22. Solmi L, Primareno AM, Gondolfi L: Ultrasound follow-up of patients at risk for hepatocellular carcinoma: Results of a prospective study of 360 cases. Am J Gastroenterol 91:1189-1194, 1996.
23. Takayasu K, Moriyama N, Muramatsu Y, et al: The diagnosis of small hepatocelluar carcinomas: Efficacy of various imaging procedures in 100 patients. AJR 155:49-54, 1990.
24. DeSantis M, Romagnoli R, Cristani A, et al: MRI of small hepatocellular carcinoma: Comparison with US, CT, DSA and Lipiodol-CT. J Comput Assist Tomogr 16:189-197, 1992.
25. Catalano O, Nunziata A, Lobianco, R, et al: Real-time harmonic contrast material-specific US of focal liver lesions. RadioGraphics 25:333-349, 2005.
26. Lencioni R, Pinto F, Armilotta N, et al: Assessment of tumor vascularity in hepatocellular carcinoma: Comparison of power Doppler US and color Doppler US. Radiology 201:353-358, 1996.
27. Tanaka S, Kitamara T, Fujita M, et al: Small hepatocellular carcinoma: Differentiation from adenomatous hyperplastic nodule with color Doppler flow imaging. Radiology 182:161-165, 1992.
28. Wilson SR, Burns PN, Muradali D, et al: Harmonic hepatic US with microbubble contrast agent: Initial experience showing improved characterization of hemangioma, hepatocellular carcinoma, and metastasis. Radiology 215:153-184, 2000.
29. Tarantino L, Francica G, Sordelli I, et al: Diagnosis of benign and malignant portal vein thrombosis in cirrhotic patients with hepatocellular carcinoma: Color Doppler US, contrast-enhanced US, and fine-needle biopsy. Abdom Imaging 31:537-544, 2006.
30. Kudo M, Tomita S, Tochio H, et al: Small hepatocellular carcinoma: Diagnosis with US angiography with intraarterial CO_2 microbubbles. Radiology 182:155-160, 1992.
31. Brannigan M, Burns PN, Wilson SR: Blood flow patterns in focal liver lesions at microbubble-enhanced US. RadioGraphics 24:921-935, 2004.
32. Dietrich CF: Characterisation of focal liver lesions with contrast enhanced ultrasonography. Eur J Radiol 51(Suppl):S9-S17, 2004.
33. Brannigan M, Burns PN, Wilson SR: Blood flow patterns in focal liver lesions at microbubble-enhanced US. RadioGraphics 24:921-935, 2004.
34. Jang HJ, Lim JH, Lee SJ, et al: Hepatocellular carcinoma: Are combined CT during arterial portography and CT hepatic arteriography in addition to triple-phase helical CT all necessary for preoperative evaluation? Radiology 215:373-380, 2000.
35. Doyle DJ, O'Malley ME, Jang HJ, et al: Value of the unenhanced phase for detection of hepatocellular carcinomas 3 cm or less when performing multiphase computed tomography in patients with cirrhosis. J Comput Assist Tomogr 31:86-92, 2007.
36. Yu SC, Yeung DT, So NM: Imaging features of hepatocellular carcinoma. Clin Radiol 59:145-156, 2004.
37. Tublin ME, Dodd GD 3rd, Baron RL: Benign and malignant portal vein thrombosis: Differentiation by CT characteristics. Am J Roentgenol 168:719-723, 1997.
38. Iannaccone R, Piacentini F, Murakami T, et al: Hepatocellular carcinoma in patients with nonalcoholic fatty liver disease: Helical CT and MR

imaging findings with clinical-pathologic comparison. Radiology 2007 Mar 13 [Epub ahead of print].
39. Choi BG, Park SH, Byun JY, et al: The findings of ruptured hepatocellular carcinoma on helical CT. Br J Radiol 74:142-146, 2001.
40. Winter TC III, Freeny PC, Nghiem HV, et al: Hepatic arterial anatomy in transplantation candidates: Evaluation with three-dimensional CT arteriography. Radiology 195:363-370, 1995.
41. Sumida M, Ohto M, Ebara M, et al: Accuracy of angiography in the diagnosis of small hepatocellular carcinoma. AJR 147:531-536, 1986.
42. Kanazawa S, Yusui K, Doke T, et al: Hepatic arteriography in patients with hepatocellular carcinoma. AJR 147:531-536, 1995.
43. Mathieu D, Guinet C, Bouklia-Hassane A, et al: Hepatic vein involvement in hepatocellular carcinoma. Gastrointest Radiol 13:55-60, 1988.
44. Fujita T, Honjo K, Ito K, et al: High-resolution dynamic MR imaging of hepatocellular carcinoma with a phased-array body coil. RadioGraphics 17:315-331, 1997.
45. Li CS, Chen RC, Lii JM, et al: Magnetic resonance imaging appearance of well-differentiated hepatocellular carcinoma. J Comput Assist Tomogr 30:597-603, 2006.
46. Ohtomo K, Matsuoka Y, Abe O, et al: High-resolution MR imaging evaluation of hepatocellular carcinoma. Abdom Imaging 22:182-186, 1997.
47. Murakami T, Kim T, Nakamura H, et al: Hepatitis, cirrhosis, and hepatoma. J Magn Reson Imaging 8:346-358, 1998.
48. Mitchell DG, Rubin R, Siegelman ES, et al: Hepatocellular carcinoma within siderotic regenerative nodules: Appearance as a nodule within a nodule on MR images. Radiology 178:101-103, 1991.
49. Mitchell DG: Focal manifestations of diffuse liver disease at MR imaging. Radiology 185:1-11, 1992.
50. Brown JJ, Naylor MJ, Yagan N, et al: Imaging of hepatic cirhosis. Radiology 202:1-16, 1997.
51. Harisinghani MG, Hahn PF: Computed tomography and magnetic resonance imaging evaluation of liver cancer. Gastroenterol Clin North Am 31:759-776, 2002.
52. Hussain SM, Zondervan PE, IJzermans JN, et al: Benign versus malignant hepatic nodules: MR imaging findings with pathologic correlation. RadioGraphics 22:1023-1036, 2002.
53. Shimamoto K, Sakuma S, Ishigaki T, et al: Hepatocellular carcinoma: Evaluation with color Doppler US and MR imaging. Radiology 182:149-153, 1992.
54. Yamamoto H, Yamashita Y, Yoshimatsu S, et al: Hepatocellular carcinoma in cirrhotic livers: Detection with unenhanced and iron-oxide enhanced MR imaging. Radiology 195:106-112, 1995.
55. Hytiroglu P, Theise ND: Differential diagnosis of hepatocellular nodular lesions. Semin Diagn Pathol 15:285-299, 1998.
56. Yu JS, Cho ES, Kim KH, et al: Newly developed hepatocellular carcinoma (HCC) in chronic liver disease: MR imaging findings before the diagnosis of HCC. J Comput Assist Tomogr 30:765-771, 2006.
57. Mitchell DG, Rubin R, Mitchell DG, et al: Hepatocellular carcinoma within siderotic regenerative nodules: Appearance as a nodule within a nodule on MR images. Radiology 178:101-103, 1991.
58. Becker CD, Grossholz M, Mentha G, al: Ablation of hepatocellular carcinoma by percutaneous ethanol injection: Imaging findings. Cardiovasc Intervent Radiol 20:204-209, 1997.
59. Lencioni R, Pinto F, Armilotta N, et al: Long-term results of percutaneous ethanol injection therapy for hepatocellular carcinoma in cirrhosis: European experience. Eur Radiol 7:514-549, 1997.
60. Okazaki M, Higashihara H, Koganemaru F, et al: Intraperitoneal hemorrhage from hepatocellular carcinoma: Emergency chemoembolization or embolization. Radiology 180:647-651, 1991.
61. Takayasu K, Wakao F, Moriyama N, et al: Response of early-stage hepatocellular carcinoma and borderline lesions to therapeutic arterial embolization. AJR 160:301-306, 1993.
62. Uchida H, Matsuo N, Nishimine K, et al: Transcatheter arterial embolization for hepatoma with Lipiodol. Semin Intervent Radiol 10:19-26, 1993.
63. Livraghi T, Salmi A, Bolondi L, et al: Small hepatocellular carcinoma: Percutaneous alcohol injection-results in 23 patients. Radiology 168:313-317, 1988.
64. Raoul J-L, Bourguet P, Bretagne J-F, et al: Hepatic artery injection of I-131-labeled Lipiodol. Part I. Biodistribution study results in patients with hepatocellular carcinoma and liver metastases. Radiology 168:541-545, 1988.
65. Bretagne J-F, Raoul J-L, Bourguet P, et al: Hepatic artery injection of I-131-labeled Lipiodol. Part II: Preliminary results of therapeutic use in

patients with hepatocellular carcinoma and liver metastases. Radiology 168:547-550, 1988.

66. Curley SA, Jones DV: Management of hepatocellular carcinoma. In Meyers MA (ed): Neoplasms of the Digestive Tract: Imaging, Staging, and Management. Philadelphia, Lippincott-Raven, 1998, pp 347-360.

67. Motoo Y, Okai T, Matsui O, et al: Liver atrophy after transcatheter arterial embolization and percutaneous ethanol injection therapy for a minute hepatocellular carcinoma. Gastrointest Radiol 16:164-166, 1991.

68. Renaro V, Merlet C, Hagege H: Fibrolamellar liver cell carcinoma. Ann Gastroenterol Hepatol 27:314-321, 1992.

69. Craig JR, Peters RL, Edmondson JL: Fibrolamellar carcinoma of the liver. Cancer 46:372-379, 1980.

70. Renaro V, Merlet C, Hagege H: Fibrolamellar liver cell carcinoma. Ann Gastroenterol Hepatol 27:314-321, 1992.

71. Berman MA, Burnham JA, Sheahan DG: Fibrolamellar carcinoma of the liver: An immunohistochemical study of nineteen cases and a review of the literature. Hum Pathol 19:784-794, 1988.

72. Friedman AC, Lichtenstein JE, Goodman Z, et al: Fibrolamellar hepatocellular carcinoma. Radiology 157:583-587, 1985.

73. McLarney JK, Rucker PT, Bender GN, et al: Fibrolamellar carcinoma of the liver: Radiologic-pathologic correlation. RadioGraphics 19:453-471, 1999.

74. Buetow PC, Midkiff RB: Primary malignant neoplasms in the adult. MRI Clin North Am 5:289-318, 1997.

75. Francis IR, Agha FP, Thompson NW, et al: Fibrolamellar hepatocarcinoma: Clinical, radiologic and pathologic features. Gastrointest Radiol 11:67-72, 1986.

76. Ross Stevens W, Johnson CD, Stephens DH, et al: Fibrolamellar hepatocellular carcinoma: Stage at presentation and results of aggressive surgical management. AJR 164:1153-1158, 1995.

77. Mattison GR, Glazer GM, Quint LE, et al: MR imaging of hepatic focal nodular hyperplasia: Characterization and distinction from primary malignant hepatic tumors. AJR 148:711-715, 1987.

78. Corrigan K, Semelka RC: Dynamic contrast-enhanced MR imaging of fibrolamellar hepatocellular carcinoma. Abdom Imaging 20:122-125, 1995.

79. Hamrick-Turner JE, Shipkey FH, Cranston PE: Fibrolamellar hepatocellular carcinoma: MR appearance mimicking focal nodular hyperplasia. J Comput Assist Tomogr 18:301-304, 1994.

80. Caseiro-Alves F, Zins M, Mahfouz A-E: Calcification in focal nodular hyperplasia: A new problem for differentiation from fibrolamellar hepatocellular carcinoma. Radiology 198:889-892, 1996.

81. Ishak KG, Glunz PR: Hepatoblastoma and hepatocarcinoma in infancy and childhood. Report of 47 cases. Cancer 20:396-422, 1967.

82. Weinberg AG, Finegold MJ: Primary malignant tumors of childhood. Hum Pathol 14:512-537, 1983.

83. Haas JE, Muczynski KA, Krailo M, et al: Histopathology and prognosis in childhood hepatoblastoma and hepatocarcinoma. Cancer 64:1082-1095, 1989.

84. Murakami T, Baron RL, Peterson MS, et al: Hepatocellular carcinoma: MR imaging with mangafodipir trisodium (MnDPDP). Radiology 200:69-77, 1996.

85. Stringer MD: The role of liver transplantation in the management of paediatric liver tumours. Ann R Coll Surg Engl 89:12-21, 2007.

86. Davey MS, Cohen MD: Imaging of gastrointestinal malignancy in childhood. Radiol Clin North Am 34:717-742, 1996.

87. Dachman AH, Parker RL, Ros PR, et al: Hepatoblastoma: A radiologic-pathologic correlation in 50 cases. Radiology 164:15-19, 1987.

88. Kaude JV, Felman AH, Hawkins IF Jr: Ultrasonography in primary hepatic tumors in early childhood. Pediatr Radiol 9:77-83, 1980.

89. Miller JH: The ultrasonographic appearance of cystic hepatoblastoma. Radiology 138:141-143, 1981.

90. Bates SM, Keller MS, Ramos IM, et al: Hepatoblastoma: Detection of tumor vascularity with duplex Doppler US. Radiology 176:505-507, 1990.

91. Helmberger TK, Ros PR, Mergo PJ, et al: Pediatric liver neoplasms: A radiologic-pathologic correlation. Eur Radiol 9:1339-1347, 1999.

92. Plumley DA, Grosfeld JL, Kopecky KK, et al: The role of spiral (helical) computerized tomography with three-dimensional reconstruction in pediatric solid tumors. J Pediatr Surg 30:317-321, 1995.

93. Smith WL, Franken EA, Mitros FA: Liver tumors in children. Semin Roentgenol 18:136-148, 1983.

94. Powers C, Ros PR, Stoupis C, et al: Primary liver neoplasms: MR imaging with pathologic correlation. RadioGraphics 14:459-482, 1994.

95. Lu M, Greer ML: Hypervascular multifocal hepatoblastoma: Dynamic gadolinium-enhanced MRI findings indistinguishable from infantile hemangioendothelioma. Pediatr Radiol 37:587-591, 2007.

96. Boechat MI, Kangarloo H, Ortega J, et al: Primary liver tumors in children: Comparison of CT and MR imaging. Radiology 169:727-732, 1988.

97. Klatskin G: Adenocarcinoma of the hepatic duct at its bifurcation within the porta hepatis. Am J Med 38:241-256, 1965.

98. Ros PR, Buck JL, Goodman ZD, et al: Intrahepatic cholangiocarcinoma: Radiologic-pathologic correlation. Radiology 167:689-693, 1988.

99. Welzel TM, Mellemkjaer L, Gloria G, et al: Risk factors for intrahepatic cholangiocarcinoma in a low-risk population: A nationwide case-control study. Int J Cancer 120:638-641, 2007.

100. Soyer P, Bluemke DA, Reichle R, et al: Imaging of cholangiocarcinoma: 1. Peripheral cholangiocarcinoma. AJR 165:1427-1431, 1995. Carr DH, Hadjis NS, Banks LM, et al: Computed tomography of hilar cholangiocarcinoma: a new sign. AJR 145:53-56, 1985.

101. Choi BI, Han JK, Kim TK: Diagnosis and staging of cholangiocarcinaoma by computed tomography. In Meyers MA (ed): Neoplasms of the Digestive Tract: Imaging, Staging, and Management. Philadelphia, Lippincott-Raven, 1998, pp 503-516.

102. Itai Y, Araki T, Furui S, et al: Computed tomography of primary intrahepatic biliary malignancy. Radiology 147:485-490, 1983.

103. Meyers MA: Cholangiocarcinoma: imaging, staging, and management. In Meyers MA (ed): Neoplasms of the Digestive Tract: Imaging, Staging, and Management. Philadelphia, Lippincott-Raven, 1998, pp 150-183.

104. Fan ZM, Yamashita Y, Harada M, et al: Intrahepatic cholangiocarcinoma: Spin-echo and contrast-enhanced dynamic MR imaging. AJR 161:313-317, 1993.

105. Adjei ON, Tamura S, Sugimura H, et al: Contrast-enhanced MR imaging of intrahepatic cholangiocarcinoma. Clin Radiol 50:6-10, 1995.

106. Carson JG, Huerta S, Butler JA: Hepatobiliary cystadenoma: A case report and a review of the literature. Curr Surg 63:285-289, 2006.

107. Teoh AY, Ng SS, Lee KF, et al: Biliary cystadenoma and other complicated cystic lesions of the liver: Diagnostic and therapeutic challenges. World J Surg 30:1560-1566, 2006.

108. Buetow PC, Buck JL, Pantongrag-Brown L, et al: Biliary cystadenoma and cystadenocarcinoma: Clinical-imaging-pathologic correlation with emphasis on the importance of ovarian stroma. Radiology 196:805-810, 1995.

109. Murphy BJ, Casillas J, Ros PR, et al: The CT appearance of cystic masses of the liver. RadioGraphics 9:307-322, 1989.

110. Ishak KG: Benign tumors and pseudotumors of the liver. Appl Pathol 6:82-104, 1988.

111. Mortele KJ, Ros PR: Cystic focal liver lesions in the adult: Differential CT and MR imaging features. RadioGraphics 21:895-910, 2001.

112. Stoupis C, Ros PR, Dolson DJ: Recurrent biliary cystadenoma: MR imaging appearance. JMRI 4:99-101, 1994.

113. Seidel R, Weinrich M, Pistorius G, et al: Biliary cystadenoma of the left intrahepatic duct. Eur Radiol 17:1380-1383, 2007.

114. Kojiro M, Nakashima T, Ito Y, et al: Thorium dioxide-related angiosarcoma of the liver. Pathomorphic study of 29 autopsy cases. Arch Pathol Lab Med 109:853-857, 1985.

115. Ito Y, Kojiro M, Nakashima T, et al: Pathomorphologic characteristics of 102 cases of Thorotrast-related hepatocellular carcinoma, cholangiocarcinoma, and hepatic angiosarcoma. Cancer 62:1153-1162, 2988.

116. Ishak KG: Mesenchymal tumors of the liver. In Okuda K, Peter RL (eds): Hepatocellular Carcinoma. New York, John Wiley & Sons, 1976, pp 228-587.

117. Ishak KG: Pathogenesis of liver diseases. In Farber E, Phillips MJ, Kaufman N (eds): International Academy of Pathology Monograph, No. 28. Baltimore, Williams & Wilkins, 1987, pp 314-315.

118. Heo SH, Jeong YY, Shin SS, et al: Solitary small hepatic angiosarcoma: Initial and follow-up imaging findings. Korean J Radiol 8:180-183, 2007.

119. Levy DW, Rindsberg S, Friedman AC, et al: Thorotrast-induced hepatosplenic neoplasia: CT identification. AJR 146:997-1004, 1986.

120. Buetow PC, Buck JL, Ros PR, et al: Malignant vascular tumors of the liver: Radiologic-pathologic correlation. RadioGraphics 14:153-166, 1994.

121. Weitz J, Klimstra DS, Cymes K, et al: Management of primary liver sarcomas. Cancer 109:1391-1396, 2007.

122. Azodo MVU, Gutierrez OH, Greer T: Thorotrast-induced ruptured hepatic angiosarcoma. Abdom Imaging 18:78-81, 1993.

123. Whelan JG Jr, Creech JL, Tamburro CL: Angiographic and radionuclide characteristics of hepatic angiosarcoma in vinyl chloride workers. Radiology 118:549-557, 1976.

124. Worawattanakul S, Semelka RC, Kelekis NL, et al: Angiosarcoma of the liver: MR imaging pre- and post chemotherapy. Magn Reson Imaging 15:613-617, 1997.

125. Stocker JT, Ishak KG: Undifferential (embryonal) sarcoma of the liver. Report of 31 cases. Cancer 42:336-348, 1978.

126. Horowitz ME, Etcubanas E, Webber BL, et al: Hepatic differentiated (embryonal) sarcoma and rhabdomyosarcoma in children. Results of therapy. Cancer 59:396-402, 1987.

127. Ros PR, Olmsted WW, Dachman AH, et al: Undifferentiated (embryonal) sarcoma of the liver: Radiologic-pathologic correlation. Radiology 160:141-145, 1986.

128. Buetow PC, Buck JL, Pantongrag-Brown L, et al: Undifferentiated (embryonal) sarcoma of the liver: Pathologic basis of imaging findings in 28 cases. RadioGraphics 203:779-783, 1997.

129. Vermess M, Collier NA, Mutum SS, et al: Misleading appearance of a rare malignant liver tumor on computed tomography. Br J Radiol 57:262-265, 1984.

130. Garcia-Botella A, Diez-Valladares L, Martin-Antona E, et al: Epithelioid hemangioendothelioma of the liver. J Hepatobiliary Pancreat Surg 13:167-171, 2006.

131. Miller WJ, Dodd GD, Federle MP, et al: Epithelioid hemangioendothelioma of the liver: Imaging findings with pathologic correlation. AJR 159:53-57, 1992.

132. Radin DR, Craig JR, Colletti PM: Hepatic epithelioid hemangioendothelioma. Radiology 169:145-148, 1988.

133. Ohtomo K, Araki T, Itai Y, et al: MR imaging of malignant mesenchymal tumors of the liver. Gastrointest Radiol 17:58-62, 1992.

134. Van Beers B, Roche A, Mathieu D, et al: Epithelioid hemangioendothelioma of the liver: MR and CT findings. J Comput Assist Tomogr 16:420-424, 1992.

135. Ferrozzi F, Bova D, Zangrandi A, et al: Primary liver leiomyosarcoma: CT appearance. Abdom Imaging 21:157-160, 1996.

136. Alberti-Flor JJ, O'Hara MF, Weaver F, et al: Malignant fibrous histiocytoma of the liver. Gastroenterology 89:890-893, 1985.

137. Conran RM, Stocker JT: Malignant fibrous histiocytoma of the liver: A case report. Am J Gastroenterol 80:813-815, 1985.

138. Reed RG, Goodman P, Soloway RD: Primary malignant fibrous histiocytoma of the liver: MRI findings. Magn Reson Imaging 11:139-143, 1993.

139. Soyer P, Bluemke DA, Riopel M, et al: Hepatic leiomyosarcomas: CT features with pathologic correlation. Eur J Radiol 19:177-182, 1995.

140. Loddenkemper C, Longerich T, Hummel M, et al: Frequency and diagnostic patterns of lymphomas in liver biopsies with respect to the WHO classification. Virchows Arch 450:493-502, 2007.

141. Levitan R, Diamond HD, Graver LF: The liver in Hodgkin disease. Gut 2:60-71, 1971.

142. Ohsawa M, Aozasa K, Horiuchi K, et al: Malignant lymphoma of the liver. Dig Dis Sci 37:1105-1109, 1992.

143. Sherlock S, Dooley J: Diseases of the Liver and Biliary System, 9th ed. Oxford, Blackwell Scientific Publications, 1993, pp 44-61.

144. Gowing NFC: Modes of death and post mortem studies. In Smithers D (ed): Hodgkin Disease. Edinburgh, Churchill Livingstone, 1973, pp 163-166.

145. Bruneton JN, Schnider M: Radiology of Lymphoma. New York, Springer-Verlag, 1986.

146. Jaffe ES: Malignant lymphoma: Pathology of hepatic involvement. Semin Liver Dis 7:257-268, 1987.

147. Shirkhoda A, Ros PR, Farah J, et al: Lymphoma of the solid abdominal viscera. Radiol Clin North Am 28:785-799, 1990. Biemer JJ: Hepatic manifestations of lymphoma. Ann Clin Lab 14:252-260, 1984.

148. Ben Haim S, Bar-Shalom R, Israel O, et al: Liver involvement in lymphoma: Role of gallium-67 scintigraphy. J Nucl Med 36:900-904, 1995.

149. Ginaldi S, Bernardino ME, Jing BS: Patterns of hepatic lymphoma. Radiology 136:427-431, 1980.

150. Zornoza J, Ginaldi S: Computed tomography in hepatic lymphoma. Radiology 138:405-410, 1981.

151. Castellino RA, Hoppe RT, Blank N, et al: Computed tomography, lymphography and staging laparotomy in colon: Correlations in staging of Hodgkin disease. AJR 143:37-41, 1984.

152. Kelekis NL, Semelka RC, Siegelman ES, et al: Focal hepatic lymphoma: Magnetic resonance demonstration using current techniques including gadolinium enhancement. Magn Reson Imaging 15:625-636, 1997.

153. Weissleder R, Stark DD, Elizondo G: MRI of hepatic lymphoma. Magn Reson Imaging 6:675-681, 1988.

154. Le Brecque DR: Neoplasia of the liver. In Kaplowitz N (ed): Liver and Biliary Disease, 2nd ed. Baltimore, Williams & Wilkins, 1996, pp 391-438.

155. Goodman ZD: Nonparenchymal and metastatic malignant tumors of the liver. In Haubrich WS, Schaffner F, Berk JE (eds): Bockus Gastroenterology. Philadelphia, WB Saunders, 1995, pp 2488-2500.

156. Golding SJ, Fletcher EWL: The radiology of secondary malignant neoplasms of the liver. In Wilkins RA, Nunnerley HB (eds): Imaging of the Liver, Pancreas and Spleen. Oxford, Blackwell Scientific Publications, 1990, pp 198-219.

157. Wilson MA: Metastatic disease of the liver. In Wilson MA, Ruzicka FF (eds): Modern Imaging of the Liver. New York, Marcel Dekker, 1989, pp 631-659.

158. Weiss L, Gilbert HA: Liver Metastases. Boston, GK Hall, 1992.

159. Baker ME, Pelley R: Hepatic metastases: Basic principles and implications for radiologists. Radiology 197:329-337, 1995.

160. Gore RM, Goldberg HI: Plain film and cholangiographic findings in liver tumors. Semin Roentgenol 18:87-93, 1983.

161. Baker SR: The Abdominal Plain Film. East Norwalk, CT, Appleton & Lange, 1990, pp 243-298.

162. Darlak JJ, Moskowitz M, Kattan KR: Calcifications in the liver. Radiol Clin North Am 18:209-219, 1980.

163. Paley M, Ros PR: Hepatic calcification. Radiol Clin North AM 36:391-398, 1998.

164. Dolan PA: Tumor calcification following therapy. AJR 89:166-168, 1963.

165. Rogers JV, Torres WE, Clements J: Plain film diagnosis of the liver. In Bernardino ME, Sones PJ (eds): Hepatic Radiography. New York, Macmillan, 1984, pp 1-49.

166. Drane WE: Nuclear medicine techniques for the liver and biliary system. Radiol Clin North Am 29:1129-1149, 1991.

167. Kinnard MF, Alavi A, Rubin RP, et al: Nuclear imaging of solid hepatic masses. Semin Roentgenol 30:375-395, 1995.

168. Delbeke D, Vitola JV, Sandler MP, et al: Staging recurrent metastatic colorectal carcinoma with PET. J Nucl Med 38:1196-1201, 1997.

169. Goldberg MA, Lee MJ, Fischman AJ, et al: Fluorodeoxyglucose PET of abdominal and pelvic neoplasms: Potential role in oncologic imaging. RadioGraphics 13:1047-1062, 1993.

170. Rappeport ED, Loft A, Berthelsen AK, et al: Contrast-enhanced FDG-PET/CT vs. SPIO-enhanced MRI vs. FDG-PET vs. CT in patients with liver metastases from colorectal cancer: A prospective study with intraoperative confirmation. Acta Radiol 48:369-378, 2007.

171. Findlay M, Young H, Cunningham D, et al: Noninvasive monitoring of tumor metabolism using fluorodeoxyglucose and positron emission tomography in colorectal cancer liver metastases: Correlation with tumor response to fluorouracil. J Clin Oncol 14:700-708, 1997.

172. Marn CS, Bree RL, Silver TM: Ultrasonography of liver: Technique and focal and diffuse disease. Radiol Clin North Am 29:1151-1170, 1991.

173. Withers CE, Wilson SR: The liver. In Rumack CM, Wilson SR, Charboneau JW (eds): Diagnostic Ultrasound. St. Louis: Mosby-Year Book, 1992, pp 45-86.

174. Parulekar SG, Bree RL: The liver. In McGahan JP, Goldberg BB (eds): Diagnostic Ultrasound: A Logical Approach. Philadelphia, Lippincott-Raven, 1998, pp 599-692.

175. Niesenbaum HL, Rowling SE: Ultrasound of focal hepatic lesions. Semin Roentgenol 30:324-346, 1995.

176. Hillman BJ, Smith EH, Gammelgaard J, et al: Ultrasonic-pathologic correlation of malignant hepatic masses. Gastrointest Radiol 4:361-365, 1979.

177. Li R, Guo Y, Hua X, et al: Characterization of focal liver lesions: Comparison of pulse-inversion harmonic contrast-enhanced sonography with contrast-enhanced CT. J Clin Ultrasound 35:109-117, 2007.

178. Marchal G, Tshibwabwa-Tumba E, Oyen R, et al: Correlation of sonographic patterns in liver metastases with histology and microangiography. Invest Radiol 20:79-84, 1985.

179. Marchal GJ, Pylyser K, Tshibwabwa-Tumba EA: Aneochic halo in solid liver tumors: Sonographic, microangiographic, and histologic correlation. Radiology 156:479-483, 1985.

180. Larsen LP, Rosenkilde M, Christensen H, et al: The value of contrast enhanced ultrasonography in detection of liver metastases from colorectal cancer: A prospective double-blinded study. Eur J Radiol 62:302-307, 2007.

181. Federle MP, Filly RA, Moss AA: Cystic hepatic neoplasms: Complementary roles of computed tomography and sonography. AJR 136:345-348, 1981.

182. Bruneton JN, Ladree D, Caramella E, et al: Ultrasonographic study of calcified hepatic metastases: A report of 13 cases. Gastrointest Radiol 7:61-63, 1982.

183. Catala V, Nicolau C, Vilana R, et al: Characterization of focal liver lesions: Comparative study of contrast-enhanced ultrasound versus spiral computed tomography. Eur Radiol 17:1066-1073, 2007.

184. Yukisawa S, Ohto M, Masuya Y, et al: Contrast-enhanced three-dimensional fusion sonography of small liver metastases with pathologic correlation. J Clin Ultrasound 35:1-8, 2007.

185. Heiken JP: Liver. In Lee JKT, Sagel SS, Stanley RJ, et al (eds): Computed Body Tomography with MRI Correlation, 3rd ed. Philadelphia, Lippincott-Raven, 1998, pp 701-778.

186. Stephens DH: The liver. In Haaga JR, Alfidi RJ (eds): Computed Tomography of the Whole Body. St. Louis, CV Mosby, 1988, pp 792-853.

187. Friedman AC, Fishman EK, Radecki PD, et al: Focal disease. In Friedman AC (ed): Radiology of the Liver, Biliary Tract, Pancreas, and Spleen. Baltimore, Williams & Wilkins, 1987, pp 151-264.

188. Baron RL, Freeny PC, Moss AA: The liver. In Moss AA, Gamsu G, Genant HK (eds): Computed Tomography of the Whole Body, 2nd ed. Philadelphia, WB Saunders, 1992, pp 735-822.

189. Foley WD, Jochem RJ: Computed tomography: Focal and diffuse disease. Radiol Clin North Am 29:1213-1233, 1991.

190. Oliver JH III, Baron RL, Federle MP, et al: Detecting hepatocellular carcinoma: Value of unenhanced or arterial phase CT imaging or both used in conjunction with conventional portal venous phase contrast-enhanced CT imaging. AJR 167:71-77, 1996.

191. Oliver JH 3rd, Baron RL, Federle MP, et al: Hypervascular liver metastases: Do unenhanced and hepatic arterial phase CT images affect tumor detection? Radiology 205:709-715, 1997.

192. Tresoldi S, Sardanelli F, Borzani I, et al: Liver metastases on serial contrast-enhanced multidetector computed tomography examinations: Was the detection possible on previous examinations? J Comput Assist Tomogr 30:378-385, 2006.

193. Pedro MS, Semelka RC, Braga L: MR imaging of hepatic metastases. Magn Reson Imaging Clin N Am 10:15-29, 2002.

194. Sica GT, Ji H, Ros PR: CT and MR imaging of hepatic metastases. AJR Am J Roentgenol 174:691-698, 2000.

195. Kim YK, Ko SW, Hwang SB, et al: Detection and characterization of liver metastases: 16-slice multidetector computed tomography versus superparamagnetic iron oxide-enhanced magnetic resonance imaging. Eur Radiol 16:1337-1345, 2006.

196. Semelka RC: Liver. In Semelka RC, Ascher SM, Reinhold C (eds): MRI of the Abdomen and Pelvis. New York, Wiley-Liss, 1997, pp 19-136.

197. Siegelman ES, Outwater Ek: MR imaging techniques of the liver. Radiol Clin North Am 36:263-287, 1998.

198. Hahn PF: Liver specific MR imaging contrast agents. Radiol Clin North Am 36:287-298, 1998.

199. Semelka RA, Mitchell DG, Reinhold C: The liver and biliary system. In Higgins CB, Hricak H, Helms CA (eds): Magnetic Resonance Imaging of the Body, 3rd ed. Philadelphia, Lippincott-Raven, 1997, pp 591-638.

200. Semelka RA, Mitchell DG: Liver and biliary system. In Edelman RR, Hesselink JR, Zlatkin MB (eds): Clinical Magnetic Resonance Imaging, 2nd ed. Philadelphia, WB Saunders, 1996, pp 1466-1512.

201. Gandhi SN, Brown MA, Wong JG, et al: MR contrast agents for liver imaging: what, when, how. RadioGraphics 26:1621-1636, 2006.

202. Reinig JW: Differentiation of hepatic lesions with MR imaging: The last word? Radiology 179:601-602, 1991.

203. Paling MR, Abbitt PL, Mugler JP, et al: Liver metastases: Optimization of MR imaging pulse sequences at 1.0 T. Radiology 167:695-699, 1988.

204. Schnall M: Magnetic resonance imaging. Semin Roentgenol 30:347-361, 1995.

205. Lee MJ, Saini S, Compton CC: MR demonstration of edema adjacent to a liver metastasis: pathologic correlation. AJR 157:499-501, 1991.

206. Outwater E, Tomaszewski JE, Daly JM, et al: Hepatic colorectal metastases: Correlation of MR imaging and pathologic appearance. Radiology 180:327-332, 1991.

207. Goldberg MA, Saini S, Hahn PF, et al: Differentiation between hemangiomas and metastases of the liver with ultrafast MR imaging: Preliminary results with T2 calculations. AJR 157:727-730, 1991.

208. Onishi H, Murakami T, Kim T, et al: Hepatic metastases: detection with multi-detector row CT, SPIO-enhanced MR imaging, and both techniques combined. Radiology 239:131-138, 2006.

209. Hamm B, Mahfouz A-E, Taupitz M, et al: Liver metastases: Improved detection with dynamic gadolinium-enhanced MR imaging. Radiology 202:677-682, 1997.

210. Bipat S, van Leeuwen MS, Comans EFI, et al: Colorectal liver metastases: CT, MR Imaging, and PET for diagnosis: Meta-analysis. Radiology 237:123-131, 2005.

211. Seneterre E, Taourel P, Bouvier Y, et al: Detection of hepatic metastases. Ferumoxides-enhanced MR imaging versus unenhanced MR imaging and CT during arterial portography. Radiology 200:785-792, 1996.

212. Oudkerk M, van den Heuvel AG, Wielopolski PA, et al: Hepatic lesions: Detection with ferumoxide-enhanced T1-weighted MR imaging. Radiology 203:449-456, 1997.

213. Soyer P: Will ferumoxides-enhanced MR imaging replace CT in the detection of hepatic metastases? Prologue to a promising future. Radiology 201:610-611, 1996.

214. Caudana R, Morana G, Pirovano GP, et al: Focal malignant hepatic lesions: MR imaging enhanced with gadolinium benzyloxypropionic-tetra-acetate (BOPTA)—preliminary results of phase II application. Radiology 199:513-520, 1996.

215. Vogl TJ, Kummel S, Hammerstingl R, et al: Liver tumors: Comparison of MR imaging with Gd-EOB-DTPA and Gd-DTPA. Radiology 200: 59-67, 1996.

216. del Frate C, Bazzocchi M, Mortele KJ, Zuiani C, Londero V, Como G, Zanardi R, Ros PR: Detection of liver metastases: Comparison of gadobenate dimeglumine-enhanced and ferumoxides-enhanced MR imaging examinations. Radiology 225:766-772, 2002.

217. Freeny PC: Angiography of hepatic neoplasm. Semin Roentgenol 18:114-122, 1983.

218. Chuang VP: Hepatic tumor angiography: A subject review. Radiology 148:633-639, 1983.

219. Reuter SR, Redman HC, Cho KY: Gastrointestinal Angiography. Philadelphia, WB Saunders, 1986, pp 128-247.

220. Jones EC, Chezmar JL, Nelson RC, et al: The frequency and significance of small (less than 15 mm) hepatic lesions detected by CT. AJR 158:535-539, 1992.

221. Paley MR, Mergo PJ, Ros PR: Characterization of focal liver lesions with SPIO-enhanced T2-weighted images: Patterns of signal intensity and liver lesion contrast change. Radiology 205:455-456, 1997.

222. Vauthey JN: Liver imaging: A surgeon's perspective. Radiol Clin North Am 36:445-457, 1998.

223. Taylor HM, Ros PR: Hepatic imaging: An overview. Radiol Clin North Am 36:237-246, 1998.

224. Namasivayam S, Martin DR, Saini S: Imaging of liver metastases: MRI. Cancer Imaging 7:2-9, 2007.

225. Rappeport ED, Loft A, Berthelsen AK, et al: Contrast-enhanced FDG-PET/CT vs. SPIO-enhanced MRI vs. FDG-PET vs. CT in patients with liver metastases from colorectal cancer: A prospective study with intraoperative confirmation. Acta Radiol 48:369-378, 2007.

226. Catala V, Nicolau C, Vilana R. et al: Characterization of focal liver lesions: Comparative study of contrast-enhanced ultrasound versus spiral computed tomography. Eur Radiol 17:1066-1073, 2007.

Focal Hepatic Infections

Pablo R. Ros, MD • Sukru Mehmet Erturk, MD

Technological advances have significantly enhanced the role of radiology in the detection, characterization, and management of focal infectious diseases of the liver. Today, all cross-sectional techniques allow highly accurate detection of focal hepatic infections. CT is particularly helpful in revealing the presence of calcifications and gas and in detailing the enhancement pattern.[1] With its multiplanar capacity and sensitivity to small differences in tissue composition, MR imaging is a very useful tool to diagnose and characterize lesions such as hepatic abscess, hydatid cyst, and candidiasis. The impact of imaging is particularly dramatic for pyogenic abscess; early diagnosis and imaging-guided percutaneous drainage have markedly reduced both the mortality rates (from 40% to 2% of cases) and the need for surgery.[1] This chapter is a review of the radiologic and pathologic findings in a variety of focal hepatic infections including abscesses, parasitic diseases, and fungal diseases.

BACTERIAL (PYOGENIC) HEPATIC ABSCESSES

Incidence

Pyogenic liver abscesses are uncommon in Western countries, accounting for 0.1% of hospital admissions and having a prevalence at autopsy series of nearly 1%. There is a slight female predominance, and individuals between age 40 and 60 years are most often affected.[2-6]

Pathogenesis

Hepatic abscess can develop via five major routes—(1) biliary: ascending cholangitis from benign or malignant biliary obstruction, choledocholithiasis; (2) portal vein: pylephlebitis from appendicitis, diverticulitis (Fig. 90-1A), necrotic colon

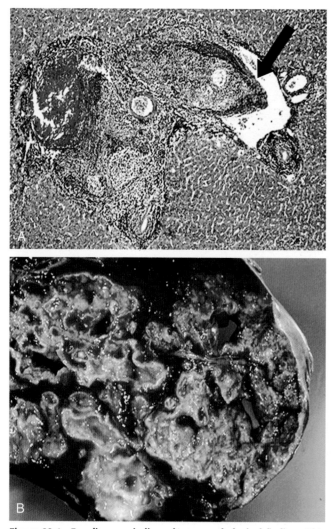

Figure 90-1. *E. coli* **pyogenic liver abscess: pathological findings.** This 76-year-old woman died of sigmoid diverticulitis and pylephlebitis of the inferior mesenteric vein and portal vein causing a liver abscess. **A.** Infected material is present within a portal vein (*arrow*). **B.** A multicompartmental suppurative liver abscess is present.

cancer, inflammatory bowel disease, proctitis, infected hemorrhoids, pancreatitis; (3) hepatic artery: septicemia from bacterial endocarditis, pneumonitis, osteomyelitis; (4) direct extension from contiguous organs: perforated gastric or duodenal ulcer, lobar pneumonia, pyelonephritis, subphrenic abscess; and (5) traumatic, from blunt or penetrating injuries. Metastatic tumor nodules can also become abscesses.[7-14]

Before the antibiotic era, pylephlebitis of the portal vein from seeding by appendicitis and diverticulitis was the most common cause of hepatic abscess.[15] Indeed, appendicitis, which was once responsible for 34% of all pyogenic abscesses, now accounts for less than 2%.[13-16] Biliary tract disease is now the most common source of pyogenic liver abscess.[15] Obstruction of bile flow allows for bacterial proliferation. Through pressurization and distention of canaliculi, portal tributaries and lymphatics are invaded, with subsequent pylephlebitic abscess formation. Cholecystitis, stricture (benign or malignant), malignancy, and congenital diseases are common inciting conditions. Approximately 50% of pyogenic abscesses are caused by an anaerobic organism, mixed anaerobic organ-

isms, or mixed anaerobic and aerobic organisms. Facultative gram-negative enteric bacilli, anaerobic gram-negative bacilli, and microaerophilic streptococci are the organisms most often responsible for liver abscesses. *Escherichia coli* is the organism most commonly isolated in culture in adults (Fig. 90-1B). Staphylococci organisms are most often isolated from hepatic abscesses in children.[5]

Pathology

Abscesses of biliary tract origin are multiple and in 90% of cases involve both hepatic lobes. Abscesses of portal origin are usually solitary; 65% occur in the right lobe, 12% occur in the left lobe, and 23% are bilateral. This distribution is explained by the streaming effect of mesenteric blood flow in the portal vein.[2]

Clinical Findings

The high morbidity and mortality of hepatic abscesses (50%-70%) before the era of cross-sectional imaging attest to the difficulty of establishing a diagnosis of pyogenic liver abscess on clinical grounds alone. The most common symptoms are fever, malaise, pain, rigors, nausea and vomiting, and weight loss. Tender hepatomegaly is the most common clinical sign, and leukocytosis, elevated serum alkaline phosphatase levels, hypoalbuminemia, and prolonged prothrombin time are the most common laboratory abnormalities. Clearly, these findings are nonspecific, and cross-sectional imaging has proved vital in the prompt diagnosis and management of hepatic abscess, resulting in improved survival.[2,5,6,17]

Radiologic Findings

Cholangiography

Ascending cholangitis is the most common cause of pyogenic hepatic abscess, and cholangiography has become an important aid to diagnosis in many cases. Percutaneous transhepatic cholangiography and endoscopic retrograde cholangiography can accurately define the level and cause of biliary obstruction; they are a first step in biliary drainage procedures and can accurately define biliary anatomy for the surgeon. These procedures increase intrabiliary pressure and can precipitate deterioration of a patient who is already septic. Accordingly, biliary drainage procedures should be anticipated.[18] Magnetic resonance cholangiopancreatography (MRCP) is a very important tool in diagnosing obstructive biliary tract lesions.

Ultrasound

Real-time ultrasound (US) can detect hepatic abscesses as small as 1.5 cm with a sensitivity of 75% to 90%. Pyogenic hepatic abscesses are extremely variable in shape and echogenicity. They are usually spherical (Fig. 90-2) or ovoid but may be lobulated or lentiform. Mural thickness is variable, and the wall typically is irregular and hypoechoic. Sonographically, abscesses appear anechoic (50%), hyperechoic (25%), or hypoechoic (25%). Septa, fluid-fluid levels, internal debris, and posterior acoustic enhancement may also be seen. Early lesions tend to be echogenic and poorly demarcated; they may evolve into well-demarcated, nearly anechoic lesions. If gas is present

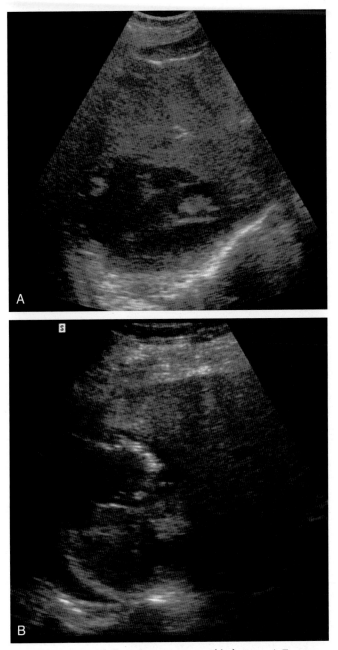

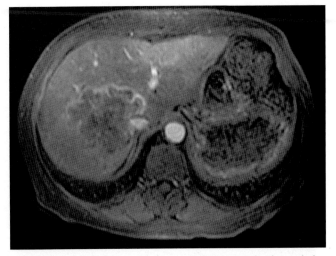

Figure 90-3. Pyogenic liver abscess: MR findings. Gd-enhanced, fat-suppressed T1-weighted image shows a predominantly low signal intensity mass with enhancing wall and septations.

Figure 90-2. Pyogenic liver abscess: sonographic features. A. Transverse sonogram of the liver shows a complex, predominately hypoechoic mass with posterior acoustic enhancement containing coarse, clumpy debris. **B.** Longitudinal sonogram of the liver in a different patient shows bright reflectors within the abscess due to gas.

in an abscess, brightly echogenic reflectors with posterior reverberation artifact may be noted.[19,20-25]

The sonographic differential diagnosis includes amebic or hydatid infection, a necrotic or cystic neoplasm, hematoma, complicated biloma, and simple cyst with infection.

Nuclear Scintigraphy

Pyogenic liver abscesses appear as rounded, cold areas on technetium Tc 99m sulfur colloid and hepatobiliary scintiscans. Occasionally, communication between the abscess cavity

and the biliary system can be demonstrated on the former study.[26-28]

Gallium citrate Ga-67 scintigraphy and imaging with ^{111}In-labeled leukocytes are the two nuclear medicine techniques that were used for the detection of pyogenic abscess in the past and abandoned today.

Magnetic Resonance Imaging

Hepatic abscesses, like most other focal hepatic processes, prolong T1 and T2 relaxation times.[29] At MR imaging, air within the abscess appears as a signal void and is therefore more difficult to differentiate from calcifications. However, the shape and location (air-fluid level) should enable the correct diagnosis. After administration of gadopentetate dimeglumine (gadolinium-DTPA), abscesses typically show rim enhancement (Fig. 90-3), which is secondary to increased capillary permeability in the surrounding liver parenchyma (the "double target" sign). Small lesions (<1 cm) may enhance homogeneously mimicking hemangiomas.[29] Abscess wall enhancement on dynamic postgadolinium images may be considered as a distinctive feature of pyogenic liver abscesses. Abscess wall shows a fast and intense enhancement that persists on portal venous and late-phase images. Some of the lesions may contain internal septations, which also reveal persistent enhancement on late phase images.[30] Perilesional edema, shown as high signal on T2-weighted images is associated with 50% of abscesses. However, it may also be seen in 20% to 30% of patients with primary or secondary hepatic malignancies. Therefore, the presence of perilesion edema can be only used to differentiate a hepatic abscess from a benign cystic hepatic lesion.[1] Resolution of perilesional edema may indicate response to therapy.[29] Limitations of MRI in the investigation of patients with abscesses include the relatively high cost and the lack of easy access for drainage procedures.[17]

Computed Tomography

By virtue of its good spatial and contrast resolution, computed tomography (CT) is the single best method for detecting hepatic abscess, with a sensitivity as high as 97% (Fig. 90-4).

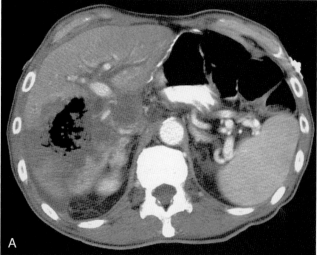

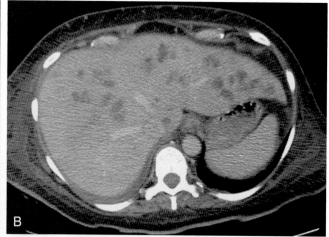

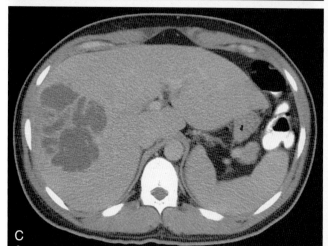

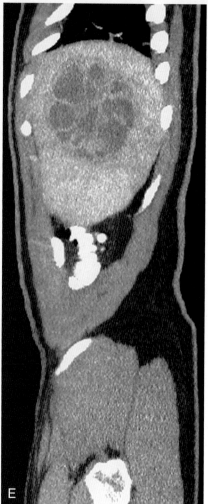

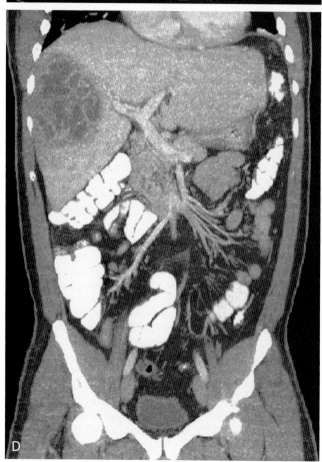

Figure 90-4. Pyogenic liver abscess: CT findings. A. Mottled gas collection is present in this right lobe abscess. **B.** A multifocal abscess is identified in this patient with cholangitis. Axial (**C**), coronal (**D**), and sagittal (**E**) images show the classic "cluster sign" of a multiloculated pyogenic liver abscess. Note the peripheral lobulations and thin enhancing wall.

On CT scans, abscesses appear as generally rounded masses that are hypodense on both contrast and noncontrast scans. The attenuation ranges between 0 and 45 Hounsfield units and thus overlaps with the appearance of cysts, bilomas, and hypodense neoplasms. Most have a peripheral rim or capsule that shows contrast enhancement in a similar pattern to that seen on MRI (see Fig. 90-2). Most abscesses are sharply defined, but a large minority have a grossly lobular contour and circumferential "transition zones" of intermediate attenuation.[24,31]

Another helpful finding is the transient segmental or wedge-shaped enhancement of the hepatic parenchyma surrounding an abscess on the arterial dominant phase of a contrast-enhanced dynamic CT scan.[32]

Some abscesses show the "cluster" sign (see Figs. 90-4C-E), in which small, pyogenic abscesses appear to cluster or aggregate in a pattern suggesting coalescence into a single large cavity.

All of these findings are nonspecific and require aspiration for diagnosis. The presence of central gas (see Fig. 90-4A), either as air bubbles or an air-fluid level, is a specific sign, but it is present in less than 20% of cases. A large air-fluid or fluid-debris level is often associated with communication with the gut.[33]

Treatment

Effective treatment of pyogenic liver abscess entails eliminating both the abscess and its underlying source. Current therapeutic options include surgical drainage, antibiotics alone, percutaneous aspiration in conjunction with antibiotics, or percutaneous catheter drainage.[2,5,34-49]

As a rule, aspiration alone is sufficient if the fluid collection is unilocular, well demarcated, and less than 5 cm in diameter and shows no communication with the gut or biliary tree. Unless the abscess is chronic and the cavity walls are fibrotic or calcified, small intrahepatic abscess cavities quickly collapse when aspirated, unlike abscesses in other organs and peritoneal spaces. In a retrospective study of 115 patients, excellent results were obtained using US-guided percutaneous needle aspiration of pyogenic abscesses followed by injection of antibiotics into the abscess cavity.[48] Cure was achieved in 98% of cases with no deaths, complications, or recurrences at 3-year follow-up.[48] Fluid drainage usually requires introducing a 16- or 18-gauge Teflon-sheathed needle into the collection, and if the fluid is extremely viscous, temporary insertion of a 5- to 8-French pigtail catheter. All fluid is aspirated, and the cavity is irrigated with normal saline or an antiseptic solution.[37,42]

Before removing the catheter, the collection is injected with contrast medium, to rule out communication with surrounding organs. Intravenous antibiotics are given before, during, and after the procedure and are changed accordingly when the infecting organism is identified.[37,42]

An indwelling drainage catheter is usually required when the fluid collection is ill defined, multiloculated, or greater than 5 cm in diameter or when communication with the gut or biliary tree is suspected. A variety of drainage catheter styles (single lumen, double lumen, sump type) and sizes (8.3-16 French) are available.[34,39] Most are made of a flexible Silastic material with a pigtail curve containing multiple side holes. Smaller catheters (8.3-10 French) are usually sufficient

to adequately drain thin fluid collections or extremely small abscesses; very large abscesses require larger catheters (12-16 French), especially if they contain particulate material. The catheter can be inserted under CT, ultrasound, or fluoroscopic guidance, using Seldinger's or trocar technique. Other chapters contain complete discussions of imaging guidance and abscess catheterization. The catheter is left in place until drainage volume has decreased to less than 20 mL/day. If there is a known or suspected fistula, a fluoroscopic sinogram is performed before catheter removal, to rule out communication with bowel, bile duct, or pancreatic duct. If no fistula is present, most hepatic abscesses require only 2 to 14 days of drainage.[37,42,49]

The failure and recurrence rates of catheter therapy are 8.4% and 8%, respectively. They are most often associated with complicated abscesses caused by fistula, phlegmons, or infected tumors.[37,42,49]

Surgery is reserved for patients who fail percutaneous drainage, those with associated intra-abdominal perforation of hepatic abscess, and those with fistula formation (e.g., biliary, colonic).

The mortality rate for pyogenic hepatic abscess has declined from 80% to less than 10%, owing to earlier diagnosis, antibiotics, and advances in surgical and percutaneous drainage techniques.[44,47]

AMEBIC ABSCESSES

Incidence

Approximately 10% of the world's population is infected with *Entamoeba histolytica*, which causes more deaths than any other parasite with the exceptions of malaria-causing plasmodia and schistosomas. Less than 10% of infected individuals, however, are symptomatic. Amebic liver abscess is the most common extraintestinal manifestation, occurring in 3% to 7% of this population.[50-56]

Although amebiasis is usually considered a disease of developing countries, certain groups are at high risk in Western nations: recent immigrants, institutionalized patients, and homosexual persons. Indeed, *E. histolytica* has been isolated in the stool of up to 30% of sexually active homosexual males; its clinical significance is unclear.[50] Worldwide, some 85% to 90% of amebic liver abscesses occur in men.

In the United States, the overall mortality rate for hepatic amebic abscess is 3%; it is less than 1% when the abscess is confined to the liver, 6% with extension into the chest, and 30% with extension into the pericardium.[57]

Pathogenesis

The cystic form of *E. histolytica* gains access to the body via oral ingestion of infected material, usually contaminated water (Fig. 90-5A). The mature cysts are resistant to gastric acid and pass unchanged into the intestine. The cyst wall is then digested by trypsin; four invasive trophozoites are released, which live and multiply in the colon, particularly the cecum. The trophozoites exist in two forms: small (10-20 μm) and large (20-60 μm). The large form usually occurs in invasive amebiasis when the mucosa is invaded. This can cause minute superficial mucosal ulcerations. With further invasion, hemorrhage, perforation, enterocolic or cutaneous fistulas,

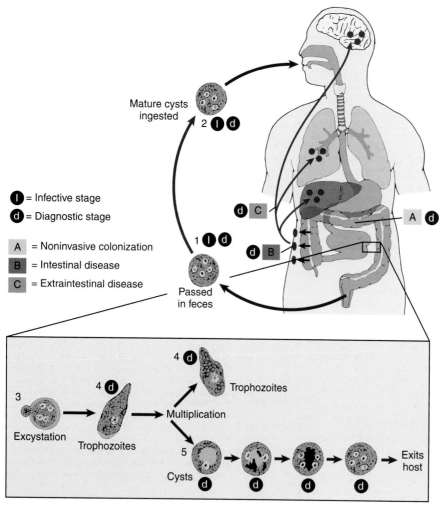

A

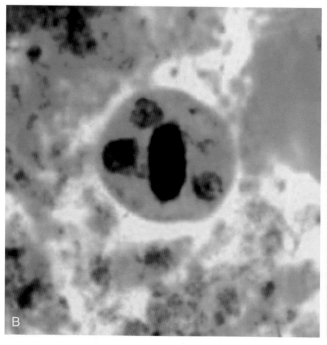

Figure 90-5. Amebiasis: pathologic finding.
A. Life cycle: Cysts are passed in feces (1).
Infection by *Entamoeba histolytica* occurs
by ingestion of mature cysts (2) in fecally
contaminated food, water, or hands. Ex-
cystation (3) occurs in the small intestine
and trophozoites (4) are released, which
migrate to the large intestine. The trophozoites multiply by binary fission and produce cysts (5), which are passed in the
feces (1). Because of the protection con-
ferred by their walls, the cysts can survive
days to weeks in the external environment
and are responsible for transmission.
(Trophozoites can also be passed in diar-
rheal stools, but are rapidly destroyed once
outside the body, and if ingested would
not survive exposure to the gastric environment.) In many cases, the trophozoites
remain confined to the intestinal lumen (A,
noninvasive infection) of individuals who
are asymptomatic carriers, passing cysts in
their stool. In some patients the trophozoites
invade the intestinal mucosa (B, intestinal
disease), or, through the bloodstream, extraintestinal sites such as the liver, brain, and
lungs (C, extraintestinal disease), with resultant pathologic manifestations. It has
been established that the invasive and
noninvasive forms represent two separate
species, respectively, *E. histolytica* and *E.
dispar*; however, not all persons infected
with *E. histolytica* will have invasive disease. These two species are morphologi-
cally indistinguishable. Transmission can
also occur through fecal exposure during
sexual contact (in which case not only
cysts, but also trophozoites could prove
infective). (Source: Centers for Disease Control and Prevention, http://www.cdc.gov/
Ncidod/parasites.) **B.** Cyst of *E. histolytica*,
permanent preparation stained with trichrome. **C.** Typical anchovy paste-like
material drained from an amebic abscess.

amebic appendicitis, or ameboma formation can occur. Amebic trophozoites can also enter the mesenteric venules and lymphatics and be carried to the liver, lungs, and other organs. The liver can be invaded in one of three ways: (1) via the portal vein (most common); (2) through lymphatics; or (3) via direct extension through the colon wall into the peritoneum and then through the liver capsule.[2,4,52]

When a sufficient number of trophozoites become lodged in small hepatic venules, thrombosis and infarction of small areas of hepatic parenchyma occur (amebic hepatitis). The host's nutritional and immune status determine whether the initial infestation heals or progresses to a macroabscess. A visible abscess results from the coalition of multiple small areas of ischemic necrosis and amebic destruction of hepatic parenchymal cells.

Trophozoites that pass into the distal colon may change into round, resistant cysts (Fig. 90-5B) that pass into the feces. Indeed, human carriers who pass amebic cysts into their stool are the primary source of infection.[2,4,54]

Pathology

The fluid of an amebic abscess is usually dark reddish brown and has the consistency of anchovy paste (Fig. 90-5C). This material is usually sterile, consisting of a mixture of blood and destroyed hepatocytes. Rarely, the trophozoites are found centrally within the paste, but they are often found in the zone of necrotic tissue adjacent to the outer abscess wall. The wall of connective tissue becomes better developed with age, and leukocyte infiltration and inflammatory reaction are characteristically absent. If the abscess is not treated, it may rupture into the peritoneum, pleural cavity, lung, or pericardium.[2,4,54]

Amebic abscesses are most often solitary (85%) and affect the right lobe more often (72%) than the left lobe (13%). Solitary liver abscesses and right lobe predominance are more marked in amebic than in pyogenic abscesses because most infestations are transmitted via the portal vein. Amebiasis most often affects the right colon, which drains into the superior mesenteric vein, which preferentially streams into the right lobe. Flow from the inferior mesenteric vein (left colon) and splenic vein streams preferentially into the left lobe.[2,4,54]

Clinical Findings

Most patients with amebic liver abscess present with a tender liver and right upper quadrant pain. When compared with persons who have pyogenic liver abscess, they are more likely to have diarrhea and hepatomegaly and less likely to have jaundice or sepsis. Amebae are not found in the stool of most patients with an amebic liver abscess.[50-52]

Because clinical features and findings of stool examination for amebae usually are nonspecific or negative, serologic tests are particularly helpful when hepatic amebic abscess is suspected. The indirect hemagglutination test is positive in more than 90% of these patients.[50-52]

Radiologic Findings

Nuclear Scintigraphy

Amebic abscesses appear as cold defects on sulfur colloid scans. They often show "rim enhancement" on hepatobiliary

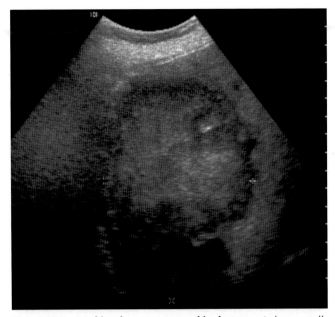

Figure 90-6. Amebic abscess: sonographic features. A large, well-defined abscess is identified in the right lobe of the liver.

scintiscans, presumably owing to inflammation of the adjacent parenchyma. A cold lesion with a hot periphery is suggestive of the diagnosis. Nevertheless, nuclear medicine techniques are not routinely used for detection of hepatic amebic abscess.

Ultrasound

Amebic abscess on ultrasound studies (Fig. 90-6) is usually a round or oval, sharply defined hypoechoic mass (Fig. 90-7) that abuts the liver capsule with homogeneous, fine, low-level echoes and distal acoustic enhancement.[15] When comparing amebic and pyogenic abscesses, amebic abscess is more likely to have a round or oval shape (82% versus 60%) and a hypoechoic appearance with fine, low-level internal echoes

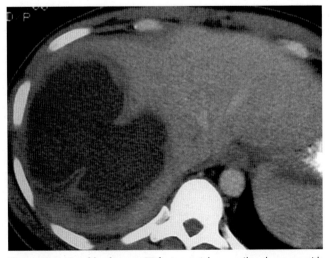

Figure 90-7. Amebic abscess: CT features. A large unilocular mass with an enhancing wall demonstrates a thin peripheral hypoattenuating rim of surrounding edema that is typical of amebic abscesses.

at high gain settings (58% versus 36%).[20,58-63] On contrast-enhanced ultrasonography, pyogenic abscess appears as a partially enhancing lesion with a thin or thick rim of dense opacification and persistently hypoechoic center.[64]

Computed Tomography

The CT appearance of amebic abscess is variable and nonspecific. The lesions are usually peripheral, round or oval areas of low attenuation (10-20 Hounsfield units). A peripheral rim of slightly higher attenuation can be seen on noncontrast scans and shows marked enhancement after administration of contrast material (see Fig. 90-7). A peripheral zone of edema around the abscess is also common and somewhat characteristic for this lesion.[1] Lesions may appear unilocular or multilocular and demonstrate nodularity of the margins. Concomitant extrahepatic abnormalities include right-sided pleural effusion, perihepatic fluid, and gastric or colonic involvement.[65,66]

Magnetic Resonance Imaging

On MR imaging (Fig. 90-8), amebic liver abscesses are spherical and usually solitary lesions with a hyperintense center on T2-weighted images and a hypointense center on T1-weighted images. The abscess wall is thick and on gadolinium enhanced images, the enhancement pattern is similar to that of pyogenic abscess.[1,30] Diffuse central inhomogeneity is often seen on T2-weighted images. Edema in otherwise normal surrounding parenchyma may be appreciated on T2-weighted images.[67,68]

After treatment, abscesses become more homogeneously hypointense on T2-weighted images. Successful treatment may show concentric rings of different signal intensity surrounding the lesion on T2-weighted images.[67,68]

Complications

Pleuropulmonary amebiasis is the most frequent complication of amebic liver abscess, occurring in 20% to 35% of patients. This may manifest as pulmonary consolidation or abscess, serous effusion, empyema, or hepatobronchial fistula.[50-52,69]

Peritoneal amebiasis occurs in 2% to 7.5% of patients with amebic liver abscess. Sudden rupture presents dramatically, in the manner of a perforated viscus. Pericardial amebiasis is the most serious complication of amebic liver abscess, because it can lead to progressive tamponade or sudden development of shock. Most abscesses responsible for this complication are located in the left hepatic lobe. Renal amebiasis is a rare complication that can result from abscess rupture.[50-52,69,70]

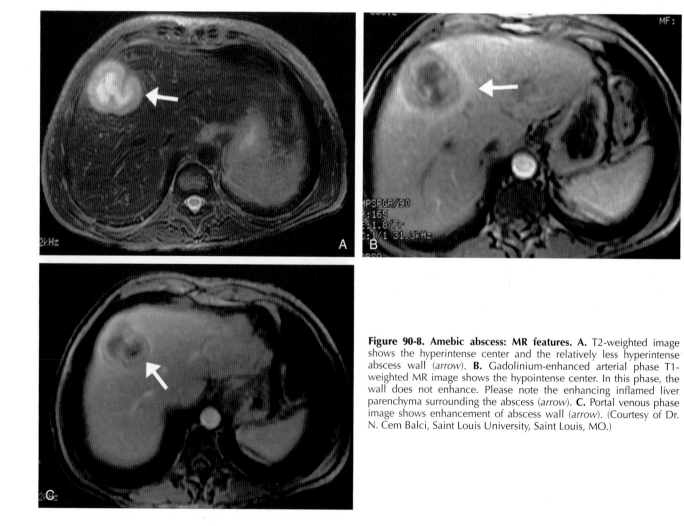

Figure 90-8. Amebic abscess: MR features. A. T2-weighted image shows the hyperintense center and the relatively less hyperintense abscess wall (*arrow*). **B.** Gadolinium-enhanced arterial phase T1-weighted MR image shows the hypointense center. In this phase, the wall does not enhance. Please note the enhancing inflamed liver parenchyma surrounding the abscess (*arrow*). **C.** Portal venous phase image shows enhancement of abscess wall (*arrow*). (Courtesy of Dr. N. Cem Balci, Saint Louis University, Saint Louis, MO.)

Treatment

The complications of amebic liver abscess just mentioned are becoming less frequent because of earlier diagnosis, improved imaging and serologic techniques, and effective medical, percutaneous, and surgical management.[71] More than 90% of hepatic amebic abscesses respond to antimicrobial (metronidazole or chloroquine) therapy alone. The efficacy of these amebicidal agents has reduced the mortality rate of hepatic amebic abscesses from 81% to 4%.[50-52,72,73]

There are, nevertheless, some circumstances in which aspiration and drainage of amebic abscess are indicated: (1) to differentiate pyogenic from amebic abscess; (2) for a large symptomatic abscess in which rupture is imminent; (3) after poor response to medical therapy; (4) with suspected bacterial superinfection; (5) in pregnancy; (6) for noncompliance with medical treatment; and (7) as an alternative to surgery when an abscess ruptures. Drainage can be accompanied by intralesional delivery of drug, which can increase mean intralesional drug levels up to 246-fold.[74-78]

Confirmation of an amebic abscess may not always be possible by percutaneous aspiration. In one series, only 50% of patients had the classic "anchovy paste" appearance, and positive diagnoses based on fluid evaluation were established in only 5% of cases. Therefore, the primary role of percutaneous aspiration and drainage in these patients is the diagnosis and treatment of superimposed bacterial infection.[74-78]

HEPATIC ECHINOCOCCAL DISEASE

Epidemiology

Hydatid disease is prevalent throughout much of the world, and the two main forms that affect humans are *Echinococcus granulosus* and *Echinococcus multilocularis*. The disease flourishes in rural areas where dogs are used for herding livestock, especially sheep. Greece, Uruguay, Argentina, Australia, and New Zealand are the countries with the highest incidence of hydatid disease.[79]

Pathophysiology

E. granulosus is a small tapeworm, 3 to 6 mm long, that lives in the intestine of the definitive host, usually the dog. The life cycle (Fig. 90-9A) depends on a primary host harboring the adult worm and an intermediate (human) host harboring the larval stage. The adult parasite sheds eggs, which may infect humans when contaminated, unwashed vegetables are ingested or through contact with infected dogs, which may carry ova on their fur or shed them onto soil where children play.[79-81]

In humans, the external shell of the egg is digested in the duodenum and the embryo is freed. The embryo actively penetrates the intestinal mucosa until it enters a blood vessel, from which it is transported until trapped by narrowing of the capillaries. Most are carried by the portal vein and trapped in the liver, but the lungs, spleen, kidneys, bone, and central nervous system can also be involved.[79-81]

Although most embryos are destroyed by host defenses, surviving embryos (Fig. 90-9B) develop into the hydatid stage in 4 to 5 days while trapped within a capillary. After 3 months, this cyst measures 5 mm in diameter. The life cycle is complete when the infected intermediate host (sheep or other

ruminant) dies and its viscera, which contain the larval form, are consumed by a definitive host.[79-81]

E. multilocularis (alveolaris) is a less common but more aggressive form of echinococcus. The disease is endemic in central Europe, the Soviet Union, Japan, and central and northern North America.[82-85] The main host of the adult parasite is the fox although less commonly domestic dogs and cats may serve as hosts.[82] The intermediate hosts, usually wild rodents, acquire infection by eating contaminated wild berries. Humans become infected either by eating wild fruits contaminated with fox feces or by direct contact with infected animals.[82-84] The larvae reach the liver via the portal vein. Here they proliferate and penetrate surrounding tissue, which causes a diffuse and infiltrative process that simulates a malignancy. *E. multilocularis* organisms induce a brisk granulomatous reaction with central necrosis, cavitation, and calcification.[79-81]

Pathology

The hydatid cyst has three layers composed of both host and parasite tissue (Fig. 90-9C). The outer pericyst is composed of modified host tissue that forms a rigid protective zone only several millimeters thick. As the cyst expands, the vessels and ductal structures of the liver become incorporated in the cyst wall; this explains enhancement of the wall on contrast CT and MR studies and angiography.

The two internal layers are formed by the parasite. The middle layer is a thicker (1-2 mm) laminated membrane that resembles the white of a hard-boiled egg and is easily ruptured with manipulation. It permits the passage of nutrients but is impervious to bacteria. Disruption of this layer predisposes to bacterial infection. The innermost or germinal layer (endocyst) is the living parasite, which is one cell thick. It produces the laminated membrane and scolices that represent the larval stage. Brood capsules are small spheres of disrupted germinal membrane that produce scolices (see Fig. 90-9C). Free-floating brood capsules and scolices form a white sediment of barely visible particles known as hydatid sand.

Cyst fluid is secreted by the germinal lining and normally is crystal clear. It is a transudate of serum that contains protein and is antigenic. The high secretion pressure is responsible for progressive cyst enlargement. Up to 60% of cysts are multiple.

In contrast to *Echinococcus* granulosus, the alveolar form has daughter cysts which arise on the outer surface of the original cyst with invasion of adjacent liver parenchyma.[86] On histologic examination, the cysts have a thick lamellated wall.[86,87] Surrounding this is the marked granulomatous reaction with hepatic necrosis, collagenous tissue, multinucleated giant cells, and lymphocytes.[78] In contrast to the cysts of *Echinococcus* granulosus, the *Echinococcus* alveolaris cysts very rarely contain scolices in human infestation.[87,88]

Clinical Findings

Most patients acquire hydatid disease in childhood but are not diagnosed until the third or fourth decade of life. Echinococcal cysts enlarge at a rate of approximately 1 cm/year. Most cysts are initially asymptomatic and remain so until they grow large enough to cause pain; erode into a moderate-sized bile duct allowing cyst fluid to enter the bile (and vice versa),

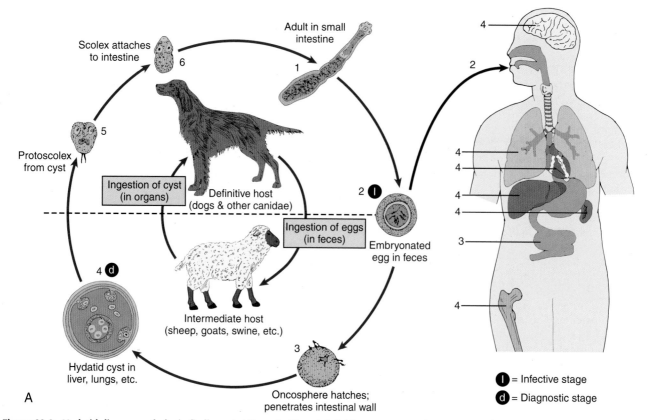

Figure 90-9. Hydatid disease: pathologic findings. A. Life cycle. The adult *Echinococcus granulosus* (3-6 mm long) (1) resides in the small bowel of the definitive hosts, dogs, or other canids. Gravid proglottids release eggs (2) that are passed in the feces. After ingestion by a suitable intermediate host (under natural conditions: sheep, goat, swine, cattle, horses, camel), the egg hatches in the small bowel and releases an oncosphere (3) that penetrates the intestinal wall and migrates through the circulatory system into various organs, especially the liver and lungs. In these organs, the oncosphere develops into a cyst (4) that enlarges gradually, producing protoscolices and daughter cysts that fill the cyst interior. The definitive host becomes infected by ingesting the cyst-containing organs of the infected intermediate host. After ingestion, the protoscolices (5) evaginate, attach to the intestinal mucosa (6), and develop into adult stages (1) in 32 to 80 days. The same life cycle occurs with *E. multilocularis* (1.2-3.7 mm), with the following differences: the definitive hosts are foxes, and to a lesser extent dogs, cats, coyotes, and wolves; the intermediate host are small rodents; and larval growth (in the liver) remains indefinitely in the proliferative stage, resulting in invasion of the surrounding tissues. With *E. vogeli* (up to 5.6 mm long), the definitive hosts are bush dogs and dogs; the intermediate hosts are rodents; and the larval stage (in the liver, lungs, and other organs) develops both externally and internally, resulting in multiple vesicles. *E. oligarthrus* (up to 2.9 mm long) has a life cycle that involves wild felids as definitive hosts and rodents as intermediate hosts. Humans become infected by ingesting eggs (2), with resulting release of oncospheres (3) in the intestine and the development of cysts (4) in various organs. (Source: Centers for Disease Control and Prevention, http://www.cdc.gov/Ncidod/parasites.)

causing fever and jaundice; or induce an allergic reaction because of leakage of cyst fluid. Large cysts can obstruct blood and bile flow, leading to portal hypertension and jaundice.[72]

Routine blood analysis is usually not helpful in establishing the diagnosis of hydatid disease. Results of serologic tests are positive in more than 80% of cases and are diagnostic of echinococcoses.[72] The clinical manifestations of *Echinococcus multilocularis* may occur 5 to 20 years after the inciting event.[86-88] Abdominal discomfort, jaundice, and hepatomegaly may be present and eosinophilia is frequently observed.[86,89] Although the serum levels of the transaminases usually remain normal, alkaline phosphatase and gamma-glutamyl tranpeptidase values are elevated.[86,88] Serologic titers are elevated in alveolar echinococcosis and aid in diagnosis.[89]

Radiologic Findings

Plain Radiographic Findings

Calcification is visible on 20% to 30% of abdominal plain radiographs (Fig. 90-10). The calcification is usually curvilinear or ring-like and lies in the pericyst. Daughter cysts may calcify, creating rings of calcification. Calcification does not always indicate death of the parasite, and small irregular areas of calcification may be secondary to dystrophic calcification in old blood clots.[90] *E. multilocularis* can cause faint or dense punctate calcification scattered throughout necrotic and granulomatous tissue.

Ultrasound

Sonographically, hepatic hydatid disease manifests in several different fashions (Fig. 90-11), depending on the stage of evolution and maturity: (1) a well-defined anechoic cyst; (2) an anechoic cyst except for hydatid sand; (3) a multiseptate cyst with daughter cysts and echogenic material between the cysts (characteristic); (4) a cyst with a floating, undulating membrane with a detached endocyst, the characteristic "water lily" sign; or (5) a densely calcified mass. Daughter cysts usually cause mural thickening as well.[15,91]

Ultrasound has been used to monitor the efficacy of medical antihydatid therapy. Findings suggesting a positive response

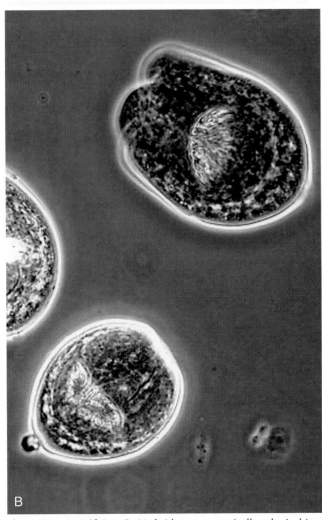

Figure 90-9, *cont'd* B to **D.** Hydatid cysts are typically spherical in shape and have the ability to achieve rather large sizes. The insides of the cysts are filled with fluid, brood capsules, daughter cysts, and protoscolices that have the capability to grow into adult worms if consumed by a definitive host. If a cyst is ruptured, which may occur through a sharp blow or during surgery, each protoscolex released may form a new cyst. Also, the fluid within the hydatids is highly allergenic and may cause anaphylactic shock and rapid death if freed inside the body.

include reduction in cyst size, membrane detachment, progressive increase in cyst echogenicity, and mural calcification.[20,92-99] When hydatid cysts become infected they lose their characteristic sonographic appearance and become diffusely hyperechoic.[20,82,92-99]

E. multilocularis produces echogenic lesions that can be single or multiple and are usually situated in the right lobe.[82] Irregular necrotic regions can be seen.[82,100] Microcalcifications have been described in about 50% of cases.[82] Intrahepatic biliary dilatation is a common sonographic finding.[82] *E. multilocularis* lesions are infiltrative with a propensity to spread to the liver hilum.[82]

Computed Tomography

On CT scans, hydatid disease appears as unilocular or multilocular, well-defined cysts with either thick or thin walls[1,30] (Fig. 90-12). Daughter cysts are usually seen as areas of lower attenuation than the mother cyst and are usually oriented in the periphery of the lesion (see Fig. 90-12). Daughter cysts can also float free in the lumen of the mother cyst, so altering the patient's position may change the position of these cysts, confirming the diagnosis of echinococcal disease. Curvilinear ring-like calcification is also a common feature.[101-107]

E. multilocularis causes geographic, infiltrating lesions without sharp margins or high-attenuation rims. These low-density

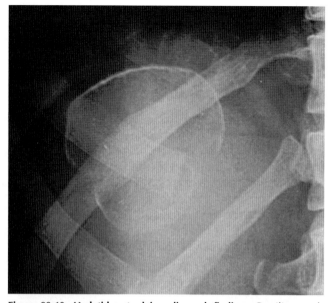

Figure 90-10. Hydatid cyst: plain radiograph findings. Curvilinear calcification of the pericyst is present in 20% to 30% of abdominal radiographs in patients with hydatid cysts.

(14-40 Hounsfield units) lesions are solid masses rather than cysts. There is little if any enhancement with intravenous contrast administration.[82-88] These are invasive rather than expansile lesions whose nonspecific appearance can simulate a primary or secondary hepatic tumor. Calcification, when present, is usually amorphous rather than ring-like. When the alveolar lesion is located centrally, it may cause hepatic lobar atrophy.[85]

Magnetic Resonance Imaging

On MR studies, the cyst component of echinococcal cysts is similar to that of other cysts, with long T1 and T2 relaxation times (Fig. 90-13). However, because of its superb contrast resolution, MR imaging best demonstrates the pericyst, the matrix or hydatid sand (debris consisting of freed scolices), and the daughter cysts.[1] The pericyst usually has low signal intensity on T1- and T2-weighted images, because of its fibrous component. This rim and a multiloculated or multicystic appearance are distinctive features. The hydatid matrix appears hypointense on T1-weighted images and markedly hyperintense on T2-weighted images. When present, daughter cysts are hypointense relative to the matrix on both T1- and T2-weighted images.[108] Floating membranes have low signal intensities on T1- and T2-weighted images.

Magnetic resonance imaging with its multiplanar capabilities is useful in displaying extrahepatic extension of *E. multilocularis* such as transdiaphragmatic spread to the pleura, lung, pericardium, and heart.[83,109] The relationship between the hepatic lesions and vessels such as the hepatic veins and inferior vena cava is well delineated on MR images.[83] The regions of fibrous and parasitic tissue are of low signal intensity on T1- and T2-weighted sequences and correspond to areas of nonenhancement on CT scans.[83] Small cystic extensions from the main lesion are shown as peripheral areas of increased signal on T2-weighted images and are thought to represent

the active portions of the disease.[83] Large regions of necrosis do not have a characteristic signal pattern.[83] Calcifications display low signal but are more difficult to identify on MR images than on CT.[83]

Complications

Rupture, the major complication of echinococcal disease, can be classified into three types: (1) contained, when only the endocyst ruptures and the cyst contents are confined by the host-derived pericyst; (2) communicating, when cyst contents escape into biliary or bronchial radicles that are incorporated into the pericyst; and (3) direct, when both the endocyst and pericyst tear, spilling cyst contents into the pleural, peritoneal, or pericardial cavity.[110]

When cyst contents enter the biliary tract (see Fig. 90-12B and C), the cyst becomes echogenic. Intrabiliary hydatid material, including echogenic or nonechogenic daughter cysts and echogenic fragmented membranes, may fill the biliary system. Cyst–bile duct communication may be manifested as interruption of the cyst wall adjacent to a bile duct wall. On CT scans, there is interruption of the cyst wall and higher-attenuation hydatid material in the biliary system. On MR studies, cyst rupture is recognized as an area of discontinuity of the low-intensity wall.[111-116] A fat-fluid level within hepatic hydatid cysts has been described on CT and MRI studies of two patients with communicating rupture of the cysts into the biliary tree.[117] Laboratory analysis of the contents of the hydatid cysts revealed elevated levels of bile confirming that the fat seen in the cysts on CT and MRI scans represented lipid material within bile.[117]

This intrabiliary hydatid material can lead to obstructive jaundice. Passage of hydatid sand or hydatid liquid can also lead to inflammation and spasm of the sphincter of Oddi.[118-121] Until surgery can be performed, endoscopic retrograde sphincterotomy can be used as a temporizing measure for decompressing the obstructed biliary system. Some 25% of cysts become infected and present clinically as abscess.

If *E. multilocularis* is left untreated, the outcome is invariably fatal within 10 to 15 years as the cyst continues to slowly grow and destroy hepatic tissue.[84,86-93] In some cases with Budd-Chiari syndrome and/or inferior vena cava thrombosis, death may be sudden due to embolic events to the heart or pulmonary arteries.[84] Another serious complication is hemorrhage from esophageal varices secondary to portal hypertension. Metastasis to the brain is a less common cause of death in patients with *E. multilocularis*.[89]

Treatment

Hepatic hydatid cysts require drainage, because medical therapy with mebendazole and albendazole is usually ineffective. There are two surgical approaches: (1) radical, in which a pericystectomy and hepatic resection are performed, and (2) conservative, with injection of scolicidal agents followed by evacuation of the cyst, removal of the germinal lining and laminated membrane, and closure, capitonnage, drainage, or omentoplasty of the remaining cyst cavity. Surgical complications are high, including a 4% mortality rate and a 50% complication rate. The recurrence rate is high for the conservative approach, and both procedures require approximately 3 weeks of hospitalization.[122,123]

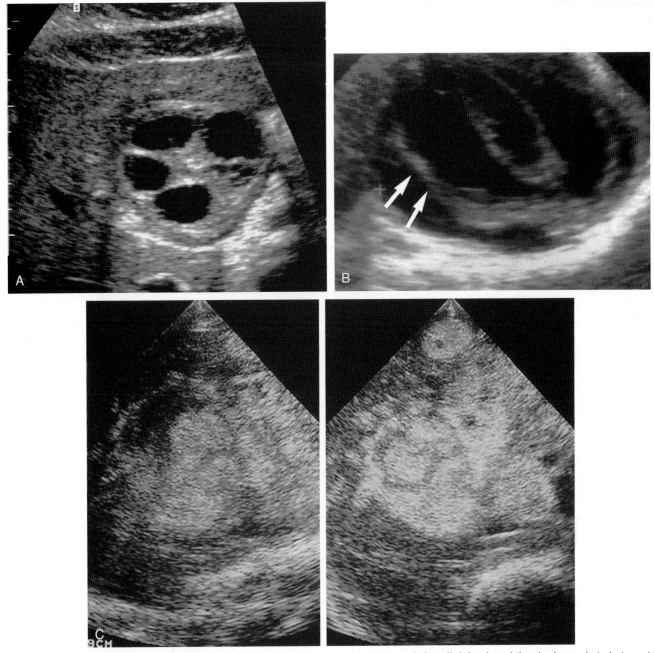

Figure 90-11. Hydatid disease: sonographic features. A. Longitudinal scan shows a rounded, well-defined, multilocular hypoechoic lesion with echogenic internal septa due to *E. granulosus*. **B.** Hydatid cyst in the right lobe with wavy bands of delaminated endocyst ("water lily sign") (*arrows*). **C.** *E. multilocularis* cysts. Transverse US images obtained at different levels of the liver show *E. multilocularis* infection with the typical hailstorm pattern, characterized by multiple echogenic nodules with irregular and indistinct margins. (**B** and **C** from Mortele, KJ, Segatto E, Ros PR: The infected liver: Radiologic-pathologic correlation. RadioGraphics 24:937-955, 2004.)

Hydatid disease of the liver has been treated percutaneously, in an effort to obviate surgery and its attendant morbidity and mortality. At one time, percutaneous drainage, or even diagnostic aspiration, of these cysts was discouraged, because of potential complications such as anaphylactic shock and spread of daughter cysts into the peritoneum. This has not proved to be the case, particularly when a transhepatic approach is used. A new cutting device has been described that can percutaneously extract laminated membranes and all daughter cysts with little chance of fluid leakage.[124-128] A single aspiration and drainage procedure using this instrument resulted in successful evacuation of cyst contents in 90% of patients with few major complications and no recurrence.[129]

A number of scolecidal agents have been used such as hypertonic (20%) saline and alcohol are effective percutaneous therapies for hepatic hydatid cysts and are associated with low complication rates.[130,131] Percutaneous therapy should be attempted only with an accessible, dominant cyst that is truly cystic and uncomplicated. Infected cysts and cysts that communicate with the biliary system require surgical drainage.[132]

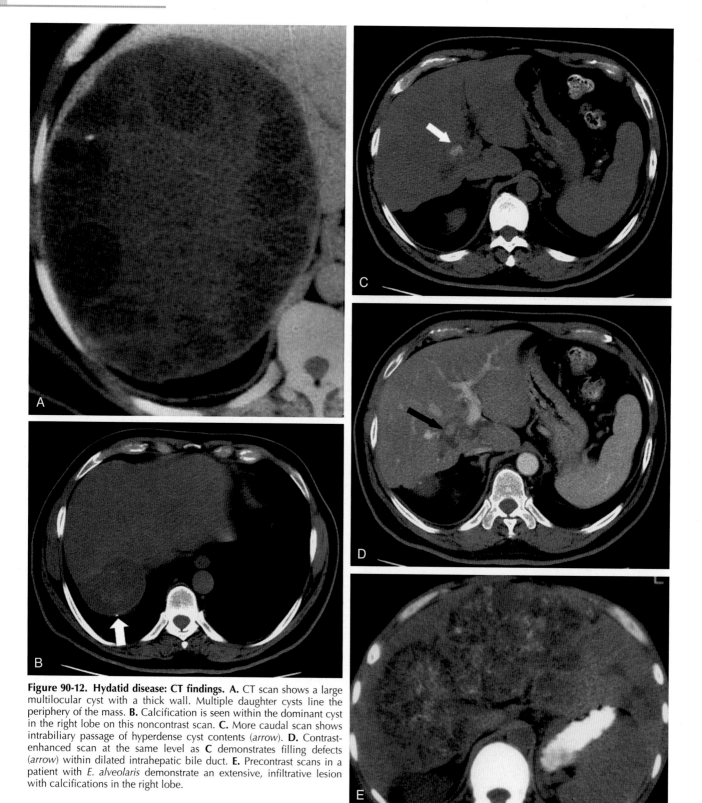

Figure 90-12. Hydatid disease: CT findings. A. CT scan shows a large multilocular cyst with a thick wall. Multiple daughter cysts line the periphery of the mass. **B.** Calcification is seen within the dominant cyst in the right lobe on this noncontrast scan. **C.** More caudal scan shows intrabiliary passage of hyperdense cyst contents (*arrow*). **D.** Contrast-enhanced scan at the same level as **C** demonstrates filling defects (*arrow*) within dilated intrahepatic bile duct. **E.** Precontrast scans in a patient with *E. alveolaris* demonstrate an extensive, infiltrative lesion with calcifications in the right lobe.

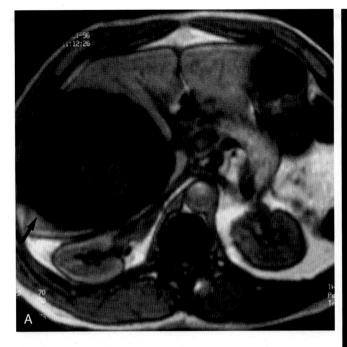

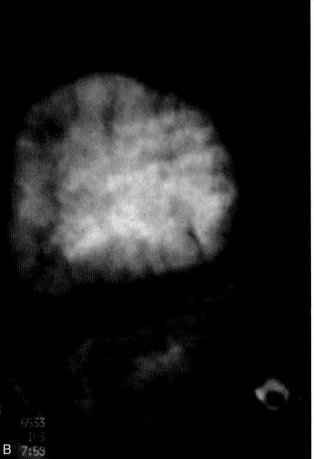

Figure 90-13. Hydatid disease: MR features. A. Axial gradient-echo T1-weighted MR image shows a hydatid cyst with a hypointense fibrous pericyst (*arrow*). The hydatid matrix has intermediate signal intensity, and peripheral daughter cysts that are hypointense relative to the matrix are seen. **B.** On an axial T2-weighted MR image, the matrix is hyperintense and the daughter cysts again relatively hypointense. (From Mortele, KJ, Segatto E, Ros PR: The infected liver: radiologic-pathologic correlation. RadioGraphics 24:937-955, 2004.)

The treatment of choice for patients with *E. multilocularis* is complete excision with partial hepatectomy where possible.[83,84,88,89] In patients with extensive disease, palliative procedures including hepaticojejunostomy, portosystemic shunts and drainage of necrotic areas or abscesses in combination with benzimidazole therapy may be undertaken to prolong survival.[84,88] Prolonged mebendazole therapy may slow disease progression and suppress metastasis.[87-89] More recent treatment strategies include hepatectomy with orthotopic liver transplantation to effect a cure.[83,84,86] However the disease can recur following liver transplantation.[86]

CANDIDIASIS AND FUNGAL INFECTIONS

Candidiasis (Figs. 90-14 and 90-15) is the most frequently encountered systemic fungal infection in immunocompromised hosts. It is becoming more common with the acquired immunodeficiency syndrome (AIDS) epidemic and with increasingly intensive chemotherapy. Indeed, hepatic candidiasis is found in 50% to 70% of patients with acute leukemia and 50% of those with lymphoma at the time of autopsy. Diagnosis is difficult on clinical grounds because blood cultures are positive in only 50% of affected patients, so cross-sectional imaging is necessary for diagnosis.[133-135]

Sonographically, four major patterns of hepatic candidiasis are seen: (1) "wheel within a wheel," in which a peripheral zone surrounds an inner echogenic wheel, which in turn surrounds a central hypoechoic nidus that represents focal necrosis in which fungal elements are found early in the disease; (2) "bull's-eye," a 1- to 4-mm lesion with a hyperechoic center that surrounds a hypoechoic rim, present when the neutrophil count returns to normal; (3) "uniformly hypoechoic," the most common appearance attributable to progressive fibrosis; and (4) "echogenic," caused by scar formation.[15,135-138] After antifungal therapy, the lesions increase in echogenicity and decrease in size often disappearing altogether, although in some cases sonographic inhomogeneity of the liver may persist for up to 3 years following treatment.[139]

On CT scans, the most common pattern is multiple small, rounded areas of decreased attenuation that may require both precontrast and postcontrast scans to appreciate. Areas of scattered increased attenuation representing calcification can be seen on noncontrast scans. Periportal areas of increased attenuation, correlating with fibrosis, may be seen as well.[140-142] Based on the available evidence, CT is more sensitive than US in detecting hepatic candidal lesions[143] (see Fig. 90-15). Although CT and US appearances may be suggestive of candidiasis, they are not specific and a definitive diagnosis is necessary before treatment since antifungal drugs may have significant side effects. Percutaneous needle biopsy achieves a definitive diagnosis in the majority of cases.[133]

On MR imaging, untreated nodules are minimally hypointense on T1-weighted pregadolinium and postgadolinium images and markedly hyperintense on T2-weighted images.[1] In the subacute presentation after treatment, lesions appear mildly to moderately hyperintense on T1- and T2-weighted

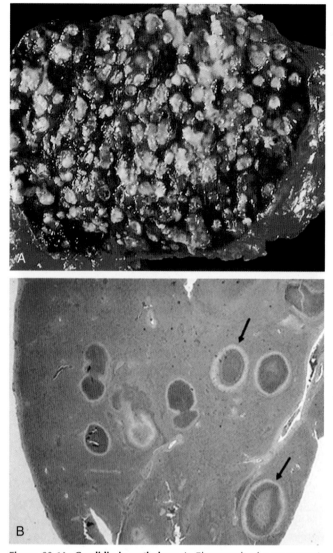

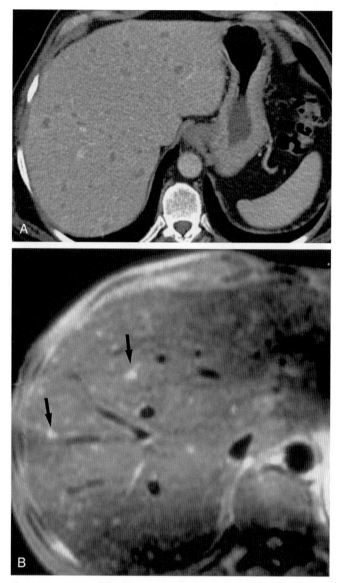

Figure 90-14. Candidiasis: pathology. A. Photograph of a gross specimen of the spleen shows multiple small, white nodules representing involvement by candidiasis throughout the parenchyma. **B.** Low-power photomicrograph shows multiple candidiasis microabscesses with a peripheral zone of fibrosis and a central area of necrosis (*arrows*). (From Mortele, KJ, Segatto E, Ros PR: The infected liver: Radiologic-pathologic correlation. RadioGraphics 24:937-955, 2004.)

Figure 90-15. Candidiasis on CT and MR. A. Contrast-enhanced CT scan of the liver shows multiple hypoattenuating microabscesses less than 1 cm in diameter disseminated throughout the hepatic parenchyma. **B.** Axial T1-weighted MR image reveals relatively hyperintense lesions less than 1 cm in diameter in the liver (*arrows*). (From Mortele, KJ, Segatto E, Ros PR: The infected liver: Radiologic-pathologic correlation. RadioGraphics 24:937-955, 2004.)

images and also demonstrate enhancement after intravenous contrast administration. A dark ring is usually seen around these lesions with all sequences. Completely treated lesions are minimally hypointense on T1-weighted images, isointense to mildly hyperintense on T2-weighted images and moderately hypointense on early postcontrast images. They become minimally hypointense in delayed-phase images.[144,145]

Candida microabscesses have been reported as cold lesions on both sulfur colloid and gallium scans.[137]

SCHISTOSOMIASIS

Epidemiology

Schistosomiasis is one of the most common and serious parasitic infections of humans. This disease affects 200 million people worldwide, and in endemic areas its prevalence is

nearly 70%. Some 10% of patients in endemic areas develop hepatosplenic involvement. *Schistosoma japonicum* occurs in the coastal areas of China, Japan, Taiwan, and the Philippines. *Schistosoma mansoni* occurs in parts of Africa, in the Middle East and West Indies, and in the northern part of South America. *Schistosoma haematobium* is seen in North Africa, the Mediterranean, and southwest Asia.[146-148]

Pathophysiology

The schistosomal larvae are shed by snails, the intermediate host, into fresh water (Fig. 90-16A). Human infection occurs in the course of bathing in or wading through contaminated irrigation canals, streams, and ponds. The schistosomal cercariae penetrate intact skin or mucous membranes and then migrate via venules and lymphatics to the heart. They pass through the pulmonary circulation to enter the mesenteric circulation. All schistosomulae die except those that enter the mesenteric arteries, where they pass through capillaries into the portal venous system and mature within intrahepatic portal venous radicles. The host responds to the ova with granulomatous inflammation, which becomes replaced by fibrous tissue, leading to periportal fibrosis. If the trematode infestation is sufficiently chronic and heavy, progressive intrahepatic portal vein occlusion, presinusoidal portal hypertension, varices, and splenomegaly result. Schistosomiasis is the most common cause of portal hypertension worldwide. These parasites (Fig. 90-16B) are also known as blood flukes, and the importance of their vascular location cannot be overemphasized.[21]

The life cycle is completed when the mature female worm, after living within the male in the portal vein for some 10 to 15 years, swims against blood flow to reach the venules of the urinary bladder (S. haematobium) or gut (S. mansoni, S. japonicum) to deposit eggs. The eggs pass through the wall of the intestine or bladder to release miracidia, which infect mollusks. Cercariae emerge after maturing in their intermediate host.

Pathology

In severe S. mansoni and S. japonicum infections, the liver is dark colored, showing a bumpy but not nodular surface that is distinct from the appearance of ordinary cirrhosis. Cut section reveals granulomas (Fig. 90-16C) with widespread

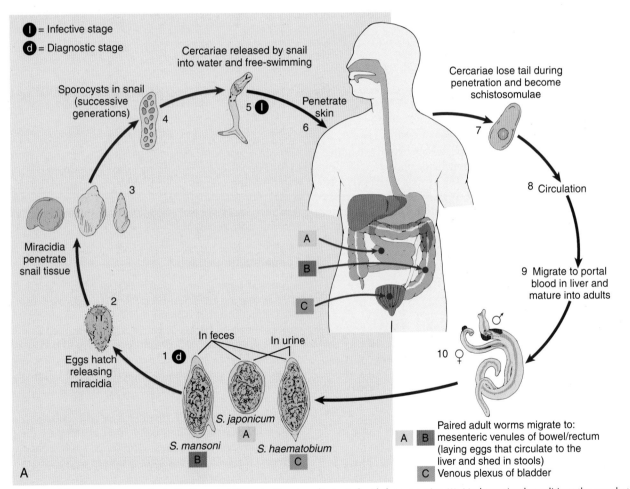

Figure 90-16. Schistosomiasis: pathologic findings. A. Life cycle. Eggs are eliminated with feces or urine (1). Under optimal conditions the eggs hatch and release miracidia (2), which swim and penetrate specific snail intermediate hosts (3). The stages in the snail include two generations of sporocysts (4) and the production of cercariae (5). Upon release from the snail, the infective cercariae swim, penetrate the skin of the human host (6), and shed their forked tail, becoming schistosomulae (7). The schistosomulae migrate through several tissues and stages to their residence in the veins (8, 9). Adult worms in humans reside in the mesenteric venules in various locations, which at times seem to be specific for each species (10). For instance, S. japonicum is more frequently found in the superior mesenteric veins draining the small intestine (A), and S. mansoni occurs more often in the superior mesenteric veins draining the large intestine (B). However, both species can occupy either location, and they are capable of moving between sites, so it is not possible to state unequivocally that one species only occurs in one location. S. haematobium most often occurs in the venous plexus of bladder (C), but it can also be found in the rectal venules. The females (size 7-20 mm; males slightly smaller) deposit eggs in the small venules of the portal and perivesical systems. The eggs are moved progressively toward the lumen of the intestine (S. mansoni and S. japonicum) and of the bladder and ureters (S. haematobium), and are eliminated with feces or urine, respectively (1). Pathology of S. mansoni and S. japonicum schistosomiasis includes: Katayama fever, presinusoidal egg granulomas, Symmers' pipe stem periportal fibrosis, portal hypertension, and occasional embolic egg granulomas in brain or spinal cord. Pathology of S. haematobium schistosomiasis includes: hematuria, scarring, calcification, squamous cell carcinoma, and occasional embolic egg granulomas in brain or spinal cord. (Source: Centers for Disease Control and Prevention, http://www.cdc.gov/Ncidod/parasites.)

Continued

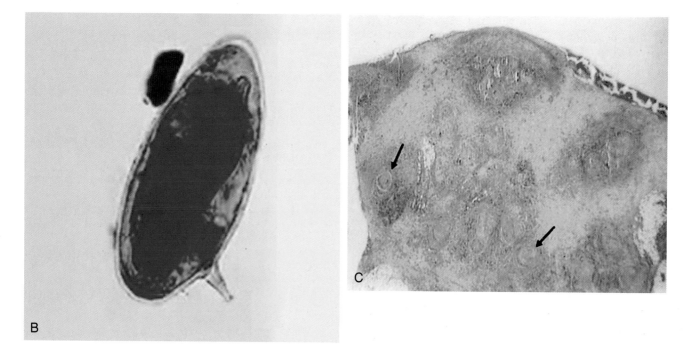

B

C

Figure 90-16, cont'd B. *S. mansoni* egg (iodine stain). **C.** Low-power photomicrograph of a liver specimen reveals calcified eggs (*arrows*) and fibrosis in the subcapsular region. (**C** from Mortele, KJ, Segatto E, Ros PR: The infected liver: Radiologic-pathologic correlation. RadioGraphics 24:937-955, 2004.)

periportal fibrosis beginning in the porta hepatis and extending peripherally. The intervening parenchyma, however, is not distorted by regenerating nodules. The fibrous triads simulate the cross section of a clay pipe stem. Some portal triads lack a perceptible vein, and latex casts demonstrate widespread distortion and blockage of the portal vascular bed. These features account for the portal hypertension. Jaundice and hepatocellular necrosis usually ensue after variceal hemorrhage.[145,147]

Clinical Findings

Schistosomiasis is an insidious and chronic disease. Because hepatocellular necrosis occurs late in its course, patients may seek medical attention for portal hypertension and variceal bleeding. Patients with *S. haematobium* infection, which affects the liver less severely, typically present with hematuria resulting from urinary tract involvement.[21]

Radiologic Findings

Conventional Studies

Calcification is usually too faint to be appreciated on abdominal plain radiographs. Splenomegaly is commonly seen, and barium studies may reveal esophageal and gastric varices.

Ultrasound

In patients with severe hepatic disease, thick, densely echogenic bands replace the portal triads. They sometimes reach a thickness of 2 cm, radiating from the porta hepatis to the periphery. When scanning is performed perpendicular to the triad, rounded foci of echogenic material with a hypoechoic rim can be identified. This produces a "network" pattern with echogenic septa outlining polygonal areas of relatively normal liver (Fig. 90-17A).[149] A "bird's claw" appearance is present at bifurcating points. Early, the liver is enlarged, but as periportal fibrosis progresses, it becomes contracted and the features of portal hypertension (varices, splenomegaly, ascites) become more apparent.[150]

Computed Tomography

Peripheral hepatic or capsular calcification is the hallmark of *S. japonicum* infection (Fig. 90-17B). The liver also shows gross septations that contain numerous calcified Schistosoma eggs resulting in bands of calcification described as a "turtle back" appearance.[151,152] Prominent periportal low-density areas may also be present. There is an increased incidence of hepatocellular carcinoma in these livers.[152] In patients with acute schistosomiasis (Katayama's syndrome), multiple hypodense nodules may develop.[152]

S. mansoni infection manifests as low-density, rounded foci with linear branching bands that encompass the portal tracts. These fibrotic bands sometimes show enhancement with contrast material but usually do not calcify.[136,149]

Magnetic Resonance Imaging

On MR imaging, the septa are of low signal on T1-weighted scans and are hyperdense on T2-weighted images and reveal enhancement on postgadolinium images.[30] The septal calcifications are depicted less well on MRI than on CT.[149,153]

Angiography

Angiography shows the hemodynamic changes of presinusoidal portal hypertension: normal hepatic venous outflow, decreased portal blood flow, and compensatorily increased

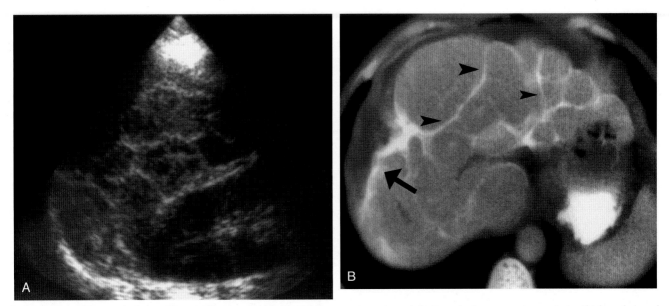

Figure 90-17. Schistosomiasis on CT and ultrasound. Hepatic *Schistosoma japonicum* infection. **A.** Sonogram demonstrates thick and densely echogenic bands producing a network pattern. **B.** Contrast-enhanced CT scan demonstrates capsular calcification (*arrow*) and gross septations (*arrowheads*).

hepatic arterial flow. Wedged hepatic venous pressure is normal or only slightly elevated, compared with portal hypertension resulting from alcoholic cirrhosis.

Treatment

Praziquantel, an isoquinoline derivative, and oxamniquine are effective against schistosomal infestation. Colchicine, an antifibrotic agent, has shown encouraging results in the treatment of schistosome-induced hepatic fibrosis.[2]

PNEUMOCYSTIS CARINII (PNEUMOCYSTIS JIROVECI) INFECTION

Pneumocystis carinii (P. jiroveci) is the most common cause of opportunistic infection in patients with AIDS. Nearly 80% of AIDS patients are affected, and extrapulmonary dissemination is becoming increasingly common.[21,154]

Sonographically, *P. jiroveci* infection of the liver can manifest as diffuse, tiny, nonshadowing echogenic foci or extensive replacement of normal liver parenchyma by echogenic clumps of dense calcification. This pattern, while very suggestive, has also been reported in *Mycobacterium avium-intracellulare* and cytomegalovirus infection.[155] On CT scans, these regions are first hypodense but then become characteristically calcified. The calcifications may be punctate, nodular or rim-like.[156-158]

References

1. Mortele KJ, Segatto E, Ros PR. The infected liver: Radiologic-pathologic correlation. RadioGraphics 24:937-955, 2004.
2. Chung RT, Friedman LS: Liver abscess and bacterial, parasitic, fungal, and granulamtous disease. In Feldman M, Friedman LS, Sleisinger MH (eds): Sleisenger & Fordtran's Gastrointestinal and Liver Disease, 8th ed. Philadelphia, WB Saunders, 2006, pp 1731-1754.
3. Doyle DJ, Hanbridge AE, O'Malley ME: Imaging of hepatic infections. Clin Radiol 61:737-748, 2006.
4. Mohan S, Talwar N, Chaudhary A, et al: Liver abscess: A clinicopathological analysis of 82 cases. Int Surg 91:228-233, 2006.
5. Lamps LW, Washington K: Acute and chronic hepatitis. In Odze RD, Goldblum JR, Crawford JM (eds): Surgical Pathology of the GI Tract, Liver, Biliary Tract, and Pancreas. Philadelphia, Saunders, 2004, pp 783-810.
6. Albrecht H: Bacterial and miscellaneous infections of the liver. In Zakim D, Boyer TD (eds): Hepatology, 4th ed. Philadelphia, Saunders, 2003, pp 1109-1124.
7. Canto MIF: Bacterial infections of the liver and biliary system. In Surawicz C, Owen RL (eds): Gastrointestinal and Hepatic Infections. Philadelphia, WB Saunders, 1995, pp 355-390.
8. Eisenberg PJ, Mueller PR, Rattner DW: Hepatic abscess. In Pitt HA, Carr-Locke DL, Ferrucci JT (eds): Hepatobiliary and Pancreatic Disease. Boston, Little, Brown, 1995, pp 81-90.
9. Cook GC: Hepatic involvement in bacterial, protozoan, and helminthic infections. Curr Opin Gastroenterol 8:458-465, 1992.
10. Block M: Abscesses of the liver (other than amebic). In Haubrich WS, Schaffner F, Berk JE (eds): Bockus Gastroenterology, 5th ed. Philadelphia, WB Saunders, 1995, pp 2405-
11. Mueller PR, White EM, Glass-Royal M, et al: Infected abdominal tumors: Percutaneous catheter drainage. Radiology 173:627-629, 1989.
12. Allard JC, Kuligowska E: Percutaneous treatment of an intrahepatic abscess caused by a penetrating duodenal ulcer. J Clin Gastroenterol 95:603-606, 1987.
13. Kandel G, Marion NE: Pyogenic liver abscess: New concepts of an old disease. Am J Gastroenterol 79:65-71, 1984.
14. Altmeir WA, Schowenger DT, Whiteley DH: Abscess of the liver: Surgical considerations. Arch Surg 101:258-267, 1982.
15. Ralls PW. Inflammatory disease of the liver. Clin Liver Dis 6:203-225, 2002.
16. Ochsner A, Debakey M, Murray S: Pyogenic liver abscess. II: An analysis of 47 cases with review of the literature. Am J Surg 40:292-319, 1938.
17. Huang C-J, Pitt HA, Lipsett PA, et al: Pyogenic liver abscess: Changing trends over 42 years. Ann Surg 223:600-609, 1996.
18. Robert JH, Mirescu D, Ambrosetti P, et al: Critical review of the treatment of pyogenic hepatic abscess. Surg Gynecol Obstet 174:97-102, 1992.
19. Kanner R, Weinfeld A, Tedesco FJ: Hepatic abscess: Plain film findings as an early aid to diagnosis. Am J Gastroenterol 71:432-437, 1979.
20. Wilson SR, Withers CE: The liver. In Rumack CM, Wilson SR, Charboneau JW (eds): Diagnostic Ultrasound, 3rd ed. Philadelphia, Elsevier Mosby, 2003, pp 77-146.
21. Sherlock S, Dooley J: Diseases of the Liver and Biliary System, 9th ed. Oxford: Blackwell Scientific Publications, 1993, pp 471-502.
22. Newlin N, Silver TM, Stuck KJ, et al: Ultrasonic features of pyogenic liver abscesses. Radiology 139:155-159, 1991.

23. Kuligowska E, Connors SK, Shapiro JH: Liver abscess: Sonography in diagnosis and treatment. AJR 138:253-257, 1982.
24. Halvorsen RA, Korobkin M, Foster WL, et al: The variable appearance of hepatic abscesses. AJR 141:941-944, 1984.
25. Rubinson HA, Isikoff MB, Hill MC: Diagnostic imaging of hepatic abscesses: A retrospective analysis. AJR 135:735-740, 1980.
26. Fawcett HD, Lantieri RL, Frankel A, McDougall IR: Differentiating hepatic abscess from tumor: Combined 111In white blood cell and 99mTc liver scans. AJR 135:53-56, 1980.
27. Zaman A, Bramley PN, Wyatt J, et al: Hodgkin's disease presenting as liver abscesses. Gut 32:959-962, 1991.
28. Moreno AJ, Battafarano NJ, Nelson PM, et al: Multiple anaerobic hepatic abscesses demonstrated on hepatobiliary scintigraphy. Clin Nucl Med 11:204-205, 1986.
29. Mendez RJ, Schiebler ML, Outwater EK, et al: Hepatic abscesses: MR imaging findings. Radiology 190:431-436, 1994.
30. Balci NC, Sirvanci M: MR imaging of infective liver lesions. Magn Reson Imaging Clin N Am. 10:121-135, 2002.
31. Heiken JP, Menias CD, Elsayes K: Liver. In Lee JKT, Sagal SS, Stanley RI, et al (eds): Computed Body Tomography With MRI Correlation, 4th ed. Philadelphia, Lippincott Williams & Wilkins, 2006, pp 829-930.
32. Gabata T, Kadoya M, Matsui O, et al: Dynamic CT of hepatic abscesses: Significance of transient segmental enhancement. AJR 176:675-679, 2001.
33. Jeffrey RB, Tolentino CS, Chang FC, et al: CT of small pyogenic hepatic abscesses: The cluster sign. AJR 151:487-489, 1988.
34. Kim SB, Je BK, Lee KY, et al: Computed tomographic differences of pyogenic liver abscesses caused by Klebsiella pneumoniae and non-Klebsiella pneumoniae. J Comput Assist Tomogr 31:59-65, 2007.
35. Robert JH, Mirescu D, Ambrosetti P, et al: Critical review of the treatment of pyogenic hepatic abscess. Surg Gynecol Obstet 174:97-102, 1992.
36. Rajak CL, Gupta S, Jain S, et al: Percutaneous treatment of liver abscesses: Needle aspiration versus catheter drainage. AJR 170:1035-1039, 1998.
37. Bret PM, Ritchie RG: Percutaneous drainage of liver abscesses and fluid collections. In Kadir S (ed): Current Practice of Interventional Radiology. Philadelphia, BC Decker, 1991, pp 481-486.
38. Do H, Lambiase RE, Deyoe L, et al: Percutaneous drainage of hepatic abscesses: Comparison of results in abscesses with and without intrahepatic biliary communication. AJR 157:1209-1212, 1991.
39. Gatewood LH, Collins TL, Yrizarry JM: Percutaneous management of multiple liver abscesses. AJR 139:390-392, 1982.
40. Bernardino ME, Berkman WA, Plemmons M, et al: Percutaneous drainage of multiseptated hepatic abscess. J Comput Assist Tomogr 8:38-41, 1984.
41. Johnson RD, Mueller PR, Ferrucci JT, et al: Percutaneous drainage of pyogenic liver abscesses. AJR 144:463-467, 1985.
42. Fernandez MDP, Murphy FB: Hepatic biopsies and fluid drainages. Radiol Clin North Am 29:1311-1326, 1991.
43. Sheinfeld AM, Steiner AE, Rivkin LB, et al: Transcutaneous drainage of hepatic, intraabdominal, and mediastinal abscesses guided by computerized axial tomography. Successful alternative to open drainage. Am J Surg 145:120-125, 1983.
44. Pitt HA: Surgical management of hepatic abscesses. World J Surg 14:498-504, 1990.
45. Gerzof SG, Johnson WC, Robbins AH, et al: Intrahepatic pyogenic abscess treatment by percutaneous drainage. Am J Surg 149:487-494, 1985.
46. Maher JA, Reynolds TB, Yellin AE: Successful medical treatment of pyogenic liver abscess. Gastroenterology 77:618-622, 1979.
47. Bergamini TM, Larson GM, Malagoni MA, et al: Liver abscess: Review of a 12-year experience. Am Surg 53:596-599, 1987.
48. Giorgio A, Tarantino L, Mariniello N, et al: Pyogenic liver abscesses: 13 Years of experience in percutaneous needle aspiration with US guidance. Radiology 195:122-124, 1995.
49. Yu SCH, Lo RHG, Kan PS, et al: Pyogenic liver abscess: Treatment with needle aspiration. Clin Radiol 52:912-916, 1997.
50. Reed SL: Amebiasis: An update. Clin Infect Dis 14:385-393, 1992.
51. Moenroe LS: Gastrointestinal parasites. In Haubrich WS, Schaffner F, Berk JE (eds): Bockus Gastroenterology, 5th ed. Philadelphia, WB Saunders, 1995, pp 3113-3198.
52. Li E, Stanley SL: Protozoa-amebiasis. Gastroenterol Clin North Am 25:471-492, 1996.
53. Lee KC, Yamazaki O, Hamba H, et al: Analysis of patients with amebic liver abscess. J Gastroenterol 31:40-45, 1996.
54. Cevallos AM, Farthing MJG: Parasitic infections of the gastrointestinal tract. Curr Opin Gastroenterol 9:96-102, 1993.
55. Remedios PA, Colletti PM, Ralls PW: Hepatic amebic abscess: Cholescintigraphic rim enhancement. Radiology 160:395-398, 1986.
56. Geslien GE, Thrall JH, Johnson MC: Gallium scanning in acute hepatic amebic abscess. J Nucl Med 15:561-563, 1974.
57. McDougall IR: The appearance of amebic abscess of liver on In-111-leukocyte scan. Clin Nucl Med 6:67-69, 1981.
58. Ralls PW, Colletti PM, Quinn MF, et al: Sonographic findings in hepatic amebic abscess. Radiology 145:123-126, 1982.
59. Missalek W: Ultrasonography in the diagnosis of amoebic liver abscess and its complications. Trop Doct 22:59-63, 1992.
60. Withers CE, Wilson SR: The liver. In Rumack CM, Wilson SR, Charboneau JW (eds): Diagnostic Ultrasound, 2nd ed. St Louis, Mosby-Year book, 1998, pp 87-154.
61. Ralls PW, Meyers HJ, Lapin SA, et al: Gray-scale ultrasonography of hepatic amebic abscesses. Radiology 132:125-129, 1979.
62. Ralls PW, Quinn MF, Boswell WP, et al: Patterns of resolution in successfully treated hepatic amebic abscess: Sonographic evaluations. Radiology 149:541-543, 1983.
63. Fujihara T, Nagai Y, Kuba T, et al.: Amebic liver abscess. J Gastroenterol 31:659-663, 1996.
64. Catalano O, Sandomenico F, Raso MM, Siani A. Low mechanical index contrast-enhanced sonographic findings of pyogenic hepatic abscesses. AJR 182:447-450, 2004.
65. Radin DR, Ralls PW, Colletti PM, et al: CT of amebic liver abscess. AJR 150:1297-1301, 1988.
66. Verhaegen F, Poey C, Lebras Y, et al: CT findings in diagnosis and treatment of amebic liver abscesses. J Radiol 77:23-28, 1996.
67. Ralls PW, Henley DS, Colletti PM, et al: Amebic liver abscess: MR imaging. Radiology 165:801-804, 1987.
68. Elizondo G, Weissleder R, Stark DD, et al: Amebic liver abscess: Diagnosis and treatment evaluation with MR imaging. Radiology 165:795-800, 1987.
69. Greaney GC, Reynolds TB, Donovan AJ: Ruptured amebic liver abscess. Arch Surg 120:555-561, 1985.
70. Tandon N, Karak PK, Mukhopadhyay S, et al: Amoebic liver abscess: Rupture into retroperitoneum. Gastrointest Radiol 16:240-242, 1991.
71. Filice C, DiPerri G, Strosselli M, et al: Outcome of hepatic amebic abscesses managed with three different therapeutic strategies. Dig Dis Sci 37:240-247, 1992.
72. DiazGranados CA, Duffus WA, Albrecht H: Parasitic diseases of the liver. In Zakim D, Boyer TD (eds): Hepatology, 4th ed. Philadelphia, Saunders, 2003.
73. Ralls PW, Barnes PF, Johnson MB, et al: Medical treatment of hepatic amebic abscess: Rare need for percutaneous drainage. Radiology 165:805-807, 1987.
74. VanSonnenberg E, Mueller PR, Schiffman HR, et al: Intrahepatic amebic abscesses: Indications for and results of percutaneous catheter drainage. Radiology 156:631-635, 1985.
75. Nordestgaard AG, Stapleford L, Worthen N, et al: Contemporary management of amoebic liver abscess. Am Surg 58:315-320, 1992.
76. Ken JG, VanSonnenberg E, Casola G, et al: Perforated amebic liver abscesses: Successful percutaneous treatment. Radiology 170:195-197, 1989.
77. Van Allen RJ, Katz MD, Johnson MB, et al: Uncomplicated amoebic liver abscess: Prospective evaluation of percutaneous therapeutic aspiration. Radiology 183:827-830, 1982.
78. Giorgio A, Amoroso P, Francica G, et al: Echo-guided percutaneous puncture: A safe and valuable therapeutic tool for amebic liver abscess. Gastrointest Radiol 13:336-340, 1988.
79. Ammann RW, Eckert J: Cestodes-echinococcus. Gastroenterol Clin North Am 25:655-689, 1996.
80. Munzer D: New perspectives in the diagnosis of echinococcus disease. J Clin Gastroenterol 13:415-423, 1991.
81. Ishak KG, Markin RS: Liver. In Damjanov I, Linder J (eds): Anderson's Pathology, 10th ed. St. Louis, Mosby-Year Book, 1996, pp 1779-1858.
82. Didier D, Weiler S, Rohmer P, et al: Hepatic alveolar echinococcosis: Correlative US and CT study. Radiology 154:179-186, 1985.
83. Claudon M, Bessieres M, Regent D, et al: Alveolar echinococcosis of the liver: MR findings. J Comput Assist Tomogr 14:608-614, 1990.
84. Bresson-Hadni S, Franza A, Miguet JP, et al: Orthotopic liver transplantation for incurable alveolar echinococcosis of the liver: Report of 17 cases. Hepatology 13:1061-1070, 1991.
85. Rozanes I, Acunas B, Celik L, et al: CT in lobar atrophy of the liver caused by alveolar echinococcosis. J Comput Assist Tomogr 16:216-218, 1992.
86. Filippou D, Tselepis D, Filippou G, et al: Advances in liver echinococcosis: Diagnosis and treatment. Clin Gastroenterol Hepatol 5:152-159, 2007.

87. DeMatteo G, Bove A, Chiarini S, et al: Hepatic echinococcus disease: Our experience over 22 years. Hepatogastroenterology 43:1562-1565, 1996.

88. Gourgiotis S, Stratopoulos C, Moustafellos P, et al: Surgical techniques and treatment for hepatic hydatid cysts. Surg Today 37:389-395, 2007.

89. Lewall DB, Nyak P: Hydatid cysts of the liver: Two cautionary signs. Br J Radiol 71:37-41, 1998.

90. Lewall DB: Hydatid disease: Biology, pathology, imaging and classification. Clin Radiol 53:863-874, 1998.

91. Friedman AC, Frazier S, Hendrix TM, et al: Focal disease. In Friedman AC, Dachman AH (eds): Radiology of the Liver, Biliary Tract, Pancreas, and Spleen. St. Louis, Mosby-Year Book, 1994, pp 169-328.

92. Gharbi HA, Hassine W, Brauner MW, et al: Ultrasound examination of hydatid liver. Radiology 139:459-463, 1981.

93. Mendez Montero JV, Arrazole Garcia JA, Lopez Lafuente JL, et al: Fat-fluid level in hepatic hydatid cyst: A new sign of rupture into the biliary tree? AJR 167:91-94, 1996.

94. Bezzi M, Teggi A, De Rosa F, et al: Abdominal hydatid disease: US findings during medical treatment. Radiology 162:91-95, 1987.

95. Choji K, Fujita N, Chen M, et al: Alveolar hydatid disease of the liver: Computed tomography with transabdominal ultrasound with histopathologic correlation. Clin Radiol 46:97-103, 1992.

96. Gürses N, Sungur R, Gürses B, et al: Ultrasound diagnosis of liver hydatid disease. Acta Radiol 28:161-163, 1987.

97. Ceramanai M, Benci A, Maestrini R, et al: Abdominal cystic hydatid disease (CHD): Classification of sonographic appearance and response to treatment. J Clin Ultrasound 24:491-500, 1996.

98. Lewall DB, McCorkell SJ: Hepatic echinococcal cysts: Sonographic appearance and classification. Radiology 155:773-775, 1985.

99. Kornaros SE, Aboul-Nour TA: Frank intrabiliary rupture of hydatid hepatic cyst: Diagnosis and treatment. J Am Coll Surg 183:466-470, 1996.

100. Czermak BV, Unsinn KM, Gotwald T, et al: Echinococcus multilocularis revisited. AJR 176:1207-1212, 2001.

101. Pandolfo I, Blandino G, Scribano E, et al: CT findings in hepatic involvement by echinococcus granulosus. J Comput Assist Tomogr 8:839-845, 1984.

102. Murphy BJ, Casillas J, Ros PR, et al: The CT appearance of cystic masses of the liver. RadioGraphics 9:307-322, 1989.

103. Kalovidouris A, Pissiotis C, Pontifex G, et al: CT characterization of multivesicular hydatid cysts. J Comput Assist Tomogr 8:839-845, 1984.

104. Acunas B, Rozanes I, Acunas G, et al: Hydatid cyst of the liver identification of detached cyst lining on CT scans obtained after cyst puncture. AJR 156:751-752, 1991.

105. Gonzalez LR, Marcos J, Illanas M, et al: Radiologic aspects of hepatic echinococcosis. Radiology 130:21-27, 1979.

106. Scherer U, Weinzerl M, Sturm R, et al: Computed tomography of hydatid disease of the liver: A report on 13 cases. J Comput Assist Tomogr 2:612-617, 1978.

107. Lewall DB, Bailey TM, McCorrell SJ: Echinococcal matrix: Computed tomographic, sonographic, and pathologic correlation. J Ultrasound Med 5:33-35, 1986.

108. Kalovidouris A, Gouliamos A, Vlachos L, et al: MRI of abdominal hydatid disease. Abdom Imaging 19:489-494, 1994.

109. Proietti S, Abdelmoumene A, Genevay M, et al: Echinococcal cyst. RadioGraphics 24:861-865, 2004.

110. Lewall DB, McCorkell SJ: Rupture of echinococcal cysts: Diagnosis classification, and clinical implications. AJR 146:391-394, 1986.

111. Marti-Bonmati L, Serrano FM: Complications of hepatic hydatid cysts: Ultrasound, computed tomography, and magnetic resonance diagnosis. Gastrointest Radiol 15:119-125, 1990.

112. Lygidakis NJ: Diagnosis and treatment of intrabiliary rupture of hydatid cyst of the liver. Arch Surg 118:1186-1189, 1983.

113. Marti-Bonmati L, Menor F, Ballesta A: Hydatid cyst of the liver: Rupture into the biliary tree. AJR 150:1051-1053, 1988.

114. Camunez F, Simo G, Robledo R, et al: Ultrasound diagnosis of ruptured hydatid cyst of the liver with biliary obstruction. Gastrointest Radiol 11:330-333, 1986.

115. Cockeram AW, Baker RJ, Sullivan SN: The echogenic echinococcal cyst. A diagnostic trap. J Clin Gastroenterol 8:100-102, 1986.

116. Grande D, Ruiz JC, Elizagary E, et al: Hepatic echinococcosis complicated with transphrenic migration and bronchial fistula: CT demonstration. Gastrointest Radiol 15:115-118, 1990.

117. Mendez Montero J, Arrazola Garcia J, Lopez J, et al: Fat-fluid level in hepatic hydatid cyst: A new sign of rupture into the biliary tree? AJR 167:91-94, 1996.

118. Shemesh E, Klein E, Abramowich D, et al: Common bile duct obstruction caused by hydatid daughter cysts: Management by endoscopic retrograde sphincterotomy. Am J Gastroenterol 81:280-282, 1986.

119. Alkarawi MA, Yasawy MI, Mohamed ARE: Endoscopic management of biliary hydatid disease: Report on six cases. Endoscopy 23:278-281, 1992.

120. Magistrelli P, Masetti R, Coppola R, et al: Value of ERCP in the diagnosis and management of pre- and postoperative biliary complications in hydatid disease of the liver. Gastrointest Radiol 14:315-320, 1989.

121. Zargar SA, Khuroo MS, Khan BA, et al: Intrabiliary rupture of hepatic hydatid cyst: Sonographic and cholangiographic appearances. Gastrointest Radiol 17:14-45, 1992.

122. Langer JC, Rose DB, Keystone JS, et al: Diagnosis and management of hydatid disease of the liver. Ann Surg 199:412-417, 1984.

123. Ozmen V, Igci A, Kebudi A, et al: Surgical treatment of hepatic hydatid disease. Can J Surg 35:423-427, 1992.

124. Saremi F: Percutaneous drainage of hydatid cysts: Use of a new cutting device to avoid leakage. AJR 158:83-85, 1992.

125. Men S, Hekimoglu B, Yucesoy C, et al: Percutaneous treatment of hepatic hydatid cysts: An alternative to surgery. AJR 172:83-89, 1999.

126. Akhan O, Dincer A, Gököz A, et al: Percutaneous treatment of abdominal hydatid cysts with hypertonic saline and alcohol. Invest Radiol 28:121-127, 1993.

127. Khuroo MS, Zargar SA, Mahajan R: Echinococcus granulosus cysts in the liver: Management with percutaneous drainage. Radiology 180:141-145, 1991.

128. Acunas B, Rozanes I, Celik L, et al: Purely cystic hydatid disease of the liver: Treatment with percutaneous aspiration and injection of hypertonic saline. Radiology 182:541-543, 1992.

129. Saremi F, McNamara TO: Hydatid cysts of the liver: Long-term results of percutaneous treatment using a cutting instrument. AJR:1163-1167, 1995.

130. Simonetti G, Profili S, Sergiacomi Gl, et al: Percutaneous treatment of hepatic cysts by aspiration and sclerotherapy. Cardiovasc Intervent Radiol 16:81-84, 1993.

131. Ustunsoz B, Akhan O, Kamiloglu MA, et al: Percutaneous treatment of hydatid cysts of the liver: Long-term results. AJR 172:91-96, 1999.

132. Giorgio A, Tarantino L, Francica G, et al: Unilocular hydatid liver cysts: Treatment with US-guided, double percutaneous aspiration and alcohol injection. Radiology 184:705-710, 1992.

133. Thaler M, Pastakia B, Shawker TH, et al: Hepatic candidiasis in cancer patients: The evolving picture of the syndrome. Ann Intern Med 108:88-100, 1988.

134. Francis IR, Glazer GM, Amendola MA, et al: Hepatic abscesses in the immunocompromised patient: Role of CT in detection, diagnosis, management, and follow-up. Gastrointest Radiol 11:257-262, 1986.

135. Gordon SC, Watts JC, Vener RJ, et al: Focal hepatic candidiasis with perihepatic adhesions: Laparoscopic and immunohistologic diagnosis. Gastroenterology 88:214-217, 1990.

136. Pastakia B, Shawker TH, Thaler M, et al: Hepatosplenic candidiasis: Wheels within wheels. Radiology 166:417-421, 1988.

137. Miller JH, Greenfield LD, Wald BR: Candidiasis of the liver and spleen in childhood. Radiology 142:375-380, 1982.

138. Callen PW, Filly RA, Marcus FS: Ultrasonography and computed tomography in the evaluation of hepatic microabscesses in the immunosuppressed patient. Radiology 136:433-434, 1980.

139. Gorg C, Weide R, Schwerk WB, et al: Ultrasound evaluation of hepatic and splenic microabscesses in the immunocompromised patient: Sonographic patterns, differential diagnosis, and follow-up. J Clin Ultrasound 22:525-529, 1994.

140. Shirkhoda A, Lopez-Berestein G, Holbert JM, et al: Hepatosplenic fungal infection: CT and pathologic evaluation after treatment with liposomal amphotericin B. Radiology 159:349-353, 1986.

141. Shirkhoda A: CT findings in hepatosplenic and renal candidiasis. J Comput Assist Tomogr 11:795-798, 1987.

142. Berlow ME, Spirt BA, Weil L: CT follow-up of hepatic and splenic fungal microabscesses. J Comput Assist Tomogr 8:42-45, 1984.

143. Anttila VJA, Ruutu P, Bondestam S, et al: Hepatosplenic yeast infection in patients with acute leukemia: A diagnostic problem. Clin Infect Dis 18:979-981, 1994.

144. Semelka RC, Shoenut JP, Greenberg HM, et al: Detection of acute and treated lesions of hepatosplenic candidiasis: Comparison of dynamic contrast-enhanced CT and MR imaging. J Magn Reson Imaging 1992:341-345, 1992.

145. Semelka RC, Kelekis N, Sallah S, et al: Hepatosplenic fungal disease: Diagnostic accuracy and spectrum of appearances on MR imaging. AJR 169:1311-1316, 1997.

146. Marcial MA, Marcial-Rojas RA: Parasitic diseases of the liver. In Schiff L, Schiff ER (eds): Diseases of the Liver, 6th ed. Philadelphia, JB Lippincott, 1987, pp 1171-1196.

147. Palmer PES: Schistosomiasis. Semin Roentgenol 33:6-25, 1998.

148. Patel SA, Castillo DF, Hibbeln JF, et al: Magnetic resonance imaging appearance of hepatic schistosomiasis, with ultrasound and computed tomography correlation. Am J Gastroenterol 88:113-116, 1993.

149. Monzawa S, Uchiyama G, Ohtomo K, et al: Schistosomiasis japonica of the liver: Contrast-enhanced CT findings in 113 patients. AJR 161:323-7, 1993.

150. Pereira LM, Domingues AL, Spinelli V, et al: Ultrasonography of the liver and spleen in Brazilian patients with hepatosplenic schistosomiasis and cirrhosis. Trans R Soc Trop Med Hyg 92:639-42, 1998.

151. Araki T, Hayakawa K, Okada J, et al: Hepatic Schistosomiasis japonica identified by CT. Radiology 157:757-760, 1985.

152. Cheung H, Lai YM, Loke TK, et al: The imaging diagnosis of hepatic Schistosomiasis japonicum sequelae. Clin Radiol 51:51-55, 1996.

153. Monzawa S, Ohtomo K, Oba H, et al: Septa in the liver of patients with chronic hepatic Schistosomiasis japonica: MR appearance. AJR 162:1347-1351, 1994.

154. Koziel MJ, Peters MG: Viral hepatitis in HIV infection. N Engl J Med 356:1445-1454, 2007.

155. Mathieson JR, Smith FJ: Hepatobiliary and pancreatic ultrasound in AIDS. In Reeders JWAJ, Mathieson JR (eds): AIDS imaging: A practical approach. London, WB Saunders, 1998, pp 188-202.

156. Sansom H, Seddon B, Padley SP: Clinical utility of abdominal CT scanning in patients with HIV disease. Clin Radiol.52:698-703, 1997.

157. Radin DR: Hepatopancreatic and biliary imaging in AIDS: computed tomography. In Reeders JWAJ, Mathieson JR (eds): AIDS Imaging: A Practical Approach. London, WB Saunders, 1998, pp 203-213.

158. Gore RM, Miller FH, Yaghmai V: Acquired immunodeficiency syndrome (AIDS) of the abdominal organs: Imaging features. Semin Ultrasound CT MR 9:175-189, 1998.

Diffuse Liver Disease

Richard M. Gore, MD

The liver has quite accurately been called the "custodian of the milieu interieur," and as such, it is vulnerable to a variety of metabolic, circulatory, toxic, infectious, and neoplastic insults. All hepatic derangements, whether primary or secondary, tend to cause similar clinical signs and symptoms. Physical examination is often inaccurate in determining liver size and detecting ascites, splenomegaly, and abdominal wall collateral veins. Liver function tests often lack diagnostic specificity, are frequently affected by nonhepatic factors, and generally do not measure any true physiologic function of the liver.[1-4]

Imaging plays a critical role in overcoming the inadequacies of laboratory and physical examination in patients with hepatic dysfunction. Dramatic advances in cross-sectional imaging have led to significant strides in the noninvasive diagnosis of diffuse hepatic disorders.

NONALCOHOLIC STEATOHEPATITIS

Hepatic fatty metamorphosis or steatosis is the metabolic complication of a variety of toxic, ischemic, and infectious insults to the liver. It is the abnormality most frequently seen on liver biopsies of alcoholics and can be seen in up to 50% of patients with diabetes mellitus. It is quite prevalent in the general population as well. Indeed, fatty infiltration of the liver has been observed in 25% of nonalcoholic, previously healthy adult males meeting accidental deaths.[5-10] With the current epidemic of obesity in the United States, hepatic steatosis has become a major source of hepatic dysfunction.

Macrovesicular fatty disorders of the liver encompass a spectrum of histologic disease that includes macrovesicular fatty liver; nonalcoholic steatohepatitis (NASH); steatohepatitis with fibrosis; and cirrhosis.[5-10]

Clinical Findings

Fatty metamorphosis is clinically silent in most cases, and liver chemistry values are usually normal as well. The liver may be slightly enlarged in an otherwise asymptomatic obese or diabetic patient. In alcoholic patients, vague right upper quadrant tenderness and pain with hepatomegaly may be present, often associated with abnormal liver function tests. One third of asymptomatic alcoholic patients have a fatty liver. In acute fatty liver associated with pregnancy, carbon tetrachloride exposure, or an alcoholic binge, patients may present with jaundice, acute hepatic failure, or even encephalopathy.[2,5,9]

Pathologic Findings

Fatty infiltration of the liver is seen in association with obesity, diabetes mellitus, alcoholic liver disease, kwashiorkor, malnutrition resulting from malignancy or tuberculosis, total parenteral nutrition, inflammatory bowel disease, severe hepatitis, hepatotoxins, carbon tetrachloride, phosphorus, chemotherapy (methotrexate), ileojejunal bypass for obesity, hyperlipidemia, endogenous and exogenous steroids, and congestive heart failure. Less common causes include cystic fibrosis, Reye's syndrome, glycogen synthase deficiency, massive tetracycline therapy, pregnancy, and trauma. Fat is deposited in the liver as a result of a number of metabolic derangements: increased hepatic synthesis of fatty acids (ethanol), decreased hepatic oxidation or utilization of fatty acids (carbon tetrachloride, high-dose tetracycline), impaired release of hepatic lipoproteins, and excessive mobilization of fatty acids from adipose tissue (starvation, steroids, alcohol).[2,6,7]

Pathologically, lipid accumulates within the cytoplasm of the hepatocyte, predominantly in the centrilobular zone (Fig. 91-1). With progressive lipid accumulation, these small vacuoles coalesce, creating large, clear, macrovesicular spaces that virtually transform the hepatocyte into a lipocyte, with a compressed and peripherally displaced nucleus. Water and protein retention add to the cellular enlargement, and the liver may weigh 4 to 6 kg and have a soft, yellow, greasy cut surface.[14,22] Although the histologic lesion of fatty infiltration caused by toxins is often reversible with substance abstinence, nonalcoholic steatohepatitis may be seen in patients with hyperlipidemia and diabetes and may lead to "cryptogenic" cirrhosis.[2,6,7]

Segmental areas of fatty infiltration of the liver may develop as a result of a variety of traumatic and ischemic insults that reduce the amount of nutrients and insulin necessary to produce glycogen, culminating in a "metabolic infarct" of the involved region. Fatty replacement occurs where glycogen is depleted from the liver. This occurs primarily in regions where portal venous blood is reduced secondary to a mass, the Budd-Chiari syndrome, and bland or tumor thrombus. Accordingly, fat often infiltrates the right lobe of the liver before the left. This is probably due to a different hormonal balance presented to each lobe: pancreatic and splenic venous blood containing higher concentrations of insulin and glycogen may stream preferentially into the left portal vein.[2,6,7]

There are several major patterns of fat deposition than can be visualized at cross-sectional imaging: diffuse; focal deposition and focal sparing; multifocal deposition; perivascular deposition; subcapsular deposition.[11]

Diffuse deposition is the most common pattern and is associated with homgenenous involvement and hepatomegaly. Focal deposition and diffuse deposition with focal sparing is a less common pattern that characteristically occurs adjacent

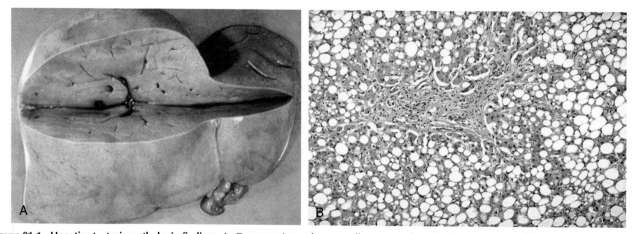

Figure 91-1. Hepatic steatosis: pathologic findings. A. Gross specimen shows a yellow, greasy liver that has undergone diffuse fatty metamorphosis. **B.** Pathologic specimen shows lipid accumulation within the hepatocytes, primarily in the centrilobular zone.

to the falciform ligament, fissure for the ligamentum venosum, porta hepatis, and gallbladder fossa. This probably relates to variant arterial supply and/or venous drainage. True masses can be differentiated from these regions of fat deposition or focal sparing because the latter occur in characteristic locations, have a geographic shape, poorly delineated margins, and absence of mass effect on blood vessels.[11]

Multifocal deposition of fat may simulate true masses such as metastases. In these patients chemical shift MR gradient-echo (GRE) imaging may be needed for confirmation. With perivascular fat deposition, halos of fat surround the hepatic or portal veins. This fat is tramlike or tubular in appearance when the course is in the imaging plane and ringlike or round for vessels with a course perpendicular to the imaging plane.[11]

Subcapsular fat deposition can be seen in patients with renal failure and insulin-dependent diabetes in which insulin is added to the peritoneal dialysate. The dialysate exposes the subcapsular hepatocytes to a higher concentration of insulin than the remainder of the liver which promotes the esterification of free fatty acids into triglycerides. This in turn results in subcapsular deposition of fat.[11]

Radiologic Findings

Plain Radiographs

Plain film radiography is relatively insensitive to the presence of fat in the liver unless marked degrees of infiltration are present. In these cases, the liver may appear hyperlucent and blend imperceptibly with the right properitoneal fat stripe. This produces a visible interface between the combined radiolucency of the fatty liver and flank stripe and the relatively radiodense abdominal musculature. A fat–fluid interface may be present if the patient has ascites. The outer wall of the gut may produce a viscus wall sign as the soft tissue density of the bowel wall is contrasted with the fatty liver. These changes, however, are most commonly seen in pediatric patients.

The imaging features of fatty metamorphosis are variable and depend on the amount of fat deposited, its distribution within the liver, and the presence of associated hepatic disease.

Ultrasound

On sonograms, the fatty liver appears diffusely echogenic and the degree of echogenicity is roughly proportional to the level of steatosis[12-15] (Fig. 91-2). These sonographic changes also tend to parallel biochemical and clinical dysfunction. The key findings sonographically are accentuation of the brightness of parenchymal echoes and an increased number of echogenic foci resulting from the proliferation of fat–nonfat interfaces. These echogenic foci are smaller than normally seen. Consequently, there is increased attenuation of the ultrasound beam, with poorer visualization of deep hepatic structures and the hepatic venous system. Normally, four to six portal and hepatic veins are seen per longitudinal section of the right lobe. With fatty infiltration, these vessels are fewer and the smaller vascular structures may disappear completely from the image. This dropout of vessels is due to physical vascular compression by parenchymal swelling, poorer sound penetration, and loss of contrast between echogenic vascular walls and the usually less echogenic surrounding parenchyma.[12-14]

Hepatic steatosis and fibrosis frequently coexist and produce similar sonographic findings. Although ultrasound is not the primary imaging modality for these disorders, the possibility of focal fat must always be considered in the differential diagnosis of space-occupying lesions seen in patients who are at risk.[12-14]

Four sonographic patterns of focal fatty infiltration have been described: (1) hyperechoic nodule, (2) multiple confluent hyperechogenic lesions, (3) hypoechoic skip nodules, and (4) irregular hyperechoic and hypoechoic areas. Occasionally focal areas of liver parenchyma may be spared from fatty metamorphosis and appear as an ovoid, spherical, or sheetlike hypoechoic mass in an otherwise echogenic liver. Its characteristic location, the lack of mass effect on surrounding vessels, a straight linear interface between normal and fatty parenchyma, and increased echogenicity of the right lobe compared with the cortex of the right kidney are useful differentiating signs. Hepatic hemangiomas, most often hyperechoic in nature, may appear hypoechoic when compared with adjacent liver parenchyma in patients with a diffusely fatty liver, necessitating other imaging modalities such as MR imaging or CT for differentiation. Focal fatty infiltration in an otherwise normal-appearing liver may also produce a hyperechoic space-occupying mass. An angular or interdigitating geometric margin is also characteristic of focal fat.[12-15]

Technical considerations are important in the sonographic diagnosis of focal fat because the operator may erroneously change the time-gain-compensation curve, so that fatty parenchyma, which should have increased echogenicity, appears normal, whereas the spared, normal liver appears abnormally hypoechoic, simulating pathologic change.

Computed Tomography

CT (Fig. 91-3) is capable of diagnosing hepatic steatosis because of the excellent correlation between hepatic parenchymal CT attenuation value and the amount of hepatic triglycerides found on liver biopsy specimens.[16,17] On noncontrast scans, the attenuation of the normal liver is generally 50 to 70 HU and the liver appears homogeneous, with the liver appearing between 8 to 10 HU greater than the attenuation of the spleen.[16,17]

In a study of potential liver donors, unenhanced CT was able to provide an accurate diagnosis of macrovesicular steatosis of 30% or greater. This can help avoid liver biopsy in those donor candidates with an unacceptable degree of macrovesicular steatosis.[16,17]

In patients with NASH the mean liver to spleen attenuation ratio is 0.66.[16,17] The craniocaudal span of the liver has a mean of 21.4 cm with hepatomegaly present in 92% of patients.[16,17] The caudate–to–left lobe ratio is usually normal (mean, 0.43) as is the preportal space (mean, 4.5 mm). Mildly prominent lymph nodes are present in the porta hepatis in 58.3% of patients with a mean dimension of 16 mm × 11 mm. The slightly higher attenuation of the liver is believed to be due to its glycogen content. Increased hepatic fat decreases the mean hepatic CT attenuation. In mild cases, the diagnosis can be made by comparing the relative CT attenuation of the liver and spleen with the liver attenuation approximating that of the spleen. In more advanced cases, the liver may appear less dense than the portal and hepatic veins on noncontrast scans, with the higher-attenuation blood vessels simulating a contrast-enhanced image of the liver.

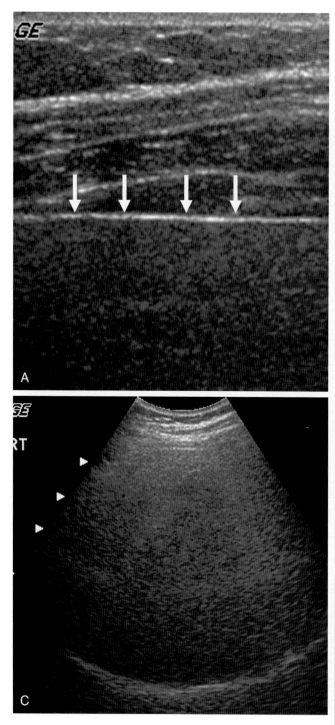

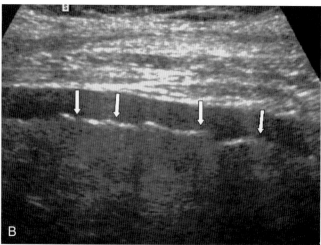

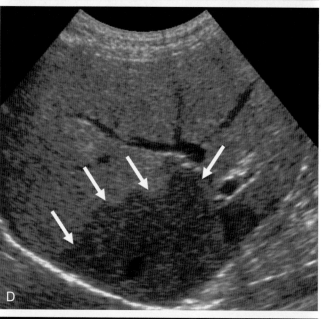

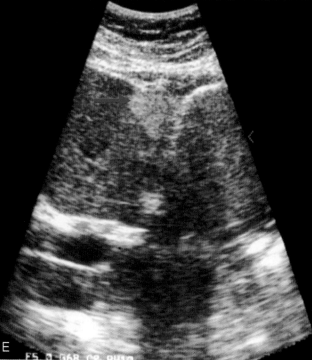

Figure 91-2. Hepatic steatosis: spectrum of sonographic findings.
A. Linear array high frequency transducer shows an echogenic liver with a smooth capsule (*arrows*) in a patient with nonalchoholic steato-hepatitis (NASH). **B.** This is in marked contrast to the nodular surface (*arrows*) of the liver in this patient with posthepatitis cirrhosis. **C.** Sagittal scan of the right lobe of the liver shows an enlarged, echogenic liver with poor sound penetration. The walls of the hepatic veins and portal veins are not defined. **D.** Oblique scan shows geographic steatosis in the anterior aspect of the liver, with focal sparing posteriorly. Note the sharp delineation (*arrows*) between the involved portions of liver. **E.** Focal fatty deposition is identified in segment IV of the liver, adjacent to the falciform ligament. (**D** courtesy of Peter Cooperberg, MD, Vancouver, British Columbia, Canada.)

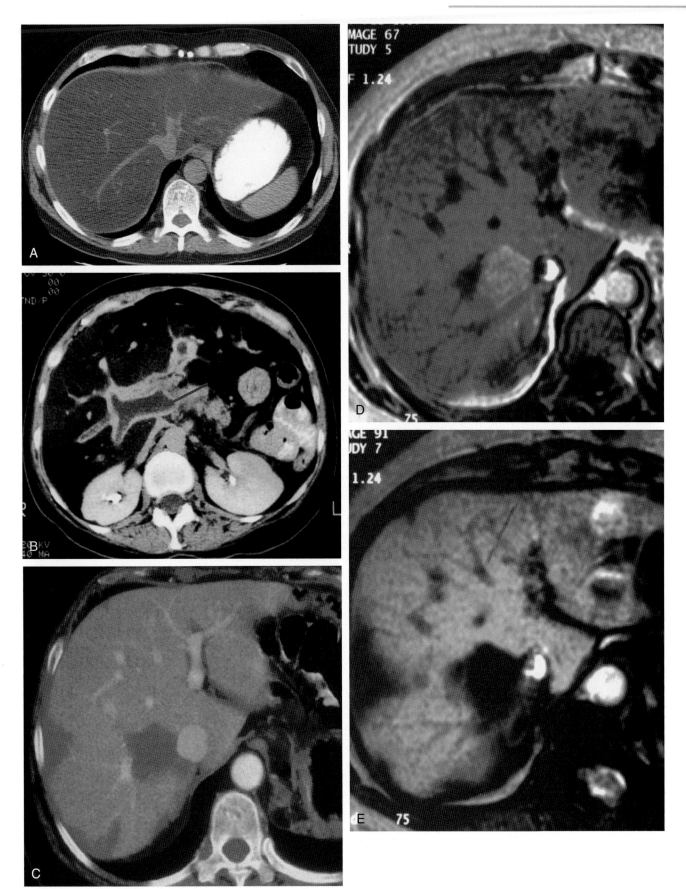

Figure 91-3. Hepatic steatosis: spectrum of CT findings. A. Diffuse hepatic steatosis. The density of the liver parenchyma is lower than that of the spleen on this unenhanced CT scan. Note how the intrahepatic blood vessels stand out as hyperattenuating structures. **B.** Although this is an enhanced CT scan, the severe hepatic steatosis is evident in this patient with portal vein thrombosis (*arrow*). **C.** CT scan shows multiple several hypodense masses in a patient with colon cancer. In-phase (**D**) and opposed-phase (**E**) MR images show that these hypodense areas represent fat.

Continued

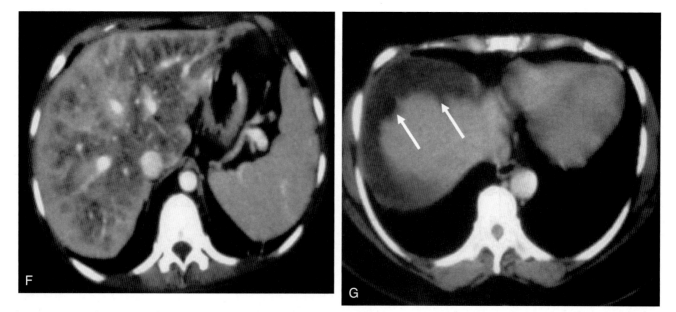

Figure 91-3, *cont'd*. F. Perivascular steatosis is a patient with cystic fibrosis. Notice the fat highlighting the hepatic blood vessels. **G.** Capsular steatosis (*arrows*) is identified in this diabetic patient with renal failure and peritoneal dialysis who had received insulin in the dialysis fluid. (**F** and **G** courtesy of Pablo Ros, MD, Boston, MA.)

The relationship of liver/spleen attenuation can reliably be compared only by using unenhanced CT images, because when large volumes of intravenous contrast medium are administered rapidly, the spleen may transiently demonstrate higher attenuation than the liver. Whereas contrast-enhanced images can be suggestive of the diagnosis of fatty infiltration, variations in degrees of liver and splenic relative enhancement are frequently encountered and vary with rate of contrast administration and scan acquisition times, resulting in a less reliable diagnosis, particularly early (<100 seconds) after initiation of contrast medium infusion.

Hepatic steatosis presents with a wide spectrum of CT appearances (see Fig. 91-3). Although diffuse parenchymal involvement is commonly seen, fat may also be deposited in a focal, lobar, or segmental fashion or scattered in a bizarre distribution. The pattern can be transient, rapidly appearing and disappearing. Fatty infiltration of the liver can obscure the detection of liver lesions, such as neoplasms or abscesses, by lowering the background liver attenuation to levels similar to that of an otherwise hypoattenuating lesion.

When fatty infiltration is lobar, segmental, or wedge-shaped, differentiation from other focal hepatic disease is straightforward. In such cases it usually has a straight-line margin, typically extending to the liver capsule without associated bulging of the contour to suggest an underlying mass. When the steatosis is focal or nodular, differentiation from metastatic disease is problematic. Absolute attenuation values are not reliable indicators because often the fatty infiltration does not cause the focus in the liver to have an attenuation value in the range of fat but merely lower than normal liver parenchyma. There are several helpful differentiating features: regions of focal deposition usually do not cause local contour abnormalities, and portal and hepatic venous branches course normally through the fatty areas, although rarely this can be simulated in metastatic tumor lesions. In addition, these lesions may improve in a matter of days, a useful differentiating feature. Indeed, complete mobilization of hepatic lipids can be seen 3 to 6 weeks after alcohol withdrawal. Occasionally,

discrete focal areas of fatty replacement have a central core of normal-appearing tissue, which is the reverse of the typical tumor necrosis pattern.

One common area of nodular focal fat deposition is adjacent to the falciform ligament. This may result from nutritional ischemia because it is a watershed of the arterial blood supply. Despite these typical features, the diagnosis may remain problematic in some cases and MR imaging techniques described below should be employed.

"Skip" areas of spared parenchyma in an otherwise fatty liver can also present a diagnostic challenge. One of the distinguishing characteristics of these focal spared areas is the sites in which they occur: inferior-medial portion of the liver, along the gallbladder fossa adjacent to the interlobar fissure, the subcapsular portions of the liver, and adjacent to the porta hepatis. Direct vascular communications to the portal system from aberrant gastric venous flow or accessory cystic veins are found in certain of these spared regions, and it is postulated that these areas are perfused by systemic blood rather than by splanchnic venous blood from the portal veins. The posterior aspect of segment IV, a common area to be spared in diffuse fatty infiltration, has been shown to have aberrant direct gastric venous flow to this region when such findings are present. Consequently, a "third blood" supply to these areas may help spare them the adverse effects of toxic agents entering through the portal circulation.[16,17]

Differentiating liver metastases from spared liver in an otherwise fatty liver is another common clinical problem, and further imaging with MR imaging may be required.[18]

Magnetic Resonance Imaging

Proton chemical shift imaging, also termed opposed-phase gradient echo imaging, can be useful in differentiating fatty metamorphosis from neoplasm (Fig. 91-4). This technique capitalizes on the difference in precession frequency between fat and water protons (3.7 ppm) and can be used with spin-echo or gradient-echo techniques. In normal liver, the lipid

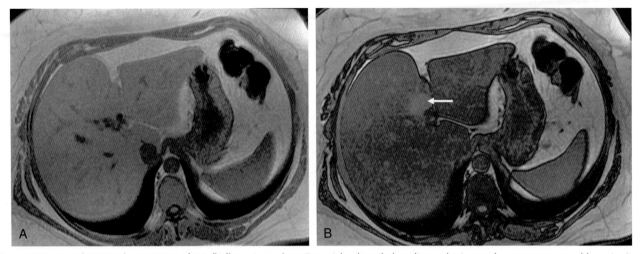

Figure 91-4. Hepatic steatosis: spectrum of MR findings. A. In-phase T1-weighted spoiled gradient-echo image demonstrates normal hepatic signal intensity. **B.** Opposed-phase image shows loss of diffuse loss of hepatic signal intensity indicating diffuse hepatic steatosis. Note the focal region of sparing (*arrow*) adjacent to the falciform ligament in the medial segment of the left hepatic lobe.

fraction is less than 10%; in areas of fat deposition in the liver, it is often greater than 20%.[19-21] Such differences can be detected with proton chemical shift imaging. In addition, liver fat can be quantitated using these imaging techniques.

Chemical shift imaging takes advantage of differences in the resonant frequency of protons in water and fat. On opposed-phase images, the fat signal is subtracted from the water signal, whereas on in-phase images, the fat and water signals are additive. Lesions containing fat and water will therefore show a loss of signal intensity on the opposed-phase images when compared with the in-phase images, readily identifying lesions as containing fat. Current gradient-echo techniques allow these two sequences to obtain complete liver images in seconds with high resolution. Because of the ease of this technique, it is rapidly becoming the imaging method of choice in the abdomen to document the presence of fat and avoid biopsy. One caveat: neoplasms such as hepatocellular carcinoma contain macroscopic fat and may show similar changes. Imaging features of focal fatty liver or focal sparing include location, wedge-shaped configuration with angulated margins, lack of mass effect, coursing of normal vascular structures, and isoenhancement with that of normal liver.[19-21]

In-phase and opposed-phase MR imaging allows reliable detection of focal steatosis hepatic due to the chemical shift cancellation artifact. Areas of steatosis show signal loss on opposed-phase images. T2* effects allow reliable detection of iron storage disease as well as metallic objects and gas filled structures due to pronounced signal loss on images with longer echo times.[19-21]

MR imaging has been shown to be useful in screening liver donors for hepatic macrosteatosis by comparing signal intensity differences on in-phase and opposed-phase images in the liver and spleen.[20]

HEPATITIS

Hepatitis is a general term used to describe acute or chronic inflammation of the liver. In general medical parlance, *hepatitis* refers to viral hepatitis, but diffuse parenchymal inflammation can occur as a result of bacterial, fungal, and rickettsial infections. It can also be seen after inhalation, ingestion, or parenteral administration of a number of agents, including alcohol, acetaminophen, carbon tetrachloride, halothane, isoniazid, chlorpromazine, oral contraceptives, alpha-methyldopa, methotrexate, azathioprine, and 6-mercaptopurine.[22-24]

Viral Hepatitis

The liver is almost invariably involved in all hematogenous viral infections, including mononucleosis, herpes simplex, cytomegalovirus infection in AIDS patients, yellow fever in tropical countries, and rubella, adenovirus infection, and enterovirus infection in children. The term *viral hepatitis* is usually reserved for hepatic infections caused by a small group of hepatotropic viruses. Viral hepatitis is responsible for 60% of cases of fulminant hepatic failure in the United States.[22-24]

Clinical Findings

Viral hepatitis type A (infectious) occurs sporadically or epidemically and is transmitted by a fecal-oral route. It has an incubation period of 15 to 50 days and has a benign self-limited course that does not cause chronic hepatitis and rarely causes fulminant hepatitis.[22-24]

Viral hepatitis type B (serum) is the most versatile hepatotropic virus and can cause an asymptomatic carrier state, acute hepatitis, chronic hepatitis, cirrhosis, fulminant hepatitis with massive hepatocyte necrosis, and hepatocellular carcinoma. Viral hepatitis type B develops within 50 to 160 days of infection by parenterally administered infected blood or by vertical transmission from mother to child. Drug addicts, dialysis patients, and health care workers are at significant risk for contracting hepatitis B infection. There are 200 million carriers of the virus worldwide and 1.5 million in the United States, where the incidence is 13.2 cases per 100,000 population.[22-24]

Hepatitis B virus infection is closely linked to the global distribution of hepatocellular carcinoma. In endemic areas, the annual incidence of hepatocellular carcinoma is 387 per 100,000 for men and 63 per 100,000 for women. In Europe and the United States, the carrier rate of hepatitis B virus is less than 1%. In Africa and Southeast Asia, the carrier rate is approximately 10%. In high-incidence locales, hepatocellular carcinoma accounts for almost 40% of all cancers, as opposed to 2.3% in the West. Vertical transmission of the virus from infected mothers is the most common means of disease spread in these regions.[22-24]

Hepatitis C is caused by a parenterally transmitted RNA virus that affects 0.5% to 1% of normal volunteer blood donors in the United States. It now accounts for 90% of the cases of hepatitis that develop after blood transfusions. A routine blood test for anti–hepatitis C antibody has been developed, greatly improving transfusion safety. The mean delay of the onset of symptoms and seropositivity is 22 weeks.[22-24]

Hepatitis C can cause either acute or chronic hepatitis; at least 50% of acute cases progress to chronic hepatitis. Chronic hepatitis C tends to be a silent, insidious disease, with 10% to 20% of patients eventually developing cirrhosis.[22-24]

Hepatitis D is a liver disease caused by the hepatitis D virus (HDV), a defective virus that needs the hepatitis B virus to exist. HDV can be acquired either as a coinfection (occurs simultaneously) with hepatitis B virus (HBV) or as a super-infection in persons with existing chronic HBV infection. HBV-HDV coinfection has a more severe acute disease and a higher risk (2%-20%) of developing acute liver failure compared with those infected with HBV alone. Chronic HBV carriers who acquire HDV superinfection usually develop chronic HDV infection. Progression to cirrhosis is believed to be more common with HBV-HDV chronic infections[22-24]

Patients with viral hepatitis typically present with fatigue, anorexia, nausea and vomiting, malaise, mild pyrexia, myalgias, photophobia, pharyngitis, cough, and coryza. These constitutional symptoms precede the onset of jaundice by 1 to 2 weeks. When jaundice appears, the patient's clinical condition improves but the liver becomes enlarged and tender in 70% of cases. Splenomegaly is present in 20% of patients. Complete clinical and biochemical recovery is usually seen in 3 to 4 months.[22-24]

If the inflammatory changes persist for more than 6 months, the patient is considered to have chronic hepatitis. The prognosis is often poor for these patients, who have jaundice and hepatosplenomegaly associated with immune-mediated multisystem disease.

Pathologic Findings

Pathologically, the changes of acute viral hepatitis are virtually the same regardless of the offending agent. The entire liver is acutely inflamed, with centrilobular necrosis, hepatocyte necrosis, periportal infiltration by leukocytes and histiocytes, and reactive changes in the Kupffer cells and sinusoidal lining cells (Fig. 91-5). Centrilobular cholestasis and bile duct proliferation also occur.[2]

In chronic active hepatitis, the chronic periportal inflammatory changes extend into the liver parenchyma, producing necrosis and formation of intralobular septa. Chronic persistent hepatitis is a relatively benign condition characterized histologically by cellular infiltrates in the necrosis. In both disorders, definitive diagnosis is made by liver biopsy.[2]

Radiologic Findings

The diagnosis of viral hepatitis can usually be made on the basis of history, serologic markers, and liver function test ab-

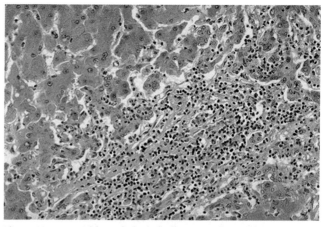

Figure 91-5. Hepatitis: pathologic findings. Liver biopsy shows so called piecemeal necrosis typical of viral hepatitis.

normalities. Imaging is usually done to ensure that there is no obstructive component of the patient's hepatic dysfunction, to confirm physical examination findings, to exclude focal hepatic abnormalities such as hepatocellular carcinoma, and to assess hepatic vascular patency.

Ultrasound

The sonographic findings correlate fairly well with the clinical and histologic severity of disease in patients with hepatitis. In acute viral hepatitis, the liver and spleen are frequently enlarged. When parenchymal damage is severe, the parenchymal echogenicity is decreased and the portal venule walls are "brighter" than normal (Fig. 91-6). The increased sonographic contrast between the parenchyma and the periportal collagenous tissue is probably due to increased hepatic water, hydropic swelling of hepatocytes, and inflammatory cell infiltration. The increased hepatic water accentuates the acoustic mismatch between the hepatocytes and the portal tracts.[3,14,15] Also, the decreased attenuation of the liver allows greater sound penetration to "highlight" these vessels, with increased echogenicity of the walls of peripheral portal veins. This has been termed the *centrilobular pattern*. It has been observed in up to 60% of patients with acute hepatitis and is best appreciated in thin patients.[3,15] This pattern has also been reported in toxic shock syndrome, cytomegalovirus infection, idiopathic neonatal jaundice, leukemia, diabetic ketoacidosis, and lymphoma. Mural thickening of the gallbladder and hepatomegaly are other nonspecific findings in patients with hepatitis.

When severe, chronic hepatitis produces increased parenchymal echogenicity and loss of mural definition of the portal veins. This is attributed to "silhouetting out" of the portal vein walls by the echogenic fibrotic and inflammatory process surrounding the lobules that abut the portal triads. These findings are nonspecific and can be seen in patients with fatty infiltration and cirrhosis. One useful differentiating feature is the presence of adenopathy in the hepatoduodenal ligament in chronic active hepatitis, which has been attributed to direct spread of the hepatic inflammatory process to these nodes.

Acute viral hepatitis is also associated with thickening of the gallbladder wall. In early hepatitis, the gallbladder is hypertonic, whereas in patients more than 9 days after disease onset, the gallbladder is hypokinetic with a large volume and diminished response to a fatty meal.[3,15]

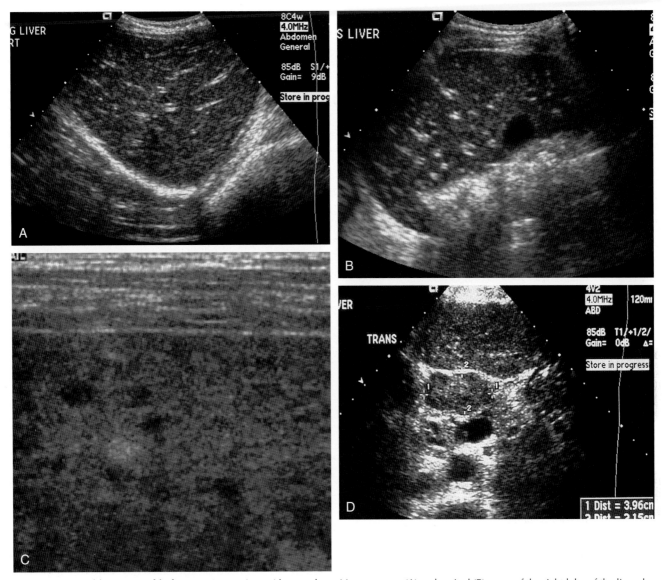

Figure 91-6. Hepatitis: sonographic features. In a patient with acute hepatitis, transverse (**A**) and sagittal (**B**) scans of the right lobe of the liver show diffusely decreased parenchymal echogenicity with accentuated brightness of the portal triads and periportal cuffing—the so-called "starry sky" appearance. **C.** In a patient with chronic active hepatitis, there is increased inhomogeneous parenchymal echogenicity due to the inflammatory process surrounding the lobules that abut the portal triads. **D.** In viral hepatitis the lymph nodes (*cursors*) draining the liver may become enlarged and serve as a useful marker as to the efficacy of antiviral therapy. (**C** courtesy of Peter Cooperberg, MD, Vancouver, British Columbia, Canada.)

The major role of ultrasound in hepatitis is to exclude biliary obstruction as the cause of liver disease.

Computed Tomography

The primary role of CT in patients with hepatitis is to exclude focal masses or a hepatocellular carcinoma. CT findings in hepatitis are usually nonspecific. Hepatomegaly, gallbladder wall thickening, and hepatic periportal lucency (Fig. 91-7) are the major CT findings in patients with acute viral hepatitis. This lucency is due to fluid and lymphedema surrounding the portal veins and has also been reported in patients with AIDS, trauma, neoplasm, liver transplants, liver transplant rejection, and congestive heart failure. Early in the disease, multiple regenerating nodules may be seen in an atrophied liver. CT has shown that hepatic necrosis is repaired by hypertrophy of regenerating nodules rather than an increase in the

number of nodules. These nodules give rise to the macronodular pattern of postnecrotic cirrhosis. Rarely, the nodules may be hypodense and simulate metastases on CT.

In patients with chronic active hepatitis, lymphadenopathy is commonly found in the porta hepatis, gastrohepatic ligament, and retroperitoneum, and may be the only CT abnormality in a patient with severe hepatic dysfunction. CT can also follow the course of immunosuppression by observing the reduction of lymph node size with therapy

Magnetic Resonance Imaging

On MR imaging, acute hepatitis may show nonspecific findings such as heterogeneous signal intensity, most apparent on T2-weighted sequences and a heterogeneous pattern of enhancement on arterial–dominant phase spoiled gradient-echo (SGE) images. This abnormal enhancement becomes more marked

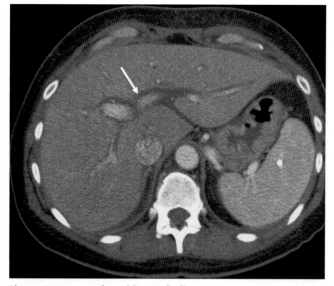

Figure 91-7. Acute hepatitis: CT findings. CT scan shows periportal edema (*arrow*) highlighting the intrahepatic blood vessels.

and can persist into the venous and delayed phases as the severity of disease increases. High signal intensity periportal edema can be on T2-weighted images. In both acute and chronic hepatitis, adenopathy in the lesser omentum may be the only abnormality identified.[25-29]

In chronic hepatitis, MR imaging can provide information on the degree of histologic activity of disease and help monitor the response to therapy. Homogeneous or heterogeneous increase in signal intensity has been described on T2-weighted images and reflects the presence of inflammation or necrosis of the liver parenchyma. Early patchy enhancement patterns in patients with chronic hepatits have been shown to be associated with significant parenchymal inflammatory reaction. Absence of this early patchy enhancement correlates with low inflammatory reaction.[26]

In patients with chronic fibrosis associated with cirrhosis, there is progressive enhancement on delayed images due to leakage of gadolinium contrast from the intravascular into the interstitial space.[27]

Alcoholic Hepatitis

Clinical Findings

Alcoholic liver disease manifests as three distinct but overlapping entities: fatty liver, alcoholic hepatitis, and cirrhosis. The first is reversible with abstinence; the latter two are progressive and shorten life. Alcoholic hepatitis is part of the spectrum of alcoholic liver disease in which a major drinking binge produces acute liver cell necrosis. These changes are usually superimposed on steatosis or already developing cirrhosis. In most cases, cessation of alcohol consumption and adequate nutrition may ameliorate the patient clinically and histologically. Repeated bouts of acute alcoholic hepatitis are associated with a 10% to 20% risk of death and a 35% risk of developing cirrhosis. Patients usually have fever and neutrophil leukocytosis and may present with malaise, anorexia, weight loss, upper abdominal pain, tender hepatomegaly, and jaundice.[30-34]

Pathologic Findings

The specific mechanism of ethanol-induced hepatotoxicity is uncertain despite an extensive literature on both biochemical and immunologic models of hepatocyte damage. Theories range from peroxidation of cell membranes to modification of membrane permeability to sensitized T cells directed against hepatocytes. The histologic hallmark of alcoholic hepatitis consists of Mallory bodies, which are eosinophilic cytoplasmic inclusions that take the form of "candle droppings" in ballooned, degenerating hepatocytes. In most cases, alcoholic hepatitis is accompanied by pericellular and perivenular fibrosis, again suggesting that this is a precursor of cirrhosis.[30-34]

Radiologic Findings

In patients with alcoholic hepatitis, imaging is done to exclude obstructive biliary disease and neoplasm and to evaluate parenchymal damage noninvasively.

Ultrasound

In acute alcoholic hepatitis, the liver is quite echogenic because of fatty infiltration. The liver may be enlarged early in the disease process, but it becomes atrophic as cirrhosis ensues. Because cirrhosis and fatty infiltration appear similar sonographically, CT is more useful in their differentiation.[3,15] Details of these sonographic findings are presented earlier in the chapter.

Computed Tomography

CT may show fatty infiltration in a normal-sized, enlarged, or atrophic liver, depending on the extent of prior liver injury.[35] For further details, see the sections on Fatty Infiltration and Cirrhosis.

Magnetic Resonance Imaging

Similar to CT, MR imaging depicts hepatic size and morphology and can be useful in depicting hepatic fibrosis and steatosis. Phosphorus-31 MR spectroscopy has shown that livers of patients with alcoholic hepatitis and cirrhosis can be differentiated from normal liver and from each other on the basis of intracellular pH and absolute molar concentration of adenosine triphosphate. In alcoholic hepatitis, the cells are more alkaline than normal, and in cirrhosis, the hepatic parenchyma is more acidic than normal.[25]

TOXIN- AND DRUG-INDUCED LIVER DISEASE

Although drug-induced liver disease represents a small proportion of all adverse drug effects, it accounts for 2% to 5% of hospital admissions for jaundice in the United States and up to 43% of admissions for "acute hepatitis." Indeed, drugs such as halothane, acetaminophen, alpha-methyldopa, and phenytoin account for 20% to 50% of cases of fulminant hepatic failure.[34]

Anesthetics (halothane, enflurane), anticonvulsants (phenytoin), anti-inflammatory agents (gold, clometacin, sulindac), analgesics (acetaminophen), hormonal derivatives (danazol), antidepressant or antianxiety drugs (amitriptyline, amineptine), antimicrobials (isoniazid, amoxicillin, sulfamethoxazole-trimethoprim), antiulcer drugs (cimetidine, ranitidine), hypolipidemic agents (nicotinic acid, gemfibrozil), drugs for inflammatory bowel disease (sulfasalazine), and cardiovascular drugs (quinidine, amiodarone) have all been associated with parenchymal liver disease.[34]

Certain drugs and other chemical agents are capable of producing virtually all types of acute and chronic liver disease. The spectrum of hepatotoxicity varies from acute, dose-related, predictable, hepatocellular necrosis to chronic inflammatory disorders ranging from mild chronic persistent hepatitis to severe chronic active hepatitis. In addition, vascular disorders such as peliosis hepatis and the Budd-Chiari syndrome and neoplastic lesions such as angiosarcomas and benign hepatic adenomas are associated with certain naturally occurring toxins such as "bush teas" and aflatoxins in peanuts; oral contraceptives and anabolic steroids; and industrial toxins such as vinyl chloride (Thorotrast); and organic arsenic found in pesticides.[34]

Chemotherapy Toxicity

The liver plays a key role in the metabolism of most medications and may be injured by many chemical agents. Hepatic deterioration resulting from chemical toxicity is particularly problematic in cancer patients with liver metastases. It is often difficult to differentiate chemotherapy-induced parenchymal injury from tumor progression, tumor necrosis, portal and hepatic venous thrombosis, hepatic ischemia and infarction, transfusion reactions, viral hepatitis, and segmental biliary obstruction by tumor. Radiology plays a key role in elucidating the cause of hepatic dysfunction in these patients.

Clinical or subclinical hepatotoxicity is quite common during systemic chemotherapy. Indeed, in a large series of patients with breast cancer, 77% of those receiving systemic adjuvant chemotherapy and 82% of those being treated for metastatic breast cancer who had normal pretreatment liver function tests developed abnormal hepatic laboratory values during and after therapy.[32-34] This hepatocellular injury is not surprising in view of the action of these agents in preventing or retarding cell division and diminishing the cellular immune response. Methotrexate is often associated with fatty change, fibrosis of the portal triads, and eventually cirrhosis. Corticosteroids and L-asparaginase may produce fatty metamorphosis. Dacarbazine and 6-thioguanine can cause thrombosis of intrahepatic portal veins, producing a Budd-Chiari type of appearance. Azathioprine and 6-mercaptopurine therapy may result in intrahepatic cholestasis and variable degrees of parenchymal cell necrosis. Intra-arterial infusion of floxuridine may cause chemical hepatitis and biliary strictures simulating sclerosing cholangitis. Mithramycin is perhaps the most hepatotoxic drug used in chemotherapy and is associated with acute parenchymal necrosis. Avastin has been associated with hepatic veno-occlusive disease.[32]

On cross-sectional images, the findings are fairly nonspecific and identical to those seen in other liver injuries: hepatomegaly, cirrhosis, and fatty infiltration. Cross-sectional imaging, however, is vital in showing that diffuse parenchymal disease rather than biliary obstruction or worsening liver metastases is the cause of the patient's hepatic dysfunction. In vitro and laboratory MR experiments have shown that carbon tetrachloride produces water and sodium retention, which can be detected by sodium Na-23 and proton imaging. The damage is most prominent in the periportal regions, which show a high proton

signal intensity on T2-weighted images and high sodium signal intensity on spectroscopy.[25]

Amiodarone Toxicity

Hepatotoxicity caused by amiodarone is well documented and is usually manifested by mild asymptomatic elevation of serum transaminase levels. When more severe injury occurs, it can simulate alcoholic liver disease with fatty metamorphosis of the liver, Mallory bodies, and cirrhosis. The length of treatment with amiodarone before recognition of hepatic damage can range from several weeks to several years.[34]

The sonographic findings in this disorder are nonspecific and related to fatty infiltration or cirrhosis. The CT appearance (Fig. 91-8), however, is distinctive. When this drug or its metabolites, which contain iodine, accumulate in sufficient quantities in the liver, increased parenchymal attenuation simulating hemochromatosis can be identified.

RADIATION-INDUCED LIVER DISEASE

Clinical Findings

Although the liver was once believed to be relatively radio-resistant, hepatic morphologic and functional alterations have been observed after radiation therapy since the 1960s.

Hepatic radiation is most often unintentional and occurs when the liver is unavoidably included in the treatment portal for breast, esophageal, gastric, and pancreatic carcinoma or lymphoma. Patients who receive a single 1200-rad dose of external beam radiation or a 4000- to 5500-rad fractionated dose over 6 weeks can develop radiation hepatitis. Nearly 75% of patients receiving whole liver irradiation have abnormal liver function tests.[1,2]

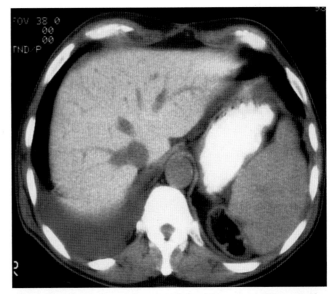

Figure 91-8. Amiodarone hepatotoxicity. Noncontrast CT scan of a cardiac patient who had been taking amiodarone demonstrates a liver with an abnormally high attenuation when compared to the spleen. Note how the hepatic blood vessels are highlighted by the dense parenchyma. The appearance is indistinguishable from that of hepatic iron overload. There is a right-sided pleural effusion.

If the area of irradiated hepatic tissue is small, the classic signs and symptoms of hepatic radiation injury, such as hepatomegaly and ascites, are not present. If the liver receives high doses of radiation during childhood, atrophy may result. If other structures such as the kidney or vertebral bodies are included in the port, they are underdeveloped as well.

Pathologic Findings

Radiation hepatitis is characterized by massive panlobar congestion, hyperemia, hemorrhage, and mild proliferative change in the sublobular central veins. Stasis secondary to injury of these veins is responsible for most of the acute findings. Complete clinical recovery is typically seen within 60 days, but there may be permanent hepatocyte loss, fat deposition, fibrosis, and obliteration of the central veins.[1,2]

Radiologic Findings

On ultrasound studies, the regions of radiation injury are hypoechoic relative to the remainder of the liver. This is probably a result of localized hepatic congestion or edema. These changes are more easily detected sonographically in patients who have fatty livers resulting from chemotherapy or other causes.[12,15]

CT scans performed within several months of the radiation therapy show a sharply defined band of low attenuation corresponding to the treatment port (Fig. 91-9). This is due to edema or fatty infiltration of the involved area. If hepatic congestion is severe, patchy congestion simulating tumor nodules may be seen. In patients with fatty infiltration of the liver, the irradiated area may appear as a region of increased attentuation. This may be due to loss of fat in the irradiated hepatocytes or regional edema, with the water content demonstrating higher attenuation than the fatty liver. Over a period of weeks, the initially sharp borders of the irradiated zone become more irregular and indistinct as peripheral areas of parenchyma regenerate. Eventually, the irradiated area may become atrophic.

Radiation hepatitis on MR imaging manifests as geographic areas of low signal intensity on T1-weighted images and high signal intensity on T2-weighted images secondary to increased water content as determined by proton spectroscopic imaging.[25]

HEMOSIDEROSIS AND HEMOCHROMATOSIS

The body normally contains 2 to 6 g of iron; 80% is functional iron in the form of hemoglobin, myoglobin, and iron-containing enzymes, and the other 20% is in the storage form as either hemosiderin or ferritin. With normal iron stores, only trace amounts of hemosiderin are found in the body, primarily in the reticuloendothelial cells of the bone marrow, liver, and spleen. When present in excess amounts, the iron is deposited in the liver, spleen, lymph nodes, pancreas, kidneys, heart, endocrine glands, and gastrointestinal tract. Increased iron deposition without parenchymal organ damage is called *hemosiderosis* and is usually seen with body iron stores between 10 and 20 g.[36-40]

Hemochromatosis is an iron-overload disorder in which there is structural and functional impairment of the involved organs. In these cases, body iron accumulation may reach 50 to 60 g. Primary hemochromatosis is an inherited disorder characterized by abnormally increased iron absorption by the mucosa of the duodenum and jejunum that leads to high plasma concentrations of iron, high transferrin saturation, and increased deposition of hemosiderin in the cytoplasm of the parenchymal cells of the liver and other organs. By contrast, when iron is liberated from red blood cells as a result of multiple transfusions or hemolytic anemias, it is deposited primarily in the mononuclear phagocyte system, so organ function is generally preserved.[36-40]

Secondary hemochromatosis develops in three groups of patients: those with high iron intake (e.g., prolonged consumption of medicinal iron, iron-laden wine, Kaffir beer, multiple blood transfusions); anemic patients with ineffective erythropoiesis and multiple blood transfusions (e.g., thalassemia major, sideroblastic anemia); and patients with liver disease in alcoholic cirrhosis and after portacaval shunts.[36-40]

Clinical Findings

The classic triad of hemochromatosis consists of micronodular pigment cirrhosis, diabetes mellitus, and hyperpigmentation. Patients with primary hemochromatosis usually present in the fourth or fifth decades of life because it takes many years to accumulate sufficient iron (20-40 g) to cause symptoms. There is a 10:1 male predominance in fully developed hemochromatosis. Women are protected from this disorder by iron loss that occurs during normal menstruation, pregnancy, and lactation.[36-40]

The liver is the first organ to be damaged in hemochromatosis, and hepatomegaly is present in 95% of symptomatic cases. Splenomegaly is present in nearly 50% of cases. Arthropathy of the small joints of the hands develops in 25% to 50% of cases and may antedate other symptoms. Cardiac involvement is the presenting complaint in about 15% of cases and

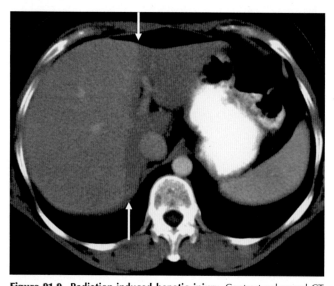

Figure 91-9. Radiation-induced hepatic injury. Contrast-enhanced CT scan shows a sharply defined (*arrows*) region of hepatic hypoattenuation near the dome of the liver. This patient had received external beam radiation therapy for lung carcinoma.

is most commonly seen as congestive heart failure in young adults. Loss of libido, loss of body hair, and testicular atrophy resulting from failure of gonadotropin production are common. Increased melanin deposition in the basal layers of the epidermis leads to hyperpigmentation, resulting in so-called bronze diabetes, in these patients.[36-40]

The life expectancy of untreated patients with idiopathic hemochromatosis after the disease becomes clinically manifest is 4.4 years. The most common causes of death in these patients are cardiac failure (30%), hepatic coma (15%), hematemesis (14%), hepatocellular carcinoma (14%), and pneumonia (12%). Removal of iron by repeated phlebotomy and use of iron chelators increases the 5-year survival from 33% to 89%. The liver and spleen decrease in size, liver function tests return to normal, pigmentation decreases, glucose tolerance normalizes, and cardiac function improves with successful therapy. Cirrhosis, however, is irreversible, and about one third of patients develop hepatocellular carcinoma as a late sequela despite adequate therapy. The risk of development of a hepatoma is increased over 200-fold in patients with hereditary hemochromatosis. It is therefore important to diagnose this disorder early, in the precirrhotic stage.[36-40]

Early diagnosis and therapy of hemochromatosis can prevent or minimize the damaging effects of the iron overload. Early diagnosis, however, is often difficult because there may be considerable hepatic iron before the patient becomes symptomatic. CT and MR imaging may fortuitously detect iron overload, and these modalities are useful in confirming the diagnosis in patients with equivocal laboratory data. Classically, the serum iron level is greater than 250 mg/dL (normal 50 to 150 mg/dL), serum ferritin value is above 500 ng/dL (normal below 150 ng/dL), and transferrin saturation approaches 100% (normal 25%-30%) in patients with hemochromatosis. Transferrin saturation is the earliest and most sensitive indicator of increased iron stores. Virtually all patients older than 20 years have levels greater than 50%.[36-40]

Serum ferritin levels, however, are nonspecific and influenced by the presence of inflammatory states, neoplastic disorders, and hepatocellular disease. Imaging or biopsy helps clarify the results of these sensitive, albeit somewhat nonspecific, tests.[36-40]

Pathologic Findings

The principal features of classic primary hemochromatosis are excessive ferritin and hemosiderin in the liver, pancreas, myocardium, joints, endocrine glands, and skin, in decreasing order of severity (Figs. 91-10 and 91-11). Because the liver contains up to one third of the total body store of iron, it is the organ most profoundly damaged in hemochromatosis. Early, the liver is slightly larger than normal, dense, and chocolate brown because of ferritin and the golden yellow granules of hemosiderin. Progressive deposition leads to slowly evolving liver damage and development of fibrous septa similar to those in alcoholic cirrhosis, ultimately producing micronodular cirrhosis. The liver size is only slightly diminished, and fat is usually absent. Liver biopsy also provides an objective measurement of hepatic iron concentration (normal 7 to 100 pg/ 100 mg). The pancreas is intensely pigmented and has diffuse interstitial fibrosis leading to exocrine but to a greater extent endocrine deficiency. Hemosiderin is found in both acinar and islet cells, and there is some correlation between the de-

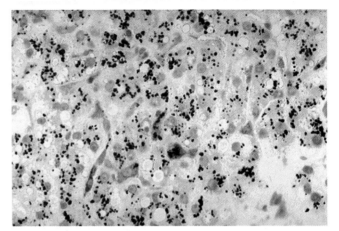

Figure 91-10. Iron overload: histologic findings. Prussian blue stain showing extensive iron deposition.

gree of iron deposition in the pancreatic islets and the severity of the diabetes.[36-40]

Radiologic Findings

Computed Tomography

CT has had a significant impact on the noninvasive diagnosis of excess hepatic iron deposition. On CT scans, the liver demonstrates homogeneously increased density with an attenuation of 75 to 135 HU (Fig. 91-12). The normal density of the liver is between 45 and 65 HU on noncontrast scans obtained at 120 kVp. In patients with hemochromatosis, the liver has diffusely increased attenuation highlighting the lower attenuation hepatic and portal veins on unenhanced CT. As discussed elsewhere in this chapter, a similar appearance can be seen in patients who are being treated with amiodarone and also in patients with glycogen storage disease. High parenchymal attenuation can also be seen in patients who have calcification resulting from shock liver, patients who have been exposed to Thorotrast and intravasated barium, rheumatoid arthritis patients receiving gold therapy, and rarely, patients with Wilson's disease and those with chronic arsenic poisoning, although

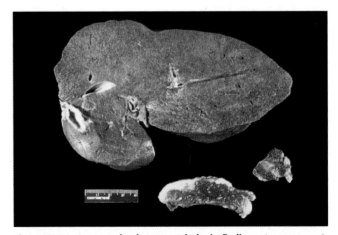

Figure 91-11. Iron overload: gross pathologic findings. Autopsy specimens show iron deposition in the liver, pancreas, and a lymph node in a patient who died with hemochromatosis. Note the dark brown hue of these organs.

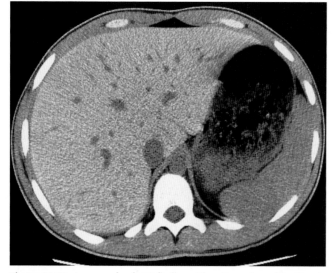

Figure 91-12. Iron overload: CT findings. The attenuation of the liver is diffusely increased secondary to intraparenchymal iron deposition.

these affected livers are usually not as homogeneous appearing as with hemochromatosis, amiodarone, or glycogen storage disease.[41]

When neoplasms in the liver are suspected in these patients, it is important to obtain noncontrast images. With the high attenuation of the background liver parenchyma, noncontrast images may best show the differences in attenuation between hypoattenuating tumors and high-attenuation liver. Contrast administration may actually decrease the inherent contrast differences between liver and tumor by increasing the attenuation of tumors.

Magnetic Resonance Imaging

MR imaging is the most sensitive and specific imaging test for the demonstration of hepatic iron overload and for follow up of patients undergoing treatment (Figs. 91-13 and 91-14). MR imaging shows dramatic reduction in the signal intensity of the liver (90%) and pancreas (20%). This signal loss is due to the large paramagnetic susceptibility of the ferritin and hemosiderin-iron-oxyhydroxide crystals, which contain ferric ions (Fe^{3+}), which profoundly shorten the T1 and T2 relaxation time of adjacent protons. The paramagnetic effect is most conspicuous on T2- and T2*-weighted images. At concentrations found in the liver, the T2-shortening effect predominates, accounting for the diminished hepatic signal intensity. Occasionally, focal iron deposition can be demonstrated by MR imaging. Iron overload can sometimes be recognized in the spleen by diminished signal intensity, as seen in the liver.[25-27,42]

MR imaging can help distinguish the parenchymal overload that occurs in hemochromatosis from reticuloendothelial cell iron overload, which occurs after blood transfusions or rhabdomyolysis (see Figs. 91-13 and 91-14). In parenchymal overload, the liver and pancreas have low signal intensity. In reticuloendothelial cell overload, the liver and spleen have low signal intensity but the pancreas, which does not contain reticuloendothelial cells, does not. This distinction is important because significant tissue damage occurs in parenchymal iron overload but reticuloendothelial cell iron overload resulting from transfusions and rhabdomyolysis is of little clinical

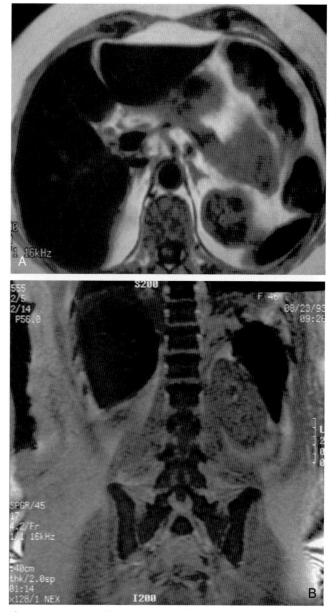

Figure 91-13. Hemosiderosis: MR findings. A. Axial T1-weighted image shows marked decrease signal intensity of the liver and spleen due to iron deposition into the Kupffer cells of the liver and the reticuloendothelial cells of the spleen. The absence of iron deposition in the pancreas is a differentiating feature from hemochromatosis. **B.** Coronal image in a different patient shows that the liver, spleen, and bone marrow of the spine have markedly decreased signal intensity due to the deposition of iron in the reticuloendothelial cells of these organs.

consequence. Another advantage of MR imaging in the diagnosis of hepatic hemochromatosis is that other disorders do not simulate the appearance of iron overload at MR imaging as occurs with CT.[25-27,42]

MR imaging can also be used to monitor the treatment of patients with hepatic iron overload. Using four gradient echo sequences and one spin-echo sequence, signal intensity of the liver is compared to paraspinous muscle. For estimated concentration of more than 85 μmol/g, the positive predictive value for hemochromatosis is 100%; for less than 40 μmol/g, the negative predictive value for hemochromatosis is 100%.[42] Complete signal loss at concentrations above 300 μmol/g precludes accurate measurements with heavy iron overload.

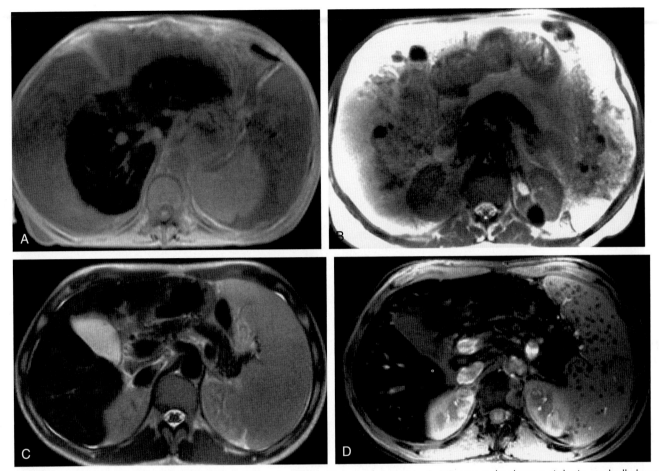

Figure 91-14. Hemochromatosis: MR findings. Two different patients with hemochromatosis. **A.** MR scan at the shows a cirrhotic, markedly hypointense liver surrounded by ascites. The spleen is spared because it is comprised primarily by reticuloendothelial cells, which do not accumulated iron in hemochromatosis, an important differentiating feature from hemosiderosis. **B.** Scan obtained caudal to **A** shows low signal intensity of the pancreas. The acinar cells do accumulate iron. In a different patient, T1-weighted (**C**) gradient-echo (**D**) images of the upper abdomen show marked hypointensity of the liver and spleen due to the deposition of iron in the hepatocytes of the liver and the acinar cells of the pancreas. Notice the low signal intensity Gamna-Gandy bodies in the spleen, secondary to hemosiderin deposition, a finding seen in portal hypertension with microhemorrhages into the splenic parenchyma.

Ultrasound

The sonographic appearance in hemochromatosis is non-specific and related to fibrosis and cirrhosis. Parenchymal iron deposits are too small to be reflective, so ultrasound has no role in the diagnosis of hepatic iron overload

Plain Radiographs

Plain abdominal radiographs in patients with hemochromatosis rarely show diffuse, homogeneously increased density of the liver. Skeletal abnormalities include chondrocalcinosis and degenerative arthritis in the second and third metacarpal heads. Chondrocalcinosis occurs in two thirds of patients and is associated with cartilage narrowing.

GLYCOGEN STORAGE DISEASE

Clinical and Pathologic Findings

The liver has a major role in the synthesis and storage of glycogen as well as its ultimate catabolism into glucose. Among inherited disorders of glycogen metabolism, von Gierke's disease (type I glycogen storage disease) is the most common

type to affect the liver. It is due to a deficiency of glucose-6-phosphatase in the liver and kidneys, which results in excessive glycogen deposition in the hepatocytes and proximal renal tubules. Pathologically, intracytoplasmic accumulations of glycogen and small amounts of lipid are found. Patients demonstrate failure to thrive, hypoglycemia, hyperlipidemia, hyperuricemia, stunted growth, hepatomegaly, and nephromegaly. Hepatic adenomas and hepatocellular carcinomas are complications of this disorder and are thought to result from chronic hormonal stimulation resulting from the chronic hypoglycemia with decreased insulin and increased glucagon levels. Imaging of these patients is necessary to exclude the development of these neoplasms.[43,44]

Radiologic Findings

Ultrasound

Sonographically, the liver is enlarged and demonstrates increased echogenicity and sound attenuation, presumably resulting from fatty infiltration and possibly from the excess glycogen deposition as well. Eight percent of all patients with glycogen storage disease and up to 40% with type I disease have hepatic adenomas. These lesions are well circumscribed and may be hypoechoic, isoechoic, or hyperechoic in relation to the remainder of the liver. Increased sound transmission with refractile shadowing at the tumor margins is commonly seen. These findings are related to the paucity of fat and glycogen in the adenomas compared with the rest of the involved liver, and these sonographic features are not observed in adenomas of patients without glycogen storage disease. Lesions with a rapidly changing sonographic appearance should be carefully monitored because this may reflect malignant degeneration or hemorrhagic necrosis.[12,14]

Computed Tomography and MR Imaging

The CT density of the liver in these patients is altered by processes that have conflicting effects: glycogen storage increases hepatic density (Fig. 91-15A and B) and fatty infiltration lowers hepatic attenuation. Which appearance is taken on by the liver depends, therefore, on the predominant underlying pathologic process. The liver, spleen, and kidneys are typically enlarged and the renal cortex may appear dense because of glycogen deposition. On noncontrast CT, hepatic adenomas (often associated with glycogen storage disease) are hypodense compared with normal liver and spuriously hyperdense if there is concomitant fatty infiltration. The adenomas should remain stable in size or show slow growth on follow-up

examination. Malignant degeneration should be suspected if there is rapid growth or density change. On MR imaging, the adenomas may show fat signal intensity (Fig. 91-15C and D).

AMYLOIDOSIS

Clinical and Pathologic Findings

Hepatic infiltration and enlargement are frequently found in patients with systemic amyloidosis, but significant liver disease is rare. Amyloids, which are proteolysis-resistant fibrils derived from monoclonal immunoglobulin light chains, are deposited in the space of Disse and then progressively encroach on adjacent hepatic parenchymal cells and sinusoids. Total replacement of large areas of liver parenchyma may occur, giving the liver a pale, waxy gray, firm appearance. Hepatic function is usually preserved despite massive amyloid infiltration. When amyloidosis is severe, the patient may present with right upper quadrant pain caused by stretching of Glisson's capsule, pruritus, ascites, malaise, weight loss, intrahepatic cholestasis, and portal hypertension.[43-46]

Radiologic Findings

CT findings in amyloidosis are nonspecific and include hepatomegaly and low-attenuation regions where amyloid deposits

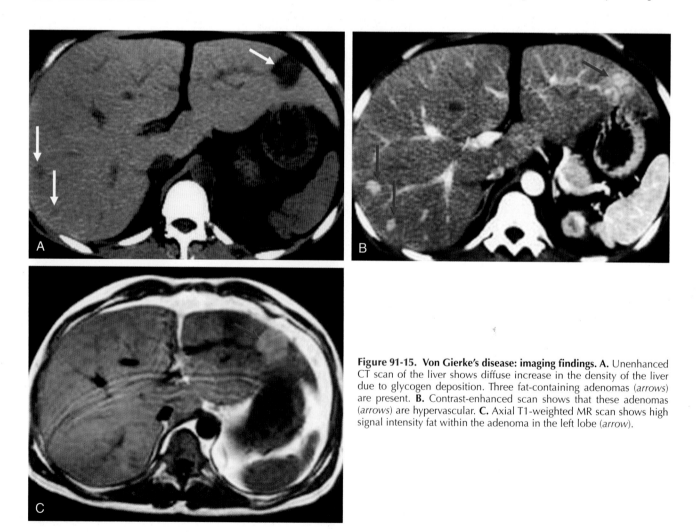

Figure 91-15. Von Gierke's disease: imaging findings. A. Unenhanced CT scan of the liver shows diffuse increase in the density of the liver due to glycogen deposition. Three fat-containing adenomas (*arrows*) are present. **B.** Contrast-enhanced scan shows that these adenomas (*arrows*) are hypervascular. **C.** Axial T1-weighted MR scan shows high signal intensity fat within the adenoma in the left lobe (*arrow*).

are found. Delayed contrast enhancement may be seen in the involved areas because of vascular and sinusoidal infiltration. Concomitant abnormalities seen in the spleen are helpful in differentiating amyloid deposition from neoplasms and fatty infiltration. Sonographically, the liver is enlarged and has inhomogeneous echoes.[47,48]

On MR imaging, the T2 values of the spleen and adrenal glands are significantly decreased, and the T2 value of the pancreas is significantly increased in patients with primary amyloidosis compared with normal individuals. T2 values are not significantly changed in the liver, subcutaneous fat, bone marrow, or kidney, so MR imaging has little role in the assessment of hepatic involvement in amyloidosis.[47,48]

WILSON'S DISEASE

Clinical and Pathologic Findings

Wilson's disease, or hepatolenticular degeneration, is a rare, autosomal recessive inherited disorder of copper metabolism. It is a result of impaired biliary excretion of copper, excessive absorption of copper from the gastrointestinal tract, abnormal urinary excretion of copper, and deficient production of ceruloplasmin, the serum protein to which 95% of body copper is tightly bound. Initially, the copper accumulates in the liver until all the hepatic binding sites are utilized. Then deposition to toxic levels occurs in the basal ganglia, renal tubules, cornea, bones, joints, and parathyroid glands.[49-51]

Clinically, most patients present in childhood or early adolescence with manifestations of liver disease (e.g., jaundice, hepatomegaly) before the onset of neurologic changes. Nearly one half of untreated patients remain asymptomatic to age 16 years. In adults, the hepatic injury usually appears insidiously after the cirrhosis evolves, clinically simulating chronic active hepatitis. If the hepatic changes remain subclinical, the patient may present in the late teens or early 20s with a Parkinson-like movement disorder and psychiatric disturbances. Kayser-Fleischer rings of green to brown copper deposits occur on the cornea.[49-51]

The serum ceruloplasmin value is low (<20 mg/100 mL) in 95% of cases, and urinary excretion of copper is elevated (>100 pg/day). Electron microscopy of liver biopsy specimens shows fat droplets, glycogen deposits, and specific mitochondrial abnormalities. Hepatic copper content is high (>200 pg/g dry weight; normal is >55 pg/g), but this can be seen in biliary cirrhosis and other liver disease.[52,53]

Imaging is needed in the 5% of patients with a normal ceruloplasmin level and high copper content. Early recognition is crucial because penicillamine and zinc are effective in chelating the copper and in preventing its toxic deposition in the liver and brain. Treatment of asymptomatic patients prevents the disease from manifesting itself, and symptomatic patients improve, sometimes dramatically.[53]

Radiologic Findings

Cross-sectional imaging has been disappointing in terms of making a specific diagnosis of Wilson's disease.[54-57] This may be related to the fact that the spectrum of hepatic injury in this disorder is nonspecific: fatty infiltration, acute hepatitis, chronic active hepatitis, cirrhosis, or massive liver necrosis.

Ultrasound and CT show changes of fatty infiltration that are indistinguishable from those of cirrhosis of other causes. Although copper has a high atomic number and can cause elevation of liver density on CT, that is an unusual finding perhaps because coexistent fatty infiltration diminishes hepatic parenchymal attenuation. There has been only one report of CT demonstration of the asymptomatic carrier state of Wilson's disease based on elevated hepatic parenchymal attenuation values.[54-57]

Although copper ions shorten the T1 relaxation time, in vitro hepatic MR imaging of patients with Wilson's disease has failed to demonstrate this effect. Hypointense nodules may be seen on T2 weighted images.[56] Phosphorus-31 MR spectroscopy offers potential in grading and disease monitoring in patients with Wilson's disease (Fig. 91-16). This technique has been shown to provide information about the pathophysiology of liver injury and can contribute to the assessment of hepatic functional state in chronic liver disease

Bone changes, including osteomalacia, chondrocalcinosis, premature degenerative joint disease with fragmentation, cystic changes and sclerosis of subchondral bone, and anterior compression of the dorsal vertebral bodies, occur in over 85% of patients.[49]

GAUCHER'S DISEASE

Gaucher's disease is a rare lysosomal storage disease caused by deficiency of glucosylceramidase that results in accumulation of the enzyme's substrate, glucosylceramide, in the reticuloendothelial cells of the body. This disease is inherited as an autosomal recessive with an incidence of 1 in 2500 births. Gaucher's disease is most common in Ashkenazi Jews. The degree of liver involvement correlates with the severity of extrahepatic disease. When there is extensive replacement of the liver by Gaucher's cells (lipid-laden macrophages), cirrhosis and portal hypertension develop.[58,59]

Plain radiographs show hepatosplenomegaly and occasionally multiple well-circumscribed calcifications. Bone changes are common and include modeling deformities of the lower femoral shafts ("Erlenmeyer flask" appearance), pathologic fractures, and vertebral body collapse. Hepatic imaging findings are nonspecific and characterized by fatty and cirrhotic changes of the hepatic parenchyma.

SARCOIDOSIS

Sarcoidosis is a systemic granulomatous disorder that affects the liver commonly, with reported series showing 24% to 79% of patients with liver involvement.[60-65] Clinically apparent liver disease is infrequent in patients with hepatic sarcoidosis, although rarely it can lead to chronic inflammation, chronic hepatitis, and cirrhosis. In such cases, patients may present with cholestatic liver disease with jaundice. Biopsy of the liver will reveal diffuse, small, noncaseating granulomas, usually less than 2 mm in size. When noncaseating granulomas are present within the liver, the differential diagnosis includes sarcoidosis and primary biliary cirrhosis. The mitochondrial antibody test can differentiate among these, as the test is negative in sarcoid and usually positive in primary biliary cirrhosis.[60-65]

The most prevalent CT finding (Fig. 91-17) of sarcoidosis in the liver is hepatomegaly, and occasionally, hypoattenuating

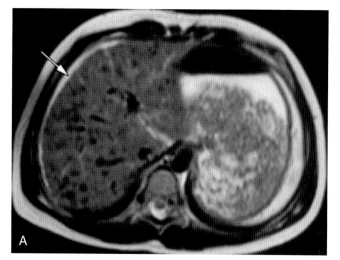

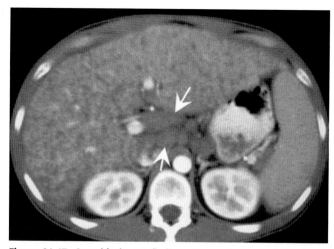

Figure 91-17. Sarcoidosis: CT findings. Contrast-enhanced CT shows hepatomegaly with innumerable small hypodense nodules. Portal adenopathy is also present (*arrows*). (From Warshauer DM, Lee JKT: Imaging manifestations of abdominal sarcoidosis. AJR 182:15-28, 2004. Reprinted with permission from the American Journal of Roentgenology.)

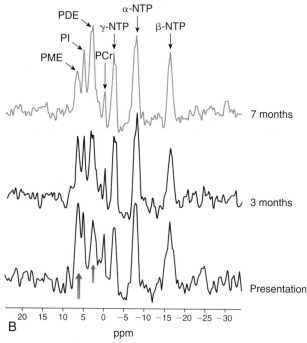

Figure 91-16. Wilson's disease: imaging findings. A. 9-year-old girl with Wilson's disease. T2-weighted axial MR image (TR/TE, 1800/90) of liver shows numerous tiny hypointense nodules in liver at presentation before medical treatment. Note hyperintense ascitic fluid (*arrow*) around edge of liver. **B.** Graph shows representative serial phosphorus-31 MR liver spectra before and after 3 and 7 months of medical treatment. Elevation in phosphomonoester (PME) resonance (*long arrow*) is concurrent with reduction in phosphodiester (PDE) resonance (*short arrow*) at presentation, followed by gradual reversal change in subsequent 3- and 7-month spectra. NTP, nucleotide triphosphate; Pi, inorganic phosphate; PCr, phosphocreatine. (From Chu WCW, Leung TF, Chan KF, et al: Wilson's disease with chronic active hepatitis: Monitoring by in vivo 31-phosphorus MR spectroscopy before and after medical treatment. AJR 183:1339-1342, 2004. Reprinted with permission from the American Journal of Roentgenology.)

nodules varying in size up to 2 cm will be seen on both unenhanced and contrast-enhanced images. Because most granulomas at pathology are small, imaging studies depict nodular changes in only approximately one third of affected patients. At ultrasound, larger granulomas can be seen as hypoechoic nodules, and at MR imaging, when visualized the nodules appear hypointense on both T1-weighted and T2-weighted

sequences (Fig. 91-18) when compared with adjacent liver parenchyma. Associated upper abdominal lymphadenopathy, as elsewhere in the body, is often present. The presence of hepatic nodules at imaging is not correlated with advanced pulmonary disease.[60-65]

BILIARY HAMARTOMAS

Biliary hamartomas are benign liver malformations characterized by bile duct duplication, surrounded by dense, hyalinized fibrous stroma. Each hamartoma, usually less than 5 mm in diameter, contains a single lumen, although no communication exists with the biliary system. These malformations are incidental findings at pathology (in approximately 2.6% of the population) or imaging, and produce no clinical symptoms.[66-71]

The larger lesions may be detected at imaging as multiple focal lesions, often simulating a multifocal or diffuse process. Sonographically, these lesions appear small, hypoechoic, heterogeneous, and well circumscribed. CT may show numerous small, hypoattenuating lesions on unenhanced scans that either persist as hypoattenuating lesions on postcontrast imaging. MR imaging (Fig. 91-19) reveals small nodules as hypointense on T1-weighted and hyperintense on T2-weighted images compared with normal parenchyma that do not show contrast enhancement with gadopentetate dimeglumine.[66-71]

PRIMARY BILIARY CIRRHOSIS

Primary biliary cirrhosis (PBC) is a chronic, usually progressive liver disease characterized by inflammation and destruction of interlobular and septal bile ducts, leading to chronic cholestasis, cirrhosis, and ultimately, hepatic failure (Fig. 91-20). This is a relentless process in which the initial destructive cholangitis is followed by proliferation of atypical bile ductules, scarring, and septum formation. The etiology of this disorder is unknown, and autoimmune, genetic, and endocrine abnormalities have been postulated.[72-77]

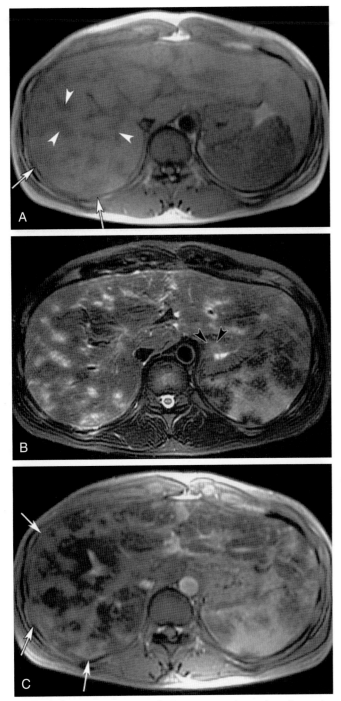

Figure 91-18. Sarcoidosis: MR findings. A. Unenhanced gradient-echo T1-weighted MR image of the upper abdomen demonstrates irregularly shaped, low signal intensity nodules peripherally in the liver (*arrows*) and widening of the periportal tract (*arrowheads*). **B.** On a T2-weighted MR image of the upper abdomen, the peripheral liver nodules demonstrate increased signal intensity. Multiple hypointense nodules in the spleen create a heterogeneous appearance. The area of focal hyperintensity (*arrowheads*) represents gastric mucosal involvement. **C.** Ferumoxides-enhanced gradient-echo T2*-weighted MR image shows multiple hyperintense nodules scattered throughout the periphery of the liver (*arrows*) and a hyperintense, widened periportal tract. (From Koyama T, Ueda H, Togashi K, et al: Radiologic manifestations of Sarcoidosis in various organs. RadioGraphics 24: 87-104, 2004.)

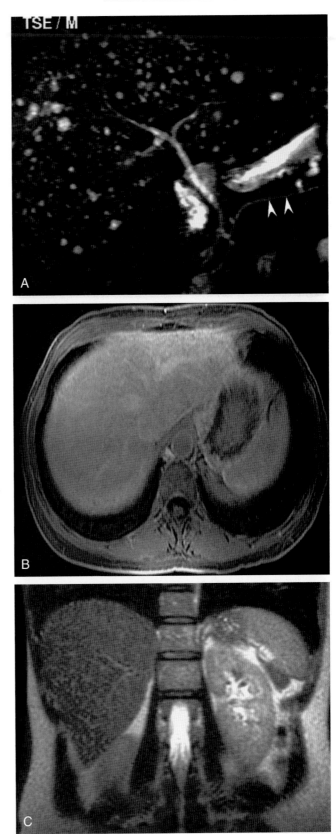

Figure 91-19. Multiple bile duct hamartomas. A. MRCP image demonstrates multiple high signal intensity bile duct hamartomas. *Arrowheads,* pancreatic duct. **B.** Axial T1-weighted image shows multiple low signal intensity hamartomas throughout the liver. **C.** Coronal T2-weighted images shows innumerable hyperintense nodules in the liver. These hamartomas should not be confused with liver abscesses or metastases.

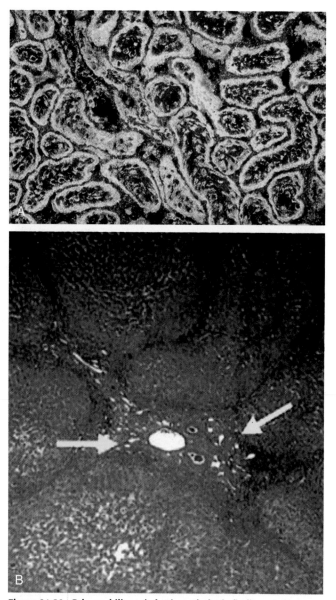

Figure 91-20. Primary biliary cirrhosis: pathologic findings. A. Immunofluorescent stain shows antimitochondrial antibodies, typical of this disease. **B.** Photomicrograph of liver tissue from 41-year-old woman with primary biliary cirrhosis with positive MR periportal halo sign. Stellate areas of hepatocellular parenchymal extinction (*arrow*) around portal triads can be seen. Larger and more variably sized regenerating nodules encircle fibrotic portal triads. (From Wenzel JS, Donohue A, Ford KL, et al: Primary biliary cirrhosis: MR imaging findings and description of MR imaging periportal halo sign. AJR 176:885-889, 2001. Reprinted with permission from the American Journal of Roentgenology.)

Clinical Findings

Patients with primary biliary cirrhosis are predominantly female (10:1) and between the ages of 35 and 65 years. This disease presents with the insidious onset of pruritus, which precedes the jaundice by months or years. Patients also demonstrate hepatomegaly (50%), hyperpigmentation (50%), and xanthelasma or xanthoma (25%).[72-77] Scratch marks caused by the pruritus are often seen, and late in the disease osteomalacia with pathologic fractures, muscle wasting, palmar erythema, spider angiomas, clubbing of the fingers, and other signs of

cirrhosis and portal hypertension are observed. Autoimmune and connective tissue disorders associated with primary biliary cirrhosis include Hashimoto's thyroiditis; scleroderma with calcinosis cutis, Raynaud's phenomenon, sclerodactyly, and telangiectasia; lupus; the sicca complex; renal tubular acidosis; and hypertrophic pulmonary osteoarthropathy.[72-77]

The diagnosis of primary biliary cirrhosis is made serologically by the detection of high titers of antimitochondrial antibody and cryoproteins composed of immunoglobulins M and G (90%-95%), antinuclear antibody (30%-50%), anti–smooth muscle antibody (30%-90%), rheumatoid factor (25%-60%), and antithyroid antibody (15%-26%).[72-77] Usually, a twofold to fivefold elevation of serum alkaline phosphatase is accompanied by normal or only slightly elevated bilirubin and transaminase levels. As the disease evolves, the bilirubin level becomes progressively elevated and may reach 30 mg/dL.[72-77]

Patients who present with jaundice and cholestatic symptoms have a mean survival of approximately 6 years, and the 10% of patients who are asymptomatic with only laboratory abnormalities may live up to 20 years. Treatment consists of anti-inflammatory agents; immunosuppressants such as steroids, methotrexate, cyclosporine, and azathioprine; and D-penicillamine, which lowers the hepatic copper concentration and reduces circulating immune complexes and autoantibodies. Cholestyramine and rifampicin are given to treat the pruritus.[72-77]

Secondary biliary cirrhosis results from long-standing partial or complete obstruction of the common bile duct or its major branches. In adults, this is usually secondary to postoperative strictures or gallstones, often with superimposed infectious cholangitis. Less common causes include idiopathic sclerosing cholangitis and the pericholangitis of ulcerative colitis. Congenital atresia of the intrahepatic or extrahepatic bile ducts induces rapidly advancing periportal fibrosis in infants.

Liver transplantation is definitive treatment in patients with advanced disease, and primary biliary cirrhosis is the second most frequent indication for hepatic transplantation in adults.

Radiologic Findings

Endoscopic retrograde cholangiopancreatography is the primary radiographic technique for establishing the diagnosis of primary biliary cirrhosis and should be used to exclude extrahepatic causes of biliary obstruction and biliary cirrhosis. The cross-sectional imaging findings in primary biliary cirrhosis are discussed in detail in Chapters 76, 77, and 82. Briefly, PBC on MR imaging manifests with characteristic hypointense regions surrounding the portal veins which correspond to areas of fibrosis (Fig. 91-21). Macroregenerative nodules may be seen and can cause peripheral biliary ductal dilatation and peripheral liver atrophy.[78,79]

SECONDARY BILIARY CIRRHOSIS

Primary sclerosing cholangitis is the most common cause of secondary biliary cirrhosis and is discussed in detail in Chapters 76, 77, and 82. There are four pathologic stages (Fig. 91-22), based on which area is involved in the inflammatory and fibrotic changes: stage 1, portal; stage 2, periportal; stage 3, septal; and stage 4, cirrhosis.[80-82]

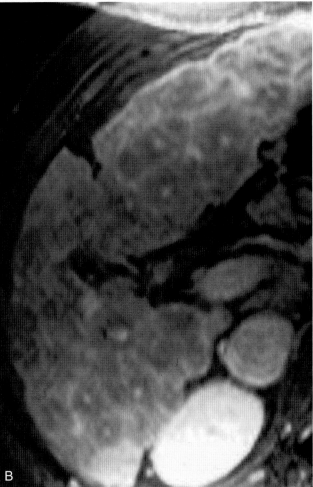

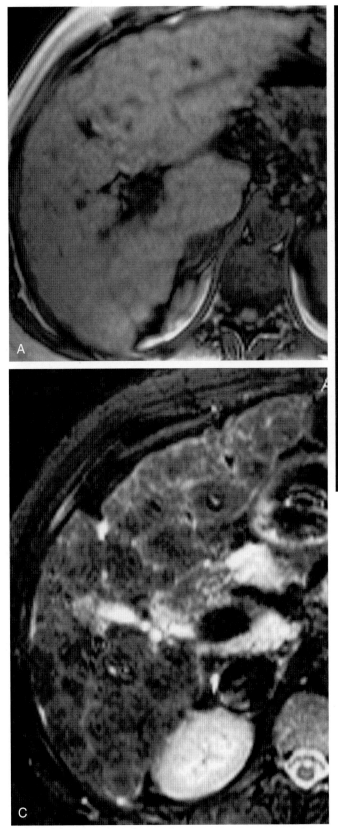

Figure 91-21. Primary biliary cirrhosis: MR findings. A. T1-weighted, unenhanced MR image shows numerous small regenerating nodules. **B.** T1-weighted MR image obtained 3 minutes after infusion shows conspicuous areas of low signal intensity around portal veins. **C.** T2-weighted single-shot fast spin-echo MR image reveals round areas of low signal intensity encircling portal veins.

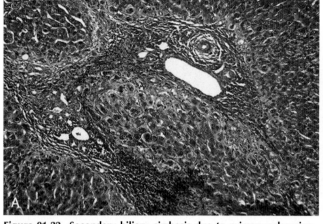

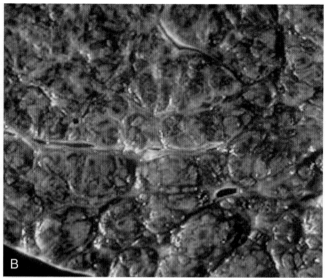

Figure 91-22. Secondary biliary cirrhosis due to primary sclerosing cholangitis: pathologic findings. A. Trichrome histologic stain shows fibrosis surrounding the bile ducts. **B.** End-stage macronodular cirrhosis is seen in this specimen. Note the greenish hue of the liver.

When cirrhosis is present there is marked lobulation of the liver contour, atrophy of the posterior and lateral segments, and hypertrophy of the caudate lobe. The atrophy of the lateral segment of the left lobe is distinctive (Fig. 91-23) because in most other forms of cirrhosis, the lateral segment hypertrophies. The caudate lobe may have a higher attenuation than the remainder of the liver on noncontrast scans, producing a pseudotumor appearance. Enlarged lymph nodes in the lesser omentum are also quite common.[83-90]

On MR imaging (Fig. 91-24), peripheral wedge-shaped zones of hyperintense signal can be seen on T2-weighted images. These triangular areas range in size from 1 to 5 cm. On T1-weighted images, areas of increased signal intensity in the liver that do not correspond to fat may be seen. Following

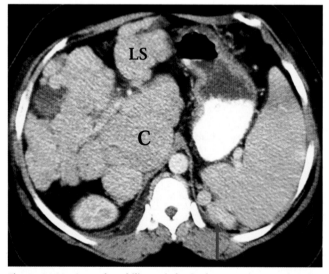

Figure 91-23. Secondary biliary cirrhosis due to primary sclerosing cholangitis: CT findings. Advanced cirrhotic changes are present with a markedly lobulated liver, enlargement of the caudate lobe (C), and widening of the fissures. There is atrophy of the lateral segment (LS) of the left lobe, which is a key differentiating feature from alcoholic and posthepatic cirrhosis. Note the splenomegaly and retrosplenic varices (*arrow*).

contrast administration, areas of increased enhancement that are patchy and/or segmental are frequently seen. These areas often remain mildly or markedly hyperintense on delayed images. Primary sclerosing cholangitis (PSC) often produces large regenerative nodules that may cause obstruction of bile ducts and ultimately segmental atrophy of peripheral liver.[83-90]

ACQUIRED IMMUNODEFICIENCY SYNDROME

Clinical Findings

With improved survival of patients, hepatic manifestations of AIDS are becoming increasingly prevalent. Recognition of specific AIDS-related liver disease is complicated by the fact that virtually all human immunodeficiency virus-positive patients have evidence of prior hepatitis B infection; indeed, the latter infection may potentiate the former. In addition, chemotherapeutic agents commonly used for patients with AIDS, such as antimycobacterial agents, acyclovir, and sulfonamides, can be hepatotoxic.[91]

Pathologic Findings

No characteristic histologic picture is seen in patients with AIDS. Nonspecific macrovesicular steatosis and portal inflammation are the most common findings. Hepatic granulomas have been reported in 16% to 100% of biopsy and autopsy specimens. These granulomas are most frequently associated with mycobacterial infection, usually *Mycobacterium avium-intracellulare*. A variety of other AIDS-related diseases may affect the liver, including lymphoma, Kaposi's sarcoma, and infection with cytomegalovirus, *Cryptococcus*, *Histoplasma*, and *Coccidioides* organisms. Liver biopsy, however, seldom affects therapeutic decisions or leads to improved survival and should be reserved for patients with unexplained fever and an elevated serum alkaline phosphatase level and those with focal mass lesions seen on imaging studies. Biliary and pancreatic changes are also quite common.

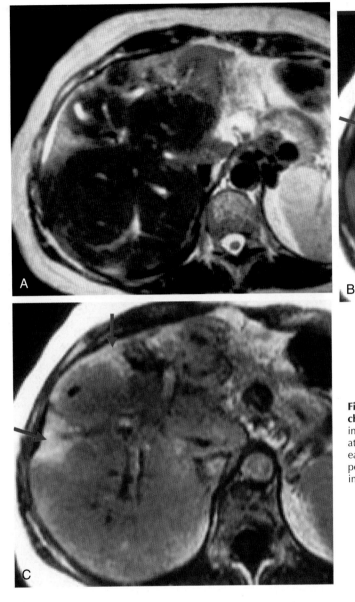

Figure 91-24. Secondary biliary cirrhosis due to primary sclerosing cholangitis: CT findings. A. T2-weighted, single-shot, fat-suppressed image shows a very lobulated liver with caudate lobe enlargement and atrophy of the lateral segment of the left lobe. In a different patient, early (**B**) and delayed (**C**) postgadolinium T1-weighted images show peripheral areas of fibrosis that show contrast accretion on the delayed images (*arrows*).

Radiologic Findings

Ultrasound

Periportal hyperechoic and hypoechoic regions associated with mural thickening of the gallbladder, cystic duct, and bile ducts can be seen in patients with AIDS and can simulate sclerosing cholangitis. This is usually seen in the presence of cytomegalovirus infection or digestive tract cryptosporidiosis. The biliary manifestations of AIDS are illustrated in Chapter 77.

On ultrasound studies, hepatic parenchymal abnormalities include a hyperechoic parenchymal echo pattern (45.5%), hepatomegaly (41%), and focal masses (9%). Hepatic steatosis and granulomatous hepatitis are responsible for the echogenic liver.[12,91] It is postulated that the tiny aggregates of histiocytes found in granulomas act as multiple reflective interfaces that produce the hyperechoic pattern. Metastatic Kaposi's sarcoma, lymphoma, pyogenic abscess, fungal or mycobacterial abscess, and preexisting benign lesions such as hemangiomas can also be seen sonographically.[12,91]

Although hepatic involvement is seen in 34% of cases of Kaposi's sarcoma at autopsy, it is uncommon to see a focal lesion sonographically. On ultrasound studies, these lesions may appear as small (5-12 mm) hyperechoic nodules and dense periportal bands. Similarly, the presence of hepatomegaly does not predict Kaposi's sarcoma involvement because the liver is commonly enlarged in patients with AIDS or AIDS-related complex even when there is no specific pathologic process.[12,25,91]

Hepatic involvement occurs in approximately 5% of AIDS patients with non-Hodgkin's lymphoma. These lesions are usually hypoechoic compared with normal liver parenchyma and may be anechoic and septate, mimicking fluid. Adenopathy in the porta hepatis and retroperitoneum may also be present as a result of AIDS, chronic hepatitis, infection, or neoplasm.[12,25,91]

Computed Tomography

On CT scans, patients with AIDS generally demonstrate hepatomegaly that is often associated with focal or diffuse fatty infiltration. Patients with long-standing hepatitis and postnecrotic change may have cirrhosis as well. Periportal lymphedema producing lucency is also commonly seen and reflects lymphadenitis, hepatitis, or malnutrition.[91]

Lymphomas are particularly aggressive in AIDS patients, and hepatic involvement is manifested on CT scans by hypodense lesions. CT abnormalities are more commonly found in affected livers in AIDS patients than in those without AIDS.

Parenchymal calcifications in the liver, spleen, lymph nodes, and kidneys can be seen in patients with healed disseminated *Pneumocystis carinii* infection. Kaposi's sarcoma commonly involves the liver in AIDS, but the lesions are usually not seen on CT scans. When present, they appear as small low-attenuation masses often located near the portal triads, so they may simulate bile ducts or fungal microabscesses. They also show enhancement on delayed scans.

Mural thickening of the gallbladder, gallbladder distention, and intrahepatic and extrahepatic biliary dilatation can also be seen in AIDS patients with cytomegalovirus or cryptosporidial infection.[91]

Cholangiography

Irregularity of the intrahepatic and extrahepatic bile duct walls with intervening strictures and dilatation simulating sclerosing cholangitis is the cholangiographic corollary of biliary abnormalities seen sonographically and by CT.

CIRRHOSIS

Epidemiology

Cirrhosis is a generic term used to describe chronic liver disease involving diffuse parenchymal necrosis, active formation of connective tissue leading to fibrosis, and nodular regeneration of liver resulting in disorganization of the hepatic lobular and vascular architecture. It is the common end response of the liver to a variety of insults and injuries. Alcohol abuse is the most common cause of cirrhosis in the West.

Cirrhosis is one of the 10 leading causes of death in the Western world and the sixth leading cause in the United States. Age-adjusted mortality is 2.3 times higher in males than in females and 1.7 times higher in black than in white persons. The mortality rate from cirrhosis has also shown a major increase in the past 20 years, and in the United States, cirrhosis is the third leading cause of death for men 34 to 54 years of age. One third of deaths from cirrhosis are secondary to hemorrhage, usually from esophageal varices.[92-95]

Pathophysiology

Although no completely satisfactory scheme for the classification of cirrhosis (Fig. 91-25) has been developed, the disorder has traditionally been divided into several categories: (1) micronodular (Laënnec's) cirrhosis, in which equal-sized nodules up to 3 mm in diameter involve every lobule; (2) macronodular (postnecrotic) cirrhosis, characterized by variable-sized nodules (3 mm-3 cm) that are focal and do not involve every lobule;

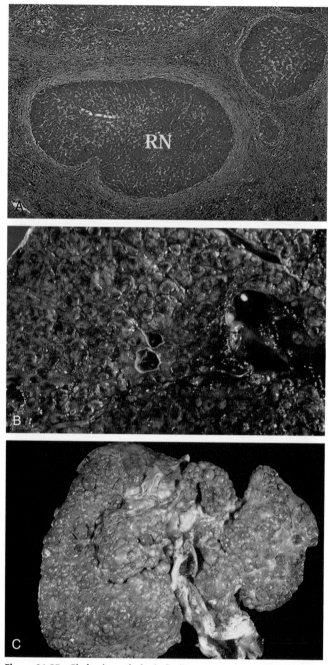

Figure 91-25. Cirrhosis: pathologic findings. A. Photomicrograph shows a regenerating nodule (RN) with surrounding fibrosis: the key pathologic finding in cirrhosis. This patient had hepatitis C cirrhosis. **B.** Micronodular cirrhosis is evident in this specimen image of a patient with alcoholic cirrhosis. **C.** Larger nodules are present in this specimen image of macronodular cirrhosis.

and (3) mixed cirrhosis. Alcoholism is responsible for 60% to 70% of cases of cirrhosis in the Western world and is associated with the micronodular pattern. Viral hepatitis, which accounts for 10% of cirrhosis in the West, is associated with the macronodular pattern. Primary biliary cirrhosis and secondary biliary cirrhosis account for 5% to 10% of cases and pigment cirrhosis (hemochromatosis) for another 5%.[92-95] A more complete listing of the causes of cirrhosis can be found in Table 91-1.

Table 91-1
Etiology of Cirrhosis

Alcoholic cirrhosis (60%-70%)
Postnecrotic: viral hepatitis (10%)
Biliary cirrhosis: primary and secondary (5%-10%)
Pigment cirrhosis: hemochromatosis (5%)
Cardiac failure
Constrictive pericarditis
Hepatic vein obstruction
Malnutrition
Hereditary: Wilson's disease, α_1-antitrypsin deficiency, galactosemia, tyrosinemia, hereditary tetany, hereditary fructose intolerance, type IV glycogen storage disease, Osler-Weber-Rendu syndrome
Drug-induced: methotrexate, oxyphenisatin, alpha-methyldopa, nitrofurantoin, isoniazid, mithramycin, 6-mercaptopurine, azathioprine

Table 91-2
Classification of Portal Hypertension

Prehepatic
Portal vein thrombosis
Splenic vein thrombosis
Node or tumor extrinsic compression of portal vein

Intrahepatic
Presinusoidal
Schistosomiasis
Biliary cirrhosis
Congenital hepatic fibrosis
Neoplasm
Arteriovenous portal fistula
Hyperkinetic portal hypertension
Sinusoidal
Laënnec's cirrhosis
Postnecrotic cirrhosis
Fatty liver
Hepatitis
Sickle cell anemia and sinus thrombosis
Postsinusoidal
Alcoholic cirrhosis
Hepatic vein obstruction
Neoplasm
Veno-occlusive disease

Posthepatic
Congestive heart failure
Constrictive pericarditis
Inferior vena cava webs or thrombosis
Rheumatic heart disease
Neoplasm

Pathologically, all forms of cirrhosis share the following characteristics: (1) the entire parenchymal architecture is disorganized by interconnecting fibrous scars formed in response to hepatocyte injury and loss; (2) the fibrosis may appear as delicate portal-central and/or portal-portal bands or constitute broad scars replacing multiple adjacent lobules; (3) the micronodules or macronodules are created by regenerative activity and the network of scars; and (4) the vascular architecture of the liver is also reorganized by the parenchymal damage and scarring with formation of abnormal arteriovenous interconnections. Cirrhosis leads to two major potentially life-threatening complications: hepatocellular failure resulting from hepatocyte damage and portal venous hypertension.[92-95]

Regenerating nodules have been further classified as siderotic or nonsiderotic, with a greater tendency for siderotic nodules to undergo malignant transformation. The increased incidence of hepatocellular carcinoma in patients with cirrhosis has been shown in part to be a transformation process with the development of dysplastic foci within dominant macroregenerative nodules. These nodules previously were termed adenomatous hyperplastic nodules, but the preferred terminology is now *dysplastic nodule*.[92-95]

Ascites is the most common complication of cirrhosis and is associated with nearly 50% of deaths. Variceal hemorrhage in patients with ascites accounts for nearly 25% of deaths, 10% are due to renal failure resulting from the hepatorenal syndrome, 5% result from spontaneous bacterial peritonitis in patients with massive ascites, and 10% are due to the complications of therapy of ascites.[92-95]

Patients with cirrhosis caused by alcoholism have an increased incidence of developing hepatocellular carcinoma. The risk is 2.5-fold greater in cirrhotic hepatitis B surface antigen-positive patients than in hepatitis B surface antigen-negative patients. Hepatocellular carcinoma has also been reported in patients with cardiac cirrhosis.[92-95]

Portal Hypertension

In chronic liver disease dramatic changes occur in the hepatic circulation. Intrahepatic vascular resistance increases and produces a decrease in the portal fraction of liver perfusion. The diminished portal perfusion is partially compensated by increased arterial flow. Additionally, capillarization of the sinusoids is observed in the form of endothelial defenestra-

tion, deposition of collagen in the extravascular Disse's spaces, and formation of basal laminas. The transit time of large and small molecules, including contrast material is significantly affected by the sinusoidal capillarization.[95]

Portal hypertension may develop in a variety of clinical conditions but is most often secondary to cirrhosis. The causes of portal hypertension (Table 91-2) have been classically divided into three major groups according to the level of obstruction: extrahepatic presinusoidal, extrahepatic postsinusoidal, and intrahepatic. In most of these disorders, increased resistance to portal flow is found. In several, there is increased flow into the portal system, so-called hyperkinetic portal hypertension.

Cirrhosis is the most common cause of intrahepatic portal hypertension. It is secondary to the mechanical effect of the regenerative nodules distorting the hepatic vascular tree, impeding the drainage of blood from the liver and ultimately producing back pressure in the portal system. The alteration in the microcirculatory route leads to portal hypertension. Presinusoidal, intrahepatic block is caused by schistosomiasis, which is the leading cause of portal hypertension worldwide. The ova of the schistosomes implant on small portal radicles within the liver carried from the mesenteric circulation and induce inflammation and granuloma formation that destroy the portal venules. Primary and secondary biliary cirrhosis, congenital hepatic fibrosis, diffuse fibrosing granulomatous disorders such as sarcoidosis, and miliary tuberculosis are other major causes.[95,96]

Sinusoidal obstruction can be seen in postnecrotic cirrhosis, Laënnec's cirrhosis, hepatitis, fatty liver, and sickle cell disease thrombosis.

Portal vein thrombosis and splenic vein thrombosis are the most common forms of prehepatic portal hypertension and are discussed in Chapter 92. Increased portal flow is a rarer cause of portal hypertension and is usually secondary to either congenital (hereditary hemorrhagic telangiectasia) or acquired (post-traumatic or aneurysm rupture) arteriovenous fistulas. Hyperkinetic portal hypertension involves increased portal flow without fistulas, splenomegaly, and increased flow in the splenic artery and vein.

Posthepatic obstruction occurs in patients with inferior vena cava webs (congenital Budd-Chiari syndrome), congestive heart failure, constrictive pericarditis, and rheumatic heart disease and is discussed more fully in Chapter 92.

In patients with portal hypertension, some of the blood in the portal venous system may reverse direction and pass through portosystemic collaterals. Varices can be classified into two groups: those that drain toward the superior vena cava and varices that drain toward the inferior vena cava.[96]

Varices

Varices That Drain into the Superior Vena Cava

The left gastric (coronary vein) is the most common visible varix in portal hypertension and it drains into the superior vena cava and is located in the gastrohepatic ligament. The normal left gastric vein drains both the anterior and posterior surfaces of the stomach and it ascends the lesser curvature within the lesser omentum to the esophageal opening when it receives the esophageal veins. The left gastric vein divides into anterior branches which feed esophageal varices and posterior branches which form paraesophageal varices. Left gastric veins typically are accompanied by esophageal or paraesophageal varices. When the left gastric vein is larger than 5 to 6 mm in diameter, portal hypertension should be considered. A left gastric vein larger than 7 mm in diameter is associated with a portoheptic gradient greater than 10 mm Hg.[96] Short gastric veins are present in the gastrosplenic ligament and drain the gastric fundus. They communicate with the splenic vein or one of its large tributaries along the greater curvature of the stomach. These vessels can also dilated in isolated splenic vein thrombosis.[96]

Esophageal varices are dilated intramural veins of the lower esophagus. Paraesophageal varices are situated outside the wall of the esophagus. They are primarly supplied by the left gastric vein which divides into anterior and posterior branches. The anterior branch fills the esophageal varices and the posterior branch fills the paraesophageal varices. Esophageal and paraesophageal varices usually drain into the azygos-hemiazygos venous system but may also enter the subclavian-brachiocephalic system through the left pericardiophrenic vein or into the inferior vena cava through the inferior phrenic vein.

Varices That Drain into the Inferior Vena Cava

The splenorenal ligament, the splenoportal vein and left renal vein communicate through the coronary vein, short gastric vein (gastrorenal shunt), or other veins that normally drain into the splenic vein (splenorenal shunt). Normally, four or five short gastric veins drain the gastric fundus and the left part of the greater curvature, traversing the gastrosplenic ligament to reach the splenic vein. Short gastric veins should be smaller than 5 mm in diameter. Gastrorenal and splenorenal shunts are seen as varices in the region of the splenic and left

renal hilum which drain into an enlarged left renal vein. This may cause fusiform dilation of the inferior vena cava at the level of the left renal vein.[96]

Umbilical (paraumbilical) veins in the ligamentum teres and falciform ligament arise from the left portal vein. These vessels may also course through the medial segment of the liver rather than the ligamentum teres. The umbilical vessels can anastomose with superior epigastric or internal thoracic veins and drain into the superior vena cava or anastomose with the inferior epigastric vein and then drain into the inferior vena cava through the external iliac vein. The paraumbilical veins can drain into the veins of the anterior abdominal wall, creating the "Medusa's head" appearance.[96]

Collateral vessels may also arise from the superior and inferior mesenteric veins within the subperitoneal space of the small bowel mesentery. They ultimately may drain into the retroperitoneal or pelvic veins. A retroperitoneal shunt may develop between the mesenteric vessels and the renal vein or inferior vena cava. Veins of Retzius are communications between the inferior vena cava and intestinal or retroperitoneal tributaries of the superior or inferior mesenteric veins and systemic veins.[96]

The intrahepatic portal veins can form collateral pathways with hepatic venous branches or direct communication with the left gastric vein. There is a loose collateral plexus over the hepatic surface and it is sometimes widely distributed over the parietal peritoneum with branches piercing the diaphragm to join pericardial, pleural, and pulmonary veins, the so-called pleuropericardial collaterals. The intercostal veins may also dilate and help drain hepatofugal blood flow through the azygos-hemiazygos system.[96]

Ultrasound: Cirrhosis

The sonographic changes (Table 91-3) in hepatic size and tissue texture observed in patients with cirrhosis are nonspecific (Fig. 91-26). There is significant sonographic overlap between fibrosis and fatty infiltration: decreased beam penetration through the liver, poor depiction of intrahepatic vessels, and increased parenchymal echogenicity are seen in both disorders[96-103] (see Table 95-10). Some authors have shown that the attenuation of sound can be normal in cirrhotic patients without fatty deposition. Nevertheless, cirrhosis should be suspected if decreased hepatic size, nodularity of the liver surface, accentuation of the fissures, marked coarsening of the hepatic

Table 91-3

Cirrhosis: Morphologic Features

Nodular hepatic contour
Enlarged caudate lobe
Enlarged lateral segment of left lobe
Atrophy of the right and quadrate lobes
Prominence of the fissures and porta hepatis
Portal hypertension: varices, ascites, splenomegaly
Fatty infiltration
Colonic interposition
Altered gallbladder angle
Increased density of mesenteric fat
Regenerating nodules
Intrahepatic arterial-portal fistulas
Fibrosis (focal confluent or lacy network surrounding nodules)

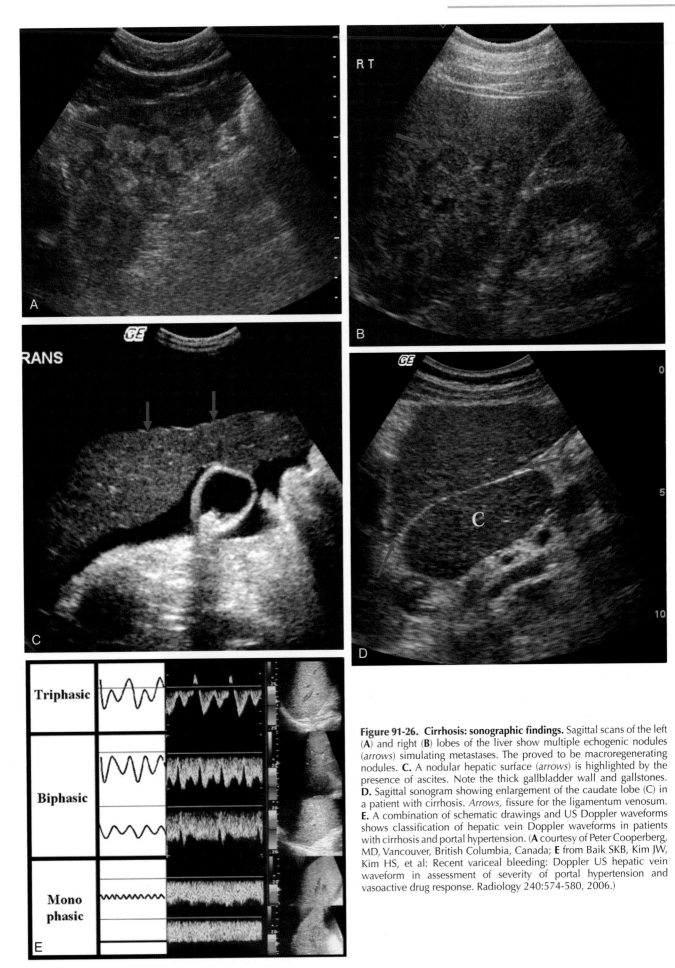

Figure 91-26. Cirrhosis: sonographic findings. Sagittal scans of the left (**A**) and right (**B**) lobes of the liver show multiple echogenic nodules (*arrows*) simulating metastases. The proved to be macroregenerating nodules. **C.** A nodular hepatic surface (*arrows*) is highlighted by the presence of ascites. Note the thick gallbladder wall and gallstones. **D.** Sagittal sonogram showing enlargement of the caudate lobe (C) in a patient with cirrhosis. *Arrows,* fissure for the ligamentum venosum. **E.** A combination of schematic drawings and US Doppler waveforms shows classification of hepatic vein Doppler waveforms in patients with cirrhosis and portal hypertension. (**A** courtesy of Peter Cooperberg, MD, Vancouver, British Columbia, Canada; **E** from Baik SKB, Kim JW, Kim HS, et al: Recent variceal bleeding: Doppler US hepatic vein waveform in assessment of severity of portal hypertension and vasoactive drug response. Radiology 240:574-580, 2006.)

architecture, regenerating nodules, ascites, or signs of portal hypertension are seen.

The reported sensitivity of ultrasound in the diagnosis of cirrhosis based on hepatic architecture varies between 65% and 95%.[96-103] Although ultrasound has up to a 98% positive predictive value in the diagnosis of diffuse parenchymal disease, it cannot reliably differentiate fat from fibrosis. Irregularity of the liver surface has been suggested as a fairly sensitive sign (88%) of cirrhosis as well. It is detected by using a high-frequency probe.[96-103] The presence of surface nodularity correlates pathologically with sinusoidal obstruction to portal flow and the development of portal hypertension. Indeed it correlates best with severe fibrosis or cirrhosis at biopsy when compared to caudate lobe hypertrophy or hepatic venous flow abnormalities.[96] In one series, high-resolution sonography was found to be useful in assessing the severity of hepatic scarring and differentiating macronodular and micronodular cirrhosis. On Doppler ultrasound, there is flattening of the hepatic venous waveforms due to decreased compliance of the fibrotic liver.[12,91-103]

As measured sonographically, segment IV undergoes atrophy in patients with cirrhosis. When compared to a normal mean diameter of 43 ± 8 mm (standard deviation), in patients with cirrhosis the mean diameter of segment 4 is 28 ± 9 mm. The cause or severity of cirrhosis had no influence on the size of segment 4.[102]

Regenerating nodules that are 2 to 3 mm to 1 to 2 cm in diameter can occasionally be appreciated sonographically as hypoechoic areas with echogenic borders resulting from fibrous and fatty connective tissue surrounding and separating the nodules. They can usually be seen only with high-frequency transducers unless they are quite large, in which case they may simulate a malignant neoplasm. For these reasons, ultrasound can be a difficult tool to use for screening in cirrhotic patients for detecting hepatocellular carcinoma. Some studies have reported that ultrasound sensitivity for detecting hepatocellular carcinoma in screening cirrhotic patients is only approximately 50%. The lack of a viable contrast agent to detect vascular changes indicative of tumor makes ultrasound a less reliable tool than CT or MR imaging for screening cirrhotic patients.[96-103]

The right lobe and left lobe lengths in longitudinal dimension have been compared sonographically. The normal right lobe/left lobe ratio is 1.44, and the ratio is less than 1.3 for patients with cirrhosis. Right lobe shrinkage with relative preservation of the left lobe was most prominent in hepatitis-associated cirrhosis (mean 1.17) as opposed to non–hepatitis-related cirrhosis (mean 1.25). A ratio of 1.40 excludes cirrhosis in 100% of cases; a ratio of 1.35 has 90% sensitivity, 82% specificity, and 81% accuracy; a ratio of 1.3 has 74% sensitivity, 100% specificity, and 93% accuracy.[96-103]

Another useful morphologic guide in the sonographic diagnosis of cirrhosis is obtained by multiplying the longitudinal, transverse, and anterior-posterior diameters of the caudate lobe and dividing them by the transverse diameter of the right lobe. The mean ratio in cirrhosis is 16.7 compared with only 3.2 for normal livers; ratios greater than 5.4 are considered abnormal. This ratio has a specificity of 95%, and its sensitivity is 94.7% compared with 73.3% for the caudate lobe/right lobe ratio.[92-106]

It should be noted when considering any of these complex measurements that Lafortune and associates found that one measurement at ultrasound of the transverse diameter of segment 4 had a sensitivity of 74% for the diagnosis of cirrhosis, with a specificity of 100%.[102] The transverse diameter was obtained from a measurement between the left wall of the gallbladder and the ascending portion of the left portal vein at the point where it gives rise to the segment 4 branch. These results were obtained using a lower limit of normal diameter of 30 mm, with atrophy below that indicative of cirrhosis.

Mesenteric, omental and retroperitoneal edema can be seen in patients with cirrhosis and portal hypertension. The increased hydrostatic pressure within the mesenteric veins causes fluid to seep into the mesentery. Liver dysfunction also produces a state of water overload due to hypoalbuminemia and decreased aldosterone catabolism. These features also play a role in the development of mesenteric edema, ascites, pleural effusion, and subcutaneous edema. With increasing severity, mesenteric edema can develop a more diffuse distribution and mass like appearance associated with recruitment of omental and retroperitoneal sites. The degree of edema correlates with other findings of severe ascites, subcutaneous edema, pleural effusions, and low mean serum albumin.[92-106]

A vascular corollary of these changes in the segmental morphology of the liver has been described. Normally, the diameter of the right portal vein is greater than that of the left portal vein because the right hepatic lobe is larger than the left lobe. When the lateral segment of the left lobe hypertrophies and the right lobe atrophies, the left portal vein diameter becomes equal to or greater than the right portal vein diameter. The sensitivity and specificity of this finding are 85% and 88%, respectively, for alcoholics without recanalization of the umbilical vein.[92-106]

Siderotic nodules, or Gamna-Gandy bodies, may rarely be identified as hyperechoic masses in the spleen.[101] These nodules, which are seen in patients with portal hypertension caused by hemorrhage into the splenic follicles, are composed of fibrous tissue encrusted with hemosiderin and calcium. Presumably, the fibrous tissue and calcium account for these echogenic splenic masses.

The incidence of gallstones is also increased in patients with cirrhosis regardless of etiology or gender. A number of mechanisms make stones more prevalent in the cirrhotic population. Ingestion of alcohol may cause spasm of the sphincter of Oddi and edema of the papilla of Vater, thus interfering with bile duct and gallbladder emptying. Bile stasis and calculus formation may result from poor food intake and excessive alcohol consumption. Indeed, ascites, encephalopathy, and varices are more common in cirrhotic patients with stones than in those without stones. Chronic hemolysis is perhaps the most significant factor in pigment stone formation. Hypersplenism is another major contributing factor. Because of functional damage to the liver, cholesterol stones are uncommon in cirrhotic patients.[92-106]

Computed Tomography: Cirrhosis

In the United States, CT[104-107] is the primary noninvasive imaging modality in the evaluation of cirrhosis (see Table 91-3). Whereas early parenchymal changes may not be visible on CT scans, fatty infiltration, which is the initial feature of alcoholic liver disease, is well displayed. The density of the liver is less than that of the spleen, and there is often hepatomegaly. The liver can be enlarged in alcoholic hepatitis as well.

Alcoholic hepatitis and hepatic steatosis are discussed more fully in other sections of this chapter.

In the later stages of cirrhosis (Fig. 91-27), the overall liver volume is diminished. Whereas all patients pathologically demonstrate regenerating nodules, these are infrequently demonstrated at CT. Nodularity of the liver contour caused by regenerating nodules, fibrous scarring, and nonuniform lobar atrophy or hypertrophy may be demonstrated, particularly in the presence of ascites. Regenerating nodules, however, are most commonly isoattenuating with liver parenchyma before and after contrast material administration. Siderotic nodules will appear of higher attenuation than liver and other soft tissue organs and be readily apparent on unenhanced CT but usually isoattenuating with contrast-enhanced liver parenchyma. Uncommonly, regenerating nodules can appear as hypoattenuating small nodules on contrast-enhanced liver CT, simulating tumor. This is most commonly seen when the etiology of cirrhosis is primary biliary cirrhosis. Because of the insensitivity of CT to depicting regenerating nodules, it is not able to depict or differentiate the transformation process of regenerative nodules to dyplastic nodules. Occasionally, large dysplastic nodules can be identified on unenhanced CT with increased attenuation, perhaps due to increased iron composition or to packed cellular material with increased glycogen content. Most often, however, these nodules go undetected by CT.[104-107]

Cirrhotic liver parenchyma often demonstrates less contrast enhancement than normal liver and appears inhomogeneous due to the underlying regeneration, fibrosis, and altered portal venous blood flow. The hepatic and portal vein radicles in the liver are often compressed and difficult to visualize. The porta hepatis and intrahepatic fissures are also unusually prominent because of the hepatic atrophy.[104-107]

Pericaval fat collections are seen in up to 25% of patients with chronic liver disease. They are located along the posterior aspect of the IVC in most cases. The rightward angulation and narrowing of the intrahepatic IVC that occur in cirrhosis causes the pericaval fat collections to appear intraluminal on axial CT scans. Also, the shrunken right lobe in cirrhosis provides a space in which fat can accumulate.[104-106]

The liver atrophy in most cirrhotic patients typically affects the right lobe and medial segment of the left lobe to the greatest degree. The lateral segment of the left lobe and the caudate lobe often undergo hypertrophy. The caudate lobe is often spared from this process in cirrhosis and other hepatic disorders because of its dual arterial blood supply and the fact that hepatic arteries and portal veins supplying the caudate have a shorter intrahepatic course than those supplying the right lobe. These vessels are therefore subject to less distortion by the fibrotic liver. It is also postulated that streaming of alcohol and other toxins in the portal vein is directed primarily toward the right lobe of the liver. Arterial and venous flow to the caudate lobe of the liver are spared from the effects of the periportal fibrosis, thus preserving blood flow that maintains function and fosters compensatory enlargement.[104-107]

Measurements of the ratio of the caudate lobe size to that of the right lobe have been determined to be accurate in diagnosing the presence or absence of cirrhosis. To determine the caudate lobe/right lobe ratio, the caudate lobe is measured transversely from its most medial aspect to the right lateral wall of the main portal vein, just caudal to its bifurcation. The right lobe is measured from the same portion of the main portal vein to the right lateral margin of the liver. If the caudate lobe/right lobe ratio exceeds 0.65, the diagnosis of cirrhosis can be made with 96% confidence. By using this sole criterion, the diagnosis can be made with a sensitivity of 84%, specificity of 100%, and accuracy of 94%. The normal caudate lobe–right lobe ratio is 0.37, and the mean ratio in cirrhotic livers is 0.83. Although these measurements do reflect the underlying morphologic changes, they are rarely used in clinical practice to diagnose cirrhosis.[104-107]

An alternative measurement uses the right portal venous bifurcation rather than the bifurcation of the main portal vein to mark the lateral boundary of the hypertrophied caudate lobe and central liver from the atrophied right lobe.[104]

Patients with biliary cirrhosis (see Fig. 91-21B), particularly those secondary to chronic changes from sclerosing cholangitis (see Figs. 91-23 and 91-24), often undergo different morphologic changes. In these patients, in addition to the marked atrophy of the right lobe, there is often marked atrophy of the lateral segment of the liver as well. These changes, coupled with marked caudate lobe hypertrophy, result in a squared or rounded appearance to the liver at CT imaging. The atrophy of the more distal parts of the liver to a greater degree in these patients is thought to be due to the effects of chronic biliary obstruction. In addition, zones of focal fibrosis in these patients can appear as peripheral bands of low attenuation.

The alterations in segmental hepatic anatomy described previously produce profound changes in the topography of the right upper quadrant. Colonic interposition between the liver and the anterior-lateral abdominal wall and/or diaphragm is seen in 25% of cirrhotic patients as opposed to 3% of control subjects on CT scans.[104-107]

The gallbladder and interlobar fissure also undergo counterclockwise rotation in patients with cirrhotic liver morphology. These topographic alterations can be quantitated by measuring the gallbladder angle. This angle is determined by drawing a line through the interlobar fissure, gallbladder neck, and/or medial aspect of the anterior segment of the right hepatic lobe (whichever is visible) and the inferior vena cava. Another line is drawn coronally through the inferior vena cava parallel to the patient's back. The gallbladder angle subtended by these lines is a useful marker of gallbladder position. In normal patients, the angle is 46 degrees, but in cirrhotics, the angle is reduced to 35 degrees. Thus, the gallbladder becomes a more lateral and superficial structure in cirrhosis, prone to inadvertent injury during "blind" liver biopsy, surgery, and percutaneous transhepatic procedures.[104-107]

The fibrosis seen in cirrhosis is usually a diffuse, lacy process surrounding regenerating nodules within the liver parenchyma. In patients with advanced cirrhosis, approximately 30% will develop collapse of normal hepatic architecture and replacement of liver parenchyma with massive, confluent regions of fibrosis, termed *focal confluent fibrosis* (see Fig. 91-30). Focal confluent fibrosis can appear at CT imaging as a focal mass, in some ways simulating tumor. It appears most conspicuous on noncontrast CT and usually becomes either isoattenuating with contrast-enhanced CT or remains slightly hypoattenuating. In some cases, the fibrosis will show irregular contrast enhancement, making it difficult to differentiate from tumors such as hepatocellular carcinoma. Fortunately, associated morphologic changes are often present that allow characterization of focal confluent fibrosis. These lesions most commonly affect the anterior segment of the right lobe and

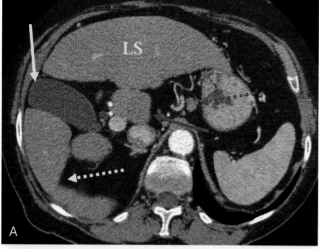

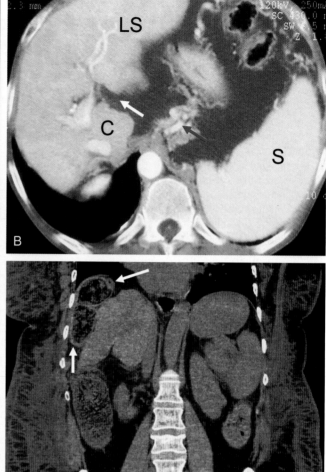

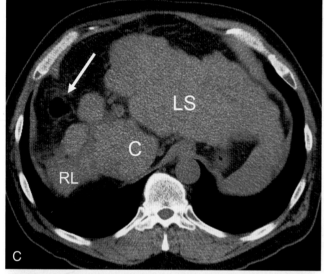

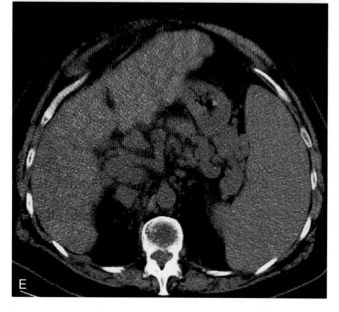

Figure 91-27. Cirrhosis: CT features. A. Contrast-enhanced CT demonstrates enlargement of the lateral segment (LS) of the left lobe, atrophy of the medial segment (*solid red arrow*) of the left lobe, and atrophy of the right lobe with a characteristic notch (*broken yellow arrow*) in the right posterior surface of the liver. Note the gallbladder (*solid yellow arrow*) is in more superficial and lateral position as a result of these morphologic changes. Several borderline size lymph nodes (*broken red arrows*) are present within the gastrohepatic ligament. **B.** Contrast-enhanced CT demonstrates widening of the gallbladder fossa (*white arrow*), enlargement of the lateral segment (LS) of the left lobe and caudate lobe (C) of the liver, ascites, varices (*red arrow*), and splenomegaly (S). **C.** Noncontrast CT scan shows diffuse nodularity of the hepatic contour associated with enlargement of the lateral segment (LS) of the left hepatic lobe and caudate lobe (C). Note the interposition of the colon (*arrow*) between the liver and lateral abdominal wall. RL, right lobe. **D.** Coronal reformatted MDCT image shows interposition of colon (*arrows*) between liver and right diaphragm (Chilaiditi's syndrome), which is much more common in cirrhosis due to atrophy of the right lobe. **E.** Noncontrast CT scan shows diffuse regenerating nodules that are hyperdense due to the presence of iron.

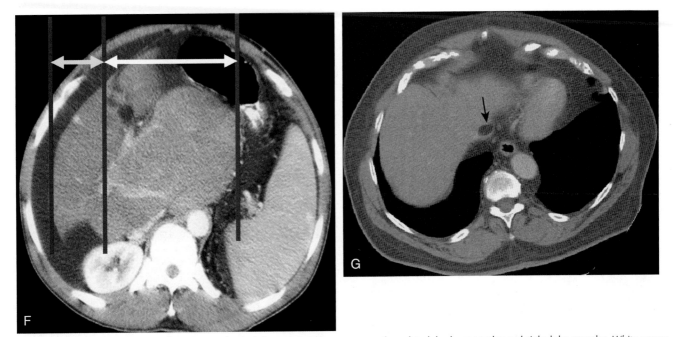

Figure 91-27, cont'd. F. Diagram depicting method of determining the presence of caudate lobe hypertrophy and right lobe atrophy. *White arrow* shows transverse diameter of the caudate lobe; *yellow arrow* depicts diameter of right lobe. If the caudate/right lobe ratio is larger than 0.9, then the diagnosis of cirrhosis can be predicted with a fairly good accuracy. **G.** Changes in the topography of the right upper quadrant commonly highlight pericaval fat in patients with cirrhosis, often simulating a fatty mass (*arrow*) in the inferior vena cava.

the medial segment of the left lobe, usually with a wedge-shaped appearance radiating from the porta hepatis. Another key differentiating feature is associated focal capsular retraction over the abnormal region due to atrophy in the fibrotic scarred region. Most untreated tumors, by comparison, cause a bulge in the overlying liver contour. When focal confluent fibrosis has an atypical appearance or location, it can be very difficult to differentiate from tumor.[104-107]

These underlying parenchymal changes distort the liver parenchyma and can simulate other masses such as hepatocellular carcinoma. In addition, the parenchymal changes can obscure subtle findings of hepatocellular carcinoma. Before the development of MDCT, it was difficult to detect even large foci of hepatocellular carcinoma in cirrhotic patients. The advent of MDCT, with the ability to optimally time contrast administration and scanning and detect arterial phase enhancement in hepatocellular carcinoma has substantially increased the ability to detect small tumors in cirrhotic patients, visualized as small enhancing foci during the arterial phase of contrast enhancement. The appearance of hepatocellular carcinoma is discussed more fully in Chapter 89. The advent of MDCT has substantially increased the accuracy of CT in screening patients with cirrhosis for hepatocellular carcinoma.

As with hepatitis, the chronic inflammation present in cirrhosis results in enlargement of abdominal lymph nodes in multiple upper abdominal locations. Such enlarged nodes range in size up to 4 cm in maximal diameter and can be found in patients with cirrhosis from all etiologies. Although most common in patients with primary biliary cirrhosis and sclerosing cholangitis, enlarged nodes have been reported with high frequency in patients with alcoholic cirrhosis (37%) and hepatitis B or C (45%-49%). The affected lymph node chains reported include (in order of frequency of involvement) the portocaval space, porta hepatis and hepatoduodenal ligament, gastrohepatic ligament, cardiophrenic angle, and celiac axis, as well as other lesser more remote abdominal chains[104-107]

Patients with cirrhosis and portal hypertension also show an increase in the density of the mesenteric fat compared with the retroperitoneal fat (−56 versus −107 HU). The CT density of the mesenteric fat is also significantly higher in these patients (−56 HU) than in normal subjects (−107 HU).[104-107]

Intrahepatic arterial-portal fistulas are occasionally seen on CT scans in patients with cirrhosis. They cause early opacification of the portal vein, which is best appreciated on dynamic scans by measuring the time-density curve in the aorta and the intrahepatic portal vein or hepatic hilum. In addition, the lobe that contains the arterial-portal fistula has higher density in the later arterial phase than the contralateral lobe.[104-107]

Magnetic Resonance Imaging: Cirrhosis

MR imaging (Figs. 91-28, 91-29, and 91-30) can often detect cirrhosis at an earlier stage than CT and ultrasound.[108-119] Early in the evolution of cirrhosis, MR imaging can demonstrate subtle changes such as fine strands of fibrosis and enlargement of the hilar and periportal space. Opposed-phase SGE images, which are heavily T1-weighted are very sensitive to the depiction of subtle fibrotic change which manifests as a lace-like hypointense network of abnormal signal intensity.[25] Linear enhancement is seen on the interstitial phase of enhancement reflecting the distribution of gadolinium in the large extracellular spaces of the fibrotic septal tissue. There is also enlargement of the hilar periportal space which lies anterior to the right portal vein. This is due to atrophy of segment IV and is visible in most patients with early cirrhosis.[108-119]

With progression of the cirrhosis, there is atrophy of the medial segment of the left lobe and right lobe with sparing

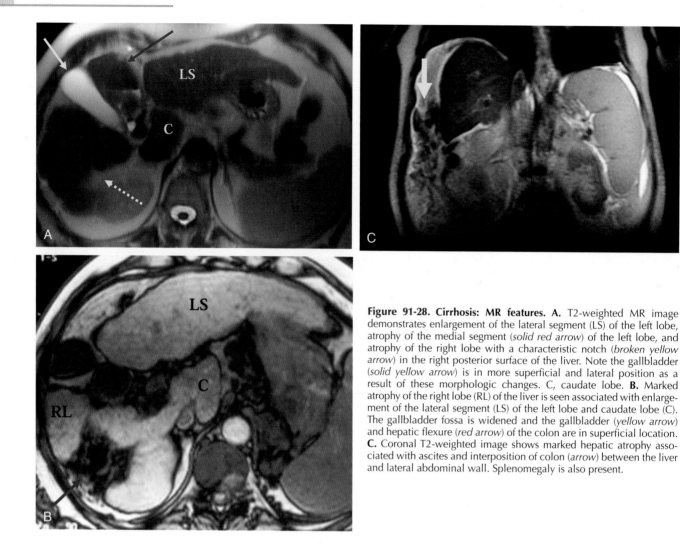

Figure 91-28. Cirrhosis: MR features. A. T2-weighted MR image demonstrates enlargement of the lateral segment (LS) of the left lobe, atrophy of the medial segment (*solid red arrow*) of the left lobe, and atrophy of the right lobe with a characteristic notch (*broken yellow arrow*) in the right posterior surface of the liver. Note the gallbladder (*solid yellow arrow*) is in more superficial and lateral position as a result of these morphologic changes. C, caudate lobe. **B.** Marked atrophy of the right lobe (RL) of the liver is seen associated with enlargement of the lateral segment (LS) of the left lobe and caudate lobe (C). The gallbladder fossa is widened and the gallbladder (*yellow arrow*) and hepatic flexure (*red arrow*) of the colon are in superficial location. **C.** Coronal T2-weighted image shows marked hepatic atrophy associated with ascites and interposition of colon (*arrow*) between the liver and lateral abdominal wall. Splenomegaly is also present.

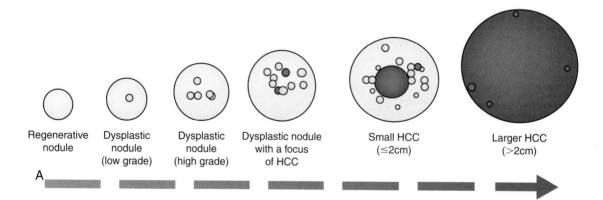

Figure 91-29. Hepatocellular nodules in cirrhosis: MR features. A. Stepwise pathway of carcinogenesis for hepatocellular carcinoma (HCC) in cirrhosis. One or more regenerative nodules may show signs of atypia and change into dysplastic nodules. Atypia indicates a number of changes in the shape and size of the nuclei and the cytoplasm of the hepatocytes. These changes often result in an increased number of cells (increased cellularity), which may be present in groups of small cells (small cell dysplasia) or large cells (large cell dysplasia). Atypia within dysplastic nodules can progress further and give rise to small and large HCCs. In addition to the cellular changes, the hepatic parenchymal structure will often be distorted in HCC.

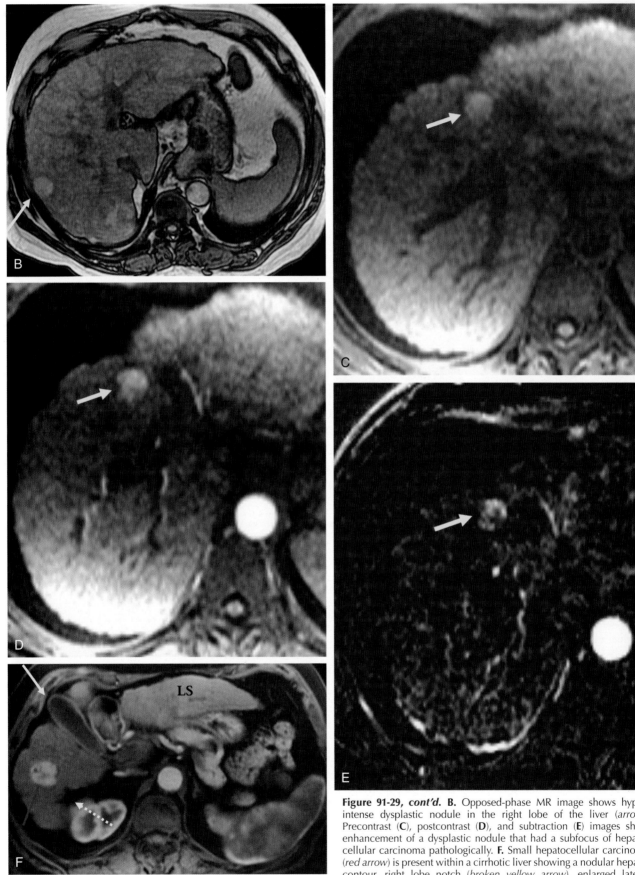

Figure 91-29, *cont'd*. B. Opposed-phase MR image shows hyperintense dysplastic nodule in the right lobe of the liver (*arrow*). Precontrast (**C**), postcontrast (**D**), and subtraction (**E**) images show enhancement of a dysplastic nodule that had a subfocus of hepatocellular carcinoma pathologically. **F.** Small hepatocellular carcinoma (*red arrow*) is present within a cirrhotic liver showing a nodular hepatic contour, right lobe notch (*broken yellow arrow*), enlarged lateral segment (LS) of the left lobe, and a superficial gallbladder (*solid yellow arrow*). (**A** from Hussain SM, Zondervan PE, Ijzermans JN, et al: Benign versus malignant nodules: MR imaging findings with pathologic correlation. RadioGraphics 22:1023-1039, 2002.)

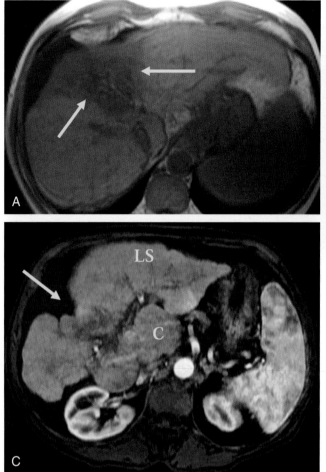

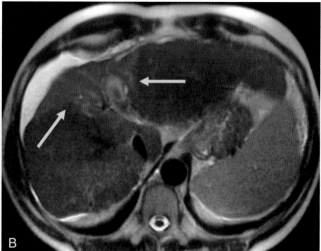

Figure 91-30. Confluent hepatic fibrosis: MR features. A. T1-weighted image shows wedge-shaped hypointense regions (*arrows*) along the anterior aspect of the right lobe and the medial segment of the left lobe. **B.** On the T2-weighted image, the areas of fibrosis are mildly hyperintense (*arrows*). This patient has ascites. **C.** Contrast-enhanced, T1-weighted MR image in a different patient shows the classic location of capsular retraction in confluent hepatic fibrosis (*arrow*). Note the hypertrophy of the caudate (C) lobe and lateral segment (LS) of the left lobe.

or hypertrophy of the central segments of the left lobe and caudate lobe. The interlobar fissure is expanded—the expanded gallbladder fossa sign. In advanced cirrhosis, atrophy of the lateral segment of the left lobe and caudate lobe may develop.[25]

The role of MR imaging in the cirrhotic patient, is to assess liver size, to evaluate the effects of portal hypertension, to screen for hepatocellular carcinoma, and to better characterize masses detected in the liver by other techniques. As with CT, MR imaging usually visualizes underlying nodular regeneration only when siderotic nodules are present. However, MR imaging does appear to be more sensitive than CT in displaying siderotic nodules, which appear as small dark nodules on T2-weighted and gradient-echo images and rarely with a similar appearance on T1-weighted images. Rarely, benign regenerating nodules can have a high signal intensity on T1-weighted images. When nodules are separated by fibrous septa, they are better appreciated. Hemosiderin deposits in these nodules are believed to account for the low MR signal because of magnetic susceptibility effects.[108-119]

MR imaging is also useful for differentiating dysplastic nodules (formerly referred to as adenomatous hyperplastic nodules) from hepatocellular carcinoma in patients with cirrhosis (see Fig. 91-29). Most small dysplastic nodules are not visualized as distinct masses on MR imaging. Many large dysplastic nodules do demonstrate a characteristic set of signal intensities, being hyperintense to adjacent liver on T1-weighted images and hypointense on T2-weighted images. This is in

distinction to most hepatomas that are hyperintense on T2-weighted images, although a substantial number of small tumors can be isointense on T2-weighted images, and they rarely can appear hypointense.[108-119]

The MR characteristics of hepatic lesions during dynamic the dynamic venous phase in conjunction with serum α-fetoprotein level and number of lesions are predictors of hepatic malignancy.[114]

MR imaging is useful in discrimination of alcoholic and virus-induced cirrhosis. The volume of the caudate lobe is significantly larger in alcoholic cirrhosis than in virus cirrhosis. Additionally, the visualization of a notch in the right posterior hepatic lobe is more commonly seen in alcoholic cirrhosis. The size of regenerating nodules is also significantly greater in patients with cirrhosis caused by hepatitis B than in those with alcoholic cirrhosis.[113]

MR elastography has shown promise as a noninvasive means of determining the degree of hepatic fibrosis. Patients with liver fibrosis have elevated MR elastographic liver stiffness measurements.[119]

Focal confluent fibrosis, as with CT, is often seen at MR imaging (see Fig. 91-30) as a focal mass. The signal characteristics of the large regions of fibrous tissue deposition are low signal intensity on T1-weighted images and high signal intensity on T2-weighted image. Unfortunately, these are signal characteristics are similar to most hepatocellular carcinomas. As with CT, the diagnosis rests with identifying the characteristic location and capsular retraction of this lesion. When focal confluent fibrosis appears round on axial images, the high signal intensity lesions on T2-weighted images replicate findings of hepatocellular carcinoma.[108-119]

MR imaging is also useful in depicting Gamna-Gandy bodies (see Fig. 91-14D) in the spleen in patients with portal hypertension. These siderotic nodules are composed of hemosiderin and calcification adjacent to thickened bundles of collagen fibers and result from repeated hemorrhages in the splenic follicles or adjacent to trabeculae. These tiny nodules have low signal intensity at virtually all pulse sequences because of their paramagnetic effect but are best seen on gradient-echo or fast low-angle shot images.[108-119]

Ultrasound: Portal Hypertension

Sonography (Figs. 91-31 and 91-32) plays a key role in the management of patients with cirrhosis in the detection of portal hypertension and the noninvasive evaluation of the portosystemic collateral circulation. The sonographic features of portal hypertension depend on changes in size and blood flow in the portal system, congestive splenomegaly, and the development of collateral pathways. Sonography is also useful in differentiating presinusoidal causes of portal hypertension from obstruction at the sinusoidal or postsinusoidal level.[12,120,121]

Measuring portal vein size and observing respiratory variations in the superior mesenteric and splenic veins are simple and sensitive methods for detecting portal hypertension. The diameter of the portal vein in normal individuals ranges from 0.64 to 1.21 cm, and the mean diameter is 1.2 cm in cirrhotic patients. There is a significant correlation between the diameter of the portal vein and maximal spleen length and the magnitude of varices seen endoscopically. A patent portal vein larger than 1.3 cm is 100% specific for portal hypertension but is seen in only 75% of cases. Other signs of portal hypertension are patency of the umbilical vein (58%), splenomegaly

with dilatation of splenic vein radicles (91.3%), and disappearance of normal splenic and mesenteric vessel caliber variation with respiration, which occurs in 78.5% and 88.4% of patients, respectively. Lack of distensibility of the portal vessels with respiration is an important sign. In normal individuals, the portal venous system distends with deep inspiration and breath holding because of diaphragmatic descent and compression of hepatic venous outflow. Indeed, the diameter of the splenic or superior mesenteric veins may increase 50% to 100%. Ninety percent of patients with manometrically proved portal hypertension fail to show this distensibility because the portal venous system is already maximally distended and respiration-induced pressure changes are poorly transmitted through the scarred liver. The caliber of these veins decreases and respiratory variation returns if therapy with various vasoconstrictors is successful.[12,120,121]

The size of the superior mesenteric and coronary veins is also affected in portal hypertension. If the superior mesenteric vein is larger than the portal vein or the coronary vein is larger than 4 mm, portal hypertension is present. The superior mesenteric vein and splenic veins should be no longer than 11 and 12 mm, respectively. A coronary vein larger than 7 mm indicates a portohepatic gradient larger than 10 mm Hg, which makes variceal bleeding likely.[12,120,121]

Collateral vessels can be seen sonographically in up to 88% of patients with portal hypertension. The most important varices involve the coronary veins and their associated esophageal varices. These varices can be identified as circular and tubular sonolucencies in the region of the gastroesophageal junction and lesser curvature of the stomach. These vessels are normally no larger than 4 mm. CT, however, more reliably depicts varices in this location.[12,120,121]

The portal circulation commonly decompresses through collaterals in the ligamentum teres. This usually echogenic structure becomes sonolucent centrally, producing a "bull's-eye" appearance in the transverse plane. A central vascular channel exceeding 3 mm in diameter is a specific sign of portal

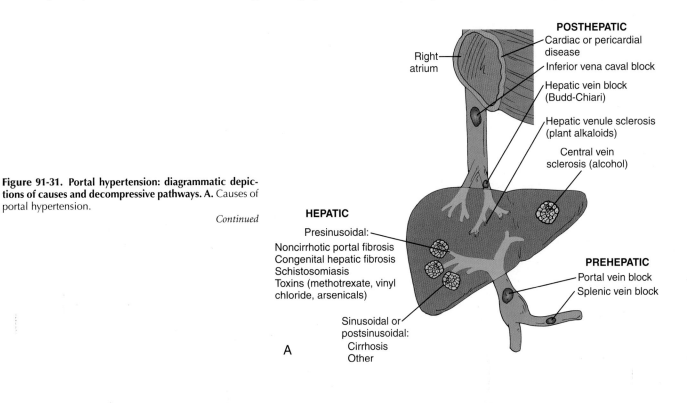

Figure 91-31. Portal hypertension: diagrammatic depictions of causes and decompressive pathways. A. Causes of portal hypertension.

Continued

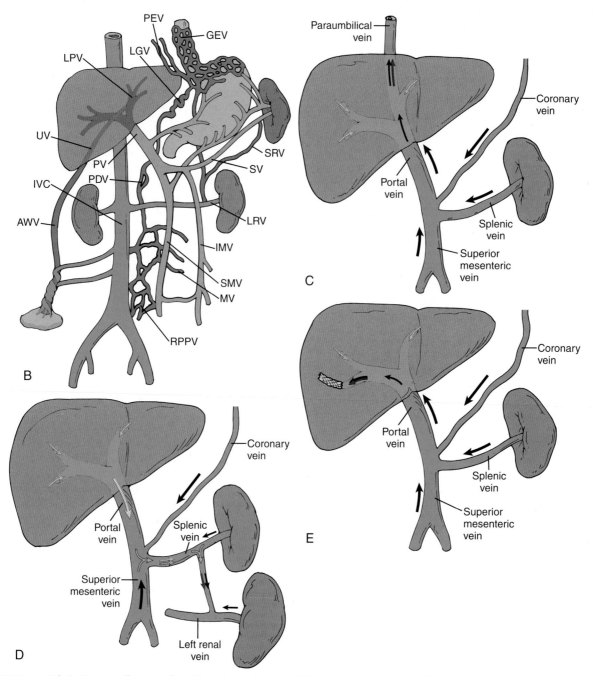

Figure 91-31, cont'd. B. Drawing illustrates the collateral vessels in portal hypertension. *awv*, abdominal wall vein; *gev*, gastroesophageal vein; *imv*, inferior mesenteric vein; *ivc*, inferior vena cava; *lgv*, left gastric vein; *lpv*, left portal vein; *lrv*, left renal vein; *mv*, mesenteric vein; *pdv*, pancreatico-duodenal vein; *pev*, paraesophageal vein; *pv*, portal vein; *rppv*, retroperitoneal-paravertebral vein; *smv*, superior mesenteric vein; *srv*, splenorenal vein; *sv*, splenic vein; *uv*, umbilical vein. **C.** Prominent paraumbilical vein in a patient with cirrhosis. Diagram shows a large paraumbilical vein associated with hepatopetal flow in the main portal vein but hepatofugal flow (*striped red arrows*) in intrahepatic portal vein branches. Both splanchnic venous blood (*blue arrows*) and hepatic artery blood are shunted to the systemic venous circulation via the paraumbilical vein. Despite hepatopetal flow in the portal vein, the hepatic parenchyma is not perfused by splanchnic venous blood because portal venous inflow is completely shunted to the paraumbilical vein. *Solid red arrow,* hepatic artery blood shunted via the paraumbilical vein. **D.** Splenorenal shunt. Diagram shows diffuse intrahepatic arterioportal shunting that drains via a portosystemic connection between the splenic and left renal veins. Note the hepatofugal flow (*striped red arrows*) in intrahepatic portal vein branches, the main portal vein, and the retropancreatic segment of the splenic vein. Superior mesenteric vein flow is also shunted via this pathway (*striped blue arrow*). Note that both hepatic artery flow and splanchnic venous flow are shunted to the systemic circulation via the splenorenal pathway, whereas only splanchnic venous blood is shunted via this pathway as shown here. *Green arrows,* sites of flow diversion; *solid blue arrows,* normally directed venous flow; *solid red arrow,* hepatic artery flow shunted via the splenorenal pathway. **E.** TIPS in a patient with cirrhosis. Diagram shows hepatofugal flow in intrahepatic portal veins (*striped red arrows*) and hepatopetal flow in the main portal vein. Note the similarity to the hemodynamics seen with a large paraumbilical vein. *Blue arrows,* splanchnic venous blood; *solid red arrow,* hepatic artery blood shunted via a TIPS. (**A** reprinted from Losowsky MS: The physician's viewpoint. In Herlinger H, Lunderquist A, Wallace S [eds]: Clinical Radiology of the Liver. Part B. New York: Marcel Dekker, 1983, pp 581-594, by courtesy of Marcel Dekker, Inc.; **B** from Kang HK, Jeong YY, Choi JH, et al: Three-dimensional multi-detector row CT portal venography in the evaluation of portosystemic collateral vessels in liver cirrhosis. RadioGraphics 22:1053-1061, 2002; **C, D,** and **E** from Wachsberg RH, Bahramipour P, Sofocleous CT, et al: Hepatofugal flow in the portal venous system: Pathophysiology, imaging findings, and diagnostic pitfalls. RadioGraphics 22:123-140, 2002.)

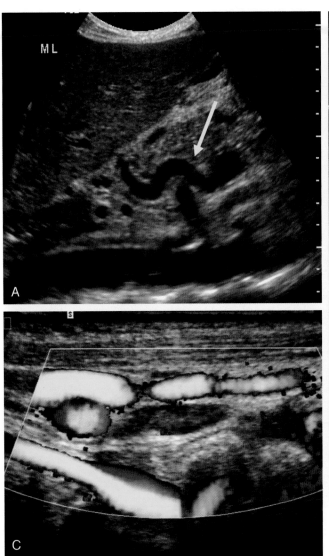

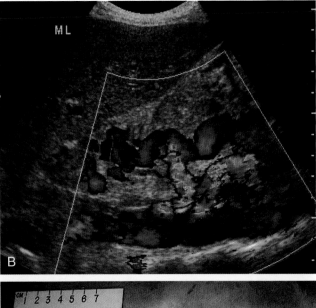

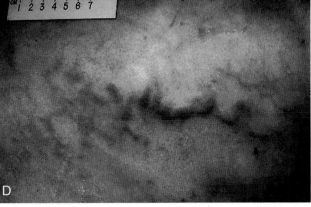

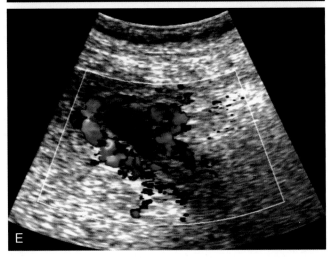

Figure 91-32. Portal hypertension: sonographic features. Coronal gray-scale (**A**) and Doppler images (**B**) obtained through the lesser omentum demonstrate varices (*arrow*) involving the coronary veins. **C.** Longitudinal color flow Doppler scan of the upper abdomen shows multiple collateral vessels. **D.** Caput medusae due to collateral vessels in the anterior abdominal wall in a patient with cirrhosis and portal hypertension. **E.** Color flow Doppler image shows multiple varices surrounding the gallbladder.

Continued

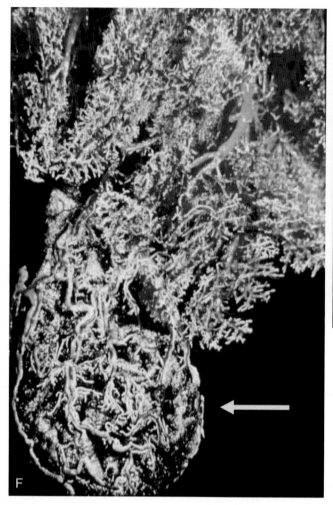

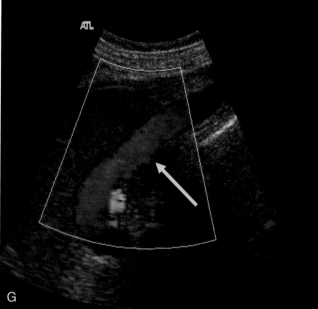

Figure 91-32, *cont'd*. F. Autopsy specimen showing multiple varices surrounding the gallbladder (*arrow*) and on the liver capsule. **G.** Sagittal color Doppler sonogram showing recanalization of the umbilical vein (*arrow*). (**A, B,** and **F** courtesy of Peter Cooperberg, MD, Vancouver, British Columbia, Canada.)

hypertension. On longitudinal scans, these recanalized para-umbilical veins can be followed caudally toward the umbilicus as a tubular lucency. A patent umbilical vein excludes an extrahepatic cause of portal hypertension because the umbilical vein arises from the intrahepatic portion of the left portal vein. This vein enables the formation of an anastomosis between the left branch of the portal vein and the veins of the anterior abdominal wall, creating a portal-systemic bypass circuit known as the *Cruveilhier-Baumgarten syndrome*. The vein may sometimes become aneurysmally dilated and simulate a pancreatic pseudocyst, so Doppler scanning of cystic structures in patients with cirrhosis should be done before biopsy. Doppler sonography can also be used to assess the hemodynamic significance of flow in the paraumbilical vein. When hepatofugal flow in the umbilical vein exceeds hepatopetal flow in the portal vein, patients are less likely to have esophageal varices and bleeding. Although it occurs more commonly in patients with severe functional impairment, it may play a protective role against variceal bleeding.[12,120,121]

The umbilical vein atrophies shortly after birth within the falciform ligament and forms the ligamentum teres. The umbilical vein, which is a three-layer structure, is obliterated in a caudal-cephalic fashion, so a short intrahepatic position may remain patent normally. The umbilicoportal junction is usually patent even in the elderly. The ductus venosus is a two-layer structure that rarely reopens because its obliteration begins on the portal side and ends at the inferior vena cava.

The inferior mesenteric vein (IMV) also dilates in patients with portal hypertension. It provides a conduit for portosystemic shunting via two major pathways: communication with the left gonadal vein and with the middle and inferior hemorrhoidal veins. The IMV is considered dilated when larger than 6 mm in diameter.

Duplex sonography and color flow Doppler sonography are extremely useful in patients with portal hypertension. Doppler provides more precise identification and characterization of vessels and flow direction than conventional sonography. It is particularly useful in patients with patent paraumbilical veins because patency of these channels can also be seen in normal patients but blood flow is hepatopetal, not heptofugal as in cirrhosis. Doppler sonography can also suggest the likelihood of a spontaneous splenorenal shunt by demonstrating hepatofugal flow and dilated splenic and renal veins. With increasingly severe cirrhosis, the hepatic veins lose their normal triphasic signature and first show lower oscillations without the reversed phase and then a completely flat waveform. This development is explained by the fact that the liver loses its compliance in cirrhosis, so it does not accommodate reverse caval flow during the cardiac cycle.[12,120,121]

Other changes in the splanchnic circulation in cirrhosis and portal hypertension can also be observed with Doppler ultrasound. Superior mesenteric, splenic, and portal venous flows are significantly increased in patients with chronic cirrhosis. This is a result of increased portal inflow in cirrhosis because of a hyperdynamic circulatory state in the splanchnic circulation of the intestine and spleen in patients with portal hypertension. Not surprisingly, splenic and superior mesenteric artery blood flow also significantly increases in patients with cirrhosis compared with normal subjects and patients with chronic hepatitis. The resistive index of hepatic arterial flow is elevated (>0.78) in patients with hepatic fibrosis and portal hypertension. Although specific for a large portal pressure gradient, the resistive index is not sensitive. Portal venous velocity is diminished in cirrhotic patients with (7.1 ± 2.3 cm/s) and without (12.0 ± 3.4 cm/s) spontaneous splenorenal shunts compared with normal subjects (16.5 ± 4.9 cm/s).[12,120,121]

The lesser omentum contains the left gastric vein and artery, lymphatics, nerves, and fatty tissue. In children with portal hypertension, its thickness on longitudinal scans increases. Measured in the longitudinal plane between the celiac axis origin and the inferior hepatic surface, the ratio of the lesser omental thickness and the anterior-posterior diameter of the aorta should not exceed 1.7. If it does, portal hypertension should be suggested except in obese patients or those with lymphadenopathy.[12,120,121]

Ultrasound cannot replace endoscopy in the diagnosis and treatment of varices, but it should be used as a screening method to identify people at risk and certainly before surgery or percutaneous procedures that may traverse these superficial varices.

Duplex Doppler sonography should be the initial screening examination in patients with shunts who present with new or recurring variceal bleeding or increasing ascites when there is a question of shunt patency. It is also ideal for routine serial follow-up. Color Doppler sonography is a superb means of guiding transjugular intrahepatic portosystemic shunt (TIPS) procedures.[12,120,121]

Sonographically, there is a correlation between hepatic venous pressure gradient and renovascular impedance. High renovascular impedance as evidenced by elevated pulsatility and resistive indices, indicates renal vasoconstriction which in turn indicates severe portal hypertension.[109]

The normal hepatic vein waveform (see Fig. 91-26) is triphasic because of central venous pressure variations that occur in the cardiac cycle. In patients with cirrhosis and portal hypertension, the waveforms become biphasic and ultimately monophasic. Monophasic waveforms are associated with severe portal hypertension with a sensitivity of 74% and specificity of 95%.[110]

Computed Tomography: Portal Hypertension

CT (Fig. 91-33) is also excellent in demonstrating portal hypertension with its attendant varices, splenomegaly, and ascites. On CT scans, portosystemic collaterals appear as tortuous, tubular, or round soft tissue masses that may be mistaken for lymph nodes on noncontrast scans. Enhancement after intravenous contrast agent administration confirms their vascular origin. By demonstrating selective vessel collateralization, CT also has the ability to diagnose and differentiate their cause. Whereas short gastric and coronary collateral vessels are seen in both portal hypertension and splenic vein occlusion, enlargement of the gastroepiploic vein is seen only in splenic vein occlusion and recanalization of umbilical veins only in portal hypertension.[122-135]

Esophageal and gastric varices can be inferred from CT scans when marked enhancement is seen in association with mural thickening. Varices can also create intraluminal esophageal protrusions, giving a scalloped appearance. Liver MDCT is useful for grading esophageal varices as well. It appears

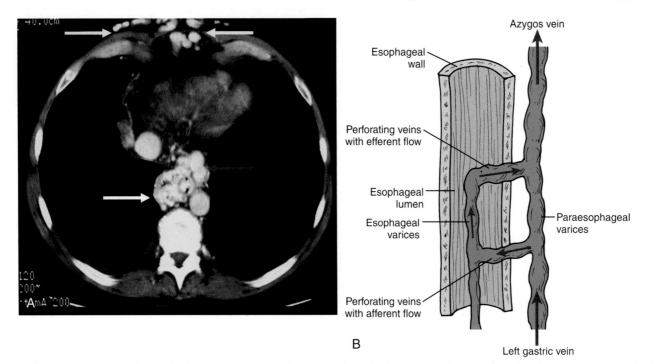

Figure 91-33. Portal hypertension: CT features. A. Axial CT scan showing esophageal (*white arrow*) and paraesophageal (*red arrow*) varices. Superficial collateral vessels are also present (*yellow arrows*). **B.** Diagram shows connections between esophageal and paraesophageal varices via perforating veins with afferent or efferent blood flow. Paraesophageal varices are formed by union of groups of dilated perforating veins, and varices connect with left gastric veins inferiorly and with azygos vein superiorly. Throughout their length, esophageal varices form connections with paraesophageal varices via perforating veins.

Continued

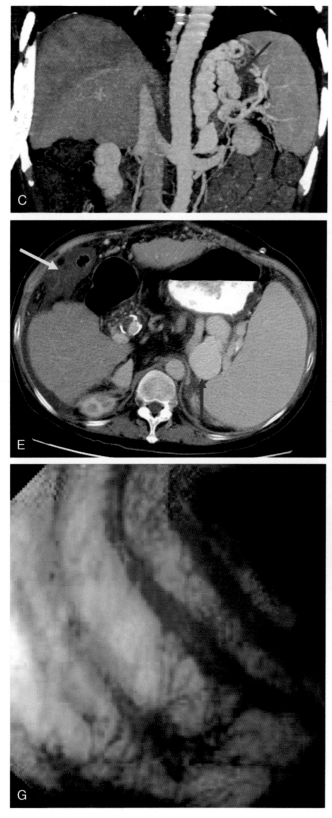

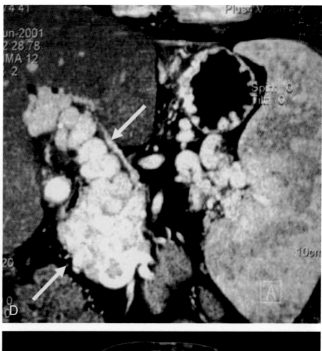

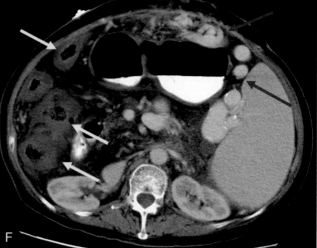

Figure 91-33, cont'd. C. Coronal reformatted multidetector CT (MDCT) image shows short gastric and perigastric varices (*arrow*). **D.** Cavernous transformation of the portal vein (*arrows*) is identified in this patient with portal vein thrombosis, hepatic steatosis, and splenomegaly. Note also the gastric wall varices. In the following patient, CT demonstrates colonic disease associated with cirrhosis and portal hypertension. **E.** There is mural thickening of the hepatic flexure of the colon (*yellow arrow*) in this patient with cirrhosis and portal hypertension. Note the atrophic right lobe, splenomegaly, calcified splenic artery aneurysm (*red arrow*), hepatic artery aneurysm. **F.** Scan obtained caudal to **E** shows mural thickening of the right colon (*yellow arrows*); the left colon (not shown) was uninvolved. Note the perisplenic and gastrocolic ligament varices (*red arrows*). **G.** Colonoscopy shows edematous and friable mucosa in a patient with portal hypertension–related colitis. (**B** from Matsuo M, Kanematsu M, Kim T, et al: Esophageal varices: Diagnosis with gadolinium enhanced MR imaging of the liver for patients with chronic liver damage. AJR 180:461-466, 2003. Reprinted with permission from the American Journal of Roentgenology; **C** and **D** courtesy of Elliot Fishman, MD, Baltimore, MD.)

that a diameter of 3 mm for the varix is useful in identifying high-risk patients who benefit most from endoscopy and prophylactic therapy.[126]

Although duplex Doppler sonography can provide information concerning variceal flow and direction, CT still offers a number of imaging advantages. It is superior in demonstrating retroperitoneal varices and in depicting azygos, hemiazygos, pericardial, and periesophageal varices that can simulate mediastinal masses.[122-135]

Hepatofugal portal venous flow in patients with cirrhosis indicates the presence of advanced portal hypertension placing the patient at increased risk for hepatic dysfunction, hepatic encephalopathy, variceal bleeding, and poorer response of the varices to endoscopic ligation when compared to cirrhotic patients with hepatopetal flow.[133]

The presence of hepatofugal flow in the main portal vein implies that the liver is being almost exclusively supplied by the hepatic artery. This has important prognostic and therapeutic implications in planning chemoembolization of tumors or placement of a transjugular intrahepatic portosystemic shunt (TIPS). A portal vein diameter less than 1 cm in the presence of cirrhosis is a highly specific but less sensitive sign of hepatofugal portal venous flow in cirrhotic patients.

The splenic index is a good indicator of the severity of esophageal varices and hepatic functional reserve in cirrhotic patients. A splenic index (= length × height × width of spleen) greater than 963 cc is a good indicatory of the presence of esophageal varices at risk for bleeding.[134]

Thickening of the all of the small bowel and colon are common in patients with cirrhosis due to the presence of portal hypertension and low protein states. There is, however, a specific right-sided colitis (see Fig. 91-33) that can develop due specifically to the portal hypertension. The increased pressure within the superior mesenteric vein leads to the release of a number of inflammatory mediators including interleukin-1 and nitrous oxide. This can lead to a colitis that simulates inflammatory bowel disease. Vascular ectasias that have a propensity to bleed may also develop. The presence of this right-sided colitis is associated with an increased risk of spontaneous bacterial peritonitis as bacteria more readily translocate through the diseased colonic wall.

Of course the imaging differential diagnosis of the submucosal edema includes inflammatory bowel disease, ischemic, and infections including pseudomembranous colitis.

Magnetic Resonance Imaging: Portal Hypertension

MR imaging (Fig. 91-34) is uniquely suited for the depiction of large vascular collaterals because of the natural contrast between flowing blood and surrounding soft tissues. The most successful MR imaging techniques for delineating abdominal blood vessels are MR angiographic techniques that can be used with or without gadolinium injection. Collateral pathways are demonstrated as tortuous structures of high signal intensity on MR angiograms. Direct sagittal scans are particularly useful for imaging the paraumbilical vein, and coronal scans are helpful for esophageal and mesenteric varices.[25,136,137]

Nodules in the Cirrhotic Liver

The cirrhotic liver is defined by the presence of both nodules and fibrosis. A spectrum of nodules (see Figs. 91-29 and 91-30) ranging from benign regenerative nodules to hepatocellular carcinoma can be visualized on pathology and cross-sectional imaging.[138-148]

Regenerative nodules, while present pathologically in all cirrhotic livers are visualized on MDCT in only approximately 25% of patients. These are seen best on unenhanced scans due to their high iron content. On MR imaging, which visualizes hyperplastic nodules in about 50% of patients, these nodules are hypointense on T2 and gradient-echo T1 images. They occasionally can appear hyperintense on T1-weighted images.[138-148]

Dysplastic nodules are felt to be an evolutionay process from a dominant large regenerating nodules associated with increased iron content. On CT these lesions can manifest as masses of high attenuation on unenhanced scans. On MR imaging, these lesions are brightly hyperintense on T1-weighted images and hypointense to liver on T2-weighted images, although a wide variety of signal intensity combinations have been reported.[138-148]

With malignant transformation of dysplastic nodules, signal intensity changes can be seen on MR imaging. The malignant foci within the larger dysplastic nodule produce a low signal intensity on T1-weighted images surrounded by the high intensity dysplastic nodule. On T2-weighted images, the malignant focus has high signal intensity surrounded by the larger hypointense dysplastic nodule. The malignant portions of the nodule may show marked contrast enhancement.[138-148]

At the time of transplantation, approximately 20% of patients with hepatitis B or C and 10% of patients with alcohol-induced cirrhosis will harbor a hepatocellular carcinoma. For detection, noncontrast, arterial-phase, venous-phase, and delayed-phase imaging following the administration of a large bolus of contrast is important. Even with optimum technique, some 35% to 40% of lesions will not be detected.[138-148]

The cirrhotic liver also demonstrates pseudotumors such as focal confluent fibrosis, which is discussed early as will as arterioportal shunts, small arteriovenous malformations, and hemangiomas.[138-148]

Transjugular Intrahepatic Portosystemic Shunt

The transjugular intrahepatic portosystemic shunt (TIPS) has become the mainstay of nonsurgical treatment of portal hypertension due to cirrhosis. This procedure is discussed in detail in Chapter 129. The goal of this procedure is to reduce portal vein–hepatic vein gradient to 12 mm Hg or less. Doppler ultrasound, CT, and MR imaging can be used to assess patency of the TIPS[149-151] (Fig. 91-35).

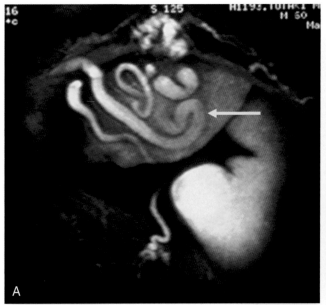

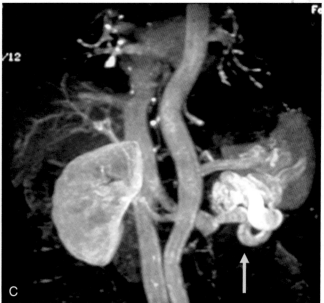

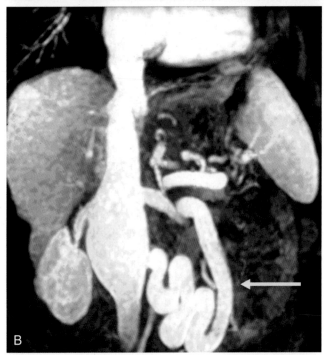

Figure 91-34. Portal hypertension: MR features. A. Superficial collateral vessels are identified in this patient with Cruveilhier-Baumgarten syndrome. **B.** Left gonadal vein varix (*arrow*). **C.** Spontaneous splenorenal shunt (*arrow*). (**A, B,** and **C** courtesy of Drs. Hiroki Haradome and Tomoaki Ichikawa, Yamanishi, Japan.)

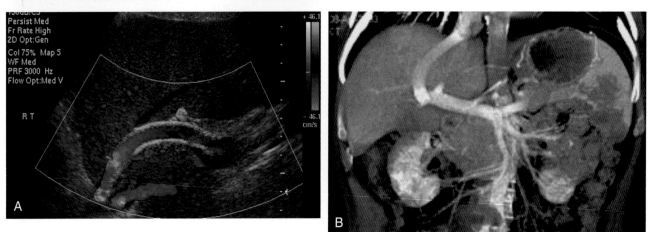

Figure 91-35. TIPS: cross-sectional imaging findings. A. Color flow Doppler image shows patency of the TIPS. **B.** Coronal reformatted MDCT image shows a patent TIPS stent (*arrow*).

References

1. Friedman SL, Rockey DC, Bissell DM: Hepatic fibrosis 2006: Report of the third AASLD Single Topic Conference. Hepatology 45:242-249, 2007.
2. Lamps LW, Washington K: Acute and chronic hepatitis. In Odze RD, Goldblum JR, Crawford JM (eds): Surgical Pathology of the GI Tract, Liver, Biliary Tract, and Pancreas. Philadelphia, Saunders, 2004, pp 863-885.
3. Stolz A: Liver physiology and metabolic function. In Feldman M, Friedman LS, Sleisenger MH (eds): Gastrointestinal and Liver Disease, 7th ed. Philadelphia, Saunders, 2002, pp 1202-1226.
4. Saxena R, Zucker SD, Crawford JM: Anatomy and physiology of the liver. In Zakim D, Boyer TD (eds): Hepatology: A Textbook of Liver Disease. Philadelphia, Saunders, 2003, pp 3-31.
5. Moscatiello S, Manini R, Marchesini G: Diabetes and liver disease: An ominous association. Nutr Metab Cardiovasc Dis 17:63-70, 2007.
6. Day CP: From fat to inflammation. Gastroenterology 130:207-210, 2006.
7. Hubscher SG: Histological assessment of non-alcoholic fatty liver disease. Histopathology 49:450-465, 2006.
8. Guha IN, Parkes J, Roderick PR, et al: Non-invasive markers associated with liver fibrosis in non-alcoholic fatty liver disease. Gut 55:1650-1660, 2006.
9. Adams LA, Lymp JF, St. Sauver J, et al: The natural history of nonalcoholic fatty liver disease: A population-based cohort study. Gastroenterology 129:113-121, 2005.
10. Miyake K, Hayakawa K, Nishino M, et al: Effects of oral 5-flourouracil drugs on hepatic fat content in patients with colon cancer. Acad Radiol 12:722-727, 2005.
11. Hamer OW, Aguirre DA, Casola G, et al: Imaging features of perivascular fatty infiltration of the liver: Initial observations. Radiology 237:159-169, 2005.
12. Wilson SR, Withers CE: The liver. In Rumack C, Wilson SR, Charboneau WR, et al (eds): Diagnostic Ultrasound, 3rd edition. Philadelphia, Elsevier-Mosby, 2005.
13. Oliva MR, Mortele KJ, Segatto E, et al: Computed tomography features of nonalcoholic steatohepatitis with histopathologic correlation. J Comput Assist Tomogr 30:37-46, 2006.
14. Cobbold JF, Wylezinska M, Cunningham C, et al: Non-invasive evaluation of hepatic fibrosis using magnetic resonance imaging and ultrasound techniques. Gut 55:1670-1672, 2006.
15. Tchelepi H, Ralls PW, Radin R, et al: Sonography of diffuse liver disease. J Ultrasound Med 21:1023-1032, 2002.
16. Park SH, Kim PN, Kim KW, et al: Macrovesicular hepatic steatosis in living liver donors: Use of CT for quantitative and qualitative assessment. Radiology 239:105-112, 2006.
17. Merkle EM, Nelson RC: Dual gradient-echo in-phase and opposed-phase hepatic MR imaging: A useful tool for evaluating more than fatty infiltration or fatty sparing. RadioGraphics 26:1409-1418, 2006.
18. Hamer OW, Aguiree DA, Casola G, et al: Fatty liver: Imaging patterns and pitfalls. RadioGraphics 26:1637-1653, 2006.
19. Hussain HK, Chenervert TL, Londy FJ, et al: Hepatic fat fraction: MR imaging for quantitative measurement and display: Early experience. Radiology 237:1048-1055, 2005.
20. Kim SH, Lee JM, Han JK, et al: Hepatic macrosteatosis. Radiology 240:116-129, 2006.
21. Khalili K, Lan FP, Hanbridge AE, et al: Hepatic subcapsular steatosis in response to intraperiotneal insulin delivery: CT findings and prevalence. AJR 180:1601-1604, 2003.
22. Hoofnagle JH, Heller T: Hepatitis C. In Zakim D, Boyer TD (eds): Hepatology: A Textbook of Liver Disease. Philadelphia, Saunders, 2003, pp 3-31.
23. Thimme R, Spangenberg HC, Blum HE: Acute viral hepatitis. In Weinstein WM, Hawkey CJ, Bosch J (eds): Clinical Gastroenterology and Hepatology. Philadelphia, Elsevier-Mosby, 2005, pp 583-594.
24. Yee HF, Lidofsy SD: Acute liver failure. In Feldman M, Friedman LS, Sleisenger MH (eds): Gastrointestinal and Liver Disease, 7th ed. Philadelphia, Saunders, 2002, pp 1202-1226.
25. Semelka RC, Braga L, Armao D: Liver. In Semelka RC (ed): Abdominal-Pelvic MRI. New York, Wiley-Liss, 2002, pp 33-318.
26. Danet I-M, Semelka RC, Braga L: MR imaging in diffuse liver disease. Radiol Clin N Am 41:67-87, 2003.
27. Martin DR, Semelka RC: Magnetic resonance imaging of the liver: Review of techniques and approach to common diseases. Semin Ultrasound CT MRI 26:116-131, 2005.
28. Lee V: Can MR imaging replace liver biopsy for the diagnosis of early fibrosis? Radiology 239:309-310, 2006.
29. Ly JN, Miller FH: Periportal contrast enhancement and abnormal signal intensity on state-of-the-art MR images. AJR 176:891-897, 2001.
30. Russmann S, Reichen J: Drug-induced and toxic liver disease. In Weinstein WM, Hawkey CJ, Bosch J (eds): Clinical Gastroenterology and Hepatology. Philadelphia, Elsevier-Mosby, 2005, pp 677-686.
31. Mookerjee RP, Jalan R: Alcohlic liver disease. In Weinstein WM, Hawkey CJ, Bosch J (eds): Clinical Gastroenterology and Hepatology. Philadelphia, Elsevier-Mosby, 2005, pp 637-646.
32. Farrell GC: Liver disease caused by drugs, anesthetics, and toxins. In Feldman M, Friedman LS, Sleisenger MH (eds): Gastrointestinal and Liver Disease, 7th ed. Philadelphia, Saunders, 2002, pp 1403-1447.
33. Maher JJ: Alchoholic liver disease. In Feldman M, Friedman LS, Sleisenger MH (eds): Gastrointestinal and Liver Disease, 7th ed. Philadelphia, Saunders, 2002, pp 1375-1386.
34. Lee WM: Drug-induced hepatotoxicity. N Engl J Med 349:474-484, 2003.
35. Colli A, Massironi S, Faccioli P, et al: "Pseudotumoral" hepatic areas in actue alcoholic hepatitis: A computed tomography and histological study. Am J Gastroenterol 100:831-836, 2005.
36. Kauffman JM, Grace ND: Hemochromatosis. In Weinstein WM, Hawkey CJ, Bosch J (eds): Clinical Gastroenterology and Hepatology. Philadelphia, Elsevier-Mosby, 2005, pp 659-664.
37. Bacon B, Britton RS: Hereditary hemochromatosis. In Feldman M, Friedman LS, Sleisenger MH (eds): Gastrointestinal and Liver Disease, 7th ed. Philadelphia, Saunders, 2002, pp 1261-1268.
38. Tavill AS, Bacon DR: Hemochromatosis and iron overload syndromes. In Zakim D, Boyer TD (eds): Hepatology: A Textbook of Liver Disease. Philadelphia, Saunders, 2003, pp 3-31.
39. Kowdley KV: Iron, hemochromatosis, and hepatocellular carcinoma. Gastroenterology 127:S79-S86, 2004.
40. Sharma N, Butterworth J, Cooper BT, et al: The emerging role of the liver in iron metabolism. Am J Gastroenterol 100:201-206, 2005.
41. Ben Salem D, Cercueil J-P, Ricolfi F, et al: Erythropoietic hemochromatosis. Radiology 233:116-119, 2004.
42. Alustiza JM, Artetxe J, Agirre A, et al: MR quantification of hepatic iron concentration. Radiology 230:479-484, 2004.
43. Mieli-Vergani G, Thompston R: Genetic and metabolic liver disease. In Weinstein WM, Hawkey CJ, Bosch J (eds): Clinical Gastroenterology and Hepatology. Philadelphia, Elsevier-Mosby, 2005, pp 687-692.
44. Thiele DL: Hepatic manifestations of systemic disease and other disorders of the liver. In Feldman M, Friedman LS, Sleisenger MH (eds): Gastrointestinal and Liver Disease, 7th ed. Philadelphia, Saunders, 2002, pp 1603-1619.
45. Maineti PP, D'Agostino L, Socia E, et al: Hepatic and splenic amyloidosis: dual-phase spiral CT findings. Abdom Imaging 28:688-690, 2003.
46. Palladini G, Perfetti V, Merlini G: Therapy and management of systemic (primary) amyloidosis. Swiss Med Wkly 136:715-720, 2006.
47. Monzawa S, Tsukamoto T, Omata K, et al: A case of primary amyloidosis of the liver and spleen: Radiologic findings. Eur J Radiol 41:237-241, 2002.
48. Georgiades CS, Neyman EG, Fishman EK: Cross-sectional imaging of amyloidosis: An organ system based approach. J Comput Assis Tomogr 26:1035-1041, 2002.
49. Gitlin JD: Wilson's disease. In Zakim D, Boyer TD (eds): Hepatology: A Textbook of Liver Disease. Philadelphia, Saunders, 2003, pp 1273-1288.
50. Ferenci P: Wilson's disease. Clin Gastroenterol Hepatol 3:726-733, 2005.
51. Medici V, Trevisan CP, D'Inca R, et al: Diagnosis and management of Wilson's disease: Results of a single center experience. J Clin Gastroenterol 40:936-941, 2006.
52. Mehta A: Epidemiology and natural history of Gaucher's disease. Eur J Intern Med 17(Suppl):S2-S5, 2006.
53. Ferenci P: Wilson's disease. Clin Gastroenterol Hepatol 3:726-733, 2005.
54. Bean MJ, Horton KM, Fishman EK: Concurrent focal hepatic and splenic lesions: A pictorial guide to differential diagnosis. J Comput Assist Tomogr 28:605-612, 2004.
55. Akpinar E, Akhan O: Liver imaging findings of Wilson's disease. Eur J Radiol Dec 7, 2006 (Epub ahead of print).
56. Chu WCW, Leung TF, Chan KF, et al: Wilson's disease with chronic active hepatitis: Monitoring by in vivo 31-phosphorus MR spectroscopy before and after medical treatment. AJR 183:1339-1342, 2004.
57. Kozic D, Svetel M, Petrovic I, et al: Regression of nodular liver lesions in Wilson's disease. Acta Radiol 47:624-627, 2006.

58. Poll LW, Koch JA, vom Dahl S, et al: Extraosseous manifestation of Gaucher's disease type I: MR and histological appearance. Eur Radiol 10:1660-1663, 2000.

59. Niederau C, Haussinger D: Gaucher's disease: A review for the internist and hepatologist. Hepatogastroenterology 47:984-997, 2000.

60. Karagiannidis A, Karavalaki M, Koulaouzidis A: Hepatic sarcoidosis. Ann Hepatol 5:251-256, 2006.

61. Ayyala US, Padilla ML: Diagnosis and treatment of hepatic sarcoidosis. Curr Treat Options Gastroenterol 9:475-483, 2006.

62. Koyama T, Ueda H, Togashi K, et al: Radiologic manifestations of sarcoidosis in various organs. RadioGraphics 24:87-104, 2004.

63. Warshauer DM, Lee JKT: Imaging manifestations of abdominal sarcoidosis. AJR 182:15-28, 2004.

64. Nguyen BD: F-18 FDG PET imaging of disseminated sarcoidosis. Clin Nucl Med 32:53-54, 2007.

65. Jung G, Brill N, Poll LW, et al: MRI of hepatic sarcoidosis: Large confluent lesions mimicking malignancy. AJR 183:171-173, 2004.

66. Zheng RQ, Zhang B, Kudo M, et al: Imaging findings of biliary hamartomas. World J Gastroenterol 11:6354-6359, 2005.

67. Mortele B, Mortele K, Seynaeve P, et al: Hepatic bile duct hamartomas (von Meyenburg complexes): MR and MR cholangiography findings. J Comput Assist Tomogr 26:438-443, 2002.

68. Lev-Toaff AS, Bach AM, Wechsler RJ, et al: The radiologic and pathologic spectrum of biliary hamartomas. AJR 165:309-313, 1995.

69. Krause D, Cercueil JP, Dranssart M, et al: MRI for evaluating congenital bile duct abnormalities. J Comput Assist Tomogr 26:541-552, 2002.

70. Mortele KJ, Ros PR: Cystic focal liver lesions in the adult: Differential CT and MR imaging features. RadioGraphics 21:895-910, 2001.

71. Brancatelli G, Federle MP, Vilgrain V, et al: Fibropolycystic liver disease: CT and MR imaging findings. RadioGraphics 25:659-670, 2005.

72. Talwalkar J, Lindor KD: Primary biliary cirrhosis. In Zakim D, Boyer TD (eds): Hepatology: A Textbook of Liver Disease. Philadelphia, Saunders, 2003, pp 3-31.

73. Angulo P, Lindor KD: Primary biliary cirrhosis. In Feldman M, Friedman LS, Sleisenger MH (eds): Gastrointestinal and Liver Disease, 7th ed. Philadelphia, Saunders, 2002, pp 1474-1486.

74. Neuberger J: Primary biliary cirrhosis. In Weinstein WM, Hawkey CJ, Bosch J (eds): Clinical Gastroenterology and Hepatology. Philadelphia, Elsevier-Mosby, 2005, pp 659-664.

75. Batts KP: Autoimmune and cholestatic disorders of the liver. In Odze RD, Goldblum JR, Crawford JM (eds): Surgical Pathology of the GI Tract, Liver, Biliary Tract, and Pancreas. Philadelphia, Saunders, 2004, pp 863-885.

76. Jacob DA, Neumann UP, Bahra M, et al: Long-term follow-up after recurrence of primary biliary cirrhosis after liver transplantation in 100 patients. Clin Transplant 20:211-220, 2006.

77. Khettry U, Anand N, Faul PN, et al: Liver transplantation for primary biliary cirrhosis: A long-term pathologic study. Liver Transpl 9:87-96, 2006.

78. Wenzel JS, Donohue A, Ford KL, et al: Primary biliary cirrhosis: MR imaging findings and description of MR imaging periportal halo sign. AJR 176:885-889, 2001.

79. Blachar A, Federle MP, Brancatelli G: Primary biliary cirrhosis: Clinical, pathologic, and helical CT findings in 53 patients. Radiology 220:329-336, 2001.

80. Mendes FD, Lindor KD: Primary sclerosing cholangitis. In Weinstein WM, Hawkey CJ, Bosch J (eds): Clinical Gastroenterology and Hepatology. Philadelphia, Elsevier-Mosby, 2005, pp 659-664.

81. Mahadevan U, Bass NM: Sclerosing cholangitis and recurrent pyogenic cholangitis. In Feldman M, Friedman LS, Sleisenger MH (eds): Gastrointestinal and Liver Disease, 7th ed. Philadelphia, Saunders, 2002, pp 1131-1152.

82. Jessurun J, Pambuccian S: Infectious and inflammatory disorders of the gallbladder and extrahepatic biliary tract. In Odze RD, Goldblum JR, Crawford JM (eds): Surgical Pathology of the GI Tract, Liver, Biliary Tract, and Pancreas. Philadelphia, Saunders, 2004, pp 863-885.

83. Dodd GD 3rd, Baron RL, Oliver JH 3rd, et al: End-stage primary sclerosing cholangitis: CT findings of hepatic morphology in 36 patients. Radiology 211:357-362, 1999.

84. Elsayes KM, Oliveira EP, Narra VR, et al: MR and MRCP in the evaluation of primary sclerosing cholangitis: Current applications and imaging findings. J Comput Assist Tomogr 30:398-404, 2006.

85. Berstad AE, Aabakken L, Smith HJ, et al: Diagnostic accuracy of magnetic resonance and endoscopic retrograde cholangiography in primary sclerosing cholangitis. Clin Gastroenterol Hepatol 4:514-520, 2006.

86. Dusunceli E, Erden A, Erden I, et al: Primary sclerosing cholangitis: MR cholangiopancreatography and T2-weighted MR imaging findings. Diagn Interv Radiol 11:213-218, 2005.

87. Bader TR, Beavers KL, Semelka RC: MR imaging features of primary sclerosing cholangitis: Patterns of cirrhosis in relationship to clinical severity of disease. Radiology 226:675-685, 2003.

88. Revelon G, Rashid A, Kawamoto S, et al: Primary sclerosing cholangitis: MR imaging findings with pathologic correlation. AJR 173:1037-1042, 1999.

89. Johnson KJ, Olliff JF, Olliff SP: The presence and significance of lymphadenopathy detected by CT in primary sclerosing cholangitis. Br J Radiol 71:1279-1282, 1998.

90. Bader TR, Beavers KL, Semelka RC: MR imaging features of primary sclerosing cholangitis: Patterns of cirrhosis in relationship to clinical severity of disease. Radiology 226:675-685, 2003.

91. Carucci LR, Halvorsen RA: Abdominal and pelvic CT in HIV-positive population. Abdom Imaging 29:631-642, 2004.

92. D'Amico G, Malizia G: Cirrhosis of the liver. In Weinstein WM, Hawkey CJ, Bosch J (eds): Clinical Gastroenterology and Hepatology. Philadelphia, Elsevier-Mosby, 2005, pp 699-706.

93. Bass NM, Yao FY: Portal hypertension and variceal bleeding. In Feldman M, Friedman LS, Sleisenger MH (eds): Gastrointestinal and Liver Disease, 7th ed. Philadelphia, Saunders, 2002, pp 1487-1516.

94. Wanless IR, Crawford JM: Cirrhosis. In Odze RD, Goldblum JR, Crawford JM (eds): Surgical Pathology of the GI Tract, Liver, Biliary Tract, and Pancreas. Philadelphia, Saunders, 2004, pp 863-885.

95. Van Beers BE, Leconte I, Materne R, et al: Hepatic perfusion parameters in chronic liver disease. AJR 176:667-673, 2001.

96. Kim M, Mitchell DG, Ito K: Portosystemic collaterals of the upper abdomen: Review of anatomy and demonstration on MR imaging. Abdom Imaging 25:462-470, 2006.

97. Colli A, Fraquelli M, Andreoletti M, et al: Severe liver fibrosis or cirrhosis: Accuracy of US for detection: Analysis of 300 cases. Radiology 227:89-94, 2003.

98. Nishura T, Watanabe H, Ito M, et al: Ultrasound evaluation of the fibrosis stage in chronic liver disease by the simultaneous use of low and high frequency probes. Br J Radiol 78:189-197, 2005.

99. Caturelli E, Castellano L, Fusilli S, et al: Coarse nodular US pattern in hepatic cirrhosis: Risk for hepatocellular carcinoma. Radiology 226:691-697, 2003.

100. Nicolau C, Bianchi L, Vilana R: Grey-scale ultrasound in hepatic cirrhosis and chronic hepatitis: Diagnosis, screening, and intervention. Semin Ultrasound CT MRI 23:3-18, 2002.

101. Martinez-Noguera A, Montserrat E, Torrubia S, et al: Doppler in hepatic cirrhosis and chronic hepatitis. Semin Ultrasound CT MRI 23:19-36, 2002.

102. Lafortune M, Matricardi L, Denys A, et al : Segment 4 (the quadrate lobe): A barometer of cirrhotic liver disease. Radiology 206:157-160, 1998.

103. Lim AKP, Patel N, Eckersley RJ, et al: Can Doppler sonography grade the severity of hepatitis C-related liver disease? AJR 184:1848-1853, 2005.

104. Awaya H, Mitchell DG, Kamishima T, et al: Cirrhosis: Modified caudate-right lobe ratio. Radiology 224:769-774, 2002.

105. Valls C, Andia E, Roca Y, et al: CT in hepatic cirrhosis and chronic hepatitis. Semin Ultrasound CT MRI 23:37-91, 2002.

106. Gibo M, Murata S, Kuroki S: Pericaval fat collection mimicking an intracaval lesion on CT in patients with chronic liver disease. Abdom Imaging 26:492-495, 2001.

107. Nakagawa H, Toda N, Taniguchi M, et al: Prevalence and sonographic detection of Chilaiditi's sign in cirrhotic patients without ascites. AJR 187:W589-W593, 2006.

108. Ito K, Mitchell DG, Gabata T, et al: Expanded gallbladder fossa: Simple MR imaging sign of cirrhosis. Radiology 211:723-726, 1999.

109. Berzigotti A, Casadei A, Magalotti D, et al: Renovasculare impedance correlates with portal pressure in patients with cirrhosis. Radiology 240:581-586, 2006.

110. Baik SKB, Kim JW, Kim HS, et al: Recent variceal bleeding: Doppler US hepatic vein waveform in assessment of severity of portal hypertension and vasoactive drug response. Radiology 240:574-580, 2006.

111. Lipson JA, Qayyum A, Avrin DE, et al: CT and MRI of hepatic contour abnormalities. AJR 184:75-81, 2005.

112. Yang DM, Kim HS, Cho SW, et al: Various causes of hepatic capsular retraction: CT and MR findings. Br J Radiol 75:994-1002, 2002.

113. Okazaki H, Ito K, Fujita T, et al: Discrimination of alcoholic from virus-induced cirrhosis on MR imaging. AJR 175:1677-1681, 2000.

114. Carlos RC, Kin HM, Hussain HK, et al: Developing a prediction rule to assess hepatic malignancy with cirrhosis. AJR 180:893-900, 2003.

115. Vitellas KM, Tzalonikou MT, Bennett WF, et al: Cirrhosis: Spectrum of findings on unenhanced and dynamic gadolinium-enhanced MR imaging. Abdom Imaging 26:601-615, 2001.

116. Hussain HK, Syed I, Nghiem HV, et al: T2-weighted MR imaging in the assessment of the cirrhotic liver. Radiology 230:637-644, 2004.

117. Mortele KJ, Ros PR: MR imaging in chronic hepatitis and cirrhosis. Semin Ultrasound CT MRI 23:79-100, 2002.

118. Aguirre DA, Behling CA, Alpert E, et al: Liver fibrosis: Noninvasive diagnosis with double contrast material-enhance MR imaging. Radiology 239:425-437, 2006.

119. Rouviere O, Yin M, Drsner MA, et al: MR elastography of the liver: Preliminary results. Radiology 240: 440-673, 2006.

120. Wachsberg RH: Inferior mesenteric vein: Gray-scale and Doppler sonographic findings in normal subjects and in patients with portal hypertension. AJR 184:481-486, 2005.

121. Farber E, Fischer D, Eliakim R, et al: Esophageal varices: Evaluation with esophagography with barium versus endoscopic gastroduodenoscopy in patients with compensated cirrhosis. Radiology 237:535-540, 2005.

122. Kang HK, Jeong YY, Choi JH, et al: Three-dimensional multi-detector row CT portal venography in the evaluation of portosystemic collateral vessels in liver cirrhosis. RadioGraphics 22:1053-1061, 2002.

123. Groves AM, Dixon AK: Superficial collateral veins on abdominal CT: Findings in cirrhosis and systemic venous obstruction. Br J Radiol 75: 645-657, 2002.

124. Kamel IR, Liapi E, Fishman EK: Liver and biliary system: Evaluation by multidetector CT. Radiol Clin North Am 43:977-998, 2005.

125. Wachsberg RH, Bahramipour P, Sofocleous CT, et al: Hepatofugal flow in the portal venous systeme: Pathophysiology, imaging findings, and diagnostic pitfalls. RadioGraphics 22:123-140, 2002.

126. Kim YJ, Raman SS, Yu NC, et al: Esophageal varices in cirrhotic patients: Evaluation with liver CT. AJR 188:139-144, 2007.

127. Lonjedo E, Ripolles T: Vascular imaging and interventional procedures in hepatic cirrhosis. Semin Ultrasound CT MRI 23:130-140, 2002.

128. Van Beers BE, Leconte I, Materne R, et al: Hepatic perfusion parameters in chronic liver disease: Dynamic CT measurements correlated with disease severity. AJR 176:667-673, 2001.

129. Merkle EM, Gilkeson RC: Remnants of fetal circulation: Appearance on MDCT in adults. AJR 185:541-549, 2005.

130. Fritz GA, Schoellnast H, Deutshmann HA, et al: Density histogram analysis of unenhanced hepatic computed tomography in patients with diffuse liver diseases. J Comput Assist Tomogr 30:201-205, 2006.

131. Annet L, Peeters F, Horsmans Y, et al: Esophageal varices: Evaluation with transesophageal MR imaging: Initial experience. Radiology 238: 167-175, 2006.

132. Annet L, Materne R, Danse E, et al: Hepatic flow parameters measured with MR imaging and Doppler US: Correlations with the degree of cirrhosis and portal hypertension. Radiology 229:409-414, 2003.

133. Bryce TJ, Yeh BJ, Qayyum A, et al: CT signs of hepatofugal venous flow in patients with cirrhosis. AJR 181:1629-1633, 2003.

134. Watanabe S, Hosimo N, Kitade Y, et al: Assessment of the presence and severity of esophagogastric varices by splenic index in patients with liver cirrhosis. J Comput Assist Tomogr 24:788-794, 2000.

135. Kamel IR, Lawler LP, Corl FM, et al: Patterns of collateral pathways in extrahepatic portal hypertension as demonstrated by multidetector row computed tomography and advanced image processing. J Comput Assist Tomogr 28:469-477, 2004.

136. Matsuo M, Kanematsu M., Kim T, et al: Esophageal varices: Diagnosis with gadolinium enhanced MR imaging of the liver for patients with chronic liver damage. AJR 180:461-466, 2003.

137. Kim M-J, Mitchell DG, Ito K: Portosystemic collaterals of the upper abdomen: Review of anatomy and deomstration on MR imaging. Abdom Imaging 25:462-470, 2000.

138. Lim JH, Kim MJ, Park CK, et al: Dysplastic nodules in liver cirrhosis: Detection with triple phase helical dynamic CT. Br J Radiology 77: 911-916, 2004.

139. Lim JH, Choi BI: Dysplastic nodules in liver cirrhosis: Imaging. Abdom Imaging 27:117-128, 2002.

140. Krinsky G: Terminology of hepatocellular nodules in cirrhosis: Plea for consistency. Radiology 224:638-639, 2002.

141. Shimizu A, Ito K, Kioke S, et al: Cirrhosis or chronic hepatitis: Evaluation of small (≤2-cm) early-enhancing hepatic lesions with serial contrast-enhanced dynamic MR imaging. Radiology 226:550-555, 2003.

142. Jeong YY, Mitchell DG, Kamishima T: Small (<20 mm) enhancing hepatic nodules seen on arterial phase MR imaging of the cirrhotic liver: Clinical implications. AJR 178:1327-1334, 2002.

143. Yu J-S, Cho E-S, Kim K-H, et al: Newly developed hepatocellular carcinoma (HCC) in chronic liver disease: MR imaging findings before the diagnosis of HCC. J Comput Assist Tomogr 30:765-771, 2006.

144. Shinmura R, Matsui O, Kobayashi S, et al: Cirrhotic nodules: Association between MR imaging signal intensity and intranodular blood supply. Radiology 237:512-519, 2005.

145. Ito K, Shimizu A, et al: Multiarterial phase dynamic MRI of small early enhancing hepatic lesions in cirrhosis or chronic hepatitis: Differentiating between hypervascular hepatocellular carcinomas and pseudolesions. AJR 183:699-705, 2004.

146. Krinsky GA, Lee VS, Theise ND: Focal lesions in the cirrhotic liver: High resolution ex vivo MRI with pathologic correlation. J Comput Assist Tomogr 24:189-196, 2000.

147. Kim YK, Kwak HS, Kim CS, et al: Hepatocellular carcinoma in patients with chronic liver disease. Radiology 238:531-542, 2006.

148. Takayasu K, Muramatsu Y, Misuguchi Y, et al: CT evaluation for the progression of hypoattenuating nodular lesions in virus-related chronic liver disease. AJR 187:454-463, 2006.

149. Tesdal IK, Filser T, Weiss C, et al: Transjugular intrahepatic portosystemic shunts: Adjunctive embolotherapy of gastroesophageal collateral vessels in the prevention of variceal rebleeding. Radiology 236:36-37, 2005.

150. Henderson JM: Surgery versus transjugular intrahepatic portal systemic shunt in the treatment of severe variceal bleeding. Clin Liver Dis 10: 599-612, 2006.

151. Laberge JM: Transjugular intrahepatic portosystemic shunt: Role in treating intractable variceal bleeding, ascites, and hepatic hydrothorax. Clin Liver Dis 10:583-598, 2006.

152. Maleux G, Verslype C, Heye S, et al: Endovascular shunt reduction in the management of transjugular portosystemic shunt–induced hepatic encephalopathy. AJR 188:659-664, 2007.

Vascular Disorders of the Liver and Splanchnic Circulation

Richard M. Gore, MD

The liver has a unique, dual blood supply in which 25% of the flow comes from the hepatic artery and 75% via the portal vein (Fig. 92-1). There is an inverse relationship between these two blood supplies. If portal flow decreases, arterial flow will increase as if an impedance has been removed. Additionally, there are several communications between these vessels that open in response to nervous and humoral factors: transinusoidal, transvasal, and transplexal. When vascular compromise develops, changes in the volume and direction of blood flow of an individual vessel will be altered. MDCT, Doppler ultrasound, and MRI are quite sensitive in the diagnosis of these perfusion disorders and are discussed in this chapter.

TRANSIENT HEPATIC ATTENUATION DIFFERENCES (THADS) AND TRANSIENT HEPATIC INTENSITY DIFFERENCES (THIDS)

Intraparenchymal perfusion disorders such as transient hepatic attenuation differences (THADS) and transient hepatic intensity differences (THIDS) are epiphenomena of alterations

of the dual vascular supply of the liver.[1-9] There is a compensatory relationship between hepatic arterial and portal venous blood supply so that arterial flow increases when portal flow decreases (Fig. 92-2). This is made possible by communication among the main vessels, sinusoids, and peribiliary venules that dilate in response to autonomic nervous system and humoral factors that are activated by hepatic demand for oxygen and metabolites. THADS and THIDS are areas of parenchymal enhancement visible during the hepatic arterial phase following the intravenous administration of contrast media. These lesions can be classified by morphology, etiology (Figs. 92-3 to 92-6), and pathogenesis.[1-4]

THADS and THIDS Associated with a Mass Lesion

Benign and malignant masses produce two morphologic types of THADS and THIDS via four pathophysiologic mechanisms: direct siphoning effect of the mass (lobar multisegmental shape) or indirectly by means of portal hypoperfusion (sectorial shape) due to portal branch compression or infiltration,

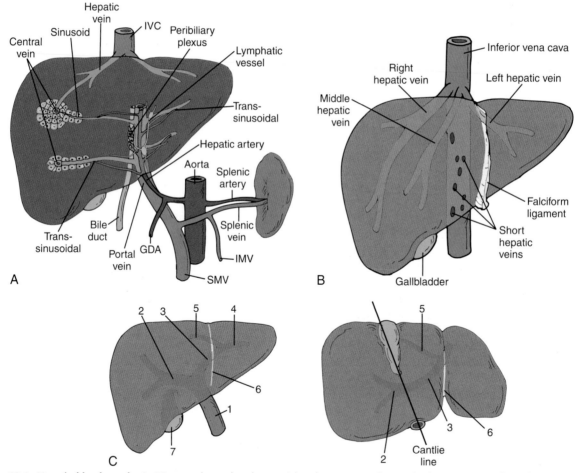

Figure 92-1. Hepatic blood supply. A. Diagram shows that the arterial and venous supplies to the liver are not independent systems. There are numerous communications between them, including the trans-sinusoidal route (between the interlobular arterioles and portal venules or sinusoids) and the transplexal route (peribiliary plexus), which play an important role when portal venous inflow is compromised. Ao, aorta; GDA, gastroduodenal artery; HV, hepatic vein; IMV, inferior mesenteric vein; IVC, inferior vena cava; SMV, superior mesenteric vein. **B.** Normal hepatic venous anatomy. Drawing shows major hepatic veins and short hepatic vein orifices. **C.** Normal branching pattern of the portal vein. Coronal (*left*) and axial (*right*) diagrams show that the main portal vein (*1*) divides into the right (*2*) and left portal veins. The left portal vein first courses horizontally (horizontal portion [*3*]), then turns anteriorly (umbilical portion [*4*] toward the ligamentum teres ([*6*]). The Cantlie line corresponds to the median fissure and extends from the gallbladder (*7*) to the inferior vena cava. It is located to the right of the umbilical ligament and divides the liver into right and left lobes. *5*, branch to segment IV.

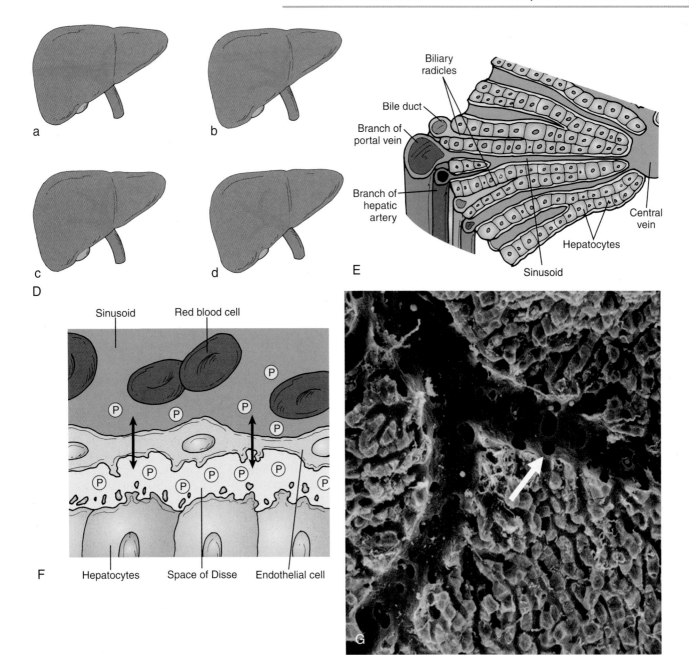

Figure 92-1, cont'd D. Four most common branching patterns of the intrahepatic portal vein. *a*, Coronal diagram shows the normal branching pattern. *b*, Coronal diagram shows trifurcation of the main portal vein. The right portal vein is not present, and the main portal vein divides into the right anterior, right posterior, and left portal veins at the same level. *c*, Coronal diagram shows the right anterior branch arising from the left portal vein. The main portal vein divides into the right posterior and left portal veins, and the right anterior portal vein arises from the left portal vein. *d*, Coronal diagram shows the right posterior branch arising from the main portal vein. The first branch to split off is the right posterior branch. The main portal vein then continues to the right for a variable distance and bifurcates into the right anterior and left portal veins. **E.** Diagram shows anatomic relationship between hepatic arterial and portal venous branches and bile duct (portal triad), biliary radicles, cords of hepatocytes, intervening sinusoid, and central draining hepatic vein. Diagram depicting hepatic blood supply at the sinusoidal level. Note that the bile ducts primarily derive their blood supply from the hepatic arteries. **F.** Diagram shows microanatomic relationship of red blood cells within sinusoid, fenestrated endothelial cells, plasma (P), space of Disse, and hepatocyte. Diagram showing the communication through the sinusoids of the hepatic veins and portal veins. **G.** Photomicrograph showing the fenestrated walls of the sinusoids (*arrow*). (**A** from Quiroag S, Sebastia C, Pallisa E, et al: Improved diagnosis of hepatic perfusion disorders: Value of hepatic arterial phase imaging during helical CT. RadioGraphics 21:65-81, 2001, p 67; **B** from Desser TS, Sze DY, Jeffrey RB: Imaging and intervention in the hepatic veins. AJR 180:1583-1591, 2003, p 1584; **C** and **D** from Gallego C, Velasco M, Marcuello P, et al: Congenital and acquired anomalies of the portal venous system. RadioGraphics 22:141-159, 2002; **E** and **F** from Pandharipande PV, Krinsky GA, Rusinek H, Lee VS: Perfusion imaging of the liver: Current challenges and future goals. Radiology 234:661-673, 2005; **E,** p 663; **F,** p. 663.)

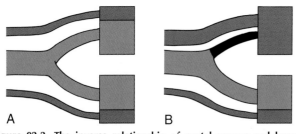

Figure 92-2. The inverse relationship of portal venous and hepatic blood flow: the origin of THADS (transient hepatic attenuation differences) and THIDS (transient hepatic intensity differences). **A.** In the normal situation, a segment of liver derives most of its blood supply from the portal vein (blue) and a minority from the hepatic artery (red). **B.** If the portal vein flow is compromised (black) by obstruction or extrinsic compression or if intraparenchymal pressure exceeds portal venous pressure, that segment of liver will derive its blood supply almost exclusively from the hepatic artery (red). The normal liver will be perfused by both the hepatic artery (red) and the portal vein (blue). This has important implications for contrast-enhanced MDCT and MRI studies. (Courtesy Dennis M. Balfe, MD, St. Louis, MO.)

by thrombus resulting in a portal branch blockade, or by flow diversion caused by an arterioportal shunt.[1-4]

Lobar multisegmental THADS and THIDS occur when a benign hypervascular lesion or an abscess induces an increase in the primary arterial inflow, which leads to surrounding parenchyma perfusion, the so-called siphoning effect. These THADS and THIDS do not assume a triangular shape but a straight border may be present between the arterial phenomenon from adjacent parenchyma.[1-4]

Sectorial THADS and THIDS follow hepatic vessel dichotomy and appear as triangular areas that result from the strict relationship between the portal hypoperfused area and the arterial reaction. These can be seen in benign and malignant tumors as well as abscesses due to the spread of inflammatory mediators. The THADS and THIDS can be wedge or fan shaped.[1-4]

THADS and THIDS Not Associated with a Mass Lesion

THIDS and THADS can be seen in the absence of a focal lesion due to three mechanisms: portal hypoperfusion due to portal branch compression or thrombosis; flow diversion by arterioportal or by an anomalous blood supply; or inflammation of the bile ducts or gallbladder.[1-4]

Sectorial THIDS and THADS are usually caused by portal hypoperfusion due to portal vein or hepatic vein thrombosis, long-standing biliary obstruction, or an arterioportal shunt that may be congenital, traumatic, or due to cirrhosis. These THIDS and THADs can have a globular shape especially when they are adjacent to Glisson's capsule.[1-4]

Polymorphous THADS and THIDS have four major causes: external compression by a rib or subcapsular collection; anomalous blood supply from atypical arteries, collateral venous vessels, or accessory veins, especially in segment IV of the liver; inflammation of adjacent organs such as cholecystitis and pancreatitis that spread inflammatory mediators and reduce portal inflow due to interstitial edema; and post-traumatic, postbiopsy, postradiofrquency ablation of hepatic tumors.[1-4]

In patients with obstruction of the superior vena cava, the medial segment of the left lobe (segment IV) of the liver

will hyperenhance due to collateral veins. The internal mammary vein connects to the left portal vein via the paraumbilical vein.

Diffuse THADS and THIDS can be seen in right-sided heart failure (see later), Budd-Chiari syndrome (see later), and biliary obstruction leading to abnormal attenuation and signal intensity adjacent to the portal triads.

BUDD-CHIARI SYNDROME AND HEPATIC VENO-OCCLUSIVE DISEASE

The term *Budd-Chiari syndrome* is applied to a diverse group of conditions associated with hepatic venous outflow obstruction, at the level of either the large hepatic veins or the suprahepatic segment of the inferior vena cava. Diagnosis of this disorder is frequently difficult because of its protean causes and clinical manifestations. Hepatic veno-occlusive disease is a subset of the Budd-Chiari syndrome in which nonthrombotic occlusion of the small presinusoidal venules occurs. This usually develops in the setting of chemotherapy, radiation therapy, and immunosuppressive therapy.[10-21]

Clinical Findings

The two major clinical presentations of Budd-Chiari syndrome are determined by the extent and speed of onset of venous occlusion. The acute form follows simultaneous obstruction of all three hepatic veins or, more frequently, obstruction of the last patent hepatic vein after previous, clinically occult thrombosis of the others. These patients experience rapid onset of abdominal pain, tender hepatomegaly, vomiting, ascites, and arterial hypotension. This constellation of findings is associated with mild or marked increase of serum bilirubin level, marked elevation of the transaminase values, and decreased clotting factors resulting from hepatocellular failure.[10-21]

Patients with the chronic form of Budd-Chiari syndrome present with ascites of insidious onset, right upper quadrant pain, hepatomegaly, normal or moderately increased transaminase values, decreased albumin and clotting factors, mild jaundice, and splenomegaly or variceal bleeding if cirrhosis develops. The diagnosis is seldom made on clinical grounds alone because clinicians tend to ignore the abdominal pain and ascribe the hepatomegaly and ascites to cirrhosis. The correct diagnosis may be inferred from the absence of a cause for the cirrhosis; episodes of abdominal pain over the preceding month; or, uncommonly, a palpable caudate lobe.[10-21]

Etiology

Budd-Chiari syndrome is classified as either primary or secondary, depending on the cause and pathophysiologic manifestations (Table 92-1). In the primary type, there is total or incomplete membranous obstruction of hepatic venous blood, either above the entrance of the hepatic veins into the inferior vena cava or between the ostium of the right hepatic vein, which remains patent, and the more superior middle and left hepatic veins. Membranous obstruction, although uncommon in Europe and North America, is the most common cause of Budd-Chiari syndrome in Japan, India, Israel, and South Africa. These membranes vary greatly in size, from wafer thin to several centimeters thick. The origin of this lesion is controversial; most are believed to be congenital malformations that

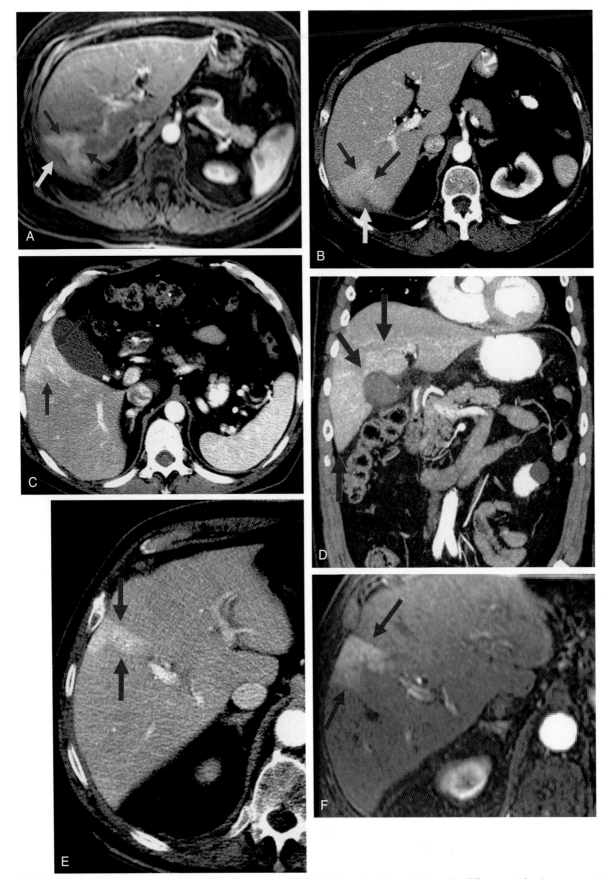

Figure 92-3. THADS (transient hepatic attenuation differences) and THIDS (transient hepatic intensity differences): benign causes. Contrast-enhanced MRI (**A**) and MDCT (**B**) in a patient with a dropped stone and pericapsular abscess. The abscess (*yellow arrow*) causes increased intra-parenchymal pressure exceeding portal venous pressure leading to hyperenhancement (*red arrows*) from compensatory hepatic arterial flow. In a patient with acute cholecystitis, axial (**C**) and coronal reformatted (**D**) CT images show hyperenhancement of the liver (*arrows*) adjacent to the gall-bladder fossa. CT (**E**) and MRI (**F**) scans in two different patients with THADS (*arrows*) (**E**) and THIDS (*arrows*) (**F**) in the right lobe of the liver without apparent cause.

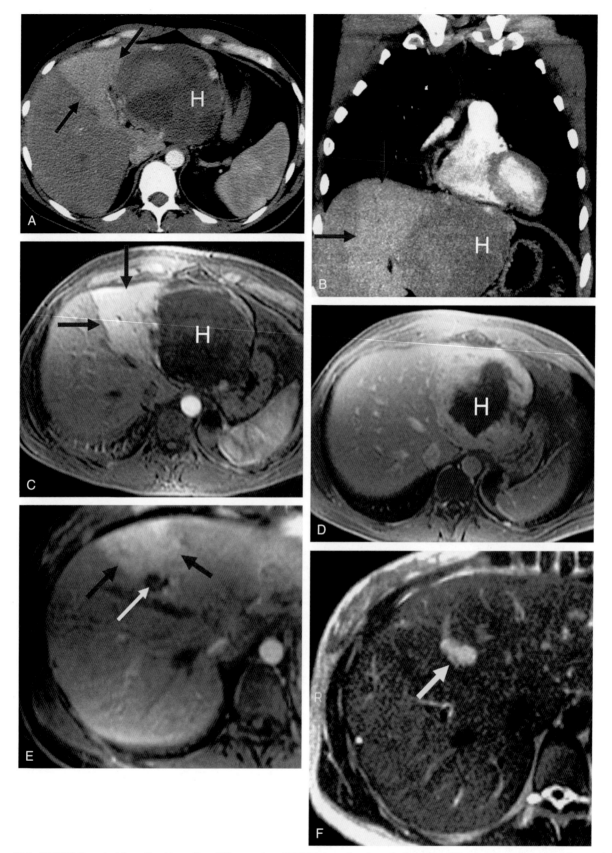

Figure 92-4. THADS (transient hepatic attenuation differences) and THIDS (transient hepatic intensity differences) resulting from hemangiomas. Axial (**A**) and coronal (**B**) reformatted MDCT images show a large hemangioma (H) in the lateral segment of the left lobe of the liver causing a large THAD (*arrows*) in the medial segment of the left lobe. **C.** MR images in the same patient show early peripheral nodular enhancement of the hemangioma (H) and a THID (*arrows*) during the arterial dominant image. **D.** On the delayed image, the hemangioma (H) has filled in with contrast and the THID has resolved. Early (**E**) and late phase (**F**) MR images in a different patient show the THID (*red arrows*) on the early phase images and resolution on the delayed scan that also shows filling in of the hemangioma (*yellow arrows*) with contrast.

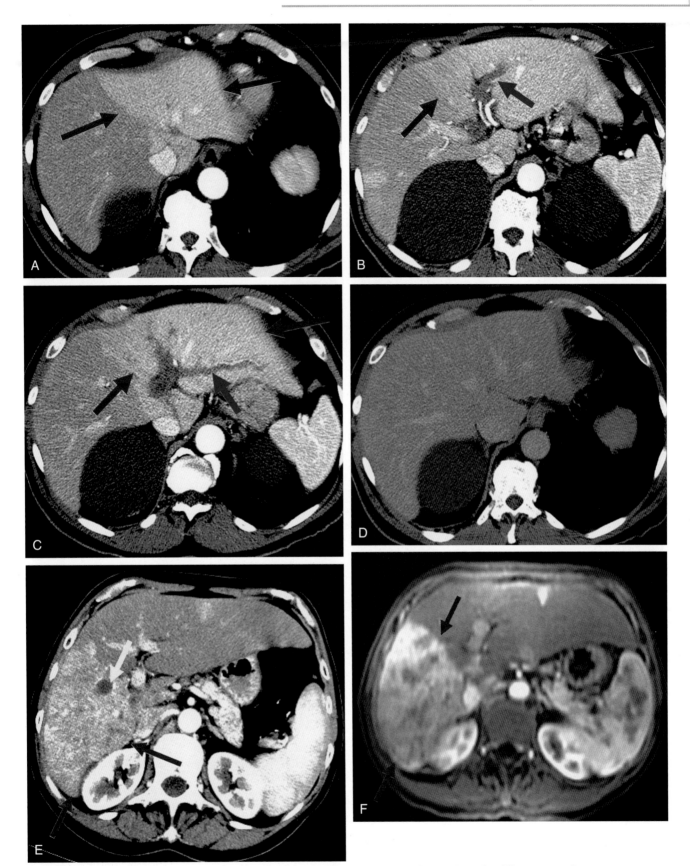

Figure 92-5. THADS (transient hepatic attenuation differences) and THIDS (transient hepatic intensity differences): malignant causes. A to D. MDCT shows a THAD (*red arrows*) in the lateral segment of the left hepatic lobe due to portal vein thrombosis (*blue arrow*) secondary to hepatocellular carcinoma (not shown). The THAD resolves on the delayed, equilibrium image (**D**). CT (**E**) and MR (**F**) images in a different patient with hepatocellular carcinoma causing portal vein thrombosis (*yellow arrow*). Notice the THID (**E**) and THID (**F**) in the right lobe of the liver,

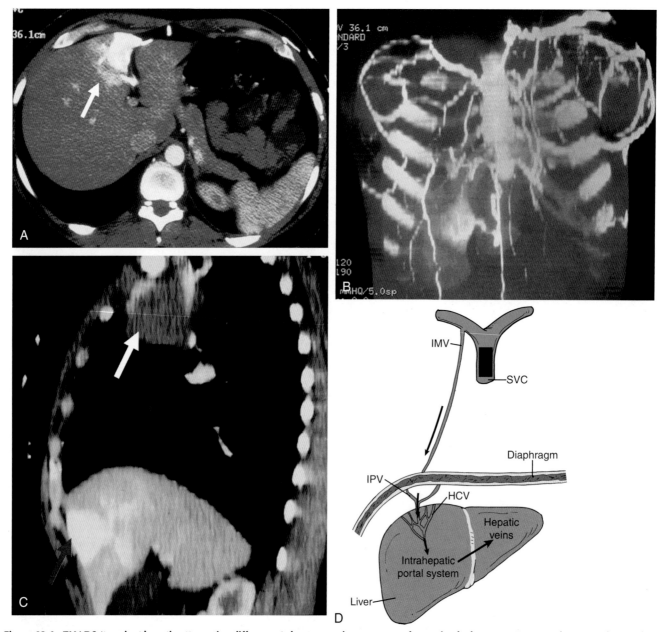

Figure 92-6. THADS (transient hepatic attenuation differences) due to superior vena cava obstruction by lung cancer. A. Axial CT scan shows robust enhancement of the medial segment of the left lobe of the liver (*arrow*). **B.** Coronal reformatted image demonstrates multiple collateral vessels. **C.** Sagittal reformatted image shows the neoplasm (*white arrow*) obstructing the superior vena cava and the hyperenhancing hepatic segment (*red arrow*). **D.** Diagram depicting the decompression pathways responsible for this THAD. HCV, hepatic central veins; IMV, internal mammary vein; IPV, inferior phrenic vein; SVC, superior vena cava. (**D** from Cihangiroglu M, Lin BH, Dachman AH: Collateral pathways in superior vena caval obstruction as seen on CT. J Comput Assist Tomogr 25:1-8, 2001.)

result from deviations of the complex embryologic process by which the inferior vena cava is formed. Other theories suggest that some of these lesions are acquired secondary to mechanical injury, infection, phlebitis, or organization of a preexisting thrombus. This origin would explain the adult presentation of the disorder.[6-21]

Membranous obstruction of the inferior vena cava is complicated by hepatocellular carcinoma in 20% to 40% of cases in South African and Japanese series. It is postulated that the obstruction renders the hepatocytes more susceptible to the action of one or more environmental carcinogens or that perhaps long-standing venous obstruction induces forma-

tion of hyperplastic nodules, which may undergo malignant transformation.[6-21]

Secondary Budd-Chiari syndrome can be classified on the basis of the site of hepatic venous obstruction. Obstruction at the level of the central and sublobular veins may follow chemotherapy with thioguanine, vincristine, cytarabine, 6-mercaptopurine, dacarbazine, internal or external hepatic radiation, chemoradiation therapy before bone marrow transplantation, azathioprine for immunosuppression, arsenic poisoning, pregnancy (particularly in the postpartum period), and oral contraceptive use. Naturally occurring toxins, such as the pyrrolizidine alkaloids found in herbal teas containing

Table 92-1
Causes of Budd-Chiari Syndrome

Hypercoagulable States
Antiphospholipid syndrome
Antithrombin III deficiency
Essential thrombocytosis
Factor V Leiden
Lupus anticoagulant
Myeloproliferative disorder
Paroxysmal nocturnal hemoglobinuria
Polycythemia rubra vera
Postpartum thrombocytopenic purpura
Protein C deficiency
Protein S deficiency
Sickle cell disease

Infection
Amebic liver abscess
Aspergillosis
Filariasis
Hepatic abscess
Hydatid cysts
Pelvic cellulitis
Schistosomiasis
Syphilis
Tuberculosis

Cancer
Adrenal cancer
Bronchogenic carcinoma
Fibrolamellar cancer
Hepatoma
Leiomyosarcoma
Leukemia
Renal cell cancer
Rhabdomyosarcoma

Miscellaneous
Behçet's disease
Celiac disease
Crohn's disease
Laparoscopic cholecystectomy
Membranous obstruction of vena cava
Oral contraceptives
Polycystic disease
Pregnancy
Sarcoidosis
Trauma

cysts, intrahepatic hematoma, Caroli's disease, large simple cysts, and amebic abscesses, can also cause obstruction.[6-21]

Pathologic Findings

In acute Budd-Chiari syndrome, the liver is markedly enlarged and reddish (Fig. 92-7). Histologically, sinusoidal dilatation is evident, and parenchymal damage ranges from mild atrophy to marked hemorrhagic necrosis in the centrilobular areas.

In chronic Budd-Chiari syndrome, the liver is nodular and irregular in shape, often with caudate lobe hypertrophy. Centrilobular fibrosis is the hallmark of this disorder, and the centrally scarred areas may link to form connective tissue bridges. Sinusoidal dilatation also predominates around hepatic venules and is associated with liver cell atrophy and peri-sinusoidal fibrosis.

Regenerative nodules are often seen in Budd-Chiari syndrome and are usually multiple, measuring between 5 and 40 mm. They develop in the setting of insufficient blood supply to the liver, leading to atrophy along with compensatory nodular hyperplasia in areas of hepatic parenchyma that have an adequate blood supply. The nodules are composed of hyperplastic hepatocytes arranged in plates of one or two cells in width. The nodules grow in an expansile fashion, compressing the surrounding liver and obliterating the central vein. There is no evidence that these nodules degenerate into malignancy.[6-21]

Radiologic Findings

Traditionally, the radiographic "gold standard" for the diagnosis of Budd-Chiari syndrome has been hepatic venography and cavography. However, these invasive angiographic procedures are not suitable for screening patients with nonspecific signs and symptoms. The cross-sectional imaging modalities have proved quite successful in the diagnosis of this disorder, and such studies can usually obviate angiography or venography.

Ultrasound

Because of its excellent sensitivity, high specificity, noninvasiveness, relatively low cost, availability, lack of contrast requirements, and multiplanar imaging ability, sonography can be the initial screening study for the Budd-Chiari syndrome. The sonographic features (Fig. 99-8) of the Budd-Chiari syndrome are stenosis of hepatic veins, which often have thick, echogenic walls and proximal dilatation; echogenic intravenous thrombi; intrahepatic collaterals or extrahepatic anastomoses; and a large inferior right hepatic vein.[22-24]

In chronic cases, the hepatic veins may not be visible. The inferior vena cava may also be narrowed by a grossly swollen liver. Ascites, abnormal hepatic shape with enlargement of the caudate lobe, and atrophy of the right lobe are present in most cases except in disease of acute onset. When both the left lobe and the caudate lobe are enlarged, confusion with cirrhosis can occur. Membranous webs are identified as echogenic or focal obliterations of the lumen.[22-24]

In patients with hepatomegaly, evaluation of the hepatic veins can be difficult because they are often compressed and may not be visible. In these patients, an abdomen distended by ascites can further interfere with sonography. Similarly, in

senecio and aflatoxins, have been implicated as well. Nonthrombotic occlusion of small central and sublobular veins is termed hepatic veno-occlusive disease (HVOD).[6-21]

Obstruction of the major hepatic veins may occur in the setting of polycythemia vera, paroxysmal nocturnal hemoglobinuria, myeloproliferative disorders, thrombocytosis, hypereosinophilic syndrome, sickle cell anemia, Behçet's disease, anticardiolipin antibodies, lupus anticoagulant, protein S or C deficiency, antithrombin III deficiency, antiphospholipid antibodies, mixed connective tissue disease, and Sjögren's syndrome.[6-21]

A variety of hepatic and extrahepatic masses can also compress the inferior vena cava and hepatic veins. These masses are the second most common mechanism of hepatic venous outflow block in Western countries. Hepatocellular carcinoma, hypernephroma, adrenal and bronchial carcinomas, leiomyosarcoma of the inferior vena cava, and hepatic adenoma or cystadenoma are the most common neoplasms associated with Budd-Chiari syndrome. Benign masses, such as hydatid

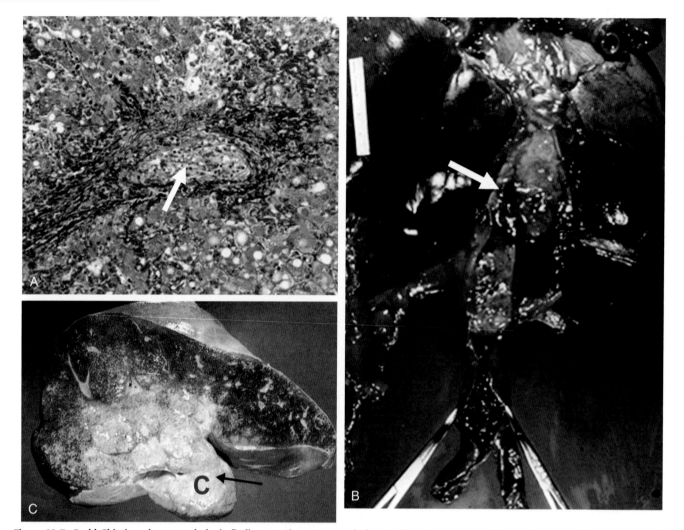

Figure 92-7. Budd-Chiari syndrome: pathologic findings. A. Photomicrograph showing thrombus (*arrow*) within a subsegmental hepatic vein in this patient with polycythemia vera. **B.** Tumor thrombus from a renal cell carcinoma has propagated superiorly to involve the inferior vena cava (*arrow*) and hepatic veins. **C.** Gross autopsy specimen reveals relative central sparing of the caudate (C) lobe (*arrow*) associated with marked hemorrhagic congestion of the periphery of the liver.

cirrhotic livers, patent hepatic veins may be difficult to identify, which precludes placement of the duplex Doppler cursor. Visualization of hepatic webs is also problematic. Color flow Doppler may be helpful in these cases.[22-24]

Absent or reversed flow in the hepatic veins or flat flow in the hepatic veins associated with reversed flow in the inferior vena cava as demonstrated by duplex Doppler ultrasound is diagnostic of Budd-Chiari syndrome. The flow in the portal vein may be slow or reversed.

Color Doppler sonography overcomes some of the limitations of real-time sonography by demonstrating reversed flow in the retrohepatic inferior vena cava, documenting the presence of intrahepatic venous collaterals, and confirming the absence of flow in presumably thrombosed vessels. Color flow imaging rapidly and accurately determines the status of the hepatic veins and inferior vena cava and the direction of flow. Areas of occlusion are also clearly depicted, as are areas of narrowing, tortuosity, and reversal of flow direction.[22-24]

In hepatic veno-occlusive disease in which there is nonthrombotic occlusion of small hepatic veins and terminal hepatic venules, the major hepatic veins show normal hepato-

fugal flow direction, and the inferior vena cava is patent with flow toward the heart. Decreased, reversed, or to-and-fro flow (flow demodulation) may be seen in the main portal vein. Other Doppler criteria include decrease in spectral density; reversed flow or maximum flow in the main portal vein of 210 cm/second, portal vein congestion index (cross-sectional area of vein divided by average velocity); hepatic artery resistive index of greater than or equal to 0.75; monophasic flow in the hepatic veins; and flow recorded in paraumbilical veins. Gray-scale criteria include hepatic vein diameter less than 3 mm; portal vein diameter greater than 8 mm in children and greater than 12 mm in adults; mural thickening of the gallbladder greater than 6 mm; and nonspecific findings, such as hepatosplenomegaly, ascites, and visualization of paraumbilical vein.[22-24]

Computed Tomography

The CT features of Budd-Chiari syndrome depend on the age and extent of the obstruction and the presence of coexisting changes in portal venous blood flow.[25,26] On noncontrast

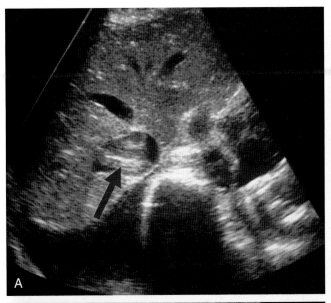

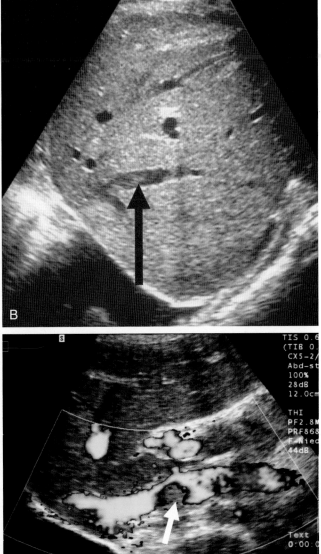

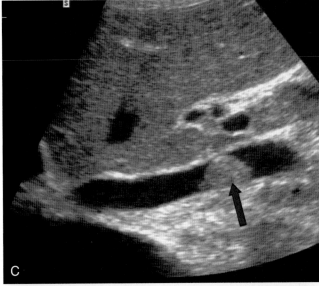

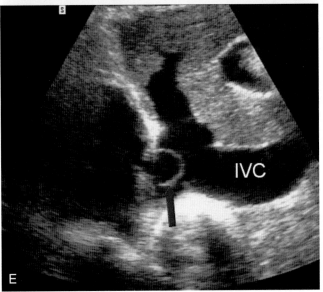

Figure 92-8. Budd-Chiari syndrome: sonographic findings. A. Axial scan shows thrombus in the inferior vena cava (*arrow*). Note the large right-sided pleural effusion. **B.** Coronal oblique scan shows thrombus within the middle hepatic vein (*arrow*). In a different patient, gray scale (**C**) and color flow Doppler images (**D**) demonstrate thrombus in the inferior vena cava (*arrow*). **E.** Sagittal sonogram shows a thin fibrous web (*arrow*) across the inferior vena cava (IVC).

scans, in the acute phase of the disease, diffuse hepatic hypodensity is associated with global liver enlargement and ascites. Presumably, the hepatic hypodensity is due to hepatic parenchymal congestion. Hyperdense thrombus with an attenuation of 38 to 42 Hounsfield units may be seen in the inferior vena cava and hepatic veins. Rarely, a calcified caval membrane is identified. After the injection of contrast material, the liver typically shows patchy enhancement; this is due to the hepatic congestion, which causes portal and sinusoidal stasis. In most patients, the central regions of the liver, including the caudate and part of the left lobe, may enhance normally and appear hyperdense compared with the more peripheral parts of the liver, which show decreased enhancement. Later, a classic "flip-flop" pattern may develop (Fig. 92-9), in which the contrast material from the normally enhanced central liver washes out so that this region becomes relatively hypodense when compared with the peripheral zones, which are slowly accreting contrast material. The subcapsular portions of the liver may enhance normally because they have independent venous drainage through systemic subcapsular veins. These differences in hepatic attenuation and morphologic changes are closely related to regional disturbances in portal flow. In

segments of the liver in which venous drainage is obstructed (the hepatic periphery), portal blood flow is diminished, if not reversed. Portal venous flow is normal in the central portion of the liver, where hepatic venous egress is uninterrupted.[25,26]

Intravascular thrombus is best seen in the acute phase of the Budd-Chiari syndrome, as a low-density mass in the lumen of the hepatic veins and inferior vena cava. The wall of the thrombosed vessel may appear dense relative to the thrombus, secondary to the enhancement of the vasa vasorum. The involved vessel also is often enlarged. Portal vein thrombus may be seen in 20% of cases. Compression of the inferior vena cava is also demonstrated[24-26] (Fig. 92-10).

In more chronic cases of Budd-Chiari syndrome, the thrombi and the hepatic veins are often difficult to visualize. Intravascular thrombus density, which is high for the first 3 weeks, also diminishes over time. As the obstruction becomes more chronic, the liver undergoes morphologic changes that are due to diminished or reversed portal blood flow in the involved hepatic segments. Portal venous blood carries certain hepatotropic agents, mainly insulin, and segments deprived of these agents experience nutritional ischemia and eventually atrophy. Accordingly, the caudate lobe exhibits hypertrophy,

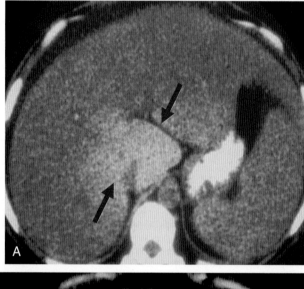

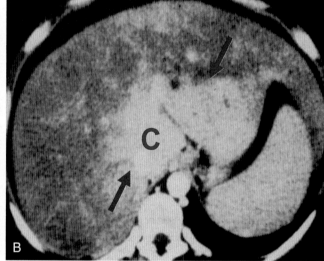

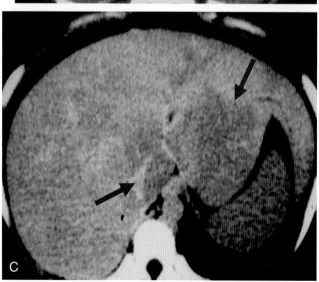

Figure 92-9. Budd-Chiari syndrome: flip-flop pattern on CT. The classic CT flip-flop pattern of hepatic contrast enhancement is shown in this patient with Budd-Chiari syndrome. Noncontrast CT scan (**A**) demonstrates normal attenuation (*arrows*) of the caudate lobe of the liver and hypodensity peripherally due to edema and steatosis from nutrional ischemia. Postcontrast CT scan (**B**) shows rapid enhancement (*arrows*) of the unobstructed central portion (C) of the liver with a delayed peripheral hepatogram. **C.** Later image shows that the central, unobstructed portion of the liver (*arrows*) has washed out, while the periphery is slowly accreting contrast.

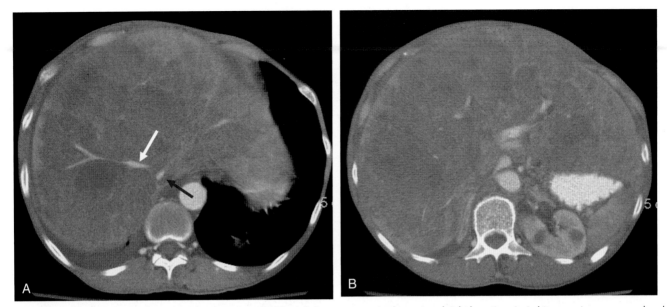

Figure 92-10. Budd-Chiari syndrome: CT features. A and **B.** The inferior vena cava (*red arrow*) and right hepatic vein (*white arrow*) are narrowed and attenuated in this patient with a swollen, inhomogeneous liver.

and the periphery of the liver tends to exhibit atrophy. These changes may take 2 to 4 months to appear. Unless the membranes are calcified, membranous obstruction of the inferior vena cava is more difficult to visualize.

On MDCT, large regenerative nodules robustly and homogeneously enhance during the arterial dominant phase and remain slightly hyperdense on the portal venous dominant phase images as well.

Magnetic Resonance Imaging

MRI is a useful screening modality for Budd-Chiari syndrome, by virtue of its ability to display directly the portal veins, hepatic veins, and inferior vena cava in numerous planes. A number of specific MRI abnormalities[27-29] are associated with this syndrome (Figs. 92-11 to 92-15): complete absence of hepatic veins or striking attenuation of their caliber, demonstration of thrombus or absent vascular flow in hepatic veins, comma-shaped intrahepatic collateral vessels, and marked constriction of the inferior vena cava. Less specific findings include enlargement of the caudate lobe, ascites, and inhomogeneity of the hepatic parenchyma. Vascular patency can confidently be confirmed when the vessel has no signal.

The multiplanar capabilities of MRI are of great value in depicting tumor thrombus in patients with Budd-Chiari syndrome secondary to neoplasm. Bland and tumor thrombus can be distinguished by the administration of gadolinium. Tumor thrombus may show contrast enhancement.[27-29]

The degree of enhancement of the liver parenchyma supplied by a thrombosed hepatic vein depends on the acuteness and duration of the thrombosis. Involved parenchyma enhances less than surrounding liver in acute thrombosis. In chronic thrombosis, enhancement is more variable and may be increased. In patients with acute Budd-Chiari syndrome, the congested liver may have a higher water content and longer T2 relaxation time than the spared caudate lobe. Also the peripheral liver enhances less than the central liver after intravenous gadolinium administration because of increased

parenchymal pressure with resultant diminished blood supply from both the hepatic artery and the portal vein.

Large regenerative nodules are bright on T1-weighted MR images and show the same enhancement pattern following the intravenous administration of gadopentetate dimeglumine (Gd-DTPA). They are predominantly isointense or hypointense relative the liver on T2-weighted images.[27-29]

Angiography

Angiography has traditionally been the radiographic gold standard for the evaluation of patients with Budd-Chiari syndrome. Now it is seldom performed for diagnosis but as a preliminary procedure to radiologic interventions, such as transjugular intrahepatic portosystemic shunt (TIPS) creation, balloon angioplasty, or stricture stenting (Fig. 92-16).

Nodular Regenerative Hyperplasia

On contrast-enhanced CT and MRI studies, multiple enhancing nodules are identified that are usually 5 to 7 mm in diameter[30-33] (Fig. 92-17).

Treatment

The treatment and prognosis of Budd-Chiari syndrome are determined by the rate and degree of hepatic outflow obstruction. In acute Budd-Chiari syndrome, survival time may be short because of acute liver failure or extension of thrombus into the inferior vena cava with resulting pulmonary emboli. Patients with chronic Budd-Chiari syndrome generally succumb to variceal bleeding secondary to severe cirrhosis and portal hypertension. Most patients require portal decompression to prevent liver failure and resolve the ascites.[34-42]

Treatment of Budd-Chiari syndrome depends on the cause. In some cases, medical management with large doses of steroids (for idiopathic granulomatous venulitis) or nutritional therapy (for an acutely enlarged, fatty liver compressing

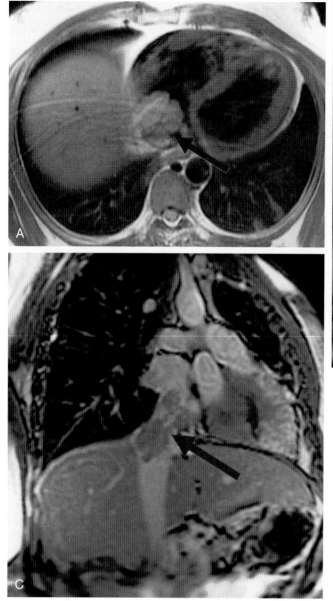

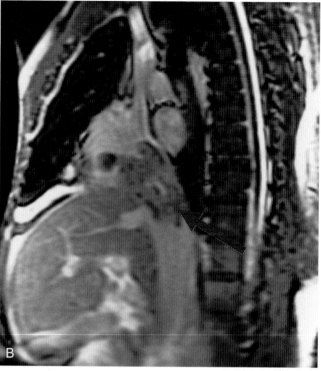

Figure 92-11. Budd-Chiari syndrome: MRI findings in a patient with hepatocellular carcinoma invading the hepatic veins and inferior vena cava. Axial (**A**), parasagittal (**B**), and coronal (**C**) images shows tumor thrombus (*arrows*) invading the inferior vena cava and right atrium.

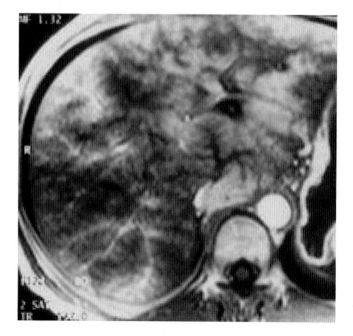

Figure 92-12. Acute Budd-Chiari syndrome: MRI findings. The liver is edematous and inhomogeneous on this MR image.

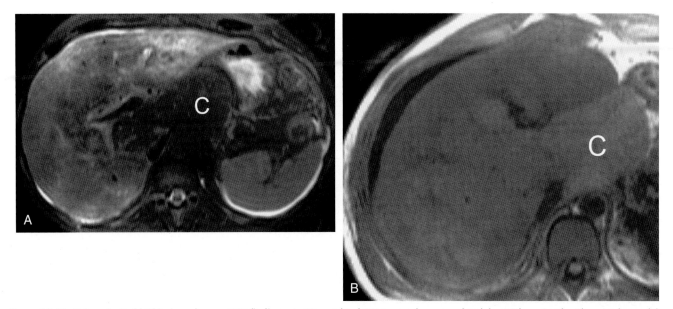

Figure 92-13. Subacute Budd-Chiari syndrome: MRI findings. A. T2-weighted MR image shows caudate lobe (C) hypertrophy. The periphery of the liver is hyperintense indicating edema. There is a small amount of ascites. **B.** T1-weighted image demonstrated the large caudate lobe (C) hypertrophy, which has higher signal intensity than the periphery of the liver. Ascites is also present.

the inferior vena cava) may suffice. However, in most cases, medical therapy is limited and is directed toward anticoagulation and the control of ascites with diuretics.

Membranous obstructions of the inferior vena cava and the hepatic veins are amenable to angioplasty with balloons or lasers and stent insertion. Before any intervention, these patients should receive anticoagulants because of the danger of pulmonary emboli from venous thrombi proximal to the

membranes. This danger is the major risk of thrombolytic therapy as well. Angioplasty is more difficult in patients with extensive thrombus, but clinical improvement may accompany dilatation and recanalization of only one hepatic vein.[34-42]

Reports suggest the utility of expandable metal stents in the treatment of Budd-Chiari syndrome resulting from tumor compression or from idiopathic obstruction of the inferior

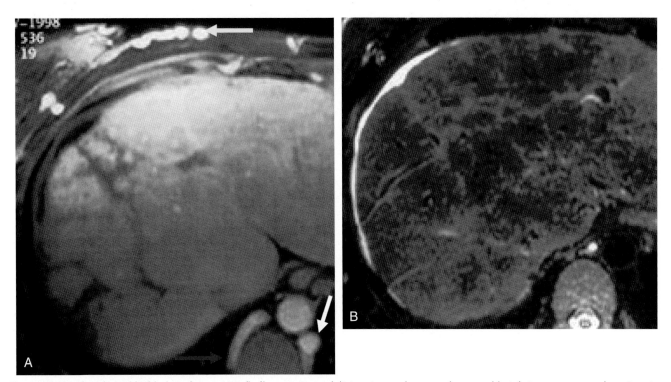

Figure 92-14. Chronic Budd-Chiari syndrome: MRI findings. A. Postgadolinium image shows no demonstrable inferior vena cava or hepatic veins. Note the dilated azygos (*red arrow*), hemiazygos veins (*white arrow*), and superficial collateral (*yellow arrow*) blood vessels. **B.** T2-weighted image shows inhomogeneous, coarsened hepatic parenchyma. Ascites is present.

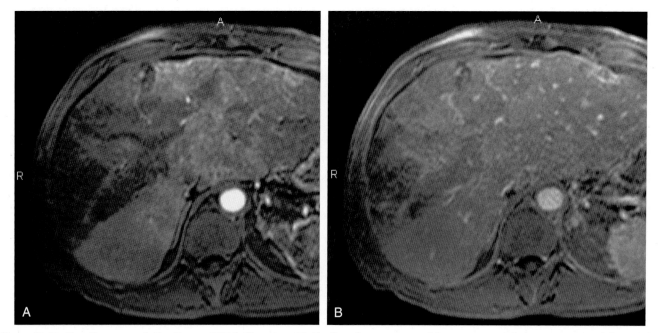

Figure 92-15. Hepatic veno-occlusive disease: MRI findings. A and B. The liver demonstrates an inhomogeneous enhancement pattern following the intravenous administration of gadolinium.

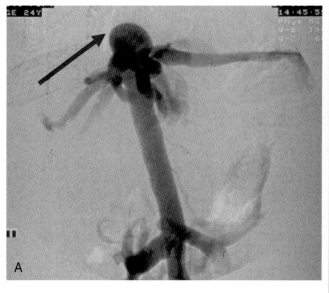

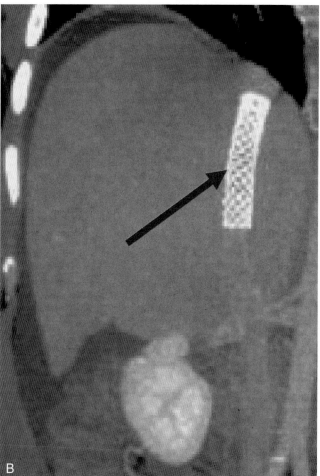

Figure 92-16. Budd-Chiari syndrome: angiographic features. A. Digital subtraction angiogram shows a web (*arrow*) obstructing the inferior vena cava. **B.** Coronal reformatted MR image demonstrates a metallic stent (*arrow*) maintaining vascular patency following balloon dilatation of the web. There is ascites present.

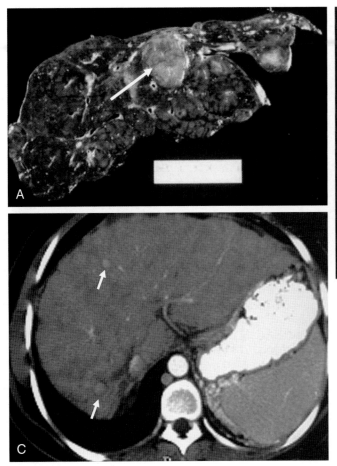

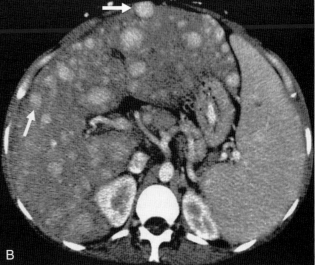

Figure 92-17. Budd-Chiari syndrome: nodular regenerative hyperplasia. A. Pathologic specimen shows a nodule (*arrow*) in a diffusely abnormal liver. In different patients, multiple hypervascular lesions (*arrows*) are identified on CT (**B**) and MRI (**C**) scans. (**A** and **B** courtesy of Michael P. Federle, MD, Pittsburgh, Pa.)

vena cava. The TIPS procedure is useful in treating Budd-Chiari syndrome as well.[34-42]

The surgical alternatives in Budd-Chiari syndrome are as follows: direct repair by membranotomy, membranectomy, or cavoplasty; portosystemic decompression by side-to-side portacaval or mesoatrial shunt; transplantation; and peritoneojugular shunt.

LIVER IN CARDIAC DISEASE

Passive hepatic congestion is caused by stasis of blood within the liver parenchyma as a result of compromise of hepatic venous drainage. It is a common complication of congestive heart failure and constrictive pericarditis, wherein elevated central venous pressure is directly transmitted from the right atrium to the hepatic veins because of their close anatomic relationship. The liver becomes tensely swollen as the hepatic sinusoids engorge and dilate with blood (Fig. 92-18). These changes may be transient, and full recovery follows once the patient's congestive heart failure is corrected. In chronic right atrial failure, cardiac cirrhosis may ensue.[43-49]

Clinical Findings

With acute congestion, the liver is enlarged and tender, and the patient may have severe right upper quadrant pain that is due to stretching of the Glisson capsule. Patients typically have hepatojugular reflux on physical examination. Liver function

abnormalities are often mild, but florid hepatic dysfunction simulating acute viral hepatitis may be seen. The diagnosis is usually not made clinically because the signs and symptoms of cardiac failure overshadow those of liver disease. In rare cases of cardiomyopathy, the patient may present with hepatic failure before cardiac disease is recognized as the cause of the hepatic dysfunction.

Radiologic Findings

Ultrasound

Ultrasound demonstrates hepatic enlargement and dilatation of the inferior vena cava and hepatic veins in the early stages of this disorder (Fig. 92-19). Normally, the maximal diameter of the main trunk of the right hepatic vein is 5.6 to 6.2 mm. In patients with congestive heart failure, the mean diameter is 8.8 mm, and it increases to 13.3 mm if there is associated pericardial effusion. Respiratory variations in the caliber of the inferior vena cava and hepatic veins are diminished.

The spectral Doppler waveform of the hepatic vein is also altered. Normally, the inferior vena cava and hepatic veins show a triphasic flow pattern: the first two peaks are toward the heart and are reflections of right atrial and ventricular diastole. The third peak is a short period of reversed blood flow, which accompanies atrial systole (the p wave of the electrocardiogram). In patients with elevated central venous pressure, the hepatic veins lose their triphasic pattern. The

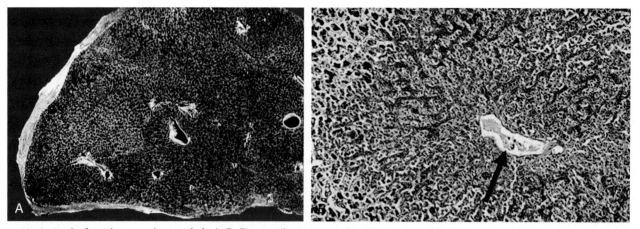

Figure 92-18. Passive hepatic congestions: pathologic findings. A. Classic "nutmeg liver" in a patient with chronic passive hepatic congestions. **B.** Dilated sinusoids are seen surrounding a dilated central hepatic vein (*arrow*).

spectral signal may have an M shape, and ultimately, in cardiac cirrhosis, a unidirectional, low-velocity continuous flow pattern may be seen.[43-49]

In tricuspid regurgitation, the normally triphasic hepatic vein demonstrates a decrease in the size of the antegrade systolic wave and a systolic/diastolic flow velocity ratio less than 0.6 (normal >4.0). The high systolic pressure of the right atrium is transmitted to the right atrium.[43-49]

In patients with severe congestive heart failure, the portal venous Doppler signal may also be altered by the mechanical events in the right side of the heart. Normally, the portal vein shows almost continuous flow except for some increase during inspiration. In passive hepatic congestion, the energy of the elevated pressure from the right atrium and hepatic vein is transmitted directly via the dilated hepatic sinusoids into the portal vein. This energy transmission causes increased pulsatility of the portal venous Doppler signal because the liver no longer prevents changes in central venous pressure from reaching the portal circulation. This pulsatility is manifested by monophasic forward flow with peak velocity at ventricular diastole and gradual diminution of velocity throughout ventricular systole, a reversal of flow during ventricular systole, or vena cava–like biphasic forward velocity peaks during each cardiac cycle.[43-49]

As cardiac cirrhosis develops, the morphology of the liver becomes similar to that observed with cirrhosis resulting from other causes. Patients with other forms of cirrhosis may also show flattening of the Doppler waveform in the hepatic veins because of impaired mural compliance of these vessels.

Computed Tomography

The CT findings (Fig. 92-20) of passive hepatic congestion include dilatation of the cava and the hepatic veins. When a bolus of contrast material injected intravenously through an arm vein reaches the failing right atrium, it may flow directly into the inferior vena cava and hepatic veins rather than flow normally into the right ventricle. The elevated central venous pressure permits retrograde opacification and enhancement of the inferior vena cava and hepatic veins. Contrast-enhanced CT scans may show an inhomogeneous, mottled, reticulated-

mosaic pattern of parenchymal contrast enhancement. The abnormal hepatogram is presumably due to impaired venous outflow leading to altered hepatic hemodynamics and hepatic parenchymal distortion. Linear and curvilinear regions of poor enhancement may be due to delayed enhancement in regions of small- and medium-sized hepatic veins. Larger patchy regions of poor or delayed enhancement in the periphery of the liver probably are a manifestation of the stagnant blood flow in these regions in patients with hepatic venous hypertension. This stagnant blood most likely affects inflow from hepatic arterial and portal venous circulations. Ancillary findings include cardiomegaly, hepatomegaly, intrahepatic periportal lucency resulting from perivascular lymphedema, pleural effusions, ascites, and pericardial effusions.[43-49]

Magnetic Resonance Imaging

On early MRI contrast-enhanced images, the liver may enhance in a mosaic fashion with a reticulated pattern of low signal intensity linear markings (see Fig. 92-20). The signal intensity of the liver becomes more homogeneous by 1 minute. There is often dilatation of the hepatic veins and suprahepatic inferior vena cava. As on CT, contrast material injected into an arm vein may reflux into the hepatic veins and suprahepatic inferior vena cava, enhancing these structures before the portal vein. On gradient-echo MR images, slow or even absent antegrade flow within the inferior vena cava may be identified.[43-49]

PELIOSIS HEPATIS

Peliosis hepatis is a rare disorder characterized by cystic hepatic sinusoidal dilatation and the presence of multiple blood-filled lacunar spaces of various sizes (1 mm to 3 cm) throughout the liver. These peliotic lesions can also occur in the spleen, bone marrow, lymph nodes, and lungs. The blood-filled spaces freely communicate with the sinusoids and are lined by a thin band of collagenous tissue and endothelial cells. Peliosis lesions can be differentiated from hemangiomas by the presence of portal tracts within the fibrous stroma of the blood spaces.[50-57]

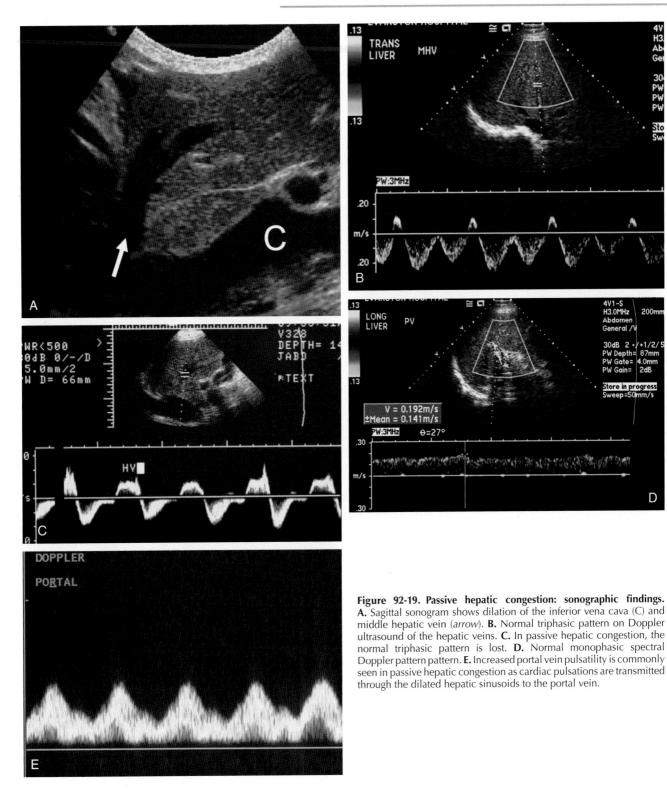

Figure 92-19. Passive hepatic congestion: sonographic findings.
A. Sagittal sonogram shows dilation of the inferior vena cava (C) and middle hepatic vein (*arrow*). **B.** Normal triphasic pattern on Doppler ultrasound of the hepatic veins. **C.** In passive hepatic congestion, the normal triphasic pattern is lost. **D.** Normal monophasic spectral Doppler pattern pattern. **E.** Increased portal vein pulsatility is commonly seen in passive hepatic congestion as cardiac pulsations are transmitted through the dilated hepatic sinusoids to the portal vein.

Pathophysiology

Numerous theories have been proposed for the cause of peliosis hepatis, including outflow obstruction at the sinusoid wall and hepatocellular necrosis leading to cyst formation. There is dilatation of a portion of the central vein of the hepatic lobule. Peliosis hepatis develops in the following settings: use of anabolic steroids, corticosteroids, tamoxifen, oral contraceptives, or diethylstilbestrol; after renal or cardiac transplantation; in association with a chronic wasting disease, such as tuberculosis, leprosy, malignancy, or AIDS; in association with sprue, diabetes, necrotizing vasculitis, or Hodgkin's disease; and after exposure to polyvinyl chloride or arsenic.[50-57]

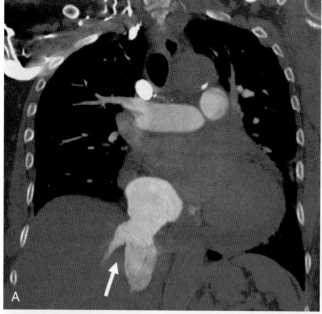

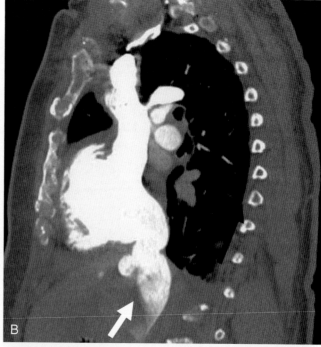

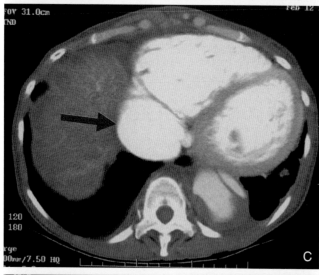

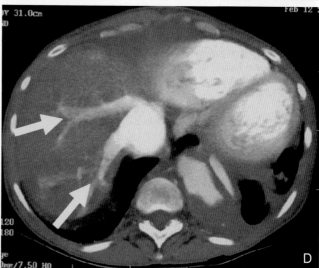

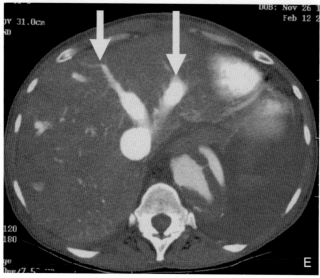

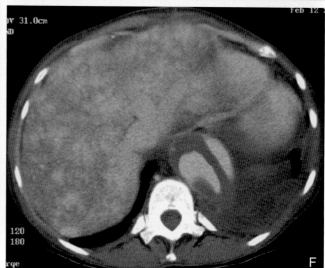

Figure 92-20. *See legend on opposite page.*

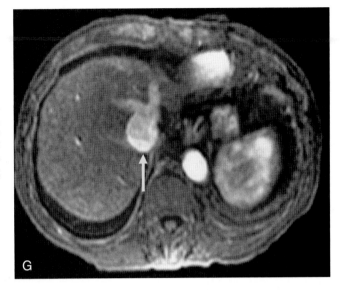

Figure 92-20. Passive hepatic congestion: CT and MRI features. Coronal (**A**) and sagittal (**B**) reformatted MDCT images demonstrates reflux of contrast into a dilated inferior vena cava (*arrows*) and hepatic veins. **C to E.** Axial scans in a different patient with a dissecting thoracoabdominal aortic aneurysm, show the dilated inferior vena cava (*red arrow*) and hepatic veins (*yellow arrows*). **F.** Delayed image on patient of **C** to **E** shows a mottled enhancement pattern typical of passive hepatic congestion. **G.** Axial MR image following gadolinium administration shows reflux of contrast into a dilated inferior vena cava (*arrow*).

Peliosis hepatis is usually found incidentally at autopsy, but it can cause hepatic failure or liver rupture with hemoperitoneum and shock. Patients sometimes present with hepatomegaly, portal hypertension, esophageal varices, and ascites.

Radiologic Findings

The diagnosis of peliosis hepatis requires a high degree of suspicion because the radiographic and sonographic findings are nonspecific. Sonographically, the hepatic echo pattern is inhomogeneous, with hyperechoic and hypoechoic regions, predominantly in the right lobe.

Detecting lesions on CT scans is difficult unless there is associated fatty infiltration to contrast the higher-density aggregation of blood-filled spaces (Fig. 92-21). After bolus administration of contrast material, these lesions may appear hypodense early and isodense with time. Angiographically,

the peliotic lesions manifest as multiple small accumulations of contrast material on the late arterial phase, which become more prominent on the parenchymal and venous phases.[50-57]

PORTAL VEIN THROMBOSIS

Portal vein thrombosis is the leading cause of presinusoidal hypertension in the United States. The patency of this vessel is of major concern in the following groups of patients: newborn infants with umbilical catheters who present with ascites, cirrhosis patients who experience sudden decompensation of their disease and exacerbation of ascites, and liver transplant recipients. In some patients, portal vein obstruction is often a diagnosis of exclusion, whereas in others it first manifests as a major variceal hemorrhage or vascular emergency. In many cases, splanchnic vein thrombosis is found incidentally in patients with mild, nondescript abdominal pain.[58-60]

Clinical Findings

The clinical presentation of portal vein thrombosis depends on how acutely the obstruction develops and its underlying cause. In most cases, the disease presents insidiously, with nonspecific abdominal pain and other manifestations of portal hypertension, including splenomegaly; varices; and massive, intractable ascites, which is a bad prognostic sign. If the thrombosis is due to septic pyelophlebitis, the patient may present with hepatomegaly, pyrexia, leukocytosis, and liver abscesses. In some cases, the disease presents catastrophically, with intestinal infarction or massive variceal hemorrhage.[58-60]

Pathophysiology

The portal vein may develop a thrombus in its intrahepatic or extrahepatic course, and in 50% of cases, no cause may be apparent (Table 92-2). The most common extrahepatic causes of portal vein occlusion in the West include cancer of the stomach or pancreas and cholangiocarcinoma; acute diverticulitis or appendicitis initiating pyelophlebitis in the portal vein or mesenteric veins; pancreatitis or carcinoma

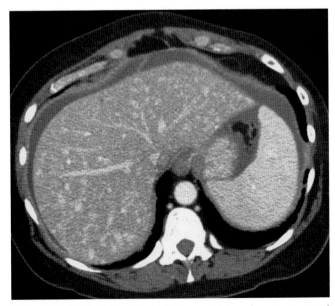

Figure 92-21. Peliosis hepatis. Multiple small lakes of contrast material are present on this CT scan. The patient also has ascites.

Table 92-2
Causes of Portal Vein Thrombosis

Hypercoagulable States
Antiphospholipid syndrome
Factor V mutations
Paroxysmal nocturnal hemoglobinuria
Myeloproliferative diseases
Oral contraceptive
Polycythemia rubra vera
Pregnancy
Protein S deficiency
Sickle cell disease

Inflammatory Disease
Behçet's disease
Crohn's disease
Pancreatitis
Ulcerative colitis

Complications of Medical Intervention
Alcohol injection
Ambulatory dialysis
Chemoembolization
Islet cell injection
Liver transplantation
Partial hepatectomy
Sclerotherapy
Splenectomy
Transjugular intrahepatic portosystemic shunt
Umbilical catheterization

Infections
Actinomycosis
Appendicitis
Candida albicans infection
Diverticulitis

Miscellaneous
Cirrhosis
Bladder cancer
Nodular regenerative hyperplasia

of the pancreas that initiates thrombosis of the splenic vein followed by propagation into the main portal vein; and postsurgical thrombosis after upper abdominal procedures, such as splenectomy, endoscopic injection sclerotherapy, liver transplantation, or trauma. Worldwide, schistosomiasis is the most common cause of portal vein obstruction and the leading cause of portal hypertension.[58-60]

Cirrhosis is the most common intrahepatic cause of portal vein thrombosis. It is estimated that 10% of patients with cirrhosis of the liver have portal vein thrombosis because stagnant intrahepatic flow predisposes to thrombus formation. These patients are likely to bleed earlier in the course of their disease than cirrhosis patients without portal vein thrombosis. Cirrhosis patients with portal vein thrombosis also tolerate portosystemic shunting better than most others because the hepatic artery supplies virtually all of their hepatic blood flow so that their hepatic hemodynamics are unaffected by portal venous diversion surgery. Less common causes of portal vein thrombosis are Budd-Chiari syndrome, congestive heart failure, intravascular invasion by primary or secondary neoplasms of the liver, cytomegalovirus infection, and Behçet's disease. The incidence of portal vein thrombosis in hepatocellular carcinoma is 26% to 34%, but at autopsy, tumor invasion of portal vein branches is seen in 70% and hepatic vein involvement in 13% of cases. Portal vein thrombosis has been

detected sonographically in 8% of patients with liver metastases. For detecting venous invasion in patients with hepatocellular carcinoma, sonography has a sensitivity of 64% and specificity of 98% as compared with arterial portography.[58-60]

Myeloproliferative disorders and blood dyscrasias account for approximately 12% to 48% of cases of portal vein thrombosis. Portal hypertension, from whatever cause, is also a major risk factor in the development of portal vein thrombosis.[58-60]

Radiologic Findings

Plain Radiographs

Calcification can occasionally be seen on plain abdominal radiographs in either the portal vein thrombus or the wall of the portal vein. The calcium is deposited diffusely in the clot, whereas mural calcifications are seen as parallel, discontinuous, radiodense lines directed along the course of the portal vein. Plain radiographs may reveal ileus; a localized sentinel loop; or, if the gut is ischemic or infarcted, thumbprinting caused by submucosal edema and hemorrhage.

Ultrasound

Failure to identify the portal vein is a significant finding and virtually diagnostic of portal vein occlusion. Ultrasound is the primary imaging modality for diagnosis and follow-up of portal vein thrombosis because of its ease of execution, sensitivity (particularly when combined with color Doppler studies), lower cost, and availability and because it does not require use of intravenous contrast material. Sonographically (Fig. 92-22), portal vein thrombosis manifests as an intraluminal echogenic reflector that can partially or completely fill the vein, obscuring normal portal vein landmarks. The portal vein may be expanded in acute thrombosis or when a neoplasm is present. Small sonolucencies may be present within tumor thrombus, but in most cases bland thrombus cannot be differentiated from tumor thrombus. Tumor thrombosis can be differentiated from bland thrombus by demonstrating color Doppler flow and arterial waveforms (often hepatofugal in direction) within the tumor thrombus on duplex Doppler. Lack of flow does not exclude tumor thrombus. Pulsatile flow is fairly specific for malignant thrombus. In these patients, the hepatic artery is dilated with increased systolic central streamline flow. In these cases, fine-needle aspiration under sonographic guidance identifies or excludes tumor. The superior mesenteric and splenic veins may dilate proximal to the thrombus as well. Although the sonographic appearance of tumor thrombus is nonspecific, neoplastic obstruction is often fairly obvious because the offending hepatic or pancreatic mass is usually quite large.[61-66]

Duplex Doppler imaging has a sensitivity of 100% and specificity of 93% in detecting thrombus of the main portal vein.[61-66] The diagnosis of intrahepatic portal vein thrombus is more difficult to establish confidently because of the high background echogenicity of the liver. Color flow Doppler sonography offers several distinct advantages over conventional spectral Doppler: it passively and automatically depicts blood flow in real time; it permits quick diagnosis of abnormal hepatofugal flow; it can reveal flow and collaterals that are invisible on gray-scale images; and it can allow diagnosis of potentially confusing helical blood flow.

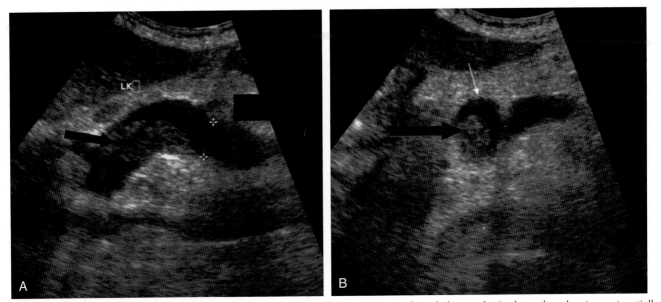

Figure 92-22. Portal vein thrombosis: sonographic findings. Sagittal (**A**) and axial (**B**) scans through the portal vein shows thrombus (*arrows*) partially occluding the lumen.

In chronic thrombosis, the portal vein can be normal sized or small, and bridging collaterals may develop in the porta hepatis, particularly when thrombus occurs early in life. These vessels are often quite prominent in cavernous transformation of the portal vein, which occurs in 30% of patients with portal vein occlusion.[61-66] Doppler examination shows a typical continuous, low-frequency portal venous flow pattern in these vessels. Secondary sonographic signs of portal vein thrombosis include splenomegaly, ascites, venous collaterals, and mesenteric vein thrombosis causing intestinal congestion or infarction. Serial scans are useful in these patients to determine the efficacy of therapy or to monitor the development of cavernous transformation after acute portal vein thrombosis.

Sonographic demonstration of normal portal and splenic vein diameter and normal vascular caliber variation during respiration excludes the diagnosis of portal vein occlusion with a high level of certainty. Ultrasound can also distinguish between tumor extension into the portal vein and extrinsic portal compression in cases of malignancy.

Computed Tomography

Portal vein thrombosis appears as a low-density central zone surrounded by an intensely enhanced periphery on contrast-enhanced scans (Figs. 92-23 and 92-24). It is not entirely clear whether this peripheral enhancement is due to flow around the clot or enhancement of the vasa vasorum of the portal vein wall. There is also transient inhomogeneous enhancement of the periportal hepatic parenchyma. Enlargement of the occluded vein increases the likelihood of the presence of tumor thrombus. There may also be streaky enhancement of the clot, which correlates with the angiographic finding of "threads" with septic thrombophlebitis and "streaks" seen in tumor thrombus (Fig. 92-25). On precontrast scans, the portal vein contents may be high in attenuation because of the high protein content of concentrated red blood cells.[61-66]

A number of indirect signs of portal vein thrombosis are related to alterations in segmental hepatic blood supply.

Portions of liver that experience segmental portal vein occlusion appear atrophic and have decreased attenuation on noncontrast scans. This appearance is caused by fatty infiltration secondary to "nutritional ischemia." Decreased parenchymal enhancement is also identified in the lobe involved by portal vein thrombosis. Increased arterial flow may be identified when scans are obtained during the arterial phase.[61-66]

Arterioportal shunting is another indirect sign of portal vein obstruction. In these cases, enhancement of the involved portal vein branch occurs early in the arterial phase. Calcification of the portal vein thrombus is also readily detected by CT.

On CT scans, portal vein thrombosis may simulate other disorders: gas in a collateral periportal vein can mimic an abscess; expansion of a thrombus-filled inferior mesenteric vein may resemble a pancreatic neoplasm or pseudocyst; segmentally occluded portal veins may simulate dilated bile ducts; and multiple intrahepatic stones may mimic calcified portal vein thrombus.

Magnetic Resonance Imaging

MRI is another excellent means of demonstrating portal vein thrombosis because of the natural contrast of moving blood (Figs. 92-26 and 92-27). A combination of black-blood techniques (e.g., spin-echo sequence with superior and inferior saturation pulses) or bright-blood techniques (e.g., time-of-flight gradient-echo or gadolinium-enhanced SGE) increases diagnostic confidence. MRI may fail to visualize the portal vein and its major branches at all in images that show flow in portal venous collaterals and hepatic veins.[61-66]

The appearance of the clot on MR images depends on its age, the oxidation state of hemoglobin, thrombus composition, organization in the thrombus, and field strength. Acute thrombus (<5 weeks old) appears hyperintense relative to muscle and liver on both T1-weighted and T2-weighted images. Older thrombi (between 2 and 18 months) appear hyperintense relative to liver but only on T2-weighted images.

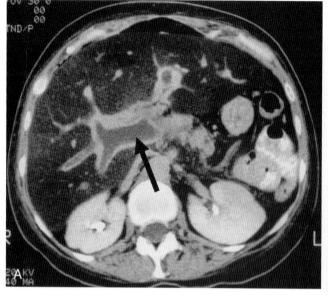

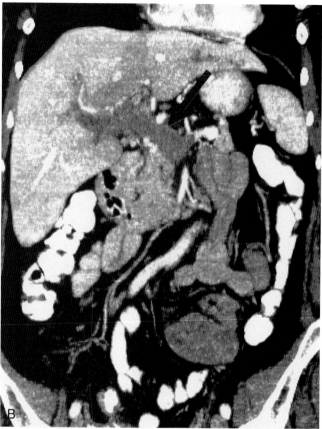

Figure 92-23. Portal vein thrombosis: CT findings. A. Axial CT image shows low attenuation thrombus (*arrow*) within the portal vein. Note the advanced hepatic steatosis. **B.** Coronal reformatted MDCT image shows thrombus in the main portal vein (*arrow*) extending into the liver.

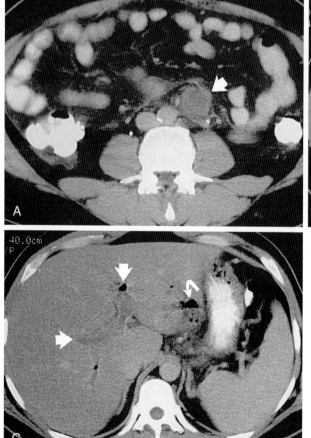

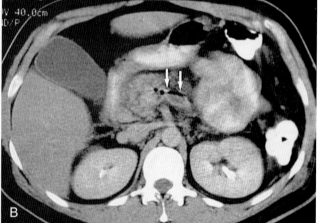

Figure 92-24. Septic portal vein thrombosis: CT findings. Acute diverticulitis-initiated septic ascending pyelophlebitis, portal vein thrombosis, and a liver abscess. **A.** Septic thrombus in the inferior mesenteric vein (*arrow*). **B.** Septic thrombus and gas are present within the splenic vein (*arrows*). **C.** Septic thrombus and gas are identified in the intrahepatic portal veins (*straight arrows*). A gas-containing abscess is visible in the left lobe of the liver (*curved arrow*).

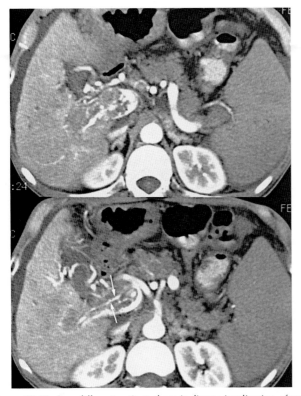

Figure 92-25. In a different patient, there is direct visualization of arterial neovascularity in tumor thrombus producing a "streaks and threads" (*arrows*) appearance. (Case courtesy of Richard L. Baron, MD, Chicago, IL.)

not enhance with gadolinium. In patients with infected bland thrombus, increased enhancement of the vein wall may be identified.

Intrahepatic portal vein occlusion can produce triangular, wedge-shaped regions in the liver that show high signal intensity on T2-weighted images and on immediate postgadolinium spoiled gradient-echo (SGE) images. The apex of this region is central, and the base abuts the liver capsule. Presumably, these changes are due to infarction or edema of the involved hepatic segment.[61-66]

As noted with CT, after the intravenous administration of gadolinium, transient increased enhancement of hepatic parenchyma may become evident in areas of decreased portal perfusion during the capillary phase of enhancement. Regions with absent or diminished portal blood supply have a commensurate increase in hepatic arterial blood supply. This autoregulatory mechanism provides that areas affected by portal vein thrombosis and increased arterial blood supply enhance intensely because the gadolinium delivered in the first phase is more concentrated in hepatic arteries than in portal veins and is delivered earlier by hepatic arteries than by portal veins. As the concentration of gadolinium in the hepatic arteries and portal veins equilibrates, this differential enhancement disappears.

Angiography

Portal vein thrombosis can usually be diagnosed angiographically, but it is better appreciated by direct cross-sectional imaging methods.

Treatment

Traditionally, the treatment of portal vein thrombosis has been based on early surgical and anticoagulant therapy. A number of percutaneous procedures in which the thrombosis is treated by angioplasty or is lysed by direct urokinase infusion have been reported.

Tumor and bland thrombus can be distinguished by the fact that tumor thrombus has a higher signal intensity on T2-weighted images, is soft tissue signal intensity on time-of-flight gradient-echo images, and enhances with gadolinium. Bland thrombus, by contrast, has a low signal intensity on T2-weighted and time-of-flight gradient echo images and does

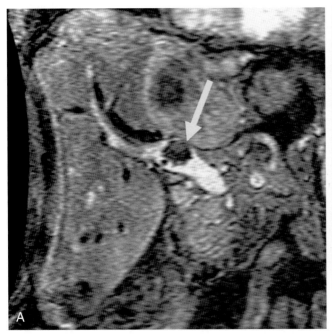

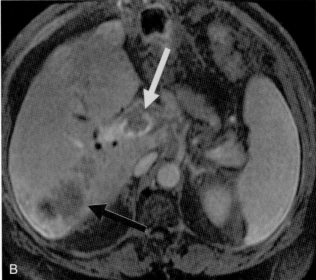

Figure 92-26. Portal vein thrombosis: MRI findings. Coronal (**A**) and axial (**B**) images show hepatocellular carcinoma (*red arrow*) that has invaded the portal vein (*yellow arrows*).

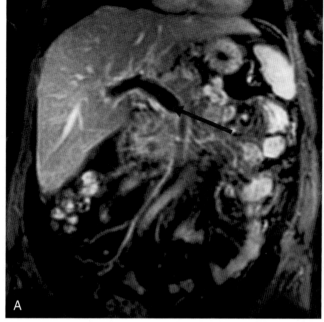

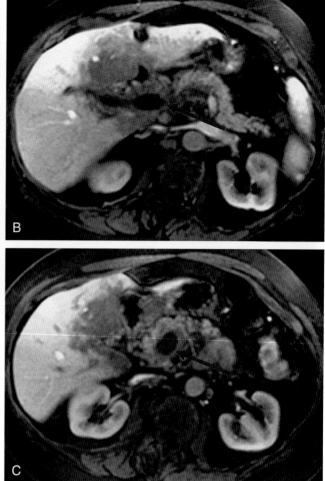

Figure 92-27. Portal and superior mesenteric vein thrombosis: MRI findings. Coronal (**A**) and axial (**B**) images show thrombus (*arrows*) in the main portal vein. **C.** The thrombus (*arrow*) continues into the superior mesenteric vein on this axial MR scan.

The surgical approach has two major difficulties: The collateral veins are often not sufficiently large to allow a bypass procedure to be performed, and there is an increased incidence of shunt thrombosis and obstruction when a bypass procedure is performed. Therefore, medical management is preferred, unless hemorrhage cannot be controlled, or there are repeated life-threatening bleeds.[61-66]

CAVERNOUS TRANSFORMATION OF THE PORTAL VEIN

Cavernous transformation of the portal vein (CTPV) develops when small collateral veins near the edge of the portal vein dilate, expand, and effectively replace the obliterated portal vein as the major hepatopetal venous conduit. These numerous wormlike vessels at the porta hepatis represent periportal collateral circulation. This transformation develops in long-standing thrombosis, requiring 12 months to occur, and thus more commonly is found in benign disease. This remarkable collateral development reflects the body's effort to maintain hepatopetal portal flow to the liver in the face of occlusion of the extrahepatic portal veins. Collaterals of this magnitude do not typically develop in cirrhotic patients because intrahepatic portal resistance is high in cirrhosis.[67-69]

In patients with CTPV, sonograms show a mass of tubular anechoic collaterals (Fig. 92-28). Normal portal venous landmarks are obliterated. Doppler evaluation of these collaterals show a slightly turbulent low-velocity venous signal with little or no respiratory or cardiac variation. It is hepatopetal in direction and has portal venous waveform. Associated findings include splenomegaly, thickening and varices of the lesser omentum, spontaneous splenorenal shunts, and gallbladder varices.

On CT (Fig. 92-29) and MRI (Fig. 92-30), CTPV appears as contrast medium-filled portal collaterals in the hepatoduodenal ligament. In addition, compensatory arterial blood flow in these patients may produce a peculiar enhancement pattern.

CTPV induces morphologic changes in the liver, the most common being atrophy of the right hepatic lobe and left lateral segment and hypertrophy of liver segment IV and the caudate lobe. It is postulated that segment IV and the caudate lobe become hypertrophic with CTPV because of their close proximity to the cavernous transformation, which results in maintained portal inflow. Similarly, the right liver lobe and the left lateral segment become atrophic with CTPV because of their greater distance from the cavernous transformation which leads to compromised portal venous flow.[68]

SUPERIOR MESENTERIC VEIN THROMBOSIS

Isolated superior mesenteric vein (SMV) thrombosis accounts for only 5% to 15% of all intestinal vascular thromboses, being

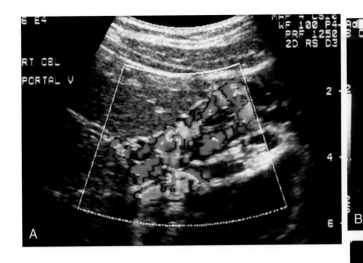

Figure 92-28. Cavernous transformation of the portal vein: sonographic features. Color Doppler scans show multiple collateral vessels in the portal vein (**A**) and splenic vein (**B**) in a patient with shistosomiasis. **C.** Multiple collateral vessels are identified in the porta hepatis in a different patient.

less common than arterial occlusion. It is most common in patients in their 50s and 60s, and 81% of patients have associated illnesses.[70-73]

Clinical Findings

Superior mesenteric vein (SMV) thrombosis can be classified into acute and chronic presentations for the purposes of management. In acute thrombosis, the patients present with symptoms of less than 4 weeks duration. The patient has pain out of proportion to the physical findings, nausea, and vomiting, with or without bloody diarrhea. Most cases are associated with metabolic acidosis and mild to moderate leukocytosis. Venous thrombosis occurs in younger patients than with arterial thrombosis.[70-73]

Chronic mesenteric thrombosis is difficult to detect as the onset is insidious and patients are asymptomatic until late complication occur, such as variceal bleeding due to portal hypertension. The patients may present with weight loss, food avoidance, postprandial pain, or distention.[70-73]

Pathophysiology

The causes of isolated SMV thrombosis include myeloproliferative disorders, peritonitis and inflammatory disorders of the abdomen, tumor compression, portal hypertension, the postoperative state, hypercoagulable states (antithrombin III

and protein C and protein S deficiencies), Weber-Christian disease, blood dyscrasias, and pancreatic neoplasms. Extensive venous collaterals in the gut prevent infarction in most cases of SMV thrombosis, so that the mortality rate is only 20%, lower than the 40% to 60% rate for arterial occlusion.[70-73]

Radiologic Findings

Plain film findings are usually noncontributory and may show only ileus. Pneumatosis intestinalis can be seen if the bowel is infarcted, and ascites may develop in patients with chronic SMV thrombosis. Bowel wall thickening and mucosal irregularity indicate intestinal ischemia. On CT scans, the SMV thrombus (see Fig. 92-31) appears as a low-density intraluminal mass with a hyperdense periphery, as is seen in portal vein thrombosis. If there is intestinal ischemia as well, mural thickening of the gut may also be seen. Selective angiography usually shows spasm of the superior mesenteric artery (SMA) and no opacification of the affected veins in the venous phase.

Ultrasound is effective in allowing diagnosis of splanchnic vein thrombosis, but if there is no associated portal vein thrombus, the diagnosis of SMV thrombosis is much more difficult, particularly in patients with a gassy abdomen. The gray-scale and Doppler characteristics of SMV thrombus are similar to those seen in the portal vein. Similarly, the CT and MRI findings are identical to those of portal vein thrombosis.

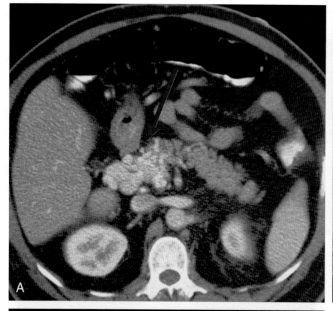

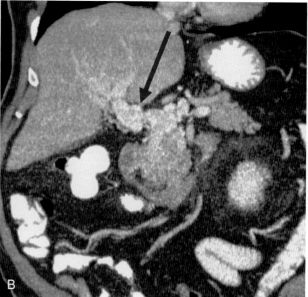

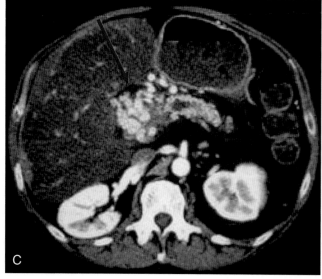

Figure 92-29. Cavernous transformation of the portal vein: CT features. Axial (**A**) and coronal (**B**) MDCT reformatted images show multiple enhancing tubular structures (*arrows*) in the hepato-duodenal ligament. **C.** In a different patient with chronic pancreatitis, axial CT image shows dilation of the pancreatic duct and cavernous transformation of the portal vein (*red arrow*). Note the diffuse hepatic steatosis.

Figure 92-30. Cavernous transformation of the portal vein: MRI features. MR portogram show multiple dilated peribiliary collaterals (*yellow arrow*) from the superior mesenteric and splenic veins to the intrahepatic portal veins. Note the dilated right gonadal vein (*red arrow*).

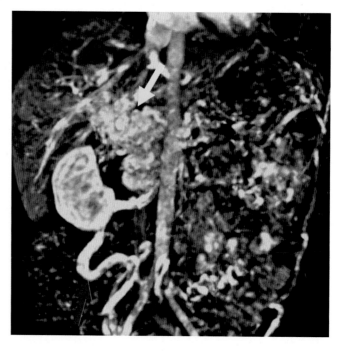

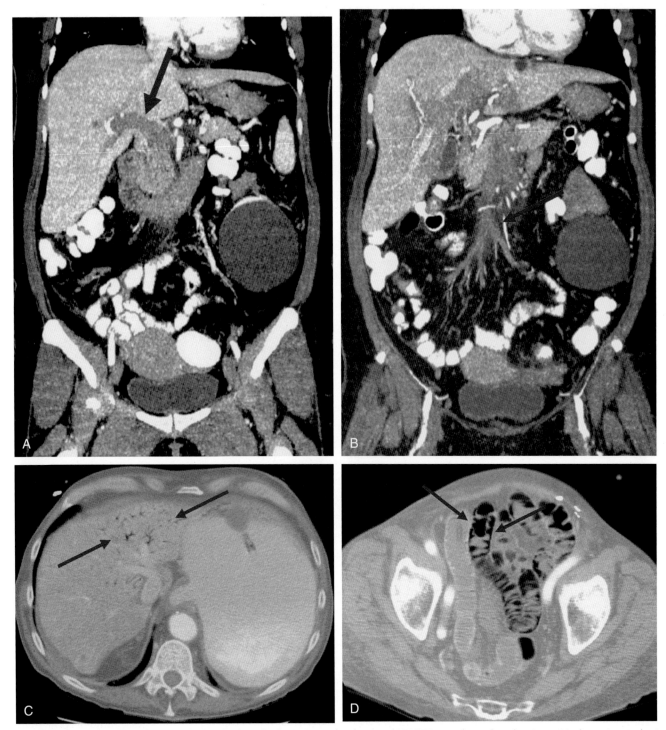

Figure 92-31. Portal and superior mesenteric vein thrombosis. A. Coronal, reformatted MDCT image shows thrombus (*arrow*) in the main portal vein in this patient with a coagulopathy. She presented with only vague, long-standing abdominal discomfort and has done well on oral anticoagulant therapy. **B.** Coronal reformatted image, dorsal to **A** demonstrates thrombus (*arrow*) extending into the superior mesenteric vein and its branches. Note the absence of ischemic or hemorrhagic mesenteric or small bowel abnormalities. Superior mesenteric venous thrombosis can have a more devastating effect. In a different patient, portal venous gas (*arrows*) is present within the left lobe of the liver (**C**) secondary to small bowel ischemia (**D**), which produced pneumatosis (*arrows*).

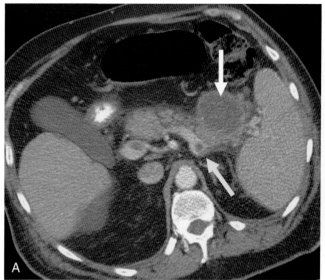

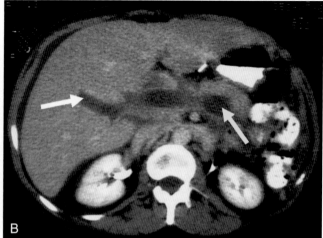

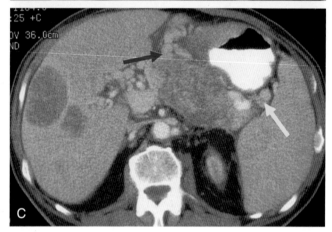

Figure 92-32. Splenic vein thrombosis. A. A small thrombus (*yellow arrow*) is present in this patient with pancreatitis and a pseudocyst (*white arrow*). **B.** Propagation of splenic vein thrombus (*yellow arrow*) into the intrahepatic portal vein (*white arrow*) following a splenectomy. **C.** The pancreas and splenic vein have been invaded by gastric carcinoma. Note the collateral blood vessels in the gastrohepatic (*red arrow*) and gastrosplenic (*yellow arrow*) as well as two liver metastases.

Treatment

Small bowel resection in patients with SMV thrombosis is associated with high rates of morbidity and mortality, so that conservative management is indicated when there are no signs of intestinal ischemia or infarction. Direct infusion of fibrinolytic agents into the mesenteric-portal system has been suggested as an alternative treatment in mesenteric vein occlusion. In this procedure, access to the portal system is gained under sonographic guidance, as in percutaneous transhepatic portography, and a large dose of urokinase is infused.[70-73]

SPLENIC VEIN THROMBOSIS

Splenic vein occlusion is usually a result of pancreatitis, pancreatic carcinoma, lymphoma, or propagation of clot from the portal vein. Chronic pancreatitis accounts for 65% of all cases of splenic vein thrombosis.[74-77] This condition is often clinically silent, but it may cause localized venous hypertension that can result in splenomegaly and bleeding gastric varices. Splenic vein thrombosis should be suspected in patients with splenomegaly and a history of gastrointestinal hemorrhage with normal liver function tests. Other causes include sclerotherapy, splenectomy, and the causes of portal vein and superior mesenteric artery (SMA) thrombosis.

Splenic vein occlusion produces rerouting of venous flow through the short gastric veins and gastroepiploic vein, causing "left-sided" portal hypertension. Gastric varices in the cardia and fundus are seen in 74% to 83% of patients with splenic vein occlusion.[74-77] They appear as broad, serpentine, redundant filling defects or clusters of polypoid defects, simulating thickened rugal folds. These represent the short gastric, gastroepiploic, and left gastric veins that drain retrogradely into the portal vein. Diagnosis is difficult because they are located primarily in the subserosa. The appearance of thrombus on CT, ultrasound, and MRI studies in splenic vein thrombosis is identical to that observed in portal or SMV thrombosis (see Fig. 92-32).

Isolated gastric varices of the short gastric and coronary vessels without esophageal varices were thought to be highly suggestive of splenic vein obstruction; however, one study has demonstrated that portal hypertension is still the most common underlying cause.[74-77] Dilatation of the gastroepiploic veins is seen only in splenic vein thrombosis.

Splenic vein thrombosis secondary to pancreatitis is now recognized as a fairly common cause of upper gastrointestinal hemorrhage in these patients. For this problem, splenectomy and gastrotomy with oversewing of bleeding varices is sufficient treatment.[74-77] Isolated gastric varices caused by splenic

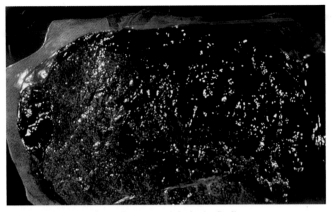

Figure 92-33. Hepatic infarction: pathologic findings. Autopsy specimen from a patient who died of septic shock shows multiple regions of hemorrhage within the liver.

vein occlusion can be cured in 90% of cases, and the incidence of recurrent bleeding is low.[74-77]

HEPATIC INFARCTION

Clinical Findings

Hepatic infarction is a relatively uncommon occurrence because of the liver's dual blood supply and hepatocytes' tolerance for low oxygen saturation. Hepatic infarction has been associated with shock (Fig. 92-33), sepsis, anesthesia, oral contraceptives, sickle cell disease or trait, polyarteritis nodosa, eclampsia, metastatic carcinoma, bacterial endocarditis, arterial emboli in rheumatic heart disease, trauma, and intra-arterial hepatic chemotherapy. The incidence of ischemic hepatitis in cirrhotic patients admitted to the intensive care unit with variceal bleeding is reported to be as high as 9% with a 60% mortality.[78-80]

The clinical diagnosis is problematic. Patients usually present with the nonspecific findings of abdominal or back pain (or both), fever, leukocytosis, and abnormal liver function tests, but they may be relatively asymptomatic.

Pathologic Findings

Ischemic hepatitis is usually diagnosed on the basis of characteristic hepatic histopathologic appearance: minimal centrilobular necrosis and seronegativity for viral hepatitis.

Radiologic Findings

It is difficult to detect hepatic infarction during its early stages by cross-sectional imaging. The region becomes sonographically hypoechoic when there is sufficient edema and round cell infiltration with indistinct margins. As the necrotic tissue is resorbed, small bile duct cysts or lakes may form. These lakes have the same microscopic appearance as the cysts seen in Caroli's disease, suggesting that the cause of the latter disorder may actually be neonatal hepatic infarction. Occasionally, large bile duct lakes can be seen on CT and ultrasound studies. Infarcts are usually well-circumscribed, peripheral, wedge-shaped lesions, but they can be round or oval and centrally located. With time, areas of infarction develop a more distinct margin and may undergo considerable atrophy (Fig. 92-34). Not all wedge-shaped areas of decreased attenuation on CT scans are due to infarction; decreased portal flow from thrombus, tumor compression, or segmental hepatic vein obstruction may produce a similar picture. Gas formation within sterile infarcts has also been described on CT and ultrasound studies. On MR images, the edema of infarction lengthens T1 and T2 relaxation times, causing lower signal intensity on T1-weighted images and higher signal intensity on T2-weighted images of the involved liver.[78-80]

HEMOLYSIS, ELEVATED LIVER ENZYMES, LOW PLATELETS (HELLP) SYNDROME

Hepatic ischemia, hemorrhage, and infarction are well-known complications of pregnancy-related HELLP (*h*emolysis, *e*levated *l*iver enzymes, *l*ow *p*latelets) syndrome. It is a variant of toxemia that occurs either antepartum or postpartum and develops in 4% to 12% of patients with severe preeclampsia.[81-83] The pathophysiology of HELLP syndrome is related to endothelial damage in the placental bed, resulting in activation of the

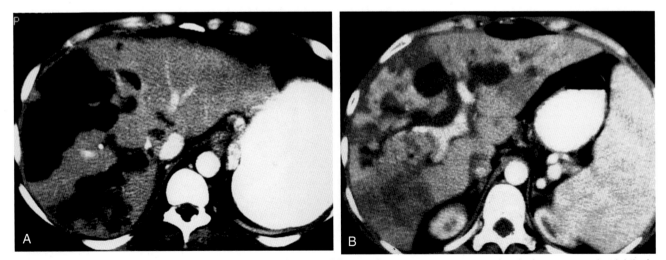

Figure 92-34. Hepatic infarction: CT features. A and B. Multiple areas of decreased attenuation are present within the liver associated with bile duct lakes.

platelets, which causes them to aggregate and the coagulation cascade, which leads to disseminated intravascular coagulation. The hemolytic anemia is due to passage of red blood cells through small vessels with damaged endothelium covered by fibrin. Fibrin deposition in the liver leads to hepatocellular damage, necrosis, and hemorrhage.

Epigastric or right upper quadrant pain is found in 90% of patients and may be associated with malaise, nausea, vomiting, headache, and nasal bleeding.[81-83] Confirmatory laboratory data include hemolytic anemia (hemoglobin <11 g/dL), elevated liver enzymes (lactate dehydrogenase >400 IU/L), and thrombocytopenia (<100,000/μL).[81-83]

The clinical course of HELLP syndrome is variable. Important complications include massive liver cell necrosis, severe disseminated intravascular coagulation, abruptio placentae, renal failure, pulmonary edema, maternal hypoglycemia, and rupture of subcapsular hematoma, with a maternal mortality rate of 3.3%. Standard treatment consists of expeditious delivery of the fetus.[81-83]

Imaging studies are usually performed in these patients to determine the cause of the abdominal complaints. Sonographically, the portions of the liver undergoing necrosis have increased echogenicity. CT scan reveals well-defined hypodense, nonenhancing areas or multiple peripheral wedge-shaped areas of low attenuation (Fig. 92-35). The CT and ultrasound appearance in these patients is nonspecific and can mimic focal areas of fatty infiltration.[84,85]

The MRI appearance in the HELLP syndrome depends on the degree of hemorrhage, necrosis, and steatosis. When edema or cellular necrosis predominates, the affected areas have a low signal intensity on T1-weighted images and high signal intensity on T2-weighted images.[84,85]

VISCERAL ARTERY ANEURYSMS

Clinical Findings

Splenic artery aneurysms account for 60% of visceral artery aneurysms followed by the hepatic artery (20%), the SMA (5.5%); celiac artery (4%); gastric and gastroepiploic arteries (4%); jejunal, ileal, and colic arteries (4%); pancreaticoduodenal and pancreatic arteries (2%); gastroduodenal artery (1.5%); and inferior mesenteric artery (<1%).[86-95]

The splenic artery is a tortuous structure due to a number of factors: the movement of the spleen and differing volumes of blood needed to supply it; the pulsatile nature of the blood flow causes excess stretching of the artery, thereby causing the loops and bends seen angiographically and on cross sectional imaging; the various branches of the splenic artery that supply the pancreas anchor and prevent the elongating splenic artery from forming one large loop instead of multiple, small excursions from the direct path. The dilated, tortuous splenic artery protects the delicate splenic pulp less forceful and more indirect.[87]

Splenic artery aneurysms are four times more common in women than in men and most are small (2-4 cm), asymptomatic, solitary, sacular, and located in the middle to distal splenic artery. There is also an association of splenic artery aneurysm and pregnancy, parity, and portal hypertension. This female predilection likely relates to the hormonal effect of estrogen and progesterone, both with receptor sites in the arterial wall. The hormone relaxin, which is responsible for elasticity of the symphysis pubis in late pregnancy, may also alter the elasticity of the arterial wall. The high flow rate associated with pregnancy and portal hypertension contribute to the deleterious effects on the arterial wall.[86-95]

Rupture is a catastrophic event that manifests with pain and hypotension. Impending rupture of a splenic artery aneurysm can produce left upper quadrant pain that radiates to the left subcapsular region. In 20% to 30% of patients, there is double rupture: the initial rupture is contained within the lesser sac followed by penetration of the lesser sac and free rupture into the peritoneal cavity. Rupture of a splenic artery aneurysm, most common during the third trimester, is a catastrophic event, with reported maternal and fetal mortality rates of 70% and 90%, respectively.[86-95]

Ruptured and symptomatic splenic artery aneurysms require treatment, as do those found in pregnant women and women of childbearing age. Patients with portal hypertension or those who undergo liver transplantation are also

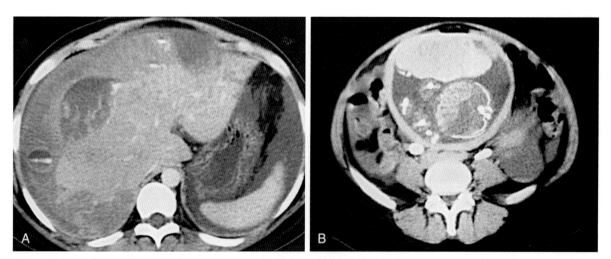

Figure 92-35. HELLP syndrome. This pregnant patient presented with acute abdominal pain, *h*emolysis, elevated *l*iver enzymes, and *l*ow *p*latelets *(HELLP)*. **A.** CT scan shows hepatic hemorrhage with active contrast extravasation from multiple sites. Hypodense areas are also present, suggesting thrombosis. **B.** CT scan obtained at a lower level shows the fetus.

candidates for treatment. Enlarging aneurysm and those larger than 2.5-3.0 cm typically require treatment.[86-95]

Hepatic artery aneurysms show a male predilection of 2:1. Most are solitary and involve the extrahepatic artery, in which case they are most often degenerative or dysplastic. Intrahepatic hepatic artery aneurysms are most frequently the result of trauma, iatrogenic injury from biopsy or intervention, infection, or vasculitis. The use of MDCT has resulted in an increased detection of post-traumatic false aneurysms of the intrahepatic arterial branches. Approximately 60% of hepatic artery aneurysms are symptomatic, and patients most often present with epigastric or right upper quadrant pain, followed in frequency by gastrointestinal hemorrhage and jaundice.[86-95] The classic triad of abdominal pain, hemobilia, and obstructive jaundice is observed in only 30% of cases.[86-95] When these findings are accompanied by an abdominal bruit or pulsatile mass, the diagnosis of hepatic artery aneurysm should be suspected. The aneurysm may rupture into the peritoneal cavity, extrahepatic bile duct, duodenum, gallbladder, portal vein, or stomach. Obstructive jaundice may result from intrabiliary clots or from extrinsic compression. The mean age at diagnosis is 38 years, and a twofold to threefold male predominance is observed. Extrahepatic aneurysms are four times more common than intrahepatic aneurysms. It is essential to diagnose and treat hepatic artery aneurysms because of the high incidence of rupture and an associated mortality of up to 82% when this occurs.[86-95]

Aneurysms and pseudoaneurysms of the gastroduodenal and pancreaticoduodenal arteries are often complications of acute and chronic pancreatitis and pancreatic surgery. Most of these aneurysms are symptomatic and manifest with gastrointestinal, intraperitoneal, or retroperitoneal hemorrhage.

Aneurysms of the superior mesenteric artery account for 5.5% of all visceral artery aneurysms and can be saccular or fusiform. Most occur within the proximal 5 cm of this vessel. Most occur in men and are most often diagnosed in the fifth decade of life. These aneurysms may be mycotic in origin or secondary to inflammation, vasculitis, trauma, arterial dissection, and dysplasia and degeneration. These aneurysms are often symptomatic, presenting with acute and colicky upper abdominal pain, nausea, and vomiting.[86-95]

Celiac artery aneurysms account for 4% of all visceral artery aneurysm and are associated with abdominal aortic aneurysms in 20% of cases and other visceral artery aneurysms in 40%. There is no gender predilection, and most present in the fifth decade of life. The risk of rupture is approximately 13% with high mortality.

In early studies, rupture of visceral artery aneurysm were reported in 22% of cases.[86-95] Now a large number are discovered incidentally when the patient is being scanned for other reasons. Indeed, the routine use of MDCT and MRI has lead to the increased diagnosis of both symptomatic and asymptomatic aneurysms. Most are degenerative, demonstrating deficiency of the arterial media. Pancreatitis with the escape of pancreatic enzymes may promote destruction of the arterial wall, resulting in pseudoaneurysms of the splenic, hepatic, gastroduodenal, and pancreaticoduodenal arteries. These aneurysms can be treated with surgical or endovascular approaches.

Radiologic Findings

Hepatic artery aneurysms (Fig. 92-36) may produce curvilinear calcification of the right upper quadrant and, when large, produce a mass effect on adjacent viscera on barium studies or on the bile ducts on cholangiograms. Duplex and color flow Doppler studies are the noninvasive screening methods of choice for hepatic artery aneurysm. A pulsatile, cystic mass with arterial flow or a sonolucent or mixed echogenic mass with dilatation of ducts proximally suggests the diagnosis. Noncontrast CT may show aneurysm wall calcification. After the bolus administration of contrast material, the residual lumen demonstrates intense enhancement. Often a low-density thrombus is seen peripherally. MRI demonstrates a tubular structure that has flow void or strong signal intensity depending on the imaging sequence used. These aneurysms must be differentiated from pancreatic pseudocysts and cystic pancreatic neoplasms.

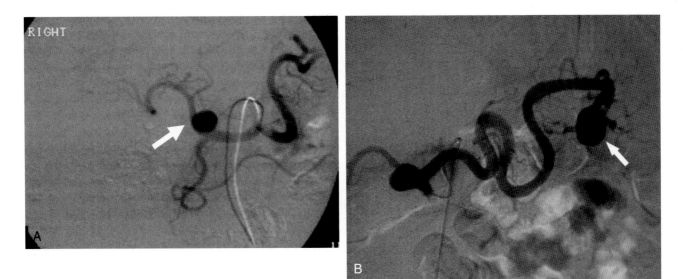

Figure 92-36. Visceral artery aneurysms. A. Digital subtraction angiogram shows an aneurysm (*arrow*) of the proximal proper hepatic artery just after the origin of the gastroduodenal artery. **B.** Aneurysm (*arrow*) of the distal portion of the splenic artery is evident on this angiogram.

Treatment of these lesions is either surgical (ligation or vein grafting) or angiographic (absorbable gelatin foam plugs for small aneurysms and Gianturco coils for larger ones). Invasive radiographic methods are becoming increasingly popular because of the high morbidity and mortality associated with surgery. Reconstructive or ablative surgery is indicated for extrahepatic aneurysm, whereas interventional techniques are favored for those in intrahepatic sites.

Aneurysms of the SMA are rare and may be congenital or associated with pancreatitis, trauma, neoplasm, mycoses, or atherosclerotic disease. Clinically, they manifest as a pulsatile mass with a systolic bruit. SMA aneurysms may be saccular or fusiform and are also always located within the first 5 cm of the SMA. The SMA is the most common site for infection of a peripheral muscular artery, which most often occurs secondary to subacute bacterial endocarditis caused by non-hemolytic streptococcal infection. Almost all patients are younger than 50 years. Over the previous four decades, infected aneurysms accounted for 58% to 63% of all SMA aneurysms. Over the past decade, this has decreased to 33% of reported aneurysms.[86-95] This decrease has been accompanied by an increase in the incidence of true aneurysms in the elderly as well as an increase in the incidence of false aneurysms associated with inflammatory processes of pancreas and biliary tract seen in 12% of SMA aneurysms. Dissection, although uncommon, affects the SMA more than any other visceral artery. Atherosclerosis is present in 25% of reported SMA aneurysms.[86-95]

In contrast to other visceral artery aneurysms, most SMA aneurysms are symptomatic, presenting with moderate to severe abdominal pain that is usually progressive in its course. A palpable mass is present in 50% of patients, who may also experience nausea, vomiting, gastrointestinal hemorrhage, hemobilia, or jaundice.[86-95]

SPLANCHNIC VEIN ANEURYSMS

Aneurysms of the portal venous system are uncommon. They represent only 3% of all aneurysm of the venous system but are the most common visceral aneurysms.[96-104] Because there are variations in the diameters in normal and cirrhotic livers, an aneurysm of the portal venous system is present if the vessel diameter larger at that point (usually 2 cm) than in the remainder of the vessel. They are usually secondary to pancreatitis and trauma but may be congenital in origin and are seen increasingly in patients with cirrhosis and portal hypertension.

The clinical features of portal vein aneurysms vary. Large aneurysms can cause duodenal compression, common bile duct obstruction, or chronic portal hypertension. Complete obstruction of the portal vein by thrombosis or aneurysm rupture can also occur. Patients who have no symptoms and no signs of portal hypertension should be followed by serial ultrasound scans.

Complications of portal vein aneurysms include rupture, thrombosis, complete occlusion of the portal vein, portosystemic shunts, or biliary tract compression.

On ultrasound (Fig. 92-37) and CT studies, a dilated portal vein can usually be identified and distinguished from other lesions. The aneurysm is anechoic, but if thrombus is present, Doppler studies are necessary for confirmation. On Doppler

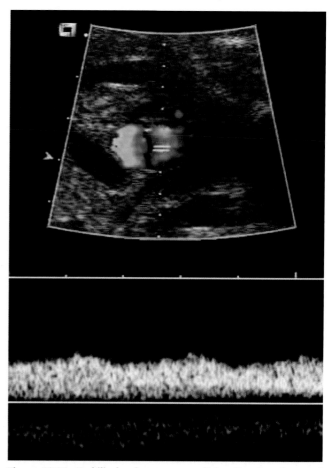

Figure 92-37. Umbilical vein aneurysm. Color Doppler ultrasound shows flow in this venous aneurysm.

ultrasound, constantly rotating blood is found in an aneurysm of the splenic vein and SMV. Contrast-enhanced CT and MRI will show robust enhancement of the aneurysm.

OSLER-WEBER-RENDU DISEASE

Osler-Weber-Rendu disease or hereditary hemorrhagic telangiectasia (HHT) is a rare (incidence of 1 to 2:100,000) autosomal dominant disorder characterized by multiple mucocutaneous telangiectasias that may involve most organ systems.[105-111] Hepatic involvement is frequent and is usually diagnosed 10 to 20 years after the first appearance of mucocutaneous telangiectasias. The typical pathologic features are angiodysplastic vascular changes, including telangiectases, cavernous hemangiomas, aneurysms of the intraparenchymal branches of the hepatic artery, and both hepatoportal and hepatohepatic arteriovenous fistula. Many patients develop high-output heart failure as a result of left-to-right intrahepatic shunts.

On Doppler ultrasound examinations in patients with HHT, the spectral waveforms show high-velocity flow (153 cm/second) in the dilated and tortuous hepatic artery and its branches. Hepatic artery-to-portal vein shunts cause pulsatility of portal flow with phasic or continuous reversal. Hepatic artery-to-hepatic vein shunts cause significant changes in the Doppler waveform of the hepatic vein only in severe stages of

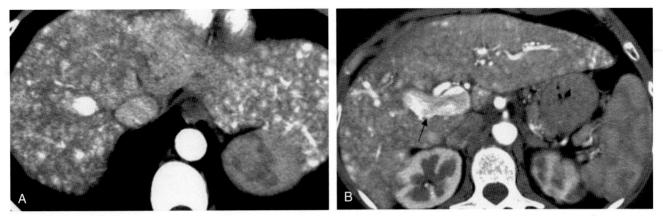

Figure 92-38. Osler-Weber-Rendu disease: CT features. A. CT angiogram shows diffuse parenchymal heterogeneity and numerous telangiectases. **B.** Dilation and early filling of main portal vein (*arrow*) during arterial phase are consistent with arterioportal shunt. (From Wu JS, Saluja S, Garcia-Tsao G, et al: Liver involvement in hereditary hemorrhagic telangiectasia. AJR 187:W399-W405, 2006. Reprinted with permission from the American Journal of Roentgenology.)

the disease. Color Doppler sonography demonstrates a large arteriovenous malformation or tangled masses of enlarged tortuous arteries or multiple aneurysms of the hepatic arterial branches within the liver.[105-111]

Contrast-enhanced CT (Fig. 92-38) shows a prominent extrahepatic or both extrahepatic and intrahepatic hepatic artery that is often associated with dilated hepatic or portal veins. Early filling of the portal venous or hepatic venous trunks on helical CT indicates the presence of an arteriovenous shunt. The intrahepatic arteriovenous fistula are being visualized with increased frequency with the use of MDCT. Other abnormalities include telangiectasias, large confluent vascular masses, and transient hepatic attenuation differences.[105-111]

MR angiograms can provide a map of the anomalous vessels. Dynamic gradient-echo imaging obtained after the injection of Gd-DTPA allows analysis of filling kinetics.

Angiograms in HHT show tortuous dilated hepatic arteries, diffuse angiectases with a diffuse mottled capillary blush, hemangiomas, and early filling of hepatic or portal veins indicating a shunt. The angiographic appearance depends on the stage of development of the hepatic arteriovenous shunt. All findings are present if the shunting is severe, whereas isolated parenchymal modifications are found only in case of mild intrahepatic shunt.

HEPATOPULMONARY SYNDROME

The hepatopulmonary syndrome (HPS) describes the clinical relationship between hepatic dysfunction and the presence of pulmonary vascular dilations, which can result in a range of arterial oxygenation abnormalities. HPS can be defined as a triad characterized by severe parenchymal liver disease, hypoxemia (an increased alveolar-arterial gradient while breathing room air), and evidence of intrapulmonary vascular dilatations.[112-116]

Pathophysiology

A number of mechanisms underlying the impaired gas exchange in the hepatopulmonary syndrome have been proposed: intrapulmonary and portopulmonary shunts, pleural spiders,

pulmonary hypertension, ventilation-perfusion mismatch, and changes in the affinity of hemoglobin for oxygen.[112-115] It now appears that vascular abnormalities known as intrapulmonary vascular dilatations are the major cause of severe hypoxemia and are the defining features of the hepatopulmonary syndrome (Fig. 92-39).

Imaging of Intrapulmonary Vascular Dilatations

Contrast-Enhanced Echocardiography

Contrast-enhanced echocardiography, although generally used to assess intracardiac right-to-left shunts, is valuable for demonstrating the presence of intrapulmonary vascular dilatations in patients with hypoxemia and liver disease. Indocyanine

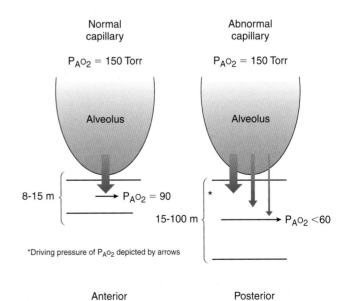

Figure 92-39. Hepatopulmonary syndrome: pathophysiology. Schematic diagram of the precapillary vascular abnormality seen in both acute and chronic liver disorders. The driving pressure of P_AO_2 is depicted by the *arrows*.

green dye and agitated saline are used to provide a stream of microbubbles 60 to 90 μm in diameter that usually opacify only the right heart chambers. The normal pulmonary capillary bed filters these microbubbles so that they do not appear in the left side of the heart. In the presence of an intracardiac or intrapulmonary shunt, microbubbles or indocyanine dye opacifies the left heart chambers.

Intracardiac intrapulmonary shunts can be differentiated by the timing of the appearance of left-sided bubbles after contrast injection. With intracardiac right-to-left shunts, microbubbles or dye is visualized within three heartbeats after the appearance of bubbles in the right heart chambers. In intrapulmonary shunts, the appearance of contrast material in the left heart chambers is delayed, occurring four to six heartbeats after the initial appearance of contrast material in the right side of the heart.[112-116]

Perfusion Lung Scanning

The perfusion lung scan (Fig. 92-40) with technetium Tc 99m–labeled macroaggregated albumin is the second major method for detecting intrapulmonary vascular dilatation. The normal pulmonary capillary bed (diameter, 8-15 μm) traps the albumin macroaggregates, which generally exceed 20 μm in diameter. The presence of isotope in the brain or kidneys indicates a right-to-left shunt through either an intracardiac or an intrapulmonary shunt. The shunt magnitude is calculated by taking the ratio of the systemic to total body activity of the isotope. Approximately 3% to 6% of the macroaggregated albumin passes through the normal pulmonary vascula-ture. Shunts ranging from 10% to 71% have been documented in patients with HPS.[112-116]

Chest Radiograph

Patients with HPS usually display the same abnormalities on the chest radiograph that may be seen in all cirrhotic patients: decreased lung volumes, pleural effusions, increased interstitial markings, and increased pulmonary vascular markings. Increased bilateral basilar interstitial markings attributed to intrapulmonary vascular dilatations and increased pulmonary vascular markings may be seen as well. These findings are nonspecific.

CT and Angiography

On CT and angiography (Fig. 92-41), the vascular dilatations are depicted as enlarged vessels that do not taper normally, extend to the pleural surface and are most numerous at the lung bases. The ratio of the segmental arterial diameter to bronchial diameter in the right lower lobe is significantly higher in patients with HPS than in cirrhotic patients with normoxemic liver cirrhosis.[112-116]

Treatment

Treatment of HPS is liver transplantation.[117,118] If the lungs are irreversibly damaged, a liver-lung transplant is in order. The TIPS procedure has been used as a temporizing measure in patients awaiting transplant.

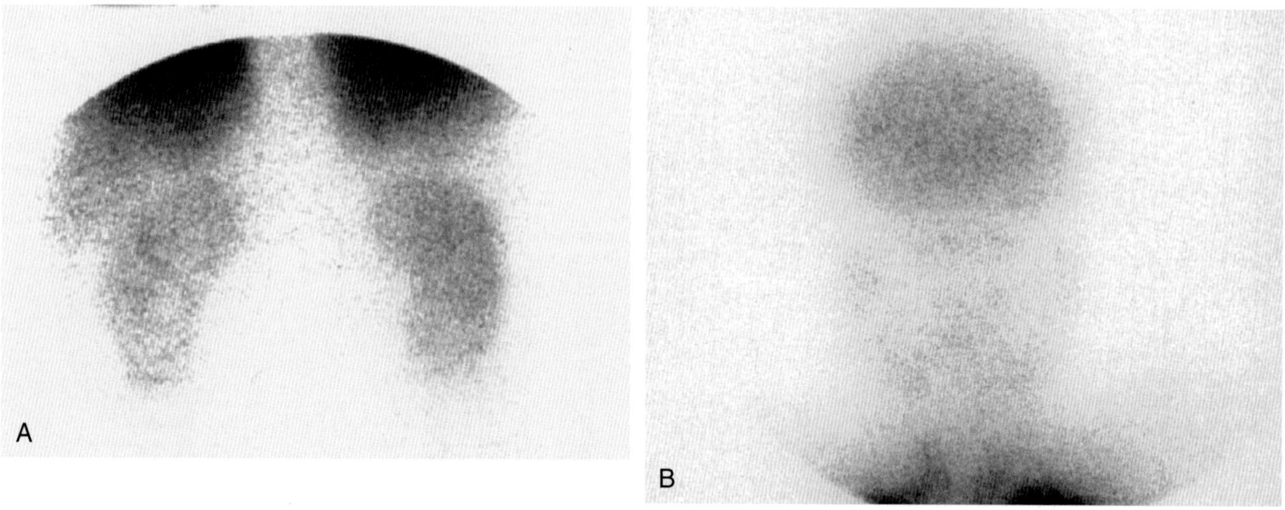

Figure 92-40. Hepatopulmonary syndrome: scintigraphy. Pulmonary perfusion images obtained with technetium 99m (99mTc) macroaggregated albumin show extrapulmonary uptake in the kidneys (**A**) and brain (**B**). This indicates right-to-left shunting.

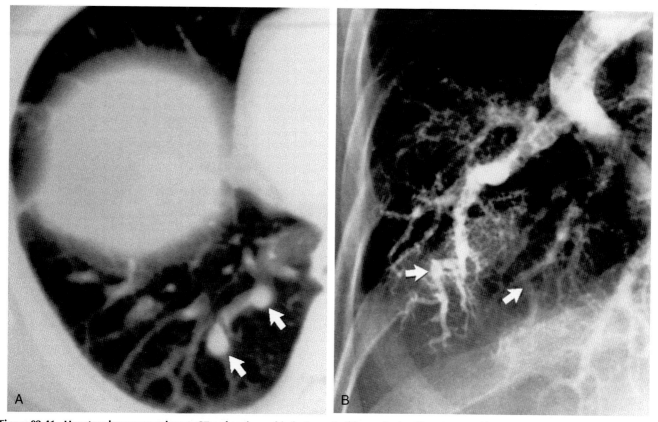

Figure 92-41. Hepatopulmonary syndrome: CT and angiographic features. A. CT scan obtained in a 64-year-old man with hepatopulmonary syndrome shows tortuous dilated peripheral vessels (*arrows*) 2 cm from the pleura. **B.** Pulmonary angiogram obtained in a 68-year-old woman with hepatopulmonary syndrome shows dilated and tortuous peripheral pulmonary arteries (*arrows*) but no evidence of arteriovenous shunting. (**A** and **B** from Lee K-N, Lee H-J, Shin WW, et al: Hypoxemia and liver cirrhosis [hepatopulmonary syndrome] in eight patients. Radiology 211:549-553, 1999.)

References

1. Colegrande S, Centi N, Galdiero R, et al: Transient hepatic intensity differences: Part 1. Those associated with focal lesions. AJR 188:154-159, 2007.
2. Colagrande S, Centi N, Galdiero R, et al: Transient hepatic intensity differences: Part 2. Those not associated with focal lesions. AJR 188:160-166, 2007.
3. Kim HJ, Kim AY, Kim TK, et al: Transient hepatic attenuation differences in focal hepatic lesions: Dynamic CT features. AJR 184:83-90, 2005.
4. Colagrande S, Centi N, La Villa G, et al: Transient hepatic attenuation differences. AJR 183:459-464, 2004.
5. Lee KH, Han JK, Jeong JY, et al: Hepatic attenuation differences associated with obstruction of the portal or hepatic veins in patients with hepatic abscesses. AJR 185:1015-1023, 2005.
6. Choi SH, Lee JM, Lee KH, et al: Relationship between various patterns of transient hepatic attenuation on CT and portal vein thrombosis related to acute cholecystitis. AJR 183:437-442, 2004.
7. Yoshimitsu K, Honda H, Kuroiwa T, et al: Unusual hemodynamics and pseudolesions of the noncirrhotic liver at CT. RadioGraphics 21:881-896, 2001.
8. Quiroag S, Sebastia C, Pallisa E, et al: Improved diagnosis of hepatic perfusion disorders: Value of hepatic arterial phase imaging during helical CT. RadioGraphics 21:65-81, 2001.
9. From Desser TS, Sze DY, Jeffrey RB: Imaging and intervention in the hepatic veins. AJR 180:1583-1591, 2003.
10. Menon KV, Shah V, Kamath PS: The Budd-Chiari syndrome. N Engl J Med 350:578-585, 2004.
11. Zimmerman MA, Cameron AM, Ghobrial RM: Budd-Chiari syndrome. Clin Liver Dis 10:259-273, 2006.
12. Erden A: Budd-Chiari syndrome: A review of imaging findings. Eur J Radiol 61:44-56, 2007.
13. Xu PQ, Dang XW: Treatment of Budd-Chiari syndrome: Analysis of 480 cases. Hepatobiliary Pancreat Dis Int 3:73-76, 2004.
14. Kamath PS: Budd-Chiari syndrome: Radiologic findings. Liver Transpl 12(11 suppl 2):S21-S22, 2006.
15. Dang XW, Xu PQ, Ma XX: Radical resection of pathologic membrane for Budd-Chiari syndrome. Hepatobiliary Pancreat Dis Int 6:157-160, 2007.
16. Cazals-Hatem D, Vilgrain V, Genin P, et al: Arterial and portal circulation and parenchymal changes in Budd-Chiari syndrome: A study in 17 explanted livers. Hepatology 37:510-519, 2003.
17. Valla DC: Hepatic vein thrombosis (Budd-Chiari syndrome). Semin Liver Dis 22:5-14, 2002.
18. Kage M: Budd-Chiari syndrome and hepatocellular carcinoma. J Gastroenterol 39:706-707, 2004.
19. Bogin V, Marcos A, Shaw-Stiffel T: Budd-Chiari syndrome: In evolution. Eur J Gastroenterol Hepatol 17:33-35, 2005.
20. England RA, Wells IP, Gutteridge CM: Benign external compression of the inferior vena cava associated with thrombus formation. Br J Radiol 78:333-557, 2005.
21. Kelleher T, Staunton M, Malone D, et al: Budd-Chiari syndrome associated with angiomyolipoma of the liver. J Hepatol 40:1048-1049, 2004.
22. Bargallo X, Gilabert R, Nicolau C, et al: Sonography of the caudate vein: Value in diagnosing Budd-Chiari syndrome. AJR 181:1641-1645, 2003.
23. Chaubal N, Dighe M, Hanchate V, et al: Sonography in Budd-Chiari syndrome. J Ultrasound Med 25:373-379, 2006.
24. Bargallo X, Gilabert R, Nicolau C, et al: Sonography of Budd-Chiari syndrome. AJR 187:W33-W41, 2006.
25. Camera L, Mainenti PP, Di Giacomo A, et al: Triphasic helical CT in Budd-Chiari syndrome: Patterns of enhancement in acute, subacute and chronic disease. Clin Radiol 61:331-337, 2006.

26. Noone TC, Semelka RC, Siegelman ES, et al: Budd-Chiari syndrome: Spectrum of appearances of acute, subacute, and chronic disease with magnetic resonance imaging. J Magn Reson Imaging 11:44-50, 2000.

27. Erden A, Erden I, Krayalcin S, et al: Budd-Chiari syndrome: Evaluation with multiphase contrast enhanced three dimensional MR angiography. AJR 179:1287-1292, 2002.

28. Mortele KJ, Van Vliergerhe H, Wiesner W, et al: Hepatic veno-occlusive disease: MRI findings. Abdom Imaging 27:523-526, 2002.

29. Erden A, Erden I, Yurdaydin C, et al: Hepatic outflow obstruction: Enhancement patterns of the liver on MR angiography. Eur J Radiol 48:203-208, 2003.

30. Brancatelli G, Federle MP, Grazioli L, et al: Large regenerative nodules in Budd-Chiari syndrome and other vascular disorders of the liver: CT and MR findings with clinicopathologic correlation. AJR 178:877-873, 2002.

31. Maetani Y, Itoh K, Egawa H, et al: Benign hepatic nodule in Budd-Chiari syndrome: Radiologic-pathologic correlation with emphasis on the central scar. AJR 178:869-875, 2002.

32. Brancatelli G, Federle M, Grazioli L, et al: Benign regenerative nodules in Budd-Chiari syndrome and other vascular disorders of the liver: Radiologic-pathologic and clinical correlation. RadioGraphics 22:847-862, 2002.

33. Rha SE, Lee MG, Lee YS, et al: Nodular regenerative hyperplasia of the liver in Budd-Chiari syndrome: CT and MR feature. Abdom Imaging 25:255-258, 2000.

34. Shirai Y, Yoshiji H, Fujimoto M, et al: Successful treatment of acute Budd-Chiari syndrome with percutaneous transluminal angioplasty. Abdom Imaging 29:685-687, 2004.

35. Ruh J, Malago M, Busch Y, et al: Management of Budd-Chiari syndrome. Dig Dis Sci 50:540-546, 2005.

36. Quateen A, Pech M, Berg T, et al: Percutaneous transjugular direct porto-caval shunt in patients with Budd-Chiari syndrome. Cardiovasc Intervent Radiol 29:565-570, 2006.

37. Gandini R, Kondra D, Simonetti G: Transjugular intrahepatic porto-systemic shunt patency and clinical outcome in patients with Budd-Chiari syndrome. Radiology 241:298-305, 2006.

38. Shirai Y, Yoshiji, H, Fujimoto M, et al: Successful treatment of acute Budd-Chiari syndrome with percutaneous transluminal angioplasty. Abdom Imaging 29:685-687, 2004.

39. Abujudeh H, Contractor D, Delatorre A, et al: Rescue TIPS in acute Budd-Chiari syndrome. AJR 185:89-91, 2005.

40. Rossle M, Oschewski M, Siegerstetter V, et al: The Budd-Chiari syndrome: Outcome after treatment with the transjugular intrahepatic portosystemic shunt. Surgery 135:394-403, 2004.

41. Klein AS, Molmenti EP: Surgical treatment of Budd-Chiari syndrome. Liver Transpl 9:891-896, 2003.

42. Mancuso A, Fung K Mela M, et al: TIPS for acute and chronic Budd-Chiari syndrome: A single-centre experience. J Hepatol 38:751-754, 2003.

43. Gieling RG, Ruijter JM, Maas AAW, et al: Hepatic response to right ventricular overload. Gastroenterology 127:1210-1221, 2004.

44. Giallourakis CC, Rosenberg PM, Friedman LS: The liver in heart failure. Clin Liver Dis 6:947-967, 2002.

45. Gore RM, Mathieu DG, White EM, et al: Passive hepatic congestion: Cross-sectional imaging features. AJR 162:71-75, 1994.

46. Holley HC, Koslin DB, Berland LL, et al: Inhomogeneous enhancement of liver parenchyma secondary to passive congestion: Contrast-enhanced CT. Radiology 170(3 Pt 1):795-800, 1989.

47. Moulton JS, Miller BL, Dodd GD 3rd, et al : Passive hepatic congestion in heart failure: CT abnormalities. AJR 151:939-942, 1988.

48. Barakat M: Non-pulsatile hepatic and portal vein waveforms in patients with liver cirrhosis: concordant and discordant relationships. Br J Radiol 77:547-550, 2004.

49. Morrin MM, Pedrosa I, Rofsky NM: Magnetic resonance imaging for disorders of liver vasculature. Top Magn Reson Imaging 13:177-190, 2002.

50. Hiorns MP, Rossi UG, Roebuck DJ: Peliosis hepatic using inferior vena cava compression in a 3-year-old child. Pediatr Radiol 35:209-211, 2005.

51. Fidelman N, LaBerge JM, Kerlan RK: Massive intraperitoneal hemorrhage caused by peliosis hepatis. J Vasc Interv Radiol 13:542-545, 2002.

52. Ferrozzi F, Tognini G, Zuccoli G, et al: Peliosis hepatic with pseudotumoral and hemorrhagic evolution: CT and MR findings. Abdom Imaging 26:197-199, 2001.

53. Iannaccone R, Federle MP, Brancatelli G, et al: Peliosis hepatis: Spectrum of imaging findings. AJR 187:W43-W52, 2006.

54. Sandrasegaran K, Hawes DR, Matthew G: Hepatic peliosis (bacillary angiomatosis) in AIDS: CT findings. Abdom Imaging 30:738-740, 2005.

55. Savastano S, San Bortolo O, Velo E, et al: Pseudotumoral appearance of peliosis hepatis. AJR 185:558-559, 2005.

56. Steinke K, Terraciano L, Wiesner W: Unusual cross-sectional imaging findings in hepatic peliosis. Eur Radiol 13:1916-1919, 2003.

57. Gouya H, Vignaux O, Legmann P, et al: Peliosis hepatis: Triphasic helical CT and dynamic MRI findings. Abdom Imaging 26:507-509, 2001.

58. Webster GJ, Burroughs AK, Riordan SM: Review article: Portal vein thrombosis—new insights into aetiology and management. Aliment Pharmacol Ther 21:1-9, 2005.

59. Sheen CL, Lamparelli H, Milne A, et al: Clinical features, diagnosis, and outcome of acute portal vein thrombosis. Q J Med 93:531-534, 2000.

60. Valla DC, Condat B: Portal vein thrombosis in adults: Pathophysiology, pathogenesis, and management. J Hepatol 32:865-871, 2000.

61. Gallego C, Velasco M, Marcuello P, et al: Congenital and acquired anomalies of the portal venous system. RadioGraphics 22:141-159, 2002.

62. Bradbury MS, Kavanaugh PV, Bechtold RE, et al: Mesenteric venous thrombosis: Diagnosis and noninvasive imaging. RadioGraphics 22:527-541, 2002.

63. Rossi S, Rosa L, Ravetta V, et al: Contrast-enhanced versus conventional and color Doppler sonography for the detection of thrombosis of the portal and hepatic venous systems. AJR 186:763-773, 2006.

64. Raab B-W: The thread and streak sign. Radiology 236:284-285, 2005.

65. Jamssen HLA, Wijnhoud A, Iwatsuki S, et al: Extrahepatic portal vein thrombosis aetiology and determinants of survival. Gut 49:720-724, 2001.

66. Ikeda M, Sekimoto M. Takiguchi S, et al: High incidence of thrombosis of the portal venous system after laparoscopic splenectomy: A prospective study with contrast-enhanced CT scan. Ann Surg 241:208-216, 2005.

67. Chang CY, Yang PM, Hung SP, et al: Cavernous transformation of the portal vein: Etiology determines the outcome. Hepatogastroenterology 53:892-897, 2006.

68. Vilgrain V, Condat B, Bureau C, et al: Atrophy-hypertrophy complex in patients with cavernous transformation of the portal vein. Radiology 241:149-155, 2006.

69. Song B, Min P, Oudkerk M, et al: Cavernous transformation of the portal vein secondary to tumor thrombosis of hepatocellular carcinoma: Spiral CT visualization of the collateral vessels. Abdom Imaging 25:385-396, 2000.

70. Bradbury MS, Kavanagh PV, Bechtold RE, et al: Mesenteric venous thrombosis: Diagnosis and noninvasive imaging. RadioGraphics 22:527-541, 2002.

71. Hatoum OA, Spinelli KS, Abu-Hajir M, et al: Mesenteric venous thrombosis in inflammatory bowel disease. J Clin Gastroenterol 39:27-31, 2005.

72. Joh JH, Kim DL: Mesenteric and portal vein thrombosis: Treated with early initiation of anticoagulation. Eur J Vasc Endovasc Surg 29:204-208, 2005.

73. Ibukuro K, Ishii R, Fukuda H, et al: Collateral venous pathways in the transverse mesocolon and greater omentum in patients with pancreatic disease. AJR 182:1825-1187, 2004.

74. Ikeda M, Sekimoto M, Takiguchi S, et al: Total splenic vein thrombosis after laparoscopic splenectomy: A possible candidate for treatment. Am J Surg 193:21-25, 2007.

75. Hiraiwa K, Morozumi K, Miyazaki H, et al: Isolated splenic vein thrombosis secondary to splenic metastasis: A case report. World J Gastroenterol 12:6561-6563, 2006.

76. Mortele KJ, Mergo PJ, Taylor HM, et al: Peripancreatic vascular abnormalities complicating acute pancreatitis: Contrast-enhanced helical CT findings. Eur J Radiol 52:67-72, 2004.

77. Mortele KJ, Mergo PJ, Taylor HM, et al: Splenic and perisplenic involvement in acute pancreatitis: Determination of prevalence and morphologic helical CT features. J Comput Assist Tomogr 25:50-54, 2001.

78. Tuvia J, Lebwohl O, Lefkowitz J: Hepatic infarction due to thrombotic angiitis; MR appearance. Clin Radiol 55:803-805, 2000.

79. Khong SY, James M, Smith P: Diagnosis of liver infarction postpartum. Obstet Gynecol 105(5 Pt 2):1271-1273, 2005.

80. Giovine S, Pinto A, Crispano S, et al: Retrospective study of 23 cases of hepatic infarction: CT findings and pathological correlations. Radiol Med (Torino) 111:11-21, 2006.

81. Basgul A, Kavak ZN, Sezen D, et al: Two cases of HELLP syndrome with fatal outcomes. Clin Exp Obstet Gynecol 33:178-180, 2006.

82. Van Runnard Heimel PJ, Franx A, Schobben AF, et al: Corticosteroids,

pregnancy, and HELLP syndrome: A review. Obstet Gynecol Surg 60: 57-70, 2005.

83. Harris BM, Kuczkowski KM: Diagnostic dilemma: Hepatic rupture due to HELLP syndrome vs trauma. Arch Gynecol Obstet 12:234-238, 2005.

84. Zissin R, Yaffe D, Fejgin M, et al: Hepatic infarction in preeclampsia as part of the HELLP syndrome: CT appearance. Abdom Imaging 24: 594-596, 1999.

85. Nunes JO, Turner MA, Fulcher MA: Abdominal imaging features of HELLP syndrome: A 10-year retrospective review. AJR 185:1205-1210, 2005.

86. Kalko Y, Ugurlucan M, Basaran M, et al: Visceral artery aneurysms. Heart Surg Forum 10:E24-E29, 2007.

87. Javors BR: Tortuosity of the splenic artery. Abdom Imaging 24:313-314, 1999.

88. Sachdev U, Baril DT, Ellozy SH, et al: Management of aneurysms involving branches of the celiac and superior mesenteric arteries: A comparison of surgical and endovascular therapy. J Vasc Surg 44: 718-724, 2006.

89. Chiesa R, Astore D, Guzzo G, et al: Visceral artery aneurysms. Ann Vasc Surg 11:440-445, 2005.

90. Carr SC, Mahvi DM, Hoch JR, et al: Visceral artery aneurysm rupture. J Vasc Surg 33:806-811, 2001.

91. Overhaus M, Lauschke H, Schafer N, et al: The coeliac aneurysm: A rare cause of abdominal pain. Vasa 35:201-205, 2006.

92. Singh CS, Giri K, Gupta R, et al: Successful management of hepatic artery pseudoaneurysm complicating chronic pancreatitis by stenting. World J Gastroenterol 12:5733-5734, 2006.

93. Sessa C, Tinelli G, Poren P, et al: Treatment of visceral artery aneurysm: Description of a retrospective series of 42 aneurysms in 34 patients. Ann Vasc Surg 18:695-703, 2004.

94. Grego FG, Lepidi S, Ragazzi R, et al: Visceral artery aneurysms. Cardiovasc Surg 11:19-25, 2005.

95. Sachdev U, Baril DT, Ellozy SH, et al: Management of aneurysms involving branches of the celiac and superior mesenteric arteries: A comparison of surgical and endovascular therapy. J Vasc Surg 44: 718-724, 2006.

96. De Gaetano AM, Andrisani MC, Gui B, et al: Thrombosed portal vein aneurysm. Abdom Imaging 31:545-548, 2006.

97. Okur N, Inal M, Akgul E, et al: Spontaneous rupture and thrombosis of an intrahepatic portal vein aneurysm. Abdom Imaging 28:675-677, 2003.

98. Kocakoc E, Kiris A, Bozgeyik Z, et al. Splenic vein aneurysm with calcification of splenic and portal veins. J Clin Ultrasound 33:251-253, 2005.

99. Laumonier H, Montaudon M, Corneloup O, et al: CT angiography of intrahepatic portal aneurysm. Abdom Imaging 30:755-757, 2005.

100. Karcaaltincaba M, Haliloglu M, Akpinar E, et al: Multidetector CT and MRI findings in periportal space pathologies. Eur J Radiol Nov 21, 2006. Epub ahead of print.

101. Hayashi S, Yi SQ, Naito M, et al: A case of spontaneous splenorenal shunt associated with splenic artery aneurysm. Surg Radiol Anat 28: 311-315, 2006.

102. Comert M, Erdem LO, Ozdolap S, et al: Splenic vein aneurysm demonstrated by magnetic resonance angiography. Dig Dis Sci 50:1344-1346, 2005.

103. Wolosker N, Zerati AE, Nishinari K, et al: Aneurysm of superior mesenteric vein: Case report with 5-year follow-up and review of the literature. J Vasc Surg 39:459-461, 2004.

104. Billaud Y, Pilleul F, Meyer X, et al: Aneurysm of the superior mesenteric vein: Imaging findings. J Radiol 84(7-8 Pt 1):857-860, 2003.

105. Jaskolka J, Wu L, Chan RP, et al: Imaging of hereditary hemorrhagic telangiectasia. AJR 183:307-314, 2004.

106. Wu JS, Saluja S, Garcia-Tsao G, et al: Liver involvement in hereditary hemorrhagic telangiectasia: CT and clinical findings do not correlate in symptomatic patients. AJR 187: W399-W405, 2006.

107. Proctor DD, Henderson KJ, Dziura JD, et al: Enteroscopic evaluation of the gastrointestinal tract in symptomatic patients with hereditary hemorrhagic telangiectasia. J Clin Gastroenterol 39:115-119, 2005.

108. Ravard G, Soyer P, Boudiaf M, et al: Hepatic involvement in hereditary hemorrhagic telangiectasia. J Comput Assisr Tomogr 28:488-495, 2004.

109. Guttmacher AE, Marchuk DA, White RI: Hereditary hemorrhagic telangiectasia. N Engl J Med 333:918-924, 1995.

110. Shovlin CL, Johanns W, Janssen J, et al: Diagnostic criteria for hereditary hemorrhagic telangiectasia (Rendu-Osler-Weber syndrome). Am J Med Genet 91:66-67, 2000.

111. Memeo M, Ianora AAS, Scaradapne A, et al: Hepatic involvement in hemorrhagic telangiectasia: CT finding. Abdom Imaging 29:211-230, 2004.

112. Leung AN: Hepatopulmonary syndrome. Radiology 229:64-67, 2003.

113. Hansell DM: Small-vessel diseases of the lung: CT-pathologic correlates. Radiology 225:639-653, 2002.

114. Engleke C, Schaefer-Prokop C, Schirg E, et al: High-resolution CT and CT angiography of peripheral pulmonary vascular disorders. RadioGraphics 22:739-764, 2002.

115. Meyer CA, White CA, Sherman KE: Diseases of the hepatopulmonary axis. RadioGraphics 20:687-698, 2000.

116. Mandell MS: The diagnosis and treatment of hepatopulmonary syndrome. Clin Liver Dis 10:387-405, 2006.

117. Swanson KL: Should we screen for hepatopulmonary syndrome in liver transplant candidates? Liver Transpl 13:183-184, 2007.

118. Herve P, Le Pavec J, Sztrymf B, et al: Pulmonary vascular abnormalities in cirrhosis. Best Pract Res Clin Gastroenterol 21:141-159, 2007.

Hepatic Trauma and Surgery

Helena Gabriel, MD • Nancy A. Hammond, MD • Mark Talamonti, MD • Riad Salem, MD • Richard M. Gore, MD

When the liver is wounded, much blood commeth out.

AMBROSE PARE

HEPATIC TRAUMA

Hepatic trauma was first graphically described in the *Iliad*, when Achilles "stabbed with his sword at the liver, the liver was torn from its place, and from the black blood drenched the fold of his tunic and he was shrouded in darkness as the light went out... ." The liver is not faring much better 2600 years later, with the increasing violence of urban life, our society's passion for high-speed travel, and the gastroenterologist and interventional radiologist constantly invading the liver.[1-3] The cross-sectional imaging modalities have dramatically improved the promptness and certainty of diagnosis in patients with hepatic trauma and have proved useful in the triage of patients to surgical or conservative management.[4-6] The single most important factor allowing for nonoperative management of blunt hepatic trauma has been the evolution of CT scanning.[7-11]

Epidemiology

The types of hepatic injury encountered in practice depend to a large degree on the location of the trauma center. In suburban and rural areas, hepatic injury is usually due to blunt trauma sustained in motor vehicle accidents and falls. In the setting of trauma, the liver is the second most commonly injured solid organ, second only to the spleen. The reported prevalence of liver injury in patients who have sustained blunt trauma ranges from 1% to 8%.[12] In large city hospitals, penetrating injuries from firearms and stabbings predominate. In this setting, the liver is the most frequently injured viscus, owing to its anterior and partially subcostal location.[13,14] Iatrogenic hepatic injuries are becoming increasingly common in all hospitals. Indeed, liver biopsy is the most common cause of subcapsular hematoma in the United States today.[15] Because of their markedly different management paradigms and prognoses, blunt, iatrogenic, and penetrating traumatic injuries are discussed separately in this chapter.

1771

Clinical Findings

Clinical features associated with hepatic trauma include right upper quadrant pain and tenderness with guarding and rebound tenderness, falling hematocrit, and hypotension. Delayed manifestations of biliary trauma, such as bilomas, are usually accompanied by right upper quadrant pain and jaundice.[15,16] Trauma is the most frequent cause of hemobilia, which is manifested by hematemesis or melena associated with right upper quadrant pain. Because of the difficulty of identifying hepatic injury by physical examination, CT is often required to avoid missing a significant injury. The mortality rate reported secondary to blunt liver trauma ranges from 4.1% to 11.7%.[13,17]

Classification of Hepatic Trauma

The management of hepatic trauma patients has evolved significantly over the last three decades and is now based on well-defined treatment algorithms. This has highlighted the need for an accurate classification system as a basis for the clinical decision-making process.[18] Fundamental to the development of these classification schemes and the subsequent treatment algorithms based upon them, is the widespread availability of rapid acquisition CT imaging in most major trauma centers. This has also led to a diminution in the role of diagnostic peritoneal lavage (DPL) in the management of the trauma patient. DPL has multiple limitations, including (1) lack of specificity regarding the source of bleeding, (2) high sensitivity to detection of small quantities of blood leading to nontherapeutic laparotomy, and (3) inaccuracy for retroperitoneal injuries. DPL fails most importantly in its ability to objectify the location and extent of intra-abdominal organ injury. DPL is valuable mainly in patients in whom ultrasonography or CT scanning is inappropriate or unavailable.[8]

Previous attempts to categorize hepatic injury were mostly anatomic in design and did not incorporate mechanism of injury or physiologic changes associated with more severe injuries. In the late 1980's, the American Association for the Surgery of Trauma (AAST) established a committee to devise an injury severity scale that incorporated etiology, anatomy and extent of injury and correlated it with subsequent clinical management and outcome. The most recently revised clinical classification is listed in Table 93-1.[19] It has been demonstrated that the CT grade of hepatic injury is not predictive of the need for surgery and that the majority of injuries can be safely managed nonoperatively.[19-24] The hemodynamic status of the patient may be the most important predictor of injury severity; patients with higher-grade injuries (IV or V) are more likely to be unstable and require surgery, whereas patients who are stable may be managed conservatively with close observation in intensive care units.[8,9,25] Correlation of mechanism of injury, radiological classification, and clinical assessment of hemodynamic stability, must all be used by the trauma surgeon to guide management decisions.

Pathophysiology

Blunt Trauma

Approximately 1% to 8% of patients who sustain blunt abdominal trauma have a liver injury.[12] Severe compressive trauma

Table 93-1
Classification of Hepatic Trauma

Grade		Injury
I	Hematoma	Subcapsular, <10% surface area
	Laceration	Capsular tear, <1 cm parenchymal depth
II	Hematoma	Subcapsular, 10%-50% surface area Intraparenchymal, <10 cm diameter
	Laceration	1-3 cm parenchymal depth, <10 cm in length
III	Hematoma	Subcapsular, >50% surface area or expanding; ruptured subcapsular or parenchymal hematoma Intraparenchymal hematoma >10 cm or expanding
	Laceration	Parenchymal fracture >3 cm deep
IV	Laceration	Parenchymal disruption involving 25%-75% of hepatic lobe or 1-3 Couinaud segments Within a single lobe
V	Laceration	Parenchymal disruption involving >75% of hepatic lobe or >3 Couinaud segments Within a single lobe
	Vascular	Juxtahepatic venous injuries, i.e., retrohepatic vena cava/central major hepatic veins
VI	Vascular	Hepatic avulsion

From Moore EE, Cogbill TH, Jurkovich GS, et al: Organ injury scaling: Spleen and liver (1994 revision). J Trauma 38:323-324, 1995.

to the liver from a steering wheel injury or direct blow can produce stellate fractures that often involve an entire lobe.[26] Rapid deceleration in motor vehicle accidents produces shearing forces that cause different degrees of parenchymal tears. The hepatic lobes may be torn from each other, or the tears may involve the supporting ligaments, hepatic veins, and inferior vena cava. The most frequent site of hepatic injury is the posterior segment of the right lobe of the liver due to its size and proximity to the ribs and spine. Although less common, left lobe injuries are more often associated with retroperitoneal injuries (duodenum and pancreas) and transverse colon injuries.[23,27] There is a high incidence of associated extrahepatic injury, including splenic rupture, head injuries, and rib, facial, and pelvic fractures.[28]

Major hepatic venous injuries occur in 13% of patients with liver trauma. These are most often a result of blunt trauma. They include, in decreasing order of frequency, right hepatic vein avulsion from the inferior vena cava, upper branch right hepatic vein avulsion, avulsion of accessory veins, avulsion of the left hepatic vein, and avulsion of the middle hepatic vein. The right hepatic vein is at greater risk for sudden acceleration-deceleration injury because it has a relatively long extrahepatic segment before it enters the inferior vena cava. The course is shorter for the middle and left hepatic veins, which usually merge to form a common channel and, thus, are less frequently injured.[29,30] Venous injuries can be suggested by multiple lacerations around the inferior vena cava or porta hepatis.[10,11] It is important to identify these findings because they may help prepare the surgeons to expect significant bleeding when the liver is lifted off the inferior vena cava.[11] Three-dimensional CT reconstruction has been advocated in the assessment of vascular involvement, especially the portal vein, hepatic veins, and retrohepatic vena cava.[31] Injuries of the bare area of the liver may not demonstrate peritoneal signs or findings on diagnostic peritoneal lavage (DPL) or screening sonography for hemoperitoneum but may show retroperitoneal blood on CT examination.[32]

Penetrating Injuries

Penetrating wounds are most commonly caused by stabbing, gunshot, or shotgun injury.[33,34] Knife stabbings usually cause superficial lacerations, whereas high-velocity projectiles generally cause injury from capsule to capsule, with massive parenchymal damage.[5]

Iatrogenic Injuries

The liver is subject to a number of iatrogenic misadventures that may be caused by any of the various needles, wires, cannulas, and catheters placed by gastroenterologists and interventional radiologists.[15,35,36] The liver can also be damaged by external cardiac compression during the course of resuscitation and by inappropriately low insertion of a chest tube.[37]

Diagnostic and interventional procedures can produce a tear of the liver capsule, subcapsular hematoma, bile leak, arteriovenous fistula, arteriobiliary or venobiliary fistula, hepatic hematoma, hemoperitoneum, and biloma.[38] The prevalence of this problem was well documented in one study in which intrahepatic (77%) and subcapsular (23%) hematomas were found sonographically in 23% of asymptomatic patients evaluated after liver biopsy.[39]

Spontaneous Rupture

Hepatic rupture and hemorrhage can occur in eclamptic or preeclamptic women during the third trimester-*h*emolysis, *e*levated *l*iver enzymes, and *l*ow *p*latelets (the HELLP syndrome).[40] The maternal mortality rate approaches 60% with hepatic rupture. Because surgery is difficult in these friable livers, hepatic artery transcatheter embolization offers a safe therapeutic alternative. One report showed good results with absorbable gelatin foam (Gelfoam) embolization in four eclamptic patients.[41,42] Bleeding from the liver may also immediately follow delivery in noneclamptic women.

Spontaneous hemorrhage can occur in patients who have sickle cell anemia, peliosis, hepatomas, hepatic adenoma, coagulopathies, B-cell lymphoma, metastases, organophosphate toxicity, or collagen-vascular disease or in patients who receive long-term hemodialysis.[43]

Radiologic Findings

Imaging can make a major contribution to the management of trauma patients who are hemodynamically stable and to the postoperative assessment of these patients.[5,10,11,14,15,44-46]

Computed Tomography of Hepatic Injuries

Multidetector computed tomography (MDCT) is the imaging technique of choice for hepatic trauma and has had an enormous impact on the detection and management of liver injuries.[5,10,11,14,15,47-49] It can reliably diagnose and stage significant hepatic and extrahepatic injuries, document interval healing of hepatic injuries, and diagnose early and delayed complications.[50] It can also detect associated and unsuspected injuries to other organs (Fig. 93-1). Patients who are hemodynamically unstable require immediate surgery; surgical delay secondary to imaging can be fatal. With the advent of MDCT and other new technologies, radiologists can now scan

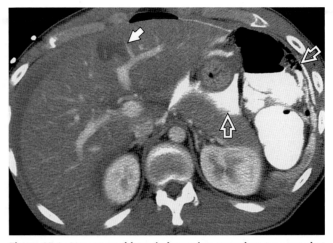

Figure 93-1. Unsuspected hepatic laceration secondary to a gun shot to the left upper abdomen resulting in colonic perforation. CT demonstrates a low-density laceration in the left hepatic lobe (*white arrow*). Free air and extravasated rectal contrast are also seen indicating bowel perforation (*open arrows*).

trauma patients in a matter of seconds, with better resolution, and with multiplanar imaging capabilities.

With any type of abdominal trauma, the first finding that should be evaluated is the presence or absence of blood, either parenchymal or intraperitoneal (hemoperitoneum). Immediately after injury, hematomas on noncontrast scans are hyperdense relative to normal hepatic parenchyma (Fig. 93-2). After intravenous contrast medium administration, unclotted blood is usually hypodense when compared with enhancing normal parenchyma but still usually has an attenuation (20-40 HU) greater than that of simple fluid (0-20 HU). Active hemorrhage is identified as contrast extravasation on contrast-enhanced CT. The attenuation values of extravasated contrast material (range 85-350 [HU]) and hematoma (range 40-70 HU) help distinguish active bleeding from clotted blood.[10,51,52] If the liver is involved by focal or diffuse fatty infiltration, a common finding in intoxicated drivers, parenchymal hematomas may appear isodense but can be usually

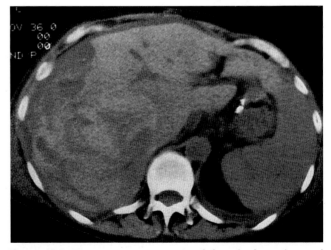

Figure 93-2. Noncontrast appearance of hepatic laceration and hematoma. Noncontrast CT demonstrates a heterogeneous masslike region in right hepatic lobe with central hyperdensity consistent with hematoma.

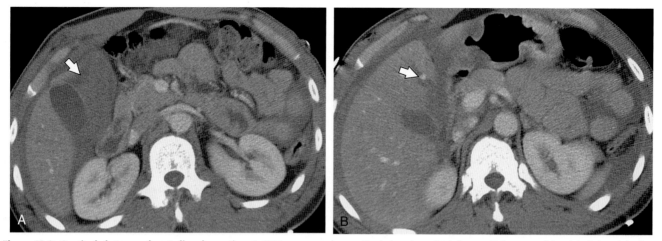

Figure 93-3. Sentinel clot secondary to liver laceration. A. CT image reveals a sentinel clot along the inferomedial aspect of the right lobe of the liver. The sentinel clot has higher density than the remainder of free fluid (*white arrow*). **B.** Scan obtained more superiorly reveals the small laceration causing the sentinel clot. A tiny hyperdense focus is suggestive of active extravasation (*white arrow*).

distinguished using narrow CT window settings. In addition, the attenuation and the distribution of fluid can serve as a clue to the site of injury. This phenomenon has been termed the sentinel clot sign.[53] The sentinel clot is the highest density blood collection seen and usually lies adjacent to the injured organ (Fig. 93-3). The evaluation of hepatic trauma should search for other fluid collections such as bile, as seen in bile leaks and bilomas, which have low attenuation due to its high cholesterol content.

When interpreting CT scans in patients with hepatic trauma, it is important to describe the anatomic site and extent of injury (superficial, deep, lobar, segmental, perihilar); the complexity of the lesion (simple or stellate laceration); and the type of hepatic injury (parenchymal laceration or subcapsular hematoma).[10,11,54,55]

The major CT findings in blunt hepatic injuries are lacerations, subscapsular and parenchymal hematomas, active hemorrhage, and juxtahepatic venous injuries.[17] Lacerations are the most common injury and appear as branching or linear low attenuation areas. Lacerations can be classified into superficial (<3 cm from the liver surface) and deep (>3 cm from the surface). Deep central parenchymal injuries seen on CT may be unrecognized at laparotomy, especially if the liver surface appears intact, and as a result, the true extent of involvement may be underestimated at surgery.[10] It is imperative to describe any potential laceration extension to the hepatic or portal veins or to the inferior vena cava (IVC) (Fig. 93-4). Hematomas can also occur in hepatic trauma and may be subcapsular or parenchymal in nature. Subcapsular hematomas can be distinguished from free hemoperitoneum by mass effect upon the liver surface creating a contour deformity (Fig. 93-5). Parenchymal hematomas follow the same attenuation values of blood as described in the preceding paragraph. Again, on contrast-enhanced CT, they may appear relatively lower in attenuation than enhancing liver parenchyma, but their attenuation values are often higher than simple fluid (Fig. 93-6). Yet another type of hepatic injury, contusion, often appears as low attenuation, sometimes ill-defined areas with intermixed areas of high attenuation representing blood.

Active extravasation on contrast-enhanced CT represents one of the more severe CT features of hepatic injury and can herald life-threatening, active bleeding (Fig. 93-7). On CT, this appears as very high attenuation approximating that of aorta compared to the density of clotted blood.[56] At times, active contrast extravasation may be difficult to distinguish from a pseudoaneurysm. Delayed contrast images are helpful in this instance, demonstrating "washout of contrast attenuation" with pseudoaneurysms and persistence of high density with active bleeding.[57] Active extravasation of contrast has been shown to be a strong predictor of potential cardiovascular collapse and failure of nonsurgical management.[58,59] Treatment of active extravasation is best performed through angiographic embolization.[60]

Vascular injuries of the liver, although relatively rare, can be fatal as well. When these occur, they are usually due to lacerations extending to the IVC, hepatic veins and portal veins; thus, it is imperative to identify and relay this extension to the clinicians (see Fig. 93-4). Alternatively, avulsion of the vessels can occur as well. IVC injuries carry a particularly high mortality rate and should be suspected when there is a laceration extending to the proximal hepatic veins and IVC and when there is a large amount of retrohepatic blood.[61] If bleeding occurs at the bare area of the liver, there may be extension of blood into the retroperitoneum as well.

Periportal zones of decreased density may be the only manifestation of hepatic trauma. These may represent linear collections of blood in the periportal regions or dilated periportal lymphatics.[62-64] Periportal low density was previously thought to be an important sign of liver injury but is actually most commonly seen due to rapid fluid resuscitation elevating central venous pressure, as suggested by a distended inferior vena cava (Fig. 93-8).[62-65] Periportal low density may also be seen in nontraumatic causes including in patients with congestive heart failure, hepatitis, liver transplant recipients, and those with AIDS. The lucency is due to a dilatation of the intrahepatic lymphatics, caused by obstruction of drainage. Intraparenchymal gas, in the absence of infection, has also been reported in patients with blunt abdominal trauma, but an abscess must always be excluded when extraluminal gas collections are present.[66,67]

A CT-based classification has been formulated from these findings (Table 93-2). CT features, however, may not correlate

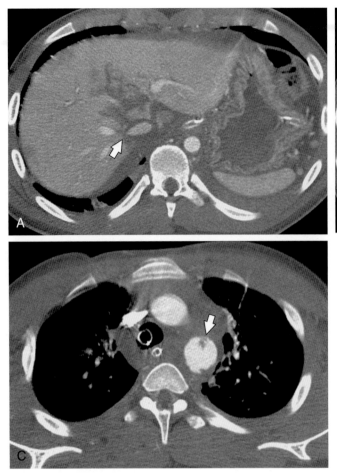

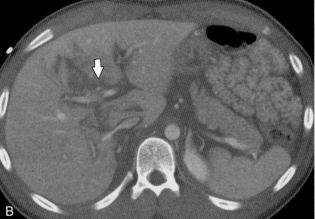

Figure 93-4. Grade IV liver laceration and traumatic aortic injury secondary to motor vehicle collision. A. CT image demonstrates a central liver laceration involving the middle hepatic vein and extending to the inferior vena cava (*arrow*). **B.** This image further depicts the degree of injury extending to the portal vein (*arrow*). **C.** CT of the chest demonstrates mediastinal hematoma and descending thoracic aortic injury (*arrow*). The patient underwent aortic grafting. Despite this extensive hepatic injury, the patient recovered with nonsurgical management of the liver injuries.

with the need for surgery.[68,69] Major hepatic injuries up to and including grade IV can usually be managed conservatively if the patient is hemodynamically stable.[21-24,51,55,68] CT findings associated with increased morbidity, mortality, and need for operation include deep perihilar lacerations; failure of the hemoperitoneum to significantly resorb within 1 week; rapid progression of hepatic injuries within hours or days of injury;

and major vascular trauma, especially injury to the confluence of hepatic veins.[13,70] Recently, it has been noted that many hemodynamically stable patients can avoid operation despite significant injuries seen on CT examination. The need for follow-up CT examination to detect delayed complications is favored by some[71-73] and opposed by others.[21,74,75] Patients with persistent or worsening symptoms should have follow-up

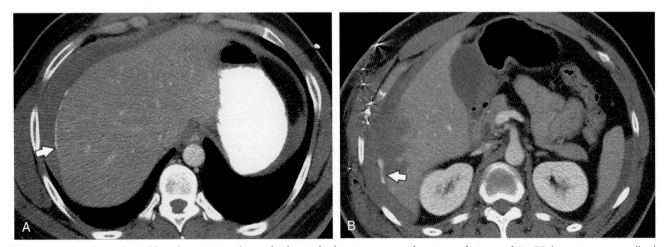

Figure 93-5. Liver laceration with active extravasation and subcapsular hematoma secondary to gunshot wound. A. CT demonstrates a small subcapsular hematoma at the superior aspect of the liver with minimal mass effect on the adjacent liver parenchyma anteriorly. A sliver of high density consistent with active extravasation of contrast material is seen (*arrow*). **B.** The site of active bleeding is noted extending into the hematoma (*arrow*); the offending bullet fragments are also visualized.

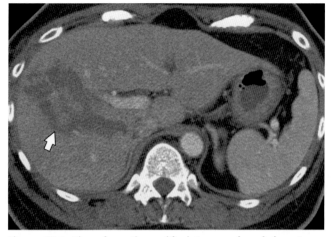

Figure 93-6. Liver laceration with intraparenchymal hematoma. Contrast-enhanced CT demonstrates a low-density hepatic laceration in the right lobe of liver with a centrally located high-density collection consistent with an intraparenchymal hematoma (*arrow*).

examinations.[74] Patients with more severe, complex hepatic injuries may also benefit from repeat CT.[76] Meredith and colleagues found that hemodynamic stability and lack of peritoneal findings were more predictive of which patients could undergo nonoperative management than the CT findings.[21]

Post-traumatic complications are not uncommon after hepatic injury and are best demonstrated by CT as well.[71,72] Delayed hemorrhage can occur and can have a high mortality rate. This may be due to several causes including an expanding injury or a biloma-induced pseudoaneurysm, a misinterpretation of contrast extravasation on the initial CT scan, or mismanagement of the patient's hemodynamic status (Fig. 93-9).[76] This should be suspected if there is a delayed drop in the hematocrit level. Post-traumatic pseudoaneurysms of the hepatic artery and its branches may occur weeks to months after the initial injury. These patients present with delayed hemorrhage and hemobilia (if the pseudoaneurysm decompresses into the biliary system) and should be evaluated with a hepatic angiogram, at which time the aneurysm

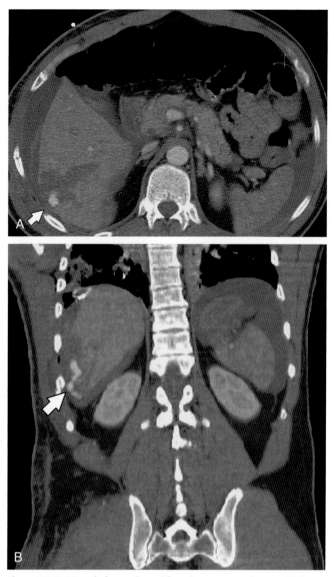

Figure 93-7. Hepatic laceration with active extravasation. A. CT shows a low-density laceration in the posterior segment of right hepatic lobe. Focal hyperdensity consistent with active extravasation of contrast and active hemorrhage is seen (*arrow*). **B.** A coronal reformatted image further reveals the extent of active extravasation (*arrow*). High-density fluid in the peritoneal cavity is consistent with hemoperitoneum.

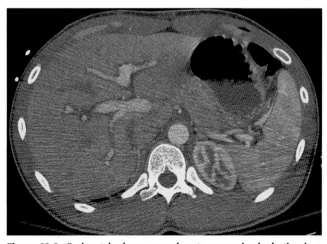

Figure 93-8. Periportal edema secondary to aggressive hydration in a patient with a stab wound. Periportal lucency extending along both sides of the intrahepatic portal veins indicates periportal edema. This is a nonspecific finding that is most commonly seen with rapid hydration.

Table 93-2

CT-Based Classification of Blunt Hepatic Trauma

Grade	Criteria
1	Capsular avulsion, superficial laceration(s) <1 cm deep, subcapsular hematoma <1 cm maximal thickness, periportal blood tracking only
2	Laceration(s) 1-3 cm deep, central/subcapsular hematoma(s) 1-3 cm diameter
3	Laceration(s) >3 cm deep, central/subcapsular hematoma(s) >3 cm diameter
4	Massive central/subcapsular hematoma >10 cm, lobar tissue destruction (maceration) or devascularization
5	Bilobar tissue destruction (maceration) or devascularization

From Mirvis SE, Whitley NO, Vainwright JR, et al: Blunt hepatic trauma in adults: CT-based classification and correlation with prognosis and treatment. Radiology 171:27-32, 1989.

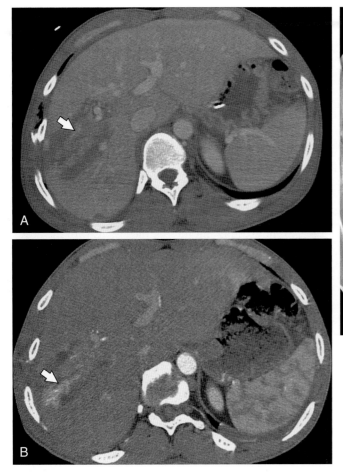

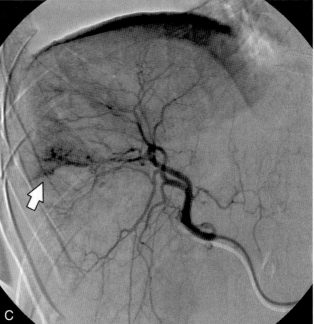

Figure 93-9. Delayed complication of arteriovenous fistula in a patient with a liver laceration. A. CT initially interpreted as a liver laceration and intraparenchymal hematoma with a potential site of active extravasation of contrast not noticed (*arrow*). **B.** Subsequent CT pulmonary artery angiogram for evaluation of pulmonary embolism performed 5 days after initial study clearly demonstrates density approximating that of the aorta consistent with active extravasation (*arrow*). **C.** Hepatic angiogram reveals a blush of contrast in the right lobe of the liver with immediate fistulization to a peripheral branch of the right portal vein consistent with a traumatic arteriovenous fistula. This fistula was embolized successfully.

can be embolized to minimize the risk of frank rupture.[77-83] Bilomas (Fig. 93-10) and intrahepatic and perihepatic abscesses are other major post-traumatic complications. Bilomas are seen in 0.5% to 20% of patients managed nonoperatively.[8,22,46,84] These fluid collections usually resolve or can be managed successfully by percutaneous drainage.[84] Aspiration

or biliary scintigraphy may be necessary for differentiating these fluid collections.[28,77] Endoscopic retrograde cholangiopancreatography can identify the bile leak and guide the insertion of a biliary endoprosthesis.

Ultrasound

Ulltrasound is being more frequently performed in the emergency room by surgeons, radiologists, and emergency room physicians. The advantages of sonography include portability, the ability to rapidly detect intraperitoneal blood, and relative inexpense. Problems include the operator-dependent nature of ultrasound and limitations in demonstrating the extent of injury.

The use of ultrasound was pioneered years ago in the European literature.[85] Ultrasound can be used either to identify parenchymal injury directly or to detect intraperitoneal fluid that in the acute setting is presumed to represent hemoperitoneum.[86,87] Ultrasound is much more accurate in the detection of hemoperitoneum than in the diagnosis of specific parenchymal or hollow viscous injury. The recent interest in ultrasound is primarily in its utility as a rapid screening test for significant intra-abdominal injury, the so-called focused abdominal sonogram for trauma (FAST).[88,89] FAST simply entails sonographic interrogation of sites in which free intraperitoneal fluid most often accumulates: Morison's pouch, the left subphrenic and subsplenic areas, and the pouch of Douglas. According to Ma and coworkers, the suprapubic view

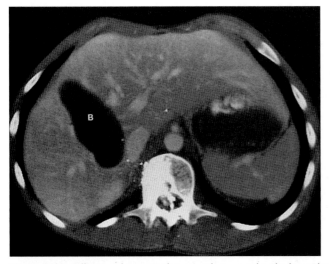

Figure 93-10. Biloma. Biloma (B) after a gunshot wound to the liver. The large low-attenuation (5 HU) collection in the liver was aspirated and proved to be a biloma.

is the single view most sensitive for hemoperitoneum (68%), but the sensitivity dramatically increases when multiple views are obtained.[8] The best use of FAST is to triage patients. A hemodynamically stable patient with a positive FAST should undergo CT scanning, whereas an unstable patient with a positive ultrasound should go to surgery emergently. Clinical management in cases with a negative FAST is more nebulous, but at a minimum, those patients should at least be observed for a period of time.

Multiple studies have been published looking at the accuracy of ultrasound and comparing it with other modalities. In general, ultrasound is relatively sensitive for the detection of free intraperitoneal fluid, but it is far from perfect. There are a wide range of values in the literature for sensitivity (81%-94%), specificity (88%-100%), and accuracy (86%-98%) for free intraperitoneal fluid.[90-100] This type of variability suggests inconsistent reproducibility of the method. In addition, to attain these values, some studies required repetitive sonographic scanning to detect developing fluid. Another confounding factor is that not all blunt abdominal trauma results in free fluid resulting in false negative results. In some studies, 26% to 34% of patients with abdominal organ injuries did not have hemoperitoneum.[101-103] Therefore, although ultrasound is very good in detecting hemoperitoneum, there are false negative and positive findings. In addition, DPL is known to be more accurate in the detection of fluid and injury than ultrasound, however, DPL is being used much less, in large part, due to the widespread use of CT.

In addition to the evaluation for hemoperitoneum, ultrasound can be used to detect other injuries. Ultrasound can demonstrate a number of traumatic lesions: subcapsular hematomas, parenchymal tears, contusions, bilomas, and hemoperitoneum. A subcapsular hematoma appears as a lentiform or curvilinear fluid collection with echogenic properties that vary with the age of the lesion (Fig. 93-11). Hematomas are initially anechoic, but as clotting proceeds, they become progressively echogenic by 24 hours. As time passes, the hematoma's echogenicity begins to decrease again.[104,105] Internal echoes and septations develop within these collections in 1 to 4 weeks. The frequency of the transducer also determines the sonographic characteristics of the hematoma. The complexity and echogenicity of the hematoma can appear greater at higher frequencies as a result of higher spatial resolution.[5,104-106]

Parenchymal contusions are normally hypoechoic at initial presentation, transiently become hyperechoic, and then hypoechoic. Lesions that occur posteriorly in the right lobe or over the spine within the left lobe are usually not sonographically demonstrable unless the patient has a slender body habitus.[81] Parenchymal tears, with or without hematoma, manifest as irregular defects with abnormal echotexture relative to the surrounding normal tissue. Intraparenchymal hematomas as small as 3.5 mL can be visualized as rounded, echogenic foci.[107]

Bilomas appear as rounded or ellipsoid, anechoic, loculated structures with sharply defined margins close to the liver and bile ducts.[108-110] Scintigraphy is an important adjunct in these cases to show communication of the lesions with the normal biliary tract. Fluid aspiration may be helpful to demonstrate bile.[111,112] Ultrasound is particularly helpful diagnostically when the collections no longer communicate with the biliary tract. Percutaneous drainage with CT or sonographic guidance may be helpful when fluid collections are symptomatic or infected.

There have been many studies evaluating the accuracy of ultrasound for detecting parenchymal hepatic and other solid organ injuries. Sensitivity for detection of all injuries ranges from 43.6% to 93%. This wide range of numbers is due to many factors including study design, technique and experience. Papers with very low sensitivities often include small bowel and mesenteric injuries, which are extremely difficult to detect by ultrasound. With respect to liver parenchymal injury, specifically, a recent article by Sato et al. comparing ultrasound examination with both the clinical outcome and CT, revealed a sensitivity for hepatic injury of 87.5% among experts and 46.2% among nonexpert sonographers.[90] This suggests that detection of injuries sonographically is more difficult than simply scanning for hemoperitoneum and can be variable. Other pitfalls of ultrasound, however, include limitations in the evaluation of retroperitoneal injuries, diaphragmatic injuries, and hollow viscous perforations.

Some authors have experimented with contrast-enhanced ultrasound in the evaluation of hepatic trauma. These contrast agents employ stabilized, encapsulated microbubbles

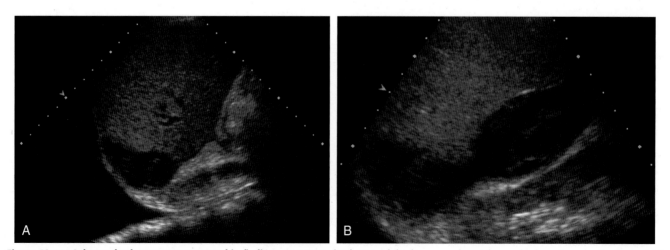

Figure 93-11. Subcapsular hematoma: sonographic findings. A. Longitudinal scan of the liver reveals a subcapsular hematoma and a large right pleural effusion. **B.** This hematoma is complex, with some areas of hyperechogenicity typical of the sonographic appearance of an acute hematoma.

which are small enough to pass through the pulmonary circulation to reach the systemic circulation and ultimately, parenchymal tissue. Contrast agents have many potential uses in the heart, vascular system, as well as in the detection of focal lesions. In the trauma setting, Catalano et al. have demonstrated that contrast enhanced sonography is a promising tool that better depicts hepatic lacerations and hematomas as echopoor areas against a background of enhanced parenchyma.[113] It also appears to demonstrate the extent of lesions better than conventional sonography. In addition, it may also have a role in detecting active extravasation of contrast and therefore, active bleeding which cannot be done with conventional ultrasound. In their study, contrast-enhanced sonography had a higher sensitivity for hepatic injury detection compared to routine ultrasound, 87% versus 65%.[113] This may potentially be a powerful tool in the emergency department setting in the future.

Nuclear Scintigraphy

Bile leaks are rare in blunt hepatic trauma. They more often follow cholecystectomy and partial hepatectomy. Hepatobiliary scans, the most sensitive means of detecting bile leakage, may identify the leak before the onset of clinical symptoms.[114] With bile leakage, the tracer may appear as a subcapsular collection or may pool freely in the peritoneal cavity. Parenchymal injuries such as lacerations and hematomas are easily identified on early hepatic phase images.[112]

Magnetic Resonance Imaging

Gadolinium-enhanced MR imaging can depict complex hepatic injuries in patients with contraindications to iodinated contrast material.[115] Contrast-enhanced MR has been shown to demonstrate traumatic hepatic injuries equal to and, occasionally, better than contrast-enhanced CT.[115] MR, however, requires a longer imaging time and cannot accommodate metallic life support and monitoring equipment. In addition, images are compromised by motion to a greater extent than CT as well as by limited evaluation of the bowel. MR imaging can help differentiate bilomas from subacute hematomas.[116] MRCP has been used for evaluation of iatrogenic bile duct injury. Its usefulness in evaluating injuries from blunt trauma has not been thoroughly investigated.[117] However, a hepatobiliary MR imaging contrast agent, mangafodipir trisodium (Telescam; Amersham Health, Princeton, NJ), using a T1-weighted sequence has been shown to provide good quality MR cholangiograms and to demonstrate the origin and extent of bile leaks.[118] Potentially, this agent may be useful in the evaluation of traumatic biliary tree injury.

Angiography

Once the mainstay of hepatic trauma imaging, angiography is now usually performed only to investigate and treat severe hemorrhage, post-traumatic fistulas, and pseudoaneurysms.[78] Angiography can help demonstrate smaller arterial pseudoaneurysms, which are difficult to identify on CT examinations. Traumatic pseudoaneurysms, arteriobiliary fistulas, arteriovenous fistulas, and portobiliary fistulas are the major sources of occult or delayed hemorrhage in the traumatized liver. These vascular abnormalities are quite amenable to

transarterial embolization with either Gianturco coils or detachable balloons. Gelfoam and Ivalon usually produce only transient hemostasis in patients who have had multiple blood transfusions.[14,78-84] Transcatheter arterial embolization has been demonstrated to be an effective alternative to surgery in patients with high-grade (Mirvis classification 3 or 4) injuries to the liver and, in one series, was successful in all patients.[84] Interventional radiologists can manage some of the most lethal venous injuries, including lacerations of the inferior vena cava, with stenting.[119]

Plain Radiographs

Plain radiographic findings are neither sensitive nor specific in patients with hepatic trauma. Nearly 50% of patients with hepatic trauma have fractures of the right lower ribs. When hemoperitoneum is present, there may be loss of the inferior liver-fat interface. Hepatomegaly, irregularity of the liver margin, and caudal displacement of the hepatic flexure all suggest liver injury. Pulmonary contusion, pneumothorax, elevation of the right hemidiaphragm, pleural effusion, hemothorax, and diaphragmatic irregularity frequently accompany hepatic trauma as well.[4,14,81,120,121]

Treatment

The majority of patients with blunt hepatic trauma and selective patients with penetrating liver injuries are now managed nonoperatively if hemodynamically stable.[7-9,20,21] Validation of conservative management has been substantiated by lower acute mortality rates and acceptable short-term morbidity and complications relative to exploratory surgery and emergent hepatic resections.[12,122,123] In patients with AAST grade I-III liver injuries, the need for surgical exploration after initial resuscitation and observation is usually less than 10% to 20%.[12,122,123] If patients with grade IV-VI injuries can be nonoperatively stabilized, a period of resuscitation and CT imaging may improve the ultimate outcome of emergent surgery by preoperatively defining the extent and location of specific hepatic injuries. In patients with severe trauma, treatment of shock and of head and thoracic injuries has priority; next, abdominal injuries should be addressed.[124] For severe liver injury (class IV or V), three main surgical principles achieve: control of hemorrhage, drainage of infection, and repair of the biliary system (Fig. 93-12). Bleeding is controlled by (1) specific ligation or direct control of bleeding points, (2) debridement and ligation, (3) hepatic artery ligation, (4) more extensive hepatic resection, (5) tamponade with packing, and (6) in extreme cases of venous avulsion, vena cava occlusion, with or without shunting, or cava resection with graft replacement. Injuries to the hepatic veins are the major cause of immediate death from hepatic trauma and are difficult to repair. Patients with a cerebral intraparenchymal bleed demonstrated on head CT scans are difficult to manage because they may be harmed by the effects of general anesthesia and the fluid shifts that accompany laparotomy, evacuation of hemoperitoneum, and repair of the liver injury.[70] Operative hemostasis and adequate debridement may be difficult, and hepatic surgery carries the risk of postoperative sepsis.[72] After operative control of hemorrhage, the liver is drained externally. Finally, biliary injury must be recognized and repaired, as it will not heal spontaneously.[125-133]

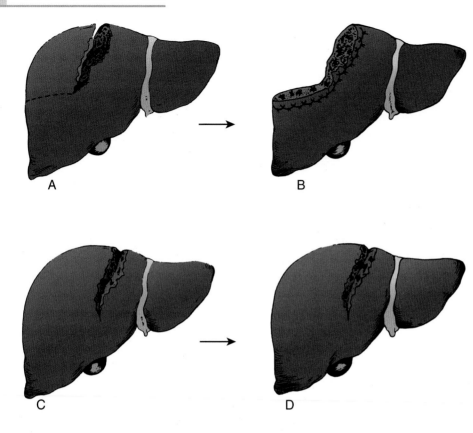

Figure 93-12. Traumatic hepatic injuries: types and treatment. A. Blunt injury in which a large defect involves the full thickness of the dome of the liver. **B.** This is treated by resectional debridement and individual vessel ligation. A less severe injury (**C**) requires only control of individual bleeders (**D**). (**A-D** from Madding GF, Kennedy PA: Trauma to the Liver, 2nd ed. Philadelphia, WB Saunders, 1971.)

Complications

Infection

Sepsis is the second leading cause of post-traumatic mortality (after hemorrhage). It is responsible for 15% of deaths resulting from liver trauma.[55] Nonpenetrating trauma is now the third most common cause of hepatic abscess in the United States.[55] These infections, however, are far more common with operative than with nonoperative management. Hematomas and bilomas are excellent media for the development of infection. In traumatized patients, bacteria may enter the body through intravenous sites, various indwelling catheters, surgical drains, and other injured areas, and by translocation from the gastrointestinal tract.[55,73] In patients with a suspected intra-abdominal source of sepsis, all intrahepatic or perihepatic fluid collections seen on imaging studies should be viewed with suspicion as a source of infection.[55]

Bilomas

Intrahepatic or extrahepatic bile cysts (bilomas) are being detected with increasing frequency in patients with hepatic trauma because of the increased sensitivity of cross-sectional imaging and hepatobiliary scintigraphy.[28,55,104,108,110] These lesions may take days to weeks to become manifest clinically, owing to the slow rate of leakage from the injured bile duct. Most bilomas are asymptomatic and detected by imaging. CT scans and sonography demonstrate nonspecific fluid collections. Often, bilomas can be adequately treated by percutaneous drainage, but in other cases, an operation is required to repair or resect the injured duct.

HEPATIC SURGERY

Hepatic surgery has been likened to an exercise in hemostasis.[134-136] No bloodless planes exist, as the liver's complex inflow and outflow tracts course at right angles. The liver parenchyma is also friable and soft and has few landmarks.[137] These factors have hindered the evolution of hepatic surgery to such a degree that, before the 1950s, segmental hepatectomy was reserved almost exclusively for trauma.[137] With advances in surgical techniques and anesthesia and a better understanding of internal vascular anatomy (Fig. 93-13) and hepatic physiology, partial hepatectomy has become a safe and accepted mode of therapy for selected patients with primary and metastatic liver tumors as well as certain benign disorders (Table 93-3).[138-142]

Two major principles are fundamental to planning hepatic resection.[143-146] First, there must be a sufficient amount of

Table 93-3
Indications for Hepatic Resection

Indication	Frequency (%)
Metastatic tumor	60
Primary malignancy	15
Undiagnosed mass	8
Benign tumor or cyst	7
Trauma	5
Localized biliary abnormality	3
Infection	2

Adapted from Meyers WC, Jones RS: Textbook of Liver and Biliary Surgery. Philadelphia, JB Lippincott, 1990, pp 391-402.

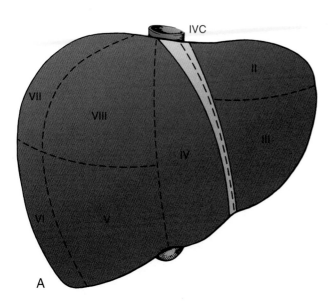

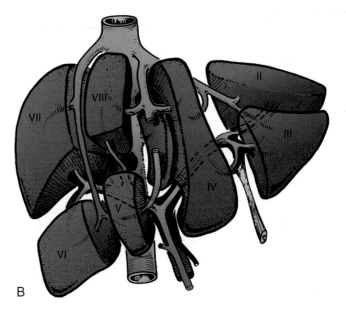

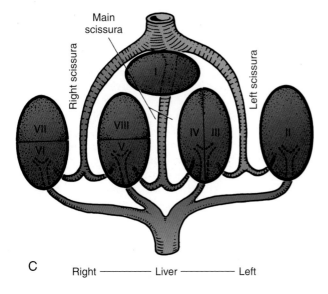

Figure 93-13. Segmental hepatic anatomy: Couinaud's nomenclature. This classification is vital to an understanding of the surgical vascular anatomy of the liver. **A.** Except for the falciform ligament, the liver has few topographic landmarks. Segment I, caudate lobe (not shown); II and III, lateral segment of the left lobe; IV, medial segment of the left lobe; V and VIII, anterior segment of the right lobe; VI and VII, posterior segment of the right lobe. **B.** Schematic representation of the segments. The three main hepatic veins lie within scissurae and divide the liver into four sections. The caudate lobe (I) is its own autonomous lobe in the French system. **C.** The segmental anatomy of **A** is depicted to show the scissurae and the caudate lobe. (**A** from Sabiston DC Jr [ed]: Textbook of Surgery, 13th ed. Philadelphia, WB Saunders, 1986; **B** and **C** from Bismuth H: Surgical anatomy. In Blumgart LH [ed]: Surgery of the Liver and Biliary Tract. Edinburgh, Churchill Livingstone, 1988, pp 1-37.)

hepatic parenchyma to sustain life after surgery. The liver possesses a remarkable capacity to regenerate itself; up to 80% can be safely removed in many patients. Regeneration of liver volume is an efficient, progressive process that in animal studies requires approximately 4 months after an 80% to 85% resection.[143,145] Coexisting hepatocellular diseases such as cirrhosis decrease the amount of hepatic reserve so much that some patients are unable to tolerate removal of any tissue. Indeed, total hepatectomy and liver transplantation may be the best way to treat patients with small hepatomas or severe cirrhosis.[147-149]

The second major principle of hepatic resection is preservation of blood supply to the liver tissue left in situ. Adhering to this principle is difficult because the vascular supply is not apparent to the surgeon on inspection of the hepatic surface. In addition, hepatic veins and arteries do not lie in parallel courses, as they generally do in other organs.

Radiology in Surgical Planning

Imaging studies play an important role in identifying the extent of disease that is important for prognosis and therapy. For example, the number and size of hepatic metastases from colorectal neoplasms and extrahepatic involvement determine long-term survival in patients with hepatic resection.[150-152] The radiologist can help the surgeon adhere to these principles by providing the following information before hepatic resection:[135,143,145,153-155]

1. The anatomic location of the lesion in relationship to the portal and hepatic veins, fissures, coronary and falciform ligaments, and the fissure for the ligamentum venosum
2. The presence of vascular invasion of the hepatic vessels by a neoplasm
3. Bland or tumor thrombus in portal and hepatic veins distant from the lesion of interest

4. Involvement and patency of the inferior vena cava
5. Spread of tumor into adjacent structures (e.g., diaphragm, colon, duodenum, lymph nodes)
6. Confirmation to the maximal extent possible that the lobe of liver to remain in situ is free of tumor

Preoperative studies should include a chest radiograph and chest CT scan, to exclude extrahepatic metastases. MDCT of the liver and the remainder of the abdomen should also be obtained. It should be noted that removal of multiple liver metastases is possible in some patients. This produces a "Swiss cheese" appearance on CT scans.

A common anomaly, the replaced right hepatic artery arising from the superior mesenteric artery, is important for the surgeon to appreciate preoperatively. The placement of hepatic artery infusion catheter for chemotherapy may require CT arterial portography to better demonstrate the arterial anatomy and lesions. Because aberrant vessels may course laterally and more posteriorly in the porta hepatis, dissection of the porta hepatis must be modified.[156]

Intraoperative Ultrasound

Intraoperative ultrasound of the liver can function as both a diagnostic and a therapeutic tool. As a diagnostic aid, intraoperative ultrasound has proved successful for the following indications: (1) to detect small (1-5 cm), nonpalpable, parenchymal liver lesions not detected by preoperative imaging studies; (2) to precisely define the topography of liver tumors and their relationship to the vessels, allowing segmental resections to be performed; (3) to guide intraoperative biopsy of impalpable lesions; and (4) to differentiate liver neoplasms from certain benign lesions such as cysts or hemangiomas.[157-163]

Several studies have documented the utility of this technique. In Conlon et al., the information provided by intraoperative ultrasound changed the preoperative surgical plan in 18% of patients and provided additional useful information not available preoperatively in 47%, including detection of subcentimeter lesions, lesion characterization, and anatomy of hepatic vasculature.[164] In another study, the sensitivity of lesion depiction with intraoperative ultrasound was 94.3% compared to MRI with a sensitivity of 86.7%. However, in this study, in only 4% of the patients did intraoperative ultrasound alter surgical management secondary to additional lesion detection.[165] Another study demonstrated intraoperative ultrasound to change surgical management in only 7% of patients.[166] In comparison to initial studies, these more recent studies demonstrate a decreased percentage of cases when intraoperative ultrasound alters surgical management. This is felt to be partly attributed to technologic advances in preoperative studies such as MRI resulting in improved patient selection.[166]

However, intraoperative ultrasound continues to be an important component of hepatic resection for purposes of lesion localization and relationship to hepatic vasculature and biliary structures, segmental localization, and further evaluation for incompletely characterized subcentimeter lesions identified on preoperative imaging studies. Intraoperative ultrasound also helps detect occult extension of hepatic tumors into vascular structures and assists in intraoperative biopsy of liver lesions.[165] Intraoperative ultrasound has also proved useful in guiding intraoperative cryotherapy and radiofrequency ablatia in the treatment of liver tumors.[167-169]

Indications

As surgical techniques become safer, the indications for hepatic surgery are broadening (see Table 93-3).

Benign Lesions

The indications for resecting a benign tumor or cyst include risk of rupture or hemorrhage, symptoms, risk of malignant transformation, and enlargement of the mass, so that it is causing pressure on bile ducts, the liver capsule, or adjacent organs. Fenestration-resection is rarely required for cosmetic or symptomatic improvement in patients with adult polycystic liver disease.[170,171]

Localized biliary abnormalities such as hepatolithiasis or segmental Caroli's disease are other indications for resection. Hepatic abscesses that do not respond to medication or percutaneous drainage may also require surgical resection.

Malignant Lesions

Resection of liver metastases is the most common indication for partial hepatectomy in the United States. Liver metastases are an enormous clinical problem in view of the fact that approximately 25% of all malignancies eventually spread to the liver (Table 93-4). It is the most common site of blood-borne metastasis and more often than not is a major contributor to the patient's demise.[172] Neoplasms grow five to seven times faster in the liver than in most other organs.[154] This is precisely why untreated liver metastases augur so ill patient survival. Colorectal metastasis is the most commonly resected hepatic tumor in the United States. Cure rates of 25% to 40% for solitary metastases confined to one lobe have been reported.[166-169]

Hepatoma is the most commonly resected tumor worldwide, owing to its prevalence in portions of the Far East and Africa. Technical improvements in hepatic resection and earlier diagnosis have increased the resectability rates. Survival rates following curative resection of hepatomas are 41% for 5 years and 32% for 10 years. The most important factor affecting long-term survival after resection is vascular invasion. Other adverse factors affecting survival include lesion multiplicity and tumor size greater than 5 cm.[149]

Hepatic Resection for Liver Metastases

With the knowledge that patients with limited metastatic disease may benefit from liver resection, there has been a marked increase in the number of hepatic resections per-

Table 93-4
Incidence of Liver Metastases at Autopsy

Primary Tumor	Percent with Liver Metastases
Pancreas	56
Colon	53
Breast	50
Melanoma	44
Stomach	42
Lung	30
Esophagus	24
Kidney	13
Prostate	70

From Foster JH: Surgical treatment of metastatic liver tumors. Hepato-gastroenterology 37:182-187, 1990.

formed during the 1980s and 1990s. Advances in the techniques of liver resection and extensive preoperative evaluation with careful patient selection have reduced operative mortality rates to less than 5%.[177-186] This improvement in operative morbidity and mortality is attributed to several different factors. Our improved understanding of the segmental anatomy of the liver and specifically its intrahepatic blood supply has made for safer hepatic resections with minimized blood loss. In addition, improved preoperative diagnostic imaging has excluded patients from operation in whom the operative risks due to major vascular involvement would have resulted in major complications. Resection techniques including vascular inflow occlusion, minimized parenchymal destruction, decreased intraoperative blood loss, and successful management of postoperative complications have improved the safety of this operation. As a result, the operative morbidity and mortality associated with hepatic surgery has significantly decreased, with most current studies reporting operative mortality rates between 2% and 7%.[177-186]

Improved long-term results after hepatic resection are due not only to decreased perioperative mortality and morbidity but also to an improved understanding of the biology of liver metastases and thus the selection criteria for surgery.

Selection of Patients for Resection

If we accept that certain patients with limited hepatic disease will benefit from surgical resection, then careful analysis of the survivors will allow us to identify specific prognostic factors useful in selecting appropriate patients for resection. Much of our knowledge regarding prognostic variables affecting patient outcome after hepatic resection is derived from the collected data of the registry of hepatic metastases by Hughes and associates.[182] This retrospective series analyzed 862 patients from multiple institutions who had undergone hepatic resection for metastatic colorectal cancer. In addition to data from the registry of hepatic metastases, other single-institutional reviews have helped to identify prognostic features related to the patient, the primary tumor characteristics, and features of the liver metastases.

Patient characteristics not thought to influence survival include gender and patient age. Currently, a patient's physiologic performance status rather than chronologic age or gender is the major determinant excluding them from consideration for resection. Patients with poor hepatic function due to advanced cirrhosis are also considered poor candidates for liver resection.[186]

The *stage and histologic grade of the primary tumor* are thought to be important prognostic factors. In Hughes and associates' registry, patients presenting with regional lymph node metastases (stage III) had a 5-year survival rate of 23% compared with 47% for patients without regional lymph node involvement (stage II).[182] In addition, other retrospective studies have suggested that patients with poorly differentiated, high-grade primary tumors have a shorter survival benefit after resection of liver metastases.[187] Finally, patients with primary tumors originating in the rectum may derive less benefit from resection of hepatic metastases. None of these primary tumor characteristics should exclude a patient from consideration for surgical resection; however, they do identify patients who will be at increased risk for hepatic or extrahepatic recurrence.

The most important prognostic factors determining survival after hepatic resection appear to be those related to the *features and characteristics of the liver metastases*. These were examined in detail in the Hughes registry and by other institutional series. Fong and colleagues have analyzed and summarized these characteristics thoroughly in their review of the literature.[188] Although controversy exists as to the influence of tumor size, disease-free interval, and number of metastases on survival, most authorities agree that the ability to achieve a pathologic-negative margin of resection and the absence of extrahepatic metastases are clearly the most important survival determinants.[189]

Some studies have shown that patients with large (>5 cm) metastases appear to have a worse prognosis than patients with smaller tumors. Survival benefit has been seen in resection of these large lesions predicated on the ability to achieve tumor-free margins of resection. Thus, size in and of itself does not preclude resection but may make the ability to achieve free vascular or parenchymal margins problematic. Similarly, it was previously thought that patients with multiple metastases should not undergo liver resection. In their review, Fong and colleagues suggest that patients with three or fewer liver metastases may have a survival advantage compared with patients undergoing resection of four or more metastatic deposits.[188] Survival differences between patients undergoing resection of a solitary metastasis versus two or three lesions is not as clear-cut. Similar to the argument regarding tumor size, the actual number of liver metastases does not appear to be the major factor limiting resection; however, as the number of metastatic deposits within the liver increases, the ability to achieve a margin-negative resection becomes impaired, as does the ability to preserve enough normally functioning liver.[182,186]

Because of these concerns, the location and distribution of multiple lesions and the extent of liver resection have been examined as prognostic variables. In the Hughes and associates' registry, the distribution of metastases comparing unilobar versus bilobar disease was not thought to be a significant predictor of survival. This has become an important factor with the advances in nonanatomic liver resections. With a greater understanding of hepatic segmental anatomy, more limited liver resections are now being performed. This allows for a reduction in the amount of normal liver resected as well as resection of disease from both lobes. When treating lesions less than 4 cm in diameter, no differences in survival are seen between more limited segmental resections compared with formal hepatic lobectomies. Formal lobectomy may be required to obtain tumor-free margins in patients with large tumors. In patients with smaller tumors undergoing segmental resection, no difference in survival has been seen as long as clear pathologic margins are obtained.[177-186]

The time interval between resection of the primary cancer and appearance of liver metastases seems to be a significant variable for survival. The 5-year survival rate for patients presenting with synchronous liver metastases was 27% in Hughes and associates' registry.[182] Similarly, patients developing liver metastases within 12 months after resection of the primary colorectal cancer had a 5-year survival rate of 31%. This difference was not significant. However, in patients developing hepatic metastases at an interval greater than 12 months, the 5-year survival rate after resection was 42%. This difference was significant and may reflect a biologically less aggressive tumor. Despite the adverse impact on survival, patients with otherwise resectable synchronous lesions should be considered for surgery.[187]

Another important variable affecting prognosis is the presence or absence of extrahepatic metastatic disease. Patients with celiac or hepatic lymph node metastases should not be considered for hepatic resection. The presence of such nodal disease is an indicator of systemic dissemination. Hughes and associates reported no 5-year survivors in 24 patients undergoing liver resection who were found to have positive intra-abdominal lymph node metastases.[182] More controversial is the role of resection of non-nodal extrahepatic metastases. Usually, this is thought to mean isolated pulmonary disease in the face of limited hepatic metastases. Although the number of patients who present with such limited pulmonary and hepatic metastases is small, there may be a role for resection in highly selected patients who demonstrate slow disease progression. In general, the presence of extrahepatic visceral metastases is a contraindication to liver resection. Despite our improved understanding of the prognostic variables related to long-term survival after liver resection, the majority of patients will ultimately succumb to metastatic cancer. Most retrospective series demonstrate 5-year survival rates between 20% and 40% after resection for hepatic colorectal metastases.[177-188]

Types of Hepatic Resection

Wedge Excision

Wedge excision, the simplest hepatic resection, consists of nonanatomic removal of a small amount of superficial tissue. It is considered nonanatomic because the tissue does not correspond to any hepatic segment or subsegment.[156]

Subsegmentectomy

Subsegmentectomy is often difficult to perform because of the difficulty of exposure and of vascular variability. For example, a solitary lesion in the caudate lobe is usually resected by removing the medial and lateral segments of the left lobe to gain access to the lesion.[156,187]

Right Hepatic Lobectomy

In this procedure (Fig. 93-14), the liver is mobilized, a cholecystectomy is performed, and the right branches of the bile duct, hepatic artery, and portal vein are dissected, ligated, and divided, while avoiding injury to branches of the left lobe. The surgical plane is lateral to the middle hepatic vein, which must be left intact to provide drainage for the medial segment of the left lobe.[156,175]

Right Trisegmentectomy

The entire right lobe and medial segment of the left lobe are removed using hilar dissection with ligation and division of the right lobe vessels plus the vessels to the medial segment (see Fig. 93-14). The right and middle hepatic veins are removed in this resection. The line of resection is just to the right of the falciform ligament, ensuring that the ascending portion of the portal vein is preserved. This extensive resec-

tion, although relatively safe for younger patients, should be used with caution in patients older than 65 years, as the associated operative mortality rate is 30.7%.[148]

Left Hepatic Lobectomy

During left hepatic lobectomy, the left lobar branches of the hepatic artery are ligated and divided in the hilum (see Fig. 93-14). The left hepatic veins are usually resected as well. The caudate lobe may be removed along with the left lobe or left in place. The surgical plane is just to the left of the middle hepatic vein, which must remain intact to drain the anterior segment of the right lobe.[156,190]

Left Lateral Segmentectomy

This procedure is technically easier than the other forms of hepatic resection because hilar dissection is usually not needed (see Fig. 93-14). The surgical plane is just to the left of the umbilical fissure, so that the ascending portion of the portal vein is left intact. Much of the left hepatic vein can be resected because the medial segment of the left lobe is drained by the middle hepatic vein.

Left Trisegmentectomy

Left trisegmentectomy is a technically difficult procedure in which both segments of the left lobe and the anterior segment of the right lobe are resected. The right hepatic vein needs to be preserved to drain the remaining posterior segment.

Right Posterior Segmentectomy

This procedure is also technically difficult. The posterior segment of the right lobe is resected, leaving the right hepatic vein intact to drain the anterior segment.[191]

LIVER-DIRECTED THERAPY

Cryosurgery

Cryosurgery refers to the in situ destruction of liver tumors by precisely and rapidly cooling the tumor and a zone of normal hepatic parenchyma to extreme subzero temperatures. By circulating a coolant such as liquid nitrogen through the core of the tumor, temperatures as low as −100°C can be achieved. The effect of such profound hypothermia on tissue results in both indirect and direct mechanisms of cell destruction. Details of the lethal effects of cryosurgery have been well described by Ravikumar and colleagues but essentially involve the formation of intracellular ice crystals leading to protein denaturation and rupture of cell membranes.[192] Indirectly, subzero temperatures result in microvascular thrombosis and tissue anoxia. Further damage occurs if the cells are allowed to slowly thaw and are then rapidly refrozen. Clinical studies have suggested that two such freeze-thaw cycles may be necessary for optimal tissue destruction. Fundamental to the implementation of cryosurgery as a viable treatment option for patients with unresectable liver metastases has been the development of intraoperative ultrasound (IOUS) and refinement of equipment used to deliver the coolant to the tumor.

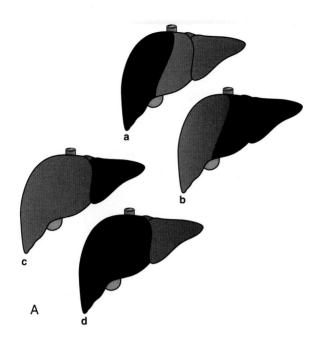

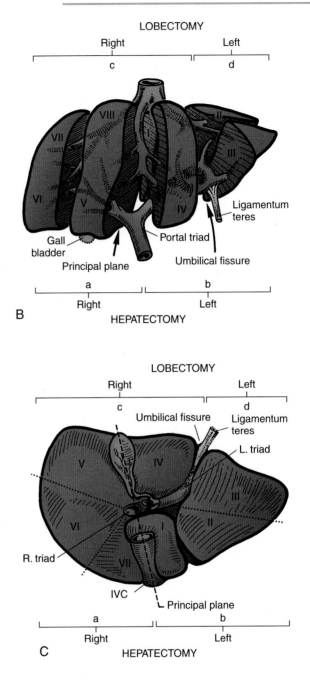

Figure 93-14. Types of hepatic resection. Traditional hepatic resections: right hepatic lobectomy (**a**); left hepatic lobectomy (**b**); left lateral segmentectomy (**c**); right trisegmentectomy (**d**). Anterior (**B**) and inferior (**C**) exploded views of the liver show the hepatic segments removed with each major form of hepatectomy. IVC, inferior vena cava; a, b, c, and d refer to surgeries in **A**. (**A** from Meyers WC, Jones RS: Textbook of Liver and Biliary Surgery. Philadelphia, JB Lippincott, 1991, p 393; **B** and **C** from Blumgart LH: Liver resection: Liver and biliary tumors. In Blumgart LH [ed]: Surgery of the Liver and Biliary Tract. Edinburgh, Churchill Livingstone, 1988, pp 1251-1280.)

Early reports demonstrated the feasibility and safety of treating liver metastases by cryosurgery, whereas follow-up series have now helped to define the indications for this modality.[192] The most significant clinical limitation of surgical resection is usually the number of lesions that can be safely removed while sparing sufficient hepatic parenchyma to avoid postoperative liver failure. Thus, the major indications for cryosurgery are either primary or metastatic lesions that are not amenable to resection due to cirrhosis or bilobar involvement in which either the number of lesions or the location of the tumors would risk sufficient postoperative hepatic function after resection.[192] For colorectal metastases, most centers with sufficient cryosurgical experience will limit this technique to patients with six or fewer metastases (generally <40% of the liver volume) and tumors smaller than 6 to 8 cm in greatest diameter and avoid large central tumors

near the hilum of the liver. Similar to other forms of liver-directed therapy, cryosurgery probably offers little advantage to patients with extrahepatic metastatic disease.

Operative technique currently involves intraoperative ultrasound localization and monitoring of the cryoprobe placement into the tumor.[193] In addition, IOUS allows detection of tumors not recognized on preoperative scans and is essential for monitoring the freeze margins of the iceball. The cryoprobes are vacuum-insulated devices that circulate supercooled liquid nitrogen through the probe's tip. A 3-mm blunt-tipped probe creates a freeze zone up to 4 cm, and the 8-mm trocar point probe creates a freeze zone of up to 6 cm. A single probe or combination of probes can be utilized to achieve complete freezing of the tumor and an additional 1 cm beyond the margin to ensure complete cryoablation. The entire process of probe introduction, freeze-thaw cycles, and probe extraction is monitored with real-time IOUS. Major complication rates are reportedly between 10% and 20% and mortality rates are less than 2%.[192-194] Complications may include hemorrhage, biliary fistula, hepatic or subphrenic abscess, and, more rarely, hepatic failure, coagulopathy, and cardiac arrest. Disease-free survival rates and patterns of failure have now been reported from several centers. With median follow-up times between 18 and 36 months, most series report 5-year actuarial disease-free survival rates between 15% and 28%.[193,194] These rates are comparable to those reported for liver resection, and in light of the reported mortality rates of less than 2%, it becomes obvious why cryosurgery has generated such interest and enthusiasm.

Radiofrequency Ablation

Radiofrquency ablation (RFA) refers to the direct thermal (heat) application (>80°C) to tumors with the intent of achieving cellular kill. The mechanisms of action of RFA include tissue heating, protein denaturation, release of water vapor, mechanical tissue destruction, breakdown of cellular membranes, vascular thrombosis.[195]

Several studies have been performed demonstrating the effectiveness of RFA in achieving local tissue destruction. The limitation continues to be disease progression at the margin of the ablated zone, as well as outside the treatment field. Although needle probes rated at 7 cm are available, there continues to be doubt whether such a large burn can truly be accomplished with a single electrode.[196,197]

RFA can be accomplished using percutaneous, laparoscopic or intra-operative means. Intra-operative ultrasound is an essential tool in the live identification of lesions intraoperatively that might not have been seen using standard cross-sectional imaging techniques. Indications for RFA include primary and metastatic liver tumors, renal tumors, osteoid osteoma, painful bony metastases, lung tumors as well as adjunct to surgery in cases of surgical debulking for neuroendocrine tumors. Complications include bleeding, pneumothorax, biliary and vascular injury, as well as tract seeding.[195,198,199]

Chemoembolization

Chemoembolization exploits the preferential blood supply provided by the hepatic artery to neoplastic lesions.[200-202] Initial attempts at ligation of the hepatic artery resulted in temporary regression of hepatic tumors. The effect was transient due to the rapid development of collateral vessels distal to the ligated vessels.[203] Chemoembolization is performed by placing a catheter into the hepatic artery followed by concomitant local delivery of chemotherapy and a vascular occlusion agent. The dual injection results in theoretical benefits above those obtained with either procedure alone. In addition to the ischemic damage created by the embolization agent, the vascular occlusion results in more confined and prolonged exposure of the chemotherapeutic agent.[204,205] Anoxic damage also causes increased vascular permeability with increased infiltration of the tumor with chemotherapy.[204] Finally, cytotoxic irritation of the vessel may result in an irritant vasculitis, leading to further occlusion and ischemia.[204] Although there is increased local toxicity with the combination of treatments, systemic toxicity is minimized by drug metabolism during first passage through the liver.[206] Clinical trials have demonstrated significant and sustained responses to chemoembolization in the treatment of unresectable primary hepatomas, metastatic colorectal cancers, and neuroendocrine tumors. In 2002, two landmark publications demonstrated the survival advantage incurred by chemoembolization in patients with intermediate stage hepatoma. These papers helped establish chemoembolization as the worldwide gold standard for treatment of hepatoma.[207,208] In summary, the mechanism of action of chemoembolization include: 1) application of chemotherapy directly into the tumor bed, 2) reduction of the blood supply to the tumor. These have the additive effect of increasing chemotherapeutic concentration within the applied area, increasing dwell time and reducing systemic toxicity.

Embolization is accomplished by using a viscous liquid, such as Lipidiol,[209-216] or particulate matter, such as Ivalon polyvinyl particles,[217,218] collagen particles,[219,220] starch microspheres,[221-225] or steel coils.[226] Although some of these agents have special properties, they have not been directly compared. Lipidiol, for example, has been shown to be taken up preferentially by hepatocellular carcinoma tumor cells. Chemotherapeutic agents that have been utilized for this procedure include 5-fluorouracil, floxuridine, mitomycin C, cisplatin, and doxorubicin. The independent relative effectiveness of these agents has not been determined.

Complications of chemoembolization include postembolization syndrome (pain, nausea, fever), elevated liver function tests, liver infarction, abscess formation, cholecystitis, renal and cardiac failure, as well as death. The likelihood of hepatic infarction is particularly elevated in patients undergoing chemoembolization in the presence of portal vein thrombosis. Hepatic abscess formation is of particular concern in patients with an incompetent ampulla of Vater (e.g., biliary stents) or in patients with a hepaticoenterostomy.[227,228]

Conventional radiologic techniques may actually not be adequate to assess response to therapy. Although changes that are consistent with liquefaction necrosis may be seen up to 1 month after chemoembolization, maximal decrease in tumor volume is obtained with scans performed 2 to 3 months after the procedure.[220] Carcinoembryonic antigen and α-fetoprotein measurements for colorectal cancers and hepatoma may be used for clinical follow-up.

The goals of chemoembolization are to improve symptom control and to increase disease-free and overall survival. Chemoembolization, in conjunction with systemic chemotherapy, may yield better results than either modality alone. Clinical parameters that predict response to treatment and survival, such as tumor vascularity and extent of liver involvement, can be used to select patients most likely to benefit from regional chemotherapy. Earlier detection and referral of patients with low-volume hepatic disease may improve outcomes.

Combination Chemoembolization and Radiofrequency Ablation

Given the effectiveness of chemoembolization and RFA as single therapeutic modalities, there has been recent interest in combining the two in an attempt to further improve on efficacy. The theory of applying both of combination in combination is analogous to the surgical pringle maneuver:

impairing blood flow to tumor (chemoembolization) with the simultaneous application of ablative heat (RFA). Results combining these therapies have been promising, with recurrence-free time of 12.5 months, >70% improvement in tumor markers and complete necrosis in >90% of tumors.[229]

Radioembolization

Radioembolization represents a new therapeutic tool for the treatment of liver malignancies. It is defined as the intra-arterial administration of radiation via an embolization vehicle. This technology capitalizes on the fact that hepatic tumors derive their blood supply from the hepatic artery rather than the portal vein. Hence, radioembolization allows the administration of microscopic radiation particles to be delivered preferentially to the tumor.

Although there have been some preliminary case reports on the use of rhenium and holmium microspheres, the most common radioembolic microsphere clinically in use is yttrium-90. Yttrium-90 is a beta emitter with a half-life of 64.2 hours. The microspheres are carried by glass or resin as the embolic carrier and range between 20 to 60 microns. They are preferentially carried to tumor by hypervascularity where they exert their local radiation effect. This technique of radio-embolization allow for the administration if high absorbed doses to hepatic tissue (>200-300 Gy). The microspheres are selectively administered by percutaneous access to the hepatic artery on a whole liver, lobar, segmental or subsegmental level.[230-232]

The use of yttrium-90 microspheres has been studied in primary and secondary metastatic tumors to the liver. With hepatoma, radioembolization has been shown to be safe and effective and, as well, been shown to permit downstaging to resection and liver transplantation. Survival in patients with hepatoma is reported to be approximately 700 days for Okuda stage I patients. In patients with metastatic disease to the liver, survival rates range between 7 to 10 months in patients who have failed standard of care polychemotherapies.[232-240]

Postoperative Radiologic Appearance of the Liver

Computed Tomography

CT is the preferred means of postoperatively evaluating the liver.[241] The CT appearance of the postoperative liver depends on what segment is resected, what operation is performed, the degree of hepatic regeneration, and the presence and nature of postoperative complications. Baseline postoperative scans are essential for future evaluation of recurrent hepatic malignancy.[241]

After resection of the right lobe, hypertrophy of the left lobe occurs with displacement of the ligamentum teres and falciform ligament to the right (Fig. 93-15). The caudate lobe also modestly enlarges, with the portal vein displaced posteriorly, so that the porta hepatis is exposed dorsally to the anterior aspect of the right renal fascia. Other common findings include migration of the colon and the small bowel into the hepatic fossa, elevation of the right kidney, posterior displacement of the inferior vena cava, and elliptical enlargement of the remaining liver.[242]

After left lobectomy, the right lobe enlarges in a rounded shape, with displacement of the porta hepatis and portal vein to the left and inferior displacement of the right kidney. The stomach or colon occupies the left hepatic fossa.[242]

Partial hepatectomy is often accompanied by a small region of low attenuation near the plane of dissection, which is due to fatty infiltration, fibrous tissue, and hepatocytes laden with bile pigment, presumably representing the sequelae of local trauma.[241-243] These changes are transient and must be differentiated from abscess and hematoma. Hypertrophy of the hepatic parenchyma can be seen on CT scans as a progressive change in contour of the hepatic parenchyma over a period of 6 months to 1 year.[242]

The greater omentum is often swung up to the operative site to provide natural "packing" material that helps diminish the frequency of postoperative complications (see Fig. 93-15). The fat in the omentum can simulate a low-density mass

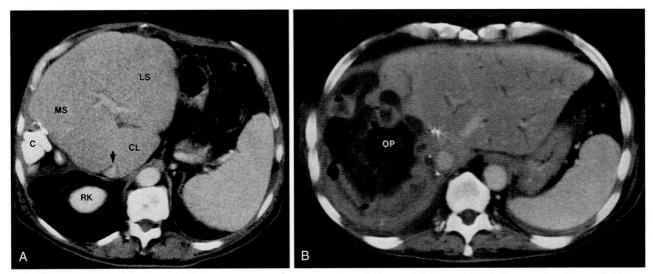

Figure 93-15. Postoperative liver: CT findings. A. Typical CT appearance after right hepatic lobectomy. There is hypertrophy of the medial segment (MS) and lateral segment (LS) of the left lobe and caudate lobe (CL). Elevation of the right kidney (RK), posterior displacement of the inferior vena cava (*arrow*), and migration of colon (C) into the hepatic fossa are seen. **B.** This patient had a trisegmentectomy with construction of a greater omental pack (OP) along the lateral aspect of the remaining lateral segment of the lobe. The patient developed a recurrent tumor, accounting for the intrahepatic biliary dilation.

lesion, so knowledge of the operative technique is useful in its identification.[244] In the early postoperative period, there can be transient fluid that accumulates between the omental pack and the resection margin. This fluid contours with the liver margin and can be differentiated from a focal collection such as a biloma or abscess.[241]

Magnetic Resonance Imaging

Although CT is the traditionally preferred primary posthepatectomy imaging technique, MR is playing an increasing role. MR can be particularly useful when CT is limited by streak artifacts caused by surgical clips or is contraindicated due to inability to administer intravenous iodinated contrast material. Regenerated liver has the same signal intensity as normal liver. Diffuse inhomogeneity of the hepatic parenchymal signal can be seen after chemotherapy and may be related to fatty infiltration or vascular damage. These irregular, ill-defined areas are in contrast to recurrent tumor, which generally has more sharply marginated regions of high signal intensity on T2-weighted images.[245] MR may be helpful in differentiating postoperative hematoma from other focal fluid collections based on the signal intensity of methemoglobin.[246]

Most hepatic regeneration occurs within 6 months, but the process may take more than 1 year. The morphologic changes of the liver and topographic alterations of the right upper quadrant are similar to those observed on CT scans.[245]

COMPLICATIONS

Complications resulting from hepatic surgery are similar to those of other major abdominal operations: abscess, hemorrhage and hematoma, and pleural effusions.[247] Biloma and hematoma are fairly common, due to the nature of the surgery and the biliary and vascular structures transected. Surgical complications occur in 25% to 30% of hepatic operations and are best diagnosed and nonoperatively treated with CT.[241,248,249] Hepatobiliary scintigraphy (Fig. 93-16) and Doppler ultrasound may be needed to help clarify biliary and vascular complications.

Postprocedural Radiologic Appearance of the Liver

Imaging of the liver following liver-directed therapy is critical in assessing response to treatment. This imaging is best performed with either CT or MRI. The normal post-therapy appearance of the liver can be confusing. An understanding of the appearance of hepatic tumors treated with liver directed therapies is crucial in differentiating normal postprocedural changes from residual and recurrent tumor.

The hallmark of positive response to chemoembolization, radiofrequency ablation and any of the liver directed therapies is loss of enhancement on postcontrast imaging. This absence of enhancement correlates with tumor necrosis and can be seen on imaging shortly after therapy (less than one month). At times, a thin, peripheral rim of enhancement may be visualized normally, which does not represent residual tumor. Areas of nodular peripheral enhancement or a thick rim of enhancement in a treated lesion should be viewed as suspicious for residual or recurrent malignancy.[250] As enhancement is one of the main determinants of tumor response, it is

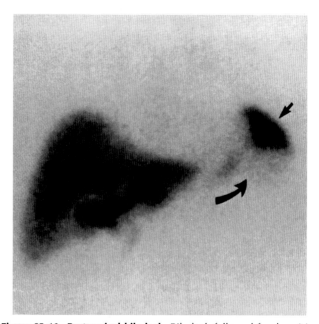

Figure 93-16. Postsurgical bile leak. Bile leak followed focal excision of a hepatic mass in the left lobe. This diisopropyliminodiacetic acid–enhanced hepatobiliary scan shows leakage of bile-containing isotope (*curved arrow*) that extends into the left subphrenic space (*straight arrow*).

important to do a triphasic exam with precontrast imaging in patients who have undergone chemoembolization. On the precontrast images, the lesion often has high density. This should not be confused with calcification but actually represents the density of the chemoembolization agents. Without precontrast images, this finding could potentially be confused with contrast enhancement. In addition to necrosis, lesion size should also be evaluated. Often no decrease in lesion size is seen in the early postprocedural period. Indeed the lesion may sometime increase in size. The intermediately timed post-therapy scans (2-3 months) show the greatest reduction in tumor volume.[251] Similar findings can be seen with MRI, which is also a reliable method of evaluating outcome of treatment.[252] In addition, chemoembolization can cause changes in the adjacent normal liver parenchyma, resulting in, low attenuation regions corresponding to areas of ischemia or infarction.[251]

The appearance of the liver following cryosurgery can vary slightly from the appearance with other therapies. Here, because the "freeze zone" is often larger than the original lesion, the resultant post-therapy low attenuation lesion is often larger. These lesions can appear rounded, oval or wedge-shaped. They can contain foci of air and hemorrhage as well. As in the other liver-directed therapies, a thin peripheral rim of enhancement may be seen.[253]

The newest liver directed therapy, radiotherapy with yttrium-90 microspheres, can cause some unique post procedural imaging changes.[254] Like the other therapies, the lack of enhancement reflects the positive response consistent with tumor necrosis (Fig. 93-17). The lesion may initially be unchanged in size or perhaps even slightly increased, but lesion volume usually decreases on subsequent imaging. Within the adjacent tumor-free liver parenchyma, there can be areas of decreased attenuation. These areas can appear very prominent and heterogeneous and be confused with tumor but they

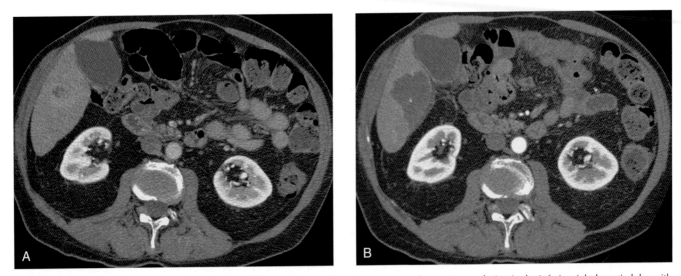

Figure 93-17. Effects of yttrium therapy on hepatocellular carcinoma. A. Pretherapy scan demonstrates a lesion in the inferior right hepatic lobe with a thick rim of peripheral enhancement and central low attenuation consistent with a small of amount of necrosis. **B.** Post-therapy image reveals complete necrosis and nonenhancement of the known tumor. A characteristic thin rim of enhancement is typically seen following therapy and is a benign finding.

do not typically enhance. They are thought to represent liver edema, congestion, and microinfarction from the radiation exposure. These hypoattenuation areas have been found to be more heterogeneous with lower radiation doses and more diffuse with higher doses. These changes tend to dissipate on later scans (four months) suggesting that they are reversible.[255] There can also be extrahepatic effects of the yttrium radioembolization on the biliary tree, gallbladder, duodenum and stomach causing radiation ischemia and necrosis.

References

1. Shanmuganathan K, Mirvis SE: CT evaluation of blunt hepatic trauma. Radiol Clin North Am 36:399-412, 1998.
2. Lee SK, Carrillo EH: Advances and changes in the management of liver injuries. Am Surg 73:201-206, 2007.
3. Pachter HL: Hepatic trauma. In Taylor MB (ed): Gastrointestinal Emergencies, 2nd ed. Baltimore, Williams & Wilkins, 1997, pp 1001-1014.
4. McNulty JG: Radiology of the Liver. Philadelphia, WB Saunders, 1977, pp 195-213.
5. Ralls PW: The liver. In Jeffrey RB, Ralls PW (eds): CT and Sonography of the Acute Abdomen, 2nd ed. Philadelphia, Lippincott-Raven, 1996, pp 17-73.
6. Eiseman B, Rainer W: Liver trauma: An old friend revisited. In Najarian JS, Delaney JP (eds): Progress in Hepatic, Biliary and Pancreatic Surgery. Chicago: Year Book Medical, 1990, pp 98-107.
7. Cushing BM, Clark DE, Cobean R, et al: Blunt and penetrating trauma: Has anything changed? Surg Clin North Am 77:1321-1332, 1997.
8. Pachter HL, Feliciano DV: Complex hepatic injuries. Surg Clin North Am 76:763-773, 1996.
9. Pachter HL, Knudson MM, Esrig B, et al: Status of nonoperative management of blunt hepatic injuries in 1995: A multicenter experience with 404 patients. J Trauma 40:31-38, 1996.
10. Shanmuganathan K, Mirvis SE: CT evaluation of the liver with acute blunt trauma. Crit Rev Diagn Imaging 36:73-113, 1995.
11. Shuman WP: CT of blunt abdominal trauma in adults. Radiology 205:297-306, 1997.
12. Matthes G, Stengel D, Seifert J, et al: Blunt liver in polytrauma: Results from a cohort study with the regular use of whole-body helical computed tomography. World J Surg 27: 1124-1130, 2003.
13. Jeffrey RB, Federle MP: Inflammatory disease and trauma of the liver. In Silverman PM, Zeman RK (eds): CT and MRI of the Liver and Biliary System. New York: Churchill Livingstone, 1990, pp 157-182.
14. Venbrux AC, Savader SJ, Friedman AC: Hepatic trauma. In Friedman AC, Dachman AH (eds): Radiology of the Liver, Biliary Tract, and Pancreas. St. Louis: Mosby, 1994, pp 329-344.
15. Janes CH, Lindor KD: Outcome of patients hospitalized for complications after outpatient liver biopsy. Ann Intern Med 118:96-98, 1993.
16. Dauterive AH, Flancbaum L, Cox EF: Blunt intestinal trauma: A modern-day review. Ann Surg 201:198-200, 1985.
17. Yoon W, Jeong YJ, Kim JK, et al: CT in blunt liver trauma. RadioGraphics 25: 87-104, 2005.
18. Oniscu GC, Parks RW, Garden OJ: Classification of liver and pancreatic trauma. HPB 8: 4-9, 2006.
19. Moore EE, Cogbill TH, Jurkovich GJ, et al: Organ injury scaling: Spleen and liver (1994 revision). J Trauma 38:323-324, 1995.
20. Sherman HF, Savage BA, Jones LM: Nonoperative management of blunt hepatic injuries: Safe at any grade? J Trauma 37:616-621, 1994.
21. Meredith JW, Young JS, Bowling J, et al: Nonoperative management of blunt hepatic trauma: The exception or the rule? J Trauma 36:529-534, 1994.
22. Croce MA, Fabian TC, Menke PG, et al: Nonoperative management of blunt hepatic trauma is the treatment of choice for hemodynamically stable patients. Results of a prospective trial. Ann Surg 221:744-755, 1995.
23. Boone DC, Federle M, Billiar TR, et al: Evolution of management of major hepatic trauma: Identification of patterns of injury. J Trauma 39:344-350, 1995.
24. Archer LP, Frederick BR, Shackford SR: Selective nonoperative management of liver and spleen injuries in neurologically impaired adult patients. Arch Surg 131:309-315, 1996.
25. Moore EF: Critical decisions in the management of hepatic trauma. Am J Surg 148:712-716, 1984.
26. Federico JA, Horner WR, Clark DE, et al: Blunt hepatic trauma. Arch Surg 125:905-909, 1990.
27. Jeffrey RB, Olcott EW: Imaging of blunt hepatic trauma. Radiol Clin North Am 29:1299-1310, 1991.
28. Zeman RK, Burrell MI: Gallbladder and Bile Duct Imaging. New York, Churchill Livingstone, 1987, pp 677-704.
29. Hollands MJ, Little JM: Hepatic venous injury after blunt abdominal trauma. Surgery 107:149-152, 1990.
30. Trunkey DD: Torso trauma. Curr Probl Surg 24:209-265, 1987.
31. Goodman DA, Tiruchelvam V, Tabb DR, et al: 3D CT reconstruction in the surgical management of hepatic injuries. Ann R Coll Surg Engl 77:7-11, 1995.
32. Patten RM, Spear RP, Vincent LM, et al: Traumatic laceration of the liver limited to the bare area: CT findings in 25 patients. AJR 160:1019-1022, 1993.
33. Hollerman JJ, Fackler ML, Coldwell DM, et al: Gunshot wounds: 2. Radiology. AJR 155:691-702, 1990.

34. Hollerman JJ, Fackler ML, Coldwell DM, et al: Gunshot wounds: 1. Bullets, ballistics, and mechanisms of injury. AJR 155:685-690, 1990.

35. Evers K, Gohel VK: Gastrointestinal system. In Schwartz EE (ed): The Radiology of Complications in Medical Practice. Baltimore, University Park Press, 1984, pp 231-288.

36. Perrault J, McGill DB, Ott BJ, et al: Liver biopsy: Complications in 1000 inpatients and outpatients. Gastroenterology 74:103-106, 1978.

37. McGrath FP, Lee SH, Gibney RG, et al: Hepatic subcapsular hematoma: An unusual complication of biliary lithotripsy. AJR 154:1015-1016, 1990.

38. Davidson B, Carratta R, Paccione F, et al: Surgical emergencies in liver disease. Baillieres Clin Gastroenterol 5: 737-758, 1991.

39. Minur GY, Sutherland LR, Wiseman DA, et al: Prospective study of the incidence of ultrasound-detected intrahepatic and subcapsular hematomas in patients randomized to 6 or 24 hours of bedrest after percutaneous liver biopsy. Gastroenterology 90:127-138, 1986.

40. Van Dyke RW: The liver in pregnancy. In Zakim D, Boyer TD (eds): Hepatology, 3rd ed. Philadelphia, WB Saunders, 1996, pp 1734-1758.

41. Riely CA, Portis MC: Pregnancy-related hepatic and gastrointestinal disorders. In Feldman MA, Scharschmidt BF, Sleisenger MH (eds): Gastrointestinal and Liver Disease, 6th ed. Philadelphia, WB Saunders, 1998, pp 1253-1264.

42. Terasaki KK, Quinn MF, Lundell CF, et al: Spontaneous hepatic hemorrhage with preeclampsia: Treatment with hepatic arterial embolization. Radiology 174:1039-1041, 1990.

43. Lubner M, Menias C, Rucker C, et al: Blood in the belly: CT findings of hemoperitoneum. RadioGraphics 27:109-125, 2007.

44. Jeffrey RB: CT diagnosis of blunt hepatic and splenic injuries: A look to the future. Radiology 171:17-18, 1989.

45. Farnell MB, Spencer MP, Thompson E, et al: Nonoperative management of blunt hepatic trauma in adults. Surgery 104:748-756, 1988.

46. Feliciano DV, Mattox KL, Jordan GL, et al: Management of 1000 consecutive cases of hepatic trauma. Ann Surg 204:435-445, 1986.

47. Federle MP: CT of upper abdominal trauma. Semin Roentgenol 19: 269-280, 1984.

48. Goldstein AS, Sclafani SJA, Kupferstein NH, et al: Diagnostic superiority of computed tomography in the evaluation of acute abdominal trauma. J Trauma 25:938-946, 1985.

49. Wolfman NT, Bechtold RE, Meredith JW: Blunt upper abdominal trauma: Evaluation by CT. AJR 158:493-501, 1992.

50. Moon KL, Federle MP: Computed tomography in hepatic trauma. AJR 141:309-314, 1983.

51. Shanmuganathan K, Mirvis SE, Sover ER: Value of contrast-enhanced CT is detecting active hemorrhage in patients with blunt abdominal or pelvic trauma. AJR 161:65-69, 1993.

52. Jeffrey RB Jr, Cardoza JD, Olcott EW: Detection of active intraabdominal arterial hemorrhage: Value of dynamic contrast-enhanced CT. AJR 156: 725-729, 1991.

53. Orwig D, Federle MP: Localized clotted blood as evidence of visceral trauma on CT: the sentinel clot sign. AJR 153:747-750, 1989.

54. Federle MP: Computed tomography of blunt abdominal trauma. Radiol Clin North Am 21:461-465, 1983.

55. Mirvis SE, Whitley NO: Computed tomography in hepatobiliary trauma. In Ferrucci JT, Mathieu DG (eds): Advances in Hepatobiliary Radiology. St. Louis: CV Mosby, 1990, pp 239-274.

56. Willmann JK, Roos JE, Platz A, et al: Multidetector CT: Detection of active hemorrhage in patients with blunt abdominal trauma. AJR 179:437-444, 2002.

57. Shanmuganathan K: Multidetector row CT imaging of blunt abdominal trauma. Semin Ultrasound CT MR. 2: 180-204, 2004.

58. Fang JF, Chen RJ, Wong YC, et al: Pooling of contrast material on computed tomography mandates aggressive management of blunt hepatic injury. AmJ Surg. 176:315-319, 1998.

59. Fang JF, Chen RJ, Wong YC, et al: Classification and treatment of pooling of contrast material on computed tomographic scan of blunt hepatic trauma. J Trauma, 49:1083-8, 2000.

60. Boy-Dranis R: Solid organ trauma. SIR 20:71-80, 2003.

61. Buckman RF Jr, Miraliakbari R, Badellino MM. Juxtahepatic venous injuries: a critical review of reported management strategies. J Trauma. 48: 978-84, 2000.

62. Shanmuganathan K, Mirvis S, Amoroso M: Periportal low density on CT in patients with blunt trauma: Association with elevated venous pressure. AJR 160:279-283, 1993.

63. Patrick LE, Ball TI, Atkinson GO, et al: Pediatric blunt abdominal trauma: Periportal tracking at CT. Radiology 183:689-691, 1992.

64. Cox SF, Friedman AC, Radecki PD, et al: Peri-portal lymphedema in trauma patients. AJR 154:1124-1125, 1990.

65. Macrander SJ, Lawson TL, Foley WD, et al: Periportal tracking in hepatic trauma: CT features. J Comput Assist Tomogr 13:952-957, 1989.

66. Panicek DM, Paquet DJ, Clark KG, et al: Hepatic parenchymal gas after blunt trauma. Radiology 159:343-344, 1986.

67. Abramson SJ, Berdon WE, Kaufman RA, et al: Hepatic parenchymal and subcapsular gas after hepatic laceration caused by blunt abdominal trauma. AJR 153:1031-1032, 1989.

68. Mirvis SE, Whitley NO, Vainwright JR, et al: Blunt hepatic trauma in adults: CT-based classification and correlation with prognosis and treatment. Radiology 171:27-32, 1989.

69. Becker CD, Gal I, Baer Hu, et al: Blunt hepatic trauma in adults: Correlation of CT injury grading with outcome. Radiology 201:215-220, 1996.

70. Hiatt JR, Harrier HD, Koenig BV, et al: Nonoperative management of major blunt liver injury with hemoperitoneum. Arch Surg 125:101-103, 1990.

71. Meyer AA, Crass RA, Kim RC, et al: Selective nonoperative management to blunt liver injury using computed tomography. Arch Surg 120:550-554, 1985.

72. Foley WD, Cates JD, Kellman GM, et al: Treatment of blunt hepatic injuries: role of CT. Radiology 164:635-638, 1987.

73. Olsen WR: Late complications of central liver injuries. Surgery 97: 733-743, 1982.

74. Davis KA, Brody JM, Cioffi WG: Computed tomography in blunt hepatic trauma. Arch Surg 131:255-260, 1996.

75. Allins A, Ho T, Nguyen TH, et al: Limited value of routine follow-up CT scans in nonoperative management of blunt liver and splenic injuries. Am Surg 62:883-886, 1996.

76. Carrillo EH, Richardson JD: The current management of hepatic trauma. Adv Surg 35:39-59, 2001.

77. Haney PJ, Whitley ND, Brotman S, et al: Liver injury and complications in the postoperative trauma patient: CT evaluation. AJR 139:271-275, 1982.

78. Casarella WJ, Martin EC: Angiography in the management of abdominal trauma. Semin Roentgenol 15:321-327, 1980.

79. Janer HP, Laws HL, Kogutt MS, et al: Emergency embolization in blunt hepatic trauma. AJR 129:249-252, 1977.

80. Sclafani SJA, Shaftan GW, McAuley J, et al: Interventional radiology in the management of hepatic trauma. J Trauma 24:256-262, 1984.

81. McIlrath EM, Thomas PS: Trauma of the upper abdomen. In Wilkins RA, Nunnerly HB (eds): Imaging of the Liver, Pancreas and Spleen. Oxford, Blackwell Scientific, 1990, pp 489-524.

82. Hagiwara A, Yukioka T, Ohta S, et al: Nonsurgical management of patients with blunt hepatic injury: Efficacy of transcatheter arterial embolization. AJR 169:1151-1156, 1997.

83. Schwartz RA, Teitelbaum GP, Katz MD, et al: Effectiveness of transcatheter embolization in the control of hepatic vascular injuries. J Vasc Intervent Radiol 4:359-365, 1993.

84. Howdieshell TR, Purvis J, Bates WB, et al: Biloma and biliary fistula following hepatorrhaphy for liver trauma: Incidence, natural history, and management. Am Surg 61:165-168, 1995.

85. Ascher WM, Parvin S, Virgilio RW, et al: Echographic evaluation after blunt trauma. Radiology 118:411-415, 1976.

86. Lentz KA, McKenney MG, Nunez DB, et al: Evaluating blunt abdominal trauma: role for ultrasonography. J Ultrasound Med 15:447-451, 1996.

87. Wherett LJ, Boulanger BR, McLellan BA, et al: Hypotension after blunt abdominal trauma: The role of emergent abdominal sonography in surgical triage. J Trauma 41:815-820, 1996.

88. Rozycki GS: Abdominal ultrasonography in trauma. Surg Clin North Am 75:175-190, 1995.

89. Rozycki GS, Stackford SR: US, what every trauma surgeon should know. J Trauma 40:1-4, 1996.

90. Sato M, Yoshii H., Reevaluation of ultrasonography for solid-organ injury in blunt abdominal trauma. J Ultrasound Med. 23:1583-96, 2004.

91. Grüessner R, Mentges B, Düber Ch, et al: Sonography versus peritoneal lavage in blunt abdominal trauma. J Trauma 29:242-244, 1989.

92. Kimura A, Otsuka T: Emergency center ultrasonography in the evaluation of hemoperitoneum: A prospective study. J Trauma 31:20-23, 1991.

93. Hoffmann R, Nerlich M, Muggia-Sullam M, et al: Blunt abdominal trauma in cases of multiple trauma evaluated by ultrasonography: A prospective analysis of 291 patients. J Trauma 32:452-458, 1992.

94. Tso P, Rodriguez A, Cooper C, et al: Sonography in blunt abdominal trauma: A preliminary progress report. J Trauma 33:39-44, 1992.

95. Liu M, Lee CH, P'eng FK. Prospective comparison of diagnostic peritoneal lavage, computed tomographic scanning, and ultrasonography for the diagnosis of blunt abdominal trauma. J Trauma 35:267-270, 1993.

96. McKenney M, Lentz K, Nunez D, et al: Can ultrasound replace diagnostic peritoneal lavage in the assessment of blunt trauma? J Trauma 37:439-441, 1994.

97. Ma OJ, Mateer JR, Ogata M, et al: Prospective analysis of a rapid trauma ultrasound examination performed by emergency physicians. J Trauma 38:879-885, 1995.

98. Boulanger BR, Brenneman FD, McLellan BA, et al: A prospective study of emergent abdominal sonography after blunt trauma. J Trauma 39:325-330, 1995.

99. Rozycki GS, Ochsner MG, Schmidt JA, et al: A prospective study of surgeon-performed ultrasound as the primary adjuvant modality for injured patient assessment. J Trauma 39:492-500, 1995.

100. Lingawi SS, Buckley AR. Focused abdominal US in patients with trauma. Radiology 217:426-429, 2000.

101. Chiu WC, Cushing BM, Rodriguez A, et al: Abdominal injuries without hemoperitoneum: A potential limitation of focused abdominal sonography for trauma (FAST). J Trauma 42:617-625, 1997.

102. Shanmuganathan K, Mirvis SE, Sherbourne CD, et al: Hemoperitoneum as the sole indicator of abdominal visceral injuries: A potential limitation of screening abdominal US from trauma. Radiology 212:423-430, 1999.

103. Brown MA, Casola G, Sirlin CB, Hoyt DB. Importance of evaluating organ parenchyma during screening abdominal ultrasonography after blunt trauma. J Ultrasound Med 20:577-583, 2001.

104. Kuligowska E, Mueller PR, Simeone JF, et al: Ultrasound in upper abdominal trauma. Semin Roentgenol 19:281-295, 1984.

105. Viscomi GN, Gonzalez R, Taylor KJW, et al: Ultrasonic evaluation of hepatic and splenic trauma. Arch Surg 115:320-321, 1981.

106. Wicks JD, Silver TM, Bree RL: Gray scale features of hematomas: An ultrasonic spectrum. AJR 131:977-980, 1978.

107. vanSonnenberg E, Simeone JF, Mueller PR, et al: Sonographic appearance of hematoma in liver, spleen and kidney: A clinical pathologic and animal study. Radiology 147:507-510, 1983.

108. Esensten M, Ralls PW, Colletti P, et al: Posttraumatic intrahepatic biloma: Sonographic diagnosis. AJR 140:303-305, 1983.

109. Ralls PW, Eto R, Quinn M, et al: Gray-scale ultrasonography of a traumatic biliary cyst. J Trauma 21:176-177, 1981.

110. Gould L, Patel A: Ultrasound detection of extrahepatic encapsulated bile: "Biloma." AJR 132:1014-1015, 1979.

111. Weissman HS, Byun KJ, Freeman LM: Role of Tc-99m IDA scintigraphy in the evaluation of hepatobiliary trauma. Semin Nucl Med 8:199-222, 1983.

112. Zeman RK, Lee CH, Stahl RS, et al: Strategy for the use of biliary scintigraphy in non-iatrogenic biliary trauma. Radiology 151:771-776, 1984.

113. Catalano O, Lobianco R, Raso MM, et al: Blunt hepatic trauma: Evaluation with contrast-enhanced sonography: Sonographic findings and clinical application. J Ultrasound Med 24:299-310, 2005.

114. Caride VJ, Gibson DW: Noninvasive evaluation of bile leakage. Surg Gynecol Obstet 154:517-520, 1982.

115. Terk MR, Rozenberg D: Gadolinium-enhanced MR imaging of traumatic hepatic injury. AJR 171:665-669, 1998.

116. Shigemura T, Yamamoto F, Shilpakar SK, et al: MRI differential diagnosis of intrahepatic biloma from subacute hematoma. Abdom Imaging 20:211-213, 1995.

117. Gupta N, Stuhlfaut JW, Fleming KW et al: Blunt trauma of the pancreas and biliary tract: A multimodality imaging approach to diagnosis. RadioGraphics 1381-1395, 2004.

118. Kapoor V, Peterson MS, Baron RL, et al: Intrahepatic biliary anatomy of living adult liver donors: Correlation of mangafodipir trisodium-enhanced MR cholangiography and intraoperative cholangiography. AJR 179:1281-6, 2002.

119. Burch JM: New concepts in trauma. Am J Surg 173:44-46, 1997.

120. Mindelzun RE, McCort JJ: Upper abdominal trauma: Conventional radiology. Semin Roentgenol 19:259-265, 1984.

121. Baker SR: The Abdominal Plain Film. East Norwalk, CT, Appleton & Lange, 1990, pp 243-298.

122. David RJ, Franklin GA, Lukan JK, Carrillo EH, et al: Evolution in the management of hepatic trauma: A 25 year prospective. Ann Surg. 232:324-30, 2000.

123. Gur S, Orsel A, Atahan K, et al: Surgical treatment of liver trauma (analysis of 244 patients). Hepatogastroenterology 50: 2109-11, 2003.

124. Federle MP, Goldberg HI, Kaiser JA, et al: Evaluation of abdominal trauma by computed tomography. Radiology 138:637-644, 1981.

125. Hollands MJ, Little JM: The role of hepatic resection in the management of blunt liver trauma. World J Surg 14:478-482, 1990.

126. Watson DI, Williams JAR: Management of the traumatized liver: An appraisal of 63 cases. Aust N Z J Surg 59:137-142, 1989.

127. Trunkey D: Initial treatment of patients with extensive trauma. N Engl J Med 324:1259-1263, 1991.

128. Chevallier JM, Jost JL, Vayre P: [Liver injuries. Anatomical lesions, an attempt at classification] [French]. J Chir 128:509, 1991.

129. Little JM, Fernandes A, Tait N: Liver trauma. Aust N Z J Surg 56:613-618, 1986.

130. Alexander JW: The mythology of hepatic trauma: Babel revisited. Am J Surg 135:1275-1276, 1978.

131. Hanna SS, Maheshwari Y, Harrison AW, et al: Blunt liver trauma at the Sunnybrook Regional Trauma Center. Can J Surg 28:220-223, 1985.

132. Brotman S, Oliver G, Oster-Granite ML, et al: The treatment of 179 blunt trauma-induced liver injuries in a statewide trauma center. Am Surg 50:603-610, 1984.

133. Sclafani SJA, Shaftan GW, McAuley J, et al: Interventional radiology in the management of hepatic trauma. J Trauma 24:256-261, 1984.

134. Blumgart LH: Liver resection-liver and biliary tumors. In Blumgart LH (ed): Surgery of the Liver and Biliary Tract. New York, Churchill Livingstone, 1988, pp 1251-1280.

135. Malt RA: Principles of hepatic surgery. In Ferrucci JT, Stark DD (eds): Liver Imaging. Boston, Andover Medical, 1990, pp 217-222.

136. Jones RS: The liver: Malignant and benign tumors, nonparasitic cysts, parasitic cysts, abscess, liver anatomy, technique of liver resection. In Moody FG, Carey LC, Jones RS, et al (eds): Surgical Treatment of Digestive Disease. Chicago, Year Book Medical, 1986, pp 377-397.

137. Foster JH: History of liver surgery. Arch Surg 126:381-388, 1991.

138. Suc B, Panis Y, Belghiti J, et al: Natural history of hepatectomy. Br J Surg 79:39-42, 1992.

139. Lambert CJ, Meydrech EF, Scott-Conner CE, et al: Major hepatic resections: A 10-year experience with emphasis on special problems. Am J Gastroenterol 85:786-790, 1990.

140. Scheele J, Stangl R, Alterdorf-Hofman A: Hepatic metastases from colorectal carcinoma: Impact of surgical resection on the natural history. Br J Surg 77:1241-1246, 1990.

141. McDermott WV: Hepatic resection. In Millward-Sadler GH, Wright R, Arthur MJP (eds): Wright's Liver and Biliary Diseases, 3rd ed. London, WB Saunders, 1992, pp 1394-1402.

142. Vetto JT, Hughes KS, Rosenstein R, et al: Morbidity and mortality of hepatic resection for metastatic colorectal carcinoma. Dis Colon Rectum 33:408-413, 1990.

143. Turner DA, Doolas A, Silver B, et al: The role of cross-sectional imaging in hepatic resections. In Ferrucci JF, Mathieu DG (eds): Advances in Hepatobiliary Radiology. St. Louis, CV Mosby, 1990, pp 209-228.

144. Soyer P, Roche A, Elias D, et al: Hepatic metastases from colorectal cancer: Influence of hepatic volumetric analysis on surgical decision making. Radiology 184:695-697, 1992.

145. Soyer P, Roche A, Gad M, et al: Preoperative segmental localization of hepatic metastases: Utility of three-dimensional CT during arterial portography. Radiology 180:653-658, 1991.

146. Gazelle GS, Haaga JR: Hepatic neoplasms: Surgically relevant segmental anatomy and imaging techniques. AJR 158:1015-1018, 1992.

147. Arii S, Yamazoe Y, Minematsu Y, et al: Predictive factors for intrahepatic recurrence of hepatocellular carcinoma after partial hepatectomy. Cancer 69:913-919, 1992.

148. Sherlock S, Dooley J: Diseases of the Liver and Biliary System, 9th ed. Oxford, Blackwell Scientific, 1993, pp 460-471.

149. Vauthey JN, Klimstra D, Franceschi D, et al: Factors affecting long-term outcome after hepatic resection for hepatocellular carcinoma. Am J Surg 169:28-35, 1995.

150. Baker ME, Pelley R: Hepatic metastases: Basic principles and implications for radiologists. Radiology 197:329-337, 1995.

151. Taylor HM, Ros PR: Hepatic imaging: An overview. Radiol Clin North Am 36:237-245, 1998.

152. Sugarbaker PH: Surgical decision making for large bowel cancer metastatic to the liver. Radiology 174:621-626, 1990.

153. Malt RA: Surgery for hepatic neoplasms. N Engl J Med 313:1591-1595, 1985.

154. Bergmark S: The surgeon's viewpoint. In Herlinger H, Lunderquist A, Wallace S (eds): Clinical Radiology of the Liver. New York, Marcel Dekker, 1983, pp 574-585.

155. Minton JP, Hamilton WB, Sardi A, et al: Results of surgical excision of one to 13 hepatic metastases in 98 consecutive patients. Arch Surg 124:46-48, 1989.

156. Hodgson WJB, Morgan J, Byrne D, et al: Hepatic resections for primary and metastatic tumors using the ultrasonic surgical dissector. Am J Surg 163:246-250, 1992.

157. Simeone JF: Intrasonography ultrasonography of the liver. In Ferrucci JT, Stack DD (eds): Liver Imaging. Boston, Andover Medical, 1990, pp 247-255.

158. Simeone JF: Intraoperative ultrasonography of liver tumors. In Ferrucci JT, Mathieu DG (eds): Advances in Hepatobiliary Radiology. St. Louis, CV Mosby, 1990, pp 229-238.

159. Bismuth H, Castaing D, Graden OJ: The use of operative ultrasound in surgery of primary liver tumors. World J Surg 11:610-614, 1987.

160. Machi J, Isomotoh I, Yamashita Y, et al: Intraoperative ultrasonography in screening for liver metastases from colorectal cancer: Comparative accuracy with traditional procedures. Surgery 105:678-684, 1987.

161. Makuuchi M: Applications of intraoperative ultrasonography to hepatectomy. In Makuuchi M (ed): Abdominal Intraoperative Ultrasonography. Tokyo, Igaku-Shoin, 1987, pp 142-161.

162. Gozzetti G, Mazziotti A: Intraoperative ultrasound during liver surgery. In Gozzetti G, Mazziotti A, Bolondi L, et al (eds): Intraoperative Ultrasonography in Hepatobiliary and Pancreatic Surgery. Boston, Kluwer Academic, 1989, pp 137-154.

163. Makuuchi M, Hasegawa H, Yamazaki S, et al: The use of operative ultrasound as an aid to liver resection in patients with hepatocellular carcinoma. World J Surg 11:615-621, 1987.

164. Conlon R, Jacobs M, Dasgupta D, et al: The value of intraoperative ultrasound during hepatic resection compared with improved preoperative magnetic resonance imaging. Eur J Ultrasound 16:211-216, 2003.

165. Sahani D, Kalva S, Tanabe K, et al: Intraoperative US in patients undergoing surgery for liver neoplasms: Comparison with MR imaging. Radiology 232:810-814, 2004.

166. Jarnagin W, Bach A, Winston C, et al: What is the yield of intraoperative ultrasonography during partial hepatectomy for malignant disease? J Am Coll Surg. 192:577-583, 2001.

167. Kane RA, Hughes LA, Cua EJ, et al: The impact of intraoperative ultrasonography on surgery for liver neoplasms. J Ultrasound Med 13:1-6, 1994.

168. Onik G, Kane R, Steele G, et al: Monitoring hepatic cryosurgery with sonography. AJR 147:665-671, 1986.

169. Weaver ML, Atkinson D, Zemel R: Hepatic cryosurgery in the treatment of unresectable metastases. Surg Oncol 4:231-236, 1995.

170. Vauthey JN, Maddern GJ, Kolbinger P, et al: Clinical experience with adult polycystic liver disease. Br J Surg 79:562-565, 1992.

171. Que F, Nagorney DM, Gross JB, et al: Liver resection and cyst fenestration in the treatment of severe polycystic liver disease. Gastroenterology 108:487-494, 1995.

172. Foster JH: Surgical treatment of metastatic liver tumor. Hepatogastroenterology 37:182-187, 1990.

173. Lise M, Da Pian PP, Nitti D, et al: Colorectal metastases to the liver: present status of management. Dis Colon Rectum 33:688-694, 1990.

174. Stehlin JS, de Ipolyi PD, Greeff PJ, et al: Treatment of cancer of the liver. Ann Surg 208:23-35, 1988.

175. Silen W: Hepatic resection for metastases from colorectal carcinoma is of dubious value. Arch Surg 124:1021-1022, 1989.

176. Griffith KD, Sugarbaker PH, Chang AE: Repeat hepatic resections for colorectal metastases. Surgery 107:101-104, 1990.

177. Adson MA, van Heerden JA, Adson MH, et al: Resection of hepatic metastases from colorectal cancer. Arch Surg 119:647-651, 1984.

178. Doci R, Gennari L, Bignami P, et al: One hundred patients with hepatic metastases from colorectal cancer treated by resection: Analysis of prognostic determinants. Br J Surg 78:797-801, 1991.

179. Rosen CB, Nagorney DM, Taswell HF, et al: Perioperative blood transfusion and determinants of survival after liver resection for metastatic colorectal carcinoma. Ann Surg 216:493-504, 1992.

180. Sugihara K, Hojo K, Moriya Y, et al: Pattern of recurrence after hepatic resection for colorectal metastases. Br J Surg 80:1032-1035, 1993.

181. Gayowski TJ, Iwatsuki S, Madariaga JR, et al: Experience in hepatic resection for metastatic colorectal cancer: Analysis of clinical and pathologic risk factors. Surgery 116:703-711, 1994.

182. Hughes KS, Simon RM, Songhorabodi S, et al: Resection of the liver for colorectal carcinoma metastases: A multi-institutional study of indications for resection. Surgery 103:278-288, 1988.

183. Nordlinger B, Jaeck D, Guiguet M, et al: Surgical resection of hepatic metastases. Multicentric retrospective study by the French Association of Surgery. In Nordlinger B, Jaeck D (eds): Treatment of Hepatic Metastases of Colorectal Cancer. Paris, Springer-France, 1992, pp 129-146.

184. Van Ooigen B, Wiggers T, Meijer S, et al: Hepatic resections for colorectal metastases in The Netherlands: A multi-institutional 10-year study. Cancer 70:28-34, 1992.

185. Fong Y, Blumgart LH, Cohen A, et al: Repeat hepatic resection for metastatic colorectal cancer. Ann Surg 220:657-662, 1994.

186. Wanebo HJ, Chu LD, Vezeridis MP, et al: Patient selection for hepatic resection of colorectal metastases. Arch Surg 131:322-329, 1996.

187. Adson MA: Resection of liver metastases: When is it worthwhile? World J Surg 11:511-520, 1996.

188. Fong Y, Kemeny N, Paty P, et al: Treatment of colorectal cancer: hepatic metastasis. Semin Surg Oncol 12:219-252, 1996.

189. Hasegawa H, Yamazaki S, Makuuchi M: Ultrasonographically guided segmentectomy and subsegmentectomy: Application in the cirrhotic liver. In Blumgart LH (ed): Pediatric Surgery of the Liver and Biliary Tract. New York, Churchill Livingstone, 1988, pp 1289-1298.

190. Bucher NLR: Liver regeneration: An overview. J Gastroenterol Hepatol 6:615-628, 1991.

191. Suenaga M, Nakao A, Harada A, et al: Hepatic resection for hepatocellular carcinoma. World J Surg 16:97-105, 1992.

192. Ravikumar TS, Kane R, Cady B, et al: A 5-year study of cryosurgery in the treatment of liver tumors. Arch Surg 126:1520-1524, 1991.

193. Ravikumar TS: Interstitial therapies for liver tumors. Surg Oncol Clin N Am 5:365-377, 1996.

194. Morris DL, Ross WB: Australian experience of cryoablation of liver tumors. Surg Oncol Clin 5:391-397, 1996.

195. Weber SM, Lee FT Jr: Expanded treatment of hepatic tumors with radiofrequency ablation and cryoablation. Oncology (Williston Park) 19(11 Suppl 4):27-32, 2005.

196. Huo TI, Huang YH, Wu JC: Percutaneous ablation therapy for hepatocellular carcinoma: Current practice and future perspectives. J Chin Med Assoc 68:155-159, 2004.

197. Pompili M, Mirante VG, Rondinara G, et al: Percutaneous ablation procedures in cirrhotic patients with hepatocellular carcinoma submitted to liver transplantation: Assessment of efficacy at explant analysis and of safety for tumor recurrence. Liver Transpl 11:1117-1126, 2005.

198. Scaife CL, Curley SA: Complication, local recurrence, and survival rates after radiofrequency ablation for hepatic malignancies. Surg Oncol Clin N Am 12:243-255, 2003.

199. Hoffman AL, Wu SS, Obaid AK, et al: Histologic evaluation and treatment outcome after sequential radiofrequency ablation and hepatic resection for primary and metastatic tumors. Am Surg 68:1038-1043, 2002.

200. Breedis C, Young C: The blood supply of neoplasms in the liver. Am J Pathol 30:969-985, 1954.

201. Sigurdson ER, Ridge JA, Kemeny N, et al: Tumor and liver drug uptake following hepatic artery and portal vein infusion. J Clin Oncol 5:1936-1940, 1987.

202. Healey JE, Sheena KS: Vascular patterns in metastatic liver tumors. Surg Forum 14:121-122, 1963.

203. Murray-Lyon IM, Parsons VA, Blendis LM: Treatment of secondary hepatic tumors by ligation of hepatic artery and infusion of cytotoxic drugs. Lancet 2:172-175, 1970.

204. Wallace S, Carrasco CH, Charnsagavej C, et al: Hepatic artery infusion and chemoembolization in the management of liver metastasis. Cardiovasc Intervent Radiol 13:153-160, 1990.

205. Chen HSG, Gross JF: Intraarterial infusion of anti-cancer drugs: Theoretic aspects of drug delivery and review of responses. Cancer Treat Rep 64:31-40, 1980.

206. Collins JM: Pharmacologic rationale for regional drug delivery. J Clin Oncol 2:498-504, 1984.

207. Llovet JM, Real MI, Montana X, et al: Arterial embolisation or chemoembolisation versus symptomatic treatment in patients with unresectable hepatocellular carcinoma: A randomised controlled trial. Lancet 359:1734-1739, 2002.

208. Lo CM, Ngan H, Tso WK, et al: Randomized controlled trial of transarterial lipiodol chemoembolization for unresectable hepatocellular carcinoma. Hepatology 35:1164-1171, 2002.

209. Chuang VP, Wallace S, Soo CS: Therapeutic Ivalon embolization of hepatic tumors. AJR 138:289-294, 1982.

210. Kobayashi H, Inoue H, Shimada J, et al: Intra-arterial injection of adriamycin/mitomycin C lipidiol suspension in liver metastases. Acta Radiol 28:275-280, 1986.

211. Inoue H, Kobayashi H, Itoh Y, et al: Treatment of liver metastasis by arterial injection of adriamycin/mitomycin C lipidiol suspension. Acta Radiol 30:603-608, 1989.
212. Tanigushi H, Takahashi T, Yamagushi T, et al: Intraarterial infusion chemotherapy for metastatic liver tumors using multiple anticancer agents suspended in a lipidiol contrast medium. Cancer 64:2001-2006, 1989.
213. Yamashita Y, Takahashi M, Bussaka H, et al: Intraarterial infusion of 5-fluoro-2-deoxyuridine-C8 dissolved in a lymphographic agent in malignant liver tumors. Cancer 64:2437-2444, 1989.
214. Kameyama M, Imaoka S, Fukuda I, et al: Delayed washout of intratumor blood flow is associated with good response to intraarterial chemoembolization for liver metastasis of colorectal cancer. Surgery 114:97-101, 1992.
215. Lang EK, Brown CL: Colorectal metastasis to the liver: Selective chemoembolization. Radiology 189:417-422, 1993.
216. Feun LG, Reddy KR, Yrrizarry JM, et al: A phase I study of chemoembolization with cisplatin and lipidiol for primary and metastatic liver cancer. Am J Clin Oncol 17:405-410, 1994.
217. Fischbach R, Gross-Fengels W, Heindel W, et al: Transcatheter hepatic artery chemoembolization of primary and secondary liver neoplasms: Response rates and survival times. Cardiovasc Intervent Radiol 15:417-422, 1992.
218. Martinelli DJ, Wadler S, Bakal CW, et al: Utility of embolization or chemoembolization as second line treatment in patients with advanced or recurrent colorectal carcinoma. Cancer 74:706-712, 1994.
219. Daniels S, Pentecost M, Reitelbaum G, et al: Hepatic artery chemoembolization for carcinoma of colon using Angiostat collagen and cisplatin, mitomycin and doxorubicin: response, survival and serum drug levels. Proc Am Soc Clin Oncol 11:171-172, 1992.
220. Meakem TJ, Unger EC, Pond GD, et al: CT findings after hepatic chemoembolization. J Comput Assist Tomogr 16:916-920, 1992.
221. Lorenz M, Hermann G, Kirkowa-Reimann M, et al: Temporary chemoembolization of colorectal liver metastasis with degradable starch microspheres. Eur J Surg Oncol 15:453-462, 1989.
222. Hunt TM, Flowerdew ADS, Birch SJ, et al: Prospective randomized controlled trial of hepatic arterial embolization of infusion chemotherapy with 5-fluorouracil and degradable starch microspheres for colorectal liver metastases. Br J Surg 77:779-782, 1990.
223. Aronsen KF, Hellkant C, Holmberg J, et al: Controlled blocking of hepatic artery flow with enzymatically degradable microspheres combined with oncolytic drugs. Eur Surg Res 11:99-106, 1979.
224. Starkhammar H, Hakansson L, Morales O, et al: Intraarterial mitomycin C treatment of unresectable liver tumors. Preliminary results on the effect of degradable starch microspheres. Acta Oncol 26:295-300, 1987.
225. Wollner IS, Walker-Andrews SC, Smith JE, et al: Phase II study of hepatic arterial degradable starch microspheres and mitomycin. Cancer Drug Del 4:279-284, 1986.
226. Allison OJ, Booth A: Arterial embolization in the management of liver metastasis. Cardiovasc Intervent Radiol 13:153-160, 1990.
227. Geschwind JF, Kaushik S, Ramsey DE, et al: Influence of a new prophylactic antibiotic therapy on the incidence of liver abscesses after chemoembolization treatment of liver tumors. J Vasc Interv Radiol 13:1163-1166, 2002.
228. Kim W, Clark TW, Baum RA, et al: Risk factors for liver abscess formation after hepatic chemoembolization. J Vasc Interv Radiol 12:965-968, 2001.
229. Yamakado K, Nakatsuka A, Ohmori S, et al: Radiofrequency ablation combined with chemoembolization in hepatocellular carcinoma: Treatment response based on tumor size and morphology. J Vasc Interv Radiol 13:1225-1232, 2002.
230. Rhee TK, Omary RA, Gates V, et al: The effect of catheter-directed CT angiography on yttrium-90 radioembolization treatment of hepatocellular carcinoma. J Vasc Interv Radiol 16:1085-1091, 2005.
231. Salem R, Lewandowski RJ, Atassi B, et al: Treatment of unresectable hepatocellular carcinoma with use of 90Y microspheres (TheraSphere): Safety, tumor response, and survival. J Vasc Interv Radiol 16:1627-1639, 2005.
232. Kennedy AS, Coldwell D, Nutting C, et al: Resin (90)Y-microsphere brachytherapy for unresectable colorectal liver metastases: Modern USA experience. Int J Radiat Oncol Biol Phys 65:412-425, 2006.
233. Lewandowski RJ, Salem R: Yttrium-90 radioembolization of hepatocellular carcinoma and metastatic disease to the liver. Semin Interv Radiol 23:64-72, 2006.
234. Lewandowski RJ, Thurston KG, Goin JE, et al: 90Y microsphere (TheraSphere) treatment for unresectable colorectal cancer metastases of the liver: Response to treatment at targeted doses of 135-150 Gy as measured by [18F]fluorodeoxyglucose positron emission tomography and computed tomographic imaging. J Vasc Interv Radiol 16:1641-1651, 2005.
235. Kulik L, Atassi B, van Holsbeeck L, et al: Yttrium-90 microsphere (TheraSphere) treatment of unresectable hepatocellular carcinoma: Downstaging to resection, RFA and bridge to transplantation. J Surg Oncol 2006. In press.
236. Kulik LM, Mulcahy MF, Hunter RD, et al: Use of yttrium-90 microspheres (TheraSphere) in a patient with unresectable hepatocellular carcinoma leading to liver transplantation: A case report. Liver Transpl 11:1127-1131, 2005.
237. Gray B, Van Hazel G, Hope M, et al: Randomised trial of SIR-Spheres plus chemotherapy vs. chemotherapy alone for treating patients with liver metastases from primary large bowel cancer. Ann Oncol 12:1711-1720, 2001.
238. Van Hazel G, Blackwell A, Anderson J, et al: Randomised phase 2 trial of SIR-Spheres plus fluorouracil/leucovorin chemotherapy versus fluorouracil/leucovorin chemotherapy alone in advanced colorectal cancer. J Surg Oncol 88:78-85, 2004.
239. Van Hazel G, Price D, Bower G, et al: Selective Internal Radiation Therapy (SIRT) plus systemic chemotherapy with FOLFOX4: A phase I dose escalation study. In ASCO GI Symposium, 2005, Miami, FL.
240. Van Hazel G, Price D, Bower G, et al: Selective Internal Radiation Therapy (SIRT) for liver metastases with concomitant systemic oxaliplatin, 5-fluorouracil and folinic acid: A phase I/II dose escalation study. In ASCO GI Symposium, 2005, Miami, FL.
241. Letourneau JG, Steely JW, Crass JR, et al: Upper abdomen: CT findings following partial hepatectomy. Radiology 166:139-141, 1988.
242. Covanet D, Shirkhoda A, Wallace S: Computed tomography after partial hepatectomy. J Comput Assist Tomogr 8:453-457, 1984.
243. Quinn SF, Bodne DJ, Clark RA: Upper abdomen: CT findings following partial hepatectomy. Radiology 168:879-880, 1988.
244. Sefczek RJ, Lupetin AR, Beckman I, et al: CT appearance of omental packs. Radiology 156:472-476, 1985.
245. Arrive L, Hricak H, Goldberg HI, et al: MR appearance of the liver after partial hepatectomy. AJR 152:1215-1220, 1989.
246. Greco A, Stipa F, Huguet C, et al: Early MR follow-up of partial hepatectomy. J Comput Assist Tomogr 17:277-282, 1993.
247. Anderson R, Saarela A, Tranberg KG, et al: Intraabdominal abscess formation after major liver resection. Acta Chir Scand 156:707-710, 1990.
248. Cole DJ, Ferguson CM: Complication of hepatic resection for colorectal carcinoma metastasis. Am Surg 58:88-91, 1992.
249. Vauthey JN: Liver imaging: A surgeon's perspective. Radiol Clin North Am 36:445-458, 1998.
250. Nghiem HV, Francis IR, Fontana R: Computed tomography appearances of hypervascular hepatic tumors after percutaneous radiofrequency ablation therapy. Curr Probl Diagn Radiol 31:105-111, 2002.
251. Meakem TJ 3rd, Unger EC, Pond GD. CT findings after hepatic chemoembolization. J Comput Assist Tomogr 16:916-920, 1992.
252. Semelka RC, Worawattanakul S, Mauro MA. Malignant hepatic tumors: Changes on MRI after hepatic arterial chemoembolization: Preliminary findings. J Magn Reson Imaging 8:48-56, 1998.
253. Kuszyk BS, Choti MA, Urban BA, et al: Hepatic tumors treated by cryosurgery: Normal CT appearance. AJR 166: 363-367, 1996.
254. Murthy R, Nunez R, Szklaruk J, et al: Yttrium-90 microsphere therapy for hepatic malignancy: Devices, indications, technical considerations, and potential complications. RadioGraphics 25:S41-S55, 2005.
255. Marn C, Andrews J, Francis I, et al: Hepatic parenchymal changes after intraarterial Y-90 therapy: CT findings. Radiology 187:125-128, 1993.

Liver Transplantation Imaging

Mitchell E. Tublin, MD • Richard D. Redvanly, MD • Robert H. Smith, MD

Advances in organ procurement and surgical techniques have made orthotopic liver transplantation (OLT) an accepted treatment for many patients with end-stage hepatic disease. Since the late 1970s, there have been several important developments that have had a significant impact on patient survival. The longer cold preservation time possible with University of Wisconsin solution makes it possible to procure organs from farther distances.[1] From a technical perspective, the development of extracorporeal venovenous bypass allows maintenance of cardiovascular stability during the anhepatic phase of transplantation and decompression of the temporarily occluded splanchnic and systemic venous systems during liver replacement.[2,3] Alternative techniques have been refined that maintain continuous systemic venous return during the anhepatic phase of liver replacement, allowing transplantation to be performed without the necessity of venovenous bypass with similar patient and graft survival.[4-6]

Perhaps the single most important factor that has improved postoperative graft and patient survival has been development of more potent immunosuppressive therapy.[7] The introduction of cyclosporine in 1980 as a primary immunosuppressive therapy quickly led to increased graft and patient survival rates. Newer immunosuppressive agents, such as

tacrolimus (Prograf, Fujisawa USA, Deerfield, IL) and mycophenolate mofetil (Cellcept, Roche Laboratories, Nutley, NJ), have largely replaced cyclosporine for primary immunosuppression in most transplant centers. The use of tacrolimus and mycophenolate mofetil has significantly improved patient survival and decreased the need for retransplantation compared with cyclosporine-based immunosuppressive regimens primarily by reducing the incidence of graft rejection.[8-15] A recent UNOS annual report shows 1-, 3-, and 5-year liver graft rates of 82%, 72%, and 65%, respectively. Adjusted patient survival rates at 1, 3, and 5 years range up to 88%, 80%, and 74%, respectively. In addition, the rate of allograft failure resulting from rejection has diminished to approximately 4% with postoperative use of tacrolimus immunosuppressive therapy.[16] Although improved survival of both the graft and the patient is primarily related to improvements in surgical techniques and immunosuppressive therapy, morbidity and mortality have also been reduced because of early detection and treatment of postoperative complications.

This chapter reviews the fundamental aspects of adult liver transplantation with an emphasis on the role of preoperative imaging of the transplant candidate, surgical aspects of liver transplantation, and detection of postoperative complications.

A separate section will be devoted to recent advances in living donor living transplantation and the role of cross-sectional imaging in the preoperative assessment of the potential donor. Preoperative radiologic evaluation is directed at selecting patients suitable for OLT and defining anatomic features that necessitate an altered surgical approach. Postoperative imaging studies are directed at detecting problems that commonly occur after liver transplantation, including biliary strictures and leaks, vascular abnormalities, infection, allograft rejec-tion, and recurrent or post-transplant malignancy. Because the radiologist is often involved with imaging of the liver transplant patient, a thorough understanding of surgical aspects of hepatic transplantation enables early diagnosis and treatment of postoperative complications.

PREOPERATIVE EVALUATION OF THE LIVER TRANSPLANT CANDIDATE

The major indications for liver transplantation are acute or chronic end-stage liver disease, inborn errors of metabolism with or without liver failure, and as an oncologic procedure in selected patients with a primary hepatic malignancy in whom resection is not an alternative. Greater than 80% of hepatic transplants are performed in patients with cirrhosis or primary cholestatic liver disease, and only 4% of transplants are performed for malignant hepatic neoplasms.[17] The percentage of transplants performed for potential curative treatment of hepatic malignancy is expected to increase with the United Network for Organ Sharing's (UNOS) adoption of the MELD (Model for End-stage Liver Disease) score as a uniform policy for organ allocation. Calculation of the MELD score is based upon serum bilirubin, international normalization ratio (INR), and serum creatinine. Additional points are allocated for patients with biopsy (or imaging) documented "early" hepatocellular carcinoma (HCC). (The parameters for what constitutes potentially resectable early HCC continue to evolve, though most centers still use Milan criteria—tumor diameter <5 cm and no more than three lesions.). The logical end result of this allocation scheme is that over the past 5 years, the percentage of "sicker" patients and patients with HCC receiving transplants has increased.[18-21]

Because the supply of donor organs is limited, preoperative clinical and radiologic evaluation of the transplant candidate is critical for appropriate patient selection. The main objective of preoperative imaging is to provide the surgeon with the necessary information needed to plan and perform liver transplantation and to exclude patients for whom surgery either is not feasible or would be of no benefit. From a surgical perspective, the main objectives of preoperative radiologic evaluation are (1) calculation of liver volume; (2) determination of the size and patency of the portal vein, superior mesenteric vein, or both; (3) detection of intrahepatic and extrahepatic malignancy; and (4) evaluation of surgical portosystemic shunts and location of varices.

In most cases, noninvasive imaging techniques provide sufficient information to the transplant surgeon for appropriate patient selection and surgical planning. Doppler ultrasound and biphasic contrast-enhanced CT are the most frequently used noninvasive imaging techniques for preoperative evaluation of the adult liver transplant candidate. MR imaging with MR angiography is an effective technique for the pre-transplant evaluation and is used as a primary imaging modality at several centers. Cholangiography is not routinely performed except in patients with biliary tract disease, such as sclerosing cholangitis. More invasive techniques such as computed tomography arterial portography (CTAP) and computed tomography hepatic arteriography (CTHA) may rarely be used to exclude hepatocellular carcinoma (HCC), although these modalities have largely been replaced by optimized multidetector biphasic CT. Specific details on techniques for each imaging modality are beyond the scope of this chapter. Rather, a discussion of these techniques, emphasizing their relative merits in the context of presurgical evaluation, is presented.

Doppler Sonography

Gray-scale, color flow, and duplex Doppler sonography are considered by some to be the most useful imaging techniques before transplantation.[22] Hepatic vasculature and hepatic parenchyma are evaluated during the examination. The most important goals are assessment of portal vein size and patency, evaluation of the inferior vena cava (IVC) and hepatic veins, and detection of malignancy.

Careful examination of the portal vein is critical because liver transplantation in patients with extrahepatic portal venous thrombosis or a small-caliber vein is difficult or sometimes impossible. Color flow and Doppler sonography are used to determine portal vein patency and direction of flow.[22-25] Grayscale images can accurately determine portal vein caliber. The normal diameter of the extrahepatic portal vein on sonography is 8 to 12 mm. The extrahepatic portal vein usually needs to be at least 4 to 5 mm in diameter for a successful portal vein anastomosis. Portal vein thrombosis is usually depicted as echogenic material within the portal vein. In this situation, evaluation with color Doppler sonography can confirm the presence of portal vein thrombus; if present, the extent of thrombus should be determined.[23,25] Specifically, the entire extrahepatic portal vein and superior mesenteric vein should be evaluated. Although extensive portal vein thrombus was considered a contraindication to OLT in the past, many patients can successfully undergo liver transplantation with modified surgical techniques. In these patients, evaluation of the superior mesenteric vein is critical. If the superior mesenteric vein is patent, placement of an interposition graft or venous jump graft from the superior mesenteric vein to the portal vein is a feasible option.[26] In addition, the nature of the thrombus is extremely important. Although patients with portal hypertension are predisposed to the development of bland portal vein thrombus because of slow or hepatofugal flow, they are also at increased risk for the development of HCC, which has a propensity for portal venous invasion. In fact, half of patients with HCC may have vascular invasion that leads to malignant portal vein thrombus.[27] Because malignant portal vein thrombus is an absolute contraindication to OLT, it is critical to characterize portal vein thrombus as either bland or malignant. Doppler sonographic demonstration of an arterial waveform within expansile thrombus is pathognomonic of a malignant thrombus; this characteristic appearance may obviate biopsy[28,29] (Fig. 94-1).

The Doppler examination also includes assessment of the hepatic veins and IVC. These veins should be evaluated for flow, presence of thrombus, and location. Budd-Chiari syndrome is occasionally the cause of hepatic failure and is diagnosed when there is occlusion of one or more major branches of the hepatic veins. The usual causes are thrombus associated with hypercoagulable states or malignant neoplasms.

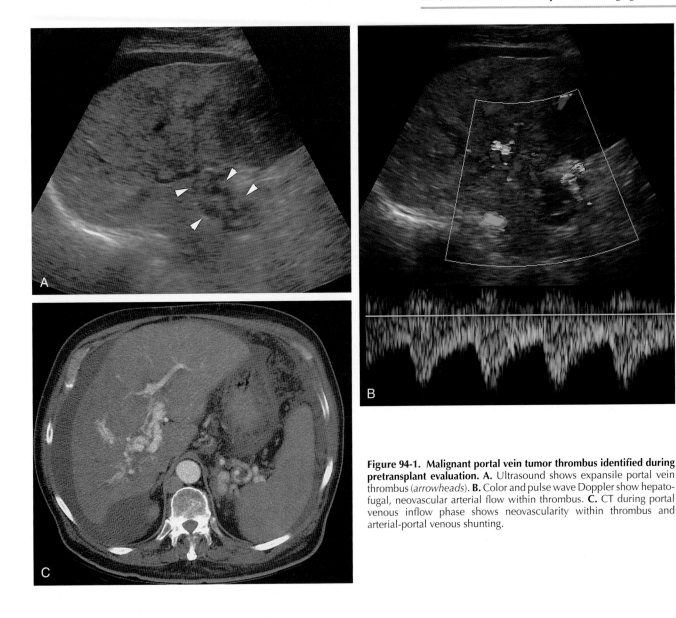

Figure 94-1. Malignant portal vein tumor thrombus identified during pretransplant evaluation. A. Ultrasound shows expansile portal vein thrombus (*arrowheads*). **B.** Color and pulse wave Doppler show hepatofugal, neovascular arterial flow within thrombus. **C.** CT during portal venous inflow phase shows neovascularity within thrombus and arterial-portal venous shunting.

When imaging patients with severe cirrhosis, color Doppler may detect flow within hepatic venous branches that are not apparent on gray-scale images.[23,30,31] Therefore, the diagnosis of Budd-Chiari syndrome is based on the absence of detectable flow in hepatic veins on color Doppler sonography.[19,23-25,30,31] Care must be taken, however, to not confuse the circuitous intrahepatic venous collaterals that develop in the setting of chronic Budd Chiari syndrome with normal hepatic veins. The IVC is examined for patency and to detect rare congenital anomalies, such as webs or an absent retrohepatic segment.

Because patients with end-stage liver disease are at increased risk for development of HCC, a thorough evaluation of the hepatic parenchyma is important. Sonographic manifestations of HCC are variable. The sonographic detection of HCC within the end-stage cirrhotic liver can be difficult.[32,33] Although a recent study with explant correlation has suggested that ultrasound may compete favorably with CT and MRI for HCC detection,[34] it has been our experience that small or infiltrating HCC is often imperceptible at ultrasound despite utilization of higher frequency probes, and incorporation of recent software upgrades such as compound or harmonic imaging (Fig. 94-2). Indeed, in one study with pathologic correlation, the sensitivity of sonography for the detection of HCC was only 50%.[32] Any solid mass found at sonography has been shown to be highly specific for malignancy, however. Therefore, any mass identified within the cirrhotic liver that does not demonstrate typical findings of a cyst should be considered HCC until proved otherwise. In particular, small echogenic—"hemangioma-like"—lesions should further characterized with either additional cross-sectional imaging or ultrasound-guided biopsy. In a recent study, half of these lesions were shown to be HCC[35] (Fig. 94-3). Additionally, sonography is a useful technique for assessment of other manifestations of portal hypertension, including ascites, varices, and splenomegaly. Preoperative sampling of ascites is essential to exclude spontaneous bacterial peritonitis in the patient presenting with fever or to exclude peritoneal tumor in those patients in whom a hepatic or extrahepatic neoplasm is suspected.

Computed Tomography

All of the goals of preoperative imaging can be accomplished with optimized multidetector biphasic contrast-enhanced CT.

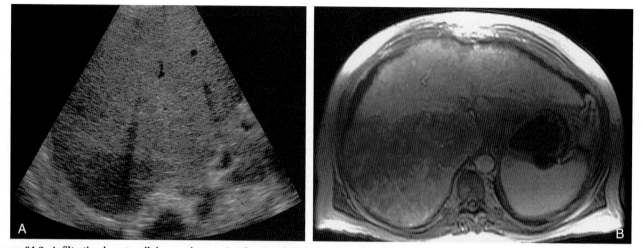

Figure 94-2. Infiltrating hepatocellular carcinoma. A. Ultrasound shows coarsened hepatic echotexture compatible with cirrhosis. No focal lesion was identified despite markedly abnormal α-fetoprotein. **B.** Enhanced fast spoiled gradient recall (FSPGR) MR image shows extensive infiltrating hepatocellular carcinoma.

Determination of liver volume is performed in an attempt to match donor to recipient organ size and to avoid a significant discrepancy of the caliber of vessels to be anastomosed. Although there is some latitude in donor organ size, transplantation of a liver that is too large makes the operation difficult if not impossible. A donor liver up to 20% larger than the optimal estimated volume is acceptable. A large liver creates problems in performing anastomoses and in controlling bleeding because retrohepatic exposure may be compromised. In addition, closure of the abdominal wall may be difficult and can result in sub capsular pressure necrosis.[36] Small donor organs are better tolerated: a donor liver as small as 50% of the optimal estimated volume is acceptable. The main problem in these situations is that the portal venous and hepatic arterial anastomoses may be difficult. Volumetric calculations using CT are relatively accurate.[37] An electronic cursor is manually traced around the margins of the hepatic parenchyma on each CT section; this process can be made less laborious using readily available semiautomatic segmentation software.[38] The cross-sectional area within the region of interest is calculated. Then the individual areas are summated, yielding the total hepatic volume. Alternatively, a three-dimensional volumetric calculation may be obtained from a spiral CT data set.[39,40]

Determination of liver volume and estimation of the amount of ascites are also useful for assigning priority to liver transplant candidates. Patients with a small liver and a large amount of ascites often have the poorest hepatic function, requiring transplantation on a more urgent basis. Patients with larger cirrhotic livers tend to have better hepatic function, allowing transplantation on a more elective basis. For those patients with end-stage liver disease that is followed with surveillance CT, a decrease in liver volume often portends a precipitous decline in hepatic reserve.

Although the direction of portal venous flow cannot be determined with CT, portal vein patency and caliber can be determined from contrast-enhanced CT in most patients. As mentioned, assessment of superior mesenteric vein patency is critical in patients with portal vein thrombosis. In patients

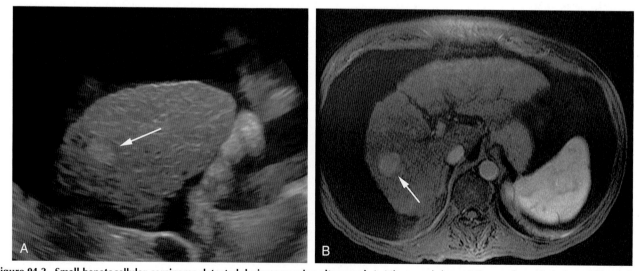

Figure 94-3. Small hepatocellular carcinoma detected during screening ultrasound. A. Ultrasound shows 1.5-cm echogenic lesion within cirrhotic liver *(arrow)*. **B.** Dynamic enhanced FSPGR MR image obtained during portal venous inflow phase shows enhancement of biopsy-proved hepatocellular carcinoma *(arrow)*.

with a hepatic mass, evaluation of the portal vein for tumor thrombus is critical. Expansile, enhancing portal vein thrombus is an accurate, pathognomonic finding of vascular invasion by HCC.[41] Similar assessments of the hepatic veins and IVC are also performed.

Preoperative assessment of recipient hepatic arterial supply is important to ensure adequate hepatic arterial inflow to the transplanted liver. The major consequence of poor hepatic arterial flow is that these patients are at risk for allograft ischemia and biliary ductal ischemia, both of which may necessitate retransplantation. Spiral computed tomography angiography (CTA) has been shown to be an accurate noninvasive technique for evaluating hepatic arterial anatomy and inflow in the transplant candidate.[42] Inadequate hepatic arterial inflow usually results from compression of the celiac trunk by the arcuate ligament or from atherosclerosis.[42] In patients with arcuate ligament compression, simple division of the ligament improves blood flow. Compromised arterial inflow resulting from atherosclerosis usually requires creation of either a supraceliac or an infrarenal aorto–hepatic artery bypass graft. Preoperative knowledge of hepatic arterial inflow is therefore extremely important so that the surgeon can ensure the allograft receives adequate hepatic arterial inflow and minimize the risk of hepatic artery thrombosis.

The major advantage of CT over sonography in the transplant candidate is its superior detection of hepatic malignancy within the cirrhotic liver.[32,33] Because most candidates for hepatic transplantation have cirrhosis and therefore have a greater chance of developing HCC, screening for malignant hepatic masses is an important aspect of preoperative imaging. Unfortunately, the detection of HCC within the end-stage cirrhotic liver is difficult with any imaging technique because of the presence of regeneration, fibrosis, and fatty infiltration. In addition, the hemodynamic changes caused by portal hypertension compromise the ability to detect lesions with contrast-enhanced techniques such as CT or MR imaging. The CT imaging technique should be specifically directed toward optimizing liver-tumor conspicuity. Because HCC is a hypervascular neoplasm, the tumor may become isodense earlier than expected with conventional dynamic bolus CT

during the portal venous (or "hepatic") phase of hepatic enhancement. These lesions may be more apparent in size and number on unenhanced images or on those images obtained during the late hepatic arterial (or "portal venous inflow") phase of hepatic enhancement[43] (Fig. 94-4). MDCT permits biphasic evaluation of the liver during the hepatic arterial phase and the portal venous phase of contrast enhancement. Therefore, unenhanced images followed by biphasic contrast-enhanced spiral CT is recommended in an effort to maximize lesion detection and to enable tumor staging if a lesion is found.[43] Other poor prognostic factors associated with an increased risk for tumor recurrence after transplantation that can be identified with CT include bilobar distribution of tumor, vascular invasion, and spread to regional lymph nodes.[44-46] These patients may have an increased risk of HCC recurrence after transplantation even after radiologically confirmed down staging (i.e., after radiofrequency ablation or chemoembolization). The combination of imaging and HCC genotyping may ultimately prove to be a more useful strategy for assessing recurrence risk in those patients transplanted with relatively limited hepatocellular tumor volume.[19,21,47,48]

Primary sclerosing cholangitis (PSC) is a common indication for liver transplantation, and these patients have an increased risk for developing cholangiocarcinoma. Traditionally, these tumors have been difficult to detect in the setting of PSC.[49,50] A study suggests, however, that a combination of contrast-enhanced helical CT and cholangiography can detect most cholangiocarcinomas that complicate the course of patients with PSC.[51] As an adjunct to contrast-enhanced CT, delayed images at 15 to 20 minutes after administration of contrast material may help detect and characterize these neoplasms.[52]

CT can precisely locate surgical and spontaneous portosystemic shunts and varices that may be encountered. In patients with cirrhosis, surgical portosystemic shunts are often created to decompress portal hypertension and varices to diminish the chance of gastrointestinal hemorrhage. When transplantation is performed, these surgical portosystemic shunts are often ligated so that portal flow to the allograft is not compromised. Likewise, the presence and location of

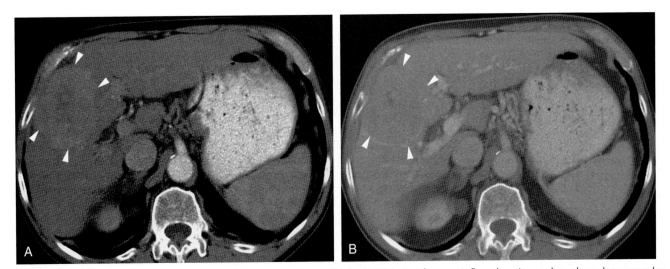

Figure 94-4. Hepatocellular carcinoma detected with contrast-enhanced biphasic CT. A. Portal venous inflow phase image shows large, hypervascular (biopsy proven) hepatocellular carcinoma (*arrowheads*). **B.** Hepatic phase image shows isoenhancement of lesion within background cirrhotic liver (*arrowheads*).

varices are helpful to the surgeon. Varices that are encountered may be ligated. Alternatively, the surgeon may choose to avoid rather than ligate certain varices, thereby reducing the potential for hemorrhagic complications.

Magnetic Resonance Imaging

MR imaging is usually reserved for complicated cases that cannot be resolved with CT or ultrasound or for patients with a contraindication to the use of iodinated contrast material. MR imaging is capable of providing all the necessary pre-operative information for planning OLT.[53-56] Although a discussion of hepatic MR techniques is beyond the scope of this chapter, routine imaging includes in- and out-of-phase fast spoiled-gradient echo imaging (to detect fatty infiltration and potential fatty metamorphosis of HCC), fast spin-echo T2-weighted images, and dynamic Gd-DTPA–enhanced breath-hold 3D gradient-echo T1-weighted images. Other additional sequences can be performed as needed. Single-shot fast spin-echo T2-weighted images and MRCP are often useful for depiction of biliary anatomy, particularly in those patients with primary sclerosing cholangitis, and possible cholangiocarcinoma. Time of flight images may confirm shunt or portal venous patency; magnetic resonance angiography (MRA) may be employed to show hepatic arterial anatomy and portosystemic shunts.

The recipient liver volume can be determined by MR imaging. Because the technique for volumetric calculation of the liver is the same for MR imaging and CT, the accuracy should be comparable. The use of dynamic Gd-DTPA–enhanced MR imaging has been shown to be slightly more sensitive than biphasic contrast-enhanced CT for detection of HCC.[57] Liver lesions may also be more effectively characterized using hepatocyte specific agents (mangofodipir trisodium), although the relative benefits of differing contrast agents is beyond the scope of this chapter.[58,59]

Invasive Imaging Techniques: CT Arterial Portography and CT Hepatic Arteriography

Angiographically assisted CT techniques, such as CTAP and CTHA, are usually reserved for patients with a high suspicion of hepatic malignancy in whom noninvasive imaging has been inconclusive.[60-62] Specifically, CTAP and CTHA may be employed in patients in whom serum α-fetoprotein levels are elevated and noninvasive imaging fails to demonstrate a hepatic lesion.

A combined study using both CTAP and CTHA may also be useful in the patient with a cirrhotic liver and multiple nodules[60-62] (Fig. 94-5). This technique can distinguish benign from malignant nodules in the cirrhotic liver by assessing the blood supply to these nodular lesions.[63] Intranodular portal blood flow tends to decrease as the grade of malignancy increases. Specifically, regenerative nodules and dysplastic nodules tend to have predominantly portal flow and little, if any, hepatic arterial flow. In contrast, intermediate lesions, such as dysplastic nodules with malignant foci and well-differentiated HCC, show a progressive decrease in portal flow and concomitant increase in hepatic arterial flow as the grade of malignancy increases. Finally, high-grade HCC has mostly hepatic arterial flow. Although this combined technique may be useful for characterizing the hemodynamic changes that occur with

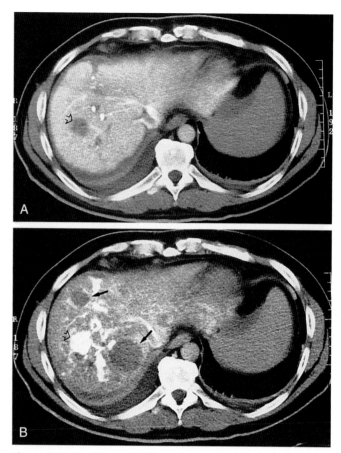

Figure 94-5. Usefulness of CT arterial portography and CT hepatic arteriography for characterization of nodular lesions within the cirrhotic liver based on assessment of blood supply. **A.** A focal lesion (open *arrow*) is detected in the dome of the liver with CT arterial portography. **B.** Corresponding section at CT hepatic arteriography shows that this perfusion defect vividly enhances and is hepatocellular carcinoma (*open arrow*). In addition, there are two large defects (*arrows*). Based on analysis of blood flow (dominant portal flow and lack of hepatic arterial supply), these lesions likely are large regenerating nodules. (**A** and **B** from Redvanley RD, Chezmar JL: Review—CT arterial portography: Technique, indications and applications. Clin Radiol 52:256-268, 1997.)

nodule dedifferentiation, the invasiveness of the procedure, adoption of organ allocation criteria that favor transplantation of patients with potential HCC, and advances in multidetector biphasic CT have significantly decreased the role of CTAP/CTHA in the preoperative evaluation of liver transplantation.

Cholangiography

Sclerosing cholangitis is the fourth most common indication for liver transplantation, accounting for approximately 10% of these procedures.[17] Patients with PSC have an increased risk for the development of cholangiocarcinoma; unfortunately, the detection of these tumors may be extremely difficult. Even with the use of cholangiography, cholangiocarcinoma can be difficult to distinguish from the benign biliary duct strictures of sclerosing cholangitis.[50] In fact, approximately 10% of patients transplanted for advanced PSC have cholangiocarcinoma that is undetected despite use of all imaging techniques.[49,64] In an attempt to identify these elusive tumors, direct cholangiography with brush biopsy of any dominant stricture or polypoid lesion may be necessary before liver transplantation.[65,66] Preoperative detection of cholangiocarcinoma is important because of the prognostic implications of even small volume (but imaging detected) tumors: patients with known cholangiocarcinoma, regardless of size, who undergo OLT have a poor prognosis with a high recurrence rate.[49,67,68] In contrast, those who have an undetectable, incidental cholangiocarcinoma (found during sectioning of the explanted liver) have a much better prognosis with a lower incidence of recurrence.[49]

SURGICAL TECHNIQUES FOR ORTHOTOPIC LIVER TRANSPLANTATION

OLT involves replacement of the diseased native liver with a suitably matched cadaver donor liver. The standard OLT procedure involves four end-to-end vascular anastomoses: the extrahepatic portal vein, the hepatic artery, and suprahepatic and infrahepatic IVC (Fig. 94-6). In this technique, the native retrohepatic segment of the IVC is replaced with that of the donor, which accompanies the transplanted liver. This technique requires temporary occlusion of the splanchnic and systemic venous systems. Consequently, venovenous bypass is necessary to prevent mesenteric congestion, maintain renal function, and drain blood from the lower portion of the body to the supradiaphragmatic venous system.[69] Venovenous bypass allows maintenance of physiologic stability during the anhepatic phase of OLT and has resulted in a significant reduction in morbidity and mortality.[69]

During the initial phase of hepatic replacement, four end-to-end vascular anastomoses are performed: the suprahepatic and infrahepatic caval anastomoses, and the hepatic artery and portal vein anastomoses.[69] First, the suprahepatic caval anastomosis is performed. Then, the infrahepatic caval anastomosis is only partially completed, which allows for flushing of University of Wisconsin preservation solution and any entrapped air out of the donor liver once the hepatic artery and portal vein anastomoses are performed and the liver is reperfused. Subsequently, the donor portal vein is cannulated, the graft is flushed with Ringer's lactate, and the venous effluent is collected from the incomplete infrahepatic caval anastomosis. Adequate flushing of the graft is necessary because reperfusion of the transplanted liver results in the washout of cold, acidic, and hyperkalemic fluid. Releasing this fluid into the systemic circulation can result in bradycardia, hypotension, and cardiac arrest.

At most transplant centers, the hepatic artery anastomosis is performed after the liver is reperfused with portal venous flow; such an approach may decrease the warm ischemia time, because the liver is supplied primarily by the portal vein.[69] Several institutions, however, prefer to perform the hepatic artery anastomosis prior to portal venous reperfusion. This approach theoretically allows earlier perfusion of oxygen-rich blood to the graft; quicker hepatic arterial flow restoration might decrease the ischemic time to the biliary tree and thus decrease the incidence of biliary complications. Variations in the arterial anatomy of the donor liver dictate the type of anastomosis that is performed. In most cases, the hepatic arterial supply to the donor liver arises entirely from the celiac axis. In these cases, the celiac trunk and a small cuff of donor aorta (Carrel patch) is excised and is anastomosed end-to-end to the recipient hepatic artery.[69] If the donor liver has a dual arterial supply, such as a replaced right hepatic artery from the superior mesenteric artery and a left hepatic artery arising from the celiac axis, a single donor arterial trunk can be created for anastomosis to the recipient hepatic artery.[69,70] As long as the recipient has a native vessel of sufficient size to

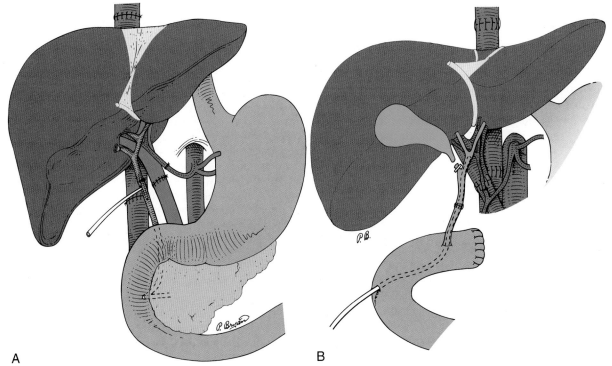

A   B

Figure 94-6. Schematic illustration of standard orthotopic liver transplant. A. Choledochocholedochostomy (common bile duct-to-common bile duct) biliary anastomosis. **B.** Choledochojejunostomy biliary anastomosis.

allow adequate arterial inflow, anatomic variants of the donor liver are of little concern.[71]

In most cases, an end-to-end anastomosis between donor and recipient portal veins is performed. The portal vein anastomosis is partially completed, and the recipient portal vein clamp is briefly released, which allows collection of hypoxic, acidic blood from the stagnant splanchnic circulation without releasing this blood into the liver and systemic circulation. The donor portal vein is then briefly clamped, the anastomosis is completed, and the portal vein is unclamped and the liver reperfused.

In patients with portal vein thrombosis, alternative techniques for portal vein anastomosis are necessary.[26,72] Depending on the extent of the portal vein thrombosis, thrombectomy with a direct donor-to-recipient portal vein anastomosis, placement of an interposition graft between the recipient splenomesenteric confluence and the donor portal vein, or placement of a venous jump graft from the superior mesenteric vein to the donor portal vein can be performed in most patients; their survival rate is comparable to that of patients with a patent portal vein. Once the allograft has been reperfused, the biliary anastomosis is performed. Biliary reconstruction is either a choledochocholedochostomy or a Roux-en-Y choledochojejunostomy.[69] An end-to-end choledochocholedochostomy (duct-to-duct) is the preferred method of biliary reconstruction in patients without preexisting extrahepatic biliary tract disease and no significant size discrepancy between the donor and recipient bile ducts.[69] A T-tube, brought out through a choledochotomy in the recipient common bile duct, may be left in place for 2 to 3 months to monitor bile and to stent the anastomosis. In addition, the T-tube provides access for cholangiography or other biliary procedures, if necessary. However, because bile leaks at the T-tube insertion site are not uncommon, some centers now perform the choledochocholedochostomy without use of a T-tube or internal stent. In one study, there were fewer biliary complications within the first 3 months after liver transplantation with duct-to-duct anastomoses without a T-tube than in patients with the same anastomosis with a T-tube.[73] If the recipient's common bile duct is diseased or there is a significant size discrepancy, the preferred method for biliary reconstruction is a Roux-en-Y choledochojejunostomy in which the donor common duct is anastomosed to a loop of recipient jejunum.[69] The choledochojejunostomy is stented either with a straight biliary tube brought out through the abdomen or with an internal biliary stent. A choledochojejunostomy is the preferred technique for biliary anastomosis in those patients with sclerosing cholangitis.

An alternative technique known as the "piggyback" OLT is performed at some centers. In fact, many transplant surgeons suggest that this technique is the procedure of choice for OLT.[4-6] Initially, the piggyback technique was developed as a method of IVC anastomosis for patients with a large discrepancy between the size of the donor and recipient IVC. The piggyback method can be technically performed in most patients undergoing OLT, however. The piggyback modification of the standard operation consists of a recipient hepatectomy whereby the entire retro hepatic IVC is preserved "in toto" allowing continuing venous return through the IVC and maintenance of hemodynamic stability[6] (Fig. 94-7). Consequently, there is no need for venovenous bypass. The piggyback IVC anastomosis is then formed by creating a vascular cuff

from the recipient hepatic veins that is anastomosed to the donor liver's suprahepatic IVC. The infrahepatic donor IVC is ligated and is essentially a blind-ending segment. There are several advantages of the piggyback procedure: (1) the procedure is technically simpler, (2) it is associated with less bleeding, and (3) venovenous bypass with its attendant potential complications is avoided.[4,74] Additionally, it has been shown that the piggyback technique maintains better hemodynamic stability and may result in better postoperative renal function than the standard technique for OLT.[4,74] The postoperative appearance of the piggyback OLT is characteristic and an understanding of the surgical procedure is necessary for proper interpretation of postoperative imaging studies. Cross-sectional imaging demonstrates a double retrohepatic IVC segment in which the ligated donor infrahepatic IVC is a blind ending segment that may eventually thrombose. Pulmonary embolism from a thrombus within the ligated donor IVC is rare. More important, thrombus within the donor infrahepatic IVC should not be confused with thrombus in the native IVC, and should not prompt performance of a venogram. In patients with suspected hepatic venous stenosis or obstruction, knowledge of the postoperative anatomy is important because hepatic venography may be technically difficult.

Orthotopic liver transplantation is the most frequently performed surgical technique for patients undergoing liver transplantation. Partial liver grafting has been increasingly used, however. Shortages of donor organs, primarily in children awaiting a suitable liver for transplantation, have driven the development of reduced size, split liver, and living related donor transplantation techniques.[75] These techniques increase the available supply of donor organs to younger recipients. Reduced size liver transplantation uses a portion of the liver as a graft but is an inefficient use of donor organs. Split liver transplantation, whereby the whole liver is used for transplantation for two recipients, is an attractive means of increasing the use of a limited supply of donor organs to both children and adults.[75] Living-related donor transplantation uses a portion of the donor liver; the lateral segment may be used successfully for small or pediatric patients with end-stage liver disease.[76] A larger graft is needed for adult living donor transplantation: whole right hepatic lobe grafts have been used successfully in many transplantation centers (the unique imaging requirements required for living right lobe donor transplantation are discussed in a later section).

Finally, auxiliary liver transplantation is a rarely used procedure in which a liver segment is placed, either heterotopically or orthotopically, without removal of the native liver. In auxiliary heterotopic transplantation, the liver graft is placed in the right upper quadrant beside the native liver. In auxiliary OLT, a portion of the native liver is removed and replaced with a reduced-size liver graft (usually the left lobe). Although OLT is the preferred treatment for patients with fulminant hepatic failure in which spontaneous recovery seems unlikely, auxiliary liver transplantation has been used in some patients with fulminant hepatic failure whose native liver is expected to recover complete function. Use of a donor liver graft as a temporizing measure in these patients is not an efficient use of a limited supply of donor organs, however. In children, auxiliary transplantation may be of benefit for those with metabolic disorders but without chronic liver disease.[75] In this situation, the auxiliary liver would alleviate the metabolic

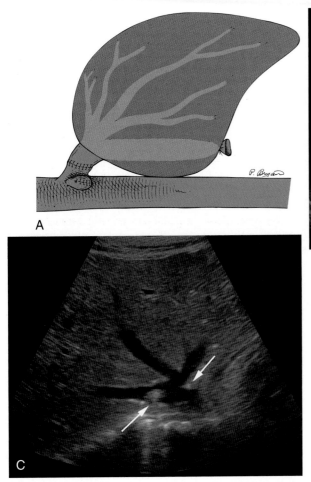
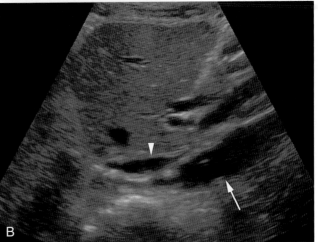

Figure 94-7. Schematic illustration and ultrasound of the "piggyback" liver transplant. After recipient hepatectomy, the allograft is implanted, and the native inferior vena cava (IVC) remains "in toto." Hepatic venous outflow is via an anastomosis connecting the donor's suprahepatic IVC to a vascular cuff formed from the native middle and left hepatic veins. The native right hepatic vein is ligated. The donor infrahepatic IVC (*hatched lines*) is ligated. **A.** Schematic lateral view. **B.** Corresponding sagittal ultrasound shows ligated donor infrahepatic IVC (*arrowhead*) and recipient IVC (*arrows*). **C.** Axial ultrasound shows vascular cuff (*arrows*).

deficiency, whereas preservation of the native liver would provide protection from liver failure should the graft fail as a result of rejection or a complication.

In the future, development of hepatocyte transplantation and biologic extracorporeal assist devices may be of benefit as a bridge to OLT for those with fulminant hepatic failure or in those with chronic end-stage liver disease.[77-80] These techniques may provide the necessary hepatic function to prevent hepatic encephalopathy and cerebral edema until a suitable donor graft is available. In addition, these techniques may be a useful temporizing technique for patients who develop fulminant hepatic failure and whose native liver is expected to recover complete function.

LIVING DONOR LIVER TRANSPLANTATION

Despite growing public awareness of the shortage of organs and well-funded campaigns mounted by hospitals, patients and UNOS, the number of cadaveric livers available for transplantation has not changed significantly over the past decade. In the meantime, the number of patients with end stage liver disease secondary to hepatitis C and nonalcoholic steatohepatitis (NASH) has markedly increased over the past several years. The often long period between initial infection with hepatitis C and clinically significant liver disease will translate into an epidemic of cirrhosis (and hepatocellular carcinoma) in baby boomers who were exposed prior to antibody screening in the early 1990s. Likewise, the current obesity epidemic

will invariably result in many new cases of NASH-related cirrhosis. This increasing demand for liver transplantation is the driving force behind the recent adoption of adult living donor liver transplantation (LDLT) at most major transplant centers in the United States.

LDLT was initially performed in the 1990s for small or pediatric patients with end-stage liver disease; procedures utilizing the left lobe or lateral segment were reported at the University of Chicago.[81] Although these techniques were attempted in adult recipients, the smaller left hepatic lobe provided insufficient hepatic mass for most adult patients. The first adult-to-adult right hepatic lobe transplant was reported by Yamaoka et al.[82,83] in Japan in 1993; the first successful donor right hepatic lobe transplantation was performed in the United States in 1997.[84] As of April 2005, 2,733 living donor transplants were performed in the United States; 323 living donor liver transplants were performed in 2004.[16] Graft survival has been reported to be up to 89% at 2 years[85]; patient survival rates at 3 years range between 70% and 93% depending upon the recipient Child status.[86]

There are several unique benefits of LDLT beyond simply increasing the potential pool of potential donors. The primary advantage of the technique is that the procedure is performed electively—detailed preoperative assessment and clinical management of often critically ill potential recipients is possible. The decreased cold ischemia time of the living donor graft (typically less than 1 hour compared to 8 to 12 hours for cadaveric transplants) may decrease allograft dysfunction and improve immediate postoperative graft performance.[87] Finally, living donor grafts are obtained from healthy donors that have been extensively screened.

Despite these advantages, there are unique risks of LDLT. There is no physical benefit for the potential donor of a right hepatic lobe graft; on the other hand, the morbidity and mortality associated with right hepatic lobe donation necessitates an extensive—predominantly imaging based—evaluation of the potential living donor.

Imaging Evaluation of the Potential Living Related Liver Donor

The ideal screening imaging modality for potential living liver donors would accurately evaluate hepatic parenchyma, provide data for split liver volume assessment, and depict intrahepatic and extrahepatic vascular anatomy prior to potential partial hepatectomy.[88,89] Rapid breath-hold, volume, parallel MR imaging is used in several centers to depict the vascular variants, hepatic volume issues, and fatty infiltration that may preclude right hepatic lobe donation. Either conventional or mangofodipir trisodium–enhanced MRCP may also be performed in order to demonstrate problematic biliary anatomy.[88,90-94] However, this technique has not been widely accepted as a substitute for intraoperative cholangiography. A comprehensive MR study of both vascular and biliary anatomy is theoretically possible with contrast media that combine the advantages of a conventional gadolinium-based extracellular agent with a hepatocyte-biliary–specific agent (e.g., gadobenate dimeglumine).[95] This approach has not been validated in large scale series, however.

The exquisite spatial resolution of multidetector CT has made it the most widely used modality for the preoperative evaluation of living donors. Protocols for obtaining vascular maps prior to potential resection continue to evolve with rapid improvements in detector technology. Accurate results have been reported in the recent literature utilizing four detector systems[89,96-101]; third-order intrahepatic branches of right and left hepatic arteries should be routinely depicted with 16- and 64-channel scanners. The extended coverage and thin collimation (0.625 mm) possible with 64-channel systems makes extremely fast, isotropic imaging possible. Rapid scanning makes bolus timing even more critical—either test boluses or automated triggering are crucial for obtaining images during peak hepatic arterial enhancement. The 2.5-mm collimated images are then obtained during a portal venous ("hepatic") phase so that portal and hepatic venous anatomy may be displayed. Both the source and reconstructed images should be meticulously reviewed. Volume-rendered images are helpful for displaying global anatomy, but many radiologists rely heavily upon sliding thick-slab maximum intensity images. Finally, radiologists involved in image interpretation and reconstruction should consult with transplant surgery colleagues often, particularly during the initial start-up phase of a living donor program—"absolute" contraindications for transplantation will vary based upon surgeon expertise.

Parenchymal Assessment

The size of the potential right lobe graft is a crucial determinant of graft viability. A sufficiently large right lobe is needed to prevent the "small for size" syndrome—transplantation of insufficient hepatic mass may result in poor allograft function, graft failure, or the death of the recipient.[102-104] Small grafts are also more prone to sinusoidal injury from increased portal pressures.[103] Several approaches for assessing sufficent liver volume for transplantation have been applied: graft weight/ recipient standard liver volumes of less than 40% or graft to recipient weight ratios of less than 85% are associated with poor outcomes.[102,104] Both MRI and CT can be used to accurately calculate split liver volumetric measurements of potential donors.[39,88]

Unenhanced CT or in-phase/out-of-phase MRI is also used to detect fatty infiltration in the potential donor graft.[88,98] It has been well shown that steatosis increases the likelihood of graft dysfunction and reduces hepatic regenerative function.[105-107] Although the degree of fat infiltration may be roughly assessed using dual voltage technique,[98] several centers still routinely perform liver donor biopsies in order to better quantify steatosis.[108]

Vascular Assessment

Anatomic variations of extrahepatic vascular anatomy (e.g., replaced left, right hepatic arteries) are common, well known, and easily demonstrated by CTA. The unique contribution of MDCT to the evaluation of the prospective right liver donor is its ability to detect variations in arterial and venous anatomy that may traverse the hepatectomy plane.[39,96,97,100,101] Although adequate hepatic mass may be procured with several techniques (left donor hepatectomy, extended right donor hepatectomy), a traditional right hepatectomy along Cantlie's line, a relatively avascular plane immediately lateral to the middle hepatic vein, is preferred in most institutions. Parenchymal dissection to the hilar plate is performed by ultrasonic dissection.[109] Accurate definition of vascular structures traversing this plane is needed to prevent inadvertent vessel injury and ischemic injury to either the graft or remaining donor liver.

Traditional hepatic arterial anatomy, in which the proper hepatic artery branches into right and left hepatic branches, is seen in only 55% of patients. Although many variants are easily shown at CT, a crucial consideration for donor graft retrieval is the blood supply to segment four. A middle hepatic artery branch that arises from the right hepatic artery will be disrupted during donor hepatectomy; inadvertent ligation of this branch during graft retrieval may cause biliary ischemic damage to the remaining donor medial segment. Other significant vascular variants that may affect donor selection include (1) a short right hepatic artery, (2) trifurcation of the common hepatic artery into the gastroduodenal artery (GDA) and right and left hepatic arteries, and (3) origination of the right or left hepatic arteries before the GDA. Replaced hepatic arteries in the recipient are not absolute contraindications for transplantation, although arterial reconstructions can be more technically demanding. Finally, recipient celiac artery stenosis either from atherosclerotic disease or a median arcuate ligament may predispose to graft infarction and biliary complications.[89]

Sliding thick-slab MIP images obtained from a second portal venous (hepatic) phase are used to display potentially significant hepatic venous variants. Variations in branching of the middle hepatic vein are particularly important because

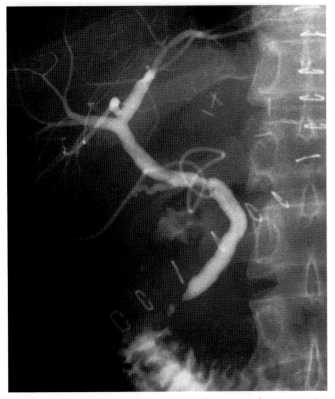

Figure 94-11. Biliary anastomotic narrowing. Normal postoperative T-tube cholangiogram demonstrates a slight focal narrowing at the anastomosis.

and intensive postoperative immunosuppressive therapy, many patients develop postoperative complications. In addition, recurrence of the primary disease, such as acute viral hepatitis or hepatic malignancy, remains a major threat to allograft and patient survival even with a technically successful procedure.[21,123] Thus, early diagnosis and treatment of these complications is critical to improve patient and allograft survival.

Vascular Complications

Clinical manifestations of vascular complications are variable. They range from mild elevation of hepatic function tests to fulminate hepatic failure, depending on how early the complication is detected and the severity of the abnormality. Vascular complications occur in 9% of cases and should be considered in patients with graft failure, biliary strictures or leaks, gastrointestinal bleeding, or septicemia.[124] Early diagnosis is important for graft salvage, with surgical intervention the primary treatment option in most circumstances. Because the clinical presentation is quite variable, imaging studies are particularly helpful for confirming and determining the exact nature of a vascular complication. Sonography is the primary screening technique; CTA[125, 126] or catheter angiography are performed to confirm and define the abnormalities detected with sonography or to evaluate patients in whom the sonographic study is indeterminate. The main arterial complications include hepatic artery thrombosis, hepatic artery stenosis, pseudoaneurysms, and arteriovenous fistulas. Venous complications are less frequent and include thrombosis or stenosis of the IVC or portal vein.

Hepatic Artery Complications

Hepatic artery thrombosis is the most common and significant vascular complication of OLT.[124,127] It occurs in approximately 7% of adult liver transplants.[124] Most patients who develop hepatic artery thrombosis require retransplantation.[124] Thrombectomy and arterial revascularization may be attempted to avoid retransplantation or to temporize the clinical condition until a suitable donor becomes available.[124,128] Risk factors for hepatic artery thrombosis include increased cold ischemic time of the donor liver, ABO blood group incompatibility, small vessels with inadequate arterial inflow, and rejection.

After liver transplantation, the donor bile duct is entirely dependent on hepatic artery blood supply; occlusion of the hepatic artery leads to biliary duct ischemia and necrosis. The natural history and clinical course of the patient with hepatic artery thrombosis is variable and can range from acute fulminate hepatic necrosis to delayed biliary leaks with septicemia. Three distinct presentations have been described for patients with hepatic artery thrombosis.[127] The first is fulminate hepatic necrosis with rapid clinical deterioration. Fulminate hepatic necrosis is a clinical emergency and requires urgent retransplantation for survival. The second is the development of delayed bile leaks as a result of biliary necrosis; biliary leaks may result in subhepatic fluid collections, bile peritonitis, bacteremia, and sepsis. The third group presents with a less dramatic clinical course characterized by recurrent episodes of bacteremia. Many of these patients develop nonanastomotic biliary strictures. Delayed intermittent episodes of septicemia are usually caused by focal hepatic abscesses from biliary necrosis and strictures or from infected bilomas (Fig. 94-12). In these patients, CT or sonography may demonstrate bilomas or infarcts.

Doppler sonography is a reliable noninvasive technique for assessing hepatic arterial patency.[22,129] In most cases of early postoperative hepatic artery thrombosis, intrahepatic and extrahepatic arterial flow is absent despite optimized Doppler technique. Occasionally, intrahepatic flow may be detected in patients with complete hepatic artery thrombosis if collateral vessels have formed; arterial collaterals may be particularly prominent in pediatric transplant recipients, although they do not develop acutely.[129,130] In most cases, the collateral flow is insufficient to prevent biliary ischemia. The absence of arterial flow at the porta hepatis and slow, low resistance, tardus-parvus intrahepatic arterial flow at Doppler interrogation should suggest collaterization after hepatic artery occlusion.[130] The tardus-parvus waveform is characterized by a resistive index less than 0.5 and a systolic acceleration time greater than 0.08 seconds.[130-133] False-positive diagnoses of hepatic artery thrombosis may occur, however, in patients with markedly diminished hepatic arterial flow secondary to severe hepatic edema, systemic hypotension, or high-grade hepatic artery stenosis, or in patients where the Doppler examination is technically compromised. CTA or angiography are performed to confirm the diagnosis of hepatic artery thrombosis (Fig. 94-13).

Hepatic artery stenoses occur most often at the anastomotic site.[130] As with hepatic artery thrombosis, decreased hepatic arterial perfusion produces biliary ischemia; biliary necrosis may result in hepatic dysfunction or frank graft failure.[134] Biliary abnormalities, as shown by cholangiography,

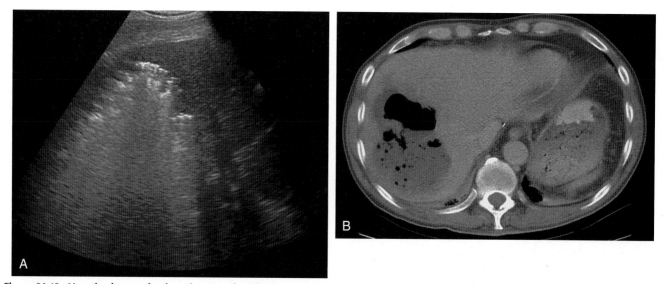

Figure 94-12. Hepatic abscess after hepatic artery thrombosis. A. Ultrasound shows dirty shadowing posterior to gas within hepatic abscess. **B.** CT shows complex, gas containing right hepatic lobe abscess.

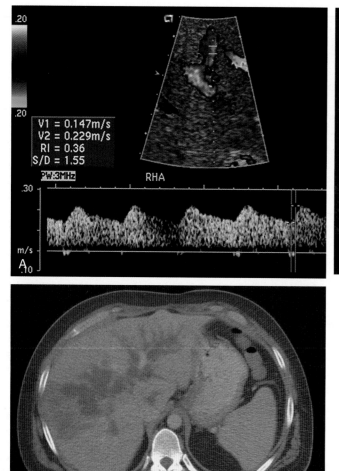

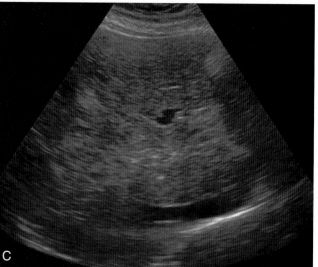

Figure 94-13. Hepatic artery thrombosis. A. Doppler ultrasound shows tardus-parvus waveform. **B.** CT shows an extensive low attenuation cast within biliary tree. **C.** Ultrasound in same patient shows subtle biliary-peribiliary echogenicity. The extent of biliary injury is often underestimated at ultrasound.

are present in more than 60% of patients with hepatic artery stenosis.[135] The most common manifestation of hepatic artery stenosis at cholangiography is multifocal intrahepatic strictures. Direct Doppler criteria employed to detect a hemodynamically significant hepatic arterial stenosis (≥50%) include a focally accelerated velocity of greater than 2 m/second with associated turbulence at or immediately distal to the stenosis.[131] Imaging the hepatic arterial anastomosis directly may be difficult, however. On the other hand, secondary, downstream manifestations of a more proximal stenosis are routinely shown using optimized Doppler. A tardus-parvus waveform detected distal to the anastomosis within an intrahepatic artery is moderately suggestive of a hemodynamically significant hepatic artery stenosis (sensitivity and specificity of 73%)[130] (Fig. 94-14). Prompt diagnosis of hepatic artery stenosis is important because most stenoses are treatable with balloon angioplasty.[136-138] If unrecognized, however, hepatic artery stenosis may progress to hepatic artery thrombosis.

Hepatic artery pseudoaneurysms after OLT are uncommon but potentially life-threatening complications that necessitate surgical intervention.[124,139] Pseudoaneurysms may be asymptomatic and detected incidentally. Rupture of a hepatic artery pseudoaneurysm causes significant arterial hemorrhage, however, and can be fatal. Patients may present with hemobilia, hemoperitoneum, or gastrointestinal bleeding if the aneurysm ruptures. Pseudoaneurysms usually occur at the anastomosis. Occasionally, intrahepatic pseudoaneurysms may occur after percutaneous biopsy or biliary procedures. In patients with hepatic dysfunction, this diagnosis requires a high index of clinical suspicion. Pseudoaneurysms can be detected with contrast-enhanced CT and color Doppler sonography.[140] At contrast-enhanced CT, hepatic artery pseudoaneurysms are depicted as a focally enhanced enlargement of the artery (Fig. 94-15). Color Doppler sonography demonstrates a periportal cystic structure with to-and-fro flow. CTHA or arteriography are used to confirm the diagnosis.[125,126,139,140] Anastomotic pseudoaneurysms require urgent surgical revascularization; symptomatic intrahepatic postbiopsy pseudoaneurysms may be effectively treated with coil embolization.

Portal Vein Complications

Portal vein complications are uncommon after liver transplantation; a prevalence rate of 2% has been reported in a retrospective series.[74] Potential causes include misalignment because of significant size discrepancy between the recipient and donor portal vein, excessive portal vein length, hypercoagulable states, thrombus from the portal vein bypass catheter, and previous portal vein surgery.[134] Patients usually present with findings of portal hypertension including gastroesophageal varices, or massive ascites.[74] Sonography may show narrowing at the anastomosis or echogenic intravascular thrombus. No portal venous flow is detected by color Doppler sonography in those patients with portal vein thrombus. Care must be taken, however, to optimize the Doppler study so that slow velocity flow may be depicted: false-positive Doppler examinations may occur if portal venous flow is extremely slow. Color Doppler evaluation of portal vein stenosis shows focal color aliasing with a threefold to fourfold increase in peak velocity at the stenosis relative to the prestenotic vein.[131] Transhepatic portography or CT venography can confirm the presence of portal vein complications (Fig. 94-16). Pressure gradients should be obtained to assess the hemodynamic significance of a stenosis. Therapeutic options for symptomatic portal vein thrombosis or stenosis include thrombectomy, surgical resection with anastomotic revision, placement of a venous jump graft, percutaneous thrombolysis and stent placement, angioplasty, and retransplantation.[26,124,138,141,142]

Inferior Vena Cava Complications

IVC thrombosis or stenosis after OLT is rare and can occur at either the suprahepatic or the infrahepatic vena caval anastomosis.[74] Patients undergoing retransplantation may have an increased risk of suprahepatic caval stenosis because of abundant fibrosis around the original anastomosis.[143] The clinical symptoms of caval stenoses are dependent upon the level and degree of obstruction to vena caval flow. Stenoses occurring at the suprahepatic anastomosis may cause hepatic venous obstruction, resulting in Budd-Chiari syndrome, renal dysfunction, and lower leg edema. In addition, venous thrombosis may develop below the caval stenosis and can extend into the hepatic veins or into the infrahepatic vena cava.

Sonography may show narrowing of the suprahepatic IVC with or without thrombus. Color Doppler shows focal color aliasing with a threefold to fourfold increase in peak velocity at the stenosis relative to the prestenotic segment.[131] Additionally, reversal of flow within the hepatic veins and an absence of periodicity in the hepatic veins are sensitive findings suggesting suprahepatic IVC anastomotic stenosis.[131]

Occasionally, the diagnosis of a caval stenosis is initially suspected based on findings from CT. Contrast-enhanced CT may demonstrate narrowing of the suprahepatic cava with dilatation of the infrahepatic IVC and caval or hepatic vein thromboses that develop below an obstruction. Multiplanar reformatted images from MDCT may be useful for noninvasive depiction of IVC stenosis.[126] Other associated findings include pleural effusions, ascites, and hepatomegaly.

Early diagnosis of a significant caval stenosis is important to prevent development of acute hepatic venous obstruction. In suspected cases, inferior venacavography and pressure gradients should be performed to assess the hemodynamic significance of a stenosis and to exclude thrombosis below the obstruction. Venography typically demonstrates narrowing at the suprahepatic anastomosis with or without thrombus (Fig. 94-17). Angioplasty and stenting have been reported to be an effective treatment for caval stenoses.[138,142-145]

Biliary Complications

Bile duct complications develop in approximately 11% to 13% of liver transplant patients.[146,147] Most biliary complications occur within the early postoperative period, although rarely biliary strictures may result in clinically significant symptoms (jaundice, graft dysfunction) years post-transplantation.[146-148] Unfortunately, the clinical symptoms of the patient with a biliary tract complication may be indistinguishable from other common causes of allograft dysfunction, such as rejection, hepatic artery occlusion, and infections. Biliary complications include either bile leaks or obstruction. Bile leaks are

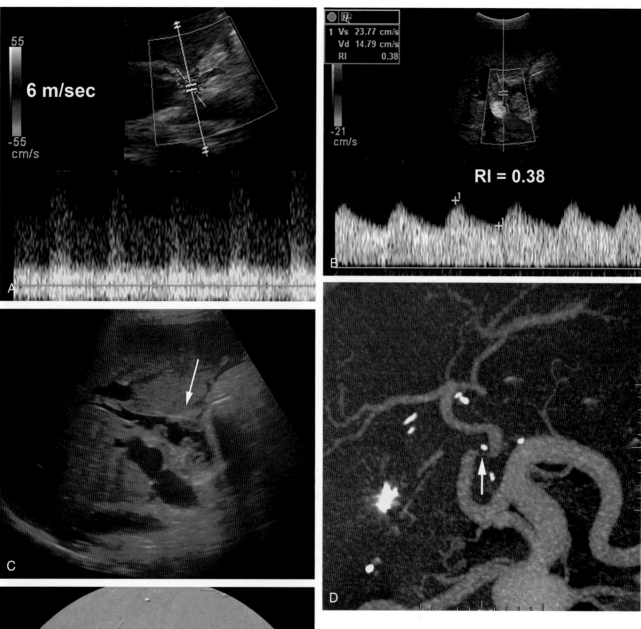

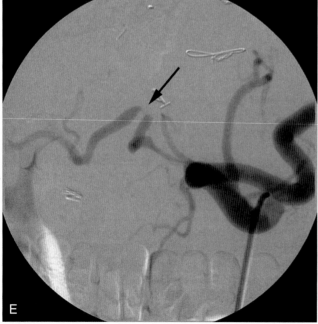

Figure 94-14. Hepatic artery stenosis. A. Doppler shows markedly elevated velocities (6 m/second) at region of focal color aliasing in a patient with graft dysfunction post–right lobe transplantation. **B.** Doppler ultrasound in another patient post–OLTX shows tardus-parvus waveform within main hepatic artery (RI = 0.38). **C.** Ultrasound shows sloughed biliary epithelium within dilated extrahepatic duct (*arrow*). **D.** Maximum intensity projection (MIP) CTA image shows high-grade anastomotic narrowing (*arrow*). **E.** Catheter angiogram shows critical hepatic arterial stenosis (*arrow*).

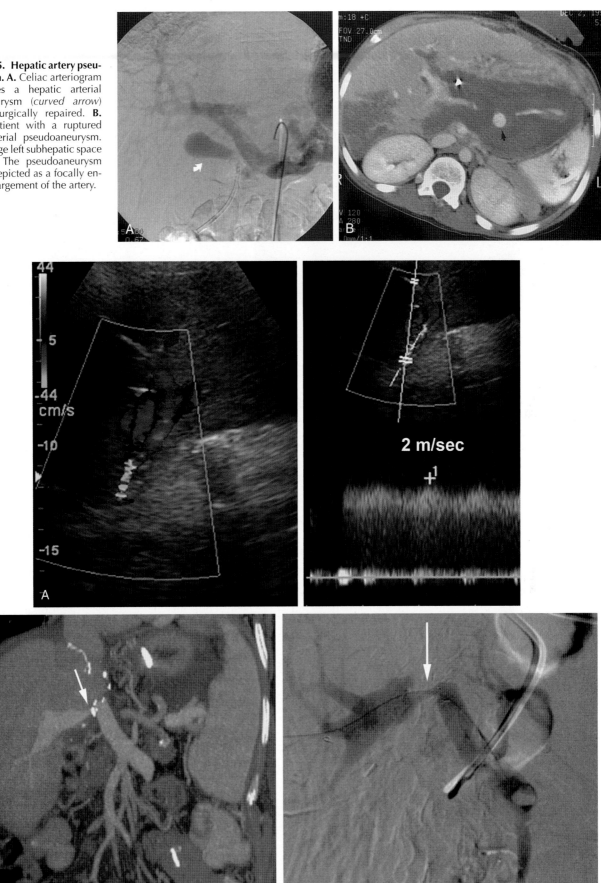

Figure 94-15. Hepatic artery pseudoaneurysm. A. Celiac arteriogram demonstrates a hepatic arterial pseudoaneurysm (*curved arrow*) that was surgically repaired. **B.** Another patient with a ruptured hepatic arterial pseudoaneurysm. Note the large left subhepatic space hematoma. The pseudoaneurysm (*arrow*) is depicted as a focally enhanced enlargement of the artery.

Figure 94-16. Portal vein stenosis. A. Doppler ultrasound shows an area of focal color aliasing at portal venous anastomosis following right lobe transplantation. Pulse wave Doppler confirms markedly elevated velocities. **B.** Coronal thick-slab maximum intensity projection image confirms a critical portal vein stenosis (*arrow*). **C.** Transhepatic portogram shows the anastomotic stenosis (*arrow*). The stenosis was successfully angioplastied.

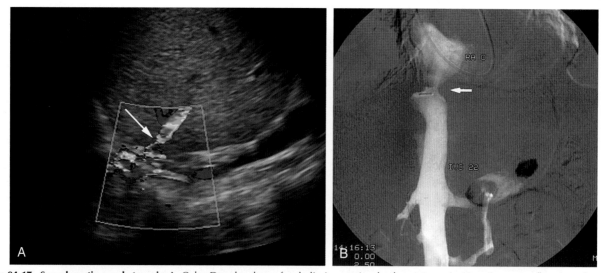

Figure 94-17. Suprahepatic caval stenosis. A. Color Doppler shows focal aliasing at piggyback anastomosis. Hepatic venous flow (not shown) was monophasic. **B.** Vena cavography in another patient shows significant narrowing at the suprahepatic caval anastomosis (*arrow*). This was successfully treated with balloon angioplasty.

usually a result of a compromised biliary anastomosis, are related to T-tubes or are a complication of hepatic artery thromboses/stenoses.[149] Biliary ductal obstruction is most frequently caused by biliary strictures and are usually related to biliary ischemia.[150] Unusual causes of biliary obstruction include occlusion or malposition of the biliary stent or T-tube, mucocele of the donor cystic duct remnant, biliary sludge and stones, papillary stenosis, and redundancy with kinking of the bile duct.[151-154]

In the immunosuppressed transplant patient, serious biliary complications are associated with a high mortality if not promptly diagnosed. Doppler sonography is performed primarily to confirm hepatic artery patency and to determine the presence or absence of biliary ductal dilatation.[129] Although sonography typically identifies secondary abnormalities, such as bilomas or ascites, it is insensitive for the early detection of bile leaks or strictures in transplant patients. Cholangiography remains the primary diagnostic technique for depiction of biliary complications and should be performed in any patient with suspected biliary complications, even if cross-sectional imaging techniques are normal.[154] Furthermore, cholangiography provides a detailed view of biliary anatomy so that appropriate therapy can be planned. Several studies have shown the potential of mangofodipir-enhanced MRI to depict biliary leaks, but this technique is not routinely performed at most centers.[155,156]

Bile Leak

The reported prevalence of post-transplant bile leaks is approximately 4%.[149] Typical clinical findings are fever with signs of cholangitis or peritonitis and elevated serum bilirubin and liver enzymes. Bile leaks may occur at the T-tube site, at the anastomosis, or in a nonanastomotic location within the donor biliary tree.[149] The most common site of bile duct leak is from the T-tube site; T-tube–related leaks are not associated with hepatic artery thrombosis. The leak usually occurs parallel to the T-tube but may also occur at the T-tube site after removal or accidental dislodgment. Most T-tube leaks are

small and are seen on cholangiograms as a contrast tract along the T-tube. Large T-tube bile leaks may be more ominous, resulting in bilomas or bilious ascites. Contrast extravasation at cholangiography typically extends into the right subhepatic space. In these cases, CT and sonography show a subhepatic fluid collection; image-guided aspiration can be performed to confirm a biloma and determine if it has become infected.

Management of a T-tube-related bile leak is based upon the size of the leak. Most small T-tube leaks resolve spontaneously[149] (Fig. 94-18). Large leaks may result in bilious ascites or bilomas. Percutaneous aspiration and potential drainage of the fluid collections are routinely performed because of the high likelihood of superinfection in immunosuppresed patients. If a fluid collection enlarges or there is a persistent bile leak, primary surgical repair of the T-tube leak or biliary reconstruction may be necessary.[147] Nonsurgical therapeutic options include transhepatic biliary drainage or endoscopic sphincterotomy with biliary stenting along with percutaneous drainage of the biloma.[157]

Anastomotic biliary leaks are technical, mechanical complications and almost always occur within 2 months after transplantation.[149] Rarely biliary necrosis due to hepatic artery thrombosis may result in an anastomotic leak, but ischemia related complications more typically occur within the donor biliary tree.[150] Cholangiography shows extravasation of contrast material from the anastomosis with pooling in the subhepatic space. Anastomotic leaks usually require surgical repair, although transhepatic biliary stenting may be successful in some cases.[149]

Nonanastomotic leaks are the least common type of biliary leak but are the most ominous biliary complication. Patency of the hepatic artery must be confirmed because a nonanastomotic bile leak is one of the most common presentations of hepatic artery thrombosis: hepatic artery thrombosis is present in almost 90% of patients with nonanastomotic bile leaks.[150] Hepatic artery thrombosis produces bile duct necrosis that leads to bile leaks, strictures, or both. Bile leaks caused by hepatic artery thrombosis may produce hilar or intrahepatic bilomas (Fig. 94-19). In patients with bile leaks from hepatic

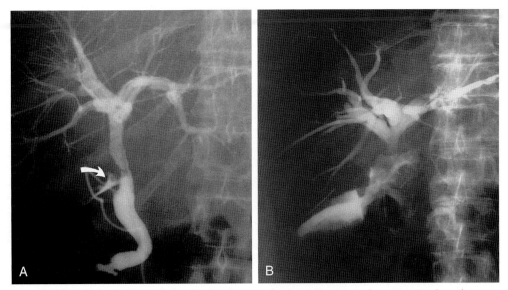

Figure 94-18. Anastomotic biliary leaks. A. T-tube cholangiogram demonstrates a small amount of extravasation from the anastomotic site (*curved arrow*). The leak resolved with conservative management. **B.** T-tube cholangiogram in another patient demonstrates a large anastomotic leak with accumulation of contrast material in the subhepatic space. This patient was treated with percutaneous biliary drainage and biloma drainage. Surgical revision was eventually necessary, however.

artery thrombosis, cholangiography may show large irregular collections of contrast material extravasating from distended, debris-filled necrotic bile ducts.

Bilomas easily become infected in these immunosuppressed patients, particularly when hepatic artery thrombosis leads to bile duct necrosis and bacteremia. Nonanastomotic leaks associated with hepatic artery thrombosis almost always require retransplantation.[149] Although rarely curative, percutaneous drainage may be palliative until a suitable donor is available so that retransplantation can be performed.[158]

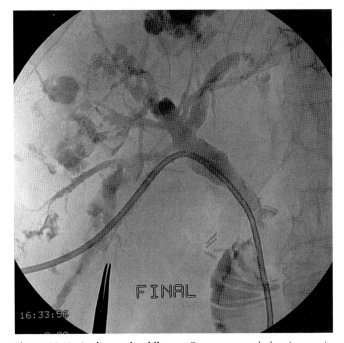

Figure 94-19. Leaks causing bilomas. Percutaneous cholangiogram in a patient with hepatic artery thrombosis who developed multiple leaks resulting in bilomas.

Biliary Obstruction

Post-transplant biliary strictures are the most common causes of biliary obstruction and occur either at the anastomosis or within the biliary tree. Anastomotic bile duct strictures typically occur within months of liver transplantation. They may be detected as a finding on routine follow-up cholangiography or they may be a cause of elevated serum bilirubin and graft dysfunction. Anastomotic strictures are usually an isolated technical problem caused by fibrosis around the anastomosis.[159,160] Mild anastomotic narrowing frequently is seen at cholangiography and is usually insignificant.[122] Careful clinical correlation is important in these patients, however. Significant anastomotic strictures present as focal concentric narrowing at the anastomosis with proximal biliary duct dilatation or a delay in bile duct emptying (Fig. 94-20). Occasionally, biliary stones or sludge may form proximal to the stricture. Anastomotic strictures may be successfully treated with percutaneous balloon dilatation.[161]

Nonanastomotic biliary strictures occur in approximately 8% of patients, are more ominous, and are typically an end result of compromise to the arterial supply of the donor bile ducts.[150,162] Biliary ischemia is usually caused by hepatic artery thrombosis or stenosis; however, long cold ischemic times of the donor liver, ABO blood type incompatibility between donor and recipient, and chronic ductopenic rejection may result in equivalent injuries.[135,150,160,163-165] Prolonged cold ischemia of the allograft produces a direct ischemic insult to the bile ducts.[164] ABO blood group incompatibility causes an immunologic injury to vascular endothelium and to biliary epithelial cells.[165] Chronic ductopenic rejection produces an arteriopathy of medium-sized hepatic artery branches.[163] Whatever the physiology, nonanastomotic biliary strictures may develop from mild or moderate ischemia, which allows the duct to heal with fibrosis and ductal stenosis. Frank biliary necrosis with intrahepatic bile leak may result from severe ischemia.

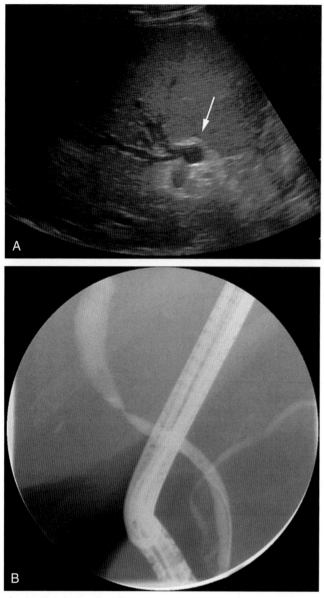

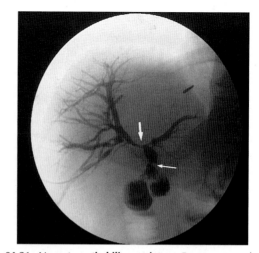

Figure 94-21. Nonastomotic biliary stricture. Percutaneous cholangiogram in a patient with hepatic artery stenosis who developed a nonanastomotic stricture at the duct bifurcation (*large arrow*). There is also an anastomotic stricture at the choledochojejunostomy (*small arrow*).

Figure 94-20. Anastomotic stricture. A. Ultrasound shows abrupt tapering of dilated common duct within the porta hepatis (*arrow*). **B.** ERCP confirms an anastomotic stricture. The stricture was successfully stented.

The evaluation of any patient with a nonanastomotic biliary stricture should begin with Doppler ultrasound to assess hepatic arterial flow. If an abnormality in hepatic arterial flow is detected, CTHA can be performed to confirm hepatic artery stenosis or thrombosis. Typically, hepatic arterial abnormalities precede biliary abnormalities by 1 to 3 weeks. Because biliary dilatation is minimal in the early stages of stricture formation, sonography is inadequate to examine the intrahepatic bile ducts.[154] Furthermore, biliary sloughing and peribiliary fibrosis that occur with biliary ischemia is often extremely subtle even with technique optimization. Therefore, cholangiography is necessary for evaluation of bile duct strictures.

Nonanastomotic strictures can occur anywhere in the donor biliary tree but usually involve the hilum with variable involvement of intrahepatic ducts (Fig. 94-21). On occasion, intrahepatic strictures may be predominant. Nonanastomotic strictures evolve over several weeks in a predictable pattern.[166] Initially, minimal irregularity in the transplanted common hepatic duct develops without proximal biliary dilatation. These abnormalities may extend proximally to involve the biliary hilum. Over days to weeks, biliary debris and mucosal casts form causing biliary obstruction. Bile duct debris may organize into stones, which may also compound the obstruction. After several weeks to months, fibrotic changes ensue, and firm obstructing strictures develop. Unrelieved biliary obstruction with biliary stasis/dysmotility and biliary ischemia may result in a cast of lithogenic material throughout the biliary tree. The so called biliary cast syndrome may occur as a result of hepatic artery stenosis/thrombosis but other causes of biliary ischemia (prolonged cold ischemia times, graft procurement from non–heart-beating donors, acute cellular rejection) have also been implicated (Fig. 94-22). Cholangiographic clearance of biliary casts may sometimes result in graft salvage, if hepatic arterial inflow is adequate.[167,168]

The treatment of nonanastomotic biliary strictures with transhepatic balloon dilatation and stenting has had variable success.[159,161,162,166] Usually, multiple stricture dilatations and long-term stenting are necessary to maintain bile duct patency. Percutaneous treatment is most successful when treating strictures not associated with hepatic artery thrombosis, PSC, or chronic rejection.[166] Often, however, if adequate hepatic function can be preserved, these techniques are successful temporizing measures until a suitable donor is available for retransplantation.

Intrahepatic and nonanastomotic strictures occur more frequently in patients undergoing liver transplantation for PSC[160,169,170] (Fig. 94-23). This finding may be related to an increased incidence of chronic rejection in patients with PSC compared with other indications for liver transplantation or to recurrence of PSC in the allograft.[171]

Obstruction from recurrent malignancy may cause biliary obstruction. Patients with cholangiocarcinoma have a recurrence rate of 66% after transplantation.[65] Cholangiocarcinoma

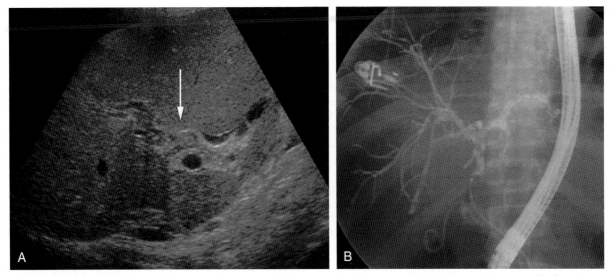

Figure 94-22. Biliary cast syndrome. A. Ultrasound shows a nonshadowing echogenic cast within the biliary tree (*arrow*). The hepatic artery was patent. **B.** Endoscopic retrograde cholangiopancreatography (ERCP) shows abundant debris within biliary system.

recurrence may occur within the liver, in porta hepatis lymph nodes, or within the bile ducts. Most biliary recurrences occur at the anastomosis, but some patients have malignant intrahepatic biliary strictures. Brush biopsy of the stricture can confirm recurrent malignancy.

On occasion, biliary obstruction may be caused by an occluded or malpositioned T-tube or internal stent.[153] Rarely, biliary obstruction may result from an allograft cystic duct mucocele that becomes distended with mucus and impinges on the common hepatic duct, biliary calculi, and common duct redundancy with kinking.[152,153]

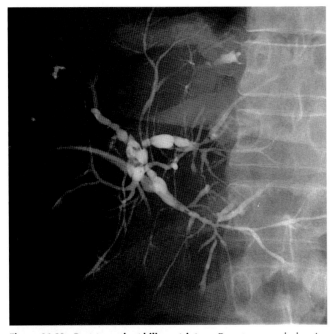

Figure 94-23. Post-transplant biliary stricture. Percutaneous cholangiogram demonstrates multiple intrahepatic biliary strictures 2 years after liver transplantation. The hepatic artery was patent in this patient with a history primary sclerosing cholangitis.

REJECTION

Rejection is a common cause of allograft dysfunction after transplantation. Hepatic allograft rejection can be classified histopathologically as either acute cellular rejection or chronic ductopenic rejection. The incidence of acute cellular rejection is variable but has been reported to occur in 50% to 100% of patients.[172] Acute cellular rejection can occur at any time but usually occurs during the first 3 weeks after OLT. Acute cellular rejection that occurs later after transplantation is usually associated with a decrease or discontinuation of maintenance immunosuppressive therapy.[172] In most cases, acute cellular rejection responds to additional immunosuppressive therapy. Chronic ductopenic rejection (vanishing bile duct syndrome) has a reported incidence of 2% to 17% in liver transplant recipients and is a major cause of late allograft failure that frequently requires retransplantation.[172] The incidence of late graft failure related to chronic ductopenic rejection appears to be decreasing, because of improved immunosuppression.[8] An increased incidence of ductopenic rejection has been reported in patients undergoing liver transplantation for PSC.[160] Most commonly, chronic ductopenic rejection occurs 6 weeks to 6 months after transplantation but it can occur at any time after OLT. It often develops after one or more episodes of acute cellular rejection that fail to respond to immunosuppressive therapy.[160] Ductopenic rejection produces a spectrum of abnormalities that range from mild loss of bile ducts and mild cholestasis, which is potentially reversible, to a severe form in which most interlobular and septal bile ducts are lost resulting in severe cholestasis that is unresponsive to therapy.[172] Severe ductopenic rejection is often associated with an arteriopathy of medium-sized hepatic artery branches.[172] In most cases, ductopenic rejection results in irreversible graft failure, and retransplantation is necessary.[160]

Biochemical and clinical markers poorly correlate with histological features of rejection.[172] Clinical findings are nonspecific and can overlap those of other conditions causing graft dysfunction. Furthermore, liver transplant rejection cannot be reliably detected with imaging techniques because the imaging findings in allograft rejection are neither sensitive nor specific. Consequently, the diagnosis of acute cellular or chronic ductopenic rejection is based on histological evaluation of liver biopsy specimens.[163,172] Because imaging is useful for the detection of vascular, biliary, and infectious complications that may clinically mimic rejection, imaging tests are frequently used for the initial evaluation of patients with graft dysfunction.

There are no specific radiologic features that affect the bile ducts or intrahepatic arteries in patients with acute rejection. Cholangiography may show variable degrees of poor filling, narrowing, or stretching of the bile ducts.[173] Similarly, arteriography may show varying degrees of narrowing, stretching, or slow flow in intrahepatic arteries.[174] Loss of hepatic artery diastolic flow is neither a specific or sensitive finding of allograft rejection.[111,113,114] Several authors have suggested that progressive dampening of hepatic venous phasicity may correlate with rejection.[175,176] The lack of specificity of this finding limits its clinical relevance, however.[177,178] A recent preliminary study has suggested that decreases in portal venous velocities and the splenic pulsatility index may be an accurate noninvasive marker of rejection, although the reproducibility of this Doppler technique has not been addressed in large-scale studies.[179]

POST-TRANSPLANT MALIGNANCY

Solid organ transplant recipients have a 100-fold increased risk for developing a malignancy as a result of immunosuppressive therapy.[180] Approximately 4% to 5% of OLT recipients develop malignant tumors; most of these are lymphomas or skin cancers.[181,182]

Development of post-transplantation lymphoma is related to an interaction of Epstein-Barr virus infection and a weakened immune system. Most patients who develop lymphoma are infected with the Epstein-Barr virus.[183] Epstein-Barr virus is thought to induce a diffuse polyclonal B-lymphocyte proliferation. Because T-cell function and other regulatory immunologic functions are suppressed, this diffuse B-cell proliferation proceeds unchecked and results in a spectrum of disease ranging from benign polyclonal lymphadenopathy to malignant monoclonal lymphoma.[183] This spectrum of disease, occurring in transplant recipients, is called *post-transplantation lymphoproliferative disorder* (PTLD). Most lymphomas are B-cell non-Hodgkin's type, but Hodgkin's, Burkitt's, and T-cell lymphomas also occur.[183]

PTLD develops in approximately 2.2% of liver transplant recipients.[183] PTLD may occur with a variety of immunosuppressive agents, but the incidence of PTLD is increased when agents are used in combination; this increased incidence is most likely related to the greater intensity of immunosuppression. In the early 1980s, most liver transplant recipients received cyclosporine as part of their postoperative immunosuppressive therapy. Tacrolimus has largely replaced cyclosporine as primary immunosuppressive therapy to prevent rejection. Tacrolimus has been found to improve patient and graft survival and reduce the incidence of rejection and is associated with a reduced frequency of infectious complications.[12,15] Furthermore, the incidence of PTLD occurring with use of tacrolimus (2.3%) is comparable to that of cyclosporine.[184] Although too few patients treated with tacrolimus have developed PTLD to allow radiologic evaluation, clinical and histopathologic features are similar to patients treated with cyclosporine.

Lymphomas in cyclosporine or tacrolimus-treated patients are characterized by their early appearance after transplantation (4-6 months), widespread involvement at presentation, and rare involvement of the central nervous system.[185-189] Without cyclosporine therapy, lymphomas occur later (48 months) and often involve the central nervous system.[186] PTLD may involve virtually any body tissue. Although nodal involvement is common, extranodal disease is significantly more frequent relative to the general population. The most common sites of involvement in patients treated with cyclosporine are lymph nodes, tonsils, gastrointestinal tract, liver, and thorax.[186]

Enteric involvement is particularly noteworthy. In the gastrointestinal tract, PTLD has a propensity for involvement in the distal small bowel and proximal colon.[186,188] Enteric lesions may have a similar appearance to those occurring in the general population but have an increased incidence of ulceration and spontaneous perforation.[186] PTLD and lymphoma involving the liver and other abdominal organs have a radiologic appearance that is similar to the general population.[187,188] Typically, solid organ disease appears as focal hypoechoic masses on sonography or low-attenuation masses on CT. Involvement of the porta hepatis and retroperitoneum are other common sites for PTLD.[188] CT/PET is a useful imaging examination for the detection of multifocal disease and for assessing responses to therapy (Fig. 94-24).

Lymphoma arising in the transplant patient is unique because if detected early and treated by a reduction in the patient's immunosuppressive agents, most cases completely resolve.[190,191] Antiviral agents, such as acyclovir or gancyclovir, are typically used in conjunction with reduced immunosuppression. A reduction in immunosuppressive therapy allows partial restitution of the immune system to combat the PTLD, and antiviral therapy is targeted at the Epstein-Barr virus infection. Large tumor masses may require surgical resection or debulking.[181] Some patients with advanced lymphoma may require systemic chemotherapy. Patients that require systemic chemotherapy have a poor prognosis and often succumb as a result of infectious complications.[190,191]

A variety of other neoplasms have been reported to occur with increased frequency after transplantation. Skin malignancies are the most common de novo tumors to develop after liver transplantation with most being either basal cell or squamous cell carcinomas.[180,182] In patients with inflammatory bowel disease and PSC, there is an increased risk for development of colorectal neoplasms, usually within a year after liver transplantation.[192] Other tumors reported to have an increased risk of development include Kaposi's sarcoma, cervical cancer, and breast cancer.[180,182]

Recurrence of primary malignant tumors is well known in those undergoing hepatic transplantation as an oncologic procedure and is accentuated because of the necessary immunosuppressive therapy. Patients with cholangiocarcinoma do poorly after liver transplantation because the tumor recurs at a high rate, usually within 2 years.[65,68] For this reason, liver transplantation for a patient with a known cholangiocarcinoma is a relative contraindication for OLT at many centers.[45,67] Patients undergoing liver transplantation for HCC are at risk for recurrence related to initial tumor stage. As mentioned, poor prognostic indicators for recurrent HCC include vascular

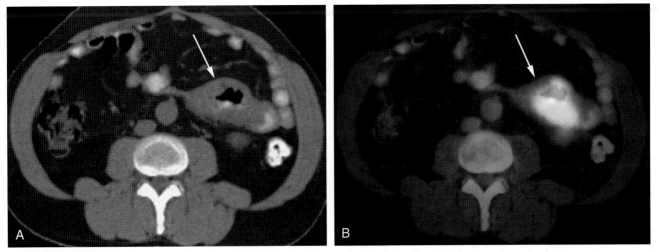

Figure 94-24. Monomorphic post-transplant lymphoproliferative disease. A. CT shows focal thickening of proximal jejunum 3 years post-transplantation (*arrow*). The patient presented with melena. **B.** CT/PET shows that the segment is markedly FDG avid (*arrow*).

invasion, spread to extrahepatic lymph nodes, bilobar tumor, and size greater than 3 cm.[19,21,44-48] Patients undergoing liver transplantation with an incidentally detected HCC found at sectioning of the explant have a low incidence of recurrence. In patients undergoing liver transplantation for HCC, recurrent tumor most commonly involves the lungs, allograft, local and distant lymph nodes, adrenal gland, and bone.[193] Recurrence of HCC involves multiple sites in approximately half of patients after transplantation. An overall 5-year survival of 42% has been reported for patients undergoing OLT for HCC.[194] Furthermore, patients transplanted for HCC who were infected with hepatitis B did poorly, with most deaths resulting from recurrent hepatitis B. Those not infected with hepatitis B had a 68% 5-year survival.[194]

FLUID COLLECTIONS

Abdominal fluid collections are frequent after liver transplantation and may be hematomas, seromas, or bilomas. These can be easily detected by CT or sonography. Small seromas are often seen on routine sonograms in the first week after OLT. These collections are perihepatic, are typically anechoic, and usually resolve spontaneously.

Hematomas usually result from operative blood loss, which is aggravated by the accompanying coagulopathy associated with end-stage liver disease. Rarely, rupture of an arterial pseudoaneurysm may cause a large perihepatic hematoma. Hematomas usually are perihepatic. The imaging appearance of hematomas reflects their gradual evolution over time. On CT, acute hematomas have areas of increased attenuation that decrease in attenuation over days to weeks. On sonography, hematomas may have a variable appearance, depending on the time at which they are imaged. The appearance may range from a predominantly complex echogenic collection to a partially echogenic collection with cystic areas.

Bilomas usually result from bile leaks and are typically located in subhepatic or perihepatic spaces.[149] Large bile leaks can result in bilious ascites. With sonography, bilomas are relatively anechoic and are difficult to distinguish from seromas.

Similarly, bilomas are of fluid attenuation on CT scans. If a bile leak is suspected, cholangiography should be performed. Mangofodipir enhanced MRI may also show large postoperative biliary leaks.[155,156] In addition, as with any biliary abnormality, patency of the hepatic artery should be determined with Doppler sonography.

Any fluid collection in the transplant recipient can become infected. As mentioned, bilomas are especially likely to become infected in an immunocompromised patient. Hematomas and areas of infarcted hepatic parenchyma can also become infected. Imaging findings often cannot differentiate infected from noninfected fluid collections. Consequently, percutaneous aspiration is necessary. If infected, image-guided percutaneous drainage is usually curative. For bile leaks, both the bile leak and the infected biloma must be treated.[154,157] The infected biloma can be treated with percutaneous drainage. Cholangiography, either through the T-tube or endoscopically, can identify the site of the bile leak. Endoscopy may be advantageous, because either a sphincterotomy and/ or placement of an internal biliary stent can be performed in the same setting.[195] Infected hematomas are difficult to treat percutaneously because of the large clots may occlude the drainage catheter. Use of large-bore catheters, frequent irrigation, and urokinase may be necessary for these collections.[196] Surgical evacuation is often necessary, however. Drainage of infected hepatic parenchyma is difficult and is usually a temporizing measure until retransplantation is feasible.[197-200]

SUMMARY

Liver transplantation has become the standard treatment for many patients with end-stage liver disease. Long-term patient and graft survival has continued to improve as a result of improved surgical techniques and improved immunosuppressive therapy.[201] Radiologic imaging has an important role in proper patient selection and providing information that may alter the surgical technique. Most importantly, early radiologic recognition and treatment of postoperative complications is necessary to lower postoperative morbidity and mortality.

References

1. McDiarmid SV, Goodrich NP, Harper AM, et al: Liver transplantation for status 1. Liver Transpl 13:699-707, 2007.
2. Shaw B, Martin D, Marquez J, et al: Venous bypass in clinical liver transplantation. Ann Surg 200:524-534, 1984.
3. Clavien PA, Petronsky H, DeOliveira ML, et al: Strategies for safer liver surgery and partial liver transplantation. N Engl J Med 356:1545-1559, 2007.
4. Jovine E, Mazziotti A, Grazi G, et al: Piggy-back versus conventional technique in liver transplantation: report of a randomized trial. Transpl Int 10:109-112, 1997.
5. Lerut J, Molle G, Donataccio M: Cavocaval liver transplantation without venovenous bypass and with temporary portocaval shunting: the ideal technique for adult liver grafting. Transpl Int 10:171-179, 1997.
6. Stieber A, Marsh J, Starzl T: Preservation of the retrohepatic vena cava during recipient hepatectomy for orthotopic transplantation of the liver. Surg Gynecol Obstet 168:543-545, 1989.
7. Said A, Einstein M, Lucey MR: Liver transplantation: An update 2007. Curr Opin Gastroenterol 23:292-298, 2007.
8. Abu-Elmagd K, Bronsther O, Jain A, et al: Recent advances in hepatic transplantation at the University of Pittsburgh. In Terasaki PI, Cecka IM (eds): Clinical Transplants. Los Angeles, UCLA Tissue Typing Laboratory, 1993, pp 137-152.
9. Abu-Elmagd K, Todo S, Fung J, et al: Hepatic transplantation at the University of Pittsburgh: New horizons and paradigms after 30 years experience. In Terasaki PI, Cecka IM (eds): Clinical Transplants, 1995. Los Angeles: UCLA Tissue Typing Laboratory, 1994, pp 133-156.
10. Bismuth H: Comparison of FK 5067- and cyclosporine-based immuno-suppression: FK 506 therapy significantly reduces the incidence of acute, steroid-resistant, refractory, and chronic rejection whilst possessing a comparable safety profile. Transplant Proc 21:45-49, 1995.
11. Cai T, Esterl R, Nichols L, et al: Improved immunosuppression with combination tacrolimus (FK506) and mycophenolic acid in orthotopic liver transplantation. Transplant Proc 30:1413-1414, 1998.
12. Fung J, Eliasziw M, Todo S, et al: The Pittsburgh randomized tiral of tacrolimus compared to cyclosporine for hepatic transplantation. J Am Coll Surg 183:117-125, 1996.
13. Jain A, Reyes J, Kashyap R, et al: Long-term survival after liver transplantation in 4,000 consecutive patients at a single center. Ann Surg 23:490-500, 2000.
14. Rudich S, Riegler J, Perez R, et al: Immunosuppression using tacrolimus, mycophenolate, and prednisone following orthotopic liver transplantation: A single-center experience. Transplant Proc 30:1417-1418, 1998.
15. Todo S, Fung J, Starzl T, et al: Single-center experience with primary orthotopic liver transplantation with FK 506 immunosuppression. Ann Surg 220:297-309, 1994.
16. UNOS Corporate Annual Report. In: United Network for Organ Sharing: Organ Donation and Transplantation, 2004.
17. Belle S, Beringer K, Defre K: Recent findings concerning liver transplantation in the United States. In Tersasaki PI, Cecka IM (eds): Clinical Transplants. Los Angeles. UCLA Tissue Typing Laboratory, 1996, pp 15-26.
18. Brown K, Moonka D: Liver transplantation. Gastroenterology 20:264-269, 2004.
19. Llovet J, Schwartz M, Mazzaferro V: Resection and liver transplantation for hepatocellular carcinoma. Semin Liver Dis 25:181-200, 2005.
20. Schulak J: What's new in general surgery: Transplantation. J Am Coll Surg 200:409-417, 2005.
21. Schwartz M: Liver transplantation for hepatocellular carcinoma. Gastroenterology 127(5 Suppl 1):S268-S276, 2004.
22. Crossin JD, Muradali D, Wilson S: US of liver transplants: Normal and abnormal. RadioGraphics 23:1093-1114, 2003.
23. Grant E, Schiller V, Millener P, et al: Color Doppler imaging of the hepatic vasculature. AJR 159:943-950, 1992.
24. Longley D, Skolnick M, Zajko A: Duplex Doppler sonography in the evaluation of adult patients before and after liver transplantation. AJR 151:687-696, 1988.
25. Ralls P: Color Doppler sonography of the hepatic artery and portal venous system. AJR 155:517-525, 1990.
26. Stieber A, Zetti G, Todo S: The spectrum of portal vein thrombosis in liver transplantation. Ann Surg 2:199-206, 1991.
27. Freeny P, Baron R, Teefey S: Hepatocellular carcinoma: Reduced frequency of typical findings with dynamic contrast-enhanced CT in a non-Asian population. Radiology 182:143-148, 1992.
28. Dodd GI 3rd, Memel D, Baron R, et al: Portal vein thrombosis in patients with cirrhosis: Does sonographic detection of intrathrombus flow allow differentiation of benign and malignant thrombus? AJR 165:573-577, 1995.
29. Tanaka K, Numata K, Okazaki H, et al: Diagnosis of portal vein thrombosis in patients with hepatocellular carcinoma: Efficacy of color Doppler sonography compared with angiography. AJR 160:1279-1283, 1993.
30. Millener P, Grant E, Rose S, et al: Color Doppler imaging findings in patients with Budd-Chiari syndrome: Correlation with venographic findings. AJR 161:307-312, 1993.
31. Ralls P, Johnson M, Radin D, et al: Budd-Chiari syndrome: Detection with color Doppler sonography. AJR 159:113-116, 1992.
32. Dodd G, Miller W, Baron R, et al: Detection of malignant tumors in end-stage cirrhotic livers: Efficacy of sonography as a screening technique. AJR 159:727-733, 1992.
33. Miller W, Federle M, Campbell W: Diagnosis and staging of hepatocellular carcinoma: Comparison of CT and sonography in 36 liver transplantation patients. AJR 157:303-306, 1991.
34. Teefey T, Hildeboldt C, Dehdashti F, et al: Detection of primary hepatic malignancy in liver transplant candidates: Prospective comparison of CT, MR imaging, US, and PET. Radiology 226:533-542, 2003.
35. Caturelli E, Pompili M, Bartolucci F, et al: Hemangioma-like lesions in chronic liver disease: Diagnositic evaluation in patients. Radiology 220:337-342, 2001.
36. Abecassis J, Paricente D, Hazebroucq V: Subscapular hepatic necrosis in liver transplantation: CT appearance. AJR 156:981-983, 1991.
37. Henderson J, Heymsfield S, Horowitz J, et al: Measurement of liver and spleen volume by computed tomograph. Radiology 141:525-527, 1981.
38. Hermoye L, Laamari-Azal I, Cao Z, et al: Liver segmentation in living liver transplant donors: Comparison of semiautomatic and manual methods. Radiology 234:171-178, 2005.
39. Kamel I, Kruskal J, Warmbrand G: Accuracy of volumetric measurements after virtual right hepatectomy in potential donors undergoing living adult liver transplantation. AJR 176:483-487, 2001.
40. Stapakis J, Stamm E, Townsend R, Thickmas D: Liver volume assessment by conventional vs. helical CT. Abdom Imaging 20:209-210
41. Tublin M, Dodd GI, Baron R: Benign and malignant, 1995, portal vein thrombosis: Differentiation by CT characteristics. AJR 168:719-723, 1997.
42. Winter T, Freeny P, Nghiem H, et al: Hepatic arterial anatomy in transplantation candidates: Evaluation with three-dimensional CT arteriography. Radiology 195:363-370, 1995.
43. Baron R, Oliver J, Dodd G, et al: Hepatocellular carcinoma: Evaluation with biphasic, contrast-enhanced, helical CT. Radiology 199:505-511, 1996.
44. Iwatsuki S, Dvorchik I, Marsh J: Liver transplantation for hepatocellular carcinoma: A proposal of a prognostic scoring system. J Am Coll Surg 191:389-394, 2000.
45. Iwatsuki S, Starzl T, Sheahan D, et al: Hepatic resection versus transplantation for hepatocellular carcinoma. Ann Surg 214:221-229, 1991.
46. Shirabi K, Kanematsu T, Matsumata T, et al: Factors linked to early recurrence of small hepatocellular carcinoma after hepatectomy: Univariate and multivariate analyses. Hepatology 14:802-805, 1991.
47. Fung J, Marsh W: The quandary over liver transplantation for hepatocellular carcinoma: The greater sin? Liver Transpl 8:775-777, 2002.
48. Kirimlioglu H, Dvorchick I, Ruppert K: Hepatocellular carcinomas in native livers from patients treated with orthotopic liver transplantation: Biologic and therapeutic implications. Hepatology 34:502-510, 2001.
49. Abu-Elmagd K, Shelby R, Iwatsuki S, et al: Cholangiocarcinoma and sclerosing cholangitis: Clinical characteristics and effect on survival after liver transplantation. Transplant Proc 25:1124-1125, 1993.
50. MacCarty R, Larusso N, May G, et al: Cholangiocarcinoma complicating primary sclerosing cholangitis: Cholangiographic appearances. Radiology 156:43-46, 1985.
51. Campbell W, Ferris J, Holbert B, et al: Biliary tract carcinoma complicating primary sclerosing cholangitis: Evaluation with CT, cholangiography, US and MR imaging. Radiology 207:41-50, 1998.
52. Lacomis J, Baron R, Oliver JI, et al: Cholangiocarcinoma: Delayed CT contrast enhancement patterns. Radiology 203:98-104, 1997.
53. Finn J, Edelman R, Jenkins R, et al: Liver transplantation: MR angiography with surgical validation. Radiology 179:265-269, 1991.
54. Naik K, Ward J, Irving H: Comparison of dynamic contrast enhanced MRI and Doppler ultrasound in the pre-operative assessment of the portal venous system. Br J Radiol 70:43-49, 1997.
55. Nghiem H, Winter T, Mountford M: Evaluation of the portal venous system before liver transplantation: Value of phase-contrast MR angiography. AJR 164:871-878, 1995.

56. Rodgers P, Ward J, Baudouin C: Dynamic contrast-enhanced MR imaging of the portal venous system: Comparison with x-ray angiography. Radiology 191:741-745, 1994.

57. Yamashita Y, Mitsuzaki K, Yi T: Small hepatocellular carcinoma in patients with chronic liver damage: Prospective comparison of detection with dynamic MR imaging and helical CT of the whole liver. Radiology 200:79-84, 1996.

58. Scharitzer M, Schima W, Schober E, et al: Characterization of hepatocellular tumors: Value of mangofodipir-enhanced magnetic resonance imaging. J Comput Assist Tomogr 29:181-190, 2005.

59. Youk J, Lee J, Kim C: MRI for detection of hepatocellular carcinoma: Comparison of mangofodipir trisodium and gadopentatate dimeglumine contrast agents. AJR 183:1049-1054, 2004.

60. Kim H, Kim T, Sung K, et al: CT during hepatic arteriography and portography: An illustrative review. RadioGraphics 22:1041-1051, 2002.

61. Oliver J, Baron R, Dodd GI: Efficacy of CT portography in the evaluation of chirrhotic patients for hepatocellular carcinoma. Radiology 181:167-168, 1991.

62. Redvanly R, Chezmar J: CT arterial portography: Technique, indications, and applications. Clin Radiol 52:256-268, 1997.

63. Matsui O, Kadoya MM, Kameyama T: Benign and malignant nodules in cirrhotic livers: Distinction based on blood supply. Radiology 178:493-497, 1991.

64. Marsh J, Iwatsuki S, Makowka L: Orthotopic liver transplantation for primary sclerosing cholangitis. Ann Surg 207:21-25, 1987.

65. Herbener T, Zajko A, Koneru B: Recurrent choangiocarcinoma in the biliary tree after liver transplantation. Radiology 169:641-642, 1988.

66. Nichols D, MacCarty R, Gaffey T: Cholangiographic evaluation of bile duct carcinoma. AJR 141:1291-1204, 1983.

67. Levy M, Goldstein R, Husburg B: Baylor update: Outcome analysis in liver transplantation. In Terasaki PI, Cecka IM (eds): Clinical Transplants. Los Angeles, UCLA Tissue Typing Laboratory, 1993, pp 161-173.

68. Stieber A, Marino I, Iwatsuki S: Cholangiocarcinoma in sclerosing cholangitis: The role of liver transplantation. Int Surg 74:1-3, 1989.

69. Makowa L, Stieber A, Sher L: Surgical technique of orthotopic liver transplantation. Gastroenterol Clin North Am 17:33-51, 1988.

70. Shaw B, Iwatsuki S, Starzl T: Alternative methods of arterization of the hepatic graft. Surg Gynecol Obstet 159:491-493, 1984.

71. Todo S, Makowa L, Tzakis A, et al: Hepatic artery in liver transplantation. Transpl Int 19:2406-2411, 1987.

72. Brancatelli G, Federle M, Pealer K, Geller D: Portal venous thrombosis or sclerosis in liver transplantation candidates: Preoperative CT findings and correlation with surgical procedures. Radiology 220:331-338, 2001.

73. Rouch D, Emond J, Thistlewaite JJ: Choledochocholedochostomy without a T-tube or internal stent in transplantation of the liver. Surg Gynecol Obstet 170:239-244, 1990.

74. Lerut J, Tzakis A, Bron K: Complications of venous reconstruction in human orthotopic liver transplantation. Ann Surg 205:404-414, 1987.

75. Broelsch C, Emond J, Whitington P: Application of reduced-size liver transplants as split grafts, auxillary orthotopic grafts, and liver related segmental transplants. Ann Surg 212:368-377, 1990.

76. Millis J, Alonso E, Piper J: Liver transplantation at the University of Chicago. In Terasaki PI, Cecka IM (eds): Clinical Transplants, 1995. Los Angeles, UCLA Tissue Typing Laboratory, 1995, pp 187-197.

77. Hoofnagle J, Carithers R, Shapiro C: Fulminant hepatic failure: Summary of a workshop. Hepatology 21:240-252, 1995.

78. Jauregui H: The technology of biological extracorporeal liver assist devices: From infancy to adolescence. Artif Organ 173:1163-1168, 1997.

79. Kerr A, Rajvanshi P, Gupta S: Percutaneous transcatheter liver cell transplantation: An emerginc modality and its clinical implications. J Vasc Interv Radiol 7:169-176, 1996.

80. Strom S, Fisher R, Thompson M: Hepatocyte transplantation as a bridge to orthotopic liver transplantation in terminal liver failure. Transplantation 63:559-569, 1997.

81. Broelsch C, Edmond J, Heffron T, et al: Liver transplantation in children from living related donors: Surgical techniques and results. Ann Surg 214:428-437, 1991.

82. Gruttadauria A, Marsh JW, Cintorino D, et al: Adult to adult living-related liver transplant. Dig Liver Dis 39:342-350, 2007.

83. Yamaoka Y, Washida M, Honda H, et al: Liver transplanation using a right lobe graft from a living related donor. Transplantation 57:1127-1130, 1994.

84. Wachs M, Bak T, Karrer F, et al: Adult living donor liver transplantation using a right hepatic lobe. Transplantation 66:1313-1316, 1998.

85. Sugawara Y, Makuuchi M, Imamura H, et al: Living donor liver transplantation in adults: Recent advances and results. Surgery 132:348-352, 2002.

86. Broering D, Sterneck M, Rogiers X: Living donor liver transplantation. J Hepatol 38:S119-135, 2003.

87. Heneghan M, Sylvestre P: Cholestatic diseases of liver transplantation. Semin Gastrointest Dis 12:133-147, 2001.

88. Sahani D, D'souza R, Kadaviegere R: Evaluation of living liver transplantation donors: Method for precise anatomic definition by using a dedicated contrast-enhanced MR imaging protocol. RadioGraphics 24:957-967, 2004.

89. Sahani D, Mehta A, Blake M: Preoperative hepatic vascular evaluation with CT and MR angiography: Implications for surgery. RadioGraphics 24:1367-1380, 2004.

90. Fulcher A, Szucs R, Bassignani M, Marcos A: Right lobe living donor liver transplantation: Peroperative evaluation of the donor with MR imaging. AJR 176, 2001.

91. Kapoor V, Peterson M, Baron R, et al: Intrahepatic biliary anatomy of living adult liver donors: Correlation of mangafodipir trisodium-enhanced MR cholangiography and intraoperative cholangiography. AJR 179:1281-1286, 2002.

92. Lee V, Krinsky G, Nazzaro C: Defining intrahepatic biliary anatomy in living liver transplant donor candidates at mangafodipir trisodium-enhanced MR cholangiography versus conventional T2-weighted MR Cholangiography. Radiology 233:659-666, 2004.

93. Lee V, Morgan G, Teperman L: MR imaging as the sole preoperative imaging modality for right hepatectomy: A prospective study of living adult-to-adult liver donor candidates. AJR 176:1475-1482, 2001.

94. Yeh B, Breiman R, Taouli B, et al: Biliary tract depiction in living potential liver donors: Comparison of conventional MR, mangafodipir trisodium-enhanced excretory MR, and multi-detector row CT cholangiography—initial experience. Radiology 230:645-651, 2004.

95. Goyen M, Barkhausen J, Debatin J, et al: Right-lobe living related liver transplantation: Evaluation of a comprehensive magnetic resonance imaging protocol for assessing potential donors. Liver Transpl 8: 241-250, 2002.

96. Erbay N, Raptopoulos V, Pomfret E: Living donor transplantation in adults: Vascular variants important in surgical planning for donors and recipients. AJR 181:109-114, 2003.

97. Guiney M, Kruskal J, Sosna J, et al: Multi-detector row CT of relevant vascular anatomy of the surgical plane in split-liver transplantation. Radiology 229:401-407, 2003.

98. Kamel I, Kruskal J, Pomfret E: Impact of multidetector CT on donor selection and surgical planning before living adult right lobe transplantation. AJR 176:193-200, 2001.

99. Lee S, Kim T, Byun J: Hepatic arteries in potential donors for living related liver transplantation: Evaluation with multi-detector row CT angiography. Radiology 227:391-399, 2003.

100. Onodera Y, Omatsu T, Nakayama J: Peripheral anatomic evaluation using 3D CT hepatic venography in donors: Significance of peripheral venous visualization in living-donor liver transplantation. AJR 193: 1065-1070, 2004.

101. Schroeder T, Nadalin S, Stattaus J: Potential living liver donors: Evaluation with an all-in-one protocol with multi-detector row CT. Radiology 224:586-591, 2002.

102. Ben-Haim M, Emre S, Fishbein T, et al: Critical graft size in adult-to-adult living donor liver transplantation: Impact of the recipient's disease. Liver Transpl 7, 2001.

103. Edmond J, Renz J, Ferrel L, et al: Functional analysis of grafts from living donors: Implications for the treatment of older recipients Ann Surg 224:544-552, 1996.

104. Suguwara Y, Makuuchi M, Takayama T, et al: Small-for-size grafts in living-related liver transplantation. J Am Coll Surg 192, 2001.

105. Hayashi M, Fujii K, Kiuchi T, et al: Effects of fatty infiltration of the graft on the outcome of living-related transplantation. Transplant Proc 31:403, 1999.

106. Marcos A, Fisher R, Ham J, et al: Selection and outcome of living donors for adult to adult right lobe transplantation. Transplantation 69: 2410-2415, 2000.

107. Selzner M, Clavien P: Fatty liver in liver transplanation and surgery. Semin Liver Dis 21:105-113, 2001.

108. Limanond P, Raman S, Lassman J: Macrovesicular hepatic steatosis in living related liver donors: Correlation between CT and histologic findings. Radiology 230:276-280, 2004.

109. Tuttle-Newhall J, Collins B, Desai D: The current status of living donor liver transplantation. Curr Probl Surg 42:144-183, 2004.

110. Kim B, Kim T, Kim J: Hepatic venous congestion after living donor liver transplantation with right lobe graft: two-phase CT findings. Radiology 232:173-180, 2004.

111. Garcia-Criado A, Gilabert R, Salmeron J: Significance of and contributing factors for a high resistive index on Doppler sonography of the hepatic artery immediately after surgery: Prognostic implications for liver transplant recipients. AJR 181:831-838, 2003.

112. Kok T, Haagsma E, Klompmaker I: Doppler ultrasound of the hepatic artery and vein performed daily in the first 2 weeks after orthotopic liver transplantation: Useful for the diagnosis of acute rejection? Invest Radiol 31:173-179, 1996.

113. Longley D, Skolnick M, Sheahan D: Acute allograft rejection in liver transplant recipients: Lack of correlation with loss of hepatic artery diastolic flow. Radiology 169:417-420, 1988.

114. Marder D, DeMarino G, Sumkin J, Sheadhan D: Liver transplant rejection: Value of the resistive index in Doppler US of hepatic arteries. Radiology 173:127-129, 1989.

115. Lautt W, Greenway C: Conceptual review of the hepatic vacular bed. Hepatology 7:952-963, 1987.

116. Chezmar J, Nelson R, Bernardino M: Portal venous gas after hepatic transplantation: Sonographic detection and clinical significance. AJR 153:1203-1205, 1989.

117. Letourneau J, Day D, Maile C: Liver allograft transplantation: Post-operative CT findings. AJR 148:1099-1103, 1987.

118. Dupuy D, Costello P, Lewis D: Abdominal CT findings after liver transplantation in 66 patients. AJR 156:1167-1170, 1991.

119. Wechsler R, Munoz S, Needleman L: The periportal collar: A CT sign of liver transplant rejection. Radiology 165:57-60, 1987.

120. Kaplan S, Sumkin J, Campbell W: Periportal low-attenuation areas on CT: Value as evidence of liver transplant rejection. AJR 152:285-287, 1989.

121. Marincek B, Barbier P, Becker C: CT appearance of impaired lymphatic drainage in liver transplant. AJR 147:519-523, 1986.

122. Campbell W, Foster R, Miller W: Changes in extrahepatic bile duct caliber in liver transplant recipients without evidence of biliary obstructions. AJR 158:997-1000, 1992.

123. Charlton M, Wiesner R: Natural history and management of hepatitis C infection after liver transplantation. Semin Liver Dis 24:79-88, 2004.

124. Langnas A, Marujo W, Stratta R: Vascular complications after orthotopic liver transplantation. Am J Surg 161:76-82, 1991.

125. Katyal S JO III, Buck D, Federle M: Detection of vascular complications after liver transplantation: Early experience in multislice CT angiography with volume rendering. AJR 175:1735-1739, 2000.

126. Quiroga S, Sebastia C, Margarit C, et al: Complications of orthotopic liver transplantation: Spectrum of findings with helical CT. RadioGraphics 21:1085-1102, 2001.

127. Tzakis A, Gordon R, Shaw B: Clinical presentation of hepatic artery thrombosis after liver transplantation in the cyclosporine era. Transplantation 40:667-671, 1985.

128. Langnas A, Marujo W, Stratta R: Hepatic allograft rescue following arterial thrombosis. Role of urgent revascularization. Transplantation 51:86-90, 1991.

129. Flint E, Sumkin J, Zajko A: Duplex sonography of hepatic artery thrombosis after liver transplantation. AJR 151:481-483, 1988.

130. Dodd GI, Memel D, Zajko A: Hepatic artery stenosis and thrombosis in transplant recipients: Doppler diagnosis with resistive index and systolic acceleration time. Radiology 192:657-661, 1994.

131. Dodd GI: Sonographic diagnosis of vascular complications of hepatic and renal transplantation. In American Roentgen Ray Society Ultrasound Categorical Course Syllabus. San Francisco, ARRS, 1993.

132. Platt J, Yutzy G, Bude R, et al: Use of Doppler sonography for revealing hepatic artery stenosis in liver transplant recipients. AJR 168:473-476, 1997.

133. Vit A, De Candia A, Como G et al: Doppler evaluation of arterial complications of adult orthoptopic liver transplantation. J Clin Ultrasound 31:339-345, 2003.

134. Wozney P, Zajko A, Bron K: Vascular complications after liver transplantation. AJR 147:657-663, 1986.

135. Orons P, Sheng R, Zajko A: Hepatic artery stenosis in liver transplant recipients: Prevalence and cholangiographic appearance of associated biliary complications. AJR 165:1145-1149, 1995.

136. Mondragon R, Karani J, Heaton N: The use of percutaneous transluminal angioplasty in hepatic artery stenosis after transplantation. Transplantation 57:228-231, 1994.

137. Orons P, Zajko A, Bron K: Hepatic artery angioplasty after liver transplantation: Experience in 21 allografts. J Vasc Interv Radiol 6:523-529, 1995.

138. Raby N, Thomas S: Stenosis of vascular anastamoses after hepatic transplantation: Treatment with balloon angioplasty. AJR 157:167-171, 1991.

139. Zajko A, Tobben P, Esquivel C, Starzl T: Pseudoaneurysms following orthotopic liver tranasplantation: Clinical and radiologic manifestations. Transplant Proc 21:2457-2459, 1989.

140. Tobben P, Zajko A, Sumkin J, et al: Pseudoaneurysms complicating organ transplantation: Roles of CT, duplex sonography, and angiography. Radiology 169:65-70, 1988.

141. Haskal Z, Naj A: Treatment of portal vein thrombosis after liver transplantation with percutaneous thrombolysis and stent placement. J Vasc Interv Radiol 4:289-792, 1993.

142. Zajko A, Sheng R, Bron K: Percutaneous transluminal angioplasty of venous anastomotic stenosis complicating liver transplantation: Intermediate-term results. J Vasc Interv Radiol 5:121-126, 1994.

143. Zajko A, Claus D, Clapuyt P: Obstruction to hepatic venous drainage after liver transplantation: Treatment with balloon angioplasty. Radiology 170:763-765, 1989.

144. Berger H, Hilbertz T, Zuhlke K et al: Balloon dilatation and stent placement of suprahepatic caval anastomotic stenosis following liver transplantation. Cardiovasc Intervent Radiol 16:384-387, 1993.

145. Pfammatter T, Williams D, Lane K: Suprahepatic caval anastomotic stenosis complicating orthotopic liver transplantation: Treatment with percutaneous transluminal angioplasty, wallstent placement, or both. AJR 168:477-480, 1997.

146. Greif F, Bronsther O, Van Thiel D: The incidence, timing, and management of biliary tract complications after orthotopic liver transplantation. Ann Surg 219:40-45, 1994.

147. Keogan M, McDermott V, Price S: The role of imaging in the diagnosis and management of biliary complications after liver transplantation. AJR 173:215-219, 1999.

148. Iwatsuki S, Starzl T, Gordon T: Late mortality and morbidity after liver transplantation. Transplant Proc 12:137-143, 1987.

149. Sheng R, Sammon J, Zajko A, Campbell WL: Bile leak after hepatic transplantation: Cholangiographic features, prevalence, and clinical outcome. Radiology 192:413-416, 1994.

150. Zajko A, Campbell W, Logsdon G: Cholangiographic findings in hepatic artery occlusion after liver transplantation. AJR 149:485-489, 1987.

151. Miller W, Campbell W, Zajko A: Obstructive dilatation of extrahepatic recipient and donor bile ducts complicating orthotopic liver transplantation. AJR 157:29-32, 1991.

152. Zajko A, Bennett M, Campbell W: Mucocele of the cystic duct remnant in eight liver transplant recipients: Findings at cholangiography, CT, US. Radiology 177:691-693, 1990.

153. Zajko A, Campbell W, Bron K: Diagnostic and interventional radiology in liver transplantation. Gastroenterol Clin North Am 17:105-143, 1988.

154. Zemel G, Zajko A, Skolnick M: The role of sonography and transhepatic cholangiography in the diagnosis of biliary complications after liver transplantation. AJR 151:943-946, 1988.

155. Bridges M, May G, Harnois D: Diagnosing biliary complications of orthotopic liver transplantation with mangafodipir trisodium-enhanced MR cholangiography: Comparison with conventional MR cholangiography. AJR 182:1497-1504, 2004.

156. Pilleul F, Billaud Y, Gautier G: Mangafodipir-enhanced magnetic resonance cholangiography for the diagnosis of bile duct leaks. Gastrointest Endosc 59:812-822, 2004.

157. Ward E, Wiesner R, Hughes R: Persistent bile leak after liver transplantation: Biloma drainage and endoscopic retrograde cholangiopancreatographic sphincterotomy. Radiology 179:719-720, 1991.

158. Kaplan S, Zajko A, Koneru B: Hepatic bilomas due to hepatic artery thrombosis in liver transplant recipients: Percutaneous drainage and clinical outcome. Radiology 174:1031-1035, 1993.

159. McDonald V, Matabon T, Patel S: Biliary strictures in hepatic transplantation. J Vasc Interv Radiol 2:533-538, 1991.

160. Sheng R, Zajko A, Campbell W: Biliary strictures in hepatic transplants: Prevalence and types in patients with primary sclerosing cholangitis vs those with other liver diseases. AJR 161:297-300, 1993.

161. Zajko A, Sheng R, Getti G. Transhepatic balloon dilatation of biliary strictures in liver transplant patients: A 10-year experience. J Vasc Interv Radiol 6:79-93, 1995.

162. Campbell W, Sheng R, Zajko A: Intrahepatic biliary strictures after liver transplantation. Radiology 191:735-740, 1994.

163. Pretter P, Orons P, Zajko A: The bile duct in liver transplantation. Semin Roentgenol 32:202-214, 1997.

164. Sanchez-Urdazpal L, Gores G, Ward E: Ischemic-type biliary complications after orthotopic liver transplantation. Hepatology 16:49-53, 1992.

165. Sanchez-Urdazpal L, Sterioff S, Janes C: Increased bile duct complications in ABO incompatible liver transplant recipients. Transplant Proc 23:1440-1441, 1991.

166. Ward E, Kiely M, Maus T: Hilar biliary strictures after liver transplantation: Cholangiography and percutaneous treatment. Radiology 177:259-263, 1990.

167. Mosca S, Militerno G, Guardascione M: Late biliary tract complications after orthotopic liver transplantation: Diagnostic and therapeutic role of endoscopic retrograde cholangiopancreatography. J Gastroenterol Hepatol 15:654-660, 2000.

168. Shah J, Haigh W, Lee S: Biliary casts after orthotopic liver transplantation: Clinical factors, treatment, biochemical analysis. Am J Gastrointest 98:1861-1867, 2003.

169. Letourneau J, Day D, Hunter D: Biliary complications after liver transplantation in patients with preexisting sclerosing cholangitis. Radiology 167, 1988.

170. Sheng R, Campbell W, Zajko A: Cholangiographic features of biliary strictures after liver transplantation for primary sclerosing cholangitis: Evidence of recurrent disease. AJR 166:1109-1113, 1996.

171. VanHoek B, Wiesner R, Krom R: Severe ductopenic rejection following liver transplantation: Incidence, time of onsent, risk factors, treatment, and outcome. Semin Liver Dis 12:41-50, 1992.

172. Wiesner R, Ludwig J, Krom R: Hepatic allograft rejection: New developments in terminology, diagnosis, prevention and treatment. Mayo Clin Proc 791:68-69, 1993.

173. Bauman J, Campbell W, Demetris A, et al: Liver transplant rejection: Angiographic findings in 35 patients. AJR 148:1095-1098, 1989.

174. White R, Zajko A, Demetris A, et al: Liver transplant rejection: Angiographic findings in 35 patients. AJR 148:1095-1098, 1987.

175. Coulden R, Britton P, Farman P, et al: Preliminary report: Hepatic vein Doppler in the early diagnosis of acute liver transplant rejection. Lancet 336:273-275, 1990.

176. Harns J, Ringe B, Pichlmayr R: Postoperative liver allograft dysfunction: The use of quantitative duplex Doppler signal analysis in adult liver transplant recipients. Bilgebung 62:124-131, 1995.

177. Jequier S, Jequier J, Hanguinet S, et al: Orthotopic liver transplants in children: Change in hepatic venous Doppler wave pattern as indicator of acute rejection. Radiology 226:105-112, 2003.

178. Zalasin S, Shapiro R, Glajchen N: Liver transplant rejection: Value of hepatic vein waveform analysis. Abdom Imaging 23:427-430, 1998.

179. Bolognesi M, Sacerdoti D, Mescoli C: Acute liver rejection: Accuracy and predictive values of Doppler US measurements: Initial experience. Radiology 235:651-658, 2005.

180. Penn I: Malignancies associated with immunosuppressive or cytotoxic therapy. Surgery 83:492-502, 1978.

181. Stieber A, Boillot O, Scott-Foglieni C: The surgical implications of the posttransplant lymphoproliferative disorders. Transplant Proc 23:1477-1479, 1991.

182. Tan-Shalaby J, Tempero M: Malignancies after liver transplantation: A comparative review. Semin Liver Dis 15:156-164, 1995.

183. Nalesnik M, Jaffe R, Starzl T: The pathology of posttransplant lymphoproliferative disorders occurring in the setting of cyclosporine A-prednisone immunosuppression. Ann J Pathol 133:173-192, 1998.

184. Reyes J, Tzakis A, Green M: Posttransplant lymphoproliferative disorders occurring under primary FK 506 immunosuppression. Transplant Proc 23:3044-3046, 1991.

185. Dodd G, Ledesma-Medina J, Baron R, Fuhrman C: Posttransplant lymphoproliferative disorder: Intrathoracic manifestations. Radiology 184:65-69, 1992.

186. Harris K, Schwartz M, Slasky B: Posttransplantation cyclosporine-induced lymphoproliferative disorders: Clinical and radiologic manifestations. Radiology 162:697-700, 1987.

187. Honda H, Barloon T, Franken E: Clinical and radiologic features of malignant neoplasms in organ transplant recipients: Cyclosporine-treated vs untreated patients. AJR 154:271-274, 1990.

188. Pickhardt P, Siegel M: Posttransplantation lymphoproliferative disorder of the abdomen: CT evaluation in 51 patients. Radiology 213:73-78, 1999.

189. Pickhardt P, Wippold F: Neuroimaging in posttransplantation lymphoproliferative disorder. AJR 172:117-1121, 1999.

190. Nalesnik M, Makowa L, Starzl T: The diagnosis and treatment of posttransplant lymphoproliferatiave disorders. Curr Probl Surg 25:371-472, 1988.

191. Starzl T, Porter K, Iwatsuki S: Reversibility of lymphomas and lymphoproliferative lesions developing under cyclosporin-steroid therapy. Lancet 1:583-587, 1984.

192. Bleday R, Lee E, Jessurun J: Increased risk of early colorectal neoplasms after hepatic transplant in patients with inflammatory bowel disease. Dis Colon Rectum 36:908-912, 1993.

193. Ferris J, Baron R, Marsh J: Recurrent hepatocellular carcinoma after liver transplantation: Spectrum of CT findings and recurrence patterns. Radiology 198:233-238, 1996.

194. Hemming A, Cattral M, Greig P: The University of Toronto liver transplant program. Clinical Transplants. Los Angeles, UCLA Tissue Typing Laboratory, 1996, pp 177-185.

195. Donovan J: Nonsurgical management of biliary tract disease after liver transplantation. Gastroenterol Clin North Am 22:317-336, 1993.

196. Vogelzang R, Tobin R, Burnstein S: Transcatheter intracavitary fibrinolysis of infected extravascular hematomas. AJR 148:378-380, 1987.

197. Colledan M, Paone G, Gridelli B: Interventional radiology of the biliary tree after liver transplantation. Transplant Proc 26:3542-3543, 1994.

198. Patenaude Y, Dubois J, Sinsky A: Liver transplantation: Review of the literature. Part 2: Vascular and biliary complications. Can Assoc Radiol J 48:231-242, 1997.

199. Safadi R, Eid A, Ilan Y: The role of ERCP in biliary complications after liver transplantation. Transplant Proc 31:1897-1898, 1999.

200. Liao JZ, Zhao O, Oin H, et al: Endoscopic diagnosis and treatment of biliary leak in patients following liver transplantation: A prospective clinical comparison. Hepatobiliary Pancreat Dis Int 6:29-33, 2007.

201. Abe K, Kiuchi T, Tanaka K, et al: Predictors of outcome after pediatric liver transplantation: An analysis of more than 800 cases performed at a single institution. J Am Coll Surg 204:904-914, 2007.

Liver: Differential Diagnosis

Richard M. Gore, MD

GENERAL IMAGING ABNORMALITIES

Table 95-1
Diffuse Hepatomegaly

Neoplastic Diseases
Metastases
Hepatoma
Lymphoma

Infectious Diseases
Viral
Hepatitis
Mononucleosis
AIDS

Bacterial
Pyogenic abscess
Tuberculosis, miliary
Histoplasmosis, miliary
Syphilis
Pneumocystis infection

Protozoan
Amebic abscess
Malaria
Leptospirosis
Trypanosomiasis
Kala-azar

Parasitic
Echinococcosis
Schistosomiasis

Fungal
Candidiasis

Degenerative Diseases
Cirrhosis
Fatty infiltration

Elevated Venous Pressure
Congestive heart failure
Constrictive pericarditis
Tricuspid stenosis
Budd-Chiari syndrome

Storage Diseases
Steatosis
Amyloidosis
Hemochromatosis
Gaucher's disease
Glycogen storage disease
Niemann-Pick disease
Histiocytosis
Weber-Christian disease
Wilson's disease
GM_1 gangliosidosis

Myeloproliferative Disorders
Myelofibrosis
Polycythemia rubra vera
Extramedullary hematopoiesis
Myeloid metaplasia
Thalassemia
Sickle cell anemia

Congenital Disorders
Riedel lobe
Polycystic disease
Wolman's disease
Reye's syndrome
Rubella syndrome
Pyruvate kinase deficiency
Osteopetrosis
Lipoatrophic diabetes
Hyperlipoproteinemia
Homocystinuria
Hepatic fibrosis-renal cystic disease
Farber's syndrome
Chédiak-Higashi syndrome
Zellweger's syndrome
Beckwith-Wiedemann syndrome
Granulomatous disease of childhood

Miscellaneous Disorders
Sarcoid
Hematoma
Felty's syndrome

Table 95-2
Hepatomegaly in the Neonate

Nutritional disorder
Heart failure
Infection
Biliary atresia
Metabolic defect
Primary neoplasm
Metastases

Table 95-3
Focal Hepatic Enlargement

Common
Anomalous lobes (Riedel)
Metastasis
Cirrhosis
Regenerating nodules or lobes
Hemangioma
Cysts
Adenoma
Focal nodular hyperplasia
Hepatoma
Lymphoma
Cholangiocarcinoma

Uncommon
Hemangioendothelioma
Actinomycosis
Abscess (fungal or pyogenic)
Biliary cystadenoma
Hamartoma
Hepatoblastoma
Sarcoma
Spindle cell neoplasm
Teratoma
Cholangioma

Table 95-5
Hepatic Capsular Retraction

Adjacent to a Hepatic Tumor
Primary malignant tumors
Hepatocellular carcinoma
Fibrolamellar hepatocellular carcinoma
Intrahepatic cholangiocarcinoma
Epitheliod hemangioendothelioma

Metastatic tumors
Adenocarcinoma of the colon, stomach, breast, lung, pancreas,
  and gallbladder

Postembolization of hepatocelluar carcinoma

Postchemotherapy of malignant tumors

Benign tumor
Hemangioma

Without an Adjacent Hepatic Tumor
Confluent hepatic fibrosis
Oriental cholangiohepatitis
Bile duct necrosis

Pseudoretraction
Accessory fissure
Normal liver parenchyma between the protruded masses

Table 95-4
Liver Atrophy with Compensatory Hypertrophy

Cirrhosis
Hepatic vein obstruction (segmental)
Portal vein obstruction (segmental)
Intrahepatic biliary obstruction (segmental)
Budd-Chiari syndrome
Radiation therapy
After chemotherapy for hepatic tumor
Surgical resection
Liver metastases
Lobar agenesis

Table 95-6
Hepatic Calcification

Infections
Histoplasmosis
Tuberculosis
Coccidioidomycosis
Brucellosis
Gumma
Echinococcal cyst, *Armillifer* infestation
Chronic amebic or pyogenic abscess
Cytomegalovirus or *Toxoplasma* infection
Chronic granulomatous disease of childhood
Clonorchis sinensis infection, cysticercosis, filariasis,
  paragonimiasis

Vascular Lesions
Hepatic artery aneurysm
Portal vein thrombosis
Hematoma

Benign Tumors
Cyst
Cavernous hemangioma
Capsule of regenerating nodules
Infantile hemangioendothelioma

Primary Malignant Tumors
Hepatoma, especially fibrolamellar
Hepatoblastoma
Cholangiocarcinoma

Metastatic Tumors
Mucinous carcinoma of the colon, breast, or stomach
Ovarian carcinoma
Melanoma
Mesothelioma
Osteosarcoma
Carcinoid
Leiomyosarcoma
Teratoma
Thyroid carcinoma
Chondrosarcoma
Neuroblastoma

Biliary Tree
Calculus
Cholangiocarcinoma
Ascariasis

Table 95-7
Neonatal Liver Calcification

Calcified venous thrombi (e.g., after umbilical vein
    catheterization)
Hematoma
Cytomegalovirus infection
Herpesvirus infection
Toxoplasmosis
Abscess
Biliary calcification
Hemangioma
Hamartoma
Hepatoblastoma
Hepatocellular carcinoma
Metastatic neuroblastoma
Ischemic infarct
Rubella

Table 95-8
Portal Venous Gas

Mesenteric infarction
Air intravasation during double contrast barium enema
Acute gastric dilatation
Percutaneous abscess drainage
Necrotizing enterocolitis
Umbilical vein catheterization
Erythroblastosis fetalis
Diverticulitis
Inflammatory bowel disease
Corrosive ingestion
Diabetic coma
Hemorrhagic pancreatitis
Hydrogen peroxide enema
Emphysematous cholecystitis
Mechanical bowel obstruction with ischemia
Necrotic colon cancer
Perforation of gastric ulcer into mesenteric vein
Abscess
Closed-loop obstruction
Pseudomembranous colitis
Gastric emphysema
Toxic megacolon
Sepsis
Corrosive gastritis
Catheterization of umbilical artery or mesenteric vein
After hepatic artery embolization

Table 95-9
Gas in the Biliary Tract

Sphincterotomy
Gallstone erosion
Patulous sphincter in elderly patient
Cholecystoenterostomy
Choledochoenterostomy
Spontaneous biliary fistula to the colon or duodenum by
    gallstones
Perforating duodenal ulcer
Trauma
Carcinoma of the gallbladder, colon, stomach, pancreas,
    duodenum, ampulla, bile duct
Diverticulitis
Crohn's disease fistula
Emphysematous cholecystitis
Cholecystojejunostomy
Pancreatitis
Strongyloides infection
Incompetent sphincter of Oddi
Ascariasis lumbricoides infection
Clonorchis sinensis infection
Ruptured amebic abscess
Common duct entry into duodenal diverticulum
Metastases
Lymphoma

Table 95-10
Hepatic Vein Dilatation

Common
Right-sided heart failure
Constrictive pericarditis
Hepatic venous thrombus
Inferior vena cava obstruction or thrombus
Tricuspid atresia or stenosis
With Valsalva maneuver in normal young patient

Uncommon
Right atrial tumor

ULTRASOUND

Table 95-11
Diffusely Increased Hepatic Echogenicity ("Bright
Liver")

Common
Fatty infiltration
Cirrhosis
Acute alcoholic hepatitis
Severe viral or drug-induced hepatitis
Diffuse malignant infiltration
Chronic right-sided heart failure
AIDS
Technical artifact

Uncommon
Glycogen storage disease
Gaucher's disease
Miliary tuberculosis
Mononucleosis
Portal tract fibrosis
Wilson's disease
Lymphoma
Sarcoidosis

Table 91-12
Focally Increased Hepatic Echogenicity

Common
Hemangioma
Metastases
Focal steatosis
Adenoma
Focal nodular hyperplasia
Abscess
Hematoma or laceration
Hepatocellular carcinoma
Fissures

Uncommon
Cytomegalovirus or *Candida* infection
α_1-Antitrypsin deficiency
Lipoma
Angiomyolipoma
Infarct
Regenerating nodules of cirrhosis
Radiation therapy
Omentum inserted into bed of hepatic resection
Echinococcus multilocularis infection
Hemangioendothelioma

Table 95-13
Diffusely Decreased Hepatic Echogenicity

Common
Acute viral hepatitis
Schistosomiasis (early)
Malignant infiltration

Uncommon
Leukemia
Lymphoma

Apparent
End-stage renal disease
Amyloid
Nephrocalcinosis
Myoglobinuric renal failure

Table 95-14
Hepatic Pseudolesions on Ultrasound Studies

Diaphragmatic leaflets: peripheral echogenic pseudolesion may
  simulate mass
Falciform ligament: echogenic "mass" (pseudolesion) in left
  lobe
Diaphragmatic leaflets: peripheral echogenic pseudolesion may
  simulate hemangiomas
Focal fatty infiltration: echogenic pseudolesion may simulate
  metastases
Focal hepatic sparing in steatosis: hypoechoic pseudolesion
  often seen in porta
Perihepatic fat may invaginate liver causing hyperechoic masses
Ligamentum venosum: fibrous tissue attenuates sound, causing
  hypoechoic pseudolesion in caudate lobe
Gallbladder inflammation: hypoechoic hepatic pseudolesion in
  adjacent parenchyma

Table 95-15
Intrahepatic Acoustic Shadowing

Linear or Branching Shadowing
Intrabiliary air
Portal venous air
Intraductal stones

Focal Shadowing
Gas: abscess, necrotic tumor, sequela of tumor embolization or
  of biopsy
Calcification: metastases, granulomas, abscess, aneurysm,
  parasites
Refractile artifacts: junction of vessels, gallbladder neck
Foreign material: surgical clips, drains, catheters, stents,
  sponges

Table 95-16
Hypoechoic or Anechoic Focal Masses

Common
Cysts
Polycystic liver disease
Bilomas
Focal sparing in steatosis
Abscesses
Hematomas (early)
Metastases, especially colon, ovary, melanoma, sarcoma
Primary hepatic tumors
Post-traumatic cysts
Hydatid cysts

Uncommon
Caroli's disease
Extramedullary hematopoiesis
Focal hepatitis
Focal hepatic necrosis
Radiation therapy (early)
Cavernous hemangiomas
Hepatomas
Intrahepatic gallbladder

Table 95-17
Multiseptate Cystic Masses

Common
Metastases
Simple cysts complicated by infection or hemorrhage

Uncommon
Teratoma
Cystic hepatoblastoma
Infantile peliosis hepatis
Hepatic hamartoma
Biliary cystadenoma

Table 95-18
Hyperechoic Masses with Acoustic Enhancement

Hemangioma
Hepatoma
Carcinoid metastases
Adenoma or hepatoma in glycogen storage disease

Table 95-19
Anechoic, Smooth-Walled Masses with Acoustic Enhancement

Cyst
Polycystic disease
Caroli's disease
Choledochal cyst
Hydatid cyst

Table 95-20
Complex Masses

Septate
Hydatid cyst
Biliary cystadenoma
Ovarian carcinoma metastases

No Septa
Abscess
Tumor

"Bull's-eye" Lesions
Metastases
Abscess
Primary neoplasm

Table 95-21
Prominent Periportal Echoes

Common
Acute cholecystitis
Chronic cholecystitis
Cholangitis
Oriental cholangiohepatitis
Cholangiocarcinoma
Sclerosing cholangitis
Hepatocellular carcinoma
Air in biliary tree

Uncommon
Cystic fibrosis
Schistosomiasis
Lymphoma
Infectious mononucleosis

In Neonates
Biliary atresia
Acute hepatitis
Cytomegalovirus infection
Nesidioblastosis
α_1-antitrypsin deficiency
Idiopathic neonatal jaundice

Table 95-22
Echo Patterns of Hepatic Metastases

Echogenic Lesions
Any carcinoma but especially from the gastrointestinal tract, pancreas, hepatoma, breast, and vascular primaries (islet cell, carcinoid, choriocarcinoma, renal cell carcinoma)

Hypoechoic Lesions
Homogeneous tumor-like lymphomas, some breast and lung cancers

Cystic Metastases
Mucin-secreting metastases from neoplasms of the ovary, colon, pancreas, or stomach
Central necrosis of any lesion, especially sarcomas

Densely Echogenic Lesions, With Shadowing
Mucinous carcinoma of the colon
Adenocarcinoma of the stomach
Pseudomucinous cystadenocarcinoma of the ovary
Cystadenocarcinoma of the pancreas
Adenocarcinoma of the breast
Melanoma

"Bull's-Eye" or Target Pattern
Lung cancer

Infiltrative Pattern
Breast cancer
Lung cancer
Melanoma

Table 95-23
Dampening of Hepatic Vein Doppler Waveform

Cirrhosis
Passive hepatic congestion
Budd-Chiari syndrome
Various parenchymal abnormalities of liver
Extrinsic compression of hepatic veins

Table 95-24
Transjugular Intrahepatic Portosystemic Shunt Malfunction

Direct Signs
No flow—consistent with shunt occlusion or thrombosis
Low-velocity flow—especially at portal venous end of shunt
Change in peak shunt velocity—increase or decrease from baseline of 50 cm/s
Reversal of flow in hepatic vein
Hepatopetal intrahepatic portal venous flow

Secondary Signs
Reappearance of varices
Reaccumulation of ascites
Reappearance of recanalized paraumbilical vein

COMPUTED TOMOGRAPHY

Table 95-25
Focal Hypodense Lesion: Precontrast and Postcontrast Scan Appearance

Lesion	Appearance after Contrast Medium Administration
Metastases	Irregular enhancement or none
Malignant primary tumors	
Hepatoma	
Hemangioendothelioma	
Hemangiosarcoma	
Intrahepatic cholangiocarcinoma	
Lymphoma	
Cholangiocarcinoma	Irregular enhancement
Benign tumors	
Hemangioma	75% Peripheral enhancement
	10% Central enhancement
	74% Progressively isodense on delayed scans
	24% Partially isodense on delayed scans
	2% Hypodense on delayed scans
Adenoma	85% Hyperdense during arterial phase but rapidly becomes isodense or hypodense (1 min)
Focal nodular hyperplasia	Most hyperdense during arterial phase but rapidly becomes isodense or hyperdense (1 min); a low-density central scar may be present, but it is also seen in fibrolamellar hepatomas and hemangiomas
Cysts	Margins of cyst are more clearly defined
Benign simple cysts	
Polycystic liver disease	
von Hippel–Lindau disease	
Abscesses	Often show peripheral enhancement
Pyogenic	May show a "spoke-wheel" enhancement pattern
Fungal	
Amebic	May show peripheral enhancement
Radiation injury	No change
Focal fatty infiltration	No change
Infarction	No change
Laceration	No change
Old hematoma	No change
Biloma	No change
Caroli's disease	No change
Choledochal cyst	No change
Focal biliary dilatation	No change
Intrahepatic extension of pseudocyst	No change

Table 95-26
Diffusely Dense Liver

Hemochromatosis
Hemosiderosis
Glycogen storage disease
Amiodarone treatment
Gold therapy
Chronic arsenic poisoning

Table 95-27
Focal Hypodense Lesion: Noncontrast Scans

Mucinous metastases: colon, ovary, stomach, pancreas (primary)
Primary hepatic tumors: hepatoma (especially fibrolamellar), hepatoblastoma, hemangioendothelioma
Benign hepatic tumors: hemangiomas
Infections

Acute Hemorrhage
Hematoma

Vascular
Budd-Chiari syndrome with spared parenchyma
Portal vein thrombosis with spared parenchyma
Fatty infiltration
Malignant infiltration
Portal vein thrombosis
Amyloidosis

Table 95-28
Focal Hyperdense Lesion: Postcontrast Scans

Hypervascular Metastases
Carcinoid tumor
Renal cell carcinoma
Islet cell tumor
Pheochromocytoma
Melanoma

Hypervascular Benign Masses
Adenoma
Focal nodular hyperplasia (dense only during arterial phase, then hypodense)

Arterioportal Shunts

Table 95-29
Patchy Hepatogram

Cirrhosis
Hepatitis
Congestive heart failure
Tricuspid atresia
Portal vein thrombosis
Budd-Chiari syndrome
Lymphomatous infiltration
Sarcoidosis
Thyrotoxicosis

Table 95-30
Hyperperfusion Abnormalities of Liver (THADs)

Lobar-Segmental
Portal vein obstruction or thrombosis
Mass effect owing to tumor, cyst, abscess within liver
Cirrhosis with arterial portal shunt
Ligation of portal vein
Hypervascular gallbladder disease

Subsegmental
Obstruction of peripheral portal branches
Percutaneous needle biopsy, ethanol ablation
Acute cholecystitis

Generalized Heterogeneous
Cirrhosis
Budd-Chiari syndrome

THADs, transient hepatic attenuation differences.

Table 95-31
Low-Density Mass Porta Hepatis

Choledochal cyst
Hepatic cyst
Pancreatic pseudocyst
Biloma
Hepatic artery aneurysm
Enteric duplication

Table 95-32
Fat-Containing Liver Mass

Hepatoma
Angiomyolipoma
Lipoma
Metastatic liposarcoma or myxoid liposarcoma
Hepatic adenoma

Table 95-33
Vascular "Scar" Tumor

Focal nodular hyperplasia
Hepatic adenoma
Giant cavernous hemangioma
Fibrolamellar hepatocellular carcinoma
Hypervascular metastases
Intrahepatic cholangiocarcinoma

Table 95-34
Periportal Lucency

Bile duct dilatation
Periportal tracking of edema fluid or blood
Cardiac failure
Hepatitis
Traumatic disruption or neoplasm invasion of hepatic lymphatics
Bone marrow transplantation
Liver transplantation
Non-Hodgkin's lymphoma
Peribiliary cysts in cirrhosis
von Meyenburg complexes of the liver

Table 95-35
Fluid-Fluid Levels within Focal Hepatic Lesions

Simple hepatic cyst
Biliary cystadenoma
Cavernous hemangioma
Cystic hepatocellular carcinoma
Hepatic metastasis (carcinoid, ovarian, lung primaries)

MAGNETIC RESONANCE IMAGING

Table 95-36
Multiple Hypointense Liver Masses: T2-Weighted Images

Common
Regenerating nodules
Multiple calcified granulomas

Uncommon
Gamma-Gandy bodies
Periportal vascular collaterals
Multifocal acute intrahepatic hemorrhages
Biliary duct gas

Rare
Portal vein gas
Osler-Weber-Rendu disease
Multiple calcified parasitic cysts

Table 95-37
Diffusely Decreased Liver Intensity

Hemosiderosis
Hemochromatosis
Superparamagnetic contrast medium
Wilson's disease

Table 95-38
Increased Periportal Signal Intensity

Cholangitis
Obstructive jaundice
Cholangiocarcinoma
Acute hepatitis
Cirrhosis
AIDS
Vigorous hydration

Table 95-39
Hepatic Lesions with Fat Signal: T1-Weighted Images

Common
Focal fatty infiltration
Hepatoma
Hepatic adenoma

Uncommon
Cavernous hemangioma

Rare
Metastatic liposarcoma or myxoid liposarcoma

Table 95-40
Wedge-Shaped Signal Alterations

T1 Hyperintensity
Irregular fatty infiltration

T2 Hyperintensity
Hepatocellular carcinoma with peripheral ischemia or infarction
Metastases with wedge pattern of edema
Primary or secondary portal infarction
THID (transient hepatic intensity difference)

Table 95-41
Liver Lesions with Circumferential Rim

Hypointense Rim on T1-Weighted Image
Chronic hematoma (hemosiderin)
Hepatocellular carcinoma (pseudocapsular rim is thin)
Hydatid cyst (thick, homogeneous rim, no perilesional edema)
Amebic liver abscess (concentric rims; rim of collagen)

Hypointense Rim on T2-Weighted Image
Metastases (peritumoral edema with double ring pattern)
Liver abscess (one or two concentric rings of mixed signal intensity)
Subacute to chronic parenchymal hematoma (white rim also seen on T1-weighted images)

No Rim
Simple cyst
Cavernous hemangioma
Adenoma
Focal nodular hyperplasia

Table 95-42
Central Scars in Primary Liver Tumors

Cavernous hemangioma: hypointense or hyperintense T2-weighted image (can be either inflammatory or fibrous scar)
Hepatic adenoma: variable signal
Focal nodular hyperplasia: hypointense T1-weighted image, hyperintense T2-weighted image (inflammatory scar)
Fibrolamellar hepatocellular carcinoma: hypointense T1-weighted image, hyperintense T2-weighted image (fibrotic repair of scar)

NUCLEAR SCINTIGRAPHY

Table 95-43
Early or Increased Flow to the Liver: Hepatic Scintiangiography

Common
Metastatic disease
Chronic liver disease
Hepatoma
Lymphoma

Uncommon
Hemangioma or hemangioendothelioma
Abscess
Adenoma
Focal nodular hyperplasia
Sequela of radiation therapy

Rare
Dilated portal vein
Massive breast shielding

Table 92-44
Focally Decreased Flow (Solitary or Multiple): Hepatic Scintiangiography

Common
Abscess, amebic or pyogenic
Cyst, of any cause
Extrinsic mass
Hemangioma
Hematoma
Hepatoma
Some metastases

Uncommon and Rare
Fatty infiltration
Lymphoma
Regenerating nodule

Table 95-45
Nonvisualization of Liver: Indium-Labeled Leukocyte Scan

Alcoholic liver disease
Neutropenia

Table 95-46
Focal Liver Uptake: PET Scan

Common
Metastases
Abscess, pyogenic or amebic
Hepatoma

Uncommon
Cirrhosis (pseudotumor)
Budd-Chiari syndrome
Acute cholecystitis
Cholangiocarcinoma
Sarcoidosis

Table 95-47
Decreased Hepatic Uptake: PET

Chemotherapy
Liver failure
Bile peritonitis

Table 95-48
Liver "Rim" Sign: Gallium Scan

Acute cholecystitis
Pyogenic abscess
Amebic abscess
Necrotic liver metastases
Primary liver cell carcinoma

Table 95-49
"Halo" Sign in Gallbladder Fossa: Indium-Labeled Leukocyte Scan

Cholecystitis
Acute acalculous cholecystitis

ARTERIOGRAPHY

Table 95-50
Single or Multiple Vascular Hepatic Lesions

Common
Cavernous hemangioma
Hepatocellular carcinoma
Hemangioendothelioma
Metastases (especially islet cell, carcinoid, renal, breast)
Focal nodular hyperplasia
Adenoma

Uncommon
Hamartoma
Hemangiosarcoma
Arteriovenous fistula, congenital, iatrogenic, or traumatic
True or false aneurysm of hepatic artery

Table 95-51
Single or Multiple Avascular Hepatic Lesions

Common
Abscess
Hydatid cyst
Cholangiocarcinoma
Metastasis
Cyst

Uncommon
Lymphoma
Hematoma
Hamartoma
Biloma
Polycystic disease

IMAGING FINDINGS IN SPECIFIC HEPATIC DISEASES

Table 95-52
Cirrhosis and Portal Hypertension

Morphologic Changes Seen on Ultrasound, CT, and MRI Studies
Large liver early
Shrunken liver late, prominent fissures
Enlarged caudate lobe and lateral segment of left lobe
Caudate-to-right lobe ratio >0.65 on transverse images
Surface nodularity and indentations (regenerating nodules)
Altered gallbladder angle
Colonic and omental interposition
Signs of portal hypertension: varices, splenomegaly, ascites

Ultrasound
Increased echogenicity
Increased sound attenuation
Heterogeneous echo architecture
Decreased definition of portal and hepatic veins
Dilated hepatic arteries, portal vein, coronary veins, superior mesenteric vein
Thick lesser omentum in children
Increased incidence of gallstones
Regenerating nodules: hypoechoic areas with echogenic borders (rare)
Siderotic nodules in spleen: hyperechoic masses (rare)
Doppler findings in portal hypertension
Dilated portal vein with decreased respiratory variation
Hepatofugal flow in portal system
Varices
Recanalized umbilical vein
Decreased variability of hepatic venous flow
Increased flow in superior mesenteric, splenic, and portal veins
Increased splenic and superior mesenteric artery flow
Resistive index of hepatic arterial flow >0.78

CT
Fatty infiltration in early cirrhosis
Dense liver in hemochromatosis
Inhomogeneous enhancement
Portal and hepatic veins possibly compressed and difficult to visualize
Intrahepatic arterial-portal fistulas
Regenerating nodules
Portal hypertension
Varices
Increased density mesenteric fat

MRI
Regenerating nodules: low-intensity areas on T2-weighted images (hemosiderin)
No appreciable change in hepatic signal in fibrosis
Siderotic nodules in spleen

Table 95-52
Cirrhosis and Portal Hypertension—*cont'd*

Angiography
Stretched hepatic artery branches
Corkscrewing: enlarged, tortuous hepatic arteries
Mottled parenchymal phase
Shunting between hepatic artery and portal vein
Delayed emptying into venous phase
Pruned hepatic vein branches

Table 95-53
Fatty Infiltration

CT
Liver less dense than spleen; spleen normally 6-12 HU less dense than liver
Rapid appearance and disappearance of fat
"Hyperdense" intrahepatic vascular structures
Possible fat deposition in a focal, lobar, segmental, or bizarre geographic distribution
Spared areas: caudate lobe, quadrate lobe, subcapsular, gallbladder fossa

Ultrasound
Increased hepatic echogenicity and increased number of echogenic foci in liver
Increased attenuation of sound with poor penetration of the posterior liver
Poor visualization of hepatic and portal veins and diaphragm
Focal fat presentations: multiple confluent hypoechoic lesions, hypoechoic ("skip") nodules, irregular hyperechoic and hypoechoic skip areas may show rapid change in time, does not produce contour abnormalities, does not alter course or caliber of regional vessels

MRI
No significant change in T1-weighted or T2-weighted images
On opposed phase images, spin-echo (Dixon's technique), fat suppression techniques, and short TI inversion recovery images, low signal intensity of fat

Table 95-54
Viral Hepatitis

Ultrasound
Acute hepatitis
Hepatosplenomegaly
Decreased hepatic echogenicity
Increased brightness of portal vein walls ("starry sky" pattern)
Mural thickening of gallbladder; hypotonic and dilated gallbladder
Chronic hepatitis
Increased hepatic echogenicity
Coarsened parenchymal texture
Loss of definition of portal vein walls
Adenopathy in hepatoduodenal ligament in chronic active hepatitis

CT
Hepatosplenomegaly
Periportal lucency
Mural thickening of gallbladder
Adenopathy in hepatoduodenal ligament in chronic active hepatitis

MRI
Hepatosplenomegaly
Periportal hyperintensity on T2-weighted images
Increased T1 and T2 relaxation times of parenchyma

Nuclear Scintigraphy
Hepatosplenomegaly
Colloid shift
Heterogeneous uptake
Delayed parenchymal clearance and blood pool tracer retention on iminodiacetic acid scans

Table 95-55
Budd-Chiari Syndrome

MRI
Constriction or loss of a signal void in the intrahepatic or suprahepatic inferior vena cava
Loss in caliber or absence of the hepatic vein signal void
Comma-shaped, intrahepatic, hypointense collateral vessels
Nodular liver, with or without hypointense regenerating nodules
Intrahepatic portal vein thrombosis
Enlarged caudate lobe, ascites, inhomogeneous hepatic parenchyma

Ultrasound
Stenosis, thrombosis, or nonvisualization of hepatic veins
Thick, echogenic hepatic vein walls
Narrowed inferior vena cava
Intrahepatic collateral vessels or extrahepatic anastomoses
Ascites, enlarged caudate lobe

CT
Noncontrast Scans
Diffuse hypodensity associated with global liver enlargement and ascites
Caudate lobe may appear hyperdense
Hyperdense thrombus in inferior vena cava

Contrast Scans
Patchy contrast enhancement because of hepatic congestion
Central liver (caudate, portions of left lobe) hyperdense; periphery hypodense

Later ("flip-flop" pattern), center washes out, becomes hypodense relative to liver periphery, which slowly accumulates contrast medium
Portal vein thrombus
Nodular regenerative hyperplasia

Angiography
Absence of main hepatic veins
"Spider web" appearance of collateral intrahepatic veins or lymphatics
Inhomogeneous, dense, prolonged, intense hepatogram with fine mottling
Stretching and draping of intrahepatic arteries with hepatomegaly
Large lakes of sinusoidal contrast medium accumulation
Bidirectional or hepatofugal portal vein flow
Thrombus in hepatic veins or inferior vena cava
Impairment of caval flow because of diffuse hepatomegaly
Membranous obstruction of the cava at the ostia of the hepatic veins
Diminished or hepatofugal flow to involved segments during arterial portography

Nuclear Scintigraphy
Enlarged caudate lobe with increased uptake
Diffusely decreased uptake in remainder of liver
Hepatosplenomegaly
Wedge-shaped focal peripheral defects
Colloid shift to spleen and bone marrow

Table 95-56
Hemochromatosis

CT
Diffuse increase in density up to 80-140 HU
Hepatic veins and portal veins stand out on noncontrast scans

MRI
Shortened T1 and T2 relaxation times; T2 shortening effect
  predominating, with significant signal loss in liver

Ultrasound
Nonspecific findings that relate to secondary fibrosis and
cirrhosis

Nuclear Scintigraphy
Discordant sulfur colloid and iminodiacetic acid scans early:
  iminodiacetic acid scan normal; sulfur colloid scan with
  diffuse parenchymal damage

Table 95-57
Hepatocellular Adenoma

CT
Round masses of decreased density, necrotic areas (30%-40%)
Hyperdense areas of fresh intratumor hemorrhage (22%-55%)
Variable patterns of enhancement; not enhanced to the same
  degree as normal liver

Ultrasound
When small, well-demarcated and solid echogenic structure
Well-defined perilesional and intralesional blood vessels with
  2-4 kHz shifts
When large, complex hyperechogenic and hypoechogenic
  heterogeneous mass with anechoic areas

MRI
Inhomogeneous on all pulse sequences
Fat within mass, producing hyperintense areas on T1-weighted
  images
Sheets of hepatocytes isointense on T2-weighted images
Areas of necrosis and hemorrhage hyperintense on
  T2-weighted images

Nuclear Scintigraphy
No gallium uptake
Photopenic area on sulfur colloid and hepatobiliary scans
  surrounded by rim of increased uptake

Angiography
Hypervascular mass that is homogeneous but does not stain
  intensely in capillary phase
Hypovascular or avascular regions because of hemorrhage or
  necrosis
Enlarged hepatic artery with feeders at tumor periphery (50%)
Neovascularity

Table 95-58
Cavernous Hemangioma

Ultrasound
Hyperechoic, homogeneous mass with discrete margins,
  usually <3 cm
When larger, possible hypoechoic center, which may appear
  lacelike or granular
Possible acoustic enhancement
Stable size and appearance

CT
Well-circumscribed, spherical to ovoid, low-density mass on
  noncontrast scans
Peripheral enhancement with vascular nodules, progressive
  centripetal flow, complete fill-in on delayed images 3-30 min
  after bolus (55-89%)
Complete (75%), partial (24%), or no (2%) fill-in isodensity in
  delayed phase

MRI
Well-marginated
Isointense or minimally hypointense signal on T1-weighted
  images
T2 relaxation time longer than 80 ms
No fibrous pseudocapsule
Peak enhancement >2 min after injection of gadolinium
  diethylenetriaminepentaacetic acid
Marked hyperintensity at 5-min delay on T1-weighted image
  after contrast medium administration
Variable central scar signal intensity on T1-weighted and T2-
  weighted images because of clot or fibrous tissue
Progressive signal hyperintensity with increased T2 weighting
No daughter nodules
Intratumoral septa uncommon
No hepatic venous, portal, or caval tumor thrombi

Nuclear Scintigraphy
Cold region during scintigraphic angiogram on technetium
  Tc 99m-labeled erythrocyte scans
Increased activity on delayed images at 1-2 h
Cold defect on sulfur colloid scans

Angiography
Dense opacification of dilated, well-circumscribed, irregular,
  punctate vascular lakes and puddles in late arterial and
  parenchymal phase, beginning at the periphery
Normal-sized feeders without arteriovenous shunting
Contrast medium persistence late into venous phase

Table 95-59
Hepatocellular Carcinoma

Ultrasound
Large tumor hyperechoic (59%)
Small tumor hypoechoic (26%), often see thin, peripheral
  hypoechoic halo corresponding to fibrous capsule
Mixed echogenicity in diffuse form (15%)
Portal vein invasion (25%-40%)
Hepatic vein invasion (16%)
Invasion of inferior vena cava
Hepatomegaly and ascites
Characteristic high-flow Doppler signals, with shifts ≥4.5 kHz
Fine blood flow network (branching pattern)

CT
Hypodense mass
Circular zone of radiolucency surrounding mass
Enhancement during arterial phase (80%)
If sufficient arteriovenous shunting, early visualization of
  hepatic veins and cava
Isodense on delayed scans (10%)

MRI
Poorly marginated
Isointense to minimally hyperintense (50%) in T1-weighted
  images owing to fat content
T2 relaxation time <80 ms
Pseudocapsule hypointense on T1-weighted and T2-weighted
  images
Moderate peak enhancement
Faint enhancement at 5-min delay after contrast administration
Hypointense central scar on T1-weighted and T2-weighted
  images
Less pronounced hyperintensity with progressive T2 weighting
Daughter nodules present
Intratumoral septa common
Intermediate signal intensity tumor thrombi in cava, portal vein,
  or hepatic vein on T1-weighted images

Angiography
Enlarged arterial feeders, coarse neovascularity, vascular lakes,
  arterioportal shunts, and dense tumor stain in differentiated
  hepatocellular carcinoma
Vascular encasement, fine neovascularity, displacement, and
  corkscrewing of vessels in cirrhosis and anaplastic hepatomas
With tumor invasion of portal vein, "thread and streaks"
  appearance, linear parallel vascular channels

Nuclear Scintigraphy
On sulfur colloid scan, single cold spot (70%), multiple defects
  (15-20%), or heterogeneous distribution (10%)
Cold nodule on iminodiacetic acid scan
On gallium scan, avid accumulation in 70%-90%

Table 95-60
Focal Nodular Hyperplasia

CT
Homogeneous mass of slightly decreased attenuation on
  noncontrast scans
Isodense or hypodense on bolus injection of contrast material
Markedly hyperdense on arterial phase, may be isodense on
  portal venous phase because of rapid washout
Central scar may be hyperdense or hypodense on arterial
  phase, hyperdense on delayed images because of delayed
  washout within myxomatous stroma

Ultrasound
Hypoechoic or hyperechoic homogeneous mass, often
  isoechoic, subtle, difficult to differentiate in echogenicity
  from adjacent liver
Central scar appears as a hypoechoic linear or stellate area
  within the central portion of the mass
Well-developed peripheral and central blood vessels creating a
  spoke-wheel appearance
Predominant arterial signals centrally with a midrange (2-4 kHz)
  shift

MRI
Isointense on T1-weighted and T2-weighted images (80%)
Isointense on T1-weighted images and slightly hyperintense T2-
  weighted images (20%)
Margins poorly defined or invisible
Central scar is hypointense on T1-weighted images and
  hyperintense on T2-weighted images (95%) (compare
  fibrolamellar hepatoma, in which central scar is hypointense
  on T1-weighted and T2-weighted images, and hepatoma, in
  which central scar is rare)

Angiography
Hypervascular mass (90%) with intense capillary blush
Enlarged main feeding artery with central blood supply (spoke-
  wheel pattern, 33%)
Decreased vascularity in central stellate fibrous scar

Nuclear Scintigraphy
Normal sulfur colloid scan (30%-55%), cold spot (40%), or hot
  spot (10%)
Iminodiacetic acid scan: normal or increased uptake (40%-70%)
  or cold spot (60%)

References

1. Dähnert W: Radiology Review Manual, 5th ed. Baltimore, Williams &
   Wilkins, 2003.
2. Reeder MM: Reeder and Felson's Gamuts in Radiology, 4th ed. New York,
   Springer-Verlag, 2003.
3. Eisenberg RL: Gastrointestinal Radiology—A Pattern Approach, 4th ed.
   New York, Lippincott-Raven, 2004.
4. Chapman S, Nakielny R: Aids to Radiological Differential Diagnosis.
   London, Bailliere Tindall, 1990.
5. Baker SR: The Abdominal Plain Film. East Norwalk, CT, Appleton &
   Lange, 1990.
6. Lee JKT, Sagel SS, Stanley RJ, Heiken J (eds): Computed Body Tomography
   with MRI Correlation. New York, Raven, 2006.
7. Rumack CM, Nilson SR, Charboneau JW (eds): Diagnostic Ultrasound,
   3rd ed. St. Louis, CV Mosby, 2006.
8. Semelka RC: Abdominal-Pelvic MRI. New York, Wiley-Liss, 2002.
9. Datz FL: Gamuts in Nuclear Medicine, 3rd ed. St. Louis, CV Mosby, 1995.

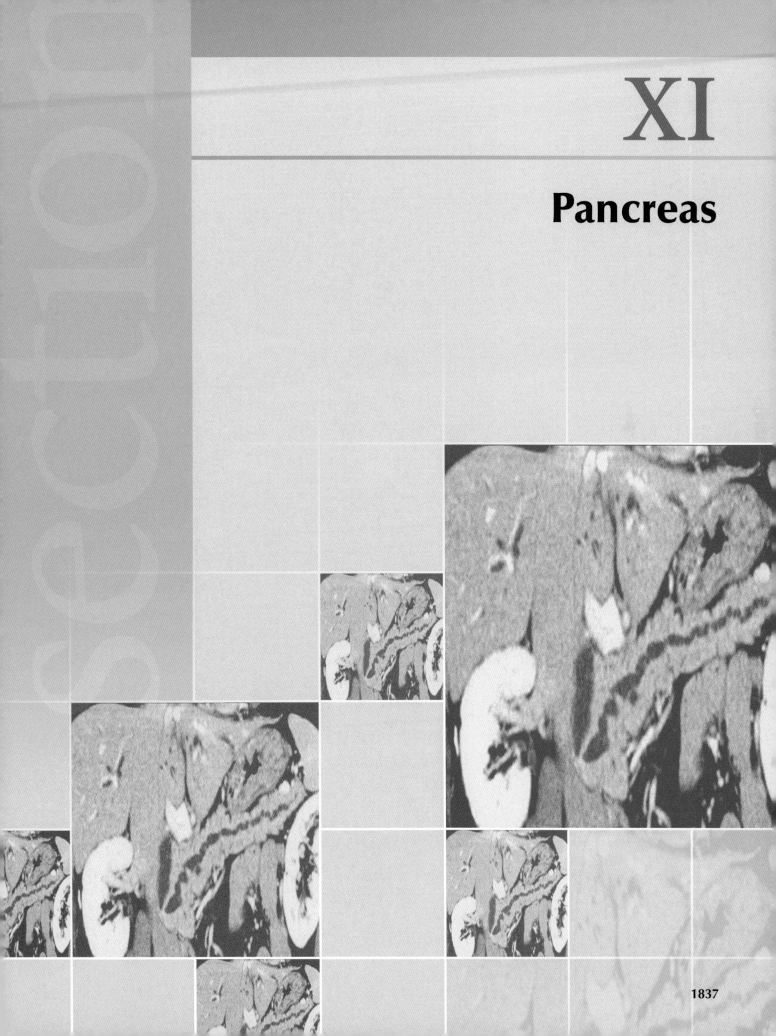

XI

Pancreas

96

Pancreas: Normal Anatomy and Examination Techniques

Frederick L. Hoff, MD • Helena Gabriel, MD • Nancy A. Hammond, MD • Richard M. Gore, MD

HISTORICAL PERSPECTIVE	RADIOLOGIC TECHNIQUES
NORMAL ANATOMY	Plain Films
Topography	Contrast Studies
Common Bile Duct	Ultrasound
Pancreatic Duct	Computed Tomography
Arterial Supply	Magnetic Resonance Imaging
Venous Drainage	Magnetic Resonance Cholangiopancreatography
Lymphatics	Endoscopic Retrograde Cholangiopancreatography
Nerve Supply	

HISTORICAL PERSPECTIVE

The pancreas was one of the last organs in the abdomen to receive the attention of anatomists, physiologists, physicians, and surgeons. Located in the "straggling mesenchyme" of the retroperitoneum, the pancreas has in the past been called the "hermit" or "hidden" organ of the abdomen.[1] The pancreas was first described in the Talmud and depicted as the "finger of the liver" between 200 BC and 200 AD. Ruphos named this organ the pancreas (Greek: *pan,* meaning "all"; *kreas,* meaning "flesh") shortly thereafter.[2] More than a millennium passed before anatomic descriptions were completed.

Wirsung of Padua demonstrated the pancreatic duct in 1642, and Santorini of Venice described the accessory duct in 1724. The papilla of Vater was described by A. Vater in 1720. In 1887, Oddi described the complex musculature of the sphincter bearing his name. The histologic structure of the pancreas was described by Langerhans in 1869. The role of the pancreas in digestion was first suggested by Bernard in 1850, and the connection between diabetes and the pancreas was established in the 1890s. Surgery for pancreatic disease was not popular until the pioneering work of Whipple in the 1930s.[3]

The pancreas also remained a hidden organ for the radiologist for decades. Indirect signs on plain films and barium studies were usually present only in advanced disease. The 1970s brought endoscopic retrograde cholangiopancreatography (ERCP) and angiography to the fore. CT, ultrasound, and MRI now routinely provide superb visualization of the gland noninvasively.[4]

NORMAL ANATOMY

The pancreas is an unpaired accessory digestive gland that has both exocrine and endocrine functions. It is a slender, soft, lobulated organ that in the adult measures approximately 15 to 25 cm in length, 3 to 5 cm in height, and 1.5 to 3.5 cm in thickness and weighs 70 to 110 g.[5,6] It has a pale, yellow-tan surface that is finely nodular and firm to palpation.

Topography

The pancreas lies within the anterior pararenal space (Fig. 96-1). The pancreatic head has a constant relationship with the

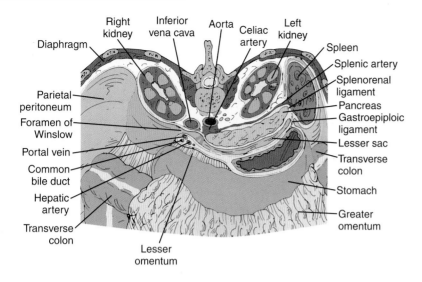

Figure 96-1. Anatomic relationships of the pancreas. (From Meyers MA: Dynamic Radiology of the Abdomen. New York, Springer-Verlag, 1988, p 57.)

duodenum, with its right lateral border nestled in the duodenal sweep.[7] The head is the thickest portion of the gland; it gives rise to the uncinate process, which projects similar to a hook, dorsal to the superior mesenteric vein. The pancreatic neck lies immediately anterior to the confluence of the splenic and superior mesenteric veins. The neck narrows behind the pylorus, then widens as it becomes the body. The body arches anteriorly and laterally to cross the spine and may be thinner than the pancreatic head and tail as it does.[8,9] The body bulges up in the pancreatic tubercle almost to the level of the celiac axis. The tail is not well demarcated from the body as it extends to the splenic hilum.[10]

The shape, position, and axis of the pancreas are quite variable and are influenced by age, body habitus, previous surgery, and organomegaly.[9] The head usually lies at the level of L1-2, and the body crosses the spine at L1; the tail is located more superiorly in the region of the splenic hilum. The longitudinal axis of the pancreas is about 20 degrees in relationship to the transverse plane[10] (Fig. 96-2). The axis of the pancreas is occasionally transverse, and even less commonly the tail

may lie caudal to the head. If the left kidney is congenitally or surgically absent, the tail often lies in a posteromedial position, adjacent to the spine. The pancreas can be shaped like an L, S, or inverted V.[10]

The gastric body and antrum lie anterior to the body and tail of the pancreas, and the pylorus is located ventral to the pancreatic neck. The duodenum lies along the right lateral border of the pancreatic head; it also passes inferior to the head, body, and tail. The spleen lies along the lateral and superior aspect of the pancreatic tail. The right kidney and adrenal gland are located posterior to the pancreatic head, and the left kidney and adrenal gland are dorsal and occasionally caudal to the tail. Depending on its size, the left lobe of the liver may lie anterior to the pancreatic body. The gallbladder is positioned ventral to the pancreatic head. The transverse colon lies anterior and generally inferior to the pancreas. The small bowel usually lies inferior to the level of the pancreas but occasionally can lie ventral to the tail.[11,12]

Nearly all of the pancreas is retroperitoneal; a nonperitonealized bare area results from the reflection of the posterior

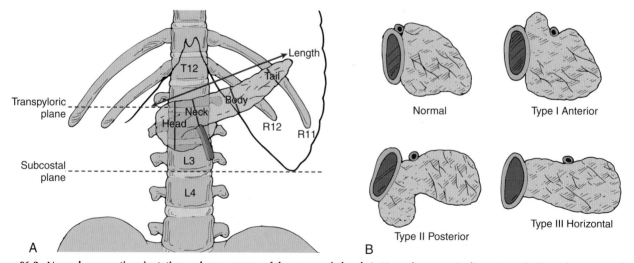

Figure 96-2. Normal pancreatic orientation and appearances of the pancreatic head. A. Normal pancreatic dimensions. **B.** Normal pancreatic head configurations. (**A** from Zylak CJ, Pallie W: Correlative anatomy and computed tomography: A module on the pancreas and posterior abdominal wall. RadioGraphics 1:61-84, 1981; **B** from Mortele KR, Rochar TC, Stretter JL, et al: Multimodality imaging of pancreatic and biliary congenital anomalies. RadioGraphics 26:715-731, 2006.)

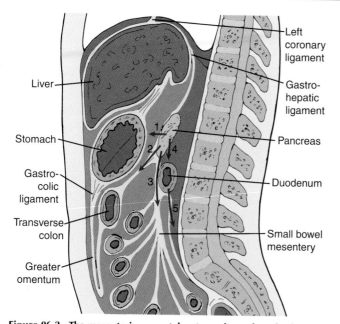

Figure 96-3. The mesenteric, omental, retroperitoneal, and subperitoneal relationships of the pancreas: sagittal perspective. Pancreatic disease may spread into the lesser sac (1), transverse mesocolon (2), root of the small bowel mesentery (3), duodenum (4), and anterior pararenal space (5). D, duodenum; L, liver; P, pancreas; S, stomach; SBM, small bowel mesentery; TC, transverse colon.

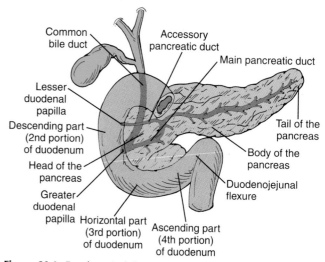

Figure 96-4. Extrahepatic biliary and pancreatic duct system. (From Tersingni R, Toledo-Pereyra LH: Surgical anatomy of the pancreas. In Toledo-Pereyra LH [ed]: The Pancreas: Principles of Medical and Surgical Practice. New York, Churchill Livingstone, 1985, pp 31-50.)

parietal peritoneum to form the two leaves of the transverse mesocolon and the posterior-inferior margin of the lesser sac (Fig. 96-3). The transverse mesocolon originates where the hepatic flexure of the colon crosses ventral to the second portion of the duodenum. The bare area begins as a broad strip across the infra-ampullary portion of the descending duodenum and continues across the head, body, and tail of the pancreas. The pancreatic tail, after extending across the left kidney, is actually an intraperitoneal structure incorporated within the leaves of the splenorenal ligament. The root of the small bowel mesentery originates inferior to the pancreatic body and is contiguous with the transverse mesocolon.[7,13] Therefore, pancreatic processes may affect the stomach and duodenum by direct spread and the small bowel loops and colon via the small bowel mesentery and transverse mesocolon (see Fig. 96-3).

Common Bile Duct

The common bile duct enters the head of the pancreas after it passes posterior to the first part of the duodenum in the hepatoduodenal ligament. It passes inferiorly and dorsally, embedded in the posterior surface of the pancreatic head to join the pancreatic duct of Wirsung. This segment runs a short intramural course before it enters the posteromedial aspect of the duodenum through the major papilla of Vater (Fig. 96-4). The common bile duct is 7 cm long and has an average diameter of 7.4 mm.[8,14,15]

Pancreatic Duct

The pancreatic duct arises from the pancreatic tail and receives 20 to 35 short tributaries entering at right angles to its long axis as it courses toward the head. The duct lies midway

between the superior and inferior margins of the pancreas and slightly more dorsally than ventrally. At the level of the major papilla, the main pancreatic duct (duct of Wirsung) courses horizontally to join the caudal surface of the common bile duct forming the ampulla of Vater. The accessory pancreatic duct of Santorini drains the anterior and superior portion of the head of the pancreas either into the duodenum at the minor papilla or into the main pancreatic duct (see Fig. 96-4). The minor papilla is often not patent, and the accessory duct may be partially or completely obliterated or have an anomalous connection with the duct of Wirsung.[16,17] These anatomic variants in ductal anatomy are discussed more fully in Chapter 98.

Arterial Supply

Although the pancreatic parenchyma is well visualized on cross-sectional imaging, it is important to recognize and define the major pancreatic vascular landmarks[18] (Fig. 96-5). The arterial blood supply of the pancreas arises from the celiac trunk and the superior mesenteric artery. After originating from the celiac artery, the common hepatic artery courses to the right in proximity to the neck and subsequently the head of the pancreas. At this point, it divides into the proper hepatic artery, which enters the free edge of the hepatoduodenal ligament, and the gastroduodenal artery, which courses caudally to lie ventral and lateral to the pancreatic head. The gastroduodenal artery gives rise to the anterior and posterior-superior pancreaticoduodenal arteries, which supply the head of the pancreas. These vessels help form the pancreatic arcade when they join the anterior and posterior-inferior mesenteric arteries that arise separately or as a common trunk from the proximal portion of the superior mesenteric artery.[5,11,14,19]

The splenic artery arises from the celiac artery and loops like a snake above and below the superior margin of the pancreas. It becomes more tortuous with age and occasionally becomes embedded within the pancreatic parenchyma. The pancreatic body and tail are supplied by the dorsal pancreatic

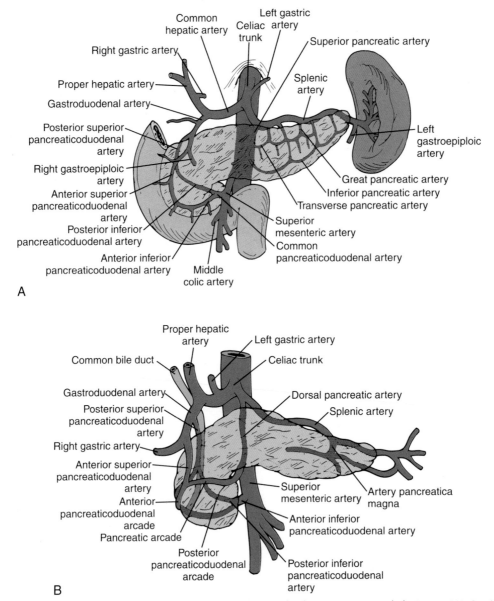

Figure 96-5. Schematic views of the arterial blood supply of the pancreas. (**A** and **B** from Tersingni R, Toledo-Pereyra LH: Surgical anatomy of the pancreas. In Toledo-Pereyra LH [ed]: The Pancreas: Principles of Medical and Surgical Practice. New York, Churchill Livingstone, 1985, pp 31-50.)

artery, which arises from the splenic artery or as a fourth branch of the celiac trunk, as well as by the splenic, hepatic, or superior mesenteric arteries. The pancreatica magna is the largest of the series of superior pancreatic branches of the splenic artery.[19,20]

The superior mesenteric artery arises from the anterior surface of the aorta, 1 to 2 cm below the celiac trunk. It courses caudal and dorsal to the neck of the pancreas, passing anterior to the uncinate process, where it serves as a major landmark for cross-sectional imaging. Displacement of the artery to the right of the aorta is a normal variant.[21]

The most frequent arterial anomaly of the upper abdomen is partial or complete replacement of either the right hepatic or the proper hepatic artery to the superior mesenteric artery. In these patients, the replaced hepatic artery passes cephalad and ventral to the pancreas, then anterior or posterior to the portal vein to reach the liver.[22]

Venous Drainage

The venous drainage of the pancreas is constant; the portal system serves as an essential landmark for localizing the pancreas on cross-sectional imaging.[11,19] In general, the veins of the pancreas parallel the arteries and lie inferior to them (Fig. 96-6). Four pancreaticoduodenal veins form venous arcades that drain the pancreatic head and the duodenum. The inferior pancreaticoduodenal veins drain into the first jejunal branch of the superior mesenteric vein. The inferior pancreaticoduodenal veins are smaller than their superior counterparts; they are not commonly visualized on cross-sectional imaging. The posterior-superior pancreaticoduodenal vein extends cephalad to join the caudal aspect of the portal vein directly.[21,22] The anterior-superior pancreaticoduodenal vein runs horizontally to drain into either the gastrocolic trunk or the right gastroepiploic vein, both of which extend to the superior mesenteric vein.[23] Three to 13 small

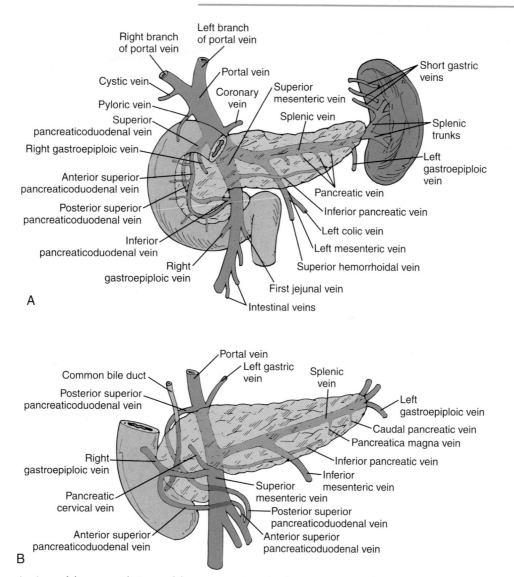

Figure 96-6. Schematic views of the venous drainage of the pancreas. (**A** and **B** from Tersingni R, Toledo-Pereyra LH: Surgical anatomy of the pancreas. In Toledo-Pereyra LH [ed]: The Pancreas: Principles of Medical and Surgical Practice. New York, Churchill Livingstone, 1985, pp 31-50.)

veins from the body and tail empty directly into the splenic vein, which follows a smooth arching course from the spleen to its junction with the superior mesenteric vein. The splenic vein parallels the splenic artery and lies in a groove along the dorsal and superior margin of the pancreas. It is a superb landmark for the posterior aspect of the pancreas, and long segments of this vessel can be seen on CT and ultrasound studies on a single image.[24] Rarely the distal tip of the pancreatic tail can lie posterior to the vein, adjacent to the adrenal gland. In these cases, it may be difficult to differentiate a mass arising in the pancreatic tail from those originating in the left adrenal gland.[25]

The splenic vein joins the superior mesenteric vein posterior to the neck of the pancreas and is seen as a round or oval dilatation to the right of the midline, posterior to the neck of the pancreas. The superior mesenteric vein courses anterior to the uncinate process just to the right of the superior mesenteric artery[11,22] (see Fig. 96-6).

The portal vein is formed behind the pancreatic neck by the union of the splenic and superior mesenteric veins and continues superiorly and laterally toward the porta hepatis as the main extrahepatic portal vein, dorsal to the common bile duct and hepatic artery. In one third of the population, the inferior mesenteric vein enters at the confluence; in another third, it joins the splenic vein close to the junction; and in the remainder, it joins the superior mesenteric vein.[8]

Lymphatics

The lymph nodes of the pancreas are distributed along the major vascular pathways (Fig. 96-7). The lymphatic channels of the pancreas form a richly branched plexus that empties in multiple directions. The anatomy of the lymphatics suggests that partial removal of the pancreas for cancer may not be sufficient because of the direct connections between different lymphatic chains.[5,8,15,19,20]

The suprapancreatic and infrapancreatic lymphatic chains receive branches from the neck, body, and portions of the pancreatic tail. Branches from the posterior surface of the head and neck drain into the pancreaticoduodenal and juxta-aortic

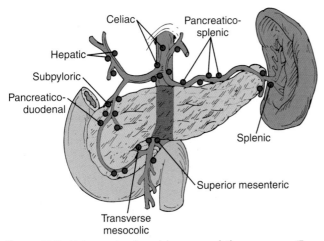

Figure 96-7. Major regional nodal groups of the pancreas. (From Tersingni R, Toledo-Pereyra LH: Surgical anatomy of the pancreas. In Toledo-Pereyra LH [ed]: The Pancreas: Principles of Medical and Surgical Practice. New York, Churchill Livingstone, 1985, pp 31-50.)

nodes. The posterior surface of the pancreatic body drains into the suprapancreatic and infrapancreatic nodes. The pancreatic tail drains into the nodes of the splenic hilum and gastropancreatic fold. Some drainage from the pancreatic head and proximal body enters the nodes in the porta hepatis and may extend inferiorly toward the superior mesenteric, mesocolic, and para-aortic nodal chains. The suprapancreatic nodes are closely related to the splenic artery and vein; the infrapancreatic chain is adjacent to the leaves of the transverse mesocolon.

Nerve Supply

It is important to appreciate the nerve supply of the pancreas (Fig. 96-8) in planning celiac nerve blocks for control of pain resulting from pancreatic carcinoma or chronic pancreatitis.[26] The pancreas receives sympathetic innervation by way

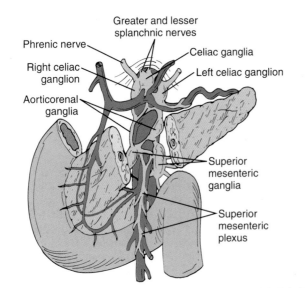

Figure 96-8. Nerve supply of the pancreas. (From Tersingni R, Toledo-Pereyra LH: Surgical anatomy of the pancreas. In Toledo-Pereyra LH: The Pancreas: Principles of Medical and Surgical Practice. Churchill Livingstone, New York, 1985, pp 31-50.)

of the splanchnic nerves and parasympathetic innervation from the vagus nerve. The sympathetic nerves carry the pain (visceral afferent) fibers. They pierce the diaphragmatic crura to enter the celiac plexus and celiac ganglion that surround the celiac artery. The superior mesenteric ganglia and plexus surround the superior mesenteric artery. Chemical extirpation of the celiac ganglion interrupts afferent pain fibers from both the sympathetic and the parasympathetic systems and can be accomplished by injection of the chemical agent between the celiac artery and the superior mesenteric artery either antecrurally or retrocrurally.[26-28]

RADIOLOGIC TECHNIQUES

Plain Radiographs

Plain radiographs are obtained on patients with suspected pancreatic disease chiefly to exclude other conditions, such as obstruction or a perforated duodenal ulcer that may simulate pancreatitis.[29-32] Oblique views are often helpful in patients with chronic pancreatitis to detect calcifications that may be obscured by the spine on the anteroposterior view.[30,32,33] More detailed descriptions of plain radiographic findings in pancreatic disease can be found in Chapters 15, 16, and 17.

Contrast Studies

Before the advent of cross-sectional imaging, angiography, ERCP, and barium studies were the major means of evaluating the pancreas. Although barium studies are less important now in evaluation of the pancreas, the following areas should still be carefully evaluated in patients with suspected pancreatic disease. The posterior gastric wall, the distal duodenum, and the duodenojejunal junction can be abnormal with lesions of the pancreatic tail and body; the greater curvature of the gastric antrum and medial aspect of the descending duodenum can provide clues for lesions arising in the pancreatic head and neck. Barium enema examination may reveal abnormalities of the colon caused by disease spread via the transverse mesocolon or at the splenic flexure caused by disease carried by the phrenicocolic ligament.[13,30,31]

Ultrasound

Sonography is a superb means of noninvasively evaluating the pancreas, particularly in thin patients. It is fast, safe, and inexpensive; it can be done portably; and it requires little preparation or cooperation of the patient and no administration of contrast medium.[34] Ultrasound examination of the pancreas is best performed on the fasting patient to reduce the amount of gas and food in overlying bowel. Real-time equipment with the highest frequency transducer (5-8 MHz) possible should be used.

Examination Techniques

Scans of the pancreas should first be performed with the patient supine and the transducer turned into a modified transverse plane angled cephalad toward the spleen (Fig. 96-9). The long axis of the pancreas is seen anterior to the splenic vein and confluence of the superior mesenteric and splenic veins. The pancreatic head and neck sweep around the superior

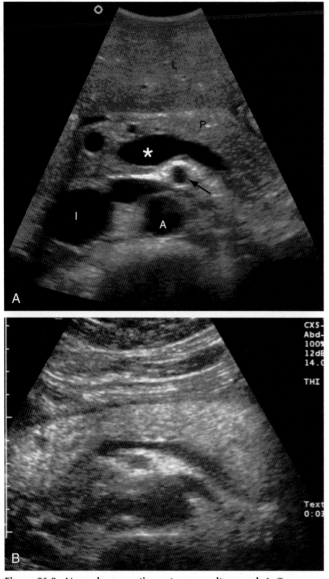

Figure 96-9. Normal pancreatic anatomy on ultrasound. A. Transverse sonogram demonstrating the majority of the pancreas. The echogenicity of the pancreas (P) is greater than that of the liver (L). A, aorta; I, inferior vena cava; *arrow*, superior mesenteric artery; *asterisk*, confluence of superior mesenteric vein and splenic vein. **B.** Transverse sonogram of a very echogenic pancreas due to fatty infiltration.

mesenteric vein, forming the retrovenous, hooklike uncinate process. The common bile duct is often imaged axially within the pancreatic head, and the gastroduodenal artery may be seen along the anterolateral aspect of the pancreatic head. The gas-filled or fluid-filled duodenum, stomach, colon, aorta, inferior vena cava, superior mesenteric artery, and left renal vein are interrogated in this projection as well. The lesser sac, which lies between the posterior gastric wall and pancreas, is best seen in this plane and should be scanned for fluid, masses, or calcifications.[35-38]

Parasagittal scans of the pancreas should begin where the portal vein merges with the longitudinally oriented superior mesenteric vein. The neck of the pancreas in transverse section is seen anterior to this confluence. The uncinate process lies posterior to the superior mesenteric vein. The pancreatic head can be seen to the right of the superior mesenteric

vein with the common bile duct located posteriorly and the gastroduodenal artery sometimes visualized anteriorly. To the left of the superior mesenteric vein, the pancreatic body and proximal portion of the tail are found anterior to the splenic vein and slightly inferior to the splenic artery.[39-43]

With meticulous technique and attention to detail, diagnostic scans of the pancreas can be obtained in 90% of cases. Several maneuvers can improve sonographic visualization of the pancreas.[44-49] Having the patient drink four 6-oz cups of degassed water can provide a sonographic window for improved visualization of the body and tail. The intravenous injection of 0.3 mg of glucagon stops peristalsis for several minutes and improves water retention by the stomach and duodenum. Deep inspiration causes the liver to move inferiorly over the pancreas, caudally displacing gas-filled bowel.

The use of oral contrast agents other than water also may be helpful in difficult examinations.[50] The oral administration of cellulose has been shown to provide improved visualization when compared to degassed water. Simethicone is used to decrease gas within the stomach, and clebopride has been used to increase emptying of gas from the stomach.[51,52]

Water or oral contrast agents are also useful in resolving pseudomasses of the pancreas produced by the stomach, duodenum, or proximal small bowel. On real-time studies, these pseudomasses change in appearance with time because of the presence of peristalsis. Gentle pressure on the transducer is also helpful in displacing overlying bowel gas. By turning the patient into the right posterior oblique position, gas in the antrum and duodenum rises into the fundus and body of the stomach; this improves visualization of the pancreatic head. The pancreatic tail is often difficult to see, and, in fact, the fat of the left anterior pararenal space can be mistaken for it sonographically. With the patient in the right decubitus position, the tail can be imaged through the spleen or left kidney.

Scanning the patient in the erect position is also helpful because it allows the liver to descend over the pancreas, displacing bowel inferiorly. It also causes gas in the duodenum and stomach to rise above the level of the pancreas.[43,47] Metoclopramide, which stimulates gastric and duodenal peristalsis, has also been shown to improve pancreatic visualization by reducing gas in the stomach.[53] Secretin stimulates water and bicarbonate secretion of the pancreas and produces fluid filling of the duodenum, giving rise to a "fluid cap" around the pancreas. These pharmacologic methods are not generally employed because they are time-consuming, and the medications are expensive.[53-56] Doppler techniques are helpful in imaging of the pancreas. Color Doppler allows quick differentiation of vascular from nonvascular structures and aids in staging of pancreatic carcinoma as well as identifying complications of pancreatitis.[57] Intravenous contrast material, generally free or encapsulated microbubbles, may aid in the Doppler examination of the pancreas.

Normal Findings on Ultrasound

Three morphologic shapes of the pancreas have been described: tadpole shaped (44%), dumbbell-shaped (33%), and sausage-shaped (23%). Absolute measurements of pancreatic size are controversial, but the maximal normal anteroposterior diameters of the pancreatic head and body are 2.6 cm and 2.2 cm.[58] The tail is much more variable in shape and size and is not measured for diagnostic purposes. In a dumbbell-shaped pancreas, the tail may be 3.5 cm; when the pancreas is sausage-shaped, the pancreatic head can be normal up to 3.5 cm.[59] The pancreatic body is usually the narrowest part of the pancreas. In general, the pancreas is proportionately larger in young people; it decreases in relative size with age.[60,61] The borders of the pancreas are usually smooth in youth and become somewhat irregular with age. Analysis of the shape of the uncinate process is particularly important because any rounding or enlargement implies disease.[58,62]

The echogenicity of the pancreas is high throughout its substance. The pancreatic tissue texture or echo size is usually coarser, more inhomogeneous, and more echogenic than that of the liver (see Fig. 96-9). It is important to compare the echo patterns and amplitudes of the liver and pancreas at the same depth because dot size and echo amplitude are closely related to the transducer beam profile.[63,64] The tissue texture of the pancreas is related to the extent of fatty infiltration.[65,66] As the pancreas ages, it undergoes progressive fatty replacement, and consequently it becomes more echogenic. Pancreatic parenchyma should be less echogenic than surrounding retroperitoneal fat. When the pancreas is completely replaced by fat in older individuals, it may be difficult to differentiate from the retroperitoneal fat.[67]

Certain caveats apply in scanning the pancreas. Gas within the stomach and duodenum can cause subtle shadowing, artifactually decreasing the echogenicity of the adjacent pancreas.[58,60] Different amounts of fat may be deposited in the ventral (head and uncinate process) and dorsal (body and tail) pancreas making the head appear hypoechoic. In some cases, demarcation of the different echogenicities can be seen to correspond to the expected fusion line of the dorsal and ventral embryologic moieties[61] (Fig. 96-10).

Considerable craniocaudal pancreatic excursion can be demonstrated from full inspiration to full expiration. The mean respiratory excursion sonographically is 1.8 cm in the supine position, 1.9 cm in the prone position, and 2.2 cm in the lateral decubitus position.[68] Pancreatic excursion also exists with changes in the patient's position from the supine to left posterior oblique position; this may cause confusion if not appreciated.[69]

Occasionally, prepancreatic fat between the stomach and pancreas can be prominent in some patients. It is usually somewhat less echogenic than pancreas and must be differentiated from fluid in the lesser sac, lymphadenopathy, and mural thickening of the stomach.[70,71] The main pancreatic duct (duct of Wirsung) is identified sonographically in approximately two thirds of patients as an anechoic space surrounded by two parallel hypoechoic lines resembling trolley tracks.[72] The maximal inner diameter is less than 2 mm; when it is larger, an obstructing mass, stricture, or stone must be suspected. The diameter of the pancreatic duct normally increases with age.[73-77]

A number of normal structures may simulate the pancreatic duct, so it is important to image the duct within the substance of the gland. The posterior wall of the stomach can mimic a dilated pancreatic duct, with normal pancreas dorsal and echogenic gastric lumen ventral, sandwiching the relatively hypoechoic gastric wall. The ingestion of water resolves this problem. A tortuous splenic artery can also simulate a dilated pancreatic duct or cystic pancreatic mass when it lies close to the pancreatic parenchyma. The use of Doppler can easily resolve the confusion.[78,79]

In patients with suspected choledocholithiasis or biliary obstruction, every effort should be made to visualize the distal common bile duct. It often is not visualized because it lies posterior to the second portion of the duodenum, which may be gas filled. This is especially true if the duct is scanned in the supine or left posterior oblique position. A superior method for visualizing the distal common bile duct sonographically is to scan the patient in an erect right posterior oblique position and to rely primarily on transverse rather than parasagittal images. The erect right posterior oblique position minimizes gas within the antrum and duodenum; the transverse scanning plane optimizes identification of the course of the intrapancreatic distal duct.[80,81] The posterior superior pancreaticoduodenal vein can mimic the distal common bile duct; color Doppler examination can easily differentiate the two structures.[82-87]

Intraoperative Ultrasound

Intraoperative sonography is a time-consuming but accurate means of localizing small islet cell tumors of the pancreas. It can also be used to guide open biopsy and aspiration.[88-92] With the increased use of laparoscopic techniques, probes for use during this procedure have also been introduced.[93]

Endoscopic Ultrasound

Ultrasound transducers have been modified so that they can be incorporated into the tip of flexible endoscopes. These

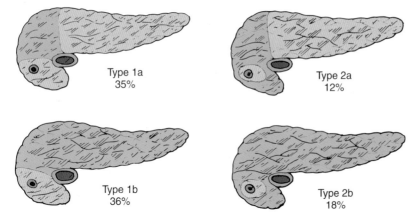

Figure 96-10. Uneven fatty replacement of the pancreas. Drawings illustrate the four different patterns of fatty replacement of the pancreas (*green areas*). The percentage of cases of uneven pancreatic lipomatosis represented by each type is also indicated. (From Mortele KR, Rochar TC, Stretter JL, et al: Multimodality imaging of pancreatic and biliary congenital anomalies. RadioGraphics 26:715-731, 2006.)

transducers have the advantage of higher frequency and spatial resolution, which may be of use in diagnosing small pancreatic tumors, in demonstrating subtle pancreatitis, and in evaluating islet cell tumors preoperatively.[94-96] This higher resolution comes at the expense of limited sound penetration and a limited field of view.[97-99] Endoscopic ultrasound is discussed in Chapter 13.

Computed Tomography

Computed tomography is the best single technique for the noninvasive imaging of the pancreas. It is unaffected by bowel gas or large body habitus, is widely available, and is relatively easily performed. CT has greatly diminished the need for diagnostic endoscopic retrograde cholangiopancreatography (ERCP) and angiography.[100-102] Multidetector row CT techniques have improved CT examination of the pancreas, allowing thinner contiguous images, overlapping images without increased radiation exposure, and freedom from respiratory misregistration. The rapidity of scanning allows several acquisitions to be made through the pancreas during different phases of a single contrast bolus.[103-121] CT scan protocols for abdominal pathology are discussed in Chapter 69.

Size, Shape, and Density on Computed Tomography

The morphologic appearance of the pancreas on CT depends on the amount of fat within the intralobular septa that separate the acinar lobules of the gland. In younger patients, the contour of the gland is smooth; the parenchyma is homogeneous, with an attenuation similar to that of spleen and muscle but less than that of liver on noncontrast scans (Fig. 96-11). With age and progressive fatty deposition, the pancreas becomes lobulated, irregular, and inhomogeneous.[103,122]

Although the size of the pancreatic head, neck, body, and tail generally correspond to normal measurements found sonographically, absolute numbers should not be used alone in diagnosing pancreatic enlargement. It is important to observe symmetry within the gland, with the head (maximal normal diameter of 3 cm) being slightly larger in anterior-posterior dimension than the body (2.2 cm) and tail (2.8 cm). The pancreatic tail can be bulbous in some normal patients and measure larger than the head. The thickness of the head of the pancreas should be less than the transverse diameter of the adjacent vertebral body; the body and tail should be less than two thirds of the size. The pancreatic body may be thinner where it crosses the spine. The lateral contour of the pancreatic head may have discrete lobulations lateral to the gastroduodenal or anterior superior pancreaticoduodenal artery in approximately one third of normal examinations.[123] The uncinate process has a triangular appearance on cross section as it projects behind the mesenteric vessels.[124-126] The pancreas moves an average of 3.2 cm craniocaudally between phases of respiration on CT scans.[127]

In patients with a surgically or congenitally absent left kidney, the pancreatic tail lies dorsomedial, adjacent to the

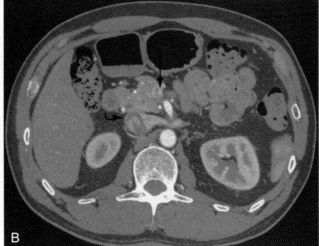

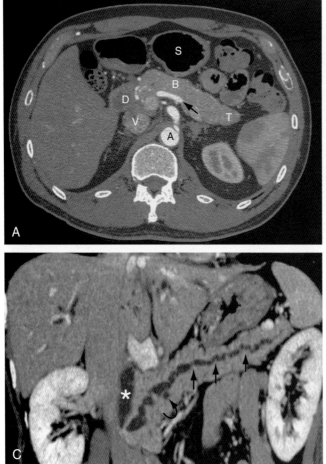

Figure 96-11. Normal pancreas on CT. Due to the oblique line of the pancreas. The entire organ is seldom seen on a single image. A. Image through the body (B) and tail (T) of the pancreas. The splenic vein (*arrow*), which lies immediately dorsal to the body of the pancreas, is an excellent landmark. A, aorta; D, duodenum; S, stomach; V, inferior vena cava. **B.** Image from the same patient obtained 1 cm caudal to A demonstrates the uncinate process of the pancreas. The superior mesenteric vein (*arrow*) is difficult to visualize on this image that was obtained early in the contrast bolus. However, the arterial anatomy is well demonstrated. *Curved arrow,* dorsal pancreatic artery. **C.** Coronal curved MPR image of the pancreas demonstrates a small, side-branch, intraductal papillary mucinous neoplasm (*curved arrow*). This technique is useful in imaging the pancreatic duct in one image (*straight arrows*), *asterisk,* common bile duct.

spine, and occupies the empty renal fossa along with bowel and spleen. The entire pancreas may rarely lie to the left of the aorta.

The pancreatic vascular anatomy is well demonstrated by MDCT. The thinner slices and overlapping reconstructions allowed by helical technique visualize many of the small named vessels. The splenic vein makes an excellent landmark for the body and tail of the pancreas. The anterior and posterior-superior pancreaticoduodenal veins are seen on 98% and 88% of scans, and the gastrocolic trunk may be visualized on 89% of scans.[128] Frequently visualized are the gastroduodenal, anterior and posterior-superior pancreaticoduodenal, and right gastroepiploic arteries. Occasionally visualized are the dorsal pancreatic, pancreatica magna, and anterior and posterior inferior pancreaticoduodenal arteries.[129]

Pancreatic Duct on Computed Tomography

The normal pancreatic duct appears as a thin, tubular region of low attenuation coursing in the center of the pancreas on CT scans. The duct can be seen at least partially in 70% of normal patients; usually, short segments are visualized on a limited number of scans. The duct is most frequently seen in the region of the pancreatic body as it arches over the spine and mesenteric vessels or in the region of the head.[130]

The normal pancreatic duct should be no wider than 2 to 3 mm, but it can occasionally be larger in older individuals. The normal fat plane between the splenic vein and pancreatic parenchyma should not be mistaken for the pancreatic duct.[131]

When CT is performed within 30 minutes of ERCP, valuable information about duct morphology and ductal obstruction can be learned by use of thin collimation. It is useful in demonstrating communication between the gut and the pancreas and in patients with prior pancreatectomy who are being considered for additional surgery. This technique should not be used routinely, however, because it adds little additional useful information in patients with a normal ERCP.[132,133]

Common Bile Duct on Computed Tomography

The internal diameter of the distal common bile duct is less than 6 to 7 mm. In older patients or those with a history of previous biliary tract disease or surgery, the duct may be as large as 10 mm in the absence of obstruction. Thus, the diagnostic significance of ducts 7 to 10 mm in size is often difficult to assess.[134] On contrast scans, the vasa vasorum of the duct may enhance.

Magnetic Resonance Imaging

Since the publication of the previous edition of this text, there has been a dramatic improvement in MR imaging of the pancreas. The pancreas had been one of the most difficult organs to image reliably on MR imaging until the development of techniques such as breath-hold imaging, chemically selective fat saturation, and gadolinium enhancement.[135] One study compared helical CT to MR imaging and found MR imaging superior in identification of small pancreatic adenocarcinomas. The authors believe that MR imaging is the modality of choice to evaluate the pancreas for small tumors.[136] The inability to demonstrate small calcifications remains a relative drawback.[137,138] MR examination protocols are discussed in Chapter 71.

Normal Pancreas on Magnetic Resonance Imaging

On MR studies (Figs. 96-12 and 96-13), the pancreas can appear smooth or lobulated and may blend in with the surrounding retroperitoneal fat if there is fatty infiltration.[139-147] The pancreas may be as bright as or slightly brighter than the liver on T1-weighted spin-echo sequences, is similar to or slightly brighter on T1-weighted spoiled gradient-echo sequences, and slightly brighter on T2-weighted images. It is relatively high in signal on T1-weighted fat-saturated sequences and enhances rapidly with gadolinium administration. The normal pancreatic duct is occasionally visualized particularly when torso coils are employed. On axial T2-weighted images, the common bile duct can be seen as a bright dot in the pancreatic

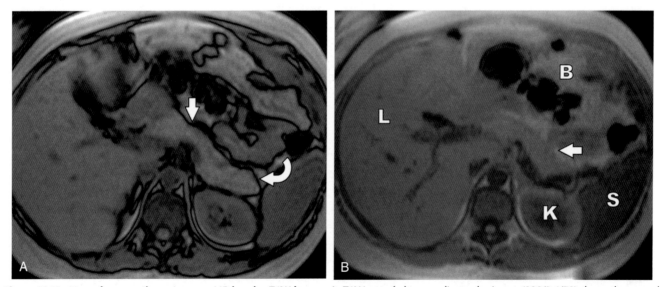

Figure 96-12. Normal pancreatic anatomy on MR imaging T1W images. A. T1W out-of-phase gradient-echo image (239/2.4/70) shows the normal appearance of the pancreatic body (*arrow*) and tail (*curved arrow*). **B.** T1W in-phase gradient-echo image (239/4.76/70) similarly shows the pancreas (*arrow*) without the chemical shift artifact. B, bowel; K, kidney; L, liver; S, spleen.

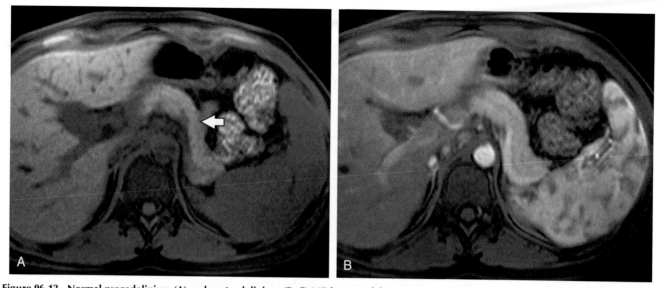

Figure 96-13. Normal pregadolinium (A) and postgadolinium (B, C) MR images of the pancreas. A. T1W fat-saturated breath-hold spoiled gradient-echo image (195/2.04/70) before the administration of contrast demonstrates the normal high signal of the pancreas relative to the rest of the parenchymal organs (*arrow*) due to proteinaceous material within the glandular elements of the pancreas. This sequence is often the single best noncontrast sequence with which to evaluate the pancreas. **B.** T1W postcontrast imaging with the same parameters shows an early and later phase of enhancement of the pancreas. Postcontrast images are routinely obtained at 60, 90, and 120 seconds after the administration of gadolinium.

head, and the gastroduodenal artery appears as a rounded, black structure as a result of flow void phenomena.[103,147]

Magnetic Resonance Cholangiopancreatography

An important new technique to examine the pancreatic and biliary tree is MR cholangiopancreatography.[148,149] The normal and abnormal pancreatic duct can be visualized without the invasiveness of ERCP[150] (Fig. 96-14). Several variations of the technique have emerged.[151-153] All have in common a heavily T2-weighted pulse sequence in which the fluid-filled ducts stand out from the surrounding low signal intensity tissues.[154] Many of these are breath-hold sequences that can easily be added to routine pancreatic imaging with little increase in overall examination time. Postprocessing using a maximum-intensity profile technique allows visualization from multiple perspectives, giving an appearance similar to ERCP. Secretin administered before the dynamic acquisition of images has been used to improve visualization of the pancreatic duct, diagnose papillary stenosis or dysfunction, and evaluate reduced pancreatic exocrine reserve.[155] MR cholangiopancreatography may be particularly valuable in postoperative patients in whom ERCP is technically impossible. This technique is discussed more fully in Chapter 77.

Endoscopic Retrograde Cholangiopancreatography

ERCP affords opacification of both the pancreatic and the bile ducts. In addition, the endoscopist can inspect and perform a biopsy of suspicious periampullary lesions, perform a sphincterotomy with or without stone extraction, and place internal biliary stents.[156-159] A more complete discussion of ERCP can be found in Chapter 76. The indications for ERCP include the following: to determine the cause of idiopathic pancreatitis (i.e., pancreas divisum); to provide a road map

for the surgeon in patients with dilated ducts and chronic pancreatitis before the Puestow procedure; to identify communication of the pancreatic duct with pseudocysts and fistulas; to detect small intraductal pancreatic neoplasms that distort ductal anatomy but do not yet cause a mass effect that can be detected by CT and ultrasound; and to identify the cause of extrahepatic biliary obstruction (e.g., stone, tumor, benign stricture, or inflammation).[160-162]

The upper limits of normal pancreatic duct diameter on ERCP are 6.5, 5.0, and 3.0 mm for the head, body, and tail, respectively. The normal duct gently tapers from the major papilla to its origin in the pancreatic tail. Slight narrowing of the pancreatic duct can be seen at the junction of the ducts of Wirsung and Santorini and at the point at which the superior mesenteric artery crosses ventral to the pancreas. Normally, 20 to 30 side branches of the pancreatic duct, which measure 0.2 mm in diameter, are filled. The duct of Santorini is opacified in about 50% of pancreatograms. A patent accessory duct orifice is present in one third to two thirds of patients but is difficult to cannulate. With aging, the diameter of the pancreatic duct increases, the number of side branches filled decreases, and cystic dilatation of the side branches may occur. The pancreatic duct moves significantly with various phases of respiration, particularly within the tail. Contrast material empties from the normal pancreatic duct in 2-7 minutes, but this figure increases in elderly patients to 10 minutes.

Injection of contrast material should be performed under fluoroscopic guidance at a pressure insufficient to cause parenchymal filling (acinarization). Injection should be terminated when acinarization occurs, if a pseudocyst is filled, if the patient complains of severe pain, or if contrast material is seen entering the duodenal lumen or wall. When a stricture or abrupt termination of the duct is encountered, heroic attempts to fill the duct upstream should be avoided. Spot films are obtained using the prone and oblique positions. Occasionally, lateral and supine views may be needed to complete the examination and to fill the duct in the tail.

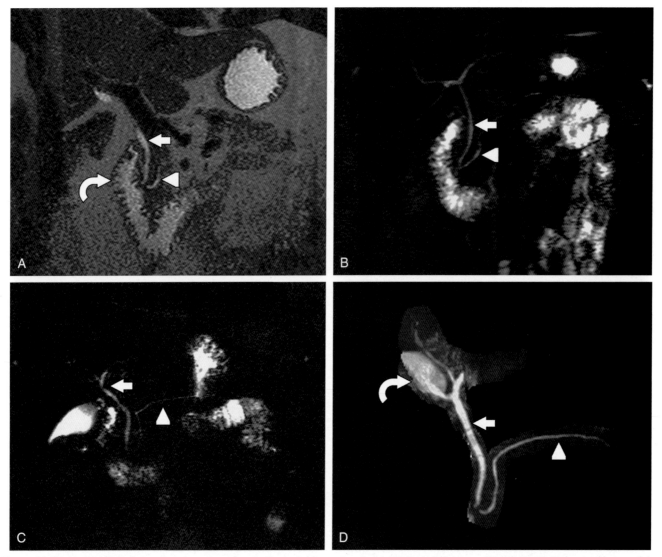

Figure 96-14. Normal MR cholangiopancreatography. A. Coronal thin-section 3-mm T2W HASTE image (1260/66/160) is the workhorse of the MRCP exam. This image displays the common duct (*arrow*) and the pancreatic duct (*arrowhead*). Fluid-filled duodenum is also seen (*curved arrow*). **B** and **C.** Coronal thick-slab RARE images (3320/1100/150) also show the common bile duct (*arrow*) and pancreatic duct (*arrowhead*). **D.** Maximum intensity projection (MIP) T2W navigator sequence (1700/705/180) is able to locate the position of the diaphragm and thus correct for diaphragmatic motion to minimize respiratory motion and artifact. This MIP image nicely displays the common bile duct (*arrow*), pancreatic duct (*arrowhead*), and gallbladder (*curved arrow*).

Pancreatic emptying should be evaluated in this position as well.[163]

PET/CT shows great promise in the staging of pancreatic carcinoma.[164-170] The applications of PET/CT in pancreatic and other abdominal malignancies are discussed in Chapter 72.

References

1. Rhoades JE, Folin LS: The history of surgery of the pancreas. In Howard JM, Jordan GL, Reber HA (eds): Surgical Diseases of the Pancreas. Philadelphia, Lea & Febiger, 1987, pp 3-10.
2. Grendell JH, Ermak TH: Anatomy, histology, embryology, and developmental anatomy of the pancreas. In Feldman M, Scharschmidt BF, Sleisenger MH (eds): Gastrointestinal and Liver Disease. Philadelphia, WB Saunders, 1998, pp 761-770.
3. Child CG: History of pancreatic surgery. In Toledo-Pereyra LH (ed): The Pancreas: Principles of Medical and Surgical Practice. New York, Churchill Livingstone, 1985, pp 1-30.
4. Quinlan RM: Anatomy and embryology of the pancreas. In Zuidema GD (ed): Surgery of the Alimentary Tract, vol III, 4th ed. Philadelphia, WB Saunders, 1996, pp 3-17.
5. Williams PL, Warwick R (eds): The pancreas. In Gray's Anatomy, 36th British ed. Philadelphia, WB Saunders, 1980, pp 1368-1374.
6. Bloom W, Fawcett DW: A Textbook of Histology, 10th ed. Philadelphia, WB Saunders, 1975, pp 726-742.
7. Meyers MA: Dynamic Radiology of the Abdomen, 5th ed. New York, Springer-Verlag, 2000, pp 32-42.
8. Skandalakis JR, Gray SW, Skandalakis LJ: Surgical anatomy of the pancreas. In Howard JM, Jordan GL, Reber HA (eds): Surgical Diseases of the Pancreas. Philadelphia, Lea & Febiger, 1987, pp 11-36.
9. Eaton SB Jr, Ferrucci JT Jr: Anatomic considerations. In Eaton SB Jr, Ferrucci JT Jr (eds): Radiology of the Pancreas and Duodenum. Philadelphia, WB Saunders, 1973, pp 1-19.
10. Zylak CJ, Pallie W: Correlative anatomy and computed tomography: A module on the pancreas and posterior abdominal wall. RadioGraphics 1:61-83, 1981.
11. Nichols MT, Russ PD, Chen YK: Pancreatic imaging: Current and emerging technologies. Pancreas 33:211-220, 2006.
12. Schneck CD, Dabezies MA, Friedman AC: Embryology, histology, gross anatomy, and normal imaging of the pancreas. In Friedman AC,

Dachman AH (eds): Radiology of the Liver, Biliary Tract, and Pancreas. St. Louis, CV Mosby, 1994, pp 715-747.

13. Meyers MA: Dynamic Radiology of the Abdomen, 4th ed. New York, Springer Verlag, 1994.

14. Mahour H, Wakim KG, Ferris DO: The common bile duct in man: Its diameter and circumference. Ann Surg 165:415-419, 1967.

15. Tersigni R, Toledo-Pereyra LH: Surgical anatomy of the pancreas. In Toledo-Pereyra LH (ed): The Pancreas: Principles of Medical and Surgical Practice. New York, Churchill Livingstone, 1985, pp 31-50.

16. Claussen M, Hellwig H, Rosch W: Anatomy of the pancreatic duct: A duodenoscopic-radiologic study. Endoscopy 5:14-17, 1973.

17. Klertsch WB: Anatomy of the pancreas: A study with special reference to the duct system. Arch Surg 71:795-802, 1955.

18. Del Frate C, Zanardi R, Mortelek, et al: Advances in imaging for pancreatic disease. Curr Gastroenterol Rep 4(2):140-148, 2002.

19. Kalra MK, Maher MM, Sahani DV, et al: Current status of imaging in pancreatic disease. J Comput Assist Tomogr 26:661-675, 2002.

20. Woodburne RT: Essentials of Human Anatomy, 5th ed. New York, Oxford University Press, 1973, pp 409-443.

21. Kahl S, Malfertheimer P: Rule of endoscopic ultrasound in the diagnosis of patients with solid pancreatic masses. Dig Dis 22:26-31, 2004.

22. Reuter SR, Redman HC, Cho KJ: Gastrointestinal Angiography, 3rd ed. Philadelphia, WB Saunders, 1986, pp 32-77.

23. Crabo LG, Conley DM, Graney DO, et al: Venous anatomy of the pancreatic head: Normal CT appearance in cadavers and patients. AJR 160:1039-1045, 1993.

24. Moncada RA, Reynes C, Churchill R, et al: Normal vascular anatomy of the abdomen on computed tomography. Radiol Clin North Am 17:25-37, 1979.

25. Abiri MM, Kirpekar M: An unusual anatomic location of pancreatic masses. J Ultrasound Med 5:703-705, 1986.

26. Haaga JR: CT-guided procedures. In Haaga JR, Alfidi RJ (eds): Computed Tomography of the Whole Body. St. Louis, CV Mosby, 1988, pp 1200-1320.

27. Buy JN, Moss AA, Singler RC: CT guided celiac plexus and splanchnic nerve neurolysis. J Comput Assist Tomogr 6:315-319, 1982.

28. Haaga JR: Improved technique for CT-guided celiac ganglia block. AJR 142:1201-1204, 1984.

29. Kelvin FM, Rice RP: Radiologic evaluation of acute abdominal pain arising from the alimentary tract. Radiol Clin North Am 16:25-36, 1978.

30. Kwon RS, Brugge WR: New advances in pancreatic imaging. Curr Opin Gastroenterol 21:561-567, 2005.

31. Gooding GAW: Conventional radiography of the pancreas. In Howard JM, Jordan GL, Reber HA (eds): Surgical Diseases of the Pancreas. Philadelphia, Lea & Febiger, 1987, pp 67-77.

32. Krabbenhoft KL: Radiologic evaluation. In Toledo-Pereyra LH (ed): The Pancreas: Principles of Medical and Surgical Practice. New York, Churchill Livingstone, 1985, pp 117-142.

33. Eaton SB, Ferrucci JT: Radiology of the Pancreas and Duodenum. Philadelphia, WB Saunders, 1973, pp 20-50.

34. Fried AM: Spleen and retroperitoneum. Ultrasound Q 21:275-286, 2003.

35. Fleischer AC: Abdominal sonography. In Fleischer AC, James AE (eds): Diagnostic Sonography. Philadelphia, WB Saunders, 1989, pp 341-433.

36. Cooperberg PL, Rowley VA: Abdominal sonographic examination technique. In Taveras J, Ferrucci JT (eds): Radiology: Diagnosis, Imaging, Intervention. Philadelphia, JB Lippincott, 1990, pp 1-11.

37. Bertolotto M, D'Onofrio M, Martone E, et al: Ultrasonography of the pancreas. 3. Doppler imaging. Abdominal Imaging 2006.

38. Loren I, Lasson A, Fork T, et al: New sonographic imaging observations in focal pancreatitis. Eur Radiol 9:862-867, 1999.

39. Fried AM: Retroperitoneum, pancreas, spleen, and lymph nodes. In McGahan JP, Goldberg BB (eds): Diagnostic Ultrasound: A Logical Approach. Philadelphia, Lippincott-Raven, 1998, pp 761-786.

40. Sample WF: Techniques for improved delineation of normal anatomy of the upper abdomen and high retroperitoneum with gray-scale ultrasound. Radiology 124:197-202, 1980.

41. Weill F, Schraub A, Eisenscher A, et al: Ultrasonography of the normal pancreas. Radiology 123:417-423, 1977.

42. Weinstein BJ, Weinstein DP: Sonographic anatomy of the pancreas. Semin Ultrasound 1:156-165, 1980.

43. Taylor KJW, Buchin PJ, Viscomi GN, et al: Ultrasonographic scanning of the pancreas. Radiology 138:211-213, 1981.

44. Crade M, Taylor KJW, Rosenfield AT: Water distention of the gut in the evaluation of the pancreas by ultrasound. AJR 131:348-349, 1978.

45. Goldstein HM, Katragadda CS: Prone view ultrasonography for pancreatic tail neoplasms. AJR 131:231-234, 1978.

46. Jacobson P, Crade M, Taylor KJW: The upright position while giving water for the evaluation of the pancreas. J Clin Ultrasound 6:353-354, 1978.

47. MacMahon H, Bowie JD, Beezhold C: Erect scanning of pancreas using a gastric window. AJR 132:587-591, 1979.

48. Warren PS, Garrett WJ, Phil D, et al: The liquid-filled stomach: An ultrasonic window to the upper abdomen. J Clin Ultrasound 6:295-302, 1978.

49. Gooding GAW, Laing FC: Rapid water infusion: A technique in ultrasonic discrimination of gas-free stomach from a mass in pancreatic tail. Gastrointest Radiol 4:139-142, 1979.

50. Harisinghani MG, Saini S, Schima W, et al: Simethicone coated cellulose as an oral contrast agent for ultrasound of the upper abdomen. Clin Radiol 52:224-226, 1997.

51. Lund PJ, Fritz TA, Unger EC, et al: Cellulose as a gastrointestinal US contrast agent. Radiology 185:783-788, 1992.

52. Varas MJ, Lopez A: Improved image quality during abdominal ultrasonography by clebopride + simethicone. Methods Find Exp Clin Pharmacol 13:69-72, 1991.

53. Kreel L, Sandin B, Slavin G: Pancreatic morphology: A combined radiological and pathological study. Clin Radiol 24:154-161, 1973.

54. Op den Orth JO: Sonography of the pancreatic head aided by water and glucagon. RadioGraphics 7:85-100, 1987.

55. Lev-Toaff AS, Langer JE, Rubin DL, et al: Safety and efficacy of a new oral contrast agent for sonography: A phase II trial. AJR 173:431-436, 1999.

56. Op den Orth JO: Pancreatic pseudomass caused by the second portion of the duodenum: A pitfall during water-aided sonography [technical note]. AJR 147:281-282, 1986.

57. Atri M, Finnegan PW: The pancreas. In Rumack CM, Wilson SR, Charboneau JW (eds): Diagnostic Ultrasound, 2nd ed. St. Louis, Mosby-Year Book, 1998, pp 225-277.

58. Mittelstaedt CA: Abdominal Ultrasound. New York, Churchill Livingstone, 1987, pp 163-220.

59. Johnson ML, Mack LA: Ultrasonographic evaluation of the pancreas. Gastrointest Radiol 3:257-266, 1978.

60. Mark WM, Filly RA, Callen PW: Ultrasound evaluation of normal pancreatic echogenicity and its relationship to fat deposition. Radiology 137:475-479, 1980.

61. Worthen NJ, Beaubeau D: Normal pancreatic echogenicity: Relation to age and body fat. AJR 139:1095-1098, 1982.

62. Kreel L, Sandin B, Slavin G: Pancreatic morphology: A combined radiological and pathological study. Clin Radiol 24:154-161, 1973.

63. Filly RA, London SS: The normal pancreas: Acoustic characteristics and frequency of imaging. J Clin Ultrasound 7:121-124, 1979.

64. Jaffe CC, Harris DJ: Sonographic tissue texture: Influence of transducer focusing pattern. AJR 135:343-347, 1980.

65. Marchal G, Verbecken E, Van Steenbergen W, et al: Uneven lipomatosis: A pitfall in pancreatic sonography. Gastrointest Radiol 14:233-237, 1989.

66. So CB, Cooperberg PL, Gibney RG, et al: Sonographic findings in pancreatic lipomatosis. AJR 149:67-68, 1987.

67. Taylor KJW, Pollock D, Crade M: Pancreatic ultrasonography: Techniques, artifacts, and clinical results. In Moss AA, Goldberg HI (eds): Computed Tomography, Ultrasound and X-ray: An Integrated Approach. San Francisco, University of California Press, 1980, pp 81-87.

68. Bryan PJ, Custar S, Haaga JR, et al: Respiratory movement of the pancreas. J Ultrasound Med 3:317-320, 1984.

69. Morgan RA, Dubbins PA: Pancreatic and renal mobility. Clin Radiol 45:88-91, 1992.

70. Chatzkel SL, Kurtz AB, Wechsler RJ: Fatty infiltration of the peripancreatic space: CT confirmation of a normal variant. Gastrointest Radiol 8:33-36, 1983.

71. Op den Orth JO: Prepancreatic fat deposition: A possible pitfall in pancreatic sonography. AJR 146:1017-1018, 1986.

72. Bryan PJ: Appearance of normal pancreatic duct: A study using real-time ultrasound. J Clin Ultrasound 10:63-66, 1982.

73. Lawson TL, Berland LL, Foley WD, et al: Ultrasonic visualization of the pancreatic duct. Radiology 144:865-871, 1982.

74. Parulekar SG: Ultrasonic evaluation of the pancreatic duct. J Clin Ultrasound 8:457-463, 1980.

75. Ohto M, Saotome N, Saishott R, et al: Real-time sonography of the

pancreatic duct: Application to percutaneous pancreatic ductography. AJR 134:647-652, 1980.

76. Gosink BB, Leopold GR: The dilated pancreatic duct: Ultrasonic evaluation. Radiology 126:475-478, 1978.

77. Hadid A: Pancreatic duct diameter: Sonographic measurement in normal subjects. J Clin Ultrasound 11:1722-1724, 1983.

78. Sanders RC, Chang R: A variant position of the splenic artery mimicking the pancreatic duct. J Clin Ultrasound 10:391-393, 1982.

79. Suramo J, Lobela P, Labde S, et al: The "ghost tail" of the pancreas in ultrasonography. Eur J Radiol 2:139-149, 1982.

80. Laing FC, Jeffrey RB, Wing VW: Improved visualization of choledocholithiasis by sonography. AJR 143:949-952, 1984.

81. Laing FC, Jeffrey RB, Wing VW, et al: Biliary dilatation: Defining the level and cause by real-time US. Radiology 160:39-42, 1986.

82. Wachsberg RH: Posterior superior pancreaticoduodenal vein: Mimic of distal common bile duct at sonography. AJR 160:1033-1037, 1993.

83. Bolondi L, Gaiani S, Casanova P, et al: Improvement of pancreatic ultrasound imaging after secretin administration. Ultrasound Med Biol 9:497-501, 1983.

84. Glaser J, Hogemann B, Schneider M, et al: Significance of a sonographic secretin test in the diagnosis of pancreatic disease. Scand J Gastroenterol 24:179-185, 1989.

85. Glaser J: Clinical perspectives of a sonographic secretin test. Gastroenterology 35:579-583, 1997.

86. Glaser J, Hogemann B, Krummeerl T, et al: Sonographic imaging of the pancreatic duct: New diagnostic possibilities using secretin stimulation. Dig Dis Sci 10:1075-1081, 1987.

87. Barbara L, Bolondi L: Functional ultrasonography in gastroenterology. Ultrasound Q 6:181-227, 1988.

88. Laing FC: Sonography of the hepatobiliary tract. In Ghahremani GG (ed): Categorical Syllabus on Gastrointestinal Radiology. Reston, VA, American Roentgen Ray Society, 1987, pp 35-43.

89. Bowerman RA, McCracken S, Silver TM, et al: Abdominal and miscellaneous applications of the intraoperative ultrasound. Radiol Clin North Am 23:107-113, 1985.

90. Smith SJ, Vogelzang RL, Donovan J, et al: Intraoperative sonography of the pancreas. AJR 144:557-562, 1985.

91. Gozzetti G, Mazziotti A: Intraoperative ultrasound during pancreatic surgery. In Gozzetti G, Mazziotti A, Bolondi L, et al (eds): Intraoperative Ultrasonography in Hepato-biliary and Pancreatic Surgery. Boston, Kluwer, 1989, pp 137-154.

92. Charboneau JW, Gorman B, Reading CC, et al: Intraoperative ultrasonography of the pancreas. Clin Diagn Ultrasound 21:121-150, 1987.

93. Bezzi M, Merlino P, Orsi F, et al: Laproscopic sonography during abdominal laproscopic surgery: Technique and imaging findings. AJR 165:1193-1198, 1995.

94. Zerbey AL, Lee MJ, Brugge WR, et al: Endoscopic sonography of the upper gastrointestinal tract and pancreas. AJR 166:45-50, 1996.

95. Caletti G, Fusaroli P: Endoscopic ultrasonography. Endoscopy 31:95-102, 1999.

96. Palazzo L: Imaging and staging bilio-pancreatic tumours: Role of endoscopic and intraductal ultrasonography and guided cytology. Ann Oncol 10(Suppl 4):25-27, 1999.

97. Matter D, Bret PM, Bretagnolle M, et al: Pancreatic duct: US-guided percutaneous opacification. Radiology 163:635-636, 1987.

98. Lees WR, Heron CW: US-guided percutaneous pancreatography: Experience in 75 patients. Radiology 165:809-813, 1987.

99. Chong WK, Theis B, Russell RCG, et al: US-guided percutaneous pancreatography: An essential tool for imaging pancreatitis. RadioGraphics 12:79-90, 1992.

100. Hessel SJ, Siegelman SS, McNeil BJ, et al: A prospective evaluation of computed tomography and ultrasound of the pancreas. Radiology 143:129-133, 1982.

101. Freeny PC: Radiology of the pancreas. Curr Opin Radiol 3:440-442, 1991.

102. Choi YH, Rubenstein WA, De Arellano ER, et al: CT and US of the pancreas. Clin Imaging 21:414-440, 1997.

103. Stanley RJ, Semelka RC: Pancreas. In Lee JKT, Sagel SS, Stanley RJ (eds): Computed Body Tomography With MRI Correlation. Philadelphia, Lippincott-Raven, 1998, pp 873-959.

104. Haaga JR: The pancreas. In Haaga JR, Lanzieri CF, Sartoris DJ, et al (eds): Computed Tomography and Magnetic Resonance Imaging of the Whole Body, 3rd ed. St. Louis, Mosby-Year Book, 1994, pp 1037-1130.

105. Smith SL, Basu A, Rae DM, Sinclair M: Preoperative staging accuracy of multidetector CT in pancreatic head carcinoma. Pancreas 34:180-184, 2007.

106. Zeman RK, Baron RL, Jeffrey RB, et al: Helical body CT: Evolution of scanning protocols. AJR 170:1427-1438, 1998.

107. Saito S, Yamamoto H, Takai S, et al: Clinical impact of multidetector row computed tomography on patients with pancreatic cancer. Pancreas 34:175-179, 2007.

108. Graf O, Boland GW, Warshaw AL, et al: Arterial versus portal venous helical CT for revealing pancreatic adenocarcinoma: Conspicuity of tumor and critical vascular anatomy. AJR 169:119-123, 1997.

109. Lu DS, Vedantham S, Krasny RM, et al: Two-phase helical CT for pancreatic tumors: Pancreatic versus hepatic phase enhancement of tumor, pancreas, and vascular structures. Radiology 199:697-701, 1996.

110. Diehl SJ, Lehmann KJ, Sadick M, et al: Pancreatic cancer: Value of dual-phase helical CT in assessing resectability. Radiology 206:373-378, 1998.

111. Kala Z, Valek V, Hiavsa J, et al: The role of CT and endoscopic ultrasound in pre-operative staging of pancreatic cancer. Eur J Radiol 62:166-169, 2007.

112. Yovino S, Darwin P, Daly B, et al: Predicting unresectability in pancreatic cancer patients: The additive effects of CT and endoscopic ultrasound. J Gastrointest Surg 11:36-42, 2007.

113. Bonaldi VM, Bret PM, Atri M, et al: Helical CT of the pancreas: A comparison of cine display and film-based viewing. AJR 170:373-376, 1998.

114. Kuroda C, Mihara N, Hosomi N, et al: Spiral CT during pharmacoangiography CT using angiotensin II in patients with pancreatic disease: Technique and diagnostic efficacy. Acta Radiol 39:138-143, 1998.

115. Hemmy DC, Zonneveld FW, Lobregt S, et al: A decade of clinical three-dimensional imaging: A review. Part 1. Historical development. Invest Radiol 29:489-496, 1993.

116. Zonneveld FW, Fukuta K: A decade of clinical three-dimensional imaging: A review. Part 2. Clinical applications. Invest Radiol 29:574-589, 1994.

117. Rubin GD, Napel S, Leung AN: Volumetric analysis of volumetric data: Achieving a paradigm shift. Radiology 200:312-317, 1996.

118. Chung MJ, Choi BI, Han JK, et al: Functioning islet cell tumor of the pancreas: Localization with dynamic spiral CT. Acta Radiol 38:135-138, 1997.

119. Novick SL, Fishman EK: Three-dimensional CT angiography of pancreatic carcinoma: Role in staging extent of disease. AJR 170:139-143, 1998.

120. Zeman RK, Davros WJ, Berman PM, et al: Three-dimensional models of abdominal vasculature based on helical CT: usefulness in patients with pancreatic neoplasms. AJR 162:1425-1429, 1994.

121. Raptopoulos V, Prassopoulos P, Chuttani R, et al: Multiplanar CT pancreatography and distal cholangiography with minimum intensity projections. Radiology 207:317-324, 1998.

122. Heuck A, Maubach PA, Reiser M, et al: Age-related morphology of the normal pancreas on computed tomography. Gastrointest Radiol 12:18-22, 1987.

123. Ross BA, Jeffrey RB, Mindelzun RE: Normal variations in the lateral contour of the head and neck of the pancreas mimicking neoplasm: Evaluation with dual-phase helical CT. AJR 166:799-801, 1997.

124. Saisho H, Yamaguchi T: Diagnostic imaging for pancreatic cancer. Pancreas 28:273-278, 2004.

125. Dupuy DE, Costello P, Ecker CP: Spiral CT of the pancreas. Radiology 183:815-818, 1992.

126. Weyman PJ, Stanely RJ, Levitt RG: Computed tomography in evaluation of pancreas. Semin Roentgenol 16:301-311, 1981.

127. Kivisaari L, Makela P, Aarimua M: Pancreatic mobility: An important factor in pancreatic computed tomography. J Comput Assist Tomogr 6:854-856, 1982.

128. Crabo LG, Conley DM, Graney DO, et al: Venous anatomy of the pancreatic head: Normal CT appearance in cadavers and patients. AJR 160:1039-1045, 1993.

129. Sim JS, Choi BI, Han JK, et al: Helical CT anatomy of pancreatic arteries. Abdom Imaging 21:517-521, 1996.

130. Callen PW, London SS, Moss AA: Computed tomographic evaluation of the dilated pancreatic duct: The value of thin-section collimation. Radiology 134:253-255, 1980.

131. Seidelman FE, Cohen WN, Bryan PJ, et al: CT demonstration of the splenic vein-pancreatic relationship: The pseudodilated pancreatic duct. AJR 129:17-21, 1977.

132. Jaffee MH, Glazer GM, Amendola MA, et al: Endoscopic retrograde computed tomography of the pancreas. J Comput Assist Tomogr 8:363-366, 1984.

133. Frick MP, O'Leur JF, Salomonowitz E, et al: Pancreas imaging by com-

puted tomography after endoscopic retrograde pancreatography. Radiology 150:191-194, 1984.

134. Donovan PJ: Technique of examination and normal pancreatic anatomy. In Siegelman SS (ed): Computed Tomography of the Pancreas. New York, Churchill Livingstone, 1983, pp 1-32.
135. Mitchell DG: Fast MR imaging techniques: Impact on the abdomen. J Magn Reson Imaging 6:812-821, 1996.
136. Schima W, Fugger R, Schober E, et al: Diagnosis and staging of pancreatic cancer. AJR 179:717-724, 2002.
137. Ly JN, Miller FH: MR imaging of the pancreas: A practical approach. Radiol Clin North Am 40:1289-1306, 2002.
138. Pamuklar E, Semelka RC: MR imaging of the pancreas. Magn Reson Clin N Am 13:313-330, 2005.
139. Gohde SC, Toth J, Krestin GP, et al: Dynamic contrast-enhanced FMPSPGR of the pancreas: Impact on diagnostic performance. AJR 168:689-696, 1997.
140. Burton SS, Liebig T, Frazier SD, et al: High-density oral barium sulfate in abdominal MRI: Efficacy and tolerance in a clinical setting. Magn Reson Imaging 15:147-153, 1997.
141. Mehmet Erturk S, Ichikawa T, Sou H, et al: Pancreatic adenocarcinoma: MDCT USMRI in the detection and assessment of locoregional extension. J Comput Assist Tomogr 30:583-590, 2006.
142. Schima W: MRI of the pancreas: Tumours and tumour-simulating processes. Cancer Imaging 6:199-203, 2006.
143. Miller FH, Rini NJ, Keppke AL: MRI of adenocarcinoma of the pancreas. AJR 187:W365-374, 2006.
144. Wang C, Gordon PB, Hustvedt SO, et al: MR imaging properties and pharmacokinetics of MNDPDP in healthy volunteers. Acta Radiol 38:665-676, 1997.
145. Ahlstrom H, Gehl HB: Overview of MNDPDP as a pancreas-specific contrast agent for MR imaging. Acta Radiol 38:623-625, 1997.
146. Kettritz U, Warshauer DM, Brown ED, et al: Enhancement of the normal pancreas: Comparison of manganese-DPDP and gadolinium chelate. Eur Radiol 6:14-18, 1996.
147. Semelka RC, Shoenut JP, Kroeker MA, et al: Chronic pancreatitis: MR imaging features before and after administration of gadopentate dimeglumine. J Magn Reson Imaging 3:79-82, 1993.
148. Verma D, Kapadia A, Eisen GM, et al: EUS vs MRCP for detection of choledocholithiasis. Gastrointest Endosc 64:248-254, 2006.
149. Asbach P, Dewey M, Klessen C, et al: Respiratory-triggered MRCP applying parallel acquisition techniques. J Magn Reson Imaging 24:1095-1100, 2006.
150. Akisik MF, Sandrasegaran K, Aisen AA, et al: Dynamic secretin-enhanced MR cholangiopancreatography. RadioGraphics 26:665-677, 2006.
151. Fulcher AS, Turner MA, Capps GW, et al: Half-Fourier RARE MR cholangiopancreatography: Experience in 300 subjects. Radiology 207:21-32, 1998.
152. Barish MA, Yucel EK, Ferrucci JT: Magnetic resonance cholangiopancreatography. N Engl J Med 341:258-264, 1999.
153. Barish MA, Soto JA: MR cholangiopancreatography: Techniques and clinical applications. AJR 169:1295-1303, 1997.
154. Jara H, Barish MA, Yucel EK, et al: MR hydrography: Theory and practice of static fluid imaging. AJR 170:873-882, 1998.
155. Schneider AR, Hammerstingl R, Heller M, et al: Does secritin enhanced MRCP predict exocrine pancreatic insufficiency? J Clin Gastroenterol 40:851-855, 2006.
156. Deviere J, Matos C, Cremer M: The impact of magnetic resonance cholangiopancreatography on ERCP. Gastrointest Endosc 50:136-140, 1999.
157. Taylor AJ, Bohorfoush AG III: Interpretation of ERCP. New York, Lippincott-Raven, 1997.
158. Classen M, Phillip J: Endoscopic retrograde cholangiopancreatography and endoscopic therapy in pancreatic disease. Clin Gastroenterol 13:819-842, 1984.
159. May G, Gardiner R: Indications for examination. In May G, Gardiner R (eds): Clinical Imaging of the Pancreas. New York, Raven, 1987, pp 11-15.
160. Varley PF, Rohrmann CA, Siluis SE, et al: The normal endoscopic pancreatogram. Radiology 118:295-300, 1976.
161. Goldberg HI, Bilbao MK, Stewart ET, et al: Endoscopic retrograde cholangiopancreatography (ERCP): Radiographic technique. Am J Dig Dis 21:270-278, 1976.
162. Jacobson IM: ERCP and Its Applications. New York, Lippincott-Raven, 1998.
163. Bilbao MK, Dotter CT, Lee TG, et al: Complications of endoscopic retrograde cholangiopancreatography (ERCP): A study of 10,000 cases. Gastroenterology 70:314-320, 1976.
164. Gross MD, Shapiro B, Thrall JH, et al: The scintigraphic imaging of endocrine organs. Endocr Rev 5:221-281, 1984.
165. Henkin RE: Selected topics in intra-abdominal imaging via nuclear medicine techniques. Radiol Clin North Am 17:39-54, 1987.
166. Shreve PD, Gross MD: Imaging of the pancreas and related diseases with PET carbon-11-acetate. J Nucl Med 38:1035-1010, 1997.
167. Heinrich S, Goerres GW, Schafer M, et al: Positron emission tomography/computed tomography influences on the management of respectable pancreatic cancer and its cost effectiveness. Ann Surg 242:235-243, 2005.
168. Sperti C, Pasquali C, Fiore V, et al: Clinical usefulness of 18-fluorodeoxy-glucose positron emission tomography in predicting survival in patients with pancreatic adenocarcinoma. J Gastrointest Surg 7:953-959, 2003.
169. Hamer OW, Feuerbach S: How useful is integrated PET and CT for the management of pancreatic cancer? Nat Clin Pract Gastroenterol Hepatol 3:74-75, 2006.
170. Blodgett TM, Melzer CC, Townsend DW: PET/CT: Form and function. Radiology 242:360-385, 2007.

chapter

97

Interventional Radiology of the Pancreas

Koenraad J. Mortele, MD • Stuart G. Silverman, MD

Percutaneous biopsy has played only a limited role in the evaluation and management of pancreatic masses historically.[1] In the past, percutaneous biopsy was reserved mostly for obtaining tissue confirmation in tumors that appeared unresectable at the time of diagnosis, for diagnosing lymphoma or metastatic disease (in whom surgery typically would be unnecessary), and for differentiating inflammatory pseudotumors from true pancreatic neoplasms.[2] In recent years, however, advanced multidetector row CT (MDCT) and MR imaging techniques have improved the detection of cystic pancreatic neoplasms and, as a result, percutaneous pancreatic mass biopsy is indicated in more patients today than ever before.[3,4]

Similarly, although traditionally the mainstay of treatment for patients with acute necrotizing pancreatitis has been surgical debridement, percutaneous image-guided catheter drainage has been proposed as a safe and alternative treatment option.[5] Many patients with pancreatic necrosis undergo fine-needle aspiration to differentiate between infected and sterile pancreatic necrosis and, if deemed necessary to control systemic toxicity, percutaneous image-guided catheter drainage of pancreatic necrosis.[6]

In this chapter, we review the specific clinical indications for pancreatic mass biopsy, summarize the reported diagnostic

efficacy of percutaneous pancreatic mass biopsy, discuss the technical factors that contribute to results and failures, and highlight the possible limitations and complications of this procedure. Finally, we will emphasize the current status of therapeutic radiology in patients with complicated pancreatitis so the practicing radiologist can understand the current role of percutaneous image-guided aspiration and catheter drainage in the diagnosis and management of patients with necrotizing pancreatitis and pancreatic pseudocysts.

ROLE OF INTERVENTIONAL RADIOLOGY IN THE MANAGEMENT OF PANCREATIC NEOPLASMS

Background

Pancreatic ductal adenocarcinoma, accounting for approximately 85% of all pancreatic neoplasms, is the fourth leading cause of cancer-related deaths in the United States; approximately 28,000 new cases of pancreatic cancer are diagnosed each year.[7,8] Percutaneous biopsy is performed typically to diagnose the cause of a pancreatic mass identified by CT scan,

MR imaging, or sonography.[9] Biopsy is useful both to diagnose malignancy, and to determine the type of malignancy.[10] For example, among malignant pancreatic tumors, including ductal adenocarcinomas, islet cell carcinomas, and lymphomas, each carries a different prognosis and is treated differently.

Percutaneous image-guided biopsy is an established means of diagnosing the cause of pancreatic masses.[8,11,12] The procedure may be performed on outpatients and complication rates are low, ranging from 3% to 6.7%.[13,14] Recently, a diagnostic rate of 97.7% was reported for CT-guided fine-needle aspiration biopsy of pancreatic masses.[15] Endoscopic sonography-guided fine-needle aspiration biopsy is an alternative technique for pancreatic masses.[16]

Indications for Pancreatic Mass Biopsy

Patients with Imaging Findings That Suggest an Unresectable Pancreatic Cancer

Percutaneous pancreatic mass biopsy is mainly indicated in patients with no known malignancy but whose imaging findings suggest an unresectable pancreatic tumor.[13] In these patients, a biopsy provides a tissue diagnosis that allows appropriate nonsurgical treatment to ensue (Fig. 97-1). Important to realize is that in patients with unresectable pancreatic cancer and other extrapancreatic lesions, such as hepatic or peritoneal/omental masses, biopsy of the extrapancreatic mass could potentially result in less morbidity than biopsy of the pancreatic tumor. For example, in a patient presenting with both a pancreatic mass and a hepatic mass(es), if biopsy of the hepatic mass revealed a metastasis of pancreatic cancer, then it would obviate subsequent biopsy of the pancreatic mass.

Patients with a Known Extrapancreatic Primary Cancer

Another indication for percutaneous biopsy of a pancreatic mass is a patient with a pancreatic mass and a known, extrapancreatic primary malignancy.[17] Percutaneous pancreatic

mass biopsy is indicated in these patients to differentiate a surgically resectable pancreatic ductal adenocarcinoma from a metastasis. A pretreatment diagnosis is needed because virtually all metastases are treated medically while resectable pancreatic carcinomas are treated surgically.[18] The importance of a pretreatment tissue diagnosis in these patients is especially emphasized in patients with lymphoma, renal cell carcinoma, and lung cancer, three tumors that spread not uncommonly to the pancreas.[19] Therefore, when a pancreatic mass is detected in a patient with an extrapancreatic primary malignancy, the mass should not be presumed to represent a metastasis; biopsy should be performed (Fig. 97-2).

Patients with a Pancreatic Mass That May Be Caused by Inflammation

Chronic pancreatitis (including autoimmune and groove pancreatitis subtypes) can appear masslike and mimic a pancreatic neoplasm.[20] Therefore, an inflammatory etiology should be considered to prevent a patient with a benign mass from going to surgery unnecessarily. Prior history of, and signs and symptoms of chronic pancreatitis are usually present. However, not infrequently, a pancreatic neoplasm with postobstructive pancreatitis induces overlapping symptomatology. Therefore, if after a careful history and laboratory evaluation, there is still the possibility of an inflammatory cause, percutaneous biopsy can be used to confirm the diagnosis of cancer, or to identify an inflammatory cause.[21]

Patients with a Cystic Pancreatic Mass

The precise role of percutaneous biopsy in the evaluation of cystic pancreatic masses is still controversial.[22-25] In the past, the majority of these masses have been considered "surgical lesions" because, with the exception of the benign serous microcystic pancreatic adenoma, (a) cystic neoplasms typically are malignant or have malignant potential (mucinous cystic tumors, intraductal papillary mucinous neoplasm, solid

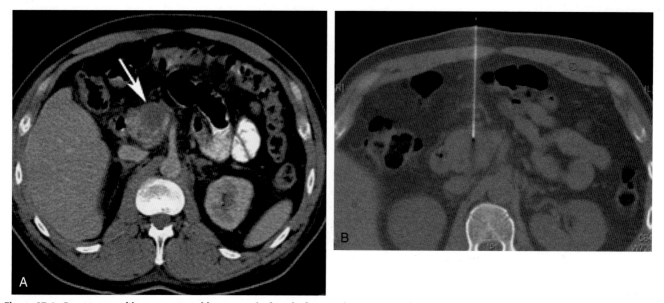

Figure 97-1. Percutaneous biopsy unresectable pancreatic ductal adenocarcinoma. A. Axial contrast-enhanced CT image shows hypovascular mass (*arrow*) in the head of the pancreas with invasion of the portal venous confluence (indicating unresectability). **B.** Axial noncontrast CT image shows needle sampling (25 gauge) of pancreatic mass; cytology revealed ductal adenocarcinoma.

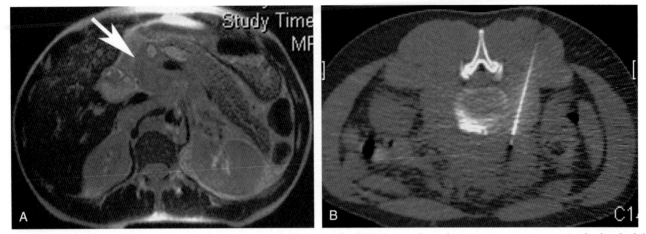

Figure 97-2. Percutaneous biopsy pancreatic lymphoma. A. Axial T2-weighted MR image shows hyperintense mass (*arrow*) in the head of the pancreas with associated ductal dilatation. Also note extensive portocaval and retrocrural lymphadenopathy. **B.** Axial noncontrast CT image (patient in prone position) shows needle sampling (25 gauge through 20 gauge) of pancreatic mass using coaxial technique and a posterior approach; cytology revealed pancreatic lymphoma.

pseudopapillary tumor of the pancreas), they cannot be characterized confidently as benign on the basis of imaging alone, and (c) they can only be diagnosed as benign with certainty if they are removed completely and examined fully at pathology.[26] As a result, biopsy specimens obtained from the cyst's wall or fluid typically contain only scant epithelial cells, inflammatory cells, and fibrous tissue; material which cannot be used to render a specific benign diagnosis. Retrieving no malignant cells still leaves the interventional radiologist, referring physician, and patient with the possibility that the lesion was improperly sampled or missed.[27,28]

Recently, helped by important advances in cyst fluid tumor markers analysis, immunohistochemistry, and molecular techniques, some authors have argued that percutaneous biopsy can be helpful in identifying patients with benign subtypes of cystic pancreatic masses, obviating surgery in these patients.[27,29,30] Indeed, new advanced MDCT and MR imaging techniques have dramatically increased the detection of cystic

pancreatic neoplasms and, although resection of all pancreatic cystic tumors would ensure that cancers are not missed, most small cystic pancreatic neoplasms grow slowly or not at all[3,4] and up to 87% of patients would undergo surgery unnecessarily.[4] As a result, percutaneous biopsy may be advocated in selected circumstances, such as in patients who have cystic pancreatic neoplasms smaller than 3 cm, patients who have comorbidities that increase the risk of surgical exploration, and patients with a cystic pancreatic mass diagnosed in the setting of acute or chronic pancreatitis (Fig. 97-3). In these patients, biopsy results can simply serve as additional data that can be combined with imaging data to render a probable clinical diagnosis.

Multiple Solid Pancreatic Masses

As pancreatic ductal adenocarcinoma is solitary in more than 95% of cases, patients without a known primary malignancy

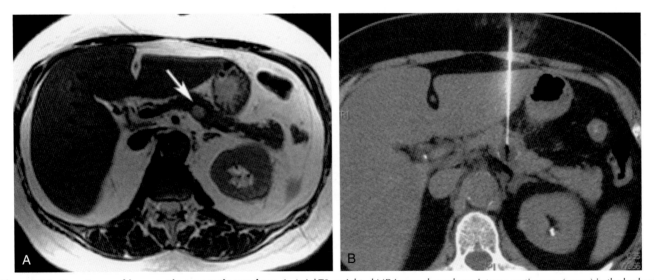

Figure 97-3. Percutaneous biopsy cystic pancreatic neoplasm. A. Axial T2-weighted MR image shows hyperintense cystic mass (*arrow*) in the body of the pancreas with surrounding rim of calcifications. **B.** Axial noncontrast CT image shows needle sampling (22 gauge) of pancreatic mass using a transhepatic approach; cytology and subsequent fluid analysis plus molecular marking revealed benign mucinous cystic tumor with indolent cytogenetics.

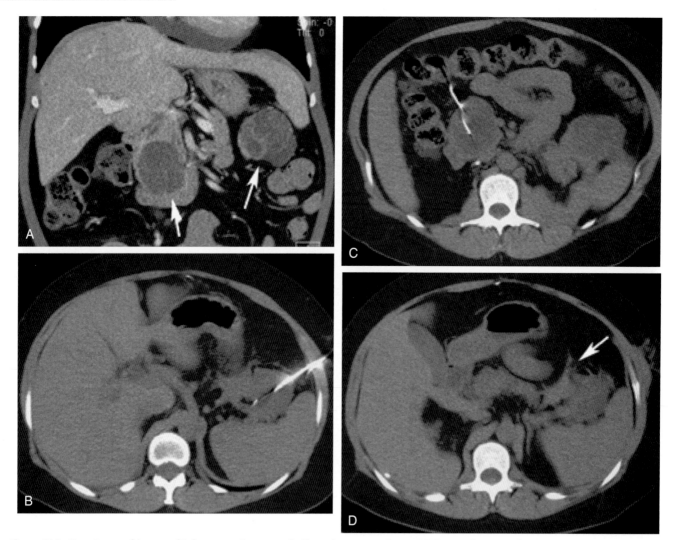

Figure 97-4. Percutaneous biopsy multiple pancreatic masses. A. Coronal contrast-enhanced CT image shows two heterogeneous masses (*arrows*) in the head and tail of the pancreas. **B.** Axial noncontrast CT image shows large needle sampling (18-gauge sidecutting device) of pancreatic mass in the tail. **C.** Axial noncontrast CT image shows fine-needle sampling (22 gauge) of pancreatic mass in the head; cytology and surgical pathology assessment of both masses revealed serous microcystic pancreatic adenoma. **D.** Axial noncontrast CT image shows small retroperitoneal hemorrhage (*arrow*) around the pancreatic tail that was self-limiting.

who present with multiple, solid pancreatic masses are also good candidates for pancreatic biopsy.[26] The differential diagnosis includes metastatic disease, but this is not likely if a primary tumor is not known. Primary lymphoma is another possibility, although lymphoma more commonly involves the pancreas secondarily and associated lymphadenopathy is usually present at time of presentation. Other differential diagnostic possibilities include multifocal nonhyperfunctioning endocrine tumors and multifocal solid-appearing microcystic pancreatic adenomas. A diagnosis of lymphoma or multifocal solid-appearing microcystic pancreatic adenomas would lead to medical treatment (Fig. 97-4). A diagnosis of multifocal nonhyperfunctioning endocrine tumors would allow the surgical treatment of each tumor to be planned such that the maximum amount of functioning pancreatic tissue can be left remaining.

Technical Considerations

Percutaneous biopsy of pancreatic masses is now most often guided by ultrasound, CT, and, rarely, MRI. To our knowledge, there are no data to support using one modality for all masses.[31,32] Ultrasound is widely available, real-time, multiplanar, portable, free of ionizing radiation, and less expensive than CT or MRI. However, not all pancreatic masses are visible with ultrasound. Due to its posterior location in the anterior pararenal space, the pancreas can not always be seen in patients with intervening bowel gas or excessive abdominal fat, and it may be difficult to visualize the location of the needletip.[31] CT can be used to visualize almost all pancreatic masses (although intravenous contrast material may be needed rarely) and is excellent in depicting surrounding normal pancreas, the hypodense/hypovascular tumor, and the needle tip.[32] MRI is typically reserved for the unusual mass that is not visualized well with CT or ultrasound. In general, we recommend using the imaging modality that depicts the mass best, and that modality with which the radiologist is most familiar.

Percutaneous biopsy of pancreatic masses can be performed using a wide range of needle sizes.[33] Percutaneous pancreatic mass biopsy refers to a procedure during which imaging is used to guide any needle into a pancreatic mass percutaneously for the purpose of obtaining a tissue diagnosis.[33] These include biopsies that utilize fine needles (20 gauge or thinner) or large needles (19 gauge or larger). Some authors distinguish between "fine-needle aspirations," during which only fine needles are used and the tissue is examined cytologically, and "biopsies," during which large needles are used to procure fragments of tissue, sometimes referred to as "cores," and examined histologically.[33] In general, fine-needle aspiration biopsies are analyzed cytologically, and large-needle biopsies analyzed histologically. Needles may also differ by type; some are end-cutting, others are side-cutting.

There are no data to suggest that pancreatic masses are better biopsied with fine needles (20 gauge or thinner) or large needles (19 gauge or larger). Diagnostic sensitivities for percutaneous biopsy procedures using only fine needles vary from 71% to 94.7%.[34-36] The reason for this range of diagnostic sensitivity might be that some studies included cystic and solid pancreatic masses while others focused on solid pancreatic masses only. As mentioned above, the diagnostic workup of most cystic pancreatic masses involves analysis of cystic fluid for biochemical and tumor markers rather than tissue sampling; thus, the accuracy of fine-needle aspiration biopsy is related both to the ability to position a needle in a mass and the accuracy of the biochemical analysis of the cystic fluid.[28]

Biopsies performed with large (typically 18 gauge) needles have yielded similar sensitivities.[37,38] These series showed that sensitivities for detecting malignancies range from 69% to 93%. Therefore, although there has been no statistically valid comparison study to draw any definitive conclusions, based on current available data, it is reasonable to conclude that fine needles are adequate by themselves to biopsy the majority of pancreatic masses. Although use of large needles may increase accuracy in selected circumstances, we believe they increase the risk of complications, particularly bleeding and pancreatitis. Therefore, in our practice, we begin with fine needles and ask our cytologists to examine one or two specimens intraprocedurally. If the preliminary cytology impression is that the specimen is adequate, the procedure is completed using fine needles alone. If there is any question as to the specimen's adequacy, we obtain large needle specimens for histologic analysis.[33]

The pancreas is located in the anterior pararenal space, and access routes that avoid traversing liver, stomach, colon, small bowel, spleen or kidney, are preferentially selected to minimize the risk of bacterial contamination and hemorrhage. If possible, an approach avoiding traversing normal pancreatic tissue is also preferred to minimize the risk of pancreatitis. Anterior routes through the liver or stomach can be used if no other routes are available. Transgressing the stomach theoretically increases the risk of infection in patients who are on H_1-receptor blockers or any other medications that raise gastric pH, as the gastric fluid is not sterile. Moreover, percutaneous biopsy of cystic pancreatic lesions using a transgastric route may impair the diagnostic accuracy of the biopsy as gastric mucin–producing cells may contaminate the smear.

Diagnostic Effectiveness

There are several studies that have evaluated the sensitivity, specificity, and overall accuracy of biopsy of pancreatic masses. These studies vary considerably with respect to patient population, tumor type, guidance modalities, and needle size.[15]

Overall, the sensitivity of biopsy for diagnosing malignancy is 71% to 97% regardless of needle size used or whether the specimens were examined using cytology, histology, or both.[15] False-negative results are most often due to failing to place accurately the needletip in a small mass, or to sampling coexistent desmoplastic reaction or pancreatitis adjacent to the mass. Even in experienced hands, false negatives do occur, suggesting that negative results should be viewed with caution in patients with a radiologically suspicious mass.

Tillou et al.[13] reported a diagnostic rate of 96.5% for diagnosing pancreatic masses via CT- and transabdominal ultrasound-guided fine-needle aspiration biopsy. In a retrospective study, Qian and Hecht[36] showed that CT-guided biopsies had sensitivity of 71%. In the study by Mallery et al.,[9] CT- and transabdominal ultrasound-guided pancreatic biopsies (80%) had a higher sensitivity than endoscopic sonography-guided biopsies (74%). In a recent study, we also found higher sensitivity for CT guidance (94.9%) compared with endoscopic sonographic guidance (85%).[15] However, the difference did not reach statistical significance. In the study of Qian et al.,[36] the negative predictive values of CT- and endoscopic sonography-guided fine-needle aspiration biopsies were similar; 41% and 45%, respectively. Mallery et al. reported negative predictive values of 23% and 27% for fine-needle aspiration biopsies performed under CT- and endoscopic sonographic guidance, respectively.[9] We found negative predictive values of 60% and 57.1% for CT- and endoscopic sonography-guided fine-needle aspiration biopsy, respectively. Also in our study, the frequency of small masses biopsied under endoscopic sonographic guidance (81.5%) was significantly higher than the frequency of those biopsied under CT guidance (32.6%).[15] In fact, since the first report of the use of endoscopic sonography-guided fine-needle aspiration biopsy for the diagnosis of pancreatic cancer in 1994,[39] it has been reported that endoscopic sonography-guided fine-needle aspiration biopsy is more accurate than CT-guided fine-needle aspiration biopsy, especially for small pancreatic masses.[34] To evaluate the effect of mass size on biopsy performance, we stratified results by mass size. There were no significant differences in test characteristics between the both guidance groups after the data were stratified by mass size; small masses were not more effectively biopsied under endoscopic sonography guidance.[15]

Since cytology is a relatively insensitive test in the diagnosis of cystic pancreatic neoplasms, advances in cyst fluid tumor markers analysis, immunohistochemistry, and molecular techniques, have been employed to improve the sensitivity for the detection of malignancy in these lesions. Cyst fluid carcinoembryonic antigen (CEA) values are uniformly low in serous pancreatic adenomas, higher in mucinous lesions and markedly elevated in mucinous cystadenocarcinomas.[27] A recent pooled analysis of 12 studies in 450 patients on the role of cyst fluid analysis in the differential diagnosis of pancreatic cystic lesions showed that a CEA greater than 800 ng/mL is strongly suggestive of a mucinous tumor.[40] Other studies confirmed that of all tested markers (e.g., amylase, mucicarmine staining, carbohydrate antigen 19-9 (CA 19-9), cyst fluid CEA is the most accurate test available for the diagnosis of mucinous cystic lesions of the pancreas.[41-43] Finally, recent studies revealed specific roles of molecular analysis of clusterin-beta and MUC4 to help distinguish reactive ductal epithelial cells from the cells of pancreatic adenocarcinoma in fine-needle aspiration samples,[44] of mutational analysis for K-ras point mutations and loss of heterozygosity in differentiating benign from malignant cystic neoplasms,[30] and of immunohistochemical staining for *MUC1* overexpression as a specific marker of invasive carcinoma in intraductal papillary mucinous neoplasm.[29]

Complications

Percutaneous pancreatic mass biopsy is a safe procedure and reported complications rates are low for both CT-guided and sonography-guided fine-needle aspiration biopsy of the pancreas.[15] Recently, in a meta-analysis, Chen et al. reported a complication rate of 4% for CT-guided procedures.[18] Bleeding is the most frequent complication, but its usually subclinical, detected only with a postprocedural CT scan, and self-limited due to the retroperitoneal location of the pancreas. Although there are no direct comparison data, we believe that peripancreatic hemorrhage is more likely with large needles.

The second most common complication is acute pancreatitis due to inadvertent transgression or biopsy of normal pancreatic parenchyma. It is almost always self-limited but may be prolonged due to pancreatic ductal disruption.[45]

Seeding of the needle track with tumor is a theoretical consequence of percutaneous biopsy of a malignant pancreatic mass, but it is extremely rare and therefore should not be a deterrent from biopsy when there is an appropriate indication. To our knowledge, only one case of needle track seeding associated with pancreatic mass biopsies has been reported.[46]

ROLE OF INTERVENTIONAL RADIOLOGY IN THE MANAGEMENT OF ACUTE NECROTIZING PANCREATITIS

Background

The International Symposium on Acute Pancreatitis held in 1992 in Atlanta defined acute pancreatitis as inflammation of the pancreas with variable secondary involvement of remote organs.[47] Acute necrotizing pancreatitis is a severe form of the disease associated with significant morbidity and mortality. Percutaneous image-guided catheter drainage is an important treatment option that can be life-saving when used alone, or as an adjunct to surgery.[5] Successful treatment outcomes depend on close cooperation and teamwork among gastroenterologists, surgeons, and interventional radiologists.[5]

Pancreatic necrosis is defined as a diffuse or focal area of nonviable pancreatic tissue.[48] Infection of the necrotic portion of the pancreas results in infected necrosis. Infected pancreatic necrosis is an "intermediate" complication of acute pancreatitis, usually occurring between the third and eighth week after onset of symptoms.[49] Infected necrosis and sterile necrosis both carry a high mortality rate.[5] Mortality rates of 30% to 35% have been reported in patients with infected necrosis, and 10% to 15% in patients with sterile necrosis.[7] Although the presence of infection increases the mortality rate in patients with pancreatic necrosis, a more recent review of 1,110 cases of acute pancreatitis demonstrated that mortality is more strongly linked to the presence of organ failure than to the presence of infection itself.[50]

Although no universally accepted treatment algorithm exists, a general consensus of indications for interventional approach to patients with acute pancreatitis has been described.[5,7,51-61] Some percutaneous drainage procedures are performed to stabilize the seriously ill patient prior to surgical debridement, while others are done with the intent to cure. In some cases, percutaneous drainage follows surgical therapy that has been only partially successful.[62] Treatment algorithms vary among medical centers and are sometimes based on expertise of both the interventional radiologist and the surgeon. The clinical status of the patient, for instance, the presence of sepsis, also influences which approach is best in any given clinical situation.[5,7]

Image-Guided Catheter Drainage: Technique

Access Route

Most pancreatic fluid collections are located in the lesser sac, the anterior pararenal space, or other parts of the retroperitoneum.[48] Access routes that avoid traversing colon, small bowel, stomach, spleen, and kidney are preferred to minimize the risk of bacterial contamination and hemorrhage. If possible, a retroperitoneal approach through the lateral flank is chosen over an anterior approach through the peritoneum.[7] Some authors suggest that anterior routes involve the theoretical disadvantage of antigravity flow of fluid through the catheter.[5,7] Anterior routes through the liver or stomach can be used if no other routes are available.[5,7] Transgressing the liver theoretically increases the risk of bleeding, but in practice, is generally safe. Transgressing the stomach is also safe, but the peristalsing stomach may result in catheter dislodgment several days after its placement. Moreover, caution should be taken in patients who are on H_1-receptor blockers or any other medications that raise gastric pH, as the gastric fluid may not be sterile. Fluid collections involving the pancreatic tail can be drained through the left anterior pararenal space, avoiding the descending colon posteriorly.[5,7] Similarly, pancreatic head collections can be drained through the right anterior pararenal space.[6] Typically, the patients' position on the interventional CT table should be adjusted to a slight posterior oblique to optimize access to the region of interest.

Catheter Selection and Placement

The fluid contained in collections caused by pancreatic necrosis is often viscous. Therefore, adequate drainage of pancreatic and peripancreatic collections typically requires catheters with multiple side holes and a minimum diameter of 12 to 14 French.[52-61] Multiple catheters may be required to drain large or multiloculated necrotic collections. If the fluid is not viscous, 12- to 14-French drainage catheters may be satisfactory.[5,7] Either tandem trocar technique or Seldinger technique can be used depending on the operator's experience. If the Seldinger technique is used, the catheter tract should be sequentially dilated over a guidewire. If the necrotic material is viscous and the collection is not drained completely, catheters larger than 14 French may be exchanged several days after a 14-French catheter is placed initially. An attempt should be made to place as much length of the catheter containing side holes as possible transversely into the necrotic pancreatic collection from the lateral flank approach to maximize drainage.[5,7]

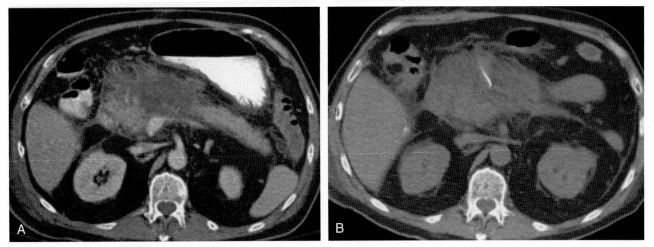

Figure 97-5. Percutaneous fine-needle aspiration of sterile necrotizing pancreatitis. A. Axial contrast-enhanced CT image shows hypovascular area in the body of the pancreas consistent with pancreatic necrosis. **B.** Axial noncontrast CT image shows needle sampling (20 gauge) of pancreatic necrotic collection via a right anterior approach. The fluid was analyzed and found to be sterile.

Management of Sterile Pancreatic Necrosis

Generally, in patients with sterile pancreatic necrosis, CT scans of the abdomen are repeated every 7 to 10 days to follow the evolution of pancreatic necrosis and to look for complications.[3] Patients who persistently show clinical instability with tachycardia, fever, leukocytosis, or organ failure may require image-guided percutaneous needle sampling to evaluate for infected pancreatic necrosis.[51] It is important that the access route avoids small and large bowel so as not to contaminate the collection or the aspiration sample[5,7] (Fig. 97-5).

If sampled pancreatic fluid is sterile, the patient is considered to have sterile pancreatic necrosis. Some of these patients recover rapidly without additional intervention while others remain persistently toxic due to pancreatic duct disruption with extravasation and accumulation of noxious pancreatic juice into peripancreatic spaces; they usually require continuous support in an intensive care unit.[63] Several years ago, patients with persistent toxicity underwent urgent surgical debridement; however, now these patients are managed nonsurgically, since early surgical debridement contributes to morbidity and mortality.[63-65] A combination of percutaneous catheter drainage and supportive care offers an alternative to surgery.[52]

Some suggest that persistently toxic patients should undergo percutaneous image-guided needle sampling every 7 to 10 days to assess for infected necrosis.[51] Instead of performing regular needle sampling, the necrotic fluid may be drained percutaneously.[66] One or more catheters may be placed and irrigated per standard radiologic protocol in order to provide a "radiologic necrosectomy" and reduce systemic toxicity.[66] Percutaneous catheter drainage of sterile necrosis is, however, still controversial. Only one clinical study is currently available that has compared the results of therapy utilizing weekly percutaneous needle sampling to assess for infection versus indwelling catheter drainage of sterile necrosis.[66]

The main rationale for not using percutaneous catheter drainage is potentially infecting a sterile pancreatic collection.[67] Although indwelling catheter colonization is common, serious clinical infection is unlikely to occur if all the fluid and material are drained within 2 to 3 days of the intervention.[5,7,66] This requires vigilant attention to follow-up CT scans and placement of additional and/or larger catheters to drain the residual fluid. Adequate drainage is achieved when no residual necrotic fluid is present on follow-up CT scans.

Management of Infected Pancreatic Necrosis

Although contrast-enhanced CT scan is excellent in assessing for pancreatic necrosis, it cannot distinguish between infected and sterile necrosis with certainty.[48] Intrapancreatic, retroperitoneal or lesser sac gas is a rare finding on CT; however, if it is present it may indicate infection.[48] Bacterial infection of necrotic pancreatic tissue is common and associated with high morbidity and mortality. The risk of infection may or may not increase with the amount of pancreatic necrosis.[50]

Infected pancreatic necrosis has traditionally been managed with surgical necrosectomy and antibiotics.[65] Percutaneous catheter drainage is often ineffective due to blockage of the catheter by necrotic tissue fragments and viscous fluid.[65] However, when patients are too unstable to undergo surgery, percutaneous catheter drainage may be successful in draining liquefied pus and minimizing the systemic manifestations of sepsis, thereby preparing patients for surgery.[68-71]

Percutaneous catheter drainage may also be successful alone.[69] In a study of 23 patients with 38 infected pancreatic fluid collections who were drained percutaneously, 65% were cured without surgery and 35% required some type of surgical intervention after drainage.[69] Catheter drainage time averaged 29 days for patients with isolated collections and 96 days for patients with pancreatic duct fistulas.[69] Success largely depends on the following factors: (1) all the collections must be drained; (2) if they are persistent after 2 to 3 days of drainage, additional catheters should be placed and large bore catheters are often required; (3) vigorous bedside catheter irrigation should be done at least three times a day with 20 mL of sterile saline injected; and (4) follow-up CT scans must be obtained frequently to assess for treatment response[69,72] (Fig. 97-6).

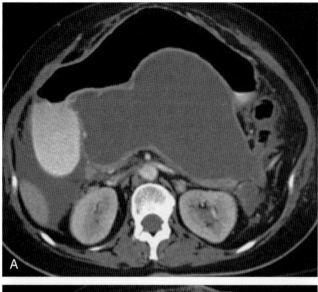

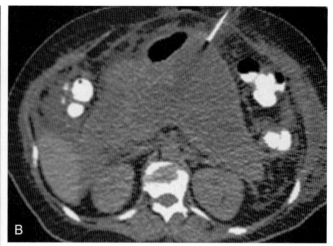

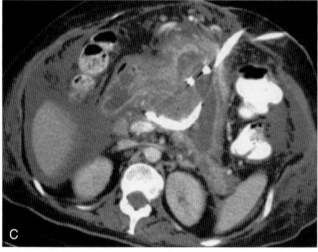

Figure 97-6. Percutaneous catheter drainage infected necrotizing pancreatitis. A. Axial contrast-enhanced CT image shows necrotic collection replacing the pancreatic gland. **B.** Axial CT fluoroscopic image obtained on the same day shows needle sampling (20 gauge) of pancreatic necrotic collection; purulent material was aspirated and 2 drainage catheters were placed. **C.** Axial contrast-enhanced CT image obtained 14 days after the drainage procedure shows two percutaneous drainage catheters (14 French and 18 French) placed via anterior approach and small residual collection.

Complications

Reported major complications of CT-guided catheter drainage are hemorrhage and injury to adjacent organs, such as bowel.[5,7] Hemorrhage is quite uncommon and may be due to pancreatitis itself rather than the drainage procedure[5,7] (Fig. 97-7). Following all percutaneous drainage procedures, CT scan of the abdomen should be done to assess for retroperitoneal hemorrhage. Venous bleeding is usually self-limiting. Arterial pseudoaneurysm or active arterial hemorrhage due to injury of adjacent vessels, such as the splenic artery, requires angiographic embolization. Fistulization to adjacent bowel is almost always due to the pancreatitis itself rather than catheter drainage.[5,7] Inadvertent insertion of the catheter through the bowel may occur when bowel loops are collapsed or unopacified. In most cases, the bowel heals without the need for surgical repair.[5,7]

Catheter Care

Daily rounds should be performed by the interventional radiologist with assessment of the patient's vital signs, white blood cell count, and clinical status.[72] Catheter(s) should be irrigated with sterile saline at least three times a day using a technique that involves aspirating and discarding all the fluid that can be withdrawn from the catheter, followed by forward flushing into the abscess cavity with 20 mL of sterile saline.[5,7] The process is repeated until the fluid is clear, typically two to three times. Finally, 10 mL of sterile saline is instilled into the catheter toward the patient, and an additional 10 mL toward the bag to prevent catheter plugging. The stopcock between the catheter and the drainage bag connecting tube should be left in the open position. It is important to document accurate drainage output amounts by subtracting the instilled volume of saline from the total drainage volume. The nurses should be familiar with drainage catheters placed by interventional radiology so that flushes are done promptly.

Abdominal CT scans should be obtained periodically, based on the clinical status and amount of drainage, to check for residual and/or undrained fluid collections.[5,7] This helps determine whether drainage is adequate or additional catheters should be placed. If a catheter is not draining and abdominal CT shows residual collection, the catheter may be blocked or the side holes may not be contiguous with the collection. In such cases, the catheter should be exchanged over a guidewire and repositioned appropriately within the collection, or removed and a new catheter placed (Fig. 97-8).

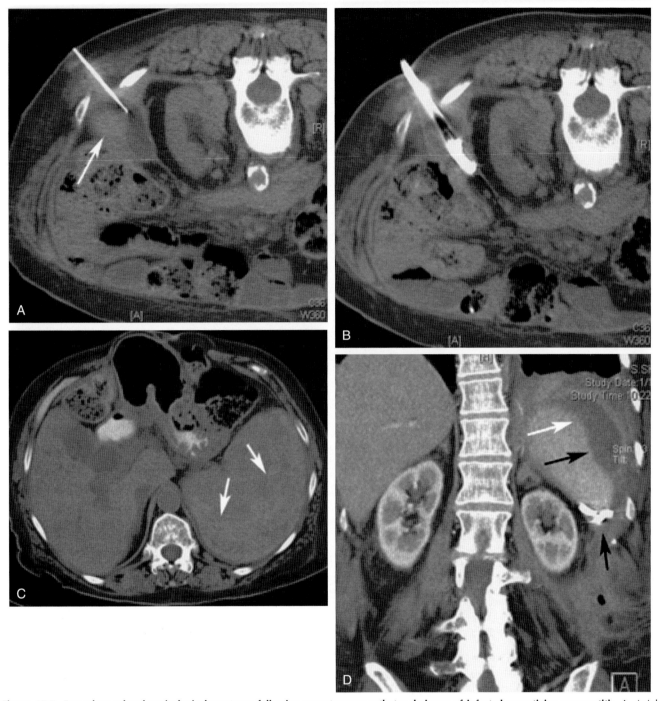

Figure 97-7. Procedure related perisplenic hematoma following percutaneous catheter drainage of infected necrotizing pancreatitis. A. Axial contrast-enhanced CT image (patient prone) shows well-defined fluid collection around the tail of the pancreas consistent with organized pancreatic necrosis. Note proximity of the collection to the spleen (*arrow*) and needle sampling (20 gauge) of pancreatic necrotic collection. **B.** Axial nonenhanced CT image (patient prone) shows percutaneous drainage catheter (14 French) placed via intercostal approach. **C.** Axial noncontrast CT image obtained 5 days later shows large subcapsular splenic hematoma (*arrows*). **D.** Coronal contrast-enhanced CT image obtained 3 weeks later shows near resolution and liquefaction of splenic hematoma (*white* and *longer black arrows*) and presence of percutaneous drainage catheter (*shorter black arrow*).

Our criteria for catheter removal include no residual collection on a follow-up CT scan and catheter output of no more than 10 mL per day of nonpurulent fluid for 2 consecutive days. It is important not to remove the catheter solely based on imaging results without assessing the amount of drainage.[5,7] Likewise it is important not to remove catheters solely because

they stopped draining; catheters may become plugged or be pulled out from the collection. As a result a CT scan will show residual fluid. In some cases, CT scan may show complete resolution of the collection; however if there is communication with pancreatic duct or its branches, the catheter may still be draining significant amounts of fluid daily.[5,7] Similarly,

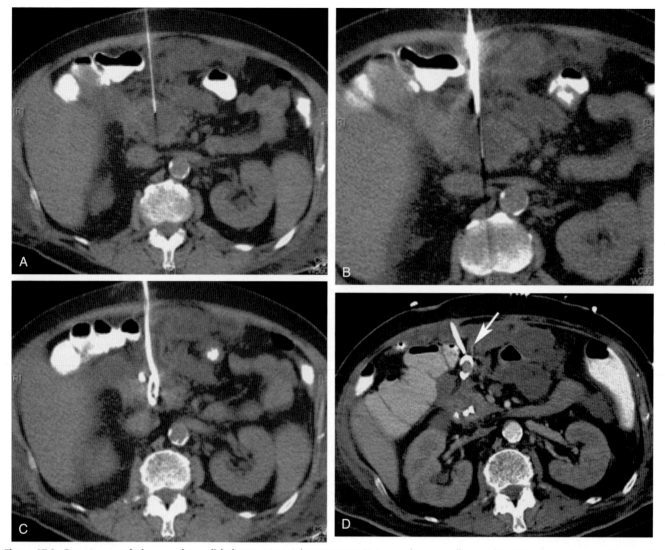

Figure 97-8. Percutaneous drainage catheter dislodgment. A. Axial noncontrast CT image shows needle sampling (22 gauge) of pancreatic necrotic collection via a anterior approach. **B.** Axial noncontrast CT image shows percutaneous drainage catheter (14 French) insertion using a tandem technique. **C.** Axial noncontrast CT image shows percutaneous drainage catheter in place and complete resolution of pancreatic fluid collection. **D.** Axial contrast-enhanced CT image obtained 14 days after the drainage procedure shows dislodgment of the catheter and spillage of pancreatic fluid in the omentum and peripancreatic tissues.

catheter output may be scant, however a fistula may still be present. Pancreatic duct fistulas usually close over time if the collection is completely drained.[73]

Patient communication and catheter education must be established, as the catheters may have to remain in place for weeks to months.[5,7] Once stabilized, patients can be discharged home with the catheter in situ and followed as outpatients. Periodic visits with the interventional radiologist are scheduled to inspect the catheter insertion site.

Ancillary Procedures

Patients with acute pancreatitis may need additional supportive procedures performed by the interventional radiologist.[5] These include image-guided thoracentesis and paracentesis, fluoroscopic-guided nasojejunal or percutaneous jejunal feeding tube placement, and angiographic embolization of pseudoaneurysms or hemorrhaging vessels.[5,7] Several studies support the use of enteral nutrition rather than parenteral nutrition in patients with acute pancreatitis.[74-76] Therefore, nasojejunal or percutaneous jejunal feeding tube placement should be attempted whenever possible.

Some patients with sterile necrotizing pancreatitis remain toxic after 3 to 6 weeks. This is often due to one or more pancreatic duct disruptions with extravasation of noxious pancreatic juice.[66] Some reports advocate endoscopic placement of a stent across a disruption.[77,78] However, there are several reasons not to recommend endoscopic pancreatic stent placement in the setting of sterile necrosis.[52] First, the duct may be obstructed and disruption may not be visualized. Second, if there is no obstruction, the injected contrast may extravasate and infect the necrotic area. Third, with extensive necrosis of the body of the pancreas, the distal portion of the duct cannot be visualized or accessed by a stent. Fourth, even if a stent can be placed across a disruption, it may act as a foreign body and result in superinfection.

If a follow-up CT scan demonstrates complete resolution of the pancreatic collection, but the catheter continues to drain significant amounts of fluid daily, there is communication with the pancreatic duct. Fluoroscopic abscessography is then used to visualize the communication and appearance of pancreatic duct.[73] This communication usually heals over time if the collection is drained completely.

ROLE OF INTERVENTIONAL RADIOLOGY IN THE MANAGEMENT OF PANCREATIC PSEUDOCYSTS

Indications

Pseudocysts are collections of pancreatic juice enclosed by a wall of granulation tissue.[79] Typically, they require 4 or more weeks to evolve and result from acute pancreatic fluid collections. Less than 10% of patients with acute pancreatitis will develop pancreatic pseudocysts.[80] They vary in size and location and are usually asymptomatic. By imaging, pseudocysts are homogeneous fluid collections with attenuation of the fluid content less than 15 Hounsfeld units (HU). The surrounding fibrous pseudocapsule is usually thin (<2 mm). Calcification of the wall, typically curvilinear in shape, is not uncommon. Chronic pseudocysts, i.e., those that do not resolve over time, may point to a persistent communication with the pancreatic duct or its side branches.[79,80] When symptomatic, pseudocysts are typically larger than 5 cm, and older than 6 weeks of age. These symptomatic pseudocysts are usually amendable to percutaneous drainage; large nonsymptomatic pseudocysts usually do not need treatment.[81,82] Secondary complications of pseudocyst formation include infection (resulting in a pancreatic abscess) and erosion into a vessel (resulting in a pseudoaneurysm).

A pancreatic abscess or infected pseudocyst is a circumscribed collection of pus, containing little or no necrosis.[83] Its incidence is far less (3%) than that of infected pancreatic necrosis; it usually occurs later in the course of the disease, and it is typically multibacterial. Importantly, the mortality of pancreatic abscess is minimal. Among many, one reason for this is that pancreatic abscesses are typically amendable to percutaneous catheter drainage[83] (Fig. 97-9). In most cases, imaging cannot be used to rule in or rule out the presence of infection in patients with localized fluid collections. Therefore, image-guided percutaneous aspiration is frequently required for diagnosis.

Outcome

Percutaneous drainage is an effective front-line treatment for most pancreatic pseudocysts;[84,85] cure is likely if fluid collections are drained adequately and if sufficient time is allowed for closure of fistulas from the pancreatic duct. In the largest series reported to date,[84] percutaneous drainage of 101 pancreatic pseudocysts (51 infected, 50 noninfected) in 77 patients is described. In this group of patients, 91 of 101 pseudocysts were cured by means of catheter drainage (90.1%) (noninfected, 43 of 50 (86%); infected, 48 of 51 (94.1%)). Six patients underwent operation after percutaneous treatment due to persistent drainage. In patients with infected pseudocysts, the infection was eradicated by percutaneous drainage before operation. Four pseudocysts recurred and were redrained percutaneously. The mean duration of drainage was 19.6 days (infected pseudocysts, 16.7 days; noninfected, 21.2 days). Four major (superinfection of sterile pseudocysts) and six minor complications occurred. Therefore, it can be concluded that percutaneous catheter drainage is a safe and valuable procedure in the management of patients with pancreatic pseudocysts.

CONCLUSIONS

Percutaneous biopsy of pancreatic masses is a safe and accurate procedure and can be used to diagnose malignancy and guide treatments. In the future, biopsy performance will undoubtedly improve as the field of cytology expands to include a more sensitive and specific array of immunocytochemical reagents and cytogenetic markers that can be used to improve the analysis of percutaneous needle biopsy specimens.

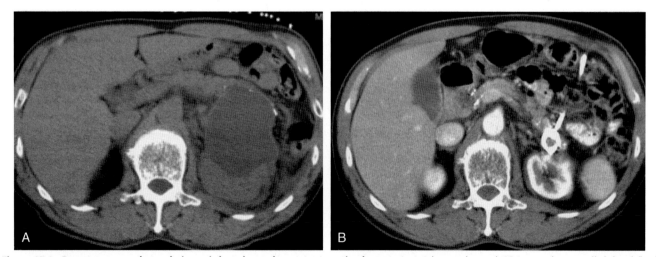

Figure 97-9. Percutaneous catheter drainage infected pseudocyst (pancreatic abscess). A. Axial nonenhanced CT image shows well-defined fluid collection adjacent to the tail of the pancreas with peripheral calcifications consistent with pancreatic pseudocyst. The collection was needle sampled via a left anterior approach; the fluid was analyzed and found to be infected. **B.** Axial contrast-enhanced CT image obtained 3 weeks later shows complete resolution of the infected pseudocyst.

Image-guided catheter drainage of fluid collections in and around the pancreas in patients with complicated pancreatitis is an important therapeutic option either alone or as an adjunct to surgery. Successful percutaneous treatment of necrotic collections of the pancreas depends on several important factors. Typically, multiple large-bore catheters are required to drain large and/or multiloculated collections. Catheters often need to remain in place for several weeks and sometimes months, hence the need for close follow-up. Daily interventional radiology rounds on inpatients, frequent vigorous bedside catheter irrigations, and willingness to place additional catheters for undrained collections are the norm in the care of these patients. Successful outcomes are best achieved when there is close cooperation among the interventional radiologist, gastroenterologist and surgeon.

References

1. Martin DF, England RE, Tweedle DEF: Radiologic intervention in the pancreatic cancer. Eur Radiol 8:9-19, 1998.
2. Dodd LG, Mooney EE, Layfield LJ, et al: Fine-needle aspiration of the liver and pancreas: Cytology primer for radiologists. Radiology 203:1-7, 1997.
3. Walsh RM, Vogt DP, Henderson JM, et al: Natural history of indeterminate pancreatic cysts. Surgery 138 :665-670, 2005.
4. Sahani DV, Soakor A, Hahn PF, et al: Pancreatic cysts 3 cm or smaller: How aggressive should treatment be? Radiology 238 :912-918, 2006.
5. Shankar S, vanSonnenberg E, Silverman SG, et al: Imaging and percutaneous management of acute complicated pancreatitis. Cardiovasc Intervent Radiol 27:567-580, 2004.
6. Ferrucci JT, Mueller PR: Interventional approach to pancreatic fluid collections. Radiol Clin N Am 41:1217-1226, 2003.
7. Wallace MB, Woodward T, Raimondo M: EUS and fine-needle aspiration for pancreatic cancer. Dig Endosc 16:193-196, 2004.
8. Harewood GC, Wiersema MJ: Endosonography-guided fine needle aspiration biopsy in the evaluation of pancreatic masses. Am J Gastroenterol 97:1386-1391, 2002.
9. Mallery JS, Centeno BA, Hahn PF, et al: Pancreatic tissue sampling guided by EUS, CT/US, and surgery: A comparison of sensitivity and specificity. Gastrointest Endosc 56:218-224, 2002.
10. Voss M, Hammel P, Molas G, et al: Value of EUS guided fine needle aspiration biopsy in the diagnosis of solid pancreatic masses. Gut 46:244-249, 2000.
11. Agarwal B, Abu-Hamda E, Molke KL, et al: Endoscopic ultrasound-guided fine needle aspiration and multidetector spiral CT in the diagnosis of pancreatic cancer. Am J Gastroenterol 99:844-850, 2004.
12. Edoute Y, Lemberg S, Malberger E: Preoperative and intraoperative fine needle aspiration cytology of pancreatic lesions. Am J Gastroenterol 86:1015-1019, 1991.
13. Tillou A, Schwartz MR, Jordan PH Jr: Percutaneous needle biopsy of the pancreas: When should it be performed? World J Surg 20:283-286, 1996.
14. Brandt KR, Charboneau JW, Stephens DH, et al: CT- and US-guided biopsy of the pancreas. Radiology 187:99-104, 1993.
15. Erturk SM, Mortele KJ, Tuncali K, et al: Fine needle aspiration biopsy of solid pancreatic masses: Comparison of CT and endoscopic sonography guidance. AJR 187:1531-1535, 2006.
16. Eloubeidi MA, Chen VK, Eltoum IA, et al: EUS-guided fine needle aspiration biopsy of patients with suspected pancreatic cancer: Diagnostic accuracy and acute and 30-day complications. Am J Gastroenterol 98:2663-2668, 2003.
17. Linder S, Blasjo M, Sundelin P, et al: Aspects of percutaneous fine-needle aspiration biopsy in the diagnosis of pancreatic carcinoma. J Surg 174:303-306, 1997.
18. Chen VK, Arguedas MR, Kilgore ML, et al: A cost-minimization analysis of alternative strategies in diagnosing pancreatic cancer. Am J Gastroenterol 99:2223-2234, 2004.
19. Mortele KJ, Ji H, Ros PR: CT and magnetic resonance imaging in pancreatic and biliary tract malignancies. Gastrointest Endosc 56:S206-212, 2002.
20. De Backer AI, Mortele KJ, Ros PR, et al: Chronic pancreatitis: Diagnostic role of computed tomography and magnetic resonance imaging. JBR-BTR 85:304-310, 2002.
21. Leung TK, Lee CM, Wang FC, et al: Difficulty with diagnosis of malignant pancreatic neoplasms coexisting with chronic pancreatitis. World J Gastroenterol 11:5075-5078, 2005.
22. MacCarty RL: Cyst fluid analysis and imaging of pancreatic cystic lesions. AJR 164:820-821, 1995.
23. Lewandrowski KB, Southern JF, Pins MR, et al: Cyst fluid analysis in the differential diagnosis of pancreatic cysts. A comparison of pseudocysts, serous cystadenomas, mucinous cystic neoplasms, and mucinous cystadenocarcinoma. Ann Surg 217:41-47, 1993.
24. Hammel P, Levy P, Voitot H, et al: Preoperative cyst fluid analysis is useful for the differential diagnosis of cystic lesions of the pancreas. Gastroenterology 108:1230-1235, 1995.
25. Khalid A, Finkelstein S, McGrath K: Molecular diagnosis of solid and cystic lesions of the pancreas. Gastroenterol Clin North Am 33:891-906, 2004.
26. Ros PR, Mortele KJ: Imaging of pancreatic neoplasms. JBR-BTR 84:239-249, 2001.
27. Brugge WR: Role of endoscopic ultrasound in the diagnosis of cystic tumors of the pancreas. Pancreatology 1:637-640, 2001.
28. Carlson SK, Johnson CD, Brandt KR, et al: Pancreatic cystic neoplasms: The role and sensitivity of needle aspiration and biopsy. Abdom Imaging 23:387-393, 1998.
29. Ueda M, Miura Y, Kunihiro O, et al: MUC1 overexpression is the most reliable marker of invasive carcinoma in intraductal papillary mucinous tumor (IPMN). Hepatogastroenterology 52:398-403, 2005.
30. Schoedel KE, Finkelstein SD, Ohori NP: K-ras and microsatellite marker analysis of fine-needle aspirates from intraductal papillary mucinous neoplasms of the pancreas. Diagn Cytopathol 34:605-608, 2006.
31. Di Stasi M, Lencioni R, Solmi L, et al: Ultrasound-guided fine needle biopsy of pancreatic masses: Results of a multicenter study. Am J Gastroenterol 93:1329-1333, 1998.
32. Amin Z, Theis B, Russell RCG, et al: Diagnosing pancreatic cancer: The role of percutaneous biopsy and CT. Clin Radiol 61:996-1002, 2006.
33. Silverman SG, Gan YU, Mortele KJ, et al: Renal masses in the adult patient: Role of percutaneous biopsy. Radiology 240:6-22, 2006.
34. Rodriguez J, Kasberg C, Nipper M, et al: CT-guided needle biopsy of the pancreas: A retrospective analysis of diagnostic accuracy. Am J Gastroenterol 87:1610-1613, 1992.
35. Edoute Y, Lemberg S, Malberger E: Preoperative and intraoperative fine needle aspiration cytology of pancreatic lesions. Am J Gastroenterol 86:1015-1019, 1991.
36. Qian X, Hecht JL: Pancreatic fine needle aspiration. A comparison of computed tomographic and endoscopic ultrasonographic guidance. Acta Cytol 47:723-726, 2003.
37. Itoi T, Itokawa F, Sofuni A, et al: Puncture of solid pancreatic tumors guided by endoscopic ultrasonography: A pilot study series comparing trucut and 19-gauge and 22-gauge aspiration needles. Endoscopy 37:362-366, 2005.
38. Storch I, Jorda M, Thurer R, et al: Advantage of EUS trucut biopsy combined with fine-needle aspiration without immediate on-site cytopathologic examination. Gastrointest Endosc 64:505-511, 2006.
39. Chang KJ, Albers CG, Erickson RA, et al: EUS-guided fine needle aspiration of pancreatic carcinoma. Am J Gastroenterol 89:263-266, 1994.
40. van der Waaij LA, van Dullemen HM, Porte RJ: Cyst fluid analysis in the differential diagnosis of pancreatic cystic lesions: A pooled analysis. Gastrointest Endosc 62:383-389, 2005.
41. Brugge WR, Lewandrowski K, Lee-Lewandrowski E, et al: Diagnosis of pancreatic cystic neoplasms: a report of the cooperative pancreatic cyst study. Gastroenterology 126:1330-1336, 2004.
42. Ryu JK, Woo SM, Hwang JH, et al: Cyst fluid analysis for the differential diagnosis of pancreatic cysts. Diagn Cytopath 31:100-105, 2004.
43. Frossard JL, Amouyal P, Amouyal G, et al: Performance of endosonography-guided fine needle aspiration in the diagnosis of pancreatic cystic lesions. Am J Gastroenterol 98:1516-1524, 2003.
44. Jhala N, Jhala D, Vickers SM, et al: Biomarkers in diagnosis of pancreatic carcinoma in fine-needle aspirates. Am J Clin Pathol 126:572-579, 2006.
45. Lee LS, Saltzman JR, Bounds BC, et al: EUS-guided fine needle aspiration of pancreatic cysts: A retrospective analysis of complications and their predictors. Clin Gastroenterol Hepatol 3:231-236, 2005.
46. Paquin SC, Gariepy G, Lepanto L, et al: A first report of tumor seeding because of EUS-guided FNA of a pancreatic adenocarcinoma. Gastrointest Endosc 61:610-611, 2005.
47. Bradley EL III: A clinically based classification system for acute pancreatitis. Summary of the International Symposium on Acute Pancreatitis, Atlanta, Ga, September 11-13, 1992. Arch Surg 128:586-590, 1993.

48. Mortele KJ, Banks PA, Silverman SG: State-of-the-art imaging of acute pancreatitis. JBR-BTR 86:193-208, 2003.

49. Steinberg W, Tenner S: Acute pancreatitis. N Engl J Med 330:1198-1210, 1994.

50. Perez A, Whang EE, Brooks DC, et al: Is severity of necrotizing pancreatitis increased in extended necrosis and infected necrosis? Pancreas 3:229-233, 2002.

51. Banks PA, Gerzof SG, Langevein RE, et al: CT-guided needle aspiration of pancreatic infection: Accuracy and prognostic implications. Int J Pancreatol 18:265-270, 1995.

52. Banks PA: Practice guidelines in acute pancreatitis. Am J Gastroenterol 92:377-386, 1997.

53. Lee MJ, Rattner DW, Legemate DA, et al: Acute complicated pancreatitis: Redefining the role of interventional radiology. Radiology 183:171-174, 1992.

54. Lee MJ, Wittich GR, Mueller PR: Percutaneous intervention in acute pancreatitis. RadioGraphics 18:711-724, 1998.

55. vanSonnenberg E, Wittich GR, Casola G, et al: Complicated pancreatic inflammatory disease: Diagnostic and therapeutic role of interventional radiology. Radiology 155:335-340, 1985.

56. vanSonnenberg E, Casola G, Varney RR, et al: Imaging and interventional radiology for pancreatitis and its complications. Radiol Clin North Am 27:65-72, 1989.

57. Balthazar EJ, Freeny PC, vanSonnenberg E: Imaging and intervention in acute pancreatitis. Radiology 193:297-306, 1994.

58. vanSonnenberg E, Wing VW, Casola G, et al: Temporizing effect of percutaneous drainage of complicated abscesses in critically ill patients. AJR 142:821-826, 1984.

59. vanSonnenberg E, Wittich GR, Goodacre BW, et al: Percutaneous abscess drainage: Update. World J Surg 25:362-369, 2001.

60. Berzin TM, Mortele KJ, Banks PA: The management of suspected pancreatic sepsis. Gastroenterol Clin North Am 35:393-407, 2006.

61. Buchler MW, Gloor B, Muller CA, et al: Acute necrotizing pancreatitis: Treatment strategy according to the status of infection. Ann Surg 232:619-626, 2000.

62. vanSonnenberg E, Ferrucci JT, Mueller PR, et al: Percutaneous drainage of abscesses and fluid collections: Technique, results and applications. Radiology 142:1-10, 1982.

63. Rattner DW, Legermate DA, Lee MJ, et al: Early surgical debridement of symptomatic pancreatic necrosis is beneficial irrespective of infection. Am J Surgery 163:105-109, 1992.

64. Bradley EL III, Allen K: A prospective longitudinal study of observation versus surgical intervention in the management of necrotizing pancreatitis. Am J Surg 161:19-24, 1991.

65. Uhl W, Warshaw A, Imrie C, et al: IAP guideline for the surgical management of acute pancreatitis. Pancreatology 2:565-573, 2002.

66. Walser EM, Nealon WH, Marroquin S, et al: Sterile fluid collections in acute pancreatitis: catheter drainage versus simple aspiration. Cardiovasc Intervent Radiol 29:102-107, 2006.

67. Isaji S, Takada T, Kawarada Y, et al: JPN Guidelines for the management of acute pancreatitis: Surgical management. J Hepatobiliary Pancreat Surg 13:48-55, 2006.

68. Adams DB, Harvey TS, Anderson MC: Percutaneous catheter drainage of infected pancreatic and peripancreatic fluid collections. Arch Surg 125:1554-1557, 1990.

69. Freeny PC, Hauptmann E, Althaus SJ, et al: Percutaneous CT guided drainage of infected acute necrotizing pancreatitis: Techniques and results. AJR 170:969-975, 1998.

70. Freeny PC, Lewis GP, Traverso LW, et al: Infected pancreatic fluid collections: Percutaneous catheter drainage. Radiology 167:435-441, 1988.

71. Endlicher E, Volk M, Feuerbach S, et al: Long-term follow-up of patients with necrotizing pancreatitis treated by percutaneous necrosectomy. Hepatogastroenterology 50:2225-2228, 2003.

72. Goldberg MA, Mueller PR, Saini S, et al: Importance of daily rounds by the radiologist after interventional procedures of the abdomen and chest. Radiology 180:767-770, 1991.

73. Singh AK, Gervais DA, Alhilali LM, et al: Imaging-guided catheter drainage of abdominal collections with fistulous pancreaticobiliary communication. AJR 187:1591-1596, 2006.

74. McClave SA, Greene LM, Snider HL, et al: Comparison of the safety of early enteral vs. parenteral nutrition in mild acute pancreatitis. J Parenteral Enteral Nutr 21:14-20, 1997.

75. Windsor AC, Kanwar S, Li AG, et al: Compared with parenteral nutrition, enteral feeding attenuates the acute phase response and improves disease severity in acute pancreatitis. Gut 42:431-435, 1998.

76. Kalfarentzos F, Kehagias J, Mead N, et al: Enteral nutrition is superior to parenteral nutrition in severe acute pancreatitis: Results of a randomized prospective trial. Br J Surg 84:1665-1669, 1997.

77. Deviere J, Bueso H, Baize M, et al: Complete disruption of the main pancreatic duct: endoscopic management. Gastrointest Endosc 42:445-451, 1995.

78. Chebli JM, Gaburri PD, de Souza AF, et al: Internal pancreatic fistulas: Proposal of a management algorithm based on a case series analysis. J Clin Gastroenterol 38:795-800, 2004.

79. Andren-Sandberg A, Ansorge C, Eiriksson K, et al: Treatment of pancreatic pseudocysts. Scand J Surg 94:165-175, 2005.

80. Singhai D, Kakodhar R, Sud R, et al: Issues in management of pancreatic pseudocysts. JOP 7:502-507, 2006.

81. Cheruvu CV, Clarke MG, Prentice M, et al: Conservative treatment as an option in the management of pancreatic pseudocyst. Ann R Coll Surg Engl 85:313-316, 2003.

82. Wittich GR, vanSonnenberg E: When should radiologists intervene in management of pancreatic pseudocysts and other complications of acute pancreatitis? AJR 166:211, 1996.

83. vanSonnenberg E, Wittich GR, Chon KS, et al: Percutaneous radiologic drainage of pancreatic abscesses. AJR 168:979-984, 1997.

84. vanSonnenberg E, Wittich GR, Casola G, et al: Percutaneous drainage of infected and noninfected pancreatic pseudocysts: Experience in 101 cases. Radiology 170:757-761, 1989.

85. Criado E, De Stefano AA, Weiner TM, et al: Long-term results of percutaneous catheter drainage of pancreatic pseudocysts. Surg Gynecol Obstet 175:293-298, 1992.

Anomalies and Anatomic Variants of the Pancreas

Ali Shirkhoda, MD • Peyman Borghei, MD

EMBRYOLOGY

VARIANTS OF NORMAL ANATOMY

CONGENITAL ANOMALIES OF THE PANCREAS

Pancreas Divisum

Annular and Semiannular Pancreas

Ectopic Pancreatic Tissue

Agenesis, Hypoplasia, and Hyperplasia of the Pancreas

Ductal Abnormalities

Congenital Cysts

In order to recognize the anatomic variants of the pancreas and understand how various pancreatic anomalies develop, it is important to be familiar with the pancreatic embryology and development. Errors or variations at several critical periods in the development of pancreas are responsible for the majority of anomalies. These anomalies can vary in their presentation from being totally asymptomatic to being inconsistent with live.[1-5] In this chapter, a brief discussion of the important events of pancreatic embryology is followed by presentation of normal variants and various types of pancreatic anomalies.

EMBRYOLOGY

The pancreatic duct develops from two buds originating from the endodermal lining of the duodenum.[6] One is the dorsal pancreatic bud, which is in the dorsal mesentery and is seen as a diverticulum of the foregut before 28 days. It grows into the dorsal mesentery (Fig. 98-1A). The other is the ventral pancreatic bud located close to the bile duct and appears as an invagination at the biliary-duodenal angle between 30 and 35 days.[1]

The dorsal and ventral pancreatic buds soon grow into a pair of branching, arborized ductal systems, each with its own central duct (Fig. 98-1B). At day 37, the ventral pancreas rotates posterior to the duodenum and comes into contact with the dorsal pancreas (Fig. 98-1C). These two anlagen fuse and, together with the duodenum, fuse with the abdominal wall. In the mature organ, the ventral primordium becomes the inferior portion of the head and the uncinate process, and the dorsal pancreas becomes the body and tail. After the fusion, a new duct connects the distal portion of the dorsal pancreatic duct with the shorter duct of the ventral pancreas

to form the main duct or the duct of Wirsung (Fig. 98-2). This main pancreatic duct, which is present in approximately 91% of adults, enters the duodenum together with the bile duct at the major papilla. The proximal portion of the dorsal pancreatic duct is pinched off during fusion and usually atrophies and disappears but may persist as the small accessory duct of Santorini, which has a variety of appearances (Fig. 98-3). This accessory duct empties into the duodenum at the minor papilla 2 to 3 cm proximal to the ampulla of Vater.[7,8] In about 10% of all cases, the duct system fails to fuse and the original double system persists.[1,9]

As the duodenum grows and differentiates, the duodenal wall resorbs the distal bile duct up to its junction with the pancreatic duct. Different degrees of resorption account for variations in the appearance and relationships of the common bile duct and pancreatic duct. If ductal resorption is minimal, a long intramural ampulla is created, and the junction is extramural. The junction becomes intramural with increasing degrees of resorption, which produces a shortened ampulla.[10-15] Maximal resorption produces separate orifices for the pancreatic duct and common bile duct (see Fig. 98-2), which no longer share a common ampulla.[7,16]

Beginning in the third month of fetal life, the islets of Langerhans develop as clusters of cells from the terminal ductules. They become intimately associated with the capillary plexus and finally separate from the ductules to become the endocrine portion of the pancreas. Insulin secretion begins at approximately the fifth month. The acini develop from terminal ductal cells. The ductal system and the acini collectively become the exocrine portion of the pancreas.[6] Secretory activity probably becomes established in the pancreas during the second trimester, although this has been disputed.[1]

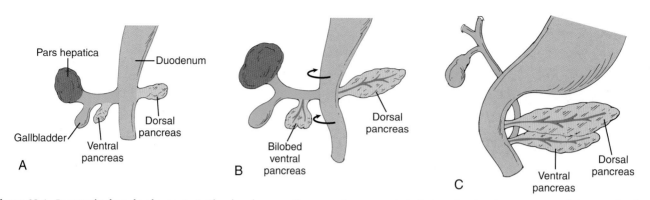

Figure 98-1. Pancreatic duct development. A. The dorsal pancreatic segment grows posteriorly into the dorsal mesentery, and the vental anlage develops as an outpouching from the base of the hepatic diverticulum and grows in the ventral mesentery. **B.** The ventral component transiently develops into a bifid structure. The ventral pancreas and the bile duct system will be carried posteriorly as the duodenum matures. **C.** The final stage of pancreatic duct maturation entails fusion of the two systems. (**A-C** from Taylor AJ, Bohorfoush AG: Interpretation of ERCP: With Associated Digital Imaging Correlation, Philadelphia, Lippincott-Raven, 1996, pp 209-210.)

The weight of the pancreas, which is 5 to 5.5 g at birth, will increase to 15 g at the end of the first year.[11]

The process of pancreatic fusion is complicated, and a wide spectrum of anomalies or anatomic variants may appear related to this process—for example, agenesis, aplasia of the pancreatic anlage, hypoplasia, annular pancreas, and pancreas divisum.[12]

VARIANTS OF NORMAL ANATOMY

The lateral aspect of the head and neck of the pancreas can have varieties of shapes and occasionally look prominent (Figs. 98-4 and 98-5). However, many of the contour variations may represent a spectrum of fusion patterns that cannot be attributed to pancreas divisum alone.[13,14] A deep cleft separating two distinct pancreatic moieties may be identified on CT scans in the head and neck of the pancreas in patients with pancreas divisum.

The pancreas is surrounded by fat that clearly defines its margin. However, owing to the lack of any pancreatic capsule, the pancreatic lobules can be outlined by fat. Such fatty infiltration can be diffuse or focal (Fig. 98-6). Focal fatty infiltration can mimic a mass on CT, particularly if there is associated lobulation (Fig. 98-7). Therefore, MRI may become necessary to differentiate this benign process from a neoplasm (Fig. 98-8). Fatty infiltration may be associated with focal sparing of pancreatic parenchyma and that should not be mistaken for tumor (Fig. 98-9).

The position and configuration of the pancreas are quite variable, and these variations may simulate pathologic conditions. For example, the pancreatic head is not fixed in position, although it almost invariably maintains a fixed relationship medial to the second portion of the duodenum and lateral to the root of the superior mesenteric vessels, even if these structures are shifted to the left of the midline. Although the splenic vein usually marks the dorsal margin of the body

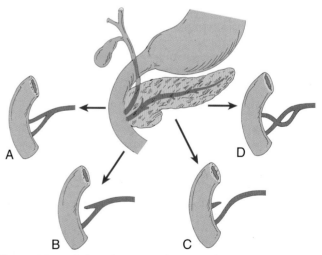

Figure 98-3. Variation of accessory duct appearance. After the dorsal-ventral system fusion, the original dorsal duct segment draining into the duodenum may (**A**) remain as the duct of Santorini, serving as a slender, narrowed connection of the main pancreatic duct (MPD) with the duodenum through the minor papilla, (**B**) maintain connection with the MPD but not drain into the duodenum, thereby becoming another MPD side branch, (**C**) maintain communication with the duodenum at the minor papilla but lose connection with the MPD, or (**D**) maintain connection with both the duodenum and the MPD but develop a circuitous course forming the ansa pancreatica. (**A-D** from Taylor AJ, Bohorfoush AG: Interpretation of ERCP: With Associated Digital Imaging Correlation. Philadelphia, Lippincott-Raven, 1996, pp 209-210.)

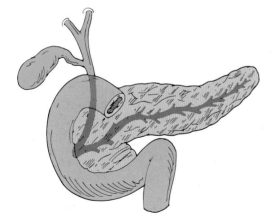

Figure 98-2. Duct of Wirsung. Notice the junction of the ventral duct and common bile duct at the ampulla with total regression of dorsal duct.

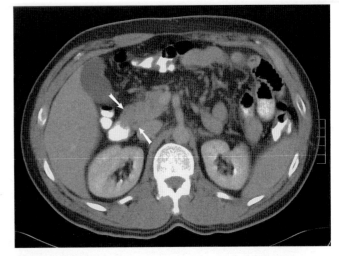

Figure 98-4. Pancreatic head lobulation: a normal variant. A 48-year-old man with lower abdominal pain was found to have a lobulated configuration of the pancreatic head with horizontal extension (*arrows*) medial to the duodenum. CT scan that was done 4 years ago showed the same finding.

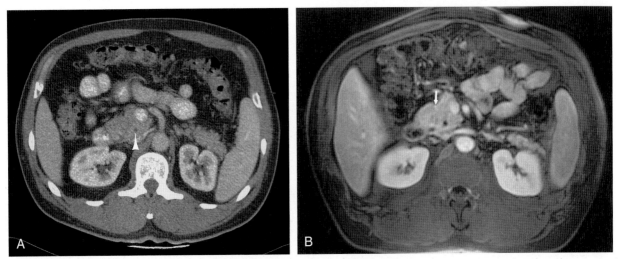

Figure 98-5. Lateral lobulation of the pancreatic head on CT and MRI. A 62-year-old man with epigastric pain was thought to have a prominent pancreatic head for which MRI was recommended. **A.** The axial CT reveals lateral lobulation of the pancreatic head with normal pancreatic and bile duct (*arrowhead*). **B.** Fat suppression postgadolinium T1-weighted image reveals homogeneous enhancement of the lobulated head with better visualization of the ducts. Notice the normal pancreaticoduodenal artery (*arrow*) between the head and lobulated part.

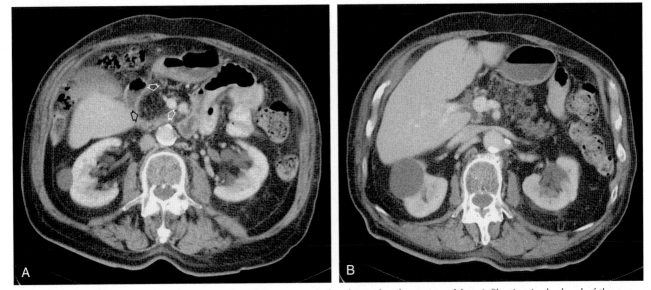

Figure 98-6. Fatty infiltration of the pancreas. A. CT of the pancreatic head reveals a large area of fatty infiltration in the head of the pancreas (*open arrows*). A portion of the uncinate process is spared from fat. Notice lack of any mass effect on the adjacent superior mesenteric vein. **B.** Fatty infiltration is also present in the pancreatic body. The tail is spared.

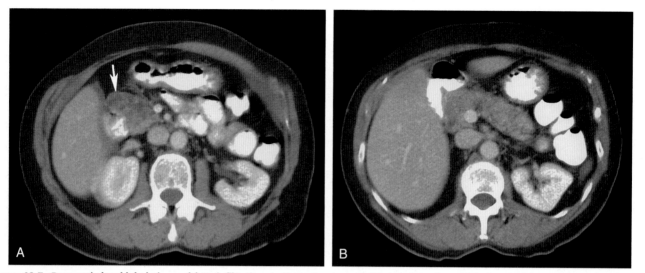

Figure 98-7. Pancreatic head lobulation and fatty infiltration. A. Contrast-enhanced CT scan shows lateral lobulation of the pancreatic head (*arrow*) with heterogeneous density due to fatty infiltration. **B.** Upper portion of the head, body, and the tail are spared fatty infiltration.

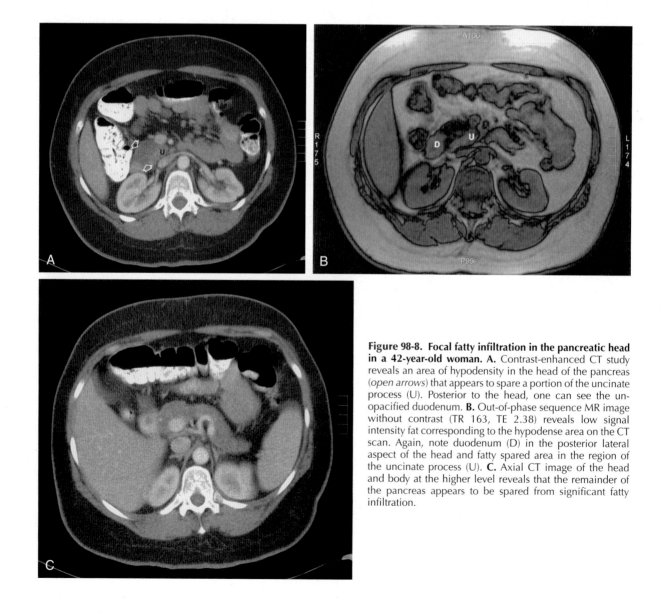

Figure 98-8. Focal fatty infiltration in the pancreatic head in a 42-year-old woman. A. Contrast-enhanced CT study reveals an area of hypodensity in the head of the pancreas (*open arrows*) that appears to spare a portion of the uncinate process (U). Posterior to the head, one can see the unopacified duodenum. **B.** Out-of-phase sequence MR image without contrast (TR 163, TE 2.38) reveals low signal intensity fat corresponding to the hypodense area on the CT scan. Again, note duodenum (D) in the posterior lateral aspect of the head and fatty spared area in the region of the uncinate process (U). **C.** Axial CT image of the head and body at the higher level reveals that the remainder of the pancreas appears to be spared from significant fatty infiltration.

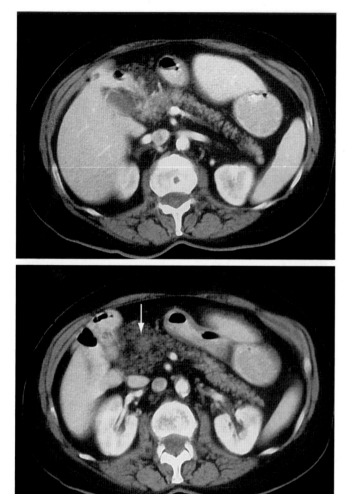

Figure 98-9. Fatty infiltration of the pancreatic head. Notice two contrast-enhanced CT images taken at 2-cm interval show sparing of lower portion of the head (*arrow*) from fatty infiltration. The body and tail are normal.

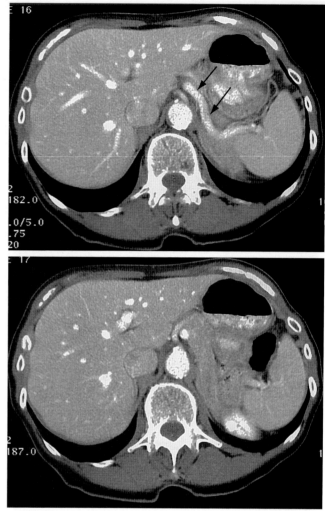

Figure 98-10. Extension of the pancreatic tail into the adrenal fossa. Notice as a normal variant, the splenic vein (*arrows*) no longer serves as the ventral pancreatic landmark. The top and bottom images are continuous 5-mm slices.

and tail of the pancreas, the tip of the gland may rarely curve dorsal to the splenic vein to simulate adrenal abnormalities (Fig. 98-10). Occasionally, even in normal persons, the pancreatic tail may be anterior-lateral to the left kidney, where it may appear as a pseudomass on excretory urography. In patients with prior left nephrectomy or in those with congenital absence of the left kidney, the pancreatic tail is often displaced into the renal fossa, which may simulate recurrent tumor or a primary retroperitoneal lesion.[15]

Kreel and colleagues[16] published a set of in vivo and in vitro measurements of pancreatic dimensions and concluded that the normal diameter of the head was up to 3 cm, that of the neck and body up to 2.5 cm, and that of the tail up to 2 cm. However, the size, shape, and position of the normal pancreas are highly variable (Fig. 98-11), and there is usually a gradual tapering from the head to the tail without abrupt alterations in size or contour. There is gradual decrease in the size of the pancreas with advancing age, sometimes becoming very small beyond the seventh decade. Fatty lobulations are more commonly observed in obese and elderly individuals. Rarely, an accessory spleen can be embedded in the tail of the pancreas, and MRI or a nuclear medicine study may be needed to differentiate this variant from a mass (Fig. 98-12).

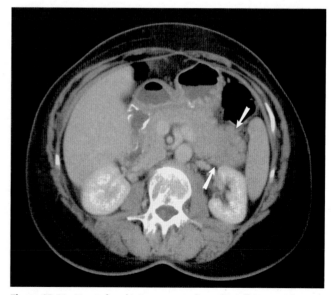

Figure 98-11. Normal variant pancreas where the tail (*arrows*) is more prominent than the head and proximal body. Notice homogeneous enhancement of pancreas and normal lobulations of its borders.

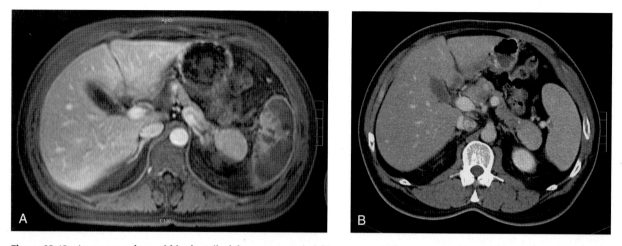

Figure 98-12. Accessory spleen within the tail of the pancreas mimicking a mass. A. The contrast-enhanced fat-suppression T1-weighted MR image that was done due to the patient's left upper quadroon pain reveals areas of infarction of the spleen. There is a well-defined homogeneous mass in the tail of the pancreas displaying similar signal intensity as the upper part of the spleen (not shown). **B.** Upon review of the contrast-enhanced CT scan that was done 2 years earlier, the mass has not changed. On a prior study, it was presumed to represent spleen and a nuclear medicine examination proved the nature of the mass to be accessory spleen in the tail of the pancreas.

Bifid pancreatic duct (Fig. 98-13) is a rare anatomic anomaly in which the main pancreatic duct is bifurcated along its length. It is associated with high incidence of pancreatitis.[17]

CONGENITAL ANOMALIES OF THE PANCREAS

Pancreas Divisum

In this anomaly, the pancreas is divided in two separate parts as a result of an absent or incomplete fusion of the ventral and dorsal anlagen. As a consequence, the pancreatic head and

uncinate process are drained by the duct of Wirsung through the major papilla; the body and tail are drained by the duct of Santorini through the minor papilla[18,19] (Fig. 98-14). This anomaly is seen in 4% to 11% of autopsy series and 3% to 4% of endoscopic retrograde cholangiopancreatography (ERCP) series.[20-23] In an analysis of 650 ERCP studies done by Uomo and coworkers,[24] 485 patients had satisfactory imaging of the pancreatic ducts, whereas in 48 cases (9.9%), anatomic variants of the duct were found. These included fusion variants in 26 cases (22 pancreas divisum and 4 functional divisum) and duplications variants in 22 patients (1 bifurcation of the main pancreatic duct, 4 loop, 2 N-shaped, and 3 ring).

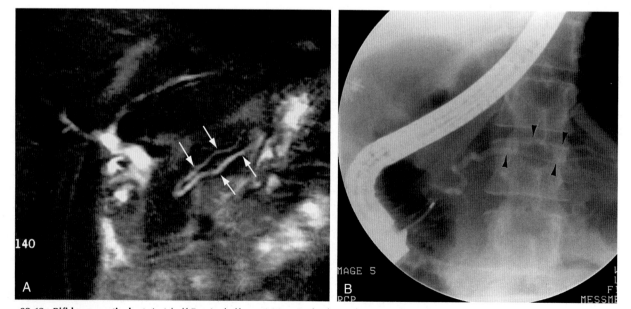

Figure 98-13. Bifid pancreatic duct. A. A half-Fourier half-acquisition single-shot turbo spin echo (HASTE) sequence was used for magnetic resonance cholangiography (MRC), which showed a dilated common bile duct due to a distal stone. However, a bifid pancreatic duct (*arrows*) was incidentally demonstrated. **B.** ERCP clearly demonstrated bifurcation of the pancreatic duct (bifid) throughout the body of the pancreas (*arrowheads*). (Courtesy of Dr. Ann S. Fulcher, Medical College of Virginia, Richmond, VA.)

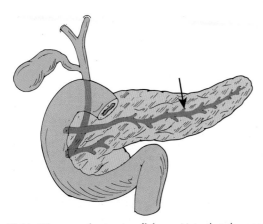

Figure 98-14. Diagram of pancreas divisum. Note that the pancreatic head and uncinate process (ventral duct) along with common bile duct are drained into major papilla while the body and tail (dorsal duct; *arrow*) drain into minor papilla.

Clinical Findings

Although the anatomic variant of pancreas divisum has been well known for some time, its clinical significance has become evident with the advent of ERCP. Most cases of pancreas divisum are asymptomatic. This anomaly may contribute to recurrent episodes of idiopathic pancreatitis in younger patients with no risk factors.[25,26] Between 12% and 26% of patients with idiopathic recurrent pancreatitis have this anomaly, as opposed to 3% and 6% in the general population.[22,26] The age at presentation varies widely but is most commonly between ages 30 and 50 years.[27] Several reports of pancreatitis associated with pancreas divisum in children have appeared, and there is a report of this anomaly occurring in multiple family members.[28]

It is postulated that in pancreas divisum, the duct of Santorini and its accessory ampulla are too small to adequately drain the volume of secretions produced by the pancreatic body and tail.[29] In a manometer study, patients with pancreas divisum had significantly higher pressure readings of the dorsal duct cannulated through Santorini than of the ventral duct cannulated through Wirsung. The study concluded that in pancreas divisum, there is chronic stasis of pancreatic fluid that, when compounded by additional factors such as alcoholism, causes greater viscosity, which increases the risk of pancreatitis.[26] Surgical sphincteroplasty of the accessory sphincter has been advocated as an important means of preventing recurrent bouts of pancreatitis in these patients.[30-33]

Association of pancreatic divisum with pancreatic tumors has been reported.[34-38] In a limited study, pancreatic tumors were detected in 12.5% of patients with divisum.[34] The authors believe that relative stenosis of minor pancreatic duct and longstanding pancreatic obstruction might be risk factors for developing pancreatic cancer.

There are some other problems associated with divisum, like santorinicele or cystic dilation of the dorsal pancreas at the minor papillae, that may indicate obstruction at the minor papilla.[39] Also, cases of multiple neuroendocrine tumors of the pancreas[40] and intestinal malrotation[41] have been reported in association with pancreas divisum.

Radiologic Findings

Endoscopic Retrograde Cholangiopancreatography

Endoscopic retrograde cholangiopancreatography (ERCP) is often considered the effective modality for confirming a diagnosis of pancreas divisum.[22-24] Often, injection of contrast material into the duct of Wirsung is met with resistance and even pain. However, after opacification, the duct is short and tapered, and acinarization commonly occurs as the endoscopist attempts to fill the "remainder" of the duct (Fig. 98-15). This duct tapers gradually from the orifice, sending branches in the pancreatic head.[21,42] It must be differentiated from a duct that appears foreshortened secondary to previous trauma, partial pancreatectomy, pseudocyst, or stricture caused by carcinoma or pancreatitis. In these cases, the pancreatic duct typically has an abrupt or irregular terminus.[21-23] The duct of Santorini is often not visualized by injection of the major papilla, and if cannulation is successful, the full-length duct of Santorini is seen without communication to the smaller duct. Otherwise, the diagnosis can be made by secretin stimulation and identification of secretions emanating from the minor papilla only. See Chapter 76 for more details.

Linear-Array Endoscopic Ultrasonography

Endoscopic ultrasonography (EUS) frequently allows detailed imaging of the pancreatic parenchyma and ductal system. It has been reported that with the use of radial instruments, if the portal vein, common bile duct, and main pancreatic duct could be demonstrated in one image, the diagnosis of pancreatic divisum would be excluded. This is considered an indirect assessment for the evaluation of pancreatic divisum.[43] Therefore, using a linear-array instrument, if the main pancreatic duct passes from the major papilla to the pancreatic body and tail, or if the duct crosses the border separating the ventral and dorsal anlagen, the diagnosis of pancreatic divisum is excluded. Lai et al.[44] reported the sensitivity, specificity, and accuracy of this method for diagnosis of pancreas divisum to be 95%, 97%, and 97%, respectively. There are some merits for EUS over MRCP, and perhaps ERCP, as it allows direct visualization and fine-needle aspiration biopsy of pancreatic masses that otherwise may lead to the ductographic phenomenon of pseudodivisum. This could conceivably result from the presence of apparently separate ventral and dorsal ductal systems due to mechanical obstruction near the expected point of connection between these two systems.[44] Also, EUS seems to be less invasive than ERCP, because EUS does not involve pancreatic duct cannulation or contrast injection, which is a risk factor for developing iatrogenic pancreatitis.[43-47] Therefore, linear-array EUS appears to be a promising, minimally invasive diagnostic imaging modality for the detection of pancreas divisum.[43,44] See Chapter 13 for more details.

Sonographic Secretin Test

In an attempt to identify patients who will benefit from surgical sphincterotomy, several tests have been proposed to assess the adequacy of the accessory papilla in transmitting pancreatic secretions. In the sonographic secretin test, the main pancreatic duct is sonographically monitored before and after the intravenous administration of secretin (1 unit/kg body

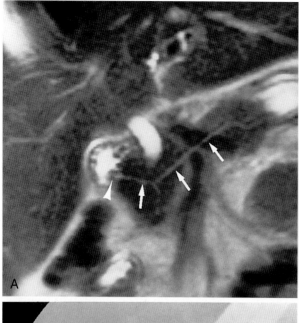

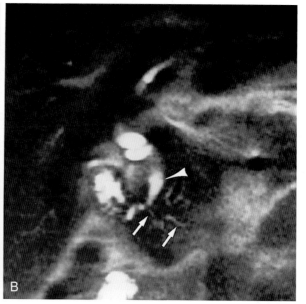

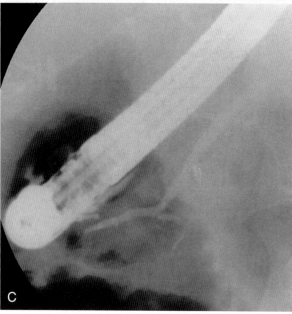

Figure 98-15. Pancreas divisum in a 36-year-old patient with recurrent pancreatitis. A. MRC demonstrates that the dorsal pancreatic duct (*arrows*) enters the minor papilla (*arrowhead*). The point of entry is cephalad to the major papilla. Additional images fail to demonstrate any communication between the ventral and dorsal pancreatic ducts. **B.** The distal bile duct (*arrowhead*) appears to join the ventral pancreatic duct (*arrows*) to enter the major papilla. **C.** ERCP was able to demonstrate the dorsal pancreatic duct by cannulation of the minor papilla. (**A-C** from Fulcher AS, Turner MA: MR pancreatography: A useful tool for evaluating pancreatic disorders. RadioGraphics 19:5-24, 1999.)

weight).[48] Secretin-induced dilatation occurs in 72% of symptomatic patients found to have a stenotic accessory papilla associated with pancreas divisum. The sonographic secretin test is also highly controversial; several authors have demonstrated that dilation of the pancreatic duct can be a normal finding.[49-51] In addition to surgery, pancreas divisum can be treated by percutaneous dilatation and stent placement.[52,53]

Computed Tomography

Contour abnormalities of the pancreatic head and neck have been identified on CT in some patients with pancreatic divisum.[54] CT can occasionally suggest this diagnosis when two distinct pancreatic moieties or an unfused ductal system is identified on thin collimation scans (Fig. 98-16). The two moieties may cause pancreatic head enlargement or may be separated by a fat cleft. Sometimes, fatty replacement of the dorsal pancreas may delineate it from the ventral moiety.[30,54] Also, the pancreatic head may be spared from atrophy and

pancreatitis affecting the body and tail, which produces a pseudotumor on CT and ultrasound studies.[55] In alcoholics, isolated ventral pancreatitis may occasionally be observed, which suggests a synergism between the effects of alcohol and bile reflux into the ventral pancreas. The dorsal pancreas is spared this reflux because of the pancreas divisum.[56] Other ductal anomalies may also produce masses on cross-sectional imaging.[57,58]

MDCT with high-resolution oblique coronal image reconstruction assists in the depiction of the continuity of pancreatic ducts. The sensitivity and specificity of this method for diagnosis of pancreatic divisum are reported to be 100% and 89%, respectively.[59]

Magnetic Resonance Cholangiopancreatography

Heavily T2-weighted, two-dimensional, fast spin-echo sequences using a body coil can often accurately depict pancreatic ductal anomaly and establish the diagnosis of pancreas

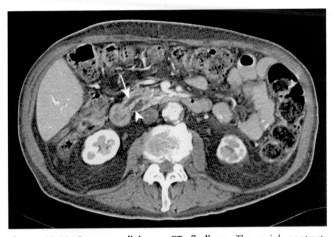

Figure 98-16. Pancreas divisum: CT findings. The axial contrast-enhanced CT study through the head of the pancreas reveals two separate pancreatic ducts draining into the duodenum. Other images prove the separate nature of these ducts, the upper one (*arrow*) draining the head and body of the pancreas into minor papilla and the lower one (*arrowhead*) only from the inferior head and the uncinate process draining into major papilla.

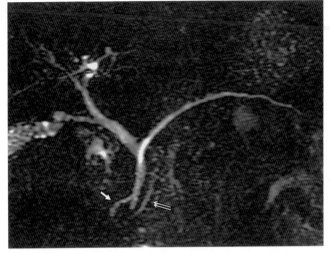

Figure 98-17. Pancreas divisum: MRCP findings. Coronal oblique thick-slab MRCP image reveals that the pancreatic duct drains through the minor papilla (*single arrow*). The duct of Wirsung is also depicted (*double arrows*) without connection between the two systems. The findings are consistent with complete pancreas divisum. This image was obtained after secretin injection. (Courtesy of Dr. Carmen DeJuan, Department of Radiology Hospital Clinic, University of Barcelona, Spain.)

divisum.[60] Gradient sequences using breath hold have been found useful for evaluation of pancreatic and biliary system. Magnetic resonance cholangiopancreatography (MRCP) is superior to ERCP for visualizing the pancreatic ducts, especially with the use of half-Fourier acquisition single-shot turbo spin-echo (HASTE) sequence.[61] However, MRCP using single-shot rapid acquisition with relaxation enhancement may be superior to HASTE for increasing pancreatic duct conspicuity.[62]

When T1-weighted sequences with fat suppression are performed,[63,64] MRCP allows visualization of not only the pancreatic ducts but also the pancreatic parenchyma around the duodenum. Indeed, MRCP may be able to replace ERCP in the diagnosis of pancreas divisum.

Secretin-stimulated MRCP has been used in the diagnosis of santorinicele or cystic dilation of dorsal pancreas at minor papillae and also for pancreas divisum[39,65,66] (Fig. 98-17). See Chapter 77 for more detail concerning MRCP.

Annular and Semiannular Pancreas

Annular pancreas is a rare congenital anomaly occurring in 1 of every 12,000 to 15,000 live births. In this anomaly, the annulus is often a flat band of pancreatic tissue completely encircling the second portion of the duodenum[21,23] (Fig. 98-18). Unusual locations of annular pancreas have also been reported to be around the third portion of duodenum.[67]

In normal pancreatic development, the ventral anlage develops as two separate buds from the hepatic diverticulum. The left ventral bud atrophies, and the right ventral bud persists to form the head and uncinate process. The ventral anlage undergoes 180-degree counter clockwise rotation while the duodenum undergoes 90-degree clockwise rotation, so that the ventral anlage occupies a position contiguous with the dorsal anlage, medial to the duodenum. There are three theories concerning the formation of the annular pancreas: (1) hypertrophy of both the dorsal and the ventral ducts, resulting in a complete ring; (2) adherence of the ventral duct to the duodenum before rotation; and (3) hypertrophy or adherence of the left bud of a paired ventral primordium.[68]

Clinical Findings

Annular pancreas is an uncommon congenital anomaly that may manifest clinically in the neonate (52%) or may be asymptomatic until adulthood (48%). This disorder does not usually manifest clinically until third to fifth decade of life[69-71] or even occasionally later.[72]

Symptoms are usually related to duodenal obstruction. Neonates present with vomiting on the first day of life, and there often is an antecedent history of polyhydramnios and other manifestation of fetal gastrointestinal tract

Figure 98-18. Annular pancreas. A and **B.** Drawings illustrate the probable embryologic basis of annular pancreas. **C.** An annular pancreas encircles the duodenum. (**A** and **B** from Moore KL: The Developing Human, 4th ed. Philadelphia, WB Saunders, 1988.)

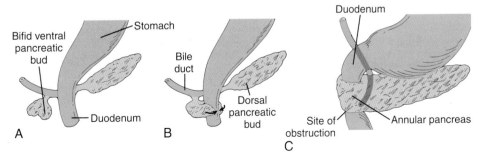

obstruction.[23,42,73,74] A number of other anomalies such as intestinal malrotation, duodenal atresias of various forms, and cardiac anomalies are often present as well.

Annular pancreas may be quiescent and not cause symptoms until adulthood. Kiernan et al.[75] reviewed 266 patients with symptoms and found that 48% were adults. In older children and adults, nausea, vomiting, and epigastric pain are the chief presenting complaints. The incidence of associated gastric and duodenal ulcers ranges from 26% to 48%, and pancreatitis develops in 15% to 30% of patients. The obstruction of the duodenum in these patients is apparently not sufficient to cause symptoms until there is supervening peptic ulcer disease or pancreatitis.[76-78] There are reports of extrahepatic biliary obstruction due to annular pancreas.[3,5]

In a 10-year review of annular pancreas in children, Jimenez et al.[79] found that among 16 patients, 12 (75%) presented within the first week of life, 5 (31%) had chromosomal anomalies and 6 had other major congenital problems. In another review of seven cases with annular pancreas, four patients (42.8%) had associated anomalies, including intestinal malrotation (42.8%), intrinsic duodenal obstruction (28.5%), trisomy 21 karyotype (14.2%), cardiac malformation (14.2%), and Meckel's diverticulum (14.2%).[80] The authors concluded that annular pancreas is most commonly associated with intestinal malrotation.

In the pediatric population, symptomatic annular pancreas is best treated by a bypass procedure such as gastrojejunostomy or duodenojejunostomy.[17,48] However, in adults, a variety of surgical, as well as interventional endoscopic procedures, are used therapeutically.

Pancreatic malignancy in the setting of annular pancreas has been reported, most often arising from the ventral bud.[81,82] However, involvement of dorsal bud has also been reported.[83,84] It is recommended to evaluate the pancreas for malignancy in cases of annular pancreas presenting with obstructive jaundice.[85]

Radiologic Findings

Plain Radiographs and Barium Studies

Pediatric patients with annular pancreas often have diagnostic findings on plain radiographs with the "double-bubble" sign (Fig. 98-19A); the proximal bubble is caused by gastric distention and the distal bubble by a dilated duodenal bulb.[23,25,75]

The radiographic findings on upper gastrointestinal barium studies are often characteristic and are best demonstrated when the duodenum is maximally distended. Stenosis is demonstrated in the periampullary region associated with an extrinsic eccentric defect on the medial margin of the second portion of the duodenum (Fig. 98-19B). The mucosa is intact unless there is associated peptic ulcer.[87] Peptic ulcer disease is quite common, so when an ulcer is seen in the periampullary duodenum in an adult, the diagnosis of annular pancreas as well as Zollinger-Ellison syndrome should be considered.[23,25]

Endoscopic Retrograde Cholangiopancreatography (ERCP)

Diagnosis of annular pancreas is most commonly suggested by ERCP, which shows typical features in about 85% of cases. In these patients, a normally located main pancreatic duct is seen in the body and tail that communicates with the small duct of the pancreatic head, which encircles the duodenum. This latter duct is seen originating on the right anterior surface of the duodenum, passing posteriorly around the duodenum and entering the main pancreatic or common bile duct near the ampulla. In some patients, biliary obstruction may be seen as well.

Computed Tomography

Findings on CT are often nonspecific, showing enlargement of the pancreatic head that has a central region of high attenuation representing contrast material within the narrowed duodenal segment. If the duodenum is not sufficiently opacified, only pancreatic head enlargement may be noted.[88] Other CT findings include apparent circumferential thickening of the duodenal wall in association with an enlarged pancreatic head. A peninsular protrusion of pancreatic tissue may also be seen in the duodenal lumen.[89,90] Review of continuous images on a monitor provides opportunity to follow the duodenum from above as it enters the encircling pancreatic head and then exits inferiorly. Occasionally, the duodenum may not be completely encircled with pancreatic tissue. This anomaly is called semiannular pancreas. Ueki et al.[91] reported that three-dimensional CT pancreatography may be useful in clarifying embryogenesis of annular pancreas.

Ultrasound

Nonspecific enlargement of the pancreatic head is the major sonographic abnormality seen in annular pancreas.[90] Endoscopic ultrasound is more accurate in making the diagnosis.[92]

Magnetic Resonance Imaging

Fat-suppressed T1-weighted sequence may show a normal appearing pancreatic tissue encircling the duodenum.[93] MR imaging as well as CT (Fig. 98-20) may be used as a problem-solving technique to supplement the conventional studies.[94,96] Because CT may only show an enlarged pancreatic head, MR imaging is able to clearly discriminate the pancreas from the duodenum.[95]

Angiography

Celiac angiography may demonstrate an anomalous branch from the posterior pancreaticoduodenal artery that courses in a right and inferior direction to supply the annular moiety.[23,42]

Ectopic Pancreatic Tissue

Heterotopic pancreas in which glandular acini ducts and well-differentiated islets can be recognized microscopically is rare. It is seen in organs derived, like the normal pancreas, from entoderm. Heterotopic pancreas is the result of heteroplastic differentiation of parts of embryonic entoderm that do not normally produce pancreatic tissue.[11] Although the embryonic origins of the pancreas and liver are close anatomically, ectopic pancreas is much more common than heterotopic liver.[1,10,97,98]

These ectopic rests of pancreatic tissue most commonly occur in the gastric antrum (25.5%) or proximal portion of the duodenum (27.7%). Less frequent sites include jejunum (15.9%), ileum, Meckel's diverticulum, colon, appendix, mesentery, omentum, liver, gallbladder, spleen, bile ducts, esophagus, ediastinal cyst,[99] fallopian tube, and bronchoesophageal fistula.[19,22,42,100-103] When present in the walls of

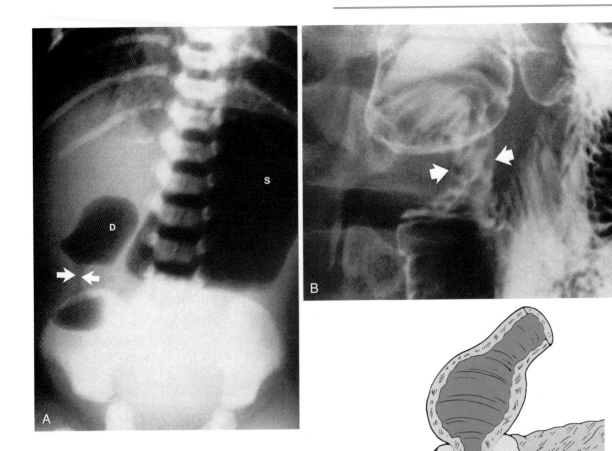

Figure 98-19. Annular pancreas. A. Annular pancreas presenting in neonatal period with narrowing (*arrows*) of descending duodenum. Duodenal bulb (D) and stomach (S) are dilated, producing the classic "double-bubble" sign. **B.** Annular pancreas manifests as concentric duodenal narrowing (arrows) in this adult patient who had nondescript epigastric pain. **C.** Diagram illustrates the pathologic process shown on the barium study. (**C** from Gray SW, Skandalakis JE, Skandalakis LJ: Embryology and congenital anomalies of the pancreas. In Howard JM, Jordan GL, Reber HA [eds]: Surgical Disease of the Pancreas. Philadelphia, Lea & Febiger, 1987, pp 37-45.)

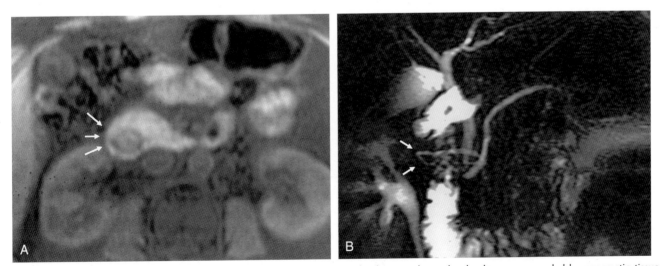

Figure 98-20. Annular pancreas: MR features. A. Axial fat-saturation T1-weighted image shows the duodenum surrounded by pancreatic tissue (*arrows*). **B.** Coronal oblique thick-slab MRCP image demonstrates the duct of the annular pancreas (*arrows*) that forms a complete loop around the duodenum. This examination was done after secretin administration. (Courtesy of Dr. Carmen DeJuan, Department of Radiology Hospital Clinic, University of Barcelona, Spain.)

the duodenum and stomach, heterotopic pancreas is usually composed of normal pancreatic tissue, including islet cells, and a small pancreatic duct. Islet cells are usually absent at other sites. The ectopic pancreatic tissue usually lies submucosally (73%), although it can be located in the muscularis mucosae or on the serosal surface of the gut.[104,105] Formation of cyst in association with duodenal heterotopic pancreas in pancreas divisum has also been reported.[104,105]

Ectopic pancreatic tissue is functional and subject to the same inflammatory and neoplastic disorders that afflict the normal pancreas. The majority of cases, however, are asymptomatic and found incidentally.[103-109] Indeed, many reported cases of pancreatic heterotopia in the duodenum are found incidentally during peptic ulcer surgery. Also, pancreatic tissue was found in the duodenum by careful sectioning in nearly 14% of autopsies, and pancreas-like tissue is also found 14.1% of postmortem studies of the biliary system. When symptomatic, ectopic pancreas may stimulate duodenal ulcer, gallbladder disease, or even appendicitis.[105,108] In the stomach, it may be a component of tumor-like lesions that cause symptoms such as pyloric obstruction.[107] Perivaterian pancreatic tissue may cause biliary obstruction and if the ectopic tissue located more distally may serve as a lead point for intussusception.[110] Symptomatic lesions tend to be larger than 1.5 cm, and malignant tumor has been reported to arise from these tissue rests.[107,109]

No specific treatment is necessary in this disorder, unless the ectopic pancreatic tissue is causing symptoms such as obstruction or hemorrhage.

Radiologic Findings

Ectopic pancreas characteristically appears as a broad-based, smooth, extramucosal or intramural lesion either along the greater curvature of the gastric antrum or in the proximal duodenum (Fig. 98-21). A small collection of barium appearing as a central niche or umbilication is diagnostic and present in 45% of cases. This represents the orifice of the rudimentary duct into which the ectopic pancreas empties.[95] This pit may be as large as 5 mm in diameter and 10 mm in length. If this feature is absent, the lesion cannot be differentiated from other submucosal tumors.[22,23,42] The differential diagnosis includes peptic ulcer disease, gastric polyp, Brunner gland adenoma, gastrointestinal stromal tumor (GIST), lymphoma, and metastasis to the stomach such as malignant melanoma or Kaposi's sarcoma.[111] Rarely, large intramural cystic collections can be seen in the stomach and duodenum on CT scans.[112]

Agenesis, Hypoplesia, and Hyperplasia of the Pancreas

Agenesis of the pancreas is rare and typically incompatible with life. A casual relationship with intrauterine growth retardation has been noted and is presumed to be due to the lack of fetal insulin necessary for development.[113]

Partial pancreatic agenesis and hypoplasia are also rare (Fig. 98-22); however, cases of agenesis of the dorsal pancreas have been reported[114] along with malrotation. Abnormal rotation of the intestine may interrupt the normal rotation of

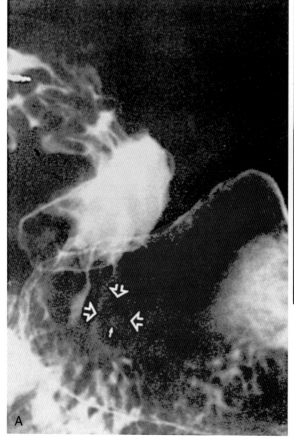

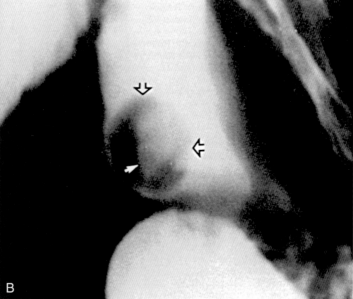

Figure 98-21. Ectopic pancreas: barium contrast studies. Ectopic rests of pancreatic tissue are present in the gastric antrum (**A**) and duodenal bulb (**B**). The mound of pancreatic tissue is signified by the *open arrows*. The *solid arrows* show the draining duct.

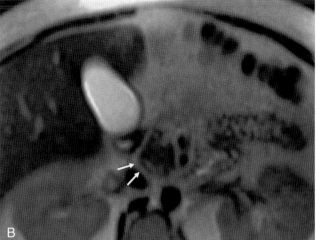

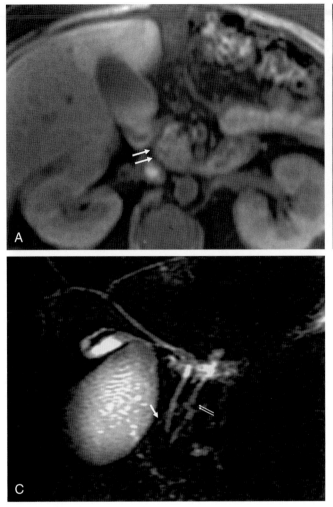

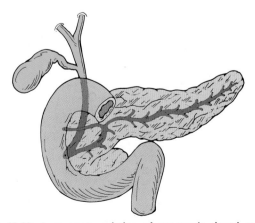

Figure 98-22.   Partial agenesis of the pancreas. Axial T1-weighted fat-saturated (**A**) and T2-weighted (**B**) images reveal the pancreatic head (*arrows*). The body and tail are not identified. **C.** Coronal oblique thick-slab MRCP reveals a short duct off the ventral pancreas joining the common bile duct (*small arrows*). There is no evidence of dorsal duct. Note that there is small duct that drains cephalic to the common bile duct, which represents the duct of Santorini draining into the minor ampulla (*single arrow*). (Courtesy of Dr. Carmen DeJuan, Department of Radiology Hospital Clinic, University of Barcelona, Spain.)

the pancreatic primordium, with malpositioning of the pancreatic buds resulting in abnormal morphology of the uncinate process.[115]

Ductal Abnormalities

The single main pancreatic duct normally connects with the accessory duct of Santorini, and then they open in conjunction with the common bile duct at the ampulla of Vater. This arrangement is seen in 60% to 70% of normal individuals.[116,117] The common variations of pancreatic ductal anatomy include (1) junction of the ventral duct and common bile duct at the ampulla with complete regression of the dorsal duct (see Fig. 98-2) (40%-50%); (2) junction of the ventral and common bile ducts at the ampulla but with persistence of the dorsal duct (Fig. 98-23) (35%); (3) persistence of both the dorsal and the ventral ducts without communication, or pancreas divisum (5%-10%); (4) common channel with a retroduct entering the common duct from 5 to 15 mm from the ampulla (5%-10%) and (5) separate entrance of the ventral duct into the duodenum with variable persistence of the dorsal duct (5%).[116-119] Variations in ductal configurations include a sigmoid configuration of the duct (Fig. 98-24) and descending course of the duct. One may rarely encounter with a loop at the point of the embryologic fusion of the ducts.

Congenital Cysts

The cystic lesions that are congenital and not related to cystic fibrosis of the pancreas are rare. Such cysts do not cause any symptoms, have a thin fibrose wall, and are lined by a columnar or cubicle type of epithelium. They are not associated with cysts in any other organs.[118-121]

Figure 98-23.   A common variation of pancreatic ductal anatomy. Junction of the ventral and common bile ducts at the ampulla with persistence of the dorsal duct.

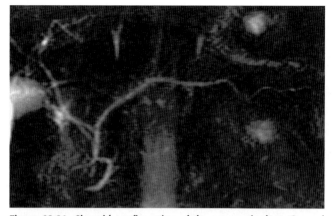

Figure 98-24. Sigmoid configuration of the pancreatic duct. Coronal oblique thick-slab MRCP reveals a normal variation seeing at the head of the pancreas as sigmoid configuration of the pancreatic duct. (Courtesy of Dr. Carmen DeJuan, Department of Radiology Hospital Clinic, University of Barcelona, Spain.)

References

1. Kozu T, Suda K, Toki F: Development of the pancreas and biliary tree. In DeMarino AJ, Benjamin SB (eds): Gastrointestinal Disease: An Endoscopic Approach. Oxford, Blackwell Science, 1997, pp 733-750.
2. Durie PR: Inherited and congenital disorders of the exocrine pancreas. Gastroenterologist 4:169-187, 1996.
3. Benger JR, Thompson MH: Annular pancreas and obstructive jaundice. Am J Gastroenterol 92:713-714, 1997.
4. Torra R, Alos L, Ramos J, et al: Renal-hepatic-pancreatic hysplasia: An autosomal recessive malformation. J Med Genet 33:409-412, 1996.
5. Tolia V, Rao R, Klein M: Annular pancreas. J Pediatr 131:14-15, 1997.
6. Skandalakis JE, Gray SW, Rowe JS, et al: Anatomic complications of pancreatic surgery. Contemp Surg 15:17-36, 1979.
7. Faerber EN, Friedman AC, Dabezues MA: Anomalies and congenital disorders. In Feldman AC, Dachman AH (eds): Radiology of the Liver, Biliary Tract, and Pancreas. St. Louis, Mosby, 1994, pp 743-762.
8. May G, Gardiner R: Clinical Imaging of the Pancreas. New York, Raven, 1987, pp 1-10.
9. Schoefl R, Haefner M, Poetzi R, et al: A case of duplication of the main pancreatic duct. Endoscopy 28:401-402, 1996.
10. Rutter WJ: Development of the endocrine and exocrine pancreas. In Fitzgerald PJ, Morrison AB (eds): The Pancreas. Baltimore, Williams & Wilkins, 1980, pp 30-38.
11. Kloppel G, Heitz PU: Pancreatic pathology. In Kloppel G, Heitz PU (eds): Pancreatic Diseases. Edinburgh, New York, Churchill Livingstone, 1984, pp 225-232.
12. Kozu T, Suda K, Toki F: Pancreatic development and anatomical variation. Gastrointest Endosc Clin North Am 5:1-30, 1995.
13. Ross BA, Jeffrey RB Jr, Mindelsun RE: Normal variations in the lateral contour of the head and neck of the pancreas mimicking neoplasm: Evaluation with dual-phase helical CT. AJR 166:799-801, 1996.
14. Dhar A, Chawla Y, Dhiman RK, et al: Bifid pancreas: A case report. Trop Gastroenterol 18:75-77, 1997.
15. Shirkhoda A: Diagnostic pitfalls in abdominal CT. RadioGraphics 11:969-1002, 1991.
16. Kreel L, Haertel M, Katz D: Computed tomography of the normal pancreas. J Comput Assist Tomogr 1:290-299, 1977.
17. Halpert RD, Shabot JM, Heare BR, et al: The bifid pancreas: A rare anatomical variation. Gastrointest Endosc 36:60-61, 1990.
18. Phillip J, Koch H, Classen M: Variation and anomalies of the papilla of Vater, the pancreas and the biliary system. Endoscopy 6:70-77, 1974.
19. Kleitsch WB: Anatomy of the pancreas: A study with special reference to the duct system. Arch Surg 71:795-802, 1955
20. Stringer DA: Pediatric Gastrointestinal Imaging. Toronto, BC Decker, 1989, pp 585-610.
21. Agha FP, Williams KD: Pancreas divisum: Incidence, detection and clinical significance. Am J Gastroenterol 81:315-320, 1987
22. May G, Gardiner R: Clinical Imaging of the Pancreas. New York: Raven, pp 50-57, 1987.
23. Schneck CD, Dabezies MA, Friedman AC: Embryology, histology, gross anatomy, and normal imaging of the pancreas. In Friedman AC, Dachman AH (eds): Radiology of the Liver, Biliary Tract, and Pancreas. St. Louis, Mosby, 1994, pp 715-742.
24. Uomo G, Manes G, D'Anna L, et al: Fusion and duplication variants of pancreatic duct system. Clinical and pancreatographic evaluation. Int J Pancreat 17:23-28, 1995.
25. Delhaye M, Engelholm L, Cremer M: Pancreas divisum: Congenital anatomy variant or anomaly? Contribution of endoscopic retrograde dorsal pancreatography. Gastroenterology 89:951-958, 1985.
26. Staritz M, Hutteroth T, Meyer Zum Buschenfelde KH: Pancreas divisum and pancreatitis, Gastroenterology 91:525-526, 1986.
27. Blair AJ, Russel CG, Cotton PB: Resection for pancreatitis in patients with pancreas divisum. Ann Surg 200:590-594, 1984.
28. Muzaffar AR, Moyer MS, Dobbins J, et al: Pancreas divisum in a family with hereditary pancreatitis. J Clin Gastroenterol 22:16-20, 1996.
29. Cotton PB: Pancreas divisum—culprit or curiosity? Gastroenterology 89:1431-1435, 1985.
30. Lehman GA, Sherman S: Diagnosis and therapy of pancreas divisum. Gastrointest Endosc Clin North Am 55-77, 1998.
31. Lehman GA, Sherman S, Nisi R, et al: Pancreas divisum: Results of minor papilla sphincterotomy. Gastrointest Endosc 39:1-8, 1993.
32. Warshaw AL, Simeone JF, Schapiro RH, et al: Evaluation and treatment of the dominant dorsal duct syndrome (pancreas divisum redefined). Am J Surg 159:59-66, 1990.
33. Lehman GA, Sherman S: Pancreas divisum: Diagnosis and therapy. In Jacobson IM (ed): ERCP and Its Applications. Philadelphia, Lippincott-Raven, 1998, pp 181-192.
34. Kamisawa T, Yoshiike M, Egawa N, et al: Pancreatic tumor associated with pancreas divisum. J Gastroenterol Hepatol 20:915, 2005.
35. Martin Fernandez J, Ratia T, Gutierrez A, et al: Intraductal pancreatic carcinoma associated with pancreas divisum. Rev Esp Enferm Dig 95:358-363, 2003.
36. Yarze JC, Chase MP, Herlihy KJ, et al: Pancreas divisum and intraductal papillary mucinous tumor occurring simultaneously in a patient presenting with recurrent acute pancreatitis. Dig Dis Sci 48:915, 2003.
37. Masatsugu T, Yamaguchi K, Chijiiwa K, et al: Serous cystadenoma of the pancreas associated with pancreas divisum. J Gastroenterol 37:669-673, 2002.
38. Outtas O, Barthet M, De Troyer J, et al: Pancreatic panniculitis with intraductal carcinoid tumor of the pancreas divisum. Ann Dermatol Venereol 131:466-469, 2004.
39. Peterson MS, Slivka A: Santorinicele in pancreas divisum: Diagnosis with secretin-stimulated magnetic resonance pancreatography. Abdom Imaging 26:260-263, 2001.
40. Raffel A, Engers R, Cupisti K, et al: Multiple neuroendocrine tumors of the pancreas associated with pancreas divisum. Eur J Endocrinol 150:837-840, 2004.
41. Bloom C, Hickey N, Haroun J, et al: Pancreatic divisum and intestinal nonrotation diagnosed with magnetic resonance imaging: Case report. Can Assoc Radiol J 50:310-313,1999.
42. Freeny PC, Lawson TL: Radiology of the Pancreas. New York, Springer-Verlag, 1982, pp 142-168.
43. Bhutani MS, Hoffman BJ, Hawes RH: Diagnosis of pancreas divisum by endoscopic ultrasonography. Endoscopy 31:167-169, 1999.
44. Lai R, Freeman ML, Cass OW, et al: Accurate diagnosis of pancreas divisum by linear-array endoscopic ultrasonography. Endoscopy 36:705-709, 2004.
45. Varshney S, Johnson CD: Pancreas divisum. Int J Pancreatol 25:135-141, 1999.
46. Gottlieb K, Sherman S: ERCP and endoscopic biliary sphincterotomy-induced pancreatitis. Gastrointest Endosc Clin North Am 8:87-114, 1998.
47. Tak WY, Kim DH, Kim H. et al: Risk factors for post-ERCP pancreatitis: A prospective study [abstract]. Gastroenterology 118:A206, 2000.
48. Warshaw AL, Simeone J, Schapiro RH, et al: Objective evaluation of ampullary stenosis with ultrasonograhy and pancreatic stimulation. Am J Surg 1549:65-72, 1985.
49. Barbara L, Bolondi L: Functional ultrasonography in gastroenterology. Ultrasound Q 6:181-227, 1988.
50. Glaser J. Hogemann B, Krummenerl T, et al: Sonographic imaging of the pancreatic duct. New diagnostic possibilities using secretin stimulation. Dig Dis Sci 32:1075-1081, 1987.
51. Hellund JC, Skattum J, Buanes T, et al: Secretin-stimulated MRCP of patients with unclear disease in the pancreaticobiliary tract. Acta Radiol 48:135-141, 2007.

52. McCarthy JH, Geenen JE, Hogan WJ: Endoscopic treatment in non-malignant pancreatic disease. In Jacobson IM (ed): ERCP: Diagnostic and Therapeutic Applications. New York, Elsevier Science, 1989, pp 189-202.

53. Soehendra N, Kempeneers I, Nam VCH, et al: Endoscopic dilation and papillotomy of the accessory papilla and internal drainage in pancreas divisum. Gastrointest Endosc 18:129-132, 1986.

54. Zeman RK, McVay LV, Silverman PM, et al: Pancreas divisum: Thin section CT. Radiology 169:395-398, 1988.

55. Silverman PM, McVay L. Silverman PM, Zeman RK, et al: Pancreatic pseudotumor in pancreas divisum: CT characteristics. J Comput Assist Tomogr 13:140-141, 1989.

56. Birnberg DE, Carr MF, Premkumar A, et al: Isolated ventral pancreatitis in an alcoholic with pancreas divisum. Gastrointest Radiol 13:323-326, 1988.

57. Halpert RD, Shabot JM, Heare BR, et al: The bifid pancreas: A rare anatomical variation. Gastrointest Endosc 36:60-61, 1990.

58. Siegel JH, Yatto RP, Vender RJ: Anomalous pancreatic ducts causing "pseudomass" of the pancreas. J Clin Gastroenterol 5:33-36, 1983.

59. Itoh S, Takada A, Satake H, et al: Diagnostic value of multislice computed tomography for pancreas divisum: Assessment with oblique coronal reconstruction images. J Comput Assist Tomogr 29:452-460, 2005.

60 Laghi A, Catalano C, Panebianco V, et al: Pancreas divisum: Demonstration of a case with cholangiopancreatography with magnetic resonance. Radiol Med (Torino) 93:648-650, 1997.

61. Fukukura Y, Fujiyoshi F, Sasaki M, et al: HASTE MR cholangiopancreatography in the evaluation of intraductal papillary-mucinous tumors of the pancreas. J Comput Assist Tomogr 23:301-305, 1999.

62. Morrin MM, Farrell RJ, McEntee G, et al: MR cholangiopancreatography of pancreaticobiliary diseases: Comparison of single-shot RARE and multislice HASTE sequences. Clin Radiol 55: 866-873, 2000.

63. Chevallier P, Souci J, Buckley MJ, et al: Annular pancreas: MR imaging including MR cholangiopancreatography (MRCP). Pancreas 18:216-218, 2000.

64. Hidaka T, Hirohashi S, Uchida H, et al: Annular pancreas diagnosed by single-shot MR cholangiopancreatography. Magn Reson Imaging 16:441-444, 1998.

65. Manfredi R, Costamagna G, Brizi MG, et al: Pancreas divisum and "santorinicele": diagnosis with dynamic MR cholangiopancreatography with secretin stimulation. Radiology 217:403-408, 2000.

66. Costamagna G, Ingrosso M, Tringali A, et al: Santorinicele and recurrent acute pancreatitis in pancreas divisum: Diagnosis with dynamic secretin-stimulated magnetic resonance pancreatography and endoscopic treatment. Gastrointest Endosc 52:262-267, 2000.

67. Rinnab L, Schulz K, Siech M: A rare localization of annular pancreas at the pars horizontalis duodeni. Zentralbl Chir 129:513-516, 2004.

68. Gray SW, Skandalakin JE: Embryology for Surgeons: The Embryological Basis for the Treatment of Congenital Defects. Philadelphia, WB Saunders, 1972, pp 263-282.

69. Ben-David K, Falcone RA, Matthews JB: Diffuse pancreatic adenocarcinoma identified in an adult with annular pancreas. J Gastrointest Surg 8:565-568, 2004.

70. Hamm M, Rottger P, Fiedler C: Pancreas annulare as a rare differential diagnosis of duodenal stenosis in adulthood. Langenbecks Arch Chir 382:307-310, 1997.

71. Urayama S, Kozarek R, Ball T, et al: Presentation and treatment of annular pancreas in an adult population. Am J Gastroenterol 90: 995-999, 1995.

72. Whittingham-Jones PM, Riaz AA, Clayton G, et al: Annular pancreas—a rare cause of gastric obstruction in an 82-year-old patient. Ann R Coll Surg Engl 87:13-15, 2005.

73. Johnston DWB: Annular pancreas: A new classification and clinical observations. Can J Surg 21:241-244, 1978.

74. Stringer DA: Pediatric Gastrointestinal Imaging. Toronto, BC Decker, 1989, pp 235-362.

75. Kiernan PD, ReMine SG, Kiernan PC, et al: Annular pancreas. Mayo Clinic experience from 1957 to 1976 with review of the literature. Arch Surg 115:46-50, 1980.

76. Godil A, McCracken GA: Images in clinical medicine. Annular pancreas. N Engl J Med 336:1794, 1997.

77. Shenoy KR, Pai US: Annular pancreas in adults—diagnostic difficulties. J Indian Med Assoc 94:242-243, 1996.

78. Gilroy JA, Adams AB: Annular pancreas. Radiology 75:568-571, 1960.

79. Jimenez JC, Emil S, Podnos Y, Nguyen N: Annular pancreas in children: A recent decade's experience. J Pediatr Surg 39:1654-1657, 2004.

80. Sencan A, Mir E, Gunsar C, Akcora B: Symptomatic annular pancreas in newborns. Med Sci Monit 8:CR434-CR437, 2002.

81. Kosai YS, Higashi IT, Setoguchi T: Annular pancreas associated with pancreatolithiasis: A case report. Hepatogastroenterology 46:527-531, 1999.

82. Shan Y, Sy E, Lin P: Annular pancreas with obstructive jaundice: Beware of underlying neoplasm. Pancreas 25:314-316, 2002.

83. Maker V, Gerzenshtein J, Lerner R: Annular pancreas in the adult: Two case reports and review of more than a century of literature. Am Surg 69:405-410, 2003.

84. Ben-David K, Falcone RA, Matthews JB: Diffuse pancreatic adenocarcinoma identified in an adult with annular pancreas J Gastrointest Surg 8:565-568, 2004.

85. Shan YS, Sy ED, Lin PW: Annular pancreas with obstructive jaundice: Beware of underlying neoplasm. Pancreas 25:314-316, 2002.

86. Urayama S, Kozarek R, Ball T, et al: Presentation and treatment of annular pancreas in an adult population. Am J Gastroenterol 90: 995-999, 1995.

87. Hamm M, Rottger P, Fiedler C: Pancreas anulare as a rare differential diagnosis of duodenal stenosis in adulthood. Langenbecks Arch Chir 382:307-310, 1995.

88. Inamoto K, Ishikawa Y, Itoh N: CT demonstration of annular pancreas: Case report. Gastrointest Radiol 8:143-145, 1983.

89. Nguyan KT, Pace R, Groll A: CT appearance of annular pancreas: A case report. J Can Assoc Radiol 40:322-323, 1989.

90. Orr LA, Powell RW, Melhem RE: Sonographic demonstration of annular pancreas in the newborn. J Ultrasound Med 11:373-375, 1992.

91. Ueki T, Yao T, Beppu T, et al: Three-dimensional computed tomography pancreatography of an annular pancreas with special reference to embryogenesis. Pancreas 32:426-429, 2006.

92. Papachristou GI, Topazian MD, Gleeson FC, et al: EUS features of annular pancreas. Gastrointest Endosc 65:340-344, 2007.

93. Desai MB, Mitchell DG, Munoz SJ: Asymptomatic annular pancreas: Detection by magnetic resonance imaging. Magn Reson Imaging 12: 683-685, 1994.

94. Reinhart RD, Brown JJ, Foglia RP, et al: MR imaging of annular pancreas. Abdom Imaging 19:301-303, 1994.

95. Mortele KJ, Rocha TC, Streeter JL, et al: Multimodality imaging of pancreatic and Biliary congenital anomalies. RadioGraphics 26:715-731, 2006.

96. Lecesne R, Stein L, Reinhold C, et al: MR cholangiopancreatography of annular pancreas. J Comput Assist Tomogr 22:85-86, 1998.

97. Yamagiwa I, Obata K, Ouchi T, et al: Heterotopic pancreas of the esophagus associated with a rare type of esophageal atresia. Ann Thorac Surg 65:1143-1144, 1998.

98. Eklof O, Lassrich A, Stanley P, et al: Ectopic pancreas. Pediatr Radiol 1:24-27, 1973.

99. Bonnard A, Lagausie P, Malbezin S, et al: Mediastinal pancreatic pseudocyst in a child. A thoracoscopic approach. Surg Endosc 15:760, 2001.

100. Ben-Baruch D, Sandbank Y, Wolloch Y: Heterotopic pancreatic tissue in the gallbladder. Acta Chir Scand 152:557-558, 1986.

101. Carr MJT, Deiranya AK, Judd PA: Mediastinal cyst containing mural pancreatic tissue. Thorax 32:512-516, 1977.

102. Eklof O: Accessory pancreas in the stomach and duodenum: Clinical features, diagnosis, and therapy. Acta Chir Scand 121:19-20, 1961.

103. Qizibash AH: Acute pancreatitis occurring in heterotopic pancreatic tissue in the gallbladder. Can J Surg 19:413-414, 1976.

104. Mizuta Y, Takeshima F, Yamao T, et al: Cyst formation of duodenal heterotopic pancreas accompanied by pancreas divisum. Dig Dis Sci 49:1412-1417, 2004.

105. Ravitch MM: Anomalies of the pancreas. In Carey LC (ed): The Pancreas. St. Louis, CV Mosby, 1973, pp 404-416.

106. Duphare H, Nijhawan S, Rana S, et al: Heterotopic gastric and pancreatic tissue in large bowel. Am J Gastroenterol 85:667-671, 1990.

107. Bedossa P, Millat B, Zrihen E, et al: Adenocarcinoma in heterotopic gastric pancreas. Gastroenterol Clin Biol 15:79-82, 1991.

108. Camunas FA, Estrada JL, Trigueros M, et al: Ectopic pancreas. Rev Esp Enferm Dig 88:672-676, 1996.

109. Ura H, Denno R, Hirata K, et al: Carcinoma arising from ectopic pancreas in the stomach: endosonographic detection of malignant change. J Clin Ultrasound 26:265-268, 1998.

110. Mito T, Nakazawa S, Yoshino J, et al: A case of adult intussusception due to the inverted Meckel's diverticulum with ectopic pancreas which showed characteristic findings of MRI. Nippon Shokakibyo Gakkai Zasshi 95:326-332, 1998.

111. Burke GW, Binder SC, Barron AM, et al: Heterotopic pancreas: Gastric outlet obstruction secondary to pancreatitis and pancreatic pseudocyst. Am J Gastroenterol 84:52-55, 1989.

112. Claudon M, Verain AL, Bigard MA, et al: Cyst formation in gastric heterotopic pancreas: Report of two cases. Radiology 169:659-660, 1988.

113. Lemons JA, Ridenour R, Orsini EN: Congenital absence of the pancreas and intrauterine growth retardation. Pediatrics 64:255-257, 1979.

114. Deignan RW, Nizzero A, Malone DE: Case report: Agenesis of the dorsal pancreas: A cause of diagnostic error on abdominal sonography. Clin Radiol 51:145-147, 1996.

115. Inoue Y, Nakamura H: Aplasia or hypoplasia of the pancreatic uncinate process: Comparison in patients with and patients without intestinal non-rotation. Radiology 205:531-533, 1973.

116. Berman LG, Prior JT, Abramow SM, et al: A study of the pancreatic duct system in man by the use of vinyl acetate casts of postmortem preparations. Surg Gynecol Obstet 110:391-403, 1960.

117. Grendell JH: Embryology, anatomy, and anomalies of the pancreas. In Haubrich WS, Schaffner F, Berk JE (eds): Bockus Gastroenterology, 5th ed. Philadelphia, WB Saunders, 1995, pp 2815-2820.

118. Taylor AJ, Bohorfoush AG: Interpretation of ERCP with Associated Digital Imaging Correlation. Philadelphia, Lippincott-Raven, 1997, pp 207-218.

119. Fulcher AS, Turner MA: MR pancreatography: A useful tool for evaluating pancreatic disorders. RadioGraphics 19:5-24, 1999.

120. Miller JC, Harisinghani M, Richter JM, et al: Magnetic resonance cholangiopancreatography. J Am Coll Radiol 4:133-136, 2007.

121. Hakime A, Giraud M, Vullierme MP, et al: MR imaging of the pancreas. J Radiol 88:11-25, 2007.

Pancreatitis

Frank H. Miller, MD • Ana L. Keppke, MD • Emil J. Balthazar, MD

Pancreatitis is one of the most complex and clinically challenging of all abdominal disorders. It remains a major diagnostic challenge because its clinical manifestations are as protean as its causes. Indeed, only one in three severe cases of acute pancreatitis is recognized to be severe at initial presentation,[1,2] and 42% of fatal cases of acute pancreatitis do not have a correct diagnosis before autopsy.[3-6]

Since the late 1970s, cross-sectional imaging and, in particular, high-resolution, bolus contrast medium–enhanced multidetector helical CT have dramatically improved the diagnosis and treatment of acute pancreatitis. MRI has proved useful in imaging patients with pancreatitis. This chapter focuses on the contribution of radiology to the assessment and management of patients with acute and chronic pancreatitis.

CLASSIFICATION OF PANCREATITIS

Pancreatitis is classified according to clinical, morphologic, and histologic criteria on the basis of the Marseille and Cambridge symposia and the 1992 International Symposium in Atlanta, Georgia[7,8] (Table 99-1).

ACUTE PANCREATITIS

Etiology

Although the causes of pancreatitis are diverse (Table 99-2), alcoholism and biliary tract disease (gallstones) account for approximately 90% of cases in the United States. The relative frequency of these causes varies with the country and population of patients examined. Alcoholic pancreatitis is more common in urban and Veterans Administration hospitals, whereas gallstone pancreatitis predominates in suburban and

rural hospitals. The incidence of acute pancreatitis is 0.005% to 0.01% in the general population.[9-14] Approximately 10% to 30% of patients with acute pancreatitis will never have the cause established and are given the diagnosis of "idiopathic" pancreatitis. Biliary sludge and microlithiasis are probably responsible for the development of pancreatitis in the majority of these cases.[12,15,16]

Table 99-1

Classification of Pancreatitis

Acute Pancreatitis

Diagnostic Criteria
1. An elevation of plasma levels of pancreatic enzymes >10 SDs above normal laboratory values
2. Evidence of acute pancreatitis from laparotomy, imaging, or autopsy

Clinical Classification
1. Etiology when known (e.g., gallstones, alcohol abuse)
2. Degree of severity: (a) mild, with no multisystem failure and an uncomplicated recovery; (b) severe (multisystem failure, pancreatic necrosis, and/or development of a complication, e.g., pseudocyst)

Chronic Pancreatitis

Diagnostic Criteria
1. Permanently impaired exocrine pancreatic function tests >2 SDs below normal levels
2. Permanent morphologic change in the gland

Clinical Classification
1. Etiology, if known
2. Absence or presence of pain
3. Complications: cysts, portal hypertension, diabetes mellitus

Table 99-2
Etiology of Acute Pancreatitis

Metabolic
Alcohol
Hyperlipidemia types I and V
Hypercalcemia
Hereditary pancreatitis
Kwashiorkor
Scorpion venom

Mechanical
Cholelithiasis
After operation (gastric, biliary, splenic)
Blunt or penetrating trauma
Pancreatic duct anomaly—pancreas divisum
Choledochocele
Perivaterian duodenal diverticulum
Retrograde pancreatography
Pancreatic, papillary tumor
Duodenal obstruction
Penetrating gastric ulcer
Ascaris or *Clonorchis* infestation

Drugs
Corticosteroids, azathioprine, thiazide, furosemide,
    aminosalicylic acid, sulfonamides, tetracycline, procainamide,
    phenformin, ethacrynic acid, estrogens, narcotic analgesics,
    opiates, cholinergic substances, chlorthalidone

Vascular
Polyarteritis nodosa
Atheroembolism
After operation (cardiopulmonary bypass)

Infection
Mumps
Measles
AIDS or human immunodeficiency virus infection
Cytomegalovirus infection
Cryptosporidiosis

Identifying the cause of pancreatitis is important because it helps determine therapy, limits further unnecessary examinations, and may improve patient's long-term outcome.[16]

Pathophysiology

The precise mechanisms of pathogenesis of acute pancreatitis are not completely understood. Alcohol increases the risk for pancreatitis through multiple mechanisms. More than 95% of heavy alcohol users never develop significant pancreatitis, however, which suggests that this is a complex syndrome, with other risk factors.[17,18] Alcoholic pancreatitis has been explained by a number of mechanisms: necrosis-fibrosis sequence, duct obstruction, leakage of enzymes from the pancreatic duct, abnormal synthesis of digestive enzymes, toxic metabolites, altered pancreatic blood flow, mitochondrial damage, and activation of pancreatic stellate cells, which produce collagen in the fibrotic pancreas.[18]

The toxic effect and chemical alterations of the exocrine secretions produced by alcohol lead to protein precipitates that obstruct the pancreatic ducts.[19,20] In addition, alcohol can lead to duodenitis, edema, and spasm of the papilla of Vater, further contributing to ductal obstruction.[19]

Alcohol also indirectly stimulates pancreatic secretion by inducing an increase in gastrin and secretin levels and decreases the level of zymogen inhibitor, resulting in the premature

activation of trypsin.[20] In acute pancreatitis, these activated pancreatic enzymes are extravasated, causing pancreatic autodigestion and necrosis.[21] In cholelithiasis-induced pancreatitis, there is obstruction of the common biliopancreatic channel by a stone (Opie stone), with resultant reflux of bile into the pancreatic duct and activation of pancreatic enzymes.[13,21] Gallstones are found in the stool of most of these patients.[22] This is the rationale for emergency cholecystectomy or endoscopic retrograde cholangiopancreatography (ERCP)-directed sphincterotomies in the treatment of gallstone pancreatitis.[12] It is interesting to note that reflux of contrast material into the pancreatic duct during intraoperative cholangiography is much more common in patients with gallstone pancreatitis than in patients undergoing cholecystectomy who do not have pancreatitis.[11,23]

Pancreas divisum, a controversial cause of pancreatitis discussed in detail in Chapter 98, is also postulated to induce this disorder by functional obstruction at the accessory papilla of Santorini.[24]

A variety of other causes, such as drugs, calcium, endotoxins, hyperlipidemia, viral infections, ischemia, anoxia, and trauma, can also activate proteolytic enzymes in the pancreas that lead to autodigestion and stimulate other enzymes such as bradykinin and vasoactive substances that cause vasodilatation, increased vascular permeability, and edema.[11,25]

Leukocytes attracted by the pancreatic injury release inflammatory mediators called cytokines, which have an important role in disease progression and multisystem complications of acute pancreatitis. Biologically active compounds such as phospholipase A2, tumor necrosis factor, polymorphonuclear cell elastase, complement factor, interleukins, and leukotrienes are released into the systemic circulation, stimulating the production of other mediators and leading to distant organ failure.[26-28] Some of these mediators, such as tumor necrosis factor, are also toxic to acinar cells and may contribute to pancreatic injury and necrosis.[28,29] These inflammatory products occur early in the course of the disease and can be used as indicators of severity and prognosis in acute pancreatitis.[28,30,31]

Pancreatitis has been shown to have an increased prevalence in AIDS patients, explained either by the effects of medication (pentamidine and 2′,3′-dideoxyinosine [ddI]) or by secondary opportunistic infections.[1,12,32]

No dependable correlation exists between the etiology and the severity of disease. In general, most cases of necrotizing pancreatitis are associated with alcoholism and hyperlipidemia, whereas severe pancreatitis is less commonly noted with other causes.

There are several major pathologic categories of acute pancreatitis. Acute interstitial pancreatitis is the mildest form of pancreatitis and is also called edematous pancreatitis. It is characterized by absent or minimal pancreatic and systemic dysfunction and a rapid response to medical therapy without complications. Only pancreatic edema and mild cellular infiltrate are present. The gland may enlarge to three times its normal size and become firm. There may be a few small, scattered foci of necrosis and saponification in the peripancreatic fatty tissue. Necrotizing pancreatitis is a far more severe form of pancreatitis in which varying degrees of systemic and distal organ failure and potentially lethal complications can occur. Extensive fat necrosis, hemorrhage, and necrotic liquefaction of the pancreatic parenchyma and adjacent peripancreatic tissues and fascial planes are seen. In addition, a variety of intermediary forms of pancreatitis occur in clinical practice. The degree and extent of injury appear to be related to the quantity, rate of production, and activity of the highly lipolytic and proteolytic extravasated enzymes.[12]

Definitions

Considerable ambiguity and overlap of pathologic features exist in describing the complications of pancreatitis, and the following are definitions of commonly encountered sequelae that are discussed in subsequent sections.[12,33]

Phlegmon: Descriptive term, formerly used, implying the presence of a heterogeneous masslike enlargement of the pancreas and retroperitoneal tissues. It does not correlate with the presence of infection or necrosis, and hence, its use should be discouraged.[12,33]

Fluid collection: A localized collection of pancreatic fluid, homogeneous or heterogeneous in attenuation, which is seen in 30% to 50% of patients with acute pancreatitis and may be located in the pancreas, lesser sac, anterior pararenal space, or subperitoneal space (see Chapters 111 and 112) or as distant as the neck, mediastinum, pleura, pericardium, or groin. Nearly two thirds of these collections resolve spontaneously; others become infected (abscess) or may persist as pseudocysts.

Pseudocysts: Localized collections of pancreatic fluid confined by a capsule of fibrous or granulation tissue. Pseudocysts develop 4 to 6 weeks after an episode of acute pancreatitis or are associated with stigmata of chronic pancreatitis. They lack a true epithelial lining, a feature that differentiates them from a cyst or cystic neoplasm. Pseudocysts smaller than 4 cm often resolve spontaneously. Fluid collections greater than 7 cm in diameter are likely to require intervention, particularly in patients with alcoholic pancreatitis.[33,34] Persistent pseudocysts often communicate with the pancreatic duct and have the potential to rupture, bleed, become infected, or cause a pseudoaneurysm.[26,35]

Abscess: Pancreatic abscess develops from infected, extravasated pancreatic secretions. It usually occurs 3 or more weeks after the initial attack or may develop as a secondary infection of a pseudocyst. The term should be used to define an encapsulated collection of pus in proximity to the pancreas without associated pancreatic necrosis.

Infected pancreatic necrosis: Infected necrotic pancreatic tissue is partially or totally liquefied. It should be differentiated from an abscess because it leads to a 48% mortality rate, compared with 25% from abscess, and is often not amenable to percutaneous drainage.[7,9,26]

Hemorrhagic pancreatitis: This term has been used synonymously with "pancreatic necrosis." It should be restricted to the intraoperative and postmortem appearance of the gland. Massive hemorrhage is a rare manifestation of acute pancreatitis, usually occurring as a late complication from a ruptured pseudoaneurysm. Gastrointestinal hemorrhage can occur if a pseudoaneurysm ruptures into the pancreatic duct directly or by way of a pseudocyst. Pseudocysts also rupture and erode into the gastrointestinal tract.

Pseudoaneurysm: A focal area of dilatation of a splanchnic artery that may occur as a result of inflammatory weakening of the arterial wall by enzymes liberated in acute pancreatitis. Pseudoaneurysms usually are found in the splenic, gastroduodenal, and pancreaticoduodenal arteries and can be free

standing or associated with a pseudocyst. Intermittent or life-threatening hemorrhage into a pseudocyst, retroperitoneum, or peritoneal cavity may occur.

Pancreatic ascites: It develops when there is outpouring of pancreatic fluid from a disrupted pancreatic duct into the peritoneal cavity by way of a fistula. Pancreatic ascites usually occurs as a complication of chronic pancreatitis but may be noted after any episode of acute pancreatitis.

Clinical Findings

The clinical diagnosis of pancreatitis is often difficult. Patients' symptoms range from mild abdominal pain, nausea, vomiting, fever, tachycardia, and abdominal distention to severe abdominal pain and shock. Most patients have abdominal tenderness and guarding. These findings are nonspecific, and the differential diagnosis usually includes acute cholecystitis, bowel obstruction or infarction, perforated viscus, renal colic, duodenal diverticulitis, aortic dissection, appendicitis, and ruptured abdominal aortic aneurysm. In very severe cases, flank ecchymosis (Grey-Turner's sign) or periumbilical hematoma (Cullen's sign) may be present.

Consequently, a battery of laboratory tests has been developed to diagnose and grade pancreatitis. These tests include evaluation of serum amylase, lipase, serum/urinary amylase ratio, pisoamylase, immunoreactive trypsin, chymotrypsin, elastase, serum cyclic adenosine monophosphate, C-reactive protein, urinary trypsinogen-2, and methemalbumin.[6,30,36] Serum amylase and lipase levels are the most commonly used measures to diagnose pancreatitis. Unfortunately, these values are elevated in only 80% to 90% of patients with acute pancreatitis.[37] Amylase is rapidly secreted by the kidneys and may return to normal levels during the first 48 to 72 hours.[33,38] Pancreatitis caused by gallstones, microlithiasis, or drugs is often associated with a greater elevation in amylase than in lipase.[39,40] The amylase level relative to lipase tends to be lower in alcoholic pancreatitis, hypertriglyceridemia-induced pancreatitis, neoplasia, and chronic pancreatitis.[16,39,40] There is no correlation between the levels of serum amylase and the severity of acute pancreatitis; patients with mild forms of disease may exhibit levels of over 1000 IU, whereas patients with severe necrotizing pancreatitis may have normal or low amylase levels.[41,42] Furthermore, hyperamylasemia may be seen in other acute abdominal conditions such as bowel obstruction, bowel infarction, gangrenous cholecystitis, and perforated ulcer.[43] An elevated lipase is more specific for pancreatitis but the level does not predict the etiology.[44]

The clinical course of acute pancreatitis varies from mild and self-limited disease to shock, overwhelming sepsis, and death. Approximately 50% of patients have mild interstitial pancreatitis and require a limited hospital stay with minor supportive therapy, 40% have a stormier course but ultimately survive, and 10% die of shock associated with early respiratory and renal failure or later sepsis. In an attempt to predict which course the patient may take, Ranson[13] has described a number of criteria linked to a poor prognosis (Table 99-3). In a study of more than 450 patients, there was good correlation between the number of risk factors and the severity of acute pancreatitis. Other scoring tests, including the Acute Physiology and Chronic Health Evaluation II (APACHE II) grading system, are similarly based on measuring physiologic and laboratory parameters routinely available in

Table 99-3
Acute Pancreatitis: Factors Associated with Poor Prognosis

At Admission or Diagnosis	During Initial 48 Hours
Age >55 years	Fall in hematocrit >10%
Leukocytosis >16,000/mm³	Blood urea nitrogen rise >5 mg/dL
Hyperglycemia >200 mg/dL	Serum calcium <8 mg/dL
Elevated lactate dehydrogenase >350 IU/L	Arterial Po₂ <60 mm Hg
Elevated serum glutamic-oxaloacetic transaminase >250 SF units/dL	Base deficit >4 mEq/L
	Fluid sequestration >6 L

Summary of 200 Patients	
Number of prognostic signs	Mortality or serious morbidity
0–2	<10%
3–4	16%
5–6	40%
≥7	100%

Adapted from JHC Ranson: Etiological and prognostic factors in human acute pancreatitis: A review. Am J Gastroenterol 77:633-638, 1982 © by The American College of Gastroenterology; and Ranson JHC, Pasternak BS: Statistical methods for qualifying the severity of clinical acute pancreatitis. J Surg Res 22:79-91, 1977.

Table 99-4
Complications of Acute Pancreatitis

Pancreatic
Fluid collections
Pseudocyst
Infected necrosis
Abscess

Local Peripancreatic
Gastrointestinal: hemorrhage, infarction, obstruction, ileus
Vascular: pseudoaneurysm formation, portal–splenic vein thrombosis, hemorrhage
Biliary: obstructive jaundice

Systemic
Pulmonary: arterial hypoxia (early), atelectasis, pleural effusion, adult respiratory distress syndrome, pneumonia
Cardiac: shock, pericardial effusion, electrocardiographic changes, arrhythmias
Hematologic: disseminated intravascular coagulation
Renal: azotemia, oliguria
Metabolic: hypocalcemia, hyperglycemia, hypotriglyceridemia, acidosis, elevation of free fatty acids
Central nervous system: psychosis, encephalopathy, Purtscher's retinopathy
Peripheral: fat necrosis (skin and bones), arthritis

Modified from Pitchumoni CS, Agarwal N, Jain NK: Systemic complications of acute pancreatitis. Am J Gastroenterol 83:597-606, 1988 © by The American College of Gastroenterology.

most hospitals. It should be stressed, however, that these scoring tests reflect only systemic alterations (renal, pulmonary, cardiovascular) and not local disease. The scoring tests do not have any diagnostic specificity, the physiologic alterations being seen in a variety of other conditions.[37,38,43] The spectrum of pancreatic, peripancreatic, and systemic complications is presented in Table 99-4.[45]

Radiologic Findings

Cross-sectional imaging has made a significant contribution to the diagnosis and staging of acute pancreatitis. Radiologic imaging of patients with suspected pancreatitis has four major objectives: (1) to exclude other abdominal disorders that can mimic acute pancreatitis, (2) to confirm the clinical diagnosis of acute pancreatitis, (3) to evaluate the extent and nature of pancreatic injury and peripancreatic inflammation in an attempt to stage the severity of disease, and (4) to determine the etiology of acute pancreatitis, if possible. Although plain radiographs and contrast studies have been used in the past for the diagnosis of pancreatitis, they have been replaced by cross-sectional studies, which have significantly greater diagnostic accuracy. Findings and signs indicative of pancreatitis on different imaging modalities are briefly discussed below. CT and MRI features of the disease are emphasized.

Abdominal Plain Radiographs

Abnormalities in the abdominal gas pattern are the most frequent findings on abdominal plain radiographs and range from a gasless abdomen to an ileus pattern. The most common findings are a small bowel ileus (42%), where an adynamic sentinel loop is seen, and the "colon cutoff" sign (56%), related to spasm of the splenic flexure with distal paucity of gas caused by spread of the pancreatic inflammation into the phrenocolic ligament.[46-50] Although originally described in abdominal plain films, the "colon cutoff" sign can also be seen on CT (Fig. 99-1).

Chest Radiographs

Approximately one third of patients with acute pancreatitis demonstrate pulmonary and chest abnormalities: elevated diaphragms, pleural and pericardial effusions, basal atelectasis, pulmonary infiltrates, and the adult respiratory distress syndrome.[51-56] Abnormal chest radiographs can be useful to determine the severity of acute pancreatitis.[57,58]

Barium Studies

Meyers and Evans[59] emphasized the importance of the ligaments and mesenteries of the subperitoneal space (Fig. 99-2) in the spread of pancreatitis. Extravasated pancreatic enzymes commonly enter the lesser sac and spread to the subperitoneal space of the transverse mesocolon, phrenicocolic ligament, and small bowel mesentery, causing serosal inflammation and irritation of the gastrointestinal tract.[46,52,59] Thickening and spiculation of mucosal folds in the stomach and duodenum can be seen on CT and barium studies. Varying degrees of atony associated with spastic segments of the duodenum, jejunum, and transverse colon can also be present.[59-62]

Cholangiography

Occasionally, the enlarged edematous pancreas causes compression and obstruction of the distal common bile duct, resulting in jaundice.[63,64] The narrowing is typically smooth and symmetric (Fig. 99-3).

Some gastroenterologists advocate endoscopic retrograde cholangiopancreatography (ERCP) with sphincterotomy to alter the course of pancreatitis when it appears that multiple

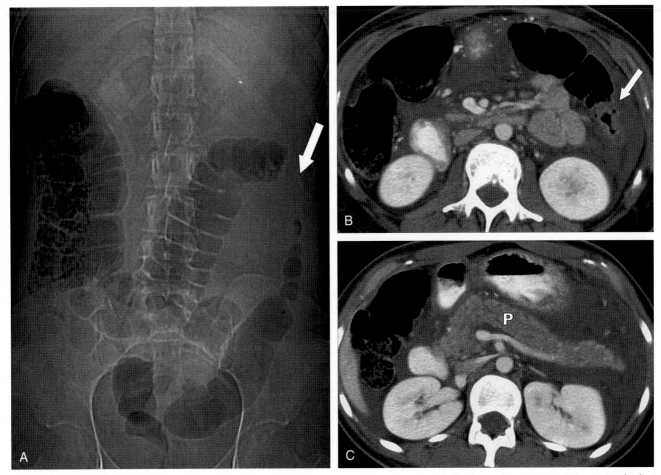

Figure 99-1. "Colon cutoff" sign on MDCT. A. Scout topogram for abdominal multidetector CT (MDCT) shows abrupt interruption (*arrow*) of colonic gas at splenic flexure in a patient with acute pancreatitis. **B.** Axial contrast-enhanced MDCT image shows narrowing (*arrow*) of the colonic lumen at the level of the splenic flexure, as a result of extension of inflammatory exudate. **C.** Axial contrast-enhanced MDCT image shows pancreas (P) surrounded by inflammatory changes and fluid.

stones are passing through the common bile duct. The pancreatic duct is usually normal but can be compressed. ERCP can also demonstrate other causes of pancreatitis, such as pancreas divisum, choledochocele, choledochal cyst, perivaterian duodenal diverticulum, pancreatic or bile duct carcinoma, and ampullary carcinoma[11] (see Chapter 76). Magnetic resonance cholangiopancreatography (MRCP) is often performed to determine the cause of pancreatitis, because it is accurate and noninvasive and avoids the complications associated with ERCP.[65,66]

Angiography

Angiography is not performed in patients with acute pancreatitis unless the presence of a pseudoaneurysm that can be treated with transcatheter embolization is suspected. It can also be helpful to elucidate vascular causes of pancreatitis such as vasculitis, polyarteritis nodosum, postaortic aneurysm resection, after transplantation, Ortner's syndrome, systemic lupus erythematosus, low-flow states, shock, and diabetes.[67-69]

In edematous pancreatitis, the vessels are stretched and displaced with increased parenchymal staining. The vessels may be beaded with an irregular caliber or show thrombosis or pseudoaneurysm formation. If there is parenchymal hemorrhage, the parenchymal stain will be mottled.[11]

Ultrasonography

Abnormal findings are seen at sonography in 33% to 90% of patients with acute pancreatitis.[70] The classic sonographic appearance of pancreatitis is a diffusely enlarged, hypoechoic pancreas.[71-73] Less commonly, focal enlargement is present. The echogenicity of the pancreas in acute pancreatitis is extremely variable and depends on a number of factors: (1) timing of the sonographic study, with maximal decrease in echogenicity occurring 2 to 5 days after the initial episode of acute abdominal pain; (2) the amount of intrapancreatic fat (with age, the pancreas is replaced by fat and becomes more echogenic); (3) the presence of hemorrhage; (4) the presence of underlying chronic pancreatitis with calcification; and (5) the degree of extrapancreatic spread of acute pancreatitis.[71,72,74] Echogenicity is also subjective because the usual internal standard employed to gauge pancreatic texture is the liver, which often has altered architecture caused by fatty infiltration, cirrhosis, or alcoholic pancreatitis. Similarly, size changes are difficult to assess without a baseline scan because the overall volume of the gland is variable and diminishes with advanced age.[75]

The pancreatic duct may dilate, particularly if the inflammation is confined to the pancreatic head. Focal intrapancreatic masses may be due to an acute fluid collection, hemorrhage, or

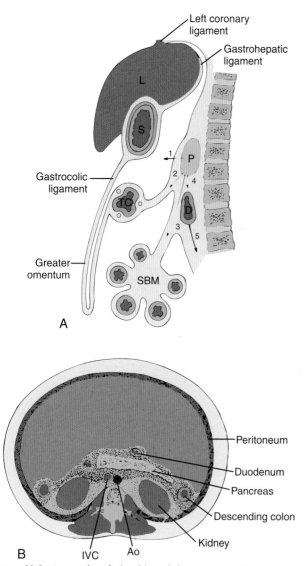

Figure 99-2. Anatomic relationships of the pancreas. These relationships explain the radiographic findings on plain films, barium studies, and cross-sectional images. **A.** Sagittal diagram of the abdomen depicts avenues of spread of the inflammation and fluid of acute pancreatitis: (1) spread into the lesser sac will deform the posterior gastric wall; (2) spread into the transverse mesocolon will cause deformity along the inferior border of the colon; (3) spread into the root of the small bowel mesentery will cause deformity of the small bowel loops; (4) extension into the duodenum will cause deformity and mucosal abnormalities; (5) spread into the remainder of the retroperitoneum will cause changes in the anterior pararenal space. D, duodenum; L, lung; P, pancreas; S, spleen; SBM, small bowel mesentery; TC, transverse colon. **B.** Axial diagram shows the intimate relationship between the pancreas and other structures in the anterior pararenal space (duodenum, ascending and descending colon). The kidneys lie in the perirenal space. Ao, aorta; IVC, inferior vena cava.

ill-defined and hypoechoic pancreatic enlargement that may sonographically simulate carcinoma. Cystic masses should be scrutinized with Doppler ultrasound studies to exclude pancreatic pseudoaneurysms.[76] Lesser sac fluid collections are often seen and may produce a "butterfly" appearance.[77]

The foregoing discussion assumes that the pancreas is well visualized. In acute pancreatitis, bowel gas and other factors will limit visualization of the gland in one fourth to one third of patients. This is one of four major limitations

of ultrasound in this clinical setting. The second is the inability of ultrasound to completely define the complex extrapancreatic spread of infection along fascial planes and within the peripancreatic compartments. It is particularly limited in visualizing spread into the transverse mesocolon. Third, ultrasound cannot specifically reveal areas of pancreatic necrosis in patients with severe pancreatitis, information that provides important prognostic information. Finally, only CT or angiography can diagnose many gastrointestinal and vascular complications of acute pancreatitis.[71,72]

What, then, is the role of sonography in acute pancreatitis? It is a good screening test in patients with suspected biliary pancreatitis and a mild clinical course. It is also useful in thin patients with mild edematous pancreatitis that promptly responds to conservative therapy. CT is preferred for patients with clinically severe pancreatitis, those whose disease fails to respond to conservative therapy, acutely ill patients who pose a diagnostic dilemma, and patients with complications such as infected pseudocyst, hemorrhage, pseudoaneurysm formation, and pancreatic necrosis.[78,79]

The use of tissue harmonic imaging improves image quality, delineation of the pancreatic tail, lesion conspicuity, and fluid-solid differentiation relative to conventional B-mode sonography.[80,81] In a recent study, tissue harmonic sonography was able to detect abnormalities in 91% of patients with acute pancreatitis.[82] The authors found that the two most useful sonographic findings were extrapancreatic inflammation and parenchymal inhomogeneity. It was difficult, however, to distinguish between fluid collections and extrapancreatic inflammation. Even with tissue harmonics, sonography does not depict necrosis or other complications as well as CT or MRI.

Computed Tomography and Magnetic Resonance Imaging

Computed tomography is the premier imaging test in the diagnosis and management of patients with acute pancreatitis. It visualizes the gland, bowel, retroperitoneum, abdominal ligaments, mesenteries, and omenta in their entirety. In addition, it may help determine the etiology, stage severity, and detect complications of pancreatitis and can be used to guide interventional procedures such as fine needle aspiration biopsy or catheter placement. However, the radiation dose delivered by CT may be a significant factor for young patients with pancreatitis who will require multiple examinations. MRI is an option for these patients, but it is more costly than CT. Other advantages of MRI include its high soft tissue contrast resolution and ability to evaluate the common bile duct, pancreatic duct, and parenchyma in a single examination.[83-86] In addition, MRI does not require iodinated contrast and thus is preferred in patients with renal insufficiency or severe pancreatitis with an increased risk for renal disease. MRI, however, is limited in the more acute setting when the patient is very ill, because patient cooperation and breath-holding may be compromised during this longer examination.

Computed Tomography Technique

The technique used in evaluating patients with pancreatitis should be individualized. Best diagnostic images are obtained with the use of multidetector CT (MDCT) by achieving optimal vascular and parenchymal enhancement and avoiding respiratory motion. A rapid 3 mL/s intravenous bolus

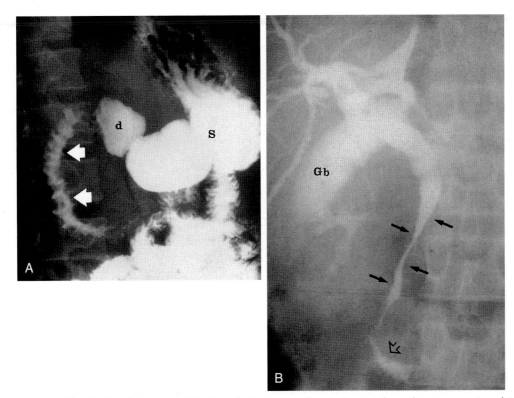

Figure 99-3. Acute pancreatitis affecting the common bile duct. A. Upper gastrointestinal series shows the reverse 3 sign of Frostberg in which pancreatic head enlargement effaces and compresses the descending duodenum (*arrows*). d, duodenum, S, stomach. **B.** Transhepatic cholangiogram performed in a patient with acute pancreatitis and elevated serum bilirubin value reveals that the intrapancreatic segment of the common duct (*solid arrows*) is narrowed and tapers smoothly into the duodenum. A small amount of contrast medium is present in the duodenum (*open arrow*). Gb, gallbladder.

of 150 mL of 60% nonionic contrast material is injected. We routinely use a two-phase imaging technique. Images in the pancreatic and venous phases are obtained using 2- to 3-mm slice thickness. Images can be reconstructed into any plane with various thickness and section intervals at any level in the scanned volume.

Magnetic Resonance Imaging Technique

The role of MRI has become increasingly more important with the advent of high-field-strength imaging, phased-array surface coils, MRI-compatible power injectors, rapid gradient-echo breath-hold techniques, and fat suppression.[86-88] These technological advances allow faster sequences with high resolution images that are largely free of artifacts. T1-weighted fat-suppressed sequences before and following gadolinium and T2-weighted sequences are essential for pancreatic evaluation. The T1-weighted fat-suppressed sequences are able to detect focal or diffuse abnormalities in the pancreas and delineate the peripancreatic fat planes. With a T1 relaxation time shorter than that of the liver, the normal pancreas has the highest signal intensity of intra-abdominal organs. This is attributed to the abundance of acinar proteins, endoplasmic reticulum, and paramagnetic ions within the pancreas.[89,90] Contrast-enhanced T1-weighted images in the arterial phase show intense enhancement of the normal pancreas, which becomes less intense on subsequent phases. T2-weighted sequences show fluid as high signal intensity, allowing assessment of the pancreaticobiliary ducts, and detection of fluid collections and peripancreatic edema.

Diagnosis

The imaging findings in acute pancreatitis are similar, regardless of etiology, with the exception of traumatic pancreatitis, in which pancreatic lacerations cause high-density (50-90 Hounsfield units [HU]) hematomas. MRI can be helpful in determining the etiology of pancreatitis, including choledocholithiasis, pancreas divisum, and underlying tumors. In the acute setting, however, the etiology may be difficulty to determine due to the significant inflammation, which may obscure stones, the pancreaticobiliary ducts, or underlying masses.

In mild forms of pancreatitis, CT and MRI may be normal or may show a slight to moderate increase in gland size. Mild inflammation may surround an otherwise normal-appearing gland (Fig. 99-4). Alternatively, the pancreas may be diffusely enlarged, with a shaggy and irregular contour, and slightly hypoenhancing heterogeneous parenchyma (Fig. 99-5). On MRI, there may be decreased pancreatic signal intensity on T1-weighted fat-suppressed sequences before and following gadolinium administration, depending on the degree of inflammation, edema, and necrosis[86,91] (Fig. 99-6).

In more advanced cases, extravasation of pancreatic fluid leads to the formation of intrapancreatic and extrapancreatic fluid collections (Fig. 99-7). Because the pancreas does not have a well-developed fibrous capsule, pancreatic secretions commonly extravasate in the retroperitoneum, most often in the anterior pararenal space (Fig. 99-8; see also Fig. 99-1), subperitoneal space, and interfascial spaces. CT superbly depicts peripancreatic inflammation, fluid, and, occasionally,

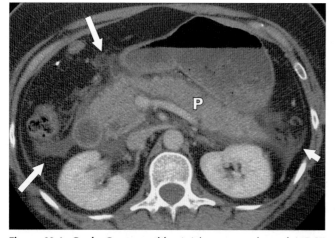

Figure 99-4. Grade C pancreatitis. Axial contrast-enhanced MDCT image shows peripancreatic inflammatory changes (*arrows*) in a patient with abdominal pain and elevated amylase levels. The pancreas (P) has normal size and enhancement.

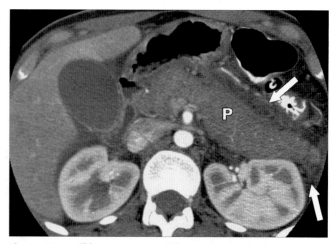

Figure 99-5. Mild acute pancreatitis. Axial arterial phase contrast-enhanced MDCT image shows diffuse enlargement and decreased enhancement of the pancreas. Note peripancreatic inflammatory changes (*arrows*). P, pancreas.

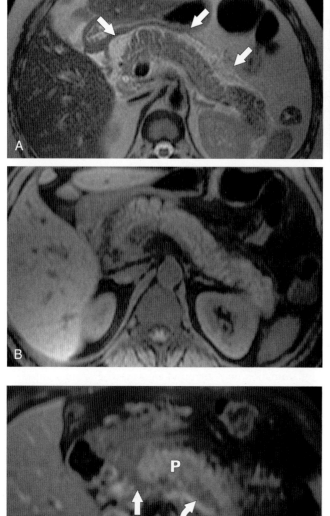

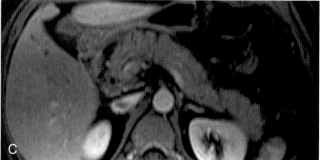

Figure 99-6. Mild ERCP-induced pancreatitis. A. Axial T2-weighted half-Fourier acquisition single-shot turbo spin-echo (HASTE) MR image shows peripancreatic fluid (*arrows*) with high signal intensity. The pancreas also has mildly increased signal intensity due to edema. **B.** Axial T1-weighted fat-suppressed spoiled gradient-echo MR image shows normal high signal intensity of the pancreas in this patient with uncomplicated pancreatitis. The peripancreatic fluid is better seen on T2-weighted images. **C.** The pancreas shows diffusely decreased enhancement during the arterial phase after administration of gadolinium. (**A, B,** and **C** from Miller FH, Keppke AL, Dalal K, et al: MRI of pancreatitis and its complications: Part 1, acute pancreatitis. AJR 183:1637-1644, 2004. Reprinted with permission from the American Journal of Roentgenology.)

Figure 99-7. ERCP-induced pancreatitis with peripancreatic fluid collections. Axial enhanced T1-weighted fat-suppressed spoiled gradient-echo MR image shows heterogeneous pancreatic enhancement and peripancreatic fluid and inflammation (*straight arrows*). Fluid (*curved arrow*) is seen between the pancreas and the splenic vein. P, pancreas. (From Miller FH, Keppke AL, Dalal K, et al: MRI of pancreatitis and its complications: Part 1, acute pancreatitis. AJR 183:1637-1644, 2004. Reprinted with permission from the American Journal of Roentgenology.)

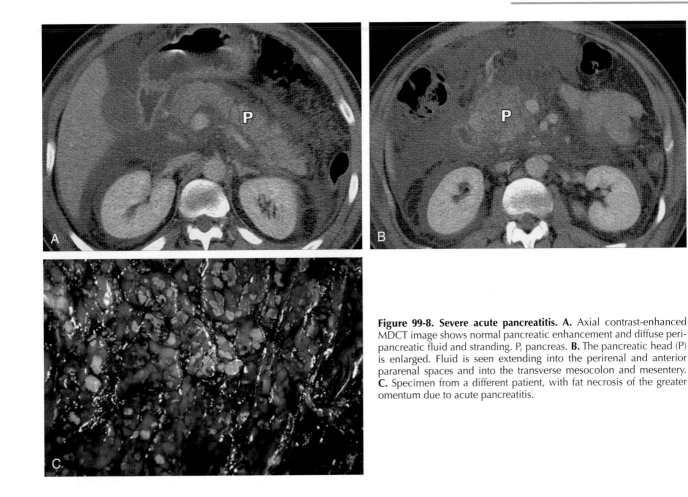

Figure 99-8. Severe acute pancreatitis. A. Axial contrast-enhanced MDCT image shows normal pancreatic enhancement and diffuse peripancreatic fluid and stranding. P, pancreas. **B.** The pancreatic head (P) is enlarged. Fluid is seen extending into the perirenal and anterior pararenal spaces and into the transverse mesocolon and mesentery. **C.** Specimen from a different patient, with fat necrosis of the greater omentum due to acute pancreatitis.

mild thickening of the adjacent fascial planes (see Figs. 99-1 and 99-4). Peripancreatic inflammatory stranding is also well seen on MRI (see Fig. 99-6).

A more unusual segmental form of acute pancreatitis occurs in as many as 18% of patients.[10,78] The CT findings are similar to those in diffuse pancreatitis; however, only part of the gland is involved either exclusively or predominantly.

The segment most often involved is the pancreatic head. This form of pancreatitis is usually mild and is most often associated with stone disease.[5,92,93] However, patients with segmental pancreatitis should be carefully evaluated to exclude an adenocarcinoma simulating pancreatitis or a mass causing pancreatitis (Figs. 99-9 and 99-10). It may be appropriate to further investigate these patients with endoscopic ultrasound,

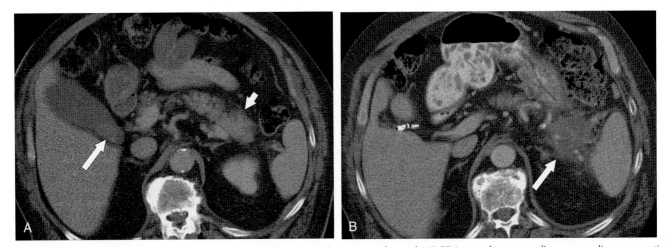

Figure 99-9. Pancreatic cancer mimicking acute pancreatitis. A. Axial contrast-enhanced MDCT image shows stranding surrounding pancreatic tail (*short arrow*) and gallstone (*long arrow*) in this patient with uncontrollable back pain who was believed to have pancreatitis. **B.** Six months after cholecystectomy, the patient had persistent pain. His amylase and lipase levels were only mildly elevated. Axial contrast-enhanced MDCT image shows a pancreatic tail mass (*arrow*) that encases vessels and was proved to be adenocarcinoma.

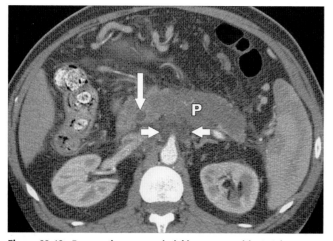

Figure 99-10. Pancreatic cancer mimicking pancreatitis. Axial contrast-enhanced MDCT image shows enlargement and lack of enhancement of the body and tail of the pancreas (P), mimicking pancreatic necrosis. Note peripancreatic stranding and soft tissue density (*short arrows*) surrounding the celiac artery, raising suspicion for cancer. There was thrombosis of the superior mesenteric vein, splenic vein, and extrahepatic portal vein (*long arrow*). Histological examination revealed pancreatic adenocarcinoma.

ERCP, or biopsy or to perform short-term follow-up CT or MRI, especially if they are older or do not have risk factors for pancreatitis.[91]

In severe forms of necrotizing pancreatitis, the gland may become enlarged, and it is commonly enveloped by high-attenuation heterogeneous fluid collections. Because of high-attenuation exudates, the presence of pancreatic necrosis cannot be assessed on CT unless the gland is imaged during the late arterial–early portal venous phase of a rapid bolus intravenous injection of contrast medium[70] (Fig. 99-11). On MRI, peripancreatic high signal intensity may be seen on T1-weighted fat-suppressed sequences related to fat necrosis and hemorrhage (Fig. 99-12). This finding is a poor prognostic sign.[94] Patchy areas of absence of enhancement, fragmentation, and liquefaction necrosis can be detected on CT and MRI (Fig. 99-13). Poorly defined peripancreatic exudates obliter-

ate the peripancreatic fat, envelop the pancreas, dissect the interfascial planes, and penetrate through fascial and peritoneal boundaries and ligaments. These collections most often occur in the anterior pararenal space around the body and tail of the pancreas and within the lesser peritoneal sac[95] (Fig. 99-14). Penetration through Gerota's fascia with involvement of the perirenal fat and kidneys occurs rarely. When fluid collections are massive, they tend to extend inferiorly along the pararenal spaces in the left flank or bilaterally. They can course over the psoas muscle, enter the pelvis (see Fig. 99-14B), and sometimes extend into the groin. Exudates can invade the small bowel mesentery, the transverse mesocolon, and the posterior pararenal spaces (see Fig. 99-8). Fluid can penetrate into solid organs such as the spleen or the liver and even the mediastinum. Splenic involvement is most common due to the close anatomic relationship of the pancreatic tail and splenic hilum. Subcapsular or intrasplenic fluid collections or pseudocysts, infarcts, and splenic hemorrhage may be seen with pancreatitis.

In about 7% to 12% of patients with acute pancreatitis, CT and MRI reveal a small amount of free intraperitoneal fluid. Massive pancreatic ascites, caused by communication of a disrupted pancreatic duct with the peritoneal cavity, is rarely seen.[26,96] This presentation is usually associated with a more severe form of pancreatitis. In most of these patients, characteristic pancreatic and peripancreatic abnormalities are recognized. Rarely, pancreatic ascites can develop in patients with a normal-appearing gland on CT scans. The patients require paracentesis with amylase determination to make the diagnosis.[97] The treatment of pancreatic ascites includes conservative management with nasogastric suction, parenteral nutrition, and repeated paracenteses.[98,99] If these measures fail, interventional or surgical procedures including pancreatic duct stenting, pancreaticojejunostomy, or distal pancreatectomy may be required.

Diagnostic Sensitivity

The accuracy of CT in the diagnosis of acute pancreatitis depends to a large extent on the severity of the disease. The reported CT sensitivity for the diagnosis of acute pancreatitis ranges from 77% to 92%.[43,100,101] The usefulness of CT is

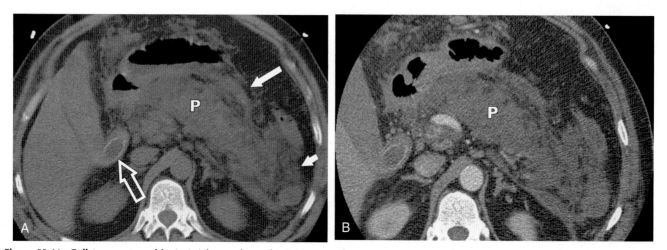

Figure 99-11. Gallstone pancreatitis. A. Axial nonenhanced MDCT image shows an enlarged pancreas (P) with indistinct borders because of peripancreatic inflammatory changes (*solid arrows*). Gallstone (*open arrow*) is seen in the gallbladder neck. **B.** Axial arterial phase contrast-enhanced MDCT image shows lack of enhancement of the pancreas (P), consistent with necrosis.

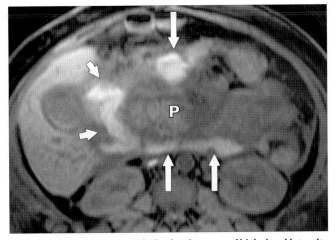

Figure 99-12. Pancreatitis with the development of high signal intensity fluid collections. Axial T1-weighted fat-suppressed spoiled gradient-echo MR image shows complex peripancreatic fluid collection (*arrows*) with predominantly high signal intensity, which extended inferiorly from the level of the pancreatic head (P). Aspiration biopsy revealed a necrotizing inflammatory process.

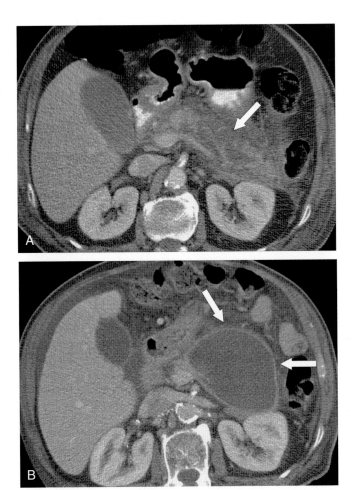

Figure 99-13. Grade E pancreatitis with necrosis evolving into pseudocyst. A. Axial contrast-enhanced MDCT image shows patchy, confluent necrotic areas (*arrow*) in pancreatic body and tail. Note peripancreatic inflammatory stranding. **B.** Axial contrast-enhanced MDCT image 4 months after the initial episode of pancreatitis shows the development of a pseudocyst (*arrows*) in previously necrotic body and tail of pancreas.

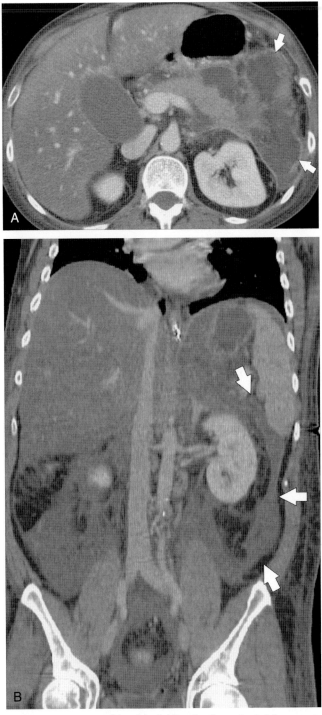

Figure 99-14. Pancreatitis with fluid collections. A. Axial contrast-enhanced MDCT image shows heterogeneous fluid collection (*arrows*) in the left anterior pararenal space involving the tail of the pancreas. Note that the fluid collection does not spread beyond Gerota's fascia. This collection extended inferiorly along the left pericolic gutter into the pelvis. **B.** Coronal contrast-enhanced MDCT image from another patient with pancreatitis shows fluid (*arrows*) extending inferiorly from the pancreatic region along the interfascial planes into the pelvis. The pathway of fluid is better demonstrated on coronal reformatted images.

further supported by its high specificity. In most series, there are few false-positive findings, and CT specificity as high as 100% has been reported.[100] In addition, by examining the entire abdomen, CT can reveal a variety of other abdominal conditions in patients with clinically suspected acute pancreatitis.

Limitations in Diagnosis

Limitations in the CT diagnosis of acute pancreatitis are related to suboptimal examinations resulting from poor technique, lack of intravenous contrast medium, or inability of the patient to cooperate. Motion or streak artifacts and paucity of retroperitoneal fat are limiting factors in some patients. In addition, in mild forms of clinical pancreatitis, morphologic parenchymal or retroperitoneal abnormalities do not develop and the gland may appear normal on CT. It occurs in patients with mild symptoms and transitory elevation of serum amylase levels. The incidence of normal CT scans in these persons is not well established because surgical or pathologic correlation is lacking, but it has been estimated to be 14% to 28%.[78,102] Experience has shown that given a good-quality CT scan, all patients with moderate or severe pancreatitis will exhibit some CT abnormality. In patients with a normal CT, pancreatitis is either absent or of minimal clinical significance.

Staging

By virtue of its ability to accurately and rapidly evaluate the pancreas, peritoneum, and retroperitoneum, CT can be used to predict the severity of acute pancreatitis.[103,104] As early as 1982, Hill and coworkers[102] correlated the initial CT findings with the clinical type of edematous or necrotizing pancreatitis. Other investigations prospectively correlated the CT appearance with the severity of disease, development of complications, and death.[19,61,95,102] Earlier studies using slower scanners, 10-mm collimation, and slow intravenous drip infusions staged pancreatitis on the basis of size, configuration of the gland, and the presence and degree of fluid collections.[78,100,105-108] With the use of helical scanners and power

injection of intravenous contrast material, the CT evaluation has concentrated on the appearance and density of the pancreatic gland in an attempt to detect or exclude pancreatic necrosis.[108-113]

Grading System

Balthazar and colleagues have initially classified the type and severity of acute pancreatitis into five grades[78,105]:

Grade A: Normal pancreas

Grade B: Focal or diffuse enlargement of the gland including contour irregularities and inhomogeneous attenuation but without peripancreatic inflammation

Grade C: Intrinsic pancreatic abnormalities associated with inflammatory changes in the peripancreatic fat (see Figs. 99-5 and 99-6)

Grade D: Small and usually single, ill-defined fluid collection

Grade E: Two or more large fluid collections or the presence of gas in the pancreas or retroperitoneum (Figs. 99-15 and 99-16)

On the basis of two consecutive prospective studies including 171 patients, it was found that patients with grade A or B pancreatitis had a mild uncomplicated clinical course, whereas patients with grade D or E disease developed a protracted clinical illness and significantly higher incidence of abscess and death.[78,102] Abscesses developed in 17% of patients with grade D pancreatitis and in 61% of those with grade E pancreatitis. Patients with grades D and E pancreatitis had 14% mortality and 54% morbidity compared with 0% mortality and 4% morbidity in patients with grades A, B, and C (Fig. 99-17). Clavien and colleagues,[100] in a prospective evaluation of 176 patients, found that most complications and a protracted clinical course developed in patients with fluid collections. Studies of patients with minimal extrapancreatic inflammation showed no deaths, whereas small areas of fluid collections led to a 4% mortality, and extensive fluid involvement resulted in a mortality of 42%. This initial CT grading system had limitations in predicting morbidity and mortality in patients with retroperitoneal fluid collections because half

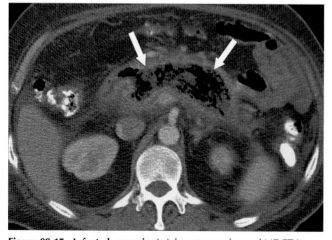

Figure 99-15. Infected necrosis. Axial contrast-enhanced MDCT image shows absence of normal enhancing pancreatic parenchyma. There are air bubbles and debris (*arrows*) in the pancreatic bed suggesting infected necrosis. The patient underwent pancreatic debridement.

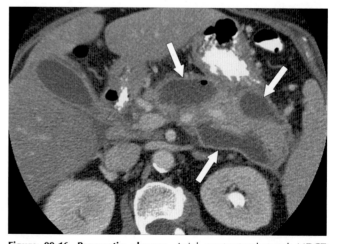

Figure 99-16. Pancreatic abscess. Axial contrast-enhanced MDCT image shows fluid collection (*arrows*) containing air bubble involving the pancreas consistent with an abscess. The patient underwent surgical drainage of the abscess and pancreatic debridement.

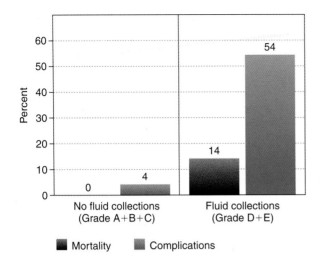

Figure 99-17. Correlation of CT staging and morbidity and mortality. Complications (morbidity) included infected fluid collections, abscesses, and pseudocysts (n = 88).

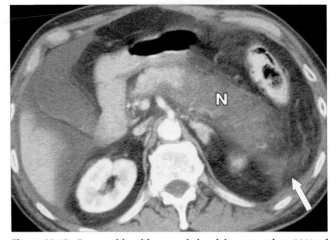

Figure 99-18. Pancreatitis with necrosis involving more than 50% of the gland. Axial contrast-enhanced MDCT image shows lack of enhancement in the body and tail of the pancreas consistent with necrosis (N). Peripancreatic inflammatory changes (*arrow*) are also seen.

of these patients did not develop complications. In addition, this grading system did not include pancreatic necrosis, which has significant prognostic implications.[78]

Delineation of Necrosis

During the arterial phase of bolus intravenous administration of contrast medium, the normal pancreas should enhance homogeneously. Mild inflammation and interstitial edema do not interfere with the expected homogeneous enhancement of the gland (see Figs. 99-1 and 99-4). When necrosis is present, there is absence of contrast medium enhancement together with liquefaction and a change in the density or signal intensity of the gland (Figs. 99-18 and 99-19). Gadolinium-enhanced T1-weighted gradient-echo MR images demonstrate pancreatic necrosis as low signal areas of nonenhancing parenchyma (Fig. 99-20). The process can be focal or segmental or can affect the entire pancreatic gland (see Figs. 99-18 and 99-19). It can be grossly quantified as involving 30% or 50% or all of the gland.[108,114,115] In Kivisaari and associates' original series using CT, mild pancreatitis was associated with a rapid rise in the density of the gland by 40 to 50 HU after

contrast administration.[116,117] Pancreatic necrosis was found at surgery in all patients who exhibited absence of enhancement or low enhancing values of less than 30 HU (see Figs. 99-18 and 99-19). Other investigators have corroborated the CT–surgical correlation in the detection of pancreatic necrosis.[118,119] In a series of 93 patients, an overall CT accuracy of 85% with 100% sensitivity for extensive glandular necrosis was found.[115] At times, MRI may be more sensitive than CT for the detection of pancreatic necrosis, because of the greater sensitivity of MRI to gadolinium than of CT to iodinated contrast medium. Many patients with pancreatic necrosis, however, may be seriously ill and may be unable to hold their breath for the required MRI sequences.

There is good correlation between necrosis and length of hospitalization, development of complications, and death[105,108]: patients without necrosis had no mortality and only 6% morbidity, whereas patients with necrosis exhibited 23% mortality and 82% morbidity (Fig. 99-21). The degree of necrosis appears to be an important factor as well (Fig. 99-22). Patients with small areas of necrosis (<30%) showed no mortality and 40% morbidity, whereas large areas of necrosis (≥50%) were associated with 75% to 100% morbidity and

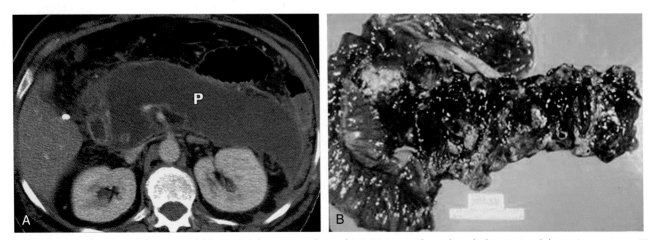

Figure 99-19. Extensive necrotizing pancreatitis. A. Axial contrast-enhanced MDCT image shows liquefied necrosis of the entire pancreas (P). Multiple surgical debridements were required. **B.** Autopsy showing necrotizing pancreatitis in a different patient.

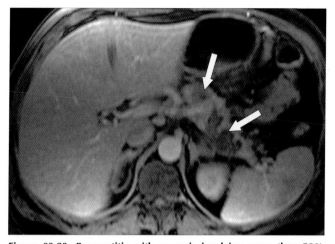

Figure 99-20. Pancreatitis with necrosis involving more than 50% of the gland. Axial gadolinium-enhanced T1-weighted fat-suppressed spoiled gradient-echo MR image shows nonenhancing necrotic areas (*arrows*) in the body and tail of the pancreas. (From Ly JN, Miller FH: MR imaging of the pancreas: A practical approach. Radiol Clin N Am 40:1289-1306, 2002.)

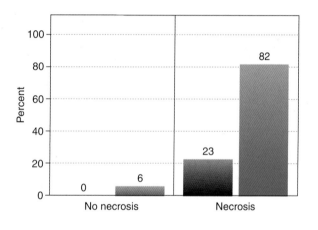

Figure 99-21. Correlation of the onset of necrosis and its association with morbidity and mortality (n = 88).

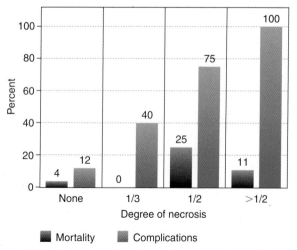

Figure 99-22. Correlation of the degree of necrosis with morbidity and mortality (n = 88). 1/3, 1/2, >1/2 refer to the amount of pancreatic tissue involved by the necrosis.

11% to 25% mortality (see Fig. 99-22). The combined morbidity of patients with more than 30% necrosis was 94%, and the mortality was 29%. There was no significant difference in prognosis between patients with up to 50% necrosis and those with more than 50% necrosis. Other studies have shown that infected pancreatic necrosis is also a significant predictor of organ failure and mortality in acute pancreatitis.[80,120,121] Garg and colleagues[80] found a mortality rate of 12% for patients with sterile necrosis and 50% for those with infected necrosis. The prophylactic use of antibiotics in patients with sterile necrosis has been recommended to avoid infection of the necrotic tissue.[122-124]

Limitations: Staging

In our experience, extensive pancreatic necrosis is detected mostly in patients with grades D and E pancreatitis.[78,108] Pancreatic necrosis, however, develops early, within the first 24 to 48 hours in the course of the disease.[109] Necrosis may be the initial CT manifestation and may precede the development of peripancreatic fluid collections. Furthermore, small patchy areas of pancreatic necrosis can be missed, particularly on the initial CT examination. These are much better defined on a follow-up examination performed a few days after the initial acute attack. Therefore, the accuracy of CT to detect and quantify pancreatic necrosis is higher 2 to 3 days after the clinical onset of disease, when there is liquefaction of the ischemic pancreatic tissue.[109] Patients with fluid collections (grades D and E disease) who do not have pancreatic necrosis still exhibit a 22% complication rate. Extravasated pancreatic enzymes leading to secondary inflammatory changes and fat necrosis in the retroperitoneum likely cause these complications. A combined CT evaluation of the pancreatitis grade plus degree of pancreatic necrosis improves the ability of CT to predict complications. For instance, the likelihood that an abscess will develop is highest (84%) in patients with associated necrosis and exudates but is significantly lower (46%) if the initial CT examination shows only exudates but no necrosis.

Severity Index

This staging method combines the two previously discussed prognostic indicators.[108] On a scale of 1 to 10, patients are assigned 0 to 4 points based on the A-to-E grading. To this, 2, 4, or 6 points are added if the initial CT scan detects up to 30%, 30% to 50%, or more than 50% necrosis. A severity index classification into three distinct categories (0-3, 4-6, and 7-10 points) more accurately reflects the prognostic value of CT as judged by the initial CT examination. As seen in Figure 99-23, there is a statistically significant increase in morbidity and mortality rates in these three groups of patients. Patients with a severity index of 0 or 1 have no mortality and morbidity. Patients with a severity index of 2 have no mortality and only 4% morbidity. In contrast, a severity index of 7 to 10 yields 17% mortality and a 92% complication rate.

Computed Tomography versus Clinical Prognostic Signs

The average number of prognostic signs (Ranson's grave signs) is higher in patients with grades D and E pancreatitis than in those with lower grades of disease.[78,108] All patients

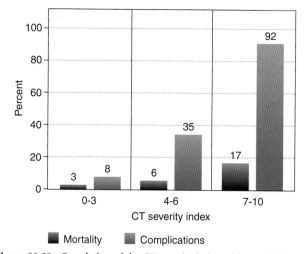

Figure 99-23. Correlation of the CT severity index with morbidity and mortality. The CT severity index takes into account CT stage as well as the degree of necrosis (n = 88).

with more than five prognostic signs have grade E pancreatitis. The correlation, however, is poor in patients with up to five prognostic signs. A study comparing Ranson criteria with the Balthazar CT criteria for detection of severe acute pancreatitis found that the CT prognostic indicators had greater sensitivity and specificity.[125] Other studies have shown that the CT severity index is superior to the APACHE II score to predict necrotizing pancreatitis and superior to the Simplified Acute Physiology score for prediction of a favorable outcome.[126,127] It should be emphasized, however, that a close correlation between CT findings and clinical scoring systems should not be expected. This is because CT evaluates local abdominal complications, whereas clinical prognostic signs are indicative of systemic complications.

A modified CT severity index has been proposed, which includes a simplified assessment of pancreatic inflammation and necrosis as well as an evaluation of extrapancreatic complications.[113] The modified CT severity index differentiates only between the presence and absence of acute fluid collections, not taking into account the number of collections. In addition, it scores pancreatic necrosis into three levels only, which are "no necrosis," "minimal necrosis," or "substantial necrosis." Last, the presence of extrapancreatic findings such as pleural effusion, ascites, vascular and parenchymal complications, and gastrointestinal tract involvement is included in the analysis. Unlike the current CT severity index, the modified index was able to predict the development of organ failure and the length of hospital stay when comparing patients with moderate pancreatitis to those with severe pancreatitis. The modified index also correlated better than the current CT severity index with the need for surgical or percutaneous procedures and the occurrence of infection.

Indications for Examination

Many patients with edematous pancreatitis have a typical clinical presentation and show rapid amelioration with limited supportive therapy. They do not require imaging examinations for diagnosis or management. On the other hand, CT imaging is needed and should be performed early when (1) the clinical diagnosis is in doubt; (2) there is failure to respond to medical treatment within 48 to 72 hours; (3) acute abdominal symptoms (distention, tenderness), leukocytosis, or fever is present; (4) patients have more than two of Ranson's grave signs; and (5) there is a change in clinical status suggesting a developing complication. Specific indications for performing MRI over CT would include (1) iodinated contrast allergy or poor renal function; (2) to detect the etiology of pancreatitis such as choledocholithiasis, pancreas divisum, and pancreatic tumors; and (3) to characterize complex fluid collections and to determine their drainability.

Complications

The complications of acute pancreatitis are legion and are summarized in Table 99-4. Most complications that develop within the first few days of disease are systemic in nature. They are likely caused by potent biochemical toxic substances released into the bloodstream by the injured pancreas. Local complications tend to develop later, within weeks or months, or even years following an episode of acute pancreatitis. The prompt detection and treatment of local complications are essential, because they are responsible for more than 50% of the mortality associated with acute pancreatitis.[27,128-130] These complications are discussed below.

Fluid Collections and Pseudocysts

Fluid collections develop in up to 50% of patients with acute pancreatitis. The fluid may be pancreatic juice, serum, or blood. They develop either from actual rupture of the pancreatic duct with liberation of enzymes and pancreatic juice or secondary to exudation of fluid from the surface of the pancreas owing to activation of pancreatic enzymes within the gland. The fluid is contained by whatever structures happen to be adjacent to the collection. Most fluid collections are absorbed within 2 to 3 weeks. Unabsorbed fluid collections can organize and, within 4 to 6 weeks, develop a fibrous capsule, forming a pseudocyst.[26,131] The lack of resorption of extravasated secretions and a communicating tract with the pancreatic duct are implicated in the development of pseudocysts. We believe that most pseudocysts in acute pancreatitis evolve at the site of parenchymal necrosis that has damaged the pancreatic duct[26] (see Fig. 99-13).

Pseudocysts develop during the initial attack of pancreatitis in 1% to 3% of patients.[78,132,133] They have been reported to occur in 12% of patients after several episodes of alcoholic pancreatitis.[12] The main causes of pancreatic pseudocysts are chronic alcoholism (75%) and abdominal trauma (13%), with cholelithiasis, pancreatic carcinoma, and idiopathic causes composing the remainder.[134] If the patient with a suspected pseudocyst has no history of pancreatitis, pancreatic trauma, or pancreatic surgery, a follow-up imaging study or aspiration biopsy may be required to exclude a pancreatic cystic neoplasm.[131]

The clinical significance of a pseudocyst is related to its size and the potentially lethal complications that may occur. Pseudocysts displace and compress adjacent abdominal organs and can produce obstruction, pain, and jaundice. Spontaneous rupture in the peritoneal cavity leads to pancreatic ascites or peritonitis. Secondary infection results in abscess formation. Erosion into an adjacent vessel leads to massive and sudden hemorrhage. Most of these complications, however, occur in pseudocysts larger than 4 to 5 cm. Small pseudocysts are often seen on CT in asymptomatic patients, have a low incidence of morbidity, and can be followed expectantly with clinical and CT examinations.[26,35] Surgical, endoscopic, or percutaneous drainage is indicated for pseudocysts that increase in size, become symptomatic, or develop complications.[26,34,135] The development of percutaneous and endoscopic techniques offers an alternative means of drainage of pseudocysts that is less invasive.[135,136] Success rates of over 90% have been reported with percutaneous drainage of pseudocysts guided by CT or sonography.[135,137] Percutaneous drainage techniques of pancreatic fluid collections are discussed in Chapter 97.

Pseudocysts vary greatly in size, are round or oval, and are located either within the pancreatic parenchyma (see Fig. 99-13) or outside it. On CT scans, they are characterized by low fluid density (<15 HU) contents and by a peripheral fibrous capsule. Higher attenuation values are indicative of secondary infection or the presence of necrotic tissue. A density greater than 40 to 50 HU are suggestive of intracystic hemorrhage. On MRI, uncomplicated pseudocysts typically show low signal intensity on T1-weighted sequences and high signal intensity on T2-weighted sequences. Complicated pseudocysts may have high signal intensity on T1-weighted images due to hemorrhagic or proteinaceous fluid and may contain solid debris, which are best depicted on T2-weighted images (Figs. 99-24 and 99-25). MRI is superior to CT and ultrasound in its ability to characterize fluid collections.[93,138]

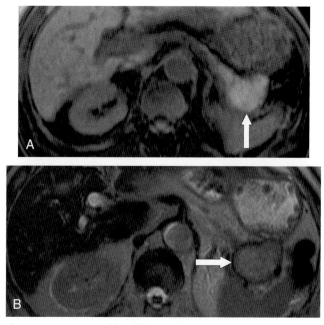

Figure 99-24. Pancreatitis with hemorrhagic pseudocyst. A. Axial T1-weighted fat-suppressed spoiled gradient-echo MR image shows pseudocyst (*arrow*) in the pancreatic tail with high signal intensity from hemorrhagic content. **B.** Axial T2-weighted HASTE MR image shows low signal intensity rim of hemosiderin in pseudocyst (*arrow*). The diagnosis of hemorrhage is easily made on MRI due to the hemosiderin rim. (**A** and **B** from Miller FH, Keppke AL, Dalal K, et al: MRI of pancreatitis and its complications: Part 1, acute pancreatitis. AJR 183:1637-1644, 2004. Reprinted with permission from the American Journal of Roentgenology.)

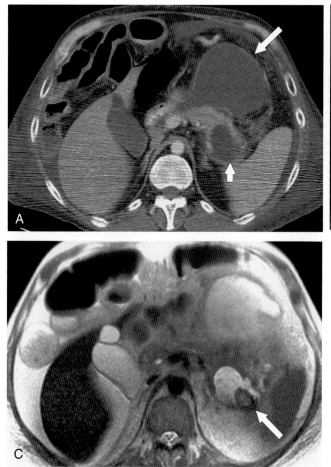

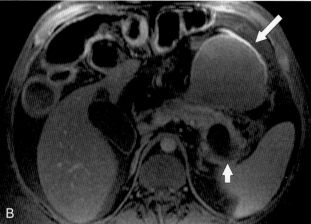

Figure 99-25. Pancreatic pseudocyst with internal debris. A. Axial contrast-enhanced MDCT image shows hypodense fluid collections in the pancreatic tail (*short arrow*) and in the lesser sac (*long arrow*), consistent with pseudocysts. **B.** Axial enhanced T1-weighted fat-suppressed spoiled gradient-echo MR image obtained 1 day after CT shows hypointense pseudocyst (*short arrow*) in the pancreatic tail and moderate signal intensity pseudocyst (*long arrow*) in the lesser sac. Note associated peripancreatic inflammatory changes. **C.** Axial T2-weighted HASTE image shows debris (*arrow*) inside the intrapancreatic pseudocyst, which were not seen on CT. Note large amount of ascites in this patient with end-stage renal failure.

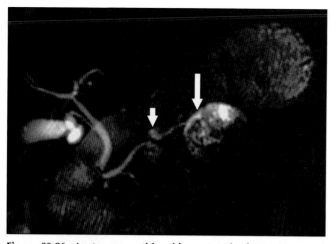

Figure 99-26. Acute pancreatitis with pancreatic duct rupture and pseudocyst. Thick-slab T2-weighted rapid acquisition and relaxation enhancement (RARE) MRCP image shows disrupted pancreatic duct (*short arrow*) and peripancreatic pseudocyst (*long arrow*) containing low signal intensity debris. (From Ly JN, Miller FH: MR imaging of the pancreas: A practical approach. Radiol Clin N Am 40:1289-1306, 2002.)

ERCP is less accurate than CT or MRI in demonstrating pseudocysts, as less than 50% of pseudocysts fill with contrast at ERCP. Conversely, MRCP is able to detect pseudocysts that do not communicate with the pancreatic duct. ERCP, however, may be required to demonstrate communication between a pseudocyst and the pancreatic duct, although sometimes it can be seen on MRI (Fig. 99-26). Communicating pseudocysts may require prolonged catheter drainage until the communication to the pancreatic duct closes and the cyst collapses. Decompression of concomitant pancreatic duct obstruction may be required.

Although many of the initial poorly defined fluid collections seen in acute pancreatitis resolve spontaneously, the natural history of pseudocysts is difficult to predict. They may persist, they can resolve, or they can even continue to grow over time. Spontaneous resolution (Fig. 99-27) even of large pseudocysts can occur and is explained by drainage into the pancreatic duct, erosion into an adjacent hollow organ (small bowel, colon), or rupture with spillage into the peritoneal cavity.

Infected Pancreatic Necrosis

Bacterial superinfection of necrotic and hemorrhagic pancreatic and peripancreatic tissue complicates severe forms of pancreatitis. Secondary infection of the necrotic tissue occurs in 40% to 70% of patients with necrotizing pancreatitis and is often the cause of death in this patient population.[139,140] The frequency of bacterial infection is proportionate to the extent of pancreatic necrosis and duration of disease.[27,141] Cultures usually reveal gram-negative organisms derived from the intestinal tract, particularly the colon, but an increase in gram-positive and fungal organisms has been observed in association with the prophylactic use of antibiotics.[27,142] On CT, sterile, partially liquefied pancreatic necrosis cannot be differentiated from infected necrosis unless gas bubbles (seen in about 12%-18% of cases) are present in the necrotic tissue[26] (see Fig. 99-15). In the absence of gas, if infected necrosis is suspected, a CT-guided percutaneous aspiration for Gram stain and culture should be performed.[26,133,134,143] This technique is safe and has a sensitivity and specificity of more than 90%.[144] Aggressive surgical treatment of infected pancreatic necrosis is recommended because it can reduce the mortality rate significantly. Surgical techniques include closed and open procedures.[7,26,142,145,146] In closed procedures the abdomen is closed after necrosectomy, and continuous postoperative retroperitoneal lavage is performed with wide-bore drains to remove residual devitalized tissue. Open procedures involve open packing or insertion of a synthetic mesh or zipper in the abdominal fascia to allow repeated, planned reoperations.[143,144,147] If possible, surgery should be delayed for at least 2 weeks after the onset of illness to allow better demarcation between viable and necrotic tissue, thus avoiding loss of viable pancreatic parenchyma. Surgical debridement with wide sump drainage has been the treatment of choice, although some studies have achieved moderate success with percutaneous drainage.[9,133,134,144,148,149] Other interventional procedures including endoscopic, laparoscopic, or retroperitoneal minimally invasive necrosectomy have been developed.[143,148,150,151] With these less aggressive procedures, the use of multiple large-bore catheters and frequent vigorous lavage are often required to ensure adequate drainage of necrotic debris.[9,143] Close monitoring of the catheter entry site and fluid output and use of periodic sinography to evaluate the residual collection are helpful to achieve favorable results.

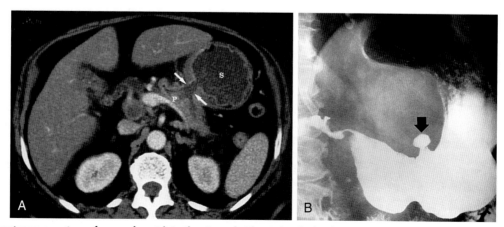

Figure 99-27. Spontaneous rupture of a pseudocyst into the stomach. The patient had a documented large pseudocyst scheduled to be surgically drained. CT examination before elective surgery shows decompression of the pseudocyst into the stomach (S) (*arrows*). P, pancreas. **B.** Upper gastrointestinal examination reveals an ulceration (*arrow*) consistent with spontaneous drainage of a pseudocyst.

Abscess

Fluid collections that fail to resorb represent an ideal medium for bacterial growth, explaining the development of abscesses. In the past, abscesses were considered the major cause of death in acute pancreatitis.[101,152] The associated high mortality was related mainly to significant delays in diagnosis. Abscesses occur in about 3% of patients after an attack of acute pancreatitis.[2,9,27,153] They develop within several weeks after the onset of symptoms in patients with severe forms of pancreatitis. Their presence is usually heralded by deterioration in the clinical course with septic systemic symptoms. They may have an inconspicuous clinical presentation initially.[154]

Abscesses are located in the peripancreatic tissues and have different sizes and configurations (see Fig. 99-16). On CT scans, they appear as poorly defined or partially encapsulated fluid collections of different densities (20-50 HU) and are often indistinguishable from residual noninfected fluid collections.[78] A more characteristic appearance, seen in about 20% of abscesses, is the presence of gas bubbles produced by gas-forming bacteria. Retroperitoneal gas may be seen in patients with enteric fistulas; however, it is always strongly suggestive of an abscess.[7,9,153] CT is more sensitive than MRI for detection of small gas bubbles, although large collections of gas or gas-fluid levels can be detected on T2-weighted MR images. CT is quite accurate in depicting the location and extent of small collections of retroperitoneal fluid and gas. This finding quickly identifies a potential life-threatening complication. Infection should be suspected in all patients with pancreatitis in whom poorly encapsulated fluid collections are still present 2 to 4 weeks after the initial attack. MRI may be able to differentiate abscesses with complex internal content from simple collections in these patients (Fig. 99-28). If the diagnosis is in doubt, CT-guided needle aspiration can rapidly and reliably establish the diagnosis, contributing greatly to the early detection, treatment, and decreased mortality in this group of patients.[135,136,155,156] It is important to differentiate infected necrosis from abscesses, because the mortality risk for infected necrosis is double that of pancreatic abscesses.[6,134] Percutaneous drainage is the therapeutic procedure of choice for pancreatic abscesses.[157-159]

Hemorrhage

Although small patchy areas of hemorrhage combined with necrotic tissue are common findings in acute pancreatitis, massive life-threatening intra-abdominal hemorrhage is seldom reported. This complication may occur within 2 to 3 weeks to several years after an acute episode of pancreatitis.[160-162] It is the result of erosion of peripancreatic vessels with the formation of a pseudoaneurysm and subsequent retroperitoneal bleeding. Commonly, the site of bleeding is located along the pancreaticoduodenal arcade or along the splenic vessels adjacent to the tail of the pancreas. Pseudoaneurysms can be located within a pancreatic pseudocyst. Hemorrhage occurs when a slowly enlarging pseudoaneurysm ruptures into the peritoneum, or erodes into an adjacent hollow viscus or into the pancreatic duct producing hemosuccus pancreaticus.[162] CT examination can identify retroperitoneal bleeding by the presence of high-density (50-100 HU) fluid collections. MRI is more sensitive than CT for the

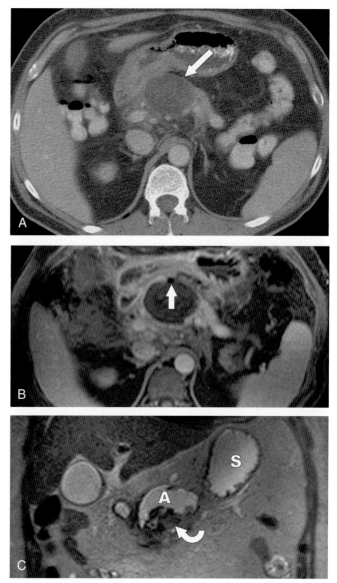

Figure 99-28. Pancreatitis with abscess. A. Axial contrast-enhanced MDCT image shows hypodense fluid collection (*arrow*) in the pancreatic head suspicious for an abscess in this patient with pancreatitis. **B.** Axial gadolinium-enhanced T1-weighted fat-suppressed spoiled gradient-echo MR image obtained 11 days after CT shows an air bubble (*arrow*) within the pancreatic abscess. **C.** Coronal T2-weighted HASTE MR image shows low signal intensity debris (*curved arrow*) within the pancreatic abscess, which were not seen on CT. The presence of necrotic debris was confirmed at surgery. A, abscess; S, stomach. (**B** and **C** from Miller FH, Keppke AL, Dalal K, et al: MRI of pancreatitis and its complications: Part 1, acute pancreatitis. AJR 183:1637-1644, 2004. Reprinted with permission from the American Journal of Roentgenology.)

detection of hemorrhage, which is depicted as high signal intensity on T1-weighted fat-suppressed images because of the presence of methemoglobin. Dynamic enhanced MDCT or T1-weighted gadolinium-enhanced MR images show a pseudoaneurysm as a rapidly enhancing mass similar in contrast density to the adjacent arteries and aorta (Fig. 99-29). Spillage of contrast material into the retroperitoneum due to active bleeding, as well as fresh blood in the peritoneal cavity, can also be diagnosed. It is important to have a high index of suspicion for pseudoaneurysm in patients with history of pancreatitis and a suspected mass in the pancreas

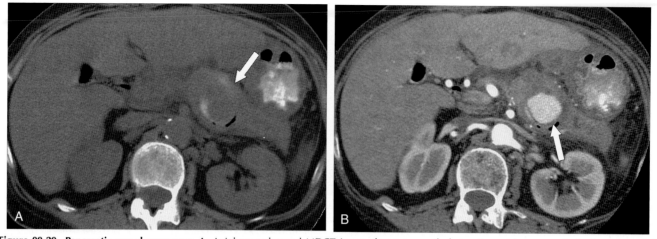

Figure 99-29. Pancreatic pseudoaneurysm. A. Axial nonenhanced MDCT image shows expansile lesion (*arrow*) in pancreatic body, surrounded by contrast material and air from previous ERCP. **B.** Axial arterial phase contrast-enhanced MDCT image clearly shows that the "mass" is a large pseudoaneurysm (*arrow*). In patients who present with suspected pseudocyst or pancreatic mass for drainage, the administration of intravenous contrast is critical, as illustrated in this example. This pseudoaneurysm was subsequently embolized.

or its vicinity. Accordingly, biopsy of these lesions should be performed only after a contrast-enhanced CT, MRI, or Doppler sonography study has excluded a pseudoaneurysm (see Fig. 99-29). If the source of bleeding is obscured by the surrounding hemorrhage, angiography is crucial in identifying the presence and precise location of the bleeding pseudoaneurysm. Therapeutic arterial embolization of the bleeding vessel is required; it is an emergency, lifesaving procedure. Massive hemorrhage from ruptured vessels or pseudoaneurysms requires surgical treatment.

CHRONIC PANCREATITIS

Chronic pancreatitis is a relatively uncommon disease that has been increasing in frequency in the Western world. It is a disease of prolonged pancreatic inflammation characterized by irreversible morphologic and functional damage to the pancreas.[163-165] The incidence of pancreatic cancer is significantly elevated in patients with chronic pancreatitis.[165,166]

Etiology

In the United States, approximately 75% of cases of chronic pancreatitis are due to alcoholism. Continued consumption of alcohol for a 3- to 12-year period is necessary before the manifestations of chronic pancreatitis develop.[166] In contrast to their major role in the development of acute pancreatitis, gallstones play little role in the etiology of chronic pancreatitis. Hyperlipidemia, hyperparathyroidism, trauma, and pancreas divisum have all been implicated as risk factors for developing chronic pancreatitis.

Clinical Findings

Pain is the predominant clinical finding in 95% of patients with chronic pancreatitis. The pain typically radiates from the epigastrium through the back and can be constant or intermittent and extremely difficult to palliate, frequently requiring narcotics or neurolysis. Weight loss often accompanies the pain, and these two findings raise the clinical suspicion of a malignancy. Endocrine and exocrine deficiencies occur

with progressive destruction of the gland. Diabetes and malabsorption with steatorrhea eventually develop in approximately half the patients with chronic pancreatitis.[166,167]

The clinical diagnosis of chronic pancreatitis, especially in its early stages, is often difficult. Histopathologic diagnosis is rarely available, because of the risks associated with pancreatic biopsy, including acute pancreatitis, fistula, and hemorrhage.[168] Therefore, the diagnosis is based on clinical, morphologic, and functional abnormalities. ERCP and pancreatic function tests are considered the gold standard diagnostic procedures, but they have limitations, and prolonged clinical follow-up is sometimes required to confirm the diagnosis.

Radiologic Findings

Plain Radiographs

Typical pancreatic calcifications are diagnostic of chronic pancreatitis. They develop in 40% to 60% of patients with alcoholic pancreatitis, and approximately 90% of calcific pancreatitis is caused by alcoholism. Unfortunately, calcifications occur late in the course of chronic pancreatitis, being associated with severe disease. Most pancreatic calculi are small, irregular calcifications that may be diffuse (Fig. 99-30) or confined to a specific region of the pancreas. Although they can appear on plain radiographs, CT is the most specific and accurate imaging modality for depicting pancreatic calcifications.

Ultrasonography

The development of high-resolution linear-array scanners has significantly increased the diagnostic accuracy of sonography in patients with pancreatitis. Although its contribution in acute pancreatitis is modest, sonography is often used in patients with suspected chronic pancreatitis and its complications. Sonography shows a 60% to 80% diagnostic accuracy rate and provides a noninvasive, inexpensive, and rapid method of evaluating morphologic changes in the pancreas. Like CT, transabdominal sonography is insensitive to diagnose early chronic pancreatitis.

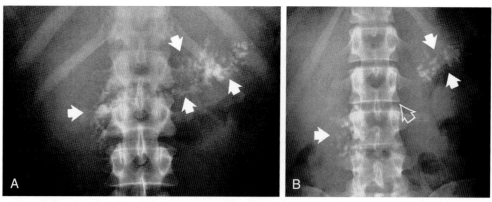

Figure 99-30. Pancreatic calcifications on plain abdominal radiographs. A. The entire gland contains numerous small calcifications located in the main pancreatic duct and its radicles (*arrows*). **B.** Pancreatic calcifications are located in the head and tail of the pancreas (*solid arrows*). The lack of calcifications in the body of the pancreas (*open arrow*) was due to displacement by a pancreatic pseudocyst.

Sonographic findings include abnormalities in gland size, irregular margins, inhomogeneous or heterogeneous echogenicity of parenchyma, and dilatation of the pancreatic duct. Calcifications are recognized as shadowing echogenic foci within the parenchyma or the main pancreatic duct. Pseudocysts are often present in chronic pancreatitis, and they are usually unilocular, anechoic, and sharply defined.[169-171] Other complications of chronic pancreatitis such as biliary dilatation and splenic vein thrombosis can also be detected with sonography.

Abnormalities in size and contour of the pancreas are the least sensitive indicators of chronic pancreatitis on ultrasound studies. Diffuse enlargement is often present early in the course of the disease, and atrophy or focal enlargement may be present later. An atrophic gland is usually difficult to appreciate, and some gland atrophy normally occurs with aging.[172]

Pancreatic parenchymal echogenicity is also unreliable in the diagnosis of chronic pancreatitis because it can be normal, increased, or decreased. Decreased echogenicity occurs when there are acute exacerbations with parenchymal edema.[168,172,173]

Dilatation of the pancreatic duct is one of the most common sonographic abnormalities of chronic pancreatitis and is seen in up to 90% of cases as a tubular, anechoic structure in the pancreatic body.

Endoscopic Sonography

Endoscopic ultrasound (EUS) overcomes many of the limitations of transabdominal sonography due to the proximity of the transducer to the pancreas and the superior image resolution provided by high-frequency transducers. Although EUS is an invasive imaging modality, it has a low risk of complications. In many cases, EUS is helpful to elucidate the cause of pancreatitis, being able to detect small pancreatic tumors and microlithiasis not seen by other imaging modalities.[174-176] EUS can demonstrate biliary sludge and tiny stones that are often masked by the contrast medium on ERCP. In 77% to 92% of cases of "idiopathic" pancreatitis, EUS is able to diagnose the cause, which are small gallstones in the majority of these patients.[176,177] EUS findings indicative of chronic pancreatitis include parenchymal calcifications, hyperechoic foci or strands, pseudocysts, heterogeneous echotexture, and lobular contour of the gland.[178-181] Ductal abnormalities include dilatation and irregularity, hyperechoic walls, intraductal stones, and visible branches.[179,181] Chronic pancreatitis is likely when more than two of these findings are present. With more than six findings, the disease is probably moderate to severe.[181] Unlike ERCP, EUS has the advantage of being able to evaluate simultaneously the pancreatic ductal system and the parenchyma. However, the diagnosis of chronic pancreatitis based on EUS changes alone is controversial.[168,178] There is usually a good correlation of EUS with ERCP in patients with moderate or severe chronic pancreatitis but not in those with mild disease.[179,182-184] Others studies reported abnormal findings at EUS in patients with normal ERCP and pancreatic function tests, suggesting that EUS may overdiagnose chronic pancreatitis or, alternatively, it may be more sensitive than ERCP and function tests to detect subtle pancreatic changes.[179,185] In a study of patients with suspected chronic pancreatitis, the addition of fine needle aspiration improved the negative predictive value but did not improve the specificity of EUS findings in patients with normal ERCP.[186] EUS can be especially helpful when combined with fine needle aspiration of a suspicious mass in patients with chronic pancreatitis. Biopsy of regional lymph nodes and assessment of tumor extension and vascular involvement can be performed with EUS to enhance staging in these patients. EUS also has therapeutic applications in chronic pancreatitis such as to perform celiac plexus blocks to alleviate pain in patients without ductal obstruction, and to guide internal stent placement for decompression of pseudocysts.[187,188] Disadvantages of EUS include its cost, limited availability, and long learning curve, being very operator-dependent. EUS is discussed in detail in Chapter 13.

Endoscopic Retrograde Cholangiopancreatography

Endoscopic retrograde cholangiopancreatography (ERCP) is a very useful technique in the diagnosis of chronic pancreatitis, although relatively invasive[189,190] (see Chapter 75). In early chronic pancreatitis, the pancreatic duct is often normal, limiting the sensitivity of ERCP. The earliest changes involve the first-order and second-order side branches of the main pancreatic duct and include dilatation and contour irregularity, clubbing, stenosis of the side branches, and opacification of small cavities. Some of these changes, however, can be seen in elderly normal patients and must be interpreted with caution in this age group.[191,192]

With disease progression, the involvement of the main pancreatic duct increases with more dilatation, mural irregularities, loss of normal tapering, and areas of stenosis or occlusion. If a solitary stricture is seen in the main pancreatic duct, the differential considerations include neoplasm or pseudocyst. Stenoses are usually shorter, smoother, and more symmetric in pancreatitis than those associated with neoplasm.[193,194] Biopsy of suspicious lesions or brushing and collection of pancreatic secretions can be performed with ERCP and may be helpful in the diagnosis of pancreatic carcinoma. In advanced chronic pancreatitis, the dilatation is more marked, and intraductal calculi can be seen. The pancreatic duct and side branches may have a "chain of lakes" appearance.

According to the Cambridge Classification or its modifications, chronic pancreatitis is considered mild if the main pancreatic duct is normal but at least three side branches are abnormal. Moderate disease requires abnormalities in the main pancreatic duct and in more than three side branches. Severe disease includes the abnormalities of moderate disease plus one of the following: a large cavity, ductal obstruction, filling defects, severe dilatation, or irregularity.[195]

ERCP is able to detect early chronic pancreatitis before morphologic abnormalities can be seen on CT.[168] There is good correlation between ERCP and histology in chronic pancreatitis. The correlation between pancreatic function tests and ERCP is not as good, however, especially in the early stages of chronic pancreatitis.[168,195,196] ERCP is also helpful in the treatment of complications of pancreatitis such as pancreatic duct strictures and pseudocysts, avoiding the complications of surgery.[190]

Magnetic Resonance Cholangiopancreatography

Endoscopic retrograde cholangiopancreatography (ERCP) is the standard imaging modality to evaluate the pancreaticobiliary tract, being a diagnostic and therapeutic procedure. Because of its invasiveness and potentially serious complications, however, ERCP is ideally reserved for patients who need intervention. MRCP has been increasingly used in patients with suspected pancreatitis or pancreaticobiliary abnormalities because it lacks ionizing radiation, does not require iodinated contrast material, and is noninvasive, sparing the patient potential complications. MRCP is also helpful in patients with anatomic abnormalities that impede cannulation of the common bile duct or pancreatic duct. Using heavily T2-weighted sequences, MRCP is able to depict fluid-filled structures such as pseudocysts and detect abnormalities of the pancreatic duct including dilatation, irregularity, intraductal stones, and multiple or severe obstructions, which may be a limitation for ERCP.[197,198] MRCP has the advantage of showing the ductal segments proximal and distal to an obstruction, being able to evaluate its character, extent, location and cause. MRCP is discussed in detail in Chapter 77.

ERCP and MRCP are helpful for evaluating the pancreatic duct for findings of chronic pancreatititis in patients with abdominal pain that is refractory to medical therapy.[198-200] The sensitivity of MRCP for ductal abnormalities and dilatation ranges from 56% to 100%, and the specificity ranges from 86% to 100%.[198-200] Strictures or obstruction of the pancreatic or bile duct by stones is a major cause of pain and one of the main indications for surgery in chronic pancreatitis.[201] In the presence of ductal dilatation, ductal drainage procedures combined with partial resection of the head of the pancreas may result in long-term pain relief in 60% to 80% of patients.

The administration of secretin during MRCP allows evaluation of the exocrine function of the pancreas, improves delineation of the pancreatic duct, and may be useful to detect abnormalities of the side branches in early chronic pancreatitis.[65,202,203] Secretin also improves detection of ductal narrowing and endoluminal filling defects in severe chronic pancreatitis.[203] Significant correlation between reduced duodenal filling scores during secretin-MRCP and impaired pancreatic exocrine function has been reported.[202,204]

Computed Tomography and Magnetic Resonance Imaging

The diagnostic criteria for chronic pancreatitis on CT and MRI examinations are based on assessment of the size and contour of the gland, dilatation and shape of the pancreatic duct, and presence of ductal calcifications[168,193,205] (Fig. 99-31). CT has reported sensitivities of 50% to 90% and specificities of 55% to 85% in the detection of chronic pancreatitis.[206]

Although CT correctly detects the morphologic alterations of chronic pancreatitis, its ability to evaluate severity of disease is more limited. These shortcomings are related to (1) the inability of CT to accurately diagnose incipient forms of chronic pancreatitis that do not exhibit gross morphologic changes and (2) poor correlation between functional exocrine and endocrine deficit and pancreatic morphology on imaging studies. When compared to ERCP and pancreatic function tests, CT is not sensitive in the diagnosis of early chronic pancreatitis. Some experts[90,207-209] believe that MRI can detect findings of chronic pancreatitis prior to CT based on signal intensity abnormalities of the pancreas. These changes are best visualized on nonenhanced and gadolinium-enhanced T1-weighted fat-suppressed images. The normal pancreas has high signal intensity due to the presence of acinar proteins and enhances markedly following gadolinium administration. Chronic pancreatitis and associated fibrosis result in loss of proteinaceous material and decreased signal intensity of the pancreas. Unlike the normal pancreas, the chronically inflamed and fibrotic pancreas shows decreased and hetero-

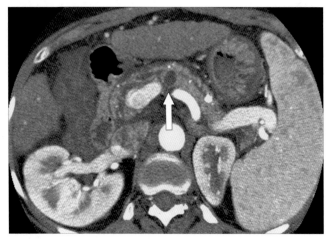

Figure 99-31. Chronic pancreatitis. Axial contrast-enhanced MDCT image shows pancreatic atrophy with diffuse calcifications, mild dilatation of the pancreatic duct and a 1.2 × 1-cm pseudocyst (*arrow*) in the pancreatic body.

geneous enhancement during the arterial phase and on later phases shows relative increased enhancement.[90,207,208,210] (Fig. 99-32). Zhang and associates[209] found a sensitivity of 92% and specificity of 75% for the diagnosis of chronic pancreatitis based on abnormal enhancement pattern, as opposed to 50% diagnostic sensitivity based on morphologic changes of the pancreas.

Alteration in the size of the pancreas is often seen in chronic pancreatitis; however, the gland may be normal or only slightly increased in size in 15% to 20% of cases. In one series, focal enlargement was present in 30% and atrophy of the gland was present in 54% of patients[206] (see Fig. 99-31). Significant atrophy of the pancreas may be seen in elderly persons without chronic pancreatitis. Evaluation of the history and clinical and functional findings may be necessary for differential diagnosis. Focal enlargement of the gland produced by a chronic inflammatory mass may simulate a pancreatic neoplasm. In cases when the CT is inconclusive, MRI may provide additional diagnostic information.[211,212] In some cases, it may be impossible to differentiate an inflammatory mass from carcinoma.

Several studies have demonstrated that focal pancreatitis and pancreatic carcinoma may have similar appearance and pattern of enhancement on CT and MRI, because of the presence of fibrosis in both types of lesions.[208,213-215] Both conditions may also cause dilatation of the pancreatic duct and common bile duct (double-duct sign), ductal strictures, arterial encasement, and peripancreatic venous obstruction.[212] In addition, carcinoma develops in 2% to 3% of cases of chronic pancreatitis, and this malignant degeneration is often difficult to appreciate on CT.[216] A new or rapidly increasing homogeneous and ill-defined pancreatic mass, which can be detected by comparison with previous CT examinations or short-term follow-up, is indicative of malignancy. Imaging features that favor the diagnosis of inflammatory mass related to chronic pancreatitis over adenocarcinoma include a nondilated or smooth-tapering pancreatic duct coursing through the mass (duct penetrating sign), the presence of pancreatic calcifications, a lower ratio of duct caliber to pancreatic gland width, and irregular ductal dilation.[208,213,215] The imaging features of adenocarcinoma and focal pancreatitis often overlap, however, and complementary studies including ERCP and EUS with fine needle aspiration biopsy may be required for definite diagnosis.

Dilatation of the pancreatic duct and its secondary radicles (>2 to 3 mm in size) is characteristic for chronic pancreatitis (Figs. 99-33 and 99-34). In advanced disease, the main duct appears beaded, irregular, or smooth, often containing stones (Fig. 99-35). These pancreatic duct abnormalities are better demonstrated on MRI than on CT. Subtle changes in side branches seen in early chronic pancreatitis, however, are best depicted on ERCP. The pancreatic duct should be

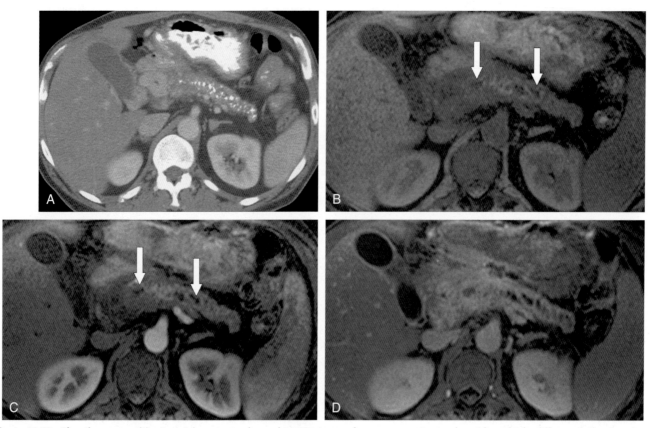

Figure 99-32. Chronic pancreatitis. A. Axial contrast-enhanced MDCT image shows pancreatic atrophy with multiple diffuse calcifications in a patient with chronic pancreatitis due to alcohol abuse. **B.** Axial T1-weighted fat-suppressed spoiled gradient-echo MR image shows decreased, heterogeneous signal intensity of the pancreas, and irregular dilatation of the main pancreatic duct (*arrows*). **C** and **D.** Axial gadolinium-enhanced T1-weighted fat-suppressed spoiled gradient-echo MR images show decreased pancreatic enhancement during the arterial phase (**C**) and delayed enhancement in the venous phase (**D**) related to fibrosis due to chronic pancreatitis. Dilated pancreatic duct (*arrows* in **C**) is more clearly visualized after gadolinium enhancement. (**B, C,** and **D** from Miller FH, Keppke AL, Wadhwa A, et al: MRI of pancreatitis and its complications: Part 2, chronic pancreatitis. AJR 183:1645-1652, 2004. Reprinted with permission from the American Journal of Roentgenology.)

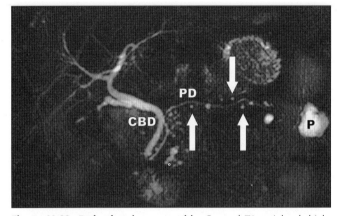

Figure 99-33. Early chronic pancreatitis. Coronal T2-weighted thick-slab RARE MR image shows mild dilatation of the secondary branches of the pancreatic duct (*arrows*) and pseudocyst (P) in the pancreatic tail. The main pancreatic duct (PD) and the common bile duct (CBD) have normal caliber. (From Miller FH, Keppke AL, Wadhwa A, et al: MRI of pancreatitis and its complications: Part 2, chronic pancreatitis. AJR 183:1645-1652, 2004. Reprinted with permission from the American Journal of Roentgenology.)

visualized entirely to the level of the papilla because small tumors of the pancreatic head may produce similar findings. The pancreatic duct may be dilated in patients with senile atrophy of the pancreas, mimicking chronic pancreatitis.

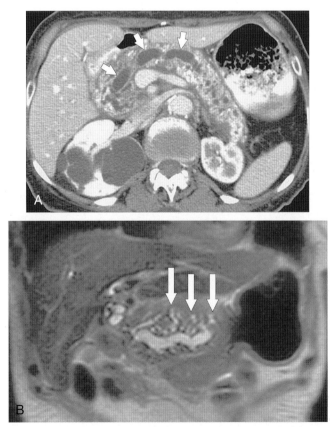

Figure 99-34. Chronic pancreatitis. A. Axial contrast-enhanced MDCT image shows diffuse calcifications in the pancreas with a dilated main pancreatic duct (*arrows*) measuring 9 mm and dilated side branches. **B.** Coronal T2-weighted MR image shows the dilated pancreatic duct and secondary radicles (*arrows*) associated with chronic pancreatitis. (**B** from Miller FH, Keppke AL, Wadhwa A, et al: MRI of pancreatitis and its complications: Part 2, chronic pancreatitis. AJR 183:1645-1652, 2004. Reprinted with permission from the American Journal of Roentgenology.)

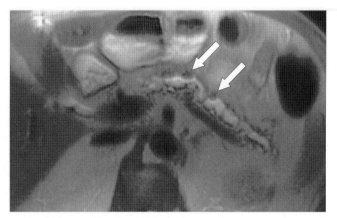

Figure 99-35. Severe chronic pancreatitis. Axial T2-weighted HASTE MR image shows dilatation of the main pancreatic duct and side branches giving a "chain of lakes" appearance. The pancreas is atrophic and contains signal void areas (*arrows*) related to calcifications from chronic pancreatitis. (From Miller FH, Keppke AL, Wadhwa A, et al: MRI of pancreatitis and its complications: Part 2, chronic pancreatitis. AJR 183:1645-1652, 2004. Reprinted with permission from the American Journal of Roentgenology.)

CT demonstrates pancreatic calcifications (see Figs. 99-31 and 99-32) in approximately 50% of patients with chronic pancreatitis.[205,206] These are the most reliable imaging features of the disease. They can be scattered throughout the gland, isolated, or focal in the head or body of the pancreas. Calcifications vary from innumerable to single and small. Chronic calcific pancreatitis are more difficult to visualize on MRI because this technique is inferior to CT in demonstrating calcifications. On T2-weighted MR images, a stone has low signal intensity compared to the high signal intensity pancreatic fluid.

Pseudocysts of various sizes may be present within the pancreas or in an extrapancreatic location. They occur in 25% to 60% of patients with chronic pancreatitis and are usually stable.[9,26]

Pseudoaneurysms and thrombosis of the splenic vein with extensive collateral circulation and gastric varices are sometimes encountered in chronic pancreatitis and can be readily diagnosed by CT and MRI (Fig. 99-36). Additionally, patients with repeated episodes of acute exacerbation may present with an acute abdominal catastrophe, dropping hematocrit, and evidence of massive intra-abdominal bleeding.

Pancreaticopleural Fistula

Pancreaticopleural fistula can occur in acute or chronic pancreatitis or as a result of pancreatic trauma. Pancreatic secretions from a ruptured pancreatic duct dissect through the aortic or esophageal hiatus or directly through the diaphragm and reach the mediastinum, pleural cavities, pericardium, or bronchial tree. Patients usually present with large pleural effusions and dyspnea. A high index of suspicion for pancreaticopleural fistula is required. CT and MRI may identify the fistula, especially when coronal reformatted images are used, as well as the changes of chronic pancreatitis (Fig. 99-37). ERCP has been considered the best imaging modality for evaluation of pancreaticopleural fistulas, but technical failures may result from incomplete opacification of the pancreatic duct or a long fistulous tract. MRCP may depict the fistula and the ductal anatomy and can be helpful

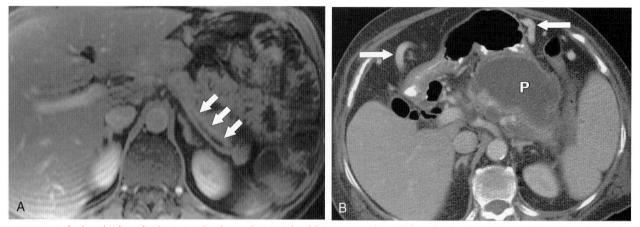

Figure 99-36. **Splenic vein thrombosis. A.** Axial enhanced T1-weighted fat-suppressed spoiled gradient-echo MR image shows low signal intensity thrombus (*arrows*) in the splenic vein. **B.** Axial contrast-enhanced MDCT image from another patient shows pancreatic pseudocyst (P) and the presence of collateral vessels (*arrows*) suggesting splenic vein occlusion. (**A** from Miller FH, Keppke AL, Dalal K, et al: MRI of pancreatitis and its complications: Part 1, acute pancreatitis. AJR 183:1637-1644, 2004. Reprinted with permission from the American Journal of Roentgenology.)

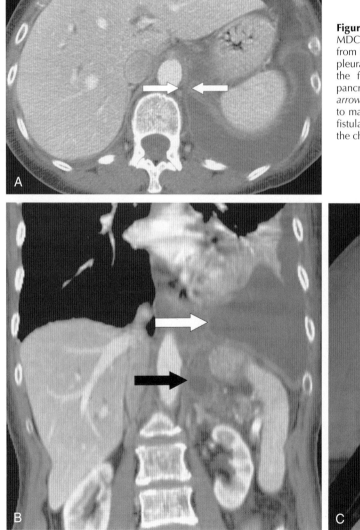

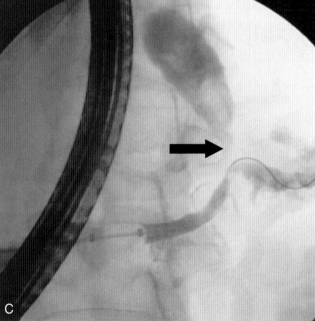

Figure 99-37. **Pancreaticopleural fistula. A.** Axial contrast-enhanced MDCT image shows fluid extending through the diaphragm (*arrows*) from the abdomen into the pleural space, in a patient with recurrent pleural effusions. **B.** Coronal contrast-enhanced MDCT image shows the fluid (*black arrow*) extending superiorly from the disrupted pancreatic duct into the chest, creating a left pleural effusion (*white arrow*). Without the coronal reformatted image, it is more difficult to make this diagnosis. **C.** ERCP confirms the CT findings showing a fistula (*arrow*) from the pancreatic duct with the fluid extending into the chest.

in the surgical planning of these patients, potentially replacing ERCP.[217]

Groove Pancreatitis

Patients who have repeated episodes of pancreatitis or acute exacerbations of chronic pancreatitis may develop a form of segmental pancreatitis described as "groove pancreatitis," in which the inflammatory reaction and fluid collection dissect into the "groove" between the duodenum and the head of the pancreas (Fig. 99-38). Because of the enzymatic action of pancreatic secretions, as many as 50% of patients develop duodenal stenosis and/or strictures of the common bile duct.[97] The recognition of groove pancreatitis is important to distinguish from pancreatic and duodenal carcinoma. Contrast-enhanced CT shows a poorly enhancing lesion extending between the duodenum and the pancreatic head. Cysts in the groove or duodenal wall and duodenal stenosis are often seen. The head of the pancreas enhances normally. MRI findings of groove pancreatitis include a sheetlike fibrotic mass between the pancreatic head and a thickened duodenal wall associated with cystic changes in the duodenal wall. This fibrotic mass has a low signal intensity on T1- and T2-weighted images. The cystic component is low signal intensity on T1-weighted images and high signal intensity on T2-weighted images and does not enhance due to its fluid content. The fibrotic component demonstrates delayed enhancement following gadolinium and is easily demarcated from the normal pancreas, which has marked enhancement initially and less intense enhancement on more delayed images[208,218] (see Fig. 99-38). Similar duodenal changes, referred to as cystic dystrophy of the duodenal wall, have been reported in patients with acute pancreatitis and heterotopic pancreatic tissue in the duodenum.[219]

Autoimmune Chronic Pancreatitis

Autoimmune chronic pancreatitis has unique clinical, histological, and imaging features that have been described.[220] It has an autoimmune mechanism and may coexist with diabetes mellitus and autoimmune diseases such as Sjögren's syndrome, primary sclerosing cholangitis, and primary biliary cirrhosis. Autoimmune chronic pancreatitis is relatively asymptomatic, predominates in middle-aged or older men, and usually shows a remarkable response to steroids.[221,222] Laboratory findings may include increased levels of serum

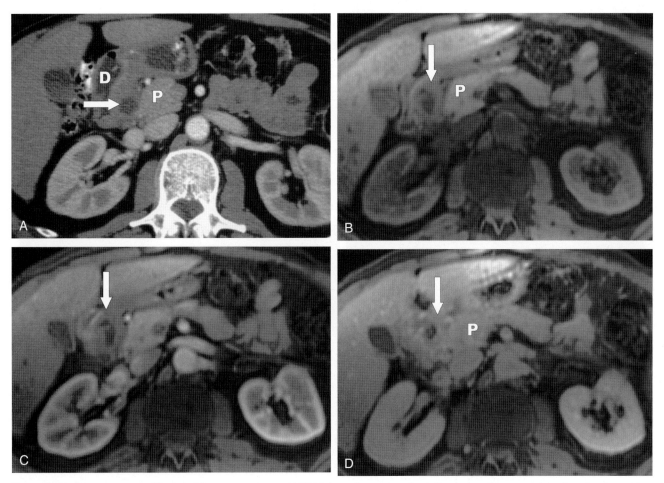

Figure 99-38. Groove pancreatitis. A. Axial contrast-enhanced MDCT shows hypoenhancing inflammatory tissue containing low-density cyst (*arrow*) in the groove between the duodenum (D) and the pancreatic head (P). **B.** Axial T1-weighted fat-suppressed spoiled gradient-echo MR image shows low signal intensity of the inflammatory mass (*arrow*) between the high signal intensity pancreatic head (P) and the duodenum. **C** and **D.** The mass (*arrow*) has decreased enhancement in the arterial phase (**C**) and delayed enhancement in the venous phase (**D**) after gadolinium administration due to fibrosis. (**A-D** from Miller FH, Keppke AL, Wadhwa A, et al: MRI of pancreatitis and its complications: Part 2, chronic pancreatitis. AJR 183:1645-1652, 2004. Reprinted with permission from the American Journal of Roentgenology.)

gammaglobulin and/or IgG, or the presence of autoantibodies. Pancreatic fibrosis with infiltration of lymphocytes
and plasma cells is seen on histopathological examination.[222]
Imaging studies show a rare association of diffuse enlargement of the pancreas with irregular narrowing of the pancreatic duct.[221] On CT and MRI, the pancreas appears diffusely
enlarged, with a "sausage-like" appearance, usually without
calcifications or stones.[221,223,224] As in chronic pancreatitis of
other etiologies, the pancreas shows decreased enhancement
in the arterial phase and increased enhancement in delayed
phases after contrast administration. A characteristic low-
density rim, likely composed of fibrous tissue, is often seen
surrounding the pancreas.[218,221] This capsule-like rim shows
delayed enhancement on dynamic imaging and low signal
intensity on T1- and T2-weighted MR images.[218] Diffuse or
segmental irregular narrowing of the main pancreatic duct
associated with strictures of the intrahepatic and extrahepatic
biliary tract is typically demonstrated on ERCP (Fig. 99-39).
MRCP shows well the biliary tract abnormalities but does
not show the stenosis of the pancreatic duct as well as does
ERCP.[218,225]

SUMMARY

Experience accumulated since the late 1970s has shown that
CT is the single most important imaging modality in evaluating patients with pancreatitis. CT has high sensitivity and
specificity in diagnosing moderate and severe pancreatitis,
as well as in detecting serious complications that are often
clinically unsuspected. In addition, CT plays a valuable role
as an early predictive indicator of disease severity. Patients
with fluid collections and pancreatic necrosis are at high
risk for developing complications. These patients should be
closely monitored clinically and with follow-up CT examinations. They require intensive care treatment and percutaneous
or surgical drainage procedures when sepsis develops.

MRI has also become an accurate imaging modality for
assessment of pancreatitis. It is especially helpful in the following situations: in patients with iodinated contrast allergy
or poor renal function; when evaluating the pancreaticobiliary tract; when characterizing complex fluid collections;
and when diagnosing early chronic pancreatitis. Sonography
is used mainly to exclude a diagnosis of gallstones and biliary

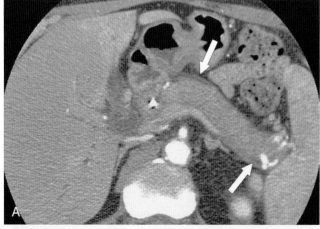
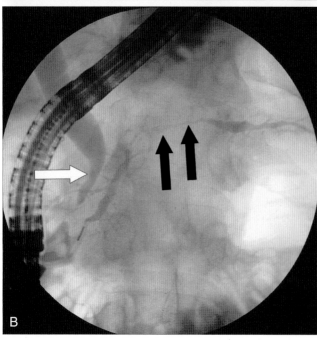
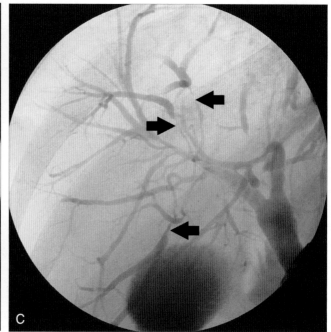

Figure 99-39. Autoimmune pancreatitis. A. Axial contrast-enhanced MDCT image shows a uniformly enlarged pancreas, with sharp outline. Note peripancreatic hypodense rim (*arrows*), which is suggestive of autoimmune pancreatitis but not diagnostic. **B.** ERCP shows segmental irregular narrowing (*black arrows*) of the pancreatic duct at the level of the body of the pancreas. The ductal segments adjacent to the stricture are minimally dilated. Stricture of the distal common bile duct is also seen (*white arrow*). **C.** ERCP shows multiple strictures (*arrows*) in the intrahepatic ducts.

obstruction. The role of ERCP has diminished, as MRCP emerged as a noninvasive alternative diagnostic tool. ERCP is mainly used for interventional procedures such as endoscopic therapy of complications of pancreatitis and ductal obstruction and to perform tissue biopsy to differentiate benign from malignant clinical and imaging features. It is occasionally used as a road map of the pancreatic duct before surgical procedures and to diagnose early side branch abnormalities in chronic pancreatitis.

References

1. Pandol SJ, Saluja AK, Imrie CW, et al: Acute pancreatitis: Bench to bedside. Gastroenterology 132:1127-1151, 2007.
2. Whitcomb DC: Acute pancreatitis. N Engl J Med 354:2142-2150, 2006.
3. Forsmark CE, Baillie J: AGA Institute Technical Review on Acute Pancreatitis. Gastroenterology 132:2022-2044, 2007.
4. Rau BM: Predicting severity of acute pancreatitis. Curr Gastroenterol Rep 9:107-115, 2007.
5. Sternby B, O'Brien JF, Zinsmeister AR, et al: What is the best biochemical test to diagnose acute pancreatitis? Mayo Clin Proc 71:1138-1144, 1996.
6. Bradley EL III: A clinically based system for acute pancreatitis. Arch Surg 128:586-590, 1993.
7. Banks PA: A new classification system for acute pancreatitis. Am J Gastroenterol 89:151-152, 1994.
8. Sarnee M, Cotton PB: Classification of pancreatitis. Gut 25:756-759, 1984.
9. Balthazar EJ, Freeny PC, vanSonnenberg E: Imaging and intervention in acute pancreatitis. Radiology 193:297-306, 1994.
10. Radecki PD, Friedman AC, Dabezies MA: Pancreatitis. In Friedman AC, Dachman AH (eds): Radiology of the Liver, Biliary Tract, and Pancreas. St. Louis, Mosby, 1994, pp 763-806.
11. May G, Gardiner R: Clinical Imaging of the Pancreas. New York, Raven, 1987, pp 57-114.
12. Karne S, Gorelick FS: Etiopathogenesis of acute pancreatitis. Surg Clin North Am 79:699-710, 1999.
13. Ranson JH: Etiological and prognostic factors in human acute pancreatitis: a review. Am J Gastroenterol 77:633-638, 1982.
14. Russo MW, Wei JT, Thiny MT, et al: Digestive and liver diseases statistics, 2004. Gastroenterology 126:1448-1453, 2004.
15. Saraswat VA, Sharma BC, Agarwal DK, et al: Biliary microlithiasis in patients with idiopathic acute pancreatitis and unexplained biliary pain: Response to therapy. J Gastroenterol Hepatol 19:1206-1211, 2004.
16. Levy MJ, Geenen JE: Idiopathic acute recurrent pancreatitis. Am J Gastroenterol 96:2540-2555, 2001.
17. Hanck C, Whitcomb DC: Alcoholic pancreatitis. Gastroenterol Clin N Am 33:751-765, 2004.
18. Oruc N, Whitcomb DC: Theories, mechanisms, and models of alcoholic chronic pancreatitis. Gastroenterol Clin N Am 33:733-750, 2004.
19. Kloppel G, Adler G, Kern HF: Pathomorphology of acute pancreatitis in relation to its clinical course and pathogenesis. In Malfertheiner P, Ditschuneit H (eds): Diagnostic Procedures in Pancreatic Disease. Berlin, Springer-Verlag, 1986, pp 11-18.
20. Singh M, Simsek H: Ethanol and the pancreas. Gastroenterology 98:1051-1062, 1990.
21. Kemppainen EA, Hedstrom JI, Puolakkainen PA, et al: Rapid measurement of urinary trypsinogen-2 as a screening test for acute pancreatitis. N Engl J Med 336:1788-1793, 1997.
22. Marotta PJ, Gregor J, Taves DH: Biliary sludge: A risk factor for "idiopathic" pancreatitis? Can J Gastroenterol 10:385-388, 1996.
23. Diehl AK, Holleman DR, Chapman JB, et al: Gallstone size and risk of pancreatitis. Arch Intern Med 157:1674-1678, 1997.
24. Kamisawa T, Egawa N, Tsuruta K, et al: Pancreatitis associated with congenital abnormalities of the pancreaticobiliary system. Hepatogastroenterology 52:223-229, 2005.
25. Draganov P, Forsmark CE: "Idiopathic" pancreatitis. Gastroenterology 128:756-763, 2005.
26. Balthazar, EJ: Complications of acute pancreatitis: Clinical and CT evaluation. Radiol Clin N Am 40:1211-1227, 2002.
27. Arvanitakis M, Koustiani G, Gantzarou A, et al: Staging of severity and prognosis of acute pancreatitis by computed tomography and magnetic resonance imaging—a comparative study. Dig Liver Dis 39:473-482, 2007.
28. Gross V, Leser HG, Heinisch A, Scholmerich J: Inflammatory mediators and cytokines—new aspects of the pathophysiology and assessment of severity of acute pancreatitis? Hepatogastroenterology 40:522-530, 1993.
29. Denham W, Norman J. The potential role of therapeutic cytokine manipulation in acute pancreatitis. Surg Clin North Am 79:767-781, 1999.
30. Rau B, Schilling MK, Beger HG: Laboratory markers of severe acute pancreatitis. Dig Dis 22:247-257, 2004.
31. Jiang CF, Shiau YC, Ng KW, Tan SW: Serum interleukin-6, tumor necrosis factor alpha and C-reactive protein in early prediction of severity of acute pancreatitis. J Chin Med Assoc 67:442-446, 2004.
32. Reisler RB, Murphy RL, Redfield RR, Parker RA: Incidence of pancreatitis in HIV-1-infected individuals enrolled in 20 adult AIDS clinical trials group studies: Lessons learned. J Acquir Immune Defic Syndr 39:159-166, 2005.
33. Behrman SW, Melvin WS, Ellison EC: Pancreatic pseudocysts following acute pancreatitis. Am J Surg 172:228-231, 1996.
34. Yeo CJ, Bastidas JA, Lynch-Nyhan A, et al: The natural history of pancreatic pseudocysts documented by computed tomography. Surg Gynecol Obstet 170:412-417, 1990.
35. Hjelmquist B, Wattsgard C, Borgstrom A, et al: Pathobiochemistry and early CT findings in acute pancreatitis. Digestion 44:184-190, 1989.
36. Yadav D, Agarwal N, Pitchumoni CS: A critical evaluation of laboratory tests in acute pancreatitis. Am J Gastroenterol 97:1309-1318, 2002.
37. Steer ML: Acute pancreatitis. In Taylor MB (ed): Gastrointestinal Emergencies, 2nd ed. Baltimore, Williams & Wilkins, 1997, pp 227-238.
38. Agarwal N, Pitchmoni CS: Simplified criteria in acute pancreatitis. Pancreas 1:69-73, 1986.
39. Gumaste VV, Dave PB, Weissman D, Messer J: Lipase/amylase ratio. A new index that distinguishes acute episodes of alcoholic from nonalcoholic acute pancreatitis. Gastroenterology 101:1361-1366, 1991.
40. Tenner SM, Steinberg W: The admission serum lipase:amylase ratio differentiates alcoholic from nonalcoholic acute pancreatitis. Am J Gastroenterol 87: 1755-1758, 1992.
41. Winslet M, Hall C, London NJ, et al: Relation of diagnostic serum amylase to aetiology and severity of acute pancreatitis. Gut 33:982-986, 1992.
42. Lankisch PG, Burchard-Recker IS, Lehrich D: Underestimation of acute pancreatitis: Patients with only a small increase in amylase/lipase levels can also have or develop severe acute pancreatitis. Gut 44:542-544, 1999.
43. De Sanctis JT, Lee MJ, Gazelle GS, et al: Prognostic indicator in acute pancreatitis: CT vs APACHE II. Clin Radiol 52:842-848, 1997.
44. Steinberg WM, Goldstein SS, Davis ND, et al: Diagnostic assays in acute pancreatitis: A study of sensitivity and specificity. Ann Intern Med 102:576-580, 1985.
45. Pitchumoni CS, Agarwal N, Jain NK: Systemic complications of acute pancreatitis. Am J Gastroenterol 83:597-606, 1988.
46. Balthazar EJ, Lutzker S: Radiological signs of acute pancreatitis. Crit Rev Clin Radiol Nucl Med 4:199-242, 1976.
47. Brascho D, Reynolds TN, Zanca P: The radiographic "colon cut-off sign" in acute pancreatitis. Radiology 79:763-768, 1962.
48. Meyers MA: Roentgen significance of phrenicocolic ligament. Radiology 95:539-545, 1970.
49. Schwartz D, Badelhoft J: Simulation of colonic obstruction at the splenic flexure by pancreatitis: Roentgen features. AJR 78:607-616, 1957.
50. Pickhardt PJ: The colon cutoff sign. Radiology 215:387-389, 2000.
51. Roseman DM, Knowlessar OD, Sleisenger MH: Pulmonary manifestations of pancreatitis. N Engl J Med 263:294-296, 1960.
52. Renert WA, Pitt MJ, Capp MP: Acute pancreatitis. Semin Roentgenol 8:405-414, 1973.
53. Ranson JH, Turner JW, Roses DF, et al: Respiratory complications in acute pancreatitis. Ann Surg 179:557-566, 1974.
54. Pastor CM, Matthay MA, Frossard JL: Pancreatitis-associated acute lung injury: New insights. Chest 124:2341-2351, 2003.
55. Lankisch PG, Droge M, Becher R: Pulmonary infiltrations. Sign of severe acute pancreatitis. Int J Pancreatol 19:113-115, 1996.
56. Heller SJ, Noordhoek E, Tenner SM, et al: Pleural effusion as a predictor of severity in acute pancreatitis. Pancreas 15:222-225, 1997.
57. Pezzilli R, Billi P, Baraket P: Peripheral leukocyte count and chest x-ray in the early assessment of the severity of acute pancreatitis. Digestion 57:25-32, 1996.
58. Raghu MG, Wig JD, Kochhar R, et al: Lung complications in acute pancreatitis. JOP 10:177-185, 2007.

59. Meyers MA, Evans JA: Effects of pancreatitis on the small bowel and colon: Spread along mesenteric planes. AJR 119:151-165, 1973.

60. Lindahl F, Vejlsted H, Backer OG: Lesions of the colon following pancreatitis. Scand J Gastroenterol 7:375-378, 1972.

61. Safrit HD, Rice RP: Gastrointestinal complications of pancreatitis. Radiol Clin North Am 27:73-79, 1989.

62. Thompson WM, Kelvin FM, Rice RP: Inflammation and necrosis of the transverse colon secondary to pancreatitis. AJR 128:943-948, 1977.

63. Rohrmann CA, Baron RL: Biliary complications of pancreatitis. Radiol Clin North Am 27:93-104, 1989.

64. Frost R, Somers S, Stevenson G: Acute biliary pancreatitis. J Clin Gastroenterol 9:4-7, 1987.

65. Fulcher AS, Turner MA: MR cholangiopancreatography. Radiol Clin N Am 40:1363-1376, 2002.

66. Masci E, Toti G, Mariani A, et al: Complications of diagnostic and therapeutic ERCP: A prospective multicenter study. Am J Gastroenterol 96:417-423, 2001.

67. Vujic I: Vascular complications of pancreatitis. Radiol Clin North Am 27:81-91, 1989.

68. Dreiling DA, Robert J, Toledano AE: Vascular pancreatitis: A clinical entity of growing concern. J Clin Gastroenterol 10:3-6, 1988.

69. Pagnoux C, Mahr A, Cohen P, Guillevin L: Presentation and outcome of gastrointestinal involvement in systemic necrotizing vasculitides: Analysis of 62 patients with polyarteritis nodosa, microscopic polyangiitis, Wegener granulomatosis, Churg-Strauss syndrome, or rheumatoid arthritis-associated vasculitis. Medicine (Baltimore) 84:115-128, 2005.

70. Balthazar EJ: Acute pancreatitis: Assessment of severity with clinical and CT evaluation. Radiology 223:603-613, 2002.

71. Jeffrey RB: Sonography in acute pancreatitis. Radiol Clin North Am 27:19-37, 1989.

72. Jeffrey RB, Laing FC, Wing VW: Extrapancreatic spread of acute pancreatitis: New observations with real-time US. Radiology 159:707-711, 1986.

73. Loren I, Lasson A, Fork T, et al: New sonographic imaging observations in focal pancreatitis. Eur Radiol 9:862-867, 1999.

74. Hashimoto BE, Laing FC, Jeffrey RB, et al: Hemorrhagic pancreatic fluid collections examined by ultrasound. Radiology 150:803-808, 1984.

75. Merkle EM, Gorich J: Imaging of acute pancreatitis. Eur Radiol 12:1979-1992, 2002.

76. Gooding GA: Ultrasound of a superior mesenteric aneurysm secondary to pancreatitis: A plan for real-time ultrasound of sonolucent masses in pancreatitis. J Clin Ultrasound 9:355-356, 1981.

77. McMahon MJ, Pickford IR, Playforth MJ: Early prediction of severity of acute pancreatitis using peritoneal lavage. Acta Chir Scand 146:171-175, 1980.

78. Balthazar EJ, Ranson JHC, Naidich DP, et al: Acute pancreatitis: Prognostic value of CT. Radiology 156:767-772, 1985.

79. Fishman M, Talner LB: Pancreatitis causing focal caliectasis. AJR 156:1005-1006, 1991.

80. Garg PK, Madan K, Pande GK, et al: Association of extent and infection of pancreatic necrosis with organ failure and death in acute necrotizing pancreatitis. Clin Gastroenterol Hepatol 3:159-166, 2005.

81. Hohl C, Schmidt T, Haage P, et al: Phase-inversion tissue harmonic imaging compared with conventional B-mode ultrasound in the evaluation of pancreatic lesions. Eur Radiol 14:1109-1117, 2004.

82. Finstad TA, Tchelepi H, Ralls PW: Sonography of acute pancreatitis: Prevalence of findings and pictorial essay. Ultrasound Q 21:95-104, 2005.

83. Gohde SC, Toth J, Krestin GP, et al: Dynamic contrast-enhanced FMPSPGR of the pancreas: Impact on diagnostic performance. AJR 168:689-696, 1997.

84. Stimac D, Miletic D, Radic M, et al: The role of nonenhanced magnetic resonance imaging in the early assessment of acute pancreatitis. Am J Gastroenterol 102:997-1004, 2007.

85. Kim MJ, Mitchell DG, Ito K, et al: Biliary dilatation: Differentiation of benign from malignant causes—value of adding conventional MR imaging to MR cholangiopancreatography. Radiology 214:173-181, 2000.

86. Ly JN, Miller FH: MR imaging of the pancreas: A practical approach. Radiol Clin N Am 40:1289-1306, 2002.

87. Kettritz U, Semelka RC: Contrast-enhanced MR imaging of the pancreas. Magn Reson Imaging Clin N Am 4:87-100, 1996.

88. Keogan MT, Edelman RR: Technologic advances in abdominal MR imaging. Radiology 220:310-320, 2001

89. Mitchell DG: MR imaging of the pancreas. Magn Reson Imaging Clin N Am 3:51-70, 1995.

90. Hakime A, Giraud M, Vullierme MP: MR imaging of the pancreas. J Radiology 88:11-25, 2007.

91. Miller FH, Keppke AL, Dalal K, et al: MRI of pancreatitis and its complications: Part 1, acute pancreatitis. AJR 183:1637-1644, 2004.

92. Piironen A, Kivisaari R, Pitkaranta P, et al: Contrast-enhanced magnetic resonance imaging for detection of acute hemorrhagic necrotizing pancreatitis. Eur Radiol 7:17-20, 1997.

93. Morgan DE, Baron TH, Smith JK, et al: Pancreatic fluid collections prior to intervention: Evaluation with MR imaging compared with CT and US. Radiology 203:773-777, 1997.

94. Martin DR, Karabulut N, Yang M, McFadden DW: High signal peripancreatic fat on fat-suppressed spoiled gradient echo imaging in acute pancreatitis: Preliminary evaluation of the prognostic significance. J Magn Reson Imaging 18:49-58, 2003.

95. Siegelman SS, Copeland BE, Saba GP, et al: CT of fluid collections associated with pancreatitis. AJR 134:1121-1132, 1980.

96. Johst P, Tsiotos GG, Sarr MG: Pancreatic ascites: A rare complication of necrotizing pancreatitis. A case report and review of the literature. Int J Pancreatol 22:151-154, 1997.

97. Balthazar EJ: CT diagnosis and staging of acute pancreatitis. Radiol Clin North Am 27:19-37, 1989.

98. Fernandez-Cruz L, Margarona E, Llovera J, et al: Pancreatic ascites. Hepato-Gastroenterology 40:150-154, 1993.

99. Fielding GA, McLatchie GR, Wilson C, et al: Acute pancreatitis and pancreatic fistula formation. Br J Surg 76:1126-1128, 1989.

100. Clavien PA, Hauser H, Meyer P, et al: Value of contrast enhanced computerized tomography in the early diagnosis and prognosis of acute pancreatitis: A prospective study of 202 patients. Am J Surg 155:457-466, 1988.

101. Ranson JH: Diagnostic standards for acute pancreatitis. World J Surg 21:136-142, 1997.

102. Hill MC, Barkin J, Usikoff MB, et al: Acute pancreatitis: Clinical vs CT findings. AJR 139:263-269, 1982.

103. Arvanitakis M, Delhaye M, De Maertelaere V, et al: Computed tomography and magnetic resonance imaging in the assessment of acute pancreatitis. Gastroenterology 126:715-723, 2004.

104. Lecesne R, Taourel P, Bret PM, et al: Acute pancreatitis: Interobserver agreement and correlation of CT and MR cholangiopancreatography with outcome. Radiology 211:727-735, 1999.

105. Ranson JHC, Balthazar EJ, Caccavale R, et al: Computed tomography and the prediction of pancreatic abscess in acute pancreatitis. Ann Surg 201:656-665, 1985.

106. Nordestgaard AG, Wilson SE, Williams RA: Early computerized tomography as a predictor of outcome in acute pancreatitis. Am J Surg 152:127-132, 1986.

107. Vernacchia FS, Jeffrey RB Jr, Federle MP, et al: Pancreatic abscess: Predictive value of early abdominal CT. Radiology 162:435-438, 1987.

108. Balthazar EJ, Robinson DL, Megibow AJ, et al: Acute pancreatitis: Value of CT in establishing prognosis. Radiology 174:331-336, 1990.

109. Balthazar, EJ: Staging of acute pancreatitis. Radiol Clin N Am 40:1199-1209, 2002.

110. Paulson EK, Vitellas KM, Keogan MT, et al: Acute pancreatitis complicated by gland necrosis: Spectrum of findings on contrast-enhanced CT. AJR 172:609-613, 1999.

111. Casas JD, Diaz R, Valderas G, Mariscal A, Cuadras P. Prognostic value of CT in the early assessment of patients with acute pancreatitis. AJR 2004; 182:569-574.

112. Vriens PW, van de Linde P, Slotema ET, Warmerdam PE, Breslau PJ. Computed tomography severity index is an early prognostic tool for acute pancreatitis. J Am Coll Surg 2005; 201:497-502.

113. Mortele KJ, Wiesner W, Intriere L, et al: A modified CT severity index for evaluating acute pancreatitis: Improved correlation with patient outcome. AJR 183:1261-1265, 2004.

114. Yassa NA, Agostini JT, Ralls PW: Accuracy of CT in estimating extent of pancreatic necrosis. Clin Imaging 21:407-410, 1997.

115. Nichols MT, Russ PD, Chen YK: Pancreatic imaging: Current and emerging technologies. Pancreas 33:211-220, 2006.

116. Kivisaari L, Kalevi S, Standertskjold-Nordenstam CG, et al: A new method for the diagnosis of acute hemorrhagic-necrotizing pancreatitis using contrast-enhanced CT. Gastrointest Radiol 9:27-30, 1984.

117. Kivisaari L, Somer K, Standertskjold-Nordenstam CG, et al: Early detection of acute fulminant pancreatitis by contrast-enhanced computed tomography. Scand J Gastroenterol 18:39-41, 1983.

118. Nuutinen P, Kivisaari L, Schroder T: Contrast-enhanced computed tomography and microangiography of the pancreas in acute human hemorrhagic/necrotizing pancreatitis. Pancreas 3:53-60, 1988.